Handbook of
Cost Accounting

Edited by
SIDNEY DAVIDSON, CPA
Arthur Young Professor of Accounting
Graduate School of Business
University of Chicago

and
ROMAN L. WEIL, CPA, CMA
Professor of Accounting
Graduate School of Business
University of Chicago

McGRAW-HILL BOOK COMPANY

New York   St. Louis   San Francisco   Auckland   Bogotá
Düsseldorf   Johannesburg   London   Madrid
Mexico   Montreal   New Delhi   Panama
Paris   São Paulo   Singapore
Sydney   Tokyo   Toronto

Library of Congress Cataloging in Publication Data

Main entry under title:

Handbook of cost accounting.

Includes bibliographies and index.
1. Cost accounting—Handbooks, manuals, etc.
2. Managerial accounting—Handbooks, manuals, etc.
I. Davidson, Sidney, date.   II. Weil, Roman L.
HF5686.C8H237   '657'.42   77-16820
ISBN 0-07-015452-X

1234567890   KPKP   7654321098

*The editors for this book were W. Hodson Mogan and Lynne Lackenbach,
the designer was Naomi Auerbach, and the production supervisor
was Teresa F. Leaden. It was set in Baskerville
by University Graphics, Inc.*

Printed and bound by The Kingsport Press.

Contents

Contributors

ANTHONY BASILE   *Arthur Young & Company* (COAUTHOR CHAPTER 9)

GEORGE J. BENSTON   *Professor of Accounting, Graduate School of Management, University of Rochester* (CHAPTER 5)

DUANE R. BORST   *Comptroller, Inland Steel Company* (CHAPTER 6)

DONALD R. BRINKMAN   *President, Valuation Systems Corporation* (CHAPTER 27)

S. THOMAS CLEVELAND   *Partner, Touche Ross & Co.* (CHAPTER 7)

JOSEPH D. COUGHLAN   *Partner, Price Waterhouse & Co.* (CHAPTER 12)

JOEL S. DEMSKI   *Professor of Information and Accounting Systems, Graduate School of Business, Stanford University* (CHAPTER 3)

NICHOLAS DOPUCH   *Professor of Accounting, University of Chicago* (CHAPTER 19)

JOHN EVERS   *Arthur Young & Company* (COAUTHOR CHAPTER 9)

ERIC G. FLAMHOLTZ   *Associate Professor of Accounting-Information Systems, and Director, Accounting-Information Systems Research Program, Graduate School of Management, University of California, Los Angeles* (CHAPTER 26)

MALVERN J. GROSS, JR.   *Partner, Price Waterhouse & Co.* (COAUTHOR CHAPTER 25)

RONALD J. HUEFNER   *Associate Professor of Accounting, State University of New York at Buffalo* (CHAPTER 17)

FELIX KAUFMAN   *Partner, Coopers & Lybrand* (CHAPTER 24)

ROBERT L. KELLY   *Director, Haskins & Sells* (COAUTHOR CHAPTER 14)

JAMES A. LARGAY III   *Associate Professor of Industrial Management, Georgia Institute of Technology* (CHAPTER 16)

JOHN D. LEWIS   *Partner, Arthur Andersen & Co.* (CHAPTER 10)

J. LESLIE LIVINGSTONE   *Fuller E. Callaway Professor, Georgia Institute of Technology* (CHAPTER 15)

D. EDWARD MARTIN   *Manager, Price Waterhouse & Co.* (COAUTHOR CHAPTER 25)

MATT G. MINOR   *Film Finance Group, Ltd.* (COAUTHOR CHAPTER 23)

JOHN L. MONTGOMERY   *Principal, Peat, Marwick, Mitchell & Co.* (COAUTHOR CHAPTER 11)

HUGO NURNBERG   *Professor of Accounting, Michigan State University* (CHAPTER 18)

LEONARD PACE   *Director, Haskins & Sells* (COAUTHOR CHAPTER 14)

RONALD J. PATTEN   *Dean, School of Business Administration, University of Connecticut* (CHAPTER 8)

WILLIAM L. RABY   *Touche Ross & Co.* (COAUTHOR CHAPTER 23)

ALFRED RAPPAPORT   *Professor of Accounting and Information Systems, Northwestern University* (CHAPTER 22)

GORDON SHILLINGLAW   *Professor of Accounting, Graduate School of Business, Columbia University* (CHAPTER 4)

DAVID SOLOMONS   *Arthur Young Professor of Accounting, University of Pennsylvania* (CHAPTER 1)

HERBERT F. TAGGART   *Emeritus Professor of Accounting, Graduate School of Business Administration, University of Michigan* (CHAPTER 21)

RUSSELL A. TAUSSIG   *Professor of Finance, Department of Accounting and Finance, College of Business Administration, University of Hawaii* (CHAPTER 2)

PETER B. B. TURNEY   *Associate Professor of Accounting, Portland State University* (COAUTHOR CHAPTER 11)

J. LOUIS WARGO   *Ernst & Ernst* (CHAPTER 13)

ROMAN L. WEIL   *Professor of Accounting, University of Chicago* (CHAPTER 20)

Preface

Accounting is an information system designed to communicate financial information about a business firm. This Handbook is designed to help both senders and receivers of accounting information. There are at least three kinds of accounting information, which we categorize as follows:

1. Information useful for managerial decision making
2. Information useful for managerial planning and control
3. Information useful (and frequently required) for external financial reporting

Senders of accounting information, the accountants working with or within a company, need to understand these three distinct uses of accounting information, why each of the three uses often requires data gathered from a different source or using a different accounting model, and, since there is some overlap in the kinds of data gathered for the three uses, how to provide data for the three different uses in an economical fashion. We believe that the senders of information, the accountants responsible for gathering and reporting accounting data, can be more effective in their jobs if they are made aware of the various uses of the data. Data gatherers will do better jobs when they fully understand the purposes that the data will serve.

Receivers of accounting information can generally be classified in one of two broad categories:

1. Managers who make decisions about the firm's operations (such as whether or not to expand a product line or to acquire some long-term asset) or who must determine whether or not operations within the firm are properly planned and controlled
2. Existing or potential investors who want to determine whether or not to expand or contract the size of their investment in a firm, whether as shareholders or lenders

We believe the receivers of accounting data can be more effective in their jobs if they are made aware of how the data have been gathered and the principles upon which they are being reported. Users of accounting data will do better jobs when they fully understand what the data do and do not show.

The editors determined that an effective *Handbook of Cost Accounting* should interweave discussion of the information needs of managers and investors with the explanation of procedures used by accountants. By our rough classification, thirteen of the twenty-seven chapters in this Handbook to some degree treat *all* three categories of accounting information: decision making, planning/control, and external reporting. Seven of the chapters integrate the decision-making and planning/control functions of accounting data. Five chapters primarily treat topics in managerial decision making, while two primarily treat planning and control. Our somewhat arbitrary classification of the chapters is as follows:

Decision making, planning/control, and external reporting—Chapters 1, 5, 8, 9, 10, 12, 15, 16, 17, 21, 22, 25, 27
Decision making and planning/control—Chapters 4, 11, 13, 14, 18, 24, 26
Decision making—Chapters 2, 3, 19, 20, 23
Planning/control—Chapters 6, 7

Most of the user-oriented material in this Handbook is directed to the managerial decision maker or to those attempting to improve the operations of the firm. There are no chapters devoted entirely to the function of external reporting. Accountants and users primarily concerned with external reporting want information about the principles and procedures underlying the numbers in published financial statements. Most such users will probably find our companion volume, the *Handbook of Modern Accounting* (also published by McGraw-Hill), to be helpful in their needs.

This Handbook seeks to provide comprehensive and authoritative information on cost and managerial accounting in a conveniently organized and succinctly stated form. Those facing accounting problems will find here helpful guidance toward answers. The Handbook contains not only practical, how-to-do-it information but also observations on the background, controversy, and likely development of each topic.

There will be occasions, of course, where the reader will wish to know more about a specific subject than is set forth here. Each chapter contains a bibliography that directs the reader to other authoritative sources.

The Handbook is the work of many people. The contributors were selected because of the knowledge they possess of the subjects assigned to them. As a group, they form a cross section of accounting thought, representing the professions of public accounting, industrial accounting, management accounting, and academic accounting. We are proud to be associated with authors of such distinction, and to each of them we express our appreciation for their contribution to this volume.

Much of the credit for the successful completion of this Handbook must be given to K. Xenophon-Rybowiak, who prepared most of the manuscript for this volume. She was aided in her efforts by Sylvia Dobray, Mary Lee Peeler, Phyllis Maxwell, Mardine McReynolds, and Raymonde Rousselot, who shared various administrative and editorial chores in preparing this book. Our McGraw-Hill contacts worked ably and cooperatively in book production. We thank Beatrice Carson, Lynne Lackenbach, Mildred Hetherington, and Margaret DeJoy, in particular.

To all who participated—authors, editors, copy editors, indexers, and publisher—goes our appreciation. Without them, this Handbook would not have been possible.

Sidney Davidson
Roman L. Weil

Chapter **1**

The Historical Development of Cost Accounting*

DAVID SOLOMONS
Arthur Young Professor of Accounting, University of Pennsylvania

*This chapter is adapted and abridged, by the editors, with permission, from "The Historical Development of Costing," in *Studies in Cost Analysis,* 2nd ed., David Solomons, ed., published by Sweet & Maxwell Limited, of 11 New Fetter Lane, London, in 1968, pp. 3–49.

INTRODUCTION

So much has been written about the early history of double-entry bookkeeping that almost everyone knows that it arose in the highly developed civilization of Northern Italy in the fourteenth and fifteenth centuries; that it was used by many merchants of the time both in Italy and in the Netherlands and Southern Germany, where the mercantile influence of the Italians was very strong; that it was not, however, until the end of the fifteenth century that the technique of the art was systematically set down by the mathematician-monk Luca Paciolo, and published in Venice in 1494 as part of a book on mathematics; and that from then on, texts on the subject appeared in Germany, the Low Countries, France, and England.

In none of these early texts is there so much as a mention of any economic activity other than buying and selling. For the merchant alone were bookkeeping texts written. The fact is, of course, that to the extent that manufacturing processes were in the hands of small craftsmen closely controlled by the rules of their guilds, there was little scope for anything worthy of the name of industrial accounting; and although it is conceivable that monastic and other large landed estates might have developed record-keeping methods that could separate the results of different activities, they do not in fact seem to have done so. The main purpose of their records was accountability of bailiff to master, not the comparison of costs and revenues, the fixing of selling prices, and the ascertaining of profit and loss.

With the enclosure of land and the growing importance in industry of capitalists who gave out materials to be worked on by artisans in their own homes, new problems emerged. There was, for instance, the need for effective methods of controlling stocks of materials in the hands of outworkers, of linking amounts earned by the workers with the amounts paid to them, and separating the financial results achieved by the capitalist on each of the separate activities.

It was only when, in the course of the great growth of capitalistic production during the Industrial Revolution, the domestic system was replaced by the factory system and the employment of costly machines and equipment was made possible, that there was added to the already-existing costing problems, which were concerned almost exclusively with the cost of labor and materials, those difficult questions concerning the treatment of overhead costs that we are still some way from having disposed of satisfactorily.

An adequate account of the evolution of record keeping into a tool of industrial management has yet to be written. Certainly nothing as brief as this chapter can hope to fill the gap. What it can hope to do, however, is to sketch the main lines of development, so that the later chapters can be better seen in perspective as the end products of a great deal of earlier thought.

That earlier thought divides rather clearly into two parts. The first part, covering the period from the early fourteenth century down to the third quarter of the nineteenth, is largely, though by no means only, concerned with bringing the records of industrial activity within the compass of double-entry record keeping, and of extending the scope of that system to cover transactions, such as the transfer of materials from process to process *within* a business, which its early practitioners had never had in view. By 1875 or thereabouts, that technical problem had been completely solved. The second part of the story, which spans the following century down to our own day, is concerned not with a rather narrow technical problem in record keeping but with the broader issue of making the accounting records flexible and capable of providing information that would be significant not for just one purpose (say, the measurement of profit or loss) or two (say, in addition, the fixing of selling prices) but for any of the purposes which, in modern business, figures may be called upon to serve.

THE BEGINNING OF THE STORY: FOURTEENTH–EIGHTEENTH CENTURY

Mrs. de Roover,[1] in her fascinating study of the accounting records of the Antwerp printer, Christopher Plantin, puts the earliest use of accounting in industry at the beginning of the fourteenth century in Italy. We have a fairly detailed picture of its state of development there two centuries later from her husband, Raymond de Roover,[2] who has given us an account of the business organization set up by members of the Medici family in Florence in the sixteenth century for the manufacture of woolen cloth. The firm was founded in 1531 and was liquidated three years later. It bought wool, put it out for processing, sometimes through factors, to artisans working in their own homes, and sold the finished cloth. Probably only a few processes, such as wool sorting, cleansing (but not washing), combing, and carding, were carried on in the firm's own workshop. The firm's books, of which there were eight, were double-entry. These included:

1. A waste book, to record transactions in chronological order as they occurred, and in considerable detail

2. A journal, which reproduced from the waste book in abridged form particulars of purchases and sales

3. A general ledger with both personal and impersonal accounts

4. A subsidiary wages ledger (which was represented in the general ledger by a control account) containing accounts for most of the factors and artisans who worked for the firm—the most independent ones, such as the dyers, had their accounts in the general ledger

5. A cash book

6–8. Three special journals, recording the materials given out to and the amounts earned by the artisans, the figures of earnings being posted to one or other of the two ledgers

Reference has already been made to the fact that neither Paciolo nor his successors for two centuries attempted to apply their record-keeping technique to industrial problems, nor, as de Roover points out, did they refer to the use of subsidiary books. It is clear, therefore, from the Medici records, that at this time practice was well ahead of theory. The record-keeping system of the Medici, writes de Roover,[3] "was not yet a cost-finding system, but it came very close to being one. The account books give enough indication to permit one to assume that the Medici had a good knowledge of their approximate cost. . . ." It is worth noting that the problem of overheads hardly obtruded itself, for such expenses represented only about 10 percent of total cost.

If we could be certain that the Plantin records were typical, we should have to conclude that the gap between practice and precept in the mid-sixteenth century was even greater than is suggested by the Medici accounts. Yet what Plantin was doing in Antwerp must have been widely practiced in Venice and elsewhere in Italy, for we know that young men from merchant families in the Low Countries were often sent to Italy to learn commercial practices. Plantin's methods would have done credit to a printer of his size three and more centuries later, for he kept separate job accounts for each book printed, he had stock accounts in value and quantity for each kind of paper used, and he kept a plant ledger. His system really was a double-entry cost-finding system of extraordinary maturity.

[1]"Cost Accounting in the 16th Century," *Accounting Review*, 12, 3 (September 1937), pp. 226–237.

[2]"A Florentine Firm of Cloth Manufacturers," *Speculum*, 16, 1 (January 1941), pp. 1–33. We cannot assume that what was done by the Medicis was necessarily widely practiced by other manufacturers of the time.

[3]*Ibid.*, p. 28.

During the next two centuries, little evidence of progress in industrial accounting has come down to us. Yet progress must have been made; for in England, James Dodson,[4] in 1750, worked out a remarkably clear illustration of a shoemaker's accounts.

When Hugh Crispin, Dodson's shoemaker, cut his 20 hides into soles and heels and his 50 skins into upper leathers and quarters, he got numbers of sets of different sizes. To each size he attached a different value, such that the total value of the parts cut exactly equaled the cost of the hides and skins used up. It would be interesting to know how the value for each size was arrived at. On this point, however, which would be of some importance in costing the different sizes of shoe made, he throws no light.

Dodson is dealing with what we would now call "job order costing." An early description of process costing in England was given by Wardhaugh Thompson[5] in 1777. He[6] takes a simplified example of the manufacture of "thread-hosiery" from flax, and shows how the cost of the finished product can be built up in a series of double-entry accounts, kept in quantities and values, process by process. Thus, there is shown a flow of values from the flax stock account through accounts for spinning, bleaching, dyeing, weaving, trimming, finally to emerge as "brown thread hose (dress'd)" at "about 2s. 7d. per pair."

Robert Hamilton devoted a chapter of his *Introduction to Merchandise*[7] to "tradesmen's," i.e., manufacturers' accounts, and made some very sensible suggestions as to the kind of subsidiary books that it would be useful to keep. Thus he recommends the use of "a book of materials, where the quantities purchased and consumed are entered in separate parts or on opposite pages," "a book of work, where the quantities of materials delivered to journeymen, the quantities of wrought goods received in return, the dates of the delivery and return, the value of the materials and wages; and the value of the wrought goods are entered in separate columns," and "a book of wages, which contains the names of the journeymen and other servants employed, the work they are employed at, the number of days, and rate per day, if they be paid by days-wages, or the quantities of work done, and rate, when paid by the piece." He also advised that the ledger should contain separate accounts for different kinds of expense, such as "materials, wages, upholding of machinery, rents, excise, incident charges, etc." And in the closing paragraphs of his chapter,[8] he shows great understanding of one of the central problems of process costing:

> When a person is engaged in several branches of manufacture, whether on different materials, or on the same materials through several successive stages, he should keep his books in such a manner as to exhibit the gain or loss on each.
>
> Take the example of a linen manufacturer who purchases or imports rough flax, dresses it by his own servants, and sells such kinds as do not suit his purpose; delivers the

[4]In *The Accountant, or The Method of Book-keeping, Deduced from Clear Principles and Illustrated by a Variety of Examples,* by James Dodson, Teacher of the Mathematics (London, 1750). Dodson was at one time employed by the Earl of Macclesfield in connection with his estates.

[5]In *The Accountant's Oracle; or Key to Science. Being a Compleat Practical System of Book-keeping. Together with the Nature and Use of Banking Business; and a plain accurate and concise method for manufacturers to keep their Books by Double Entry,* by Wardhaugh Thompson, many years an accountant in London (York, 1777). Extracts from this book are given by Edwards, "Early Literature and Development of Cost Accounting in Great Britain, *The Accountant,* vol. 97 (July–December 1937), pp. 229–231.

[6]Thompson. *The Accountant's Oracle,* vol. 2, pp. 243–253.

[7]Edinburgh, 1788, pp. 486–488. Part IV of the book is on "Italian Book-keeping" and part V is on "Practical Book-keeping." Hamilton was Professor of Philosophy in the Marischal College, Aberdeen.

[8]*Ibid.,* pt. 5, chap. 5, pp. 487–488.

rest to be spun, and receives the yarn from the spinners; weaves part in his own work-house by journeymen, and delivers the rest to other weavers; gives out the linen to be bleached, and receives and sells it when white.

If all these branches of business were necessarily connected, and the manufacturer had no other choice than to purchase the rough flax, and carry on the successive operations, it would be sufficient to keep his books in a form that should exhibit the gain or loss on the whole; but if he has an opportunity of beginning or desisting at any stage of the manufacture, his books should exhibit the gain or loss on each operation separately. He may purchase dressed flax or yarn; he may sell the linen before it be bleached; and, since he chooses to unite the several trades of flax-dresser, spinner, weaver, and bleacher, it is proper he should have a separate view of the success of each. This is the leading principle by which his books should be regulated.

THE EARLY NINETEENTH CENTURY IN ENGLAND

Both Dodson and Thompson record transactions with persons external to the firm, i.e., with outworkers, suppliers, and customers; and Hamilton does not actually give an illustration of a set of manufacturers' accounts. There is no question yet, therefore, of any of these writers showing how to record an internal flow of values from process to process *within* the firm. That was to come, naturally, only with the development of the factory system, in the nineteenth century. Still, there was no justification for the sweeping assertion by F. W. Cronhelm in the preface to his book, *Double Entry by Single,*[9] that "from the pale of the Italian System, Retailers and Manufacturers have ever been excluded." Yet he is probably fairly reflecting the opinion of his day when he says[10] that "it is a common prejudice that, from the very nature of his business, and the numerous processes through which his goods pass, the Manufacturer is unable to keep his Accounts on the same systematic principles as those of the Wholesale Dealer or the Merchant." This certainly suggests that at the beginning of the nineteenth century in England systematic records for manufacturing transactions were by no means in common use. Unfortunately, although Cronhelm[11] claimed that his own "New Method enables [manufacturers] to obtain that PROOF of their Books which has hitherto been deemed impracticable," his achievement falls far short of his promises.

Cronhelm ascertains the profit or loss for the business monthly in a "Merchandise Account," which is really a detailed trading account written up from day to day, being debited with the opening inventory, purchases, and expenses and credited with sales and closing inventory. Except for the frequency of the balancing, there is nothing at all advanced in this. We can certainly agree with Littleton[12] that Cronhelm's illustration of manufacturers' accounts was "deficient."

As the country that led the Industrial Revolution in Europe, England might have been expected to lead the way in industrial accounting during the early nineteenth century. Yet to judge from the surviving literature, this was a period of sterility compared with the stream of advanced thinking that came out of France. One English writer of this period, an eminent mathematician, must, however, claim our attention. This is Charles Babbage, Lucasian Professor of Mathematics in the University of Cambridge from 1828 to 1839. In two famous paragraphs of his book *On the Economy of Machinery and Manufactures,*[13] he puts forward a case for the devotion of time and attention to costing that has hardly been improved since:

[9]London, 1818, p. viii.
[10]*Ibid.,* p. 125.
[11]*Ibid.,* p. viii.
[12]A. C. Littleton, *Accounting Evolution to 1900* (American Institute Publishing Co., Inc., New York, 1933), p. 334.
[13]London, 1832. The quotation that follows is from chap. 21, "On the Cost of Each Separate Process in a Manufacture," p. 203, pars. 253 and 254.

The great competition introduced by machinery, and the application of the principle of the subdivision of labour, render it necessary for each producer to be continually on the watch, to discover improved methods by which the cost of the article he manufactures may be reduced; and, with this view, it is of great importance to know the precise expense of every process, as well as of the wear and tear of machinery which is due to it. The same information is desirable for those by whom the manufactured goods are distributed and sold; because it enables them to give reasonable answers or explanations to the objections of inquirers, and also affords them a better chance of suggesting to the manufacturer changes in the fashion of his goods, which may be suitable either to the tastes or to the finances of his customers. To the statesman such knowledge is still more important; for without it he must trust entirely to others, and can form no judgment worthy of confidence, of the effect any tax may produce, or of the injury the manufacturer or the country may suffer by its imposition.

One of the first advantages which suggests itself as likely to arise from a correct analysis of the expense of the several processes of any manufacture, is the indication which it would furnish of the course in which improvement should be directed. If a method could be contrived of diminishing by one-fourth the time required for fixing on the heads of pins, the expense of making them would be reduced about 13 percent.; whilst a reduction of one-half the time employed in spinning the coil of wire out of which the heads are cut, would scarcely make any sensible difference in the cost of manufacturing of the whole article. It is therefore obvious, that the attention would be much more advantageously directed to shortening the former than the latter process.

Babbage did not give any guidance in his book as to how industrialists were to achieve these admirable objectives, though he[14] did refer later to the necessity, in any but the smallest factory, "to establish an accountant's department, with clerks to pay the workmen, and to see that they arrive at their stated times; and this department must be in communication with the agents who purchase the raw produce, and with those who sell the manufactured article." Whether contemporary accountants were commonly able to provide the cost information that Babbage so clearly saw to be desirable must be open to doubt.

THE FRENCH CONTRIBUTION TO INDUSTRIAL ACCOUNTING

This rather barren period in British accounting coincided, oddly enough, with a period of considerable advance in French thought on industrial, and more especially, agricultural accounting. One has only to compare Cronhelm's work in England with that of Anselme Payen[15] in France, published a year earlier, to see the difference in quality. As illustrations, Payen takes three quite different types of business: a carriage maker, a glue manufacturer, and a producer (apparently) of certain chemical products. The records distinguish among "accounts in money," which we might call the financial accounts; "accounts in kind," which are broadly what we would call cost accounts; and materials accounts, which show the movement of materials in quantities. The accounts in money and the accounts in kind are not formally linked together, though the figures in the two sets of accounts can be easily shown to agree. The costs which are taken account of include the depreciation of utensils and furnaces, rent, and interest. Payen's system, although stopping short of the neat tie-up between cost and financial accounts that was achieved by the end of the nineteenth century, was a considerable step on the way toward it.

[14]*Ibid.*, p. 216, par. 268.
[15]*Essai sur la Tenue des Livres d'un Manufacturier* (Paris, 1817). Payen was himself a manufacturer.

The work of the Frenchman M. Godard,[16] whose treatment of industrial accounting appeared in 1827, is in some respects remarkably modern. Godard was a glass manufacturer who had, he says, been much occupied with accountancy in a long administrative career, and he certainly describes process costing with great skill. He discusses the depreciation and maintenance of buildings and plant, he recognizes the problem of pricing out materials that have been purchased at varying prices—he favors a single average price for the year for each material— and he includes interest on capital among the expenses in his profit-and-loss account. He also describes a system of perpetual inventory. He is writing, unlike the eighteenth-century writers in England, about *factory* accounting.

Louis Mézières,[17] some 30 years later, brings us several steps along the road to modern job costing. His book on *Industrial and Manufacturing Accounts,* which had run five editions by 1862, was written primarily for technical schools, and he claimed to be the first to concern himself with an elementary text on industrial accounting. "The factories," he says, "have long cried out for a book-keeping system more appropriate to the needs of industry," and he addresses himself not only to students but to industrialists.

As a method of accounting for materials, he illustrates a form of stock record showing, on a single page, with one line for each type of material used, the quantity in stock at the beginning of the month, the quantity and value received, the quantity and value issued *to jobs completed during the month,* and a balance in quantity only. Particulars of materials received are obtained from a purchases recapitulation that he illustrates, and materials issued are also summarized to give the figures needed for the stock record. Next, labor, in days of work, is analyzed by means of a monthly summary of workman's time, over the jobs worked on each month. In the cost ledger, each job has its account, in which is recorded the materials and labor used on it. The cost ledger is said to be written up from notes made by the foreman. Whenever he issues material to a workman, he notes the job on which it is to be used and also how workmen's time is to be charged. The foreman's notes are made from day to day and are summarized before entry in the cost ledger, because in each job account there is only one entry for each type of material and one entry for each workman engaged on the job. The costs recorded against the job are added to the profit on it to give the selling price. Finally Mézières has a "Work Executed" book, which shows in chronological order, on the left-hand page, particulars of completed work and the selling price charged or to be charged. Articles sold during the month are extended into the money column, the total of which must agree with that of the sales column of the (analyzed) journal: the item is shown as sold by having the journal folio entered against it. Articles made for stock and unsold at the end of the month are extended into one of the columns on the right-hand page—there is one column for each month of the year—which thus shows for each month the total finished stock on hand, at selling price.

Mézières' system has certain serious shortcomings. He has no record of work in progress, and he admits that his raw material stock balances include materials in process. He appears not to recognize the existence of overhead expenses, for no mention is made of them. Moreover, by using constant purchase prices through-

---

[16]*Traité Général et Sommaire de la Comptabilité Commerciale* (Paris, 1827). Section III is devoted to manufacturers' accounts. Edwards gives extracts in his *Survey of French Contributions to the Study of Cost Accounting during the 19th Century* (Accounting Research Association, London, 1937), pp. 9–17.

[17]*Comptabilité Industrielle et Manufacturiére,* 5th ed. (Paris, 1862). I have not been able to ascertain when the book first appeared. Mézières was the accountant of and also taught accounting at the Technical College at Châlons.

out his illustrations, he evades entirely the problem of valuing issues of material bought at fluctuating prices. Yet for all this, he shows a clear grasp of the kind of records that a job cost system demands. He adds nothing to the theory of costing, but he displays considerable facility in its practice.

Payen, Godard, and Mézières are only three of several French writers who, during the first 60 years or so of the nineteenth century, carried forward the study of industrial accounting at a time when, as the premier industrial country of the time, England might have been expected to lead the way. England did, as a matter of fact, take over the lead again for a short time toward the end of the century, but by that time America was beginning to lay claim to the preeminent position both in industry and in industrial accounting that it has since attained.

FARM ACCOUNTING IN THE EIGHTEENTH AND NINETEENTH CENTURIES

One of the earliest and most delightful works in English to deal with farm accounts was *The Gentleman Accomptant: or an Essay to Unfold the Mystery of Accompts* by "a Person of Honour."[18] The author directs his reader to open separate accounts for husbandry and for pasture, as well as for a separate farm that is supposed to be under the management of a bailiff. He further shows how, "if a Gentleman will condescend to traffick with Butchers, etc.," it is easy to subdivide the accounts still further, and he opens a separate account for a flock of sheep. Each activity is debited with the opening value of live or dead stock, is charged with its expenses, credited with sales or the value of produce taken by the household, and also with the closing value of the stock. The balance is transferred to Profit and Loss Account. In his account for personal chattels, he writes off £100 "by Profit and Loss, failure of values." In the accounts for husbandry, sheep, etc., however, opening and closing stocks are maintained at constant amounts, so that no question of depreciation arises.

Thought on farm accounting in France seems to have made substantial progress, as the work of de Cazaux, Godard, and a host of later writers testifies. De Cazaux's book[19] was first published in 1824, and an expanded version of it appeared in 1825 as Book III of his *Eléments d'Economie Privée et Publique*. It shows a remarkable mastery of the principles of agricultural accounting. Although in its original form it is quite short, it would take too long to summarize all the interesting things it contains; some of them, however, must be mentioned. De Cazaux sees the desirability of distinguishing profits on cultivation from speculative profits from holding produce after it has been raised. Long-maturing investments, like vineyards and woods, are to be charged with 5 percent per annum compound interest while maturing, and credited with the value of the produce obtained, so that it can easily be seen whether the annual return on the investment is more or less than 5 percent. Depreciation of equipment, buildings, and improvements is taken account of by writing off the cost over the expected lives of the assets (at different rates even for different parts of the same asset, according to the durability of the part), with an adjustment if it should be found that the actual asset life differs from expectations. The depreciation is charged proportionately to each of the activities that the assets serve.

As for the records, de Cazaux recommends that an account be opened for each

---

[18]London, 1714. The author has since been identified as the Hon. Roger North, youngest son of the fourth Lord North and author of *Lives of the Norths*. See David Murray, *Chapters in the History of Book-keeping* (Jackson, Wylie & Co., Glasgow, 1930), p. 261.

[19]L. F. G. de Cazaux, *De la Comptabilité dans une Entreprise Industrielle et specialement dans une Exploitation Rurale* (Toulouse, 1824).

field, each crop, each herd or flock, and each fixed asset. Each field account is opened with a debit for its capital value at the beginning of the year, this being put at 20 times its rental value (i.e., the capitalization rate is put at 5 percent). It is then debited with the costs of cultivation, including a due proportion of any general costs such as depreciation of equipment. The value of its crop is credited to the field and debited to the crop account, which is in turn credited with its realized price when sold, or its value when used as forage for animals. The animals are charged with the value of forage fed to them. And so on. But this does not exhaust de Cazaux's subtlety; for crops that increase the fertility of the soil are to be further credited with the value of a quantity of manure equal to two-thirds of the weight of dry fodder produced when they are cropped, and this value increment is to be debited to the field account. The converse treatment is given to crops that use up fertility. Finally, all accounts are credited with the closing inventory valuation, so as to show final profits or losses.

Perhaps enough has been said to suggest how mature de Cazaux's work was. But he was not content with accounting after the event and, in the 1825 edition of his book, he goes on to consider budgeting. I shall return to this aspect of his work later.

ENGLISH COSTING IN THE MID-NINETEENTH CENTURY

It is interesting to compare the standard of the French works with what was available in England in the middle of the century. For farmers, there appeared in 1851 *An Improved System of Farm-Book-Keeping.*[20] The author[21] saw that it was not enough to ascertain the total profit or loss on the farm for the year, for "no comparative judgment can be found of the value of different modes of culture, or different kinds of stock, without keeping a separate account of each, in order to see how the profit or loss arises, and to enable the farmer to determine on the propriety of continuing or abandoning the one or the other." To this end accounts are opened in the ledger and posted from the cash account. Much of the book is devoted to specimen rulings for the various accounts, which make the ledger more a record of operations than a mere book of account. The explanations of the accounting aspects of the system, however, are defective, whatever its agricultural virtues may have been, and there is none of the subtlety that marks the French works on the subject.

Little seems to have been published in England in this period that could be dignified by the name of industrial accounting. It may well be that English practice at this time had once more run ahead of theory. We need first-hand studies of the industrial accounts of the period to enable us to judge what practical people were doing and to compare it with the impression of feebleness that is conveyed by contemporary accounting literature. Certainly all the signs point to a lack of interest among industrialists in the application of accounting to industrial pro-cesses—at least in England. Before long, the pressure of events was to bring about a change.

THE COSTING RENAISSANCE

The last three decades of the nineteenth century were marked by a costing renaissance in the English-speaking world. In the 1880s and 1890s a growing number of writers on costing explained "new" ideas. Yet to a great extent they

---

[20]By "The Author of 'British Husbandry'" (Longmans, London, 1851).
[21]*Ibid.,* p. 4.

were only rediscovering ideas that were becoming of great practical importance for the first time but that could certainly have been found, though perhaps in an undeveloped state, in earlier works.

The impact of the new writing on industrialists was, however, not dramatic. There is plenty of evidence that even at the turn of the century anything that could be called a costing system was still to be found only exceptionally both in British and American industry. The typical situation was for a manufacturer to compute product costs on some rough-and-ready basis, whereas distribution costs were largely ignored altogether. Alexander Hamilton Church[22] wrote in 1900:

> the majority of firms of any size have some sort of cost method, however rough and home-made, which enables them to tell how much labour and what value of material have been expended on any particular job. Between this elementary stage and the next there is a very wide gap which is bridged over by comparatively few firms even in the go-ahead United States.

And a year later he wrote:[23]

> No board would think of carrying on operations without a set of commercial books arranged by an accountant in whom they had confidence, yet the equally important technical records are nearly always treated in an amateur spirit. . . . So far is this attitude carried that many otherwise experienced business men really and conscientiously do not believe that shop accounts are of any use at all.

E. J. Smith, a pioneer of uniform costing in Great Britain, wrote in 1899, after referring to a number of industries of which he had had experience:[24] "Speaking for these and of these, I have no hesitation in saying that one evil in each and all which has most impressed me is the marvellous absence of really useful and practical knowledge as to the cost of the article produced."

Reasons for the Growing Interest in Costing.   It is from this time, however, that we can begin to detect a growing interest among practical business people in the industrial uses of accounting. Doubtless the increasing scale and complexity of business and the administrative problems that resulted had much to do with this. In the iron industry, for example, the size of business and the degree of integration had ceased to be limited by the availability of water power. The coal mining industry had developed similarly; the sinking of deep shafts, construction of galleries, ventilation and pumping equipment, and transport all called for large capital investment. The textile industries had been transformed by the introduction of power machinery. Thus the importance of buildings, plant, equipment, and supervision, i.e., of overhead costs, had rapidly increased in relation to the prime costs of materials and labor. Larger bodies of labor had to be paid and controlled, complex processes to be organized and administered. Moreover, the development of railways, with their enormous volume of fixed equipment, had brought the problem of overhead to the fore. These factors doubtless played a part in the development of cost accounting. And their effect was reinforced around the end of the century by the steady absorption of small businesses by large ones, giving rise to a demand for means of controlling operations by managers and directors divorced from their actual execution.

Perhaps the most important factor, however, leading to a growth of interest in costing was the increasing difficulty of setting prices in the engineering industry. As the industry grew and as it became more competitive, so the interest in cost

---

[22]"The Meaning of Commercial Organisation," *Engineering Magazine*, 20, 3 (December 1900), p. 394.

[23]"The Proper Distribution of Establishment Charges," *Engineering Magazine*, July 1901, pp. 510–511.

[24]*The New Trades Combination Movement*, p. 21.

accounting developed. This interest is marked by references to the subject in the trade and professional journals in the second half of the century. For example, in 1869 a leading article in *The Engineer* pointed out that an "estimate right within 20 percent of the actual cost is . . . regarded as a very good estimate, and one reflecting much credit on the engineer and all concerned." And the same article goes on to say that[25] "it is not to negligence, however, that we are inclined to ascribe the thoroughly unsatisfactory state in which the practice of estimating now is, but rather to incapacity. There is no good treatise on the subject. . . ." A year later, a correspondent in the same journal[26] wanted to know of a "good system of getting out cost price," and subsequent correspondence showed a very real and practical interest in the subject. An editorial on "Practical Prime Costs" in *Engineering* in 1891 remarked:

> The present-day conditions of the engineering and manufacturing trades, as regards keenness of competition and consequent narrowness of profit, render this subject of an increased importance.

Up to 20 years ago, it said,[27] conditions had been different.

> Selling prices could generally be fixed at figures leaving good margins, and a "rough and ready" cost of a certain article or piece of work, upon which could generally be fixed a fancy profit, with a liberal contingency allowance, was as a rule found all that was required. . . . It is during the past 15 or 20 years that prime costing has been developed to the elaborate systems in operation in many of our large and well-managed firms.

Here, then, was a practical reason, a reason that would appeal to business people, for the quickening interest in cost accounting. Writing in 1904, John Mann went so far as to say that:[28]

> Records of costing doubtless originated in the need of data required in estimating, especially in engineering and kindred trades where the work is specially contracted for, and where there is no scale of market prices.

Although it would be going too far to say that costing originated in this way, it was the growing recognition that careful records of past experience might improve price estimating in this type of industry that persuaded business people that it was worth spending money on.

During the period 1875–1900 the typical costing system (where such a thing existed at all) in the engineering industry relied on the foreman for details of time spent by workers on each job and also often for details of materials used. A check on total wages was kept by the use of a time book kept at the works gate by a timekeeper to record employees' arrival and departure times; or sometimes this was done by giving each worker a disk with the works number, the disk being taken from a board and put in a box by the worker on arrival and departure. A latecomer would find only a "late box" in which to put the disk. By changing the box at 15- or 30-minute intervals the approximate time of arrival by latecomers could be ascertained and recorded. Overhead would be added to the prime costs of each job usually by adding a flat percentage to labor cost or to prime cost. This percentage would be ascertained from the previous year's financial accounts by expressing the total overhead costs for the year as a percentage of the year's total direct wages or the total prime costs.

The total of these three amounts—direct wages, direct materials costs, and overhead—gave a figure that was accepted as the "actual" cost of the job. But it was

[25] *The Engineer,* London, September 3, 1869, p. 166.
[26] *The Engineer,* November 25, 1870, p. 363.
[27] *Engineering,* London, December 4, 1891, pp. 665–666.
[28] *Encyclopaedia of Accounting,* vol. 2, p. 260, on "Cost Records or Factory Accounting."

not long before the concept of "actual" cost became clouded by doubts. There were differences of opinion as to whether items such as interest on capital, plant obsolescence, and development expenditure ought to be included in costs? Again, how should materials bought at different prices be charged into costs? Should overtime pay be averaged over all jobs or charged only to those done during overtime hours? How should overhead be allocated, and, especially, how should the burden of unused plant capacity be dealt with? These and other difficulties obscured the apparently clearcut nature of "actual" costs. They certainly made their value somewhat doubtful, whether for purposes of setting prices or for controlling efficiency. It was, however, only slowly that this came to be generally realized.

In escaping from some at least of the limitations of crudely ascertained "actual costs" there can be distinguished three main lines of advance:

1. Refinements in the apportionment of overhead were introduced, in an endeavor to make the cost records more accurately reflect the facts of the situation.

2. Methods were devised to isolate the effect on costs of changes in the scale of output, so that the effect of changes in other factors could be detected, while at the same time breaking the vicious circle of contracting demand and increasing unit costs.

3. Finally, a technique was developed to separate and quantify the effect of *all* significant changes in the factors that determine costs.

Any further major advance along the first of these lines seems unlikely, but the movement away from "actual cost" to "standard cost," which is what the second and third of the above developments amount to, is still going on. It may be useful, therefore, to consider the way in which these developments have come about.

Methods of Attaching Overhead Cost to Prime Cost.   The treatment of overhead costs was, in the 1880s, still often incredibly crude. Henry Roland,[29] writing in 1898, describes the method of estimating used by a drop-forging firm. The firm used the "Beecher rule," devised by one of the early American drop-forgers, Beecher of Meriden, Connecticut. This rule was to take the cost of materials plus the flat labor cost and double the total of these two items for other costs. The firm claimed that for average work the rule gave "a wonderfully close approximation to accuracy," although as it had no clearly formulated system of record keeping, it is difficult to see how anyone could know what "accuracy" was.

A considerable variety of estimating methods was listed by Thomas Battersby,[30] a Manchester public accountant, who published a small book on the subject in 1878. They included such methods as:

1. Charging actual materials and wages, 100 percent on wages to cover overhead, and 25 percent on the total for profit.

2. Charging a flat daily rate for the use of each machine or tool; to the sum of this charge and the actual wages is added a percentage for indirect costs and profit; materials are included at cost plus the same percentage addition.

3. Charging a percentage of wages for the use of tools and to cover all costs.

4. Machines and tools are rated according to their purchase price, power costs, and operative's wages, and to this charge plus actual wages and materials a percentage addition is made for other indirect costs. (But these tool rates, said Battersby, were not based on actual costs, being to a great extent "assumed.")

5. Machines and tools are rated according to their purchase price only. This

[29]"An Effective System of Finding and Keeping Shop Costs," *Engineering Magazine*, 15 (May 1898), p. 241.

[30]*The Perfect Double Entry Book-keeper (abridged) and the Perfect Prime Cost and Profit Demonstrator (on the Departmental System), for Iron and Brass Founders, Machinists, Engineers, Shipbuilders, Manufacturers, etc.* (Manchester, 1878).

gives a selling price for the work done, although some deduction might be made to secure a particular order.

6. A percentage is added to prime cost (i.e., materials and wages) for overhead, and a further percentage is added to the total for profit.

7. A single percentage is added to prime cost to cover overheads and profit. "The *amount* of percentage varies very considerably in different establishments, according to the opinions of the principals."

This last method, said Battersby,[31] was "the general method in use." That it was still a standard practice 20 years after Battersby's book appeared is certainly implied by Roland[32] in 1898. On the other hand, Hamilton Church[33] in 1901 refers to the "percentage on wages" method as the most usual one, "at any rate in Great Britain," and so does John Mann.[34]

The "percentage on prime cost" method regarded all jobs with equal prime costs as being responsible for an equal amount of overhead. This, of course, was open to criticism on the ground that the cost of materials used on a job (an important part of its prime cost) might be no indication at all of the load that the job imposed on supervision, equipment, and factory space.

This was not the only criticism leveled against this basis of allocating overhead, but it was the one peculiar to it. In an attempt to meet it, allocation of overhead on the basis of direct labor cost was often practiced. It was argued that labor cost would reflect the time spent by a job in the works and that this in turn reflected the call it made on production facilities. But this method also attracted criticism. Products using a relatively high proportion of low-paid labor would, even though they occupied as much time in the factory as products using more highly paid labor, be allocated less overhead because the rate per hour paid to the labor was lower. In fact, so the argument ran, such low-paid labor might be the cause of proportionately more rather than proportionately less overhead. For example, it might need more supervision, it might waste more material and damage more equipment than high-grade and more expensive labor.

In an attempt to defend the use of wages as a basis for allocating production overhead, and to counter the criticism that this was inequitable to work done by expensive skilled labor, the refinement of departmental overhead rates was introduced.[35] This only met the criticism to the extent that the labor employed in each department was more or less homogeneous. But so long as this was broadly true, much of the sting was taken out of this particular criticism.

In so far as the labor *within* a department was of varying degrees of skill (and consequently of cost), even the use of a different overhead rate (i.e., overhead expressed as a percentage of total direct labor) for each department was still apt to charge a disproportionate amount of overhead to certain jobs. The adoption of labor *time* instead of labor cost as the basis for charging overheads was intended to circumvent this difficulty. By relating a department's overhead to the total direct labor hours worked in it, a departmental overhead rate per labor hour was calculated. This would bear with equal weight on any two jobs that occupied a department for the same time, even though one job demanded expensive skilled labor and the other did not.

---

[31] *Ibid.,* p. 34.

[32] "Cost Keeping Methods in Machine-shop and Foundry," *Engineering Magazine,* 14 (January 1898), pp. 626–627.

[33] "The Proper Distribution of Establishment Charges," *Engineering Magazine,* July 1901, p. 725.

[34] *Encyclopaedia of Accounting,* vol. 5, p. 208.

[35] Departmental rates were certainly in use as early as 1870. See, e.g., *The Engineer,* December 23, 1870, p. 428.

The direct-labor-hour basis for charging overheads got round one difficulty only to draw attention to another. It made no allowance for differences in the kind of equipment that different jobs employed. One hour of an operative's time on a light, inexpensive machine would attract the same charge for overhead as an hour on a costly piece of equipment. Although the direct-labor-hour rate might serve well enough for purely manual operations, for mechanized operations it clearly left much to be desired.

Early Attempts at a Machine-Hour Rate.   It was quite obvious to a number of writers by the last decade of the century that no single basis of overhead allocation could be satisfactory. In 1891, for instance, Sir John Mann[36] was arguing for a division of overhead cost into (a) buying costs which vary with the cost of goods bought, (b) selling costs which vary with the sales, and (c) production costs. So far as the last were concerned, he dismissed quantity or value of material as a suitable basis of allocation and pointed out the danger of using wages as a basis when some workers are paid more than others. He emphasized time as the significant factor and put forward some proposals for machine-hour rates.

The use of machine-hour rates had been noted years earlier by Battersby in his list of estimating methods, but only as a means of allocating those expenses which were directly associated with the machine, such as depreciation, machine maintenance, and power. His main criticism of the practice of his day had been that the engineering firms concerned had inadequate data on which to calculate the rates. They were based on opinion and assumption rather than facts. He therefore had elaborated a procedure for working out rates to be charged for work done in each separate production department. They included rates per ton of casting in the iron foundry, a rate per indicated horsepower per year for allocating the cost of the steam power department, and rates per day to be charged for the different machine tools. In the last case the total cost of machine upkeep was divided among individual machines on the basis of capital value, and power cost was allocated on the basis of horsepower. The addition of wages gave the "prime cost rate per day to be charged upon work."

ALEXANDER HAMILTON CHURCH AND THE IDEA OF PRODUCTION CENTERS

In the last decade of the century, other advocates of machine-hour rates were to be heard. But they were overshadowed by one, of whom a former President of the Institute of Cost and Works Accountants[37] has said that he "probably did more than anyone, both directly and indirectly, to promote costing as it is now known, chiefly because he promoted thought." This was Alexander Hamilton Church,[38] whose six articles[39] in the *Engineering Magazine* on "The Proper Distribution of Establishment Charges" in 1901 "at once took rank as a standard reference work on one of the most difficult questions of cost-finding."[40]

His analysis starts with a clear division of overhead between what he calls shop charges and general establishment charges. He relates the different categories of costs and profits in this way:

[36]*The Accountant,* August 29 and September 5, 1891.

[37]Roland Dunkerley, in a paper entitled "A Historical Review of the Institute and the Profession," read to the eighteenth National Cost Conference of the I.C.W.A. on May 10, 1946.

[38]Church was an English electrical engineer. At one time he had worked for the National Telephone Company in Britain. He settled in the United States around the turn of the century.

[39]Vol. 21 (July–September 1901), pp. 508–517, 725–734, 904–912, and vol. 22 (October–December 1901), pp. 31–40, 231–240, and 367–376.

[40]From the Editor's preface to the articles, reprinted in book form in 1916.

Material
Wages   } Prime Cost   } Works Cost
Shop Charges

General Establishment
   Charges   } Inclusive Cost   } Selling Price

Profit

Church precedes his own contribution to the problem of allocating overheads by a searching criticism of the methods most common in his own day. Very little of importance has been added to his criticism by subsequent discussion. The "percentage on wages" method he declared[41] to be "not alarmingly incorrect" if "machines are all of a size and kind performing practically identical operations by means of a fairly average wages rate." But in general it was[42] "really quite arbitrary and without any real relation to the actual problem." He turns next to the "Hourly Burden Plan," by which shop costs are allocated to jobs in proportion to the labor time spent on them. This method has two virtues that the first lacks. It shows up the cost of cheap labor prolonging and bungling a job; and it brings into full prominence the essential fact that to have work hanging about is costly. But it is too simple. It does not discriminate between jobs using large and costly machines and those using cheap and light machines. It works well enough where all the machines used and all the jobs done are fairly uniform. In similar circumstances, the "percentage on wages" method also works well enough. In such simple conditions almost any method will serve. What is wrong with both the "labor-cost" and the "labor-time" bases is that they produce an averaged result, for which there is as little justification in all but exceptional circumstances as there would be for using average instead of actual wage rates to give the labor cost of a particular operation.

He turns to the machine-hour rate of earlier days only to dismiss it as hopelessly crude. But it does have one advantage over other methods: it does take into account the variation in the cost of work done on different types of machine. It is this idea that Church takes and develops. "What does the expression 'shop' really signify?" he asks. We get no nearer to disentangling costs so long as we look at the shop as an organic whole. But if we regard it as a collection of "little shops" or production centers, the problem suddenly becomes clear. Each "little shop," consisting of a machine, or a bench at which a handcraftsman works, must be charged with its own depreciation, rent, and other running expenses. The cost of each production center is then loaded on to the work passing through it, at an hourly rate, which he calls the "scientific machine rate." There will still be certain general shop overhead, such as supervision, which cannot be charged other than by an average rate applicable to all work in the shop. But to a great extent costs that were formerly averaged over all jobs will now be made to bear on different jobs with differing weight as the facts demand.

The Problem of Idle Capacity and the Supplementary Rate. The development of the idea of the "production center" made possible the refinement of the machine-hour rate into something very like its modern form. But Church did not stop there. He was much concerned with the problem of idle capacity. He saw clearly the absurdity of showing the cost of a particular operation as varying greatly in successive months simply because the shop was fully employed one month and only half-employed the next, the monthly level of overhead remaining steady. The remedy he proposed for this situation was the *supplementary rate*. All shop costs for the month, both those allocable to specific production centers and those of a

[41]Church, "The Proper Distribution of Establishment Charges," p. 726.
[42]*Ibid.*, p. 727.

general nature, such as supervision, were in the first instance to be charged to a shop charges account. "Scientific" machine-hour rates would be calculated for each production center on the basis that each would operate full time throughout the month. Actual work passing through each center would be charged at the "scientific" hourly rate, these charges going to the credit of the shop charges account. If at the end of the month all the centers proved to have been fully occupied throughout the period, there would be left to the debit of the account a sum representing the *general* shop overhead (i.e., those not allocated to production centers). If all the production centers had *not* been fully occupied, the debit left on the shop charges account would be swollen by the proportion of the allocable costs not taken up by the "scientific" machine-hour rates. It was this debit balance that was disposed of by means of the supplementary rate. The charges made to jobs by the application of the "scientific" rates had now to be supplemented by further charges, which bore the same proportion to the normal charges as the total unabsorbed costs bore to the total already absorbed.

It is easy to criticize Church's "supplementary rate." In the first place, the net effect on job costs was to bring them back to the "actual costs" that they would have shown had the "scientific" machine rate and the supplementary rate not been kept separate in the first place. Second, the fact that the supplementary rate was made up not only of unabsorbed machine costs but also of the unallocable general shop costs made nonsense of Church's claims that the supplementary rate was a barometer of shop efficiency: for a rise in the general costs would raise the supplementary rate even if all machines were being fully utilized. Even a rise in allocable machine costs caused by a sharp rise in the price level would raise the supplementary rate irrespective of the degree of capacity usage. And, finally, Church's use of the word "efficiency" is highly confusing. If the production centers of his system were run for the maximum number of hours, the supplementary rate would fall to a minimum. This for him was the sign of "efficiency." But, of course, the volume of production *per machine hour* might fall away very seriously without the slightest effect on the supplementary rate. He seems to regard the full use of plant capacity as synonymous with full efficiency. The distinction in the records between the two, which, at least, is attempted by modern standard costing, belongs to a later period.

It is hardly surprising that, after gaining some support, Church's supplementary rate faded out. But it was not on that account a wholly abortive innovation; for it drew attention to the distinction between "normal" costs and abnormal losses. In his book, published almost 30 years later, he writes[43] about his original proposals that "no element of the new method was more criticized than the 'supplementary rate.' It was (somewhat to the author's surprise) generally recognized that it was no part of true cost and that, therefore, wasted capacity should be charged off to profit and loss." Church's original solution of this problem was clearly not the right one; but it stimulated others to do better. One such other was John Whitmore, to whom further reference will be made below. He is of particular interest to us in connection with the development of standard costing, but another aspect of his work is relevant here. Church's "scientific" machine-hour rate was worked out on the basis that machines were worked at their maximum capacity. Whitmore saw that this went too far and excluded too much from what he called "proper costs." He saw the danger of "assuming an impossibly perfect standard of working." This

[43]*Overhead Expense* (McGraw-Hill Book Company, New York, 1930), p. 384. For an example of this kind of criticism, see John Whitmore, "Factory Accountancy as Applied to Machine Shops," *Journal of Accountancy,* August 1906–January 1907, especially at pp. 254–258 (August 1906). These articles were reprinted in *The Accountant,* vol. 35 (1906), pp. 605–610, 646–651, 675–680, 746–751, and vol. 36 (1907), pp. 160–163 and 220–223.

is well on the way to substituting normal machine usage for maximum usage as a basis for spreading overheads.

Other Methods of Dealing with Overhead.   Before leaving the problem of how overhead ought to be apportioned among products in a multiproduct firm, we should note that the machine-hour rate was not left unchallenged as the best method of apportioning works expenses in all circumstances. In 1907 we find a writer[44] on the motor industry advocating the use of not one method but a combination of methods. The shops in a motor works are to be divided into two groups, the machine departments (foundries, plating, lacquering, etc.), each department being again subdivided into production centers. Overhead in the production centers of the machine departments is apportioned by a machine-hour rate, which in the special departments is dealt with by rates per labor hour, percent on labor costs, per-pound weight of output, and so on, according to the nature of the operation carried on in each production center. These suggestions are only a refinement of proposals made by Battersby and others many years earlier.

A still more elegant combination of methods was proposed by Dr. William Kent[45] in 1916. Recognizing that no one basis could conceivably be right for apportioning all the costs incurred in a works, he suggested that overhead could be classified as one of four types, according as the incidence was related to:

1. Labor hours
2. Machine hours
3. The job
4. Materials used

As an example of the way in which costs might be allocated to each of these categories, he suggested the classification shown in Exhibit 1. The rate per labor hour would be the same for each job; the machine-hour rate would be calculated separately for each class of machine—in effect, there would be a separate rate for each production center; the job rate would be a flat charge per job; whereas the materials rate would be differentiated for different classes of materials, and loaded directly on to the cost of the materials.

EXHIBIT 1   Kent's Basis for Overhead Allocation

	Expenses apportioned on the basis of		
Labor hours	Machine hours	Jobs	Materials
Shop supervision	Tool makers	Cost clerks	Storekeeper
Bookkeeper's wages	Oil, waste, and other supplies	Planners	Stationery, postage Truckmen, cranemen
Blacksmith's wages	Supervisors		Interest and deprecia-
Millwright's wages	Interest and		tion on stores
Laborer's wages	depreciation on equipment Power		

Adapted from Dr. William Kent, "New Methods of Determining Factory Costs," *Iron Age,* 98 (August 24, 1916), pp. 392–394.

With this development we can say that the process of attaching overhead costs to units of product had been brought more or less to completion. From the application of a simple percentage to prime costs we have seen the treatment of overhead costs become more and more complex, first by the replacement of the simple idea of a homogeneous works by the more realistic concept of a group of production

[44]D. C. Eggleston, "Motor Manufacturing Costs," *Business Man's Magazine,* October 1907.
[45]"New Methods of Determining Factory Costs," *Iron Age,* 98 (August 24, 1916), pp. 392–394.

centers; then by a distinction first between works overhead and general overhead; and later between different classes of works overhead. Again, from the more or less accidental short-period relationship of actual overhead and actual output, we have seen emerge the calculation of overhead rates first on maximum output and then on normal output. The idea of "normal" cost replaces that of "actual" cost. We shall see later on how that idea in turn is replaced by the concept of a "standard" cost.

Critics of Overhead Allocation. First let us pick up another thread that can be detected running through the discussions and disputations over the treatment of overhead costs. The writers we have considered so far differed about how over-head should be attached to units of product. They entertained few doubts as to the desirability of making such an attachment somehow. For if selling prices were to be based on costs, and if the revenue from sales was to be sufficient to cover both prime costs and overhead, what was more natural than that goods should be sold only at prices that showed some margin over and above the cost accountant's computation of average cost, i.e., prime cost plus allotted overheads? It was the very necessity of fixed selling prices that caused such importance to be attached to the choice of the "correct" method of spreading overheads. Cost accountants have, on the whole, continued to attach importance to it for the same reason right down to our own day. Nevertheless, there have always been critics to attack the conventional treatment of overhead. Several different grounds for criticism can be distinguished.

First, there have been those who have argued that overhead cost allocation was not necessary for price-setting purposes, and that so long as each product made *some* contribution to overhead and profit, while all products together covered the total overhead and desired profit, it was neither possible nor necessary to say how much over and above prime costs each product should earn. On this view, of course, prices are regarded as determined by market conditions; entrepreneurs can only respond to prices; they cannot dictate them. This view was supported by Harrington Emerson[46] in an article on foundry costs in 1904. After discussing the application of a uniform percentage of overhead to prime cost for different kinds of foundry work, which in the case he is discussing works out at 82 percent., he goes on:[47]

> Selling prices are, however, not made at the whim of the foundry owner, but by competition. It may, therefore, happen that 82 per cent will carry certain classes of work above competition prices, and carry other classes unnecessarily below competition prices. The foundry owner may therefore . . . assign a different percentage to each (class) provided the totals of all classes, with percentages added, equal his bookkeeper's totals. . . . *The overcharges are distributed, not by some fancy accounting method, but according to the exigencies of competition.*

The second group of critics of overhead allocation have been those who dismissed it as arbitrary and therefore useless. We may represent the views of this group by quoting from a paper by W. R. Hamilton,[48] writing in 1910:

[46]"Percentage Methods of Determining Production Costs," *The Foundry,* October 1904, pp. 80–81.

[47]*Ibid.,* p. 31. Italics added.

[48]"Some Economic Considerations Bearing on Costing," *The Accountant,* February 5, 1910. The words of an earlier Hamilton might also be aptly quoted at this point: "When we import a cargo of different kinds of goods which could not well be separated, such as iron and deals, of which the one is necessary for ballast, and the other to complete the lading, it is proper to join them in one accompt, and complete the profit or loss on the whole together. . . . Perhaps there might be gain on the one and loss on the other; but as we were obliged to import both together, it is the success of the whole that we should inquire into." Robert Hamilton, *Introduction to Merchandise* (1788), p. 408.

It is easy to carry this division [of overheads between departments] to a point at which it ceases to correspond to any useful fact. What, for instance, is the use of splitting up a manager's salary between departments? If a department be shut up, can a portion of the manager be dispensed with? If such divisions have any value it is a relative one only, as between one year and another. They have no absolute value for they do not answer to facts which confirm past action, or give rise to new—the only facts worth having in business.

That Hamilton is referring here to the allocation of overhead between departments rather than between units of product does not, of course, diminish the force of his criticism.

Both the views which have just been quoted tended to be rather negative. Those who held them were right to point out the shortcomings of overhead allocation. But they did little to put anything in its place. There was, however, a third line of thought, more constructive in nature, which it is interesting to watch developing into what we now know as "marginal costing."

VARIATION OF COST WITH OUTPUT

The way in which the cost of producing an article would vary with the amount of it that was produced engaged the attention of a number of economists in the nineteenth century and even earlier, but they were usually more concerned with the output of an industry than of a firm. The notion of "diminishing returns" in agriculture was first stated by Turgot[49] in France as early as 1768, and was taken up by Malthus in England in 1814. It was in the sphere of railway economics, young as the transportation industry was in 1850, when an Irishman, Dionysius Lardner, wrote about it, that the nature of the problem which faced the individual producer was most clearly seen. In his *Railway Economy,* Lardner[50] clearly perceived that in fixing railway tariffs it was necessary to have regard to the way in which costs reacted to changes in traffic, for an alteration in railway rates would result in a change in the amount of traffic carried and in the total receipts. Only by comparing the change in receipts with the change in total costs could the effect on profits of any tariff change be judged.[51] To do this it was necessary to distinguish between fixed and variable costs, which he does in the following passage:[52]

> ... the cost of production of the objects of industry, at present, may always be regarded as consisting of two parts, one of which is quite independent of the number of articles produced, and being, therefore, equally divided among them, will render one element of their price precisely in the inverse ratio of their number; but still there will be another component which, depending on the direct application of manual or other labour, and on the immediate consumption of raw materials, will be in the direct ratio of the number of articles produced.

Far from opposing the practice of allocating overhead, Lardner worked out a most elaborate system of allocation, classifying railway overhead into a number of categories according to the way they behaved when the volume of traffic changed. But in emphasizing what we should now call the "marginal approach," as in other matters, Lardner was in advance of his time. His views have become the commonplace of twentieth century economics; and they are still well ahead of much that is written about cost accounting.

Alfred Marshall[53] gave prominence to the distinction between what he called

[49]In his *Observations on the Effects of the Corn Laws.*
[50]Born in Dublin 1793, died 1859. He was for some years Professor of Mathematics in University College, London.
[51]*Railway Economy,* pp. 249–253.
[52]*Ibid.,* p. 216.
[53]*Principles of Economics,* pp. 359–362, 394–402.

"prime" and "supplementary" costs in developing his theory of business behavior in 1890. He obviously learned something from *Factory Accounts,* by Garcke and Fells, first published in 1887, for he refers to it in approving footnotes in both his *Principles*[54] and in *Industry and Trade.*[55] *Factory Accounts* was by far the best-known English work on costing to be published during the last quarter of the nineteenth century, the period I have described as the costing renaissance, and it reached seven editions by 1922. Its main interest lies in the fact that it integrated the cost accounts into the double-entry system, and it really does represent, as its authors claimed,[56] "the first attempt to place before English readers a systematized statement of the principles regulating Factory Accounts." It has, however, this further subsidiary interest for us, that its authors clearly assert the futility of allocating "fixed" overheads, and must be counted among the founders of the "marginal cost" school of thought. The passage which follows sets forth their view on this point with admirable clarity:[57]

> The establishment expense [salaries of clerks, office rent, stationery] and interest on capital should not, however, in any case form part of the cost of production. There is no advantage in distributing these items over the various transactions or articles produced. They do not vary proportionately with the volume of business. A large increase in the value of orders received would not necessitate a like augmentation of the office staff, nor would a sudden and serious falling off in trade enable a firm to effect an immediate or proportionate reduction of general expenditure. The establishment charges are, in the aggregate, more or less constant, while the manufacturing costs fluctuate with the cost of labour and the price of material. To distribute the charges over the articles manufactured would, therefore, have the effect of disproportionately reducing the cost of production with every increase, and the reverse with every diminution of business. Such a result is greatly to be deprecated, as tending neither to economy of management nor to accuracy in estimating for contracts. *The principals of a business can always judge what percentage of gross profits upon cost is necessary to cover fixed establishment charges and interest on capital.*

There is a good deal of oversimplification in this passage. The distinction between fixed and variable costs (itself an oversimplification) is identified with that between establishment expenses and manufacturing costs. In fact, of course, factory rent is hardly less fixed than office rent. Nevertheless, Garcke and Fells were pretty much on the right lines here. Taken to task by Professor W. J. Ashley[58] for seeming "specifically to exclude establishment expenses and interest as items in the cost of production," the authors agreed that these charges must be elements in the cost of production in the wider sense, but that from the [59]

> . . . commercial standpoint of a manufacturer desirous under competitive conditions of obtaining business data on which he could act as to the price of the product, establishment charges, and in some measure interest, would not be regarded as items in the cost of production of particular commodities in so far as it regulates price.

The Breakeven Chart.   A favorite method nowadays of representing the relationship between total costs and output in a department, works, or firm is by the use of a breakeven chart. There is nothing very modern about this device. Sir John Mann[60] knew about it in 1904. We find a much fuller account of it in 1903 in a

---

[54]*Ibid.,* p. 360n.
[55]*Industry and Trade,* p. 369n.
[56]Emile Garcke and John Manger Fells, *Factory Accounts,* 1st ed. (1887), p. v.
[57]*Ibid.,* p. 74. Italics added.
[58]Garcke and Fells, *Factory Accounts,* 7th ed. (1922), p. 119 (footnote).
[59]*Ibid.*
[60]*Encyclopaedia of Accounting,* vol. V, pp. 217–218.

remarkable article by Henry Hess.[61] In this article, Hess takes a set of imaginary figures and divides them into fixed and variable costs. He then plots these costs for various levels of output (measured in terms of people employed and tons produced), together with the total net receipts for each output, and gets a breakeven point at which total costs equal total revenue. Because of the incidence of fixed costs, at zero output costs exceed revenue. But as output increases, total revenue increases faster than total costs, and eventually overtakes them. This gives the breakeven point. As output increases beyond this point, profits appear and increase proportionately with the growth in output. The effect of output changes on profits, assuming that the underlying assumptions as to the behavior of costs and prices are not falsified, is clearly shown.

Hess's article has another interest for us, for it contains the germ of what we now call a flexible budget. I shall return to this aspect of his work later.

It was only subsequently that the excessive simplification of dividing costs into fixed and variable categories was recognized and that the need for at least a third category of semifixed costs was seen. John H. Williams,[62] in America, wrote on this in 1922, and suggested that the amount of any semifixed cost which could be expected to be associated with any particular scale of output could be found by interpolating between the amounts of expense appropriate to the maximum and minimum outputs. By doing this for each expense, and aggregating, the total expense for any chosen output level could be predicted. The economist J. M. Clark[63] represents another point of view. He recommends an empirical approach to the problem of relating costs to output: for various scales of output, the amount of each category of cost would be estimated, and the total cost for each level of output arrived at by aggregation. Incremental cost could then be ascertained by taking the differences between the cost totals for each level of output.

The subsequent literature is full of references to the necessity of distinguishing between fixed and variable costs in order to assess the effect of production policy on profits, and a number of empirical studies of cost behavior were made.[64] But most of these studies were somewhat crude, and it was not until the late 1930s that refined techniques for relating cost to size of output in the short run were developed.

STANDARD COSTS

We have seen that the concept of the "actual" cost of a particular product or unit of product had to be replaced by the idea of normal cost. We now trace the further movement from normal cost to standard cost.

The possibility of setting up norms of cost, with which "actual" product and process costs might be compared, is implied by one or two of the nineteenth-century writers on costing. For instance, Garcke and Fells suggest that:[65]

[61]"Manufacturing: Capital, Costs, Profits and Dividends," *Engineering Magazine,* December 1903, p. 367. Hess was born in Darmstädt, Germany, in 1864, and went to the United States as a small boy. He became a member of the American Society of Mechanical Engineers, 1906, and was its Vice-President, 1914–1916. He was associated with the Hess-Bright Manufacturing Co., 1902–1912, and the Hess Steel Corporation of Baltimore from 1912 until his death in 1922.

[62]"A Technique for the Chief Executive," *Bulletin of the Taylor Society,* VII (1922), pp. 47–68.

[63]*The Economics of Overhead Cost* (University of Chicago Press, Chicago, 1923), p. 180.

[64]For a survey of such studies between 1920 and 1936, see Joel Dean, "Statistical Determination of Costs, with Special Reference to Marginal Costs," University of Chicago *Studies in Business Administration,* vol. VII, October 1936, no. 1, pp. 13–23.

[65]Garcke and Fells, *Factory Accounts,* 1st ed., pp. 52–53.

Before any order to manufacture is given it is advisable, as tending to produce greater economy in cost of production, that the person best acquainted with its processes and details should estimate the probable cost to be measured in wages and materials, in the production of the articles in question. This estimate should be a minimum rather than a maximum one, and the storekeeper having been furnished with particulars of it, should not issue more material for the order than is estimated without special authority.

Another early work which deserves mention in this connection is *Textile Manufacturers' Book-keeping,* published in 1889 by G. P. Norton. This book had a great success, running into four editions by 1900. The cost records, which were kept quite separate from the commercial accounts, were designed to allocate costs to departments and processes in such a way that the costs could be compared with the prices that would have been charged by outside specialists, i.e., the trade or "country" prices, as they were called. The results of the undertaking are summarized in a Manufacturing Account, the first part of which compares the actual sales with the work done valued at the trade prices, any difference after stock adjustments being the amounts of profit that would have been made if the work had been carried out at the trade rates. In the second section of the account the "actual" costs (i.e., the costs arrived at after allocations of overhead) of each of the processes, spinning, weaving, dyeing, and finishing, are compared with the work valued at trade prices, the difference showing the "profit" or "loss" on each department. The sum of these profits and losses plus the profit from the first section of the Manufacturing Account shows the net profit of the business subject to deduction of certain costs not allocated between the processes. This comparison of the firm's costs with "outside" values seems to be the nearest that the nineteenth century came to standard costing as we know it. Later, as the practice of putting work out on commission fell out of use, "country" prices ceased to be available, and in his *Cost Accounting and Cost Control,* published in 1931, Norton replaced them by full-blooded standard costs. The evolution in Norton's own mind from "country" prices to standard costs is thus quite clear.

It is impossible to take any discussion of the origins of standard costing far without acknowledging its close connection with the "scientific management" movement in America generally, for standard costs mean little without standard processes and standard operating times, such as F. W. Taylor and his followers developed. No one can read Taylor's famous paper on "Shop Management"[66] of 1903 without seeing that many of the essential elements of standard costing are there, including what is perhaps the first reference to "management by exception."[67]

Credit for the earliest detailed description of a system of standard costing has been given to an American, John Whitmore,[68] who, in a lecture delivered before the New York University School of Commerce in February 1908, gave a clear account of the use of standards in a shoe factory. In some earlier lectures given by him[69] in the winter of 1905–1906, he makes no reference to standard costing. It

---

[66] *Transactions of the American Society of Mechanical Engineers,* paper 1003, vol. XXIV (1903), pp. 1337–1456.

[67] "What may be called the 'Exception Principle' in management is coming more and more into use; although like many of the other elements of this art, it is used in isolated cases, and in most instances without recognizing it as a principle which should extend throughout the entire field." (*Ibid.,* p. 1408.)

[68] John Whitmore, "Shoe Factory Cost Accounts," *Journal of Accountancy,* May 1908. This article has been described by Dr. W. B. Macfarland, of NACA, as "the first of its kind to appear in accounting literature"—see J. Hugh Jackson, "A Quarter-Century of Cost-Accounting Progress," *NACA Bulletin,* 28, 19 (June 1, 1947).

[69] John Whitmore, "Factory Accountancy as Applied to Machine Shops," *Journal of Accountancy,* August 1906–January 1907, reprinted in *The Accountant,* 1906, pp. 605, 646, 675, 746, and 1907, pp. 160 and 220.

looks, therefore, as if either his ideas on the subject developed between these two dates or, what is more likely, that during this period he saw a standard costing system in operation and decided to write it up.

Before turning to Whitmore's contribution, however, there is an earlier one that deserves mention, an article on foundry costs by an American engineer, Percy Longmuir,[70] that appeared in 1902. Longmuir asserts quite clearly the value of controlling the cost to *functions* (as distinct from products) by comparison with certain standards of what these functions ought to cost. He proposes that the labor costs of each class of work undertaken in the foundry should be ascertained, each type of labor, e.g., molders, laborers, etc., being kept separate. These labor costs are then related to the weight of the class. "Experience," he says, "will readily give standard factors for each class of work and these standards may be plotted on a chart as a fair curve (straight line), the departure from which of the actual weekly cost line will instantly show the degrees of good or bad working." We need not stop to examine this claim. It is sufficient to acknowledge that Longmuir is expressing an important and, for his time, a novel idea. His strictures on the uselessness of job costs that are often worked out too late to be of service to the foundry manager, and his assertion of the necessity of providing management with cost information on the completion of every payment of wages, also strike a surprisingly modern note.

Turning back to Whitmore, it would seem that some of his more developed ideas stem direct from Hamilton Church, to whom, therefore, some of the credit for the development of the idea of standard costs must go. In his earlier lectures, as we have already said, Whitmore does not mention standard costs in the accepted sense. But he does there discuss Church's supplementary rate. He disapproved of Church's treatment of idle capacity costs and proposed instead that they should be charged to an idle capacity account and written off.

In his 1908 lecture he returns to the same theme. But now he takes it and develops it into something of much wider application. If the cost of idle capacity is not a part of the "true cost" of a product, may there not be other costs that ought to be similarly excluded? In the following passage we have the crux of his arguments:[71]

> I would say that true or correct cost does not necessarily include every expense incurred in the course of producing an article. Accidents or blunders occur and the cost, as in some instances the cost of unused factory capacity, may be so great that it would be absurd to state it as part of the cost of the product. If this is established, it establishes the principle that improper costs may be separated and stated under a heading which will distinguish between these and manufacturing expenses properly and necessarily incurred. This principle is rather far-reaching; its application may be of the greatest practical value; and it is susceptible of abuse. The danger is of assuming an impossibly perfect standard of working and of failing to allow for an inescapable average of accident and failure. Or again of applying in complex work the standards that are fair where work is simple, or in special work where new means of working to a new end have to be developed, the standards that are fair where processes are throughly established.
>
> It is possible to carry the application of distinguishing between proper and improper cost so far as to use calculations of proper cost, and then to direct the cost accounting to showing the variations of actual from calculated costs. This involves the setting up of complete standards for quality in materials and efficiency in working, and is not be confused with estimates of probable cost which are arrived at by any superficial method or except with the idea of continuously testing actual and calculated costs by each other.

It would be difficult to find a passage written in our own time, of comparable length, that expresses more clearly the basic ideas of standard costing.

[70]"Recording and Interpreting Foundry Costs," *Engineering Magazine,* September 1902, p. 887.
[71]Whitmore, "Shoe Factory Cost Accounts."

Harrington Emerson and Standard Costs.   When we turn to Harrington Emerson, the American efficiency engineer, we move on only 12 months in time but we come closer still to the outlook and terminology of our own day. His series of articles,[72] entitled "Efficiency as a Basis for Operation and Wages," revised and published as a book in 1909, are said to have taken place[73] "at once as one of the classics of the literature of industrial engineering."

The first thing that strikes one about Emerson's work is the very clearcut way in which he distinguishes between standard costing and all that has gone before:[74]

> There are two radically different methods of ascertaining costs, the first method to ascertain them after the work is completed, the second method to ascertain them before the work is undertaken. The first method is the old one, still used in most manufacturing and maintenance undertakings, the second method is the new one, beginning to be used in some very large plants, where its feasibility and practical value have already been demonstrated.

The old methods are wrong because the information they provide is hopelessly delayed; and it is[75] "wholly and absolutely incorrect, mixing up with costs incidents that do not have the remotest connection with them, so that analysis of cost statements . . . does not lead to elimination of wastes." Also,[76] "the acceptance of the haphazard is the main characteristic of the old method, still in full and orthodox standing in cost accounting." And,[77] " . . . because costs are not standardized, the variations due to inefficiency under identical conditions are in the records either increased or lessened by the much larger variations due to change of conditions."

Two other points are notable. One is his advocacy of the use of the standard hour as "the real standard unit of cost." "The cost of repairing a particular locomotive for a particular mile run," he says,[78] in the course of describing the application of standard costing to a locomotive repair shop,

> never has been, never can be ascertained, but the rate of pay for a man for a given hour and his speed of work can be as definitely determined as the length of a race track and the time required by a horse to go round it. . . . Costs of locomotives or of locomotive miles, or of track maintenance, or of anything else will take care of themselves when the unit hours of each man and machine are operating at highest efficiency for standard cost. . . .

A further noteworthy point about Emerson's approach is his reluctant acceptance of the necessity to tie in standard costs with actual current expenditure. He described efficiency engineers as having found this "to their sorrow" and that without tying-in they could not[79] "convince those on whose support they must rely that the methods used are really producing the results promised."

As with Whitmore, so with Emerson. It is impossible to say how much originality is embodied in his articles. In an earlier article,[80] published in 1904, there is no sign of the advanced ideas that he is found advocating in 1908. In his later articles he is describing a system he has seen in operation. We do not know how much he contributed to its devising.

[72]*Engineering Magazine,* July 1908–March 1909.
[73]Editor's note to the book, p. iv.
[74]*Engineering Magazine,* XXXVI, p. 336.
[75]*Ibid.,* p. 336.
[76]*Ibid.,* p. 337.
[77]*Ibid.,* p. 339.
[78]*Ibid.,* p. 683.
[79]*Ibid.,* p. 678.
[80]"Percentage Method of Determining Production Costs," *The Foundry,* October 1904.

There are two great weaknesses in Emerson's system, or at least in his account of it. First, his idea of what constitutes a standard is confusing and confused. In one place he talks of it as being[81] "always elusively ahead of the actual" and again,[82] "The worker is limited by conditions as they are, but standard time presupposes standard power and maintenance conditions—ideal, not actual, conditions for the worker." Yet later he says[83] that "predetermined standard costs can be attained through the direct and indirect assistance given to the line by the staff." Thus he seems to vacillate between an ideal and an attainable standard. A second weakness in his work is that he makes no attempt to arrive at anything more detailed than an overall variance between actual and standard costs. There is no suggestion of the possibility of analyzing the total variance into its component parts. Thus his repeated claim that his system enables waste to be "located" is hardly justified. That it would come near to enabling the total dollar wastage during any period to be *measured* is probably true enough. But for the *location* of waste in any sense of the word that is at all significant we must look not to Harrington Emerson but to others whose work lies a little nearer to our own time.

THE CHANGE OF EMPHASIS FROM ASCERTAINING COST TO COST CONTROL

It will be seen by comparing the summarized account of Longmuir's ideas with that of Whitmore's that they approach the idea of standard costing from somewhat different angles. Longmuir wants standards as a check on the economy with which various functions in the business are being performed. Whitmore is more concerned with the elimination from "actual" costs of wasteful expenditure in order to arrive at a "true" cost, and this brings him also to standards. It will be seen from this that the extension of the use of standard costs was not immediately accompanied by a change of emphasis away from the use of costing as a technique for the ascertaining of product costs toward the control of expenditure and the location of wastes. The introduction of standards seemed more satisfactorily to serve both these functions. The suggestion that the two functions may be incompatible and that there should be a change of emphasis from ascertaining cost to cost control was to be heard only somewhat later.

Budgetary Control. Budgeting, in the sense of forecasting and acting on forecast, is a very old practice. Joseph, in Egypt, made a budget of corn supplies and planned Pharaoh's investment and consumption policy in the light of it. In less remote times, in Great Britain the practice of drawing up a government budget each year is about 200 years old. In the United States it dates back only to 1921.

Even in the humbler sphere of business, budgeting is of respectable antiquity. De Cazaux, whose work on agricultural accounting was referred to earlier, is the first writer I have found to show an interest in accounting for the future as well as for the past, and in the 1825 edition of his book he devotes a chapter to budgeting.[84] "Future conduct," he says, "is to be traced from an account of successes and failures of the past. Thus one can determine one's needs in the coming year and can compare them with the resources one will have. This statement of resources and needs is called a budget." And he goes on to explain[85] that it is desirable to foresee not only what demands on one's resources will be encountered but also exactly when these demands will arise. "Hence the necessity to establish *monthly budgets,* elements of the *general* or *annual budget.*"

[81] *Engineering Magazine,* XXXVI, p. 174.
[82] *Ibid.,* p. 178.
[83] *Ibid.,* p. 178.
[84] *Élements d'Économie Privée et Publique,* book II, chap. III, pp. 105–108.
[85] *Ibid.,* p. 105.

Budgeting today serves several different purposes. It may function, as in government, primarily as part of the machinery of financial procurement. It may serve, in business, as a device to aid systematic planning. Or it may aid the delegation of authority, by fixing limits up to which subordinates may be allowed to spend. It is, however, in the incorporation of budgets into the cost records for the purpose of controlling expenditure that we are specially interested here. This practice seems to have developed early in the present century.

S. H. Bunnell[86] described such a system in 1911. He explained that each item of overhead was to be budgeted and charged into costs at this budgeted figure. Subsequently, actual expenditure under each head would be compared with the budget and the differences examined. He claimed two advantages for the system. First, costs did not fluctuate as a result of the purely arbitrary incidence of actual expenses. Second, the differences between budgeted and actual expenses gave a control over efficiency.

We have here an early example of standard costing coupled with budgetary control. The budget, however, is a fixed budget. Like all fixed budgets, it does not take account of fluctuations in output, so that differences between actual and budget expenditure that might at first glance look like excess spending might in fact have been justified by an expansion of output. On the other hand, the complete agreement of budget and actual expense would be quite compatible with the existence of wasteful expenditure.

Bunnell's claims for his system of budgetary control—for that is what it is, though he does not use the term—cannot therefore really be substantiated. His budget lacked flexibility in that the figures were not adjusted in the light of changes of circumstance that supervened during the period for which the budget was drawn up. The basic idea of what we now call a flexible budget had, as a matter of fact, already been expressed by Henry Hess[87] in his remarkable article of 1903 to which reference has already been made. Discussing the use of expense forecasts, Hess says:[88]

> Forecasting is quite useful but far more important is to make sure that results agree materially with such forecasts and to find the causes for whatever divergencies there may be. . . . There is nothing new in the idea of following up costs in detail and by groups and comparing these with some ideal; rarely do the results agree with that, and very often are discrepancies attributed to the influence of a fluctuating output; there is generally just enough truth in that excuse to prevent the responsibility for a falling off being definitely located, owing to the haziness of knowledge of the actual influence of such fluctuation.

THE LATER DEVELOPMENT OF STANDARD COSTING

From about 1912 on, the literature of standard costing becomes richer, and it becomes increasingly difficult to trace the genealogy of new ideas. We find a growing volume of criticism of retrospective costing; and the change of emphasis, to which I have referred, from the ascertaining of what it costs to make something to the control of what it costs to carry out an industrial process or function can be seen developing. The newer view is put thus by W. E. McHenry,[89] writing in 1914: "'What it costs to *do* things' and 'What it cost per HOUR' may some day supplant

---

[86]"Standardizing Factory Expense and Cost," *Iron Age,* November 16, 1911.
[87]"Manufacturing: Capital, Costs, Profits and Dividends," *Engineering Magazine,* December 1903.
[88]*Ibid.,* pp. 376–377.
[89]"Cost per Ton," *Engineering Magazine,* February 1914, p. 791.

much present detail, laboriously worked out 'per ton'." And the same writer,[90] two years later, gives us an admirably clear illustration of the application of standard costing techniques to the operation of a blast furnace. In this illustration he separates what we would now call volume, efficiency, and spending variances, and he shows how a straight calculation of cost per ton would give an unfavorable (and misleading) impression of the efficiency of a works in a month in which the blast is off for seven days out of 30, without a corresponding fall in the monthly costs of operation. McHenry makes no claim to originality. "The general method of distributing indirect expense by means of 'standard' rates, so that the product is only charged with its *proportion of the services actually used*, has been before the public for several years," he says. But it is[91] "little understood."

One more pioneer of standard costing must be mentioned. This is G. Charter Harrison.[92] Becoming associated with Harrington Emerson in 1909, he took up his ideas and developed them in 1911 into the first *complete* standard costing system known to exist.[93] A series of articles[94] which he wrote in 1918 have a sureness of touch and a comprehensiveness in their treatment that shows standard costing to have left the experimental stage and to have attained the status of established practice. In these articles he[95] produced the first set of formulas for the analysis of cost variances.

Any detailed account of Harrison's ideas would encroach too far into the field of modern costing, for his articles and his book are not only milestones in the development of the subject—they are still part of its current literature. Harrison viewed the growth of standard costing, not as a new departure but rather as a return to the principle of predetermining costs that in earlier times had found general acceptance but had become obscured by the complexity of modern business. And for justification of his view he quotes from St. Luke's Gospel: "for which of you intending to build a tower sitteth not down first and counteth the cost."

UNIFORM COSTING

The development by trade associations of uniform costing definitions and methods for adoption by all member firms and others in the industry is the last costing evolution that I shall try to describe.[96] It is by no means a recent development. We first encounter it in America, where the National Association of Stove Manufacturers, formed in 1872, had by 1889 developed a uniform "formula" for costing the industry's products. Similar activities in the printing industry were afoot before 1887 but only resulted in the formal adoption of the Standard Uniform Cost Finding System for Printers by the United Typothetae of America in 1910.[97]

---

[90]"Is Your Cost System Scientific?" *Engineering Magazine,* August 1916, pp. 681–683.

[91]*Ibid.,* p. 686.

[92]Born in London, 1881, became an Associate of the Institute of Chartered Accountants in England and Wales in 1905, and forthwith settled in America. From 1911 to 1916 he was head of the Systems Department of Price, Waterhouse & Co. From 1918 he practiced independently as a management consultant for over 30 years in Madison, Wis. He kindly prepared some notes for me about his early work.

[93]This was for the Boss Manufacturing Co., of Kewanee, Ill., makers of work gloves.

[94]"Cost Accounting to Aid Production," *Industrial Management,* October 1918–June 1919.

[95]In an article entitled "Scientific Basis for Cost Accounting," *Industrial Management,* December 1918, p. 459ff.

[96]For a fuller study of this subject, see my "Uniform Cost Accounting—A Survey," *Economica,* August and November 1950.

[97]On this, see Leona M. Powell, "Typothetae Experiments with Price Maintenance and Cost Work," *Journal of Political Economy,* February 1926, pp. 78–99.

Following World War I, uniform systems had a checkered career in the United States. In 1925, adverse decisions by the Supreme Court in the Hardwood Lumber and Maple Flooring Cases brought under the Sherman Antitrust Law made trade associations wary about developing this side of their activities. On the other hand, the National Recovery Administration under the New Deal, during the period 1933–1936, had power to prohibit sales below cost—and uniform costing was greatly encouraged as a result. In 1950 there were probably about 150 *effective* schemes in the United States, though a vastly greater number certainly existed on paper.

In Great Britain, it was in the Birmingham iron bedstead trade that uniform costing seems to have been first tried out in the 1890s. The prime mover in this development was E. J. Smith, a bedstead manufacturer. Having organized his own trade, he set out to spread the light elsewhere by starting the New Trades Combination Movement. This was to ensure a quiet life for industrialists by fostering price agreements based on cost within each industry, and uniform costing was to play its part. "It is part of my scheme," he wrote,[98] "to establish in every trade a system of cost taking which, while it may not be all that could be desired when tested by the special circumstances of any individual business, is still all that is needed for the purpose of fixing throughout an entire trade a selling price for each manufactured article which will bring a legitimate and reasonable profit to each maker without unduly taxing the purchaser." Smith was active in a number of trades, but virtually nothing is left of his work for uniform costing, for, so far as I know, none of the still-extant schemes owes anything to him.

The oldest existing British scheme is that of the British Federation of Master Printers. The Federation was founded in 1900, and almost from the start costing occupied much of its executives' time. A form of printers' cost system was issued in 1909, and in 1911 a representative of the Federation went to America to learn what he could from experience there. Two years later, after further discussions, the first edition of the present scheme was issued as a cost manual after formal adoption by a Cost Congress held in London.[99]

Since 1913, the printers have been followed by many other trade associations. Not all the schemes launched have survived. There were in 1950 probably not more than 25 in effective operation.

CONCLUSION

This survey of cost accounting history makes no pretensions to completeness. A full history would have to concern itself with many aspects of the subject that have been omitted here, such as the development of mechanized means of keeping cost records, the growing integration of costing and production control, the application of costing to selling and distribution functions, and its application to governmental activities.

If there is one conclusion to be drawn from the foregoing study, it is that there is remarkably little in modern costing that our fathers did not know about. What can be fairly claimed for the period 1910–1950, however, is that great strides were made in converting ideas into widely adopted practices. In that process, two world wars played no inconsiderable part. But that there is room for further advance both in the theory and practice of industrial accounting hardly needs to be said.

[98] *The New Trades Combination Movement,* p. 30.

[99] For a detailed account of these developments, see Ellic Howe, *The British Federation of Master Printers, 1900–1950* (University Press, Cambridge, England, 1950).

BIBLIOGRAPHY

American Accounting Association: "Report of the Management Accounting Committee," *Accounting Review,* 37 (July 1962), pp. 523–537.

Chapin, Ned: "The Development of the Break-Even Chart: A Bibliographical Note," *Journal of Business* (1955), pp. 148–149.

Chatfield, Michael: *Contemporary Studies in the Evolution of Accounting Thought,* Dickenson Publishing Company, Belmont, Calif., 1968.

——: *A History of Accounting Thought,* Dryden Press, Hinsdale, Ill., 1974.

Church, Alexander Hamilton: "The Meaning of Commercial Organisation," *Engineering Magazine,* 20, 3 (December 1900), p. 394.

——: "The Proper Distribution of Establishment Charges," *Engineering Magazine,* July 1901, pp. 510–511.

de Roover, Mrs.: "Cost Accounting in the 16th Century," *Accounting Review,* 12, 3 (September 1937), pp. 226–237.

de Roover, Raymond: "A Florentine Firm of Cloth Manufacturers," *Speculum,* 16, 1 (January 1941), pp. 1–33.

Emerson, Harrison: "Percentage Methods of Determining Production Costs," *The Foundry,* October 1904, pp. 80–81.

Garner, S. Paul: *Evolution of Cost Accounting to 1925,* University of Alabama Press, University, Ala., 1954.

Hamilton, W. R.: "Some Economic Considerations Bearing on Costing," *The Accountant,* February 1910.

Jackson, J. Hugh: "A Half Century of Cost Accounting Progress," In *Contemporary Studies in the Evolution of Accounting Thought,* M. Chatfield, ed., Dickenson Publishing Company, Belmont, Calif., 1968, pp. 222–236.

Julius, M. J.: "Historical Development of Uniform Accounting," *Journal of Business,* 16 (1943), pp. 219–229.

Kent, Dr. William: "New Methods of Determining Factory Costs," *Iron Age,* 98 (August 1916), pp. 392–394.

Most, Kenneth S.: "The History of Uniform Cost Accounting," pp. 40–48 of his *Uniform Cost Accounting,* Gee, London, 1961.

Parker, R. H.: *Management Accounting: An Historical Perspective,* Augustus M. Kelley, New York, 1969.

Raymond, Robert H.: "History of the Flexible Budget," *Management Accounting,* 47 (August 1966), pp. 9–15.

Sizer, J.: "The Development of Marginal Costing," *Accountants' Magazine,* 72 (January 1968), pp. 23–30.

Solomons, David, ed.: "The Historical Development of Costing," in *Studies in Cost Analysis,* 2nd ed., Sweet & Maxwell, London, 1968.

Sowell, Ellis Mast: *The Evolution of the Theories and Techniques of Standard Costs,* University of Alabama Press, University, Ala., 1973.

Stephens, R. J.: "A Note on an Early Reference to Cost-Volume Profit Relationships," *Abacus,* 2 (September 1966), pp. 78–83.

Villers, Raymond: "The Origin of the Break-Even Chart," *Journal of Business,* 28 (1955), pp. 296–297.

Weber, C.: *The Evolution of Direct Costing,* Center for International Education and Research in Accounting, Urbana, Ill., 1966.

Whitmore, John: "Shoe Factory Cost Accounts," *Journal of Accountancy,* May 1908.

Williams, John H.: "A Technique for the Chief Executive," *Bulletin of the Taylor Society,* VII (1922), pp. 47–68.

Wing, G. A.: "Capital Budgeting, Circa 1915," *Journal of Finance,* 20 (1965), pp. 472–479.

Chapter **2**

The Nature and Classification of Costs

RUSSELL A. TAUSSIG

Professor of Finance, Department of Accounting and Finance, College of Business Administration, University of Hawaii

NATURE OF COST

This chapter is devoted to the different, sometimes conflicting, meanings of cost, and to the various classifications of costs that have proven useful to management.

Cost Varies with Purpose. It has been recognized that at least since 1923 different costs are needed for different purposes. It was at that time that J. M. Clark wrote:[1]

> The general idea of cost covers a number of different meanings. . . . A great deal of controversy [exists] as to whether certain items are properly costs at all. Most of this controversy will disappear if we carry our study far enough to recognize that there are different kinds of problems for which we need information about costs, and the particular information we need differs from one problem to another.

Simon, Guetzkow, Kozmetsky, and Tyndall, in their classic research on the control function, found that cost data are used:[2] (1) as a *score-card* for the appraisal of an operating unit; (2) to *direct attention* to problems that need to be solved; and (3) to aid in the *solution of problems.*

They found that different costs are required for different purposes; moreover, they argued that the same cost data often should be reported differently to different management levels. Modern information systems store and analyze data on a multiplicity of dimensions, but dimensionality increases at a price. Accordingly, cost classification can be appraised only by balancing its value against the price paid to acquire it.

Alternative Definitions of Cost. *Cost* has many meanings, differing among accounting, economics, and engineering. A charge to a "cost" account under traditional accounting theory is a debit to an asset, whereas the expiration of a "cost" is an "expense." For example, a purchase of raw materials is a "cost," but the payment of current advertising is an "expense."

Davidson, Schindler, and Weil express this dichotomy succinctly:[3]

> An expense is an expired asset. A firm acquires assets to obtain the services of future benefits that the assets provide. All acquisitions are acquisitions of assets, that is, of future benefits. As the services are used up, as the future benefits disappear, assets become expenses. Expenses may thus be described as "gone assets," that is, as benefits or resources used up in the process of securing revenue. To decide when an asset (or its synonym, a cost) loses its power to provide future benefits and, hence, has become an expense is one of the most difficult problems in accounting.

Thus, a traditional accounting definition of "cost" is limited to the amount expended to acquire an asset. A more general concept equates cost with any sacrifice, past or future. It is the price paid for the selection of one alternative over another. Or, as Shillinglaw states this broader economic/accounting definition:[4] "a cost represents the resources that have been or must be sacrificed to attain a particular objective."

The concept of cost is multifaceted. A useful approach for understanding the various aspects of costs consists of examining alternative cost classification schemes, starting with the usual general ledger classification of costs for a typical manufacturing concern.

[1]J. Maurice Clark, *Studies in the Economics of Overhead Costs* (University of Chicago Press, Chicago, 1923), p. 35.

[2]Herbert A. Simon, Harold Guetzkow, George Kozmetsky, and Gordon Tyndall, *Centralization vs. Decentralization in Organizing the Controller's Department* (Controllership Foundation, New York, 1954), p. 3.

[3]Sidney Davidson, James S. Schindler, and Roman L. Weil, *Fundamentals of Accounting*, 5th ed., (Dryden Press, Hinsdale, Ill., 1975).

[4]Gordon Shillinglaw, *Cost Accounting: Analysis and Control*, 3rd ed. (Richard D. Irwin, Homewood, Ill., 1972), p. 11.

COST ACCOUNT CLASSIFICATIONS

In his excellent treatise on the historical development of costing, David Solomons[5] points out that the impact of the Industrial Revolution was of major importance in creating a need for more advanced methods of cost determination and control, particularly for manufacturing concerns. These advances have been abetted by a systematic approach to cost classification. Generally, costs incurred by manufacturers are classified usefully in three different ways:

1. By object of expenditure (machinists' labor, maintenance, etc.)
2. By program (such as cost of Job No. 1, No. 2, etc.)
3. By responsibility center (machining, packing, etc.)

Classification by Object of Expenditure. The most primitive classification of costs is by object of expenditure, that is, descriptive charges such as direct labor, raw materials, manufacturing overhead, and subdivisions of these categories. This classification "by natural elements" is generally used for external reports. It is simple to implement in small organizations. Often it is the only common denominator available for uniform classification of expired costs in larger multiproduct organizations.

Classification by object of expenditure is useful for overall company planning because data are in a convenient form for establishing trends. The cost elements in a given set should be homogeneous; they should respond to volume changes in the same way. If payroll tax varies with output while property tax varies with the value of equipment, putting them together will confuse their relationship to the amount of goods produced. Accordingly, a single account for taxes would not be appropriate.

Incidentally, some cost accountants define a *cost object* as any alternative, activity, or part of an organization for which a separate cost determination is wanted. Thus, the "classification of cost by costing objective" differs from the "classification of costs by object of expenditure." Managers classify costs by different objects depending on the problem to be solved. They need the cost of an activity, such as filling an order, for pricing. They need the cost of holding inventories for ascertaining the economic lot size of those inventories. Classification of costs by object is a sophisticated concept for breaking costs down into small building blocks that can later be reassembled in a variety of ways. It is an approach for constructing a data base according to the specific needs of management. This sophisticated approach to the storing of costs by *cost object* differs from the simple classification of costs by *object of expenditure*. Examples of the classification of costs by cost object are included in this chapter in the section "Costs for Operations Research Models." The general theory is considered in Chapter 24 on management information systems.

Classification by Program. Cost classification by program, or project, plays a major role in planning. A builder of custom homes, for example, accumulates costs for each job. Costs are tabulated by stages of construction from initial excavation to final painting. These figures assist the builder in planning future construction activities. They help signal cost overruns, and they are useful for short-run pricing.

Job costs also show what work is in process at any time; thus they enable the accountant to prepare financial reports without physical inventories. They simplify income measurement and determination of financial position.

Classification by Responsibility Center. Control is the primary objective in the classification of costs by responsibility centers or departments. Additionally, departmentalization improves the accuracy of cost measurement.

[5]David Solomons, "The Historical Development of Costing," in *Studies in Cost Analysis,* 2nd ed., David Solomons, ed. (Richard D. Irwin, Homewood, Ill., 1968).

Control of direct labor and raw material is effected at the departmental level as work proceeds through a factory. On the other hand, control over many indirect charges is effected at a higher level. However, even when cost classification by department is not useful for control, it facilitates a reasonable allocation of charges to jobs. Responsibility centers used for cost classification are generally operating departments or smaller subdivisions used solely for costing. The subdivisions are appropriate for an operating department containing basically different kinds of subsections, some using expensive machinery and others not. The smaller cost centers improve the accuracy of cost measurement when some work requires expensive machine time whereas other work does not.

Control is implemented through departmental cost reports. These are attention-getting devices. They signal the need for immediate corrective action, and they provide the facts for long-term decisions such as changes in methods and equipment.

Master Coding System.   The cross-classification of costs by object, project, and department is facilitated by a master coding system. Modern account codes for use with data processing facilities generally are numbering plans with sections of digits reserved for object, project, and department.

An example of a master coding system is provided by Construction Corporation, which uses a 15-digit identification code for its costs comprising four elements: general ledger, cost center, project, and detail expense. The 15 digits are assigned as follows:

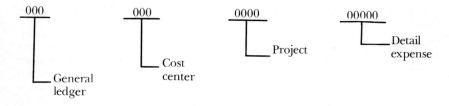

The general ledger code, by object, is established at the corporate level. All reports submitted for consolidation by the centralized computer facilities are coded using the standard chart of general ledger accounts. The cost center code can be modified at the group level to show programs and services. On the other hand, the project code and the detail expense code are determined entirely at the operating level and may be applied in various ways to meet the needs of management. Detailed data processing is available for construction reporting, including estimating, progress reporting, payroll, equipment programs, and accounting. The last five digits are used to provide further detail of expense accounts included in the general ledger code according to the dictates of the particular division. One such list analyzes costs by specific kinds of materials, labor, and other costs, such as techkote resins, hose assemblies, and so on. A quite different list, prepared by another division, shows costs by excavation labor, framing lumber, and so on, to meet the perceived needs of the managers in that division.

Process and Service Industries.   The foregoing classification illustrated the chart of accounts for a job-order firm, one manufacturing a heterogeneous mix of products, such as a construction company or a print shop. A similar threefold classification by object of expenditure, by project, and by responsibility center is also applicable for process firms such as oil refiners or fruit canners.

Some special adaptations may be dictated. Process firms, characterized by long runs and repetitive production, are well suited to the use of departmental performance indicators. Costs are identified conveniently with aggregate output for a specific period such as a week or month. Management focuses on average costs for control and pricing. Minor differences arise because activity measures are broader. Manufacturing supplies charged to overhead in a job shop may be charged directly against the product in a process plant.

In fact, the same costing techniques are applicable in a wide variety of nonmanufacturing situations, such as department stores, banks, and hotels. In each of these, costs can be classified by object, project, and responsibility.

SUBDIVISION OF COST CLASSIFICATION BY OBJECT OF EXPENDITURE

When costs are classified by object of expenditure, the three basic categories are (1) direct materials, (2) direct labor, and (3) manufacturing overhead.

Direct materials are those materials, parts, and subassemblies whose cost can be identified conveniently with a particular job or process. Relatively minor items are charged to manufacturing overhead as indirect materials. The distinction between direct and indirect materials is pragmatic, based on whether the expense of controlling the expenditure by job is justified by the savings. Accordingly, materials are classified as direct because of their importance rather than physical inclusion in the end product. For instance, a catalyst used to effect the chemical reaction between caustic soda and animal fat in the making of soap is classified as a direct cost, although the catalyst does not remain in the final bar of milled soap. On the other hand, the cost of nails used in building a house may be charged as an expedient to overhead rather than to the job. Materials are classified as direct when their cost warrants identification with a job, or process, for managerial control and planning.

The cost of materials includes all charges necessary to acquire and prepare them for use. Freight, drayage, taxes, and other acquisition charges are properly included. Also logically included are carrying costs such as storage and insurance when inventories are aged or normally kept on hand for a time before being put into production. Many incidental charges are classified as overhead in practice, however, because they are small. Cost means spot cash price. Interest charged is a financial expense, not part of the cost of materials. Cash discounts are properly deducted from the invoice price whether taken or not. Discounts lost represent a nonmanufacturing expense.

The cost of scrap and defective materials is charged to the job unless due to an abnormal cause such as a power outage, in which event it is classified as a loss of the period. Proceeds from scrap should be credited against the job, although they are often deducted from overhead because of the difficulty of identifying the recovery by jobs.

Direct labor is the category charged for workers whose time can be readily identified with specific jobs. The pay of a cutter in a garment factory constitutes direct labor; the salary of a sweeper is indirect labor.

It is often useful to include supplementary payments such as payroll taxes, pension payments, and other fringe benefits in the cost of direct labor. This gross labor cost is meaningful for a number of management decisions, including make-or-buy and markup pricing decisions; nevertheless, fringe benefits often are charged to factory overhead as a matter of expediency. It is important for a manager to know whether labor is being accounted for on a gross or net basis. If the industry price-quoting rule is "materials and labor plus a given percentage," a firm can go broke omitting fringe benefits when they are included in labor cost as a general industry practice.

The outlay for overtime premium pay is classifiable as overhead unless caused by a specific job. When a job worked on during overtime hours is not responsible for extra work, the overtime premium is attributable to all jobs, because aggregate demand caused the extra cost. Moreover, charging the overtime premium to manufacturing overhead isolates the cost for managerial attention.

Time spent on correcting defective production should be singled out as "rework," often a critical cost. Like defective materials, this cost should be charged to the job if product related and to manufacturing overhead if process related.

Setup cost is generally separated from other labor charges. It is needed for economic lot-quantity calculations. The cost of a setup remains the same regardless of the size of a production run, and its inclusion would destroy the proportionality between direct labor and the number of units produced, a useful relation for cost analysis. Setup labor can be charged to jobs with a coding that permits segregation for cost analysis. Alternatively, it can be charged to manufacturing overhead. The first approach is generally preferable because it facilitates relating setup costs to run sizes.

Manufacturing overhead comprises all manufacturing costs other than direct materials and direct labor. Manufacturing overhead costs include items such as depreciation of factory buildings, property taxes, and machinery repairs that are not readily identifiable with any one contract or product. They are costs incurred jointly for all jobs during the fiscal period. Manufacturing overhead is also known as *burden, on-cost,* and, imprecisely, *manufacturing expense.*

Distinction Between "Cost" and "Expense."   Manufacturing costs are sharply distinguished from selling and administrative expenses for financial reporting. Manufacturing overhead is a cost (an asset). Selling and administrative overheads are expenses (current period deductions from revenues).

Manufacturing costs are assets because they are deemed to measure added utility for goods produced. Thus the charge for depreciation of factory machinery constitutes an increase in an asset (work-in-process inventories). Conversely, selling and administrative overheads are expenses, deductible from revenues when incurred.

Depreciation of a factory building is a cost; however, depreciation of a corporate office building is an expense. This dichotomy between manufacturing cost and nonmanufacturing expense, though simple in concept, entails problems in application. For instance, it is generally recognized that the salary of a divisional controller who is responsible for the plant is part of manufacturing overhead. However, it is not so often apparent that the cost of the same type of financial executive whose office is located at corporate headquarters is also a product cost. Estimating and design costs incurred in bidding a job clearly are manufacturing costs. Not so clear, but arguably includable as manufacturing costs, are promotional expenditures incident to the securing of a specific contract.

Incidentally, some of the language of accounting on "cost" and "expense" is confusing. "Cost of goods sold," for example, is an operating expense title in the income statement. The reader may wonder how a "cost" can be an "expense." Actually, "cost of goods sold" designates the expired cost of products sold, which is an expense. Also, in practice, the word "cost" sometimes is attached loosely to what is in fact an "expense" item. Managers refer to the "cost of advertising," which actually is an expense of the current period.

Interest as a Manufacturing Cost.   Should interest be included as a manufacturing cost? The question has not been definitely settled. Those who argue in favor of inclusion point out that capital is as important as labor for production and that the cost of capital should be included along with the cost of labor. They also maintain that aging is often an essential part of manufacturing, as in the production of fine wines. When included it must logically be a weighted average of the cost of debt and equity funds, not just the cost of borrowed funds alone.

Those who oppose inclusion state that it has been customary to distinguish financial expenses from manufacturing costs in accordance with generally accepted accounting principles. They further point out the difficulty of measuring imputed interest with precision. Some also argue that, following an entity theory of the firm, interest payments are distributions of net income, not part of its determination.

Thus, interest is generally not capitalized except when the aging function is significant. Regardless of the disposition of interest for financial reporting, it is always included as a cost for economic analyses such as inventory planning and make-or-buy decisions.

Extensions of the Object Classification. The classification of costs into the threefold categories of materials, labor, and overhead may be expanded. For example, a category "buyouts" sometimes is added for purchases of services from subcontractors. Again, special test equipment without salvage value is sometimes charged separately to jobs, particularly when records are designed to meet disclosure requirements of the Cost Accounting Standards Board for government contractors.[6]

Materials, labor, and overhead are combined in various ways. The sum of direct labor and manufacturing overhead, called *conversion cost,* is useful in process costing because conversion cost generally varies with the number of units finished during a period, whereas material cost varies with the number of units started. The sum of materials and labor is called *prime cost.* Prime cost is charged directly to jobs, whereas manufacturing overhead is allocated indirectly on the basis of some index of activity. Prime cost plus an appropriate markup covering other expenses and profits is frequently used for short-term pricing decisions.

Although the classification of costs by object of expenditure is simple and may be applied to a wide variety of industries, it may not be the most useful one for cost control and managerial planning. Accordingly, modern costing systems generally classify costs at the outset according to the way in which they vary with changes in output.

COST-VOLUME CLASSIFICATION

Costs are classified according to how they change with output for a variety of planning decisions, including the setting of prices and negotiation of budgets.

Fixed costs remain the same in total dollar amount for various levels of output. Typical fixed costs are property taxes, superintendence, and depreciation. *Variable costs* increase in total dollar amount as output increases. Examples include the costs of materials and power. Fixed costs per unit diminish as volume increases, whereas variable costs per unit remain constant.

Economic Theory. The fixed-variable dichotomy is crucial for output planning in the short run according to economic theory. The law of diminishing marginal productivity postulates that as variable inputs are added to a fixed input, the incremental output, or marginal product, eventually declines. *Marginal cost* is the additional cost per unit of output. Because of diminishing marginal productivity (and possibly increasing input prices), marginal cost rises with increases in output. An entrepreneur expands output so long as marginal revenue exceeds marginal cost. Under pure competition, where market price cannot be affected, the producer expands output until marginal cost equals market price.

This economic theory is helpful for several management decisions, including short-term pricing. In practice, average variable cost often can be substituted for marginal cost. Statistical studies of cost behavior, by Dean[7] and others, show that

[6]Cost Accounting Standards Board, "Standards, Rules and Regulations as of June 30, 1975" (U.S. Government Printing Office, Washington, D.C., 1975).

[7]Joel Dean, *Statistical Determination of Costs, with Special Reference to Marginal Costs* (University of Chicago Press, Chicago, 1936).

marginal cost is generally constant for a broad range of output. Thus, average variable cost is also constant, and total cost varies directly with output. These empirical cost studies imply that output should be set at plant capacity for pure competition, and at that output which brings marginal revenue down to average variable cost for other than pure competition.

The economic theory of cost-volume behavior is also relevant for planning and control. Flexible budgeting recognizes that costs vary with output—but not necessarily in a linear fashion. Accordingly, costs are analyzed into fixed and variable elements to establish meaningful budgetary allowances.

Practical Modification.   The fixed-variable cost dichotomy must often be modified when put into practice. An intermediate classification, *semifixed costs,* is useful for fixed costs that increase stepwise. (Some writers refer to these costs as *semivariable* costs.) Salaries of foremen is a typical example. Each new gang of workers requires an additional foreman. One may consider these costs fixed throughout a given range for many analyses. For other analyses ranging over a wider domain the stepwise pattern must be recognized.

Semifixed is also applied to costs that increase with volume by small amounts at short, possibly irregular, intervals. One can approximate these by a continuous function for most practical purposes.

A "semivariable" cost plots as a straight line with a positive intercept indicating a fixed charge plus a variable component. Telephone bills, for example, typically include a fixed monthly charge plus variable charges based on use. Semivariable costs frequently indicate a lack of homogeneity in the underlying classification. For example, one firm found that an account titled heat, light, and power was fixed as to heat and light but variable as to power. Either the initial charges should be classified more precisely, or the category heat, light, and power should be decomposed for profit-volume analyses.

Subdivision of Fixed Costs.   It is useful to classify fixed costs further for planning and decision making. *Committed costs* are fixed costs that result from decisions of prior periods. They are the costs of basic operating capacity that continue at zero output. Examples include depreciation, insurance, property taxes, and the salaries of general managers. *Discretionary costs* are fixed costs that result from decisions in the current period. Examples include promotional expenditures, legal expenses, and research and development. Discretionary costs can be eliminated when a plant is temporarily closed, say by a strike, whereas committed costs cannot be eliminated. Discretionary costs sometimes vary with volume, simply because management budgets them that way. However, they do not perforce increase with output.

The committed/discretionary dichotomy is useful for managerial control because discretionary costs are controlled annually, but committed costs are controllable only when a project is approved. The distinction is also pertinent for output reduction decisions. Management may decide it is cheaper to retain skilled workers than to dismiss them and retrain new ones when demand is curtailed temporarily as a result of a recession.

Alternative Terminology.   Additional terms have been invented by cost accountants and management consultants either to describe more vividly the cost components used in profit-volume analyses or to identify their nature more precisely. Beyer[8] created the term *standby costs* for those planned costs that would be incurred at zero output. He designated *programmed costs* as those planned costs that will be incurred for some particular period as a result of a management policy decision. Once this decision is made, the costs become established for that period,

---

[8]Robert Beyer, *Profitability Accounting for Planning and Control* (Ronald Press, New York, 1963), p. 53. The terms are continued in use in the second edition by Beyer and Trawicki published by Ronald Press in 1972.

unless and until they are reduced by a revision which may be required by a change in business conditions. Standby costs are essentially synonymous with committed costs; they are costs such as the compensation for key supervisory personnel who would be retained when a plant is shut down. Programmed costs are essentially synonymous with discretionary costs; they are costs such as advertising that can be cut back if need be.

Standby costs and programmed costs are classified further by Beyer as *specific* or *general.* They may be specifically attributable to a product line, and would cease if the line were discontinued, or they may be applicable to general corporate activities and would continue unaffected.

The costs of providing capacity also are known as *capacity costs,* that is, costs which do not increase with volume. These are fixed costs planned at a specific amount for a period, and they are sometimes called period costs. They may be viewed as costs that expire during the current period, as opposed to product costs, which may be viewed as attaching to units produced. Essentially, period costs are the costs of standing ready to produce. They are charged against revenues in the current period. Product costs are inventoriable costs. (The distinction is particularly applicable in connection with the subject of "direct costing," which is discussed in Chapter 11.)

Nature of Fixed Costs.   What makes a cost fixed? The determination, at least to some extent, depends on organization policy and the time span being considered. Most costs are not inherently fixed or variable in nature. If management cuts the work force because of a drop in demand, labor cost is variable; otherwise it is fixed.

However, the argument that costs acquire the characteristics of being fixed or variable through operating decisions by management is quite different from the contention that costs become fixed or variable depending on management's choice of accounting method. The managerial significance of a cost is not changed by the way in which it is reported. Some accountants have asserted that when depreciation is calculated by the straight-line method it is fixed, but when it is calculated by the unit-of-production method it is variable. Management does control how reported depreciation varies with volume, but the actual cost is determined by expiration of an asset's utility. As Keynes has noted,[9] one component of depreciation relates to physical wear and tear, and is a variable cost. A second component is brought about by obsolescence and inadequacy, and is a fixed cost, unrelated to the use of the asset.

Measuring the Cost-Volume Relation.   Four methods are available for measuring the functional relation between costs and output: (1) engineering introspection, (2) high-low approximation, (3) visual scatter plot, and (4) regression analysis.

(1) Under the engineering introspection approach, the cost analyst determines how costs should increase with work load. Time and motion studies and generalized productivity data are examined. An engineering estimate of fixed and variable costs emerges. (2) Using the high-low approximation, the analyst plots a representative number of weekly or monthly costs against output, then sketches a line through the high and low points. (3) The visual scatter plot is similar, except the line is fitted by sight to an average of the points. (4) Regression analysis is a mathematical method for fitting a line to the data so as to minimize the squared differences of the points from the line of best fit. The function may be linear or nonlinear.

Costs may be expressed as a function of more than one variable for greater reliability. Dean[10] found in a study of department store costs that they correlated

[9]John Maynard Keynes, *The General Theory of Employment Interest and Money* (Harcourt, Brace and Company, New York, 1935), pp. 53–55.
[10]"Department Store Cost Functions," in *Studies in Mathematical Economics and Statistics,* Oskar Lange, ed. (Cambridge University Press, London, 1942).

highly with both the number of transactions and the average value per transaction. Multiple regression analysis can be applied when an analyst believes that cost is related to variables in addition to volume.

RESPONSIBILITY ACCOUNTING AND CONTROLLABLE COSTS

Reports for division managers are of most use when they clearly set out the costs that these executives can control. Departmental statements in the past often included both controllable and uncontrollable expenses without separation. A busy manager then had to sort out controllable variances from a confused list. Many are completely outside the manager's sphere of influence. For example, depreciation of machinery often has been viewed as an unfair charge by a manager who had no voice in the acquisition of the machine.

Responsibility Accounting. *Responsibility accounting* focuses a manager's attention on controllable costs. It is a system for organizing and reporting data according to the responsibilities of individuals. Higgins[11] defines responsibility accounting as a system for reporting only controllable costs to a manager.

> In effect, the system personalizes the accounting statements by saying, "Joe, this is what you originally budgeted and this is how you performed for the period with actual operations as compared against your budget." By definition it is a system of accounting which is tailored to an organization so that costs are accumulated and reported by levels of·responsibility within the organization. Each supervisory area in the organization is charged *only* with cost for which it is responsible and over which it has control.

Responsibility accounting is based on the hypothesis that cost reports are designed primarily to motivate managers to maximum performance. It is assumed that standards have been set with the aspiration levels of managers in mind, and it is believed that reporting of exceptions will motivate managers to pursue actions congruent with the overall goals and objectives of an organization.

The reports under a system of responsibility accounting begin with statements to foremen, who are in charge of only a few workers, and continue with statements to each higher level of management that incorporate the figures of more and more underlying statements as the pyramid rises. An executive at any level can review the results obtained by each lower level.

Practice differs among accountants in the reporting of uncontrollable costs. Some omit them entirely from reports to lower-echelon executives. Others include them in a separate section. The second procedure shows an executive that directly controllable costs are not the only concern of an enterprise. However, the first approach does not confuse the manager with uncontrollable variances.

Controllable and Uncontrollable Costs.   The success of responsibility accounting depends on the ability of a company to identify correctly which costs are controllable at each level of management. Fundamentally, a cost is *controllable* when a manager exerts spending authority over it. That is, *controllable costs* are those which can be curtailed at a given organizational level. The manager of a machining department controls indirect labor and manufacturing supplies used in that department. Such a manager does not control his or her own salary or the salary of higher-level managers. These salaries, which would be allocated as a charge against departments under traditional methods, would be separated from them under responsibility accounting.

Locus of control is relatively clear for some costs; for others it is not. Some costs are only partly controllable by a given manager. The control of maintenance costs

---

[11]John A. Higgins, "Responsibility Accounting," *Arthur Andersen Chronicle*, April 1952.

depends both on the ability of a production manager to prevent abuse of equipment and on the proficiency of a maintenance manager to supervise repairmen.

Jointly controllable costs are encountered in many organizations, service as well as manufacturing. Branch managers of a large New York City bank had little to say about the hiring of their employees; nonetheless, they did control scheduling and assignment of work. Accordingly, the expense for branch salaries was shown as controllable on branch statements. Cost classification is a practical art. Absence of scientific precision has not been a bar to the effectiveness of responsibility accounting.

Cost controllability has a time as well as a place dimension. Costs resulting from decisions of prior periods are not controllable in the short run by anyone; in the long run, however, these costs, like all others, are controllable. The control over a fixed-asset acquisition, for example, is exercised when its purchase is approved. The subsequent depreciation expense is not controllable.

All costs are controllable by someone, at least to some extent, at some time. Occasionally, costs are managed jointly by several executives, and such costs should be reported to each of them. As a general rule, however, one person should ultimately be responsible for each expenditure. The existence of jointly managed costs may signal to management the need for a restructuring of its table of organization. The installation of responsibility accounting system frequently forces management to define its lines of authority more sharply.

Controllable, Variable, and Direct Costs.   Variable costs are not necessarily identical to controllable costs. Most variable costs are controllable at the lowest level of management. For example, cloth in a garment factory is both a variable cost and a controllable cost. However, controllable costs are not limited to variable costs. Some fixed costs are also controllable. Heat and light is controllable at the shop level. A watchful manager may effect savings even though usage is unrelated to output.

Conversely, variable costs are not necessarily controllable costs. A cost is controllable by one who monitors it. A cost is variable when it is a function of output. The two are not the same. For example, a brewery found that the cost of cans varied with beer packaged; but with little wastage of cans, the cost of containers was not controllable by the manager of the container department. As a matter of fact, the cost of the cans varied mostly with the price of aluminum rather than with production.

Also, direct costs may not be controllable. Responsibility statements include controllable costs and exclude (or show separately) direct costs that are not controllable. "Direct costs" are generally costs incurred in a department, as opposed to indirect costs, which are prorated to a department. (The term "direct costs" is also used as a synonym for prime costs. One can usually tell by context what is meant.) The direct costs of a machining department include the salary of the manager and depreciation of machinery, as opposed to joint departmental costs, such as building occupancy and corporate overheads, which are prorated to departments on some basis such as floor space. Depreciation of machinery is a direct cost but not controllable. Likewise, the manager's salary is direct but not controllable, because it is approved by a higher authority. Direct costs may, or may not, be controllable at the departmental level. Controllable and uncontrollable direct costs are comingled in conventional statements. Controllable costs are listed separately under responsibility accounting.

COSTS FOR DECISION MAKING

Costs for decision making differ from those for managerial control. Costs for decisions are expected sacrifices arising from specific actions. Costs for control are monetary expenditures from general operations.

The essence of decision making is the sorting out of options and the attaching of payoffs to them. Action is based on an evaluation of the payoffs ordered in some fashion, possibly by expected values. The information specialist measures the expected costs and benefits that determine the payoffs.

Incremental Versus Sunk Cost.   Costs relevant for the making of decisions are those that change as a consequence of selecting one option as opposed to another. When a manufacturer with unused capacity in the short run decides whether to make or buy a component, the pertinent costs are for the additional materials, labor, and direct supervision required to fabricate the component. The costs for rent, taxes, and insurance, which continue whether the component is manufactured or not, are irrelevant. The difference in total cost from selecting one option over another is called *incremental cost,* or differential cost.

Marginal cost is the increase in total cost for one additional unit of output. In other words, marginal cost is a special kind of incremental cost. It is the rate of incremental cost per unit of output at any given level of activity. Marginal cost is used for expansion and pricing decisions. Generally, a firm expands until marginal cost equals marginal revenue. That is, a firm expands so long as the increase in cost is less than the increase in revenue.

A *sunk cost* is one that is not affected by a particular decision. It is the opposite, or complement, of an incremental cost. Amounts that have already been spent on research and development are sunk costs for purposes of considering whether or not to go ahead with the manufacture and marketing of a product. The expenditures of prior years are sunk costs. They do not change with the decision to produce, and thus are irrelevant for that decision. However, when a company is making an economic analysis, and has not as yet done research and development work, R&D is an incremental cost properly chargeable against the project.

Fixed costs are not always sunk costs. Salaries of supervisors, though fixed over a broad range of output, do eventually increase. Hence, these fixed costs are not sunk costs for capital budgeting. Also, sunk costs are not restricted to fixed costs. Variable costs can be sunk costs under some circumstances. For example, when a company is deciding whether to lease or buy a plant, the variable cost of power is not likely to be affected; hence it is irrelevant and may be termed a sunk cost for this decision.

In the context of an abandonment decision, an *avoidable cost* is one that is eliminated when part of the activities of an organization are discontinued. A sunk cost is unavoidable. Avoidable costs from elimination of activities may be less than the incremental costs from their addition because of union agreements and other contractual obligations that preclude the reduction of some costs, at least in the short run.

Shillinglaw suggests the concept of *attributable cost* for studying whether segments of a business should be discontinued.[12] He defines an attributable cost as

> the cost per unit that could be avoided, on the average, if a product or function were discontinued entirely without changing the supporting organization structure. The costing unit may be either a physical product or a unit of service performed.

Attributable cost (which may be accumulated by an organization as part of its management information system) is more suited than full cost or variable cost for decisions to discontinue a given cost center, activity, or product. It is the long-run analogue to the short-run concept of avoidable cost. In other words, when a manager is considering whether to discontinue a product, the attributable cost is the relevant cost because it includes the variable out-of-pocket costs and fixed departmental costs that would be eliminated if the product were abandoned.

---

[12]Gordon Shillinglaw, "The Concept of Attributable Cost," *Journal of Accounting Research,* Spring 1963, p. 77.

Opportunity Cost Versus Monetary Cost.   *Opportunity cost* is the net benefit that would have been received from an asset if put to its next best use. The concept of opportunity cost is implicit in any comparison of alternatives. The merit of any course of action is its relative merit, the difference between one action and another.

For example, a decision of whether to make or buy a product requires a determination of opportunity cost. Suppose that the unit cost of material, labor, and variable overhead is $24 per unit, whereas fixed overhead in the department amounts to another $6 per unit, for a total of $30. Suppose further that a vendor agrees to supply the component for $28. Should the company make or buy the product? The answer depends on what could be done with the manufacturing facilities released from production. If this plant is to remain idle, the $24 out-of-pocket payment is the only relevant cost, and it is cheaper to make the component. On the other hand, if the facility can be rented to an outsider for the equivalent of $5 per unit, $29 is an opportunity cost per unit and it is cheaper to buy the component. The opportunity cost for the plant is the maximum that could be earned if it were put to another use.

The explicit introduction of opportunity cost is indicated when some of the resources for a proposal are already owned by a company. For example, when management decides to replace machinery with a book value of $60,000 and a resale value of $100,000, it is the resale value that is relevant. Though no money is paid, the cash foregone from resale (net of tax effects) is a cost. It is an opportunity cost: the sacrifice of the benefits that would have been received if the asset were put to its next best use.

Costs for Operations Research Models.   Costs for operations research (OR) have three characteristics: (1) they are incremental costs; (2) they are opportunity costs; and (3) they are projected costs.

Management information systems are being extended gradually to include some costs relevant for OR; however, the vast majority of costs now being accumulated are not useful for this purpose without transformation. They are historical costs. These are relevant for OR only to the extent that they help to predict future costs. Opportunity costs, such as the cost of lost sales needed for inventory decisions, are generally not accumulated in accounting records. To understand the nature of costs for OR, let us consider three OR models.

Linear programming (LP) is a common model employed to optimize a constrained objective function. In applying LP to optimize product mix, one must specify the unit profit for each product. This profit is the incremental profit, which excludes fixed costs. It is forward looking, based on expected factor prices for the planning period. Additionally, it is based on the opportunity costs of the inputs, that is, what they would bring in their next best use. Thus the costs required are incremental, opportunity, and projected.

Experimentation is now being conducted on the feasibility of using OR models to derive relevant costs for certain classes of decisions. For example, an attempt has been made to use the LP model to solve the transfer-price problem (what price to bill transfers of goods and services from one division to another).

A mathematical transformation of the original LP problem, called the dual, provides *shadow prices,* the unit worth of each input used. Some writers have suggested these shadow prices, or imputed opportunity costs, should be used for valuing products transferred from one division to another, that is, for solving the transfer-price problem.[13]

Another illustration of costs for OR is provided by a queuing model. A sugar

[13]Nicholas Dopuch and David Drake, "Accounting Implications of a Mathematical Programming Approach to the Transfer Price Problem," *Journal of Accounting Research,* Spring 1964, pp. 10–24.

refiner wanted to determine whether another truck loading dock should be constructed. It was to be justified by a reduction in idle time of trucks waiting for a position to unload. The relevant cost of idle time for the trucks is the opportunity cost as measured by the best alternative use of the trucks. In this queuing model, as in the LP model, the required costs are other than the historical costs available from traditional accounting records. The relevant costs are incremental, opportunity, and projected.

Management information systems can be designed to capture some opportunity costs, particularly for probabilistic inventory models. Failure to order in sufficiently large quantities may result in stock-outs, the costs of which are largely measurable in terms of unfilled orders. An information system can be tailored to capture data on unfilled orders; however, for most OR applications, costs must be gathered for specific models.

Let us consider a replacement model as a final example. Some equipment, such as transformers and pumps, runs at almost 100 percent efficiency for their economic lives, then suddenly fail. Other equipment gradually deteriorates with age, and results in increasing maintenance and operating costs. This discussion is concerned with equipment of the second type.

Equipment never would be replaced if the annual operating and maintenance costs (including obsolescence) did not increase, because the longer an asset is held, the lower is its annual amortization cost. However, after a number of years, this decrease in amortization cost is offset by an increase in maintenance and operating (M&O) costs.

This can be demonstrated by a simplified illustration for a fleet of taxis, as shown in Exhibit 1. The discounting of cash flows is ignored to facilitate exposition and to focus on relevant costs. Each taxi costs $6,600 and is depreciated on a straight-line basis to a zero residual at the end of each year (to simplify discussion further). Operating costs, which are $600 the first year, increase by $600 annually. Thus, if a cab is held for two years, average annual M&O is ($600 + $1,200)/2 = $900. For three years it is ($600 + $1,200 + $1,800)/3 = $1,200, and so on.

EXHIBIT 1   Average Annual Costs per Cab

Years held	Capital amortization	Maintenance and operating	Total
1	$6,600	$ 600	$7,200
2	3,300	900	4,200
3*	2,200	1,200	3,400 (low)
4	1,650	1,800	3,450
5	1,320	2,400	3,720

*Optimum replacement life.

Although a replacement model could include probabilities, and could otherwise be made mathematically more formidable, the model illustrated is sufficiently complex to demonstrate the nature of costs required for implementation of its generalized form. The basic difficulties encountered in its practical application arise largely in the specification of maintenance and operating costs. The general principles of costs for OR apply. They should be incremental costs, they should be opportunity costs, and they should be prospective costs.

Data gathering is simplified by reason of the fact that only incremental costs are significant. Costs that remain the same from year to year can be ignored. For example, although oil needs to be changed periodically, this cost can be ignored so long as usage does not increase with the age of the cabs. The addition of a constant to the cost figures for each year will not change the year that the total annual cost reaches a minimum.

Part of M&O cost must be ascertained from sources other than company records. As taxis age they become less attractive, and fail to draw as much traffic. A significant part of M&O cost is the opportunity cost of lost revenue. This cost can be measured by a statistical sampling of traffic generated as related to age of cabs.

Last but not least, relevant costs are prospective; they are the expected costs over the future life of the cabs expressed in common-purchasing-power dollars. Historical data must be rectified for changes in factor prices. M&O costs increase each year not only because taxis require more repairs as they wear, but also because monetary costs increase due to inflation. Labor costs from company records must be restated by use of a specific wage-rate index to express them in terms of a common dollar. Costs adjusted for changes in factor prices are called *real costs,* as opposed to *nominal costs* or monetary costs. Costs for OR are economic costs measured by the sacrifices of the next best alternatives foregone.

This chapter has summarized the different meanings of cost and the various cost classifications that have proven useful to management. Cost analysts have developed a number of different cost constructs to guide them in the classification of costs for a variety of managerial applications. Different cost constructs are appropriate for different purposes.

BIBLIOGRAPHY

Beyer, Robert, and D. J. Trawicki: *Profitability Accounting for Planning and Control,* 2nd ed., Ronald Press, New York, 1972.

Clark, J. Maurice: *Studies in the Economics of Overhead Costs,* University of Chicago Press, Chicago, 1923.

Cost Accounting Standards Board: "Standards, Rules and Regulations as of June 30, 1975," U.S. Government Printing Office, Washington, D.C., 1975.

Davidson, Sidney, James S. Schindler, and Roman L. Weil: *Fundamentals of Accounting,* 5th ed., Dryden Press, Hinsdale, Ill., 1975.

Dean, Joel: *Statistical Determination of Costs, with Special Reference to Marginal Costs,* University of Chicago Press, Chicago, 1936.

Dopuch, Nicholas, and David Drake: "Accounting Implications of a Mathematical Programming Approach to the Transfer Price Problem," *Journal of Accounting Research,* Spring 1964, pp. 10–24.

Higgins, John A.: "Responsibility Accounting," *Arthur Andersen Chronicle,* April 1952.

Horngren, Charles T.: *Cost Accounting: A Managerial Emphasis,* 4th ed., Prentice-Hall, Englewood Cliffs, N.J., 1977.

Shillinglaw, Gordon: "The Concept of Attributable Cost," *Journal of Accounting Research,* Spring 1963, pp. 77–85.

————: *Cost Accounting: Analysis and Control,* 3rd ed., Richard D. Irwin, Homewood, Ill., 1972.

Simon, Herbert A., Harold Guetzkow, George Kozmetsky, and Gordon Tyndall: *Centralization vs. Decentralization in Organizing the Controller's Department,* Controllership Foundation (now Financial Executives Institute), New York, 1954.

Chapter **3**

Mathematical Concepts in Cost Accounting*

JOEL S. DEMSKI

Professor of Information and Accounting Systems, Graduate School
of Business, Stanford University

INTRODUCTION

Mathematics is used extensively in the theory and practice of cost accounting. Unfortunately, a single chapter in a handbook, indeed a single handbook, cannot possibly capture the various aspects of mathematics used, let alone the purposes

*The considerable help of Professors Charles A. Holloway and Charles T. Horngren in the preparation of this chapter is gratefully acknowledged.

for and manners in which they are employed. In addressing the topic of mathematical concepts in this *Handbook* we must, therefore, adopt a less ambitious goal than that of a coherent treatment or general survey.

Our strategy is to concentrate on a central use of mathematics in cost accounting, that of building models and using the models to analyze issues in cost accounting. References will be provided for the reader interested in more specific techniques or uses. As such, we do not provide a chapter dealing with the techniques of, say, statistics, matrix algebra, or the relationship of linear programming to cost accounting. Rather, we concentrate on some conceptual underpinnings that may be applied to a host of cost accounting issues.

The general model-building theme is explored in the first section of the chapter. In the second section, we turn to an exploration of probability as a model of uncertainty. This provides an opportunity to explore a useful concept as well as to illustrate the model-building theme. Finally, in the third section we explore decision theory as a model of choice behavior under uncertainty. Besides providing an additional model-building illustration, this provides a theoretical basis for systematically resolving numerous cost accounting dilemmas, such as "proper" methods of product cost measurement.

MATHEMATICS AND COST ACCOUNTING

Mathematics is an integral part of cost accounting. Combining, relating, and allocating costs rests on the theory of numbers. In fact, if we view mathematics in a broad sense of "systematic treatment of relationships among symbolic expressions," it becomes clear that cost accounting is a part of mathematics. It is not entirely surprising, then, that we find a fairly large literature that employs mathematics to analyze cost accounting practices.

Mathematics has, for example, been used to *analyze* various *cost accounting procedures.* Discounting techniques, an application of time series, have been used to compare various depreciation patterns with conventional capital budgeting procedures.[1] Calculus has been used to analyze cost behavior patterns when significant learning patterns are present.[2] Algebra has been used to analyze standard cost variance analysis procedures[3] and to compare direct with full costing procedures depending on whether LIFO or FIFO inventory procedures are employed.[4] Linear algebra has been used to explore allocation procedures.[5] And the basic double-entry framework has been analyzed as a network[6] as well as a functionally represented information structure.[7]

[1]C. T. Horngren, *Cost Accounting: A Managerial Emphasis,* 4th ed. (Prentice-Hall, Englewood Cliffs, N.J., 1977); or G. Shillinglaw, *Cost Accounting: Analysis and Control,* 4th ed. (Richard D. Irwin, Homewood, Ill., 1977).

[2]A. W. Corcoran, *Mathematical Applications in Accounting* (Harcourt, Brace and World, New York, 1968); N. Dopuch, J. G. Birnberg, and J. S. Demski, *Cost Accounting: Accounting Data for Management's Decisions,* 2nd ed. (Harcourt Brace Jovanovich, New York, 1974); Horngren, *Cost Accounting;* and Shillinglaw, *Cost Accounting.*

[3]See Chapter 16.

[4]Y. Ijiri, R. K. Jaedicke, and J. L. Livingstone, "The Effect of Inventory Costing Methods on Full and Direct Costing," *Journal of Accounting Research,* Spring 1965.

[5]Corcoran, *Mathematical Applications;* R. S. Kaplan, "Variable and Self-service Costs in Reciprocal Allocation Models," *Accounting Review,* October 1973; and J. K. Shank, *Matrix Methods in Accounting* (Addison-Wesley, Publishing Co., Reading, Mass., 1972).

[6]A. Charnes, W. W. Cooper, and Y. Ijiri, "Breakeven Budgeting and Programming to Goals," *Journal of Accounting Research,* Spring 1963; and Y. Ijiri, *Management Goals and Accounting for Control* (North Holland Publishing Co., Amsterdam, 1965).

[7]J. S. Demski and G. A. Feltham, *Cost Determination: A Conceptual Approach* (Iowa State University Press, Ames, Iowa, 1976).

Similarly, various mathematical techniques have been used to *examine the use of cost accounting data.* Application of algebra and probability in breakeven analysis is, perhaps, the most familiar example.[8] Calculus and classical optimization techniques have been used to examine various transfer pricing schemes[9] as well as allocation procedures in a single-entity setting.[10] They have also been used to analyze when standard cost variances warrant investigation.[11] And probability theory has been employed to determine consistent manners of revising cost expectations in the light of recent events.[12]

Even more common, however, is the examination of formal decision models that represent or describe management's resource allocation decisions in order to determine what costing procedures ought, in some sense, to be provided. Capital budgeting, cost-volume-profit analyses, and inventory control procedures, for example, are often examined in this light. The classic study of cost accounting, J. M. Clark's *Economics of Overhead Costs* (published in 1923 by the University of Chicago Press) employed this technique; and it provides the structure of present-day textbooks as well as this *Handbook.*

Finally, mathematics is also used to *characterize the process of selecting among cost accounting alternatives.* We continually face the question of trading off costliness of costing procedures for the quality of the resulting data. (As developed on pp. 3-12–3-16, quality is assessed in terms of the decisions that are made on the basis of the data provided.) For example, the questions of how many cost elements to aggregate in a common overhead pool or how detailed a recording of scrap to employ are dealt with, in one way or another, by trading off costliness and quality of the data. And mathematics has been used to analyze such choices, employing the same techniques as when we analyze management's allocation decisions.[13]

A central theme in these various applications is that of *modeling* the process and using the model to analyze specific issues. In particular, we model various data generating, data use, and choice processes in cost accounting. Put differently, we construct symbolic representations of the processes in question. (And in this sense any cost accounting system, because it purports to be a representation of some economic phenomenon, is a model.)

The essential idea here is deceptively simple. We merely detail the relationship between some independent and dependent variables. We might depict this as follows:

$$z = f(c, u) \tag{1}$$

where z is the dependent variable or variables of interest, c and u are the independent variables, and f is the detailed functional relationship in question. Often we distinguish the independent variables in terms of whether they are controllable, c, or uncontrollable, u.

---

[8]Chapter 19; Dopuch, Birnberg, and Demski, *Cost Accounting;* Horngren, *Cost Accounting;* R. K. Jaedicke and A. Robichek, "Cost-Volume-Profit Analysis Under Uncertainty," *Accounting Review,* October 1964; and G. Johnson and S. Simik, "Multiproduct C.V.P. Analysis Under Uncertainty," *Journal of Accounting Research,* Autumn 1971.

[9]A. Abdel-Khalik and E. Lusk, "Transfer Pricing—A Synthesis," *Accounting Review,* January 1974; Dopuch, Birnberg, and Demski, *Cost Accounting;* Horngren, *Cost Accounting;* and J. Hirshleifer, "On the Economics of Transfer Pricing," *Journal of Business,* July 1956.

[10]R. Weil, Jr., "Allocating Joint Costs," *American Economic Review,* December 1968.

[11]R. S. Kaplan, "The Significance and Investigation of Cost Variances: Survey and Synthesis," *Journal of Accounting Research,* Autumn 1975.

[12]Dopuch, Birnberg, and Demski, *Cost Accounting;* and Demski and Feltham, *Cost Determination.*

[13]Demski and Feltham, *Cost Determination;* and H. Itami, *Evaluation of Adaptive Behavior and Information Timing in Management Control* (American Accounting Association, New York, 1977).

Of course, specifying the variables and their relationship is the key to successful representation. We seek to study, say, the relationship between alternative costing procedures but find carefully controlled actual use of the competing procedures impracticable. The alternative is to construct a model and use it to gain some insight into how the procedures differ. In specifying the model, however, we must keep it simple enough to be able to address the question of interest, but rich enough to capture a sufficient amount of "reality" so that we retain confidence that results obtained by using the model bear some relationship to the real phenomena in question. Otherwise, the model is too complex to be manageable (either in terms of data required or ability to take advantage of existing mathematical techniques of analysis) or so nonrepresentative that its usefulness is relegated to entertainment. The key, in other words, is to balance tractability with representativeness in specifying the variables and their relationship.[14]

Example. A simple inventory model is indicative of this philosophy. Suppose that we face a problem of determining how much of a raw material to keep in stock. Two classes of assumptions will provide for a particularly straightforward analysis of such a question. First, we presume a known constant rate of usage for the material and do not allow any stock-outs to occur. Let D denote the known annual usage. Second, we presume a known linear cost structure consisting of ordering and storage cost components. The ordering cost increases directly with the number of units acquired during the year and with the number of orders placed during the year. The storage cost increases directly with the average level of inventory during the year.

Suppose that q units of the raw material are ordered each time an order is placed and that the orders are timed to arrive just as the inventory on hand is fully depleted. D/q orders will then be placed each year; and with the inventory on hand varying uniformly between zero and q, the average inventory throughout the year will be $q/2$. Hence the presumed cost structure is linear in D, D/q, and $q/2$.

Now let F denote the fixed component of the total cost, P the variable cost per unit of material (e.g., price and shipping cost), C_p the variable cost per order placed and received (e.g., order and payment processing cost), and C_s the variable cost per unit of average inventory on hand (e.g., capital cost and insurance). We then have the following total cost structure:

$$\text{Total Cost} = F + PD + C_p \left(\frac{D}{q}\right) + C_s \left(\frac{q}{2}\right) \tag{2}$$

Relating back to our basic description of a model, we now have total cost as the dependent variable, D, F, P, C_p, and C_s as the independent uncontrollable variables, and q as the independent controllable variable. And the functional relationship is specified in relation (2) above.

Moreover, the presumed structure is readily analyzed with calculus. In particular, we seek an order policy, q, that will minimize the total cost of acquiring D units of raw material per year. Differentiating total cost with respect to q, setting the result equal to zero, and solving for q produces the familiar economic order quantity or EOQ model:[15]

---

[14]R. L. Ackoff, *Scientific Method: Optimizing Applied Research Decisions* (John Willey & Sons, New York, 1962); R. L. Ackoff and M. W. Sasieni, *Fundamentals of Operations Research* (John Wiley & Sons, New York, 1968); and V. C. Hare, Jr., *Systems Analysis: A Diagnostic Approach* (Harcourt, Brace and World, New York, 1967).

[15]
$$\frac{d \text{ Total Cost}}{dq} = 0 = \frac{-C_p D}{q^2} + \frac{C_s}{2}$$

and second-order conditions ensure a minimizing solution:

$$\frac{d^2 \text{ Total Cost}}{dq^2} = \frac{2 C_p D}{q^3} > 0$$

$$q^* = \sqrt{\frac{2DC_p}{C_s}} \tag{3}$$

Several comments are in order. First, we term q^* an *optimal controllable variable* in that it produces the most desirable value of the dependent variable. Whether q^* is a good or "optimal" solution to the problem actually at hand depends on how well the model in (2) represents that problem. We have carefully chosen a structure that, in this case, is amenable to straightforward analysis. In other words, by endowing the model with requisite properties, we are able to appeal to mathematical techniques in order to perform the desired analysis. More specifically, the precise cost structure assumed provides for a straightforward, easy determination of the optimal controllable variable. Of course, alternative assumptions could be made (e.g., allow for stock-outs, recognize an uncertain or time varying demand, or recognize quantity discounts). But the basic point of trading off tractability and representativeness remains.

Second, even when a decision is to be made, we do not always formulate the model so that an optimal solution can be determined. Required complexity may be such that *simulation*[16] is used to locate the optimal solution approximately, or extensive search procedures may be only partially implemented.[17] Also, interactive models may be employed, in which the model is used to predict implications of various configurations of the controllable variables, but a decision maker directly intervenes and selects the controllable variables to be analyzed and ultimately implemented.[18] For example, rather than directly express the benefits and costs of various stock-out admitting policies in some summary profit or utility measure, we might use a model to predict the pattern of costs and stock-outs associated with the various policies and then allow the manager to decide which of the possible trade-offs is most desirable (or least undesirable).

Third, we see that the motivation for some types of cost measurements may arise in contexts much broader than that of traditionally construed cost analysis. Here, for example, an ability to analyze the inventory model has an impact on the basic form of cost function that is sought. Indeed, some of the cost elements, such as capital charges imbedded in the C_s term, are not measured in conventional costing systems.

PROBABILITY AS A MODEL OF UNCERTAINTY

In this section we discuss the notion of probability. This is an extremely important element in many models with which the cost accountant deals.[19] And it is, in itself, an example of a model. We begin with a simple motivating example.

Example.   Consider a situation in which a fair die is to be tossed. We assume that the die will come to rest on one of the six sides, and thus the possible outcomes are the first six positive integers: 1, 2, 3, 4, 5, 6. Before the die is tossed we do not know which of the six outcomes will obtain. However, because the die is fair, we

[16]Ackoff and Sasieni, *Fundamentals of Operations Research;* and H. M. Wagner, *Principles of Operations Research*, 2nd ed. (Prentice-Hall, Englewood Cliffs, N.J., 1975).

[17]Ackoff and Sasieni, *Fundamentals of Operations Research;* and Wagner, *Principles of Operations Research.*

[18]C. A. Holloway and R. T. Nelson, "Job Shop Scheduling with Due Dates and Overtime Capability," *Management Science,* September 1974; C. A. Holloway, et al., "An Interactive Procedure for the School Boundary Problem with Declining Enrollment," *Operations Research,* March–April, 1974; and A. H. Packer, "Simulation and Adaptive Forecasting as Applied to Inventory Control," *Operations Research,* July–August 1967.

[19]Probability is used, for example, in the determination and interpretation of production standards, in the determination of overhead budgets, in determination of warranty and pension related costs, and so on.

regard each outcome as being equally likely. In other words, no outcome is more likely to occur than any other outcome. We then say in this case with six equally likely outcomes that the probability of observing "die face up = 1" is 1/6, the probability of observing "die face up = 2" is 1/6, and so on. Alternatively, if you prefer the language of betting odds, we say that the odds of observing "die face up = 1" are 1 to 5. Similarly, in tossing a fair coin that is assumed always to come to rest on one of its faces, we would say that the probability of observing a "head" is 1/2.

Probability, then, is a familiar concept with a straightforward interpretation. This interpretation is not, however, unique.[20] (There are, in fact, three different interpretations of probability: the "classical" view expressed above, a "relative frequency" view based on repeated trials of an experiment, and a "subjective view" that emphasizes information aspects of probability.) And from a mathematical point of view, probability is merely a special type of model.

Definition of Probability.   To explore the meaning of probability, we envision some primitive experiment or uncertain event that will eventually result in some *outcome*. For example, throwing a die in the above illustration will result in one and only one of the first six positive integers being observed. The essential point here is that one and only one of the outcomes will eventually obtain. Let $X = \{x_1, x_2, \ldots, x_N\}$ be a mutually exclusive and collectively exhaustive collection of possible outcomes from some experiment. One and only one member of X will obtain (and N is positive and finite).

A probability measure is merely a rule that assigns—in a manner prescribed below—numbers to these outcomes and their various combinations. Let $\phi(x_j)$ denote the assigned probability of observing outcome x_j, $j = 1, \ldots, N$. We may also be interested in various groupings of these possible outcomes and the probability that any outcome in a particular grouping will obtain. Any such grouping of outcomes is termed an *event*. (Alternatively, an event is a subset of X.) For example, observing "die face up = 1" *or* "die face up = 2" is an event in our die-tossing experiment. Denote this event by $E_1 = \{1, 2\}$. Other examples of events in the die-tossing experiment are $E_2 = \{4, 5\}$, $E_3 = \{5, 6\}$, and $E_4 = \{1\}$, where E_1 and E_2 are mutually exclusive events in the sense that if the actual outcome is a member of E_1 it is not a member of E_2 and vice versa.

In somewhat formal terms, now, a probability measure is a rule that assigns a number $\phi(x_j)$ to each possible outcome x_j, $j = 1, \ldots, N$ such that (1) each number is nonnegative, $\phi(x_j) \geq 0$; (2) their sum is unity, $\sum_{j=1}^{N} \phi(x_j) = 1$; and (3) the assignments are additive across mutually exclusive events, such as $\phi(x_i \text{ or } x_j) = \phi(x_i) + \phi(x_j)$ where $i \neq j$.

In a strict sense, then, probability is a model, expressing a relationship between numbers (the dependent variable) and outcomes (the independent variables). The only requirements are nonnegativity, a total of unity, and additivity across mutually exclusive events. But no meaning is attached to these assignments. Hence, all of the assignments for our die-tossing experiment in Table 1 are correctly termed probabilities. Of course, we may have strong feelings about which make more sense than others. And this is an issue to which we now turn.

Objective and Subjective Probabilities.   The pure theory of probability, in other words, is silent on the related questions of how one should assign probabilities (e.g., which of the probability assignments in Table 1 is "best") and how they should be interpreted. One answer to these questions is the assignment and

---

[20]B. de Finetti, "Probability: Interpretations," in *International Encyclopedia of the Social Sciences* (The Macmillan Company, New York, 1968); and L. J. Savage, *The Foundations of Statistics* (John Wiley & Sons, New York, 1954).

TABLE 1   Possible Probability Assignments for Die-Tossing Experiment

Outcome	Probabilities			
	Case 1	Case 2	Case 3	Case 4
1	1/4	1/16	0	1/6
2	1/4	1/16	0	1/6
3	1/8	1/2	0	1/6
4	1/8	1/16	0	1/6
5	1/8	1/16	0	1/6
6	1/8	1/4	1	1/6

interpretation that arise from a simple counting operation that, presumably, independent observers would agree upon. That is, if a die were tossed a *large* number of times, we would assign the relative frequencies as equal to the probability assignments. This is an *objective* assignment and interpretation of probability. It relies on the properties of the experiment for its justification.

Of course, the concept of probability is not limited to situations in which counting operations are available or where a large number of repeated trials of the experiment is conceivable. Conceptually, for example, it is possible to speak of the probability of an undiscovered element, the probability that changes in the money supply are systematically related to inflationary forces in the economy, or the probability that division Z will experience a cost overrun next year. These are examples of another answer to the assignment and interpretation questions and are known as *subjective* probabilities. We do not necessarily expect interobserver agreement here. And we interpret such an assignment as a "degree of belief" that the respective events will obtain.

To illustrate, suppose that you are offered a choice of two bets. Either way, winning provides you a $10,000 gain whereas losing gives you nothing. The first is betting on heads on the flip of a fair coin. The second is betting on the Democratic candidate winning a particular election. If you are truly indifferent between which bet you take, it is perhaps reasonable to presume that you assign subjective probability 1/2 to the Democratic candidate winning. Alternatively, if you strictly prefer the latter, then you assign subjective probability in excess of 1/2 to the Democratic candidate winning. (We assume here that your personal wishes for who wins do not influence your thinking about who is likely to win, or that you bet on a particular football team because you think it is more likely to win and not because you want it to win.)

Uncertainty Representation and Summary Measures.   Now consider a situation in which management wants to know the cost of two alternative product-redesign plans. No one knows for sure what the respective costs will be. Rather the possible cost outcomes have been determined, and beliefs as to the various likelihoods have been encoded in an assignment of (subjective) probabilities to the various possible cost outcomes. A particular example is displayed in Table 2. Thus, with alternative a_1, the probability of the cost being $90,000 is .10; with alternative a_2, the probability of the cost being $60,000 is .20; and so on.

It may, at this point, be useful to summarize the distribution of outcome possibilities with some summary measures.[21] A common measure of central ten-

---

[21]Numerous summary measures, applicable to either probability distributions or summarizations of large numbers of data, are discussed in statistics textbooks. See W. L. Hayes, *Statistics for the Social Sciences*, 2nd ed. (Holt, Rinehart and Winston, New York, 1973); and W. A. Spurr and C. P. Bonini, *Statistical Analysis for Business Decisions*, rev. ed. (Richard D. Irwin, Homewood, Ill., 1973).

TABLE 2   Possible Outcomes and Probability
Assignments for Product-Redesign Example

Possible cost	Probability assignments	
	Plan a_1	Plan a_2
$ 20,000	.05	—
30,000	.10	.10
40,000	.10	.10
50,000	.15	.20
60,000	.20	.20
70,000	.15	.20
80,000	.10	.20
90,000	.10	—
100,000	.05	—
	1.00	1.00

dency is the mean or expected value, which we denote μ. For a discrete set of outcomes it is defined as

$$\mu = \sum_{j=1}^{N} x_j \phi(x_j) \tag{4}$$

For the two alternatives in Table 2, we have

$$\mu_1 = \$20,000(.05) + \$30,000(.10) + \cdots + \$100,000(.05)$$
$$= \$60,000$$
$$\mu_2 = \$20,000(.00) + \$30,000(.10) + \cdots + \$100,000(.00)$$
$$= \$59,000$$

Observe that computation of this measure requires summation over all possible outcomes, weighting each by its respective probability. The mean, in other words, is merely a weighted average of the outcomes.[22]

Further note that summarizing the two distributions in Table 2 with their respective means tells only part of the story. A remaining question is how "disperse" each is about its mean or measure of central tendency. A common measure of dispersion is the *variance*. It is denoted σ^2 and is computed as the expected value of the square of the difference between the possible outcomes and their mean:

$$\sigma^2 = \sum_{j=1}^{N} (x_j - \mu)^2 \phi(x_j)$$

And for each of the distributions in Table 2, we have

$$\sigma_1^2 = (\$20,000 - \$60,000)^2(.05) + (\$30,000 - \$60,000)^2(.10) + \cdots$$
$$+ (\$100,000 - \$60,000)^2(.05)$$
$$= \$450,000,000$$
$$\sigma_2^2 = (\$20,000 - \$59,000)^2(.00) + (\$30,000 - \$59,000)^2(.10) + \cdots$$
$$+ (\$100,000 - \$59,000)^2(.00)$$
$$= \$249,000,000$$

The positive square root of the variance is termed the standard deviation. It summarizes the same dispersion tendency, but in the same measurement units as the variable itself. Thus, we might summarize the two distributions in Table 2 by

---

[22]Such a procedure requires that the outcomes be represented numerically. (The technical term here is that the outcome be a random variable.) We do not compute the expected value of flipping a coin; but we do compute the expected value of a dollar bet based on the outcome of flipping a coin.

observing that the first has a mean of $\mu_1 = \$60,000$ and a standard deviation of $\sigma_1 = \$21,213$ whereas the second has a mean of $\mu_2 = \$59,000$ and a standard deviation of $\sigma_2 = \$15,780$. That is, although the second has a lower mean, its possible outcomes are more tightly distributed about that mean.

Use of Probability Theory. Numerous extensions of the cost measurement example in Table 2 are possible. In particular, by representing the uncertainty with a probability measure, we gain access to the many results of probability theory. We might, for example, elect to represent the uncertainty with one of the standard probability distribution functions that are extensively studied. By adopting the normal distribution, for example, we would be admitting to extremely large (indeed unbounded) negative and positive cost outcomes—though with extremely small and likely negligible probability. But we would also gain use of all known results concerning the normal distribution, such as the probability that the cost is within one standard deviation of the mean is .68.[23]

Similarly, we might consider conducting experiments to better determine the nature of the cost distributions. By invoking appropriate assumptions as to the underlying process and the manner in which the experiments are performed, we gain access to the rich results of sampling theory and classical hypothesis testing.[24]

Finally, by observing events that are correlated with the process in question, we may also be able to systematically revise the probability assignments that were originally assigned.[25]

DECISION THEORY AS A MODEL OF CHOICE BEHAVIOR

A mathematical model, recall, is a symbolic representation of some system or process. In turn, probability is a particular type of model that, by specifying conditions the posited relationship must satisfy, provides a rich set of theoretical results. Decision theory makes extensive use of probability theory and also provides a representation of choice behavior in terms of maximizing the value of a particular function. This, in turn, allows us to use the theory of optimization to study choice behavior.

The central features of decision theory and its relationship to cost accounting are explored in this concluding section. We begin with the setting of decision theory—a formally represented choice problem.

A Model of a Choice Problem. Many of the central features of decision theory can be developed by focusing on a setting in which some act must be selected from some set of available acts. (Presumably, at least two alternatives are present, otherwise there is nothing to choose.) Our purpose, however, will be better served if we specifically construct the type of setting to be explored.

We focus on a model relating dependent to controllable and uncontrollable independent variables. The basic problem is to specify or select the controllable independent variable that, in conjunction with the uncontrollable independent variables, results in the "best" or "most desirable" dependent variable value. This is a cumbersome description, and it is not surprising that we find a more specialized language in the decision theory literature.

The controllable variables are termed *acts* and, as noted above, the basic problem is to select an act from a specified set of available acts that is, in some sense, best. The uncontrollable variables are termed *states*. If more than one state is

[23]Hayes, *Statistics for the Social Sciences;* and Spurr and Bonini, *Statistical Analysis.*
[24]Hayes, *Statistics for the Social Sciences;* and Spurr and Bonini, *Statistical Analysis.*
[25]R. Schlaifer, *Analysis of Decisions Under Uncertainty* (McGraw-Hill Book Company, New York, 1969); and Spurr and Bonini, *Statistical Analysis.*

conceivable, but precisely which one is or will be present is unknown at the time of act selection, the problem is one of *choice under uncertainty*. (Otherwise, it is choice under subjective certainty.) The dependent variable of interest, in turn, is termed an *outcome*. Thus, a decision problem consists of a set of acts, set of states, and set of outcomes and a relationship specifying the outcome that will obtain for each possible act and state combination. Table 3 provides a symbolic representation of the assumed structure: m acts are available (denoted $a_1, \ldots, a_m$), n possible states are conceivable (denoted $s_1, \ldots, s_n$), and outcome x_{ij} will obtain if act a_i is selected and state s_j is present.

TABLE 3   Model of Choice Problem

		Possible states				
		s_1	s_2	$\cdots$ s_j	$\cdots$	s_n
Possible acts	a_1	x_{11}	x_{12}	$\cdots$ x_{1j}	$\cdots$	x_{1n}
	a_2	x_{21}	x_{22}	$\cdots$ x_{2j}	$\cdots$	x_{2n}
	$\cdot$	$\cdot$	$\cdot$	$\cdot$		$\cdot$
	$\cdot$	$\cdot$	$\cdot$	$\cdot$		$\cdot$
	a_i	x_{i1}	x_{i2}	$\cdots$ x_{ij}	$\cdots$	x_{in}
	$\cdot$	$\cdot$	$\cdot$	$\cdot$		$\cdot$
	$\cdot$	$\cdot$	$\cdot$	$\cdot$		$\cdot$
	a_m	x_{m1}	x_{m2}	$\cdots$ x_{mj}	$\cdots$	x_{mn}

Example. An example will illustrate the nature of this structure. Consider a manager who must decide whether to accept an offer to construct a variant of one of the firm's major products. Accepting or rejecting the offer will have no effect on the firm's normal activities (excess capacity is present, no demand effects will materialize if the offer is accepted, and so on). The question therefore reduces to one of whether the offered revenue exceeds the incremental cost of production. If the offer is accepted, the incremental revenue, labor cost, and material cost will be

Incremental revenue		$800,000
Incremental labor	$300,000	
Incremental material	200,000	500,000
Contribution to other costs and profit		$300,000

The only other cost in question is incremental overhead, and this amount is not known. All the manager knows is that it might total $100,000 or $400,000. Thus, accepting the offer will result in either an incremental profit of $200,000 or an incremental loss of $100,000. Rejection, on the other hand, will result in neither gain nor loss. Table 4 summarizes these data.

TABLE 4   Special Order Choice Problems

		Possible states	
		Low overhead: s_1	High overhead: s_2
Possible acts	a_1: accept	$200,000	$-$100,000
	a_2: reject	0	0

Representation of Choice Behavior.   The state-act-outcome model, then, is used to represent a decision problem. We must now introduce the concept of preference in order to be able to specify which act is "best." Two classes of assumptions are important here: consistency and expected value representation. We discuss them in turn.

Consistency essentially requires that choice be a meaningful concept. We require that, when confronted with a pair of choices, individuals be able to determine whether one is better than the other or whether they are truly indifferent. Otherwise we have no concept of preference and cannot meaningfully engage in systematic analysis of the decision problem posed in Table 3.

Consistency also requires that these expressions of preference be *transitive*. If confronted with three alternatives with the first valued at least as good as the second and the second valued at least as good as the third, the individual must also rank the first as good as the third. Otherwise, the choice process may whirl about in circles, needlessly consuming resources in the process.[26] (Imagine attempting to select a tree in a large Christmas tree lot without transitive preferences.)

Consistency, then, refers to the desire or ability to rank all choices in a transitive manner. Of course, if this consistency requirement could be readily met for all problem representations, the choice problem would be easily resolved. The individual would simply know, after looking at the choices available, which act or set of acts is best. However, additional assumptions allow us to represent these consistent preferences in an expected value manner. And this, in turn, allows us systematically to analyze the question of which act or set of acts is best. Thus, by moving to the expected value representation, we are able to use analysis to support this oblique and demanding concept of consistent preference among acts.

Basically, these additional assumptions require that the individual assign probabilities to the various outcomes and then choose among the acts in a manner consistent with these probability assignments.[27] To illustrate, return to the example in Table 4 and suppose that the manager assigns a probability of .6 to the low incremental overhead event, $\phi(s_1) = .6$, and .4 to the high incremental overhead event, $\phi(s_2) = .4$. (This implies a mean incremental gain of $\mu_1 = \$80,000$ with a standard deviation of $\sigma_1 = \$146,969$.) Further suppose that the manager's preferences for acts leading to incremental gains and losses are such that the act with the maximum *expected value of incremental gain* is always selected. With the assigned probabilities we then have:

Expected gain with $a_1 = \mu_1 = \$80,000$
Expected gain with $a_2 = \mu_2 = \$0$

And given the preference for acts that maximize expected value of incremental gain, the offer is clearly accepted.

Once a choice problem is properly specified, then, we introduce a concept of preference in order to be able to tell which act is best (relative to the specified preferences). With an expected value representation of these preferences, however, we have *decomposed* the analysis so that beliefs and risk-taking preferences are assessed separately. In turn, arithmetic operations are used to evaluate each possible act; and this, in its turn, allows us to use optimization theory in locating the best act. In particular, it is relatively easy to satisfy the consistency requirement, because our preferences are expressed in terms of the maximum expected value measure.

Expected value representation, however, is not confined to reliance on the expected value of the outcomes. Such behavior is, in fact, an extreme form in which only the outcome's expected value is relevant in assessing the respective act's

[26]More specifically, suppose that a_1 is better than a_2, a_2 is better than a_3, but (violating transitivity) a_3 is better than a_1. It is now conceivable that the individual could be in possesion of a_3, pay $100 to switch to a_2, then pay $100 to swith to a_1, and finally pay another $100 to switch to a_3—thereby winding up at the initial position minus $300!

[27]See Demski and Feltham, *Cost Determination;* S. Kassouf, *Normative Decision Making* (Prentice-Hall, Englewood Cliffs, N.J., 1970); and Schlaifer, *Analysis of Decisions Under Uncertainty.*

desirability. No attention whatever is paid to the dispersion of the possible out-comes about their respective means. For example, a_1 would be preferred to a_2 in this case as long as it had a positive expected outcome value, regardless of the variance of the outcome distribution. Such behavior is truly indifferent toward risk (where risk is defined in terms of the variability or dispersion of the possible outcomes about their expected value). More technically, such behavior is termed *risk-neutral* behavior.

It may, therefore, be desirable to account for the "riskiness" of the alternatives in selecting among them. The act a_2 guarantees a zero outcome here and therefore is riskless. The act a_1, on the other hand, guarantees an outcome of either $200,000 or $-$100,000 and is clearly risky. The question is whether its riskiness is too great.

We account for risk-taking attitudes in the analysis by introducing a utility function. This function represents the individual's outcome preferences. If the marginal utility of the outcome in question decreases as more of the outcome is provided, we have risk-avoiding or *risk-averse* behavior. For example, the man-ager's risk-taking behavior might be represented by the following utility function:

$$U(x) = (100,000 + x)^{1/4}$$

This particular function represents risk-taking behavior that demands a payment of at least $375 to accept a 50–50 gamble on winning or losing $10,000. That is, if the individual is paid $375 to accept such a gamble and wins, the outcome will be $375 + $10,000 = $10,375. And if the individual loses, the outcome will be $375 - $10,000 = -$9,625. The expected value of the utility of these outcomes is

$$.50(100,000 + 10,375)^{1/4} + .50(100,000 - 9,625)^{1/4} = 17.78$$

which is precisely equal to the utility of not participating in the gamble,

$$(100,000)^{1/4} = 17.78$$

Now analyze the choices in Table 4 with this particular attitude toward incre-mental gain and its risk. We see that the offer would be deemed too risky:

Expected Utility with $a_1 = .60(100,000 + 200,000)^{1/4} + .40(100,000 - 100,000)^{1/4}$
$= 14.04$

Expected Utility with $a_2 = (100,000)^{1/4} = 17.78$

Conversely, with less risk aversion it would not be deemed too risky. For example, with $U(x) = (100,000 + x)^{1/2}$ it would be accepted:[28]

Expected Utility with $a_1 = .60(100,000 + 200,000)^{1/2} + .40(100,000 - 100,000)^{1/2}$
$= 328.63$

Expected Utility with $a_2 = (100,000)^{1/2} = 316.23$

In sum, expected value representation allows for separate encoding of beliefs (in the probability function) and risk attitudes (in the utility function) in such a manner that the best act is the one that results in the maximum expected value of the utility function.[29] With uncertainty represented by the probability measure, we also have access to probability theory and, in particular, well-defined procedures for analyzing information-gathering options. This is discussed below.

Information. In analyzing the choice problem in Table 4, the manager com-pared the "accept" and "reject" acts in terms of the risks and returns each

[28]This utility function requires a payment of $250 to accept a 50–50 gamble on winning or losing $10,000.
[29]Further note that procedures exist for assessing utility functions and there is no inherent reason to use a "standard" function such as a square root, logarithmic, or exponential.

promised. It may, however, be possible to find out more about the uncertain outcomes associated with the various acts before committing to a particular act.

An extreme form of this question arises when we entertain the possibility of a clairvoyant revealing—with absolute certainty—which state will obtain before the manager must select an act. Quite obviously, if it were revealed that overhead would be low (s_1), the manager would accept the offer (select a_1). If it were revealed that overhead would be high (s_2), the manager would reject the offer (select a_2). Of course, before the clairvoyant's revealing, the manager would not know what message (s_1 or s_2) would be provided. Hence, before the clairvoyant's revealing, the manager faces an outcome structure of $200,000 incremental gain if s_1 is revealed and 0 if s_2 is revealed. Using the risk-neutral case, the manager would then perceive an expected outcome of

$$.60(\$200,000) + .40(\$0) = \$120,000$$

Conversely, because the manager would select a_1 (with an expected outcome of $80,000) without a clairvoyant, the manager would pay a maximum of

$$\$120,000 - \$80,000 = \$40,000$$

for a clairvoyant's services. This amount is termed *the expected value of perfect information*. It is the maximum amount the manager would pay to learn more about the cost structure in this particular setting.[30]

We term the clairvoyant's message *information* because it causes the manager to revise the state occurrence probability assignments. Moreover, it derives its value from the fact that the manager's act choice depends on which message is observed. That is, a_1 is selected if the message is s_1 and a_2 is selected if the message is s_2. Compare this with the case where a_1 results in only a $100 incremental *gain* if s_2 obtains; all other data remain as before. In this case, the manager will select a_1 regardless of what the clairvoyant reveals. Without any information, the manager selects a_1 with an expected outcome of

$$.60(\$200,000) + .40(\$100) = \$120,040$$

The manager will not use the information or outcome to alter behavior:

$$.60(\$200,000) + .40(\$100) = \$120,040$$

Thus, the information has no value in this particular case. Information will surely alter the manager's beliefs, but the act selected is unaffected and we have therefore no reason to commit resources to altering the beliefs.

Finally, this type of analysis is readily extended to questions of gathering less than perfect information. The information is again modeled in terms of probability revision. The only difference is that we do not alter the state probability assignments to the 0 or 1 extremes.

To illustrate, consider a situation in which the manager in the above example may, before selecting between the two options, commission a special accounting study to analyze some similar products in the firm. Such a study will result in one of two conclusions. Either the cost experience was above expectations (High Cost) or below expectations (Low Cost). Moreover, the recent experience and current production possibilities are related in such a manner that observing the High Cost event will convince the manager that s_2 will obtain for certain, whereas observing the Low Cost event will convince the manager that s_1 will obtain with probability .75 (and s_2 with probability .25).

[30]In the $U(x) = (100,000 + x)^{1/4}$ risk-averse case, we have an expected value of perfect information of $80,000 because $(100,000)^{1/4} = .60(300,000 - z)^{1/4} + .40(100,000 - z)^{1/4}$ when $z \cong 80,000$. Also see Chapter 19 for additional discussion of the expected value of perfect information.

Evaluating this information option requires that the manager decide what will be done upon receipt of either message and then, in conjunction with the message probabilities, evaluate the various possible outcomes. Given that the manager is using probability as a model of uncertainty, however, the message probabilities must be consistent with his or her other probability assignments. In particular, the manager must assign ϕ(High Cost) $= .20$ and ϕ(Low Cost) $= .80$.[31] These assignments are summarized in Table 5.

TABLE 5   **Probability Assignments for Special Order Example**

State

		s_1	s_2	
Signal	High Cost	$\phi(s_1$ given High Cost obtains) $= 0$	$\phi(s_2$ given High Cost obtains) $= 1$	ϕ(High Cost) $= .2$
	Low Cost	$\phi(s_1$ given Low Cost obtains) $= .75$	$\phi(s_2$ given Low Cost obtains) $= .25$	ϕ(Low Cost) $= .8$
		$\phi(s_1) = .6$	$\phi(s_2) = .4$	1

Observe, now, that if the study reports High Cost, the manager knows for certain that s_2 will obtain. In that event, the offer will *be rejected* (select a_2). Conversely, if the study reports Low Cost, the offer will be accepted.

Expected outcome if Low Cost reported and a_1
$$= .75(\$200,000) + .25(-\$100,000) = \$125,000$$
Expected outcome if Low Cost reported and $a_2 = 0$

Clearly, then, if the High Cost event obtains, the manager faces an outcome of $0; and if the Low Cost event obtains, the expected outcome is $125,000. Hence, prior to receiving the message [recalling that ϕ(Low Cost) $= .80$], the manager faces the following expected outcome:

$$.80(\$125,000) + .20(\$0) = \$100,000$$

Thus, recalling an expected outcome of $80,000 without any additional information, the manager will pay a maximum of $100,000 $-$ $80,000 = $20,000 for this special cost study. See Exhibit 1.

We see, in other words, that by employing probability as a model of uncertainty, questions of additional information are addressed systematically by consistent revision of probability assessments.

[31]Recall that $\phi(s_1) = .6$ and $\phi(s_1$ given Low Cost) $= .75$. Also, the High Cost event cannot— by assumption—occur in conjunction with s_1. Consistency in the probability assignments then requires that ϕ(Low Cost) $= .60/.75 = .80$. Moreover, we now encounter use of probability theory to revise probability assignments consistently. By Bayes' theorem, we have

$$\phi(s_1 \text{ given Low Cost}) = \frac{\phi(\text{Low Cost given } s_1)\phi(s_1)}{\phi(\text{Low Cost})}$$
$$= \frac{1 \times .6}{.8} = .75$$

and similarly, $\phi(s_2$ given Low Cost) $= .25$.

EXHIBIT 1 Diagrammatic Structure of Special Order Example

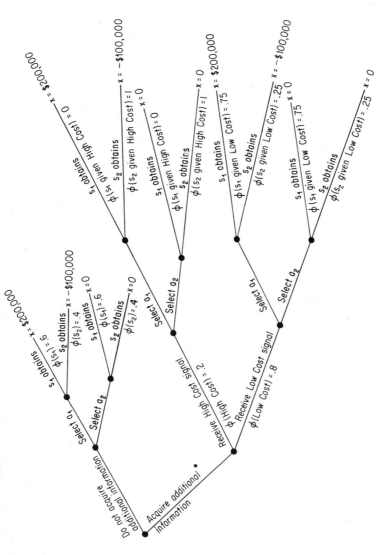

Design of Cost Accounting Systems.   Questions of how to measure costs are, in fact, information questions. The above example of whether to perform a special cost study illustrates that cost measurement is a question of information. Another is whether the use of departmental overhead charging rates is superior to a firm-wide rate. In both cases we analyze the cost measurement alternatives in terms of whether the outcomes they will ultimately produce, by influencing various decisions within the firm, are desirable. This is, by systematically specifying and analyzing the design question, we are able to analyze accounting alternatives explicitly in terms of the costs and benefits to which they give rise. At a conceptual level, then, decision theory provides a model of how one should, if preferences satisfy the requisite assumptions, resolve cost accounting controversies.[32]

SUMMARY

We have concentrated on the use of models in exploring mathematical concepts in cost accounting. Models have been used to analyze cost measurement procedures, the manner in which cost data are used, and selection among alternative methods of cost measurement. Ultimately, however, we must recognize a model for what it is. By endowing the model with sufficient mathematical properties, we are able to bring the results of mathematical development to bear *on the model*. But what such analyses tell us about the problem at hand depends on how faithfully the constructed model represents that problem. Models are not perfect; and in using them we must seek a proper balance between our ability to analyze them and our ability to learn from what that analysis produces.[33]

BIBLIOGRAPHY

Bergamini, D.: *Mathematics,* Time-Life Books, New York, 1963.

Emerson, L. S., and L. R. Paquette: *Linear Algebra, Calculus, and Probability: Fundamental Mathematics for the Social and Management Sciences,* Allyn & Bacon, Boston, 1971.

Howell, J. E., and D. Teichroew: *Mathematical Analysis for Business Decisions,* rev. ed., Richard D. Irwin, Homewood, Ill., 1971.

Livingstone, J. L.: *Management Planning and Control: Mathematical Models,* McGraw-Hill Book Company, New York, 1970.

Rappaport, A.: *Information for Decision Making: Quantitative and Behavioral Dimensions,* Prentice-Hall, Englewood Cliffs, N.J., 1975.

Williams, T. H., and C. H. Griffin: *Management Information: A Quantitative Accent,* Richard D. Irwin, Homewood, Ill., 1967.

---

[32]This approach to the resolution of cost accounting issues is described in Demski and Feltham, *Cost Determination.*

[33]Interestingly, the problem of model construction can itself be analyzed as a decision problem. That is, model selection is subject to cost-benefit tests.

Chapter **4**

Economic Concepts in Cost Accounting

GORDON SHILLINGLAW
Professor of Accounting, Graduate School of Business,
Columbia University

INTRODUCTION

Cost accounting springs mainly from the needs of managers and others to make decisions affecting the allocation of economic resources. This might suggest that cost accounting is based directly on a fairly well-defined set of concepts drawn from economic theory. The truth is something else. Cost accounting does use some economic concepts directly, particularly in cost estimation, but in many areas approximations of economic concepts are all the cost accountant can hope for.

This chapter deals with economic concepts, not economic principles. A concept is an idea, a description of a presumed phenomenon or relationship. Economic principles, on the other hand, are intended to serve as a basis for certain kinds of action. They include economic decision rules (e.g., maximization of present value) and analytical techniques (e.g., linear programming) as well as presumed laws of economic behavior (e.g., the law of supply and demand).

The line between concepts and principles is often indistinct. Principles embody concepts, and some concepts are so strong that they are virtually principles. Extension of the scope of this chapter to include a discussion of major economic principles, however, would cross the line into topics that can be dealt with more effectively in context in later chapters.

INTERFACES BETWEEN ECONOMICS AND COST ACCOUNTING

Although economics and cost accounting deal with the same phenomena, they sometimes approach these from different points of view. It would be tempting to say that economists prescribe and cost accountants measure, but it is not as simple as that. At least four groups of economists have had some impact on cost accounting or use some of its output:

1. Microeconomists, focusing on the forces that affect the allocation of resources within the economy

2. Managerial economists, concerned with making economic theory a useful tool in managerial planning and decision making

3. Industrial organization economists, interested in the public policy implications of microeconomic theory

4. Macroeconomists, interested in relationships among aggregate economic variables for regions, nations, or the world

The economic concepts embodied in most aspects of cost accounting come mainly from microeconomics and managerial economics. In fact, where cost accounting leaves off and managerial economics takes up is not very clear, and the distinction is not really important.

The affinity between cost accounting and theoretical microeconomics is far less clear. The microeconomist is interested in developing theoretical models to predict the behavior of individual firms and the markets in which they operate. The cost relationships in these models have been based mainly on logical reasoning, although some attempts have been made to identify them empirically.[1] Abstractions are both inevitable and necessary for this purpose. It makes little difference whether anyone can measure any of the variables in a theory—the theory is expected to stand or fall on its internal logic and the consistency of its predictions with observable conditions.

The cost accountant's interest in cost is more mundane, at least in part because

---

[1] J. Johnston, *Statistical Cost Analysis* (McGraw-Hill Book Company, New York, 1960), chaps. 4 and 5; also P. J. D. Wiles, *Price Cost, and Output* (Basil Blackwell & Mott, Oxford, 1956), chap. 12, apps. A and B.

the cost accountant traditionally is not concerned with revenues. Management wants to know what things cost. Management wants this information partly to help it set prices on its products, partly to decide whether new products are worth introducing or old products are worth keeping, and partly to find out whether costs are greater than they should be. Management is not interested in abstractions—it wants numbers.

Cost accountants have found that they cannot provide these numbers without some theory of what they are measuring, and so they, too, have built up a theoretical structure.[2] This structure does not try to answer any major questions; instead, it helps the practicing accountant define costs in each of a number of situations. These definitions in effect paraphrase the questions that the measures of cost are supposed to answer. The question, "What would happen to cost if we were to use our present facilities to fill customer order 4276 for delivery to customer A in location B at time C?" calls for an entirely different answer from the question, "What would happen to cost if we were to acquire, equip, and staff new facilities to make repeated deliveries to a number of customers in different locations over a period of years?" The theoretical structure of cost accounting consists of guides to the answers to these questions and others like them.

The cost accountant's task is more difficult than the economist's in that the cost accountant must resolve the measurement problems that the microeconomist can assume away. The economist can, if the model's objective permits, ignore multi-product situations and other complicating elements; the cost accountant must deal with costs as they are encountered, in all their complexity. Cost accounting is simpler in another sense, however, in that the cost accountant can accept any kind of cost behavior, unrestricted by any *a priori* assumptions as to the kinds of cost behavior that are consistent with a specific model.

The industrial organization economist, interested in such questions as the desirability of antitrust action or the need for government regulation, starts with the same models the microeconomist uses. The industrial organization economist, unlike the microeconomist, however, needs data drawn from actual experience, and given full power to intervene, can specify how these data are to be constructed. Otherwise, reliance must be placed on accounting data supplied by the firms, classified as they choose to classify them.[3]

The macroeconomist has far less interest in the work of the cost accountant and less power to influence it. The input-output models of macroeconomics are likely to call for data on physical quantities that emerge from other parts of business information systems. National income statistics use data on business income and inventories, both of which are affected by cost accounting, but so many others are interested in these same quantities that the macroeconomist cannot prescribe the accounting methods to be used.

MEASUREMENT CONCEPTS

Some economic concepts merely describe situations that pose problems for any economist or accountant who has to make or interpret accounting measurements. These "situational concepts" are discussed briefly in the next section. This section

---

[2]A partial theoretical structure is summarized in the American Accounting Association Committee on Concepts and Standards, "Tentative Statement of Cost Concepts Underlying Reports for Management Purposes," *Accounting Review*, XXXI, 2 (April 1956), pp. 182–193.

[3]The U.S. Federal Trade Commission prescribes the data to be submitted to it in its Line of Business Program, but the instructions were changed many times while the program was being formulated and implemented. A major purpose of these changes was to reduce the respondents' need to modify their existing record-keeping systems. *FTC Form LB*, Federal Trade Commission, Washington, D.C., 1975.

concentrates instead on nine measurement concepts—that is, those that provide some guidance to the cost accountant by describing quantities that might be expected to be measured or how they should be measured. These include:

1. Variable cost
2. Fixed cost
3. Short-run marginal cost
4. Incremental cost
5. Marginal contribution
6. Opportunity cost
7. Long-run average cost
8. Current cost
9. Present value

One additional pair of economic concepts, the concepts of the short run and the long run, must also be included in this group because they are fundamental to understanding some of the others. We shall begin with them.

Short Run and Long Run.   The capacity of any organization to carry out its activities can be changed only slowly. It takes time to conceive of the need for new facilities, arrange for financing, complete facilities construction or acquisition, provide the necessary staff and personnel, and put all of these resources to work. Capacity reductions also take time. This means that during any short period of time, the firm must operate with a relatively constant stock of productive resources.

This fact provides the basis for the distinction the economist makes between the short run and the long run. The short run is a period long enough to permit management to change the volume of production of goods or services but too short to enable management to increase or decrease the amount of productive capacity. The long run is a period long enough to permit management to increase or decrease the organization's operating capacity so that average cost at capacity will be the lowest permitted by the available technology for that volume of activity.[4] Short-run capacity may consist of a mixture of facilities of varying age, condition, and efficiency; in the long run all facilities can be assumed to be brand new, of the latest design, and operated smoothly by well-trained, efficient personnel.

Variable Cost.   Costs that change as a necessary response to small changes in the rate of utilization of existing capacity are known as variable costs. Variable cost, in other words, is a short-run concept.

Exhibit 1 shows two of the many possible patterns of cost variation. The straight

[4]Charles E. Ferguson and J. P. Gould, *Microeconomic Theory*, 4th ed. (Richard D. Irwin, Homewood, Ill., 1975), p. 183.

EXHIBIT 1   Variable Costs

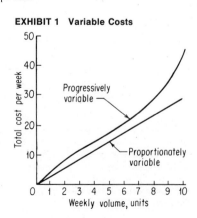

line in Exhibit 1 represents a cost that changes in direct proportion to changes in volume, for example, a royalty charge computed at a constant amount per unit sold. In contrast, the curved line shows costs rising sharply at first, then more gradually as volume achieves normal operating levels, and then sharply again as operations began to approach capacity limits.

Exhibit 1 illustrates two possible relationships between total volume and total variable cost in a specified period of time. Exhibit 2 shows two possible relationships between total volume and average variable cost per unit of activity. The

EXHIBIT 2   Average Variable Cost

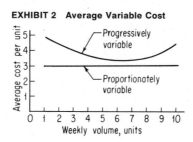

horizontal line in this exhibit corresponds to the straight line in Exhibit 1. If total variable cost always increases in proportion to changes in volume, then average variable cost must remain constant as volume changes. For a variable cost described by the curved line in Exhibit 1, however, average variable cost will vary. This is illustrated by the figures in column (3) of Exhibit 3. The variable cost of the first 1,000 units produced is quite high, $5.00. As the total variable cost curve levels off, the increase in cost is less than proportional to the increase in volume and average variable cost decreases. Total variable cost begins to climb more rapidly again at a volume of 7,000 units per week, and after this happens average variable cost starts to increase.

EXHIBIT 3   Average Variable Cost

(1) Weekly volume (units)	(2) Weekly variable cost	(3) Average variable cost (2)/(1)
1,000	$ 5,000	$5.00
2,000	9,000	4.50
3,000	12,000	4.00
4,000	15,000	3.75
5,000	18,000	3.60
6,000	21,000	3.50
7,000	24,500	3.50
8,000	29,200	3.65
9,000	36,000	4.00
10,000	46,000	4.60

Volume in this illustration has been measured in "units," with no indication of what kinds of units are referred to. The most obvious choice is the number of units of goods or services produced. This can be used for operations that produce only a single product or service, but when output is diverse something else must be found. The usual solution is to use some form of input measure, such as direct labor hours or pounds of materials used.

Fixed Cost.   Fixed cost, like variable cost, is a short-run concept. The economist defines fixed cost as any cost that will be the same in total whether existing capacity is fully utilized or left completely idle.[5] This ignores two highly significant phenomena: (1) indivisibilities in the short-run cost structure; and (2) activities whose scope is not technologically determined by the current volume of activity. As a result, the accountant is likely to define as fixed any cost that does not change as a necessary response to small changes in the rate of utilization of existing capacity.

Costs that fit this second definition fall into two categories: capacity costs and programmed costs. Economists initially recognized only the former, but both exist and the distinction is so important that a separate discussion of each is necessary.

Capacity Costs.   Many of the resources consumed in a period are consumed to provide or maintain the organization's capacity to produce or sell. These are known as capacity costs or supportive overheads.

If total capacity costs are the same at all volumes, average capacity costs will decline as volume increases. A cost that will amount to $2,000 a month, no matter what the operating volume, will average $1.00 a unit if volume is 2,000 units a month or $0.50 a unit at a volume of 4,000 units. The effect on average total cost will depend on the relative importance of capacity costs and the shape of the variable cost function. If variable costs tend to be proportional to volume, average total cost will decline almost indefinitely as output expands. If average variable cost increases with increases in volume, however, this increase will offset the decline in average capacity cost at some stage, and average total cost will begin to rise.

Capacity costs can be classified further into standby costs and enabling costs. Standby costs are those that will continue to be incurred if operations or facilities are shut down temporarily. Examples are depreciation, property taxes, and some executive salaries. Enabling costs are those that can be avoided by a temporary shutdown but that must be incurred if operations are to take place. Some of these are likely to be constant over the entire output range; others are likely to vary in steps. For example, one departmental supervisor may be adequate for single-shift operation, but operation of a second shift will require a second supervisor.

Step-variable capacity costs would be classified by an economist as variable costs; executives and accountants classify them as fixed within the capacity range they support.

Programmed Costs.   Many discussions of fixed costs focus entirely on the relationships between volume and total or average capacity costs. Fixed costs also include a second category, however, that is fundamentally different from the first. These are costs designed neither to maintain current operating capacity nor to meet the demands placed on the system for the production and delivery of goods and services. Instead, they are established by autonomous management decisions to meet objectives other than the fulfillment of service demands.

Costs in this group are known by a variety of names, including programmed costs, discretionary costs, and managed costs. Some programmed costs are incurred to obtain and retain sales orders; the cost leads to volume rather than the other way around. Some are incurred to achieve other kinds of results unrelated to current operating volume—ideas for new products, for example. Still others yield services to management and can be justified only by management's perception of the value of these services—for example, financial reporting systems.

Programmed costs tend to be budgeted at specified levels for individual time periods. Once the budget is set, programmed cost per unit will be low if volume is high and high if volume is low. The size of the programmed cost budget, however, should be determined by estimates of the effectiveness of these costs in achieving the objectives desired by management. If increases in budgeted spending seem likely to increase volume by a larger percentage than the increase in spending,

[5] Paul A. Samuelson, *Economics,* 10th ed. (McGraw-Hill Book Company, New York, 1976), p. 457.

average cost will fall. If additional spending produces a less than proportional increase in volume, however, average cost will rise. This is illustrated in the following table:

Total programmed cost	Volume achieved	Average programmed cost
$10	50	$.20
20	125	.16
30	200	.15
40	250	.16
50	280	.18
60	300	.20
70	310	.23

Short-Run Marginal Cost. The fourth economic concept underlying cost accounting is short-run marginal cost, defined as the change in cost that results from increasing the rate of output by one unit of goods or services per period of time. (More precisely, it is the rate of change in cost for an infinitely small change in the volume of activity, the derivative dc/dv of the relationship between total cost (c) and volume (v). The cruder definition cited above is easier to illustrate and perfectly adequate for the purposes of this chapter.)[6]

A key question in economic theories of how business firms behave is whether marginal cost is likely to be the same at different volumes or whether it will increase or decrease as volume increases. This depends on the shape of the relationship between volume and total cost. If total cost is strictly proportional to volume, it will show up as a straight line on a cost-volume chart like the one illustrated earlier in Exhibit 1. A straight line indicates that each unit change in volume produces exactly the same change in total cost as every other unit change in volume. Only if cost does not trace a straight line on a cost-volume chart will marginal cost vary with volume.

The curve in Exhibit 4 traces a different marginal cost curve, one that is familiar to most students of economics. This shows marginal cost decreasing at first due to economies achieved by production in larger quantities. This corresponds to the steep portion at the left-hand side of the total variable cost curve in Exhibit 1. In fact, marginal cost at any volume can be calculated by measuring the slope of the total cost curve at that point.

As volume increases, the total cost curve flattens out and marginal cost remains constant for a while. In practice, this seems likely to cover a larger portion of the total output range than in this simple illustration. Finally, diseconomies set in as the organization approaches the limits of its capacity, meaning that additional output gets harder and harder to achieve. When this happens, the total cost curve begins to climb more and more sharply, and marginal cost goes up.

The marginal cost curve always crosses the average total cost curve at the lowest point on the average cost curve, as in Exhibit 4. This makes sense. If an amount smaller than an existing average is added to any total, the average will be dragged down. If the increment is greater than the previous average, then the average will rise.

The concept of marginal cost has no meaning in connection with programmed fixed costs. Marginal costs measure the effects of increasing volume; programmed costs do not change as a result of changes in volume and therefore cannot be marginal with respect to those changes.

Marginal Contribution. Managerial economists are seldom interested in cost behavior alone. In studying possible ways of allocating any scarce resource, they

[6]*Ibid.*, p. 468.

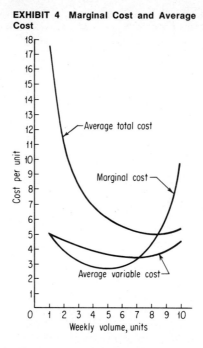

EXHIBIT 4   Marginal Cost and Average Cost

look instead at the marginal contribution the resource can make in each use. Marginal contribution is the spread between the amount of revenue to be received from one additional unit of the scarce resource and the amount of incremental cost necessary to produce that revenue. The cost of the scarce resource itself does not enter into this calculation because it is unaffected by the way the resource is used.

Some economic models reflect the assumption that marginal contribution declines as capacity usage increases. A relationship of this kind is illustrated in Exhibit 5. Marginal contribution is the spread between marginal revenue and marginal cost at any volume. In this case, as volume increases, marginal cost rises and marginal revenue falls. When the lines cross, marginal contribution is zero.

The microeconomist's definition of marginal contribution is a by-product of the definitions of fixed and variable cost that exclude programmed fixed costs.[7] The

[7]Chamberlin was one of the first microeconomic theorists to give explicit recognition to programmed costs. See Edward H. Chamberlin, *The Theory of Monopolistic Competition*, 7th ed. (Harvard University Press, Cambridge, Mass., 1956), chaps. 6 and 7.

EXHIBIT 5   Declining Marginal Contribution

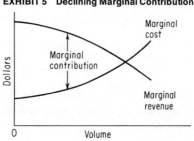

managerial economist may use this definition or combine it with an estimated relationship between programmed cost and sales volume. Exhibit 6 illustrates a relationship of this sort. In this case marginal contribution is assumed to be constant, which is the same as saying that the total contribution is proportional to volume.[8] The total amount of programmed fixed cost necessary to obtain volume is not linear, however. As more and more programmed cost is pumped in, additional volume becomes more and more difficult to obtain. This makes the additional programmed cost curve rise more and more steeply as volume increases, as in Exhibit 6a. (Additional programmed cost is the cost of obtaining one more unit of volume.) These two curves can be combined in one, as in Exhibit 6b.

EXHIBIT 6   Marginal Contribution

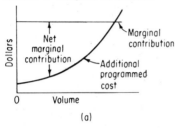

(a)

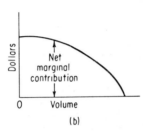

(b)

Incremental Cost.   Most of the concepts in this list are definitional—that is, they describe a phenomenon or set of conditions, and their purpose is to help people discuss the implications of these phenomena or conditions. One concept that goes beyond description to prescription is incremental cost, or differential cost, defined as the difference in total cash outlays that will result from choosing one alternative course of action instead of another. Incremental cost is a prescriptive concept in that it is based on the presumption that management is indifferent to the choice between two alternatives with identical anticipated cash flows but is not indifferent to other choices. (This is not precisely correct, because one set of cash flows may be more uncertain than the other. The implications of differences in uncertainty are explored in Chapter 3.)

For example, a cafe proprietor is studying the profitability of reopening a billiard room in the rear of his cafe. The billiard tables have been unused for several years but are in usable condition. The monthly cost estimates are shown below:

	Operate the billiard room	Do not operate the billiard room
Food and beverages	$4,500	$4,000
Salaries and wages	1,600	1,200
Supplies	150	100
Utilities and heat	60	50
Rent	500	500
Insurance	80	80
Miscellaneous	110	70
Total	$7,000	$6,000

[8]Dean used this concept frequently in his early work in managerial economics. See, for example, Joel Dean, *Managerial Economics* (Prentice-Hall, Englewood Cliffs, N.J., 1951), chap. 6.

The incremental cost in this case is $7,000 minus $6,000, or $1,000 a month. This is the cost that is relevant to the decision to be made.

The term "incremental cost" is often used in another sense, to refer to the elements of cost that will change as a result of the decision. For example, in this illustration the only costs affected by the decision are the costs of food and beverages, salaries and wages, supplies, utilities and heat, and miscellaneous resources consumed. The analysis can be simplified slightly in this case, significantly in others, by eliminating the unaffected items completely. The simplified comparison would be as follows:

	Operate the billiard room	Do not operate the billiard room
Food and beverages	$4,500	$4,000
Salaries and wages	1,600	1,200
Supplies	150	100
Utilities and heat	60	50
Miscellaneous	110	70
Total	$6,420	$5,420

Sunk Cost.   Any cost element that is unaffected by management's choice between alternatives is a sunk cost. In the first table above, two of the elements were sunk: rent $500 and insurance $80. Reopening the billiard room would leave these costs unchanged, and they are therefore irrelevant to the decision.

Negative Increments.   The cost differences in the preceding example were additions to cost. Incremental cost may also be negative; that is, a management decision may reduce costs. This reduction may be referred to as a cost saving, but the analytical method is still incremental. For example, if the cafe proprietor is now operating the billiard room and wishes to know how much could be saved by closing it, the incremental cost should be measured by the amounts of cash outlays that will be made only if the billiard room remains open.

Opportunity Cost.   Management's decisions often affect the use of resources the organization already controls. No cash outlay has to be made to obtain them. They have an incremental cost, however, measured by the net cash inflow that will be lost if they are diverted from their best alternative use. This differential cost is known as the opportunity cost of these resources. It is the value of an opportunity foregone. It belongs in the analysis because an action that eliminates a cash inflow is exactly equivalent to an action that requires a cash outflow. The effect on the organization's cash position is identical.

For example, a variety chain paid $500,000 ten years ago for a plot of land as a site for a shopping center. Uncertainty as to state highway relocation plans forced management to postpone the project, and the land has lain idle ever since. The route of the new highway has now been established, and the company is again considering the possibility of using the land as a shopping center site.

The original purchase price of the land is a sunk cost, irrelevant to the decision. The shopping center proposal must be charged for the land, however, because building the shopping center would prevent the company from using it to generate cash in other ways. If we find that the land can be sold for a net price of $800,000, after deducting all commissions, fees, and taxes, and if the chain has no other use for the land, then $800,000 is its opportunity cost and this amount should be included in the calculations in deciding on the shopping center proposal.

We would not need the opportunity cost concept if we always listed all the alternatives available to the decision maker. In the illustration we could simply have labeled one alternative "build shopping center" and another "sell land" and compare the two. We cannot always do this, however. The owned resources to be incorporated into a particular project are often a small part of the total project, and there may be several such resources. A full set of alternatives would include one for each possible combination of resource uses, and the number could get so large as to be unwieldy. The better procedure ordinarily is to compute an opportunity cost for each resource.

Long-Run Average Cost.   All of the cost curves in the preceding diagrams reflected short-run conditions. A comparable set of cost curves can also be drawn to represent long-run cost behavior. For example, each of the small U-shaped curves in Exhibit 7 represents the average total cost (ATC) for one possible size of the firm, operating at all possible volumes for a firm of that size.[9] In this case the

EXHIBIT 7   Average Total Cost for Firms of Different Sizes

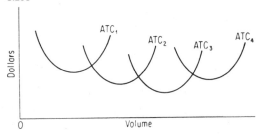

diagram pictures a situation in which average total cost decreases as capacity is increased from size 1 to size 2 and from size 2 to size 3, then rises again as the firm expands to size 4. The downward-sloping section of the diagram represents a phenomenon known to economists as *increasing returns to scale,* meaning that larger plants or firms are more efficient than smaller plants or firms. When the costs of operating larger plants or firms are greater than those of smaller plants or firms, as in the right-hand portion of the exhibit, the organization is said to be subject to *diminishing returns to scale.* If the low point on the average total cost curve does not change as plant size or firm size is changed, then the situation is one of *constant returns to scale.*

If enough short-run cost curves are drawn on a single diagram, a line tracing the lowest cost of operating at each possible level of activity might very well be a smooth curve like the one in Exhibit 8. Long-run marginal cost is the cost of increasing volume by one unit, including the costs of providing production capacity. Once again, average cost falls as long as marginal cost is lower than the average and rises after marginal cost rises above the average. When long-run

[9]Samuelson, *Economics,* p. 471; Ferguson and Gould, *Microeconomic Theory,* pp. 198–204.

EXHIBIT 8   Long-Run Average Cost

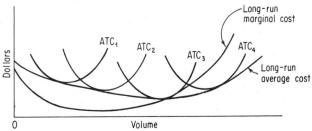

marginal cost is declining, the firm has an incentive to take actions that will expand its markets. That is, an efficient large firm will have lower costs and a competitive advantage over efficient smaller firms. When this situation prevails over a large portion of the possible output range, the industry is likely to be dominated by one or a few large firms.

Current Cost.   An economic concept of an entirely different order is the concept of current cost. Economic theory ordinarily postulates stable prices. Economists tabulating actual data usually attempt to adjust these data for changes in prices that have taken place.[10] This can be done in different ways, but one way is to measure the resources consumed in any period at their current cost—that is, the amount that would have had to be paid at the moment of consumption to obtain a quantity identical to the quantity consumed.

Current cost sometimes can be measured directly, sometimes must be approximated by the application of index numbers to historical cost data. Current cost is more relevant than historical cost for decisions about use of an existing resource if use of the resource will require immediate replacement. For example, a company bought 50,000 pounds of a certain material last year at $.50 a pound. The company uses this material as a raw material for several products. If 20,000 pounds are used to fill an order for a special product, the company will have to buy 20,000 pounds at the current price of $.60 a pound to rebuild its inventories to the desired level. In this case, the cash outlay required by the special order would be 20,000 pounds × $.60 = $12,000. The historical cost figure of $.50 a pound has no relevance because it does not measure the current cash outlay that acceptance of the order would entail.

Current cost is not always the same as opportunity cost, however, and it is not always used to help management decide how to use available resources. Instead, it is matched against current revenues to determine the margin between benefits received and the costs of obtaining these benefits. This is intended to show how attractive a given product or other business segment is likely to be on a continuing basis.[11]

Present Value.   The economic sacrifices (costs) made to reach specific cost objectives do not always take place immediately. When a cash outlay is deferred, the economic sacrifice is smaller than if a payment of the same amount had to be made immediately. The reason is that the organization can use or invest the amount of the outlay to earn a return until the payment actually has to be made.

The economic concept that allows the accountant to deal with this phenomenon is present value. The present value of an anticipated future cash sum at a specified future date is the amount that, if invested at a specified rate of return, will grow to an amount equal to the anticipated cash sum at the specified future date.

Calculation of Future Value.   The best way to begin to learn how present value is calculated is to look at a related concept, future value. To illustrate, if a bank will pay $1,050 one year from now in return for a $1,000 deposit today, it is paying interest at the rate of 5 percent a year. This relationship can be expressed mathematically in the following equation:

$$F_1 = P(1 + r) \tag{1}$$

where P = present outlay or deposit in the bank, r = rate of interest, and F_1 = future value at the end of the year. If P = $1,000 and r = 0.05, then F_1 = $1,050.

[10]Thomas F. Dernburg and Duncan M. McDougall, *Macroeconomics,* 4th ed. (McGraw-Hill Book Company, New York, 1972), pp. 70–71.

[11]See Chapter 22 for a more complete discussion of the meaning of figures on segment profitability.

Continuing the example, if the $1,050 is left in the bank for another year, it will build up by the end of two years to a balance of $1,050 + ($1,050 × .05) = $1,102.50. Interest in this second year amounts to $52.50 and is greater than the first year's interest because the bank is now paying interest not only on the original investment but also on the interest earned during the first year.

The mathematical formula for computing the future value of a present sum two years later is

$$F_2 = F_1(1 + r) = P(1 + r)(1 + r) = P(1 + r)^2 \qquad (2)$$

In general, it can be shown that if an amount P is invested at interest r percent each period, at the end of n years it will grow to

$$F_n = P(1 + r)^n \qquad (3)$$

The process of calculating interest not only on the original sum but on the interest of any previous periods as well is known as *compounding*. In this case, interest has been compounded annually, meaning that interest is added to the bank balance only once a year. It is more likely that interest will be compounded quarterly or even more frequently. The shorter the interest period, the sooner the interest is added to the amount on which interest is earned and the faster the amount will grow.

Conversion to Present Value. Because future value is the compounded future amount equivalent to a present sum, present value can be calculated simply by transposing the terms in equation (3). Because $F_n = P(1 + r)^n$, then

$$P = F_n \frac{1}{(1 + r)^n} \qquad (4)$$

This shows that the present value of any future sum can be determined by dividing the latter by $(1 + r)^n$ or by multiplying it by $(1 + r)^{-n}$. If n is two years, r is 5 percent, and an asset is expected to yield a cash inflow of $1,000 two years from now, then its value today is

$$P = \frac{\$1,000}{(1.05)^2} = \frac{\$1,000}{1.1025} = \$907.03$$

In other words, $907.03 will grow to $1,000 in two years if it is invested now at 5 percent interest, compounded annually; it is therefore the present value of that future amount.

The process of finding the present value of specified future sums is known as discounting, and present value for this reason is sometimes referred to as discounted value or the discounted cash flow. The relationship between present and future values is shown graphically in Exhibit 9. Starting with $1,000, the depositor's account will build at 5 percent to $1,050 in one year, $1,102.50 in two years, and so on, up to $2,653.30 at the end of 20 years. Therefore, $1,000 can be said to be the present value at 5 percent of $1,628.90 to be received 10 years from now or $2,653.30 to be received in 20 years' time, and so on.

Present Value of a Series of Cash Payments. Some cost objectives are reached by making not one but a series of cash payments. Cost in such cases is measured by the sum of the present values of the various cash outlays to be made.

For example, suppose that the cash required to complete a certain contract will be $20,000 immediately, $10,000 a year from now, and $5,000 a year after that.

EXHIBIT 9   Future Values Equivalent to Present Value of $1,000 (Annual Compounding at 5 Percent a Year)

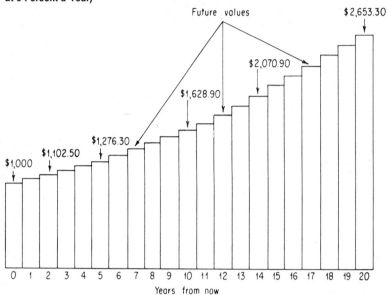

The appropriate discounting rate is 10 percent. In this case cost can be calculated as follows:

(1) Years now	(2) Cash outlay	(3) Present value multiplier	(4) Present value at 10% [(2) × (3)]
0	$20,000	1.0000	$20,000
1	10,000	1/1.10	9,091
2	5,000	1/(1.10 × 1.10)	4,132
Total	$35,000		$33,223

With $33,223 in cash, the company could buy someone's promise to pay the amounts shown in column (2) if that person demanded interest at a 10 percent rate, compounded annually. The $1,777 difference between this amount and the $35,000 total cash flow is the interest applicable to this two-year period. The acquisition cost is $33,223.

SITUATIONAL CONCEPTS

Two other economic concepts the cost accountant uses more aptly describe problems to be solved rather than quantities to be measured directly. These are the concepts of "common cost" and "joint cost."

Common Cost.   A common cost is a cost incurred for the support of two or more cost objectives, not traceable to any one of them. Accountants refer to these as indirect costs or, more clearly, as nontraceable costs.

As this may suggest, a cost can be classified as a common cost only after the cost objectives have been specified. For example, if the cost objective is the operation of factory department X, then the salary of the department's supervisor is not a common cost because it can be traced unequivocably to the department. If attention is shifted to one of the several products the department makes, however, then the supervisor's salary is a common cost. The supervisor is there to support and oversee everything the department does; no part of the supervisor's salary can be traced to any one product.

Joint Cost. One class of common costs poses special analytical problems. These costs are the cost of joint products, otherwise known as joint costs. Joint products are any two or more products emerging simultaneously from a single set of inputs. Joint costs are the costs of all the inputs that are necessary for the manufacture of all the joint products as a group. Costs incurred for the production of an individual joint product are known as separable costs or specific costs. Livestock, purchasing, and slaughtering costs are true joint costs of all the products that will eventually be marketed by a meat packer, but tanning costs are specific costs of the tanned hides produced.

Joint costs are tabbed for special attention because they can never be traced directly to individual products. This poses difficult analytical problems both for the economist and for the accountant. The problems are discussed in Chapter 18.

APPLICATIONS IN COST ACCOUNTING

Merely describing the concepts in this short list does not indicate how each one is used in cost accounting, or to what extent. In general, the remaining chapters of this book must supply this information, but a thumbnail description here may be a useful guide to the chapters that follow. We shall try to indicate how the cost accountant relies on each measurement concept, both in measuring the costs of things that the organization has done and in estimating the costs of things it may or will do in the future. For convenience, we shall refer to the first of these as cost assignment and to the second as cost estimation.

Fixed and Variable Costs. Cost accountants use the concepts of fixed and variable costs extensively in cost estimation. The cost estimates needed for periodic financial planning and flexible budgeting, for example, are estimates of the absolute levels of costs that will prevail at specified volumes during the next short-term operating period. These cannot be prepared in the absence of information of some sort on short-run cost behavior.

The cost estimates for specific decision choices, on the other hand, are estimates of differential or incremental costs. Despite this difference, knowledge of cost variability is useful here, too, to the extent that the available alternatives lead to different levels of activity. The cost accountant also uses estimates of cost variability in analyzing differences between actual profit performance and the profit plan.

The distinction between fixed and variable costs is recognized in cost assignments by manufacturing firms that develop product costs on a variable costing or direct costing basis. Statistical data on the incidence of the direct costing approach to product costing are lacking, but the amount of attention devoted to it in practitioners' publications indicates that it is widespread. Direct costing is not an acceptable procedure, however, for external financial reporting, for taxation, or in most contract costing situations.

Incremental Cost and Opportunity Cost. By their very nature, incremental cost and opportunity cost cannot be used in historical cost assignments. They are decision concepts, reflecting comparisons between specified future courses of action. As such, they are an indispensable part of the cost accountant's working vocabulary and form an integral part of the cost accountant's methodology in cost estimation for managerial decisions.

Short-Run Marginal Cost. The uneasy and ambiguous relationship between cost accounting and economics is nowhere more apparent than in the application of the concept of short-run marginal cost. One problem is that marginal cost in its purest sense refers to the cost increment accompanying an infinitesimal change in volume, whereas management's volume-determining decisions always relate to significant volume differences. If marginal cost is not constant throughout the entire range affected by the change, then point values of marginal cost cannot be used to estimate incremental cost.

An economist's solution to this problem would be to integrate, or add, all the marginal costs for the volume units affected by the decision. The cost accountant would accept this, but would first have to make sure that steps in fixed costs were included in the marginal cost function. Economists define fixed costs as those that are fixed for all possible levels of activity, including zero. Most microeconomic models also postulate nonfluctuating marginal cost curves, thereby leaving out steps in fixed costs entirely. The cost functions the cost accountant encounters in practice are more complex because the conditions postulated by the economist do not exist. As we have seen, this has led to the recognition of steps in fixed costs within the limits of existing capacity. These must be included in estimates of incremental cost when volume differentials are sufficient to move volume from one segment of the range to another with a different level of fixed costs.

Closely related to this problem is the one raised by the presence of programmed fixed costs. Because these were rare in the firms familiar to the early microeconomists, the classification of costs into fixed and variable categories did not take them into consideration. To the extent that they relate to volume at all, they produce volume rather than result from it. Because this excludes them from the marginal cost function, increments in these cost elements will not be reflected in the integral of marginal costs.

Another serious barrier to the direct adoption of the marginal cost concept by the cost accountant is the lack of tools sensitive enough to trace a marginal cost function with any precision. Few attempts to find close correlations by analytical means between marginal cost and volume have succeeded.[12] The result of these measurement difficulties is that cost accountants usually assume that marginal cost is constant over wide portions of the operating range. Partly for this reason, the marginal cost concept does not enter into historical cost assignment systems. Variable costing is sometimes regarded as an effort to measure short-run marginal cost, but it can do this only under one particular set of circumstances. Variable costing is based on an assumption that average variable cost is constant. If this is in fact true, then product cost calculated on this basis will measure marginal cost. If average variable cost is not constant, however, the variable costing figures will not measure marginal cost.

Marginal Contribution.   Marginal contribution is subject to many of the same difficulties as marginal cost. It is approximated in cost accounting by the contribution margin. The inversion of the word order represents more than a trivial difference. Contribution margin is always a total or an average, whereas marginal contribution always refers to an incremental response to a change in volume. Nonlinearities in marginal cost and marginal revenue create disparities between marginal contribution and the average contribution margin.

Attempts have been made in cost accounting to identify something like marginal contribution by relating period-to-period changes in contribution margin to period-to-period changes in other factors, such as advertising expenditures.[13] Changes in economic conditions or competitors' actions make these comparisons difficult to interpret, but management may find them useful.

[12]Published studies on this question generally summarize efforts to verify the microeconomist's hypotheses on cost behavior rather than attempts to provide management with useful information. A number of these studies are summarized in Johnston, *Statistical Cost Analysis*, chaps. 5 and 6.

[13]Richard A. Feder, "How to Measure Marketing Performance," *Harvard Business Review*, XLIII, 3 (May–June 1965), pp. 132–142.

Aside from calculations of this sort, the marginal contribution concept comes into play only in profit estimation, in which cost accountants and others attempt to estimate the response of costs and profits to changes in various variables. In most such cases the contribution margin is used to approximate marginal contribution. Linear programming decision models are an obvious example of this practice.

Long-Run Average Cost. Much cost accounting reflects a full costing approach. Tax and financial reporting, for example, require the cost accountant to state inventories at their average full cost of production up to the time of revenue recognition. Contract costing typically takes the same approach, and in the case of government contract costing in the United States goes even farther by including the average cost of nonmanufacturing administrative and supportive activities in contract cost.[14] Cost figures given management for use in catalogue pricing are also likely to reflect a full costing approach.

When the irrelevance of these figures to short-run decisions is pointed out to cost accountants, the usual response is to shift the focus of the discussion to the long run. Full-cost accounting figures, it is argued, represent long-run average cost, and perhaps long-run marginal cost as well. If this is true, they show (1) the average cost of keeping the product or service in the line on a continuing basis; (2) the costs competing organizations are likely to face if they enter the market; or (3) the long-run incremental cost of expanding capacity and increasing the volume of operations.

It is not the function of this chapter to decide whether long-run average cost either is or should be used in any particular decision model. Our purpose is to describe the economic concepts the cost accountant tries to implement and indicate how closely they are likely to be approximated in cost accounting practice. In this case, three influences may keep accounting average cost from having the long-run meanings attributed to it. First, average cost may vary with the size of the firm (as in Exhibit 7), meaning that expanding or contracting capacity would either increase or decrease average cost. Second, production takes place under conditions leading to common costs, and the allocations of these costs may not correspond to their long-run response to changes in capacity. Third, the average costs produced by cost accounting systems reflect the organization's existing facilities, location, and personnel. These are the cumulative result of hundreds, perhaps thousands, of past decisions or historical accidents. Even in the absence of any economies or diseconomies of scale, there is no reason to expect these to produce average costs identical to those for new facilities of equal capacity. Only if none of these three influences seems particularly strong can the cost accountant's average cost figures be interpreted as equivalent to long-run average cost.

To implement the concept of long-run average cost, the cost accountant has developed a related concept. Most cost accounting texts suggest that factory overhead costing rates represent the costs necessary to run the plant at "normal volume" rather than at full capacity or at estimated actual volume.

The argument is that because total capacity costs vary with the size of the plant, management will build plants that will minimize the average cost of serving customers not in one year but over the life of the plant. No one can expect average cost to be as low as it would be at full-capacity operation because no plant is expected to operate at that level all the time. If anticipated volume had been equal to full capacity, a larger plant would have been built to accommodate volume fluctuations. Similarly, the higher cost of lower-than-normal usage does not measure what management wants cost to represent, because if anticipated volume had been that low, a smaller plant would have been built and average costs would have been lower.

[14]Cost Accounting Standards Board, *Restatement of Objectives, Policies and Concepts* (Washington, D.C., 1977), p. 5.

Not all cost accounting systems implement this concept. In fact, government contractors even go so far as to calculate their burden rates on the basis of the volume actually achieved, mainly because that is the basis on which contract cost is calculated. Systems that use normal volume, however, do so because this is presumed to give management a better measure of long-run average cost than other volume bases.

Current Cost. Current cost is seldom represented explicitly in cost accounting systems in the United States. External financial statements reflect historical costs, and cost accounting systems are designed to provide the data for these statements. The result is that macroeconomists attempt to adjust reported inventory and depreciation figures to allow for differences between historical cost and current cost.

Cost figures available to management often approximate current cost, however. Although some of the systems for producing such figures are highly informal, most of them are standard costing systems. Standard costs that are revised annually, or more often, are likely to be reasonably good approximations of current cost. If management wants greater accuracy than this, it must go to the more detailed records of current purchases.

Present Value. The concept of present value plays no role in the historical-cost assignment side of cost accounting. Whether the cost accountant uses it in preparing cost estimates is likely to depend on how the issue is presented. If the cost accountant is asked to evaluate a capital expenditure proposal and the company uses present value in screening such proposals, present values will enter into the calculations. But asked to estimate the annual cost of manufacturing and marketing a new product, the cost accountant is unlikely to reflect the present value concept. Capital carrying charges, or interest, are typically excluded from the cost accounting records, and cost accounting estimates of annual operating costs are consistent with this. They will include depreciation as an undiscounted average annual cost, with no provision for interest.

SUMMARY

Cost accounting uses a number of economic concepts. More of these enter into *ex ante* cost estimation than into *ex post* cost assignment, but they appear in both.

The relationship between cost accounting and economics is closer for some branches of economics than for others. The industrial organization economist and the macroeconomist are likely to play a relatively passive role in cost accounting, with little power to prescribe what the cost accountant does. Those with the greatest influence on cost accounting are the managerial economists. In cost estimation, the cost accountant and managerial economist build on the same concepts, and the work of one leads directly into the work of the other. The microeconomist, on the other hand, deals with abstract models and therefore can adopt simpler versions of certain concepts than the cost accountant or managerial economist, who must work within the real world.

By far the most pervasive economic concepts in cost accounting are incremental and opportunity cost, present value, and long-run average cost. The first three of these enter into cost estimation; the latter is behind both *ex ante* and *ex post* measurements. The concepts of variable cost and fixed cost are also important, but the cost accountant is likely to apply these in ways the microeconomist would regard as unacceptable.

One problem is that neither the cost accountant nor anyone else has tools sharp enough to measure the relationships the microeconomist knows are there. Another difficulty is that the cost accountant, in adopting the terminology of microeconomics, has redefined some of the terms to reflect practical complexities.

But the main source of difference probably lies in the differing orientation of the two disciplines. Cost accounting deals with a specific organization and centers on the needs of the management of that organization. Microeconomics deals with abstractions relating to the behavior of prices, output, and the sizes of the firms in individual markets. The cost accountant must overcome measurement difficulties, even at the sacrifice of some theoretical elegance; the microeconomist can assume these measurement difficulties away. In the end, however, it is hard to imagine a cost accounting system divorced from a substantial underpinning of economic concepts.

BIBLIOGRAPHY

American Accounting Association Committee on Cost Concepts and Standards: "Tentative Statement of Cost Concepts Underlying Reports for Management Purposes," *Accounting Review,* XXXI, 2 (April 1956), pp. 182–193.

Baumol, William J.: *Economic Theory and Operations Analysis,* 3rd ed., Prentice-Hall, Englewood Cliffs, N.J., 1972.

Chamberlin, Edward H.: *The Theory of Monopolistic Competition,* 7th ed., Harvard University Press, Cambridge, Mass., 1956.

Clark, John Maurice: *Studies in the Economics of Overhead Costs,* University of Chicago Press, Chicago, 1923.

Dean, Joel: *Managerial Economics,* Prentice-Hall, Englewood Cliffs, N.J., 1951, especially chap. 5.

Ferguson, Charles E., and J. P. Gould: *Microeconomic Theory,* 4th ed., Richard D. Irwin, Homewood, Ill., 1975.

Horngren, Charles T.: *Cost Accounting: A Managerial Emphasis,* 4th ed., Prentice-Hall, Englewood Cliffs, N.J., 1977.

Johnston, J.: *Statistical Cost Analysis,* McGraw-Hill Book Company, New York, 1960.

Shillinglaw, Gordon: *Managerial Cost Accounting,* 4th ed., Richard D. Irwin, Homewood, Ill., 1977.

Staubus, George J.: *Activity Costing and Input-Output Accounting,* Richard D. Irwin, Homewood, Ill., 1971, chaps. 6 and 10.

Chapter 5

Cost Measurement

GEORGE J. BENSTON
Professor of Accounting, Graduate School of Management,
University of Rochester

BASIC PURPOSES OF MEASURING COST BEHAVIOR

The purpose for which an estimate of costs is to be used must be stated before determining what measurements are to be taken. Although this requirement is obvious, it often is not followed. As a consequence, numbers are produced that not only do not provide answers to the questions asked, but may misinform the user of the numbers.

Three basic uses of cost data may be delineated. First, the manufacturing cost of units produced and not sold and of work in process is required for inventory valuation. Second, cost estimates may be used for decisions on pricing and output, such as pricing a new product, bidding on a contract, make-or-buy decisions, and deciding how much to offer suppliers. Third, cost data are used to measure efficiency and evaluate performance.

Inventory Valuation. The first use—inventory valuation—requires numbers that meet the approval of the regulatory, quasiregulatory, and tax authorities. In general the SEC, AICPA, CASB, and FASB insist on full cost allocation. All manufacturing overhead costs, whether variable or fixed, must be allocated to units produced. The Internal Revenue Service also generally insists on full cost allocation. Last-in, first-out (LIFO), first-in, first-out (FIFO), or some other cost-flow assumption must be selected. The cost-flow assumption chosen need not be that which best reflects the economic (opportunity) cost of production, but often is the one that is expected to minimize taxes. In any event, procedures for costing inventories are prescribed by regulations and must be applied consistently from period to period. Consequently, they often will provide inadequate estimates of costs for price and output decisions or for determining efficiency and evaluating performance.

Price and Output Decisions. Price and output decisions require estimates of the expected consequences of the specific decision in question. Thus, although the price charged for a new product may be primarily a function of the prices of substitute products available in the market, the decision maker also must estimate the amount of resources that will be used as a consequence of the product's production and distribution. This "cost" of the product depends on the specific circumstances under which it is expected to be produced and sold. For example, all other things being equal, the relevant cost of the product will be greater if the prices of raw materials are expected to go up. It does not matter whether the inventory is costed at LIFO or FIFO: the relevant cost of raw materials is the opportunity cost of using or purchasing the materials, the value of resources given up as a consequence of the decision to produce the product. Furthermore, the cost of raw materials used also may depend on the type of machinery used, the length of production run, etc. Thus, the amount by which costs change may vary according to factors other than the numbers of units produced.

Costs that are not expected to change as a consequence of the decision to produce the product are irrelevant to the decision. Such costs may include insurance, real estate taxes, depreciation on the plant, and depreciation on the machinery used if the value of the machine is not expected to change because it is or is not used. However, the amount of costs that are fixed depends on the specific decision. For example, a production run of 100 units when the plant is operating well below capacity may not affect the amount paid for supervisory labor, or even for direct labor. But were the amount 1,000 units or were the plant operating near full capacity, another supervisor might have to be engaged and overtime might have to be paid. When the plant already is operating at peak capacity, production of additional units might require the displacing of other production. In this event, the cost of the additional units is the amount given up because of the displacement. Thus the cost of production depends on the specific circumstances. Unlike costing for inventory, cost estimating for decisions is not simply a matter of following the rules laid down by an authority.

Similarly, an estimate of the amount it would cost to fulfill a contract, should a bid be successful, depends on the specific circumstances under which the work is done. For example, materials that otherwise would be sold as scrap or thrown away might be used in a special order. Their cost, then, would not be the amount originally paid for them, but the amount that would be given up were they not used for the order. This amount may be zero or even negative, if the next best alternative is to pay someone to dispose of the materials.

Make-or-buy decisions also require costs that are specific to the circumstances under which production is expected to take place. The cost of making a product may be very high if other profitable production must be foregone or delayed. But if workers and plant could not be otherwise employed, the cost would be lower. The question is, what is the opportunity cost of resources that will be expended as a consequence of the decision to make rather than buy a product?

Estimates of how much to offer suppliers depend largely on the cost of alternative products or services and on the least amount the buyer believes that suppliers will accept (adjusted for nonprice aspects, such as quality and reliability). The amount that suppliers might accept depends, in part, on how much it will cost them to produce the product. Estimates of these amounts require knowledge about each supplier's special circumstances. It would be most unusual were the suppliers to have exactly the same production facilities, labor availability, etc., as did the customer. Therefore, the customer's own estimate of monetary or opportunity costs should not be taken as an adequate measure of the supplier's costs. Rather, the purchasing agent must estimate the supplier's opportunity cost of resources that will be expended to produce the order. Often it is nearly impossible to get detailed information concerning each supplier's special circumstances. As a surrogate measure, an estimate of the dollar amount of resources that the supplier will use may suffice.

Measurement of Efficiency and Performance.   The costs estimated for measuring efficiency and for evaluating performance are similar in concept to those estimated for price and output decisions. Measurement of efficiency requires a yardstick or standard against which actual performance can be compared. For evaluating the performance of an economic entity, such as a division, a department, or an operation, this standard is the cost expected or predicted as a consequence of some decision. Thus if the decision was to produce 1,000 additional units in a plant at a time when it was underutilized, the expected (standard) amount against which actual costs incurred are compared should include only those amounts that were expected to vary. As is discussed above, the expected and actual amounts of cost are likely to be different if the decision to produce 1,000 units was made when the plant was operating near full capacity. Similarly, if the decision was to bid on a contract (and the bid was accepted), the efficiency with which the contract was fulfilled would depend on the circumstances that were expected to prevail.

Evaluation of the performance of a person additionally involves consideration of the effect of measuring past performance on the person's future performance.[1] Although there is some controversy on the question, it is generally accepted that the people being evaluated should not be charged with costs over which they have no control. Rather, a report of performance should give the actual versus the expected consequences of the decision maker's actions.

Thus, cost estimation for decision making, including the decision that a process or department is being operated efficiently, requires estimates of the amounts that are expected to change (and not change) as a consequence of the decision. On the other hand, costs recorded for inventory valuations that will be used for external reports made pursuant to the authority of the SEC, AICPA, FASB, IRS, CASB, etc., must be measured in accordance with the authorities' regulations. This task often is expensive and difficult. Nevertheless, the problem is not conceptual: rather, cost measurement for inventory valuation consists essentially in following a set of prescribed rules which are better described elsewhere. The balance of this chapter, therefore, is concerned with cost estimation for decision making. Cost estimation for authorities is considered only to the extent that it is economically efficient to combine the procedures for estimating costs for authorities with those used for estimating costs for decisions.

THE USEFULNESS OF RECORDED ACCOUNTING DATA FOR COST ESTIMATION

The discussion above concludes that the numbers relevant for measuring the cost of a specific decision depend on the specific circumstances in which it will be effected. Because recorded accounting data necessarily refer to past occurrences (and, to an extent, past expectations of future events, such as the expected useful life of an asset), it would seem that these numbers are not useful for decision making. An example of this situation is a decision concerning a new manufacturing, distribution, or other process or procedure. Changes in prices for labor or raw materials may make past labor or materials costs irrelevant. Adaptation of new procedures and achievement of increased efficiencies also may make past data not useful for decisions about future production. Indeed, because most decisions require estimates of future cost behavior, recorded accounting data often provide inadequate estimates.

Nevertheless, data on past cost behavior can be useful for estimating future cost behavior. In many important situations the best estimate of the future is that it will be like the past, such as when past conditions are not expected to change very much. Where conditions are expected to change, past data may be adjusted to account for these changes. For example, although the hourly rate of labor has changed, the hours required to produce a part may remain the same. If the same quantity of labor will be used, the adjustment of the past data will be easy if past labor hours were recorded or can be estimated. Thus it is important to record past data so that it can be adjusted for the types of changes that are expected.

Past data also can be useful when alternative sources of information either are not available or are much too expensive to acquire and use. As with any other decision, the decision about how to estimate cost behavior should equate the marginal cost of the decision with the marginal revenue expected from it. In many instances, the additional cost of analyzing each decision to determine the specific situation relevant to it and the effect on costs of each situation may exceed the additional revenue that can be achieved from the information. For example, a

[1]See George J. Benston "The Role of the Firm's Accounting System for Motivation," *Accounting Review*, April 1963, pp. 347–354.

make-or-buy decision may involve use of facilities that are not currently engaged. However, it is likely that these facilities might be used for other production. Rather than attempt to determine which alternative is likely to occur when the item would be made, it may be best just to assume that past levels of use will continue into the future.

Finally, for many operations, particularly routine manufacturing and distribution activities, the future is expected to be like the past. Furthermore, for the very important efficiency measurement and control decision, deviation of the costs from those incurred in the past (adjusted at least for volume changes) may be an important indication of a change in efficiency or loss or gain of control. Thus past costs are relevant for a wide range of decisions.

Keeping in mind that circumstances may change such that the past is a misleading indicator of the future, this chapter proceeds on the assumption that recorded costs are useful for estimating future costs and, hence, for decision-making purposes.

THE LEVEL AT WHICH COSTS ARE AGGREGATED

One reason that costs are aggregated for a company as a whole is to prepare financial statements. Generally, costs (and expenses—expired costs) are grouped according to a natural classification, such as salaries and wages, materials, depreciation, and real estate taxes. Costs and expenses also may be aggregated according to broadly defined functions, such as manufacturing expenses or cost of goods sold, selling expenses, and administrative expenses. Companies subject to the SEC's and the FASB's line of business rules also must report revenues, expenses, and assets according to lines of business (generally those whose revenues exceed 10 percent of total revenues for corporation with over $50 million in sales). However, these levels of aggregation are too broad for most purposes for which cost estimates are wanted. Rather, costs and expenses may be grouped by responsibility area, such as a department. They often are also grouped by product or product line. Selling and distribution expenses also may be grouped by geographic area. The particular level of aggregation depends on the purpose for which the data will be used and the expense of recording and reporting the numbers.

In general, expenses are aggregated at a level where someone can be held responsible for the amount of expenses incurred. As mentioned above, evaluation of persons is aided by distinguishing between costs and expenses over which the responsible supervisor has direct or indirect control from those over which no control can be exercised. Thus, the supervisor of an assembly department would be charged with the cost of the direct labor managed, the direct materials used, and the items of overhead chargeable to the department. (Methods of estimating and assigning overhead are discussed below.) The department also might be charged with maintenance expenses even though these are directly controlled by another department, because the supervisor who controls the amount of maintenance used thus has indirect control over these charges. However, it would not be useful to charge the supervisor with a portion of general company administrative costs if the supervisor could in no way affect the amount incurred or be influenced by that amount. For purposes of measuring the cost of an activity, department, etc., however, the effect of the activity on general company administrative costs would be relevant.

Expenses also are aggregated by product. As the product passes through each department—parts, assembly, painting, inspection, packaging—the costs of each operation are assigned to the products produced to arrive at the total product cost. As is discussed above, this procedure is followed in part to determine inventory valuation. But because these amounts usually include amounts that are allocated arbitrarily to units, such as costs that are fixed with respect to the production of the units, the cost per unit is likely to provide a misleading estimate for decisions. Many companies aggregate costs only for inventory valuation purposes and then attempt to use these numbers to solve decision problems. As a consequence, the data have to be adjusted, often informally. Other companies reduce the extent of this problem by using direct costing, where inventory is charged only with direct labor, direct materials, and variable overhead. The resulting number is much more likely to provide the decision maker with a useful estimate of the incremental cost of producing units of inventory.

METHODS OF RECORDING COSTS

Costs usually are identified in three ways: (1) by type (such as salaries and supplies), (2) by department or other responsibility unit, and (3) by product. The types generally are grouped by direct labor, direct material, and variable and fixed overhead. Each group includes a number of subtypes. Direct labor may be subdivided into grades of labor or skills. Different types of direct materials usually are accounted for separately. Overhead may consist of dozens of accounts, including, for example, indirect labor, indirect materials, power, depreciation on machinery, and supplies of various types. Often overhead is grouped into costs that are directly related or allocated to a department or activity, costs that are directly related or allocated to a plant or division, and costs that are related to the corporation as a whole (such as central administrative expenses).

Direct labor, direct materials, and overhead may be charged to a department and thence to products (or subparts of products) or directly to products as well as to departments. The charge to products generally is made when the amount that is incurred because of the production of the product is clear and where the record-keeping cost is not excessive. For example, where workers sign on and off jobs and charge materials used to jobs, the hours incurred and materials used can easily be charged to products. The task is even easier where the department works on only one type of output. Some overhead items also may be incurred only for the production or distribution of a particular product. For example, a supervisor may be in charge of a single product. However, even where the association between cost and a specific output is direct, the expense of recording the amounts may not be worthwhile. Thus, although the electricity used by a machine may be determined if the machine is metered and the meter is read, it may be preferable to charge electricity to departmental or plant overhead. The cost of electricity and other overhead costs then may be assigned to products in some other way (as described below).

ASSIGNMENT OF DIRECT COSTS TO DEPARTMENTS AND PRODUCTS

The direct costs of accomplishing an activity or producing or distributing a product generally are routinely charged to that activity or product by the company's accounting system, unless the record-keeping costs exceed the value of the information. For example, direct labor would be charged to a product if activity time cards are kept routinely as part of the labor control process. However, where time cards are not kept (as would be the case in most nonproduction situations, such as a bank or an accounting department of a manufacturer), direct labor would be charged to a department or other unit under someone's control. The amount charged to a product or activity then can be determined by a special time study or by some other sort of formal or informal analysis. Time studies can be used to determine the average amount of time that a unit or subunit takes to process a unit. The times may be estimated by stopwatch time and motion studies or by logging the time required to process a number of units. (When an activity is newly undertaken, "learning" time should be taken into account.) Once the direct time per unit is estimated, it is multiplied by a labor rate to arrive at a standard direct labor cost per unit. Alternatively, the time required to process output may be estimated by an engineer or by the supervisor of the process. Again, the estimates are converted into a standard time and direct labor cost per unit. (Some writers suggest that the labor standards be set stringently to motivate improvements in performance; this is, however, a controversial subject.)

Direct material costs also may be routinely charged to products. Where the required record keeping is considered too costly, however, engineering analyses may be used. This procedure consists of listing and pricing the materials required for production plus an allowance for expected wastage.

Where a department processes only one product, the average product direct cost can be determined by dividing the total amount of charged direct cost of the department by the number of units produced (adjusted for work in process).

ASSIGNMENT OR ALLOCATION OF OVERHEAD COSTS TO DEPARTMENTS AND PRODUCTS

Overhead costs are more difficult to assign because they are not assumed to be directly associated with a department or product, either because there is no obvious relationship or because the cost of analysis and record keeping is considered too great. Some items of overhead, however, may be incurred directly by a department for a product; examples are depreciation on special-purpose machines and the cost of supervisory labor. These overhead amounts may be charged to the applicable departments or products in a manner similar to the charge for direct labor and materials. In many (perhaps most) instances where the overhead is incurred by another department (e.g., engineering and maintenance services), cost assignment is more difficult.

Two types of outside department overhead costs may be distinguished: (1) the costs of service (and administrative) departments that perform tasks for production departments and for other service departments, and (2) general plant and company overhead, such as administration and real estate taxes. Service department costs may be allocated to other departments or directly to products in any of the ways described in the following paragraphs. (In that discussion, it is assumed that cost measurement is undertaken primarily for decision making rather than for motivation.)

The *effort related transfer price* method assigns service costs to a department or product according to the amount of effort incurred, as it is incurred. Thus the cost of the engineering department would be charged to a particular department or product according to the number of engineering hours it used. The amount charged could be that which, it is expected, would fully allocate the total costs of the engineering department or would charge the receiving department for variable costs only or would reflect the market price at which the service could have been purchased outside the firm, etc. An obvious difficulty with this procedure is that it requires the company to maintain records of the amount of effort incurred.

A second method, *estimated effort allocation,* assigns overhead costs to departments or products periodically, according to an estimate of the effort incurred. The procedure requires the manager of each overhead department to estimate the percentage of the department's efforts during the period expended on behalf of other departments and products. (The percentages estimated may be reviewed by the receiving department and product managers, who may challenge them.) The total or variable costs of the overhead departments then are allocated to the departments and products that received their efforts. Where an overhead service department does work for another overhead service department (e.g., the personnel department serves the accounting department which, in turn, serves the personnel department), a procedure must be chosen to deal with cross-allocations. The simultaneous method states the percentages in the form of simultaneous equations, which are solved using matrix algebra.[2] The step method, though less accurate, is more prevalent. The overhead service departments are ordered in terms of the amount of their expenses and the number of other service departments to which their costs can be allocated. The expenses of the departments that serve others but are not served by others are allocated first. Then the expenses of the departments that serve others are allocated completely one at a time. Some companies find it easier to charge out the smaller departments first; others find it preferable to begin with the departments that serve the largest number of other departments.[3]

A third method allocates service costs according to some *base number,* such as direct labor dollars, machine hours, or total department or product direct costs. Multiple bases may be employed where it is felt that they are applicable and worth the additional expense. If the service costs vary according to the base number(s) chosen, the assigned costs will provide useful estimates for decision purposes. However, the base number used often is chosen because it has been recorded for some other purpose (such as direct labor dollars recorded because of payroll accounting requirements) and, hence, is readily available. Consequently, the amounts allocated may bear little, if any, relationship to the amount of service costs incurred because of a production or other decision.

Other overhead items not assigned directly to departments and/or products may also be allocated according to some base number. For example, plant and central office administrative expense might be allocated as a percentage of departmental direct costs, departmental labor costs, or even as an amount per square footage occupied. A refinement of this procedure allocates individual types of overhead costs to departments or products on different, presumably sensible, bases such as square footage for building maintenance and number of employees for the personnel department. However, where variations in the bases for allocating overhead do not result in variations in the costs incurred in the overhead departments, the departmental and unit product costs reported will provide misleading estimates of economic (opportunity) costs.

When service-related overhead costs are assigned to departments first, a procedure must be adopted to assign departmental costs to products (if product cost data are wanted). If more than one product is worked on by the department, a basis is chosen on which to allocate overhead costs. This basis preferably should reflect the incurrence of overhead. If direct labor hours is the base (as is common), overhead should vary according to the number of direct labor hours worked. If some part of overhead (say personnel expenses) varies according to some other base (say direct labor dollars), that portion should be allocated according to that base number. Thus overhead may be allocated to products on more than one base. However, some portions of overhead do not vary according to some base number because the costs are fixed or the relationship may not be clear between overhead and the base number that is available in the records. Furthermore, the choice of

[2]See Robert S. Kaplan "Variable and Self-Service Costs in Reciprocal Allocation Models," *Accounting Review,* 48 (October 1973), pp. 738–748; and Appendix 20.1, "Matrix Allocation of Service Department Costs," in S. Davidson, J. S. Schindler, and R. L. Weil, *Fundamentals of Accounting* (Dryden Press, Hinsdale, Ill., 1975), pp. 636–639.

[3]See, for example, Chapter 12 in Sidney Davidson, James S. Schindler, Clyde P. Stickney, and Roman L. Weil, *Managerial Accounting: An Introduction to Concepts, Methods, and Uses* (Dryden Press, Hinsdale, Ill., 1978).

allocation base may essentially be arbitrary because it is easier to use a single available number (such as direct labor dollars or total direct costs) than to undertake a detailed analysis. In these rather common situations, the amount of overhead charged to a particular product may not provide decision makers with useful information, because a change in output will not result in a change in costs that is implied by the amount of overhead charged in the accounting records.

DETERMINATION OF THE AMOUNT BY WHICH COSTS VARY

A key aspect of cost measurement for decision making is the assessment of the amount by which costs are expected to vary as a consequence of a decision. As is discussed above, the amount of cost variation depends on the specific conditions expected to prevail when the decision is carried out. However, because the effect of these conditions on costs often is very difficult (and hence costly) to measure, the amount by which recorded costs varied in the past may be used to estimate the amount by which they are expected to vary in the future. The assumption made is that all things other than the past decision variable, such as the level of output, are expected to remain constant.

The following procedure is commonly used to estimate cost variability. Each type of recorded costs is assigned to two or sometimes three groups: fixed, variable, and semivariable. Variable costs are those that are expected to change, approximately proportionately, with expected changes in output. Direct materials almost always are variable costs. Direct labor also is usually considered a variable cost. In some manufacturing processes, however, such as chemical production, the amount of labor required does not vary much over wide ranges of production, and hence would be classified as partially or completely fixed. Overhead costs may be variable, partially variable, or fixed.

The type of cost (e.g., wages, supplies, depreciation) and the amounts classified as partially or completely variable or fixed depend, of course, on the activity being costed and the range of expected variation of the activity. Some costs, such as plant building insurance, may be fixed with respect to the output of the plant but not with respect to a management decision to change the insurance coverage. Supervisory wages may be fixed with respect to the output over a certain range but will increase at some increased level of output. The degree of variability of a cost item also depends on the time over which an activity changes. For example, a rapid increase in output might result in greater total labor costs (including overtime) than would a gradual increase.

Nevertheless, the usual procedure followed is to assume a level and rate over which the activity costed is expected to range. Given this assumption, cost accounts are classified as variable or fixed. The entire amount of a given type of cost—direct labor, direct material, power, heat, supervisory labor, supplies, depreciation, etc.— is usually classified as variable or fixed. However, each type of cost can be individually analyzed. Generally, an experienced supervisor, engineer, or cost accountant reviews each cost item. Given a projected range of changes in activity, the amount that is expected to be incurred regardless of the changes is labeled "fixed." The balance is considered variable. Thus a portion of the monthly power cost may be categorized as fixed even though the cost of power would drop to near zero if production were stopped. The analysis may be at the department level or at a higher organization level, such as a plant or division. The variable costs per unit of activity then may be used to prepare flexible budgets and statements of performances that account for changes in activity. As is discussed above, if product cost variability is to be estimated, the costs also must be assigned or allocated to products. Unit average variable costs then are calculated by dividing total variable costs for a period (often a year) by the number of units produced during that period. The assumption underlying this procedure is that variable costs are the same per unit produced over the range of production that was experienced. Therefore marginal costs also are assumed to be constant.

LIMITATIONS OF THE ACCOUNTING PROCEDURES
FOR COST MEASUREMENTS

Before considering the limitations of the commonly practiced procedures for measuring costs described above, their advantages should be reviewed. First, the system of recording direct costs by departments and products is a relatively inexpensive aspect of the record-keeping procedures that must be used to fulfill tax and public reporting requirements. Second, the determination of cost variability is relatively simple, because all one has to do is identify a cost item as "variable" or "fixed." But this simplicity gives rise to several limitations.

One limitation of the accounting procedure is that many costs may not be easily associated with departments or products. This usually is the case for those overhead costs that are not clearly due to the operations of a department or to the production of a product. But even direct costs may not be assignable to a specific product without a detailed engineering analysis. This analysis may require time studies and detailed material specifications, procedures that may be expensive. (Statistical procedures, such as multiple regression analysis, discussed below, may provide a cost-efficient alternative.)

Overhead allocations may be a problem for two reasons: one is that many operations are commonly undertaken; the other is that overhead may not vary proportionately with the base on which it is allocated. Where an overhead cost is incurred for the common production of several products (or departments), it may not be easy even for a skilled engineer or supervisor to estimate how much of the overhead would be saved (or increased) if the production of the product or combination of products is reduced (or increased). Without such estimates, however, the amount of overhead that should be asigned to individual products so that the costs would be useful for decisions cannot be determined (assuming that past costs are good predictors of future costs). The "solution" to this problem is to allocate overhead as an amount per unit of a base number, such as direct labor hours or dollars. Obviously, an important limitation is that the amount of overhead incurred may be very imperfectly related to the amount of the base number incurred. In addition, it is difficult to determine the accuracy of the allocation procedure.

The accounting procedures also provide no way of determining whether the accountant's subjective separation of costs into variable and fixed is reasonably accurate. Dividing output during a period into total variable cost during that period yields a single number (unit average variable cost) whose accuracy cannot be assessed. If the procedure is repeated for several periods, it is likely that different unit variable costs will be computed. But the accountant cannot determine if the average of these numbers (or some other summary statistic) is a useful number.

Another possibly important shortcoming of this method is the assumption of a linear relationship between variable cost and output. (Variable costs are the same per unit regardless of the number of units produced.) Although this assumption may be valid for relatively small ranges of activity, it often is a poor description of cost behavior over the range from zero to the present output. Separation of a variable cost account into a "fixed" and a variable portion (the "fixed" portion being the amount that is not expected to change over the range of expected variation) is a means of dealing with this problem. However, variable costs still may not be linear.

COST ESTIMATION[4]

The purpose of cost estimation is to estimate for various types of costs (for examples, raw material, labor, utilities, insurance) their fixed cost amount and their variable cost amount. Of course, some costs, such as rent and insurance, will have only a fixed portion. Others, such as raw materials and direct labor, will have only a variable portion. Many costs however are mixed, having both fixed and variable components.

The total cost of an item can be expressed as

Total Cost During Period = Fixed Cost During Period
+ (Variable Cost per Unit of Activity
× Units of Activity Carried Out During Period)

or, using briefer but fairly standard notation,

$$TC = a + bx$$

where a is total fixed cost, b is variable cost per unit of activity, and x is the number of units of activity carried out. For example, assume that the total cost of utilities per month is determined to be $400 plus $.008 per kilowatt-hour used. If 100,000 kilowatt-hours of use is anticipated next month, utilities cost is estimated to be $1,200 (= $400 + $.008 per hour × 100,000 hours).

The activity represented by x is often called the *independent variable* and the amount of total costs is the *dependent variable*. In some sophisticated analyses, more than one activity or independent variable is presumed to influence total cost. The symbolic representation of such a relation might be

$$TC = a + bx_1 + cx_2 + \cdots$$

where a is total fixed cost, b is the variable cost per unit of activity x_1 carried out, c is the variable cost per unit of activity x_2 carried out, and so on. The activities might be direct labor hours worked and number of units produced. Multiple independent variables are discussed in a later section.

There are essentially two approaches to estimating costs—engineering estimates of what costs *should be* and analysis of historical data showing what costs *have been*. Both approaches can be useful; both are used in practice.

Engineering Method of Estimating Costs.   The engineering method is probably so-named because it was first used in estimating manufacturing costs from engineer's specifications of the required inputs to the manufacturing process for a unit of manufactured output. The method is not, however, confined to manufacturing, as the frequent use of time-and-motion studies of certain administrative or selling activities attests.

Virtually all business activities are designed to produce a defined output from a variety of labor, material, and capital equipment inputs. The engineer's cost estimates are based on a study of the physical relation between the quantities of these inputs and each unit of output (what the economist calls the "production function"). It is then a relatively simple matter to assign costs to each of the physical inputs (wages, material prices, insurance charges) in order to estimate the cost of the outputs.

[4]The material in this section is taken from S. Davidson, J. S. Schindler, C. P. Stickney, and R. L. Weil, *Managerial Accounting: An Introduction to Concepts, Methods, and Uses* (Dryden Press, Hinsdale, Ill., 1978), chap. 5.

There are several problems with using the engineering method to estimate costs. The cost estimate will be of low quality to the extent that the actual amounts of inputs used, such as materials and labor, vary during the production process because of waste, spoilage, and varying labor efficiency. Another problem with this method is that labor comes in varying degrees of skill with correspondingly varying wage rates. The engineering estimate of the appropriate skill level and wage rate may be subject to large errors. It is usually difficult to estimate using the engineering method the indirect costs of production—the cost of utilities, supervision, maintenance, security—so that the method tends to be reliable only when most costs have a direct relation to output, such as for labor and materials. Finally, the engineering method is surprisingly costly to use. Analysis of time, motion, materials, operating characteristics of equipment, and the ability of labor with varying skills requires an expert. Expert engineers are costly.

We suspect that the engineering method of estimating costs is used only when direct costs are a large proportion of total costs and when input-output relations are fairly stable over time. The engineering method must be used, however, when there are no historical data to analyze.

Estimation of Costs Using Historical Data.   When a firm has been carrying out activities for some time and future activities are expected to be similar to those of the past, then the firm can analyze the historical data to estimate the components of total cost and to determine likely future costs. There are several methods used to estimate costs from historical data; these range from the simple to the sophisticated. Whatever method is used, the manager should take some preliminary steps before relying on cost estimates based on historical data.

Preliminary Steps in Analyzing Historical Cost Data.   In the several decades since computers have become a cost-effective tool for analysis, the expression GIGO, "garbage-in, garbage-out," has become well known to data analysts. The results of an analysis cannot be better than the input data. Before using cost estimates, the analyst should be confident that the estimates make sense and are based on valid assumptions.

Keep in mind that we are trying to determine fixed costs per period, a, and variable cost, b, per unit of some activity or independent variable in the relation

$$TC = a + bx$$

The historical data will consist of several observations. An observation is the amount of total costs for a period and the level of activity carried out during that period. Thus, we might have total labor costs by months (the dependent variable) and the number of units produced during each of the months or the number of direct labor hours worked during each of the months (the independent variable). We do not provide here an exhaustive list of all the steps to take in analyzing historical data, but the following are some of the more important.

1. *Review Alternative Activity Bases (Independent Variables).*   In deciding which measure of activity to use, there are often several alternatives. The total cost for an item might be a function of number of units produced, labor hours used, labor costs incurred, machine hours used, quantities of materials used, cost of materials used, and so on. The objective in selecting an activity base is to find one that varies, or is most closely associated, with the cost item being estimated. In principle, there is no reason not to use more than one activity base or independent variable, but a given cost estimation usually focuses on just one. (In order to have more than one independent variable, the number of observations must be large if the statistical relations are to be robust and reliable.) The activity base chosen should have some logical relation to the cost item.

2. *Plot the Data.*   One of the simplest procedures, but one often omitted by careless analysts, is to plot each of the observations of total costs by activity levels.

Such plots will often indicate an "outlier" observation—one that is significantly different from the others. Such outliers may indicate faulty data collection, incorrect arithmetic, or merely a time period when production was so far out of control that it would make sense to ignore the observation in determining the average relationships among total, fixed, and variable costs. Moreover, plotting the data may make it clear that no relation or only a nonlinear relation exists between the activity base and actual costs.[5]

3. *Examine the Data and Method of Accumulation.*   Do the time periods for the cost data and the activity correspond? Occasionally, accounting systems will record costs actually incurred late on a given day as occurring on the following day. It is difficult to deduce valid relations when the data for the dependent variable (total costs in our case) are not compiled for the same period as the data for the independent variable (activity base, in our case). Are the time periods covered by each observation of total costs and the activity base long enough to be meaningful, but short enough to allow for variations in activity levels? If, for example, observations are hourly, the time of day may be the reason why there is a no relationship between the dependent and independent variables. Workers may be more efficient in the morning and less so in the late afternoon. On the other hand, observations by month may smooth over meaningful variations of activity level and cost that could be observed if the data were based on weekly observations.

4. *Examine the Constancy of the Production Process.*   Do the observations (of total cost and activity level) all refer to times when production processes were approximately the same? Comparisons of total costs and activity level are not likely to be meaningful if there have been technological changes in production processes, changes in the skill or wages of the labor force, or changes in the prices of materials. The data analyst must constantly make trade-offs between having more observations, which increases the reliability of the cost estimates, and keeping the total time span covered by the observations short enough so that the production process remains relatively constant.

Once the independent variable is chosen for the activity base, the data have been gathered and plotted to see if there are outlier observations that should be discarded, the production process is determined to have been roughly constant over the time of the observations, the actual cost estimation procedure can begin.

Methods of Cost Estimation Using Historical Data.   This section presents some of the methods used in estimating historical relationships between total costs and activity levels. The methods are illustrated for the data shown in Exhibit 1 and plotted in Figure 1. These data show the total manufacturing overhead costs of the Chicago Manufacturing Company for each month during the previous year. Manufacturing overhead costs include all manufacturing costs except those for direct materials and direct labor. The overhead costs include, among others, utility costs, property taxes on the factory building, supervisors' wages, wages for security and maintenance staff, and insurance on the factory building. The problem here is to determine the relationship between total overhead costs and activity for the Chicago Manufacturing Company.[6] The activity base that initially is suspected to correlate, or relate, best with total overhead costs per month is the number of direct hours worked during the month. Exhibit 1 shows total overhead costs and direct labor hours worked during the month.

---

[5]The cost estimation methods discussed in this section assume that a linear relationship exists between the dependent and independent variables. If a nonlinear relationship is found to exist, more sophisticated estimation methods are required.

[6]Alternatively, we could estimate the amount of each of these overhead costs individually and aggregate the fixed and variable cost components to obtain an estimate of total overhead costs. These alternative approaches normally yield approximately the same results.

EXHIBIT 1

CHICAGO MANUFACTURING COMPANY
Overhead Cost Data by Month

Month	Total overhead costs incurred during month	Direct labor hours worked during month
January	$ 5,580	6,000
February	4,330	5,500
March	4,080	3,500
April	2,830	3,000
May	2,455	2,500
June	3,080	2,000
July	3,580	4,000
August	4,455	4,500
September	5,330	5,000
October	6,580	6,500
November	5,580	7,000
December	6,930	7,500
	$54,810	57,000

FIGURE 1   Chicago Manufacturing Company: Scatter Plot of Total Monthly Overhead Costs and Direct Labor Hours Used during Month (based on data in Exhibit 1). The outliers are plotted for purposes of illustration.

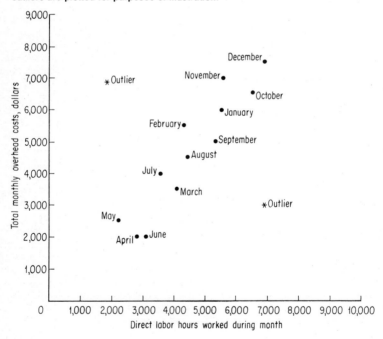

The cost relationship to be estimated is

Total Overhead Costs per Month = Fixed Costs per Month
    + (Variable Overhead Cost per Direct Labor Hour
        × Direct Labor Hours Worked during Month)

or
$$TC = a + bx$$

Before estimating the cost relationsip, we plot the data, as in Figure 1. There are no apparent outliers for the 12 observation pairs in Exhibit 1. Two outliers are drawn on the plot so that you can see what is meant by an outlier.[7] If there were one or two months with outliers such as those shown, we should investigate what happened during those months and discard the observations once we understood their cause.

Three common methods of estimating the cost relationship, that is, identifying a and b in the above equation, are illustrated next.

High-Low Method.   The high-low method estimates the fixed and variable cost components using the observations with the highest and lowest total costs (ignoring outliers). Although this method is easy to apply, its principal weakness is that it uses only two of the observations. First, identify the observation with the largest total cost, December in this example. Then identify the observation with the smallest total cost, May in this example. Next compute the difference in total costs between these two extreme observations, $4,475 (= $6,930 − $2,455) in the example. Then compute the change in activity base levels between the two extreme observations, 5,000 hours (= 7,500 hours − 2,500 hours) in the example. Then estimate b, the variable cost per unit of activity base by dividing the cost difference by the activity difference. In our example, the variable cost would be estimated at $.895 (= $4,475/5,000 hours) per direct labor hour worked. The general formula, using subscript h and l to represent high and low, respectively, is

$$b = \frac{TC_h - TC_l}{x_h - x_l}$$

The estimate of the fixed cost, a, can then be determined from either of the following two relationships (both will give the same estimate of a):

$$\text{Fixed Costs} = a = TC_h - bx_h \quad \text{or} \quad \text{Fixed Costs} = a = TC_l - bx_l$$

In the example, the high-low method would estimate the fixed cost to be $217.50. The calculation of this amount is as follows:

$$\begin{aligned}
\text{Total Costs} &= a + bx \\
\$6,930 &= a + b\,(7{,}500 \text{ hours}) \\
-[2{,}455 &= a + b\,(2{,}500 \text{ hours})] \\
\hline
\$4,475 &= b\,(5{,}000 \text{ hours})
\end{aligned}$$

$$b = \frac{\$4,475}{5,000 \text{ hours}} = \$.895 \text{ per hour}$$

$$a = \$6,930 - (\$.895 \text{ per hour} \times 7{,}500 \text{ hours}) = \underline{\$217.50}$$

or

$$a = \$2,455 - (\$.895 \text{ per hour} \times 2{,}500 \text{ hours}) = \underline{\underline{\$217.50}}$$

Thus, in the example, we estimate fixed overhead costs to be $217.50 per month and variable overhead costs to be $.895 per direct labor hour worked. This relationship is drawn in Figure 2. The line seems to fit the data points reasonably well but, as we shall see when we examine a line fit with statistical methods, the results in Figure 2 are quite different from those given by those methods. The main shortcoming of this method is that it uses only two of the observations, the

[7]One of the outliers, the one corresponding roughly to 7,000 hours and $3,000 of total costs, is a "good" outlier in the sense that total costs are much less than they apparently should be. We suspect that the cause is faulty recording of data, but if not, then we would want to know what happened that month. Then we might change operations to incur costs each month that are this small relative to activity levels. Investigation of outliers illustrates the concept called "management by exception." Understanding the cause of outlier observations is particularly important for managerial control.

FIGURE 2   Chicago Manufacturing Company: High-Low Method of Estimating Fixed Overhead Costs per Month and Variable Overhead Costs per Direct Labor Hour Worked (based on data in Exhibit 1)

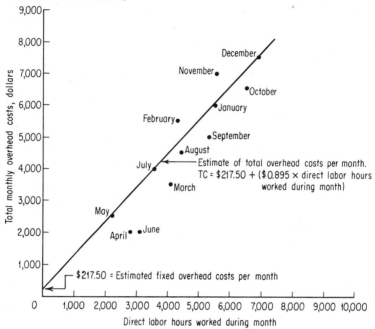

highest and the lowest. The accuracy of the estimates of *a* and *b* depends on how representative the high and low data points are of all the data.

Visual Curve-Fitting Method.   Another method of estimating cost from data such as those in Exhibit 1 is visual curve fitting. In contrast to the high-low method, visual curve fitting uses all of the available observations. In visual curve fitting a straight line is drawn through the data points that seems to "fit" well. By "fit," we mean a straight line that goes through the middle of the data points as closely as possible. Draw in such a line in Figure 1. The line we visually fit to these data intercepts the vertical axis at $1,000 and has a slope of $.75 per hour.[8] The chances are that the line you drew is not exactly the same as ours. Yours and ours would each give roughly the same estimate of total costs for 3,000 hours to 6,000 direct labor hours per month, but probably give significantly different estimates of total costs for 2,000 or 8,000 direct labor hours per month. The shortcoming of this method has, we hope, been demonstrated by the difference between your visually fit line and ours. The visually fit line is subjective, and different analysts may reach different conclusions from examining the same data.

Once you have drawn a line to fit the data, the estimate of the fixed cost component, *a*, is the total cost for a zero level of activity, the amount at the point where the line crosses the vertical axis. The estimate of the variable cost per unit of activity can be found by reading the numbers for any two points *on the line*. The relation is as follows, where subscripts 1 and 2 refer to the two points:

[8]That is, we drew a line indicating $1,000 per month of fixed costs, *a*, and variable costs, *b*, or $.75 per direct labor hour. (You may reproduce our visually fit line by drawing a line on Figure 1 between the point $1,000 on the vertical axis and a total cost of $7,000 for 8,000 hours.)

Variable Cost per Unit of Base Activity $= b$

$$= \frac{TC_1 - TC_2}{x_1 - x_2} = \frac{\text{Change in Costs Between Two Points}}{\text{Change in Activity Between Two Points}}$$

In our case, we use the points

Point 1:	8,000 hours; $7,000 total costs
Point 2:	0 hours; $1,000 total costs

Using the formula, we find that

$$b = \frac{\$7,000 - \$1,000}{8,000 \text{ hours} - 0 \text{ hours}} = \frac{\$6,000}{8,000 \text{ hours}} = \$.75 \text{ per hour}$$

Thus, total overhead cost is as follows:

Total Overhead Costs per Month $= \$1,000 + \$.75$ per direct labor hour

Statistical Methods. When computing facilities are available, by far the most cost-effective and accurate method for determining cost relations is *regression analysis*. Rather than estimating the cost relationship by the high-low or visual curve-fitting methods, the regression analysis "fits" a line to the data by the method of least squares. That is, a line is fit to the observations in such a way that the sum of the squares of the vertical distance of the observation points from the point on the regression line is minimized. In other words, the statistical regression locates the line that best goes through the center of the data points using the least squares criterion. (The sum of the absolute deviations might just as well be minimized, but the computational problems are somewhat more difficult. Nearly all "canned" computer library programs use the least-squares criterion.) The remainder of this chapter discusses statistical methods.

MULTIPLE REGRESSION ANALYSIS—GENERAL DESCRIPTION[9]

Many of the limitations of the accounting procedures for cost measurement can be overcome with the statistical procedure of multiple regression. A rough description of the method is that it measures the increases (or decreases) in cost resulting from a change in one variable, say output, while holding the effects on cost of other variables, say the season of the year or the size of batches, constant.

For example, consider the problem of analyzing the costs incurred by the shipping department of a department store. The manager of the department believes that these costs are primarily a function of the number of orders processed. However, heavier packages are more costly to handle than are lighter ones. The manager also considers the weather an important factor (rain or extreme cold slows down delivery time) and might want to eliminate the effect of the weather, because it is not controllable. But the manager would like to know how much each order costs to process and what the cost of heavier against lighter packages is. If such costs can be estimated, then the accountant can prepare a flexible budget for the shipping department that takes account of changes in operating conditions, and thus leads to better managerial decisions. A properly specified multiple regression equation can provide the required estimates.

The procedure essentially consists of estimating mathematically the average relationship between costs (the "dependent" variable) and the factors that cause

[9]The material on multiple regression analysis is taken largely from the author's article, "Multiple Regression Analysis of Cost Behavior," *Accounting Review*, XLI (1966), pp. 657–672, by permission of the publisher. Professor Mel Krasney provided valuable suggestions.

cost incurrences (the "independent" variables). The analysis provides the accountant with an estimate of the expected marginal cost of a unit change in output, for example, with the effects on total cost of other factors accounted for. These are the data required for costing many decisions.

The regression technique also can allow the accountant to make probability statements concerning the reliability of the estimates made.[10] For example, the analysis may indicate that the marginal cost of processing a package of average weight is $.756, when the effects on cost of different weather conditions and other factors are accounted for. If the properties underlying regression analysis (discussed below) are met, the reliability of this cost estimate may be determined from the standard error of the coefficient (say $.032) from which the accountant may assess a probability of .95 that the marginal cost per package is between $.692 [= $.756 − (2 × $.032)] and $.820 [= $.756 + (2 × $.032)].

In the past, a valid objection to multiple regression was that it was too costly. Analysts, therefore, would plot cost data and output from many periods on graph paper. A line then was fitted by eye, the slope being taken as the variable cost per unit of output. When the least-squares method of fitting the line is used, the procedure is called "simple linear regression" because only one independent variable (output) is specified as a determinant of costs. Until the advent of computers, even simple regression was considered to be quite sophisticated.[11] Although it was recognized that its use neglects the effects on cost of factors other than output, it was defended on the then-reasonable grounds that multiple regression with more than two or three variables was too difficult computationally to be considered economically feasible.

At present, the cost and computational difficulty of multiple regression is no longer a valid argument. Today, with high-speed computers and library programs, most regression problems ought to cost less than $10 to run. Unfortunately, this ease and low cost of using regression analysis may prove to be its undoing if analysts are tempted to use the technique without adequately realizing its technical data requirements and limitations. The "GIGO" adage, "garbage-in, garbage-out," always must be kept in mind. A major purpose of this section is to state these requirements and limitations explicitly and to indicate how they may be handled.

THE TECHNIQUE OF MULTIPLE REGRESSION ANALYSIS: A NONTECHNICAL DISCUSSION

The usefulness of multiple regression analysis can be appreciated best when the essential nature of the technique is understood. It is not necessary that the mathematical proofs of least squares or the methods of inverting matrices be learned, because library computer programs do all the work. However, it is necessary that the assumptions underlying use of multiple regression be fully understood so that this valuable tool is not misused.

Multiple regression analysis presupposes a linear relationship between the contributive factors and costs.[12] The functional relationship between these factors,

[10]This and the following statements are made in the context of a Bayesian analysis in which the decision maker combines sample information with a prior judgment concerning unknown parameters. In the examples given, a jointly diffuse prior distribution is assumed for all parameters.

[11]National Association of Accountants, *Separating and Using Costs as Fixed and Variable,* June 1960.

[12]A curvilinear or exponential relationship also can be expressed as linear relationship. This technique is discussed below.

$x_1, x_2, \ldots, x_n$, and cost, C, that arise in time period t is assumed in multiple regression analysis to be of the following form:

$$C_t = \beta_0 x_0 + \beta_1 x_{1t} + \beta_2 x_{2t} + \cdots + \beta_n x_{nt} + \mu_t \tag{1}$$

where β_0 = a constant term ($x_0 = 1$ for all observations and time periods)
      β_i = a fixed coefficient that expresses the marginal contribution of x_1 to C
      μ = the sum of unspecified factors, the disturbances, that are assumed to be randomly distributed with a zero mean and constant variance
      $t = 1, 2, \ldots, m$ = time periods

The β coefficients are estimated from a sample of C's and x's from time periods 1 through m. For example, assume that the cost (in whole dollars) recorded in a week is a function of such specified factors as x_1 = units of output, x_2 = number of units in a batch, and x_3 = the ratio of the number of "deluxe" units to total units produced. Then the right-hand side of equation (2) is an estimate of the right-hand side of equation (1), obtained from a sample of weekly observations, where the b's are estimates of the β's and u is the residual, the estimate of μ, the disturbance term:

$$C_t = b_0 + b_1 x_{1t} + b_2 x_{2t} + b_3 x_{3t} + u_t \tag{2}$$

If the values estimated for coefficients of the constant term and three independent variables, x_1, x_2, and x_3, are $b_0 = 100$, $b_1 = 30$, $b_2 = -20$, and $b_3 = 500$, the expected cost ($\hat{C}$) for any given week (t) is estimated by

$$C = 100 + 30x_1 - 20x_2 + 500x_3$$

Given estimates of the β's, one has, in effect, estimates of the marginal cost associated with each of the determining factors. In the example given above, the marginal cost of producing an additional unit of output, x_1, is estimated to be $30, with the effects on costs of the size of batch (x_2) and the ratio of the number of deluxe to total units (x_3) accounted for. Or, β_2, the marginal reduction in total cost of increasing the batches by three units, given fixed values of the number of units and the relative proportions of deluxe units produced, is estimated to be $-$60 (= $20 × 3).

It is tempting to interpret the constant term, b_0, as fixed cost. But this is not correct unless the linear relationship found in the range of observations applies for all levels of output down to zero.[13] This can be seen best in the two-dimensional graph of cost on output shown in Figure 3. The line was fitted with equation $C = b_0 + b_1 x_1$, where the dots are the observed values of cost and output. The slope of the line is the coefficient, b_1, which is an estimate of the marginal change in total cost (C) with a unit change (z) in output (x_1) if the assumed linear relationship shown is correct. The intercept on the C axis is b_0, the constant term. It would be an estimate of fixed cost if the range of observations included the point where output were zero, and the relationship between total cost and output were linear as shown. However, if more observations of cost and output (as represented by the square blocks) were available, it might be that the dashed curve would be fitted and b_0 would be zero. Thus the value of the constant term, b_0, is not the costs that would be expected if there were no output; it is only the value that is calculated as a result of the regression line computed from the available data.

The data for the calculations are taken from the accounting and production

[13]Fixed cost is defined here as avoidable cost related to time periods and not to output variables.

FIGURE 3 Linear Relation with Nonzero Fixed Costs Fit to Observations (Dots) when True Relation Is Nonlinear with Zero Fixed Costs

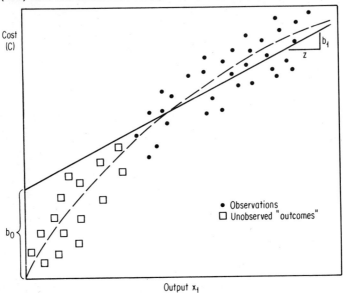

records of past time periods. The coefficients estimated from these data are averages of past experience. The fact that the b's are averages of past data must be emphasized, because their use for decisions is based on the assumption that the future will be like an average of past experience.

The mathematical method usually used for estimating the β's is the least-squares technique. It has the properties of providing best, linear, unbiased estimates of the β's. These properties are desirable because they tend "to yield a series of estimates whose average would coincide with the true value being estimated and whose variance about that true value is smaller than that of any other unbiased estimators."[14] Although these properties are not always of paramount importance, they are valuable for making estimates of the expected average costs, assuming that past cost experience is considered a meaningful guide for decisions.

Another important advantage of the least-squares technique is that when it is combined with the assumptions about the disturbance term (μ_t) that are discussed below, the reliability of the relations between the explanatory variables and costs can be determined. Two types of reliability estimates can be computed. One, the standard error of estimate, shows how well the equation fits the data. The second, the standard error of the regression coefficients, assesses the probability that the β's estimated are within a range of values. For example, if a linear cost function is used, the coefficient (b_1) of output (x_1) is the estimated marginal cost of output. With an estimate of the standard error of the coefficient, s_{b1}, we can say that the true marginal cost, β_1, is within the range $b_1 \pm s_{b1}$, with a given probability.[15]

---

[14]J. Johnston, *Statistical Cost Analysis* (McGraw-Hill Book Company, New York, 1960), p. 31.

[15]The interpretation of the confidence interval is admittedly Bayesian. As the data depart from the mean values, the confidence interval widens. See Johnston, *ibid.*, or a similar text for the relevant formula.

REQUIREMENTS OF MULTIPLE REGRESSION AND IMPLICATIONS FOR RECORDING COSTS

Although multiple regression is an excellent tool for estimating recurring costs, it does have several requirements that make its use hazardous without careful planning.[16] Most of the data requirements of multiple regression analysis depend on the way cost accounting records are maintained. If the data are simply taken from the ordinary cost accounting records of the company, it is unlikely that the output of the regression model will be meaningful. Therefore, careful planning of the extent to which the initial accounting data are coded and recorded is necessary before regression analysis can be used successfully. This section of the chapter is organized into four groupings that include several numbered subsections in which the principal technical requirements are described, after which the implications for the cost system are discussed. In the first group, (1) the length and (2) number of time periods, (3) the range of observations, and (4) the specification of cost-related factors are described, following which their implications for cost recording are outlined. In the second group, (5) errors of measurement and their cost recording implications are considered. The third group deals with (6) correlations among the explanatory variables and the important contribution that accounting analysis can make to this problem. Finally, (7) the requirements for the distribution of the nonspecified factors (disturbances) are given. The implications of these requirements for the functional form of the variables are taken up in the following section.

1. Length of Time Periods.   The time periods $(1, 2, 3, \ldots, m)$ chosen should be long enough to allow the record-keeping procedures to match output produced in a period with the cost incurred because of that production. For example, if 500 units are produced in a day but records of supplies used are kept on a weekly basis, an analysis of the cost of supplies used cannot be made with shorter than weekly periods. Lags in recording costs must be corrected or adjusted. Thus, production should not be recorded as occurring in one week while indirect labor is recorded a week later when the pay checks are written.

The time periods chosen should be *short* enough to catch variations in production within the period. Otherwise, the variations that occur during the period will be averaged out, possibly obscuring the true relationship between cost and output.

2. Number of Time Periods (Observations).   For a time series, each observation covers a time period in which data on costs and output and other explanatory variables are collected for analysis. As a minimum, there must be one more observation than there are independent variables to make regression analysis possible. (The excess number is called "degrees of freedom.") Of course, many more observations must be available before one could have any confidence that the relationship estimated from the sample reflects the "true" underlying relationship. The standard errors, from which one may determine the range within which the true coefficients lie (given some probability of error), are reduced in inverse proportion to the square root of the number of observations.

3. Range of Observations.   The observations on cost and output should cover as wide a range as possible. If there is very little variation from period to period in cost and output, the functional relationship between the two cannot be estimated effectively by regression analysis.

4. Specification of Cost-Related Factors.   All factors that affect cost should be specified and included in the analysis. This is an important requirement that is

[16]Proofs of the requirements described may be found in many econometrics textbooks, such as J. Johnston, *Econometric Methods,* 2nd ed. (McGraw-Hill Book Company, New York, 1972).

often difficult to meet. For example, observations may have been taken over a period when input prices changed. The true relationship between cost and output may be obscured if high output coincided with high input because of price changes. If the higher costs related to higher prices are not accounted for (by inclusion of a specific price index as an independent variable) or adjusted for (by stating the dependent variable, cost, in constant dollars), the marginal cost of additional output estimated will be meaningful only if changes in input prices are proportional to changes in output and are expected to remain so.

It should be noted, however, that complete specification is not mandatory if requirement 7 (below) is met. However, requirement 7 is not likely to be fulfilled if the specification is seriously incomplete.

Implications for Cost Recording of 1, 2, 3, and 4.   In general, the time period requirement calls for the recording of production data for periods no longer than one month and preferably as short as one week in length. Although quarterly data could be used, there is a danger that there will not be a sufficient number of observations available for analysis because, as a bare minimum, one more period than the number of explanatory variables is needed. Even if it is believed that only one explanatory variable (such as units of output) is needed to specify the cost function in any one period, requirement 4 (that all cost related factors be specified) demands consideration of differences among time periods. Thus, such events as changes in factor prices and production methods, whether production is increasing or decreasing, and the seasons of the year might have to be specified as explanatory variables.

The necessity of identifying all relevant explanatory variables, such as those just mentioned, can be met by having a journal kept in which the values or the behavior of these variables in specific time periods is noted. If such a record is not kept, it will be difficult (if not impossible) to recall unusual events and to identify them with the relevant time periods, especially when short time periods are used.

For example, it is necessary to note whether production increased or decreased substantially in each period. Increases in production may be met by overtime. However, decreases may be accompanied by idle time or slower operations. Thus, we would expect the additional costs of production increases to be greater than the cost savings from decreases. This situation can be accounted for with a dummy variable that represents qualitative values, such as $P = 1$ when production increased and $P = 0$ when production decreased.[17] From the coefficient of P, we can estimate the cost of differences in the direction of output change and also reduce contamination of the coefficient estimated for output.

Other commonly found factors that affect costs are changes in technology, changes in capacity, periods of adjustment to new processes or types of output, and seasonal differences. The effect of these factors may be accounted for by including variables in the regression equation, by specific adjustment of the data, or by excluding data that are thought to be "contaminated."

The wide range of observations needed for effective analysis also argues against observation periods of longer than one month. With long periods, variations in production would more likely be averaged out than if shorter periods were used. In addition, if stability of conditions limits the number of explanatory variables other than output that otherwise would reduce the degrees of freedom, this same stability probably would not produce a sufficient range of output to make regression analysis worthwhile. Thus, weekly or monthly data usually are required for multiple regression.

5. Errors or Measurement.   It is difficult to believe that data from a "real-life" production situation will be reported without error. The nature of the errors is

---

[17]If the data are in logarithmic form, the dummy variable would be coded to yield logs of 1 and 0 (common log 10 = 1, natural log 2.7183 = 1, common and natural log 1 = 0).

important, because some kinds will affect the usefulness of regression analysis more than others. Errors in the dependent variable, cost, are not fatal, because they affect the disturbance term, μ.[18] The predictive value of the equation is lessened, but the estimate of marginal cost (β_1) is not affected.

Where there are errors in measuring output or the other independent variable (x's), however, the disturbance term, μ, will be correlated with the independent variables.[19] If this condition exists, the sample coefficient estimated by the least-squares procedure will be an underestimate of the true marginal cost. Thus, it is very important that the independent variables be measured accurately.

The possiblity of measurement errors is intensified by the number of observations requirement. Short reporting periods increase the necessity for careful classification. For example, if a cost caused by production in week 1 is not recorded until week 2, the dependent variable (cost) of both observations will be measured incorrectly. This error is most serious when production fluctuates between observations. However, when production is increasing or decreasing steadily, the measurement error tends to be constant (either in absolute or proportional terms) and hence will affect only the constant term. The regression coefficients estimated and, hence, the estimates of average marginal cost, will not be affected.[20]

Another important type of measurement error is the failure to charge the period in which production occurs with future costs caused by that production. For example, overtime pay for production workers may be paid for in the week following their work. This can be adjusted for easily. However, the supervisor may not be paid directly for overtime. Rather, there might be a year-end bonus or a raise in pay many months after the work. These costs cannot easily be associated with the production that caused them but will be charged in another period, thus making both periods' costs incorrect.[21] This type of error is difficult to correct. Usually, all that one can do is eliminate the bonus payment from the data of the period in which it is paid and realize that the estimated coefficient of output will be biased downward. Average marginal costs, then, will be understated.

A somewhat similar situation follows from the high cost of the careful record keeping required to charge such input factors as production supplies to short time periods. In this event, these items of cost should be deducted from the other cost items and not included in the analysis. If these amounts are large enough, specific analysis may be required, or the decision not to account for them carefully may be reevaluated.

This separation of specific cost items also is desirable where the accountant knows that their allocation to time periods bears no relation to production. For example, such costs as insurance or rent may be allocated to departments on a monthly basis. There is no point in including these costs in the dependent variable because it is known that they do not vary with the independent variables. At best,

---

[18]Let γ stand for the measurement errors in C:

$$C + \gamma = \beta_0 + \beta_1 x_1 + \mu$$
$$C = \beta_0 + \beta_1 x_1 + \mu - \gamma$$

[19]In this event, where ψ stands for the measurement error in x_1:

$$C = \beta_0 + \beta_1(x_1 + \psi) + \mu$$
$$= \beta_0 + \beta_1 x_1 + \beta_1 \psi + \mu$$

The new disturbance term $\beta_1\psi + \mu$, is not independent of x_1 because of the covariance between these variables.

[20]If the error is proportionally constant (i.e., 10 percent of production), transformation of the variables (such as to logarithms) is necessary.

[21]Actually, the present value of the future payment should be included as a current period cost.

their inclusion will only increase the constant term. However, if by chance they are correlated with an independent variable, they will bias the estimates made (requirement 7). This type of error may be built into the accounting system if fixed costs are allocated to time periods on the basis of production. For example, depreciation incurred as a function of time may be charged to production on a per-unit or direct-labor-hours basis. The variance of this cost, then, may be a function of the accounting method and not of the underlying economic relationships.

6. Correlations Among the Explanatory (Independent) Variables. When the explanatory variables are highly correlated with one another, it is very difficult, and often impossible, to estimate the separate relationships of each to the dependent variable. This condition is called "multicollinearity," and it is a severe problem for cost studies. When we compute marginal costs, we usually want to estimate the marginal cost of *each* of the different types of output produced in a multiproduct firm. However, this is not always possible. For example, consider a manufacturer who makes refrigerators, freezers, washing machines, and other major home appliances. If the demand for all home appliances is highly correlated, the number of refrigerators, freezers, and washing machines produced will move together, all being high in one week and low in another. In this situation it will be impossible to disentangle the marginal cost of producing refrigerators from the marginal cost of producing freezers or washing machines by means of multiple regression. However, the computed regression can provide useful predictions of total costs if the past relationships of production among the different outputs are maintained.

Problems similar to that of our manufacturer can be alleviated by disaggregation of total cost into several subgroups that are independent of each other. Preanalysis and preliminary allocations of cost and output data may accomplish this disaggregation. This is one of the most important contributions the accountant can make to regression analysis.

If the total costs of the entire plant are regressed on outputs of different types, it is likely that the computed coefficients will have very large standard errors and, hence, will not be reliable. This situation may be avoided by first assigning costs to cost centers, where a single output is likely to be produced. This allows a set of multiple regressions to be computed, one for each cost center. The cost assignment procedure (which may be followed for inventory costing) also reduces the number of explanatory variables that need be specified in any one regression.[22] Care must be taken to assure that the assignment of costs to cost centers is not arbitrary or unrelated to output. For example, allocation of electricity or rent on a square footage basis can serve no useful purpose. However, assigning the salary of the supervisor on a time basis would be meaningful for the supervisor who spends varying amounts of time per period supervising different cost centers and whose time could otherwise be used.

A further complication arises if several different types of outputs are produced within the cost centers. For example, the assembly department may work on different models of television sets at the same time. In most instances, it is neither feasible nor desirable to allocate the cost center's costs to each type of output. Cost, then, should be regressed on several output variables, one for the quantity of each type of output. If these independent variables are collinear, the standard errors of their regression coefficients will be so large relative to the coefficients as to make the estimates useless. In this event, an index of output may be constructed, in which the different types of output are weighted by a factor (such as labor hours)

---

[22]The author used this procedure with success in estimating the marginal costs of banking operations. See "Economies of Scale and Marginal Costs in Banking Operations," *National Banking Review,* 1965, pp. 507–549.

that serves to describe their relationship to cost. Cost then may be regressed on this weighted index. The regression coefficient computed expresses the average relationship between the "bundle" of outputs and cost and cannot be decomposed to give the relationship between one output element and cost. However, because the outputs were collinear in the past, it is likely that they will be collinear in the future, so that knowledge about the cost of the "bundle" of outputs may be sufficient.

A valid objection to the allocation of costs to cost centers is that one can never be sure that the allocations reflect the effect of cost-related activities. Nevertheless, some allocations must be made for multicollinearity to be overcome. Therefore, the statistical method cannot be free from the accountant's subjective judgment; in fact, it depends on it.

A limitation of analysis of costs by cost centers also is that cost externalities among cost centers may be ignored. For example, the directly chargeable costs of the milling department may be a function of the level of operations of other departments. The existence and magnitude of operations outside of a particular cost center may be estimated by including an appropriate independent variable in the center regression. An overall index of production, such as total direct labor hours or total sales, is one such variable. Or, if a cost element is allocated between two cost centers, the output of one cost center may be included as an independent variable in the other cost center's regressions. The existence and effect of these possible intercost center elements may be determined from the standard error and sign of the coefficient of this variable.

Some types of costs that vary with activity cannot be associated with specific cost centers because it is difficult to make meaningful allocations or because of bookkeeping problems (as discussed above). In this event, individual regression analyses of these costs probably will prove valuable. For example, electricity may be difficult to allocate to cost centers although it varies with machine hours.[23] A regression can be computed such as the following:

$$E = b_0 + b_1 M + b_2 S_1 + b_3 S_2 + b_4 S_3$$

where E = electricity cost
  M = total machine hours in the plant
  S = seasonal dummy variables
with S_1 = 1 for summer, 0 for other seasons
  S_2 = 1 for spring, 0 for other seasons
  S_3 = 1 for winter, 0 for other seasons
    (A dummy variable for the fall season is not included because there are only four seasons; when three seasons are explicitly represented in the dummy variables, the effect of the fourth season is automatically included in the constant term.)
  b_0, b_1, b_2, b_3, b_4 = the computed constant and coefficients

If the regression is fully specified, with all factors that cause the use of electricity included (such as the season of the year), the regression coefficient of M, b_1, is the estimate of the average marginal cost of electricity per machine hour. This cost can be added to the other costs (such as materials and labor) to estimate the marginal cost of specific outputs.

For some activities, physical units, such as labor hours, can be used as the dependent variable instead of costs. This procedure is desirable where most of the activity's costs are a function of such physical units and where factor prices are

---

[23]Machine hours may not be recorded by cost center although direct labor hours are. If machine hours (M) are believed to be proportional to direct labor hours (L), so that $M_i = k_i L_i$ where k is a constant multiplier that may vary among cost centers, i, $k_i L_i$ is a perfect substitute for M_i.

expected to vary. Thus, in a shipping department, it may be best to regress hours worked on pounds shipped, percentage of units shipped by truck, the average number of pounds per sale, and other explanatory variables. Then, with the coefficients estimated, the number of labor hours can be estimated for various situations. These hours can be costed at the current labor rate.

7. Distribution of the Nonspecified Factors (Disturbances)

Serial Correlation of the Disturbances.   An important requirement of least squares is that the disturbances not be serially correlated. When this requirement is violated, both the coefficients and the estimates of their reliability are affected. For a time series (in which the observations are taken at successive times), this means that the disturbances that arose in a period t are independent from the disturbances that arose in previous periods, $t - 1$, $t - 2$, etc. The consequences of serial correlation of the disturbances are that (1) the standard errors of the regression coefficients (b's) will be seriously underestimated, (2) the sampling variances of the coefficients will be very large, and (3) predictions of cost made from the regression equation will be more variable than is ordinarily expected from least-squares estimators. Hence, the tests measuring the probability that the true marginal costs and total costs are within a range around the estimates computed from the regression are not valid.

Independence from Explanatory Variables.   The disturbances that reflect the factors affecting cost that cannot be specified must be uncorrelated with the explanatory (independent) variables, $x_1, x_2, \ldots, x_n$. If the unspecified factors are correlated with the explanatory variables, the coefficients will be biased and inconsistent estimates of the true values. Such correlation often is the result of record-keeping procedures. For example, repairing equipment in a machine shop is a cost-causing activity that often is not specified because of quantification difficulties. These repairs may be made, however, when output is low, because the machines can be taken out of service at these times. Thus, repair costs will be negatively correlated with output. If these costs are not separated from other costs, the estimated coefficient of output will be biased downward, so that the true extent of variation of cost with output will be masked.

Variance of the Disturbances.   A basic assumption underlying use of least squares is that the variance of the disturbance term is constant; it should not be a function of the level of the dependent or independent variables.[24] If the variance of the disturbance is nonconstant, the standard errors of the coefficients estimated are not correct, and the reliability of the coefficients cannot be determined.

When the relationship estimated is between only one independent variable (output) and the dependent variable (cost), the presence of nonconstant variance of the disturbances can be detected by plotting the independent against the dependent variable. Where more than one independent variable is required, the residual values ($\hat{u}$) can be plotted against each independent variable and the dependent variable. If these tests indicate that the variance of the residuals is not approximately constant, the data should be transformed to a form in which constant variance is achieved. At the least, the accountant should decide if the disturbances are likely to bear a proportional relationship to the other variables (as is commonly the situation with economic data). If they do, it may be desirable to transform the variables to logarithms. The efficacy of the transformations then may be tested by replotting the independent variables against the residuals.

Normal Distribution of the Disturbances.   For the traditional statistical tests of the regression coefficients and equations to be strictly valid, the disturbances should be normally distributed. Tests of normality can be made by plotting the residuals on

---

[24]Constant variance is known as *homoscedasticity.* Nonconstant variance is called *heteroscedasticity.*

normal probability paper, an option available in many computer library regression programs. Although requirement 7 does not have implications for the accounting system, it does determine the form in which the variables are specified. These considerations are discussed in the following sections.

FUNCTIONAL FORM OF THE REGRESSION EQUATION

Thus far we have been concerned with correct specification of the regression equation rather than with its functional form. However, the form of the variables must fit the underlying data well and be of such a nature that the residuals are distributed according to requirement 7 above.

The form chosen first should follow the underlying relationship that is thought to exist. Consider, for example, an analysis of the costs (C) of a shipping department. Costs may be a function of pounds shipped (P), percentage of pounds shipped by truck (T), and the average number of pounds per sale (A). If the accountant believes that the change in cost due to a change of each explanatory variable is unaffected by the levels of the other explanatory variables, a linear form could be used, as follows:

$$C = a + bP + cT + dA + u$$

where u is the residual whose expected value = 0 and whose variance is a constant amount. In this form, the estimated marginal cost of a unit change in pounds shipped (P), $\partial C/\partial P$, is b.

If the marginal cost of each explanatory variable is thought to be a function of the levels of the other explanatory variables, the following form would be better:

$$C = aP^b T^c A^d v$$

where v is the residual whose expected value = 1 and whose variance is a constant proportion of total costs. In this case, a linear form could be achieved by converting the variable to logarithms.

$$\log C = \log a + b \log P + c \log T + d \log A + \log v$$

Now, an approximation to the expected marginal cost of a unit change in pounds shipped (P) is $\partial C/\partial P = baP^{b-1}\bar{T}^c\bar{A}^d$, where the other explanatory variables are held constant at some average values (denoted by bars over the letters). Thus, the estimated marginal cost of P is a function of the levels of the other variables.

The logarithmic form of the variables also allows for estimates of nonlinear relationships between cost and the explanatory variables. The form of the relationships may be approximated by graphing the dependent variable against the independent variable. (The most important independent variable should be chosen where there is more than one, although in this event the simple two-dimensional plotting can only be suggestive.) If the plot indicates that a nonlinear rather than a linear form will fit the data best, the effect of using logarithms may be determined by plotting the data on semilog and log-log ruled paper.

If the data seem curvilinear, even in logarithms, polynomial forms of the variables may be used. Thus, for an additive relationship between cost (C) and quantity of output (Q), the form fitted may be $C = a + bQ + cQ^2 + cQ^3$. If a multiplicative relationship is assumed, a curvilinear form that fits the data may be $\log C = \log a + \log Q + (\log Q)^2$. Either form describes a large family of curves that can have two bends.

When choosing the form of the variables, attention must always be paid to the effect of the form on the residuals, the estimates of the disturbances. Unless the variance of the residuals is constant, not subject to serial correlation, and approximately normally distributed (requirement 7), inferences about the reliability of the coefficients estimated cannot be made. Graphing is a valuable method for determining whether or not these requirements are met. (The graphs mentioned usually can be produced by the computers.) Three graphs are suggested. First, the residuals should be plotted in time sequence. They should appear to be randomly distributed, with no cycles or trends.[25] Second, the residuals can be plotted against the predicted value of the dependent variable. There should be as many positive or negative residuals scattered evenly about a zero line, with the variance of the residuals about the same at any value of the predicted dependent variable. Finally, the residuals should be plotted on normal probability paper to test for normality.

If the graphs show that the residuals do not meet the requirements of least squares, the data must be transformed. If serial correlation of the residuals is a problem, transformation of the variables may help. A commonly used method is to compute first differences, in which the observation from period $t, t - 1, t - 2, t - 3$, and so forth, are replaced with $t - (t - 1), (t - 1) - (t - 2), (t - 2) - (t - 3)$, and so forth. With first difference data, one is regressing the change in cost on the change in output, etc., a procedure that in many instances may be descriptively superior to other methods of stating the data. However, the residuals from first difference data also must be subjected to serial correlation tests, because taking first differences often results in negative serial correlations.[26]

Where nonconstant variance of the residuals is a problem, the residuals may increase proportionally to the predicted dependent variables. In this event transformation of the dependent variable to logarithms will be effective in achieving constant variance. If the residuals increase more than proportionately, the square root of the dependent variable may be a better transformation.

AN ILLUSTRATION

Assume that a firm manufactures widgets and several other products, and that the services of several departments are used. Analysis of the costs of the assembly department will provide us with an illustration. In this department, widgets and another product, digits, are produced. The widgets are assembled in batches, whereas the larger digits are assembled singly. Weekly observations on cost and output are taken and punched on cards. A graph is prepared, from which it appears that a linear relationship is present. Further, the cost of producing widgets is not believed to be a function of the production of digits or other explanatory variables. Therefore, the following regression is computed:

$$\hat{C} = 110.3 + 8.21N - 7.83B + 12.32D + 235S + 523W - 136A$$
$$(40.8) \quad (.53) \quad (1.69) \quad (2.10) \quad (100) \quad (204) \quad (154)$$

where $\hat{C}$ = expected cost
N = number of widgets
B = average number of widgets in a batch
D = number of digits
S = summer dummy variable, where $S = 1$ for summer, 0 for other seasons
W = winter dummy variable, where $W = 1$ for winter, 0 for other seasons

[25]A more formal test for serial correlation is provided by the Durbin-Watson statistic, which is built into many library regression computer programs. (J. Durbin and G. J. Watson, "Testing for Serial Correlation in Least-Squares Regression," Parts I and II, *Biometrika*, 1950 and 1951.)

[26]If there are random measurement errors in the data, observations from period $t - 1$ might be increased by a positive error. Then $t - (t - 1)$ will be lower and $(t - 1) - (t - 2)$ will be higher than if the error were not present. Consequently, $t - (t - 1)$ and $(t - 1) - (t - 2)$ will be negatively serially correlated.

A = autumn dummy variable, where A = 1 for autumn, 0 for other seasons
R^2 = .892 (the coefficient of multiple determination)
Standard error of estimate = 420.83, which is 5 percent of the dependent variable, cost
Number of observations = 156

The numbers in parentheses beneath the coefficients are the standard errors of the coefficients. These results may be used for such purposes as price and output decisions, analysis of efficiency, and capital budgeting.

For price and output decisions, we would want to estimate the average marginal cost expected if an additional widget is produced. From the regression we see that the estimated average marginal cost, $\partial C/\partial N$ is 8.21, with the other factors affecting costs accounted for. The standard error of the coefficient, .53, allows us to assess a probability of .67 that the "true" average marginal cost is between 7.68 and 8.74 (8.21 ± .53) and a probability .95 that it is between 7.15 and 9.27 [8.21 ± (2 × .53)].[27]

The regression also can be used for flexible budgeting. For example, assume that the following production is reported for a given week:

$$W = 532$$
$$B = 20$$
$$D = 321$$
$$S = \text{summer} = 1$$

Then we expect that, if this week is like an average of the experience for past weeks, total costs would be

$$110.3 + (8.21 \times 532) - (7.83 \times 20) + (12.32 \times 321) + (235 \times 1) = \$8,511.14$$

The actual costs incurred can be compared to this expected amount. Of course, we do not expect the actual amount to equal the predicted amount, if only because we could not specify all of the cost-causing variables in the regression equation. However, we can calculate the probability that the actual cost is within some range around the expected cost. This range can be computed from the standard error of estimate and a rather complicated set of relationships that reflect uncertainty about the height and tilt of the regression plane. These calculations also reflect the difference between the production reported for a given week and the means of the production data from which the regression was computed. The greater the difference between given output and the mean output, the less confidence we have in the prediction of the regression equation. For this example, the adjusted standard error of estimate for the values of the independent variables given is 592.61. Thus, we assess a probability of .67 that the actual costs incurred will be between $7,918.53 and $9,103.75 ($8,511.14 ± $592.61) and probability .95 that they will be between $9,696.36 and $7,325.92 ($8,511.14 ± 2 × $592.61). With these figures, management can decide how unusual the actual production costs are in the light of past experience.

LIMITATIONS OF MULTIPLE REGRESSION ANALYSIS

Although multiple regression is a very powerful tool, it is not applicable to all cost situations. Its use of past data necessarily requires that these numbers be relevant for predicting the future. If the process that is being costed has changed radically or if future factor prices and cost relationships are expected to change substan-

---

[27]The statements about probability are based on a Bayesian approach, with normality and diffuse prior distributions assumed.

tially, the calculated regression coefficients will not be useful. Furthermore, such decisions as the cost of new products that are different from products produced in the past normally cannot be based on an analysis of past recorded data. Although these limitations also apply to the usual accounting procedures for estimating costs, it is useful to mention that they also limit the usefulness of regression analysis.

A second limitation has been described above. Multiple regression requires relatively large amounts of data that have been carefully recorded. Often such data do not exist or are very costly to obtain.

Another important limitation of multiple regression analysis is that it appears to be complicated and so is thought difficult to "sell" to management and supervisory personnel. This is a valid concern that evidently has restricted the use of regression analysis in practice. However, it should be noted that the method allows for a more complete specification of "reality" than does the accounting procedure. Essentially arbitrary allocations of overhead costs and subjective separation of costs into fixed and variable items also are hard to sell to production supervisors and managerial decision makers. Although they may not reject the accounting numbers as too complicated, they may, however, disregard them. Worse yet, they may use the numbers for decisions without realizing when they provide very poor estimates of expected costs. Therefore, it would seem essential that the accountant learn to use multiple regression analysis, at least as a means of checking on the assumptions about cost behavior that underlie the usual accounting cost reports.

Linear Programming. Another procedure for estimating costs that should be mentioned, though briefly, is linear programming.[28] Use of this method requires the assumption that the contribution margin (revenue less variable costs) expected from a unit of output is constant over the range of production expected. It also assumes that the amount of an essential, scarce resource cannot be expanded within the time frame of the decision. Such a resource might be machine hours, warehouse floorspace, or salesperson's time. Therefore, use of the resource for the production of one product or activity may be at the expense of limiting the production of other products. Linear programming provides a means for determining the production plan that is expected to yield the maximum contribution to profits.

Linear programming requires inputs from the accountant's cost estimates as well as mathematical descriptions of the production technology(ies) and the availability of scarce inputs. Most solution methodologies provide the accountant with estimates of the economic (opportunity) cost of the limiting scarce resources. The inputs required are the average variable costs (where marginal costs are assumed to be constant) of the alternative products that can be produced with the scarce resource. These numbers are needed to calculate the contribution margin. One output of the linear programming solution is "shadow prices," the *ceteris paribus* increase in the maximum total contribution margin associated with an additional unit of a limiting scarce resource. These opportunity costs can be used by the decision maker (along with other information) for estimating the net benefits from expanding the amount of the scarce resource.

CONCLUSIONS AND SUMMARY

Cost estimation for decision making requires consideration of the context in which the decisions are made and the environment in which they will be carried out.

---

[28]A description of the mathematics and techniques of linear programming is beyond the range of the chapter. See, however, Chapter 19 in this *Handbook*. Computer library programs that perform the required operations are readily available.

Often, recorded costs are not a useful source for cost estimation because the future is expected to be very different from the past. For many decisions, however, such as whether a process or department is in control, past costs generally are highly useful. Costs that provide useful estimates for price and output decisions also may be derived from past cost experience where the environment within which the decisions take place is not expected to change significantly or where recorded costs can be adjusted for significant changes.

The manner in which costs are recorded influences their usefulness for cost estimation. The level of cost aggregation obviously affects the availability of the data for preparing budgets and reports of performance, and for estimating the costs of a particular activity. The detail in which costs are categorized affects the extent to which they can be identified as variable or fixed. The frequency with which they are recorded also affects their usefulness for estimating cost variability with multiple regression analysis.

In practice, cost estimation procedures generally are based on an analysis of recorded costs adjusted by the estimator (often informally) for changes that are believed to affect costs significantly. Multiple regression analysis and linear programming can be used to supplement this procedure. Exhibit 2 shows a summary of the methods, along with their strengths and weaknesses, used to estimate costs.

EXHIBIT 2   Strengths and Weaknesses of Cost Estimation Methods

Method	Strengths	Weaknesses
Engineering method	Based on studies of what future cost should be rather than what past costs have been.	Not particularly useful when the physical relationship between inputs and outputs is indirect. Can be costly to use.
High-low method	Easy to understand and apply. Provides reasonably good cost estimates when the high and low observations are representative.	Uses only two of the available observations of cost data.
Visual curve-fitting method	Uses all the observations of cost data. Relatively easy to understand and apply.	The fitting of the line to the observations is subjective. Difficult to do where several independent variables are to be used.
Regression method	Uses all of the observations of cost data. The line is statistically fit to the observations. A measure of the goodness of fit of the line to the observations is provided. Relatively easy to apply with "canned" regression programs.	The regression model requires that several relatively strict assumptions be satisfied in order for the results to be valid. More difficult to understand than the preceding methods.

SOURCE: S. Davidson, J. S. Schindler, C. P. Stickney, and R. L. Weil, *Managerial Accounting: An Introduction to Concepts, Methods, and Uses* (Dryden Press, Hinsdale, Ill., 1978).

BIBLIOGRAPHY

Benston, G. J.: "Economies of Scale and Marginal Costs in Banking Operations," *National Banking Review,* 1965, pp. 507–549.

————: "Multiple Regression Analysis of Cost Behavior," *Accounting Review,* XLI (1966), pp. 657–672.

————: "The Role of the Firm's Accounting System for Motivation," *Accounting Review,* April 1963, pp. 347–354.

Davidson, Sidney, James S. Schindler, Clyde P. Stickney, and Roman L. Weil: *Managerial Accounting: An Introduction to Concepts, Methods, and Uses,* Dryden Press, Hinsdale, Ill., 1978.

Davidson, Sidney, James S. Schindler, and Roman L. Weil: *Fundamentals of Accounting,* Dryden Press, Hinsdale, Ill., 1975.

Durbin, J., and G. J. Watson: "Testing for Serial Correlation in Least-Squares Regression," *Biometrika,* Parts I and II, 1950 and 1951.

Johnston, J.: *Econometric Methods,* 2nd ed., McGraw-Hill Book Company, New York, 1972.

————: *Statistical Cost Analysis,* McGraw-Hill Book Company, New York, 1960.

Kaplan, R. S.: "Variable and Self-Service Costs in Reciprocal Allocation Models," *Accounting Review,* 48 (October 1973), pp. 738–748.

National Association of Accountants: *Separating and Using Costs as Fixed and Variable,* June 1960.

Chapter **6**

Operating Budgets

DUANE R. BORST
Comptroller, Inland Steel Company

INTRODUCTION

An operating budget is a short-range (usually one year) quantitative expression of management's expectations of future revenues, costs, and profits for the entire company. This forecasted income statement is generally supported by projections of relevant marketing, production, and financial factors. The budget's expected impact on the firm is explained by certain key statistics such as turnover ratios, return on sales, and return on investment. For example, return on investment is an important means of measuring management's success in profitably investing the firm's assets.

The concept of return on investment (ROI) and its use for investment decision analysis are well known, and the literature abounds with rich material. One aspect of the use of ROI for internal profit measurement has received little attention in the literature. This aspect, which was developed by Du Pont in the early part of the twentieth century, is probably the most important contribution of the ROI system. The management of Du Pont discovered a link between the objectives of the firm and the goals and decision criteria of the separate functions of the business by relating every function (marketing, production, distribution, credit, financing, etc.) to the ROI goal of the firm. The famous Du Pont ROI chart (Exhibit 1) illustrates this principle.

For example, most manufacturing companies have the classic conflict of goals among the departments of sales (sales volume maximization), production (manufacturing cost minimization), and credit (receivable investment minimization plus minimum bad debt losses). These three subgoals conflict with one another. The

EXHIBIT 1   Relationship of Factors Affecting Return on Investment

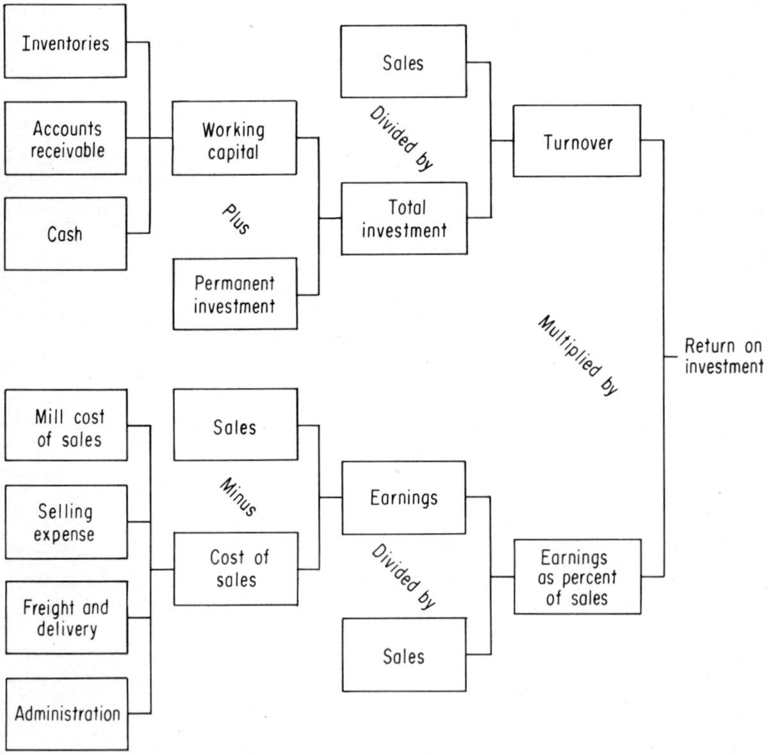

$$\frac{\text{Net profit } \$5,000}{\text{Sales } \$50,000} \quad \text{X} \quad \frac{\text{Sales } \$50,000}{\text{Capital } \$25,000} \quad = \quad \frac{\text{Return on}}{\text{investment}}$$

$$10\% \qquad \text{X} \qquad 2 \qquad = \qquad 20\%$$

Du Pont ROI approach replaces these subgoals with the common goal of the firm, ROI. This approach does not settle all arguments or differences of opinion, but it focuses the attention of the managers on the ROI goals of the firm rather than discrete, conflicting subgoals.

In general, operating budgets are designed to reflect management's short-range business plans, to facilitate the implementation and control features of the plan, and to provide a tool for the evaluation of managerial performance. The total budgetary process provides a means for integrating and coordinating planning activities of the entire company. It also serves to improve communications among the various levels of management and among the different functions of the company (e.g., the marketing, production, purchasing, and finance functions).

The operating budget is not merely an accounting technique; rather, it is a crucial element of the overall management process. The operating budget fulfills its objective when it becomes an integral tool of management rather than a periodic drudgery that management is forced to "suffer" through.

A successful budget system requires a disciplined approach to planning with the participation and acceptance of both top and middle management. In order to monitor events effectively during the time period covered by the budget, the budgetary process must provide a feedback system to management comparing actual results with the appropriate budgeted allowances at all levels of activity.

The operating budget should not be confused with two other (though related) planning tools: the financial budget and the long-range plan. The financial budget consists of *pro forma* statements of financial position and changes in financial position. The purpose of this budget is to assist management in evaluating alternative courses of action regarding such matters as liquidity, methods of financing, and dividend policy through projections of important balance sheet accounts, simulation models (manual or computerized), and other tools of financial planning.

Although the structure and formality of long-range planning vary considerably among companies, the essential functions of this activity are to (1) establish corporate objectives such as minimum acceptable return on investment for new capital projects, desired market share, earnings per share goal, and sales and earnings growth targets; (2) identify new opportunities and challenges such as determining which markets and products have the potential for achieving the desired sales growth; (3) evaluate alternative strategies by comparing the characteristics of various investment proposals to the corporate objectives; and (4) make decisions determining the overall direction of the company.

With their relatively short time horizon, operating budgets are obviously inappropriate for planning activities involving several years or longer. Consequently, the emphasis of operating budgets should be on improving the utilization of the company's existing organization and resources. However, the long-range planning process should be in harmony with the operating budgets; otherwise management actions may be at cross purposes.

In this chapter we shall discuss the components of an operating budget, the steps involved in preparing the budget, and the administration of a budgeting system within the corporate organization.

FLEXIBLE BUDGETS

A flexible budget is a budget that is prepared for a range rather than a single level of activity, and that can be geared automatically to changes in the level of volume. The flexible budget is structured so that, given any reasonable level of operations, a specific determination can be made as to what the costs should have been for that level of output. The flexible budget is also known by other names, such as variable budget, sliding-scale budget, step budget, expense formula budget, and expense control budget.

The concept of a flexible budget, applicable to a range of operating activity, is in contrast to a static (or fixed) budget, which is tailored to a single target level of volume. For example, assuming that a manufacturing operation is expected to produce 10,000 units of output, a static budget could be created that would develop the estimated manufacturing costs at this specific level of activity. However, if the actual production decreased to 9,000 units, then under a static budget the manager would be comparing the actual costs of producing 9,000 units with the budgeted cost of producing 10,000 units. Clearly the idea of comparing performance at one activity level with a plan that was developed at some other activity level is nonsense from the viewpoint of judging how efficiently the manager has produced any given output.

The more logical approach for budgeting production costs would be to develop a flexible budget that can provide budgeted costs within any reasonable range of the estimated production output. Thus, as in the above example, a flexible budget might be developed that would apply to a "relevant range" of production, say 8,000 to 12,000 units. Under this approach, if actual production slips to 9,000 units from a projected 10,000 units, the manager has a specific tool (i.e., the flexible budget) that can be used to determine what budgeted costs should have been at 9,000 units of output. The flexible budget provides a dynamic basis for comparisons because it is automatically geared to changes in production activity.

Definition of Fixed, Variable, and Semivariable Costs.   As discussed above, flexible budgeting is an important management tool because significant variations from planned volume are almost certain to occur, and variable standards that can be applied under such conditions become necessary. In order to develop a flexible budget, it is necessary first to classify each cost into one of three categories: variable costs, fixed costs, or semivariable costs.

Variable costs are costs that are expected to change in direct proportion to sales, production, or some related measure of activity. Variable costs can be visualized as the costs required to place an additional unit of product in the hands of the customer. For example, raw materials are variable costs.

Fixed costs remain constant over short periods of time irrespective of changes in production or sales volume. Normally, for planning and control, fixed costs are subdivided into committed (sometimes referred to as "sunk") and discretionary costs.

Committed fixed costs include those fixed costs derived from the possession of plant and equipment and the continuation of the company organization itself. Examples are depreciation, property taxes, rent, insurance, and the salaries of key personnel. These costs reflect primarily the long-run capacity needs of the firm. Committed costs are all those organization and plant costs that continue to be incurred and cannot be reduced without injuring the organization's ability to stay in business.

Discretionary fixed costs are fixed costs that arise from periodic (usually yearly) appropriation decisions made by management. Discretionary costs often have no particular relation to volume of activity. Examples include research and development expenditures, management consulting fees, and the costs of many employee training programs. These costs can generally be reduced in a year of poor profits, whereas the committed costs would be much more difficult to reduce.

As the name implies, a semivariable cost has both fixed and variable elements. The fixed portion reflects the minimum cost of supplying a service. The variable portion is that part of the semivariable cost that is influenced by changes in production. An example of a semivariable cost is the lease of a piece of equipment for a fixed cost per month plus a variable cost based on usage. Theoretically, semivariable costs should be subdivided into two portions, one for the variable portion and one for the fixed portion. Such a separation of costs can be accomplished by using relatively simple techniques such as scatter charts or the high-low, two-point method of analysis. However, because these methods are based entirely on historical data, there is a danger of depending too much on the past and not considering future changes in cost behavior. In practice, a semivariable cost might be assumed to be either all fixed or all variable depending on its size and characteristics in relation to total costs.

The Cost-Volume Relationship. Defining the relationship between cost and volume is probably the most difficult phase of developing the flexible budget. This is because the relationship is not a precise one, and the various costs do not vary at the same rate. Fixed and variable costs represent extremes of cost behavior. Few costs are purely fixed or purely variable. Some costs increase in a "stepwise" manner, and others increase in a varying manner over the relevant range so that the assumed linearity of the variable cost as a function of production is not entirely correct. Many factors contribute to the variability of costs. Among these are the nature of the relationship between a given cost and the production activity itself, the relationship of that cost with time, the controllability of a variable cost, and the degree of discretion permitted in the control of fixed costs. The imprecise nature of these factors is not conducive to defining the variability of costs precisely.

Two major methods are available to management for quantifying these relationships. The first is the use of industrial engineering studies to develop cost standards for various levels of output. This method produces discrete costs associated with given volumes. The second means of determining cost variability is to use historical data as a basis for regression analysis in order to establish a relationship, usually linear, between cost and volume. However, such cost analysis methods are only the first step in the budgetary process. The budgeted figures are expected *future data,* so analysis must be altered to reflect anticipated changes in prices, efficiency, technology, and other important factors.

When the cost-volume relationship is determined for the relevant range of output, cost standards are available against which actual performance can be measured even if the targeted sales volume is not achieved.

Cost-Volume-Profit Analysis. A firm's cost-volume-profit relationship is an important extension of the flexible budget. The flexible budget defines the relationship between cost and volume. Cost-volume-profit analysis adds dollar or unit sales (or both) to the analysis in order to determine expected profit at each point within the relevant range. Two means are used to present cost-volume-profit analyses, the graphic method and the mathematical equation method.

The graphic method dynamically reflects the key concepts of "breakeven point" and contribution margin. In Exhibit 2, costs and revenue are shown on the vertical axis and volume produced and sold is shown on the horizontal axis. Fixed costs (i.e., those that remain the same regardless of the number of units produced) are represented as a horizontal line. Variable costs are represented as that component of total costs lying above the fixed cost line (note the linearity of variable cost as it varies directly in proportion to the volume of activity). Total sales equals the price per unit times the number of units sold. In Exhibit 2, fixed costs are assumed to be $270,000, variable costs are $70 per unit, and the selling price is $100 per unit.

The breakeven point is defined as that level of sales volume at which total revenues are equal to total expenses (see Exhibit 2). Any sales level below the breakeven point will result in a loss, and sales above the breakeven point will result in a profit.

This leads to the key concept of "contribution margin," or "marginal income." Contribution margin is defined as the excess of sales price over variable expense.

EXHIBIT 2   Breakeven Chart

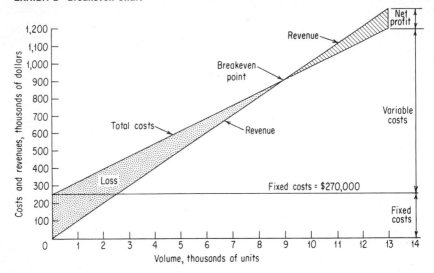

For example, in Exhibit 2 the sales price per unit is $100 and the variable cost per unit is $70. The difference between these two numbers ($100 − $70 = $30) is the contribution margin per unit or that portion of the selling price which "contributes" toward covering fixed costs and making a profit.

An alternative graphic presentation illustrates the contribution margin concept more clearly (Exhibit 3). By first graphing variable costs and then adding fixed costs to them, it is easy to see that the total contribution margin, which is the vertical distance between revenue and variable costs, increases with increasing unit sales. The contribution margin initially is insufficient to cover fixed costs. At the

EXHIBIT 3

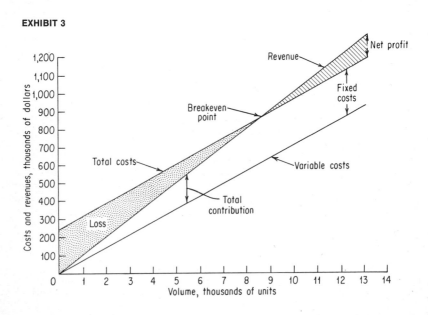

EXHIBIT 4   Algebraic Solution for Breakeven Point in Sales

1. The breakeven point is where total revenue equals total costs.
2. Sales price and variable cost per unit are assumed to be constant; therefore, the ratio of variable costs to sales is assumed to be constant. This is referred to as the variable cost ratio.
3. Subtraction of the variable cost ratio from unity (1) determines the contribution of each sales dollar to cover fixed costs and profit.
4. Thus:

$$\text{Breakeven} = \frac{\text{Total Fixed Costs}}{1 - (\text{Total Variable Costs}/\text{Total Sales Volume})}$$

5. Example:

$$\begin{aligned} \text{BE} &= \frac{\$270,000}{1 - (\$700,000/\$1,000,000)} \\ &= \frac{\$270,000}{.30} \\ &= \$900,000 \end{aligned}$$

breakeven point, the contribution margin exactly equals fixed cost and total revenue equals total costs. Then, at any level of production above the breakeven point, profit results.

The concept of contribution margin is the key to the algebraic solutions of breakeven point illustrated in Exhibits 4 and 5. Fixed costs divided by contribution margin per unit sold (i.e., $30) determines the breakeven point in units, whereas fixed costs divided by contribution margin per dollar of sales determines the breakeven point in terms of total dollar sales. The level of sales necessary to achieve a given level of profits can easily be determined by adding the desired level of profits to total fixed costs in the numerator of the algebraic equations and then solving.

A word of caution is necessary in cost-volume-profit analysis. The graphic presentation of Exhibit 2 seems to indicate that the cost-volume relationship is valid over the full spectrum of sales from $0 up to any maximum limit. However, this is seldom true; the many assumptions that underlie the graph are subject to

EXHIBIT 5   Algebraic Solution for Breakeven Point in Units

1. The breakeven point is where total revenue equals total costs.
2. Total costs equals fixed costs plus variable costs.
3. Variable costs divided by units to be produced equals variable cost per unit.
4. Let:

$$\begin{aligned} P &= \text{sales price per unit} \\ S &= \text{quantity produced and sold} \\ FC &= \text{total fixed cost} \\ VC &= \text{variable cost per unit} \end{aligned}$$

5. Thus:

$$\begin{aligned} P \times S &= FC + VC \times S \\ (P \times S) - (VC \times S) &= FC \\ S(P - VC) &= FC \\ \text{At breakeven, } S &= \frac{FC}{(P - VC)} \end{aligned}$$

6. Example:

$$\begin{aligned} S &= \frac{270,000}{\$100 - \$70} \\ &= 9,000 \text{ units} \end{aligned}$$

change if actual volume falls outside the "relevant range" that is the basis for drawing the chart. The relevant range is the range in which cost-volume relationships can be expected to hold, usually a range in which the firm has had some recent experience. If volume falls outside the relevant range, then the cost-volume-profit relationship is unlikely to hold. For example, at extremely low levels of activity, some fixed costs may be avoided (i.e., there would be no fixed heating costs associated with a closed plant).

It should be noted that the goal of cost-volume-profit analysis is generally not the calculation of the breakeven point. The real purpose of the analysis is to determine how sensitive profitability is to changes in volume. Hence, the term "cost-volume-profit analysis" is preferred to "breakeven analysis."

The assumptions underlying cost-volume-profit analysis are as follows:

1. The behavior of costs and revenues has been accurately determined and is linear over the relevant range.
2. All costs can be broken down into fixed and variable elements.
3. Fixed costs remain constant over the volume range on the breakeven chart.
4. Variable costs fluctuate in proportion to volume.
5. Selling prices are constant.
6. Efficiency and productivity are constant.
7. The analysis covers a single product, or the same sales mix is maintained as volume changes.
8. *Volume* is the only factor affecting cost.

Standard Costs.   The concept of "standard" cost is of key importance in comparing planned with actual performance. Standard costs are predetermined costs based on reasonably attainable performance at a given level of volume under anticipated operating conditions. Standard costs for direct materials, direct labor, and manufacturing overhead represent the company's best estimate of attainable production costs. Standard costs of direct materials, direct labor, and variable overhead per unit of output are the determinants of the variable portion of the flexible budget when multiplied by expected production.

After a given period of production, the actual costs for that production are determined. Comparison of these actual costs with the standard costs identifies the cost variances associated with the period's production. Significant variances from standard costs should be investigated to discover better ways of adhering to standards, of altering the standards, or of accomplishing objectives.

Currently attainable standards (i.e., standards that are difficult but possible to achieve) are used most prevalently because they usually have the most desirable motivational impact and because they may be used for a variety of accounting purposes in addition to monitoring performance. (For example, standard costs are frequently used in product pricing decisions.) When standards are currently attainable, there is little difference between standards and the flexible budget. A standard is a unit cost concept, whereas a budget is a total cost concept (i.e., the standard cost can be visualized as the budget for one unit). Standard costs are the backbone of the budgeting and feedback system.

Material and labor variances basically are divided into two categories: (1) quantity or efficiency variance and (2) price or wage variance.

Exhibits 6, 7, and 8 illustrate the calculation of standard costs, their comparison with actual costs, and the calculation of the associated variances. Exhibit 8 shows the variance analysis appropriate for manufacturing overhead. Two methods are shown: the three-variance method and the two-variance method.

Variance analysis should be performed in a manner consistent with "responsibility accounting." That is, managers should be held responsible only for those costs over which they have the requisite authority and ability to control. The concept of "responsibility accounting" will be discussed later in the chapter.

EXHIBIT 6   Standard Costs

Example of Computation of Material Variances
Data: Standard unit price as per standard cost card: $5.00
      Purchased: 5,000 units @ $4.94
      Requisitioned: 3,550 units
      Material allowed as per standard production order: 3,500 units

Material quantity variance (computed when material is issued or used)
   3,550 actual units × $5.00 standard cost   = $17,750
   3,500 standard units × $5.00 standard cost =   17,500
     Unfavorable quantity variance   = $ 250 debit

Because 50 units in excess of the standard quantity were used, the quantity variance of $250 is unfavorable.
This variance can also be computed as follows:
   50 units × $5.00 = $250

Material price variance (calculated at time of purchase)
   5,000 units × $4.94 = $24,700 actual cost
   5,000 units × $5.00 =   25,000 standard cost
     Favorable price
     variance   = $ 300 credit

Because the purchase price $4.94 is lower than the $5.00 standard cost, the price variance of $300 is favorable.
This variance can also be computed as follows:
   5,000 units × $.06 = $300

Overall, it must be remembered that variances raise questions; they do not provide answers. The variances must be investigated to determine (1) what caused the variances, (2) who is responsible for the variance, and (3) how to improve performance in the future. Thus, it is the investigation of the causes of variances and the follow-up action to improve operations that provide the real value of variance analysis.

EXHIBIT 7   Standard Costs

Example of Computation of Labor Variances
Data: Actual hours worked   8,500
      Actual rate paid $4.70
      Standard hours allowed   8,600
      Standard rate $4.60

Labor efficiency (labor quantity) variance
   8,500 actual hours @ $4.60 standard labor rate   = $39,100
   8,600 standard hours @ $4.60 standard labor rate =   39,560
     Favorable efficiency variance   = $ 460 credit

Because 100 hours less than the standard allowed were used, the efficiency variance of $460 is favorable.
This variance can also be computed as follows:
   100 hours (difference between actual and standard hours) × $4.60 = $460

Labor rate (price or wage) variance
   8,500 actual hours @ $4.70 actual labor rate   = $39,950
   8,500 actual hours @ $4.60 standard labor rate =   39,100
     Unfavorable labor rate variance   = $ 850 debit

Because the actual labor rate $4.70 is higher than the $4.60 standard cost, the rate variance of $850 is unfavorable.
This variance can also be computed as follows:
   8,500 actual hours × $.10 (difference between actual and standard rates) = $850

EXHIBIT 8   Standard Costs

EXAMPLE OF COMPUTATION OF MANUFACTURING EXPENSE VARIANCES

Data	Direct labor hours	Total cost	Overhead rate per hour
Attainable capacity	10,000	$40,000	$ 4.00
Consists of: Fixed costs		$10,000	$ 1.00
Variable costs		30,000	3.00
Actual performance	8,500	34,680	
Standard (allowed) hours for actual production	8,600		
Budget allowance for	9,000	37,000	
Budget allowance for	8,000	34,000	

The Two-Variance Method:
(1) Controllable variance:

Actual manufacturing expenses		$34,680
Budget allowance based on allowed (standard) hours		35,800
Fixed cost = $10,000		
Variable cost = 25,800 (8,600 hours × $3.00)		
$35,800		
Favorable controllable variance (credit)		$ 1,120

(2) Volume variance:

Budget allowance based on allowed (or standard) hours		$35,800
Standard hours × standard overhead rate (8,600 hours × $4.00)		34,400
Unfavorable volume variance (debit)		$ 1,400

The volume variance consists of fixed costs only.

The Three-Variance Method: Using the three-variance method with a flexible budget the following variances are computed:

(1) Budget variance:

Actual manufacturing expenses		$34,680
Budget allowance based on the actual 8,500 hours worked		35,500
Fixed cost = $10,000		
Variable cost = 25,500 (8,500 hours × $3.00)		
$35,500		
Favorable budget variance (credit)		$ 820

(2) Capacity variance:

Budget allowance based on actual hours		$35,500
Actual hours × standard overhead rate (8,500 × $4.00)		34,000
Unfavorable capacity variance (debit)		$ 1,500

(3) Efficiency variance:

Actual hours × standard overhead rate (8,500 × $4.00)		$34,000
Standard hours × standard overhead rate (8,600 × $4.00)		34,400
Favorable efficiency variance (credit)		$ 400

THE FIXED (STATIC) BUDGET

All departments of a company do not necessarily incur expenses that are functions of either sales or production. The expenses of some departments may be determined solely by management discretion and may not fluctuate within the budget period. Examples of such departments are the administrative staffs and the general executive offices of the firm. For such departments, a variable budget is obviously inappropriate and an approved fixed budget should be used as a means of planning, controlling, and evaluating the performances of these departments.

Fixed Budget Worksheet. Although it is less complicated, the process of estimating operating costs for general and administrative departments, whose expenses are not a function of production or sales, must be performed just as carefully as the estimates of departments having variable budgets. One type of budget estimate sheet used for fixed departmental budgets is shown in Exhibit 9.

Column A describes the various expense accounts. Each departmental expense should be classified into the appropriate account. Column G shows the budgeted expense for each account for the current year. Column H shows the amount by which the next year's budgeted expense in each account either exceeds or falls below the current year's budgeted amount.

The current year's expenses under each account should be carefully reviewed and analyzed in order to determine where greater efficiencies can be implemented. This is the starting point for estimating next year's expenses. It is at this time that proposed changes in programs, systems, responsibilities, etc., are evaluated and their cost savings and/or performance improvement are quantified. If approved, the expected annual expenses related to these changes should be incorporated into the upcoming year's budget. It is important to have the approved budget for the current year (column G) and the increase/(decrease) therefrom expected in the following year's budget (column H) because they call attention to significant cost trends and patterns that might require further investigation.

Alternatively, the practice of a zero-based budget may be used. The zero-based budget starts with a budget of $0 and adds individual items of expense only as they are scrupulously analyzed and justified as a necessary cost in the upcoming year. In this manner, no unjustified cost is allowed to "slip through" into the current year's budget merely because it was included in last year's budget. This technique may be used selectively for departments where management is concerned with costs versus benefits of a particular function or periodically, say every three or four years, as a continuing review of the cost/benefit trade-offs available to the management of the firm.

Columns B, C, D, and E show the proposed expenses for the upcoming year by quarter, and column F shows the budget for each expense account for the year in total. It is necessary to break down the proposed budget into quarterly (or even monthly) amounts in order to illustrate trends and seasonal costs if they exist and also to aid management in the cash-budgeting process. For example, there may be a gradual buildup of personnel during the year in order to implement a new program within a department. Departments may have one-time seasonal expenses (e.g., association dues, conventions, major meetings, etc.) that are included in one quarter but do not recur during the remainder of the year. There may be a change in duties or responsibilities among departments in the middle of the year. If the proposed budget was shown only as annual figures, then these changes and trends would not be nearly as apparent as they are in the quarterly (or monthly) data.

Not all general and administrative areas should necessarily be budgeted on a fixed basis. For example, a data handling department or a clerical unit may have a paperwork load that is directly dependent on a volume factor such as sales or invoices. Such areas should follow a variable rather than a fixed budgeting procedure. Thus, it is necessary to analyze the cost behavior of each department to determine whether the fixed or variable budget is applicable, rather than to make a broad statement that all "general and administrative" areas should use a fixed budget.

EXHIBIT 9 Example of a Budget Estimate Sheet

AMERICAN IRON & STEEL, INC. 19X2 BUDGET ESTIMATE SHEET

	A	B	C	D	E	F	G	H	I	
	Account	Budget for the year 19X2					19X1 budget	Over or under(−) 19X1	Comments	
		1st qtr.	2nd qtr.	3rd qtr.	4th qtr.	Year				
1	Base salaries	48,000	50,000	60,000	60,000	218,000	190,000	28,000	3 new employees in 3rd qtr.	1
2	Overtime	9,000	9,000	3,000	3,000	24,000	30,000	6,000 −	New employee in 3rd qtr.	2
3	Indirect comp.	5,400	6,000	7,000	7,000	25,400	21,300	4,100	Increased pension costs	3
4	Total empl. comp.	62,400	65,000	70,000	70,000	267,400	241,300	26,100		4
5										5
6	Office supp. and equip.	90	90	90	90	360	360	—		6
7	Rent and utility	3,750	3,750	3,750	4,200	15,450	15,000	450	Rent increase in 4th qtr.	7
8	Machine rental	225	225	225	225	900	900	—		8
9	Outside services	225	300	300	300	1,125	900	225	Increase in computer time-sharing	9
10	Postage	30	30	30	30	120	150	30 −		10
11	Repairs and alter.	105	105	1,000	105	1,315	500	815	Remodel manager's office in 3rd qtr.	11
12	Misc. office exp.	120	120	120	120	480	450	30		12
13										13
14	Training and educ.	225	600	225	225	1,275	900	375	Special training program in 2nd qtr.	14
15										15
16										16
17										17
18										18
19	Total expenses	67,170	70,220	75,740	75,295	288,425	260,460	27,965		19

Approved: PAYROLL DEPT. ______ Budget Center ______ Date ______ Manager ______ Date ______ 601 Budget Center Code

BUDGETING FOLLOWS LINES OF AUTHORITY

The structure of the budget is subject to the organizational lines of authority of the company because it reflects the quantification of delegated responsibility. Departmental budgets are prepared for every unit of authority down to the lowest section that has distinct operating accountability. Summaries are made for each higher level of authority in order to facilitate the formal review and approval process.

It is important that managers of each department prepare their own budgets with the assistance of the budget staff (rather than the other way around). When the original estimates are summarized and reviewed by higher-level management, the department manager should be informed and consulted if changes seem warranted. Even in the event of drastic revisions of the proposed departmental budget, the manager should be kept informed and participate in all major changes so that each manager is committed to the budget. Ideally this process should occur within the normal chain of command, but the budget staff must close any gaps in communication. This should gain the acceptance and cooperation of the managers, provide better information, and improve the probability of success of the entire budget program.

BUDGET CENTER REPORT AND CONTROL

Preparation and approval of the departmental budget, although of key importance, do not represent the end of the budgeting process. Organizing and setting up a budget is not sufficient to assure that it is properly implemented. For control purposes, it is necessary that some sort of monitoring procedure be instituted to compare the actual results for the budgeted period with the approved budget.

Exhibit 10 illustrates a Budget Center Report for a department with a fixed operating budget. Column E gives a description of each expense account applicable to the particular department. Columns A, B, and C show the actual expenditures made for each month of the current quarter. Column D contains the budgeted amount for each of the three months in the current quarter.

By comparing the actual amounts in columns A, B, and C with the budgeted amount in column D, a determination can be made as to which costs are out of line with the budget. Column F of Exhibit 10 shows the actual year-to-date expenses incurred by account, column G shows the amount of planned expense per the approved budget, and column H shows the variance of the actual expense from budget. Totals are summarized at the botton of the page, and the appropriate name, budget code, and other appropriate identifying information are shown at the top of the page.

Copies of the Budget Center Report for each department should be sent to the manager of the department and to his or her supervisor. The manager of the department should study the Budget Center Report for the department in order to determine those areas in which greater cost controls are needed or areas that have been subject to unusual or unforeseen expenses during the budgeted period. The Budget Center Report should help the manager (1) to improve control over the remaining periods of the current budget year and (2) to improve cost planning for the following year.

The group manager of several departments should receive the Budget Center Report for each department supervised in order to evaluate properly the performance of the department managers. The group manager can then work with the department manager in seeking better cost controls and more efficient operations. The group manager must be careful in evaluating the performance of the department manager. The group manager should remember that an unfavorable variance is not necessarily bad and that a favorable variance is not necessarily good.

EXHIBIT 10   Budget Center Report

BUDGET CENTER REPORT

PAYROLL DEPT | 601 | 1 | 3 | 19X2
Budget Center | Code | Qtr. | Mo. | Yr.

A	B	C	D	E	F	G	H
Current quarter by months					Year to Date		
Actual			Budget (1/3 of qtr.)	Description	Actual	Budget	Over or under (−) budget
1st mo. of qtr.	2nd mo. of qtr.	3rd mo. of qtr.					
17,030	16,500	16,010	16,000	Base salaries	49,540	48,000	1,540
2,700	3,000	2,900	3,000	Overtime	8,600	9,000	400 −
2,000	1,900	1,800	1,800	Indirect compensation	5,700	5,400	300
21,730	21,400	20,710	20,800	Total empl. comp.	63,840	62,400	1,440
100	25	30	30	Office supp. and equip.	155	90	65
1,100	1,100	1,280	1,250	Rent and utility	3,480	3,750	270 −
75	75	75	75	Machine rental	225	225	−
45	80	25	75	Outside services	150	225	75 −
10	8	15	10	Postage	33	30	3
15	30	175	35	Repairs and alter.	220	105	115
18	15	32	40	Misc. office exp.	65	120	55 −
0	100	50	75	Training and educ.	150	225	75 −
23,093	22,833	22,392	22,390	Grand totals	68,318	67,170	1,148
103%	102%	100%		Percent of actual to budget	102%		

Thus, the group manager must take into account the cause of the variance when assessing the performance of the department manager, rather than blindly assigning responsibility for all variances to the manager.

The vice president in charge of the group managers should receive a summarization of departmental actual performance compared with budget. The vice president can then work with the general managers in a more general manner, but similar to the interface between the general manager and department managers. If this kind of review process of actual versus budgeted performance is followed carefully, the desired control feature of the budgeting process will permeate the organization from the president's level down to the manager of the smallest department.

STEPS IN THE DEVELOPMENT OF AN OPERATING BUDGET

The first step in developing an operating budget is to obtain the demand forecast for the firm's products and services (in units) over the course of the upcoming operating cycle. This will be the result of extensive research and analysis by the sales and marketing staffs. The demand forecast serves as the framework on which all other parts of the budget are hung. Although the forecast will rarely prove to be 100 percent accurate, it does serve as the central point of the relevant range of activity for purposes of deriving cost behavior patterns.

The second step is the preparation of a master operating plan or production budget. This plan will be a statement of targeted numbers of unit production, usually by month. Basically, it is determined by adding demand in units to desired ending finished goods inventory and subtracting beginning finished goods inventory. It is often advantageous in the development of the master operating plan to stabilize production during the year even though the demand pattern may be erratic. This stabilization of production is desirable in order to avoid using relatively unprofitable facilities, overtime penalties, and the hiring and training of temporary employees. Inventory serves as a cushion that may be built or liquidated in order to keep production stable during periods of erratic demand. This inventory planning process requires a careful analysis (one or possibly two years in advance) to determine the inventory position target at year-end.

The master operating plan is used by the managers of individual processing units to prepare their own operating plans. Here again, planned inventory levels at the beginning and end of each process are used to help smooth production.

At the same time as the operating plans are being developed, the sales department will be determining product prices for the year. The prices will be based on controllable factors such as product mix, quality, and customer service rendered, and certain uncontrollable factors relating to market conditions and government "price control" pressures. These prices will then be multiplied by their respective demand forecasts to arrive at monthly dollars sales projections.

The combination of a master operating plan and various subplans, all stated in units of production, defines the flow of products and the mix of facilities needed to meet the demand forecast. Once the level of production for each operating unit and the required facilities are known, several steps may be taken simultaneously.

The group of unified operating plans makes it possible to estimate raw material needs. The level of raw material purchases and/or production can be set and costs of materials determined. Again, desired inventory levels play important roles in the planning process.

It is important that the development of all subplans be properly coordinated in order that the interrelationships of requirements and productive capabilities of all operating units and staff departments be considered carefully. As a hypothetical illustration: unit B requires 1,000 tons of raw materials from unit A to meet its demand forecast. If unit A can produce only 900 tons, unit B must find an alternative source of raw materials or scale down its sales forecast.

Because approximate production levels are known, standards for product yield, productivity, and materials mix can be set for the various producing processes. These form the basis for costing materials on a unit basis for each stage of production. These costs will be used to derive material costs at the forecast level of production and will be used later to calculate the standard material costs at actual levels of production.

The level of production and the product mix determine the amount and type of labor required. By applying labor rates, direct labor costs are estimated. The direct labor budget is, of course, adjustable to differing levels of production.

After the prime costs of production are developed, attention is focused on the various overhead items. Some are related to the operating plan and others are independent of the operating plan. Estimates are developed for such items as rent expense, salaries for supervisory personnel, repair and maintenance budgets, utilities expense, depreciation expense, supplies expense, property tax, etc. Variable overhead items are allocated to individual cost centers based on a method such as budgeted direct labor hours or units produced. The others are simply held in a factory overhead account and are not allocated.

The development of the operating plan does, as mentioned earlier, affect the mix of facilities in use. A given plan may call for the closing of old facilities or the opening of new facilities, or both. These changes in facility usage affect the assignment of costs such as rent, utility, and depreciation expenses to individual products. Also, if new facilities are required, the overall financial budget will be affected by additional capital expenditures.

The direct and indirect costs are then combined into a cost-of-goods-sold budget for the plant or division. The next step will be to determine the amounts of selling, general, and administrative expenses that are consistent with the operating plan. Then, after computing the applicable taxes, a budgeted income statement can be compiled for the plant or division.

The operating budget for a division will have been approved by the various levels of management within the division, including the general manager. The review will be done at whatever level of detail is necessary to satisfy the managers. Next, the budget will be submitted to corporate management for review, approval, and consolidation into the annual corporate profit plan.

The form of this submission will vary depending on the needs of the individual situation. In general, there will be a summary statement of income accompanied by detail of the operating plan, the labor and materials budgets, the overhead items, as well as selling, general, and administrative expenses.

One helpful way to illustrate the key components of either the total income statement or components thereof is to show a reconciliation of the current year's actual performance to the proposed plan for next year. This format highlights items that are expected to change. Exhibit 11 is an example of how an income statement reconciliation might look. The differences shown on this exhibit could be explained further by using footnotes and narrative explanations or by doing supportive detailed reconciliation of individual items, such as the higher raw material costs.

EXHIBIT 11

AMERICAN IRON & STEEL, INC.
STEELMAKING DIVISION
Reconciliation of 19X2 Operating Budget to Actual 19X1 Results
(in Thousands)

Actual (or estimated) 19X1 Pretax Income	$25,000
Differences due to:	
Sales volume and product mix	4,000+
Selling prices	1,500+
Higher raw material costs	2,000−
Higher labor costs	1,000−
Higher depreciation expense	500−
Other overhead items	500−
All other items, including S, G & A	500+
19X2 operating budget pretax income	$27,000
Estimated taxes on income	13,500
19X2 operating budget net income	$13,500

This type of reconciliation is also useful at the other end of the planning cycle. By reconciling actual 19X2 performance to the 19X2 budget, management can be shown how certain budgets were met and others missed. It tends to force managers to practice management by exception.

The final step of presenting the budget to corporate management for review and approval may be done by the line managers themselves or by the corporate budget director. In either case the budget director usually reviews individual budgets for consistency, clarity, and mathematical accuracy. The budget director will have the responsibility for consolidating the individual budgets into the corporate plan.

If the line managers are present at the budget review session, they will respond to questions from top management regarding their budgets. Otherwise, the budget director must have sufficient knowledge of the individual budgets to field questions.

After the chief executive or the budget review committee has approved the budget for each division, it is important that managers at all levels of each entity be informed of the final approved plan so that they can be confident that they are participating in the implementation of the budget as well as its development.

ORGANIZATIONAL AND BEHAVIORAL IMPLICATIONS OF THE BUDGETING PROCESS

By its very nature, the process of developing and using operating budgets involves the entire organization. The corporate organization and the budgeting process interact in two directions. First, the given structure of the firm and the preferences and personalities of individuals within the firm largely determine the scope and type of the budgeting system that will be feasible. Simultaneously, the budgeting system itself formalizes certain patterns of organization and affects the behavior of managers throughout the chain of command.

Prerequisites for Effective Budgeting.   Experience has shown budget executives that certain conditions are essential if a given budget is to be successful.

First, the structure of the organization must be conducive to the budget process. The key aspects of the organization that must be examined here are responsibility and authority. How the various entities fit into the corporation is not as important as knowing who is responsible for a given operation and who has the power to reward or remedy performance in a given situation. Ambiguities in the lines of responsibility and authority make the control function extremely difficult. A clear and sound organizational structure makes it possible to identify who is responsible for specific performance and who is able to correct deficiencies.

A secondary benefit of the development of a budgeting system is often the realization that the chain of command is vague or contradictory. The budgeting process may then provide the necessary stimulus for correcting the situation.

The second prerequisite is an adequate accounting system. Because one phase of the budgeting process is the comparison of actual performance with planned performance, the accounting and budgeting systems must be compatible. The accounting system must be capable of providing data that are timely so that corrective action may be taken before the actual data are obsolete. Also, the data must be assembled in sufficient detail to enable the assignment of revenues and costs to managers responsible for them. The notion of responsibility accounting will be discussed later, but it should be noted here that managers can be expected to improve performance only with respect to costs and revenues that are controllable by them. Items that the managers cannot control should be isolated or omitted from their budget reports.

The third condition necessary for effective budgeting is the interest and support of top management. The chief executive need not oversee the entire budgeting process, but should be involved in a meaningful way for three major reasons. First, the development of an operating budget is not strictly a financial exercise. It involves sales forecasting, production scheduling, personnel requirements, etc. The chief executive is best able to ensure the participation and interest of these diverse groups in the budgeting process. Second, after the budgeting system has pointed out actual departures from the budgeted performance and the reasons for them, the decision to take corrective action and the nature of that action will ordinarily be determined at a high level in the organization. The budget director does not normally have the authority to take corrective action. Third, those managers being evaluated by the budgeting process are more likely to take serious interest if they know that top management considers the budget to be a very important management tool.

This leads to the fourth prerequisite: acceptance by middle management. Many executives feel that a budgeting system will succeed only to the extent that middle management supports it. Managers are more likely to accept and support a budget system when they feel that they have had a voice in determining what goes into it. The involvement of all levels of management in the planning process is important for its success.

This involvement can be encouraged if several guidelines are followed. A "top-down, bottom-up" approach should be used. The budget director and top management develop the ground rules and format of the planning process and pass these down to managers at all levels. Then, at each level of responsibility, a budget is developed and passed up the line for review and approval. All data that the managers require along the way should be made available to them by the accounting department. The budget staff should be available to assist managers with any necessary analysis. The review process should be adequate and meaningful at all levels. It is important that all levels of management be informed of the final approved plan. The resulting control reports and explanations should be timely, informative, and constructive.

The final prerequisite for effective budgeting is that the budget system should meet the specific company's needs. In order to make sure that this is the case, the system should be created with a thorough knowledge of how management *wants* to plan, control, and evaluate. The review and reporting process should be as concise as possible. The amount of detail contained in various reports should be tailored to the needs of the user. The reports should be timely and meaningful, and should stress conditions that are out of the ordinary so that "management by exception" can be practiced. Finally, the budgeting process should be sensitive to change and flexible enough to adapt to new situations.

Dealing with Manager Resentment.   Some managers consider budgets as constraints on their ability to react to changing situations during the period covered by the budget. To the extent that managers have such feelings, they will probably not enthusiastically support the budgeting effort.

Several steps can be taken to avoid or overcome this problem. The use of flexible budgets shows the manager that budgets can adapt to changing conditions. The revision of budgets when necessary has the same effect. The importance of having managers participate in the planning process cannot be overemphasized as a deterrent to managerial resentment. Care should be taken not to measure individual performance on factors that are not controllable. On a more qualitative level, comparison of actual performance with plan should be reasonable, showing managers that justifiable deviations are permissible and that each situation will be dealt with based on its own circumstances.

Management's Role in Budget Preparation.   It has already been noted that the participation of top management is vital to successful budgeting. However, the degree and type of participation by management must be tailored to the individual company.

In general, top management sets guidelines for submission of the budget and then reserves for itself the final review and approval of the corporate annual plan. It is important that each operating unit's plan be reviewed and approved by each level of management above it. This process ensures that top management reviews an operating budget which is consistent with those of other corporate entities and which meets the approval of people along the chain of command. Top management can then deal with the budget in total and be confident of the detail behind it.

The presentation of the budgets to top management takes many forms. In some companies all budgets are presented by the budgeting executive, who supplies supplementary information and gives the recommendations of the budget group. In other companies the heads of operating units present their own budgets and the budget executive serves as a collecting point for the budgets, consolidating and making recommendations. However, the actual presentation is made by personnel of the operating units. Also, in some companies, a budget committee, rather than the chief executive, reviews the budgets. The form of this review process must be determined by such factors as the size and complexity of the corporation, the number of operating units, and the degree of decentralization of responsibility and authority.

Controlling Operations Through Budgeting.   A major reason for installing a budget system is to provide a means of control. Control is the process of ensuring that actual performance goes according to plan or better than plan. A common error in planning and control systems applications is the *separation* of the planning and control functions. What may appear to be a semantic subtlety is crucial to the success of an operating budget system. The planning and control functions are part of a total management process. Conceptually, this is a circular, iterative system, not a straight-line continuum from step 1 through step X. Thus, the real value of the system comes in the constant "looping" or "cycling" from plans to implementation of plans to actual results to variance analysis of actual versus budget and to the next planning step. It consists of reporting actual performance versus the budget, pinpointing reasons for variances, and taking action to correct unfavorable situations. The taking of action is a line-management responsibility, whereas the reporting of actual versus plan is a function of the budget and accounting staffs. Determining the reasons for variances is generally a duty shared by line and staff personnel.

Not only must line management take action to correct unfavorable variances, but the budget itself must be changed when necessary to keep up with new situations. This may consist of revising the original budget for purpose of variance reporting or simply reforecasting the current year periodically to inform management of the results that can be expected based on the current situation and also continuing to report based on the original budget.

Responsibility Accounting.   Responsibility accounting is based on the theory that costs and revenues should be assigned to the manager most responsible for making decisions about them. This idea can be incorporated into the organization by instituting cost centers or profit centers, or both. A cost center is a decision point within the organization at which an individual manager has primary responsibility for the costs in question. A profit center is an extension of the cost center in which the manager has responsibility for sales and investments in addition to costs.

The organization of a responsibility accounting system follows closely the structure of authority and responsibility within the firm. The complex network of organization, communication patterns, and decision-making processes must be incorporated into the system. The assignment of responsibility for costs and profits is not easy. If the assignment is not strictly defined, it will be easy for individual managers to pass the buck when unfavorable results appear. However, if responsibility is too rigidly defined, gaps will occur where no explicit assignment of responsibility has been made. Thus, care must be taken to arrive at the correct balance between competition and cooperation among the various managers.

The effectiveness of responsibility accounting is determined by how successfully costs can be segregated into controllable and noncontrollable costs at each level of management. A manager's performance versus budget can best be measured by evaluating those costs (and revenues) over which he or she has some control. It is important to note that costs which are not controllable at one level of management are controllable at others. For example, rent expense may not be controllable by a supervisor but will be controllable by a plant manager. Therefore, rent expense should be excluded or segregated from controllable costs in evaluating the supervisor but should be included in the evaluation of the plant manager.

It must be emphasized that controllability is a matter of degree. In some cases certain costs may be shared by several cost centers. In these cases care should be taken (1) to allocate these costs in a fair manner if they are to be allocated, and (2) to recognize that these costs are not completely controllable by the given manager so that the evaluation is fair. Throughout this process it should be remembered that the primary goal of responsibility accounting is to motivate individual managers in a manner which is beneficial to both the company and the manager responsible for the operation.

BIBLIOGRAPHY

Ackoff, Russell L.: *A Concept of Corporate Planning,* John Wiley & Sons, Wiley-Interscience Division, New York, 1970.

Bacon, Jeremy: *Managing the Budget Function,* National Industrial Conference Board, New York, 1970.

Bunge, Walter R.: "Budgeting," in *Handbook of Modern Accounting,* 2nd ed., McGraw-Hill Book Company, New York, 1977, chap. 40.

Butler, W. F., R. A. Kavesh, and R. B. Platt, eds.: *Methods and Techniques of Business Forecasting,* Prentice-Hall, Englewood Cliffs, N.J., 1974.

Charnes, A., W. W. Cooper, and Y. Ijiri: "Breakeven Budgeting and Programming to Goals," *Journal of Accounting Research,* 1, 1 (Spring 1963), pp. 16–41.

Dopuch, Nicholas, Jacob G. Birnberg, and Joel Demski: *Cost Accounting: Accounting Data for Management Decisions,* Harcourt Brace Jovanovich, New York, 1974.

Gershefski, George: "Building a Corporate Financial Model," *Harvard Business Review* (July–August 1969), pp. 61–72.

————: *The Development and Application of a Corporate Financial Model,* Planning Executives Institute, Oxford, Ohio, 1968.

Gorman, Thomas: "Corporate Financial Models in Planning and Control," *Price Waterhouse Review,* 15, 2 (Summer 1970), pp. 7–12.

Horngren, Charles T.: *Cost Accounting: A Managerial Emphasis,* 4th ed., Prentice-Hall, Englewood Cliffs, N.J., 1977.

Ijiri, J., J. C. Kinard, and F. B. Putney: "An Integrated System for Budget Forecasting and Operating Performance with a Classified Budgeting Bibliography," *Journal of Accounting Research,* 1, 2 (Autumn 1963), pp. 198–212.

Jaedicke, Robert K.: "Improving Break-Even Analysis by Linear Programming Techniques," *N.A.A. Bulletin,* XLII, 7 (March 1961), pp. 5–12.

Knight, W. D., and F. H. Weinwurm: *Managerial Budgeting,* 3rd ed., Macmillan, Riverside, N.J., 1968.

Koontz, Harold, and Cyril O'Donnell: *Principles of Management: An Analysis of Managerial Functions,* 5th ed., McGraw-Hill Book Company, New York, 1972.

Lucado, William E.: "Corporate Planning—A Current Status Report," *Managerial Planning* (November/December 1974), pp. 27–34.

Mahn, John E.: "The Techniques and Application of Profit Planning," *Managerial Planning* (November/December 1975), pp. 25–32.

Mattessich, Richard: "Budgeting Models and Systems Simulation," *Accounting Review,* XXXVI, 31 (July 1961), pp. 384–397.

McVay, H. L.: "Detailed Cost Planning in a Manufacturing Environment," *Managerial Planning* (January/February 1975), pp. 30, 31, 35.

Stedry, Andrew C.: *Budget Control and Cost Behavior,* Prentice-Hall, Englewood Cliffs, N.J., 1960.

Tosi, Henry L., Jr.: "Human Effects of Budgeting Systems on Management," *MSU Business Topics* (Autumn 1974), pp. 53–63.

Vickers, Douglas: "On the Economics of Break-Even," *Accounting Review,* XXXV, 3 (July 1960), pp. 405–412.

Welsch, Glenn A.: *Budgeting: Profit Planning and Control,* Prentice-Hall, Englewood Cliffs, N.J., 1976.

Wilson, James D.: "Practical Applications of Cost-Volume-Profit Analysis," *N.A.A. Bulletin,* XLI, 7 (March 1960), pp. 5–18.

Chapter **7**

Cash Budgets and Cash Management

S. THOMAS CLEVELAND
Partner, Touche Ross & Co.

INTRODUCTION

The artful skill of cash management requires attention to certain classical details and the judicious use of new techniques. After a brief historical perspective, these methods and techniques (accompanied by some helpful tips) are presented.

Cash management has always received attention, but the intensity of interest increased in the late 1960s. A primary reason was adverse publicity from situations where corporations such as Penn Central were reporting "profits" but suffering severe hardships and, in some cases, bankruptcy due to cash shortages. It was typical that these troubled companies had their cash tied up in old receivables, slow-selling inventory, and other non-income-producing assets. In more recent years, other organizations such as the City of New York have been publicized for their cash shortcomings in the media, much to their discomfort.

Increased understanding of effective management methods helped to give credibility to the operating budget techniques discussed in the last chapter. Obviously, operating budgets alone have not provided the "final" answer to improved profits and better understanding of the business environment. The ultimate management approaches deal with the coordination of the operating budgets, capital expenditure plans, and management of cash discussed in this chapter.

Current thinking identifies the cash management process as a set of techniques to:

- Accelerate the inflow of cash
- Minimize the status of cash as an asset
- Maximize the use of cash as an "earning" asset

The rest of this chapter describes the techniques to optimize the gains from this management process.

ON BECOMING A SUPERIOR CASH MANAGER

The motivation for this chapter and certainly the best interest of the reader is served by presenting techniques to improve the cash management process and results. At recurring intervals, or as a first serious attempt, pursuit of the following initial steps are necessary elements of superior cash management:

Identify special needs. Certain requirements for cash management will be unique to the industry, geographical location or other special factors. For instance, financial institutions such as banks have fiduciary responsibilities that may make cash management more significant than operating management. Many municipalities are experiencing embarrassing cash shortfalls for which the public has demanded immediate attention. Commercial enterprises have to work their resources, including cash, much harder to remain competitive.

Require more planning objectives. After recognizing the special needs, realistic objectives of cash management must be established. Appropriate plans are needed for assigning responsibility, measuring performance, and the formalization of techniques to make decisive, informed decisions.

Improve controls through budgets and decision reporting. Preparation of budgets helps to quantify the planned objectives and provide useful information. Reports should be devised and distributed in such a way that timely decisions can be made.

Use classical and new techniques for significant cash management gains. Taking advantage of methods to make cash available faster and work idle cash harder will show immediate results. An example is the use of a "lock box" (explained in another section) that efficiently gathers customer checks to accelerate the availability of cash from receivable collections.

Exercise cash psychology. A final element is the development of shrewdness in selecting cash management techniques to meet the needs without creating conflicts. The "lock box" idea may be advantageous to the collecting firm but not to the customer who may take measures to meet cash needs by slowing payments. Sometimes resolution of these conflicts can be critical to the success of a particular cash management technique.

PLANNING AND OBJECTIVES OF CASH MANAGEMENT

The final objective of cash management is to maximize the use of cash as an earning asset. Effective cash management calls for organized planning effort and cooperation among departments. The result of planning should be a cash budget including estimates of the sources and uses of cash over a definite period of time. The cash estimates usually involve consideration of both operational and capital project objectives.

To complement *operational planning,* the cash management objectives must gauge the minimum amount of cash necessary to sustain the flow of cash through the specific business cycle and to identify the peaks and valleys in the cycle. This enables cash managers to spot trouble periods well before they arise and solve the cash problems with optimal efficiency and benefits.

In *capital project planning,* several cash management objectives are obvious. Cash planning can help identify the best time to borrow or invest needed or idle cash. It can help obtain favorable financing by showing lenders a definite forecast of repayment plans.

Cash planning also provides overall financial control. Comparisons of actual and budgeted cash reports can assist in decision making. This can identify problem areas for decision reports, detailing the actions required to correct the cash problem.

As previously mentioned, cash planning is an estimate of cash sources and uses involving either operations or capital projects. Poor cash planning is a major cause of business failure. Not to be confused with profits, cash management is the basis for short- and long-term decisions. A major tool in cash planning is the budget or cash forecast.

On a short-term or operational basis, the forecast estimates day-to-day business operations. This includes all aspects of the sales and collections cycle as well as the purchase and payment cycle. This budget is often on a daily or weekly basis and can extend up to a year or more. This is an invaluable aid to the cash manager in that the financing of operations can be carefully planned and implemented as the actual transactions take place and the forecast is updated.

When the cash needs of longer-term capital budgets are considered, the forecast is often less exact. Even with anticipated lack of accuracy, the capital budget is an excellent way to plan for such projects as divisional expansion, equipment replacement, securing long-term debt or financing of various capital projects. Due to the wide range of variables such as future market conditions, the availability of tax credits, and interest rates, it is difficult to plan significant capital projects with a high degree of accuracy very far into the future. The budgets, however, are necessary. The uncertainties only limit the amount of detail one can forecast.

By combining the operating and capital budgets over the same period of time, one can prepare the respective cash forecasts that can be used to estimate cash balances at any point in the future. The development of such a cash budget is discussed in the next section. The result of such a cash budget is the foundation for effective decision reporting which follows the cash budget preparation concepts.

PREPARING A CASH BUDGET

There are basically two methods of preparing a cash budget: the "adjusted net income" method and the more commonly used "cash receipts and disbursements" method.

Cash Receipts and Disbursements Method. The cash receipts and disbursements method is a projection of an entity's cash position from past experience to future periods. Before any projections can be made about the future, a thorough study and understanding of past experience are required. One must have a knowledge of sales history in terms of collection periods, seasonal fluctuation, collectibility of credit sales, and discount policies. But all this must be applied to estimates without neglecting prevailing trends in business.

In addition to sales, one must consider all other sources of cash, such as dividends, interest, rents, and royalties. Seasonal borrowings are also a typical source and are not to be neglected in the cash budget. Another major source of cash is often from the sale of capital assets. However, one must scrutinize projected sales of capital assets because of the many variables involved in such sales. It is appropriate not to overestimate on the receipts side because such errors create a disproportionate credibility gap and directly affect the important operating budget. In developing estimates of cash disbursements, it is often helpful to segregate fixed and variable costs. This will facilitate simple and accurate revisions to disbursements if sales projections prove inaccurate. Once again, a knowledge of past experience is necessary. This is where cost to sales percentages can prove extremely helpful in analyzing disbursement estimates.

In addition to operational disbursements, consideration must be given to capital expenditures, dividends, debt requirements, and unforeseen cash outlays such as litigation. Contrary to sales, realistic but slightly high estimates provide for a buffer against unforeseen cost increases or unexpected expenditures.

As with receipts, it is necessary to map out accurately when cash disbursements are to be made. The entity's payment policies must be considered to analyze the lag time between the acquisition of goods and services and the payment for them. All this must be reviewed in addition to contractual commitments and new actions voted by the board of directors.

As previously mentioned, a "buffer" will provide a safeguard against unforeseen cash shortages. One way to produce such a buffer is to build into the budget a minimum allowable cash balance. Such a buffer can be estimated by plotting deviations from monthly standards over the past.

Once all the elements of the cash budget are known, they are easily presented in chart form. The example in Exhibits 1 and 2 illustrates a cash receipts and disbursement budget for a six-month period (by month).

The example illustrates that proper cash management could avoid the problems this company otherwise must anticipate. Cash shortages appear at the beginning of production and a large excess occurs at the end of the peak season. It is possible that the company may have to defer its dividend payment, borrow needed funds on 60- to 90-day terms, or possibly negotiate an alternative means of paying for the equipment in the first month.

Adjusted Net Income Method. The second method to be discussed is the adjusted net income method of cash budgeting, which generally focuses on

EXHIBIT 1 Cash Receipts and Disbursements Budget by Month

	1	2	3	4	5	6
Receipts						
Cash sales	$ 70,000	$ 62,500	$ 60,000	$ 62,500	$ 97,500	$ 87,500
Collections on credit sales						
Two months prior	12,500	15,000	16,250	12,800	10,000	33,000
One month prior	90,000	97,500	112,000	100,000	90,000	75,000
Current	195,000	140,000	125,000	150,000	150,000	162,500
Royalties	10,000	10,000	10,000	10,000	10,000	10,000
Interest	8,000	8,000	8,000	8,000	8,000	8,000
Note installments					80,000	
Total	$385,500	$333,000	$331,250	$343,000	$445,500	$376,000
Disbursements						
Variable costs[a]						
1. Material	$ 67,760	$ 59,500	$ 66,600	$ 59,800	$ 82,600	$ 90,080
2. Labor	67,760	59,500	66,600	59,800	82,600	90,080
3. Overhead	33,880	29,750	33,300	29,900	41,300	45,040
Fixed costs[b]	125,000	125,000	125,000	125,000	125,000	125,000
Loan payments	15,000	15,000	15,000	15,000	15,000	15,000
Interest	6,000	6,000	6,000	6,000	6,000	6,000
Taxes	32,500			32,500		
Dividends	15,000			15,000		
Equipment[c]	40,000					40,000
Total	$402,900	$294,750	$312,500	$343,300	$352,500	$411,200

[a]Based on ratio of total variable costs to sales of 50 percent. Labor applied at 100 percent of materials, overhead 50 percent of materials.
[b]Fixed costs excludes depreciation on production equipment and other noncash charges.
[c]Purchase terms—one-half down, one-half in five months.

EXHIBIT 2 Summary of Receipts and Disbursements by Month

	1	2	3	4	5	6
Receipts	$ 385,500	$ 333,000	$ 331,250	$ 343,300	$ 445,500	$ 376,000
Disbursements	(402,900)	(294,750)	(312,500)	(343,000)	(352,500)	(411,200)
Increase (decrease)	$ (17,400)	$ 38,250	$ 18,750	$ 300	$ 93,000	$ (35,200)
Cash balance at beginning	15,000	(2,400)	(4,150)	14,600	14,900	107,900
Buffer	(20,000)	(20,000)	(20,000)	(20,000)	(20,000)	(20,000)
Cash excess (need)	$ (22,400)	$ (15,850)	$ (5,400)	$ (5,100)	$ 87,900	$ 52,700

changes in balance sheet accounts, particularly the working capital accounts including cash. This method should yield the same budget results as the receipts and disbursements method if the estimates used are accurate.

The first step in this method is to estimate net income over the desired period. The net income is adjusted for noncash transactions to arrive at net income on a cash basis.

Examples of noncash income and expense items are depreciation and amortization of plant and equipment, amortization of bond premium and discount, insurance and bad debt write-offs, and changes in deferred taxes.

The above items are estimated in the same way as are the items in the cash receipts and disbursements method. They are also subject to the same review and analysis. However, this method is less often used because it requires stable operations to offer good cash control over short periods (less than three months). It can be a valuable check against the receipts and disbursements method and does provide cash budgeting over longer periods such as three months to a year.

Exhibit 3 provides an illustration for a three-quarter period of a cash budget using the net income method. Careful analysis of this example will show that there

EXHIBIT 3   Net Income Budget

	1	2	3
Net income	$45,000	$50,000	$60,000
Add:			
Depreciation	10,000	10,000	10,000
Amortization of patent	2,000	2,000	2,000
Write-off of insurance	1,000	1,000	1,000
Net income cash basis	$58,000	$63,000	$73,000
Add:			
Reduction in inventory	2,000	4,000	3,000
Increase in payables	8,000	2,000	—
Sale of capital assets	—	4,000	—
(Less):			
Excess of sales over collections	(12,000)	(16,000)	(4,000)
Decrease in payables			(6,000)
Purchase of capital assets		(30,000)	(35,000)
Dividends	(50,000)		
Increase in cash	$ 6,000	$ 27,000	$ 31,000
Cash at beginning of month	75,000	81,000	108,000
Cash at end of month	$81,000	$108,000	$139,000
Less minimum cash requirement	(50,000)	(50,000)	(50,000)
Cash excess	$31,000	$ 58,000	$ 89,000

is little control over cash disbursements on an item by item basis. However, assuming that items comprising net income are analyzed elsewhere, this method has merit as a planning model for accounts that affect cash over a longer period of time than three months.

In summary, each of the two methods discussed and illustrated is a valuable tool to the cash manager. They provide a means to anticipate cash shortages or surpluses and when they may occur. Of major concern, however, is that (1) both methods are subject to estimates, (2) prevailing business conditions may change at any time, and (3) the needs of the entity may be difficult to anticipate.

Effective use of either method would dictate that projections be limited to a period over which meaningful estimates can be made. This period usually is a year. The refinement and sophistication of the budget estimates depend on the needs of the entity. Some companies, such as retail enterprises, need to analyze their cash balances on a daily basis, and do so with great accuracy.

EFFECTIVE DECISION REPORTING

With the development of a cash budget, one has the information necessary to prescribe effective action in the way of decision reports. These reports should be more than informational. The format must be designed for ease of analysis and exceptions, if any, must be apparent. Thus, the descriptive term "decision reporting."

Just what kind of action is detailed in a decision report depends, of course, on how the cash forecast is used. Compared to the results of actual transactions, the forecast may be used to identify exceptions from the plan and action can be taken to correct deficiencies or put excess cash to use as a working asset. The type of decision report used in this instance should be timely and directed to those capable of initiating the necessary corrective steps.

The cash forecast can also be used as an experiment to discover what course of action would be best over a given period before any actual transactions take place. Here the decision report is the result of a study instead of actual exceptions from plans. This type of decision report may involve the use of statistical probabilities and advanced quantitative techniques.

The users of decision reports are sometimes as many as there are prescribed courses of action. Financial managers such as treasurers use the reports to determine optimum cash management policies. Other high-level officials may use the reports to schedule the availability of cash to meet the special needs of the company, such as funding expansions. Even outsiders such as lending agencies may use the reports in deciding on whether or not to lend money.

The Cash Forecast as a Decision Report. Cash forecasts, such as the ones illustrated in the previous section, can point out many courses of action to help improve a company's cash position or assist in making critical management decisions. A few examples can further illustrate how they are used.

Illustration A. Over the past three years, a new high-technology company experienced cash shortages during its early production periods but has had a surplus of cash during peak sales seasons. Based on three years of seasonal trend analysis, a forecast for the coming year was developed. It showed that for three months at the beginning of its production period, a large cash deficit would occur if no action was taken to obtain the needed cash. However, it was also noted that by the end of four months, the cash shortage would reverse and the company would have a large amount of idle cash. There was also a plan to pay dividends in a month when it would create an additional burden on financing needed production.

The company's treasurer prepared a detailed report outlining the company's current cash position, including immediate and future needs and charts of expected cash flows under several alternative courses of action. One alternative called for borrowing the necessary funds for production on an installment basis, repaying them over a one-year period. Another plan was to borrow on a term loan, for a 90-day period, the amount to be repaid out of the expected sales revenues to follow. The third alternative was to obtain a line of credit that could be paid at any time after 60 days and to provide an acceptable limit. In each case, the dividend was postponed one quarter but increased in amount.

Based on the recommendations from the board, the company's treasurer was able to take the best alternative to the bank and obtain the needed financing on favorable terms.

Illustration B. A medium-sized manufacturer-leasing company was experiencing cash shortages during certain periods of each month. In fact, the shortage had developed a pattern. A cash forecast was developed day by day, for a three-month period. From this, it was determined that billing and payment cycles did not coincide so that in certain periods of each month shortages occurred. It was also possible to narrow the problem down to a few departments that were consistently spending more than budgeted. Appropriate action was taken to accelerate the billing process and curb certain departmental excess spending. Subsequently, each department was provided with an updated weekly budget showing expenditures to date, actual to planned and remaining estimated costs with funds available. This proved helpful in reducing departmental spending.

Illustration C. A large steel fabricating company was considering expanding its operations to include another product. Three other companies that produced such a product were for sale by their parent companies. In addition to the usual financial data, the buying company requested from each of the smaller firms a five-year cash projection, the first year by months and the remainder by years. The projections were analyzed and used in determining which company would best be able to support itself with necessary funds for its own operations. The results of the analysis, in conjunction with other data, were used in preparing the final bids for purchase.

As can be seen from the three examples above, cash projections are an important part of the cash management decision making process. The decision report is used by almost everyone involved in financial management and can be effective as a means of producing the desired results concerning cash management.

Comparative Decision Reports.   The cash budgets in the previous section can be compared to actual performance for a fixed period of time (usually on a weekly or monthly basis). See Exhibit 4. The manager might note an increase in disbursement on accounts payable offset by better than expected collections.

EXHIBIT 4

Weekly Cash Report
July 13, 198X

	Forecast	Actual	Difference
Balance July 8, 198X	$ 42,000	$ 36,000	$(6,000)
Receipts:			
Cash sales	66,000	68,000	2,000
Accounts receivable collections	75,000	81,000	6,000
Other cash income	12,000	12,000	-0-
Total receipts	$153,000	$161,000	$ 8,000
Expenditures:			
Payroll	61,000	62,000	(1,000)
Accounts payable	43,000	49,000	(6,000)
Supplies and materials ...	8,500	9,000	(500)
Taxes	4,000	4,200	(200)
Other expenses	7,500	7,000	500
Total expenditures ..	$124,000	$131,200	$(7,200)
Balance July 13, 198X	$ 29,000	$ 29,800	$ 800

EXHIBIT 5

Daily Financial Position Report
July 16, 198X

Receivables:		
Balance forward		$66,000
Add daily billings	+	9,500
Subtract credits issued	−	1,200
Subtract cash receipts	−	16,500
Add adjustments	+	500
Subtract adjustments	−	200
New balance		$58,100
Payables:		
Balance forward		$42,500
Add invoices posted	+	10,600
Subtract debits issued	−	1,300
Subtract bills paid	−	12,500
Add adjustments	+	-0-
Subtract adjustments	−	700
New balance		$38,600
Cash:		
Balance forward		$23,000
Add cash received	+	16,500
Subtract cash disbursed	−	12,500
New balance		$27,000

Daily Financial Position Reports.   A daily report for quick comparisons can be a valuable management tool, although the figures usually are not very accurate because of the short span of time. See Exhibit 5. This daily report can be compared to the forecasts for possible action.

CLASSICAL AND USEFUL APPROACHES TO CASH MANAGEMENT

The first step in an improved cash management program is the implementation of certain classical procedures to accelerate the inflow of cash:

- Improve billing and collection activities
- Reduce inventory investment
- Control disbursements

Improving Billing and Collection Procedures.   A delay in billing of even one day can be costly (approximately the internal interest rate times the average daily billings). Ideally, billing occurs every day upon shipment. This typically means a refinement of the paper flow so that discount information, shipping papers, and other billing data are available for invoices to be prepared. In addition, excuses for customers to hold up payment should be minimized by an evaluation of the clarity of any explanations written on the invoice or the need for additional information.

An initial important step in evaluating various improved collection strategies is to forecast accurately the monthly collections. Considerations include the average sales per month, average increase in sales, collection patterns, uncollectibles, and anticipated variances in each estimate.

Exhibit 6 shows a format to compute monthly collections.

Many companies and governmental units have benefited from a centralization of their cash functions and banking relationships. Consolidating the cash function helps eliminate the situation where one division or department is borrowing at 9 percent and another is investing excess funds at 7 percent. The centralization of banking activities tends to accelerate the collection process and help control disbursements. Exhibit 7 illustrates the process.

The obvious major concern in evaluating the benefits of bank centralization is the cost of maintenance.

In addition to centralizing the banking system, other banking activities related to the collection process can be streamlined, including the following.

Area Concentration.   It may be profitable to regionalize the collection of checks in a market area by requesting that customers send their checks to a regional office. Because checks drawn usually are from banks within the region, the collection process is accelerated by depositing all the checks in a regional bank.

Lock Box System.   A lock box system refines the area concentration concept by requesting that customers send their payments to a locked post office box instead of the regional office. The regional bank handles the collection of checks at the post office box and sends them on to the drawee banks with copies to the regional company office. This technique may be costly unless the regional office has a heavy volume of checks with large amounts. A typical computation on the potential savings from a lock box system is shown in Exhibit 8.

Reducing Inventory Investment.   Budgets and forecasts cannot be used as efficient management tools if inventory cash needs are undisciplined. Purchases of material, a significant use of cash in production situations, need consistent monitoring because of revisions in production plans, delivery problems, and other changes in operations. Price changes that occur during inflationary periods can be disastrous to cash management as well as the more obvious effects on the costs of production.

EXHIBIT 6 Forecast of Monthly Sales and Collections

Prior year actual	Month	Current year forecast	Jan.	Feb.	Mar.	Apr.	May	June	July	Aug.	Sep.	Oct.	Nov.	Dec.	Collection trend[a]
$ 230,000	Jan.	$ 220,000	(Oct.) 11,500	132,000	$ 66,000	$ 11,000									60-30-5
170,000	Feb.	175,000	(Nov.) 136,000	(Nov.) 17,000	105,000	52,500	$ 8,750								60-30-5
135,000	Mar.	140,000	(Dec.) 190,000	(Dec.) 152,000	(Dec.) 20,900	70,000	56,000	$ 7,000							50-40-5
250,000	Apr.	250,000					150,000	75,000	$ 12,500						60-30-5
300,000	May	300,000						180,000	90,000	$ 15,000					60-30-5
340,000	June	325,000							195,000	97,500	$ 16,250				60-30-5
300,000	July	280,000								140,000	112,000	$ 16,800			50-40-6
240,000	Aug.	250,000									125,000	100,000	$ 10,000		50-40-4
275,000	Sep.	300,000										150,000	90,000	$ 33,000	50-30-10
230,000	Oct.	250,000											150,000	75,000	60-30-5
340,000	Nov.	325,000												162,500	50-40-5
380,000	Dec.	350,000													50-40-5
$3,190,000	Total	$3,165,000	$337,500	$301,000	$191,900	$133,500	$214,750	$262,000	$297,500	$252,500	$253,250	$266,800	$250,000	$270,500	

Collections

aCollection trends for January, as an example, were 60 percent in the first month (February), 30 percent in the second month (March), and 5 percent in the third month (April). The remaining accounts are either very slow paying or represent accounts expected to be written off.

EXHIBIT 7 Centralized Banking System

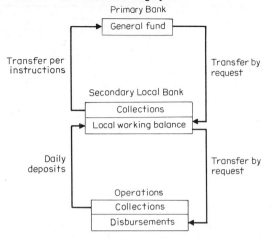

EXHIBIT 8 Potential Annual Savings from Lock Box System

	Mail days			Average	
	Current situation	With lock box	Potential reduction	daily receipts	Mail float reduction
Western	2.5	1.5	1.0	$125,000	$125,000
Central	3.0	1.5	1.5	185,000	277,500
Eastern	3.5	1.5	2.0	90,000	180,000
				$400,000	$582,500

Potential benefits
Earnings on reduction of mail float ($582,500 × .07) $41,000
Earnings on reduction of collection float ($400,000 daily receipts × .5 days × .07) ... 14,000
In-house processing costs (mail room, cashier) 10,000

    Benefits $65,000

Estimated costs
Per-item charges, based on 29,000 remittances annually (29,000 × .30) .... $ 8,700
Wire transfer charges, based on two lock boxes (430 × $3.00) 1,300

    Costs $10,000

    Net potential benefits.. $55,000

The organizational techniques to control and anticipate the production needs are not the subject of this chapter. However, the decision reports outlined in a previous section highlight the need for accurate communication of any changes in the plan. It is recommended that inventory investment be a part of these reports.

Controlling Disbursements. Asserting management control through centralizing the payables function frequently has improved the cash balance by timing cash disbursements to match available cash and directing attention to the taking of discounts when offered. As noted with other centralization schemes, the cost of monitoring the payables system must be evaluated. Management also must cooperate with the purchasing function to better time deliveries with cash availability. Exhibit 9 is a typical analysis of the cash disbursement function demonstrating how improved procedures can increase the availability of cash.

EXHIBIT 9   Potential Increase in Cash Available

Purchase terms	Type of purchase	Annual dis- bursements ($000)
1/10 net 30	Manufacturing supplies	$13,700
Upon receipt of invoice	Rent, utilities, insurance, travel	6,000
Net 7	Freight and warehousing	3,300
Net 10	Services	3,000
Net 25	Advertising	7,000
Net 30	Office and plant supplies	3,000
		$36,000

Daily disbursements	Current paying practice (days)	Potential extension (days)	Additional cash available
$37,500	10	-0-	-0-
16,400	10	10	$164,000
9,000	7	-0-	-0-
8,200	10	-0-	-0-
19,200	25	-0-	-0-
8,200	22	8	65,000
			$229,000

REFINED ELEMENTS OF CASH MANAGEMENT

The previous section provided ideas on accelerating the inflow of cash and slowing down disbursements. Contemporary refinements include the *minimization* of the time cash remains a dormant asset, and, *maximizing* its use as an "earning asset." The problem of converting cash assets into earning assets may be called "float control." This section discusses the refined elements to achieve better float control.

Knowing What to Look for.   Knowing the problem areas that will need evaluation is a necessary first step. The following problems require attention:

- Existence of large cash balances anywhere
- Unusual requirements for large cash flows
- Lack of a viable cash planning and forecasting function
- No knowledge of "float" or funds in transit
- Decentralized cash receipts
- Existence of many bank accounts and compensating balance requirements
- Little change in procedures
- No system for analyzing profit relating to cost
- Environment conducive to "emotional" decisions

Analyzing these problem areas and providing recommendations for improvement are receiving the most current cash management attention.

Good Reporting.   Many of these problem areas will require new detailed decision reports from those discussed in a previous section. Careful format design and attention to appropriate distribution of the reports will make both the current assessment and the basis for improvement much easier.

Improved Monitoring of Bank Accounts.   Techniques to improve float control by regulating the bank balances can best be illustrated by the decision report shown in Exhibit 10. The cash management recommendation to lower the average balance (by about $190,000) is obvious from this decision report.

Maximum Use of Available Investments.   At one time, converting cash to an earning asset required a level of aggressive supervision available only to organizations that employed money market specialists. The ability to take advantages of favorable short-term yields with adequate risk, liquidity, and maturity is now available even to small cash managers through consulting services.

EXHIBIT 10   Establishing Target Bank Balances

Name of bank	Central Regional		
Year ended	3/31/X1		

Services Provided	Volume	Unit cost	Total cost (nearest $)
Checks deposited	200	.05	$ 10
Checks paid	20,754	.11	2,283
Deposits and credits			
Account maintenance	12	5.00	60
Account reconciliation	21,200	.03	636
Stop payments	60	2.00	120
Total activity charges			$ 3,109 (1)

Calculation of Average Bank Balance Required	
Divide (1) by earnings credit rate (90-day T-bill rate)	.068
Balance available for investment	$ 45,700 (2)
Divide (2) by (1 − reserve requirement of *18* percent)	.82
Collected balance required	55,800
Add: Uncollected funds	-0-
Required average *bank* balance	$ 55,300
Balance Adjustment and Profit Impact	
Actual average balance	$246,000
Less: Required average bank balance	55,800
Excess (shortage)	$190,200
Times: Earnings credit rate	× .068
Annual savings (cost)	$ 12,900

Consultants and money managers try to take advantage of yield differentials among several securities as well as to adjust maturities of the securities. Foreign investments have been used to respond to currency changes. A representative list of reasonable low-risk investments used by cash managers might include the following:

1. Commercial paper
2. U.S. Treasury bills and other Treasury obligations
3. Federal agency issues
4. Federal funds
5. Tax-exempt obligations
6. Bank time deposits and negotiable certificates of deposit
7. Banker's acceptances
8. Repurchase agreements
9. Canadian time deposits
10. Eurodollar deposits

Improved Control Procedures.   It should be apparent that a successful management program to convert cash to an earning asset requires concentrated control procedures. The cash manager should look for situations similar to the following illustration where controls can be improved.

Illustration D.   A medium-sized company had a large volume of checks written on four bank accounts. In order to improve controls and increase their concentration on larger transactions, they decided to institute the following new program:

1. *Imprest fund transactions*—all transactions less than $1,000 were transferred to an imprest bank account. The balance was kept at $50,000 in $25,000 increments. It was discovered that 80 percent of the checks were written on this account with about 20 percent of the total dollar volume. Specific procedures were followed and it was possible to limit management involvement to less than 25 percent of the previous activity.

2. *Regular Deposit Account*—all transactions over $1,000 were carefully monitored as to timing of disbursement and size of deposit. Management time was increased by 25 percent.

The final result was a reduction of two bank accounts, better controls, decreased overall management involvement, and an increase in cash as an earning asset of $28,000 over a year.

NEW TECHNIQUES FOR OPTIMIZATION

A current interest of money managers is to make "optimum" improvements in maximizing the use of cash as an earning asset. The techniques involved are quantitative and usually require the use of a computer to search for the optimum result. The conceptual background for the techniques is beyond the scope of this chapter, but some comments on a representative list of contemporary methods follow.

Linear Programming.   The format for linear programming problems include an "objective" to be optimized and a series of constraints on this objective. Search techniques have been developed to locate the optimum solution, if one exists, within the given restraints. Computer programming vendors have prepared cash management models using the linear programming format and suggest search techniques for the "best" solutions. These programs have been used with success by money managers.

Dynamic Programming.   Dynamic programming is useful where time is a significant variable to be optimized, there are a large number of constraints, and certain objectives and constraints are nonlinear. Cash managers have found a strong analogy between the well-researched inventory problems and cash management problems. Therefore, some models already are available for use.

Simulation.   Simulation in cash management is a useful, but expensive, technique to reproduce the cash management system in quantitative terms. Computer program vendors have developed special programming languages to facilitate the creation of a simulation model. The models, as an example, can be used from year to year to provide information to the cash manager about uncertainty in some of the expected future events.

Bayesian Analysis.   Uncertainty always exists in the cash management process. Bayesian statistics is a field where past results are continuously used to help predict the future. A "memory" for probabilities in the past using Bayesian techniques may help reduce the risk factors in making cash decisions.

Sensitivity Analysis.   All of the above techniques, as well as some specialized methods not mentioned here, can be used to test the sensitivity of the "optimum" result. Changes in probability structure of the objective function or constraints on these objectives can be manipulated to test the changes. The "sensitivity analysis" techniques have been used to identify the most critical circumstances in cash management.

CASH PSYCHOLOGY

There is a definite "psychology" related to optimization, or more generally to improvements, and refinements in cash management. A shrewd choice among alternative cash management techniques is required so that the plan creates awareness and benefits but not internal or external conflicts.

Avoiding Internal Conflicts.   It is necessary to gain cooperation from at least the operating departments, the treasury function, and the accounting area to ensure the success of cash management programs. Experience indicates that their involvement in the planning stage and the tailored design of the decision reports can reduce interference. Frequent reporting of the benefits from the techniques is useful feedback to those involved.

Avoiding External Conflicts.   For every cash management plan there is a potential external reaction that might confound the expected achievements. More frequent billing may have no collection effect on customers who pay on a computerized disbursement cycle no matter when they receive the invoice. Changes in the discount structure may be required to meet the desired objective. It is not necessary to show more cases of this "force-counterforce" situation to stress the idea that the potential reaction should always be considered during the formulation of the cash management plan.

RECOVERY FROM THE UNEXPECTED

What should happen if the decision reports indicate that unexpected results have occurred? Recovery from this situation is best handled by planning appropriate contingency actions in advance.

Illustration E.   The cash manager for W-L Company remembered a severe cash shortage when the price of plywood rose sharply in a recent year. A contingency plan for actions necessary to counteract such a rise in price has now been developed. The plan was discussed with plant supervisors, the treasurer (who arranged a contingent line of credit at no charge), and appropriate management. The contingency plan included notification of the above people when the plan needed to be activated.

The Ultimate Coordination.   The objectives of this chapter have been met if the cash manager has discovered techniques to improve the availability and use of cash as an earning asset. Ultimately, significant achievements and continued improvement cannot occur without the coordination of the operating and capital expenditure budgets and the cash management function. Cooperation among the managers in these areas and recognition of ways to benefit mutually from coordinated activities are important management responsibilities.

BIBLIOGRAPHY

Archer, Stephen H.: "A Model for the Determination of Firm Cash Balances," *Journal of Financial and Quantitative Analysis*, 1, 1 (March 1966), pp. 1–11.

Baumol, William J.: "The Transactions Demand for Cash: An Inventory Theoretical Approach," *Quarterly Journal of Economics*, November 1952.

Eppen, Gary D., and Eugene F. Fama: "Cash Balance and Simply Dynamic Portfolio Problems with Proportional Costs," *International Economic Review*, 10, 2 (June 1969), pp. 119–133.

Miller, Merton H., and Daniel Orr: "A Model of the Demand for Money by Firms," *Quarterly Journal of Economics*, August 1966.

Orr, Daniel: *Management and the Demand for Money*, Praeger Publishers, New York, 1971.

Sastry, A. S. Rama: "The Effect of Credit on Transactions Demand for Cash," *Journal of Finance*, September 1970.

Smith, Keith V.: *Management of Working Capital*, West Publishing Company, St. Paul, Minn., 1974.

Chapter **8**

Material Costs

RONALD J. PATTEN
Dean, School of Business Administration, University of Connecticut

INTRODUCTION

Materials—a term used in manufacturing to cover raw commodities, fabricated parts, and subassemblies—represent a large investment of capital and a substantial percentage of the cost of production in many companies. As a consequence, materials should be carefully accounted for and controlled. The functions of controlling and accounting are distinct, yet they are interrelated and interdependent. Materials are both a responsibility of management and a responsibility of the accountant. Management is responsible for (1) the proper storage and protection of the materials inventory and (2) having sufficient quantities of inventory on hand to meet the production schedule while managing to avoid carrying expensive excess quantities. The accountant is responsible for maintaining an accurate record of the materials inventory which (1) can help management maintain the proper quantity of material at all times and (2) can provide the proper costing of materials received and issued and the proper valuation of inventories for financial reporting purposes. This chapter attempts to emphasize the interrelationship of these responsibilities throughout.

Material costing and control encompasses (1) the managerial and accounting problems that accompany the purchase, receipt, and storage of materials needed in the manufacturing process and (2) the managerial and accounting problems pertaining to the issue and use of these materials.[1]

CONTROL AND MATERIAL COSTS—AN OVERVIEW

In order to achieve the maximum managerial control over material costs in a manufacturing firm, the following organizational and operating procedures should be followed:

1. *Budgeting* of the sales, finished goods inventory, and production schedules on both a long- and short-run basis so that guidelines will be available for the operation of a *centralized* purchasing department

2. *Routinizing and systematizing* the ordering, purchasing, receiving, storing, and issuing of all materials

3. Preventing errors and fixing responsibility through the use of a well-integrated series of *printed forms*

4. Protecting the investment in inventory by means of an adequate *system of internal checks and balances* that ensures accurate accounting as well as the prevention of fraud and theft

5. *Maintaining* efficient inventory records of the quantities received and issued and the balance on hand of all materials along with the costs thereof

6. *Pricing* of all requisitions and inventory balances in such a way as to provide reliable costs of manufacturing and effective planning for income tax purposes

7. *Controlling and summarizing* the accounting for the acquisition and use of materials by means of control accounts, subsidiary ledgers, and reports of materials used, returned, and spoiled

8. *Organizing* the material cost control section's administrative and supervisory staff so that decisions can be made promptly and efficiently[2]

9. *Setting standards* for material costs in standard cost systems

ORGANIZATION FOR ACCOUNTING AND CONTROL OF MATERIAL

In part, control is achieved by means of an organization structure that permits specialization while it defines authority, fixes responsibility, and provides a system of checks and balances. One such organization structure would comprise an engineering, planning, and routing department, a purchasing department, a receiving department, a stores department, and an accounting department.

[1]John J. W. Neuner, *Cost Accounting: Principles and Practice,* 8th ed. (Richard D. Irwin, Homewood, Ill., 1973), p. 186.
[2]*Ibid.,* pp. 186–187.

The engineering, planning, and routing department or departments would be responsible for the design of the product being manufactured. Consequently, it would prepare material specifications prior to the actual purchase of materials. In carrying out its responsibility, the department would probably study the effects of the use of various materials and their substitutes and make appropriate recommendations. The department would also need to draw up bills of materials for issuance with the various kinds of production orders. Lastly, the department would be responsible for controlling the flow of production through the plant.[3]

A centralized purchasing department would be headed by a purchasing agent who is familiar with prices and conditions. Depending on the specific organizational structure used, the department would either receive or prepare purchase requisitions for all materials used in the plant. The department would be responsible for placing orders with reliable sellers, at the proper time, and at the right price. Upon receipt of an invoice from the seller, the department would approve the invoice and send it to the accounting department for recording.

The receiving department would be responsible for actually receiving goods from various carriers and signing the authorized receipts. All of the incoming shipments would be verified as to quantities received and inspected for quality and breakage. The department would move the goods to the storeroom and would send copies of the receiving report to appropriate departments.

The stores department would receive the goods from the receiving department and verify the quantities received. The department would be responsible for protecting material against theft and physical deterioration. Material would be issued only upon the receipt of a properly authorized request, and an appropriate record would be kept of both receipts and issuances of material.

Record keeping would be centered in the accounting department, where transactions would be entered in the accounting records after appropriate documents had been received from the other departments. Entries would be made to record the purchase of materials, the return of materials purchased to the supplier, the use of materials, the return of excess materials to the storeroom, and defective production or spoilage. It should be noted that neither the purchasing department nor the accounting department would pay the invoices. Typically, such payment would be made through the treasurer's office. Because each department would be independent of the others, a control system would be provided.

FORMS

In the preceding section one possible organization was described. In addition, certain procedures were indicated and an occasional reference was made to certain forms and reports. These forms and reports, and a number of others, are described in this section.

Regardless of the specific documents involved, one purpose of the documents used is to assist in safeguarding the inventories by making it possible to identify at all times the persons responsible for them and to insure against their unauthorized use. A second purpose is to transmit instructions that describe an appropriate action to be taken. Another purpose is to provide a basis for data accumulation and information reporting. The information contained in the forms and reports constitutes the input to cost accounting.

One form used is a *purchase requisition*. This written request can be issued to the purchasing department by a foreman for special materials needed in the department; by an inventory clerk for material needed to replenish the inventory; or by a person in the engineering, planning, and routing department for material needed for planned production. Usually, the purchase requisition indicates the type and

[3]*Ibid.,* p. 187.

quality of the item to be purchased as well as the quantity. As noted earlier, the source of supply and the price are left to the judgment of the purchasing agent.

A *purchase order* is a form prepared by the purchasing department authorizing the shipment of goods by a supplier. Enough copies are made to meet the requirements of all interested departments. Typically, the purchase order indicates in detail the amounts and specifications of the materials being ordered and requests a certain delivery date.

When materials are shipped, the seller sends an *invoice* to the purchasing department along with other shipping documents. Among other things, the invoice lists the actual quantities shipped, the prices charged, and the total amount due the supplier.

When materials are received, they are inspected and counted by the receiving department and a *receiving report* is prepared. This report indicates the quantity and kind of materials received in reply to specific purchase orders. Sometimes the receiving report is a separate report, whereas at other times it is the receiving department's copy of the original purchase order on which the goods received have been entered.

A *stores* or *inventory ledger card* carries the name of the material being accounted for and its code number. One such card is kept for each type of material that is held in inventory. The cards collectively comprise the subsidiary ledger for the materials inventory accounts. Predetermined maximum and minimum quantities may be noted on the card, as well as the point at which an order should be placed and the most economical quantity to buy on a single order.

A *materials requisition* is a written request to a stock clerk prepared by a foreman or other authorized person requesting that material of a specified kind and quantity be issued to a certain department. This requisition is used whenever any materials are withdrawn from the stores department by another department in a plant.

Other forms may be used in individual companies, but the ones discussed previously constitute the foundation of a documentary system of accounting for materials.

Having discussed the organization and forms used in the accounting for and control of material, it is now possible to examine in further detail the various controls utilized and accounting records made as materials move from production planning stage through the finished product stage.

SPECIFICATIONS

The establishment of specifications or standards for materials is the point of origin for the control of costs of materials. Although the company setting will bear heavily upon the exact delineation of duties of employees, it can be said that technical experts determine the kinds of materials to be used and the yields to be expected. Such determinations consider such things as the chemical and physical characteristics of materials, the formulas by which they will be joined together, and the chemical reaction that results. In establishing the expected yields, consideration is given to such things as processing losses resulting from spillage, adherence to containers, and possible processing damage. If chemical characteristics are dominant, the laboratory may set the yield; whereas if physical measurements are dominant, the engineering department may do so.

The accounting function relating to the area of specifications is one of evaluation. Prior to the establishment of a specification or standard, the accounting department determines its effect on the product's profitability. This determination encompasses the cost of material, production speeds, capacity, equipment for processing and handling, and customer acceptance. As I. Wayne Keller has observed, "such evaluation cannot be limited to simple application and addition of unit costs, but calls for the exercise of sound business judgment and consideration of economic factors."[4]

ACCOUNTING FOR THE COST OF ACQUIRING MATERIALS

Once specifications have been established, the purchasing department is responsible for the procurement of materials in accordance with the specifications and at the best price possible. No accounting entry is made at the time a purchase requisition is received by the purchasing department. However, an accounting entry is made at the time purchased materials are placed in the stores department following their receipt and inspection. In accounting for the cost of the materials purchased, all costs incurred in obtaining a unit of material and placing it into production should be included. Although the inclusion of all such costs may be theoretically sound, implementation may be impracticable. The vendor's invoice price and the transportation charges are obvious items to be included in the materials cost. However, the costs of ordering, receiving, unpacking, inspecting, insuring, storing, and accounting for materials received are also part of the cost of materials used in production. Theoretical justification and pragmatism must both be weighed in making a decision on which costs to include and which to exclude. The typical journal entry made to record the purchase of materials is as follows:

```
Materials ...................   XXXX
    Accounts Payable .......          XXXX
    Purchase of materials.
```

In essence, the major decision made with regard to the inclusion or exclusion of costs involves a judgment as to whether or not the additional clerical expense involved exceeds the benefits to be derived from the increased accuracy. In many instances materials are carried at the vendor's invoice price, with all of the other acquisition costs mentioned earlier being charged to overhead and then allocated to production indirectly.

Purchase Discounts.   Purchase discounts are cash discounts allowed on the purchase of materials used in manufacturing. From a theoretical standpoint, the amount of the purchase discount should be subtracted from the vendor's invoice price and the materials recorded net of the discount. If the invoice is paid after the discount period has expired, the extra cost should be recognized as a discount lost, which is a financing cost. Illustrative journal entries using the so-called net price method of recording purchase discounts in this event are as follows:

```
Materials ....................   19,800
    Accounts Payable ........            19,800
    Materials invoiced at $20,000
    less 1% discount.

Purchase Discount Lost .......      200
Accounts Payable .............   19,800
    Cash....................            20,000
    Invoice paid after the discount
    period has expired.
```

Sometimes, the materials are recorded at invoice price and the purchase discount is recognized at the time the invoice is paid. Using the same purchase that

[4]I. Wayne Keller, "The Critical Areas of Material Cost Control," *NACA Bulletin,* July 15, 1948, p. 1411.

was considered earlier, the entries using the so-called gross price method and assuming that the bill was paid within the discount period would be:

```
Materials .....................   20,000
       Accounts Payable .........          20,000
Materials purchased.

Accounts Payable .............   20,000
       Purchase Discounts .......             200
       Cash ...................          19,800
Invoice paid within discount
period; discount is 1%.
```

Purchase discounts are treated in the financial statement as a deduction from the gross purchase price of materials (credited to the Materials Inventory Account), or occasionally as an item of other revenue or as a financial management item. The practice of accounting for cash discounts as items of other revenue is objectionable. Revenue is produced by selling an item, not by buying it. Although the cash discount can assist in widening the margin between the cost and sales price of an item, income is not produced until the end product is sold.

Transportation.   Earlier it was noted that some acquisition costs are charged to overhead rather than to particular units of materials inventory. The costs of transporting materials from the seller's warehouse or factory to the buyer's inventory location constitute an item that is charged to overhead in many instances. Yet when a seller quotes a delivered price to a prospective buyer, it is obvious that the transportation cost, which is buried in the *quoted* price, will be included in the cost charged to particular units of materials inventory. If, however, the price is quoted f.o.b. shipping point, the quoted price does not include the transportation and the transportation costs incurred for purchases should be charged to inventory but might be charged to overhead and then allocated to production. It is up to the company management to decide the policy to be followed regarding costs of transportation.

Applied Cost of Acquiring Materials.   If management decides to adhere to the theoretically sound position of carrying materials at the net invoice price plus incoming freight charges plus other acquisition costs, an appropriate rate can be determined and added to each invoice and to each item. If this procedure of accounting for the costs of the various acquisition functions is not practicable, a single, predetermined amount can be added to the total materials cost for a given lot, order, or department. For example, if a company has found that a close relationship exists between material acquisition costs, other than the invoice price, and labor hours, a rate based on labor hours may be used to apply the cost of acquiring materials. If the material acquisition costs incurred by a company, other than the invoice price, are estimated at $240,000, and if the labor is budgeted at 1 million hours, material acquisition costs may be applied to each production order at a rate of $.24 per estimated labor hour. An order that called for 200 hours of direct labor would not only be charged for the invoice cost plus transportation of materials used, but would also be charged $48 for other materials acquisition costs. A single rate can be used for these combined costs, or separate rates can be computed for each class of costs. For example, the estimated receiving department costs for a period of time can be divided by the estimated number of items to be received during the period and the resultant rate used in applying receiving costs to the materials account. Actual receiving department expenses will also be accumulated, and the difference between the expenses incurred and the expenses applied to materials represents under- or overapplied expenses and is closed to an appropriate account and treated as a period expense. Although the application of other materials acquisition costs to production as just described seems to be desirable, it may be extremely difficult to select an appropriate application base.

Insurance charges will fluctuate with the dollar value of the materials inventory. The cost of processing purchase requisitions and purchase orders and of posting to inventory ledger cards will be related to the number of documents used and the notations that must be made on them. Materials handling labor costs will be related to the number of units handled, probably weighted in such a way as to recognize differences in bulk or the difficulty of handling. In short, it is very difficult to find a single base that will be perfectly satisfactory. Yet the use of several bases to allocate the different kinds of costs may entail prohibitive clerical costs. The treatment of materials acquisition costs, other than the invoice cost and possibly transportation, is a perplexing problem to which no standard solution can be prescribed. Careful study, theoretical understanding, and pragmatic thinking must be combined in such a way as to produce a feasible answer.

ACCOUNTING FOR MATERIALS PLACED IN PRODUCTION

In the preceding section, the issue of "cost inclusiveness" was discussed: that is, how many different kinds of cost elements should be included in the cost of materials placed in inventory storage. Once the problem of cost inclusiveness has been resolved, management must decide in what sequence costs should be transferred from the materials inventory accounts into production. The ultimate objective is to produce cost figures that are accurate and meaningful and that can be matched against revenues generated so as to determine net income from operations.

> In costing materials placed in production, the method chosen makes the assumption that the cost to be charged against revenue produced is related to (1) the physical flow of goods—for example, materials are used in the same order in which they are purchased, or (2) the flow of costs—for example, the most recent costs are related to materials issued and therefore should be charged to products completed, with the earlier costs related to items remaining in inventory.[5]

Some of the assumptions for costing materials issued and inventories are (1) average cost, (2) first-in, first-out (FIFO), (3) last-in, first-out (LIFO), (4) market price at date of issue (sometimes called NIFO—next-in, first-out), (5) month-end average cost, and (6) standard costs.

Before a journal entry is recorded for the cost of materials issued, the various costs must be classified. The format of the entry depends on whether the materials issued are direct materials, indirect materials, or packing supplies. For the direct and indirect materials issued, the following entry would be made:

```
Work in Process—Materials ...................     vvvv
Manufacturing Overhead (Indirect Materials Used)   uuuu
    Materials  ..............................            tttt
Entry to record issuance of direct and indirect
materials where a standard cost system is not used.
```

Appropriate entries would also be made on the various stores or inventory ledger cards or computer records to reflect the precise quantity and cost of each type of material issued. Because the costing of materials issued also affects the costing of remaining inventories of materials and work in process, a detailed discussion of costing methods will take place in the section relating to valuation of inventory at the end of an accounting period.

---

[5]Adolph Matz and Milton F. Usry, *Cost Accounting: Planning and Control,* 6th ed. (South-Western Publishing Co., Cincinnati, 1976), p. 334.

CONTROL OF MATERIALS IN PROCESS

The costing of materials into the production process signals a continuation of the responsibility for materials cost control that was started at the time the items were received and stored. Until such time as a product is finished, packaged, sold, and shipped, inventory control problems exist. In general, emphasis is placed on maintaining materials and finished goods inventory levels that are based on either maximum production or lowest unit cost. As a consequence, the control of in-process inventory is neglected. This neglect can be rectified, in part, by the computation of turnover rates. If turnover rates are computed, it will be easier to identify inventory problems and measure the effectiveness or lack thereof of control procedures. Turnover rates can be computed for each manufacturing department, cost center, or production process by dividing the cost of units transferred to the next department by the average cost of inventory of the transferring department. Because these turnover rates will vary among departments, the focus should be placed on changes in the rate of turnover. A change in the rate of turnover should be analyzed so as to ensure that problems in scheduling and production are minimized and that appropriate corrective action is taken.

VALUATION OF MATERIALS IN INVENTORY AT END OF PERIOD

The accounting department is responsible for the valuation of materials in inventory at the end of an accounting period. The valuation of the ending inventory, of course, affects the cost of goods sold. Earlier, mention was made of the fact that there are several cost-flow assumptions for materials issued and ending inventories. The studies made by the American Institute of Certified Public Accountants (AICPA) and published periodically in *Accounting Trends and Techniques* indicate the assumptions used. Over the period extending from 1950 to 1970, of the companies studied by the AICPA, 30 percent used LIFO, 30 percent used FIFO, 25 percent used average cost, 5 percent used standard cost, 3 percent used actual cost, and the remaining 7 percent used a variety of other methods.

During the inflation of the mid-1970s, there was a sharp increase in the number of firms using LIFO. The 1976 edition of *Accounting Trends and Techniques* showed that in 1975, 53 percent used LIFO for at least part of their inventories.

It should be noted that if all purchases of materials are made at the same price, the valuation of ending inventory and materials issued is a simple matter. However, because purchases of materials are typically made at different times, different prices are usually involved with each purchase. Thus, the accountant must make an assumption as to the flow of costs from the stores department to the producing departments. Each of the major methods (assumptions) is reviewed briefly at this point.

Average Cost. The average cost method assumes that each batch of materials taken from the stores department is comprised of uniform quantities from each purchase shipment that is on hand at the issue date. Frequently, it is not practicable to mark items of materials so as to identify them with their cost of acquisition. Further, it might be said that units of materials are used in a somewhat accidental manner as far as the specific units and specific costs are concerned. Thus, an average cost of all units on hand at the time of use may be a satisfactory measure of the cost of materials issued.

The average cost is calculated in a variety of ways. One way (a periodic method) divides the total cost of a particular class of materials by the number of units on hand in order to find the average cost per unit. This unit cost is used both to cost the unit used into production and to cost the items remaining in the materials inventory. For example, if a materials inventory consists of 400 units purchased on February 1, each costing $.20, and 1,200 units purchased on June 1, each costing $.24, the average cost per unit is $.23 (400 units @ $.20/unit plus 1,200 units @ $.24/unit = $368/1,600 units = $.23). Each unit of materials issued to production will be assigned a cost of $.23, and the materials remaining in inventory at the end of an accounting period will be costed at $.23 per unit, assuming no additional purchases during the remainder of the period.

Under a moving average (perpetual) method, the average cost is computed after each purchase of materials by dividing the total cost of all of the materials on hand by the total number of units on hand. Each issue of materials is costed at this unit amount until a new purchase of materials is made. With the new purchase, a new calculation is made by dividing the total cost of all of the materials then on hand by the total number of units.

A somewhat simpler average cost method than the one just described calculates an average cost at the start of each month and uses that unit cost for all materials issued during that month.

FIFO. The first-in, first-out method of costing materials issued and ending inventories is based on the concept that materials used in production should be issued in the order and at the price of their original purchase. It is assumed that materials are issued from the oldest supply on hand and that the cost of those materials when issued to a producing department is the cost of those materials when placed in stock.

For example, assume a beginning balance of material of 400 units each of which costs $.20 when purchased on February 1 and 1,200 units purchased on June 1 each of which costs $.24. The first 1,200 units issued to production would be costed at $272 (= 400 units @ $.20, $80, + 800 units @ $.24, $192). The remaining 400 units will be costed at $.24 each or $96. In theory, it is assumed that the 400 units are physically segregated from the 1,200 units and are issued first. In reality, because both lots of material are identical, the goods are not segregated. It is the costing information that is segregated, because each lot (both number of units and unit cost) is accounted for separately. If a sizable number of lots comprise the balance of materials on hand at any point in time, the record keeping could become cumbersome. Practicably speaking, this cumbersome situation seldom arises because few concerns have more than a few lots of materials on hand at one time unless they anticipate rising prices.

FIFO appears to be a satisfactory costing method when: (1) materials inventory has a high rate of turnover, (2) the nature of the materials inventory changes often, and (3) the materials inventory is not a major factor in the current asset situation.

LIFO. The last-in, first-out assumption for costing materials issued and ending inventories assumes that units of materials issued to production departments should be assigned the cost of the most recent purchase. The objective is to charge the cost of the most recent purchase to production. An inherent assumption exists that the most recent purchase costs are the most significant in terms of matching costs with revenues in the process of determining net income.

Some say that the LIFO cost-flow assumption for materials results in costs that are both realistic and systematic. Further, reported operating profits are stabilized in those industries that are subject to sharp fluctuations in the price of materials. Lastly, because the higher prices of the most recent materials purchases are charged to operations during periods of rising prices, profits are reduced and there is a resultant tax saving.

As was noted in the section relating to FIFO, there are mechanical difficulties when two or more lots exist in an inventory of materials that is accounted for on the LIFO basis.

As an example of LIFO costing, assume that the balance of material at the beginning of a period is 400 units purchased on February 1 costing $.20 each and 1,200 units purchased on June 1 costing $.24 each. The first 1,200 units issued to production would be assigned a cost of $288 (= 1,200 units @ $.24 each). The remaining units issued to production would be assigned a cost of $80 (= 400 units @ $.20 each).

The LIFO assumption can be applied in several alternative ways. Because each way results in different costs for the materials issued and for the ending inventory of materials, a different net income figure results as well. As in all of accounting, consistency in following a selected alternative is mandatory.

The alternative ways of applying the LIFO method are differentiated by the amount of time that passes between inventory computations. Specifically, the inventory balance can be computed after each receipt and each issue of material (perpetual method) or at the end of the period (periodic method) with the day-to-day receipts and issues of materials being ignored. Both of these procedures would be appropriate applications of the LIFO costing method despite the fact that they would produce different cost of materials used and different ending inventory balances. Because LIFO is used, at least in part, to reduce taxes in times of rising prices, most firms would probably prefer to combine LIFO with a periodic method. A LIFO, periodic method will always lead to cost of goods sold at least as large as a LIFO, perpetual method in times of rising prices.

The LIFO assumption works well in process cost systems where individual materials requisitions are seldom used and the materials move into process in bulk lots.[6] Examples of such systems include oil refineries, sugar refineries, spinning mills, and flour mills.

Other Methods.   Two other assumptions for cost of materials issued and inventories, the market-price-at-date-of-issue method and the standard cost method, are mentioned by some writers. The market-price-at-date-of-issue, also referred to as the next-in, first-out assumption (NIFO), is discussed first. This assumption substitutes the market price existing at the date of issuance of materials to production (replacement cost or the cost of the next units of materials that will be purchased) for the cost that was actually incurred when the materials were purchased. The cost of replenishing the materials inventory receives the focus of attention under this method. Advocates of the market-price-at-date-of-issue assumption claim that by charging production with the cost of replenishing the materials inventory at the current market price, a matching of current costs with current revenues is achieved.[7] The ending inventory absorbs the difference between NIFO cost and acquisition cost of materials issued, and soon becomes a meaningless figure. In a period of rapidly rising prices, it may have a credit balance, requiring an adjustment that is unspecified by its advocates. The assumption never achieved a substantial following, however.

A large number of companies carry materials inventory at standard rather than actual costs. The standard cost method charges units of materials into production at a budgeted, estimated, or predetermined figure set by the purchasing department which represents a price that should be paid for the various kinds of materials. The difference between actual and standard cost is recorded in a variance account at the time of purchase. Materials then are costed at the standard cost while in inventory and when issued for production.

By keeping the materials inventory at standard costs, record keeping is simplified. Because all units are brought in and issued at a single cost figure, there is no

---

[6]*Ibid.,* p. 337.

[7]W. Asquith Howe, *Cost Accounting* (International Textbook Co., Scranton, Pa., 1969), p. 55.

need to spend as much time on the task of pricing materials requisitions as when assumptions such as average cost, LIFO, and FIFO are used. As a consequence, clerical costs are reduced.[8] This savings in clerical costs may be an important reason why some companies use the standard cost method.

As noted earlier, the difference between actual and standard cost is recorded in a variance account at the time of purchase. To illustrate, assume that the standard cost of material is $.10 per unit. Because of an error on the part of an employee, a rush order was made at the price of $.12 per unit. The purchase of 2,000 units of material would be recorded as follows:

Materials	200	
Materials Price Variance	40	
Accounts Payable		240
To record purchase of materials.		

Note that the materials inventory account is charged at the standard cost of $.10 per unit. The extra $.02 per unit that resulted from an employee's error is charged to a variance account. The several methods of treating the materials price variance at the end of the accounting period are described in the chapter on the operation of standard cost systems (Chapter 16).

Cost or Market.   In the United States, year-end inventories are usually valued at cost or market, whichever is lower. (Lower of cost or market may not be combined with a LIFO cost-flow assumption in tax reporting, however. See Chapter 23.) This departure from a purely cost basis is justified when the utility of an inventory item is no longer as great as its cost. Where evidence exists that the utility of an item of inventory, in its disposal in the ordinary course of business, will be less than its cost, the difference is recognized as a loss of the period in which the diminution in utility takes place. This loss would be recognized whether it is caused by physical deterioration, obsolescence, changes in price levels, or other causes. Recognition of the loss is accomplished by stating the inventory item at a level lower than cost that is designated as "market."[9] Conservatism is cited as the rationale for this departure from incurred cost. Davidson, Schindler, and Weil point out, however, that[10]

> An examination of the effects of using the lower of cost or market over a series of accounting periods shows why the "conservatism" argument is questionable. For any one unit of goods, there is only one income or loss figure—the difference between the original cost and the selling price—and the valuation rule merely determines how this figure of income or loss is to be spread over the accounting periods. When the lower-of-cost-or-market price is used, the net income of the present period may be lower than if the original cost basis were used, but the net income of the period when the units is sold will then be higher.

The official accounting literature specifies that market means market replacement cost or reproduction cost, except that the amount should not exceed the expected sales price less costs to be incurred in completing and selling the item. Likewise, this figure, which is lower than cost, should not be less than the amount expected to be realized in the sale of the item, reduced by a normal margin of profit.[11]

[8]Gerald R. Crowningshield and Kenneth A. Gorman, *Cost Accounting: Principles and Managerial Applications,* 3rd ed. (Houghton Mifflin, Boston, 1974), pp. 192–193.

[9]Committee on Accounting Procedure, *Accounting Research Bulletin No. 43* (AICPA, New York, 1953), chap. 4, statement 5.

[10]Sidney Davidson, James S. Schindler, and Roman L. Weil, *Fundamentals of Accounting* (Dryden Press, Hinsdale, Ill., 1975), p. 359.

[11]Committee on Accounting Procedure, *Accounting Research Bulletin No. 43,* chap. 4, statement 5.

TRANSFER OF COST OF MATERIALS TO FINISHED GOODS

It is intended that ultimately all units of raw materials will end up as finished goods that are sold and delivered to customers. As was pointed out earlier, the materials requisition contains a record of the cost of materials issued to a production department. The total of all of the materials requisitions is entered on a cost sheet along with the cost of direct labor and manufacturing overhead. These costs collectively comprise the cost of the work in process inventory. When production is completed, a journal entry similar to the following is made:

Finished Goods XXX
Work in Process XXX

SCRAP

In a number of manufacturing operations, the very nature of the raw materials used results in scrap. Scrap is a recovery of materials that have separated from the main product, but that have suffered a decline in value as a result of the separation. The accounting for scrap is described in Chapter 17.

CONCLUSION

As I. Wayne Keller has noted, "Material is the one inert element of cost. It is completely controllable, but, because it is inert and inarticulate, it does not force itself upon the attention of management."[12] In the final analysis, however, vast amounts of the firm's resources flow through the materials accounts. The control and accounting for materials deserve close management attention. In a well-run company, they receive it.

BIBLIOGRAPHY

Crowningshield, Gerald R., and Kenneth A. Gorman: *Cost Accounting: Principles and Managerial Applications,* 3rd ed., Houghton Mifflin, Boston, 1974.

Davidson, Sidney, James S. Schindler, and Roman L. Weil: *Fundamentals of Accounting,* 5th ed., Dryden Press, Hinsdale, Ill., 1975.

Howe, W. Asquith: *Cost Accounting,* International Textbook Co., Scranton, Pa., 1969.

Keller, I. Wayne: "The Critical Areas of Material Cost Control," *NACA Bulletin,* July 15, 1948, p. 1411.

Matz, Adolph, and Milton F. Usry: *Cost Accounting: Planning and Control,* 6th ed., South Western Publishing Co., Cincinnati, 1976.

Neuner, John J. W.: *Cost Accounting: Principles and Practice,* 8th ed., Richard D. Irwin, Homewood, Ill., 1973.

Orlicky, Joseph: *Materials Requirements Planning,* McGraw-Hill Book Company, New York, 1975.

[12]Keller, "The Critical Areas of Material Cost Control," p. 1420.

Chapter **9**

Labor Costs

JOHN EVERS
Arthur Young & Company

ANTHONY BASILE
Arthur Young & Company

OBJECTIVES OF LABOR ACCOUNTING

Cost accounting for labor has two primary objectives beyond documenting payment of employee compensation and related taxes, benefits, and miscellaneous costs:

1. Determining labor costs components in product or service costs
2. Reporting labor costs for management planning and control

For the typical manufacturer or similar organization engaged in making or assembling a specific product, labor costs can be accumulated as incurred and charged to the assemblies and end products as they are manufactured. The labor cost components are included in recorded inventories, and such costs may be used as a basis for pricing considerations and for calculation of gross margins by product.

For service organizations engaged in providing a service or special activity as contrasted with a product, labor costs can be accumulated by function to determine costs of performing specific services or activities. The labor cost portions of transaction costs in banking or of correspondence handling in insurance, for example, might be key factors for customers or subscribers. For pricing decisions, and for gross margin calculations, it is just as important for a service organization to determine labor costs accurately for its services as it is for the typical manufacturer to do so.

The second objective in cost accounting for labor is to provide management with the information necessary for effective planning and control of human resources in making products or offering services. Depending on the type of organization and its management, actual labor costs are accumulated by department, job order number, machine unit, supervisor area, process, or other cost center. When accumulating labor costs, it is important to be specific about the activities and locations involved and the goods or services produced.

Additional detail about the type or classification of labor skills and experience or job titles will be helpful in subsequent payroll distribution and analysis. In order to obtain the most effective control of labor costs, management should compare actual costs to objective targets or to engineered standards. This comparison will highlight what labor costs should have been (given a specific set of conditions) and will guide management in planning for improvement in actual labor cost expenditures in future periods.

MANAGEMENT CONSIDERATIONS IN ACCOUNTING FOR LABOR

Accounting for labor involves calculating and recording wages earned by each employee, the pertinent tax deductions (FICA and income tax withholding), and other related deductions that may be part of the wage rate plan such as contribution to a pension plan, a U.S. Savings Bond program, or union dues. Although the narrow definition of labor costs as wages paid to employees is often questioned, there is significant justification for management to consider the wider definition of all of those costs associated with maintaining employees. Examples of such costs are the employer's share of FICA, group health insurance plans paid by the employer, company-paid life insurance premiums, etc. Although these expenditures can be separated into different accounts, grouping them together for reporting purposes under the common caption of labor costs is important, especially for the budgeting and planning process.

Having decided on the labor cost classifications, management should consider the degree of detailed reporting necessary, both for external and internal purposes. Typically, external reporting requirements are specifically directed toward ensuring the proper payment of related liabilities, both to the government and to other organizations such as labor unions. The degree of detailed internal labor costs reporting can vary significantly from industry to industry, and from company to company within an industry. The degree of labor cost information required by management is usually influenced by the following factors:

1. The number of employees
2. The relative importance of labor costs to total costs
3. The needs of the cost accounting system

Once management has determined the degree of labor reporting needed for internal purposes, it should decide how the labor activity will be analyzed and controlled. Common approaches to analyzing labor activity include:

1. Cost per unit
2. Hours per unit
3. Period costs to operate a process
4. Overtime activity
5. Employee turnover
6. Productive labor versus total labor

Another important consideration in the accumulation and tabulation of labor costs is the division of responsibility for the initial capturing, transmitting, summarizing, and reporting of labor costs. A determination must be made about each employee's responsibility in reporting total time and activities in a given day. Additionally, management should define the production foreman's or departmental supervisor's responsibility for accumulating and verifying the accuracy of labor information reported by the employee (time, product, operation, etc.). Special consideration must be given to describing clearly the roles of the timekeeping, payroll, and cost accounting departments in accumulating, tabulating, and analyzing labor costs in resolving discrepancies or problems. Individual responsibilities and points of interface must be defined clearly to assure that labor costs are properly accumulated (timekeeping), tabulated (payroll), and analyzed (cost accounting).

A further consideration is the level of automation that is appropriate for the labor accounting activity. A cost/benefit analysis of automation versus the manual effort in the accumulation tabulation, and reporting aspects of labor accounting should be undertaken before a final decision is made.

SOME PROBLEMS IN ACCOUNTING FOR LABOR

Careful thought needs to be given in designing the system to collect labor information in enough detail for product or service cost control. Installing a system that collects extraneous and unnecessary information creates an unwieldy monster that increases unit costs instead of decreasing those costs. At the other extreme, however, attempting to collect minimal data, highly summarized, leaves management without meaningful information needed for good planning and control. A balanced system will accumulate easily gathered labor data, group and summarize labor cost detail, compare the information to objectives or standards, and feed the analysis back to management for effective action.

The reporting system for labor hours should have built-in checks to assure relative accuracy in labor information. Because of other pressures on production management, there may be a tendency to report some production hours in such categories as setup time, repairs, or machine downtime. If labor distributions or subsequent overhead allocations are based on production hours only, and inaccurate reporting has occurred, artificial errors will be introduced into the system. Accounting will need to assure also that reconciliations of total hours by each product or job order match total payroll hours paid.

In some organizations, labor is the only basis for allocation of other costs to products or jobs. This may be an easy solution,' but it introduces significant inaccuracies for those costs that really tend to depend on such measures as machine hours, tonnage, customers, items purchased, space, and so forth. An index that is based only on direct labor will fluctuate as productivity varies and as the percentage of direct labor to total cost changes. Even basing the index on total labor may result in inequitable cost allocation.

LABOR CLASSIFICATIONS

The design or selection of a labor classification scheme for a particular organization can have a significant impact in the manner of accumulating labor costs. Depending on the type of classification used, actual labor costs can be wholly contained in the Labor account, or can be distributed in different ways to Labor, Materials, and Overhead. Before an organization can compare its labor cost components to those of a competitor or another similar organization, it will need to know how labor is classified.

Exhibit 1 shows the relationship among labor classifications as a company might progress from generalized classifications (direct labor and overhead) to more detailed and specific classifications (variable direct, semivariable, semifixed, and fixed). Although the illustration is for a sample manufacturing plant, the same information is applicable to different industries or to service organizations.

In addition to the elements of direct/indirect or variable/fixed, at least two other groups of terms are used in describing labor costs and classifications: productive/nonproductive and controllable/noncontrollable. Usually the terms productive/nonproductive are used to describe the way labor hours are used, rather than how labor is classified. If the employee hours are spent working directly or indirectly to produce a product, then that time is productive. If the employee hours are spent waiting, repairing a breakdown, reworking off-quality production, or similarly doing something other than producing quality items, then that time is nonproductive.

The terms controllable/noncontrollable are most often used in connection with management budget and variance report analysis, to describe costs that are either controllable or noncontrollable within the role of a department or plant management position. These terms are also used within particular time periods, to reflect whether costs are controllable in the short term or whether they will require long-term action. In the design of standard costs systems, it is important to guide management activity toward controllable areas of responsibility.

TIMEKEEPING

Objectives of Timekeeping Function. Generally, the timekeeping department has three major objectives:

1. To report the presence and amount of time, or the lack of employees on the job and in the plant.

EXHIBIT 1   Descriptions and Representative Job Titles for Illustrative Labor Classifications (for a Sample Manufacturing Plant)

General	Specific	Detailed
Direct labor	*Direct labor*	*Variable direct labor*
Employee works directly with or on product XYZ	Employee works directly on product XYZ	Employee works directly on product XYZ and hours vary directly with XYZ units produced
Grinder	Grinder	Grinder
Assembler	Assembler	Assembler
Polisher	Polisher	Polisher
Inspector	Inspector	
Fork lift operator		
	Indirect labor	
Overhead labor	Employee works in support of other labor employees	*Semivariable labor*
Employee does not work on product XYZ itself		Employee works in support of making product XYZ and hours vary directly with something other than number of XYZ units
Receiving clerk	Fork lift operator	
Storeroom attendant	Receiving clerk	
Foreman	Storeroom attendant	
Accountant		Inspector
Plant manager	*Fixed labor*	Fork lift operator
	Employee hours do not vary except for multishift operations	Receiving clerk
	Foreman	*Semifixed labor*
	Accountant	Employee works in support of making product XYZ and hours vary indirectly or in a stepwise fashion with production volumes
	Plant manager	
		Storeroom attendant
		Foreman
		Fixed labor
		Employee hours do not vary but are fixed for every level of production
		Accountant
		Plant manager

2. To maintain employee activity records for purposes of satisfying requirements set by the Fair Labor Standards Act. The Act requires that basic records that reflect the total daily hours worked be maintained for each employee.

3. To ensure that the time reported by each employee for a given job or order is stated properly.

Assurance that the employee is on the job can be obtained through a review of the daily clock cards (see Exhibit 2) and verification of the employee's presence with the department supervisor. Verifying the accuracy of time reported for a given job or process by an employee is more difficult, but it can be done by inspecting the work performed before the labor-reporting documents are approved. This would be done by the employee's supervisor rather than the timekeeper.

Organization of the Timekeeping Department.   In larger companies, the timekeeping department is usually decentralized, with time clerks located in or responsible for each production department and reporting to a single head timekeeper or supervisor. Those performing the timekeeping function are usually indirectly responsible to the factory superintendent and directly responsible to the supervisor of the cost accounting or payroll departments.

Time clerks can be classified into two categories: traveling or stationary. A traveling timekeeper moves from one department to another, noting the activities of each employee and verifying the presence of the employee, the job being

EXHIBIT 2   Daily Clock Card

Employee No. _____

Employee Name _____

Pay End. _____

EARNINGS

Reg. Hrs. _____ Rate _____ Amt. _____

Overtime Hrs. _____ Rate _____ Amt. _____

Total Earnings _____

DEDUCTIONS

W.T. _____

FICA _____

Insurance _____

Other _____

Total Deductions _____

Net Payroll Check _____

SUN	MON	TUES	WED	THUR	FRI	SAT

worked on, the operation being performed, and the start and stop times. A stationary timekeeper usually remains in a single location (usually the timekeeper's office located in the plant) to perform the timekeeping duties. Employees go to the timekeeper to record any changes in their work status. It is a good policy for the stationary timekeeper to make occasional visits to the various departments to ensure that workers are present and that situations have not changed without notification.

The specific production or processing characteristics of a given location will influence the decision to use traveling or stationary timekeepers. A work environment that is characterized by constant jobs or processes over a relatively long time span is usually served more efficiently by a stationary timekeeper. However, the stationary timekeeper is responsible for removing the clock cards from the time-card racks for review and tabulations at the end of each shift or day.

Relationship of Timekeeping to Payroll and Cost Departments.   Timekeeping is the first function in the labor accounting process. The payroll department is an intermediary step between the timekeeping and the cost accounting departments. The function of the payroll department is to compute each employee's earnings, withholdings, and the company's share of labor-related liabilities, and to record labor changes by specific classification—department, area, or operation. This information comes from the timekeeping department (hours worked by employee) and personnel department (number of exemptions, savings plans, union dues, etc.). The cost accounting department is generally responsible for the accumulation and classification of all cost information, of which labor is one element. The amount of effort put forth by the cost accounting department in accumulating and analyzing labor cost data usually depends on whether the industry is labor-, material-, or overhead-intensive. In those industries where labor is an important cost element, some companies decentralize their accounting activities to have the cost accountant direct how payroll information is accumulated.

PAYROLL ACCOUNTING

Objectives of Payroll Department. The payroll department (tabulation) is an intermediate function between the timekeeping (accumulation) and the cost accounting (analysis) departments. The objectives of the payroll department are, quite simply,

1. To compute employee compensation
2. To pay employees
3. To maintain individual employee payroll records
4. To prepare departmental payroll summaries
5. To calculate payroll taxes and other related payroll liabilities

The responsibilities of the payroll department in controlling and accounting for labor costs are described by Blocker and Weltmer[1] as follows:

1. To maintain a record of the job classification, department, and wage rate for each employee
2. To verify and to summarize the time of each worker as shown on the daily time cards
3. To compute the wages earned by each worker
4. To prepare the payroll for each department showing the total amount earned for the period by each employee
5. To compute the payroll deductions required by the federal Social Security Act, state unemployment compensation laws, and the federal Internal Revenue Code
6. To compute the payroll deductions authorized by the employee for union dues, credit union, charitable donations, savings bonds, and health and accident insurance
7. To maintain a permanent payroll record for each employee
8. To distribute salary and wage payments

Methods of Accumulating Labor Hours for Payroll Purposes. There are three basic classifications of labor for payroll purposes: (1) salaried personnel compensated on a semimonthly or monthly basis (including executive compensation plans), (2) weekly salaried personnel, and (3) hourly personnel compensated either on a daily or weekly basis. Within each of these classifications, the specific method of accumulating labor hours will depend on various factors, such as whether or not the employee is (1) exempt or not from overtime compensation, (2) qualified for a profit incentive, such as a piece rate or a bonus arrangement, and (3) compensated for excused leaves.

One method commonly used to compensate salaried employees, whether exempt or not, is the use of the prepunched time card illustrated in Exhibit 3. With a prepunched time card, the salaried employee does not have to make any

[1]John G. Blocker and W. Keith Weltmer, *Cost Accounting* (McGraw-Hill Book Company, New York, 1954), p. 82.

EXHIBIT 3   Prepunched Time Card for Salaried Employee

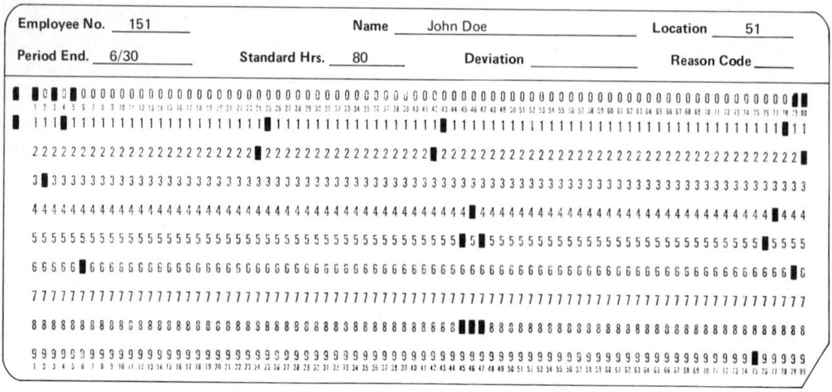

notations on the card if he or she worked regular hours. At the end of the pay period, the prepunched card is sent to the data processing department to update the employee's master file and prepare the compensation. Only differences from standard time for the period (such as extra hours for nonexempt employees, sick time, vacation, etc.) are noted on the prepunched card.

A method commonly used to accumulate labor hours for hourly personnel is the use of the clock card, which also may have certain data elements prepunched, such as employee name, social security number, and home department number (see Exhibit 2). After entering the plant or office, the employee goes to a clock station, picks up his or her time card from a rack, punches in, and puts the card in an "in" rack. At the end of the day, the employee pulls the time card from the "in" rack, punches into the clock, and then puts the card into an "out" rack. Companies that do not use a time card system often have a "sign-in" sheet which is controlled by the timekeeping department. Employees sign in on arrival and out on leaving. In smaller companies, neither of these systems may be in use. Rather, the department supervisor may report directly to the payroll department on an exception basis hours not worked by an employee or overtime hours.

Methods of Accumulating Labor Activity for Costing Purposes.   There are four commonly used methods of accumulating labor activity for costing purposes:

1. Daily production and time report by crew—often maintained and controlled by the crew leader or department supervisor; see Exhibit 4.
2. Combined daily labor ticket/time card by employee; see Exhibit 5.
3. Daily labor ticket by employee; see Exhibit 6.
4. Use of time recorders to record time by groups of employees performing related duties, as well as each individual's activities.

When the daily production and time report is used to accumulate labor cost by product and/or process, controls should be in effect to assure that all employees in a given department are included in the crew size. Without controls, total hours reported on a crew report for a given period may not match the total hours reported by employees on their time cards. This method of accumulating labor activity is most suitable where jobs or processes do not change frequently.

A combined daily labor ticket/time card is useful in situations where employees move between jobs during the day. If all employees are responsible for recording their activities by job or process, one form can serve several purposes. It can both track movement of an employee between jobs and total time worked and facilitate the reconciliation of labor charges to earnings. The advantages of the combined daily labor ticket/time card have been described as follows:[2]

[2]*NAA Bulletin,* vol. 38.

EXHIBIT 4 Daily Production and Time Report by Crew

Date _____

Shift _____

Extruder _____

Crew _____

Approved _____

DAILY PRODUCTION AND TIME REPORT

(Computed only at product change or end of shift)

Product line/ activity	Crew size per extruder	Activity start time	Activity stop time	Total activity time	Downtime* code	Machine hours		Remarks	Total tons	Labor hours		Actual labor hours per ton	Standard labor hours per ton	Standard labor hours	Percent efficiency
						Down	Run			Non-prod.	Prod.				
TOTAL															

*DOWNTIME CODES — PROCESSING

A — System changeover

B — Startup/shutdown

C — Out of feed

D — Processing system

E — Other (see remarks)

Machine hours scheduled

Machine efficiency (run: Scheduled)

Machine hours available

Machine utilization (scheduled: Available)

EXHIBIT 5   Combination Clock Card and Labor Ticket

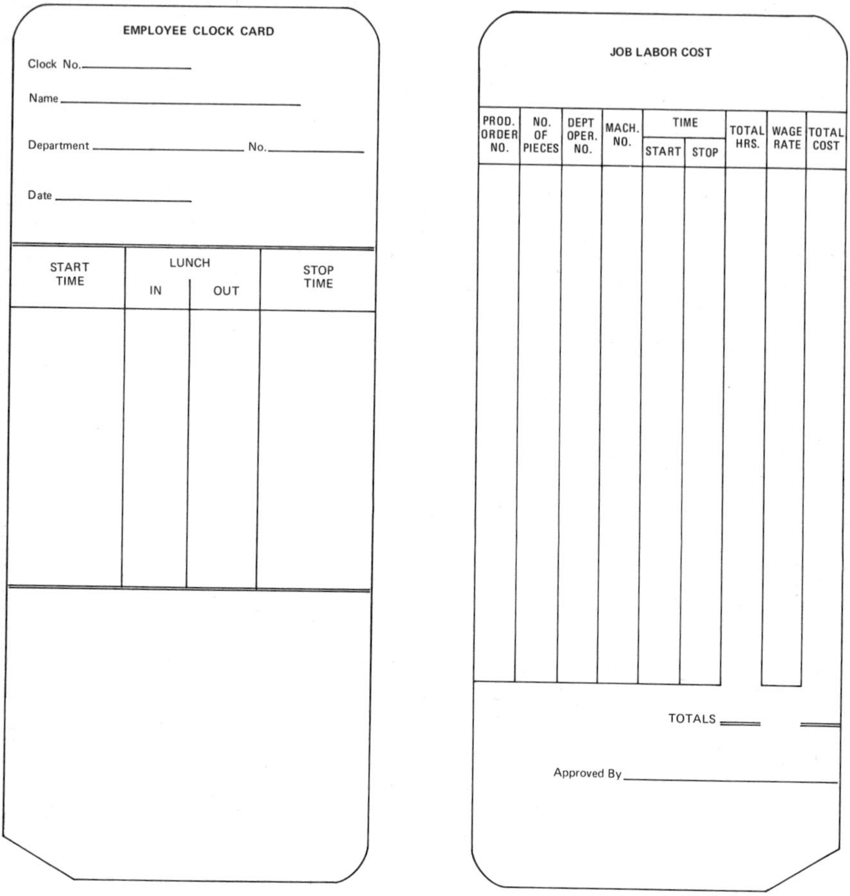

EMPLOYEE CLOCK CARD

Clock No._____

Name_____

Department _____ No._____

Date_____

| START TIME | LUNCH | | STOP TIME |
	IN	OUT	

JOB LABOR COST

| PROD. ORDER NO. | NO. OF PIECES | DEPT OPER. NO. | MACH. NO. | TIME | | TOTAL HRS. | WAGE RATE | TOTAL COST |
				START	STOP			

TOTALS _____

Approved By_____

Because the cards are available to them in their departmental areas, supervisors are aided in their control of personnel. They can detect absence and lateness sooner and can adjust work assignments more quickly to compensate for the missing employees. Time-keepers find it easier to reconcile differences between total job time and hours worked because they now do this daily. There is no longer need to ask people to try to remember time data for previous days. The single card system makes it practical to produce timely reports of absence and analysis of the reasons for the absence from the same sources from which payrolls are prepared. Also, it helps to relieve congestion at the plant entrance by eliminating the necessity for putting cards back in the card rack at the clock area, both at the beginning and ending of the shift.

Another method of accumulating labor activity by job is by using a daily labor ticket, which is usually put in the clock card rack behind the clock card. After entering the plant or office, the employee punches his or her clock card and takes the labor ticket to the work station. For each change of job, the employee records the job number and start and stop times (or just elapsed time) on the labor ticket. The use of the daily labor ticket is desirable in companies where employees change jobs or processes several times during the day. Some companies pay the employee

EXHIBIT 6   Daily Labor Ticket

EMPLOYEE LABOR TICKET

Date_____ Employee No._____

Employee Name _____

PROD'N ORDER NO.	DEPT. OPER. NO.	NO. OF PIECES	MACH. NO.	TIME						TOTAL TIME
				PRODUCTIVE		NON-PRODUCTIVE			CODE	
				START	STOP	START	STOP	NO.		

TOTAL TIME ═══

Approved by _____

based on the lower total number of hours on either the labor ticket or the clock card. This procedure assures that all time paid for is charged to a specific operation or product, or both.

A fourth method of accumulating labor activity involves time records located at fixed points in the plant or office. These machines may do nothing more than record start and stop times for each employee and job. Others can be very sophisticated, with an on-line arrangement where the insertion of the time ticket into the time recorder automatically transmits data to a computer.

Preparation of Payroll Distribution. Clock cards are the most commonly used input into the payroll department for the preparation of payrolls. In companies with an automated payroll system, the labor activity is usually keypunched directly from the clock card into the computer. Daily computerized departmental payroll sheets recapitulate data appearing on the clock card. Similarly, weekly and monthly computerized payroll sheets are prepared from the monthly payroll sheets. Where prepunched time cards are used for salaried employees, the cards serve as the basic input into the payroll journals.

An example of the monthly journal entries that a payroll department would be involved in is as follows:

Journal Entries to Record Liabilities Connected with Payrolls

Labor	XXXX	
Vouchers Payable (amount paid employees) .		XXXX
Federal Income Tax Withheld		XXXX
State Income Tax Withheld		XXXX
Federal Old Age Tax Withheld		XXXX
Group Insurance Premium Withheld		XXXX
Union Dues Withheld		XXXX
To record payroll per register.		
Vouchers Payable	XXXX	
Cash		XXXX
To record payment to employees.		
Federal Old Age Tax Expense (FICA)...........	XXXX	
State Unemployment Tax Expense	XXXX	
Federal Unemployment Tax Expense	XXXX	
Welfare Fund Contribution Expense	XXXX	
Federal Old Age Tax Payable (FICA)		XXXX
State Unemployment Tax Payable		XXXX
Federal Unemployment Tax Payable		XXXX
Welfare Fund Contribution Payable		XXXX
To record employers contributions to social		
security and welfare programs.		

These entries are commonly found in companies that use only a general (financial) accounting system. The accounts reflecting the employer's share of labor-related expenses are typically closed out to the profit and loss accounts at the end of each period. In those companies where a cost accounting system is also used, these expense accounts are further classified into departmental or cost center accounts. The basis for the distribution is normally the labor dollars paid within each department or cost center.

Payroll Changes, Additions, or Deletions. In addition to translating hours worked and pieces produced by employee (where incentive systems are in use) into dollars of pay, the payroll department is typically charged with retaining current employee status files. The payroll department is usually responsible for the preparation of external reports, such as the Employer's Quarterly Federal Tax Return, Form 941 (see Exhibit 7), the Employer's Annual Federal Unemployment Tax Return, Form 940 (see Exhibit 8); quarterly deposit tickets of withheld taxes and employer's portion of payroll taxes (see Exhibit 9); and employment applications and other reports to governmental agencies (see Exhibit 10).

The initiating document to put an employee on the payroll is usually forwarded from the personnel department to the payroll department. This document, sometimes called the Employment Report, transmits data about the employee's status. It usually contains the following information:

1. Name
2. Address
3. Number of exemptions
4. Base hourly rate
5. Exempt or nonexempt status
6. Immediate supervisor's title or occupational code
7. Marital status
8. Social security number

The payroll department should be notified of any changes in the status of an employee that affect his or her withholdings, compensation computation, or residency. The Payroll Changed Status Report (see Exhibit 11) transmits the following types of changes to the payroll department:

EXHIBIT 7   Employer's Quarterly Federal Tax Return

Form **941**
(Rev. April 1976)
Department of the Treasury
Internal Revenue Service

Employer's Quarterly Federal Tax Return

Schedule A—Quarterly Report of Wages Taxable under the Federal Insurance Contributions Act—**FOR SOCIAL SECURITY**

List for each nonagricultural employee the WAGES taxable under the FICA which were paid during the quarter. If you pay an employee more than $15,300 in a calendar year, report only the first $15,300 of such wages. In the case of "Tip Income," see instructions on page 4. IF WAGES WERE NOT TAXABLE UNDER THE FICA, MAKE NO ENTRIES IN ITEMS 1 THROUGH 9 AND 14 THROUGH 18.

1. Total pages of this return including this page and any pages of Form 941a ►	2. Total number of employees listed ►	3. (First quarter only) Number of employees (except household) employed in the pay period including March 12th ►

4. EMPLOYEE'S SOCIAL SECURITY NUMBER	5. NAME OF EMPLOYEE (Please type or print)	6. TAXABLE FICA WAGES Paid to Employee in Quarter (Before Deductions) Dollars Cents	7. TAXABLE TIPS REPORTED (See page 4) Dollars Cents
000 00 0000			

If you need more space for listing employees, use Schedule A continuation sheets, Form 941a.
Totals for this page—Wage total in column 6 and tip total in column 7 ——➤

8. TOTAL WAGES TAXABLE UNDER FICA PAID DURING QUARTER. $ _____
(Total of column 6 on this page and continuation sheets.) Enter here and in item 14 below.

9. TOTAL TAXABLE TIPS REPORTED UNDER FICA DURING QUARTER. $ _____
(Total of column 7 on this page and continuation sheets.) Enter here and in item 15 below. (If no tips reported, write "None.")

Name _____   Date Quarter Ended _____

Address _____   Employer Identification No. _____

IMPORTANT.—Keep this copy and a copy of each related schedule or statement. Before filing the return, be sure to enter on this copy your name, address, and identification number, and the period for which the return is filed.

10. Total Wages And Tips Subject to Withholding Plus Other Compensation . . . . . ——➤	
11. Amount Of Income Tax Withheld From Wages, Tips, Annuities, etc. (See instructions)	
12. Adjustment For Preceding Quarters Of Calendar Year	
13. Adjusted Total Of Income Tax Withheld . . . . ——➤	
14. Taxable FICA Wages Paid (Item 8) . . $ _____ multiplied by 11.7% = TAX	
15. Taxable Tips Reported (Item 9) . . . $ _____ multiplied by 5.85% = TAX	
16. Total FICA Taxes (Item 14 plus Item 15) . . . . ——➤	
17. Adjustment (See instructions)	
18. Adjusted Total Of FICA Taxes . . . . ——➤	
19. Total Taxes (Item 13 plus Item 18)	
20. TOTAL DEPOSITS FOR QUARTER (INCLUDING FINAL DEPOSIT MADE FOR QUARTER) AND OVERPAYMENT FROM PREVIOUS QUARTER LISTED IN SCHEDULE B (See instructions on page 4) . . . . Note: If undeposited taxes at the end of the quarter are $200 or more, the full amount must be deposited with an authorized commercial bank or a Federal Reserve bank in accordance with instructions on the reverse of the Federal tax deposit form. This deposit must be entered in Schedule B and included in item 20.	
21. Undeposited Taxes Due (Item 19 Less Item 20—This Should Be Less Than $200). Pay To Internal Revenue Service And Enter Here	
22. If Item 20 is More Than Item 19, Enter Excess Here ► $ _____ And Check If You Want It ☐ Applied to Next Return, Or ☐ Refunded.	
23. If not liable for returns in the future, write "FINAL" (See instructions) ► _____ Date final wages paid ►	

1. Change in residence
2. Name change
3. Change in marital status
4. Change in title
5. Change in hourly rate
6. Change in incentives
7. Change in authorized deductions
8. Change in departmental or occupational code
9. Change in employee's status, such as part-time to full, temporary to regular
10. Termination of employment

Internal Control in Accumulating, Tabulating, and Accounting for Labor. Sound internal controls dictate separation of the functions of accumulation, computation,

EXHIBIT 8 Employer's Annual Federal Unemployment Tax Return

Form 940
Department of the Treasury
Internal Revenue Service

Employer's Annual Federal Unemployment Tax Return

1976

Name of State 1	State reporting number as shown on employer's State contribution returns 2	Taxable payroll (As defined in State act) 3	Experience rate period 4		Experience rate 5	Contributions had rate been 2.7% (col. 3 × 2.7%) 6	Contributions payable at experience rate (col. 3 × col. 5) 7	Additional credit (col. 6 minus col. 7) 8	Contributions actually paid to State 9
			From—	To—					
	Totals ▶								

10 Total tentative credit (Column 8 plus column 9).
11 Total remuneration (including exempt remuneration) PAID during the calendar year for services of employees

Exempt Remuneration	Approximate number of employees involved	Amount paid
12 Exempt remuneration. (Explain each exemption shown, attaching additional sheet if necessary):		
13 Remuneration in excess of $4,200. (Enter only the excess over the first $4,200 paid to individual employees exclusive of exempt amounts entered on line 12)		

14 Total exempt remuneration (line 12 plus line 13) . . . .
15 Total taxable wages (line 11 less line 14) . . . .
16 Gross Federal tax (3.2% of line 15) . . . .
17 Enter 2.7% of the amount of wages shown on line 15 . . . .
18 Line 10 or line 17 whichever is smaller . . . .
19 Amount, if any, of wages on line 15 attributable to the following States:
    (a) Vermont $_____ × .003 . . .
    (b) Washington $_____ × .003 . . .
    (c) Total (add lines 19(a) and (b)) . . . .
20 Credit allowable (line 18 less line 19(c)) . . . .
21 Net Federal tax (line 16 less line 20) . . . .

Record of Federal Tax Deposits for Unemployment Tax (Form 508)

Quarter	Liability by period	Date of deposit	Amount of deposit
First			
Second			
Third			
Fourth			

22 Total Federal tax deposited . . . .
23 Balance due (line 21 less line 22—this should not exceed $100). Pay to "Internal Revenue Service" . . ▶
24 If no longer in business at end of year, write "FINAL" here ▶

Under penalties of perjury, I declare that I have examined this return, including accompanying schedules and statements, and to the best of my knowledge and belief it is true, correct, and complete, and that no part of any payment made to a State unemployment fund, which is claimed as a credit on line 20 above, was or is to be deducted from the remuneration of employees.

Date ▶   Signature ▶   Title (Owner, etc.) ▶

T
FF
FD
FP
I
T

(If incorrect make any necessary change.) ▶

Name (as distinguished from trade name)

Trade name, if any

Address and ZIP code

Calendar Year
1976

Employer Identification No.

EXHIBIT 9 Federal Tax Deposit Ticket

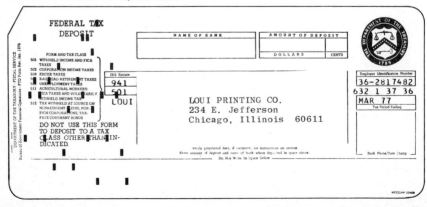

EXHIBIT 10 Employment Application

EMPLOYMENT APPLICATION
Administrative

XYZ COMPANY
An equal opportunity employer

XYZ COMPANY DOES NOT DISCRIMINATE ON THE BASIS OF RACE, RELIGION, ORIGIN, AGE, OR SEX.
YOU ARE NOT REQUIRED TO GIVE INFORMATION WHICH IS PROHIBITED BY LAW.

PERSONAL

Date _____

Name _____ Tel No. ( ) _____ Area Code
Last / First / Middle Initial

Address _____ Social Security No. _____
No. / Street / City / State / Zip

Previous Address _____ Date of birth _____ (Not applicable where prohibited by law)
No. / Street / City / State / Zip

Marital Status: ☐ Single ☐ Married ☐ Widowed ☐ Divorced

Are you a U.S.A. citizen? _____ If not, type of visa _____ (Not applicable where prohibited by law)

Date of and reason for your last physical examination _____

Describe any health problems or limitations. _____

(a) Has your application for bond ever been rejected or do you have any reason to believe your application for a fidelity bond might be rejected?
_____ (b) Have you ever been convicted of a felony? _____ If your answer to (a) or (b) is "yes", please explain. _____

In case of emergency or illness, whom should we notify? _____ Tel. No. ( ) _____ Area Code
Address _____
No. / Street / City / State / Zip

EDUCATION

| | Dates of Attendance | | | | |
Name and address of school	From	To	Course or Major	Date Graduated	Degree or Diploma
High School or Prep					
College					
Graduate, Technical, Business or Other School					

Extra-curricular activities & honors (social, scholastic, athletic) _____

Foreign language ability:	French	German	Italian	Spanish		
Speak	☐	☐	☐	☐	Office skills, speeds:	
Read	☐	☐	☐	☐	Steno. _____	
Write	☐	☐	☐	☐	Typing _____	

MILITARY

Branch of service _____ From Mo. ___ Yr. ___ To Mo. ___ Yr. ___ Rank _____

Specialization _____ Type of discharge _____ Selective Service status and other military commitments: _____

EMPLOYMENT

What kind of work are you applying for _____

By whom were you referred to XYZ Company _____

Please list the record of your employment beginning with present or most recent:

Dates of Employment	Names and addresses of employers	Position & Supervisor's name	Salary	Reason for leaving
From: Mo. ___ Yr. ___ To: Mo. ___ Yr. ___	Name of Company _____ Address _____		$ Starting $ Ending	
From: Mo. ___ Yr. ___ To: Mo. ___ Yr. ___	Name of Company _____ Address _____		$ Starting $ Ending	
From: Mo. ___ Yr. ___ To: Mo. ___ Yr. ___	Name of Company _____ Address _____		$ Starting $ Ending	
From: Mo. ___ Yr. ___ To: Mo. ___ Yr. ___	Name of Company _____ Address _____		$ Starting $ Ending	

In making this application for employment with XYZ Company I affirm that all information is true and complete and I grant permission for the firm to contact all references and former employers, obtain school transcripts, and make inquiries regarding character, personal attributes, general reputation, etc. Information about the nature and scope of any such inquiries will be provided upon written request. I understand that any misrepresentation in this application will be sufficient cause for rejection of this application or my dismissal after employment.

Signature _____ Date _____

DO NOT WRITE BELOW THIS LINE

COMMENTS _____

Employment date _____
Position title _____
Department _____
Salary _____
Exemption status: ☐ Exempt ☐ Non-exempt
Replacement for: ☐ Addition
Agency fee _____
Recruiting source _____

EXHIBIT 11   Payroll Changed Status Report

```
┌──────────────────────────────────────────────────────────────────────┐
│                       PAYROLL CHANGE STATUS                            │
│                                                                        │
│                                             DATE _____             │
│  Name _____  Soc. Sec. No. _____  │
│                                                                        │
│  Dept. _____ No. _____ Shift _____ Clock No. _____  │
│                            REASON                                      │
│  □ New hire, effective date _____ time _____   │
│  □ Rate change, from _____ per _____ to _____ per ____ │
│  □ Transfer, from _____ to _____     │
│  □ Termination, effective date _____ time _____   │
│  □ Suspension, from _____ to _____    │
│  ════════════════════════════════════════════════════════════════     │
│  Remarks  ─────────────────────────────────────────────────────        │
│  _____   │
│  _____   │
│  _____   │
│  _____   │
│  _____   │
│                                                                        │
│  Approved by _____ Entered _____    │
│                                                  TIMEKEEPING           │
└──────────────────────────────────────────────────────────────────────┘
```

payment of wages earned, and analysis of the labor activity. A paymaster who distributes employees' checks should not also prepare the employees' checks or reconcile the payroll bank account. The person who sends payroll checks to employees' homes should not prepare the check or receive any checks returned as undeliverable. Workers paid in cash should get a pay envelope containing a detachable receipt, which they should sign and give to the paymaster. An alternative approach requires the employee to sign a payroll sheet when receiving his or her compensation. To ensure that the proper person is given the payroll check, the paymaster should request identification, either personal by the department foreman or union steward or by the employee's presentation of a company identification card.

LABOR COST ACCOUNTING

For ease of presentation, subsequent sections in this chapter describe three types of cost systems: process cost, job cost, and standard cost. In actual practice, there is considerable overlap among these systems, and many organizations will use elements of each system in accounting for labor.

The first two systems are actual cost systems, differing primarily by whether the production or service organization is organized for continuous production in a process flow, or for intermittent, batch production in a special order or job flow. The third system uses standard costs, varying from estimates to sophisticated engineered calculations for material, labor, and overhead components.

The process cost system, with modifications, is used by many mass-production or processing industries and large service industries. Accumulation of actual costs by cost center is relatively simple, once the definitions of cost centers and the chart of accounts have been completed. It is important that the accounting system parallel the production or process steps, from the input of materials, labor, and overhead, through cost centers to finished goods and inventory. Labor costs are accumulated by cost center (often identical to organizational groups reporting to a single supervisor or manager) and reported daily or weekly to accounting.

The job cost system, also generally with modifications, is used when costs for jobs, or batches, or groups of items or activities need to be known. Maintenance groups almost always use a modified job cost system to accumulate labor and materials costs for individual work orders as the maintenance activities are performed. Industries that frequently use a job cost system include construction, printing, subcontractors, foundries, heavy fabrication, aircraft, and furniture. Professional service firms and a number of special service companies also use job cost systems in accounting for their costs. Labor cost accounting in the job cost system requires more detailed accumulation of data for fewer units of production or service than in process cost systems. In some organizations dual sets of documents will be used to collect both job or order cost detail and departmental or cost center detail.

The standard cost systems are usually better than the actual cost or historical cost systems because they emphasize planning for future events. The standards, whether established through agreed estimates or through detailed engineering studies (which in themselves vary from simple and low cost to complex and costly), define what costs *should be* for a given set of conditions in the production or service organization. Actual labor costs are also accumulated in a standard cost system and are compared to the standard or "should be" costs through variance reports and analysis. The standard cost system may be used with either the process or job cost system to provide effective planning and cost control.

LABOR COST ACCOUNTING IN A PROCESS COST SYSTEM

The installation of a process cost accounting system usually indicates a relatively continuous production flow. In such an environment, costs are accumulated by process, and no attempt is made to determine the cost of a particular job or batch of products. Additionally, the accumulation of labor costs is more directly related to periods of time rather than to production quantities. Products and activities remain substantially unchanged from day to day, as opposed to a job (custom) environment. At the end of a set reporting period, total actual labor costs for a given operation are compared to the actual units of production to determine the average actual cost per unit for that period.

The technique for costing direct labor into work in process by the cost accounting department depends on the specific plant and products produced. Some companies with a limited number of products have a single work-in-process inventory account which receives the direct labor charge. Other companies with more complex processes and large numbers of products may have separate work-in-process inventory accounts for each department or cost center. In this latter situation, the labor distribution prepared at the end of a month charges each of the work-in-process inventory accounts for the appropriate amount of direct labor incurred in that department or cost center. A typical journal entry of this case debits the work-in-process inventory account for each of the departments or cost centers and credits the payroll or direct labor accounts.

Some production processes are characterized by a few basic products produced in the initial operation(s), which then branch out into many different products having minor differences from each other. In such processes, a careful review should be made to determine if the production environment can better be reported and controlled through the use of a job cost accounting system. A process cost system best serves an environment with these characteristics: continuous production flow, recurring manufacturing of the same product without specification changes, not a made-to-order production environment.

LABOR COST ACCOUNTING IN A JOB COST SYSTEM

Job cost accounting systems are appropriate for companies that specialize in the manufacture of products to customers' specifications or companies that are too small, or whose production runs are too small, to set up separate production lines for each product. These companies control and record the cost of production as a series of separate, identifiable jobs. A job may be a single unit, such as a large piece of equipment, or a batch of items, such as a hundred small motors. Each job must be specifically defined, usually by the product engineer on a Work Order (see Exhibit 12), and assigned a job number that identifies it throughout the manufacturing process.

EXHIBIT 12   Work Order Sheet for a Job Cost System

WORK ORDER					
				Job No. _____	
Product _____				Quantity _____	
Customer _____					
Delivery Scheduled _____					
Description:					
DATE	EMPLOYEE	HOURS	RATE	AMOUNT	

The movement of a job through the various operations in a plant is specified by the industrial engineer on a Labor Route Sheet (see Exhibit 13). This route sheet accompanies the job through the plant. It specifically identifies for a particular job the product, quantity, and engineering specifications, as well as the sequence of operations, and possibly the individual machines that will be used in the manufacturing process.

EXHIBIT 13   Labor Route Sheet for a Job Cost System

LABOR ROUTE SHEET

Job. No. _____

Product _____   Quantity _____

Customer _____   Date to
start _____

Delivery scheduled _____   Date to
complete _____

Specifications: Drawing No. _____

Pattern No. _____

Materials:

	SCHEDULED OPERATIONS		COMPLETED OPERATIONS		
OPER. NO.	DESCRIPTION	MACHINE	DATE	EMPLOYEE	FOREMAN

Direct labor is typically charged to the job through labor tickets, which are kept by each employee as his or her record of time spent on each job. The employee lists the job number and time worked on each job throughout the day. At the end of the day, a cost accounting clerk (1) posts the hours for each job to the cost accounting department's copy of the work order and then (2) extends the hours by the individual's wage rate to determine the total direct labor costs to charge to the job.

Other elements of labor are not readily identifiable as chargeable to specific jobs. Material handling employees in the receiving department are an example of an indirect labor category, for they usually cannot charge their time specifically to individual jobs. Yet this type of labor cost must be allocated to individual jobs if the accounting system is expected to reflect actual costs for each job. Typically, indirect labor categories are included in the manufacturing overhead accounts, and all overhead is allocated to the various jobs in process.

To allocate overhead to jobs in a job order cost system, the total overhead costs incurred during a month are normally divided by the direct labor hours (or dollars) recorded in the month. Then the overhead per hour (or per labor dollar) is applied to the jobs on the basis of actual direct labor charged to each job during the month.

A separate Job Order Cost Summary (see Exhibit 14) should be maintained by the cost accounting department for each job until the job is completed. In addition to showing direct labor costs, a Job Order Cost Summary should list the raw material and manufacturing overhead charges to the job. In this way, all costs directly related to the job are recorded in the summary for reporting total costs per job, for pricing decisions, and in estimating future cost.

EXHIBIT 14   Job Order Cost Summary

JOB ORDER COST SUMMARY							
Product _____			Job No. _____				
Customer _____			Quantity _____				
			Date started _____				
Delivery scheduled _____			Date completed _____				
MATERIAL			DIRECT LABOR		FACTORY OVERHEAD		
DATE	REQ. NO.	COST	DATE	COST	DATE	RATE	COST APPLIED
						TOTAL JOB	PER UNIT
TOTAL COSTS:	Material						
	Direct labor						
	Factory overhead						
	TOTAL						

LABOR COST ACCOUNTING IN A STANDARD COST SYSTEM

The basic objectives of a standard cost accounting system for labor are to maintain control over and isolate problems associated with the labor activity expense categories. The accumulation of labor cost and preparation of payrolls are recorded in a manner similar to an "actual cost" accounting system. However, the amount charged to the cost of a product is different. The standard labor cost is a predetermined amount of time required for each operation to produce a part, extended at a set labor rate. Standard labor cost (based on standard cost per unit times number of units produced) is charged to the production cost. The difference between the actual labor cost incurred and the amount charged into production cost (standard cost) is a *variance*. The variance is the quantification of factors that cause the process to be running "off standard." An analysis of the reasons for the variance provides management with information to control the process.

Standard labor cost charged to production is calculated in the following way: the number of units produced in each cost center is multiplied by the standard labor hours or minutes allowed per unit. The result is then multiplied by the standard direct labor wage rate for the cost center. The result of these extensions is the standard labor cost for the cost center attributed to the production of that center for the period. Obviously, the starting point in the establishment of a standard cost system should be the determination of standards. The following discussion describes commonly followed approaches in establishing and using standards.

Types of Standards. Standard costs are predetermined unit costs for each product produced. In determining standard costs, a company calculates the amount and cost of direct materials, direct labor, and overhead required to produce each unit of product by a predetermined process within a specific facility. Once a standard cost system is operating, management accumulates actual costs by product and compares the actual costs with standards to determine where costs are running high or low (variances). This system stresses costs that are out of line and permits analysis to locate and deal with trouble spots. Two basic approaches to establishing standards are:

1. To establish estimates based on historical costs under favorable conditions (estimated standards), or
2. To have industrial engineers determine what the various cost elements should be (engineered standards).

A company establishing a standard cost system should first consider the practicability of measurement against estimated and engineered standards. In a job shop, for instance, estimates are more practical than engineered standards, because the production of a specific product typically involves a single run. Because an engineer would find it difficult to set standards in this environment through time and motion studies of the physical operations, estimated standards are the most practical means of measuring actual performance. However, in an environment where there is a continuous flow of product with minimal change, industrial engineering (IE) standards would be more practicable. Where IE standards are utilized, it is not uncommon to find that the standards are changed during the course of a year to meet changing conditions, such as the introduction of new production methods, the acquisition of new machinery, or the modification of the materials used which change the amount of labor required in a particular cost center.

When standards can change during an accounting period, the following problem must be solved. How should the differences between inventory costs charged with one standard but relieved with another because a standard is changed during the interim be accounted for? The answer to this question focuses on two concepts: *budget standards* and *operating standards*. At the beginning of a year when standards are established, both the budget and the operating standards are the same. The two become different during the year when a new standard is established for operating purposes. It is impracticable for operating management to measure the effectiveness of production personnel against a standard based on a work environment that no longer exists. Because of the impact on carrying inventories, once a standard is established for accounting purposes at the beginning of a year, the budget standard is held constant until a physical inventory is taken at the end of the accounting year. In this situation, there can be two different points of measurement for determination of variances, one for accounting purposes (budget standard) and one for purposes of reporting production efficiency (operating standard). The following journal entries illustrate the use of both budget and operating standards for a given product.

(1)

Direct Labor Cost XXXX
    Payroll Payable XXXX
To record actual payroll cost based on
timekeeper's reports or time cards.

(2)

Work-in-Process Inventory XXXX
    Direct Labor Cost XXXX
To record labor transferred to work-in-process
inventory based on reported production ×
standard labor cost (budget standard) per unit of
production.

(3)

Direct Labor Efficiency Variance XXXX
    Direct Labor Cost XXXX
To record direct labor efficiency variance: (budget
standard hours × standard wage rate) − (actual
labor hours × standard wage rate).
Note: The variance can be a debit or credit,

(4)
Memo Entry

Direct Labor Methods Change Variance XXXX
    Contra-Direct Labor Methods Change
      Variance XXXX
To record the labor variance caused by methods
changes: (budget standard hours − operating
standard hours) × standard wage rate.
Note: The variance can be a debit or credit.

This set of entries would normally be prepared on a monthly basis to reflect the results of the total activities within each department.

Memo entry (4) allows the accounting department to prepare labor efficiency reports for the production department, reflecting the labor efficiency variance stated in dollars resulting from the most recent standard established. This approach can be illustrated in the following example:

XYZ Company establishes a standard labor cost of $10 per unit at the beginning of the year (budget standard). Two months later, methods changes reduce the amount of labor required for each unit, resulting in a new standard cost of $8 per unit (operating standard). At the end of the second month, actual labor costs are computed at $12 per unit. Because the budget standard cost per unit must be held constant for financial accounting purposes unless a physical inventory is taken, journal entries (2) and (3) above will be based on $10 per unit. However, from the production department's point of view, the actual variance (and base of measuring production personnel) is the difference between the most recent standard established ($8 per unit) and the actual cost per unit of $12.

Setup Time. Often, machinery and support equipment must be adjusted before a particular operation or job can be started. The time involved in getting the equipment ready for production is usually traceable to a specific operation or job; however, the cost in preparing for operations is typically not related to the quantity of product to be produced. A question typically raised is whether the setup costs should be treated as direct or as part of the overhead factor. In situations where the production runs fluctuate widely in units produced, the impact of the setup cost can be more significant than the actual direct labor production time. The cost per unit of product can vary solely because of the length of the production run, rather than the efficiency of production personnel. In many standard cost systems, standard lot sizes are determined in computing the standard product cost. The standard cost buildup is often figured containing a standard cost setup factor for each operation and cost center. A drawback of this practice for cost control purposes is that it mixes two different labor elements, each subject to different causes and cost controls. Where this practice is followed, setup costs should be identified within both the standard and the actual labor cost accumulations, so that measurement of labor efficiency can be made independently for the productive and setup labor elements.

Spoiled Work (Scrap). The control and reporting of spoilage are important aspects of any cost system in manufacturing. The initial point of control rests with the inspector, who should, when rejecting a particular job, write the number of the last operation completed on the scrap report. The inspector's report serves the following two functions for management: (1) a point of reference for determining the cause of the spoilage (use of defective materials, machine problems, operator errors, etc.); (2) relieve the cost of the product accumulated through the point it is scrapped from the work-in-process inventory and charge the spoiled work inventory with the appropriate dollar accumulation. At the end of the month, the inspector's report can be costed to relieve the work-in-process inventory, and the following journal entry can be prepared:

```
Spoiled Inventory ...................  XXXX
        Work-in-Process Inventory .......          XXXX
To record cost of spoiled work per
inspector's report.
```

This entry is calculated by multiplying the standard cost of the product up to the last operation before scrapping by the number of units scrapped.

Recording Direct Labor Costs in a Standard Cost System.   After labor costs in a standard cost system are accumulated, the labor distribution is prepared from the actual time tickets accumulated and the payroll liability is recorded. However, only the standard direct labor cost is charged to the work-in-process inventory account or accounts. The difference between the actual direct labor cost and the standard direct labor cost remains in the labor variance accounts (efficiency or time and wage rate variances). An example of the labor journal entries to be recorded under a standard cost system is as follows:

```
                          (1)
Direct Labor Cost ...............................  XXXX
Indirect Labor Cost ............................  XXXX
        Payroll Payable ...............................          XXXX
To record actual payroll cost based on timekeeper's
reports or time cards.

                          (2)
Work-in-Process Inventory ......................  XXXX
        Direct Labor Cost ...........................          XXXX
To record labor transferred into work-in-process
inventory based on reported production × standard
labor cost per unit of production.

                          (3)
Direct Labor Rate Variance ......................  XXXX
        Direct Labor Cost ...........................          XXXX
To record direct labor rate variance: (actual hours ×
actual rate) − (actual hours × standard rate).

Direct Labor Efficiency Variance ..................  XXXX
        Direct Labor Cost ...........................          XXXX
To record direct labor performance variance: (actual
hours × standard wage rate) − (standard labor hours
× standard wage rate).
Note: The variance can be a debit or credit,
depending on the computations.
```

More sophisticated standard cost systems often have the labor efficiency variance further detailed in the accounts or management reports, to reflect those elements creating the variance, such as off-line operations, malfunctioning machines, and material shortages.

WAGE INCENTIVE SYSTEMS

Organizations have had differing degrees of success with wage incentive and bonus payment plans. Because selection or design of an appropriate system involves many factors, it should not be undertaken casually by inexperienced personnel. Traditionally, wage rates or base compensation amounts have been established according to the general qualifications, skills, and experience an individual brings to a defined job. Although the definition usually covers responsibilities and assigned tasks, output volumes and performance quality may be stated only subjectively, if at all, in nonincentive applications.

Incentive plans have been developed because of management desires for greater productivity and higher quality, and because of employee desires for greater pay. The successful, or good, incentive plan will be one that both management and employees like and understand. Employees will want:

- Extra pay for extra effort, in direct proportion to that effort
- High minimum guarantees and job security
- Prompt individual payments, easily calculated in advance

Management will want:

- High production levels, with the best producers paid the most
- Easily verified and simple production and payment records

Incentive payments, and therefore one component of labor costs, will be determined by the type of incentive plan in use and the actual units (goods or services) produced compared to the expected units of production. Note that incentive systems require management to establish standard or target levels of production volumes and quality criteria. These standards may be established by different techniques, ranging from less accurate but simple estimates to more accurate and sophisticated industrial engineering studies.

For accounting purposes, incentive plans can be described in five major groups:

1. Piecework or unit rate plans
2. One hundred-percent participation plans
3. Sharing plans
4. Step-rate plans
5. Bonus plans

Straight piecework plans pay an agreed number of minutes or hours or dollars for every piece or item produced. It is a simple and common incentive plan, with various modifications added in the event of inflationary spirals or other contractual adjustments that erode the relationships between time and money. With straight piecework plans the labor portion of product or service costs is highly predictable.

One hundred-percent participation plans vary in name, but consistently begin with standards expressed in earned hours per unit and end with payment calculated at earned hours multiplied by the individual's wage rate. For example, an individual who produces at 25 percent more than normal earns 125 percent of the base wage rate (for a 25 percent bonus). This plan is similar to straight piecework plans, but avoids the recalculations required with general wage increases and some of the problems associated with different wage rates.

Sharing plans provide that employees producing at a rate greater than the agreed standard (usually defined as 100 percent) share with management in the amount in excess of standard. If the plan is defined as a 50–50 plan, for example, the employee producing at 25 percent more than normal earns $12\frac{1}{2}$ percent bonus in addition to the base wage rate. This type of plan is less appealing to hourly employees for obvious reasons, even though management may claim that such a program costs money to maintain and that therefore some of the savings should be reserved for administering the plan.

Step-rate plans simplify pay computations and help meet employee requests for better continuity of incentive earnings. In these plans, the typical employee starts at a hiring rate for the job and progresses on promotion by merit through several rate levels. The employee may be expected to produce at up to 100 percent of standard to earn the rate at the first step. Depending on the number of steps in the plan, an employee may earn, for example, 10 percent extra each pay period at step 2 for continued productivity in the range of 100 to 115 percent of standard. Stepwise promotion criteria can also include quality and other measures, but are established primarily on the basis of productivity percentages better than standard or normal.

There are many other enhancement or bonus plans in industry, often including supervisory and management personnel. These plans may be on an individual or a group basis, but are characterized by lump-sum payments made at periodic intervals (sometimes at each pay period, but sometimes at longer intervals) after calculating productivity or even subjective results of performance. Such plans make it more difficult to allocate labor costs to the proper product or service unit.

Other considerations in accounting for labor costs in an organization using wage incentive systems should not be overlooked. Some plans provide for extra wage payments to employees on the basis of improved machine or process efficiencies (particularly in capital-intensive companies) or improved materials yields (when materials and ingredients are a high percentage of total costs). In these cases, higher labor productivity results in increased labor costs, and decreased capital or materials costs, for each unit produced. Other incentive plans provide base guarantees of 100-percent payment for lower productivity (with increased unit labor costs) or ceilings on incentive payments for exceptionally high productivity.

Another consideration in accounting for labor costs in an organization using an incentive plan is the handling of training costs for employees, both in classrooms and on the job. Learning curves, whether for an individual or a group, have important application in planning and controlling labor costs. Although the rate at which an individual learns a new job is highly dependent on several factors (instruction techniques, individual qualifications, job design and methods, tooling and equipment, cycle times, etc.), the expected time for average people to progress from a beginner level to a trained level can be determined for typical jobs with learning curves. Often, an 80-percent curve is used, which means that every time the quantity of production doubles, the direct labor allowance per unit reduces to 80 percent for all units. If the first 10 units require 1 labor hour each to produce at the start of production or with a new employee, then the first 20 units (the first 10 plus the second 10) will require eight-tenths of a labor hour each. With new employees and with new products or services, labor costs per unit volume begin high and decrease to a steady level as learning is completed.

LABOR CONSIDERATIONS IN THE BUDGETING PROCESS

The budget is management's tool for controlling and coordinating a firm's resources. It states in accounting terms management's goals regarding mix of product outputs, capital expenditures, product cost, product sales and, above all, profit.

In virtually all lines of business, labor costs represent a significant portion of total production cost and are, therefore, of great concern in developing a budget. The budget provides management with a tool for controlling and evaluating the effectiveness and efficiency with which labor is deployed.

Treatment of Labor in Fixed Budgeting.   Fixed (or static) budgeting implies the establishment of an activity level (labor required) for a given level of operations. This process requires identification of a target level of production output. Management can extract the budget for labor from the target by estimating the amount of labor required to produce a unit of output and the expected labor wage rate. When actual labor costs are obtained, they can be compared to the labor cost estimates used in the budget. Differences and the reasons for them can be analyzed. A simple example serves to demonstrate this process.

Disregard material costs and assume that the following estimates for labor costs have been determined:

Estimated labor rate	$5.00/hour
Estimated labor usage	2 hours/unit of output

Clearly, to produce 10,000 units of output should require 20,000 labor hours with a total labor cost of $100,000.

Further, assume the following actual results from operations:

Units produced	10,000 units
Labor hours used	21,000 hours
Total labor cost	$107,000

The labor wage rate implied in these data is $5.10 per hour. The excess of actual cost over budget is caused both by the higher-than-estimated wage rate and by higher-than-estimated labor usage. The amount attributable to each can be determined by computing the following variances.

Wage rate variance:

$$(\text{Actual Rate} - \text{Estimated Rate}) \times \text{Actual Hours} = \text{Variance}$$
$$(\$5.10/\text{hour} - \$5.00/\text{hour}) \times 21{,}000 \text{ hours} = \$2{,}100$$

Labor efficiency variance:

$$(\text{Actual Hours} - \text{Estimated Hours}) \times \text{Standard Rate} = \text{Variance}$$
$$(21{,}000 \text{ hours} - 20{,}000 \text{ hours}) \times \$5.00/\text{hour} = \$5{,}000$$

With these variances in hand, management can assign responsibility for the variances from budget. Furthermore, a variance can be analyzed to determine whether it resulted from inefficiencies, one-time unusual occurrences, or faulty estimates, and the appropriate action taken.

Treatment of Labor in Flexible Budgeting.   Flexible budgeting provides a method for comparing actual costs for any given activity level to budgets for those same activity levels.

Such a system of comparison works well for labor that is directly involved in the production process but not for labor employed in service and support activities. For instance, how can expenditures for janitorial services or repair and maintenance workers be controlled? It is unlikely that usage of these services will vary in direct proportion to output.

A simple approach is to set a target level of output and determine the amount of indirect labor that will be needed to produce that output. After the budget period is ended, actual expenditures can be compared to budget. This technique is known as a *fixed* or *static* budget (discussed in the previous section). But suppose that the target output is not reached? Can we compare expenditures that *should* have been made at one level of output with those that actually *were* made at a different level of output? Imagine the following situation:

	Actual	Budget	Variance
Units produced	9,000	10,000	1,000 (U)
Indirect labor	$2,100	$2,500	$400 (F)

Even though production goals were not met, there appears to be a favorable variance for indirect labor. But less indirect labor should have been used to produce the smaller output. A method is needed to determine how much less should be used to evaluate the efficiency of indirect labor personnel.

Flexible budgeting provides a solution to the problem. Under flexible budgeting, a formula is developed for the target amount of indirect labor that should be used for a given range of outputs. For instance, the target may be $1 of indirect labor for each 2 hours of direct labor. Indirect labor can also be based on machine hours or any other activity measure that is related to the cost of service and support functions. An estimate of indirect labor costs can then be made and the actual cost of overhead items, such as indirect labor hours, judged in relation to this estimate.

An obvious problem with flexible budgeting is that indirect manufacturing costs may not vary directly with activity measures, such as direct labor hours or machine hours. It is likely that an activity measure such as direct labor hours could be doubled without a commensurate increase in indirect labor costs. An alternative is to develop a variation factor that expresses the response of semivariable costs, such as indirect labor to changes in activity. This technique requires that a budget be prepared for some target level of output and indirect costs budgeted for that level. Then for each cost classification, an index number of 0 to 100 is assigned. An index of 0 implies that the costs would not vary at all with changes in output. As a fixed cost, it is not the responsibility of any individual department and is not included in setting operating budget goals. A factor of 100 implies that the cost varies in direct proportion with output and can be handled as part of direct labor. Only those costs with factors 1 through 99 vary with output, but in less than direct proportion. The factor is applied in the following way:

1. Determine indirect labor costs at the target volume. (Assume that these costs are $750 for a planned direct labor expenditure of $3,000.)
2. Determine how much direct labor actual activity differs from the targeted level. (Assume that an additional $1,000 of direct labor will be used.)
3. Identify a variation factor for indirect labor by answering the question, how much will indirect labor costs change (percentage variation) for every $1 change in direct labor costs. (Assume it to be .80.)
4. Compute the budgeted amount of indirect labor using the formula:

$$\frac{\text{Indirect Labor}}{\text{Direct Labor}} \times \text{Difference from Target Activity} \times \text{Variation Factor}$$

$$= \frac{\$750}{\$3,000} \times \$1,000 \times .80$$
$$= \$200$$

The result of these calculations is the additional amount of indirect labor cost that should be budgeted as a result of the increased use of direct labor. The indirect labor budget should be $950 for a direct labor budget of $4,000. It should be noted that estimated hours and estimated rates should be used in determining the direct labor budget. If actual direct labor costs are used, the indirect labor budget will be increased by exceeding target amounts and diminished as a result of beating the target. Such a result is not desirable.

Treatment of Labor in Zero-Base Budgeting. Another budgeting technique gaining increasing acceptance is known as *zero-base budgeting*. Under this technique costs are defined as discretionary or nondiscretionary. Such costs as direct labor are considered nondiscretionary because they are determined largely by the state of technology. Management cannot significantly alter the amount of labor required to produce a given amount of output. For these costs, preparation of the budget is largely a computational process.

Zero-base budgeting has its primary impact on the discretionary costs, such as wages for maintenance and repair personnel, supervisory personnel, and other indirect labor. For those departments that employ indirect labor, department managers first define alternative ways of performing the department's function and choose the best method. Next, the operating manager defines various levels of activity for performing the function and the cost of each additional level. These include a base level of activity, below which it would be inadvisable to continue the function, and any number of additional levels up to and exceeding the current level of activity. When these "decision packages" are prepared, they are accumulated, and the various activity levels are ranked in priority. A cutoff point on this listing is then defined, and all activity level packages above the cutoff receive a budget allotment. A possible result of this process might be that an additional activity level would be added to production planning (i.e., an additional person), reducing the current activity level in materials handling (because of more economical scheduling of production runs). This technique allows management to evaluate discretionary costs, such as indirect labor, as packages of activities instead of dollar value allotments.

Explanation of Differences from Budget. Regardless of how the budget for labor items is determined, variances from the budget should be computed and analyzed for control purposes. For direct labor, both wage rate and efficiency variances are computed.

Typical factors causing wage rate variances include:

1. A wrong or unrealistic wage rate estimate
2. Unanticipated overtime required to complete work
3. A more expensive grade of labor required than in the estimate

Efficiency variances generally occur more frequently than wage rate variances. Following are some common factors that cause a labor efficiency variance:

1. Stated labor effort per unit of output may be deliberately set low or high.
2. Poor scheduling or shortages of materials may cause delays and idle time.
3. Machine breakdowns may lose time.
4. Inexperienced or apprentice labor may need longer learning time.
5. Defective or below-standard quality material may result in abnormal lost time spent on spoiled parts.
6. A greater number of workers may be involved in a process than anticipated in the budget.

Whatever the causes of the variance, they should be calculated and explained on a timely basis.

TYPES OF LABOR REPORTS

The primary objective of an accounting system is to generate information in a format that is useful. Although labor cost information, which is usually a significant portion of a product's or cost center's total cost, is important to many groups, two user groups predominate: external, such as unions and government agencies, and internal, from the shop foreman to the company president.

Internal Reports. Internal reports provide the information on which the firm depends to control the operation, as well as to base important forecasting and planning strategy decisions. The decisions range from day-to-day choices, such as production scheduling, to long-range planning, in which only the top management of the company is involved. Because of the diversity of user groups; the reports present information in various ways. The simplest is probably the informational report, although it can vary greatly in scope and content. Exhibit 15 is an example of an informational report. It conveys information about labor hours

EXHIBIT 15   Labor Information Report

Date _____

Shift _____

DAILY PROCESSING SUMMARY

Plant _____

Production data	Product A	Product B	Product C	Product D	Product E	Product F	TOTAL
MACHINE #1							
Total tons produced							
Machine hours:	xxxxxx	xxxxxx	xxxxxx	xxxxxx	xxxxxx	xxxxxx	
Down							
Run							
Scheduled							
Machine efficiency							
Labor hours:	xxxxxx	xxxxxx	xxxxxx	xxxxxx	xxxxxx	xxxxxx	
Nonproductive							
Productive							
Actual labor hours/ton							
Standard labor hours/ton							
Standard labor hours							
Percent efficiency							
MACHINE #2							
Total tons produced							
Machine hours:	xxxxxx	xxxxxx	xxxxxx	xxxxxx	xxxxxx	xxxxxx	
Down							
Run							
Scheduled							
Machine efficiency							
Labor hours:	xxxxxx	xxxxxx	xxxxxx	xxxxxx	xxxxxx	xxxxxx	
Nonproductive							
Productive							
Actual labor hours/ton							
Standard labor hours/ton							
Standard labor hours							
Percent efficiency							
MACHINE #3							
Total tons produced							
Machine hours:	xxxxxx	xxxxxx	xxxxxx	xxxxxx	xxxxxx	xxxxxx	
Down							
Run							
Scheduled							
Machine efficiency							
Labor hours:	xxxxxx	xxxxxx	xxxxxx	xxxxxx	xxxxxx	xxxxxx	
Nonproductive							
Productive							
Actual labor hours/ton							
Standard labor hours/ton							
Standard labor hours							
Percent efficiency							

used in the production of several products on each of three machines. Comparative data or interpretive comments are not emphasized. Because this report is intended primarily for the foreman supervising these machines, it presents only the information relevant to the decisions at the foreman level. The report is issued at the end of each shift, so that the foreman may alter the next day's work assignments and avoid unfavorable work conditions.

Although foremen control daily work assignments, a production scheduling department usually handles longer-term scheduling of production runs. Because the decisions made in production scheduling are different from those made by foremen, the timing and content of the information that production schedulers receive are also different. An exception report may be most useful in this instance. As the name implies, exception reports are issued only when actual results deviate from some predefined goal by a certain amount. For instance, production scheduling may be informed of production delays only if a department falls behind scheduled production activity by more than one full day. It may be that delays of less than one day can be made up without serious consequences. For delays longer than one day, the scheduling department may be forced to consider rescheduling.

EXHIBIT 16   Illustrative Labor Report for Middle Management

COMPANY NAME

WEEKLY COST CENTER LABOR VARIANCE REPORT

BY PRODUCT AND COST CENTER

Plant _____

| | DIRECT LABOR | | | | | | | |
| | Labor hours | | | Dollars | | | | |
PRODUCT/COST CENTER	Actual	Std.	Var.	Actual	Std.	Total var.	Effic.	Rate
Product A								
Raw material receiving and storage								
Processing dept.								
Packaging dept.								
Total Product A								
Tons produced								
Per ton								
Shipping and warehouse								
Tons shipped								
Per ton								
Product B								
Raw material receiving and storage								
Processing dept.								
Packaging dept.								
Total Product B								
Tons produced								
Per ton								
Shipping and warehouse								
Tons shipped								
Per ton								

Because no report is issued unless there are serious problems, the timing of the report is coordinated with the decisions. The report presents only the specific problem areas that require attention. Departments that are operating within one day of schedule are not mentioned in the report.

Labor reporting to managerial levels higher than the production foreman in the organization requires still different timing and report content. Exhibit 16 shows a weekly cost report, relating information to product costs. It accumulates more detailed informational reports and relates the cost of a number of activities to units of output. The report is stated in both dollars and labor hours to avoid changes resulting from fluctuations in the value of the dollar. Intended for plant management, this information emphasizes managerial control by the actual versus standard comparisons. When coupled with selling price information, it is useful for an analysis of product-line profitability. This information is needed by those levels of management responsible for overall product profitability. Such a report may also provide the impetus to search for new, labor-saving machinery or methods to hold down labor costs.

External Reports.   Many labor reports are required by external organizations, most notably government agencies. Some of the better-known reports deal with FICA taxes withheld by employers, determination of workmen's compensation benefits, payment of head taxes on employees, etc.

Unions also use external reports. In almost all unionized companies, union dues are withheld from wages and remitted to the union at regular intervals. A report showing at least the name of the employee, the social security number, and the amount of dues withheld is prepared periodically for the union. In addition, pension plan administrators and pension plan participants receive periodic notification of benefits accrued, allocation of benefits among the participants, employee contributions, and employer contributions to the plans.

The major distinction between internal and external reports is the intended use. In most cases, internal reports are generated to provide input for making operating or planning decisions. Even the simple informational report issued to department foremen is clearly intended to influence future decisions on work arrangements. However, most reports to government and unions are not immediately used for decision making.

BIBLIOGRAPHY

Dearden, John: *Cost and Budget Analysis,* Prentice-Hall, Englewood Cliffs, N.J., 1962.

Gillespie, Cecil: *Cost Accounting and Control,* Prentice-Hall, Englewood Cliffs, N.J., 1957.

Matz, Adolph, Othel J. Curry, and George W. Frank: *Cost Accounting,* South-Western Publishing Co., Cincinnati, 1962.

Maynard, H. B., ed.: *Industrial Engineering Handbook,* 3rd ed., McGraw-Hill Book Company, New York, 1971.

Neuschel, Richard F.: *Management Systems for Profit and Growth,* McGraw-Hill Book Company, New York, 1976.

Reitell, Charles, and Gould L. Harris: *Cost Accounting,* International Textbook Co., Scranton, Pa., 1948.

Willoughby, Theodore C., and James A. Senn: *Business Systems,* Association for Systems Management, Cleveland, 1975.

Chapter **10**

Overhead Accumulation and Distribution

JOHN D. LEWIS
Partner, Arthur Andersen & Co.

INTRODUCTION

Preceding chapters have treated the direct material and direct labor cost groups in a manufacturing operation. This chapter describes various methods used in practice for accumulating and distributing the third and final cost group.

Overhead is becoming an increasingly large portion of total manufacturing cost in today's environment as a result of several influences. The continuing expansion of technology in many industries has resulted in increased automation. Increased automation generally reduces direct labor costs and increases an enterprise's investment in productive equipment and in supervisory personnel necessary for the efficient use of this equipment. Energy costs have expanded dramatically in recent years, and there are few industries where these increases have not had a significant effect on overhead costs. The requirements of the Occupational Safety and Health Act (OSHA) and other governmental regulations have also contributed significantly to increased overhead.

The measurement and control of overhead costs have traditionally received the least attention among the three basic cost groups. The changing business environment warrants much greater focus on this cost group and the development of new methods and systems to monitor these costs and to respond quickly to changes. New corporate financial statement disclosure requirements and income tax regulations are also imposing increased data needs on costing systems, including the overhead component. Many progressive companies are modifying their costing systems to provide greater responsiveness, and some of these new practices are described here, together with the more traditional approaches.

COMPOSITION OF OVERHEAD

Stated simply, overhead in a classical cost accounting sense includes all of those manufacturing or production costs that have not been classified by the business unit as direct material or direct labor. More specifically, the overhead cost group relates to indirect manufacturing costs that cannot be identified in a practical manner with specific units of production and, therefore, cannot be included in specific product cost as direct material or direct labor. Other common labels for the overhead cost group include *burden, production overhead, manufacturing overhead,* and (less precisely) *factory expense.* What the cost group is called is not important. Understanding its composition and relationship to the production process, how it behaves under differing conditions, and its effect on end product cost is important.

The three common and conventional classifications within the manufacturing overhead cost group are indirect materials, indirect labor, and other indirect manufacturing costs. The criteria for distinguishing between direct and indirect costs must necessarily depend on the particular business unit and its needs. The various alternatives available in practice are discussed later.

The distinction between manufacturing overhead and general business overhead is also important. Managers often intend the term "overhead" to encompass both categories, because both are certainly important costs of doing business and must be taken into account in making informed business decisions. General business overhead includes marketing, selling, and distribution costs as well as general and administrative expenses. Such costs are, however, generally not accommodated within the boundaries of a product costing system for several reasons, some of which may not be valid for a particular business unit.

The prime reasons for excluding general business overhead from the scope of a cost accounting system are certain conventions regarding the periodic valuation of inventories. Cost accounting system objectives with regard to treatment of overhead for product sales pricing and for inventory valuation are usually not compatible. The traditional solution is to include overhead in product costs to the point of acceptability for inventory valuation and no further. It is possible, however, to accommodate both the inventory and the pricing objectives by simply indicating total inventoriable costs in cost buildup records and continuing the cost determination to incorporate all other costs to be recovered in setting selling prices.

This technique can logically be extended to accommodate differing overhead inclusion objectives for financial statement and income tax valuation of inventories and to deal with some of the inadequacies of present accounting methods in an inflationary environment. The technique will be characterized in the remainder of this chapter as multistep overhead costing, and it is illustrated in Exhibit 1.

EXHIBIT 1   Illustration of Product Cost Determination Using Multistep Overhead Costing Technique

PRODUCT COST SHEET	Unit	Product No: 1234				Possible use of
Cost elements	Each	V	F	T	Cum.	cumulative total
Direct materials		4.00	–	4.00		
Direct labor		2.00	–	2.00		
Manufacturing overhead						
Group I		1.00	.75	1.75	7.75	Book valuation of inventories
Group II		.90	.60	1.50	9.25	Tax valuation of inventories
Group III		.25	.50	.75	10.00	Total manufacturing cost
General business overhead						
Direct		.80	.20	1.00		
Indirect		.20	1.50	1.70		
Inflation adjustments						
Replacement depreciation		–	.50	.50		
Other		.20	.30	.50		
Total product cost		9.35	4.35	13.70		Total product cost recovery
V = Variable F = Fixed		T = Total		Cum. = Cumulative		

OVERHEAD CLASSIFICATIONS

Overhead is segregated in numerous ways depending on the size and complexity of the business unit, the type of industry, and the degree of management control required. As indicated earlier, precisely what costs are included as part of overhead and at what point they are included in the buildup of product overhead cost also varies. Some businesses treat certain material or labor costs as indirect costs for inclusion in overhead, whereas others include the costs as direct costs.

In whatever manner overhead costs are treated by a particular business unit, the conventional costs can be conveniently examined here in three basic categories:

1. Indirect material costs
2. Indirect labor costs
3. Indirect manufacturing costs

As discussed earlier, certain businesses use multistep overhead costing to improve visibility of other overhead costs or to assist in the determination of inventoriable and other costs on different bases. The costs and special determinations can be broadly grouped as follows:

- Marketing, selling, and distribution costs
- General and administrative costs
- Depreciation on replacement-cost basis
- Other current cost determinations

Some businesses include research and product development costs in the indirect manufacturing costs category for product cost and inventory determination. Others consistently exclude these and other indirect manufacturing costs (such as depreciation, factory administrative costs, etc.) for product costing and inventory valuation purposes. The compensating factor in either case is naturally the business' policy regarding "markup" from product unit cost, however it is determined, to arrive at target unit selling price.

The section that follows deals with each of the three conventional overhead cost categories:

Indirect Materials.   Indirect material is material that is not used directly in or incorporated into the item or group of items being produced. It also includes all tangible materials used in the manufacturing process that have not been treated as direct materials due to an inability to identify the materials with specific units of production, or an inability to do so in a practical manner. Examples of indirect material costs are:

- Operating supplies—lubricating oils, detergents, abrasives, polishing, buffing, welding materials, paint, and low-cost direct materials such as fasteners, screws, washers, nuts, bolts, dyes, and starches.
- Nondurable tools—small portable standard tools, dies, jigs, fixtures, and gauges that have a comparatively short effective life and are consumed in current operations; where such costs are significant they would be capitalized and amortized to production on basis of elapsed time or units produced.
- Repairs and maintenance supplies—gears, machine belts, pulleys, screws, washers, nuts, bolts, and paint used in repairing and maintaining machinery, equipment, and facilities. Major maintenance projects would typically be performed under a project authorization and cost accumulation system.
- Safety and OSHA supplies—protective work clothing, masks, hearing loss prevention supplies, etc.
- Other supplies—janitorial supplies and materials, light bulbs, cleaning rags, and other less significant indirect materials.

Indirect Labor.   Similarly, indirect labor represents the cost of labor that cannot be related directly to or identified with specific units of production in a practical manner. This would include all labor used in the manufacturing process that has not been handled as direct labor in the cost accounting system. The various classifications that can be used are as follows:

- Supervision—the salaries of operating officers, managers, and supervisors clearly associated with production.
- Working supervisors—the wages of all section leaders and other factory personnel below the rank of foreman who are engaged in part-time supervisory activities. Time spent on direct production would be charged to direct labor.
- Material handling—the wages of personnel involved in receiving (sometimes segregated as material overhead), handling, and moving materials within and between departments.
- Setup—The labor cost of setting up production machines to work on a specific product item, whether performed by a regular setup worker, an operator, or some other worker. The time could be included in relation to the time taken to manufacture the product item or where the machine operator always sets up the machine.
- Inspection—the labor cost of inspection or quality-control work performed by inspectors not assigned to specific production departments. Inspection time would usually be included in direct labor cost where inspection is performed by department floor inspectors or by an inspection department through which production is routed as part of standard operations.
- Repairs and maintenance—the labor cost of repairing and maintaining machinery, equipment, tools, jigs, fixtures, gauges, and dies. Major maintenance

projects would typically be performed under a project authorization and cost accumulation system.

■ Moving and rearranging—the labor costs of routine moving of machinery and equipment and rearranging departments.

■ Technical and clerical—salaries and wages of personnel not directly supervising production but nevertheless associated with production by performing ancillary tasks or services such as production scheduling, production reporting, timekeeping, and engineering.

■ Other indirect labor—all indirect labor not specifically provided for by other accounts including, for example, janitors, security personnel, safety inspectors, first aid, inventory counters, tool crib attendants, and supplies stores personnel.

There are certain other labor costs that are usually segregated from other indirect labor costs for control purposes, as follows:

■ Overtime premium—the premium portion of overtime costs incurred, usually on both direct and indirect wages. When this account is used, descriptions of all other accounts would be revised to include the words "straight-time costs."

■ Shift differential—the premium paid to induce personnel to work night shifts, usually on both direct and indirect wages.

■ Fringe benefits—FICA taxes, unemployment taxes, group life and health insurance premiums, workmen's compensation, wage continuation, vacation and holiday pay, sick leave pay, and retirement plan contributions. Alternatively, fringe benefits are often "loaded" into the basic labor distribution rates and amounts and the actual fringe benefits are charged against the credit that arises from such treatment.

The final group of indirect labor costs represents what might be viewed as unproductive time of both direct and indirect workers. Under some costing systems and to the extent associated with direct laborers, these costs might appear as direct labor variances rather than being distributed to indirect manufacturing overhead. These costs are as follows:

■ Idle time—labor cost of workers who are temporarily idled by machine breakdown, material shortage, insufficient work, injury, or other reasons.

■ Employee allowances—time spent by direct and indirect workers engaged in company-sponsored or union meetings and events on company time.

■ Rework and salvage—time spent by direct workers repairing, reworking, and salvaging off-quality production.

■ Extra or substitute operations—additional labor incurred in performing nonstandard or substitute operations on a product. These costs might appear as methods or substitution variances rather than in overhead accounts.

It should be noted that certain of the overhead cost elements included in the indirect labor cost group would be candidates for multistep overhead cost handling. Factory administrative expenses, production officers' salaries, and safety and medical costs considered to be employee benefits, certain other employee benefits, and rework labor may be excluded from inventory valuation for federal income tax purposes (see page 10-22) if excluded for financial statement reporting purposes and such treatment is not inconsistent with generally accepted accounting principles. Exclusion of these costs can have a favorable cash conservation effect through minimizing current income tax expense. However, from a managerial cost accounting viewpoint, inclusion of these overhead costs in product cost determination may be desirable if full cost visibility is required. Both objectives can be met by including these costs below the inventory valuation line in product cost buildups.

Other Indirect Manufacturing Costs.   All other manufacturing costs not directly identifiable with specific units of production, and not included as indirect material or labor, would be included in this classification. Examples of other indirect manufacturing costs include the following:

- Outside services—such costs as help-wanted advertising, clerical outside service, employment agency service, vermin extermination, and towel service.
- Professional services—the costs of outside professional services required by the production facilities of the organization, such as engineering and management consulting.
- Contracted moving and rearranging—the costs of contracted services for routine moving and rearranging.
- Contracted repairs and maintenance–tools, fixtures, gauges, and dies—the cost of contracted services used for the repair of all tools, fixtures, gauges, and dies. This would include tool sharpening and other work done by outsiders on a contract basis.
- Contracted repair and maintenance–building, machinery, and equipment—the cost of contracted services used for repair and maintenance of buildings, machinery, and equipment. This would include electrical work, plumbing, servicing of machines and other work done by outsiders on a contract basis.
- Scrap or quality loss—the total cost (material, labor, and overhead) of production items scrapped due to quality or other defects where rework or salvage is not feasible or desirable. All billings or receipts from the sale of off-quality materials might be credited against these costs. If off-quality production is routinely sold to customers at reduced prices and such revenues are significant, the differential between first-quality production cost and estimated net realizable value (reduced by costs to complete, where applicable) might be charged to this account and the related sales revenues included in the revenue accounts.
- Purchase cancellation charges—the penalty cost of cancelling outstanding purchase orders with vendors.
- Rent—rentals of buildings, parking lots, machinery, and equipment used in the normal operation of the plant.
- Property taxes—all real estate and personal property taxes connected with manufacturing operations.
- Insurance—all insurance, except payroll-oriented insurance (such as group insurance and workmen's compensation insurance) connected with manufacturing operations.
- Depreciation and amortization—all depreciation and amortization on buildings, machinery, and equipment, and leasehold improvements related to manufacturing operations and determined using the depreciation method and lives used for financial reporting purposes.
- Energy costs—electricity, natural gas, fuel oil, petroleum, coal, other fuel or water used in manufacturing operations for driving equipment, for heating, drying, cooling, or washing the production item and for lighting, heating, or cooling the factory space.
- Freight-in—freight on incoming shipments that cannot be identified with direct material or indirect material. Freight-in on returned sales would be distributed to the shipping department. Freight-in on fixed assets would be capitalized with the assets.
- Freight-out—freight and expense on outgoing shipments if not classified as a sales deduction or a selling and distribution expense. One or the other of the latter two treatments is more common.
- Other transportation—the cost of hauling material and other manufacturing operation items between company plants.
- Travel and entertainment—the cost of reimbursing manufacturing employees for travel and entertainment costs incurred on company business.
- Other—there are numerous other potential indirect overhead expense classifications, which may be combined or segregated depending on the degree of visibility warranted for control purposes.

Again, it should be noted that multistep overhead costing may be useful with respect to certain of the above overhead cost elements. Certain overhead costs, such as insurance costs, may be omitted from inventory valuation for income tax purposes under conditions described earlier and in more detail on page 10-23.

The three basic overhead cost categories have now been examined. These are the costs that are traditionally included to some degree or another in a so-called full-absorption costing system.

General Business Overhead.   The less inclusive the product cost determination, the greater the "markup" margin in pricing has to be to achieve recovery of all enterprise costs and to earn a profit for its owners. If all products cause or benefit from the excluded overhead structure on a *pro rata* basis, the costs included in each product item or group can be marked up consistently to determine a minimum adequate selling price.

If, however, one product or group of products generates or requires a disproportionate amount of other overhead (marketing, selling, distribution, general and administrative expenses), uninformed pricing decisions might result by application of a uniform rate.

This business problem can be addressed in different ways. The simplest, but probably the least accurate, remedy is to weight the company's markup margin toward the product or product group believed to warrant such treatment. This approach then relieves the other products or product groups of a disproportionate share of total enterprise costs and prevents the item or items from being "priced out of the market." The mathematical determinations of overall weighting factors are sometimes based on special cost studies for that purpose or, in the more rudimentary situations, are based on the intuitive judgment of appropriate executives.

A more thorough approach is to extend the product costing system (using the multistep technique described earlier) by incorporating those elements of general business overhead believed necessary to address the business problem, if one exists. These overhead costs are then subjected to the discipline of detailed cost performance analysis and are accumulated and distributed to products like any manufacturing overhead item in the manner believed most suitable in the circumstances.

A simple example may serve to illustrate this point effectively. An apparel manufacturer produces denim jeans and pantyhose in equal dollar volumes. Denim jeans are in great demand and this product group requires minimal promotional expenditures, primarily youth magazine advertisements. Pantyhose, however, although also popular, are sold in a more competitive market and require substantial point-of-sale and television advertising expenditures. It would be misleading to allocate aggregate selling costs equally to the two product groups in establishing the minimum adequate selling prices of the respective product groups to recover enterprise costs and earn a desired profit. Rather, management should have accurate information available on the total costs associated with each of the two product groups. This calls for accumulation of these costs in a manner that enables identification with each product and requires distribution of such costs to product units in a meaningful manner.

Classification of general business overhead into direct and indirect groups where possible may provide additional insight into disproportionate cost relationships among products.

Special Cost Determinations.   In an inflationary environment, the net assets retained because of depreciation based on the historical acquisition cost of machinery and equipment do not adequately provide the necessary funds for replacement of these assets at the required time. A particular machine acquired five years ago for $100,000 may cost $150,000 to replace today. Conventional straight-line depreciation over, say, a ten-year life would state that $10,000 of capital a year is consumed in operations. The fallacies of present-day financial reporting do not necessarily have to weaken a cost accounting system as they would if a business attempts to recover only $10,000 capital consumption in this example in establishing an appropriate product selling price.

Those managers who recognize this problem of capital and profit erosion use the multistep overhead cost technique to include in product cost determinations the incremental amount necessary to state depreciation on a replacement-cost basis. Thus, an additional $5,000 depreciation would be included in the accumulation and distribution of overhead for price-setting purposes in our example. This incremental amount would be included below the inventory valuation line and would not, under today's accounting principles, be reflected in the financial accounting records.

Common arguments against incorporating replacement-cost depreciation into product costing systems include the inability of a business to set selling prices at a level adequate to recover the incremental charge, and the difficulty and cost associated with the practice. Inability to maintain the integrity of capital and earn a reasonable rate of return on invested capital is a fundamental business problem. It would seem that the more information available to managers when setting sales prices and the more focus on this problem, the better off a company and its owners would be. Ignoring the issue of inability to recover automatically the additional cost can only perpetuate the problem.

With regard to the difficulty and cost associated with incorporating replacement-cost depreciation into product costing systems, two points are relevant. First, a business may not be able to afford to ignore the problem. Second, the Securities and Exchange Commission requires (Accounting Series Release No. 190) the disclosure by certain public companies of the replacement cost of their productive capacity and the related depreciation. The not inconsiderable expense of determining replacement costs may be incurred anyway, and taking maximum advantage of the resulting information seems desirable.

Another special cost determination required by the Securities and Exchange Commission in the same release has various ramifications for the accumulation and distribution of overhead in product costing systems. Briefly, supplemental disclosures are required with regard to cost of goods sold stated on the basis of current costs in effect at the time of the sale. This requires duplicate costing of goods sold—once in the financial records using accounting policies and methods in effect, and again on a basis adjusted for subsequent cost changes. The necessary modifications for the overhead cost element are particularly difficult and should certainly be considered by companies presently designing or redesigning product costing systems.

OVERHEAD BEHAVIOR CHARACTERISTICS

Each of the categories of indirect material, indirect labor, and other indirect manufacturing costs can be further subdivided according to the extent that the costs in each category vary with production. The subdivisions used are
1. Fixed costs
2. Variable costs
3. Semivariable costs

Fixed Costs.   Fixed overhead costs are costs that are not affected by changes in the volume of activity, at least within a broad range of activity. They are costs incurred to provide plant capability for anticipated business volume and are sometimes referred to as "capacity costs," "standby costs," "constant costs," or "period costs." Included in the fixed cost category would be certain supervisory salaries, depreciation, real estate taxes, insurance, and basic maintenance.

EXHIBIT 2   Scatter Chart: Fixed Costs

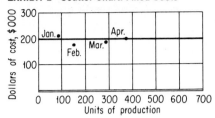

Exhibit 2 illustrates a scatter chart of fixed costs. Units of production are shown along the horizontal line, and the dots indicate the fixed costs incurred at various levels of production. As can be seen, the monthly fixed costs remain fixed around the $200,000 level independent of the level of production.

Variable Costs.   Variable overhead costs are costs that fluctuate directly with a change in volume. Strictly variable costs will be zero if current volume is zero. Where several different products are produced so that volume cannot be easily measured by units of production, such costs can usually be related to an activity basis, such as direct labor hours or machine time.

The scatter chart for variable costs shown in Exhibit 3 illustrates how variable overhead costs increase proportionately with the number of units produced.

Direct material and direct labor generally have this direct relationship, and many manufacturing overhead costs closely follow this same pattern. An example of manufacturing overhead costs in this category would be factory operating supplies.

Semivariable Costs.   Semivariable costs are costs that vary with volume but not in direct proportion to the changes in volume. There are two main types of semivariable costs:

1. Partially fixed and partially variable costs—Partially fixed and partially variable costs are actually a combination of fixed costs and variable costs. One can see from Exhibit 4 that at zero units of production, the minimum cost is $200,000.

EXHIBIT 3   Scatter Chart: Variable Costs

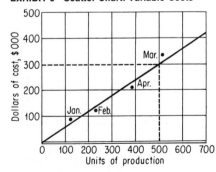

EXHIBIT 4   Scatter Chart: Partially Fixed and Partially Variable Costs

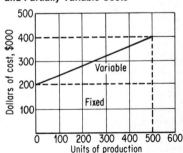

This is the fixed portion of the cost. As production increases, the cost increases in proportion to the increase in units of production. An example of this type of cost would be electricity costs, which are subject to a minimum demand charge.

2. Step-type semivariable costs (semifixed costs)—This type of cost remains constant over a narrow range of production levels. At a certain level of production, however, there is an increase in cost that then remains constant until the next step in costs is reached. This is often the case with supervisory or other indirect labor

EXHIBIT 5   Scatter Chart: Step-type Semi-variable Costs (Semifixed Costs)

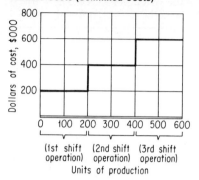

costs. For instance, Exhibit 5 shows that if one shift is operated, one group of supervisors is required; if two shifts are operated, two groups of supervisors are required; and at three shifts, three groups of supervisors are required. From this scatter chart it is apparent that the base on which items vary may not be units of production but the number of shifts worked or some other factor.

Practical Application.   Unfortunately, it is easier to define fixed, variable, and semivariable costs than to make this segregation in practice. This is primarily because most cost or expense accumulation accounts have some element of each in them.

This problem is usually approached by refining the definitions of the accumulation accounts, where appropriate, and by determining their characteristics by means of the scatter charts illustrated and other cost behavior analyses. However, judgment is usually required to make these determinations, because many costs cannot be readily classified even after thorough analysis.

The major benefit that results from segregating overhead costs according to their sensitivity to volume is the ability to perform breakeven analyses and to use flexible budgeting techniques.

Breakeven analysis is a most useful tool, particularly for profit-planning purposes. Virtually all its uses are aimed at comparing the cost-volume-profit relationship of alternatives. Such alternatives include evaluating capital spending decisions, optimization of product mix, and product pricing decisions. In each of these cases, the availability of overhead data separated into fixed and variable cost categories enables management to predict cost behavior and make decisions based on facts rather than "guesstimates."

Flexible budgeting, as contrasted with static budgeting, techniques permit comparison of actual overhead with a budget that is geared to changes in production volume. This technique, when combined with responsibility reporting, provides greater accountability for performance in that the budget remains realistic regardless of activity levels.

To summarize, overhead accumulation systems that segregate costs according to volume sensitivity provide substantial benefits. These benefits should be considered when designing product costing systems.

OVERHEAD COST ACCUMULATION

This section concentrates on the accumulation of manufacturing overhead cost data and describes the common sources of such data found in practice.

The accumulation procedure itself is basically a simple concept, which does not vary much regardless of the complexity of the particular business unit. What does vary greatly, however, is the system for the coding of transactions and events at the point of origin or entry into the accumulation system. For example, assume that management wants routinely available information regarding the cost of time spent on moving and rearranging machinery. Then the manufacturing overhead chart of accounts must provide the account name and code, which must be known by the personnel involved in the activity to accumulate and later distribute this cost item properly. If fixed and variable costs are to be accumulated separately in the overhead-reporting system, provision must be made for this in the chart of accounts. Thus, if electricity is a significant cost item, the monthly power company billing may have to be segregated into the two elements (minimum demand charge and variable portion) for separate accumulation.

In summary, it is essential that the objectives and format of the overhead control and reporting systems and the supporting coding structure be defined before deciding on the source data collection procedures. Also, the nature and complexity of the production process and departmental organization will obviously play an important part in these deliberations.

Overview.   The overhead cost accumulation overview shown in Exhibit 6 illustrates very simply how indirect manufacturing costs are accumulated, reports are generated, and the final journal entries are produced to record the absorption or recovery of manufacturing overhead and the charge to make to work-in-process inventories. Overhead costs are accumulated in established departments or cost centers through the coding structure and the normal accounting process of sorting and summarizing transactions. Certain of these costs may be incurred by service departments such as a steam plant, storeroom, or toolroom and periodically reallocated to user departments. Overhead costs are usually applied to work-in-process inventories through monthly journal entries that record production costed out to include the overhead elements on some predetermined basis. Once recorded in work-in-process, the costs follow the product flow throughout finished goods inventories and the sales process.

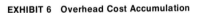

EXHIBIT 6   Overhead Cost Accumulation

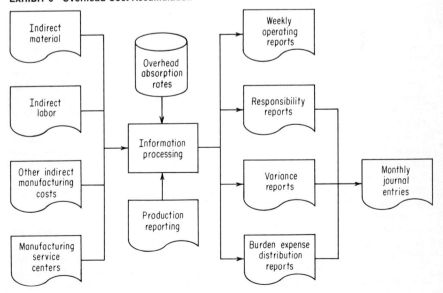

Sources of Overhead Costs.   Input to the overhead accounts varies depending on which of the various cost elements—indirect material, indirect labor, or other indirect manufacturing costs—is being handled. Where these costs relate to departments that provide manufacturing services, such as maintenance, the costs will usually be accumulated in the service center before being charged into user departments' overhead accounts. This allows service department managers and others to review service department cost performance even though such costs are ultimately allocated to operating departments.

Indirect Material Input.   When purchased, indirect materials are charged to a material stores account as inventory. When the material is drawn, a requisition is prepared to be used as the basis on which to relieve the material stores account and to charge the department requesting the material. The paperwork flow is portrayed in Exhibit 7, which shows that these requisitions are summarized periodically before being put into the accounting system in the normal way.

EXHIBIT 7   Data Flow in Overhead Accounting: Indirect Materials

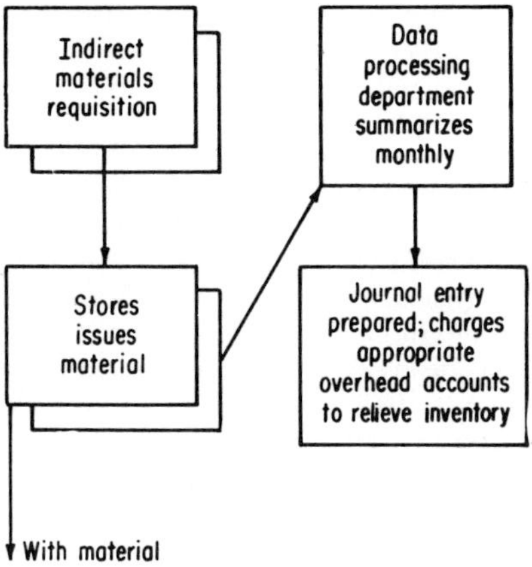

The stores' requisition tickets can be priced out in several different ways depending on volume, significance, and other considerations. In the simplest circumstance, unit prices of supply items might be determined through manual reference to vendor invoices or to a card index system. Extensions and additions would also be performed manually in this environment. At the other end of the spectrum, quantities issued and the part or item code are keypunched or entered in some other manner for data processing, and the transactions are priced through access to a master file of cost unit prices.

For less significant indirect materials or as an alternative to using the material requisition system, an enterprise may choose to charge the cost of indirect materials directly to the user departments as the materials are received through the accounts payable system. Where more than one department uses the same indirect material item or group of items, the costs could be allocated among the user departments in some equitable manner.

Indirect Labor Input.   Indirect labor costs are generally reported on labor time cards or tickets by indirect workers or direct workers performing indirect functions. Accumulation of such costs within the using departments is based on the work codes recorded on the time cards by the employees. A typical time card would show the employee name and number, hours worked, job description, and the department or work code to which the time should be charged. An example of indirect labor data flow is shown in Exhibit 8.

EXHIBIT 8   Data Flow in Overhead Accounting: Indirect Labor

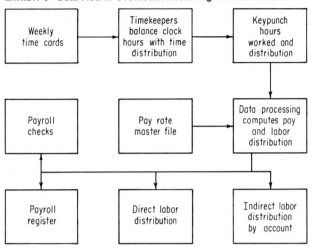

Two common problems are often experienced in accumulation of labor costs, both direct and indirect. The accurate reporting of time is largely dependent on the human element, and the indirect classifications can become "catch-alls" for nonproductive time, with resulting distortions of the overhead category. Supervision and training are usually the only effective remedies if this becomes a problem. The other common difficulty arises from discrepancies between hours paid and hours distributed, particularly when data collection of each is captured on separate input documents. The key to elimination of this problem is to balance the two categories of hours frequently and to pursue exceptions with those responsible.

The indirect labor distribution report, as illustrated in Exhibit 8, forms the basis for the charge to the user and service departments' overhead accounts for indirect labor incurred during the period by means of appropriate journal entries.

Other Indirect Overhead Input.   Purchases of items and services included in the other indirect manufacturing overhead cost group are generally charged directly to the user departments and other overhead accounts through the accounts payable system distribution. The degree of refinement in the coding structure will influence the volume of separate charges to individual overhead accounts in each department and the manner in which the data are accumulated, i.e., manually or by means of electronic data processing.

Other indirect overhead costs, such as depreciation and amortization, property taxes, and insurance, are usually charged periodically to each department and to the overhead accounts within the department on a predetermined basis using standard journal entries.

DISTRIBUTION OF OVERHEAD

The techniques to be used for distribution or allocation of manufacturing overhead to production and specific units of production can be decided upon once the particular business unit has had its cost performance characteristics evaluated, the desired basic coding (or reporting) structure is defined, and the cost accumulation procedures are available.

There are two basic approaches that can be used in assigning overhead to production. Both permit specific product cost determination but differ significantly in the degree of control management can obtain over product costs.

As with direct material and labor costs, it is possible to charge actual manufacturing overhead costs to the actual goods produced during the period. The costs for the period are summarized and are then charged in total to the inventory accounts. The total costs incurred flow through the inventory accounts and eventually to cost of sales when the products are sold. This approach provides management with minimum control over manufacturing overhead costs. Also, final product costs generally cannot be determined until some time after the end of the accounting period when actual overhead costs for the period are known. This also reduces cost reporting effectiveness and complicates current product pricing and inventory valuation.

The other basic approach for actual overhead costs in a manufacturing company is temporarily to substitute for actual overhead costs predetermined or standard costs based on overhead expense budgets and predetermined activity levels. This approach permits routine, timely, and more effective monitoring and control of performance. The trade-off is perhaps less accurate information regarding actual specific product costs, but this approach, within reasonable limits, is usually acceptable.

More specifically, predetermined or standard overhead costs are included in the unit prices used to cost out both production and the input to work-in-process inventories and to record the transfer of the product into finished goods and ultimately to cost of goods sold. When this method is used, overhead is absorbed into inventories by multiplying the actual levels of activity during the period by the predetermined overhead rates.

Standard or predetermined overhead rates are usually established by the cost accounting department in conjunction with budget and production planning departments. The rates are normally set annually and are not changed during the year. In times of rapid inflation in overhead costs, it may, however, be desirable to update the various related budgets and the rates on a more frequent basis.

A simple definition of manufacturing overhead (absorption) rates might be as follows: the ratio, percentage, or unit dollars amount obtained by dividing the total manufacturing overhead costs for a segment of a business by a measure of activity or volume level such as direct labor hours. Other activity bases could be direct labor dollars, machine hours, product units, direct materials units or dollars, or a combination of two or more.

As is the case with direct material and labor standard costing, the difference between actual costs and predetermined costs are reported as overhead variances, also sometimes referred to as under- or overabsorptions. These amounts quantify departures from plans established by management for control purposes and enable action that might not otherwise be perceived as necessary.

The factors that should be considered in establishing an overhead rate and that will be examined in this section are as follows:

- Activity indicators
- Volume assumptions
- Overhead costs

Each of these three components enters into the determination of the overhead rate in the manner shown simply in this equation:

$$\frac{\text{Overhead Costs}}{\text{Volume Assumptions} \times \text{Activity Indicator}} = \text{Overhead Rate}$$

It should be recognized that in order to select the most appropriate activity indicators and overhead rate methods, a detailed analysis must be made of the company's product lines and the manufacturing steps or processes required to produce each product. As an example, a company makes one product from purchased subassembly parts requiring high assembly labor costs and also manufactures another product from raw materials requiring significant machine processing time and little labor. It is unlikely that one method of allocating manufacturing overhead to both products would provide accurate and meaningful cost data.

Typically, either a plant-wide or departmental activity indicator will be used to develop the overhead rates. A third alternative, a product class rate, is in substance a weighted average rate used for a particular class of products as if it were a plant-wide rate. Factors to be considered relative to each are as follows:

■ Plant-wide rate—this is simple to calculate and administer in a cost system. This type of rate may be all that is necessary to provide a satisfactory product cost and give a measure of control of overhead costs. Usually, this would apply only in a one-product, one-process plant.

■ Departmental rates—these rates might result in a better indication of product costs. Practical conditions indicating that such a refinement might be appropriate are that burden is a significant element of cost, the actual rates differ significantly by department, and the various products proportionately require a different amount of time in each department. Departmental rates allow the costs of different departments to be compared accurately and will allow more accurate costing of products. It may be necessary to refine departmental rates further into cost center, operational, or machine rates where there are significant variations in machines or because of variations in products.

■ Product class rate—these are rates established for each product class unit. They take into account the different times and efforts necessary in each department, on each machine, etc., for each different product. These different costs are merged into one rate and applied to the product. This method is simple to apply because only one rate is necessary for each product, thereby reducing clerical computations. For example, when a departmental rate is used, a product may go through several departments, thus requiring several separate rate extensions to cost the product. One product class rate would provide the same cost information with only one calculation. A product class rate would be used when there are only a few variations in a few product classes. If many variables exist, this concept is difficult to apply.

■ Separate rates for material and labor—in certain situations, it may be desirable to use two burden rates, one based on labor and the other based on material. A separate material burden rate should be considered when there are some products that are principally purchased and on which little direct labor is incurred. Some products may be assembled from purchased parts or purchased complete and resold. Other products are manufactured complete, including the fabrication of all or most of the component parts. If burden were applied only to direct labor, the purchased items would not be charged with any burden even though they had to be purchased, received, inspected, handled, warehoused, and shipped.

In deciding on the best distribution methods to be used by a particular business unit, management's primary objective should be to select those that provide the most logical and accurate application of overhead costs to the products manufactured. An important secondary and often overlooked objective should be to keep the distribution methods as simple as possible. This achieves maximum understanding on the part of operating personnel held accountable for performance and minimizes clerical and data processing effort and related costs. There is a fine line between these two objectives, and too often operating personnel are heard in practice to disclaim responsibility for indirect overhead costs in their departments because they are unable to comprehend their composition and view them as theoretical absurdities.

Activity Indicators. Some of the more commonly used methods in computing an overhead rate base or activity indicator, their advantages, and guidelines for application are as follows:

▪ Direct labor hours—generally used when labor is the main productive element and significant pay rate differences preclude using direct labor dollars. Advantages: relates well with the time factor involved in many indirect costs. Disadvantages: direct labor hours are sometimes not readily available and must be compiled, and the method ignores contribution of value by factors other than direct labor, such as machinery.

▪ Direct labor dollars—generally used when labor is the main productive element and there are no significant pay rate differences among employees within the production department. Advantages: the requisite payroll data is generally readily available, and the method is simple and economical to use. Disadvantages: like direct labor hours, it ignores the contribution of value by factors other than direct labor, and the method rests on costs expended and tends to ignore fixed expenses that are functions of time.

▪ Equivalent units of production—generally used when only one product is produced or the product line consists of similar items that can be reduced to a common unit of measure. For example, pounds of fiber in different yarn production or of copper in a copper wire drawing mill, or one unit A equals two unit B's. Ten unit A's and ten unit B's equal total units produced of 15 unit A equivalents. Advantages: it is the most direct method of allocation. Disadvantages: the application of the method is limited to situations where only one or similar products are produced, and actual overhead costs must be closely related to the equivalent unit of production chosen.

▪ Machine hours—generally utilized when machinery and equipment comprise the primary productive element and there is no consistent relationship between machine time and labor time. Advantages: where machinery is the main factor in production, it is perhaps the most accurate method of allocating overhead to production, and from a management point of view, it provides a basis for measuring idle machine time.

▪ Total direct costs—this is an example of a method that may be acceptable where there is uniformity of material and labor cost and processing among products. Advantages: simplicity of use. Disadvantages: the method does not give adequate recognition of expenses which are functions of time; the method does not allocate overhead properly when part of the materials passes through all processes and part through some processes; and, where there are multiple products each using materials or requiring labor having wide differences in cost, high-cost products may be weighted with more than their share of overhead.

It should be noted at this point that the use of activity indicators is not limited to the distribution of total plant or department overhead to production. They may also be used to allocate or spread specific overhead cost elements to departments during the accumulation process depending on their compatibility with the cost characteristics. Thus, maintenance supplies not subject to a stores inventory requisition system might be distributed to production departments based on machine hours in each; safety and OSHA supplies might be distributed based on direct labor hours. Further examples of activity indicators used for allocation of indirect manufacturing costs to departments are as follows:

▪ Square footage—this method is generally used to allocate certain elements of overhead such as utilities, depreciation, rent, and property taxes to service and production departments and to allocate certain service department costs, such as security costs, to production departments.

▪ Value of installed equipment—this method can be used to allocate depreciation and also costs from the maintenance service department to production departments.

Volume Assumptions. The next factor to be considered in developing the manufacturing overhead rate is the volume assumption to be applied to the chosen activity indicator. The volume assumption also affects the third component of the overhead rate equation, i.e., the estimated overhead cost itself to the extent it includes variable or semivariable costs.

There are many different volume assumptions that can be made, but only four merit consideration. The first, maximum theoretical capacity, is generally not used in practice, because it is impossible to achieve. It assumes round-the-clock operation of all plant facilities with no allowances for machine downtime. The other three reasonable volume assumptions are as follows:

■ Practical capacity—this capacity is measured by deducting from maximum capacity the normal downtime interruptions due to repairs, waits, breaks, machine failures, etc. It is a measure of the organization's actual ability to produce if it were running on a target of 24 hours, each day, but was still part of an organization that is not perfectly coordinated. Some organizations may use this concept on a shift basis so that practical capacity could relate to production for one, two, or three shifts per day, perhaps varied by department to portray a "balanced" operation through assuming extra shifts in bottleneck departments.

■ Normal activity—normal activity is usually based on a capacity-to-make-and-sell concept. A sales budget is set. If it is within the practical production capacity, and the product has not reached the stage of diminishing profit returns, the sales budget will determine normal activity. This activity level is usually based on a period longer than one year. The activity level in the long-range forecast is then used as the basis for the calculation of normal activity.

■ Expected activity—this is the budgeted activity for the year. It can be more or less than the normal activity level, but will never be more than the practical capacity level.

The normal activity level is generally considered the most realistic volume assumption for product cost determinations used in establishing selling prices and in valuing inventories in financial statements. Use of the expected activity level tends to inflate product unit costs when lower than normal activity levels prevail. Such higher unit costs are usually not recoverable from the customer, primarily because of the market conditions that caused the lower level of activity in the first place. The use of the practical capacity activity level has certain advantages in the valuation of inventories for income tax purposes, but this approach can be used on a memorandum basis outside of the integrated cost accounting system.

Overhead Costs.   The final component of the overhead rate equation is the amount of overhead to be used in the formula. This aggregate overhead amount may be determined on the basis of budgeted costs or, in the absence of such information, historical costs. In either event, certain overhead costs may be excluded, as explained below, or, if multistep overhead costing is used, additional overhead cost groups or other elements may be added below the inventory valuation line.

When historical overhead figures are used, care should be taken to exclude nonrecurring costs or the effects of abnormal business conditions, and to reflect planned changes expected in the forthcoming year.

The use of budgeted overhead amounts will normally provide the most realistic rate available to absorb overhead into product cost. The budgeted amounts, when such data are available, will have been based on the aggregate of variable costs for the assumed volume and fixed costs. The forecasted status of the business is taken into account and variances from this plan can be highlighted for management review and action.

As indicated earlier, some business units exclude certain overhead costs from the amount used in overhead rate determination. Such exclusion might be viewed as a planned variance, and this is best illustrated by idle plant capacity. The fixed cost of maintaining idle facilities or equipment is not realistically an element of product cost and should be segregated to provide a clearer picture of the absorption of fixed costs of capacity that is in use. Other examples include excessive scrap or rework costs realistically included in the annual operating budget as cost of doing business but excluded from standard costs to provide tighter control over operating departments. Such costs might be considered for "below the line" treatment in a multistep overhead costing system to maintain their visibility in overall pricing decisions if market conditions warrant.

Allocation of Service Center Costs.   Before proceeding to the important control considerations inherent in the use of a predetermined overhead absorption system, one final aspect of distributing accumulated overhead costs needs to be examined. This can be done briefly, because it represents one of the most overworked procedures in cost accounting. It is the "chicken and the egg" question of whether the accumulated cost of service centers should be allocated directly to production departments or whether a portion of this cost should first be allocated to other service centers with that cost then being allocated to production departments on some appropriate activity-level base.

The answer here is that it generally does not make a major difference to final product unit cost whichever way the allocation is performed. Unless some material distortion were to result in a specific and unusual circumstance, the second objective of distribution methods, simplicity, should usually prevail. That is, allocate service center costs directly to production departments. Kaplan[1] provides a comprehensive, mathematical treatment of the service department problem.

Overhead Variances.   However precise or refined a predetermined overhead absorption rate may be, it is certain that actual overhead incurred during a period of time will differ from the amount absorbed into the inventory accounts. Timely analysis of the difference presents management with opportunities to take corrective action that may affect the business unit's profit performance. The purpose of this section is to discuss the practical business and financial reporting significance of overhead variances. Some degree of definition is appropriate here, but comprehensive guidelines and explanations regarding variance determination may be found elsewhere in this book.

The distribution of manufacturing overhead to production and to inventory accounts on a predetermined basis leaves a positive or negative residue of accumulated overhead that must also be accounted for and distributed in some manner. No such residue results from an overhead distribution system that distributes actual overhead to actual production. The residue goes by many names in practice, including overhead variances and under- or overabsorbed, recovered or applied overhead.

Most managements prefer what are often termed "tight" standards, which tend to provide an incentive to operate efficiently if such predetermined criteria are in fact realistic and attainable. The variance, more often than not, is a net negative amount, which usually signals lost profit to the enterprise relative to what it believed was attainable. This condition can result from any or all of the three components of an overhead rate being established with minimum margin or cushion for unnecessary or wasteful expenditures or practices.

In whatever manner standards may be set, there are three basic manufacturing overhead variance categories that comprise the difference between actual and absorbed overhead. Exhibit 9 shows the relationship of overhead variances and provides a simple explanation of the method of calculating each variance.

A simple example of the dollar computations of the three basic overhead variances follows:

[1]Robert S. Kaplan, "Variable and Self-Service Costs in Reciprocal Allocation Models," *The Accounting Review,* 48 (October 1973), pp. 738–748.

Plant—single-product operation
Activity indicator—direct labor hours (DLH)
Volume assumptions:
   Capacity concept—normal (and expected) volume
   Production and sales plan—200,000 units
   Direct labor standard—2 units per direct labor hour
   Indicator volume—100,000 DLH
Overhead budget—$150,000
Plant-wide overhead rate—$1.50 (= $150,000/100,000)
Actual volume—160,000 units
Actual direct labor hours—96,000 units
Actual overhead—$160,000
Standard direct labor hours
   allowed for actual production—80,000 DLH (= 160,000/2)
Overhead absorbed—$120,000 (= 80,000 DLH × $1.50)
Total negative variance—$40,000 (= $160,000 − $120,000)
Budget variance—$10,000 (= $160,000 − $150,000)
Volume variance—$30,000 (= $150,000 − $120,000)
Volume portion—$6,000 [= $150,000 − (96,000 × $1.50)]
Efficiency portion—$24,000 [= $144,000 − (80,000 × $1.50)]

The computation of the variance components can be more easily understood by reference to Exhibit 9.

EXHIBIT 9   Disaggregation of Overhead Variance

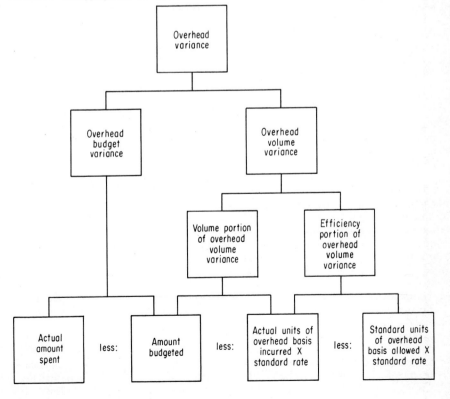

Some of the possible causes of these variances and action that might be taken in practice by management include the following:

■ Budget (or spending) variance—cause: inflation in overhead such as energy costs; action: a combination of tighter control over spending (energy conservation measures, etc.) and adjustment of overhead rate and product selling prices. Cause: excessive or wasteful use of operating and other supplies or overstaffing of indirect labor functions; action: increased or more disciplined supervision. Cause: poor budgeting or higher production levels causing absorption distortion due to fixed cost content of overhead rate; action: closer review of budgeting process, use of responsibility reporting format and flexible budgeting techniques.

■ Volume variances—cause: tight supply of qualified direct workers in labor market: action: initiate thorough review of direct labor variances but this symptom could indicate need for competitive wage rate adjustment. Cause: product marketing problems, demand, etc.; action: product review, market analysis, promotional efforts, overhead reduction program, etc.

■ Efficiency variance—cause: use of underqualified direct workers, labor turnover, equipment or scheduling problems; action: same as probably initiated in action regarding direct labor and material variances.

There are many combinations of causes of overhead variances and possible corrective actions that might be taken. This limited discussion does, however, set the stage for a review of the ultimate accounting disposition or distribution of overhead variances.

Accounting Disposition.   The bookkeeping aspects of manufacturing overhead distribution are relatively simple and do not warrant much focus here. The following accounting entry would be made at the end of the accounting period using the amounts contained in the earlier illustration of variance determination:

Work-in-Process Inventory	120,000	
Budget Variance Expense	10,000	
Volume Variance Expense	6,000	
Efficiency Variance Expense	24,000	
Manufacturing Overhead		
Accumulation Account		160,000

The accounting principles involved in the distribution of manufacturing overhead do, however, warrant discussion. Note that in the above accounting entry each of the variances has been expensed in the period incurred. It can be argued that these variances represent a portion of the actual cost of the goods that remain in inventory at period-end and should therefore be restored to inventories on the balance sheet.

There is little published on this matter in the authoritative literature of the accounting profession and what, therefore, constitutes generally accepted accounting principles in this regard is a matter of some judgment. As a general statement, variances arising from abnormal operating conditions or inefficiencies are, in practice, expensed in the period in which they arise. This treatment, although often not recognized as such, flows from application of the inventory valuation principle of stating inventories at the "lower of cost or market." The relevant definition of market here is that of "reproduction cost." If the overhead variances in question were caused by abnormal operating conditions or inefficiencies, it follows that the related inventories could be reproduced at standard cost and that the variances should therefore be expensed as representing a write-down from actual cost to reproduction cost.

Thus, the plant alluded to earlier that experienced efficiency variances due to abnormal labor-force turnover would properly expense such variances. This is a proper disposition if the standards were realistic or attainable given a "normal" degree of labor turnover. The judgment decision here is, of course, whether the turnover or other operating problem experienced is normal or abnormal. It should be remembered that the assumptions made in setting standards are subject to the discipline of being used ultimately in setting product selling prices. This tends to keep the necessary judgments in balance with the facts.

A similar argument is used in practice with respect to volume variances. Expected and actual capacity use may fall below "normal" capacity (see page 10-17) for periods of time. The definition of normal here is associated with the longer-term view and is usually not a month-to-month or even year-to-year determination. Thus, volume variances are also usually expensed currently in practice by applying the reproduction cost limitation on carrying value of inventories. Again, the judgment applied is the test of normality. Production experience and volume over several years and anticipated in the future are certainly factors that can be used as evidence in support of the judgments made. In any event, the costs of idle productive capacity or equipment should be expensed directly whether it is included in the overhead absorption rate or not.

Budget or spending variances should also be subjected to the same tests of abnormality. Components of this variance group often fail this test, and as a result, if material, are included on a proportionate basis in ending inventories. For example, if energy costs are a significant indirect overhead item and rates increase substantially to a level not anticipated in setting the annual operating budget, the associated budget variance would usually not represent an abnormal or erratic excess cost.

In the past, the most common practice has been to adjust overhead rates annually for then-current conditions. If inventoriable variances for the year just ending are significant, such revised rates are often used in valuing ending inventories. If not, the new rates are placed in effect for the next year. Today's environment probably warrants more frequent adjustment to budgeted overhead amounts included in overhead rate determinations for two reasons. First, the effects of inflation are resulting in more significant budget variances than in the past. Second, quarterly financial reports to stockholders and to the Securities and Exchange Commission are subject to standards of accuracy that did not prevail several years ago.

Accounting Principles Board Opinion No. 28 states[2]

> Companies that use standard cost accounting systems for determining inventory and product costs should generally follow the same procedures in reporting purchase price, wage rate, usage or efficiency variances from standard cost at the end of an interim period as followed at the end of a fiscal year. Purchase price variances or volume or capacity cost variances that are planned and expected to be absorbed by the end of the annual period, should ordinarily be deferred at interim reporting dates. The effect of unplanned or unanticipated purchase price or volume variances, however, should be reported at the end of an interim period following the same procedures used at the end of a fiscal year. . . .

For certain public companies, the requirements of the Securities and Exchange Commission[3] regarding quarterly financial reports and review thereof by auditors may precipitate quarterly adjustment of overhead rates with resulting effects on the valuation of inventories at quarter-end.

OTHER CONSIDERATIONS

The design of product costing systems, including the manufacturing overhead segment, has traditionally been a free-form internal matter with very personalized results and reports. The complex business environment faced by most enterprises

[2]Accounting Principles Board, Opinion No. 28, "Interim Financial Reporting" (AICPA, New York, 1973).

[3]Securities and Exchange Commission, *Accounting Series Release No. 177, 1975.*

today requires that several external reporting requirements be considered in developing or enhancing the overhead segment of a costing system. To ignore them means a foregone opportunity to minimize the cost of obtaining data for compliance with these requirements.

These requirements come largely from various governmental and other standards-setting bodies and include the following:

▪ Internal Revenue Service—the IRS has issued regulations dealing with the determination of inventoriable costs for income tax reporting purposes and often referred to as the "Full Absorption Inventory Costing" regulations.

▪ Cost Accounting Standards Board—this governmental body has established several cost accounting standards affecting the accumulation and distribution of overhead to certain governmental procurement contracts.

▪ Federal Trade Commission—this agency has requirements for detailed reporting of revenues, costs, and profits of various lines of business of larger corporations.

▪ Securities and Exchange Commission—this regulatory body requires certain disclosures of revenues and profits of lines of business in annual and other reports and registration statements filed by public companies.

▪ Financial Accounting Standards Board—this private-sector standards-setting body requires disclosure in annual financial statements of assets, revenues, and profits of segments of a business (Statement of Financial Accounting Standards No. 14).

It is not feasible to explore here the practical effect of each of these external influences on methods of overhead accumulation and distribution. Those that deal with lines or segments of business reporting do, however, need to be coordinated by knowledgeable people to minimize inconsistencies in allocating manufacturing overhead. Although of considerable significance to many corporations, these and the Cost Accounting Standards Board requirements do not have the same widespread effect as the Full Absorption Costing regulations of the IRS. They are discussed next.

Income Tax Aspects. The Internal Revenue Service has issued regulations (Reg. Sec. 1.471-11) dealing with the determination of inventoriable costs for income tax reporting purposes. The direct cost method (discussed in Chapter 11) is specified as not being acceptable and the "full absorption" inventory costing method is mandatory. The result for many companies is that more cost items are included in inventory costing for income tax purposes than before the regulation was issued in 1974. All direct production costs and certain indirect production costs "incident to and necessary for production" must be included in the computation of inventory cost. Although these regulations do not require taxpayers to modify their cost accounting systems significantly, the provisions of the regulations should be considered in the system to the extent that financial data might require significant modification to conform with income tax reporting requirements.

These regulations specify the rules for determining how specific overhead and other costs are to be treated in the computation of inventoriable costs. The approach of the regulations in determining inventoriable costs is to segregate typical overhead costs into three classifications as follows:

▪ Category One costs—overhead costs that must be included in the computation of cost of inventory, regardless of the treatment of such items in the financial statements.

▪ Category Two costs—overhead items that need not be included in cost of inventory, regardless of their treatment in the financial statements.

▪ Category Three costs—overhead items that for income tax reporting purposes must be treated the same as in preparing financial statements, provided that the financial statements are prepared in accordance with generally accepted accounting principles.

The specific elements of overhead for each of the foregoing categories apply to taxpayers whose general method of accounting for production costs is comparable for both tax and financial reporting purposes and are as follows:

- Category One:
  Repair costs
  Maintenance
  Utilities
  Rent
  Indirect materials and supplies
  Tools and equipment not capitalized
  Quality control
  Inspection
  Indirect labor and production supervision wages, including:
    Basic compensation
    Overtime pay
    Vacation and holiday pay
    Sick leave pay (with exceptions)
    Shift differential
    Payroll taxes
    Contributions to supplemental unemployment benefits plan
- Category Two:
  Marketing costs
  Advertising costs
  Selling costs
  Other distribution costs
  Interest
  Research and development
  Specified casualty and other losses
  Excess of percentage depletion over cost
  Excess of tax over book depreciation
  Income taxes on inventory sales
  Past service cost of pension contributions
  General and administrative overall activities
  Officers' salaries, overall management activities
- Category Three:
  Taxes, property, and other local and state
  Book depreciation and cost depletion
  Costs attributable to strikes, rework labor, scrap, and spoilage
  Factory administrative costs
  Production officers' salaries
  Insurance costs
  Employee benefits:
    Current pension service costs
    Workmen's compensation
    Wage continuation
    Nonqualified pension, profit-sharing, stock bonus (to extent taxable to employees)
    Life and health insurance premiums
    Safety, medical treatment
    Cafeteria
    Recreational facilities
    Membership dues

Inclusion of Category One items in the computation of inventoriable costs is governed by the general concept that an item is includable to the extent that it is "incident to and necessary for production or manufacturing operations or processes." Category Two items allow exclusion from the computation of inventoriable costs and tend to follow the guidelines for financial reporting discussed previously in this chapter (for example, selling and marketing expenses should be excluded from inventory valuation). Category Three items are included or excluded from inventory valuation depending on the treatment used for financial reporting purposes, subject to the further requirement that "the treatment not be inconsistent with generally accepted accounting principles."

Generally accepted accounting principles are not specific as to which overhead elements are to be considered as inventory costs. *Accounting Research Bulletin No. 43,*[4] makes a general statement that exclusion of all overheads from inventory cost does not constitute an accepted accounting procedure. Even though this pronouncement prohibits use of direct or prime costing methods, the guidelines that it provides are so general and vague that companies have exercised considerable latitude as to which elements of overhead they have included in inventory cost. Accounting Principles Board Opinion No. 20[5] provides that a company may not change its method of accounting unless it changes to a preferable method. Although the types of costs to be included in overhead for inventory purposes are not well defined under generally accepted accounting principles, it would generally be difficult to conclude that a decision to omit certain costs previously included for financial reporting purposes would be a change to a preferable method under the full absorption concept. This means that insofar as Category Three items are concerned, there will continue to be inconsistency of treatment of such items between taxpayers depending on their accounting practices prior to change for full absorption for tax purposes. Some enterprises that previously inventoried only minimum amounts of overhead costs will be able to continue to include in inventory fewer costs than other enterprises that were closer to full absorption of production overhead costs.

As support for principles applied in costing inventories, under Revenue Procedure 75-40, taxpayers must represent to the Internal Revenue Service that the financial statement treatment of Category Three items is not inconsistent with generally accepted accounting principles, and that immateriality of inventory costs, in a financial reporting sense, was not relied on as a basis for making this representation. Taxpayers may, as further support, submit statements from their independent accountants regarding the consistency of the principles applied in valuation of inventories in the financial statements with generally accepted accounting principles.

The regulations specify special rules for those taxpayers whose general method of accounting for overhead costs is not comparable for tax and financial reporting purposes, or who do not maintain inventories for financial reporting purposes. These rules will not be summarized here because of their rather limited application.

The regulations further prescribe the allocation methods to be used to distribute overhead costs to goods produced and remaining in inventory at year-end. Overhead items that must be included in inventoriable costs are to be allocated by the method that fairly apportions such costs among the items produced. Acceptable methods include the manufacturing burden rate method and the standard cost method. In addition, a practical capacity concept can be used with either of these methods to account for fixed overhead costs.

Variances arising from the use of the standard cost or manufacturing burden

---

[4]Committee on Accounting Procedure, *Accounting Research Bulletin No. 43* (AICPA, New York, 1953), chap. 4, statement 3.

[5]Accounting Principles Board, Opinion No. 20, "Accounting Changes" (AICPA, New York, 1971).

rate methods must be reallocated to units in ending inventory on a *pro rata* basis with certain exceptions. This need not be done (1) for practical capacity or volume variances; (2) for those variances that in total (net) are not significant in amount to total actual indirect production costs for the year, and not allocated to inventories in the company's financial statements; and (3) where both overabsorbed and underabsorbed variances are treated consistently for financial reporting and income tax purposes.

These regulations are significant, and in order to conform to them in a manner designed to minimize additional income taxes, a company may have to modify its present cost accounting system. Also, significant advantages may result from careful treatment of variances. The use of the practical capacity concept for tax purposes can be more beneficial from a cash-flow viewpoint than the "normal" or "expected" capacity concepts of developing a volume base for application of overhead to production described on page 10-17.

SUMMARY

There are two key points that need to be made in summarizing the concepts and practicalities of overhead accumulation and distribution.

The quantity of data entering this portion of a product costing system, the variety of displays of the accumulated data, and opportunities for meaningful summaries and reports virtually mandate extensive use of electronic data processing facilities in a typical large manufacturing enterprise. Timeliness of reporting and variance information is essential if the data are to be used effectively. Yet there are relatively few businesses that have developed systems that accomplish all of the objectives enumerated in this chapter. Overhead cost accumulation and distribution practices, by and large, have not kept pace with the changing technological and business environment or the data explosion resulting from governmental and other external influences.

Finally, there is no more vivid illustration of the need for coordinated teamwork of various disciplines in designing, implementing, or enhancing product costing systems than in the overhead cost module. In years past, a team of experienced cost accountants could get the complete system operating effectively, perhaps in conjunction with industrial engineers. The manufacturing overhead area is a microcosm of the total enterprise. It involves forecasting where operations research personnel can be helpful, income tax savings opportunities requiring income tax specialists on the team, data processing systems analysts and programmers to achieve maximum computerization benefits, financial accountants and independent auditors to cover financial reporting and disclosure requirements and, above all, management must be involved to ensure that full consideration is given in the costing system to the needs of the business and the industry in which it operates.

BIBLIOGRAPHY

Accounting Principles Board: Opinion No. 20, "Accounting Changes," AICPA, New York, 1953.
———: Opinion No. 28, "Interim Financial Reporting," AICPA, New York, 1973.
Committee on Accounting Procedure: *Accounting Research Bulletin No. 43,* AICPA, New York, 1953, chap. 4, statement 3.
Dopuch, Nicholas, Jacob G. Birnberg, and Joel Demski, *Cost Accounting: Accounting Data for Management's Decisions,* 2nd ed., Harcourt Brace Jovanovich, New York, 1974.

Horngren, Charles T.: *Cost Accounting: A Managerial Emphasis,* 4th ed., Prentice-Hall, Englewood Cliffs, N.J., 1977.

Kaplan, Robert S.: "Variable and Self-Service Costs in Reciprocal Allocation Models," *The Accounting Review,* 48 (October 1973), pp. 738–748.

Securities and Exchange Commission: *Accounting Series Release No. 177,* 1975; *No. 190,* 1976.

Shillinglaw, Gordon: *Cost Accounting: Analysis and Control,* 3rd ed., Richard D. Irwin, Homewood, Ill., 1972.

Chapter 11

Direct Costing

PETER B. B. TURNEY
Associate Professor of Accounting, Portland State University

JOHN L. MONTGOMERY
Principal, Peat, Marwick, Mitchell & Co.

INTRODUCTION

Scope.   For over forty years, direct costing has been a controversial and disputatious topic. Since 1936, numerous articles and monographs have exposed the fundamental issues underlying the direct costing controversy. Much of the disagreement has stemmed from a failure to agree upon the real purpose of direct costing. To some, direct costing is a simple exposition of the management tool of cost-volume-profit analysis. To others, direct costing is viewed as an unwelcome candidate for status as a generally accepted accounting principle.

This introductory section defines direct costing and other pertinent terms and discusses the two major purposes of direct costing—management decision making and financial reporting. A contrast between direct costing and absorption costing demonstrates the reporting consequences of direct costing. The use of direct costing for planning and control is outlined in the next major section, which also notes the limitations on its use for decision-making purposes. The following major section considers financial accounting theory as it relates to direct costing and discusses its effect on direct costing as a possible generally accepted accounting principle for published financial statements, SEC and IRS purposes.

The current status of direct costing makes it likely that a company using it for internal reporting purposes will adjust its financial statements to an absorption costing basis before release for external use. An outline of such a system of adjustment is provided. Examples of internal direct costing reports are provided. The accounts required for adjustment to an absorption costing basis are presented and described.

It has often been said that direct costing is more than an accounting system; it is a management philosophy. This philosophy is spelled out as the advantages and disadvantages of direct costing are documented. The concluding section provides a summary of the current position of direct costing and provides some thoughts on its future development and acceptability.

Definition, Terminology. In an area of controversy, it is important to take care in definition and choice of terminology. The term "direct costing" is somewhat misleading. Preferred terminology would be *variable costing,* which more correctly reflects the underlying matching assumptions of direct costing. Because direct costing has significant financial and management accounting implications, we shall start by defining all pertinent terms.

1. *Direct Costing.*   Direct costing is a reporting system that values inventory and cost of sales at its manufacturing variable cost. It is frequently used as an internal management reporting system. It is advocated for use in external reporting but does not appear to be a generally accepted accounting principle.

2. *Variable Cost.*   A variable cost is one that increases linearly with volume. Exhibit 1 shows the relationship between variable cost and volume. The important assumption of variable cost is its proportionate or linear relationship to volume. It differs from marginal cost, which may have a nonlinear relationship to volume.

EXHIBIT 1   Variable Cost

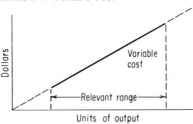

3. *Fixed Cost.*   A fixed cost is one that does not vary within a certain range of output fluctuation (Exhibit 2). Fixed cost is thus excluded from product cost under direct costing.

4. *Relevant Range.*   The assumptions of cost behavior, variability or fixity, can be made only with respect to a limited range of output fluctuations. Outside that range capacity may be inadequate or variable labor and material rates may change.

EXHIBIT 2   Fixed Cost

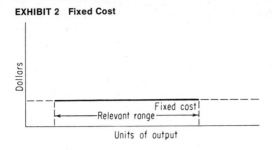

The range of volume within which the assumptions do hold is known as the relevant range.

5. *Semivariable and Semifixed Costs.*   Direct costing makes a dichotomy between variable and fixed costs. Unfortunately, not all costs fall neatly into these two categories. Costs that contain both a variable and a fixed element are known as semivariable costs (Exhibit 3). An example of a semivariable cost is a worker who is paid a basic wage supplemented by a piecework rate. Semifixed costs are sometimes referred to as step-fixed costs (Exhibit 4). Unlike purely fixed costs, which remain totally fixed within the relevant range, semifixed costs increase in a stepwise progression within the relevant range. The hiring of a new production quality inspector for each 5 percent increase in production is an example of a semifixed cost where these production increases are within the relevant range.

EXHIBIT 3   Semivariable Cost

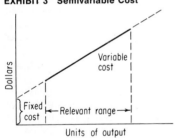

EXHIBIT 4   Semifixed Cost

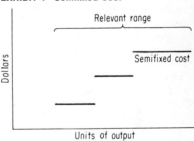

6. *Variable Margin.*   An important subtotal in the direct costing statement is the variable margin. The variable margin represents the contribution to overhead and profits resulting from the spread between the selling price and the variable cost per unit. Arithmetically, it is the selling price per unit less the variable cost per unit multiplied by the number of units sold. The variable margin may alternatively be described as contribution margin or marginal income. Sometimes a distinction is made between the manufacturing variable margin (selling price less manufacturing variable cost) and the total variable margin (selling price less manufacturing and selling variable cost).

7. *Direct Costs.*   Costs that are incurred because a certain decision is made are known as the *direct costs* of that decision. Direct costs are incremental or additional costs. The concept of direct or incremental costs is not, however, equivalent to variable costs. Variable costs are incremental to production-level decisions. Fixed costs may also be incremental when the decision affects the level of fixed cost. Direct cost, therefore, is not equivalent to direct costing, which utilizes the concept of variability.

Purpose of Direct Costing. There are two major purposes of direct costing: planning and control for management; and inventory valuation and income determination. Direct costing statements provide a methodology for quite a number of management planning decisions. Comparative statements may be prepared for historical and budgeted results under a number of different circumstances. Management may use such analyses to answer a variety of "what if?" questions on volume changes, cost changes, pricing decisions, and product mix analyses. The direct costing statement may also serve as an evaluative tool for corporate manufacturing departments or divisions. As a part of the responsibility accounting system, it serves as an incentive to revenue planning and cost control. The use of direct costing as an integral part of the historical accounting system will affect periodic computed income and the balance sheet valuation of inventory. Financial statements that are direct costing based are consistent with internal reports generated for management. They may, however, need to be adjusted to absorption costing to be in conformance with generally accepted accounting principles.

Direct Costing and Absorption Costing Contrasted—A Historical Perspective. Early accounting systems for manufacturing enterprises were limited to recording line-item expenditures, such as material and labor costs. Some companies made informal estimates of product costs as an aid to setting prices or valuing inventories. It was only at a later time that these informal cost estimates were incorporated into the financial accounting system.

The integration of cost estimates into the accounting system was primarily an attempt to improve the accounting valuation of inventory and the measurement of periodic income. Manufacturing accounting developed under the predominant theory that "attached" all historical manufacturing costs to the product. Good matching of costs and revenues, therefore, required that all variable and fixed manufacturing costs be included in the cost of the product. These costs became the basis of valuation of inventory and became expensed when the inventory was sold. All other costs were treated as period costs and expensed in the period of incurrence or amortization.

The matching process described above is known as *absorption costing*. It has been, and still is, the one recognized method of inventory valuation for external reporting purposes. Its early and broad acceptance for external reporting, however, somewhat belies the technical problems involved in applying the theory. Under absorption costing, the valuation of output requires the assignment or "allocation" of fixed costs to the product. This allocation is performed by prorating the fixed capacity costs over a normal level of volume. Each unit of output, therefore, bears a predetermined amount of fixed costs. The purpose of predetermining the fixed cost per unit is to avoid the problem of a historical fixed cost per unit that varies inversely with volume. Each unit of output is charged only the standard rate even if actual volume is greater or less than the normal volume. If actual output is more or less than normal volume, there will be an overabsorption or underabsorption of fixed costs, respectively. Generally, an unfavorable volume variance (underabsorption) is treated as a period cost. A favorable volume variance (overabsorption) is usually applied to reduce inventory and cost of sales so that inventory will not be valued in excess of historical cost. Under- and overabsorption may also result from variances other than the volume variance; the appropriate allocation will depend on the type and nature of the variance.

In direct costing, matching is based on cost behavior. Manufacturing costs are classified as either variable or fixed. The variable manufacturing costs are treated as product costs. The fixed manufacturing costs are treated as period costs. Unlike absorption costing, there is no requirement for allocating the fixed manufacturing cost to the product.

Despite its apparent simplicity and utility as a management tool, direct costing has failed to supplement absorption costing as a generally accepted accounting principle of inventory valuation. This lack of acceptance in financial accounting theory is related to the origin of direct costing as a cost accounting and management tool. Early developments in cost accounting were outside the accounting system. Breakeven analysis, for example, was conducted as a special study. The cost accountant would make assumptions about future cost, volume, and revenue relationships. The breakeven concept would be the model for measuring the effect on profit of a change in any of the cost, volume, and revenue assumptions.

As cost accounting developed, its concepts became incorporated into the chart of accounts and financial reports. The breakeven chart became the basis of the direct costing statement. This permitted managers to view cost-volume-profit relationships in the light of an accounting statement. Their confusion was understandable, however, when they found that the direct costing statement did not predict the direction or measure changes in net income as computed under absorption costing.

Much of the pressure to change financial accounting theory from absorption to direct costing has come from managers and cost accountants who wish to make the income statement consistent with their direct costing statement. Consistency with a cost behavior format, however, has never been viewed by financial accounting theorists as sufficient reason for general acceptance. Although direct costing is popular today as a management accounting tool, absorption costing remains the dominant basis for valuing output for external reporting purposes. For the foreseeable future, many companies will report on a direct costing basis for internal reporting purposes and on an absorption costing basis for external reporting purposes. An important requirement for these companies will be ease of adjustment from a direct to an absorption costing format. A method for making this adjustment is presented in a later section of this chapter.

In addition, it is important that the relationship between direct and absorption costing be clear. Exhibit 5 illustrates the principal differences between direct costing and absorption costing. Absorption costing and direct costing will generally report the same net income when production and sales are in balance. In Exhibit 5, production exceeds sales for the year by 10 units. Absorption costing values these 10 units at the sum of their variable and fixed manufacturing costs. Direct costing values the inventory units at only their variable costs. The $40 of fixed manufacturing cost included in the inventory under absorption costing is an expense of the period under direct costing. It is the treatment of this $40 of fixed manufacturing costs that explains the difference in net income of $40.

The absorption costing income statement in Exhibit 5 does not group costs according to cost behavior. If the volume of sales changes, the gross margin does not vary proportionately with sales. In contrast, the direct costing format deducts only variable manufacturing cost from sales to produce the variable margin. The variable margin varies proportionately with changes in sales.

It is clear from the example in Exhibit 5 that absorption costing and direct costing net income will not be the same when sales and production differ. This difference is complicated in periods of changing prices and by choice of inventory cost-flow assumption, LIFO and FIFO, for example. Let us first establish some generalizations about comparative income effects in the simplest circumstances when prices remain constant (and all flow assumptions produce the same result). When we have established these generalizations, we shall introduce price changes and observe the effect on income under LIFO and FIFO.

The following information is assumed for the second example in Exhibit 6. The company has no inventories at the beginning of the first year and goes out of

EXHIBIT 5 Comparison of Absorption and Direct Costing Income Statements for Year Ending 12-31-19X0

Facts

Beginning inventory: 0 units
Production: 110 units
Sales: 100 units
Ending inventory: 10 units

Fixed manufacturing cost at volume of 110 units: $440 or $4 per unit
Variable manufacturing cost: $12 per unit
Selling price: $20 per unit
Variable selling and administrative costs: $1 per unit; fixed selling and administrative costs: $150

Absorption Costing			*Direct Costing*		
Sales		$2,000	Sales		$2,000
Variable manufacturing costs	$1,320		Variable manufacturing cost of goods produced	$1,320	
Fixed manufacturing costs .	440		Less ending inventory at variable manufacturing cost	120	1,200
Cost of goods available for sale	$1,760		Manufacturing variable margin		$ 800
Less ending inventory	160	$1,600	Less variable selling and administrative expense ..		100
Gross margin		$ 400	Net variable margin		$ 700
Less total selling and administrative expense ..		250	Less fixed costs: Fixed manufacturing costs	$ 440	
			Fixed selling and administrative	150	590
Net income		$ 150			$ 110

EXHIBIT 6 Comparison of Assumption and Direct Costing When There Are No Price Changes

	Year 1	Year 2	Year 3	Year 4
Sales (units)	30,000	30,000	50,000	60,000
Production (units)	40,000	50,000	50,000	30,000

Comparative Income Statements over a Four-Year Period

	Year 1	Year 2	Year 3	Year 4
	Absorption Costing			
Sales	$600,000	$600,000	$1,000,000	$1,200,000
Less: cost of sales	450,000	450,000	750,000	900,000
Gross margin	$150,000	$150,000	$ 250,000	$ 300,000
Less: volume variance*	—	(50,000)	(50,000)	50,000
Net income	$150,000	$200,000	$ 300,000	$ 250,000
	Direct Costing			
Sales	$600,000	$600,000	$1,000,000	$1,200,000
Less: cost of sales	300,000	300,000	500,000	600,000
Manufacturing variable margin	$300,000	$300,000	$ 500,000	$ 600,000
Less: fixed manufacturing expenses	200,000	200,000	200,000	200,000
Net income†	$100,000	$100,000	$ 300,000	$ 400,000

*Parentheses reflect a favorable volume variance.
†Assumes no spending or performance variances.

business at the end of the fourth year. Only one product is manufactured and is sold at a price of $20 per unit. Variable costs are $10 per unit. Budgeted fixed costs are $200,000 per year. A normal volume of 40,000 units provides a fixed cost per unit at normal volume of $5. Realistically, most companies also have fixed and variable selling and administrative expenses. The choice between direct and absorption costing, however, has no effect on the amount of selling and administrative costs that are expensed. We, therefore, ignore selling and administrative costs to simplify the example. Units of sales and production for the four years are as shown at the top of Exhibit 6.

The income figures in Exhibit 6 assume no variances from standard. The total income over the four years is $900,000 for both methods, because all units are sold by the end of year 4. Like all choices between competing methods in historical cost accounting based on nominal dollar measuring units, the differences between absorption and direct costing are timing differences in income rather than permanent differences in income. It is possible to make the following conclusions about the timing effects of absorption and direct costing from Exhibit 6.

1. When sales and production are equal, as in year 3, net income is the same under both methods.

2. When production exceeds the level of sales, as in years 1 and 2, net income will be greater under absorption costing.

3. When sales exceed production, as in year 4, direct costing will produce a higher level of net income.

4. In years 1 and 2, sales remain constant. In these two years direct costing reports the same net income. Absorption costing reports higher net income in year 2 because of the inventory effect of higher production. Absorption costing will, therefore, report different net incomes for the same level of sales as production fluctuates.

The above differences relate to the attachment of fixed manufacturing costs to inventory under absorption costing. In years when production exceeds sales, the portion of fixed cost that is attached to inventory is relieved from the current income statement. Absorption costing income is, therefore, higher in such years. When sales exceed production, the inventory is sold and the previously deferred fixed cost is now expensed. Absorption costing income is thus lower in such years. Some advocates of direct costing describe this phenomenon by saying that absorption costing "sells profits to inventory."

A problem in absorption costing relates to the need to prorate fixed manufacturing costs over a normal volume. The prorated fixed cost is the amount of fixed cost charged to each production unit. When actual production exceeds or falls short of normal volume, however, there is an overabsorption or an underabsorption, respectively, of fixed cost. In years 2 and 3, production exceeds normal volume by 10,000. There is, therefore, an overabsorption of fixed cost of $50,000 (= $5 × 10,000 units). In year 4, actual production falls short of normal volume by 10,000 units, resulting in an underabsorption of $50,000 (= $5 × 10,000 units). In Exhibit 6, the volume variance is treated as an adjustment to income; cost of sales is effectively increased or decreased by the volume variance. (Some accountants prefer to prorate the volume variance between cost of sales and inventory. This would change the amount of the differences shown but would not affect the principle.)

Exhibits 5 and 6 ignore the possibility that the costs of manufacturing may vary with changing prices. When manufacturing costs change over time, it is necessary to deal with the problem of cost flow. Accounting uses several inventory methods for handling the cost-flow problem, including average cost, FIFO, LIFO, and standard cost. Recent research has demonstrated that the above generalizations under stable prices regarding direct and absorption costing profit are correct under changing prices only under the LIFO and standard cost inventory cost-flow assumptions. Under FIFO and average cost, the profit effects of direct and absorption costing are somewhat more complex.

Under both the FIFO and the average inventory methods, it is possible for inventory quantity to increase and for direct cost and full cost profit to be the same or for direct cost profit to exceed full cost profit. Conversely, it is possible under FIFO or average cost for inventory quantity to decrease with direct cost showing a lower profit than full cost, contrary to the usual generalizations.[1]

For a complete analysis of the impact of inventory costing methods on direct and absorption costing profit, the reader is referred to the Ijiri, Jaedicke, and Livingstone article.[2] Exhibit 7 is reproduced from this article and summarizes the differences between direct and absorption costing profit.

EXHIBIT 7   Differences Between Direct and Absorption Costing Profit

Inventory cost-flow assumption	$P(AC) - P(DC)$
Average	$\dfrac{es}{e+s}\left(\dfrac{MN}{s} - \dfrac{BN}{e}\right)$
FIFO with $s \geq b$	$e\left(\dfrac{MN}{q} - \dfrac{BN}{e}\right)$
FIFO with $s \leq b$	$s\left(\dfrac{MN}{s} - \dfrac{BN}{e}\right)$
LIFO with $s \leq q$	$(e - b)\dfrac{MN}{q}$
LIFO with $s \geq q$	$(e - b)\dfrac{BN}{e}$
Standard	$a^*(e - b)$

where $P(AC)$ = profit under full absorption costing
$P(DC)$ = profit under direct cost
MN = fixed-cost portion of current period's manufacturing cost
BN = fixed-cost portion of beginning inventory
e = ending inventory quantity
b = beginning inventory quantity
s = current period's quantity sold
q = quantity produced in current period
a^* = standard fixed cost per unit

SOURCE: Yuji Ijiri, Robert K. Jaedicke, and John L. Livingstone, "The Effect of Inventory Costing Methods on Full and Direct Costing," *Journal of Accounting Research*, 3, 1 (Spring 1965), p. 71.

DIRECT COSTING AS A TOOL FOR PLANNING AND CONTROL AND FINANCIAL REPORTING

Planning and Control.   Direct costing is most easily justified when used for profit planning and control. A study by the National Association of Accountants (NAA) indicated that the majority of companies ranked profit planning as the prime reason for adopting a direct costing system.[3] The choice of direct costing for internal reporting can also be made without regard to generally accepted accounting principles, SEC and IRS guidelines.

[1] Y. Ijiri, R. K. Jaedicke, and J. L. Livingstone, "The Effect of Inventory Costing Methods on Full and Direct Costing," *Journal of Accounting Research*, 3, 1 (Spring 1965), pp. 63–74.
[2] *Ibid.*
[3] National Association of Accountants, "Current Applications of Direct Costing," *Research Report 37* (NAA, New York, 1961), p. 22.

This section first discusses the role of direct costing in the planning and control of profits in a manufacturing enterprise. Most companies establish profit objectives for the coming accounting period or periods. Profit planning is the active process of decision making to coordinate operations toward achievement of the overall profit goal. Direct costing assists in this process by restructuring the information within the annual profit budget to emphasize cost behavior and to highlight the contribution margin. The variable margin, the spread between the selling price and the variable costs of manufacture, provides information on the impact of short-run changes in the levels of variable and fixed costs and changes in the volume and price of sales. The research that is required to develop a cost accounting classification by cost behavior improves a company's knowledge of its own cost structure. A classification by cost behavior requires the identification and grouping of costs into variable and fixed categories. In some cases, this increased understanding of cost behavior permits increased emphasis on the principles of responsibility accounting in assigning organizational responsibilities. In addition, the clarification of performance reports can encourage behavior consistent with increased profit.

This section also presents some caveats regarding the use of a direct costing internal reporting system. The apparent simplicity of direct costing may in some cases be misleading and even dangerous. Direct costing is not suitable for all kinds of decisions and all time frames. There are technical problems to be dealt with in determining the classifications of cost. There are necessary simplifications to be made in assigning costs to each cost class. There are all the drawbacks of using historical cost for the purposes of making decisions about the future. There may also be legal problems in using direct cost information for pricing purposes, particularly in multinational companies.

1. *Managerial Uses of Direct Costing.*   The characteristic that distinguishes direct costing profit statements from the more conventional absorption cost statements is the calculation of the variable margin. On a per-unit basis the variable margin is the difference between the variable cost per unit and the selling price per unit. The total variable margin for all sales of a product is simply the variable margin per unit multiplied by the number of units sold. The variable margin quantifies and highlights a very simple relationship between profit and volume. For every sale that is made, a surplus, the variable margin, is earned above and beyond the variable cost of the product. This surplus is available to cover the fixed costs of production and sale and to provide a profit. The more units that are sold, or the higher the variable margin per unit, the greater will be the contribution to fixed costs. On a firm-wide basis, a profit is made when the total variable margin from the sale of all products exceeds the total fixed costs of the company.

a. Segment Reporting.   Direct costing statements provide planning information for any definable segment of sales within the company. Typical segments for which direct costing statements would be appropriate include product, product line, salesperson, sales territory, department, and division. The direct costing statements facilitate profit analysis and planning by highlighting certain key figures:

1. The variable manufacturing costs associated with segment sales are reported separately. Because these costs are proportionately variable with sales volume, the reader of the statement can easily identify the relationship between sales revenue and variable manufacturing costs for the achieved sales or any prospective level of sales.

2. The difference between the revenues and variable manufacturing costs of the segment represents the manufacturing variable margin generated by the segment during the reporting period.

3. The deduction of nonmanufacturing variable costs from the manufacturing variable margin provides the segment variable margin. This variable margin is the segment contribution to segment and firm fixed costs for the period.

4. The amount of fixed costs traceable directly to the segment operations are treated as period costs and are deducted from the segment variable margin. The separable fixed costs of the segment represent those period costs that must be covered by the segment margin before any surplus is available to cover the unallocated fixed costs of the company as a whole.

5. The bottom line of the direct costing statement at the segment level is the net of variable margin and the segment fixed costs of the period. This net amount is the segment income, the amount of segment contribution to unallocated company fixed costs. The amount of segment income is an additional guide to the adequacy of segment margins, even though it does not bear an easily recognizable relationship to the volume of sales. Direct costing segment income is not affected by volume variances and by changes in inventory levels as would be the case under absorption costing.

b. SHORT-RUN DECISION MAKING.   The identification in the direct costing statement of the five figures discussed above facilitates segment and company short-run decision making. The separation of variable and fixed costs is the key to cost-volume-profit analysis. Cost-volume-profit relationships are in turn the basis for answering many frequently asked questions. The following is a partial list of the kinds of questions and decisions to which direct costing statements may contribute information:

(1) VOLUME CHANGES.   A critical factor in profit planning is forecasting the volume of sales and the effect of volume fluctuations on the achieved levels of profits. The direct costing statement plays a role in this by highlighting the relationship between volume and profit at historical price and cost levels. (Cost-volume-profit analysis requires an assumption of a constant product mix for multiproduct firms because the variable margin differs from product to product.)

If price and cost relationships have changed, it is a fairly simple task to adjust the direct costing statement to incorporate prospective selling prices and cost levels. The effect of volume changes can then be calculated by adding or subtracting the appropriate amount of variable margin that will be gained or lost by increasing or reducing volume. The direct costing statement format is consistent, in other words, with the demands of breakeven analysis (Exhibit 8).

(2) COST CHANGES.   Different decisions affect different kinds of costs. By segregating those costs that change with volume, the variable costs, the direct costing statement provides the starting point for analyzing the effect on profit of changes in variable cost levels. A reduction in unit variable costs widens the variable margin per unit of sale and decreases the breakeven point; an increase in variable cost per unit, of course, has the opposite effect. Decisions regarding changes in capacity costs and other costs not variable in the short run can be related to the size of the variable margin. An investment in fixed costs to reduce variable costs (for example, an investment to mechanize a manual process) involves a trade-off between the variable and fixed cost components of the direct costing statement. The trade-off may or may not affect total costs at a given volume level, but it certainly changes the responsiveness of profit to changes in volume levels by changing the slope of the contribution line. The variable/fixed dichotomy of the direct costing statement is not limited to manufacturing costs but extends to marketing costs as well. The interrelationships among selling price, volume, variable marketing costs, and fixed marketing costs can also be handled in terms of their effect on the size and adequacy of the variable margin. An increase in fixed advertising costs, for example, would affect the adequacy of the variable margin at

EXHIBIT 8   Breakeven Analysis

Sales in units	25,000	50,000	75,000
Sales @ $3	$75,000	$150,000	$225,000
Variable costs @ $2	50,000	100,000	150,000
Variable margin @ $1	$25,000	$ 50,000	$ 75,000
Fixed costs	50,000	50,000	50,000
Net income	$(25,000)	$ —	$ 25,000

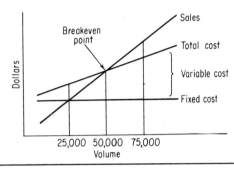

	Per Unit
Selling Price	$3
Variable costs	2
Variable margin	$1

Fixed costs $50,000 per year.

current volume levels, but if volume levels increased at the same margin per unit, the effect on segment net income might be positive.

(3) PRICING DECISIONS.   Pricing a product involves a great number of complexities ranging from marketing considerations to long-run full cost recovery and the generation of an adequate rate of return on investment. An adequate return on investment is a long-run goal. In the short run, most companies price flexibly to meet changing market conditions. Under the very worst conditions a company can still make a positive contribution to covering the fixed period costs if the selling price exceeds variable cost. Variable cost serves as the pricing floor for most products. In situations where the company has excess capacity, sales may be priced with reference to the variable margin. In all of these cases, the direct costing statement identifies the scope of short-run pricing decisions. In all pricing situations, care must be taken to avoid violating the antitrust laws.

(4) PRODUCT MIX ANALYSES.   In situations where excess capacity exists, the appropriate short-run solution is to try to fill that excess capacity with the product that will provide the greatest variable margin.[4] If it is possible to use the excess capacity to make a product that is normally contracted to an outside company, a comparison of the variable costs of making versus the cost of buying outside should be the basis of the decision. In cases where all products make equal use of the fixed resources, a ranking of the products by variable margin will indicate their relative contribution to firm overhead. In cases where products fail to cover either their separable fixed costs or their share of firm fixed costs, an analysis of their

[4]Excess capacity refers to a general ability to produce more. The lack of excess capacity may result from a machine constraint, labor constraint, space constraint, or any other kind of manufacturing bottleneck.

variable margin will indicate the impact on firm profitability of dropping the product. In all these cases, the direct costing format emphasizes the marginal impact of adding, dropping, expanding, or contracting the volume of products. In contrast, the full-cost absorption costing statement emphasizes the profitability of a product for a given level of volume.

The incremental effects of short-run product decisions are not readily visible in an absorption cost framework. An illustrative ranking of product profitability under both systems is given in Exhibit 9. Products A, B, and C share common manufacturing facilities but are sales independent. Products A and B both appear to be unprofitable. Both statements make it clear that neither are covering their share of period costs. In the short run, however, the dropping of these two products would have a detrimental effect on company profits equal to their combined variable margin of $8,000. The effect of capacity constraints and lengthening time horizons are discussed in the next section.

EXHIBIT 9   Product Profitability: Illustration of Superior Information from Direct Costing Report Where Three Products Share Common Facility

	Product A		Product B		Product C	
Sales		$20,000		$15,000		$30,000
Variable expenses	$15,000		$12,000		$20,000	
Fixed costs	8,000		5,000		8,000	
Cost of sales		23,000		17,000		28,000
Net income		$ (3,000)		$ (2,000)		$ 2,000

c. "WHAT IF?" QUESTIONS.   Because the format of the direct costing statement lends itself to cost-volume-profit analysis, it provides the starting point for analyzing management's "what if" questions. What will happen to profit if volume increases 10 percent? What will happen to profit if we increase selling prices 5 percent and volume stays constant? How much additional volume do we need to cover additional fixed advertising costs? Comparative direct costing profit statements provide variable margin information to answer management's questions.

d. INTERSEGMENT PRICING PROBLEMS.   The problem of pricing intrafirm transactions is a somewhat controversial one. It is necessary, however, to choose some accounting basis for pricing these transfers to ensure that the right products and amounts of the products are transferred between segments of the firm. Additionally, the transferred costs affect the performance reports of the segments involved. One recommended method of transfer pricing is to price transfers at variable cost. The advantage of the variable cost method is to eliminate the need to allocate segment fixed manufacturing cost to the transfers. It also avoids the danger of including the fixed costs of one division in the price charged to the second division. Because the transfer price to the buying division is all variable, it will make decisions on that basis. The cost to the company, however, is partially fixed. Transfers at variable cost avoid these problems and are consistent with direct costing performance statements.

e. MANAGEMENT CONTROL.   The direct costing performance report highlights volume-related cost changes by segregating variable and fixed costs. The process of classifying costs into their fixed and variable components is a learning experience for all concerned. The controller's department, the sales manager, the production manager, and the industrial engineer may all acquire an improved understanding of cost behavior. Persons interviewed in an NAA research study, for example, stated that top executives were astounded when they first learned the amount of period cost associated with being ready to do business.[5] A better understanding of cost behavior should produce related improvements in cost control.

A segment performance report prepared in a direct costing format highlights volume-related cost changes and their effect on the variable margin. The variable margin becomes, therefore, a basis for divisional or departmental evaluation and control. Whether or not this emphasis produces positive results is a matter of some dispute. The absorption costing school believes that emphasis on the variable margin reduces the pressure on a manager to earn a sufficient margin to cover separable segment fixed costs and to provide a contribution to company overhead. They believe that a departmental manager should be responsible for bottom-line performance. The direct costing statement does, however, emphasize volume-related cost and revenue changes. Also, it does not ignore the period costs; it deducts them from the variable margin to obtain segment income. If the segment manager's responsibility is clear regarding the adequacy of segment margin and income, the danger of maintaining inadequate long-run margins should be minimized. In the short run, managerial responsiveness should be greatly improved.

2. *Limitations of Direct Costing for Planning and Control.*

a. THE HISTORICAL COST PERSPECTIVE. Planning is a prospective venture. Decisions are made about the future and not about the past. The use of the direct costing statement as a planning tool is limited by its historical perspective. It is a report on historical revenues, variable costs, and period fixed costs. The report should not be used for planning purposes unless it has been adjusted for any current or expected changes in the cost and revenue relationships. Increases or decreases in the selling price, variable cost per unit, or the expected level of fixed period costs should be incorporated into the direct costing statement before it is used as a breakeven tool. The new cost and revenue assumptions can be built into a *proforma* performance statement that restates the variable margin and net income at the historical volume levels. This *proforma* statement will show the amount of income that would have been earned in the preceding period if prospective cost and revenues had been in force.

b. COST BEHAVIOR ASSUMPTIONS. The classification of costs into their variable and fixed components is not a simple or clear process. Cost behavior analysis requires certain assumptions to be made, simplifications to be accepted, and the risk accepted of misclassification and lack of completeness. The use of variability as a basis for classification requires assumptions regarding proportionality, the relevant range of production, the time horizon involved, and the possible interdependency of cost and volume.

Variable cost is a simplification of what economists refer to as "marginal cost." Both terms imply cost changes relative to volume changes. Marginal cost may imply a nonlinear relationship between cost and volume. Variable cost implies a linear relationship, a proportionality between cost and volume. Rarely is proportionality a completely valid assumption. If production remains within the relevant range, however, it is approximately valid. Where this is the case, the direct costing statement is a sufficiently accurate representation of cost variability. The user of direct costing statements should be aware, however, that proportionality is an assumption that cannot hold true in all situations. Examples of factors that might affect the proportionality assumption include quantity discounts on materials, material, and labor efficiency variances with changing volume levels and learning curve effects.

Departure from the relevant range of production requires reconsideration of

[5]National Association of Accountants, "Current Applications of Direct Costing."

cost behavior. The assumptions of variability and fixity cannot hold through all possible ranges of production volume. Outside the relevant range, it is still possible to make forecasts, but the inappropriateness of the assumptions of the performance report will make a special analysis of the situation necessary.

Any good planning model defines a time horizon to limit the scope of uncertainty. The length of this planning horizon has important implications for the use of the direct costing statement. The definition used for variability in the direct costing statement is a short-run definition. In the short run, it is possible that only the direct costs of production and sales are variable with volume. In the long run, any cost not already sunk is variable. Machines must be replaced and new facilities must be constructed. Costs that appear to be fixed in the performance report may require funds to be expended within the planning time horizon.

The separate classification of the cost and revenue types might lead the reader to the erroneous conclusion that each item was independent of all the others. A correct understanding of cost and revenue interdependencies is essential if the performance report is to be used correctly. An increase in variable cost might increase quality and permit a per-unit price increase. An increase in fixed cost might lower the variable cost per unit by improving productivity. An increase in fixed advertising costs might increase per-unit prices and sales volume.

c. OPPORTUNITY COSTS.   The variable/fixed dichotomy presents a proposition to the uninformed reader that only those costs classified as variable will actually be increased when a decision increasing the volume of the product is made. There are many situations when this will not be true. In these situations, the information in the direct costing performance statement will be only a starting point for a complete analysis. A complete analysis is one that includes all costs, including opportunity costs, that will be incurred or avoided as a result of a particular decision. Opportunity cost is the incremental net revenue or cost saving derivable from an opportunity that is sacrificed by accepting the next best alternative opportunity.

The availability of excess capacity for increasing the volume of a product affects the existence of opportunity costs. As long as there is excess capacity, the incremental cost of increasing the volume of a product is the variable cost; the variable margin represents the increase in profits per unit of the product. If the company is operating at the limits of capacity, the cost of increasing production of one product must include the indirect opportunity cost of reducing the volume of another product. The cost of expanding product A will be the sum of the variable cost of product A plus the variable margin of product B that is produced in lesser volume to make room for product A. As long as there is only one capacity constraint, and each product uses an equal amount of the capacity, the decision rule is simply to produce those products with the highest per-unit variable margin. The decision becomes a little more complicated if products use different amounts of the limited capacity resource to produce units of the products. The decision rule is then to produce those products that contribute the highest variable margin per unit of the limited capacity resource. A further complication occurs where there are two or more capacity constraints. An example would be where a product passes through two production processes. The decision rule here is to maximize the total variable margin from all products given the limitations of capacity. The analysis for this decision requires a linear programming model (see Exhibit 10). Note that the source of information for the linear programming objective function is the variable margin in the direct costing performance statement.

The direct costing statement may also provide an incomplete analysis for decisions to retain or drop a product. The variable/fixed dichotomy does not necessarily parallel the division of costs into an avoidable/unavoidable classification. The dropping of a product may permit the sale of machinery and tooling, the

EXHIBIT 10   Linear Programming

	Product X	Product Y
Selling price	$8.00	$8.00
Variable cost	4.00	5.00
Variable margin	$4.00	$3.00
Maximum estimated sales demand per month	100 units	80 units
Woodworking time per unit	4 hours	5 hours
Assembly time per unit	3 hours	5 hours

Combined fixed manufacturing cost for X and Y: $200 per week.
Maximum time in woodworking, 500 hours; in assembly, 450 hours.

$$\text{Objective function} = \text{maximize } \$4X + \$3Y$$

$$
\begin{aligned}
\text{Subject to: } X &\leqslant 100 \\
Y &\leqslant 80 \\
4X + 5Y &\leqslant 500 \\
3X + 5Y &\leqslant 450 \\
X &\geqslant 0 \\
Y &\geqslant 0
\end{aligned}
$$

The optimum solution is 100 units of X and 20 units of Y, yielding a variable margin of

$$\$4 \times 100 + \$3 \times 20 = \$460$$

SOURCE: Adapted from Jack Gray and Kenneth S. Johnston, *Accounting and Management Action* (McGraw-Hill Book Company, New York, 1973).

dropping of advertising campaigns, and the abandonment of market and product research programs. If this is the case, then some of the costs classified as fixed by direct costing will be avoidable when the product is dropped. This does not mean that the classifications of direct costing are wrong. It does indicate, however, that direct costing cannot and does not provide the right information for all short-run decisions.

d. TECHNICAL PROBLEMS.   Classifying costs by behavior raises some technical problems. As noted earlier, a general assumption of direct costing is that certain costs vary proportionately with volume. A preliminary task in implementing a direct costing system is to identify the variable costs. This identification may be performed via an engineering study or by examining historical accounting data. In either case, the researcher is looking for a positive correlation between the cost incurred and volume. Costs vary in their degree of variability, however, and this will be evidenced by a stronger or weaker correlation. The classification of costs as fixed or variable may vary according to the strength of correlation that is desired. A further problem is that the basis for variability may not always be volume. Some costs might vary more closely with direct labor hours than with the number of units produced. In this case, the assumption that the cost varies proportionately with volume will hold true only if the efficiency with which the cost is incurred remains constant. A significant labor efficiency (or quantity) variance would affect this assumption.

Direct costing distinguishes between variable and fixed costs. How then should one account for semivariable and semifixed costs? One determining factor is the degree to which the cost departs from pure variability or fixity. If the cost is predominantly variable, it should be classified as such. If it is predominantly fixed, it should be classified as fixed. A large number of stepwise progressions within the relevant range may suggest that classification as variable is a reasonable assumption. Fixed may be a better approximation if the steps are small and infrequent. Where it is not possible to classify the cost as either variable or fixed, it may still be possible to separate its component parts. The hourly wage of a piecerate worker may be classified as fixed, for example, and the piecerate may be classified as variable.

e. Institutional Problems.

(1) antitrust.   The variable cost of a product represents, in certain circumstances, the minimum price that may be accepted for that product. A price that is collected above the variable cost represents at least a partial contribution to overhead. A company may, for example, accept a low price for a special order that provides a positive variable margin. If this special price is not available to other customers, however, the company may be in violation of the antitrust laws. The Robinson-Patman Act of 1936 was passed to prohibit certain kinds of price discrimination. The preamble to the Bill states that its purpose is

> To make it unlawful for any person engaged in commerce to discriminate in price or terms of sale between purchasers of commodities of like grade and quality; to prohibit the payment of brokerage or commission under certain conditions, to suppress pseudoadvertising allowances; to provide a presumptive measure of damages in certain cases; and to protect the independent merchant, the public whom he serves, and the manufacturer from whom he buys, from exploitation by unfair competitors.[6]

Price discrimination is not prohibited when costs differ because methods or quantities of sale differ. The cost proviso of the Act states:

> That nothing herein contained shall prevent differentials which make only due allowance for differences in the cost of manufacture, sale, or delivery resulting from the differing methods or quantities in which such commodities are to such purchasers sold or delivered.[7]

Clearly, the definition of cost is crucial to the question of lawful price differential. Wright Patman defined what he believed to be cost:

> Costs enjoy the paradoxical position of being definite and at the same time variable. Every article in commerce has accumulated certain definite elements of cost in the process of its production and distribution. At the same time the elements of pricing with which we are concerned must include also a forecast of what costs will accumulate in an article by the time it passes out of our hands into the hands of a purchaser. Thereupon we encounter the variable factor arising out of future processes.
>
> ... It is not sound to argue that, because present overhead is absorbed by present production, a producer could make 10,000 extra units at no cost for overhead and hence could sell them to a favored buyer at a less cost than other units sold. The increased production merely reduces the overhead cost on all units equally. The same applies to the cost of handling or warehousing.
>
> As the volume of business increases, the cost per unit recedes all along the line. Every unit handled must bear its share. As the units increase in number, the individual share becomes less and the selling price may be lowered in direct proportion to the decrease in cost of each unit.[8]

From this definition, it is clear that Wright Patman intended cost to include all costs of manufacture, sale or delivery, excluding the return on invested capital, but including a prorated share of all overhead costs.

It would probably be unlawful for a company to sell to one customer based on full cost and to another based on variable cost where the methods or quantities of sale do not differ. This does not mean, however, that direct costing cannot be used as a guide to pricing. Prices may be set below full cost, but care must be taken not to violate the Robinson-Patman Act. Using direct costing as a basis for pricing is not the same as setting the price equal to variable cost.

(2) direct costing and transfer pricing.   Companies structured on a divisional basis need divisional performance statements and rules for pricing interdivi-

---

[6]Wright Patman, *The Robinson-Patman Act* (Ronald Press, New York, 1938), p. 3.
[7]*Ibid.*, p. 70.
[8]*Ibid.*, pp. 13–14.

sional transactions. The choice of direct costing as the format for divisional performance reports does not preclude the choice of a transfer price from the several types available. It does, however, provide a simple opportunity to transfer price at variable cost.[9]

In multinational companies, intra- and interdivisional transactions may cross international boundaries. Tax and customs duty minimization may dictate transfer at variable cost. Penrose, for example, developed a model that utilizes transfer prices to make optimal use of differing treatments of incomes and different tax rates between countries.[10] Before any transfers are made at variable cost, careful evaluation should be made of local tax laws, customs regulations, antidumping provisions, and the social responsibilities of multinational companies.

Inventory Valuation and Income Determination

Accounting Theory and Generally Accepted Accounting Principles. The analysis of direct and absorption costing in preceding section found significant income differences in certain situations. These income effects were the result of a difference in the application of the matching of costs to revenues. In absorption costing a distinction is made between manufacturing and nonmanufacturing costs. The manufacturing costs are treated as costs of the product. The nonmanufacturing costs are treated as costs of the period. Direct costing, in contrast, distinguishes between variable and fixed manufacturing costs. Direct costing treats only the variable manufacturing costs as costs of the product. It is this difference in the application of the matching concept that is central to the choice between direct and absorption costing for financial statement purposes.

Advocates of direct costing find support for their matching concept in the principle of cost obviation.[11] The principle of cost obviation states that a cost incurred in the production of revenue, in this or some future accounting period, may be capitalized only to the extent that it results in the avoidance of costs in some future period. The use of raw material, labor, and variable overhead to make a unit of the product obviates the need to use those resources in the future to produce one unit of the product. The production of this unit has no effect, however, on the fixed costs of manufacture. Variable costs, according to this theory, are appropriately treated as product costs. Fixed costs are period costs.

Absorption costers counter this argument by demonstrating that an opportunity cost may be associated with capacity and by stating further that historical fixed costs represent the most acceptable measure of these opportunity costs. Where there are capacity limitations, the failure to produce will result in lost sales. The lost variable margin on these sales represents an opportunity cost to the firm. This opportunity cost does not, however, appear in the accounting system. As an imputed cost it lacks the objectivity of a historical cost and is not acceptable as a basis for asset valuation. Absorption costers, therefore, take the opportunity cost only as evidence of the value of capacity. Fixed cost should, it is argued, be included in inventory cost as an objective approximation of opportunity cost.

There are some theoretical problems with this argument. If there is excess capacity, opportunity cost will be zero. Where capacity is limited, opportunity cost may be higher than historical fixed cost. Only coincidentally will opportunity cost equal historical fixed cost. Valuation based on opportunity cost would produce a fluctuating inventory valuation from zero to some positive figure. Sorter and

---

[9]If transfers at variable cost are purely intracompany transactions, it is not thought that the Robinson-Patman Act applies.

[10]Edith Penrose, *The Large International Firm in the Developing Countries: The International Petroleum Industry* (MIT Press, Cambridge, Mass., 1968).

[11]David Green, Jr., "A Moral to the Direct Costing Controversy," *Journal of Business,* XXXIII, 3 (July 1960), pp. 218–226.

Horngren recognized this and proposed a partial solution to the problem.[12] In this solution, inventory would be valued from an available range of historical cost from full cost at the upper end to variable cost at the lower end. The amount of opportunity cost would determine the valuation from within the range.

A switch from historical cost accounting to some form of current price accounting will not end the direct/absorption costing controversy. General price-level adjustments will not affect the need for attachment of cost classes to inventory. The effect on inventory will be merely an inflation of the historical cost of each manufacturing cost class to reflect the current value of the dollar. The introduction of replacement cost accounting will require the adjustment of manufacturing costs to current levels.[13] This affects the timing and measurement of income but does not affect the matching principle.

In attempting to determine the acceptability of direct costing as a generally accepted accounting principle, the only authoritative literature is Chapter 4 of *Accounting Research Bulletin No. 43,* Paragraph 5, which states:

> . . . the exclusion of all overhead from inventory costs does not constitute an accepted accounting. The exercise of judgment in an individual situation involves a consideration of the adequacy of the procedures of the cost accounting system in use, the soundness of the principles thereof, and their consistent application.[14]

The difficulty with Paragraph 5 is that it does not specify which particular overhead cost components are to be included or excluded from inventory. A result of this ambiguity is that alternative methods of allocating overhead costs to inventory under absorption costing are acceptable. In addition, because direct costing requires the capitalization of variable overhead, it could be argued that Paragraph 5 recognizes direct costing as a generally accepted accounting principle.

An examination of inventory valuation practice may shed some light on how this ambiguity is handled. A 1961 survey of 50 companies by the NAA found 17 companies using direct costing for external reporting purposes.[15] None of the 17 companies received qualified opinions. Unfortunately, it is not possible to verify that this frequency continues, because there is no disclosure of direct costing in financial statements. *Accounting Trends and Techniques* does not mention the use of direct costing.[16] A search of the annual reports of approximately 3,100 companies in the National Automated Accounting Research System (NAARS) yielded no disclosure of the use of direct costing.[17] One annual report from 1974 yielded a change from variable costing (an alternative term for direct costing) to absorption costing. The footnote and management's explanation of the effect of the change are reprinted in Exhibit 11. This change was treated as a change in accounting method rather than a correction of an error. The auditors indicated in their opinion that the financial statements were

> . . . in conformity with generally accepted accounting principles consistently applied during the period except for the changes, with which we concur, in the methods of accounting for overhead cost in inventory. . . .

[12]G. Sorter and C. T. Horngren, "Asset Recognition and Economic Attributes—A Relevant Costing Approach," *Accounting Review,* XXXVII, 3 (July 1962), pp. 391–399.

[13]Lawrence Revsine, *Replacement Cost Accounting* (Prentice-Hall, Englewood Cliffs, N.J., 1973).

[14]American Institute of Certified Public Accountants, *Accounting Research Bulletin No. 43* (AICPA, New York, 1953).

[15]National Association of Accountants, "Current Applications of Direct Costing," pp. 86–96.

[16]American Institute of Certified Public Accountants, *Accounting Trends and Techniques* (AICPA, New York, 1977).

[17]American Institute of Certified Public Accountants, National Automated Accounting Research System.

EXHIBIT 11   Disclosure of Change from Direct to Absorption Costing

NORTHWEST ENGINEERING COMPANY AND SUBSIDIARY
From Notes to Consolidated Financial Statements
Years Ended December 31, 1974 and 1973

Note B—Changes in accounting principles:
Effective January 1, 1974, the Company changed its methods of accounting for overhead costs in
inventory, vacation pay, and insurance dividends relating to the Company's pension plan to more
properly match revenues and expenses. The proforma amounts shown on the statement of consolidated
earnings give the retroactive effect of these changes.
Effective January 1, 1974, the valuing of overhead costs in inventory was changed from a variable costing
method (the treatment of certain manufacturing costs as period expenses) used in prior years to a full
absorption method. The $961,117 cumulative effect (net of income taxes of $625,000, which are to be
paid principally over a ten year period) of this change on prior years is included in earnings for the year
ended December 31, 1974.

From Management's Analysis of the Summary of Operations:
Cumulative effect of accounting changes on prior years earnings of $919,000 is primarily the result of a
change by the Company in its method of valuing overhead costs in inventory from a variable costing
method used in prior years to a full absorption method. This change was made so manufacturing
overhead would be ratably allocated to products sold and ending inventories, thereby resulting in a
better matching of costs and revenues in the statement of earnings. The effect of this change for the year
1974 was to increase net earnings by $276,399 ($.30 per common share). . . .

A company that has used direct costing for years might be able to justify
continuing its use on the basis of consistency. *Accounting Research Bulletin No. 43*
mentions consistency as an important consideration in determining the acceptability of an inventory valuation method. It would not be possible, however, for a
company to switch from absorption costing to direct costing. Absorption costing is
the predominant method.

Securities and Exchange Commission.   The SEC has the authority to determine its
own accounting principles but has usually relied on the accounting profession to
set generally accepted accounting principles. A material departure from generally
accepted accounting will usually require an adjustment to the financial statements.
Mere disclosure is generally not sufficient.[18]

Because absorption costing is the predominant generally accepted accounting
principle, it should be the basis for inventory valuation in SEC filings. Some
companies, however, apparently file their financial statements omitting a portion
of indirect cost from inventory. If this does not have a material effect, disclosure
alone has been accepted by the SEC:

> Sometimes the omission of overhead from inventory does not have a material effect
> either on the financial position or on the results of the operations during the period
> under report. In that case the SEC has accepted registration statements containing
> financial statements which disclosed the facts and stated that the statements had not been
> adjusted.[19]

Accounting Reports for Tax Purposes.   Section 471 of the Internal Revenue Code
governs the determination of inventoriable costs. The IRS did not issue definitive
regulations under Section 471 until 1973. Prior to that date, there was considerable variability in the determination of inventoriable costs, including some acceptance of direct costing in the courts of law. The regulations issued in 1973
(1.471.11) specifically require absorption costing. Regulation 1.471.11 spells out in
detail the types of cost that must or must not be capitalized to inventory. There is,
however, some discretion available to the taxpayer in the choice of treatment for
certain categories of cost.

[18]Louis H. Rappaport, *SEC Accounting Practice and Procedure*, 2nd ed. (Ronald Press, New
York, 1963), p. 93.
[19]*Ibid.*, p. 21.20.

The requirement for capitalizing inventory costs is stated as follows in Section 471:

> Whenever in the opinion of the secretary or his delegate the use of inventories is necessary in order clearly to determine the income of any taxpayer, inventories shall be taken by such taxpayer on such basis as the secretary or his delegate may prescribe as conforming as nearly as may be to the best accounting practice in the trade or business and as most clearly reflecting the income.

Attempts by the IRS to require full absorption costing under this section were somewhat frustrated by the courts. In *Photo Sonics, Inc.* [42 T.C. 926 (1964)], the tax court found prime cost to be unacceptable. The 9th Circuit Court reaffirmed this decision but left the door open for approval of direct costing. The consistent use of direct costing over a period of years was approved in *McNeil Machine and Engineering Co.* [Ct. Cl. Commissioner's Report, (3-29-67)] and in *Geometric Stamping Company* [26 T.C. 301 (1956)]. A taxpayer could justify exclusion of cost from inventory under the "immutability theory" expounded in *All Steel Equipment Co.* [54 T.C. 1749 (1970)]. Under this theory, currently deductible specific expenses expressly authorized by the Code could be deductible and excluded from inventory.

Regulation 1.471.11 was issued in 1973. Its effect was to require the use of absorption costing and prohibit the use of direct costing. Paragraph 1 of 1.471.11 states in part:

> In order to conform as nearly as may be possible to the best accounting practices and to clearly reflect income (as required by section 471 of the Code), both direct and indirect production costs must be taken into account in the computation of inventoriable costs in accordance with the "full absorption" method of inventory costing.

The inclusion of indirect production cost in inventory cost is required. Not all indirect production costs, however, must be included. Regulation 1.471.11 defines three categories of indirect production cost (Exhibit 12). Category I costs, such as repairs and maintenance, must be capitalized. Category II costs, such as marketing and advertising, are includable at the taxpayer's option. The treatment of category III costs, such as "factory administrative expenses," is governed by the financial statements where the statements follow generally accepted accounting principles. The taxpayer who follows generally accepted accounting principles has considerable discretion in the treatment of category II and category III items for tax purposes.

Where the taxpayer uses different accounting methods for financial reporting purposes and tax purposes, the regulations are somewhat different. Regulation 1.471.11(c)(3) would apply, for example, where the taxpayer uses direct costing for financial reporting and absorption costing for tax purposes. Under this regulation there are only two categories of cost, those that are includable inventoriable costs and those that are excluded. The excludable costs are those in category II (Exhibit 12) plus employee benefits and the cost of strikes, rework labor, scrap, and spoilage from category III. Includable costs are category I costs, and the remaining are category III costs.

Segment Reporting.   Segment reporting has always been an internal management reporting tool. The Financial Accounting Standards Board (FASB) requires external reporting of segment profit data.[20] The use of direct costing statements in segment reporting would be an unambiguous method of stating segment results. No allocation of fixed costs would be required to compute the segment variable

---

[20]Financial Accounting Standards Board, Statement of Financial Accounting Standards No. 14, "Financial Reporting for Segment of Business Enterprises" (FASB, Stamford, Conn., 1976).

EXHIBIT 12   Categories of Indirect Production Cost
(Adapted from Section 1.471.11)

Category I	*Costs Which Must Be Recognized*
	Repairs
	Maintenance
	Utilities
	Rent
	Indirect labor
	Production supervisory wages
	Indirect materials and supplies
	Small tools and equipment
	Quality control and inspection
Category II	*Costs Which Are Includable at Taxpayer's Option Regardless of Treatment in Financial Reports*
	Marketing
	Advertising
	Selling
	Other distribution expenses
	Interest
	Research and experimental
	Section 165 losses
	Percentage depletion in excess of cost depletion
	Depreciation and amortization for federal tax purposes in excess of financial statement depreciation
	Local and foreign income taxes
	Past service costs/pensions
	Administrative (general)
	Officers' salaries (general)
Category III	*Costs Governed by Financial Statements*
	(If statements follow generally accepted accounting principles and the financial statements use absorption costing)
	Taxes (under Section 164, other than local and foreign income taxes)
	Financial statement depreciation and cost depletion
	Factory administrative expenses
	Officers' salaries (manufacturing)
	Insurance costs (manufacturing)
	Employee benefits (e.g., current service costs of pension and profit sharing plans, workmen's compensation, etc.)
	Cost of strikes, rework labor, scrap, and spoilage

margin. The FASB does not, however, take this approach. The "profit contribution" defined in the statement is an absorption costing gross margin less other direct costs.

DIRECT COSTING AS AN INTEGRATED REPORTING SYSTEM

A company that contemplates designing a direct costing system must expect to devote much effort to the development of the system and its integration into the accounting and reporting system. The design of a direct costing system is an opportunity to improve and consolidate the company's financial reporting structure. If a thorough job is done, the result should be to improve cost controls, pricing decisions, planning, and budgeting efforts.

A direct costing system should not be viewed as an adjunct to the accounting system but as a component of an integrated management and financial reporting system. In addition to its basic tasks of inventory and cost-of-sales valuation, the direct costing concept should be tied into the following:

- Standard costs
- Margin variance analysis by division, by product group or product, and by product mix
- Reconciliation with absorption costing.

A brief description of a general system designed to accomplish all of the above objectives follows.

Standard Costs. In a standard cost system, the primary document for capturing actual cost will be the Manufacturing Work Order. The work order is issued to the plant by the production department, authorizing a certain kind of manufacturing activity and providing a control number against which labor and material are charged.

Raw materials and purchased parts are brought into inventory at standard purchased prices, with variances from these standards written off to a material price variance account in the period in which the purchase is recorded. When a Manufacturing Work Order is issued, the parts are transferred via a requisition into Work in Process at their standard cost. Labor expended to assemble these parts into finished units is reported on the Manufacturing Work Order and charged to Work in Process at variable departmental budget rates. Upon completion of the order, a transfer is made to Finished Units Inventory via a Move Order. The transfer will be at the standard material and standard labor cost for the assembled units. Variances will be written off in the period of completion. The difference between actual material charged to the Manufacturing Work Order and the standard material cost is written off to Material Usage Variance. The difference between the actual labor charged to the work order and the standard labor cost is written off to the Labor Efficiency Variance.

Note that the procedure charges only variable costs, at standard, to the work-in-process and completed inventory. Exhibit 13 presents the format of a Division Earning Statement using this standard direct costing system. The cost of sales contains two components, the standard cost of sales and the material and labor variances. Cost of sales is, therefore, the variable manufacturing cost of sales at actual for the period.

Margin Variance Analysis. In Exhibit 13, the variable margin is stated at both planned and actual for the division. The difference between planned and actual for each product line or for total sales is the variable margin variance. These variable margin variances are net indicators of divisional success in meeting planned margins.

The variable margin variances in Exhibit 13 are computed using standard cost. We assume that standard costs have not been adjusted during the budget period and that the component specifications of each product remain the same. If these assumptions hold true, the margin variances are the net result of three factors: the performance, volume, and mix variances. The performance variance, either by product line or for total sales, results from differences between planning and actual selling prices. The volume variance is caused by differences between planned and actual total sales. A mix variance occurs when more or less than planned high- or low-margin products are sold.

Exhibit 14 is a simplified version of a Performance, Volume, and Mix Analysis Report. Data are shown for only two products, one high-margin and one low-margin product. The total margin variance for both products is favorable; actual margins exceed planned margins by $1,000. The analysis of this variance is shown in Exhibit 15. The adjustments are all done at standard. The annual budgeted amounts for capacity costs and direct manufacturing cost must be reviewed monthly or quarterly to ensure that the Fixed Complement Standard Rate reflects current and projected budgeted amounts.

Reconciliation with Absorption Costing. Our analysis of generally accepted accounting principles, SEC and IRS regulations, indicates that direct costing is not usually acceptable for external reporting purposes. It is, therefore, necessary to build into a direct costing system a simple adjustment mechanism to convert to full absorption costing. Exhibit 13 contains a "fixed complement adjustment" that effectively adjusts the earnings to an absorption costing basis. The conversion of inventory values to a full absorption basis requires the computation of the proportion of fixed capacity cost to be capitalized to the inventory. The method described involves using the ratio of Capacity Costs to Direct Manufacturing Costs on a budgeted basis.

The adjustment from direct to absorption costing requires two accounts, the Fixed Complement Inventory to adjust the inventory accounts, and the Fixed Complement Adjustment to adjust earnings.

1. *Fixed Complement Inventory:* Manufacturing Capacity Costs to be reflected in inventory to convert to a full absorption basis of inventory valuation.

2. *Fixed Complement Adjustment:* Adjustment to earnings and inventory as a result of a change in variable direct cost inventory.

The first step in applying this method is to compute the ratio of Capacity Costs to Direct Manufacturing Costs in order to derive the Fixed Complement Standard Rate. The following figures are assumed for purposes of illustration.

$$\frac{\text{Annual Budgeted Manufacturing Capacity Costs}}{\text{Annual Budgeted Direct Manufacturing Costs}} = \frac{\text{Fixed Complement}}{\text{Standard Rate}}$$

$$\frac{\$11,000,000}{\$10,000,000} = \$1.10 \text{ of capacity costs per dollar of direct cost}$$

The second step is to compute the change in the standard labor inventory accounts as follows:

	Standard Direct Cost Inventory Accounts	
	Work-in-process	*Finished goods*
Ending balance	$175,000	$500,000
Beginning balance	200,000	400,000
Net change	$ (25,000)	$100,000

These amounts are then multiplied by the Fixed Complement Standard Rate:

$(25,000)	$100,000
× 1.10	× 1.10
$(27,750)	$110,000

These then are the amounts by which the Fixed Complement Inventory Accounts for Work in Process and Finished Goods should be adjusted. The net amount of this adjustment reflects the net effect upon earnings for the period. The entry in this example would be

Finished Goods Fixed		
Complement Inventory	110,000	
Work-in-Process Fixed		
Complement Inventory		27,750
Fixed Complement Adjustment . .		82,250

Thus, the net valuation of Work in Process is decreased while that of Finished Goods is increased. Earnings for the period are adjusted upward by the credit of $82,250.

EXHIBIT 13   Division Statement of Earnings

Date_____
($000)

	Current month			Year-to-date	
	Actual	Forecast	Variance from plan	Actual	Plan	Variance from plan
Sales						
Consumer products						
Other						
Industrial products						
Sales, returns, & allowances						
Net sales						
Standard cost of sales						
Material						
Direct labor & variable O/H						
Standard variable margin						
Other variable costs						
Material price variance						
Material usage variance						
Efficiency variance						
Spending variance						
Other						

Cost of sales				
Variable margin				
Capacity costs				
Manufacturing cost				
Engineering cost				
R&D cost				
Selling cost				
Advertising cost				
Administrative cost				
Total capacity costs				
Operating earnings				
Fixed complement adjustment				
Other income				
Interest				
Royalty				
Miscellaneous				
Other expense				
Interest				
Royalty				
Miscellaneous				
Earnings before taxes				
Provision for taxes				
Net earnings				

EXHIBIT 14 Performance, Volume, and Mix Analysis

Product line	Planned			Actual			Actual sales at planned margin (%)	Variance			
	Sales	Variable margin	Percent of sales	Sales	Variable margin	Percent of sales		Performance	Volume	Mix	Total
Consumer products	$10,000	$5,000	50.0%	$15,000	$6,000	40.0%	$ 7,500	$(1,500)			
Industrial products	12,000	3,000	25.0	10,000	3,000	30.0	2,500	500			
Total sales	$22,000	$8,000	36.4%	$25,000	$9,000	36.0%	$10,000	$(1,000)	$1,100	$900	$1,000

Performance variance (product line and total sales)
  Actual sales at actual margin percent *less* actual sales at planned margin percent
Volume variance (total sales only)
  Actual sales in total at planned margin percent *less* planned sales at planned margin percent
Mix variance (total sales only)
  Actual sales by product line at planned margin percent *less* actual sales in total at planned margin percent

EXHIBIT 15   Analysis of Performance, Volume, and Mix Variances

Performance variance

Consumer products			
Actual sales at actual margin percent	$6,000		
Less actual sales at planned margin percent	7,500	$(1,500)U	
Industrial products			
Actual sales at actual margin percent	$3,000		
Less actual sales at planned margin percent	2,500	500F	
Unfavorable total performance variance			$(1,000)U

Volume variance

Actual sales in total at planned margin percent = $25,000 × 36.4%		$ 9,100	
Less planned sales in total at planned margin percent		8,000	
Favorable volume variance			1,100F

Mix variance

Actual sales by product line at · planned margin percent		$10,000	
Actual sales in total at planned margin percent		9,100	
Favorable mix variance			900F
Total margin variance			$1,000F

CONCLUSION

Direct costing is a management reporting system for planning and control and for financial reporting. Recent and prospective developments in financial statement, SEC, and IRS reporting are likely, however, to reduce the role of direct costing for financial reporting for external purposes. The following developments suggest a reduced role for direct costing in financial reporting:

■ Absorption costing is the inventory method preferred in generally accepted accounting principles.

■ The SEC's position is that absorption costing is the generally accepted accounting principle.

■ The issue of Regulation 1.471.11 of the Internal Revenue Code greatly strengthens the use of absorption costing for tax purposes.

■ Future developments in the area of segment profit reporting are likely to be on an absorption costing basis despite the many years of use of direct costing for internal segment reporting.

The importance of direct costing in the years to come is likely to remain in the management accounting area. For many controllers, direct costing is an indispensable management tool. The highlight of the direct costing statement is the variable margin, an item that is widely recognized in management accounting textbooks and literature. It is the cornerstone of breakeven analysis and related linear programming problems. Direct costing is not a prerequisite to using either the variable margin or breakeven analysis. It does, however, incorporate the concept into internal management reports. The direct costing format, if used with care, lends itself to straightforward analysis. Without it, it would be difficult to perform the margin variance analysis that distinguishes performance, volume, and mix effects.

Chapter **12**

Inventories and Inventory Models

JOSEPH D. COUGHLAN
Partner, Price Waterhouse & Co.

VALUATION OF INVENTORIES[1]

In accounting literature, the term "valuation" is the one most commonly used in any discussion of inventories. In the majority of instances, however, the amount assigned to a particular inventory for accounting purposes is fundamentally a reflection of cost rather than a determination of value.

There are times when the value of an inventory is of primary significance. For example, where there is to be a forced bulk sale when liquidation of a business is contemplated, value is the only significant figure. This value will be the amount that a purchaser will pay for all the goods on hand. Value is also significant when a sale of a continuing business is contemplated. For this purpose, the value of the inventory is normally the aggregate of the replacement cost for the individual items on hand that will be useful to the purchaser plus the scrap value of excess quantities and obsolete items.

It may also be necessary to establish the value of an inventory when considering appropriate insurance coverage, the extent to which the inventory will be recognized as collateral for a loan, or the amount on which property tax assessments are based. In these situations, the amount assigned to the inventory in the course of normal accounting procedures may or may not be the answer. For example, in determining the appropriate base for a property tax, primary consideration must be given to the statutory requirements, local practices, and possibly the equalization factors that are part of the assessor's procedures.

Except for additions and revisions necessitated by recognition of the last-in, first-out (LIFO) method, there have been no substantive changes in the sections pertaining to inventories in the Internal Revenue Code for several decades. The only significant change in the Regulations is discussed below under "Tax and Other Influences on Overhead Absorption."

The Internal Revenue Code contains the general requirement that, "Whenever in the opinion of the Secretary or his delegate the use of inventories is necessary in order clearly to determine the income of any taxpayer, inventories shall be taken by such taxpayer. . . ." This section of the law concludes with the requirement that the inventories be taken on the basis that is prescribed by regulations "as conforming as nearly as may be to the best accounting practice in the trade or business and as most clearly reflecting income." The regulations reflect this statutory provision by the conclusions that (1) inventory rules cannot be uniform and (2) an inventory that can be used under the best accounting practice in a balance sheet showing the financial position of the taxpayer can, as a general rule, be regarded as clearly reflecting income.

The federal income tax regulations contain only a few general paragraphs to state the meaning of the term "cost." In the case of merchandise on hand at the beginning of the year, cost means the balance sheet valuation of the inventory at the end of the previous year. In the case of merchandise purchased since the beginning of the taxable year, cost means the invoice price less trade or other discounts (except strictly cash discounts approximating a fair interest rate, which may be deducted or not at the option of the taxpayer, provided that a consistent course is followed) *plus* transportation or other necessary charges incurred in acquiring possession of the goods. In the case of merchandise produced by the

---

[1]Although this *Handbook* is directed to specific facets of cost accounting, this chapter on inventories necessarily broadens the approach to reflect the influence of general reporting principles and tax requirements. Much of the material closely follows the format presented in Chapter 16 of the *Handbook of Modern Accounting*, 2nd ed., by R. H. Hoffman and J. D. Coughlan (Sidney Davidson and Roman L. Weil, eds., McGraw-Hill Book Company, New York, 1977).

taxpayer since the beginning of the year, the general rule is that cost means the aggregate of[2]

> (1) the cost of raw materials and supplies entering into or consumed in connection with the product, (2) expenditures for direct labor, (3) indirect expenses incident to and necessary for the production of the particular article, including in such indirect expenses a reasonable proportion of management expenses, but not including any cost of selling or return on capital, whether by way of interest or profit.

Use of general language in the income tax regulations is a recognition of the fact that there is no single concept of cost that is appropriate in all businesses.

The Lower of Cost or Market.   From the standpoint of modern accounting practice, the concept of value is primarily involved in the principle of stating inventories at the "lower of cost or market." The general rule is that there should be a departure from the cost basis of stating an inventory when the utility of the goods is no longer as great as its cost. The premise is that whether the difference between the cost and the expected utility of the goods is due to physical deterioration, obsolescence, changes in price levels, or other causes, the difference should be recognized as a loss of the period in which the determination of expected utility is made.

As used in the phrase "lower of cost or market," the term "market" means current replacement cost (by purchase or by reproduction, as the case may be) subject to the limitations that (1) market should not exceed the net realizable value, i.e., selling price in the ordinary course of business less reasonably predictable cost of completion and disposal; and (2) market should not be less than the net realizable value reduced by an allowance for an approximately normal profit margin. In many instances, the lower-of-cost-or-market rule for stating inventories will be applied, as a practical rather than a theoretical matter, in accordance with the federal income tax regulations. The general rule in the regulations is that, under ordinary circumstances and for normal goods in an inventory, cost is to be compared with replacement cost. The regulations also provide, whether cost or the lower-of-cost-or-market inventory method is used, the amount assigned to goods that are "unsalable at normal prices or unusable in the normal way because of damage, imperfections, shop wear, changes of style, odd or broken lots, or other similar causes, including second-hand goods taken in exchange" should not exceed net realizable value. In applying the rule of lower of cost or market, the scrap value of the items included in the inventory constitutes a *minimum* amount.

The federal income tax regulations state that where an inventory is valued on the basis of cost or market, whichever is lower, the market value of each article on hand at the inventory date shall be compared with the cost of the article, and the lower shall be taken as the inventory amount for the article. There are many instances in practice where this absolute statement in the regulations is not complied with, and there is accounting authority for a broader view of the basis for making comparisons between cost and market.

The purpose of reducing inventory to market is to reflect fairly the income of the accounting period. Although probably the most common practice is to compare cost with market separately for each item in an inventory, there are a number of situations in which the comparison of the aggregate cost with the aggregate value is more significant.

Where a single category of end product is being produced, the reduction of the cost of individual items to market value would ordinarily not be justified if the value to the business of the total inventory is in excess of the aggregate cost. This

[2]Reg. §1.471-3(c).

would be particularly true in a case where selling prices are not affected by temporary or relatively small fluctuations in current costs.

When no loss of income is expected to take place as a result of a reduction in cost prices of certain goods because others forming components of the same general category of finished products have a market equally in excess of cost, it is generally held that the components need not be adjusted to market if they are included in the inventory in balanced quantities. If the stock on hand of particular inventory items is excessive in relation to others, clear reflection of income will normally require the direct comparison of cost and value for the excess quantities.

If an item is included in inventory that had been written down to market for purposes of the preceding year's inventory, the comparison should be between the opening inventory value and market at the end of the year. Normally, income should be recognized only from the *disposition* of goods.

In Some Businesses Value May Be an Appropriate Basis for Stating Inventories. Mining companies may inventory gold and silver at current value when there is an effective viable market. The general rule of modern financial accounting that inventories should not be stated at amounts in excess of cost reflects a practical realization of the uncertainties inherent in doing business in a free competitive economy. Where metals have a fixed monetary value and the sale of the quantities on hand at the end of any particular period at such fixed amounts is practically mechanical, it is appropriate to base the inventory on such value. Any expenditures that will be incurred in the disposition of the inventory should, of course, be taken into account so that the inventory is not stated at an amount in excess of net realizable value. The exception to the general rule sometimes made by mining companies is also justified, at least in part, by the difficulty of establishing the cost for the particular goods in the inventory. The metals may have been extracted from several mines that have been operated over a long period of time with numerous shutdowns. In this situation, the determination of the provision for depreciation that should be appropriately allocated to any particular production may be subject to a wide range of difference in opinion, to say nothing of the difficulty of establishing the appropriate amount of the provision for depletion.

Agriculture is another industry in which value may be an appropriate basis for stating inventories. As a practical matter, many farmers do not maintain adequate records to establish clearly appropriate costs for the products that may be on hand at the end of a year. For federal income tax purposes, this fact is recognized in the permission granted to farmers to report income on a cash receipts and disbursements basis. Where the farm accounting is placed on an accrual basis for financial reporting because the units are interchangeable and the immediate marketability at established prices is recognized in the normal course of business, value may be accepted as an appropriate basis for stating inventories without the necessity of establishing costs. The "farm price method" of stating inventories thus provides for a valuation at market price less the estimated direct cost of disposing of the products on hand.

The federal income tax regulations provide that a dealer in securities may use an inventory based on market values as an alternative to stating inventories at either cost or the lower of cost or market. The only requirement in the regulations is that the method used for tax purposes be the same as the method regularly used in the dealer's books of account.

AMOUNTS ASSIGNED TO INVENTORIES TO DETERMINE PERIODIC RESULTS FROM BUSINESS OPERATIONS

If the results of operating a business were determined only at the time of completion of a venture, there would be no need for inventory accounting. Modern business, however, is conducted on a "going-concern" basis. With securities being actively traded on established markets, the relationship between the owners and operators of a business is largely impersonal, and there is a constant change in some portion of the owner group. For these reasons, as well as to make possible some degree of management control, it is accepted (quite aside from the requirements of income tax laws) that the income or loss from operating a business should be determined at least annually. The determination of periodic operating results requires the recognition of inventories.

Treatment of Supplies.   The federal income tax regulations recognize the fact that income cannot be stated fairly without giving proper regard to inventories by inclusion of the following paragraph:[3]

> In order to reflect taxable income correctly, inventories at the beginning and end of each taxable year are necessary in every case in which the production, purchase, or sale of merchandise is an income-producing factor. The inventory should include all finished or partly finished goods and, in the case of raw materials and supplies, only those which have been acquired for sale or which will physically become a part of merchandise intended for sale, in which class fall containers, such as kegs, bottles, and cases, whether returnable or not, if title thereto will pass to the purchaser of the product to be sold therein. Merchandise should be included in the inventory only if title thereto is vested in the taxpayer. Accordingly, the seller should include in his inventory goods under contract for sale but not yet segregated and applied to the contract and goods out upon consignment, but should exclude from inventory goods sold (including containers), title to which has passed to the purchaser. A purchaser should include in inventory merchandise purchased (including containers), title to which has passed to him, although such merchandise is in transit or for other reasons has not been reduced to physical possession, but should not include goods ordered for future delivery, transfer of title to which has not yet been effected.

The foregoing quotation from the current federal income tax regulations is more restrictive than the concept of inventory as reflected in modern accounting practice. Modern accounting practice will include supplies that are to be *consumed* in the production of the goods or services to be sold in the ordinary course of the business. Normally the accounting concept of supplies being part of the inventory is accepted in practice for income tax purposes. In recognition of the fact that the income tax law applies to all businesses, regardless of the size of the operation or the sophistication of its accounting records, the regulations include the following paragraph.[4]

> Taxpayers carrying materials and supplies on hand should include in expenses the charges for materials and supplies only in the amount that they are actually consumed and used in operation during the taxable year for which the return is made, provided that the costs of such materials and supplies have not been deducted in determining the net income or loss or taxable income from any previous years. If a taxpayer carries incidental material or supplies on hand for which no record of consumption is kept or of which physical inventories at the beginning and end of the year are not taken, it will be permissible for the taxpayer to include in his expenses and to deduct from gross income the total cost of such supplies and materials as were purchased during the taxable year for which the return is made, provided the taxable income is clearly reflected by this method.

The foregoing statement recognizes that, for federal income tax purposes, as a practical matter, smaller businesses may expense all supplies as purchased, and in the case of the larger businesses certain items, if not material in amount, may be so treated.

Assumptions of Movement of Goods.   In addition to a difference in the concept of cost in various businesses, there can be a difference in the concept of the

---

[3]Reg. §1.471-1.
[4]Reg. §1.162-3.

assumption applied with respect to identification of the goods on hand. It is only in the most exceptional case that there will be specific identification of the goods. Generally this will be practical and needed for a fair reflection of income only with respect to items of relatively high individual value, such as rare violins, jewels, and valuable paintings. In the operation of a business, identification of particular lots of similar goods is not only impractical but may also distort rather than aid in a fair reflection of income on a going-concern basis. The common practice, therefore, is to reflect in the accounting records average costs, and there is a wide variety of procedures for determining an average. The average may be computed by reference to production or acquisitions during a week, month, or year; or a procedure based on the theory of a moving average may be developed and applied in particular cases.

In further recognition of the fact that specifically identified costs are not always the most appropriate, an assumption is commonly made that goods move through the business on a first-in, first-out basis, so that the most recent costs can be applied to the quantities on hand at the inventory date. Since approximately 1940, the last-in, first-out assumption as to the movement of goods has been acceptable for federal income tax purposes, and there has been an increasing proportion of business inventories determined on this basis. The mechanics of determining the cost for an inventory on the last-in, first-out basis are described below in some detail.

Another type of assumption as to the movement of goods is reflected in the retail inventory method, which is commonly used in the retail trade and was developed to meet the practical problems inherent in that industry. Inasmuch as the retail method embraces some of the principles of the lower-of-cost-or-market philosophy and does not involve the detailed questions inherent in establishing a cost for a manufacturing concern, this method is specifically considered in the following section.

Retail Inventory Method.   Under the retail inventory method, the total of the retail selling price of the goods on hand at the end of the year in each department is reduced by applying a single percentage based on the operations of that department during the period. The determination of this percentage adjustment to the retail value and the mechanics of the computation are illustrated in Exhibit 1.

In the operation of the retail inventory method, the records required to be maintained, with respect to each department, are those showing the aggregate cost and initial retail sales price for all purchases, incoming freight where not included in cost, aggregate sales made, markdowns, discounts allowed to employees and others, and additional markups, if any. It is important that markdowns and additional markups be based on actual changes in retail sales prices.

Shortages are recognized as inevitable in retail store operations, so that a provision therefor must be made. These shortages can result from errors in the preparation of sales slips as well as from shoplifting. Frequently, a monthly provision will be made for shortages measured by a fixed percentage of sales during the period as reflected by the experience of each department. Inasmuch as the inventory control records are kept in terms of retail selling prices, the amount of shortage is initially measured at that level.

In order that the inventory determined under the retail method will be stated at an amount that will approximate the lower of cost or market, markdowns are not included in the computation of the adjustment percentage. The adjustment percentage is multiplied by the ending inventory at retail to derive ending inventory at cost. The percentage is cost divided by retail price. Markdowns potentially reduce the denominator of the adjustment percentage. Hence, excluding markdowns from the denominator makes it larger and the adjustment percentage, and

EXHIBIT 1   Retail Inventory Method

	Computation approximating					
	Lower of cost or market			Cost		
	Selling price	Inventory		Selling price	Inventory	
		Amount	%		Amount	%
Opening inventory	$ 10,000	$ 6,000	60.00	$ 10,000	$ 6,000	60.00
Purchases	100,000	52,000		100,000	52,000	
Incoming freight, etc	—	2,000		—	2,000	
Additional markups	1,000	—		1,000	—	
	$111,000	$60,000	54.05			
Markdowns	$ 3,000			(3,000)	—	
				$108,000	$60,000	55.56
Sales	92,000			$ 92,000		
Discounts	1,500			1,500		
Shortages	2,500			2,500		
	$ 99,000			$ 96,000		
Closing inventory:						
At retail	$ 12,000			$ 12,000		
Amount approximating: Lower of cost or market (54.05 % of $12,000)		$ 6,486				
Cost (55.56 % of $12,000)					$ 6,667	

ending inventory, smaller. If the last-in, first-out inventory method is used in conjunction with the retail computation, federal income tax regulations require that retail selling prices be adjusted for markdowns as well as markups in order that the determination will approximate the cost of the goods on hand at the end of the year rather than the lower of cost or market.

Concepts of "Cost" for Manufactured Goods.   Just as there are several concepts of value, there are many concepts of cost. For purposes of establishing selling prices, all amounts expended in the conduct of the business must be recovered in the proceeds of sales in order to make a profit. It is unimportant for this purpose whether expenditures are classified as a cost or an expense. Use of the word "cost" to embrace any and all expenditures can, however, lead to misunderstandings. Categorizing expenditures is important when the cost of an inventory is being established for the purpose of determining income derived from business operations during a stated period. The basic accounting principle in the measurement of income involves the "matching" of costs and expenses against related revenues. The unabsorbed costs properly chargeable against future sales are carried forward.

Inasmuch as assigning a dollar to an inventory defers an expense, it is fundamental that an actual expenditure or a commitment resulting in an accrued liability has occurred. From the standpoint of the determination of the cost of an inventory for federal income tax purposes, no amount should be included that does not constitute at least an accrued obligation under the federal income tax rules. For example, the general practice is not to include any portion of a provision for vacation pay not recognized as an accrued liability for tax purposes in determining the cost of goods included in an inventory.

Inclusion of Overhead. Subject to the adoption of an acceptable practice as to the averaging of costs and a stated assumption as to the flow of goods, generally little difficulty is encountered in determining the appropriate amount to be allocated to an inventory for the cost of materials purchased and expenditures for direct labor. Greater differences of opinion exist with respect to overhead.

Expenditures that do not further a productive activity are not part of overhead includable in cost computations; and the extent to which expenditures are included in any particular instance will depend on such factors as the complexity of the organization, the attitude and sophistication of the individuals compiling and using the economic data, and the availability of information. Not every business is equipped to analyze its expenditures in the same detail. Further, costs are computed to meet a particular situation, and no one amount can be said to be "correct" to the exclusion of all others.

There are several viewpoints as to the extent to which the costs relating to production should be included in inventory cost as a matter of principle. The alternatives for inclusion of overhead in production costs may be grouped broadly in four classes:

1. Prime costing, under which no overhead is included
2. Direct costing, under which costs that are attributable directly to production and that tend to increase and decrease in proportion to changes in the operating rate are included but no fixed overhead is included
3. Analytical costing, under which overhead attributable to production is included, except for the portion not taken into account because of the production facilities not being fully utilized
4. Full absorption costing, under which all overhead attributable to production is included

Circumstances may make it appropriate and useful to apply procedures falling into any of these four categories in preparing statements and reports for management purposes; and management should understand what procedures have been followed. This is particularly important where the computed costs are utilized in establishing selling prices.

Prime costing has the advantage of simplicity and is applied most frequently where the overhead costs are of little significance. The suitability of this concept of cost for financial statement purposes (in contrast with operating statements prepared for management control purposes) is, however, subject to question. Chapter 4 on "Inventory Pricing" in *Accounting Research Bulletin No. 43* specifically states that "the exclusion of *all* [emphasis supplied] overheads from inventory costs does not constitute an accepted accounting procedure."

Direct costing implies that none of the recurring and continuing overhead items are to be included in cost of inventories. The major items are frequently depreciation and plant maintenance. The reasoning is that the expenses were incurred as a consequence of decisions that had nothing to do with any particular units of production; that the expenses would have been incurred whether or not any specific units had been produced; and that corresponding amounts of expense will be incurred in subsequent periods regardless of the quantity of the current production. The practice of not including in overhead certain items considered to be period expenses is a partial application of the direct costing principle. Among the items frequently not included in overhead under this concept are research and development, product guarantees, defective parts and rework, pensions, inventory-taking labor, employee training time, downtime, overtime and shift premiums (where abnormal and incurred to effect shipments rather than to produce the goods in the inventory), and plant rearrangement.

Analytical costing measures the proportion of the recurring and continuing items to be included in the computations of inventory cost by comparing the actual rate of activity with a predetermined norm. Overhead for a particular period is included in inventory cost to the extent that available capacity was actually utilized. Overhead allocable to the unused capacity is considered to represent a loss. This is an economic loss attributable to the lower-than-normal level of production during the period, and is not part of the cost of the units actually produced.

Both the direct costing and analytical costing procedures are premised, in part, on a recognition of the fact that, in addition to variable expenses, overhead includes costs that are recurring and necessary merely to provide the capacity to carry on production activities. The assumption of a certain level of recurring and continuing costs is essential to being in a position to carry on any activities. During a particular period, however, production may be all or only a part of the total possible with the available capacity. Judgment is exercised in determining how much of the costs required to provide the existing capacity to produce should be considered part of the cost of the goods produced.

Full absorption costing is most frequently applied in smaller enterprises where detailed analyses of the various production cost accounts are not available. It may also be appropriate where a plant is consistently operated at capacity or where the aggregate amount of overhead is relatively small. It shares with prime costing the advantage of simplicity; however, special attention must be given to any elements of overhead attributable to events that are not customarily a part of plant operations, and the full absorption costing concept will not be literally applied where the amount of cost resulting from such events can be identified. Examples of events that could justify special recognition in determining the overhead to be included in cost computations are shortages of materials, receipt of defective materials, labor slowdowns and strikes, and interruptions of production caused by a flood, fire, or other casualty. In a business that does not have a regular program for model or product changes, special recognition might also be given to the effect on expenses of disruptions caused by such factors as the introduction of a new product, the training of an expanded labor force, and the realignment of facilities incident to equipping a plant to manufacture a different product.

All the authoritative pronouncements on the subject of accounting for inventories uniformly emphasize that greater weight is to be given to consistency than to the use of any particular method.

Illustration of Analytical Costing.   In applying the analytical costing concept, it is necessary first to establish a normal operating rate or practical capacity. Practical capacity is usually determined by starting with a theoretical capacity and allowing for normal interruptions. Capacity may be measured in terms of tons, pounds, yards, labor hours, machine hours, or any other standard appropriate to the particular operating unit—sometimes a plant, but frequently a department within the plant or other type of "cost center."

The application of this concept may be illustrated on the basis of the following assumptions:

Plant A has a theoretical capacity of 105,000 units per week if operated continuously; however, in determining an annual practical capacity, recognition must be given to the fact that the plant operates on a 5-day week at 8 hours a day. Also, allowances must be made for scheduled holidays, vacation shutdown, and other normal interruptions due to such causes as power failures and shutdowns for repairs. The plant is closed completely for five annual holidays (equivalent to one week of operation) and for two weeks during the vacation period. In this case, a reasonable allowance for breakdowns is 5 percent.

		Production units
Theoretical capacity (105,000 units for 52 weeks)		5,460,000
Reductions to recognize operations:		
On an 8-hour day ($^{16}/_{24}$ of 5,460,000)	3,640,000	
On a 5-day week ($^2/_7$ of 1,820,000)	520,000	4,160,000
Capacity on basis of 5-day week at 8 hours per day		1,300,000
Allowances for:		
Scheduled holidays ($^1/_{52}$ of 1,300,000)	25,000	
Vacation shutdown ($^2/_{52}$ of 1,300,000)	50,000	75,000
Capacity on basis of scheduled operating time		1,225,000
Allowance for normal interruptions (5%)		61,250
Practical capacity		1,163,750

Practical capacity is

$$5,460,000 \times \quad \tfrac{1}{3} \quad \times \quad \tfrac{5}{7} \quad \times \quad \tfrac{49}{52} \quad \times \quad .95 \ = \ 1,163,750$$

to recognize only 8 hours of 24 per day worked	to recognize only 5 days of 7 per week worked	to recognize only 49 of 52 weeks per year worked	to recognize that only 95% of "operating time" is production

If 1,100,000 units were produced during the year, the basis on which the fixed overhead would be allocated to production would be 1,100,000/1,163,750, or 94.52 percent. The total of the variable overhead would also be allocated to production. Assuming that the inventory consisted of 110,000 units and the first-in, first-out (FIFO) cost-flow assumption is applied, 10 percent of the aggregate fixed overhead allocated to production would be included in the computed cost for the inventory.

Even if the actual production exceeded 1,163,750 units as a result of favorable operating conditions and not as a result of additions to or improvements made in the facilities that would increase the theoretical capacity, only 100 percent of the fixed overhead would be allocated to production. Allocating more than 100 percent would result in including "phantom dollars" in cost rather than actual expenditures.

For purposes of this simple illustration, the rate of activity has been computed on an annual basis; however, depending on the circumstances, a more significant computation might have been based on the operations during the last month or final quarter in the year during which the particular articles in the inventory are assumed to have been produced.

Tax and Other Influences on Overhead Absorption.   The foregoing discussion of the problems in allocating overhead to inventory should be considered fundamental in nature and is explained in more detail in Chapter 11. Emphasized is the fact of differing approaches and the need for judgment as well as the validity of various procedures under differing circumstances. More detailed explanations and analyses of major inventory accounting practices, including diversity of procedures, environmental influences, and continuing questions, are clearly presented in the comprehensive 1973 AICPA Research Study No. 13, entitled "The Accounting Basis of Inventories," by Horace G. Barden.

The Cost Accounting Standards Board exerts considerable influence in the costing of inventories of companies engaged in government contracting through its published Standards applicable to accounting techniques and objectives, record keeping, definitions and methods of overhead allocation and criteria for allowable costs and expenses.

Actual practice seems to be reflected in the following general conclusions of Paragraph 3.5 of Statement No. 6 issued in 1973 by the Committee on Management Accounting Practice of the National Association of Accountants:

> (a) Where it is practical and meaningful to do so, expenditures for materials, supplies, labor, and services which are necessary for and indirectly associated with producing the goods should be included in the inventories as part of the inventory amount. In some instances it is neither practical nor meaningful to make allocation to the inventory of charges for depreciation, taxes, and certain other classes of expenditures. However, the judgment as to whether or not a particular class of expenditure is included in the amount of inventories should be applied on a consistent basis.
>
> (b) Many companies adopt what they consider a conservative posture in treating as period expenses certain items which might reasonably be associated with a product amount, if only rather indirectly. The principal reasons for this attitude given by respondents to an NAA research study on allocation of indirect charges are:
>
> a. Method of allocation would be too arbitrary.
> b. Results would be misleading.
> c. Amounts are often insignificant.
>
> Out of 1,200 responses which were included in the tabulation, 671 indicated the firms do not allocate all expenditures indirectly related to production (at least on a broad-brush basis) in preparation of their annual financial statements (for the general public). For purposes of management (internal) reporting, 691 companies do not allocate.

In recognition of the complexities in this area and the practical need to rely on consistent industry accounting practices, the U.S. Treasury and Internal Revenue Service issued so-called full absorption regulations for manufacturers in 1973[5] that most practitioners consider "enlightened." In extending the book/tax conformity objective required for the approval of changes in the accounting methods, the government made mandatory for most manufacturers the inclusion of *direct* production costs (category I), permitted exclusion of certain indirect costs (category II), and authorized other indirect items (category III) to be included or excluded depending on their treatment for financial accounting purposes, provided that the treatment was not inconsistent with generally accepted accounting principles. For the few taxpayers who do not have comparable methods of determining inventory for both book and tax purposes, two categories of expenses were mandated: category I must be included whereas category II may be excluded. A liberal, two-year implementation period was established under which the effects on taxable income were spread over 10 years after giving effect to a specific "pre-1954 adjustment." Special provisions also applied to significant standard cost variances, LIFO computations, and the practical capacity method discussed above under analytical costing.

Exhibit 2 illustrates the treatment of typical items of overhead for manufacturers depending on their particular tax status under these (almost) full absorption regulations.

LIFO

Reasons for Development of the LIFO Assumption as to the Movement of Goods. The acceptance of conventional accounting procedures that recognize cost, or the lower of cost or market, in stating inventories appears to have been a natural consequence of the thought that the principal financial statement is the balance sheet. In reflecting the financial position of a business, it is logical to determine the shareholders' equity by deducting the total of the liabilities from the valuation of the assets.

[5]Reg. §1.471-11(a).

EXHIBIT 2   Analysis of Indirect Production Costs for Full Absorption Purposes

Description of Cost	Situation A: Taxpayers using comparable methods of accounting for inventory for tax and financial reporting purposes			Situation B: Taxpayers not using comparable methods of accounting for inventory for tax and financial reporting purposes	
	Category 1: Required to be included in inventory cost	Category 2: Not required to be included in inventory cost	Category 3: Required to be treated same as financial statements	Category 1: Required to be included in inventory cost	Category 2: Not required to be included in inventory cost
Repairs and maintenance	X			X	
Utilities	X			X	
Rent	X			X	
Indirect labor and production supervisory wages, including basic compensation, overtime pay, vacation and holiday pay, sick leave [other than payments pursuant to a wage continuation plan under section 105(d)], shift differential, payroll taxes, and contributions to a supplemental unemployment benefit plan	X			X	
Officers' salary related to business activities as a whole		X			X
Officers' salary related to production			X	X	
Pension contributions representing past service cost		X			X
Pension contributions representing current service cost			X	X	
Profit-sharing contributions			X	X	
Other employee benefit costs, including workmen's compensation expenses, payments under wage continuation plan described in section 105(d), amounts includible in income of an employee under nonqualified pension, profit-sharing, and stock bonus plans, premiums on life and health insurance, and miscellaneous employee benefits			X	X	
Indirect materials and supplies	X			X	
Tools and equipment not capitalized	X			X	
Costs of quality control and inspection	X			X	
Marketing, advertising, and distribution expenses		X			X
Interest		X			X
Research and experimental expenses		X			X
Losses under section 165		X			X
Depreciation and depletion reported in financial statements			X	X	
Depreciation and depletion in excess of amount reported in financial statements		X			X
Income taxes attributable to income received on sale of inventory		X			X
Taxes allowable as a deduction under section 164, excluding state, local, and foreign income taxes, attributable to assets incident to production or manufacturing			X	X	
General and administrative expenses incident to business activities as a whole		X			X
Factory administrative expenses			X	X	
Costs attributable to strikes, rework labor, scrap, and spoilage			X	X	
Insurance incident to production			X	X	

The development and acceptance of the LIFO (last-in, first-out) inventory method resulted from increasing emphasis being placed on the income statement. Under currently accepted accounting concepts, the statement of financial position is conceived of as reflecting amounts for the assets (other than cash, receivables, and sundry assets from which the maximum cash realization is fixed) that merely represent the unabsorbed portion of expenditures incurred in the past but applicable to the future and to be charged against the revenue of some future period. From this viewpoint, it was logical to develop an accounting convention relative to inventories designed to result in a more appropriate charge being made against current sales for the cost of goods sold. The basic principle of LIFO is that current income is better determined by deducting from the sales of the accounting period the cost of replacing the merchandise used in making the sales; in view of the difficulty of computing the cost for each sale, however, the desired end result is approximated by stating the inventory on a LIFO basis.

The physical quantity of goods may remain constant from year to year, but the number of dollars invested in that inventory may increase or decrease solely as a result of changes in prices. So long as a manager relies on continuous turnover of inventory to produce income, it is important that the effects of mere changes in prices be distinguished from profits attributable to the sale of merchandise.

If there is on hand at the beginning and end of any year the same physical quantity of goods, but solely as a result of changes in prices the dollar amount attributed to those goods for inventory purposes has increased 10 percent, this 10 percent increase in the dollar amount represents an unrealized inventory profit. This profit cannot be used to pay taxes or wages or dividends but must be retained in the business in order to permit its very continuation by replacing the goods that have been sold. If these unrealized inventory profits continue and are taxed, the business can be forced to secure additional capital to finance the higher-cost purchases, even though there has been no actual growth.

It is equally significant that a decline in the value of an inventory can, under the FIFO inventory method, depress the operating results; the LIFO method similarly attempts to distinguish this type of charge against income from the normal results of current business operations.

Wherever the quantities in the closing inventory equal or exceed the volume of the opening inventory, the desired result of charging against current income a cost for the goods sold based on contemporary prices is accomplished within reasonable limits. In the event of a reduction in inventory volume, however, the present-day LIFO method departs from the objective of reflecting current replacement costs and yields to the conventional accounting practice of dealing only with recorded costs.

From the standpoint of those who use the balance sheet, LIFO is unsatisfactory because the amount assigned to the inventory may have no relationship to current value and may reflect an aggregation of prices during several unidentified years depending on the number of "layers" in the inventory. Similarly, from the standpoint of those who believe that true income can be stated only if all the factors of income, costs, and expenses are expressed in terms of a unit with the same monetary value, LIFO is admittedly deficient where there has been a reduction in the volume of goods on hand at the end of the year.

As a result of taxpayer persistence, in the Revenue Act of 1938, Congress authorized the use of LIFO for specified raw materials used by tanners and the producers and processors of certain nonferrous metals. The following year Congress expanded the use of LIFO and removed the restrictions as to the industries and classes of inventories to which LIFO could be applied. Under the Revenue Act of 1939, any taxpayer could elect the LIFO method with respect to any of the goods in inventory.

The present provisions of the Internal Revenue Code do not permit either (1) the "replacement" of inventories and the restoration of previous costs, even where a portion of the inventory has been liquidated as a result of causes entirely beyond the taxpayer's control, or (2) the write-down of inventories to market where market is lower than LIFO costs. A write-down to market is permitted by the regulations for financial reporting purposes only.

Timing the Adoption of LIFO.   The decision as to when LIFO should be adopted depends on many factors, which will be different in every case. Generally, the principal factors governing the question of "when" include:

1. Anticipated rise in prices, because price increases cause paper profits in the inventory

2. High taxes, because a tax saving (or deferment) is the most tangible benefit from electing LIFO

3. No foreseeable conditions that could cause the liquidation of the inventory during the high-price and high-tax period, because such liquidation would mean that the recognition of income was only temporarily deferred and the income may actually be taxed at a higher rate.

After LIFO is once adopted, it will normally be advantageous, so long as high prices continue, to maintain normal inventory quantities and avoid a liquidation at the end of any year. Inventory liquidations at an interim date are immaterial to the LIFO computations, but the necessity to maintain quantities at each year-end may result in the accounting department of a business temporarily directing the volume of purchases and shipments near the close of the year.

Consequences of Cost Reductions.   If the LIFO method is applied to the aggregate of the elements of the cost of an inventory of manufactured goods and a procedure is developed for substantially reducing production costs, it may be that the cost savings effected through an improvement in production methods are being offset against the price increases attributable to material in the product. This has prompted some companies to limit the application of the LIFO method to the material content of the inventory. Where the LIFO method is applied to manufacturing costs as well as the material content, the volume of inventoriable production costs is commonly measured in terms of direct labor hours or some other unit in order to preserve the benefits of increased efficiency.

There may also be unforeseen consequences of LIFO in the event of product changes. Such changes can result from using a different raw material or the production of items that had previously been purchased, as well as a distinct change in the finished product. As an illustration, members of the wool industry adopted LIFO and subsequently began to substitute artificial fibers for natural wool. Where the inventory volume is measured in terms of yards and LIFO is applied to one particular type of material, such a change in material means the complete liquidation of the original inventory and the inclusion in income of the entire amount previously deferred through election of the LIFO method. With the passage of time, almost every business may expect that new lines will be added and old ones dropped.

In the case of a business anticipating that it may resort to a different type of raw material, it may be helpful to use the dollar-value principle in which the aggregate investment in inventory is considered rather than the quantity of particular items. Where the substituted material has not been the subject of a price increase similar to that of the original material, the dollar-value method does not provide a completely satisfactory solution but is of some benefit.

Conditions to the Use of LIFO for Income Tax Purposes.   The two principal conditions to be complied with if LIFO is to be used for federal income tax purposes are (1) the filing of appropriate election forms with the federal income tax return covering the year in which the method is first used and (2) the statutory requirement that no other method be used in determining income for the purpose of annual reports to shareholders, creditors, and other interested parties. Of significance is the fact that the LIFO election need not be made until after the close of the year in which the method is to be used for federal income tax purposes. Although the state income tax laws do not in all cases provide specifically for an exception to the general rule for securing advance approval of changes in accounting methods, the general practice is to follow substantially the same procedure in the state returns as in the federal return.

The requirement in the Internal Revenue Code that no method other than LIFO be used in stating inventories for the purpose of *determining income in annual reports* to shareholders, creditors, and others must be recognized by management and is not a matter of mere detail. Reports to shareholders are frequently prepared before it is necessary to file the federal income tax return and make the final decision as to adoption of the LIFO method for tax purposes. Consequently, it may be necessary to use that method in the annual report going to shareholders even though there is a possibility that the decision will be against the adoption of LIFO for tax purposes.

It is not necessary that the inventory amount as computed for purposes of the financial statements be the same as that later used in the tax return. For example, there may be a difference in the classification of the inventory as used in the financial statement computation. The Internal Revenue Code merely requires that no method other than LIFO be used in computing income in financial statements covering a taxable year. The restriction does not apply to interim statements.

Interim Financial Statements and Statements of Product or Departmental Results. Questions naturally arise as to whether, from a practical standpoint, the LIFO principle can be incorporated in a cost accounting system and the commonly used form of statements of product or branch results and of departmental operations. It is reasoned that if the LIFO method results in a better reflection of income, it should be used for all management purposes. In practice, however, LIFO is generally appended to previously used operating statements and cost systems.

In reporting profits of the business as a whole, "ideal" conditions for using LIFO are simple, i.e., when closing inventories equal opening inventories and the goods sold are equivalent to the purchases for each accounting period throughout the year. Because such conditions are rarely, if ever, found in practice, the accounting system must provide for reflecting all possible developments.

If at the end of an interim accounting period the inventory of any LIFO group is below the opening inventory for the year, an estimate must be made of the amount of closing inventory for the year. Assuming that at the interim date no reduction is expected for the year, cost of sales for the interim period should be charged with the cost of goods purchased plus an estimated amount to cover the cost that will be incurred in making good the temporary decrease in inventory. An account should be established (ordinarily shown on the balance sheet among current liabilities) for the difference between the estimated replacement cost and the LIFO inventory cost for the quantities liquidated to the interim date.

The opposite situation is where a reduction is expected in the closing inventory as compared with what was on hand at the beginning of the year. Should a substantial difference exist between LIFO cost and current replacement cost and should the major part of the liquidation occur in one interim period, the charge to cost of sales for the goods liquidated may be abnormally low (or high) and, assuming no proportionate change in selling prices, may result in a significant effect on income for the period. Because of the increasing attention to the determination of income for interim periods, it is important to report fairly the effect, if significant, of charging to cost of sales the "old" inventory costs. This is usually done by a footnote disclosing the fact that LIFO inventories have been reduced and an estimate of the effect on cost of sales.

Estimates of the year-end inventory volume may also be needed when there is an increase in inventory at the interim date. If an increase is expected for the year, such an increase will be reflected in the year-end inventory at current year costs (first-purchase, last-purchase, or average costs). If a decrease, or at least no substantial increase, is expected for the year as a whole, the problem is more difficult but remains: how to price the interim increase in inventory. At the interim date the general objective is to use, insofar as possible, the conventional principles applicable at year-end, thereby minimizing subsequent adjustments. Adjustments will sometimes be necessary because of differences between the costs attributed to the increase in inventory at the interim date and the costs at which the increase will be included in the year-end LIFO inventory; using the general objective above, such an adjustment should normally be taken into cost of sales in the interim period in which the need for the adjustment occurs. If significant effects on net income result, again they should be disclosed.

LIFO Computations Where Quantities Are Determined by Weight or Count. The classification of inventories into groups for LIFO purposes depends primarily on the character of the goods involved and the complexity of the inventories. Although a LIFO computation wherein quantities are determined directly by weight or count is simple and involves the least amount of clerical effort and expense, the chief disadvantage of this procedure is its limited application in a business that has a variety of raw materials and manufactures many types of goods. If the quantity method were adopted in such a business, there would be numerous LIFO groups, and over a period of years, as quantities increased and decreased, there would be a tendency to restore to income some of the inflationary profit that LIFO was designed to eliminate.

The dollar-value principle of measuring the volume of goods in a LIFO inventory is usually applied except where the inventory as a whole consists of relatively few raw material commodities or products that can be measured and expressed in units of quantity.

When the LIFO method is first adopted, the opening inventory of the year may have to be adjusted. The goods must be reflected in the beginning inventory at *cost* and are considered as having been acquired at the same time. In stating the opening inventory at cost, any write-down to market values with respect to the closing inventory of the preceding year must be restored. Such restorations create additional income or reduce the loss, whichever the case may be, for the preceding year. When the write-down to market is restored, the cost of the goods in the opening inventory will be the cost determined by the method previously used, i.e., the cost determined by reference to specific invoices, by the assumption of first-in, first-out (FIFO), by the use of an average of the opening inventory and purchases during the year, or by any other procedure consistently followed by the company under the lower-of-cost-or-market rule.

The opening inventory for the first LIFO year is the basic "layer." At the close of the year the quantity on hand is compared with the quantity at the beginning. If there is no increase in quantity, the average cost of the basic layer is applied to the quantity on hand at the end of the year to obtain the inventory amount. If there is an increase in quantity, a current-year's cost must be established. The methods commonly used to establish the current-year's cost are generally described as first-purchase costs, last-purchase costs, or the average cost for the year. Many companies that elect to price quantity increments by reference to the actual cost of goods most recently acquired, or by reference to the actual cost of goods acquired during the taxable year in the order of acquisition, determine an average cost for each month during which acquisitions are made, the aggregate of which equals or exceeds the increase in inventory, and then treat the quantity acquired and average cost as a single "layer" for inventory pricing.

Decreases in quantities are taken from the most recent year's acquisitions.

An illustration of LIFO inventory computations where bushels are the unit for measuring the quantity of goods on hand is set forth in Exhibit 3.

LIFO Computations Where Relative Quantities Are Determined by the Retail Inventory Method. The procedures for applying the LIFO concept to the determination of amounts to be assigned to retail department store inventories were developed to meet a specific business need. To superimpose the LIFO principle on the retail method, price fluctuations are adjusted by application of a series of nationwide price indexes to the total dollar value of each departmental inventory.

The LIFO problem peculiar to retailers arises from the fact that because of the nature of the business there is rarely a record of the specific identity of individual inventory items. The retail method consists of accumulating the aggregate retail value of all items in a department at the inventory date and reducing this departmental total by applying an adjustment representing the average gross markup on that department's goods.

The series of inventory price indexes approved by the Treasury Department for federal income tax purposes is based on data furnished by the Bureau of Labor Statistics (BLS) exclusively for the use of retail stores. Because the tabulations published by the Bureau of Labor Statistics use either January or July 1941 as 100 percent, department stores electing LIFO as of later dates compute their own accumulative percentage of price change. To aid in these computations, the government statistics show the percentage of price change during each year.

A form of worksheet for the computation of departmental LIFO inventories is illustrated by Exhibit 4. It will be noted that the BLS index is applied to the retail value of the inventory rather than to the cost.

LIFO Computations Where Relative Quantities Are Determined by the Dollar-Value Principle. The dollar-value principle is that the volume of the goods in annual inventories can be measured in terms of total dollars reflecting cost levels for the inventory items as of a particular year. The appropriate unit of measure for the various items may be yards, tons, gallons, or any combination of these and similar measures, but the common denominator for determining the total volume of goods in the inventories from year to year is dollars.

The term "base-year cost" is the aggregate of the cost (determined as of the beginning of the year for which the LIFO method is first adopted) for all terms in the inventory, and the term "base-year unit costs" refers to the individual costs as of that date for the various items. Liquidations and increments for a particular LIFO inventory are reflected only in terms of a net liquidation or increment for the inventory as a whole. Fluctuations will occur in quantities of items within the inventory. New items may be added and discontinued items may be dropped without necessarily effecting a change in the dollar value of the inventory as a whole.

In the case of a manufacturer or processor, the entire inventory that is considered to relate to a "natural business unit" is commonly reflected in a single LIFO computation. Where an enterprise is composed of more than one business unit, a separate inventory must be recognized for each. What constitutes a natural business unit is considered in the following excerpt from the federal income tax regulations:[6]

> Whether an enterprise is composed of more than one natural business unit is a matter of fact to be determined from all the circumstances. The natural business divisions adopted

[6]Reg. §1.472-8(b)(2)(i).

EXHIBIT 3   LIFO Computations Where Quantities Are Determined by Weight or Count

	LIFO base	Inventories at end of				
		First year	Second year	Third year	Fourth year	Fifth year
1. Inventory quantities	10,000 bu	12,000 bu	11,000 bu	9,000 bu	10,500 bu	10,000 bu
2. Current-year cost per bushel	$2.00	$2.046	$2.107	$2.090	$2.111	$2.143
Inventory on LIFO basis:						
In bushels, attributable to:						
3. Base year	10,000 bu	10,000 bu	10,000 bu	9,000 bu	9,000 bu	9,000 bu
4. First year		2,000	1,000			
5. Fourth year					1,500	1,000
6. Total	10,000 bu	12,000 bu	11,000 bu	9,000 bu	10,500 bu	10,000 bu
At LIFO cost, attributable to:						
7. Base year (3 × $2.00)	$20,000	$20,000	$20,000	$18,000	$18,000	$18,000
8. First year (4 × $2.046)		4,092	2,046			
9. Fourth year (5 × $2.111)					3,167	2,111
10. Total LIFO inventory cost	$20,000	$24,092	$22,046	$18,000	$21,167	$20,111
11. Inventory on current cost basis (1 × 2)		24,552	23,177	18,810	22,166	21,430
12. Cumulative inventory effect from use of LIFO method (10 – 11)		$ (460)	$ (1,131)	$ (810)	$ (999)	$ (1,319)

12-18

EXHIBIT 4 LIFO Computations Where Relative Quantities Are Determined by the Retail Inventory Method

Department: _____
No.: _____

	LIFO base	Inventories at end of				
		First year	Second year	Third year	Fourth year	Fifth year
Conversion factors:						
1. Percentage change in BLS index during the year	100.00%	2.30%	3.00%	(0.80)%	1.00%	1.50%
2. Index of price-level change from LIFO base		102.30	105.34	104.50	105.55	107.13
Percentage of cost to retail value:						
3. As of base year	60.00					
4. As of current year		59.56	59.80	61.00	59.20	60.70
5. Inventory at retail value	$10,000	$12,000	$11,000	$9,000	$10,500	$10,000
6. Inventory at base-year price level (5 ÷ 2)	10,000	11,730	10,442	8,612	9,948	9,334
Inventory on LIFO basis:						
At base-year price level, attributable to:						
7. Base year	$10,000	$10,000	$10,000	$8,612	$8,612	$8,612
8. First year		1,730	442			
9. Fourth year					1,336	722
10. Total	$10,000	$11,730	$10,442	$8,612	$9,948	$9,334
At LIFO cost, attributable to:						
11. Base year (7 × 60.00%)	$ 6,000	$ 6,000	$ 6,000	$5,167	$ 5,167	$ 5,167
12. First year (8 × 102.30% × 59.56%)		1,054	269			
13. Fourth year (9 × 105.55% × 59.20%)					835	451
14. Total LIFO inventory cost	$ 6,000	$ 7,054	$ 6,269	$5,167	$ 6,002	$ 5,618
15. Inventory on current cost basis (5 × 4)		7,147	6,578	5,490	6,216	6,070
16. Cumulative inventory effect from use of LIFO method (14 – 15)		($ 93)	($ 309)	($ 323)	($ 214)	($ 452)

by the taxpayer for internal management purposes, the existence of separate and distinct production facilities and processes, and the maintenance of separate profit and loss records with respect to separate operations are important considerations in determining what is a business unit, unless such divisions, facilities, or accounting records are set up merely because of differences in geographical location. In the case of a manufacturer or processor, a natural business unit ordinarily consists of the entire productive activity of the enterprise within one product line or within two or more related product lines including (to the extent engaged in by the enterprise) the obtaining of materials, the processing of materials, and the selling of manufactured or processed goods. Thus, in the case of a manufacturer or processor, the maintenance and operation of a raw material warehouse does not generally constitute, of itself, a natural business unit. If the taxpayer maintains and operates a supplier unit the production of which is both sold to others and transferred to a different unit of the taxpayer to be used as a component part of another product, the supplier unit will ordinarily constitute a separate and distinct natural business unit. Ordinarily, a processing plant would not in itself be considered a natural business unit if the production of the plant, although saleable at this stage, is not sold to others, but is transferred to another plant of the enterprise, not operated as a separate division, for further processing or incorporation into another product. On the other hand, if the production of a manufacturing or processing plant is transferred to a separate and distinct division of the taxpayer, which constitutes a natural business unit, the supplier unit itself will ordinarily be considered a natural business unit. However, the mere fact that a portion of the production of a manufacturing or processing plant may be sold to others at a certain stage of processing with the remainder of the production being further processed or incorporated into another product will not of itself be determinative that the activities devoted to the production of the portion sold constitute a separate business unit. Where a manufacturer or processor is also engaged in the wholesaling or retailing of goods purchased from others, the wholesaling or retailing operations with respect to such purchased goods shall not be considered a part of any manufacturing or processing unit.

Inventories of wholesalers, retailers, jobbers, and distributors are classified for the purpose of LIFO computations by major lines, types, or classes of goods. Customary business classifications of the particular trade generally provide a satisfactory basis for determining the extent to which items can be combined into a single inventory by application of the dollar-value principle. In some cases operations of other than a manufacturer or processor may constitute a single natural business unit.

A wide variety of procedures have been developed for determining an appropriate index to be used in dollar-value LIFO inventory computations. As a general rule, however, a "double-extension method" is used for computing the base-year and current-year cost. Under this method, the quantity of each item in the inventory at the close of the year is extended at both its base-year unit cost and the current-year unit cost. The comparison of the relative volume of the opening and closing inventories, as reflected by the totals of the extensions at the base-year unit costs, indicates whether there has been an increment or liquidation for the year. The relationship between the totals of the extensions of the closing inventory at the current-year unit costs and at the base-year unit costs can be used as the factor to be applied in converting an increment from base-year cost to current-year cost. This conversion factor may be measured by whichever procedure was selected for costing increments, i.e., on the basis of the earliest acquisitions during the year, the most recent acquisitions, or an average for the entire year.

Under the double-extension method, a base-year unit cost must be established for each new item. In many instances it is most practicable to use the earliest actual cost recorded for the item, but a base-year unit cost may be constructed. For an item that was in existence, the base-year unit cost should be the price that would have been paid by the company had the item been used. Where the new item is a product or raw material not in existence in the base year, an amount should be constructed that represents what the cost would have been in the base year had the item been in existence. Frequently the base-year unit cost for a new item is computed by applying to the current-year cost of such item the percentage relationship between the base-year unit cost and current-year unit cost for an item sufficiently similar in physical characteristics to justify an assumption that the changes in unit cost would have been comparable.

With the passage of time, the proportion of the items in an inventory that were not included in the base-year inventory will increase. In recognition of the facts that the base-year unit costs established for LIFO inventory computation purposes can often be utilized for management control purposes and that reasonably current costs are more significant and accurate than reconstructed costs, the double-extension method of applying the dollar-value principle is frequently modified to permit the use of a substitute base year. The updating of the base-year costs does not change the cost for the inventory, but merely permits the use of the more current and reliable unit costs for purposes of measuring the relative volume of the goods included in the inventories.

Exhibit 5 illustrates LIFO inventory computations where the volume of goods is measured by the dollar-value principle.

Link Chain. In recognition of the reliability and practicality afforded by the comparison of current costs to costs of the immediately preceding year, many companies, especially those with changing products, adopt the "link chain" method of determining an annual index. The overall change in cost levels is determined by multiplying the last previously determined cumulative index by the most recent annual index as illustrated in Exhibit 6 using the same assumption as in Exhibit 5. This procedure, which produces slightly different results from the base-year double-extension method, is used in compiling the BLS indexes for the computation of LIFO inventories by retail stores.

INVENTORY MODELS

Inventory management including the use of models has as its three major objectives:

- Maximum customer service
- Minimum inventory investment
- Low cost plant operations

Customer service is improved if inventories are raised to very high levels and production schedules are kept flexible to meet changing demands. Inventory is minimized if production is scheduled to meet exact requirements of customer orders. Plant costs are kept low by stable production levels. Thus, the second and third objectives run counter to the first. It is the function of inventory management to balance these competing objectives.

In most large organizations, the responsibility for customer service rests with one organizational group, the sales department, which seldom recognizes much responsibility on its part for plant efficiency; conversely, manufacturing people usually have little responsibility for the levels of inventory. The last group in the triangle, finance, has as its major concern minimization of inventory levels for maximum use of funds.

Reconciling these conflicting objectives in a modern company where responsibilities have been sharply divided becomes a challenging problem. Although there are many techniques that can be employed, all rely on a forecast of sales or usage.

There are four basic inventory classes, defined by function, and each is dependent on sales or usage forecasts:

- Fluctuation inventories: caused because sales and production time for the inventory cannot always be predicted accurately. These are commonly called *reserve stock* or *safety stocks*.

EXHIBIT 5   LIFO Computations Where Relative Quantities Are Determined by the Dollar-Value Principle

		Inventories at end of				
	LIFO base	First year	Second year	Third year	Fourth year	Fifth year
Conversion factors:						
Inventory extended at:						
1. Current-year unit costs	$100,000	$120,000	$110,000	$90,000	$105,000	$100,000
2. Base-year unit costs	100,000	117,300	104,420	86,120	99,480	93,340
3. Percentage of total base-year cost to total current-year cost (2 ÷ 1)	100.00%	97.75%	94.93%	95.69%	94.74%	93.34%
Inventory on LIFO basis:						
At base-year costs, attributable to:						
4. Base year	$100,000	$100,000	$100,000	$86,120	$86,120	$86,120
5. First year		17,300	4,420			
6. Fourth year					13,360	7,220
7. Total	$100,000	$117,300	$104,420	$86,120	$99,480	$93,340
At LIFO cost, attributable to:						
8. Base Year (4 × 100.00%)	$100,000	$100,000	$100,000	$86,120	$86,120	$86,120
9. First year (5 ÷ 97.75%)		17,698	4,522			
10. Fourth year (6 ÷ 94.74%)					14,102	7,621
11. Total LIFO inventory cost	$100,000	$117,698	$104,522	$86,120	$100,222	$93,741
12. Inventory on current cost basis (line 1)		120,000	110,000	90,000	105,000	100,000
13. Cumulative inventory effect from use of LIFO method (11 − 12)		$ (2,302)	$ (5,478)	$ (3,880)	$ (4,778)	$ (6,259)

EXHIBIT 6 LIFO Computations Where Annual Index Is Determined by the Link Chain Method

				Inventories at end of		
	LIFO base	First year	Second year	Third year	Fourth year	Fifth year
Conversion factors:						
Inventory extended at:						
1. End of current-year unit costs	$100,000	$120,000	$110,000	$90,000	$105,000	$100,000
2. Beginning of current-year unit costs	100,000	117,300	106,832	90,729	103,961	98,520
3. Percentage of total beginning of current-year costs to total end of current-year costs (2 ÷ 1)	100.00%	97.75%	97.12%	100.81%	99.01%	98.52%
4. Cumulative index (previous year's cumulative × current index)	100.00%	97.75%	94.93%	95.70%	94.75%	93.35%
5. Ending inventory at base-year cost (1 × 4)	$100,000	$117,300	$104,423	$86,130	$99,488	$93,350
Inventory on LIFO basis:						
At base-year costs, attributable to:						
6. Base Year	$100,000	$100,000	$100,000	$86,130	$86,130	$86,130
7. First year		17,300	4,423			
8. Fourth year					13,358	7,220
9. Total	$100,000	$117,300	$104,423	$86,130	$99,488	$93,350
At LIFO cost, attributable to:						
10. Base year (6 ÷ 100%)	$100,000	$100,000	$100,000	$86,130	$86,130	$86,130
11. First year (7 ÷ 97.75%)		17,698	4,525			
12. Fourth year (8 ÷ 94.75%)					14,098	7,620
13. Total LIFO inventory cost	$100,000	$117,698	$104,525	$86,130	$100,228	$93,750
14. Inventory on current cost basis		120,000	110,000	90,000	105,000	100,000
15. Cumulative inventory effect from use of LIFO method (13) − (14)		$ (2,302)	$ (5,475)	$ (3,870)	$ (4,772)	$ (6,250)

- Anticipation inventories: buildups in advance of a peak selling season, a promotion program, or a plant shutdown.
- Lot-size inventories: it is frequently impossible or impractical to manufacture or purchase items at the same rate at which they will be sold. These items are therefore obtained in larger quantities than needed; the resulting inventory is the lot-size inventory.
- Transportation inventories: inventories that exist because material must be moved from one place to another.

The expenses and losses incident to owning and caring for inventories include:

- Earnings from alternative investments of the working capital applied (commonly computed at current interest rates or at the average earning rate of the company)
- Personal property taxes
- Insurance premiums
- Storage expense, which may represent additional rental payments or an allocated portion of maintaining a warehouse or storeroom
- Employee compensation payments, which are increased because of the handling of excess goods and reduction in efficiency caused by the inconvenience of "working around" the extra bulk
- Losses due to deterioration and obsolescence, which are continuing risks inherent in ownership of goods and which tend to be higher with respect to finished goods than to raw materials

Inventory Management Through "Classification."   The objective of an inventory management system including the "control" of the above expenses and losses is portrayed in Exhibit 7. Exhibit 8 depicts the commonly accepted ABC concept of the classification of goods included in an inventory for the purpose of establishing the appropriate inventory control procedure.

EXHIBIT 7   Objective of Inventory Management System

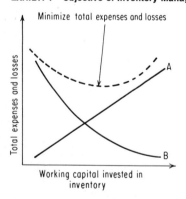

A   Factors which vary directly with level of inventory:

Possible earnings from alternative investments
Personal property taxes
Insurance premiums
Storage expense
Added employee payments
Deterioration and obsolescence

B   Factors which vary inversely with level of inventory:

Lost sales
Production delays
Inefficiency of small purchase orders and short production runs

The distribution of annual dollar usage is established by listing the various items in descending order. In a typical manufacturing inventory, it is found that approximately 70 percent of the items carried account for only 5 percent of the annual dollar usage. These items are referred to as the *C* items. Another 15 percent of the items may account for 15 percent of the annual dollar usage; they may be referred to as *B* items. The remaining 15 percent of the items would account for 80 percent of the annual dollar usage and would be referred to as *A* items.

EXHIBIT 8   Typical Distribution of Inventory—Manufacturing Company

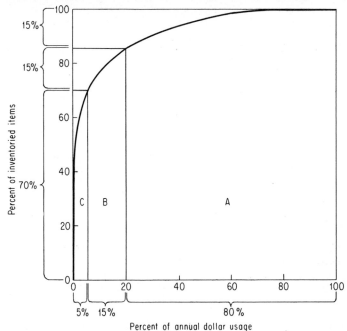

Percent of annual dollar usage

It is necessary to vary the type of control procedures according to the particular characteristics of the items included in the inventory. No single method of inventory control would be appropriate for all items.

Items classified as *A* will justify maximum control measures, such as perpetual inventory records, product identification, and precisely determined reorder quantities. In many cases, the economic order quantity will be established by applying an adaptation of the classical economic order quantity (EOQ) formula described later.

The control techniques for the *B* items will be less sophisticated than for the *A* items. The updating of perpetual inventory records, if maintained for the *B* items, may not be as frequent; e.g., such updating may be on a weekly basis whereas the records for the *A* items may be maintained on a daily basis.

The primary objective in the control of *C* items may be to minimize the expense involved in maintaining the control. Some minimum procedures for these items are, however, essential for any inventory control system. Safety stocks for *C* items can be relatively high, and in many cases a "two-bin" system can be used to eliminate the necessity of maintaining a perpetual inventory record. Items are used out of one of the bins, and the reorder point is identified when the storeroom must go to the reserve stock in the alternate bin to fill an order. When a new shipment is received in the stock room, the reserve stock bin is filled with a quantity equal to the reorder point, and the excess is placed in the primary storage bin.

Formula for Establishing Economic Order Quantity.   The principal factors taken into account in establishing the EOQ for a particular item are reflected in Exhibit 9. The minimum point on the total variable cost curve, TVC, is where the two solid lines intersect or where the annual carrying cost equals the annual ordering cost.

EXHIBIT 9   Economic Order Quantity

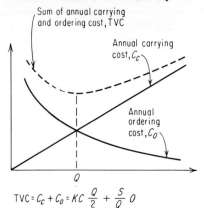

Sum of annual carrying and ordering cost, TVC

Annual carrying cost, C_c

Annual ordering cost, C_o

Q

$$\text{TVC} = C_c + C_o = KC\,\frac{Q}{2} + \frac{S}{Q}\,O$$

Minimum TVC occurs where $C_c = C_o$ giving:

$$Q = \sqrt{\frac{2SO}{KC}}$$

Where:

Q = order quantity in units

S = annual demand in units

O = cost per order in dollars

K = annual carrying cost as a percentage

C = unit cost in dollars

EXHIBIT 10   Economic Order Quantity Modified

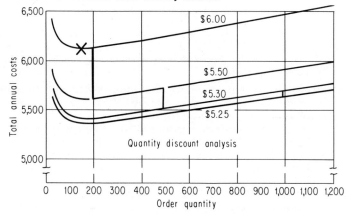

Total annual costs

$6,500 — $6.00

$6,000

$5.50

$5.30

$5,500 — $5.25

Quantity discount analysis

$5,000

0   100   200   300   400   500   600   700   800   900   1,000   1,100   1,200

Order quantity

	EOQ	First price break	Second price break	Third price break
Order quantity	150	200	500	1,000
Unit price	$6.00	$5.50	$5.30	$5.25
Annual costs				
Material	$6,000	$5,500	$5,300	$5,250
Ordering	67	50	20	10
Inventory carrying	67	83	199	394
Total........	$6,134	$5,633	$5,519	$5,654
Annual savings	--	$501	$615	$480

Annual usage _____ 1,000 units
Ordering costs _____ $10 per order
Inventory carrying cost _____ 15%

In any particular instance, the basic formula for establishing the economic order quantity must be expanded and modified. For example, Exhibit 10 illustrates a situation in which the material costs vary according to the quantity ordered. In this example, it is assumed that (1) the annual usage is 1,000 units; (2) the ordering cost is $10 per order; and (3) the inventory carrying expenses amount to 15 percent per annum of the working capital tied up in inventory. It is further assumed that for an order under 200 units the cost is $6; this becomes lower as larger quantities are ordered; e.g., the per-unit cost is $5.50 if the order is for between 200 and 500 units.

Exhibit 10 reflects the aggregate annual cost and expense curves for the four unit prices examined. The perpendicular lines on the upper portion of the exhibit show how the analyst moves from one curve to the next at points where a new discount takes effect, such as 200, 500, and 1,000 units. It will be noted that both the per-unit purchase cost and the per-unit expense decrease as order quantities increase, but that the expense of carrying the inventory increases with the order quantity. The annual savings at the three price breaks relative to the economic order quantity levels are $501, $615, and $480, which means that the indicated optimum order quantity is 500 units.

Timing of Orders.   After establishing the optimum quantity of goods to be covered by an order, it is essential to determine when orders should be placed. Exhibit 11 reflects the relationship among stock levels, reorder points, order quantities, lead times, and safety stocks. The reorder point R is defined as (1) the lead time (replenishment time) in days multiplied by the demand per day plus (2) the safety stock. When the stock level reaches the reorder point, action is initiated to issue an order. The lead time L is the elapsed time from the moment the stock level reaches the reorder point until the new order is received. If both the lead time and demand per day were constant, the stock level would reach the safety

EXHIBIT 11   General Inventory Decisions

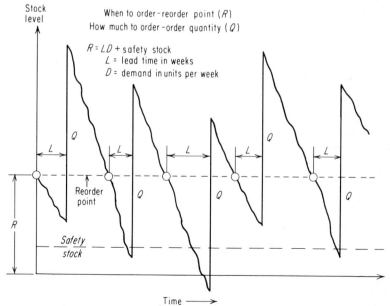

stock level just as the new order is received. However, both lead times and demand rates represent averages with statistical variations about these averages. If total demand during a lead time period is greater than the average, the stock level will be below that of the total safety stock. The second cycle on the graph shows a case where the demand rate increased above the average and resulted in the stock level being in the safety stock before the new order arrived. The third cycle reflects a stockout situation that came about as a result of an extended lead time.

The size of the safety stock is based on two factors: (1) the likely variability in total demand from the forecast demand during the lead time period, and (2) the acceptable rate of stockouts. If management wants to reduce the number of stockouts, the safety stock must be increased or the variability from forecasted lead time demand must be controlled through improved forecasting of demand and by reducing the number of past-due production or purchase orders.

Other Methods and Techniques.   The foregoing approaches to typical inventory management models can be tailored to a particular situation using the following methods:

Statistical
- Correlation analysis (for leading series)
- Time-series analysis
- Moving averages
- Seasonal analysis
- Exponentially smoothed moving averages

Judgmental
- Managerial estimates
- Salesperson estimates
- Surveys
- Market research

BIBLIOGRAPHY

Barden, Horace G.: AICPA Accounting Research Study 13, "The Accounting Basis of Inventories," AICPA, New York, 1973.

Brown, R. C.: *Statistical Forecasting for Inventory Control,* McGraw-Hill Book Company, New York, 1959.

Committee on Accounting Procedure: *Accounting Research Bulletin No. 43,* AICPA, New York, 1953, chap. 4, "Inventory Pricing."

Cost Accounting Standards Board, Published and Proposed Standards, Washington, D.C.

Davidson, S., J. S. Schindler, and R. L. Weil: *Fundamentals of Accounting,* 5th ed., Dryden Press, Hinsdale, Ill., 1975.

Dopuch, Nicholas, and Joel Demski: "Mathematical Models and Accounting," in *Handbook of Modern Accounting,* 2nd ed., Sidney Davidson and Roman L. Weil, eds., McGraw-Hill Book Company, New York, 1977.

General Service Administration: The Economic Order Quantity Principle and Applications, Federal Stock No. 7610-543-6765, Washington, D.C., 1966.

Hoffman, R. A., and J. D. Coughlan: "Inventories," in *Handbook of Modern Accounting,* 2nd ed., Sidney Davidson and Roman L. Weil, eds., McGraw-Hill Book Company, New York, 1977.

Hoffman, R. A., and H. Gunders: *Inventories—Control, Costing and Effect on Income and Taxes,* Ronald Press, New York, 1970.

Institute of Chartered Accountants in England and Wales: Recommendations on Accounting Principles No. 22, "Treatment of Stock-in-trade and Work in Progress in Financial Accounts," London, 1960.

Magee, John F., and David M. Boodman: *Production Planning and Inventory Control,* 2nd ed., McGraw-Hill Book Company, New York, 1967.

National Association of Accountants: Statement Number 6 on Management Accounting Practices, "Guidelines for Inventory Management," NAA, New York, 1973.

Plosal, G. W., and O. W. Wight: *Production and Inventory Control,* Prentice-Hall, Englewood Cliffs, N.J., 1967.

Prichard, James W., and Robert H. Eagle: *Modern Inventory Management,* John Wiley & Sons, New York, 1965.

U.S. Internal Revenue Code provisions with respect to inventories and related regulations: Code sec. 471 and 472 and Reg. sec. 1.471 and 1.472.

Chapter **13**

Job Order Cost Accounting

J. LOUIS WARGO
Ernst & Ernst

GENERAL

A Dictionary for Accountants defines job order costing as "a method of cost accounting whereby costs are compiled for a specific quantity of products, equipment, repairs or other service that move through the production process as a continuously identifiable unit. . . ."[1] Job order costing is used in those manufacturing processes where it is necessary or desirable to identify the costs related to a specific amount of production. The quantity of production could be a single unit, a batch, a factory order, a sales order, or any other accumulation of the amount produced.

---

[1]Eric L. Kohler, *A Dictionary for Accountants,* 5th ed. (Prentice-Hall, Englewood Cliffs, N.J., 1975), p. 278.

Generally, the job order system is used by manufacturing concerns where an order is produced to a customer's specifications. Usually, no two orders are exactly alike and frequently, not all orders are processed in the same manner. Consequently, it is necessary to accumulate the costs for each order or job so that the total cost of each job can be determined and a proper matching of cost and revenues can be made. Some companies manufacture on a process basis, but for purposes of factory orders and cost accounting, group the products, which are essentially standard stock items, into separate, clearly distinguishable groups, usually called batches or lots. Examples are mastics or machine tools.

PRODUCTION ORDERS

The job order method of accumulating costs usually parallels the manufacturing method used, i.e., the way the production order is routed through the plant by production planning. The job order cost accounting system makes use of the system of routing the production order to accumulate the related costs. Raw material is withdrawn from stores to be used on the job and also coded for accounting purposes. Employees are assigned to perform the various operations that are specified and are required to code their time tickets for these operations for accounting purposes. Variations of the job order system are used by production planning to minimize the costs (usually setup costs) and maximize the lot size. For example, a manufacturer may use one job order with the same basic structure for several customer orders that have variations in the accessories that apply. An example would be turning machines with different machine tools for each final product. In this situation there would be one job order for the basic machines and individual job orders for each of the machine tools.

The purpose of the job order system is to see that the costs of the items used in the manufacturing process, the direct material, the direct labor, and the manufacturing overhead, are identified to each of the jobs involved. These costs are then transferred to the applicable inventory accounts and finally to cost of goods sold. Because of this method of identifying costs, it is unusual with a job order cost system to have a sizable physical inventory adjustment. Job order cost systems are also used by concerns that provide service and have no inventory of their own. That is, ownership of the material is retained by the customer while the material is being processed. Examples of this are heat treating and plating. In such a situation, it is not unusual to have the various customers' materials comingled in the processing cycle. The following industries might be expected to use a job order cost system: construction, foundries, machine tools, mastics, printing, and ship building.

JOB ORDER COST VERSUS PROCESS AND STANDARD COSTS

The job order cost system can be contrasted to two other systems that are normally encountered, process cost and standard cost. Process costing is used primarily when the product is manufactured in a relatively continuous operation. It is more closely identified with those industries in which the same type or similar materials are run through the same process or same pieces of equipment with the result that the products are very nearly fungible. Costs are collected by the process performed and distributed to the units manufactured. An example of this would be steel making, chemicals, plastics, and industrial fasteners. Standard costs are used primarily to generate data for the management's use in controlling costs, usually on the basis of management by exception. Standard cost accounting is thought by some to be unusable with job order costing; however, standard costs can be used in a job order system. To do so requires the establishment of standards for each of the elements involved: the quantities and prices of direct material and the hours and rates of direct labor or machine time. The individual job orders are costed at predetermined rates and then compared to actual costs incurred in computing the variances from standard.

Advantages and Disadvantages.   A job order cost system provides the primary advantage of a complete capture of the costs applicable to each specific order. The use of the word "complete" in this area involves only the direct costs, i.e., direct labor and direct material.

Job order costing has the following advantages: it is precise, complete, historical, simple, and enables comparisons. The precision results from all direct costs being identified to particular orders. The completeness results from all costs, direct and indirect, being correlated to production and then being cleared to cost of sales. Job order costing provides a historical record by accumulating all the charges that are incurred in the manufacture of a specific order. The simplicity results from the fact that the recording of direct materials and direct labor hours is along the lines of a reporting system that already exists, either for production planning or scheduling purposes. The job order system also provides a basis for comparing one job cost to another or for comparing a job cost to a cost estimate.

The disadvantages of a job order system are as follows: Any inefficiencies that occur in the manufacture of a batch or a lot are captured in the job cost. They are not segregated, thus not allowing a comparison to what the costs should have been. Costs cannot be segregated for the individual items in a lot. For example, if 15 machines are started through on a job order, the total costs that are accumulated will be spread over each one of the 15 machines even though the production of one or two specific machines may have increased the costs disproportionately among the others. Different costs may occur for producing similar, if not identical, products at different points in times. The lack of detail does not enable a ready identification of the reasons for these differing costs. A comparison of details for direct material and direct labor is usually not facilitated. These details, relative to yields, rejections, setup costs, run sizes, efficiency by operation, etc., are not required in order to accumulate costs for a job order.

REPORTING OF COST DATA

A job order cost accounting system requires the reporting of direct material and direct labor used for each of the job orders. This is accomplished by using job order numbers that are assigned by production planning for orders to be processed. Job orders may be originated in response to customers' orders or they may be originated in anticipation of customers' orders (stock production). The specifications for each job order are transmitted to the production floor by means of a production or shop order (see Exhibit 1). Production orders provide the details describing the product, the direct material to be used, and the operations to be performed. These descriptions can be in narrative form, or they can be in numerical form (coding pattern). These details are reported to accounting to allow a computation of the related costs. These orders include various descriptive data including the date of the order, the job order number, the product description, the quantity to be produced, the date the work is to be started, and the completion date. The production order packet will usually include a production routing

EXHIBIT 1   Production or Shop Order (National Acme Co.)

```
I05800-P192                    NATIONAL  ACME  PRODUCTION  ORDER         DATE 03/02/78      PAGE NO.  1

   ORDER NO. A-47032-17    MTL NO. RB- 70667-     MTL DESC ADPTR BLK,CYL,HYDR        MTL SIZE

   PART NO. BW- 70667-         PART DESC  ADAPTOR,CYL,HYDR              ORDER QTY      2       EDITION  06
```

OPER NUMBER	DEPT CODE	OPERATION DESCRIPTION	TOOLING DATA	MACHINE CODE	FULL SETUP	PARTIAL SETUP	STANDARD MINUTES	DNP
1	1700	ORDER MATERIAL						
3	4301	DIP PAINT RED						
6	1701	BORE,REAM,TRN,		LTV360	75.00	R	90,000R	
9	1701	CBR,FACE,TURN		LTV360	27.00	C	50,000R	
12	2201	BORE,DRL,TAP,RM,	BW-70667NC-1	DS1XQT	170.00	60.00R	160,000R	
15	2201	DRL,RM,BORE,CBR,	BW-70667NC-2	DS1XQT	80.00	30.00R	65,000R	
18	2807	BURR		BENCH	4.50	A	27,900A	
21	4401	SPRAY PAINT RED					14,310C	
24	4601	INSPECT						
27	4701	STORE						

identifying the part name, the part number, the job order number, the date, the operation numbers, the sequence of those operation numbers, the department or cost center performing the operation, and the time involved.

The job order number is used by the storeroom workers on material requisitions and by the factory employees through the timekeeping or payroll system. These job order numbers are usually assigned sequentially as sales orders are received. However, some systems do attach significance to the digits to provide additional information about each job or about similar jobs. This frequently occurs when it is desirable to obtain information about a particular line or class of product. For example, in a foundry it may be desirable to accumulate statistics relative to steel grades, product lines, casting weight, or casting dimensions.

The disbursement of materials requires a recording of the raw materials used on each job order. This is done by using material requisition forms (see Exhibit 2) for each item disbursed or by using a bill of material (see Exhibit 3) that lists all of

EXHIBIT 2   Material Requisition Form (National Acme Co.)

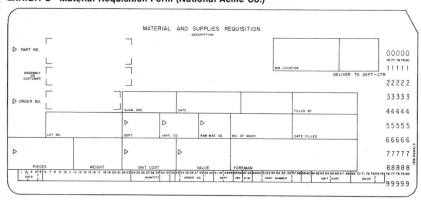

EXHIBIT 3   Bill of Material (National Acme Co.)

ITEM NO	LEVEL	PART NO	DS	DESCRIPTION	QTY/UNIT	U/M	PA	SC	REMARKS
10	1	562- 1	C	BODY AY,CYLINDER CYDY	1	PC	D	M	
20	1	562- 2	C	PISTON AY 5.997 PTDY	1	PC	A	M	
30	1	2753-90	C	CAP,CYLINDER CYCO	1	PC	C	M	
40	1	1727-50	P	PIPE PLUG,FL 0.062 PEPF	4	PC	P	P	
50	1	562-46	C	STEM AY,DISTR,HYDR DTSY	1	PC	A	M	
60	1	1727-51	P	PIPE PLUG,FL 0.125 PEPF	2	PC	P	P	
70	1	562-19	B	PISTON RING,6.000 P100	3	PC	P	P	
80	1	562- 7	A	PKG,V-RING,OD 1.750 PPWO	1	PC	P	P	
90	1	562- 6	A	RETAINER,PKG 1.266YRPO	1	PC	P	M	
100	1	XA- 4159-	S	PIN,STR .312X0.562FPBO	1	PC	P	M	
110	1	50790-	S	SET SCR,FP 3/8-16FTOF	2	PC	P	P	
120	1	A- 17084-	A	BRG,BALL,RDL 111L0028BRO	1	PC	P	P	
130	1	51634-	A	PIN,STR 0.188X1.500FPSR	1	PC	P	M	
140	1	562-24	A	PIN,MISC FPZO	1	PC	P	M	
150	1	562-18	B	GASKET PG00	1	PC	P	P	
160	1	1151-	S	C'SCR,SCH 5/16-18FCSO	10	PC	P	P	
170	1	1837-24	S	O-RING, 224 PR00	1	PC	P	P	
180	1	1837-22	S	O-RING, 222 PR00	1	PC	P	P	
190	1	562-13	A	NUT,HEX 1-1/2-12 FNWO	1	PC	P	M	
200	1	562-10	B	SEAL,1 LIP,ID 2.000 PS40	1	PC	P	P	
210	1	562-15	A	SHIM,DISC TYPE 1.375SMDO	1	PC	P	P	
220	1	562-14	A	COVER,SHAFT END CV90	1	PC	P	M	
230	1	562-17	A	C'SCR,HEX HD 1/4-20FCHO	2	PC	P	M	
240	1	562-22	A	GASKET PG00	1	PC	P	P	
250	1	562-42	A	COVER DISC 3.375 CV40	1	PC	P	M	
260	1	50134-	S	C'SCR,HEX HD 1/4-20FCHO	4	PC	P	P	
270	1	77771-	S	SET SCR,CUP 1/4-20FTDG	1	PC	P	P	

BILL OF MATERIAL MACHINERY NATIONAL ACME Div of Acme-Cleveland Corp DATE 01/24/78

DESCR: CYLINDER AY,HYDR,RD CYJY PAGE NO 1 ASSEMBLY NO - 562-27 X DS

DS = Drawing Size   U/M=Unit of Measure
PA Column: P=Part; A=Assembly; R=Raw Material C=Casting; F=Forging; S=Semi-finished
SC=Source Code P =Purchase; M=Manufacture
FIN   1   - 562-27

the materials to be used. The use of a bill of materials expedites the release of material to the shop floor, but it also provides the disadvantage of having material on the floor prior to the time that it is required. The use of the bill of materials also alerts the storeroom to the fact that required materials or parts may be out of stock and thus enables the purchasing department to expedite the delivery or ordering of the required material. Coordination of the job order system with the inventory control system will aid in avoiding stock-out situations by correlating purchase lead times to the delivery time quoted to the customer or by stocking material in anticipation of orders.

Labor or machine time is recorded on a job ticket (see Exhibit 4) according to the job order number established by the production planning department. The identifying information for the job ticket is obtained from the job order. Setup time and run time also may be separately identified.

EXHIBIT 4   Job Ticket (National Acme Co.)

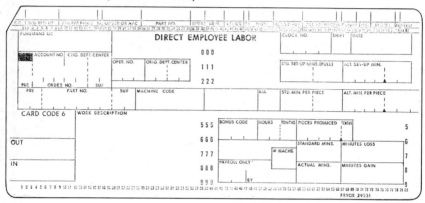

Job order costs may also include those elements of indirect material that can be identified directly to a particular job order. Such materials would include manufacturing supplies, packaging supplies, or loading supplies. If these items are included in manufacturing overhead, instead of being charged directly, their distribution will be accomplished on the basis of machine hours or labor hours through the use of standard overhead rates. The use of standard overhead rates will result in variances or underabsorbed or, less frequently, overabsorbed overhead.

Accounting for Direct Materials Costs.   In the job order system, direct material purchases must be accounted for as well as requisitions, scrap or waste, rejections, and returns. In those situations where material is not stocked in anticipation of an order, the purchasing department will purchase the material for each job order. A typical purchase order form is shown on Exhibit 5. The purchase order, in addition to identifying the job order to which the material applies, also provides the raw material code to facilitate costing. Material can be requisitioned through the disbursement of materials on the basis of individual requests from the storeroom, or they can be made on the basis of the (previously mentioned) bill of materials. Under either method, the completed requisition form is provided to the Accounting Department to allow accumulation of the proper costs for each order. Material issues that are to be charged to different jobs should not be recorded on the same material requisition. This will facilitate the recording of costs by the Accounting Department.

In the manufacturing process, not all material that has been requisitioned will become part of the final product. This loss of material can be due to the unintentional production of scrap, or it can be the result of natural waste or design scrap. It is typical to continue to record the total cost amount of the material requisitions to the job order and not to decrease the costs reported for the amount of related

EXHIBIT 5   Purchase Order Form (National Acme Co.)

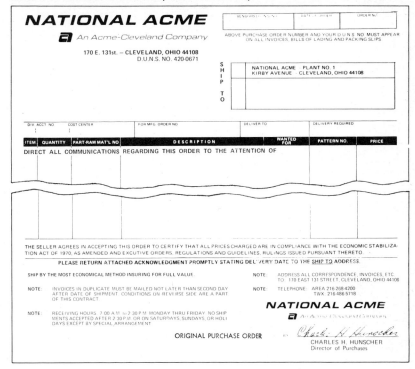

scrap. The scrap that is generated is combined with scrap from other orders and carried in a scrap account. This account is cleared when the scrap is sold or reprocessed in the manufacturing process.

Rejections that occur in the production process are recorded against the production order. When rejects occur, additional materials are requisitioned from the storeroom to replace the amount that has been scrapped and the additional materials are charged to the job order. If excessive material is ordered for the job order or if the wrong material is obtained, the material should be returned to the storeroom. This return is then recorded on a material credit slip (see Exhibit 6) to provide the correct costs for the job order and also to see that the storeroom balances are maintained.

Direct Labor.   As mentioned earlier, a job order cost system is usually correlated to the production planning process. With such a system employees charge their time worked to each job order. Timekeeping systems combined with a job order system generally make use of two cards. One, a daily card (see Exhibit 7) to record the employee's time for the daily eight hours, and the second to accumulate the time for each job order. The former is used for payroll control purposes, whereas the latter is used for cost control purposes. The job order time cards identify the operations performed and the cost center involved. This permits a subsequent calculation of the direct labor and related overhead costs.

The job card tickets are sent to the Accounting Department for accumulation of the cost for the job order. This accumulation may be posted to a Kardex record

EXHIBIT 6   Material Credit Slip

RETURNED MATERIAL SLIP

DATE: _____

ISSUE DATE	ORDER NO.	PART NO.	DESCRIPTION	UNIT/MEAS.	QUANTITY	EXPLANATION

_____
FOREMAN

_____
MATERIALS MANAGER

EXHIBIT 7   Daily Card (National Acme Co.)

DAY	MON.	TUE.	WED.	THUR.	FRI.	SAT.	SUN.
SHIFT							
ACTUAL HRS.							
HALFTIME HRS.							
	A.M.			P.M.			
1							
2							
3							
4							
5							
6							
7							

REG. HRS.   BASE EARNINGS

1-1/2 HRS.   BONUS

DBL. HRS.

TOTAL HRS.   TOTAL EARNINGS

DEDUCTIONS	F.O.A.B.		
	WITHHOLDING TAX		
	BONDS		
	INSURANCE HOSP.		
	MISC'L.		
			$

NET AMOUNT OF PAY $ _____

NAMCO NO. 6-017797

(see Exhibit 8), or it may be done by computer with a subsequent report printout (see Exhibit 9).

The use of the previously described routing enables the Accounting Department to determine that all work has been performed by comparing the reported

EXHIBIT 8   Kardex Record (National Acme Co.)

CA-14 REV.1-22-77

NAME: _Clutch Arem_   LIST NO. _SM- 71966_

ORDER NUMBER	DATE ISSUED	QUANTITY	REMARKS	DATE FINISHED	UNIT HOURS	UNIT MATERIAL	UNIT LABOR	UNIT BURDEN	TOTAL UNIT COST
23313	4/13/77	16		3/8/78	3 19	193 10	16 28	19 69	229 08
24015	8/24/77	8		7/10/78	3 22	193 10	15 84	20 05	229 08
41330	8/30/77	8		9/2/78	3 23	203 15	16 92	22 19	241 26
24337	12/16/77	4		1/5/78	2 75	207 46	16 09	21 32	244 76
94810	5/6/78	24		2/23/79	3 06	236 11	17 72	24 41	278 24

EXHIBIT 9   Report Printout

		PRODUCTION ORDER COST			DATE 03 31 78	SELLING PRICE 16068	TYPE ORD. 2	TOOL CLASS 0900	ORDER 550556	ITEM 010

CLOCK NO.	WORK GROUP NO	SEQUENCE NO.	COST CENTER	QUANTITY	PRICE PER 100	SET-UP	HOURS	BASE INCENTIVE LABOR	CURRENT INCENTIVE LABOR	NON-INCENTIVE LABOR	OVERHEAD	TOTAL LABOR AND OVERHEAD INCLUDING DAY WORK INSPECTION
0635	000	020	508	13	30000	850		1240	406		434	840
0529	002	030	585	13	00100	051 S		051	20		38	58
0064	056	040	529	13	37000	500		981	335		918	1253
0277	003	050	585	13	00100	147 S		147	60		113	173
0840	000	060	570	13			55			306	505	811
0963	000	070	512	13	1200	350		366	125		176	301
0264	002	071	505	13	0000	051 S		051	21		40	61
0091	026	080	534	13	17700	350		580	198		164	362
0160	000	090	546	13	0000	258		258	88		260	348
1057	000	100	546	13	1300	100		117	39		115	154
0370	072	110	552		0000	000		054	19		38	57
		120	562	13	2000	050		076	25		25	50
1326	000	130	553	13	1500	060		080	26		23	49
	0	150	552		0000	000		054	19		38	57
0711	001	160	585	2	0000	105 S		105	43		81	124
0292	061	170	565	13	1240	056 S		072	29		55	84
0762	070	171	562	13	22500	040		333	113		112	225
0762	070	171	562	1	22500	040		063	21		21	42
0762	070	171	562	1	22500	040		063	21		21	42
0292	001	172	585	13	1240	056 S		072	29		55	84
	0	180	552		0000	000		054	19		38	57
0255	000	190	540	13			26			94	93	187
0253	000	200	570	13			127			747	1233	1980
0240	198	210	575	13			107		556		701	1257
0322	190	220	594	13			46 S		227		241	468
0300	193	230	595	13	27500	350		708	242		305	547
1230	200	240	596	13	52500	350		1033	353		402	755
0151	198	250	595	9			118		634		799	1433
0248	198	251	595	1	64700	150		214	73		92	165
0539	006	260	589	65	5410	000 S		352	146		123	269
0248	198	261	595	3	13300	200		241	82		103	185
0162	006	270	589	65	9470	000 S		616	275		231	506
0162	006	271	589	6	9470	000 S		057	25		21	46
0646	005	280	536	26	5090	000 S		132	48		44	92
088	8888	8888					13					

| | | | | | | 13051 TOTAL COST | | 13 TOTAL MATERIAL | 4275 TOTAL CUR. IN. LABOR | 1147 TOTAL N. I. LABOR | 7616 TOTAL O. H. | 13038 TOTAL LABOR & O.H. |

operations to the routing. In some cases, the routing that has been specified on the order may be replaced or supplemented by an alternative routing. When this occurs, it is necessary to determine if the operations that were performed were either substituted for or in addition to the regular routing operations. This is necessary to ensure that all operations have been reported and properly accounted for.

Two areas related to the recording of direct labor must be considered, rework and overtime. The amount of rework that occurs usually is related to the experience in the production process. The amount of overtime that is incurred on a job order may be related to the sequence in which the jobs are scheduled. It would seem inequitable to apply rework and overtime only to those jobs that happen to be worked on at a point in time. For this reason, rework and overtime, instead of being applied to specific job orders, should be spread over all job orders by including them in the overhead rate. For expense control purposes it is desirable to have both rework and overtime reported on natural expense codes different from those used for direct labor.

Indirect Identifiable Overhead.   As was mentioned earlier, some indirect materials can and should be identified directly to particular job orders; included in this category are lumber for blocking and loading, special packaging, and special tooling required to complete the processing. In addition, outside processing may be classified as identifiable overhead because it does not relate directly to direct materials. Such outside processing would include machining or heat treating. These costs should be accumulated directly against the applicable job order.

Manufacturing Overhead.   Manufacturing overhead, as a rule, is distributed on the basis of standard overhead rates, although in some systems an overhead rate is computed for each accounting period involved. The accounting period may be a calendar month or a four-week period, although quarterly and semiannual rates are more often used. Generally, the more detail that is involved in the computation of the overhead rates, the more exact and precise will be the accumulation of costs. Overhead rates may be developed on a plant-wide basis or on the basis of departments or production cost centers. The most realistic results will be obtained by developing the rates along the same lines used to report costs. If production cost centers are used, then to the extent possible, manufacturing overhead costs should be accumulated for those cost centers. This will facilitate a comparison of the actual overhead rate to the standard overhead rate.

The use of standard or predetermined overhead rates will result in a difference between the amount of overhead that is charged through inventory and the amount of overhead incurred. This difference is caused by some combination of three factors:

1. Rate of spending
2. Production volume
3. Labor or machine efficiency

These differences, usually called variances or unabsorbed overhead, may be charged directly to cost of sales without identification to particular job orders. The direct charge to cost of sales, while providing the convenience of simplicity, will result in a misstatement of the gross margin that is applicable to each of the specific orders. To overcome this, variances may be allocated to individual job orders and inventory on the basis of the direct labor or machine hours incurred.

Spending variance is difficult to match to a particular order. Variances that result from seasonal effects such as increased or decreased spending for heating and lighting are difficult to match to specific orders, as are effects of repairs or vacations scheduled at a given time. These items can significantly affect the amount of underabsorption that takes place in a given month. For this reason overhead rates should be computed on the basis of the overhead for a year to ensure that seasonality effects and periodic spending are being properly recognized.

Under a job order cost system, efficiencies or inefficiencies are generally captured and related directly to the order. Other factors such as scheduling can also affect job costs by the amount of setup costs and teardown costs that are identified to jobs. The specific sequence that has been established by the production planning department can result in an allocation of costs that is quite arbitrary. This effect can be overcome by using a standard setup rate. That is, a standard amount of time is charged for each setup at a standard cost rate for the hours involved. Here again, another variance will be generated and must be charged to cost of sales.

INVENTORY ACCOUNTS

In the job order cost accounting system, there are usually several inventory accounts:
1. Raw Material
2. Work-in-Process
3. Finished Goods
The information is accumulated for each of these from:
1. Purchase orders
2. Material requisitions
3. Time cards
4. Shipping notices or bills of lading
The appropriate data are sent to the Accounting Department, where the proper costs are applied to the materials and appropriate rate to the labor hours. This information then is recorded against the job order in either a manually maintained file or a computer-maintained file. The computer-maintained file provides a relatively faster retrieval of information, but unless the production planning process is integrated in the data base this approach may result in a duplication of files maintained in the production planning department. The computer file also provides ease of analysis and identification of problems in a particular area by comparing actual against preestablished parameters for the generation of exception reports. To perform an analysis in a manually maintained inventory requires the review of detailed records, which usually involves considerable clerical effort.

JOURNAL ENTRIES

The standard journal entries that are required by a job order system are detailed below. As can be seen from the general ledger flow charts (see Exhibit 10), all expenses related to the various job orders are accounted for in either raw material inventory, work-in-process inventory, finished goods inventory, or cost of goods sold. The only exception is the difference between incurred factory overhead costs and applied factory overhead costs. The journal entries that are required are the same for both the manually maintained system and the computer-maintained system. That is, reports are obtained for material usage and labor cost incurred. The job status of each of the job orders can be obtained by either a review of the manually prepared cards or by obtaining a computer printout.

(1)   Dr.   Raw Material Inventory XX
       Dr.   Work-in-Process Inventory XX
               Cr. Accounts Payable....................................   XX
               To record the purchase of direct material for stocking purposes and also specific job orders.

(2)   Dr.   Work-in-Process Inventory XX
               Cr. Raw Material Inventory   XX
               To record the disbursement of direct material to the shop floor for use on specific job orders.

EXHIBIT 10 Flow of Accounting Transactions: Job Order Cost System. The numbers in parentheses relate to the journal entries on pages 13-11 and 13-13.

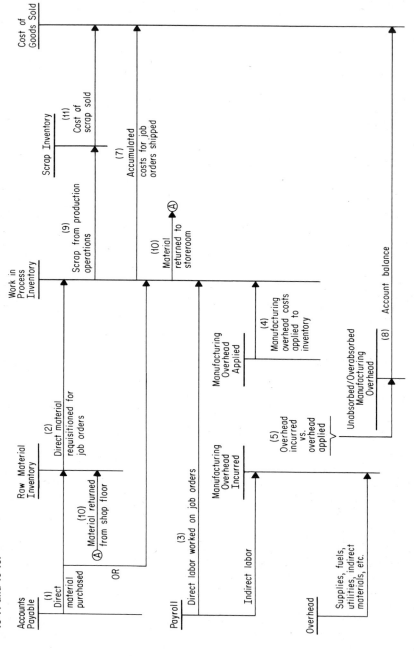

(3)   Dr.   Work-in-Process Inventory XX
                  Cr. Payroll Payable   XX
               To record the incurrence of direct labor in performing operations
               for specific job orders.

(4)   Dr.   Work-in-Process Inventory XX
                  Cr. Manufacturing Overhead Applied   XX
               To apply manufacturing overhead to specific job orders on the basis
               of operations reported.

(5)   Dr.   Manufacturing Overhead Applied XX
                  Cr. Manufacturing Overhead—Incurred   XX
       Dr./Cr.   Manufacturing Overhead—Unabsorbed .... XX XX
               To record the difference between manufacturing overhead
               incurred and manufacturing overhead applied.

(6)   Dr.   Finished Goods Inventory XX
                  Cr. Work-in-Process Inventory   XX
               To record the transfer of finished product from work in process to
               finished goods (this entry is not required when products are
               shipped from work-in-process inventory to the customer).

(7)   Dr.   Cost of Sales XX
                  Cr. Work-in-Process Inventory/Finished Goods Inventory ...   XX
               To record the shipment of specific job orders and to relieve
               inventory for the related costs.

(8)   Dr./Cr.   Cost of Sales .... XX YY
       Dr./Cr.   Manufacturing Overhead—Unabsorbed .... YY XX
               To charge cost of sales with the difference between applied and
               incurred overhead.

(9)   Dr.   Scrap Inventory XX
                  Cr. Work-in-Process Inventory   XX
               To record the accumulation of scrap in the production process.

(10)   Dr.   Raw Material Inventory XX
                  Cr. Work-in-Process Inventory   XX
               To record the return of material from the shop floor to the store
               room.

(11)   Dr.   Cost of Sales XX
                  Cr. Scrap Inventory   XX
               To record the shipment of scrap accumulated in the production
               process.

INVENTORY RECORDS

Job order costs may be accumulated manually on a cost sheet or Kardex record, or they may be accumulated through a computer. The mechanics with either method are similar: data reported from the shop floor by job order number are accumulated until the job is completed. The use of manual record involves posting from material requisitions and time tickets. Overhead is applied on the basis of the hours reported on the time tickets. Proper maintenance of the manual cost records requires daily posting of the cost information.

The use of a computer provides a more efficient system because it allows the processing of the same data for more than one purpose: the updating of raw material inventory, work-in-process inventory, open-order file, computation of payroll, etc. The use of a computer also facilitates the preparation of summary reports or cost-to-date reports by job order number.

Usually a monthly summary of costs to date by job order number is prepared for management reporting purposes. A typical job order cost summary form is shown on Exhibit 11.

Monthly summaries are also prepared for raw material status, material requisitions, rejects or defective work, direct labor, rework, cost of sales, and purchases.

EXHIBIT 11　Job Order Cost Summary Form (National Acme Co.)

```
A51600-CS00A                                    N A T I O N A L

                                       COST HISTORY 11/01/75
```

PART NUMBER	DATE CLOSED	ORDER NUMBER	QUANTITY	UNIT HOURS
A- 14343-00	4/04/77	A9566215	20	.64
	4/04/77	A9566215	20	.64
	5/22/77	A9574915	35	.53
	5/22/77	A9574915	35	.53
	10/03/77	A9513317	25	.59
	10/03/77	A9513317	25	.59
	12/06/77	A9535117	47	.48
	12/06/77	A9535117	47	.48
A- 14346-00	12/28/76	A9500115	15	.95
	12/28/76	A9500115	15	.95
	10/31/77	A9538515	24	1.15
	10/31/77	A9538515	24	1.15
A- 14347-00	6/21/76	A1083214	18	.06
	1/04/77	A5006615	8	.26
	1/04/77	A5006615	8	.26
	2/13/77	A3999114	12	.38
	2/13/77	A3999114	12	.38
	8/14/77	A3136117	9	.43
	8/14/77	A3136117	9	.43
	11/21/77	A4610917	4	.33
	11/21/77	A4610917	4	.33
	2/06/78	A4349417	6	.52
A- 14348-00	6/14/76	A1084914	18	.41
	12/10/76	A3928814	8	1.05
	12/10/76	A3928814	8	1.05
	1/04/77	A3001115	12	.67
	1/04/77	A3001115	12	.67
	6/20/77	A3136217	9	.58
	6/20/77	A3136217	9	.58
	10/24/77	A4613117	4	.80
	10/24/77	A4613117	4	.80
	11/14/77	A4310717	12	1.43
	11/14/77	A4310717	12	1.43
- 14348-00	11/30/75	A9656114	560	.00
	8/16/76	A4181612	325	.00
	3/14/77	A9537115	433	.05
	3/14/77	A9537115	433	.05
A- 14349-00	6/21/76	A9800714	18	.47
	11/15/76	A9500215	8	.34
	11/15/76	A9500215	8	.34
	2/13/77	A9523115	12	.30
	2/13/77	A9523115	12	.30
	4/04/77	A9538615	8	.39

A C M E   02/24/78   PAGE: 1000

THRU   2/06/78

UNIT MATERIAL	UNIT LABOR	UNIT BURDEN	TOTAL UNIT COST	DEL
1.274	4.695	11.588	17.557	
1.274	4.695	11.588	17.557	
1.274	3.914	8.659	13.847	
1.274	3.914	8.659	13.847	
1.274	4.612	9.640	15.526	
1.274	4.612	9.640	15.526	
1.274	3.711	8.887	13.872	
1.274	3.711	8.887	13.872	
4.835	6.650	13.064	24.549	
4.835	6.650	13.064	24.549	
4.629	7.813	21.145	33.587	
4.629	7.813	21.145	33.587	
46.451	.369	.810	47.630	
24.306	1.954	3.344	29.604	
24.306	1.954	3.344	29.604	
41.859	2.728	7.138	51.725	
41.859	2.728	7.138	51.725	
52.357	3.228	6.667	62.252	
52.357	3.228	6.667	62.252	
65.578	2.543	5.983	74.104	
65.578	2.543	5.983	74.104	
85.295	4.137	9.182	98.614	
16.300	2.730	4.867	23.897	
17.945	7.496	12.600	38.041	
17.945	7.496	12.600	38.041	
20.936	4.973	8.000	33.909	
20.936	4.973	8.000	33.909	
22.534	4.342	8.603	35.479	
22.534	4.342	8.603	35.479	
22.535	6.448	11.910	40.893	
22.535	6.448	11.910	40.893	
25.228	10.982	24.367	60.577	
25.228	10.982	24.367	60.577	
.281	.373	.585	1.239	
.000	.000	.000	.000	
.425	.352	.802	1.579	
.425	.352	.802	1.579	
10.606	3.071	6.217	19.894	
10.606	2.289	4.658	17.553	
10.606	2.289	4.658	17.553	
10.606	2.133	4.140	16.879	
10.606	2.133	4.140	16.879	
10.606	2.584	7.448	20.638	

                LAST PART ON THIS PAGE: A- 14349-00

Such summaries are facilitated when the source documents have been processed by a computer.

BIBLIOGRAPHY

Buckley, John W., and Kevin M. Lightner: *Accounting: An Information Systems Approach,* Dickenson Publishing Co., Encino, Calif., 1973.

Crowingshield, Gerald R., and Kenneth A. Gorman: *Cost Accounting: Principles and Managerial Applications,* Houghton Mifflin Company, Boston, 1974.

Editorial staff: *Handbook of Successful Operating Systems and Procedures with Forms,* Prentice-Hall, Englewood Cliffs, N.J., 1964.

Fremgen, James M.: *Accounting for Managerial Analysis,* Richard D. Irwin, Homewood, Ill., 1972.

Horngren, Charles T.: *Cost Accounting, A Managerial Emphasis,* 4th ed., Prentice-Hall, Englewood Cliffs, N.J., 1977.

Neuner, John J. W., and Edward M. Deakin, III:-*Cost Accounting,* 9th ed., Richard D. Irwin, Homewood, Ill., 1977.

Rossell, James H., and William W. Frasure: *Managerial Accounting,* Charles E. Merrill Publishing Co., Columbus, Ohio, 1972.

Schmiedicke, Robert E., and Charles F. Nagy: *Principles of Cost Accounting,* South-Western Publishing Co., Cincinnati, Ohio, 1973.

Shillinglaw, Gordon: *Cost Accounting: Analysis and Control,* Richard D. Irwin, Homewood, Ill., 1977.

Summers, Edward L.: *Introduction to Accounting for Decision Making and Control,* Richard D. Irwin, Homewood, Ill., 1974.

Chapter **14**

Process Cost Systems*

ROBERT L. KELLY AND LEONARD PACE
Directors, Haskins & Sells

*This chapter contains certain materials adapted by the editors from Sidney Davidson, James S. Schindler, and Roman L. Weil, *Fundamentals of Accounting,* 5th ed. (Dryden Press, Hinsdale, Ill., 1975), chap. 21.

INTRODUCTION

Process costing and job order costing are the two principal approaches to cost accounting in the manufacturing environment. The principal difference between the two may be stated as follows, in a simplified form. In job order costing (except for repair work, and certain other applications) the basis for accumulating the relevant costs is a job or work order that normally specifies a quantity of a particular product to be manufactured. The costs required to perform specified operations are accumulated against the job order as they are incurred and these costs are attributed to the quantity of the item produced under the job order. In process costing the basis for accumulating the relevant costs is a process or cost center. These costs are then attributed to the quantity produced of the homogeneous product output of the process during the time period over which the costs have been accumulated. A key difference in concept between these two approaches is thus seen to be their bases for cost accumulation. In a job order system all relevant costs for a particular lot specified by the job order are accumulated against that order regardless of the period in which they are incurred; in a process costing system all relevant costs incurred in a particular process or cost center are accumulated against the process itself for a specified period. In either approach accumulated costs can be divided by recorded production to yield unit cost of production.

To develop the concept of process costing requires further consideration of what is meant by process, homogeneous product output, and quantity produced. First, however, it may be useful to cite briefly some of the circumstances of the manufacturing environment and accounting conventions within which process costing may usually be applied.

Process costing is particularly well suited to industries using continuous production technology such as paper making, petroleum refining, and certain chemical processing (e.g., manufacturing sulfuric acid, ammonia, and many petrochemicals). In such instances process costing may represent the only logical and practical approach to use. It is also well suited to many other applications that reflect batch processing technology. It may be used for coal mining or other extractive processes, batch production processes in the chemical, baking, canning, and brewing industries, as well as many others. The common elements appear to be production of a product in one or a series of processing steps, over a reasonable period of time (usually days, weeks, or even longer), and units of product that are essentially homogeneous or indistinguishable from each other (obviously with appropriate consideration of nonstandard production).

Process costing is an underlying concept broadly applied. Its use in the implementation of a cost accounting system requires the selection of specific complementary techniques from among many available. Thus a process costing system may be based on actual or standard cost principles; it may be used in direct cost systems or cost systems reflecting overhead cost accumulations or allocations. In many of the industries where it is applicable, the treatment of joint products is inherent. As examples one can cite petroleum refining or the production of caustic soda and chlorine from salt. By-product costing is an essential element of cost accounting in the chemical and other industries. From another viewpoint, the selection of a particular set of inventory conventions is obviously an important consideration in implementing any cost system. Each of these matters and others of importance such as scrap, spoilage, and waste are treated in detail elsewhere in this *Handbook* and therefore are not developed in this chapter. Process costing as a concept does not dictate a selection among these alternatives nor does it, of itself, solve some of the difficult problems implied by such selection. It suffices to say that any selection of compatible techniques from among these can be accommodated in the underlying process costing approach.

Features of the Process Costing Method. The essential characteristics of the accounting for the process costing method are as follows:

1. Each process or stage of production becomes a center for cost accumulation. For example, a product may go through the following steps or processes: (a) cutting, (b) assembling, (c) finishing, (d) painting, and (e) inspection. Under the process method, the cost of carrying out each of the five processes is determined separately.

2. Costs are accumulated by process for the duration of a production run on a particular product, or for a shorter period consistent with the normal accounting reporting periods.

3. The number of units produced in each process must also be determined, and the unit cost for the process is calculated by dividing the total costs for the period by the total number of units produced. If some units are only partially completed, the total work done or completed on partially completed units is translated into an *equivalent number of completed units.*

4. The determination of the final or total unit cost of the product is essentially one of adding together the unit costs of each process through which the product flows.

PROCESS

One of the ideas cited above for further development is the concept of *process.* As used in this chapter, it refers to an operation or series of operations performed in the course of manufacturing an identifiable product, the quantity of which is susceptible to measurement. Further, we assume that all relevant elements of cost associated with the input to the operation, whether related to materials, labor, or overhead, are also measurable.

At one extreme, a total plant or significant portion thereof may be considered the process. In many cases, however, the process consists of a relatively limited complement of equipment together with the associated labor and elements of overhead. Regardless of the extent of the process it is important that the quantities of material, labor, and as applicable, overhead elements that represent input to the process be measurable over any required time span.

The accounting concept of process is then derived from the physical concept described above and the process is designated as a cost center, or process center, for the accumulation of the costs. Within the cost center, of course, the various elements of cost may be stated in whatever degree of detail is necessary or desirable to fulfill all of the purposes for which the cost system is designed.

HOMOGENEOUS PRODUCT OUTPUT

Reference is made above to homogeneous product output. By this it is meant that the output resulting from the process over a given period of time should be identifiable as intrinsically the same product. This does not imply the absence of any and all variations associated with normal manufacturing output. Rather it requires conformance within acceptable tolerances that might be established by specifications, commercial acceptability, or other means.

Further, there is no implication that necessarily only one such product may be made in a given process or cost center. From time to time many different products might be manufactured in the same process or cost center, but normally these would be manufactured one at a time. Simultaneous production of more than one item, where such is the inevitable result of the particular technology, requires treatment on a joint product or by-product basis.

Finally, the product resulting from a given process is not necessarily to be construed as a finished item for sale. In many industries where process costs are used, the products of many intermediate processes are never sold in an outside market but are used internally in successive processes from the last of which there is produced a finished item for sale. Unit costs of these intermediate products are treated (on whatever basis employed, e.g., actual or standard) as transfer costs at the next process or cost center. Naturally, there are instances in which some units of a given product might be sold and other units of that used in further processes to produce other products.

QUANTITY PRODUCED

In a process cost system, costs are accumulated by process or cost center for a period of time. To convert such accumulated process costs to product cost per unit, it is necessary to have a reliable measurement of the quantity of product made during the period. The quantity may be expressed, variously, by weight, length, area, volume, or count, depending on the physical process of production, the nature of the product, and the form in which unit costs are required. In the process industries, analysis or assay of the physical product to establish the composition of the product output may be required in order to determine quantity in the reporting terms used in the accounting system. The quantities of product to be reworked, rejected material, scrap, and the like may also require identification to provide a proper basis for calculating the quantity of production meeting the requirement of homogeneous units of product output. Where joint products or reportable by-products are produced, their quantities must also be determined for the period.

One of the several criteria that establish the boundaries of a particular process is the ability to determine the quantity of output with accuracy and with reasonable effort and expense. Additional criteria may relate to the organizational responsibility for control of operations, the physical or even geographical relationship between successive operations, the inherent nature of the operations, and other factors. These, taken as a whole, are the basis for establishing the number of process or cost centers (and the boundaries between them) used in a particular accounting system. In any case, it is a requirement that the quantity of output from each process or cost center be determinable and reportable in homogeneous units of some kind.

It has been emphasized that process costing is characterized by the collection of all relevant costs in a process or cost center for a period of time. Ideally the time should be that of the production cycle during which a particular product (or set of joint products) is manufactured. However, only by coincidence would such intervals correspond to normal accounting reporting periods (month, quarter, or year). As a result, the ends of the normal reporting periods frequently occur during the course of manufacturing runs. One consequence of this fact is that some units of production are in an incomplete state at the end of a reporting period. In order to report properly the quantity produced, it is necessary to estimate the degree of completion of that material which is incomplete within each process.

In process costing, degree of completion and percentage incomplete are complementary concepts. If a product is 30 percent complete with respect to a particular process, it is also 70 percent incomplete. The objective is to estimate the equivalent of completed units to which the cost of the process incurred in the reporting period is to be attributed. This is accomplished by properly adjusting for changes in the equivalent full units in process at the beginning and end of the period. The percent complete, or its complement percent incomplete, is normally understood to relate to costs incurred in the particular process. Accordingly, the percent complete represents the estimated costs incurred for the incomplete units as a percent of the total cost normally incurred for a similar number of completed units. The estimated cost incurred may involve consideration of time, supplies, or any relevant combination of factors, weighted as necessary.

Application of the above rationale has led to development of two methods for stating production quantity, the completed units method and the incomplete units method. Either yields the same result, and selection between them would normally be made on the basis of the relative ease of application where any differential exists. Both methods are illustrated in the first illustration, on pages 14-5 and 14-6.

It should be noted that, as a practical matter, in certain large-scale continuous processes, changes in the inventory quantity of incomplete product from the beginning to the end of a period are sometimes (and without material error) disregarded. This approach is based on several factors. First, the characteristics of the physical processes inherently tend to make the quantity and state of incomplete units during operation constant over time. Second, the quantity involved is often small compared to the throughput during the period. Additionally, the cost and effort required to establish the quantity and state of the incomplete units is deemed excessive compared to the benefit to be derived therefrom. If an approach based on a simplifying assumption of this nature is used for interim reporting but not year-end reports, special care needs to be taken to avoid unacceptable differences in reports published or filled with regulatory agencies.

ILLUSTRATION OF COMPLETE/INCOMPLETE UNIT COMPUTATION

In the most general terms, process costing consists of accumulating the processing and material costs by process or cost center for a specified time period. The processing cost may then be divided by the quantity produced to develop an actual unit processing cost. When the actual unit cost of material is added to the actual unit processing cost, the total represents actual unit cost of the product resulting from the particular process involved. In an actual cost system, this may be the unit valuation for transfer of current period production either to the next succeeding process or to finished goods inventory. (In contrast, of course, in a standard cost system the unit valuation for transfer is the appropriate standard cost and differences between standard and actual costs are debited or credited suitably to variance accounts.)

A simple demonstration is sufficient to show the arithmetic principle of process cost accounting. The information required is the number of units in process at the beginning and end of the period and their degree of completion, the number of units of product started or finished in the period, and the costs chargeable to the process for the period.

The underlying principle is not changed by expanding material and processing costs into as many functional accounts as desired, or by repeating the calculations for any number of successive processes.

Computation of Equivalent Production.   The computation of equivalent production is necessary to give effect to any change in the work-in-process status at the beginning and end of the time period. It may be developed by either the completed units method or the incomplete units method.

For purposes of this example the following assumptions are made:

Beginning work in process (estimated 25 percent complete) .... 800 units
Production started .... 2,200 units
Production completed .... 2,000 units
Ending work in process (estimated 30 percent complete) .... 1,000 units

All items are expressed in terms of units of the product that is the output produced by the particular process. The equivalent units of completed work in this illustration are 2,100 units. This answer can be computed in either of two ways. These are illustrated next.

Completed Units Method

Units of completed production .... 2,000 units
Equivalent units in ending inventory (1,000 × .30) 300
                                                                                    2,300 units
Less: Equivalent units in beginning inventory (800 × .25) .... (200)
        Equivalent units of production .... 2,100 units

Incomplete Units Method

Units started in production .... 2,200 units
Equivalent incomplete units in beginning inventory (800 × .75) 600
                                                                                    2,800 units
Less: Equivalent incomplete units in ending inventory (1,000 × .70) .... (700)
        Equivalent units of production .... 2,100 units

Cost Computation.   Let us assume that processing costs (i.e., exclusive of material cost) for the period have been accumulated in the amount of $8,400. Applying the equivalent production developed above of 2,100 units, the unit cost of processing for the period is

$$\frac{\$8,400}{2,100 \text{ units}} = \$4 \text{ per unit}$$

The total cost per unit transferred to finished goods or further processing steps would be $4 per unit plus the material costs per unit.

Material cost, including both raw material cost and transfer cost from any previous process, is often considered to have been incurred completely at the start of production and to be expressed in terms of the units of the product in which completed production in the subject cost center is measured. (Where product shrinkage takes place along with processing, the assay and valuation methods used may effect the conversion of the input data into homogeneous output units.) Application of this method to the example would require that the cost of raw materials and transfers, excluding beginning inventory, charged to the process during the period be attributed to the quantity started, 2,200 units.

Costs for raw materials and transfers may sometimes be incurred over time as processing is carried out. In such a case it may be advisable to employ a procedure for relating this incurred cost to the units of production. This procedure would be similar to the one utilized for developing equivalent production for determining unit processing cost.

Value computations on transfers of finished material should appropriately reflect the inventory-flow assumptions that are inherent in the system. If the system in use is an actual cost system based on the FIFO cost-flow assumption, then the transfer values computed should reflect these facts. Any transfers made at nominal values that are at variance with the conventions employed will entail later correction or adjustments.

APPLICATION ILLUSTRATION

The foregoing illustration is intended to demonstrate the fundamental concept of process costing without introducing the complications that arise from the selection of a particular set of the additional conventions (inventory, etc.) required to implement a cost accounting system.

The illustration is useful to the intended purpose. However, an expanded illustration, as follows, will further demonstrate the concept in more conventional terms. To provide this illustration, specific assumptions have been made regarding the cost system and inventory treatment. These particular assumptions should not be viewed as inherent or limiting in the development of process costing systems. Further, because the matter of incomplete units has been treated previously, the following illustration omits such consideration in the interest of clarifying other points.

Simplified Illustration of the Process Costing Method. The schedule of production costs shown in Exhibit 1 indicates the accumulation of process costs and the

---

EXHIBIT 1   Process Costing Illustration

LESTER METAL PRODUCTS COMPANY
Production Costs
Month of July 19X0

	Units	*Amount*	*Unit costs*
Process A			
Raw material used		$10,800	
Direct labor		35,100	
Overhead costs (details omitted)		5,400	
Units started and completed during July ...	27,000	$51,300	
Units on hand 7/1 at $2.024	5,000	10,120	
Total units available during July	32,000	$61,420	$1.919
Units on hand 7/31 at $1.919	1,000	1,919	$1.919
Transferred to Process B	31,000	$59,501	$1.919
Process B			
Transferred from Process A	31,000	$59,501	$1.919
Direct labor		9,920	
Overhead costs (details omitted)		3,410	
Units started and completed during July ...	31,000	$72,831	
Units on hand 7/1 at $2.563	1,500	3,845	
Total units available during July	32,500	$76,676	$2.359
Units on hand 7/31 at $2.359	500	1,180	$2.359
Transferred to Process C	32,000	$75,496	$2.359
Process C*			
Transferred from Process B	32,000	$75,496	$2.359
Parts used		1,600	
Direct labor		4,800	
Overhead costs (details omitted)		1,280	
Total cost of units available (started and completed) during July	32,000	$83,176	$2.599

*No units were on hand at the start of July in Process C.

---

method of computing unit costs for the Lester Metal Products Company. The significant features of the illustration are as follows:

1. The plant produces a single product, which passes through three successive processes.

2. The nature of the production technique is such that at the end of the month all products have just completed one or more of the processes. (This assumption precludes ending inventories of work only partially complete for a process and the resulting difficulties in accounting for the equivalent units of work done. This assumption is one of those that makes this illustration "simplified.")

3. Units that have completed Process A and Process B are held at those points until needed in the next process. Those that have completed Process C are immediately transferred to the warehouse, where they are held until sold.

4. The weighted-average cost-flow assumption is used in valuing inventories in all processes.

Comments on Illustration. In Process A, the unit costs are determined by dividing the total of all costs, $61,420, including cost of units on hand at the start of the period, by 32,000, the number of units of product on hand at the beginning of the period plus the number made during the month. In Process B and Process C, the unit costs are similarly calculated in accord with the weighted-average cost-flow assumption. That is, unit cost is determined by dividing total costs incurred plus costs of units on hand at the start of the period by the total number of units on hand during the period, 32,500 in Process B and 32,000 in Process C.

"Overhead costs" include all of the costs of production except the direct material and labor that are chargeable to the three processes. Indirect labor, depreciation, maintenance, insurance, taxes, supplies, light, heat, and power are common examples. (The sum of direct labor costs and these "overhead costs" is often called *conversion costs.*)

Accounting Under the Process Costing Method. Recording the ordinary daily transactions under the process method involves nothing new in the way of accounting procedure. Costs are assigned directly to individual processes whenever it is feasible to do so. Certain overhead costs (i.e., those not directly associated with the process centers) may be charged to general overhead cost accounts that are later allocated to the production processes.

The following selected transactions indicate the typical requirements of accounting analysis under this method. It is assumed that controlling accounts are used for each group of process accounts and for the general production-overhead accounts. Appropriate detail accounts are, of course, maintained in each case. (These transactions involve operations of the Lester Metal Company for the month of July 19X0.)

(1) Raw material is acquired on account from the Northwest Steel Company. The invoice totals $15,725.

Raw Material Inventory	15,725	
Accounts Payable		15,725

(2) When materials, parts, or supplies are needed for production, they are requisitioned from the stock room. A summary of the requisitions issued during the month is as follows:

Raw Material, Process A	$10,800
Parts, Process C	1,600
Supplies, Process A	150
Supplies, Process B	475
Supplies, Process C	50
Janitors' Supplies	25

Supplies are treated as overhead costs. The entry, omitting detail accounts, would be

Process A Control	10,800	
Process C Control	1,600	
Production Overhead Control	700	
Raw Material Inventory		10,800
Parts Inventory		1,600
Supplies Inventory		700
Raw materials, parts, and supplies used are debited to production cost accounts.		

(3) The payroll distribution for the month provides the following information:

Direct Labor, Process A	$35,100
Direct Labor, Process B	9,920
Direct Labor, Process C	4,800
Superintendence	550
Maintenance Labor	600
Janitors' Wages	500
Nightwatchman's Wages	200

The entry, omitting detail accounts, is

Process A Control	35,100	
Process B Control	9,920	
Process C Control	4,800	
Production Overhead Control	1,850	
Wages and Salaries Payable		51,670
Labor costs for month are debited to production		
cost accounts.		

(4) Depreciation for the month is as follows:

Machinery and Equipment, Process A	$ 675
Machinery and Equipment, Process B	1,125
Machinery and Equipment, Process C	125
Building	100

The entry would be

Process A Control	675	
Process B Control	1,125	
Process C Control	125	
Production Overhead Control	100	
Accumulated Depreciation of Machinery and Equipment		1,925
Accumulated Depreciation of Building		100
Depreciation for month is debited to production		
cost accounts.		

At the end of the month, the production overhead accounts are allocated to the various processes and a statement of production costs is prepared (such as the one in Exhibit 1). If the total costs shown in that statement are to appear in the process control accounts, the entry to close the Production Overhead Control account is

Process A Control	4,725	
Process B Control	2,285	
Process C Control	1,155	
Production Overhead Control		8,165

Overhead costs amounting to $5,515 in addition to those shown in entries (2) to (4) will, of course, have been entered if the balance in Production Overhead Control is $8,165. Note that Process A shows in Exhibit 1 total overhead cost of $5,400 (= $675 depreciation + $4,725 production overhead). Process B shows $3,410 (= $1,125 depreciation + $2,285 production overhead), and Process C shows $1,280 (= $125 depreciation + $1,155 production overhead).

The cost of the units transferred from one process to another is recorded, the transfer from Process C being made to the Finished Goods account.

Process B Control (Transfers from Process A)	59,501	
Process A Control (Transfers to Process B)		59,501
Units completed in Process A transferred to Process B		
Process C Control (Transfers from Process B)	75,496	
Process B Control (Transfers to Process C)		75,496
Units completed in Process B transferred to Process C		
Finished Goods	83,176	
Process C Control (Transfers to Finished Goods)		83,176
Units completed in Process C.		

EXHIBIT 2

LESTER METAL PRODUCTS COMPANY
Control Accounts
July 19X0

Process A Control

7/1/X0	Balance, 5,000 at $2.024	10,120	July	Transferred to Process B	59,501
July	Raw material	10,800	7/31/X0	Balance, 1,000 at $1,919	1,919
	Direct labor	35,100			
	Depreciation	675			
	Other production				
	overhead	4,725			
		61,420			61,420
8/1/X0	Balance, 1,000 at $1.919.	1,919			

Process B Control

7/1/X0	Balance, 1,500 at $2.563	3,845	July	Transferred to Process C	75,496
July			7/31/X0	Balance, 500 at $2.35	1,180
	Direct labor	9,920			
	Depreciation	1,125			
	Other production				
	overhead	2,285			
	Transferred from				
	Process A	59,501			
		76,676			76,676
8/1/X0	Balance, 500 at $2.35 ...	1,180			

Process C Control

July	Parts	1,600	July	Transferred to Finished Goods .	83,176
	Direct labor	4,800			
	Depreciation	125			
	Other production				
	overhead	1,155			
	Transferred from				
	Process B	75,496			
		83,176			83,176

Finished Goods Inventory

July 1		Balance	July	Transfer to Cost of Goods Sold
				not shown here
July		83,176		

The T-accounts shown in Exhibit 2 summarize the illustration for the Lester Metal Products Company.

Diagram of the Process Costing Method.   Exhibit 3 indicates how costs of production flow through the accounts and finally emerge in the Cost of Goods Sold account when goods are sold to customers. It is stated in general terms rather than corresponding to the illustration for Lester Metal Products.

IMPLEMENTATION CONSIDERATIONS

Three major objectives of any cost accounting system are to provide assistance in (1) controlling costs, (2) valuing inventory, and (3) establishing prices. Selection from among the available implementation options is conditioned by these objectives and by the nature of the plants, processes, and activities to which the system is applied. Further criteria are the cost of operation of the system and the timeliness with which results are available.

Selection of process costing as an underlying approach is one step in establishing the overall system. In some cases it may represent the only practicable and logical alternative. Large-scale, continuous processes, by their nature, almost eliminate consideration of other available approaches. In other cases, process costing is

EXHIBIT 3 Process Costing Method: Diagram of Cost Flows

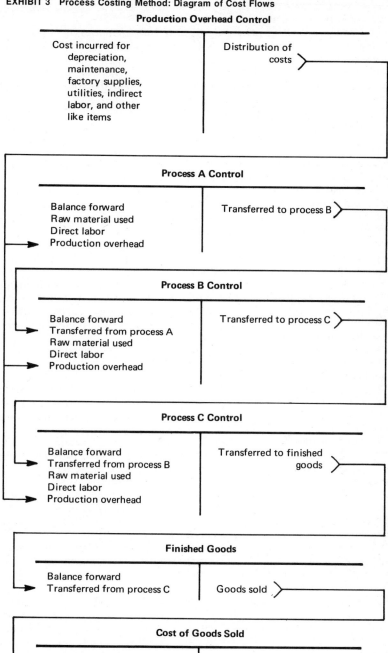

Production Overhead Control

Cost incurred for
depreciation,
maintenance,
factory supplies,
utilities, indirect
labor, and other
like items

Distribution of
costs

Process A Control

Balance forward
Raw material used
Direct labor
Production overhead

Transferred to process B

Process B Control

Balance forward
Transferred from process A
Raw material used
Direct labor
Production overhead

Transferred to process C

Process C Control

Balance forward
Transferred from process B
Raw material used
Direct labor
Production overhead

Transferred to finished
goods

Finished Goods

Balance forward
Transferred from process C

Goods sold

Cost of Goods Sold

Transferred from finished
goods

established only because it is judged to be the most desirable approach after due consideration of the available alternatives.

Process costing is well adapted to developing information useful in the control of costs of operations. When used appropriately, it is usually perceived by management personnel as coinciding with the realities of plants and processes.

When process costing has been selected as the underlying approach, it is necessary to select additional specific techniques whereby the approach is implemented. This involves such choices as actual versus standard costs and direct cost systems versus those with allocated overhead absorption. It must be determined whether the system must accommodate by-products or joint products, or both. A specific inventory-flow assumption, such as FIFO, LIFO, or weighted average, must be chosen. These aspects of cost accounting are all addressed elsewhere in this *Handbook,* so it is not appropriate that they be fully developed here. However, some limited comments, relating these to process costing but not intended to be exhaustive, may be helpful.

Actual and Standard Costs.   Selection between actual and standard costs is made on the basis of many factors. Among these are the handling of transfer costs and the identification of costs for control purposes.

Whenever process costing is employed, it is necessary to establish costs for the transfer of goods either to the next process or to finished goods inventory. In an *actual* cost system where multiple sequential processes are involved, this implies that the costs from each process can be developed only in the same sequential pattern as the physical processes. In a *standard* cost system all such transfers can be made at standard, and therefore costing for all processes can be carried on concurrently. This normally results in better timeliness for reports and often reduces the cost of operating the accounting system.

In controlling costs, the use of standard costs permits the identification of variances at the point of incurrence. This appears to be the best basis for establishing cost control.

A hypothetical advantage of actual cost systems in price establishment results from carrying forward all actual costs to salable products. This purpose can also be fulfilled in standard cost systems by periodic analysis of the variance accounts with attribution to particular products.

Direct and Absorption Costing.   Product costing systems vary substantially in the degree that they associate indirect costs with specific products. At one extreme, only direct variable costs are identified with products; at the other, all or almost all costs are allocated on some basis or other to specific products. Most systems fall some place in between, depending on a variety of considerations and trade-offs. Process costing systems facilitate the inclusion in product costs of some indirect costs that would be excluded in a strict direct cost approach, but they do not require all overhead to be assigned to products.

For example, utility costs, especially power or fuel costs, may be treated satisfactorily as period expenses when such costs are relatively small in impact. However, they should be assigned directly to products on a realistic basis if they are substantial and vary by product.

FIFO, LIFO, and Other Inventory Flow Assumptions.   Inventory conventions are oriented toward preparation of historical cost financial statements, whereas process cost accounting systems are likely to emphasize control of current operating costs. Accordingly, some special attention to coordinating the cost accounting records with the financial accounting needs is usually required. Frequently, the coordination consists of establishing counts for costing that also serve to provide the basis for controlling the layers of inventory. When the inventory cost-flow assumption treats acquisitions during one year as a layer with equal costs for all homogeneous elements, standards reviewed annually can be used as a convenient bridge between the cost accounting system and the inventory-flow assumption adopted for external reporting.

Items transferred from process to process are normally recorded at transfer prices per unit that do not separate material cost from processing costs incurred. If it is required, or desired, to prepare a report on these separate components of inventory cost, a standard cost system is normally capable of reducing the drudgery of such work substantially.

Production Reporting.   The concept has been developed earlier in this chapter that all production from a given process should be reported in units of the product or products produced. Some further comments on this point, for emphasis and clarification, may be helpful.

The processes involved may be either physical or chemical in nature and almost invariably entail losses of material. To develop appropriate unit costs it is necessary that the production be reported in terms of the homogeneous product or products produced considering losses that would be deemed normal. These units may be and often are different from the units charged as input. In chemical operations an entirely different material may be produced. In certain physical operations, such as evaporation, the change from input to output may involve, primarily, a change in strength or concentration. In cither of these instances statements of the literal physical quantity (e.g., a weight or volume) produced may require adjustment by assay. At the other end of the scale, simple weight or count may fully define the quantity produced.

In any case, the production to be reported and used in the cost accounting system should be consistent with the predetermined basis defined as the homogenous product output.

Consistent with the above, it is necessary to treat units that are incomplete at the end of accounting periods. For this purpose it is often necessary to state incomplete production in expected units of the homogeneous product output so that the percentage of completion (or alternatively, percentage incomplete) may be applied.

Some special attention is required in reporting production to cover such events as abnormal spoilage, off-standard production, extraordinary loss (as from fire, spillage, etc.), and the like. The production represented in such cases and the costs associated therewith are often not included in the cost of the "good" production of the homogeneous product output but may instead be charged to loss or other accounts.

A more complete treatment of these matters is presented in other chapters of this *Handbook,* including those on spoilage, waste and scrap, and standard costs.

Frequency and Extent of Reports.   The selection of an appropriate set of components for an overall reporting system does not determine the detailed decisions regarding frequency of reporting. It is generally advisable to prepare operating cost reports as often as financial reports to facilitate intracompany communications. It is evident that statistical reports, even though used for cost control purposes, may need to be prepared at different times. The decisions relating to frequency and extent of departmental and cost center reports should be reviewed from time to time so that they can be modified to fit in with changing conditions. Some processes are inherently predictable and stable. Others change over time with resultant alteration in the degree of control required or the relative importance of expenses. In cases where both random fluctuation and trends are involved, some statistical analysis may well be a valuable adjunct to the process cost center reports. Evaluation of trade-offs between frequency and report preparation costs is normally a matter for management decision.

Features.   Although no system of reporting will resolve all the communications difficulties among accountants, engineers, and plant management, process cost accounting provides an excellent basis for common understanding. As seen by operating personnel, process costing provides substantial realism, despite the convention of equivalent units which is incorporated to satisfy the needs of financial accounting.

Actual costs, or standards and the latest variances posted, give ready access to current expense and unit cost levels for control, pricing, or other purposes.

In any operation except perhaps where an entire factory is designated as a cost center, process costing can provide a basis for recording and controlling costs in a manner consistent with technological and organizational considerations. Especially where process costing and standards have been combined, the accounting pattern lends itself to easy assessment of current trends.

The cost centers established for a process cost system provide a convenient organization of accounting for operations, logically related to the products that generate sales. This in turn assists in analysis of current operations and products or of specific costs likely to be incurred in projected future activity. It is, of course, reasonable to combine activities that are related in making projections so as to simplify calculations without unnecessary sacrifice of realism. Organization of costs by cost center can also be designed to support cash-flow projections by stating depreciation and other noncurrent outlays separately from labor, materials, and supplies. The purpose of the projection will, of course, have a strong bearing on the kind of grouping that is likely to be most suitable and helpful.

BIBLIOGRAPHY

Backer, Morton, and Lyle E. Jacobsen: *Cost Accounting: A Managerial Approach,* McGraw-Hill Book Company, New York, 1964.

Davidson, Sidney, and Roman L. Weil, eds.: *Handbook of Modern Accounting,* 2nd ed., McGraw-Hill Book Company, New York, 1977, chap. 41, pp. 14–21.

Franke, Reimund: "A Process Model for Costing," *Management Accounting,* January 1975, pp. 45–47.

Horngren, Charles T.: *Cost Accounting: A Managerial Emphases,* 4th ed., Prentice-Hall, Englewood-Cliffs, N.J., 1977.

Neuner, J. J. W., and E. G. Deakin, III: *Cost Accounting: Principles and Practice,* 9th ed., Richard D. Irwin, Homewood, Ill., 1977.

Schwan, Edward S.: "Process Costing via Reaction Accounting," *Management Accounting,* September 1974, pp. 45–50.

Chapter **15**

The Setting of Standard Costs

J. LESLIE LIVINGSTONE
Fuller E. Callaway Professor, Georgia Institute of Technology

THE CONCEPT OF COST STANDARDS

Dictionaries define *standard* as "a measure of comparison," "a criterion of excellence," "a norm," and "a model or example for comparison." In the accounting literature, "standard cost" has been described as "a yardstick," "a bench mark," "a sea level from which to measure cost altitudes," and "a gauge." Each of these definitions focuses on the basic attribute of being able to *compare* in a valid manner against an established *baseline*.

The notion of comparison makes it clear that standard costs are not meant to supplant historical costs. Rather, they complement historical costs. This is illustrated by the simple formula underlying the structure of any standard cost accounting system, namely:

Actual cost

Less standard (or allowed) cost

Equals standard cost variance

This, in turn, is the basis for the major functions of management accounting, such as the scorecard role and the attention-directing role. Also, it provides the basis for a management-by-exception system, and for delegation of authority by means of accountability.

The Uses of Cost Standards. *Effectiveness* and *efficiency* are important objectives for management. Therefore we need to define clearly what we mean by each of these terms. Effectiveness is the attainment of a given objective, for example producing an output of 2,000 units this week, or keeping absenteeism below 4 percent. Efficiency is the relationship between output and input, for example, miles per gallon, or number of widgets produced per machine.

We note that it is possible to be effective without necessarily being efficient. Normally, management strives to be effective and efficient. However, it is possible to fail in both aspects, or to attain one without the other. For example, consider an operation that should produce 1,000 widgets from 200 tons of raw material. If only 900 widgets are produced but 250 tons of raw material are used up, performance has not been effective or efficient. If 1,000 widgets are produced using 250 tons of raw material, this is effective but not efficient. Finally, if 500 widgets are produced using only 90 tons of raw material, the performance is efficient but not effective.

In order to determine the effectiveness and the efficiency of performance, it is necessary to have standards of comparison. Cost standards provide these comparisons, so that the important objectives of effectiveness and efficiency can be specified, and so that their degree of attainment can be measured.

The Nature of Cost Standards. Cost standards are predetermined targets, usually based on desired performance. They reflect acceptable levels of effectiveness and efficiency. Cost standards are a means of communicating goals for satisfactory performance, so that both employees and their supervisors are made aware of what is expected from them. Further, cost standards provide a means of comparison that serves to evaluate actual performance. This is the basis for a system of management control, for which a proper monitoring of performance is a key factor. Also, cost standards are a useful aid in predicting the financial outcomes of alternative plans (such as varying the existing product mix) and in putting together budgets.

The existence of standards allows actual performance to be measured against a consistent, valid goal. In the absence of standards, only historical comparisons of performance can be made: this month's costs against last month's or against the same month last year. The drawback of historical performance comparisons is that they lack a proper *norm*. For instance, past costs may represent efficient or inefficient performance and it is difficult to say which is the case. Also, changes in conditions, in technology, in materials, or in equipment weaken the usefulness of historical comparisons. Therefore, we see that the existence of cost standards serves important purposes in management planning, control, and decision making.

Types of Standards.   At what level should standards be set? Should they represent ideal or faultless performance, or, at the other extreme, easily attainable or low-effort performance? Accountants usually classify standards into three main categories, as follows:

1. *Basic standards* are constant standards that are left unchanged over very long periods. Their principal advantage is to allow consistent comparison with the same baseline. This reveals multiperiod trends over time in efficiency and effectiveness. Such information is valuable so long as conditions remain stable. However, when changes occur in technology, price levels, or other relevant factors, basic standards lose their significance. Therefore basic standards are seldom used, because there are few situations where conditions remain sufficiently stable over a long time.

2. *Theoretical or ideal standards* represent perfect performance. Ideal standards reflect the very best performance theoretically possible under the most favorable operating conditions. For the most part such perfection exists only in the mind of the most zealous industrial engineer, and it is rarely attained in actual practice. Nevertheless, ideal standards may be used by management where it is felt that they provide the best motivation, or are otherwise psychologically productive. It is rare, however, to find ideal standards in use.

3. *Currently attainable standards* are those that should be achieved under reasonably expected levels of efficiency. These standards are lower than ideal standards because of normal waste and spoilage, ordinary equipment failures, and lost time. However, attainable standards may still represent performance that is difficult (although quite possible) to achieve and that is above average.

In actual practice, currently attainable standards are most often used. There are two main advantages to the use of currently attainable standards. First, most accountants probably support the following view:

> Interview results show that a particular figure does not operate as a norm . . . simply because the controller's department calls it a standard. It operates as a norm only to the extent that the executives and supervisors whose activity it measures accept it as a fair and attainable yardstick of their performance. Generally, operating executives were inclined to accept a standard to the extent that they were satisfied that the data were accurately recorded, that the standard level was reasonably attainable, and that the variables it measured were controllable by them.[1]

A similar position is expressed in a research report of the National Association of Accountants, which says the following in favor of attainable performance standards:

[1]Reproduced by permission from the Financial Executives Research Foundation; H. A. Simon, H. Guetzkow, G. Kozmetsky, and G. Tyndall, *Centralization vs. Decentralization in Organizing the Controller's Department* (The Controllership Foundation, New York, 1954), p. 29. But for an opposite view, see Andrew Stedry, *Budget Control and Cost Behavior* (Prentice-Hall, Englewood Cliffs, N.J., 1960).

Such standards provide definite goals which employees can usually be expected to reach and they also appear to be fair bases from which to measure deviations for which the employees are held responsible. A standard set at a level which is high yet still attainable with reasonably diligent effort and attention to the correct methods of doing the job may also be effective for stimulating efficiency.[2]

Three phrases from the quotation merit emphasis: "high yet still attainable"; "reasonably diligent effort"; "attention to correct methods." A good performance is something more than an ordinary performance.

Second, there is an economy associated with the use of standards that closely represent expected actual performance. Such attainable standards can be used in planning and budgeting as well as in the control process. Where standards are not close to expected actual performance, they may be applicable for control purposes, but are not realistic for planning and budgeting uses. Also, the knowledge that different standards are used for different purposes can lead to resentment against a "double standard" and employee resistance to possible feelings of being fooled or psychologically manipulated by management.

As Horngren[3] points out, we should keep in mind that in some cases terminology can mislead us. For example, an ideal standard can be used as a currently attainable standard under certain conditions. Such a case would occur when components such as auto tires or batteries are purchased on the outside by firms engaged in auto manufacturing or repair. For these components no substandard units need be accepted from venders and hence, with proper quality-control inspection procedures, assembly or repair operations should not be slowed down by faulty components.

PSYCHOLOGICAL IMPACT OF STANDARDS

Just because a standard is set does not necessarily mean that it will become a goal. In order for a standard to function as a target, it must first be accepted as such by the worker. Then, and only then, will it motivate the desired behavior. For this reason we need to ask what are the factors that affect the motivational power of standards?

Psychologists have suggested the following major factors:

1. The Basis on Which Performance Is Measured and on Which Rewards Are Assigned. When the important aspects of performance are validly measured, and equitably rewarded, motivation for high performance is enhanced. However, if the accounting system fails to measure, or incorrectly measures, important performance factors, then problems tend to arise. Most people wish to look good on what is measured and will therefore attempt to score high on aspects that are measured while neglecting activities that—although important to the job—are not measured.

For example, Berliner[4] has described the behavior of Soviet plant managers who have been given unreasonably high production targets. He notes practices such as the concealment of production capacity, falsification of reports, deterioration of quality, overordering of supplies, hoarding of material, and the use of "expediters" to make black market purchases. Cohen[5] observes similar tendencies

[2]Reproduced by permission from the National Association of Accountants, *Standard Costs and Variance Analysis* (NAA, New York, 1974), p. 9.

[3]Charles T. Horngren, *Cost Accounting: A Managerial Emphasis,* 3rd ed. (Prentice-Hall, Englewood Cliffs, N.J., 1972), pp. 188–189.

[4]J. S. Berliner, "The Situation of Plant Managers." In *Soviet Society: A Book of Readings,* A. Inkeles and K. Geiger, eds. (Houghton Mifflin Company, Boston, 1961), pp. 361–381.

[5]A. K. Cohen, *Deviance and Control* (Prentice-Hall, Englewood Cliffs, N.J., 1966).

in some American managers to look good on the scorecard measures, while neglecting or subverting unmeasured but desirable organizational functions. Cohen calls this "bureaucratic" behavior.

We may ask whether certain individuals are more likely to respond to inadequate performance measures with bureaucratic behavior. People who have high F-scale (dogmatism) scores are more likely to exhibit bureaucratic behavior than low F-scale individuals. High F-scale persons tend to have a low tolerance for ambiguity and a strong regard for authority, rules, and regulations. From these values, it is predictable that F's would adhere rigidly to the formal control system even where it is clearly dysfunctional.[6]

2. The Difficulty of the Standard.   For this section we need to distinguish between *extrinsic* rewards, such as pay and promotion and other tangible gains, and *intrinsic* rewards, such as feelings of satisfaction at a job well done and the respect of other people. Atkinson[7] and McClelland[8] have found that for persons with high need for achievement (achievement motivation), the greatest intrinsic motivation tends to result when effort is believed to have about a 50–50 chance of leading to good performance. Specifically, feelings of accomplishment, competence, and growth are associated with achievement of performance that is only in the 50 percent range of likelihood.

It seems that easier targets do not present a high enough challenge for such persons, whereas more difficult targets are rejected as being too high to have much chance of attainment. These findings are not easy to apply in practice. Even if we know which employees have high need for achievement,[9] it may be impossible to personalize custom standards for different individuals. On the other hand, where this *is* possible (e.g., say in setting sales quotas for individual salespersons), it can produce worthwhile results.

Intrinsic rewards can be significant motivators, as has been found to be the case in several studies, for instance Galbraith and Cummings,[10] Hackman and Porter,[11] and Porter and Lawler.[12] The importance of this factor in relation to control has been recognized in the concept of "self-control" used by Dalton,[13] who distinguishes three types of control systems operating in organizations:

1. *Organizational or systems control:* the formal accounting control system of rules, procedures, standards, variance reporting, etc.

2. *Social control:* the influence of peer group relations on individual behavior.

3. *Self-control:* the intrinsic motivation of the individual to perform well.

[6]Edward E. Lawler, III, *Motivation in Work Organizations* (Brooks Cole Publishing Company, Monterey, Calif., 1973), pp. 182–185. See also Richard M. Steers and Lyman W. Porter, "The Role of Task-Goal Attributes in Employee Performance," *Psychological Bulletin*, 81, 7 (1974), pp. 439–447.

[7]J. W. Atkinson, *An Introduction to Motivation* (D. Van Nostrand Company, Princeton, N.J., 1964).

[8]D. C. McClelland, *The Achieving Society* (D. Van Nostrand Company, Princeton, N.J., 1961).

[9]This can be measured on a standard test.

[10]J. Galbraith and L. L. Cummings, "An Empirical Investigation of the Motivational Determinants of Task Performance: Interactive Effects Between Instrumentality-Valence and Motivation-Ability," *Organizational Behavior and Human Performance*, 2 (1967), pp. 237–257.

[11]J. Richard Hackman and L. W. Porter, "Expectancy Theory Predictions of Work Effectiveness," *Organizational Behavior and Human Performance*, 3 (1968), 417–426.

[12]L. W. Porter and Edward E. Lawler, III, *Managerial Attitudes and Performance* (Irwin-Dorsey Press, Homewood, Ill., 1968).

[13]Gene W. Dalton, "Motivation and Control in Organizations," in *Motivation and Control in Organizations*, Gene W. Dalton and Paul R. Lawrence, eds. (Richard D. Irwin, Homewood, Ill., 1971).

In order for self-control to operate strongly, a high level of trust between managers and subordinates is needed. Without trust it is hard to believe that difficult goals would be set and accepted.

Stedry[14] found that performance was high for subjects who formulated high aspiration levels. Hofstede[15] concluded that standards will have the most positive effect on motivation when they are tight and attained with difficulty. These studies are congruent with the work of Locke and Bryan[16] on the motivating power of setting challenging goals. Also, standards can provide useful goal clarification, which, in turn, can improve performance. Locke and Bryan[17] also report results that indicate that when specific goals are set, subjects perform better than when they were simply enjoined to "do your best."

3. *Participation.*   We now turn to *participation*, which involves the mutual communication of information. It has been argued by several researchers that participation tends to enhance self-control and hence increase motivation. For instance, participation in the setting of standards may lead employees to feel a sense of ownership of the standards and to be more motivated to live up to the standards. A number of studies[18] confirm this view that participation facilitates "ego involvement,"[19] self-control, and hence higher intrinsic motivation. Participation may lead to expectancies that successful implementation of the participative decision will lead to heightened feelings of competence and self-esteem even if no extrinsic rewards are involved. Also, Vroom[20] has found that participation can lead to better-quality decisions, especially when individuals possess special skills or knowledge that are not otherwise available to their superior and that are of value to the decision in question.

The effects of participation on motivation vary according to individual differences. As Vroom and others have shown, the positive relationship does not hold for highly authoritarian people who prefer directive leadership and controlled, unambiguous situations. It should be pointed out that the participative approach focuses on intrinsic motivation, and does not give extrinsic rewards a significant role in motivation. Also, it has little to say about motivating people who do not desire interesting work, involvement in decisions, or other higher-order need-fulfillment. Where organizations tend to have members with diverse characteristics, participation may be effective only if used discriminately and not applied across the board.

4. *Feedback.*   An important aspect of communication is *feedback* on performance. Feedback on performance appears to have two important functions. It supplies the individual with the information needed to improve performance.

---

[14]Stedry, *Budget Control and Cost Behavior.*

[15]G. H. Hofstede, *The Game of Budget Control* (Van Gorcum, Assen, Netherlands, 1967).

[16]Edwin A. Locke and J. F. Bryan, *Goals and Intentions as Determinants of Performance Level, Task Choice and Attitudes* (American Institute for Research, Washington, D.C., 1967).

[17]Edwin A. Locke and J. F. Bryan, "Cognitive Aspects of Psychomotor Performance: The Effects of Performance Goals on Level of Performance," *Journal of Applied Psychology,* August 1966, pp. 286–291.

[18]K. Lewin, R. Lippitt, and R. K. White, "Patterns of Aggressive Behavior in Experimentally Created Social Climates," *Journal of Social Psychology,* 10 (1939), pp. 271–299. See also W. F. Whyte, ed., *Money and Motivation: An Analysis of Incentives in Industry* (Harper & Row, New York, 1955); Nancy J. Morse and E. Reimer, "The Experimental Change of a Major Organizational Variable," *Journal of Abnormal Social Psychology,* 52 (1956), pp. 120–129; and V. H. Vroom, *Some Personality Determinants of the Effects of Participation* Prentice-Hall, Englewood Cliffs, N.J., 1960).

[19]V. H. Vroom, *Work and Motivation* (John Wiley & Sons, New York, 1964).

[20]V. H. Vroom, *Some Personality Determinants of the Effects of Participation* (Prentice-Hall, Englewood Cliffs, N.J., 1960).

Also, it tends to contribute to intrinsic motivation. The enhancement of intrinsic motivation may occur partly through the greater degree of self-control that the feedback information provides the worker, and partly through feelings of competence and achievement aroused by knowledge of what has been accomplished, especially when a challenging goal has been met or surpassed. Several studies have shown that persons provided with knowledge of results will work longer and harder without added extrinsic rewards.[21] The importance to managers of adequate "scorecard" accounting information has been very clearly and usefully described by Simon et al.[22]

Although the point seems obvious, it is not unusual to find situations in which employees do not receive feedback either while they are performing or soon after they have completed their task. Some control systems provide feedback too late to allow the person to exercise self-control. Learning theory clearly shows the importance of prompt feedback on performance, if not during the task, at least while the memory of past performance is still fresh. Some accounting control systems fail to meet this requirement and thereby lose effectiveness.

DISTINCTION BETWEEN STANDARDS AND BUDGETS

How does a standard cost differ from a budgeted cost? It will differ unless the standard represents expected actual performance, because that is what budgets usually reflect. There is another kind of difference also, which is more of terminology than of concept. Standards usually refer to *single units* of output, for instance, standard labor hours per widget. A budgeted cost normally applies to multiple-product units, such as a department or a project, for example, total monthly labor cost for the machining department.

Thus the latter difference between a standard and a budget is one of unit versus total. It may be helpful to consider a standard as a budget for a single unit. Then the terms standard performance and budgeted performance become the same in meaning.

Where standards in use are not currently attainable, there is a difference between standard and budgeted amounts. In such cases, it will be necessary to use a different set of standards for budgeting purposes, or to make predetermined allowances for expected variances between budgets and actual performance.

QUANTITY AND PRICE STANDARDS

Quantity, or physical, standards are the core of a standard cost system. By quantity standards, we mean the relationship between resources used in production and the quantity of output produced. Such standards might be stated in yards, pounds, gallons, square feet, etc., for each of the various raw materials used. For labor, they would be expressed in terms of hours for each of the various types of labor needed to produce the output. For other costs, such as manufacturing overhead, the measure may be in terms of hours of machine time (of each kind required), hours of direct labor (again of each kind used), square feet occupied, kilowatts of electric power used, etc.

---

[21]G. F. Arps, "Work with Knowledge of Results versus Work without Knowledge of Results," *Psychological Monographs*, 28 (3, Whole No. 125, 1920). See also A. F. Smode, "Learning and Performance in a Tracking Task Under Two Levels of Achievement Information Feedback," *Journal of Experimental Psychology*, 56 (1958), pp. 297–304.

[22]Simon et al., *Centralization vs. Decentralization.*

These physical quantity standards are often arrived at by systematic engineering studies, based on careful specifications of materials, equipment, and processes and on controlled observation of operations. Sometimes a less formal approach, based more on judgment and estimation, is used and may be adequately accurate depending on circumstances. The point to be stressed, however, is that the physical standards are the fundamental efficiency ratios for the productive process. They are the essential building blocks of any standard cost system. Therefore it is essential that they be soundly derived, and sufficiently accurate. If not, the resulting standard cost system will be no better than its underlying efficiency ratios, or physical quantity standards.

Standard costs are established by multiplying the physical cost standards by applicable price factors. For example, assume that the physical cost standards for a widget require:

3 gallons of raw material X
2 square feet of raw material Y
4 hours of labor type A
7 hours of labor type B
5 hours of overhead, cost center G
6 hours of overhead, cost center H

Assume also that the standard prices of these resources are as follows:

Raw material X, $11.00 per gallon
Raw material Y, $5.60 per square foot
Type A labor, $6.00 per hour
Type B labor, $7.75 per hour
Overhead, cost center G, $27.00 per hour
Overhead, cost center H, $36.40 per hour

Then the standard manufacturing cost per widget would be

Raw material		
X: 3 × $11.00	$ 33.00	
Y: 2 × 5.60	11.20	$ 44.20
Labor		
A: 4 × $ 6.00	$ 24.00	
B: 7 × $ 7.75	54.25	78.25
Overhead		
G: 5 × $27.00	$135.00	
H: 6 × 36.40	218.40	353.40
Total		$475.85

Although physical quantity standards are in diverse units, such as gallons, or feet, or hours, the use of price standards enables standard costs to be computed in the common denominator of dollars. The use of dollars in turn allows various physical operations to be aggregated into overall financial results for a department, a division, a company, or a group of companies. By translating physical quantities into dollars, priority can be given to the more expensive items that merit greater managerial attention.

Note that each separate standard for physical quantity and for price is a basic building block. These building blocks are combined into product costs, department costs, and increasingly more aggregated levels by the accounting system. However, planning and control are difficult to exercise at the aggregate level. Typically, planning and corrective action must be executed in relation to the specific individual elements of cost in order to be effective. Thus the existence of the individual physical quantity and price standards allows planning and control activities to be focused precisely to the relevant source elements. This is an important function of cost accounting, which tends to focus on individual elements of the firm's activities, in contrast to financial accounting, which generally reflects the firm as a whole.

Having pointed out the critical importance of the individual standards, both for physical quantity and for price, we now discuss how these standards are created.

MATERIAL QUANTITY STANDARDS

A material quantity standard is defined as "a preestablished measure, expressed in physical terms of the quantity of material."[23] Material quantity standards can be set either by use of engineering methods or by examination of past data. The former method is usually much more rigorous and exact and also much more expensive than the latter. Which approach is used depends to a large degree on the technical complexity of the operation in question. For example, it is equally difficult to imagine engineering methods being used for the Crisp Pizza Parlor as it is to envisage examination of past data being relied upon by the Supercolossal Nuclear Reactor Corporation.

Engineering Methods. The starting point is usually the product specifications. To understand these may require considerable technical knowledge. For instance, the specifications may call for CA-610, SAE 1020, or M-type HSS materials, all of which are standard technical designations and meaningless to the nonexpert. Numerous other technical aspects of materials specifications may also be involved.

In addition to the type and characteristics of the materials, correct quantities must be specified. This requires careful analysis of yields, scrap, wastage, evaporation, shrinkage, etc. The standard quantities usually do not provide for loss of materials due to careless handling, damage to units in process, or other undesirable circumstances. Indeed, these are the kinds of materials losses that use of standards is intended to identify and stop.

Examination of Past Data. Sometimes "past data" may be nothing more than the accumulated experience of seasoned personnel. A skilled garment cutter, for instance, can usually estimate very closely the quantity of cloth required to make a certain number of a given kind of garment.

Where past data are examined, the existence of good records is most helpful. Good records will enable an accurate identification to be made between raw materials used and output produced, on a batch-by-batch basis or over a particular time period. Inability to match materials used closely with output due to poor records can result in very inexact "standards." Also, care must be taken to check whether product characteristics, raw material characteristics, or other conditions may have changed over the period being examined. Any such changes may, of course, affect the raw material usage.

Bill of Materials. Whether set by engineering methods or examination of past data, material quantity standards are usually reflected on a bill of materials. The bill of materials describes and states the required quantity of each of the materials and parts that go into the completed product. A simple example is shown in Exhibit 1.

The bill of materials can be much more complex than indicated in our first example. Even an uncomplicated product may have a lengthy bill of materials. For example, Exhibit 2 shows just the dyestuff for a particular type of carpeting, and Exhibit 3 shows just the adhesives for the back of the carpeting.

Material Loss Standards. The development of material loss standards normally results in a Material Loss Specification, which would include information on

---

[23]Cost Accounting Standards Board, Standard 407, "Use of Standard Costs for Direct Material and Direct Labor," 1974.

EXHIBIT 1   Bill of Materials

STANDARD MATERIALS REQUIREMENTS

ITEM BASE PLATE NO. 423   DRAWING NO. 9463
STANDARD QUANTITY 1,000   DATE 11/14/—

MATERIALS			REMARKS
No.	Description	Required for Standard Lot	
176	Steel plate	4,200 lbs	

PARTS

Part No.	Description	Specs. per Unit	Required for Lot	Part No.	Description	Specs. per Unit	Required for Lot
201	Anchor	1	1,010				
217	Brace	2	2,080				

Reproduced by permission from Gordon Shillinglaw, *Cost Accounting: Analysis and Control,* 3rd ed. (Homewood, Ill., Richard D. Irwin, 1972), p. 259.

EXHIBIT 2   Dyestuff Specification and Cost Calculation

Material description	Standard price per pound	Pounds material per 100 pounds of carpet	Standard cost per 100 pounds of carpet
Carpet: nylon			
Color: green			
Chemicals			
Chemical A	$0.20	1.75	$0.35
Chemical B	0.06	3.00	0.18
Chemical C	0.22	0.50	0.11
Dyestuffs			
Yellow	$1.70	0.20	$0.34
Scarlet	3.20	0.10	0.32
Blue	6.00	0.20	1.20
Total cost/100 pounds of carpet dyed	—	—	$2.50
Cost per pound			$0.025

Issued by:	Approved by:	Superseded date None	Effective date: xx-xx-xx	Specification No. 980

Reproduced by permission from Frank C. Wilson, *Industrial Cost Controls* (Prentice-Hall, Englewood Cliffs, N.J., 1971), p. 58.

product, department, type of material, standard loss formula, allowed loss per unit of production, allowed loss per week, cost per unit of material loss. Exhibit 4 provides an example. Specifications of this type can usually be developed. The key factor is determination of a valid formula for calculation of the expected material loss. In certain cases, this poses a complex problem for which sophisticated

EXHIBIT 3   Adhesive Specification and Cost Calculation

Material code	Description	Wet weight	Dry weight	Unit	Std. price	Total cost
	Adhesive for jute-back carpet					
6121	Base adhesive	420	180	lb	$0.30	$54.00
6211	Filler	600	600	lb	0.01	6.00
6434	Chemical A	10	1	lb	1.20	1.20
6315	Thickener	20	1	lb	1.00	1.00
	Total/batch	1,050	782	—	—	$62.20

Cost/pound dry

$$\frac{\$62.20}{782} = \$0.080/\text{lb}$$

Issued by:	Approved by:	Superseded date None	Effective date: xx-xx-xx-	Specification No. 324

Reproduced by permission from Frank C. Wilson, *Industrial Cost Controls* (Prentice-Hall, Englewood Cliffs, N.J., 1971), p. 60.

EXHIBIT 4   Material Loss Specification

Department: Adhesive
Type Waste: Selvage trim waste
Description: Trim waste cut off each side of carpet
Collection of waste: Waste collected each shift, weighed, and recorded on Waste Record Sheet

Calculation of standard per linear yard of carpet $= \left[\left(\frac{A}{36} \times \frac{B}{16} \right) + C + D + \left(\frac{E}{36} \times \frac{F}{16} \right) \right] \times 2$

Example: A = standard width of primary back trim waste, 3"
　　　　 B = ounces per square yard of primary back
　　　　 C = pounds per linear yard of latex determined by Waste Study, = .075
　　　　 D = pounds per linear yard of yarn determined by Waste Study − 2 rows, = .010
　　　　 E = standard width of secondary back trim waste, 3"
　　　　 F = ounces/square yard of secondary back

Allowed pounds
Per lin. yd. latexed $= \left[\left(\frac{3}{36} \times \frac{9}{16} \right) + .075 + .010 + \left(\frac{3}{36} \times \frac{7}{16} \right) \right] \times 2$

$$= (0.047 + .075 + .010 + .036) \times 2$$
$$= 0.168 \times 2 = 0.336 \text{ pounds linear yard}$$

Allowed pounds/week: linear yards double jute back × 0.336

Waste cost:

Primary back:　0.168 SY × 0.200 = $0.0336
Latex:　　　　 0.150 lb × 0.080 = $0.0120
Yarn:　　　　　0.020 lb × 1.170 = $0.0234
Secondary back: 0.168 SY × 0.160 = $0.0269
　　　　　　　　　　　　　　　　　　$0.0959

$$\text{Waste cost/pound} = \frac{\$0.0959}{0.336} = \$0.286$$

Reproduced by permission from Frank C. Wilson, *Industrial Cost Controls* (Prentice-Hall, Englewood Cliffs, N.J., 1971), p. 64.

mathematical and statistical analysis is required, for instance, the trim problem in the pulp and paper industry. Note that material loss standards may not seek to minimize material losses: studies and experience may show that it is profitable to lose more material than the minimum in order to improve machine or operator performance, or both.

MATERIAL PRICE STANDARDS

A material price standard is defined as "a preestablished measure, expressed in monetary terms, of the price of material."[24]

Standard materials prices are usually gathered from supplier price lists and catalogues. To these prices should be added freight and other shipping costs, whereas both quantity and cash discounts should be subtracted.

External factors can significantly affect materials prices, and therefore careful predictions of price trends are important in setting or revising material price standards. Therefore the strong participation of the purchasing department is desirable. However, price standards are also a check on the performance of the purchasing department. For instance, effective standards help to counter any tendency of purchasing agents to play favorites among suppliers. To help ensure objectivity in setting price standards, therefore, the purchasing department may be required to substantiate their recommendations to a standards committee or to the accounting department.

Normally price standards take into account the advantages to be obtained by determining the most economical purchase quantity, the best method of delivery, the lowest-cost storage, and the most favorable credit terms. However, consideration also is given to vendor reliability with respect to material quality and meeting scheduled delivery dates. In addition, the timing and lot sizes of purchases may be varied in relation to anticipated price increases and/or shortages.

STANDARD MATERIAL COST

Having established quantity and price standards for materials, the building blocks for material cost standards have been created. Material cost at standard is defined as "a preestablished measure of the material element of cost, computed by multiplying material price standard by material quantity standard."[25] This concludes our discussion of material cost standards, and we now proceed to discuss labor cost standards. As we did for material, we first deal with quantity (or time) standards, and then with price (or rate) standards.

LABOR TIME STANDARDS

A labor time standard has been defined as "a preestablished measure, expressed in temporal terms, of the quantity of labor."[26] Labor time standards are sometimes also called labor efficiency or labor performance standards.

Several methods may be used to develop labor time standards. Most widely used is time and motion study, which may make use of direct observation of operations or which may employ predetermined time standards. Less prevalent, but becoming more frequently used, is work sampling.

Time and Motion Study.   A better name would be motion and time study, because normal procedure is first to analyze each operation in order to eliminate unnecessary elements and to determine the most efficient method. Second, methods, equipment, and operating conditions are standardized. Then, and only then,

[24] *Ibid.*
[25] *Ibid.*
[26] *Ibid.*

are time measurements made to determine the number of standard hours required for an average worker to do the job.

Time and motion study is usually performed by industrial engineers. It is the backbone of many standard cost systems. Because a human factor is involved, the process is complicated and subject to disputes. Worker resentment and resistance may be encountered.

There are vivid examples of information distortion in the setting of time standards. Gardner[27] supplies the following case:

> In one case, a group, who worked together in assembling a complicated and large sized steel framework, worked out a system to be used only when the rate setter was present. They found that by tightening certain bolts first, the frame would be slightly sprung and all the other bolts would bind and be very difficult to tighten. When the rate setter was not present, they followed a different sequence and the work went much faster.

Another example is given by Whyte:[28]

> ... you got to outwit that son-of-a-bitch! You got to use your noodle while you're working and think your work out ahead as you go along! You got to add in movements you know you ain't going to make when you're running the job! Remember, if you don't screw them, they're going to screw you! ... Every moment counts! ...
> ... When the time-study man came around, I set the speed at 180. I knew damn well he would ask me to push it up, so I started low enough. He finally pushed me up to 445, and I ran the job later at 610. If I'd started out at 445, they'd have timed it at 610. Then I got him on the reaming, too. I ran the reamer for him at 130 speed and .025 feed. He asked me if I couldn't run the reamer any faster than that, and I told him I had to run the reamer slow to keep the hole size. I showed him two pieces with oversize holes that the day man ran. I picked them out for the occasion! But later on I ran the reamer at 610 speed and .018 feed, same as the drill. So I didn't have to change gears.

Falsification of information on *actual* performance also is known to occur. Again, it is difficult to say how prevalent this is. One may conjecture that it does not happen as frequently as invalid estimation in standard setting because it is normally easier to police the accuracy of actual performance measurement than to detect erroneous estimates of future events. Usually, unchallenging standards become self-fulfilling forecasts of actual performance because employees fear that superior performance will cause management to tighten up on future standards.

Examples of the feeding of incorrect performance data into control systems are given by Argyris,[29] Pettigrew,[30] and Roethlisberger and Dickson.[31] The last-mentioned study showed a classic example of a work group manipulating information on their output. The employees were on an incentive wage plan and wished to show a level daily production figure. They did so by not reporting extra output produced on some days and by inflating actual output figures on days of low production. For these reasons, it is advisable to take care to obtain worker (and

[27]B. B. Gardner, *Human Relations in Industry* (Richard D. Irwin, Chicago, 1945).

[28]Reproduced by permission from *Money and Motivation: An Analysis of Incentives in Industry.*

[29]C. Argyris, "Management Information Systems: The Challenge to Rationality and Emotionality," *Management Science,* 17 (1971), pp. 275–292.

[30]T. F. Pettigrew, "Social Evaluation Theory: Convergence and Applications," in *Nebraska Symposium on Motivation* D. Levine, ed., (University of Nebraska Press, Lincoln Neb., 1967), vol. 15, pp. 241–311.

[31]F. J. Roethlisberger and W. J. Dickson, *Management and the Worker* (Harvard University Press, Cambridge, Mass., 1939).

Timed by R. Van Jones	Checked by Geo Davis	Workplace or mach. 673X	Mach no. 1
Operators name Remold Jeffer	Clock No. 303-9709	Material See side note	R.P.M.
Time study no.		Lubricant —	Strokes per min. 1
Special tools used None			Feed
Part name Electrical receptacle	Part No 1050		Operation No. 40
	Dept. No. Electrical assembly		
Remarks			

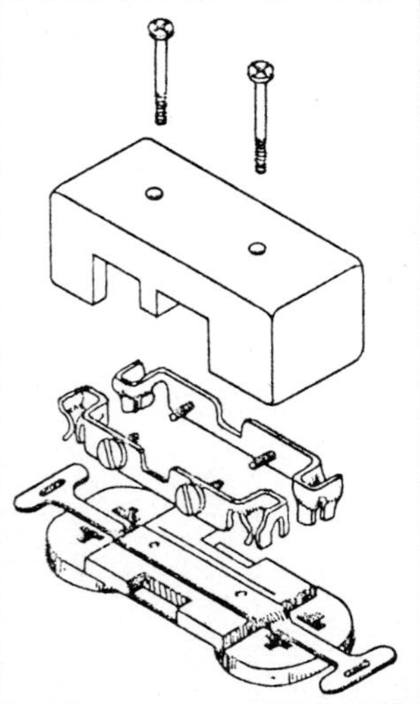

DETAILED DESCRIPTIONS OF ELEMENTS

1. Right hand reaches for back plate at bin A and grasps.
2. Moves to left hand, reaches for mounting ear at B and grasps, mounting ear and inserts. Left hand holds.
3. Right hand reaches for contact and inserts (from C).
4. Right hand reaches for contact and inserts (from C).
5. Right hand reaches, grasps, transports, and places back plate over back plate. Left hand holds.
6. Reaches for A screw at F, grasps, transports, positions with right hand. Left hand holds.
7. Same as 6.
8. Right hand reaches for screwdriver at H, grasps and transports to back plate, and tighting screw. Left hand assembles, right hand returns screwdriver.

EXHIBIT 5 (above and below) Time and Motion Studies

Reproduced by permission from Phillip F. Ostwald, *Cost Estimating and Management* (Prentice-Hall, Englewood Cliffs, N.J., 1974), pp. 69–70.

Time study observation

Date __Sept 23__
Time start __9:00 A.M.__
Time stop __9:15 A.M.__
Elapsed time __.15__

Elements

1. Pick up back plate
2. House car to back plate
3. Goldbock w back plate
4. Contacts w back plate
5. Place plate over back plate
6. Place screw in back plate
7. Rock screw in back plate
8. Tighten screw and assemble

Line	1 T	1 R	2 T	2 R	3 T	3 R	4 T	4 R	5 T	5 R	6 T	6 R	7 T	7 R	8 T	8 R
1	.03	.06	.03	.06	.08	.16	.05	.21	.05	.26	.09	.35	.04	.39	.21	.60
2	.03	.03	.06	.05	.11	.03	.14	.06	.20	.04	.24	.05	.29	.17	.46	
3	.02	.02	.04	.06	.04	.10	.04	.14	.08	.22	.04	.26	.05	.31	.16	.47
4	.02	.02	.04	.06	.04	.10	.04	.14	.06	.20	.04	.24	.05	.29	.16	.45
5	.02	.02	.06	.07	.05	.12	.03	.15	.05	.20	.04	.24	.05	.29	.15	.44
6	.01	.02	.03	.06	.05	.10	.04	.14	.04	.18	.06	.24	.04	.28	.16	.43
7	.01	.02	.03	.06	.06	.10	.05	.15	.06	.21	.04	.25	.06	.31	.16	.47
8	.04	.03	.01	.05	.12	.05	.17	.04	.21	.06	.21	.06	.27	.14	.49	
9	.02	.02	.04	.06	.05	.11	.04	.15	.05	.20	.04	.24	.08	.32	.15	.47
10	.04	.04	.04	.08	.04	.12	.04	.16	.05	.21	.06	.27	.06	.32	.16	.48
11	.01	.02	.07	.07	.14	.07	.21	.05	.26	.04	.09	.19	.14	.63		
12	.03	.03	.08	.07	.15	.07	.22	.05	.27	.04	.31	.04	.35	.21	.56	
13	.01	.02	.06	.05	.05	.11	.03	.14	.08	.22	.06	.21	.05	.12	.15	.47
14	.03	.03	.07	.02	.09	.06	.15	.12	.27	.06	.33	.05	.38	.18	.56	
15	.03	.03	.06	.05	.11	.03	.14	.08	.22	.04	.27	.05	.32	.16	.48	
16																

Summary

	1	2	3	4	5	6	7	8
Total time	.39	.59	.76	.67	.92	.75	.63	2.45
No. of readings	15	15	15	15	15	15	15	15
Av. of readings	.026	.039	.051	.045	.061	.050	.055	.163
Frequency	One out	OP	One out					
Average time	.026	.039	.051	.045	.061	.050	.055	.163
El. rating factor	1.05	1.00	1.00	.95	.90	1.00	1.00	1.05
El. normal time	.027	.039	.051	.043	.055	.060	.055	.171

Sum = 0.1491

$\sum$ T = 7.35
$\sum$ UM = 7.35

Av. cycle time 7.35/15 = .49
Cycle rating factor 1.05
Normal cycle time .516

Percent allowances

SYM	Pers.	Fat	Delay	Total	Description
A					
B					
C					
D					
E					
F					
G					
H					
I					
	5%	5%	5%	15%	

Std time per unit 0.543
Pieces per hour 101
Std hours per 100 0.953

Allowances in minutes

Pers.	Fat	Delay	Total

Avail prod min per hr
Pieces per hour
Std hrs per 100

union, if there is one) cooperation in the making of time and motion studies. Well-trained and experienced engineers should be used.

Examples of time and motion study procedures are shown in Exhibit 5.

In developing time standards, allowance is usually made for rest time, fatigue, vacation time, machine breakdown or preventative maintenance, and other routine factors.

For certain operations, it is necessary for equipment to be adjusted or set up before a particular job can be commenced. Setup time is seldom affected by the number of units subsequently produced. Therefore, setup time is usually kept separate from operating time so that it will not distort the average time taken per unit produced. Many standard cost systems have standard lot sizes for production runs. So long as these are regularly adhered to, setup times may be allowed for in the standard labor time for production runs. Where setup time is kept separate, it is sometimes treated as part of overhead rather than as direct labor. This is an acceptable alternative.

Work Sampling.   Work sampling is a technique suitable for economically gathering data about large sectors of a sizable work force, engaged in nonrepetitive work activities. It has been used in the U.S. Postal Service and in the study of office workers. It is convenient and relatively inexpensive.

A work sampling study consists of obtaining observations at random moments of time of actual activities being carried out by individual workers at the given moment. These observations are classified into preestablished categories related to the work situation.

By taking a large number of "snapshot" observations over a reasonably long period of time (to iron out unusual conditions), a statistically valid analysis of activities can be obtained. From this, the average percentage of time spent on each designated activity can be computed. It must be remembered that such informa-

EXHIBIT 6   Standard Operations List

STANDARD OPERATIONS LIST

ITEM   Base Plate No. 423   DRAWING NO.   9463
STANDARD QUANTITY   1,000   DATE   11/14/—

| Dept. | Operations | | Job Class | Hours Allowed | Remarks |
	No.	Description			
P	1731	Setup	1	2.0	
M	2146	Cut	2	5.5	
M	2172	Drill	2	21.0	
M	2175	Bevel	3	6.0	
M	2304	Polish	3	14.5	
A	2903	Press	5	2.5	
A	2905	Slip	5	2.5	

Reproduced by permission from Gordon Shillinglaw, *Cost Accounting: Analysis and Control* (Richard D. Irwin, Homewood, Ill., 1972), p. 260.

tion reflects "what is" and not necessarily "what ought to be," and thus may require adjustment before being adopted as a set of standards.

Predetermined Time Data.   Predetermined time data are preexisting information for standard operations, and can be purchased from suppliers. Usually they provide standards for very short elements of activity, and their greatest applications are for the mass production industries. Their accuracy is superior, but their applicability is normally limited to small human motions such as assembly-line tasks.

Standard Operations List.   The operations required to manufacture a product, and the standard time for each, are usually summarized on a standard operations list. An example is shown in Exhibit 6. The column headed "Job class" states the skill level of employee normally assigned to each operation.

LABOR RATE STANDARDS

A labor rate standard is defined as "a preestablished measure, expressed in monetary terms, of the price of labor."[32] Labor rates are frequently determined by union negotiations, in which case labor rate standards are usually revised following labor contract changes.

If rate standards are kept current, they should be closely in line with actual labor rates. Differences will then tend to be minor, and will probably arise mainly from the use of a worker with a wrong rate for the given job or unexpected use of overtime.

Labor rate standards normally reflect a single average rate for a particular operation. Individual workers who carry out this operation may, of course, earn above or below the average rate because of seniority above or below average. But these differences should even out.

Note that standard labor cost per unit of output is a function of both the labor time and the labor rate standards. Therefore, both labor time and labor rate should be considered in combination when labor standards are set. Consider the following example:[33]

The engineers of the American Family Hi-Fi Systems Company have determined the number of hours required to assemble a finished loudspeaker system for labor of varying skills. The labor negotiator has reported an estimate of wages per hour for the next year by skill level. The information is as follows:

Skill level	Wage rate per hour	Hours to complete one unit	Unit labor cost
A	$2	11.0	$22.0
B	3	7.2	21.6
C	4	5.2	20.8
D	5	4.1	20.5
E	6	3.5	21.0

[32]Cost Accounting Standards Board, Standard 407.
[33]Reproduced by permission from Sidney Davidson, James S. Schindler, and Roman L. Weil, *Fundamentals of Accounting,* 5th ed. (Dryden Press, Hinsdale, Ill., 1975), p. 709.

Clearly, the standard should be set at skill level D, which has the lowest total labor cost of $20.50 per unit. Even though skill level D is neither the lowest labor rate standard nor the lowest labor time standard, it does represent the minimum labor cost per unit produced. It is the job of the cost accountant to insure, so far as possible, that standards are set at the minimum cost per unit produced. Otherwise, performance that is less than optimal will go unnoticed. For example, if standards are set for skill level E with unit cost $21 and 100 units are produced for $2,100 of labor costs, then there will be no signal from the labor variances that total labor costs are $50 [= ($21.0 − $20.5) × 100] larger than necessary.

Labor rate standards generally cover hourly and piecework labor, but not salaried employees whose compensation normally is budgeted as overhead rather than direct labor.

A major component of the labor rate consists of fringe benefits, which may constitute 30 percent or more of the base labor rate. Fringe benefits include payroll taxes, workmen's compensation insurance, employer pension contributions, holiday, vacation, and sick pay, employer contributions to group insurance plans, profit-sharing payments, and wash-up and travel time.

Some of these fringe benefits, such as the Social Security payroll tax, may vary in rate from time to time and then the fringe benefit component of the standard labor rate will require periodic updating. It should be noted that some fringe benefits are straight percentages of the base labor rate, but that others are not (e.g., Social Security tax is payable only up to a ceiling amount of earnings, thereafter it does not apply). Therefore the labor rate consists of both fixed and variable elements. This may lead some accountants to prefer treating fringe benefits as overhead rather than as part of the direct labor rate. The disadvantage of doing so is to risk overlooking the substantial portion of labor costs represented by fringe benefits.

STANDARD LABOR COSTS

Standard labor times and standard labor rates are the elements that determine standard labor costs. Labor cost at standard is defined as "a preestablished measure of the labor element of cost, computed by multiplying labor rate standard by labor time standard."[34] This concludes our discussion of labor cost standards, and we now proceed to deal with standards for manufacturing overhead costs.

OVERHEAD COST STANDARDS

Standard costs for material and labor have a direct relationship to the number of units of output produced. Overhead is, however, by definition, identified only indirectly with physical output. Although overhead cost standards can be developed, the indirect nature of overhead costs requires methods of developing standards for overhead that are different from those used to establish material and labor standards. The main difference is that we do not have clear cut separate standards for quantity and for price. Therefore overhead standards consist only of dollar amounts per unit of activity or of output.

Predetermined Overhead Rates.   The fundamental notion of a standard is that of a *predetermined* measure. In the case of overhead, the formulation of cost

[34]Cost Accounting Standards Board, Standard 407.

standards requires predetermination of overhead as a total dollar amount for a future period, usually a year.

Overhead items are first classified as being either fixed or variable. Then the variable items are forecast for the coming year on the basis of a suitable measure of activity (such as direct labor hours or machine hours, for example). To this variable overhead dollar total the fixed overhead is added to arrive at total budgeted overhead for the coming year.

The budgeted overhead is divided by the activity measure to give a predetermined, or standard, overhead rate per direct labor hour, or per machine hour or per whatever the activity unit is.

This brief overall description is vastly oversimplified, and was included only as a quick preview of the discussion to follow. We shall now begin to fill in the gaps.

Flexible Budgets.   The predetermined overhead rate described above applies only to a single level of activity. This is known as a *static* budget. If actual activity turns out to be different from the planned level, there is no way to provide a standard applicable to the level of actual activity: the only available comparison between actual and standard is to use the single standard that exists.

In order to overcome this problem, flexible budgets are prepared. A flexible budget is applicable to range of activity levels rather than a single level because it is automatically related to any volume level within the selected range. Let us consider a highly simplified example. Assume the following facts:

Overhead item	Budget for July	Actual
Factory rent	$10,000	$10,000
Electric power	6,250	4,700
Supplies	1,750	1,300
Total	$18,000	$16,000
Units to be produced	2,000	
Units actually produced		1,500
Overhead per unit	$9.00	$10.67

Using a static budget, we find that actual volume is below budget and actual overhead per unit is over budget. In other words, the department concerned has not been *effective*. But, given the effectiveness level, has it been *efficient*? We cannot say.

However, let us now use a flexible budget. The key element is to separate fixed and variable costs. Presumably, factory rent is fixed but electric power and suppliers are variable. Therefore we expect overhead cost for any level of output within a reasonable range to be

Fixed overhead: factory rent	$10,000
Variable overhead: electric power	$ 6,250
supplies	1,750
	$ 8,000
Divided by 2,000 units =	
Variable overhead per unit	$4

Then the flexible budget for output of 1,500 units is

$$\$10,000 + (1,500 \times \$4) = \$16,000$$

This budgeted amount of $16,000 is equal to the actual overhead incurred of $16,000, which indicates that although the department was not effective, it did operate at standard efficiency. If actual overhead had been $17,000 ($15,000), we would know that efficiency had been below (above) standard.

Therefore the flexible budget, being applicable to any level of output, enables us to separate effectiveness from efficiency, which—as we stated at the beginning of this chapter—is a major objective of using cost standards.

The heart of the flexible budget is proper separation of costs into their fixed and variable elements. This in turn is based on reliable information on cost behavior with respect to volume. A detailed treatment of that topic is given in Chapter 5, on cost estimation. A useful introduction and practical guide on this subject is "Separating and Using Costs as Fixed and Variable," Accounting Practice Report 10, National Association of Accountants.[35]

We have discussed flexible budgets in relation to levels of activity. Clearly the proper definition and use of activity measures is vital to the flexible budget process. We now therefore consider this factor.

How to Measure Activity.   Our simplified example above measured activity in terms of units of output produced. Where only one uniform product is manufactured, this is an adequate measure. But in practice, life is seldom so simple. There may be multiple products, or at least varying sizes and types of a single product. In that case, a common denominator is needed. In selecting a suitable measure, the following should be taken into account:

1. *Causal factor:* individual items of cost should be linked to whatever activity it is that causes that cost item to fluctuate. For example, factory electric power is probably related to number of machine hours. Other frequently used activity measures are direct labor hours and weight of materials handled.

2. *Independence:* the activity measure should be as free as possible of influencing factors other than the level of activity. For example, use of direct material costs or direct labor dollars as an activity measure is not independent of variations of materials prices or wage rates. These price or rate influences are neutralized by using standard material costs or direct labor hours.

3. *Simplicity:* easily understood measures are to be preferred and are usually less expensive to develop and record.

4. *Output-oriented:* the activity measure should be insulated from fluctuations in efficiency. Therefore it would be better to use standard labor hours allowed than actual labor hours used, because the latter is affected by efficiency. Actual labor hours used is an effort, or input, measure rather than the more desirable output-oriented measure of standard labor hours. Standard hours is an output measure because it is based on the number of hours allowed, at standard, to produce a given output. Unless that output is known, the standard labor hours cannot be derived.

Cost Allocation.   Before costs can be identified with the appropriate activity measures, it is usually necessary to select and assemble these costs in relation to a cost objective. A cost objective[36] is defined by the Cost Accounting Standards

---

[35]National Association of Accountants, "Separating and Using Costs as Fixed and Variable," Accounting Practice Report 10 (NAA, New York, 1960).

[36]Sometimes also referred to as "cost centers." Cost objective is the preferred, modern term.

Board as "a function, organizational subdivision, contract or other work unit for which cost data are desired and for which provision is made to accumulate and measure the cost of processes, products, jobs, capitalized projects, etc."[37]

Cost allocation consists of three steps:

1. Selecting the appropriate cost objectives
2. Selecting and accumulating the relevant cost data pertaining to the respective cost objectives.
3. Determining a basis of allocation (i.e., an activity measure) with which to assign the accumulated costs from cost objections to products, processes, or jobs by means of appropriate activity measures.

The accumulation of costs resulting from step 2 above is referred to as a *cost pool.* The term *allocate* is defined as "to assign an item of cost, or a group of items of cost, to one or more cost objectives. This term includes both direct assignment of cost and the reassignment of a share from an indirect cost pool."[38] An example of the allocation process is given in Exhibits 7(a) and 7(b).

Exhibit 7(a) shows the accumulation of costs to various cost objectives, which in this case are productive departments and service departments. This illustrates step 2 above. Then, Exhibit 7(b) shows for one particular productive department (Dyeing) the allocation basis by means of an activity measure (machine hours) to products.

Cost Pools and Homogeneous Allocations.   Pooled costs may be homogeneous. For example, a product may have a standard overhead cost of $50 per unit for buffing and $50 per unit for polishing. If these costs are pooled and are assigned collectively at $100 per unit of product, this is equivalent to assigning them separately at $50 each per unit of product. In this case, the allocation is said to be perfectly homogeneous. Thus the cost pooling achieves a computational saving at no loss of precision in assigning costs to products.

However, usually cost pooling combines costs that are not homogeneous. Rather than assigning each item of cost individually (which is the most precise method), costs are pooled and a single method is used to assign the entire pool to units of activity. The loss of precision is then regarded as balanced off by the saving of expense, because a more aggregated cost system is more economical to maintain than a more detailed cost system.

On the one hand, it is hard to say just where the ideal trade-off between precision and system expense lies. There is no quick or easy answer, or even a general answer. This is a universal problem in accounting. Even though the ideal point is not exactly determinable, it is often worthwhile to test the *sensitivity* of the level of homogeneity in use. This is done by also making a more detailed cost assignment, giving individual assignment to at least the major items in the cost pool for a number of sample periods. The difference in product costs under the respective allocations may or may not be judged to be significant. If judged insignificant, this indicates that sufficient homogeneity has been attained through the existing cost pooling. However, a significant difference signals the need for considering a less aggregative level of cost pooling.

Blanket or Specific Standard Overhead Rates.   The different products produced in a single plant may require varying labor and equipment. These variations may, in turn, justify more specificity of overhead allocation in order to determine more valid product costs. An excellent example to illustrate this point is furnished by Horngren.[39] He says:

---

[37]Cost Accounting Standards Board, Part 400.
[38]*Ibid.*
[39]Horngren, *Cost Accounting: A Managerial Emphasis,* pp. 410–411.

EXHIBIT 7(a) Annual Manufacturing Expense Summary

Expense	Receiving & tufting	Dyeing	Drying	Adhesive	Inspection & packing	Shipping	Maint.	Steam generation	Total	Basis
Variable manufacturing expense:										
Operating supplies	$ 40,000	$ 30,000	$ 7,500	$ 5,000	$ 5,000	$ 7,500	$11,500	$ 5,000	$111,500	Supply specifications
Fuel & gas	8,000	135,000	22,000	25,000	2,000	6,000	2,000	—	200,000	Steam consumption analysis
Water	—	20,750	—	1,250	—	—	—	3,000	25,000	Direct charge
Electricity	10,500	6,250	12,250	7,750	2,250	4,000	1,500	2,000	46,500	Direct charge
Subtotal: variable	$ 58,500	$192,000	$41,750	$39,000	$ 9,250	$ 17,500	$15,000	$10,000	$383,000	
Distribution										
Steam	$ 1,000	$ 6,000	$ 500	$ 1,000	$ 500	$ 1,000	—	($10,000)	0	Steam consumption
Maintenance	6,000	2,000	1,500	2,500	2,000	1,000	(15,000)	0	0	Utilization of maint. svcs.
Total/year	$ 65,500	$200,000	$43,750	$42,500	$11,750	$ 19,500	0	0	$383,000	
Total/week	$ 1,310	$ 4,000	$ 875	$ 850	$ 235	$ 390	0	0	$ 7,660	
Fixed manufacturing expense:										
Manufacturing mgrs.	$ 12,000	$ 10,000	$ 5,000	$12,000	$12,000	$ 12,000	$12,000	—	$ 75,000	Department managers $
Dept. managers	12,000	10,000	5,000	12,000	12,000	12,000	12,000	—	75,000	Direct charge
Fixed Soc. Security & other payroll taxes	1,600	1,200	400	1,600	1,600	1,600	1,600	—	9,600	Department managers $
Depreciation	135,500	54,500	20,000	25,000	20,000	35,000	21,150	18,250	329,400	Direct calculation
Methods & Stds. dpt.	39,000	11,000	6,000	9,000	9,000	11,000	6,000	4,000	{ 60,000	Number of employees
Personnel dept.									35,000	Number of employees
Insurance	1,500	1,000	500	500	500	1,000	500	250	5,950	Building & equipment replacement value
Property tax	25,000	12,500	5,000	5,000	5,000	15,000	6,000	4,000	77,500	Building & equipment replacement value
Salary & pension plan	5,000	1,500	750	1,250	1,250	1,500	750	500	12,500	Direct calculation
Hospital & major medical program	30,000	8,000	4,000	6,000	6,000	8,000	4,000	2,500	68,500	Direct calculation
Building maintenance	12,000	6,000	1,500	3,000	3,000	15,000	1,000	500	42,000	$0.20 per square foot
Subtotal: fixed	$273,600	$115,700	$48,150	$75,350	$70,350	$112,100	$65,000	$30,000	$790,250	
Distribution										
Steam	$ 3,000	$ 18,000	$ 1,500	$ 3,000	$ 1,500	$ 3,000	—	($30,000)	0	Steam consumption
Maintenance	26,000	8,500	6,500	11,000	9,000	4,000	($65,000)	—	0	Utilization of maint. svcs.
Total/year	$302,600	$142,200	$56,150	$89,350	$80,850	$117,100	0	0	$790,250	
Total/week	$ 6,052	$ 2,844	$ 1,123	$ 1,787	$ 1,617	$ 2,382	0	0	$ 15,805	

Reproduced by permission from Frank C. Wilson, *Industrial Cost Controls* (Prentice-Hall, Englewood Cliffs, N.J., 1971), p. 103.

EXHIBIT 7(b)   Complete Cost Center Worksheet for the Dyeing Department

	Labor cost		Variable labor benefits	Cost/week mfg. expense	Fixed mfg. expense	Total cost
	Methods & standard summary	Service dept.				
Cost/week	$2,400	$780	$710	$4,000	$2,844	$10,734
Number of machines	12					
Operating hours: 2 shifts, 40 hours each	× 80					
Total machine hours	= 960	960	960	960	960	960
Cost per machine hour	$2.50	$0.81	$0.74	$4.17	$2.96	$11.18
		$3.31		$4.91		

Reproduced by permission from Frank C. Wilson, *Industrial Cost Controls* (Prentice-Hall, Englewood Cliffs, N.J., 1971), p. 104.

Assume that one job is routed through two departments: machining and finishing. The machining department is heavily mechanized with costly semiautomatic and automatic equipment. The finishing department contains a few simple tools and is dependent on painstaking skilled workmanship. Overhead costs would be relatively large in machining and small in finishing.

Now consider two jobs. The first requires one hour of machining time and ten hours of finishing time. The second requires nine hours of machining time and two hours of finishing time. If a single, plant-wide, blanket overhead rate based on labor-hours is used, each job would receive the same total-overhead application. But this probably would not be a sufficiently accurate measurement of the underlying relationship, because Job No. 1 made light use of overhead-incurring factors while Job No. 2 made heavy use of such services. Departmental rates result in a more accurate linking of overhead with specific jobs when products do not move uniformly through the plant.

It may be appropriate, within a single firm, to use different overhead allocation bases for different departments. In Exhibit 8, direct labor hours are used as the base for the machining department on the assumption that direct labor hours are proportional to machine hours. If this is not the case, machine hours should be the base for the machining department, but direct labor hours would still be the base for the finishing department.

Alternative Allocation Bases.   Following are the most commonly used bases of overhead allocation and their respective advantages and disadvantages. Note that more than one base may be used within a single organizational unit for assigning different categories of overhead.

1. *Physical units produced:* this base is acceptable where only one product is produced, and each unit is identical or almost identical.

2. *Direct standard labor hours:* this is probably the most widely used base. Most items of overhead cost are related to time (e.g., rent, depreciation, property taxes, insurance, supervisory and other indirect labor). Use of this base assumes that overhead generally does vary proportionately with labor hours.

3. *Standard machine hours:* for highly automated operations, or processes using expensive equipment, machine time probably better represents overhead accrual than an alternative base such as labor hours. Capital equipment carrying costs such as depreciation, rentals, property taxes, and insurance are likely to be related closely to machine usage.

EXHIBIT 8   Plant-Wide Overhead Rate Versus Departmental Overhead Rates

	Plant-wide rate		Departmental rates		
	Machining	Finishing	Machining	Finishing	
Budgeted annual overhead	$100,000	$ 8,000	$100,000	$ 8,000	—
Direct labor hours (DLH)	10,000	10,000	10,000	10,000	
Blanket rate per DLH:					
$108,000 ÷ 20,000		$ 5.40			
Departmental rates per DLH			$ 10.00	$ .80	
Overhead application:					
Job no. 1					
Labor time, 11 hours @ $5.40		$59.40			
or					
Labor time:					
Machining, 1 hour @ $10.00			$ 10.00		*Total*
Finishing, 10 hours @ $.80				$ 8.00	$18.00
Job no. 2					
Labor time, 11 hours @ $5.40		$59.40			
or					
Labor time:					
Machining, 9 hours @ $10.00			$ 90.00		
Finishing, 2 hours @ $.80				$ 1.60	$91.60

Reproduced by permission from Charles Horngren, *Cost Accounting: A Managerial Emphasis* (Prentice-Hall, Englewood Cliffs, N.J., 1972), p. 411.

4. *Direct standard labor cost:* where the wage rates for the different activities are very nearly uniform, this base achieves a result similar to direct labor hours. Otherwise, it is probably preferable to use labor hours rather than dollars. However, where overhead includes fringe benefits (which are proportionate or nearly so to labor costs), or high-cost employees tend to make the most use of expensive equipment, then this dollar basis is suitable. It is frequently used for professional service firms, such as public accountants, consulting engineers, lawyers, and management consultants.

5. *Direct standard material weight or cost:* these are not valid bases unless material storage and handling costs are a predominant portion of overhead. Alternatively, and probably preferably, material-related overhead costs may be accumulated separately from other overhead and then allocated on this basis. Sometimes, however, it does happen that material weight will achieve allocation results very similar to those obtained by more generally accepted methods. In that case, material weight may be used because of its simplicity and ease. An example of this occurs in the consumer products operations of the paper converting industry (e.g., paper towels, napkins, tissues, toilet paper, etc.).

STANDARD COST SHEET

We have now discussed all three elements of standard cost, namely, materials, labor, and overhead. These are the components of standard product cost, and they are usually recorded on a standard cost sheet. Such a sheet will exist for each product, and normally it gives the product description, the standard batch size, and the individual elements and total of standard cost. Exhibit 9 illustrates an example.

EXHIBIT 9   Standard Cost Sheet

STANDARD COST SHEET

Description: <u>Base Plate No. 423</u>   Standard Cost per Batch: <u>$915.60</u>
Batch Quantity: <u>1,000 pieces</u>   Standard Cost per Unit: <u>$0.9156</u>

Operation or Item	Dept.	Materials			Labor			Overhead			
		Quan-tity	Price	Cost	Hours	Rate	Cost	Base	Quan-tity	Rate	Cost
Setup	P				2.0	3.50	7.00	LH	2.0	4.00	8.00
Steel plate	M	4,200	0.06	252.00							
Cut	M				5.5	3.00	16.50	MH	5.5	2.40	13.20
Drill	M				21.0	3.00	63.00	MH	32.0	2.40	76.80
Bevel	M				6.0	3.00	18.00	MH	5.0	2.40	12.00
Polish	M				14.5	3.00	43.50	MH	41.5	2.40	99.60
Anchor	A	1,010	0.14	141.40							
Press	A				2.5	2.00	5.00	LH	2.5	1.80	4.50
Brace	A	2,080	0.07	145.60							
Slip	A				2.5	2.00	5.00	LH	2.5	1.80	4.50
Total		—	—	539.00	—	—	158.00	—	—	—	218.60

Reproduced by permission from Gordon Shillinglaw, *Cost Accounting: Analysis and Control* (Richard D. Irwin, Homewood, Ill., 1972), p. 261.

THE LEARNING CURVE

Operations that start out as new or unfamiliar usually require progressively less time with repetition. This is the learning effect. The first, and perhaps most well-known, production applications of learning were in airframe manufacture. It was found that the number of direct labor hours required to build an aircraft body declined at a constant rate as the number of units built increased. A commonly observed constant rate of decline gave rise to the so-called 80-percent learning curve. (80 percent represents the reduction in cumulative average labor cost per unit.) Exhibit 10 shows an example of an 80-percent learning curve.

The learning curve is a well-established, practical occurrence. It is applicable to setting labor time standards and overhead cost standards. Note that the learning effect tends to level out as transition is made from the startup, or learning phase of

EXHIBIT 10   An 80 Percent Learning Curve

Quantity		Time in minutes	
Per lot	Cumulative	Cumulative	Cumulative average per unit
10	10	300	30.0
10	20	480	24.0 (30.0 × 80%)
20	40	768	19.2 (24.0 × 80%)
40	80	1,232	15.4 (19.2 × 80%)
80	160	1,968	12.3 (15.4 × 80%)

Reproduced by permission from Charles T. Horngren, *Cost Accounting: A Managerial Emphasis* (Prentice-Hall, Englewood Cliffs, N.J., 1972), p. 210.

production, to the steady-state phase. Thus, standards are affected only during the learning phase. During this phase, standards should progressively reflect the learning changes. Care should be taken not to apply standards during the startup phase that are based on steady-state production and that may be either too easy or impossibly difficult to attain.

Expanded discussion of this topic will be found in Baloff and Kennelly and in Ostwald.[40] We present here only the bare essentials on this specialized topic. Exhibit 11 presents an example plot of a learning curve, linear in the logarithms.

EXHIBIT 11   Log-Log Plot of Industry Average Unit Curve for Century Series Aircraft

Reproduced by permission from Phillip F. Ostwald, *Cost Estimating and Management* (Prentice-Hall, Englewood Cliffs, N.J., 1974), p. 272.

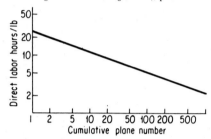

The learning curve expression is

$$T_N = KN^s$$

where T_N = effort, such as labor hours, required to produce the Nth unit
   N = unit number
   K = a constant, the effort such as labor hours required to produce the first unit
   s = learning rate, a negative constant, equal to $-.80$ for an 80-percent learning curve

Then

$$\log T_N = \log K - s \log N$$

which is the log-linear expression plotted in Exhibit 11.

It is important that standards based on a projected learning curve be carefully checked against actual experience at frequent intervals. Adjustments can then be made if necessary. This can be done by plotting actual observations against the projected learning curve, usually on log-log graph paper. Better yet, with sufficient observations, a least-squares fit can be determined by means of standard regression techniques.[41]

---

[40]Nicholas Baloff and John W. Kennelly, "Accounting Implications of Product and Process Start-ups," *Journal of Accounting Research*, 5, 2 (Autumn 1967), pp. 131–143. See also Phillip F. Ostwald, *Cost Estimating for Engineering and Management* (Prentice-Hall, Englewood Cliffs, N.J., 1974).

[41]See Chapter 5, "Cost Estimation," for discussion of these regression techniques in relation to cost behavior.

REVISION OF STANDARD COSTS

Material quantity and labor time standards generally require less frequent revision than material price and labor rate standards, which are subject to inflationary pressures. Changes in quantity and time standards usually are made only in recognition of altered specifications, different methods, or new equipment.

Nevertheless, the real issue is not whether standards will be revised, but rather how often this will be done. There are clear benefits to keeping standards current, which results in more meaningful information for planning, control, and decision making. Also, however, there are definite costs attached to revision. Thus standards are not as a rule changed to reflect only minor differences. There is no simple rule for all purposes about when to change a standard. Many firms will review their standards as frequently as once a quarter, but actual revision is seldom made more than once a year unless highly unusual conditions occur.

NONMANUFACTURING STANDARDS

The greatest use of cost standards is found in manufacturing industry. However, this is not the only area in which standards are used. The work measurement techniques that were first used in the factory have since been extended into clerical, logistical, and selling activities, and also into service areas such as nursing. Often the standards developed in these newer areas are less precise than those in the more routinely structured manufacturing activities. But they still do represent a considerably more methodical approach than the more informal and intuitive one that previously prevailed.

Due to the nature of the work being performed, the success of such techniques is usually limited. Difficulties are task diversity, discretionary latitude on the part of employees, and difficulties in measuring output. Nevertheless, significant progress has been made in some areas.[42]

RESPONSIBILITY FOR DEVELOPING COST STANDARDS

The development of cost standards is an undertaking that requires time, talent, and good organization. An approach has been designed for this purpose by Price Waterhouse and Company, based on the use of two sets of forms—network analyses and organizational task lists. We reproduce some excerpts from illustrative samples of these forms.

Exhibit 12 shows a network analysis for the steps involved in developing standard product costs. Note that in an actual application the time estimates would be shown on the network chart. In fact, establishing time schedules would have been a primary objective of the preliminary survey, which is event 1 in the network chart.

Illustrative organizational task lists are shown in Exhibit 13. Note that these are excerpts only, and they do not represent a full coverage of the tasks of each organizational unit concerned.

---

[42]For more detailed discussion, see Chapter 5, "Cost Estimation." For description of clerical work study techniques, see H. W. Nance and R. E. Nolan, *Office Work Measurement* (McGraw-Hill Book Company, New York, 1971).

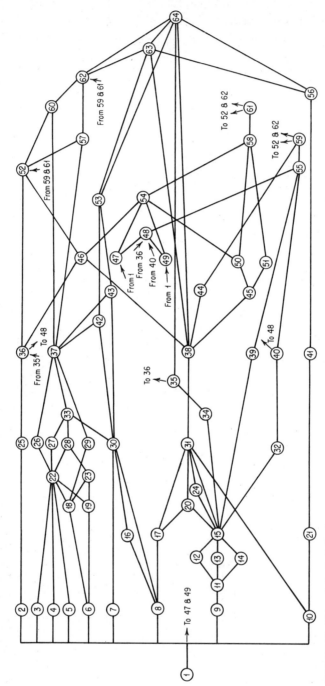

EXHIBIT 12   Network Analysis for Designing and Installing a Standard Cost System. Chart No. 1: Developing Standard Product Costs. The list of events for the chart is given on page 15-29.

List of Events for Exhibit 12.

1 Preliminary survey of organization and methods completed
2 Product numbers assigned
3 Accounting treatment of cash discount decided
4 Direct labor defined
5 Accounting treatment of freight-in decided
6 Organization charts reviewed and revised as necessary
7 Normal work week determined
8 Machine groups established
9 Parts numbering system established
10 Standard labor grades established
11 Parts numbers assigned
12 Unit of measure codes assigned
13 Engineering level codes assigned
14 Source codes assigned
15 Parts number identification files set up
16 Standard downtime allowances set
17 Standard manning tables prepared
18 Service centers established
19 Production centers established
20 Standard production rates set
21 Wage rate ranges assigned to labor grades
22 Expense account classes reviewed and revised
23 Factors of variability selected
24 Raw material content determined—piece parts
25 Annual sales forecasted
26 Procurement burden analysis completed
27 Bases for amortizing capacity costs revised as necessary
28 Fixed-variable expense analyses made
29 Bases for redistributing service center costs determined
30 Practical capacity determined
31 Operation sheets available
32 Vendors chosen for purchased parts
33 Flexible budgets prepared
34 Bills of material available
35 EDP bill of material file established
36 Annual parts requirements determined
37 Budgeted costs in service centers redistributed
38 EDP operation sheet data file established
39 Standard freight rates set for purchased parts
40 Tentative standards set for purchased parts
41 Standard labor rates set for all grades
42 Variable manufacturing burden rates computed
43 Fixed manufacturing burden rates computed
44 Standard prices set for outside operations
45 Vendors chosen for raw materials
46 Annual raw material requirements established
47 Inventory carrying costs estimated
48 Economic order quantities established—purchased parts
49 Cost of placing a purchase order estimated
50 Tentative standards set for raw materials
51 Standard freight rates set for raw materials
52 Standard cost of annual purchases computed
53 EDP file, manufactured burden rates, established
54 Economic order quantities established—raw materials
55 Standard prices determined—purchased parts
56 EDP file, standard labor rates, established
57 Standard procurement burden rates set—raw materials
58 Standard prices determined—raw materials.
59 EDP file, standard cost of purchased parts and outside operations (excluding procurement burden), established
60 Standard procurement burden rates set—purchased parts
61 EDP file, standard cost of raw materials (excluding procurement burden), established
62 Procurement burden added and standard purchase price files combined
63 EDP file, standard cost of fabricated parts, established
64 EDP file, standard cost of assemblies, established

Reproduced by permission from Price Waterhouse & Co. pamphlet entitled "A Program for Designing and Installing a Standard Cost System," in the 1974-MAS/PACE *Cost Accounting Systems,* (a Price Waterhouse & Co. manual for continuing education programs), pp. H-218–219.

Note that a task force is appointed, usually consisting of key people, representing at a minimum accounting, design engineering, industrial engineering, production control, and purchasing. If the firm has a methods group, its head should be included. Any consultants hired should also be members of the task force.

Each task list shows the events for which each organizational unit is responsible. Where the completion of an event depends on the completion of certain other events, these events are indicated in Exhibit 13 as interfaces "in." Those events that are constrained by the events being described are shown as interfaces "out." These lists serve also to record the personnel resources required and the status of the project.

The development of cost standards is a complex undertaking, and the approach for organizing it described above should be of significant assistance in bringing about a successful system.

EXHIBIT 13

Event		Interfaces			
No.	Description	In	Out	Org. unit	Pg.
Primary responsibility for the following events should be assigned to the Standard Cost Task Force					
1	Preliminary survey of organization		2	G	20
	and methods completed		3	H	20
			4	H	20
			5		20
			6	A	14
			7	F	19
			8	C	17
			9	B	16
			10	D	18
			47	H	21
			49	E	18
6	Organization charts reviewed and	1		A	14
	revised as necessary		18	A	14
			19	A	14
18	Service centers established	6		A	14
			22	H	20
			23	H	20
			29	H	21
19	Production centers established	6		A	14
			22	H	20
			23	H	20
			94	A	14
66	Procedures for making vendor	65		E	19
	returns established		69	A	14
67	Procedures for accounting for mate-				
	rial in hands of vendors revised		69	A	14
68	Format and frequency of purchase				
	price variance report determined		69	A	14
69	Procedures established for determin-	66		A	14
	ing purchase price variance and	67		A	14
	applying procurement burden	68		A	14
			70	H/J	22/25
		79		H	22
		80		A	15
Primary responsibility for the following events should be assigned to the Industrial Engineering Department					
8	Machine groups established	1		A	14
			16	C	17
			17	C	17
			30	C	17
16	Standard downtime allowances set	8		C	17
			30	C	17
17	Standard manning tables prepared	8		C	17
			20	C	17
			31	C	17
20	Standard production rates set	15		J	23
		17		C	17
			31	C	17
24	Raw material content determined-	15		J	23
	piece parts		31	C	17
30	Practical capacity determined	7		F	19
		8		C	17
		16		C	17
			33	H	21
			42	H	21
			43	H	21
31	Operation sheets available	10		D	18
		15		J	23
		17		C	17
		20		C	17
		24		C	17
			38	J	23

EXHIBIT 13 (Continued)

Event		Interfaces			
No.	Description	In	Out	Org. unit	Pg.
Primary responsibility for the following events should be assigned to the Accounting Department					
3	Accounting treatment of cash discount decided	1		A	14
			22	H	20
4	Direct labor defined	1		A	14
			22	H	20
			94	A	15
5	Accounting treatment of freight in decided	1		A	14
			22	H	20
22	Expense account classes reviewed and revised	3		H	20
		4		H	20
		5		H	20
		18		A	14
		19		A	14
			26	H	20
			27	H	20
			28	H	22
23	Factors of variability selected	18		A	14
		19		A	14
			28	H	21
26	Procurement burden analysis completed	22		H	20
			37	H	21
			78	H	22
27	Bases for amortizing capacity costs revised as necessary	22		H	20
			33	H	21
			117	H	22

Reproduced by permission from Price Waterhouse & Co. pamphlet entitled "A Program for Designing and Installing a Standard Cost System," in the 1974-MAS/PACE *Cost Accounting Systems* (a Price Waterhouse & Co. manual for continuing education programs), pp. H-226, 229, 232.

BIBLIOGRAPHY

Argyris, C.: "Management Information Systems: The Challenge to Rationality and Emotionality," *Management Science,* 17 (1971).

Atkinson, J. W.: *An Introduction to Motivation,* D. Van Nostrand Company, Princeton, N.J., 1964.

Baloff, Nicholas, and John W. Kennelly: "Accounting Implications of Product and Process Start-ups," *Journal of Accounting Research,* 5, 2 (Autumn 1967), pp. 131–143.

Berliner, J. S.: "The Situation of Plant Managers," in *Soviet Society: A Book of Readings,* A. Inkeles and K. Geiger, eds., Houghton Mifflin Company, Boston, 1961.

Cohen, A. K.: *Deviance and Control,* Prentice-Hall, Englewood Cliffs, N.J., 1966.

Cost Accounting Standards Board, Standard 407, "Use of Standard Costs for Direct Material and Direct Labor," 1974.

Dalton, Gene W.: "Motivation and Control in Organizations," in *Motivation and Control in Organizations,* Gene W. Dalton and Paul R. Lawrence, eds., Richard D. Irwin, Homewood, Ill., 1971.

Davidson, Sidney, James S. Schindler, and Roman L. Weil, *Fundamentals of Accounting,* 5th ed., Dryden Press, Hinsdale, Ill., 1975.

Gardner, B. B.: *Human Relations in Industry,* Richard D. Irwin, Homewood, Ill., 1945.

Hofstede, G. H.: *The Game of Budget Control,* Van Gorcum, Assen, Netherlands, 1967.

Horngren, Charles T.: *Cost Accounting: A Managerial Emphasis,* 3rd ed., Prentice-Hall, Englewood Cliffs, N.J., 1972.

Lawler, Edward E., III: *Motivation in Work Organizations,* Brooks Cole Publishing Company, Monterey Calif., 1973.

Nance, H. W., and R. E. Nolan: *Office Work Measurement,* McGraw-Hill Book Company, New York, 1971.

National Association of Accountants: *Separating and Using Costs as Fixed and Variable,* Accounting Practice Report 10, NAA, New York, 1960.

———: *Standard Costs and Variance Analysis,* NAA, New York, 1974.

Ostwald, Phillip F.: *Cost Estimating for Engineering and Management,* Prentice-Hall, Englewood Cliffs, N.J., 1974.

Porter, L. W., and Edward E. Lawler, III: *Managerial Attitudes and Performance,* Irwin-Dorsey Press, Homewood, Ill., 1968.

Price Waterhouse & Co., "A Program for Designing and Installing a Standard Cost System," in the 1974-MAS/PACE *Cost Accounting Systems.*

Shillinglaw, Gordon: *Cost Accounting: Analysis and Control,* 3rd ed., Richard D. Irwin, Homewood, Ill., 1972.

Simon, H. A., H. Guetzkow, G. Kozmetsky, and G. Tyndall: *Centralization vs. Decentralization in Organizing the Controller's Department,* Financial Executives Research Foundation, New York, 1954.

Stedry, Andrew: *Budget Control and Cost Behavior,* Prentice-Hall, Englewood Cliffs, N.J., 1960.

Vroom, V. H.: *Work and Motivation,* John Wiley & Sons, New York, 1964.

Whyte, W. F., ed.: *Money and Motivation: An Analysis of Incentives in Industry,* Harper & Row, New York, 1955.

Wilson, Frank C.: *Industrial Cost Controls,* Prentice-Hall, Englewood Cliffs, N.J., 1971.

Chapter **16**

Operation of a Standard Cost System

JAMES A. LARGAY III
Associate Professor of Industrial Management, Georgia Institute of
Technology

INTRODUCTION

Cost accounting systems have two basic functions. The first is to measure *product costs* for purposes of income determination and inventory valuation. The second is to aid in *cost and production control* so that management is better able to identify problem areas and formulate corrective action. Systems that accumulate only *actual* production costs are generally adequate for product costing but are often inadequate for control purposes. Control is usually facilitated by the existence of some *standard* or *yardstick* against which actual results may be compared. If the standard or yardstick is reasonable, the favorable or unfavorable deviations shown by a comparison of standard and actual results provide important data to management. For example, if such a comparison suggests that costs are "too high" relative to the standard, investigation and corrective action may be undertaken quickly. On the other hand, if costs are "too low" relative to the standard, investigation may ascertain the existence of increased efficiency, which may lead to significant cost savings.

Standards may appear in the form of production costs, budgets, and sales targets. Broadly speaking, they represent management's plans. If management can easily determine when actual results differ from planned results, a higher degree of control is possible. The task of this chapter is to describe the role of standards in an accounting system, with particular emphasis on the cost accounting system. We shall also discuss the use of standards as control devices in areas outside the cost accounting system.

REVIEW OF STANDARD COSTS

Chapter 15 discusses the setting of standards in detail. These standards are, in effect, estimates of what *should* occur under given operating conditions. They reflect assumptions about the level of production, prices of input resources, specifications of materials, competence of the labor force, production technology, and, perhaps, the state of the economy. The most useful standards are those viewed to be *currently attainable,* given input prices, the production process, normal efficiency, and so forth. Such standards are revised periodically so that they reflect current conditions. They should reflect the firm's goals in the production area and should be capable of being achieved. Other concepts of standards include *basic standards* and *theoretical standards.* Basic standards are rarely changed and, over a long period of time, can be used to highlight trends. Theoretical standards are those reflecting ideal conditions such as maximum capacity, no downtime, no absenteeism, and so forth. Theoretical standards may be useful as ideal benchmarks but may never be attained. Basic standards, on the other hand, may soon become obsolete in a world of rapidly changing prices and technology.

Currently attainable standards, then, appear to have the greatest potential for motivating employees and for effectively controlling operations. We shall concentrate on these kinds of standards in this chapter.

Standards are most relevant when they are formulated for operations or processes that are relatively uniform. Many manufacturing operations are characterized by large numbers of identical, repetitive operations and by the use of materials and parts having fairly inflexible specifications. Jobs on an assembly line, steel sheets used in stamping appliance cabinets, and sorting operations in a clearinghouse all provide sound bases for the establishment of standards.

To develop standards, one usually starts at the most detailed level possible to estimate the cost of a direct labor hour and a unit of material. Then, by determining the number of direct labor hours and units of material to be used in fabricating a unit of final product, the *standard direct cost* can be calculated. The standard direct cost is then augmented by an appropriately determined share of variable and fixed manufacturing overhead to develop the standard cost of a unit (or batch) of product. To prepare a production *budget,* standard unit costs are multiplied by planned production levels. The following example illustrates these points.

EXAMPLE. The Argosy Corporation produces widules. The standard costs of producing the "Regular" and the "Super" models are shown in Exhibit 1. If Argosy expects to produce 10,000 of both the Regular and Super models next period, the production budget would be $405,000 [= (10,000 × $16.50) + (10,000 × $24.00)].

ANALYSIS OF DEVIATIONS FROM STANDARD: VARIANCE ANALYSIS

Evaluation of deviations of actual results from the standards that have been formulated is accomplished using the techniques of *cost variance analysis.* Cost variances are of two general types: price or rate variances and quantity or efficiency variances. These variances merely express the differences between an actual cost and a standard cost. The price/quantity differentiation is employed to show the portions of the total variance attributable to (1) deviations from standard input prices and (2) deviations from standard input quantities. This is known as the *two-factor variance model.*

Two-Factor Variances in General. Let P_a = actual price, Q_a = actual quantity, P_s = standard price, and Q_s = standard quantity. Then

$$\text{Actual Cost} = P_a Q_a$$
$$\text{Standard Cost} = P_s Q_s$$
$$\text{Total Variance} = \text{Actual Cost} - \text{Standard Cost}$$
$$= P_a Q_a - P_s Q_s$$

This total variance is represented graphically in Figure 1.

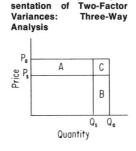

FIGURE 1   Graphic Representation of Two-Factor Variances: Three-Way Analysis

Three-Way Analysis.   The total variance is $P_a Q_a - P_s Q_s = A + B + C$. This total variance has three components.[1] These are enumerated below.

[1]Symbolically we can show that the total variance is equal to the sum of the three component variances. To show this, we set the total variance (left-hand side) equal to the three component variances (right-hand side), expand all terms, and cancel where appropriate.

$$P_a Q_a - P_s Q_s = (P_a - P_s) \times Q_s + (Q_a - Q_s) \times P_s + (P_a - P_s) \times (Q_a - Q_s)$$
$$P_a Q_a - P_s Q_s = P_a Q_s - P_s Q_s + Q_a P_s - Q_s P_s + P_a Q_a - P_a Q_s - P_s Q_a + P_s Q_s$$
$$P_a Q_a - P_s Q_s = P_a Q_a - P_s Q_s$$

EXHIBIT 1 Per-Unit Standard Costs

Input resource	Units required (how determined)		Price (source)		Extensions
		Regular Model			
Direct labor	1½ hours	(time and motion studies)	$4.00/hour	(union contract)	$ 6.00
Direct materials:					
A	2 lb	(engineering specifications and	$2.00/lb	(current replacement cost	4.00
B	2 lb	material usage studies)	1.00/lb	from suppliers)	2.00
Variable overhead	—		$1.75/DLH	(flexible budget)[1]	2.625
Fixed overhead	—		$1.25/DLH	(flexible budget and	1.875
				normal activity estimate)[2]	
Total					$16.50
		Super Model			
Direct labor	2 hours	(time and motion studies)	$4.00/hour	(union contract)	$ 8.00
Direct materials:					
A	5 lb	(engineering specifications and	$2.00/lb	(current replacement cost	10.00
		material usage studies)		from suppliers)	
Variable overhead	—		$1.75/DLH	(flexible budget)[1]	3.50
Fixed overhead	—		$1.25/DLH	(flexible budget and	2.50
				normal activity estimate)[2]	
Total					$24.00

NOTES:

[1]The company has determined that variable overhead is closely related to the number of direct labor hours (DLH) worked. The flexible overhead budget formula is: Overhead Cost = $43,750 + $1.75 × DLH, where $43,750 is the estimated fixed overhead for the period and variable overhead is estimated to increase by $1.75 for each direct labor hour worked.

[2]Normal activity is estimated at 35,000 DLH. Therefore, the fixed overhead rate per DLH is $1.25 (= $43,750/35,000 DLH).

Pure Price Variance A = (Actual   Price $-$ Standard   Price)
$\times$ Standard   Quantity
$= (P_a - P_s) \times Q_s$
Pure Quantity Variance B = (Actual Quantity $-$ Standard Quantity)
$\times$ Standard Price
$= (Q_a - Q_s) \times P_s$
Joint or Mixed Variance C = (Actual Price $-$ Standard Price) $\times$ (Actual Quantity
$-$ Standard Quantity)
$= (P_a - P_s) \times (Q_a - Q_s)$

The pure price variance isolates the deviation resulting from the difference between actual price and standard price at standard quantity. The pure quantity variance isolates the deviation due to the difference between actual quantity and standard quantity at standard price. The joint variance isolates the deviation attributable to both the difference between actual price and standard price *and* the difference between actual quantity and standard quantity. This breakdown is useful because it suggests that responsibility for the pure price variance should perhaps be assigned to the purchasing department and that the pure quantity variance is perhaps the responsibility of the production foreman. Because the joint variance is the result of deviations in both prices *and* quantities, some managements prefer to keep it separate and not attempt to assign the responsibility for it arbitrarily.

These variances are *favorable* or *unfavorable*, depending on their sign. A *positive* variance indicates that actual quantities and/or prices exceeded their standard amounts and is therefore *unfavorable* (denoted by U). Conversely, a *negative* variance is *favorable* (denoted by F) because it indicates that actual prices and/or quantities were less than their standard amounts.

Two-Way Analysis.   In most practical applications, the joint variance arising in the three-way analysis is assigned to either the price or the quantity factor. The advantages of doing so include (1) the desire to do away with the troublesome and sometimes confusing joint variance and (2) the belief that clearly defined areas of responsibility contribute to more effective control. Thus, by assigning the joint variance to one of the two factors, the rules of the game are established and there is no joint variance to serve as a point of contention or friction.

By convention, the joint variance is most often assigned to the price factor, although there is no compelling reason for doing so in all cases. When this is done, the resulting analysis of cost variances is two-way rather than three-way. Figure 2 shows this graphically, using the symbols described earlier. Again, the total variance is $P_aQ_a - P_sQ_s = A' + B$, and $A' = A + C$ in Figure 1. It now has two rather than three components.

FIGURE 2   Graphic Representation of Two-Factor Variances: Three-Way Analysis

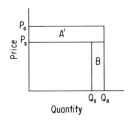

Price Variance A' = (Actual Price − Standard Price) × Actual Quantity
$= (P_a - P_s) \times Q_a$ (see footnote 2)
Quantity Variance B = (Actual Quantity − Standard Quantity) × Standard Price
$= (Q_a - Q_s) \times P_s$

Offsetting Variances.   Variances that offset one another often arise when an input resource having different quality and price than called for by the standards is used in production. For example, when a higher-priced, higher-quality resource is used, an unfavorable price variance and a favorable quantity variance may be reported, leading perhaps to a small total variance. Similarly, the use of a lower-priced, lower-quality resource would tend to generate favorable price variances and unfavorable quantity variances. Figure 3 shows the offsetting variances arising when the higher-priced, higher-quality resource is used.

FIGURE 3   Partially Offsetting Two-Factor Variances

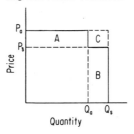

Referring to Figure 3, three-way analysis leads to an unfavorable pure price variance ($A + C$), a favorable quantity variance (B), and a favorable joint variance (C). Two-way analysis yields an unfavorable price variance (A—the pure price variance less the joint variance) and a favorable quantity variance (B).

The point of this exercise is that price and quantity variances should *not* be considered independently. If in fact the offsetting variances were caused by the substitution of a better-quality, higher-priced resource, it would be unfair to penalize the purchasing manager and reward the production manager solely on the basis of the reported variances. Indeed, if the substitution resulted in an overall favorable variance, the standards should be revised accordingly.

Throughout the remainder of this chapter, we adopt the convention that assigns the joint variance to the price factor (i.e., the two-way analysis). Now we turn to some specific applications.

Raw Material Variances.   Raw material variances are designed to show: (1) the dollar impact of deviations in actual prices paid for raw materials from the predetermined standard prices and (2) the dollar impact of deviations in actual quantities of raw materials used in production from the predetermined standard quantities.

Raw Material Price Variance.   There are two ways to calculate the raw material price variance. The method selected will depend on how quickly management wants price variance information.

[2]To show that this is equal to the sum of the pure price and joint variances, observe that

$$(P_a - P_s) \times Q_a = (P_a - P_s) \times Q_s + (P_a - P_s) \times (Q_a - Q_s)$$
$$(P_a - P_s) \times Q_a = P_aQ_s - P_sQ_s + P_aQ_a - P_aQ_s - P_sQ_a + P_sQ_s$$
$$(P_a - P_s) \times Q_a = P_aQ_a - P_sQ_a$$
$$(P_s - P_s) \times Q_a = (P_a - P_s) \times Q_a$$

1. The price variance may be computed and recorded when the material is *purchased,* rather than when it is *used.*

2. The price variance may be computed and recorded when the material is used in production.

Method 1 will obviously generate material price variance information more quickly than method 2. In addition, the choice of method affects the actual computation. In method 1, the actual quantity employed in the calculation is the actual quantity *purchased.* In method 2, the actual quantity in the calculation is the actual quantity *used* in production. These amounts are not necessarily identical. Therefore, the choice of method will affect the magnitude of the raw material price variance. The formula is

Raw Material Price Variance = (Actual Price − Standard Price)
$$\times \text{ Actual Quantity Purchased (or Used)}$$

The two methods can now be illustrated. Recall the standard cost data for the Argosy Corporation (Exhibit 1). Let us assume that 100,000 pounds of material A were purchased for $205,000 and that 76,232 pounds were used in production. In addition, 25,000 pounds of material B were purchased for $27,500 and 19,800 pounds were used in production. Under method 1 (based on quantity purchased), the total raw material price variance is $7,500 *U* as shown below.

Method 1

Price variance (material A) = ($2.05 − $2.00) × 100,000 = $5,000 *U*
Price variance (material B) = ($1.10 − $1.00) ×   25,000 =   2,500 *U*
Total raw material price variance (method 1) $7,500 *U*

With method 2, however, the total raw material price variance is

Method 2

Price variance (material A) = ($2.05 − $2.00) × 76,232 = $3,812 *U*
Price variance (material B) = ($1.10 − $1.00) × 19,800 =   1,980 *U*
Total raw material price variance (method 2) $5,792 *U*

Raw Material Quantity Variance.   In calculating the quantity variance, we are interested only in actual quantities *used* as compared with the standard quantities that should have been used. Therefore, there is only one method to be considered; the formula is

Raw Material Quantity Variance
$$= \text{(Actual Quantity − Standard Quantity)} \times \text{Standard Price}$$

The calculations for the Argosy Corporation follow. We assume that 11,000 "Regular" models and 9,600 "Super" models were produced. The standard quantity of material A was 70,000 [= (11,000 × 2) + (9,600 × 5)] pounds and 22,000 (= 11,000 × 2) pounds of material B.

Quantity variance (material A) = (76,232 − 70,000) × $2.00 = $12,464 *U*
Quantity variance (material B) = (19,800 − 22,000) × $1.00 = −2,200 *F*
Total raw material quantity variance $10,264 *U*

Observe that analysis of the individual variances, as opposed to an aggregation, can provide useful information. The total raw material quantity variance is $10,-264 *U*. This amount is the result of partially offsetting quantity variances for the two materials. In particular, the total quantity variance alone would conceal the unfavorable quantity variance for material A and the favorable quantity variance for material B. In other situations, reporting a single total raw material variance might conceal large offsetting price and quantity variances.

Direct Labor Variances.   Deviations between actual and standard direct labor cost can also be analyzed by determining the direct labor variances. The total direct labor variance (actual minus standard) has two dimensions, analogous to the raw material case. The price dimension is isolated through the calculation of a *wage rate variance,* and the quantity or efficiency dimension is highlighted by a *labor efficiency* variance. Let W_a = the actual wage rate, W_s = the standard wage rate, H_a = the actual direct labor hours worked, and H_s = the standard direct labor hours. Using the two-way analysis, the formulas for the two variances are

$$\text{Wage Rate Variance} = (\text{Actual Wage Rate} - \text{Standard Wage Rate})$$
$$\times \text{Actual Hours}$$
$$= (W_a - W_s) \times H_a$$
$$\text{Labor Efficiency Variance} = (\text{Actual Hours} - \text{Standard Hours})$$
$$\times \text{Standard Wage Rate}$$
$$= (H_a - H_s) \times W_s$$

For a numerical example, return to the Argosy Corporation. Actual direct labor cost incurred on the total of 20,600 units produced amounted to $154,836 (34,408 hours worked at an average wage rate of $4.50). The standard number of direct labor hours for the assumed output of 11,000 Regular models and 9,600 Super models was 35,700 [= $(11,000 \times 1\frac{1}{2}) + (9,600 \times 2)$]. The variances are calculated below.

Wage rate variance = ($4.50 − $4.00) × 34,408	= $17,204 *U*	
Labor efficiency variance = (34,408 − 35,700) × $4.00	= −5,168 *F*	
Total direct labor variance	$12,036 *U*	

In this case it is interesting to speculate about the causes of the variances. The unfavorable wage rate variance is obviously caused by a wage rate in excess of standard. This in turn might imply that better-qualified workers were employed. Indeed, the highly favorable labor efficiency variance lends credence to the suggestion that better-qualified workers were employed. If the total variance was favorable, then we should consider resetting standards to call for fewer hours of higher-paid labor.

Flexible Budget Preparation.   Setting standards for overhead is usually tied in with preparation of a *flexible budget* for overhead. The flexible budget expresses the relationship between total cost and levels of activity and is of the form

$$TC = a + bX$$

where TC = total cost
  a = estimated fixed portion of total cost
  b = estimated variable cost per unit of activity
  X = units of activity, such as direct labor hours or machine hours

To prepare a flexible budget for overhead, one collects the level of total overhead cost at various levels of activity. A scatter diagram prepared from these observations is shown in Figure 4. Once the data have been collected, a straight line is fit to the data points by means of regression analysis, visual curve fitting, or a similar method. The line through the data points in Figure 4 illustrates the relationship between total overhead cost and level of activity. The interpretation of this line is that for activity levels between X_1 and X_2, the fixed portion of overhead cost is a, the intercept, and the variable overhead cost per unit of activity is b, the slope of the estimated budget line. The total budgeted overhead for any amount of production between levels X_1 and X_2 can now be readily calculated, hence, the title *flexible* budget.

For the Argosy Corporation, the flexible budget equation for overhead is $TC = $43,750 + ($1.75 \times \text{DLH})$. Normal capacity is given as 35,000 DLH. The budgeted fixed overhead is $43,750; therefore the standard fixed overhead rate is

FIGURE 4   Illustration of Scatter Diagram and Estimated Flexible Budget Line

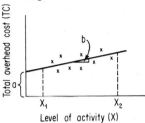

$1.25 (= $43,750/35,000) per DLH, and the standard variable overhead rate is $1.75 per DLH.

The flexible budget for overhead, then, provides us with standard cost data for variable and fixed overhead. We now proceed to develop and compute the overhead variances arising in a standard cost system.

Variable Overhead Variances.   Variable overhead includes all those indirect manufacturing costs that vary with the level of manufacturing activity. Because variable overhead is a production cost, it must be allocated to units produced on some reasonable basis. To do so, the historical relationship between overhead cost and various measures of activity is studied. The measure of activity that bears the closest relationship to movements in overhead costs is selected as the basis for allocating the overhead. Typical bases are direct labor hours worked or machine hours used. Preparation of a flexible budget will indicate the estimated variable overhead rate per unit of activity.

The total variable overhead variance will have two dimensions. One will result from a difference between the actual and standard overhead rates. We identify this as the *variable overhead budget variance* or, alternatively, the *variable overhead rate variance*. The second is the result of a deviation between the actual and standard measures of production activity on which the overhead allocation is based (e.g., direct labor hours). It is known as the *variable overhead efficiency variance*. Let $V_a =$ the actual variable overhead rate and $V_s =$ the standard variable overhead rate derived from the flexible budget. H_a and H_s are actual and standard direct labor hours, respectively. The formulas for the variable overhead variances follow.

Total Variable Overhead Variance = Actual Variable Overhead − Standard Variable Overhead Applied to Production

$$= V_a H_a - V_s H_s$$

Variable Overhead Budget Variance = (Actual Variable Overhead Rate − Standard Variable Overhead Rate) × Actual Direct Labor Hours

$$= (V_a - V_s) \times H_a$$

Variable Overhead Efficiency Variance = (Actual Direct Labor Hours − Standard Direct Labor Hours) × Standard Variable Overhead Rate

$$= (H_a - H_s) \times V_s$$

Observe that the variable overhead budget variance reduces to the difference between actual variable overhead (that is, $V_a H_a$) and budgeted variable overhead ($V_s H_a$). Similarly, the variable overhead efficiency variance is the difference between budgeted variable overhead (that is, $V_s H_a$) and variable overhead applied to production (that is, $V_s H_s$).

For the Argosy Corporation, actual variable overhead was $61,246 ($V_a =$ $61,246/34,408 = 1.78). Calculation of these variances yields the following.

Total variable overhead variance	= ($1.78 × 34,408) − ($1.75 × 35,700)	= $-1,229$ F
Variable overhead budget variance	= ($1.78 − $1.75) × 34,408	= $ 1,032 U
Variable overhead efficiency variance	= (34,408 − 35,700) × $1.75	= −2,261 F
		$-1,229$ F

Fixed Overhead Variances.   Fixed manufacturing overhead consists of indirect manufacturing costs that remain invariant over the relevant range of production. Examples include depreciation allocated on the basis of time (rather than units of production), rent on factory plant and equipment, and supervisors' salaries. Generally accepted accounting principles require that product costs be based on *full* or *absorption costing* in which fixed manufacturing costs are charged to production. Chapter 11 of this *Handbook* discusses an alternative product costing method, known as *direct* or *variable costing*. Under direct costing, fixed manufacturing overhead is considered to be a *period* rather than a *product* cost; the setting of fixed overhead standards and the calculation of fixed overhead variances therefore become unnecessary. Given current accounting principles, however, we proceed to discuss the fixed overhead variances that will arise when absorption costing is used.

There are two major fixed overhead variances. A *fixed overhead budget variance* shows the difference between actual and budgeted fixed overhead. The *fixed overhead volume variance* (sometimes referred to as the *idle capacity variance*) indicates the extent to which fixed overhead charged to production differs from budgeted fixed overhead.

Fixed overhead is allocated to production based on the activity measure employed in constructing the flexible budget. Because the flexible budget provides an estimate of total fixed manufacturing overhead, the standard fixed overhead rate per unit of activity still must be determined. Letting F_s = the standard fixed overhead rate, the formula is

$$F_s = \frac{\text{Budgeted Fixed Overhead}}{\text{``X,'' an activity level}}$$

Because the objective is to allocate fixed overhead to production, the denominator should represent some measure of capacity utilization. Further, the level of capacity utilization chosen will affect the size of F_s and hence the standard cost of production. The following measures of capacity utilization have been suggested as candidates for "X," the activity level in the denominator of the formula for computing the standard fixed overhead rate.

Expected capacity is the expected activity level for next period's production.

Theoretical capacity represents the activity level which would occur under the ideal conditions of full capacity utilization and no "downtime."

Normal capacity is an annual measure of the average production required to meet consumer demand over some intermediate time horizon, usually three to five years, assuming efficient operation of the plant and the usual amount of downtime.

Normal capacity is typically preferred over the alternative activity measures suggested above. Theoretical capacity represents an ideal that is rarely attained. Its use would seem to lead to consistent underabsorption of fixed overhead to production. Expected capacity is usually not suitable for this purpose because, if fixed overhead is relatively constant while production varies, the standard fixed overhead rate will also vary. Therefore, the use of a fixed overhead rate based on expected capacity could lead to variations in product cost at the same time as general cost conditions remained the same. Normal capacity, then, seems to provide the best basis for standard fixed overhead rates. It should lead to more consistent product costs without consistent underabsorption of fixed overhead.

We now present the fixed overhead variances using the following notation, assuming that the basis for allocation is normal capacity, measured in direct labor hours.

$$H_a = \text{actual direct labor hours worked}$$
$$H_s = \text{standard direct labor hours for the actual production}$$
$$H_n = \text{normal capacity in direct labor hours}$$
$$F_s = \text{standard fixed overhead rate}$$
$$= \frac{\underline{\text{Budgeted Fixed Overhead}}}{H_n}$$
$$F_a = \text{actual fixed overhead rate}$$

The total fixed overhead variance = actual fixed overhead less standard fixed overhead applied to production = $F_a H_a - F_a H_s$. It has two dimensions. One results from the difference between actual and budgeted fixed overhead and leads to the *fixed overhead budget variance.* The second, known as the *fixed overhead volume variance* (also called the *idle capacity variance*), arises from the difference between normal capacity in direct labor hours and standard direct labor hours for the actual production.[3]

The fixed overhead budget variance will measure the extent to which the *actual* fixed manufacturing overhead for a period differs from the amount *budgeted.*

Fixed Overhead Budget Variance = Actual Fixed Overhead
$$- \text{Budgeted Fixed Overhead}$$
$$= F_a H_a - F_s H_n$$

The fixed overhead volume variance, on the other hand, measures the over- or underabsorption of fixed overhead.

Fixed Overhead Volume Variance = Budgeted Fixed Overhead
$$- \text{Fixed Overhead Applied to Production}$$
$$= F_s H_n - F_s H_s = (H_n - H_s) \times F_s$$

The Argosy Corporation reported actual fixed overhead of $45,763 ($F_a = $45,763/34,408 = 1.33); the fixed overhead variances are as follows:

Total fixed overhead variance	= ($1.33 × 34,408) − ($1.25 × 35,700)	= $1,138 *U*
Fixed overhead budget variance	= ($1.33 × 34,408) − $43,750	= $2,013 *U*
Fixed overhead volume variance	= (35,000 − 35,700) × $1.25	= __875 *F*__
		$1,138 *U*

[3]Some authors choose to identify three, rather than two, fixed overhead variances. According to this scheme, the volume variance as explained in the chapter is broken into two components: a fixed overhead efficiency variance (= $F_s H_a - F_s H_s$) and a different overhead volume variance (= $F_s H_n - F_s H_a$). In this way, over- or underabsorption of fixed overhead is attributed to both direct labor performance as reflected in off-standard hours [for example, $F_s(H_a - H_s)$] and the over- or underutilization of capacity as measured by the difference between normal activity (hours) and hours actually worked [that is, $F_s(H_n - H_a)$]. See, for example, Gordon Shillinglaw, *Cost Accounting: Analysis and Control,* 3rd ed. (Richard D. Irwin, Homewood, Ill., 1972), pp. 478–479; and Sidney Davidson, James S. Schindler, and Roman L. Weil, *Fundamentals of Accounting,* 5th ed. (Dryden Press, Hinsdale, Ill., 1975), pp. 697–701.

These variances arose because (1) actual fixed overhead exceeded the budgeted amount and (2) standard DLH for the actual activity of the period exceeded normal activity. It has been argued that an unfavorable volume variance measures the cost of idle capacity. This would be true only by coincidence; the actual "cost" of the idle capacity is best represented by its *opportunity cost*—the net profit to be derived from its best alternative use, if any.

Three-Way Analysis of Overhead Variances.   It is often convenient to combine variable and fixed overhead variances into a single analysis for purposes of management review. This is readily accomplished by combining the variable and fixed overhead budget variances and presenting them along with the variable overhead efficiency variance and the fixed overhead volume variance.

We first observe that the total overhead variance is equal to the sum of the variable and fixed overhead budget variances, the variable overhead efficiency variance, and the fixed overhead volume variance. This is shown below.

$$
\begin{aligned}
\text{Total Overhead Variance} &= (V_a + F_a) \times H_a - (V_s + F_s) \times H_s \\
&= [(V_a - V_s) \times H_a + F_a H_a - F_s H_n] \\
&\quad + (H_a - H_s) \times V_s + (H_n - H_s) \times F_s \\
&= \text{Total Overhead Budget Variance} \\
&\quad + \text{Variable Overhead Efficiency Variance} \\
&\quad + \text{Fixed Overhead Volume Variance}
\end{aligned}
$$

These variances can be illustrated quite effectively by developing an exhibit similar to the one that follows.

Actual overhead		Budgeted overhead at actual output		Budgeted overhead at standard output		Overhead applied to product
$[(V_a + F_a) \times H_a]$	$(-)$	$(V_s H_a + F_s H_n)$	$(-)$	$(V_s H_s + F_s H_n)$	$(-)$	$[(V_s + F_s) \times H_s]$

Total overhead budget variance $(V_a - V_s) \times H_a + F_a H_a - F_s H_n$ Variable overhead efficiency variance $(H_a - H_s) \times V_s$ Fixed overhead volume variance $(H_n - H_s) \times F_s$

Substituting the numbers in the formulas, we see that

$$
\begin{aligned}
\text{Total Overhead Variance} &= 34{,}408 \times (\$1.78 + \$1.33) \\
&\quad - 35{,}700 \times (\$1.75 + \$1.25) \\
&= 107{,}009 - 107{,}100 \\
&= -91\ F \\
&= 1{,}032\ U + 2{,}013\ U - 2{,}261\ F - 875\ F \\
&= -91\ F
\end{aligned}
$$

Three-Factor Variances in General.   One limitation of two-factor variances is that they are restricted to analyzing the price and quantity dimensions of a single resource input. Even though two-factor variances can be individually computed for any number of, say, raw materials, they are not capable of recognizing the *interaction* between input resources, especially when these resources may be *substituted* for each other. Therefore, a given variance may be partially attributed to a difference between the actual and standard *mix* of input resources as well as to deviations between actual and standard prices and quantities. In the three-factor model, then, mix is the third factor to be considered.

To illustrate the general three-factor approach to cost variances, consider the following notation. We assume that two substitutable input resources are being used in production of an output product.

P_{xa}, P_{xs} = actual and standard unit prices of resource X
P_{ya}, P_{ys} = actual and standard unit prices of resource Y
Q_{xa}, Q_{xs} = actual and standard quantities of resource X
Q_{ya}, Q_{ys} = actual and standard quantities of resource Y
M_{xs}, M_{ys} = standard mix percentages for the resources X, Y

$$\left(= \frac{Q_{xs}}{Q_{xs} + Q_{ys}}, \frac{Q_{ys}}{Q_{xs} + Q_{ys}} \right)$$

Actual Cost = $P_{xa}Q_{xa} + P_{ya}Q_{ya}$
Standard Cost = $P_{xs}Q_{xs} + P_{ys}Q_{ys}$
Total Variance = $(P_{xa}Q_{xa} + P_{ya}Q_{ya}) - (P_{xs}Q_{xs} + P_{ys}Q_{ys})$

This total variance can be subdivided into three variances, assuming that the "joint variances" for the two resources are included in their price variances (as in the two-way analysis of the two-factor model).[4]

Price Variance $= (P_{xa} - P_{xs}) \times Q_{xa} + (P_{ya} - P_{ys}) \times Q_{ya}$
Quantity Variance $= [M_{xs} \times (Q_{xa} + Q_{ya}) - Q_{xs}] \times P_{xs}$
$+ [M_{ys} \times (Q_{xa} + Q_{ya}) - Q_{ys}] \times P_{ys}$
Mix Variance $= [Q_{xa} - M_{xs} \times (Q_{xa} + Q_{ya})] \times P_{xs}$
$+ [Q_{ya} - M_{ys} \times (Q_{xa} + Q_{ya})] \times P_{ys}$

The first term in each of the variances is for resource X, and the second is for resource Y. In the quantity variance, price and mix percentages are held constant; the deviation between actual quantity given the standard mix and standard quantity is highlighted. In the mix variance, price and quantity are held constant and the difference between actual quantity and actual quantity given the standard mix is shown.

The three-factor variance model has two main applications—production price, mix, and yield variances; and sales (or profit) price, mix, and quantity variances. These applications will be discussed in the next two sections. Note that three-factor variances may be computed in several different ways;[5] the method presented here is the general formulation.

Production Mix and Yield Variances. When various raw materials or types of labor are combined in production, it is often possible to vary the proportions of

---

[4]Notice that the price variance in the three-factor model is identical to that in the two-factor model. The quantity variance in the two-factor model has two components in the three-factor model—quantity *and* mix. Recall that the two-factor quantity variance for two resources = $(Q_{xa} - Q_{xs}) \times P_{xs} + (Q_{ya} - Q_{ys}) \times P_{ys}$. To show that this is equivalent to the combined three-factor quantity and mix variances, observe that

$$(Q_{xa} - Q_{xs}) \times P_{xs} + (Q_{ya} - Q_{ys}) \times P_{ys} = [M_{xs} \times (Q_{xa} + Q_{ya}) - Q_{xs}]$$
$$\times P_{xs} + [M_{ys} \times (Q_{xa} + Q_{ya}) - Q_{ys}] \times P_{ys} + [Q_{xa} - M_{xs} \times (Q_{xa} + Q_{ya})]$$
$$\times P_{xs} + [Q_{ya} - M_{ys} \times (Q_{xa} + Q_{ya})] \times P_{ys}$$

Expanding all terms yields

$$Q_{xa}P_{xs} - Q_{xs}P_{xs} + Q_{ya}P_{ys} - Q_{ys}P_{ys} = M_{xs}P_{xs} \times (Q_{xa} + Q_{ya})$$
$$- Q_{xs} \times P_{xs} + M_{ys}P_{ys} \times (Q_{xa} + Q_{ya}) - Q_{ys}P_{ys} + Q_{xa}P_{xs} - M_{xs}P_{xs}$$
$$\times (Q_{xa} + Q_{ya}) + Q_{ya}P_{ys} - M_{ys}P_{ys} \times (Q_{xa} + Q_{ya})$$

Cancellation of the M terms leaves

$$Q_{xa}P_{xs} - Q_{xs}P_{ys} + Q_{ya}P_{ys} - Q_{ys}P_{ys} = Q_{xa}P_{xs} - Q_{xs}P_{xs} + Q_{ya}P_{ys} - Q_{ys}P_{ys}$$

Thereby proving the equivalency.

[5]For a further discussion of the three-factor variance model, see Charles T. Horngren, *Cost Accounting*, 3rd ed. (Prentice-Hall, Englewood Cliffs, N.J., 1972), chap. 26.

these input resources by substituting plastic for wood, highly skilled for lesser-skilled labor, and so forth. These substitutions affect the quantities of resources used and may affect the quantities of outputs produced. In the two-factor variance model, the quantity variance reports resource usage that deviates from standard but does not attempt to explain this usage in terms of changes between the budgeted and actual mix of input resources. Nor does it focus on changes in quantities of finished product yielded by given amounts of input resources. The three-factor variance model permits disaggregation of the quantity variance into its *mix* and *yield* components that, in conjunction with the price variance, explain the total cost variance. The formulas are the same as those presented in the discussion of the three-factor variance model.

EXAMPLE.[6]   A paint company utilizes several liquid materials that are blended to yield base paint to which pigment may later be added as the various colors on the color chart are custom-mixed for customers in retail outlets. The company has the following standards.

Per 9-gallon batch of paint:

5 gallons of material X @ $ .70 =	$3.50
3 gallons of material Y @ 1.00 =	3.00
2 gallons of material Z @ .80 =	1.60
Total (10 gallons of input for 9 gallons of output; $.90 per gallon of output)	$8.10

During a recent production period, the following materials were purchased and used.

45,000 gallons of X at actual cost of $.72 =	$32,400
33,000 gallons of Y at actual cost of .99 =	32,670
22,000 gallons of Z at actual cost of .80 =	17,600
100,000	$82,670
Good output was 92,070 gallons at a standard cost of $.90 per gallon	82,863
Total material variance	$ − 193 F

Management has requested a complete analysis of the total material variance in terms of its price, mix, and yield components. Exhibit 2 shows the computations.

What can we say about mix and yield variances? Their primary function is to provide more detailed information for decision making, information that might be concealed if only two-factor quantity variances are computed. Where materials (and other factors of production) have different qualities or specifications and the production process permits some substitution, management can determine the effects of changes in the mix of inputs and whether such changes affect the finished-product yield of input resources. In the example, the fact that the actual mix of inputs deviated from the standard mix generated an unfavorable mix variance of $1,100. However, this was more than offset by an increase in yield, as shown by the favorable yield variance of −$1,863 F.

Sales and Profit Variances.   Up to this point, the chapter has concentrated on the determination, treatment, and evaluation of standard production cost variances. Such variances may be useful in highlighting potential problem areas as well as opportunities for cost savings. The technique of variance analysis is sufficiently general to be applied in an attempt to identify the various components of deviations from other types of standards or plans as well. For example, variance analysis

[6]This problem is adapted from one appearing in *ibid.*, pp. 888–890.

EXHIBIT 2   Computation of Material Price, Mix, and Yield Variances

Material Price Variances

Material	$(P_a - P_s) \times Q_a$
X	($.72 - $.70) \times 45,000 = 900 *U*
Y	$(.99 - 1.00) \times 33,000 = -330$ *F*
Z	$(.80 - .80) \times 22,000 = 0$
	Total material price variance $\underline{\$570}$ *U*

Material Yield Variances

Material	$[M_s \times (Q_{xa} + Q_{ya} + Q_{za}) - Q_s] \times P_s$
X	$[(.5 \times 100,000) - {}^*51,150] \times \$.70 = \$-805$ *F*
Y	$[(.3 \times 100,000) - {}^*30,690] \times 1.00 = -690$ *F*
Z	$[(.2 \times 100,000) - {}^*20,460] \times .80 = -368$ *F*
	Total material yield variance $-\$1,863$ *F*

$*51,150 = 50,000 \times (92,070/90,000)$
$30,690 = 30,000 \times (92,070/90,000)$
$20,460 = 20,000 \times (92,070/90,000)$

Material Mix Variances

Material	$[Q_a - M_s \times (Q_{xa} + Q_{ya} + Q_{za})] \times P_s$
X	$[45,000 - (.5 \times 100,000)] \times \$.70 = -\$3,500$ *F*
Y	$[33,000 - (.3 \times 100,000)] \times 1.00 = 3,000$ *U*
Z	$[22,000 - (.2 \times 100,000)] \times .80 = 1,600$ *U*
	Total material mix variance $\$1,100$ *U*

Total material variance = $\$570 - \$1,863 + \$1,100 = -\$193$ *F*

Note that the mix and yield variances sum to $-\$763$ *F*. This agrees with the material quantity variances computed using the two-factor model as shown below.

Material Quantity Variances (Two-Factor Model)

Material	$(Q_a - Q_s) \times P_s$
X	$(45,000 - 51,150) \times \$.70 = -\$4,305$ *F*
Y	$(33,000 - 30,690) \times 1.00 = 2,310$ *U*
Z	$(22,000 - 20,460) \times .80 = 1,232$ *U*
	Total material quantity variance $-\$763$ *F*

can be applied to comparisons between actual and planned sales, this year's and last year's net income, and so forth. Unlike production cost variances in a standard cost accounting system, sales and profit variances do not enter the accounts; they are supplementary analytic devices only. This section illustrates the use and computation of sales variances.

Sales variances are another application of the three-factor variance model. The total sales variance is the difference between actual and planned sales revenue. It can be broken down into three subvariances: sales mix variance, sales price variance, and sales quantity variance. The formulas are based on those developed in the section dealing with three-factor variances in general. However, the order of the terms (and their signs) in each variance is reversed here. This is to permit use of the convention that positive variances are unfavorable and negative variances favorable. In the sales case, if actual sales exceed budgeted (or standard) sales, the variance is *favorable* rather than *unfavorable* and should have a negative sign. The following notation will be used in the discussion of these variances for a two-product firm:

$$P_{xs}, P_{ys} = \text{standard unit price for products X, Y}$$
$$P_{xa}, P_{ya} = \text{actual unit price for products X, Y}$$
$$Q_{xs}, Q_{ys} = \text{budgeted sales quantity for products X, Y}$$
$$Q_{xa}, Q_{ya} = \text{actual sales quantity for products X, Y}$$
$$M_{xs}, M_{ys} = \text{budgeted mix percentages for products X, Y}$$
$$\left(= \frac{Q_{xs}}{Q_{xs} + Q_{ys}}, \frac{Q_{ys}}{Q_{xs} + Q_{ys}} \right)$$

Sales mix variances identify that portion of the total sales variance attributable to the actual product mix differing from the budgeted mix. The formula is

$$\text{Sales Mix Variance} = [M_{xs} \times (Q_{xa} + Q_{ya}) - Q_{xa}] \times P_{xs}$$
$$+ [M_{ys} \times (Q_{xa} + Q_{ya}) - Q_{ya}] \times P_{ys}$$

The two expressions in the formula are the sales mix variances for products X and Y, respectively. Observe that, for example, $M_{xs} \times (Q_{xa} + Q_{ya})$ is the amount of sales of product X that should have been made based on the budgeted mix. The difference between that quantity and the actual quantity of X that was sold, Q_{xa}, is attributable to a change in the mix.

Sales price variances show how much of the total sales variance is due solely to actual prices differing from their budgeted amounts; the formula is

$$\text{Sales Price Variance} = (P_{xs} - P_{xa}) \times Q_{xa} + (P_{ys} - P_{ya}) \times Q_{ya}$$

The two parts of the formula are the sales price variances for products X and Y, respectively.

Sales quantity variances are used to highlight the portion of the total sales variance arising because actual quantities sold differed from those budgeted. The formula is

$$\text{Sales Quantity Variance} = [Q_{xs} - M_{xs} \times (Q_{xa} + Q_{ya})] \times P_{xs}$$
$$+ [Q_{ys} - M_{ys} \times (Q_{xa} + Q_{ya})] \times P_{ys}$$

For the Argosy Corporation, we assume that product X is the Regular model and product Y is the Super model. Sales data appear in Exhibit 3. The variance calculations follow.

EXHIBIT 3   Sales Data for the Argosy Corporation

	Price		Quantity		Budgeted mix percentage
	Budget	Actual	Budget	Actual	
Regular model	$20.00	$19.00	10,000	11,000	50
Super model	30.00	30.50	10,000	9,600	50

$$\text{Sales Mix Variance} = [.5 \times (20{,}600) - 11{,}000] \times \$20 + [.5 \times (20{,}600) - 9{,}600] \times \$30$$
$$= \$7{,}000 \ U$$
$$\text{Sales Price Variance} = (\$20 - \$19) \times 11{,}000 + (\$30 - \$30.50) \times 9{,}600$$
$$= \$6{,}200 \ U$$
$$\text{Sales Quantity Variance} = [10{,}000 - .5 \times (20{,}600)] \times \$20 + [10{,}000 - .5 \times (20{,}600)] \times \$30$$
$$= -\$15{,}000 \ F$$

These three variances sum to $\$-1,800$ F, which agrees with the total sales variance = $[(10,000 \times \$20) + (10,000 \times \$30)] - [(11,000 \times \$19) + (9,600 \times \$30.50)] = \$-1,800$ F.

Sales variances can be especially useful when compared over time, because the relationship between selling prices and quantities sold may be revealing. Observe that the difference between this year's and last year's sales revenue may be analyzed by using last year's *actual* data as this year's *standards*. Some insight into the nature of the demand curve facing the firm may be gained, in terms of general price-quantity trade-offs as well as the *sensitivity* of sales volume to small (or large) price changes.

ACCOUNTING ENTRIES IN A STANDARD COST SYSTEM

Standard cost systems are usually characterized by valuation of inventories at standard cost. Hence, amounts charged and credited to raw materials, work-in-process, and finished goods inventories will be at standard. The variances will arise and be recorded when actual amounts differ from their standard amounts. Journal entries to record the production-related transactions of the Argosy Corporation are presented in Exhibit 4. Only the production cost variances, based on the two-factor model, are recorded. Sales variances do not enter the accounts.

Accounting Disposition of Variances.   At the end of the accounting period, firms employing standard cost systems must decide how to treat the variances that arise during the year. Materiality aside, the issue is whether the variances should be included in inventory or entered directly into income determination for the period. On the one hand, it can be argued that the cost of inefficient operations is not something that should be included in the valuation of inventories. Hence, quantity and efficiency variances are not viewed as inventoriable product costs and should be carried directly to the income statement. On the other hand, price variances are normally not a function of the internal organization of the firm but rather of the external market. Because the firm normally has no control over the external market, it appears that price variances do affect this period's product costs and should be inventoried by prorating them across the appropriate inventory accounts. In a hypothetical world characterized by accurate, currently attainable standards and no measurement errors in the accounting process, these arguments seem reasonable. In practice, however, the causes and subsequent treatment of variances may become arbitrary. A case can be made, therefore, for closing all the variances directly to income, normally through cost of goods sold. If, however, the variances are judged to be *material*, then the standard cost of production is frequently not viewed as an adequate measurement of production cost and the variances are used to adjust standard production cost to actual by a proration process. This proration process will now be illustrated.

Proration of Production Cost Variances.   Once it is decided to prorate standard cost variances across the inventory accounts, the mechanics are straightforward. Each variance is allocated to the various inventory accounts in accordance with the proportion of total cost in each account. For example, assume an unfavorable raw material price variance of $\$10,000$ U. The variance was based on total standard raw material purchases of $\$800,000$, of which $\$100,000$ remains in raw material inventory, $\$60,000$ in work in process, $\$150,000$ in finished goods inventory, and $\$490,000$ in cost of goods sold. The journal entry to prorate the price variance would be

Raw Material Inventory	1,250	
Work in Process	750	
Finished Goods Inventory	1,875	
Cost of Goods Sold	6,125	
Raw Material Price Variance		10,000

To allocate the unfavorable raw material price variance of $10,000 to the appropriate inventory accounts.

Other variances to be prorated would, of course, be treated in a similar manner.

EXHIBIT 4   Accounting Entries in the Argosy Corporation's Standard Cost System

Raw Material Inventory	225,000		(1)
Raw Material Price Variance	7,500		
Accounts Payable		232,500	

To record purchase of raw materials, charging inventory for their standard cost [$225,000 = (100,000 × $2) + (25,000 × $1)], crediting accounts payable for their actual cost ($232,500 = $205,000 + $27,500), and charging raw material price variance (using method 1) for the amount previously calculated.

Work in Process	162,000		(2)
Raw Material Quantity Variance	10,264		
Raw Material Inventory		172,264	

To record usage of raw material in production, charging work in process for the standard cost of the *standard* quantity [$162,000 = (70,000 × $2) + (22,000 × $1)], crediting raw material inventory for the standard cost of the *actual* quantity [$172,264 − (76,232 × $2) + (19,800 × $1)], and charging raw material quantity variance for the amount previously calculated.

Work in Process	142,800		(3)
Wage Rate Variance	17,204		
Labor Efficiency Variance		5,168	
Wages Payable		154,836	

To record direct labor production cost, charging work in process for the standard cost of the standard number of direct labor hours ($142,800 = 35,700 × $4), crediting wages payable for the actual direct labor cost ($154,836 = 34,408 × $4.50), and entering the variances as previously calculated.

Factory Overhead Control	107,009		(4)
Various Credits (Supplies, Payables, etc.)		107,009	

To record the actual factory overhead for the period, charging the overhead control account, and crediting asset and liability accounts.

Work in Process	107,100		(5)
Factory Overhead Applied		107,100	

To record the factory overhead applied to production, based on standard rates and standard direct labor hours [$107,100 = 35,700 × ($1.75 + $1.25)].

Factory Overhead Applied	107,100		(6)
Total Overhead Budget Variance	3,045		
Variable Overhead Efficiency Variance		2,261	
Fixed Overhead Volume Variance		875	
Factory Overhead Control		107,009	

To close out the factory overhead *control* and *applied* accounts. The difference of $91 is the total overhead variance which is composed of the three overhead variances previously calculated in the three-way analysis.

Finished Goods Inventory	411,900		(7)
Work in Process		411,900	

To transfer completed production at standard cost [$411,900 = (11,000 × $16.50) + (9,600 × $24)].

INTEGRATED FORMAT FOR PRESENTATION OF
SALES AND PRODUCTION COST VARIANCES[7]

This section illustrates a form of reporting to management for a standard cost system in which budgeted, standard, and actual results of operations can be readily grasped and reconciled. Such a report not only aids in the understanding of a standard cost system but is also a valuable tool for evaluation and control purposes.

The Argosy Corporation's data are used for illustration. To simplify the analysis, we assume no beginning or ending inventories and that all standard cost variances are charged to cost of goods sold. Furthermore, we illustrate this comprehensive analysis as applied to both a conventional absorption costing system and a variable costing system (discussed in Chapter 11 of this *Handbook*).

Shortly after the close of the reporting period, the following summary data were developed for managerial analysis.

	Budget	*Actual*	*Variance*
Sales	$500,000	$501,800	−$ 1,800 *F*
Cost of goods sold	$405,000	$441,609	$36,609 *U*
Selling, general, and administrative expenses	50,000	48,540	− 1,460 *F*
Total expenses	$455,000	$490,149	$35,149 *U*
Net income	$ 45,000	$ 11,651	$33,349 *U*

These data are based on the detailed information appearing in Exhibit 5. Exhibit 6 shows the calculation of all relevant variances described in the preceding sections of the chapter. Exhibits 7 and 8 provide the disaggregation of the summary data and variances into their respective components for the absorption and variable costing systems, respectively.

Examination of Exhibits 7 and 8 discloses that overall variance analysis is facilitated by including budget data at the forecast level of operations (column A) as well as budget data at the actual level of operations (flexible budget—column B). In this way, we are able to isolate variances due solely to the difference between the planned and actual *level* of operations (column D—these could be called operating volume variances) from the conventional cost and sales price variances (column E). Notice that there is no fixed overhead volume variance in the variable costing system; the totals in column E differ by the amount of the fixed overhead volume variance, −$875 *F*.

EX POST VARIANCE ANALYSIS

As we have seen, standard cost and profit variances derived from comparisons between actual and standard costs and prices are useful devices for monitoring and controlling operations. In many situations, however, traditional cost variance analysis is of limited value. Although it will disclose deviations between planned and actual results, it does not incorporate the *revision of plans* to fit the actual circumstances as they unfold. In other words, traditional variance analysis does not disclose the difference between actual results and *what should have been done* had all facts known at the end of the period been incorporated into the planning process.

Joel Demski has developed a framework for a variance system distinguished by its ability to encompass *ex post analysis*.[8] *Ex post* analysis refers to incorporation of

---

[7]The author thanks Professor L. Todd Johnson for his help in developing this integrated format.

[8]Joel S. Demski, "Analyzing the Effectiveness of the Traditional Standard Cost Variance Model," *Management Accounting*, October 1967, and Joel S. Demski, "An Accounting System Structured on a Linear Programming Model," *Accounting Review*, October 1967.

EXHIBIT 5   Argosy Corporation: Sales—Production Data

Product	Budget forecast		Actual	
	X	Y	X	Y
Sales (physical units)	10,000	10,000	11,000	9,600
Average unit selling price	$20.00	$30.00	$19.00	$30.50
Production (physical units)	10,000	10,000	11,000	9,600
Unit production cost	$16.50	$24.00	$17.144	$26.1788

Unit Production Cost of X

	Standard	Actual
Pounds of material A	2.0	2.2
Cost per pound of material A	$ 2.00	$ 2.05
Pounds of material B	2.0	1.8
Cost per pound of material B	$ 1.00	$ 1.10
Materials cost	$ 6.00	$ 6.49
Hours of direct labor (DLH)	1.5	1.4
Wage rate per hour	$ 4.00	$ 4.50
Labor cost	$ 6.00	$ 6.30
Variable overhead per DLH	$ 1.75	$ 1.78
Fixed overhead per DLH	$ 1.25	$ 1.33
Variable overhead cost	$ 2.625	$ 2.492
Fixed overhead cost	$ 1.875	$ 1.862
Total unit production cost	$16.50	$17.144

Unit Production Cost of Y

Pounds of material A	5.0	5.42
Cost per pound of material A	$ 2.00	$ 2.05
Material cost	$10.00	$11.111
Hours of direct labor (DLH)	2.00	1.98
Wage rate per hour	$ 4.00	$ 4.50
Labor cost	$ 8.00	$ 8.91
Variable overhead/DLH	$ 1.75	$ 1.78
Fixed overhead/DLH	$ 1.25	$ 1.33
Variable overhead cost	$ 3.50	$ 3.5244
Fixed overhead cost	$ 2.50	$ 2.6334
Total unit production cost	$24.00	$26.1788

Other Data

1. Fixed overhead is estimated at $43,750. The standard fixed overhead application rate is based on normal capacity of 35,000 DLH.
2. Selling, general, and administrative expenses have estimated fixed and variable components of $30,000 and $1 per unit sold, respectively.

results based on what should have been done into a variance analysis. To be a valid tool of analysis in a given firm, the following basic conditions should exist:

1. The firm employs a relatively formal and explicit decision-making process.
2. Management is capable of determining whether observed variations are controllable and avoidable or not.
3. Feedback information is viewed as being useful.
4. The search for alternative decisions is structured by the decision-making process.

The discussion here is intended to introduce the reader to the technique and motivate its use in practice. Interested readers should consult Demski's original papers for further details.

Ex Post Analysis in a Simple Marginal Analysis Model.   Chapter 4 of this *Handbook* reviews the economic theory of the firm. Among other things, the theory concludes that maximum profits are earned when production is set at the point where marginal cost (MC) = marginal revenue (MR) and the price is set at the point where a vertical line from the optimum production point (X^*) intersects the

EXHIBIT 6   Argosy Corporation: Calculation of Variances

Sales Variances

Sales price variance:

Product X: ($20.00 − $19.00) × 11,000	=	$11,000 *U*
Product Y: ($30.00 − $30.50) × 9,600	=	−4,800 *F*
		$ 6,200 *U* (1)

Sales mix variance:

Product X: [(.5 × 20,600)−11,000] × $20	=	−$14,000 *F*
Product Y: [(.5 × 20,600)− 9,600] × $30	=	21,000 *U*
		$ 7,000 *U*

Sales quantity variance:

Product X: [10,000 − .5 × (20,600)] × $20	=	$−6,000 *F*
Product Y: [10,000 − .5 × (20,600)] × $30	=	−9,000 *F*
		−$15,000 *F*
Total sales operating volume variance	=	$−8,000 *F* (2)
Total sales variance = $6,200 *U* − $8,000 *F*	=	−$1,800 *F* (3)

Cost Variances

Material price variance:

Material A: ($2.05 − $2.00) × 100,000	=	$ 5,000 *U*
Material B: ($1.10 − $1.00) × 25,000	=	2,500 *U*
		$ 7,500 *U*

Material quantity variance:

Material A: (76,232 − 70,000) × $2.00	=	$12,464 *U*
Material B: (19,800 − 22,000) × $1.00	=	−2,200 *F*
		$10,264 *U*
Total material cost variance	=	$17,764 *U* (4)
Wage rate variance: ($4.50 − $4.00) × 34,408	=	$17,204 *U*

Labor efficiency variance:

(34,408 − 35,700) × $4.00	=	$−5,168 *F*
Total labor cost variance	=	$12,036 *U* (5)

Overhead budget variance:

Variable overhead: ($1.78 − $1.75) × 34,408	=	$ 1,032 *U*
Fixed overhead: ($1.33 × 34,408) − $43,750	=	2,013 *U* (8)
Total overhead budget variance		$ 3,045 *U*

Variable overhead efficiency variance:

(34,408 − 35,700) × $1.75	=	−$2,261 *F*

Fixed overhead volume variance:

(35,000 − 35,700) × $1.25	=	−875 *F*
Total variable overhead variance = $1,032 *U* − $2,261 *F*	=	−$1,229 *F* (7)
Total fixed overhead variance = −$2,013 *F* + $875 *U*	=	1,138 *U*
Total overhead variance		−$ 91 *F* (6)

demand curve (*D*). Figure 5 shows these relations, assuming constant marginal cost.

Suppose that $P^* = \$7$, $MC = \$4$ (assumed not to vary over the range of production possibilities), and $X^* = 100,000$. If selling price is set at $7, then 100,000 units can be sold and the highest profit will be earned. If fixed costs are $120,000, profit will equal $180,000 [= ($7 − $4) × 100,000 − $120,000]. The firm's budget, therefore, would project a standard selling price of $7, a standard variable cost of $4, and net profit of $180,000.

Now suppose that, shortly after the end of the period, the final accounting reports are received. All projected plans were carried out except that cost during the period was less than the standard by $.20 and actual profit was $200,000. Thus there was a favorable profit variance of −$20,000 (= $180,000 − $200,000) caused by a favorable cost variance of −$20,000 [= ($3.80 − $4.00) × 100,000].

EXHIBIT 7 Argosy Corporation Comprehensive Variance Analysis—Absorption Costing

	A	B	C	D	E	F
					Variances	
	Forecast budget X: 10,000 units Y: 10,000 units	Flexible budget X: 9,000 units Y: 11,000 units	Actual X: 9,600 units Y: 11,000 units	Operating volume (A—B)	Sales price—cost (B—C)	Total (A—C)
Sales	$500,000	$508,000	$501,800	$8,000 F (2)	$ 6,200 U (1)	$ 1,800 F (3)
Less:						
Cost of sales						
Materials	$160,000	$162,000	$179,764	$2,000 U	$17,764 U (4)	$19,764 U
Labor	140,000	142,800	154,836	2,800 U	12,036 U (5)	14,836 U
Overhead	105,000	107,100	107,009	2,100 U	91 F (6)	2,009 U
Total	$405,000	$411,900	$441,609	$6,900 U	$29,709 U	$36,609 U
Less:						
Selling, general, and administrative expenses	$ 50,000	$ 50,600	$ 48,540	$ 600 U	$ 2,060 F	$ 1,460 F
Net Income	$ 45,000	$ 45,500	$ 11,651	$ 500 F	$33,849 U	$33,349 U

NOTE: Numerical references to the right of the variances are to the detailed variance calculations in Exhibit 6.

EXHIBIT 8 Argosy Corporation Comprehensive Variance Analysis—Variable Costing

	A	B	C	D	E	F
					Variances	
	Forecast budget X: 10,000 units Y: 10,000 units	Flexible Budget X: 9,600 units Y: 11,000 units	Actual X: 9,600 units Y: 11,000 units	Operating volume (A—B)	Sales price—cost (B—C)	Total (A—C)
Sales	$500,000	$508,000	$501,800	$8,000 F (2)	$ 6,200 U (1)	$ 1,800 F (3)
Less:						
Variable cost of sales						
Materials	$160,000	$162,000	$179,764	$2,000 U	$17,764 U (4)	$19,764 U
Labor	140,000	142,800	154,836	2,800 U	12,036 U (5)	14,836 U
Overhead	61,250	62,475	61,246	1,225 U	1,229 F (7)	4 F
Less:						
Variable selling, general, and administrative expenses	20,000	20,600	19,800	600 U	800 F	200 F
Total variable costs	$381,250	$387,875	$415,646	$6,625 U	$27,771 U	$34,396 U
Contribution margin	$118,750	$120,125	$ 86,154	$1,375 F	$33,971 U	$32,596 U
Less:						
Fixed overhead	$ 43,750	$ 43,750	$ 45,763	—	$ 2,013 U (8)	$ 2,013 U
Fixed selling, general, and administrative expenses	30,000	30,000	28,740	—	1,260 F	1,260 F
Total fixed costs	$ 73,750	$ 73,750	$ 74,503	—	$ 753 U	$ 753 U
Net income	$ 45,000	$ 46,375	$ 11,651	$1,375 F	$34,724 U	$33,349 U

NOTE: Numerical references to the right of the variances are to the detailed variance calculations in Exhibit 6.

FIGURE 5   Illustration of *Ex Ante* Optimal
Price-Quantity Policy.

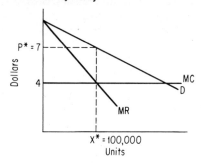

However, if the firm had known about and reacted to the decline in its cost, it
would have projected a different price/quantity policy, as shown in Figure 6. Profit
under this new policy would have been $221,000 [= ($6.90 − $3,80) × 110,000 −
$120,000]. Traditional variance analysis, however, would report only the favorable
profit variance of −$20,000 (= $180,000 − $200,000) and would attribute it to the
favorable cost variance of −$20,000 [= ($3.80 − $4.00) × 100,000].

FIGURE 6   Illustration of *Ex Post* Optimal
Price-Quantity Policy

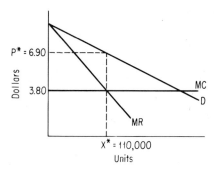

Ex post analysis explicitly recognizes the existence of the revised optimal policy
given the actual data for the period. Symbolically, let

$$NI_a = ex\ ante\ \text{or planned profit} = \$180,000$$
$$NI_o = actual\ \text{or observed profit} = \$200,000$$
$$NI_p = ex\ post\ \text{or revised profit} = \$221,000$$

Therefore,

$$NI_a − NI_o = (NI_a − NI_p) + (NI_p − NI_o)$$
$$\$180,000 − \$200,000 = (\$180,000 − \$221,000) + (\$221,000 − \$200,000)$$
$$−\$20,000 = −\$41,000 + \$21,000$$

The term on the left-hand side, $NI_a − NI_o$, is the traditional profit variance
equal to the difference between planned and actual profit. The first term on the
right-hand side, $NI_a − NI_p$, the difference between *ex ante* and *ex post* optimum
profit, is a rough indicator of the accuracy of the planning or forecasting process.
It should highlight the need for additional forecasting and estimation effort. The
second term on the right-hand side, $NI_p − NI_o$, is the difference between what the
firm could have accomplished with the additional information (in this case the

lower production cost) and what actually was accomplished. It is a measure of *opportunity cost,* or the cost of following a nonoptimal policy. The forecasting variance, $NI_a - NI_p$, although "favorable," suggests considerable room for improvement. The opportunity cost variance, $NI_p - NI_o$, is unfavorable.

Before attempting to use these variances for the purpose of performance evaluation, care must be taken to distinguish between those factors that are controllable (and avoidable) and those factors that are noncontrollable (and not avoidable). For example, determination that the decline in cost was random and, therefore, not controllable, may relieve forecasting personnel of responsibility for the forecasting variance. Similarly, if institutional arrangements limit the flexibility to revise selling prices, personnel involved in pricing decisions may be exonerated of responsibility for the opportunity cost variance.

One might object that *ex post* analysis is "second-guessing" and should be discouraged because it is unfair. On the other hand, regular and continuing use of *ex post* analysis may aid in identifying these functions where systematic and recurring problems are evident and could be corrected.

THE DECISION TO INVESTIGATE COST VARIANCES

Cost variances provide signals to management. These signals are typically used in a "management by exception" context. "Significant" variances suggest areas where corrective action may be needed to reduce excessive costs and areas where standards may be tightened and cost savings achieved. Of course, reaction to reported variances for one of the purposes mentioned above usually involves a commitment of time, effort, and financial resources. Each manager is therefore faced with a decision to be made—when is a variance "significant" enough to justify the cost of an investigative and perhaps corrective undertaking? This problem is further complicated by the unfortunate circumstance that management rarely knows with certainty whether a given variance is due to a random fluctuation or to an underlying systematic problem.

Many firms have developed rules of thumb to assist them in determining the significance of variances. Such rules may dictate investigations if the absolute size of the variance is greater than a certain amount or if the ratio of the variance to the total standard cost exceeds some predetermined percentage. These rules, of course, are the outcome of a heuristic approach to coping with the *significance* and *uncertainty* aspects of evaluating the signals provided by cost variances.

In this section, two more formal methods for dealing with this problem are developed.[9] Bear in mind that there are lessons to be learned from studying these methods, even if their practical application seems limited. The methods are most helpful in suggesting ways to think about the structure the problem that may not be self-evident.

The "In-Control–Out-of-Control" Dichotomy. Any decision to investigate the causative factors behind a cost variance should be based on the belief that the process generating the variance is, in some sense, *out of control.* Both favorable and unfavorable variances can signal an out-of-control process; hence both are candidates for investigation.

A cost variance can have many different values, some of which are more likely to occur than others. Indeed, the outcomes of a process generating cost variances can be visualized as a *frequency* or *probability* distribution. Figure 7 illustrates graphically the in-control–out-of-control dichotomy with probability distributions.

[9]See Mohamed Onsi, "Quantitative Models for Accounting Control," *Accounting Review,* April 1967, pp. 321–330, for a more rigorous discussion and comparison of the quantitative approaches to investigating cost variances introduced in this section.

FIGURE 7   In-Control–Out-of-Control Distributions of Cost Variances

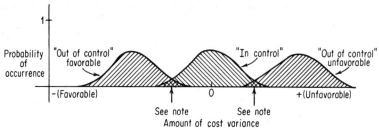

Note: Observed variances lying in these ranges can result from either an in-control or out-of-control process. The uncertainty stems from whether such observations are random and in control or systematic and out of control.

Variances having values lying with the *in-control* (middle) distribution arise as a result of normal random fluctuations in a well-behaved process. Values lying within either the favorable or unfavorable *out-of-control* (outer) distributions are not the random outcomes of a well-behaved process. Rather, they represent the outcomes from a process different from that specified by the standards. Thus it may be necessary to revise the standards or correct an underlying problem in order that the process once again is well-behaved. Uncertainty exists with respect to values lying within either crosshatched area. The process may be *either* in control *or* out of control when such values occur.

Costs and Benefits from Investigating Variances.   The decision to investigate a process reporting a cost variance should follow from a consideration of the potential costs and benefits likely to flow from an investigation. An attempt must be made to estimate these costs and benefits as accurately as possible.

Cost of an Investigation.   Obtaining additional information is rarely costless. Additional personnel may have to be hired or overtime paid. Expensive engineering studies and disassembly of equipment or manufacturing configurations may be required. If the investigation is performed and a problem discovered, correction of the problem may necessitate further outlays. Once the extent of the physical resources required is determined, the additional or incremental *out-of-pocket* costs associated with the investigative effort must be computed. Only incremental outlays, not including allocated costs or any other nonavoidable costs, are relevant here. A correct analysis balances the incremental cost of the investigative effort against the incremental benefits from correcting an out-of-control process (or the incremental cost of permitting an out-of-control process to continue).

Benefits from an Investigation.   What is to be gained if an out-of-control process is discovered and corrected? There are two main considerations here: the amount to be saved each period and the number of periods the savings are expected to continue.

Reduction in an unfavorable variance means that the gap between actual and standard cost is being decreased by a reduction in actual cost each period. Correction of a favorable variance causes the gap between actual and standard cost to narrow as standard costs are reduced and actual costs each period are subsequently held at their low level. In the event the entire variance cannot, on the average, be eliminated, only that portion that can be eliminated is a savings. Furthermore, only reductions in *out-of-pocket* costs are true savings. Changes in rates of nonavoidable and allocated costs generally have no economic benefit.

Once the expected benefit per period is estimated, the number of periods for which the benefit will continue must be determined. This is a crucial consideration. If variances are reported frequently, perhaps monthly or quarterly, correction of an out-of-control process should produce savings in several of these periods. Although the single-period saving may appear unimpressive, the *present value* of a series of periodic savings may be much more impressive. If the savings are expected to occur over more than three to six months, the time value of money begins to play a role. The cost of an investigation is an immediate outlay; it must be balanced against the expected savings in present value terms.

The Control Chart Approach.   The techniques of *statistical quality control* provide a useful tool that can be of use to management in attempting to evaluate cost variances. This tool is the *control chart* and is often used to monitor physical processes through a comparison of certain critical output specifications with the predetermined acceptable tolerances. So long as measurements of these specifications lie between the upper and lower control limits on the chart, the process is assumed to be in control.

The control chart is a useful device for checking whether reported cost variances indicate that the underlying physical process is in or out of control. If it can be assumed that observed variances are distributed in accordance with the normal or bell-shaped probability distribution (like those displayed in Figure 7), the mean and standard deviation of a group of observations can be used to set upper and lower central limits for the variance. In a normal distribution, about 68.3 percent of the observations lie within one standard deviation (σ) on either side of the mean ($\overline{X}$), about 95.5 percent lie within $\overline{X} \pm 2\sigma$, and about 99.7 percent lie within $\overline{X} \pm 3\sigma$. The control limits will be set at $\overline{X} \pm k\sigma$, where k reflects management's beliefs about the relative costs and benefits from an investigation. If costs are high relative to benefits, k will be large (e.g., 3), ensuring that relatively few investigations will be made and that some out-of-control situations may remain uncorrected. If benefits are high relative to costs, k will be lower (e.g., 1.5 or 2), ensuring that more investigations will be made and that some in-control situations will be investigated.

EXAMPLE.   Labor efficiency variances over the past 12 months are listed below.

Month	Labor efficiency variance
1	$ 400 U
2	700 U
3	1,000 U
4	−500 F
5	−100 F
6	1,000 U
7	−1,100 F
8	−1,000 F
9	600 U
10	800 U
11	−900 F
12	−900 F
	0

The mean of these outcomes is $0 and the estimated standard deviation is $838.[10] If these outcomes follow a normal distribution with $\overline{X} = 0$ and $\sigma = 838$, then, for example, 2σ control limits would be $1,676 (upper) and −$1,676 (lower). So long as the periodic labor efficiency variances remain inside these limits, the probability that the process is in control is .95, on the grounds that, according to chance, 95 percent of the "in-control" periodic variances fall within these limits.

[10]The estimated standard deviation, s, is calculated as follows:

$$s = \sqrt{\sum_{i=1}^{12} \frac{(X_i - \bar{X})^2}{n - 1}} \approx 838$$

The control chart is most useful when it is based on a large sample of observations.[11] If weekly variances are reported, a large sample may be easily obtained. Otherwise, monitoring the underlying physical process with a control chart may help in explaining unusually large variances when they occur. When control charts are used to monitor physical processes and each "observation" is a sample of physical measurements, the following statistics are called for:

$\overline{X}_i$ = arithmetic mean of the ith sample

$\overline{\overline{X}}$ = arithmetic mean of the sample means (the $\overline{X}_i$'s)

R_i = range of the ith sample (high value minus low value)

$\overline{R}$ = arithmetic mean of the sample ranges (the R_i's).

It is not necessary to compute the standard deviations, as conversion tables are available for various "σ limits" and based on the normal probability distribution.[12] The formulas for the upper and lower control limits (UCL and LCL) of $\overline{X}$ and R follow.

$$\text{UCL}_{\overline{X}} = \overline{\overline{X}} + A_2\overline{R} \qquad \text{UCL}_R = D_4\overline{R}$$
$$\text{LCL}_{\overline{X}} = \overline{\overline{X}} - A_2\overline{R} \qquad \text{LCL}_R = D_3\overline{R}$$

The A and D factors are taken from the appropriate table on the row corresponding to the number of items in each sample.

The Decision-Theoretic Approach. The main weakness of the control chart approach to assessing the significance of cost variances is that it fails to dictate a course of action. By remaining silent on the cost-benefit aspects of a variance investigation situation, the chart does not disclose when the economics of the situation justify an investigation. The chart can suggest that a process is out of control, but it cannot suggest whether an investigation is warranted.

Over the last 15 years, the application of statistical decision theory to investigation decisions has been discussed by a number of authors.[13]

Central to the approach is the use of a *payoff table* or *matrix*, which explicitly considers costs and benefits. Such a table appears in Exhibit 9. There are two possible states of nature—the process is in control or out of control—and two possible actions—investigate or do not investigate.

This formulation rests on several simplifying assumptions. First, the costs, *C, M,* and *L,* are assumed to be constant. Second, an out-of-control process will always be

---

[11]The assumption that the observations follow a normal probability distribution may not be justified when a small sample is involved. If normality cannot be assumed, *Chebyshev's inequality* may be used to determine control limits where the underlying distribution is unknown. This inequality states that $1 - (1/k^2)$ of the distribution lies between $\overline{X} \pm k\sigma$ for $k > 1$. If, in the numerical example, we desired 95 percent control limits, then

$$.95 = 1 - 1/k^2$$
$$.05 = 1/k^2$$
$$k^2 = 20$$
$$k \approx 4.5$$

The upper control limit would be $3,771, and the lower control limit would be −$3,771. These limits are 225 percent as wide as those computed under the assumption of normality!

[12]See Eugene Grant, *Statistical Quality Control,* 3rd ed. (McGraw-Hill Book Company, New York, 1964), for a complete treatment of statistical quality control and as a source of the conversion tables.

[13]See, for example, chap. 2 of Harold Bierman, Jr., and Thomas R. Dyckman, *Managerial Cost Accounting* (The Macmillan Company, New York, 1971).

EXHIBIT 9   Cost Payoff Table for Variance Investigation Decision

	States	
Actions	In control	Out of control
Investigate	C	$C + M$
Do not investigate	0	L

C = cost of an investigation
M = cost of correcting an out-of-control process
L = cost of permitting an out-of-control process to continue (or benefits foregone by not investigating and correcting an out-of-control process)

detected by an investigation and can always be corrected. Third, once the process goes out of control, it remains out of control until corrected.

Our objective here will be to compute the expected cost associated with each action and select that action having the lowest expected cost. To perform the calculations, we need estimates of the probabilities that the process is in control, P, and out of control $(1 - P)$. These probabilities will normally be based on the decision maker's experience that the process is in control, say, 90 percent of the time (that is, $P = .9$, $1 - P = .1$).

$$\text{Expected Cost (Investigation)} = PC + (1 - P)(C + M)$$
$$= C + (1 - P)M$$
$$\text{Expected Cost (No Investigation)} = 0 + (1 - P)L$$
$$= (1 - P)L$$

If $C + (1 - P)M$ is less than $(1 - P)L$, investigation is dictated; otherwise, do not investigate.

Note that by setting the expected costs of the two actions equal to each other, we can solve for the value of P for which the decision maker is indifferent between the two actions. Calculation of this breakeven probability, P^*, follows.

Let

$$C + (1 - P)M = (1 - P)L$$
$$C = (1 - P)(L - M)$$
$$\frac{C}{L - M} = 1 - P$$
$$1 - \frac{C}{L - M} = P^*$$

Given the costs C, M, and L, the decision maker who believes that the in-control probability is less than P^* knows that investigating has the lowest expected cost and may proceed accordingly.

EXAMPLE.   An unfavorable raw material quantity variance of $10,000 has been reported. If the cause of the variance can be found and corrected, estimated cost savings of $4,000 can be realized (L). Out-of-pocket costs for investigation (C) and correction (M) are $600 and $1,500, respectively. Management believes that the process is in control 80 percent of the time. What action, if any, should be taken?

Expected Cost (Investigation)
$$= \$600 + .2 \times \$1,500$$
$$= \$900$$
Expected Cost (No Investigation) $= (1 - P)L$
$$= .2 \times \$4,000$$
$$= \$800$$

Therefore, the model suggests that the variance should not be investigated.

Knowledge of the breakeven probability, P^*, can be of value here.

$$P^* = 1 - \frac{C}{L - M}$$
$$1 - \frac{\$600}{\$4,000 - \$1,500}$$
$$= 1 - .24$$
$$= .76$$

Suppose that the manager feels that the estimate of $P = .8$ is too high given recent material usage trends. If it is closer to .7 than .8, and less than P^*, the manager may decide to investigate anyway.

If C and M are fairly constant over time and for various types of investigations, it is possible to prepare a decision chart using values of P^* computed at various amounts of L to identify combinations of P^* and L for which investigation leads to the lowest expected cost.[14]

EXAMPLE.   Suppose that L is typically 40 percent of a reported variance if the underlying process is out of control. Then for variances of $8,000, $10,000, $12,000, and $14,000, L becomes $3,200, $4,000, $4,800, and $5,600. The values of P^* for $C = \$600$, $M = \$1,500$, and the above amounts of L are computed below. The decision chart is shown in Figure 8.

FIGURE 8   Cost Variance Investigation
Decision Chart

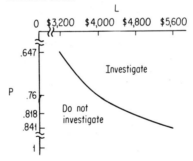

$$P^*{}_{3,200} = 1 - \frac{\$600}{\$3,200 - \$1,500} = .647$$

$$P^*{}_{4,000} = 1 - \frac{\$600}{\$4,000 - \$1,500} = .76$$

$$P^*{}_{4,800} = 1 - \frac{\$600}{\$4,800 - \$1,500} = .818$$

$$P^*{}_{5,600} = 1 - \frac{\$600}{\$5,400 - \$1,500} = .841$$

[14]See Nicholas Dopuch, Jacob Birnberg, and Joel S. Demski, *Cost Accounting*, 2nd ed. (Harcourt Brace Jovanovich, New York, 1974), pp. 505–506; and Harold Bierman, Jr., Lawrence E. Fouraker, and Robert K. Jaedicke, "A Use of Probability and Statistics in Performance Evaluation," *Accounting Review*, July 1961, pp. 409–417.

The interpretation of this chart is that for combinations of P and L to the left of the indifference line, either P is too large or L is too small to trigger an investigation. The converse is true to the right of the indifference line.

Extensions of the Basic Decision-Theoretic Approach.   Admittedly, the model presented here is a simplified one. Some of the extensions to this approach are listed below.[15]

1. Periodic revision of the in-control and out-of-control state probabilities, based on the use of Bayes' theorem
2. Consideration of both exploratory and complete investigations
3. The use of transition probabilities to allow for the chance that an out-of-control process may correct itself
4. Expansion from a one-period to a multiperiod framework

These extensions are beyond the scope of this *Handbook*. The interested reader should consult the works cited in footnote 15.

SUMMARY AND CONCLUSION

A properly functioning standard cost system provides both consistent product costs and signals to management regarding potential trouble spots in the firm's operations. When augmented by sales variances, traditional production cost variances can be used to analyze the difference between budgeted and actual net income by disaggregating the total variance into its several components. Formal consideration of the costs and benefits likely to flow from an investigative and corrective action can help management employ its investigative resources effectively. Finally, the use of *ex post* analytical techniques can further assist in measuring opportunity costs and the general accuracy of the firm's forecasting activity.

BIBLIOGRAPHY

Anton, Hector R., and Peter A. Firmin, eds.: *Contemporary Issues in Cost Accounting,* 2nd ed., Houghton Mifflin Company, Boston, 1972.

Benston, George J., ed.: *Contemporary Cost Accounting and Control,* Dickenson Publishing Company, Encino, Calif., 1970.

Bierman, Harold, Jr., and Thomas R. Dyckman: *Managerial Cost Accounting,* The Macmillan Company, New York, 1971.

Bierman, Harold, Jr., Lawrence E. Fouraker, and Robert K. Jaedicke: "A Use of Probability and Statistics in Performance Evaluation," *Accounting Review,* July 1961, pp. 409–417.

Demski, Joel S.: "An Accounting System Structured on a Linear Programming Model," *Accounting Review,* October 1967.

———: "Analyzing the Effectiveness of the Traditional Standard Cost Variance Model," *Management Accounting,* October 1967.

———: *Information Analysis,* Addison-Wesley Publishing Company, Reading, Mass., 1972.

Dopuch, Nicholas, Jacob Birnberg, and Joel S. Demski: *Cost Accounting,* 2nd ed., Harcourt Brace Jovanovich, New York, 1974.

Grant, Eugene: *Statistical Quality Control,* 3rd ed., McGraw-Hill Book Company, New York, 1964.

Horngren, Charles T.: *Cost Accounting,* 4th ed., Prentice-Hall, Englewood Cliffs, N.J., 1977.

Kaplan, Robert S.: "Optimal Investigation Strategies with Imperfect Information," *Journal of Accounting Research,* Spring 1969, pp. 32–43.

Onsi, Mohamed: "Quantitative Models for Accounting Control," *Accounting Review,* April 1967, pp. 321–330.

Rappaport, Alfred, ed.: *Information for Decision Making,* 2nd ed., Prentice-Hall, Englewood Cliffs, N.J., 1974.

[15]See Harold Bierman, Jr., and Thomas R. Dyckman, *Managerial Cost Accounting;* and Robert S. Kaplan, "Optimal Investigation Strategies with Imperfect Information," *Journal of Accounting Research,* Spring 1969, pp. 32–43.

Chapter **17**

Spoilage, Waste, and Scrap

RONALD J. HUEFNER

Associate Professor of Accounting, State University of New York at
Buffalo

INTRODUCTION

Definitions. The terms "spoilage," "waste," and "scrap" have not been consistently defined in the literature. In some cases, two terms may be used interchangeably by an author. In other cases, usage among authors will differ. Additional categories are sometimes employed. However, an examination of the literature does suggest a set of prevalent definitions, which will be used here. In defining each term, it is necessary to distinguish between the physical phenomenon (i.e., what is happening in the production process) and the accounting for it (i.e., what costs are associated with the occurrence).

Spoilage.   Spoilage signifies manufactured product that is defective in some manner. Because spoilage may be detected at any time during the production process, spoiled product may be only partially complete, or it may be complete. Depending on the circumstances, spoiled product may be discarded, sold for a nominal value (reflecting perhaps any recoverable materials), sold as "seconds," or reprocessed into product of acceptable quality. The term "spoilage" could be reserved for materials, work in process, etc., that are spoiled beyond repair. A separate term, "rework," is then used for costs of repairing or correcting otherwise defective (but not spoiled) items. This precision in terminology is seldom used, however.

Because spoilage involves manufactured product, its cost normally includes all elements of manufacturing cost (material, labor, and overhead). However, the question of what happens to the spoiled product has some bearing on the costs associated with it. If spoiled product is discarded or sold for a nominal amount, the spoilage cost is the amount of manufacturing costs incurred, less any recovery. If spoiled product (which is presumably complete) is sold as seconds, the spoilage cost may be viewed as the reduction in revenues (the difference between normal selling price and the price for seconds). Finally, if spoiled product is reprocessed, spoilage cost is the additional amount of manufacturing cost incurred to rework the item. Thus, the determination of spoilage cost is dependent on what happens to spoiled product. The further question of how one accounts for spoilage cost will be treated in later sections.

Waste.   Waste signifies the loss of input, with no output resulting. Resources are consumed, but no economic benefit is obtained. Input loss may be either physical or economic. A physical loss suggests the disappearance of materials, either prior to production (e.g., loss or evaporation during storage) or during the production process (e.g., shrinkage or destruction during processing). An economic loss suggests that, although the material or some residual may physically remain, its value has disappeared (e.g., damaged materials). The notion of economic loss also applies to the input of labor or overhead resources without a resulting output.

The term "waste" is also used to signify the presence of worthless input residuals, such as gases, dust, toxic residues, and so forth. Here, the inputs have yielded their intended output, plus these wastes. Often, these wastes are not only worthless, but costly to dispose. To distinguish these items from the waste described in the preceding paragraph, we shall adopt the commonly used term "industrial waste."

The cost of waste is generally the cost of the inputs that have been lost plus, if appropriate, disposal costs. The cost of industrial waste is typically disposal cost only. Because the inputs yielded the intended output, input costs are charged to product. Disposal costs for industrial wastes may be significant. Nuclear wastes, for example, require careful and costly disposal. Many other industrial wastes require treatment before they may be discharged into sewers, waterways, or the atmosphere. Again, the question of accounting for waste costs will be treated in later sections.

Scrap.   Scrap signifies an input residual of minor value. Output of minor value can also be called scrap, although the term "by-product" is commonly used. Examples of scrap include leftover pieces of material (cuttings, filings, etc.) and damaged or worn-out materials (e.g., waste oil). Scrap may be either sold, or reused in some manner.

Although it is possible to assign input costs to scrap, it is more common to use recovery value as the cost of scrap. Several accounting procedures are possible, and will be discussed in later sections.

Other Terms.   As mentioned previously, consistency of definition is not always found in the literature. "Scrap" and "waste" are sometimes used interchangeably, as are "scrap" and "spoilage." The term "shrinkage" is sometimes used in place of "waste." Some authors use the term "defective units" to identify spoiled product that is capable of reprocessing. Although we recognize the presence of alternative terminology, the definitions above will be maintained throughout this chapter.

Significance to Cost Accounting. Although spoilage, waste, and scrap may appear to be a minor element of manufacturing cost, there are many indications in today's economy that this is indeed an important area. Many firms find that this element of manufacturing cost must be carefully controlled if profitability is to be achieved. Government figures indicate that about 20 percent of all iron, steel, aluminum, and copper going into production comes out as scrap. Thus, in many industries, the collection and recycling of scrap materials formerly discarded is becoming increasingly significant. Even household garbage is being used in the production of energy. On another dimension, concerns with safety and environmental quality have brought increased attention to the handling and disposition of wastes. Thus, on several dimensions, spoilage, waste, and scrap constitute an important cost consideration, in terms of controlling the occurrence, maximizing the recovery of valuable items, and achieving proper disposition.

Subsequent sections of this chapter will deal, first, with the accounting procedures for spoilage, waste, and scrap and, second, with the control of these costs.

ACCOUNTING FOR SPOILAGE, WASTE, AND SCRAP

Development of Accounting Procedures. The accounting treatment of spoilage, waste, and scrap has had a mixed, and comparatively brief, history. Little attention was given to the subject prior to 1900. Early concern focused on recovery, with little indication of whether the accounting credit should be made to materials, overhead, a job account, or miscellaneous revenue. Garner's *Evolution of Cost Accounting to 1925* traces some of the early development of this topic.[1] A summary is useful here, to observe the variety of possible treatments, several of which are still popular.

Spoilage. Early treatment centered on those items capable of being reworked into salable product. Here it was suggested that the rework costs be charged to overhead. Later, recognition was given to spoilage that could not be reworked, but was either sold for recovery value or discarded. Three alternatives were suggested. The total production cost could be divided by the number of good items produced, thereby spreading the total cost of spoiled units over all good units. Any recovery would be credited to a revenue account. Or total production cost less recovery value could be divided by the number of good items, thereby spreading the spoilage *loss* over all good units. As a third alternative, the full cost of spoiled goods could be charged to a separate account and, after reduction by any recovery, written off as a loss. After several years, the concepts of *normal* (expected as a natural part of the production process) and *abnormal* spoilage were developed. Normal spoilage was viewed as a part of production cost, whereas abnormal spoilage was variously viewed as a charge to overhead, a noninventoriable production cost, a charge to the specific job on which incurred, or a loss.

Waste. Essentially, only two alternatives were developed for waste. One possibility was that the waste (typically a material cost) be charged to the specific production order on which it was incurred. The other possibility was that the waste be charged to a separate account, and then either averaged over all production (as part of overhead) or written off as a loss. A variation of this latter approach involved a budget-and-allowance system. Estimated waste (or other) losses for the

[1] S. Paul Garner, *Evolution of Cost Accounting to 1925* (University of Alabama Press, University, Ala., 1954).

period would be charged to overhead and credited to the allowance account. As actual losses occurred, the allowance would be charged (with a credit to work in process).

Scrap.   Treatment of scrap again centered around the issue of recovery. Various treatments of the recovery credit were proposed. Some viewed scrap recovery as a reduction of materials cost, and thus specific materials accounts were credited. Others held that, if the scrap could be associated with a particular job, the job cost should be credited; otherwise, the recovery credit would go to a miscellaneous revenue account. A hybrid proposal called for the establishment of a shop scrap account, to which handling costs would be charged and recovery values credited; the net result would then be charged (or credited) to the materials account.

Summary.   Early accounting practice focused largely on the treatment of recovery from spoilage and scrap. Somewhat less concern was directed to the determination of the cost of spoilage, waste, or scrap, and the effect on product costs. Similarly, early accounting treatments did little to promote control of spoilage, waste, and scrap costs.

Issues in Accounting for Spoilage, Waste, and Scrap.   The accounting treatment of spoilage, waste, and scrap involves three issues: the assignment of cost to these items, the disposition of the cost, and the treatment of recovery value. Each will be briefly discussed below, and then considered more extensively in the context of the major cost accounting systems.

Cost Assignment.   The first issue involves the question of how to assign cost to items of spoilage, waste, or scrap. Three general answers are possible: (1) no cost may be assigned; (2) the item may be costed in a manner similar to a finished product, that is, have material, labor, and overhead costs associated with it; or (3) the item may be assigned a cost equal to its net realizable value. The selection from among these three generally depends on the item involved, its significance, and the type of product costing system employed.

Disposition of Cost.   If a nonzero cost is assigned to spoilage, waste, and scrap items, the disposition of this cost must then be resolved. One possibility is to treat the cost as a production cost, either directly (as a charge to a specific job or product) or indirectly (as a charge to overhead). The alternative possibility is to view the cost as a nonproduction cost, or loss. Frequently, "normal" spoilage, waste, or scrap costs are viewed as production costs, whereas "abnormal" costs are viewed as losses.

Treatment of Recovery Value.   Scrap, and in some cases spoilage, have recovery values upon disposition. Thus, in addition to handling the cost of these items, an accounting treatment for recovery value must be chosen. The major alternatives are as follows: (1) treat the recovery as miscellaneous income and make no cost assignment; (2) treat the recovery as a reduction of production cost (this may have several variations, including credits to specific jobs, materials, overhead, or cost of goods sold); or (3) treat the recovery as sales revenue from a joint product, and assign full costs to the item. Again, considerations of significance and the product costing system will influence the choice.

Job Costing.   In job costing, spoilage, waste, and scrap costs, and any recovery values, may or may not be associated with the job on which they arose. Considerable variation of practice exists; the following sections describe what appears to be predominant practice.

Spoilage.   The treatment of spoilage under job costing generally takes one of three possible forms. Spoilage cost may be charged to the specific job, to all production (by a charge to manufacturing overhead), or to a separate loss account. There is, however, no unanimity in the literature on which treatment applies in which circumstances.

Spoilage is generally charged to job costs if it is identifiable with, and is due to some particular characteristic of, that job. For example, if a particular job has unusually precise specifications to be met, more than a routine amount of spoilage would be expected, and thus should be included in the job cost. On the other hand, spoilage that occurs randomly due to non-job-specific causes is generally charged to overhead, even though the jobs on which the spoilage occurred can be identified. Accounting for spoilage costs that will be charged to a particular job is straightforward. Because the production costs of both good and spoiled work have already been charged to the job, no further cost entry is necessary. If the spoiled units have a recovery value, the job cost should be credited with the net realizable value, as follows:

Inventory (spoilage, at net realizable value) ..	XX	
Work in process (specific job)		XX

"Normal" spoilage is generally charged to manufacturing overhead, so that its cost is spread over all jobs. Normal spoilage is that expected as a regular aspect of operations, rather than being caused by the particular requirements of a given job. Routine machine malfunctions, operator error, material defects, and the like, would give rise to normal spoilage. Although this cost should be borne by all production, the cost is likely to occur on some jobs and not on others. Thus the spoilage cost must be reclassified from individual job costs to manufacturing overhead, by the following entry:

Inventory (spoilage, at net realizable value)	XX	
Manufacturing Overhead (spoilage cost less recovery) ..	XX	
Work in Process (specific jobs)		XX

Because this addition to overhead cost is anticipated, it should be reflected in the calculation of the predetermined overhead rate. Thus, all jobs would bear a proportionate share of normal spoilage cost.

Abnormal spoilage is caused by the same operating factors that cause normal spoilage (machine malfunctions, operator error, etc.). However, abnormal spoilage signifies a much greater than expected rate of occurrence. It is generally suggested that these costs be written off as a loss. The entry would be:

Inventory (spoilage, at net realizable value)	XX	
Spoilage Loss (abnormal spoilage cost less recovery) ..	XX	
Work in Process (specific jobs)		XX

Undoubtedly, the distinction between job-related spoilage, normal spoilage, and abnormal spoilage becomes, in many cases, a matter of judgment.

Although the above treatments of spoilage cost are in common use, criticism has been directed at the practice of charging spoilage costs to overhead. Koch[2] argues that only the material and labor elements of the cost of spoiled goods should be charged to manufacturing overhead, because these are the only out-of-pocket costs. If the overhead element of spoilage cost is charged back to the manufacturing overhead account, these costs are being recorded twice, because the original overhead cost items (indirect labor, depreciation, repairs, etc.) have already been entered. Thus Koch argues that the overhead component of spoilage cost should be charged to the applied overhead account, in effect reversing the entry originally made to charge overhead to the job. The result is that overhead is applied to good production only, and the overhead attributable to spoiled goods will be included in the underapplied variance.

Laimon[3] takes exception to the ideas presented by Koch. He argues that the material and labor components of spoilage cost should not be charged to overhead, because they do not represent the incurrence of additional *overhead* costs.

---

[2]Alfred P. Koch, "A Fallacy in Accounting for Spoiled Goods," *Accounting Review,* XXXV, 3 (July 1960), pp. 501–502.
[3]Samuel Laimon, "Accounting for Spoiled Goods" (unpublished working paper, University of Saskatchewan).

Further, the overhead component of spoilage cost should not be charged to applied overhead, because the propriety of the original application is not changed by the fact that some output is of lesser quality. Moreover, the procedures suggested by Koch fragment the cost of spoilage, reducing the effectiveness of cost control. Laimon suggests that spoilage cost be charged to a separate "cost-of-spoiled-goods" account, and then allocated either to jobs (for normal spoilage) or a loss account (for abnormal spoilage). No entries would be made to overhead accounts. Despite the criticisms discussed above, however, charging spoilage to overhead still appears to be a common practice.

Reworked Spoilage.   The preceding section assumed that spoiled goods would be disposed of at their recovery value (which may be zero). It is also possible that spoiled goods may be reworked into salable product. Reworking involves additional inputs, and so the treatment of these costs must be considered. The same alternatives exist as for spoilage cost: specific-job-related rework is charged to job costs, normal rework is charged to manufacturing overhead, and abnormal rework is written off as a loss. Thus, the entry to record rework costs would be:

Work in Process (specific job)	XX	
or Manufacturing Overhead (normal rework) ..	XX	
or Spoilage Loss (abnormal rework)	XX	
Materials		XX
Labor		XX
Overhead Applied		XX

Waste.   It would be possible to classify waste in the same manner as spoilage (specific-job-related, normal, and abnormal), and to adopt the corresponding accounting treatments. This, however, seems to be infrequently done. Rather, waste costs are often ignored, which has the effect of assigning the cost to the job on which the waste occurred. Waste disposal costs are generally charged to manufacturing overhead, although these too could employ the three-part classification discussed above.

Scrap.   Common practice is to ignore the costs of scrap, and to focus on accounting for its recoverable value. If scrap occurrence is a minor factor, no reduction of production cost may be recorded. Rather, a miscellaneous revenue account would be credited with the proceeds upon sale. More frequently, however, the recovery value of scrap is credited either to the specific job on which it was generated, or to manufacturing overhead. The credit to manufacturing overhead is generally employed in cases where it is not feasible or not cost-beneficial to maintain scrap-recovery records by specific jobs.

When scrap is recognized at time of recovery, the debit to Inventory is based on estimated recovery value. The determination of recovery value depends on the intended disposition of the scrap. If the scrap is to be sold, then net realizable value should be used, as in the case of spoilage. If, however, the scrap will be reused, it should be valued at its estimated material value.

Process Costing.   In job costing, spoilage, waste, and scrap can be associated either with an individual job or with all production. Process costing, on the other hand, is an averaging method, which does not separately recognize individual jobs. Thus, there is no counterpart in process costing to job-specific spoilage, waste, or scrap; all must be considered as related to general production. The distinction between normal and abnormal, however, continues to be used.

Most of the literature on this subject deals with the treatment of spoilage under process costing. Waste and scrap receive little attention, because it is rarely suggested that costs be assigned to these items. Thus, the majority of the following discussion will focus on spoilage.

Spoilage—Basic Approaches.   Two basic approaches are found for spoilage accounting in process cost systems. The first is essentially to ignore the presence of spoilage. All costs are associated with good output (both finished goods and ending inventory), and no costs are assigned to spoiled goods. Thus, the cost of spoilage is absorbed by the good production. To illustrate, assume the following data:

Completed goods—10,000 units
Ending inventory in process—3,000 units (complete as to material and
   two-thirds complete as to labor and overhead)
No beginning inventory
Spoiled goods—650 units (inspection occurs when goods are complete
   as to material and half complete as to labor and overhead)
Costs incurred:

Material ···	$13,650
Labor and overhead ····································	27,730
Total ··	$41,380

One approach to the computation of equivalent units, and the assignment of costs to product, is as follows:

	Total	Material	Labor and overhead
Completed goods	10,000	10,000	10,000
Ending inventory	3,000	3,000	2,000
Total equivalent units	13,000	13,000	12,000
Total costs		$13,650	$27,730
Cost per equivalent unit		$1.05	$2.31
Cost assignment:			
Completed goods			
10,000 × ($1.05 + $2.31)			$33,610 (adjusted for
Ending inventory			rounding error)
3,000 × $1.05		$3,150	
2,000 × $2.31		4,620	7,770
			$41,380

Under this approach, the effect of greater (or lesser) amounts of spoilage (assuming total costs move in the same direction) is higher (or lower) costs per equivalent unit.

The alternative approach is to include spoiled units in the calculations. Costs are assigned to spoiled units in the same manner as they are assigned to completed goods and ending inventory. Then, a determination must be made as to the disposition of the spoilage cost—it may be charged to completed production, to all production, or written off as a loss. Using the same data as above, this approach operates as follows:

	Total	Material	Labor and overhead
Completed goods	10,000	10,000	10,000
Ending inventory	3,000	3,000	2,000
Spoiled goods	650	650	325
Total equivalent units	13,650	13,650	12,325
Total costs		$13,650	$27,730
Cost per equivalent unit		$1.00	$2.25
Cost assignment:			
Completed goods			
10,000 × ($1.00 + $2.25)			$32,500
Ending inventory			
3,000 × $1.00		$3,000	
2,000 × $2.25		4,500	7,500
Spoiled goods			
650 × $1.00		$ 650	
325 × $2.25		730	1,380
			$41,380

Here, specific recognition has been given to the presence of spoiled goods, resulting in lower costs per equivalent unit, and an assignment of costs to the spoiled goods. Disposition of the $1,380 spoilage cost would now have to be considered. If the spoilage is considered normal, the cost would either be assigned to completed goods (resulting in a total cost of completed goods of $33,880), or assigned to all production—both completed goods and ending inventory (and resulting in cost assignments of $33,610 and $7,770, respectively, as obtained under the first approach). If the spoilage is considered abnormal, the $1,380 cost would be written off as a loss. If the spoilage is considered partially normal and partially abnormal, each component is treated in the manner just described.

Evaluation of Approaches.   The first approach described above (absorbing spoilage cost directly by all units produced) is simple to apply, and requires no details as to the extent of completion of spoiled units. Some authors suggest that this method be used when spoilage is deemed normal.

There are, however, several deficiencies to this simple approach. If the items in ending inventory have not yet reached the inspection point (at which spoilage is detected), it is inappropriate to assign part of the cost of spoilage to them. These items will be charged for spoilage now, and again in the period in which they are completed. If spoilage costs are fairly uniform over time, however, no great distortion will result. To remedy this deficiency, some authors suggest that this method be employed only when spoilage occurs early in the process (so that ending inventory units are past the inspection point, and thus are properly charged with a share of spoilage).

A second objection involves the effect on cost control. The simple approach reflects spoilage cost in the form of increased unit costs. No separate cost of spoilage is presented, which may reduce management's attention to this element of manufacturing cost. Similarly, factors other than spoilage may cause changes in unit costs from period to period. By failing to analyze the components of these changes separately, cost control may become less effective.

Thus, except for cases where the benefits of simplicity outweigh the deficiencies discussed above, the second approach (involving a specific cost assignment to spoiled goods) is preferred. Although somewhat more work is involved, the cost of spoilage is determined separately for control purposes. Moreover, the cost can then be treated in one of several manners. Normally, a distinction is first made between normal and abnormal spoilage. Normal spoilage is charged to those goods that passed the inspection point during the period, whereas abnormal spoilage is charged to a loss account.

FIFO Versus Weighted-Average Process Costing.   Both the first-in, first-out and weighted-average inventory methods are commonly used in process costing systems. These procedures are covered in Chapter 14, and hence will not be described here. The interaction of these procedures with spoilage accounting, however, should be briefly mentioned.

Weighted-average costing presents no particular problem with respect to spoilage, because both prior-period (beginning inventory) and current-period costs are combined to form a single set of equivalent-unit costs. Assignment of cost to spoiled goods, and disposition of spoilage cost, proceeds as previously illustrated. When FIFO is used, however, *current* (rather than average) cost per equivalent unit is determined. Thus, cost assigned to spoiled goods is based solely on costs incurred this period, and does not include any of the costs carried in the beginning inventory. This distortion of spoilage cost (which may be insignificant) violates the strict assumptions of the FIFO technique. To remedy this deficiency would require identification of spoiled items as coming either from beginning inventory or from units currently started, with appropriate FIFO accounting used in costing both good units and spoilage. As suggested above, however, the improvement in information may not be sufficient to merit the more refined procedure.

Recovery Values and Rework Costs.   The discussion up to this point has assumed that spoiled units are simply discarded. Two alternative assumptions merit brief mention. One is that the spoiled goods have a recovery value. If so, after the assignment of cost to spoiled goods, the net realizable value should be deducted before the allocation of (net) spoilage cost occurs (i.e., to good units, loss, etc.).

A second possibility is that spoiled units may be reworked into units of acceptable quality. If rework occurs within the process (which is unlikely in many process-type manufacturing activities), the additional material, labor, and overhead costs may simply be absorbed into the determination of unit costs. Although this approach has the same deficiencies as the first approach to spoilage accounting described previously, segregation of the rework costs incurred within the process may well be difficult. A more likely situation, however, is that spoiled units would be transferred to a separate department for rework. In this situation, process costs can be assigned to spoiled goods as previously described. These costs would then be transferred (with the spoiled goods) to the rework department, where the additional rework costs would be added.

Comprehensive Illustration.   The topics discussed in the preceding sections are illustrated in the following analysis. Assume the following data:

25,000 good units completed.

4,000 units in ending work-in-process inventory (complete as to material and 50 percent complete as to labor and overhead).

3,000 units spoiled owing to an undetected equipment malfunction over two days during the month. These units were complete as to material and 10 percent complete as to labor and overhead. The units cannot be reworked. Management considers this occurrence to be unusual and will regard it as abnormal spoilage. The expected recovery value is $.50 per unit.

1,300 units failed to pass inspection at the end of the process. This number is within expected limits and thus is considered normal. It is determined that 600 units can be reworked (at an additional cost of $1.25 per unit) and sold as "seconds." The other 700 spoiled units cannot be reworked and have an expected recovery value of $.50 per unit.

Cost data for the beginning inventory plus current costs of the process are (weighted-average costing is used):

Materials	$ 58,275
Labor and overhead	128,700
Total	$186,975

The computation of equivalent units, and the assignment of costs to product, is as follows:

	Total	Material	Labor and overhead
Completed goods	25,000	25,000	25,000
Ending inventory	4,000	4,000	2,000
Abnormal spoilage	3,000	3,000	300
Normal spoilage-rework	600	600	600
Normal spoilage	700	700	700
Total equivalent units	33,300	33,300	28,600
Total costs		$58,275	$128,700
Cost per equivalent unit		$1.75	$4.50

Cost assignment:

Completed goods		
25,000 × ($1.75 + $4.50)		$156,250
Ending inventory		
4,000 × $1.75	$7,000	
2,000 × $4.50	9,000	16,000
Abnormal spoilage		
3,000 × $1.75	$5,250	
300 × $4.50	1,350	6,600
Normal spoilage (to rework)		
600 × ($1.75 + $4.50)		3,750
Normal spoilage		
700 × ($1.75 + $4.50)		4,375
		$186,975

The disposition of the spoilage costs would be as follows. The cost of abnormal spoilage, less the expected recovery value, would be written off as a loss for the period. The cost of spoiled goods capable of being reworked would be transferred to the Rework Department. This cost, plus the added rework costs, would become the cost of the completed "seconds." Finally, the cost of spoiled goods that could not be reworked, less expected recovery value, would be charged to the good units completed during the period. Ending inventory would not be charged, because these items had not yet reached the inspection point. The results would be:

Cost of completed goods ($156,250 assigned cost, plus $4,375 cost of normal spoilage, less $350 recovery value)	$160,275
Ending inventory	16,000
Spoilage loss ($6,600 assigned cost of abnormal spoilage, less $1,500 recovery value)	5,100
Cost of completed goods—seconds ($3,750 assigned cost, plus $750 rework cost)	4,500

Scrap and Waste.   Little attention is normally given to scrap and waste in process cost accounting (except in standard cost systems, which are described in the next section). Costs are typically not allocated to scrap and waste; rather, these are absorbed into the unit cost of materials. Scrap recovery values are credited to material or overhead cost, if it is convenient to identify scrap generation by process; otherwise, miscellaneous revenue is credited.

Standard Costing.   Standard costing is not a costing system independent of the two previously discussed, but rather a system of predetermined costs that may be used in conjunction with job or process costing. Standards for spoilage, waste, and scrap are established, so that normal amounts become part of product cost, and deviations from normal (either higher or lower) appear as cost variances. Because the preceding chapters have dealt extensively with the establishment of standards and the operation of a standard cost system, this section will focus only on the particular elements of standard costing applicable to accounting for spoilage, waste, and scrap. Further discussion of standard costing for control purposes appears later in this chapter.

Spoilage.   A standard allowance for spoilage is typically expressed in terms of output expectations from given input. That is, material, labor, and overhead standards per unit of product are established. The spoilage standard is then expressed as a percentage, either of total production or of good units produced.

The selection of total production versus good production as the base for the calculation of standard spoilage does make some difference. It is generally recommended that total production not be used as the base, because this figure includes any abnormal spoilage. For a given amount of good output, the higher the total spoilage, the higher the amount considered normal under this approach. To illustrate, assume that of each 100 units produced, 95 are expected to be good.

Thus the standard for normal spoilage could be expressed as 5/100 of total production, or 5/95 of good production. If no abnormal spoilage exists, the two standards give identical results. For example, if 10,000 units are produced, and 9,500 pass inspection, 500 units of normal spoilage are calculated in either case. Suppose, however, that 12,000 units are produced and only 9,500 pass inspection. The standard based on total production would indicate 600 units of normal spoilage, whereas the standard based on good production would indicate 500 units. Although some logic can be attached to each approach, the predominant recommendation in the literature is the use of a standard based on good production.

To illustrate, assume that input standards for a unit of product are:

Material (3 pounds at $12.00)	$36.00
Labor (4 hours at $6.00)	24.00
Overhead (4 hours at $5.00)	20.00
Standard cost per unit	$80.00

Assume further that the standard spoilage allowance is 5 percent of good output. That is, 105 units must be produced to yield 100 good units. Incorporating the spoilage allowance gives a standard cost per good unit of $84.00 [$80.00 × (105/100)]. Assume that during a particular time period 540 units were produced and 500 passed inspection. The analysis of costs shows the following:

Total manufacturing costs incurred	
(540 units at $80.00)	$43,200
Standard cost of good units	
(500 units at $84.00)	42,000
Variance (unfavorable)	$ 1,200

In this illustration, the entire variance is attributable to abnormal spoilage (15 units at $80.00). The cost of normal spoilage (25 units) has been absorbed by costing each good unit at $84.00.

Waste.   Waste has been defined as the loss of input, with no economic benefit resulting. This normally involves materials, but it may also involve labor and overhead if the loss occurs during production. Again, allowances for expected waste may be incorporated into the cost standards.

Provision for materials waste would be incorporated into the material usage standard, and excess waste would appear as part of the material quantity variance. Provision for waste during production (loss of partially completed products) would be treated in a similar manner as spoilage, that is, by recognition in the various input standards. Standard waste disposal costs are generally included in overhead.

Scrap.   Scrap, like waste, is usually associated with the material usage standard. Allowances are made for expected scrap generation in the production process, thereby increasing the standard material input required per unit of output. In addition, because scrap has a recovery value, the standard material cost must be reduced by the estimated recovery. Thus the material standard may appear as in the following illustration:

Material in a finished unit	4.0 pounds
Scrap allowance	0.4
Standard input	4.4 pounds
Cost of standard input	
(4.4 pounds at $11.50)	$50.60
Less scrap recovery	
(0.4 pounds at $3.30)	1.32
Net cost	$49.28
Net cost per pound	
($49.28/4.4)	$11.20

Thus, a material standard including a scrap allowance and scrap recovery value would be expressed as 4.4 pounds of material at $11.20 per pound.

Variations in scrap generation would appear as part of the material quantity variance, whereas variations in recovery value would be included in the material price variance. If desired, the joint variance could be computed to show the effects of both generation and recovery value differences.

Continuing the illustration above, assume that 1,000 units of product were manufactured, using 4,580 pounds of material having a net cost of $51,754. Variances would be calculated as follows:

Material price variance	
$51,754 − (4,580 × $11.20)	$ 458.00 U
Material quantity variance	
(4,580 − 4,400) × $11.20	2,016.00 U
Total material variance	$2,474.00 U

One possible factor contributing to the material price variance is the price received for scrap, whereas a possible factor contributing to the material quantity variance is the amount of scrap generated. Suppose that it is known that 470 pounds of scrap was generated, and was sold for a total of $1,410 (average of $3.00 per pound). Thus, the gross cost of material was $53,164 ($51,754 plus $1,410). The above variances could be further analyzed as follows:

Material price variance:	
Variance in gross purchase price	
$53,164 − (4,580 × $11.50)	$494.00 U
Variance in scrap recovery[4]	
$1,410 − (4,580 × $.30)	(36.00) F
	$458.00 U
Material quantity variance:	
Due to excess scrap	
(4,470 − 4,400) × $11.20	$ 784.00 U
Due to other factors	
(4,580 − 4,470) × $11.20	1,232.00 U
	$2,016.00 U

CONTROL OF SPOILAGE, WASTE, AND SCRAP

The control of spoilage, waste, and scrap may be divided into three main subareas: (1) its occurrence; (2) its recovery, handling, and storage; and (3) its disposition.

Spoilage occurs in the process of production. Its recovery involves the identification of spoiled goods, and their segregation for later action, which may involve reworking into a unit of acceptable quality, or direct disposition (either as "seconds," scrap materials, or worthless discard). Thus, spoilage control involves production quality control (the occurrence stage) as well as control over the recovery and disposition of spoiled goods.

Waste occurs when inputs fail to yield an economic benefit. In many cases, no physical output will result, and so only the occurrence stage of control will be relevant. This involves control over the acquisition, storage, and use of inputs (primarily materials, although labor and other inputs are also subject to waste), as well as production control. In some cases, waste may take the form of worthless residuals requiring disposition. For these "industrial wastes," control over recovery, handling, and disposition may be very important, not so much for economic reasons as for safety (in the case of toxic wastes) or environmental (in the case of potential pollutants) reasons.

[4]The expected recovery per pound of input is $1.32/4.4, or $.30.

Scrap involves input residuals having some value. The occurrence of scrap is normally controlled at the production stage. In addition, recovery and disposition controls are necessary lest the recoverable value be diminished or lost through carelessness or misappropriation.

General Aspects of Control Systems.   The establishment of a control system for spoilage, waste, and scrap requires, first, a distinction between controllable and uncontrollable losses. For example, some degree of spoilage may be inherent in the production process, as may be a certain level of scrap occurrence; some material waste via evaporation may be unavoidable; and complete recovery of all scrap may not be feasible. Thus, the system must first establish feasible levels of performance with respect to occurrence, recovery, handling, storage, and disposition. Care must be taken in establishing these levels, as losses that may initially appear as uncontrollable may in fact be somewhat controllable. For example, loss of a certain material by evaporation may be a natural phenomenon that is uncontrollable. The total amount of the loss, however, may be minimized by appropriate storage facilities, proper handling, rotation of stock, and avoidance of excessive inventory levels. Thus, any loss initially designated as "uncontrollable" should be carefully reviewed to determine the feasible level at which control may begin.

A control system also requires measurement and reporting of activity. Thus, data must be collected on a regular basis concerning occurrence, recovery, transfers to and from storage, disposals, and so forth. Considerations of materiality and economic benefit must be applied to determine the appropriate level of frequency and detail of data collection. Periodic reports must then be prepared, with distribution to relevant individuals for evaluation and any required corrective action.

Finally, a control system requires a basis for the evaluation of performance. Thus, standards may be established for the occurrence, recovery, and disposition stages. Variances may be calculated to serve as an indication of those areas of performance requiring further analysis and possibly corrective action.

Control over Occurrence.   The objective of occurrence control is to minimize, subject to the limitations and requirements of the manufacturing system, the generation of spoilage, waste, and scrap. This area of control is intertwined with the nature of the product, the design of the manufacturing system, desired quality control, and so forth. Although some broad aspects of occurrence control will be discussed here, it must be recognized that the design of an occurrence control system cannot be done in isolation, but must involve the other areas as well.

Causes of Spoilage, Waste, and Scrap Occurrence.   A relatively long list of potential causes for the occurrence of spoilage, waste, and scrap may be developed. These may be grouped into broad categories as follows:

1. Labor-related causes: lack of training as to proper work methods; inadequate supervision; machine operator error, handling damage; carelessness

2. Material-related causes: defective or incorrect materials; evaporation; deterioration; obsolescence

3. Manufacturing-system-related causes: defective or improper tooling and equipment; deficiencies in product design; engineering changes and problems of new product introduction; tolerance restrictions; machine jams, trials, and adjustments; overutilization of facilities causing malfunctions and errors due to operator fatigue

4. Other causes: overzealous inspection; theft

As indicated previously, several of these causes must be viewed in conjunction with other aspects of manufacturing operations. Also, no attempt has been made in the above list to separate the causes of spoilage, causes of waste, and causes of scrap. Some of the causes cited may apply only to one area (e.g., evaporation is a cause of waste), whereas others may apply to two or three areas (e.g., handling damage could cause spoilage, waste, or scrap).

Control Devices.   Some type of performance standards serve as the basic device for the control of the occurrence of spoilage, waste, and scrap. Because occurrence may be connected to one of several areas of manufacturing operations, the performance standards may take different forms.

For example, some of the causes of waste and scrap derive from the handling and usage of materials. One important control device in this area is the *standard bill of materials.* This document specifies, for each product, the description and quantity of materials required and perhaps also the manufacturing methods to be employed. Material requisitions for production are prepared from the standard bill of materials. Thus, the proper types and quantities of materials should be issued, thereby reducing losses due to issuance of the wrong materials, or of excessive quantities. The responsibility of the production department is also fixed. Additional materials required due to losses in the production stage (operator error, machine malfunctions, etc.) will have to be separately requisitioned, and the presence of an exception will therefore be noted. This latter feature may well encourage production personnel to exercise better control over issued material, rather than have to make additional requisitions which will be reported as variances in the performance report.

Different types of standards must be applied to the generation of spoilage, waste, and scrap in the process of production. Here, input and output standards must be designed to reflect the amount of spoilage, waste, or scrap that is to be considered "normal," that is, inherent in the process, or not economical to eliminate. Determination of what is normal may involve considerations of engineering design, production methods, quality control, and so forth. However determined, these normal allowances will then be incorporated into the appropriate input-output standards. A subsequent section presents an illustration of such standards.

Measurement and Reporting.   A system of occurrence control requires the occurrence of spoilage, waste, and scrap be measured with reasonable accuracy, and be reported to management on a periodic basis. One author has suggested formats for several types of reports.[5] Two examples serve to illustrate the general approach:

1. The occurrence of spoilage should be reported on a document containing items of information such as the following:
    a. Part number and description
    b. Kind of material
    c. Quantity
    d. Last operation completed
    e. Cause of rejection
    f. Foreman's and/or inspector's signature
    g. Department to be charged
    h. Disposition instructions and approval
    i. Cost (material, labor, overhead)
    j. Salvage value and net loss
2. The discovery of defective materials should be reported on a document containing items of information such as:
    a. Identification of material
    b. Vendor's name
    c. Purchase order number

[5]John G. Barrett, "A Frontal Attack on the Scrap Accounting Problem," *NACA Bulletin,* XXXIV, 6 (February 1953), pp. 791–796.

d. Date and quantity received
e. Quantity rejected
f. Reason for rejection
g. Inspector's signature
h. Disposition instructions and approval

In general, any reporting system on the occurrence of spoilage, waste, or scrap should present data on quantities (subdivided between normal and abnormal, if standards are in existence), causes, responsibility, and costs. Frequent reports are desirable so that prompt action may be taken to reduce excessive losses.

An Illustration of Performance Standards and Variances.   Assume that a company manufactures a standard product, P-1. The product requires a single material, MX. Each unit of P-1 requires 1.85 pounds of MX. Two percent of this input is expected to be left as scrap material. Upon completion of the manufacturing process, 10 percent of the units are, on the average, not of acceptable quality. Of these spoiled units, half can normally be reworked, requiring one additional pound of material MX each. The remaining spoiled units are sold as salvage.

Relevant cost and recovery prices are:

Material MX, cost per pound	$6.50
Scrap material, recovery per pound	1.43
Spoiled units, recovery per item	.76

Assume that during a particular period's operations, the following occurred:

1. Purchases of material MX: 1,000,000 pounds at a total cost of $6,500,000.
2. Production of product P-1: 478,000 total units of which 50,000 did not meet specifications. 28,000 were reworked and 22,000 were sold as salvage for $.76 per unit.
3. Scrap material recovered and sold for $1.43 per pound: 18,200 pounds.
4. Inventory of material MX at end of period (assume no beginning inventory): 80,000 pounds.

These data do not include price variations so that the illustration may focus exclusively on quantity variations for spoilage, waste, and scrap.

The standard input of material per finished unit of product is determined as follows. For convenience, we initially consider 100 units.

	Units of P-1	Pounds of MX
100 units into process	100	185
10% spoilage	(10)	
Units reworked (half of spoilage)	5	5
End result	95	190

Thus, 95 units of P-1 require 190 pounds of MX, and the standard input per finished unit is 2 pounds (190/95).

The standard cost of material per finished unit is determined as follows:

Standard input of material, 2 pounds at $6.50	$13.00
Recovery of spoiled units [for each 95 good units, have 5 spoiled units yielding $.76 each. Recovery per finished unit is ($.76 × 5)/95)]	(.04)
Recovery of scrap [2% of input: 2 pounds per unit standard input times 2% equals .04 pounds, times recovery of $1.43 per pound. Recovery per finished unit is .04 × $1.43 × (100/95)]	(.06)
Standard cost of material per finished unit	$12.90

Given these standards and the operating results above, the total material usage variance for the period may now be determined.

Total material purchased		
(1.000,000 pounds at $6.50)		$6,500,000
Materials accounted for:		
Ending inventory		
(80,000 pounds at $6.50)	$ 520,000	
Finished units		
(456,000 units at $12.90)	5,882,400	
Spoilage recovered		
(22,000 units at $.76)	16,720	
Scrap recovered		
(18,200 pounds at $1.43)	26,026	
Total accounted for		6,445,146
Materials usage variance		$ 54,854 *U*

This total usage variance may be analyzed in terms of its spoilage, waste, and scrap components, as follows:

1. Rework variance:

Actual units reworked	28,000
Standard rework (because 456,000 good units were produced, which should be 95% of total production, implied total production is 480,000 (450,000/.95), and standard rework is 24,000 (5% × 480,000)	24,000
Excess of actual rework over standard	4,000
Material required per unit	× 1
Additional pounds of material	4,000
Cost per pound	× $6.50
Rework variance	$ 26,000 *U*

2. Spoilage variance:

Actual units spoiled (net of rework)	22,000
Standard spoilage (5% of total implied production of 480,000)	24,000
Excess of actual spoilage over standard	(2,000)
Material input per unit	× 1.85
Pounds of material saved	(3,700)
Cost per pound	× $6.50
Spoilage variance	$(24,050) *F*

3. Spoilage recovery variance:

Underrecovery of spoilage (as per above), units	2,000
Recovery value per unit	× $.76
Spoilage recovery variance	$ 1,520 *U*

4. Scrap recovery variance:

Actual pounds of scrap recovered	18,200
Standard scrap (478,000 units produced, times .04 pounds per unit)	19,120
Underrecovery of scrap, pounds	920
Recovery value per pound	× $1.43
Scrap recovery variance	$ 1,316 *U*

5. Waste variance:

Pounds of material purchased		1,000,000
Material accounted for		
Ending inventory	80,000	
Entered into production		
(478,000 × 1.85)	884,300	
Used for rework		
(28,000 × 1.00)	28,000	
Pounds accounted for		992,300
Materials lost		7,700
Cost per pound		× $6.50
Waste variance		$ 50,050 *U*

6. Summary of variances:

Rework variance	$ 26,000 U
Spoilage variance	(24,050) F
Spoilage recovery variance	1,520 U
Scrap recovery variance	1,316 U
Waste variance	50,050 U
	$ 54,836 U
Rounding errors	18 U
Total materials usage variance	$ 54,854 U

As this illustration demonstrates, material usage variances can be analyzed into spoilage, waste, and scrap components. This information can then be used to identify occurrences of spoilage, waste, and scrap, to evaluate performance, and to determine those areas requiring immediate action. The extent of separate identification of the elements of the variance must of course, be cost-effective: the benefits of extra record keeping should be compared with its cost.

Control over Recovery, Handling, and Storage.   The control objectives at this stage are to maximize the recovery (of spoilage and scrap, primarily) and to handle and store the items involved so as to achieve maximum value from these goods.

Recovery of spoilage and scrap begins at the occurrence stage in the production process. A system for recording quantities (and other data) concerning spoiled goods or scrap materials establishes an initial control point for recovery. Quantities recovered may be compared to quantities generated, to determine that losses of these items are minimized. It may also be desirable to provide means for segregation of different types of spoilage or scrap at the point of occurrence (e.g., provision of separate, labeled containers). A regular collection procedure should be followed.

In designing recovery and handling procedures, concern must be directed to the objective of achieving the maximum economic benefit from spoilage and scrap that has occurred. Items that can be reworked, reconditioned, reused, or sold must be identified. As suggested above, separation (by type, grade, etc.) is generally desirable. If several kinds of scrap material, for example, are mixed together, the sales price is likely to approximate that of the least valuable material in the mix. Other handling procedures, such as cleaning, bundling, and the like, may also serve to increase the recoverable value.

Control over storage involves the typical problems of protecting the goods from theft, damage by the elements, and so forth. Procedures are necessary to ensure the separation of materials is maintained, and that good, reusable, or returnable materials are not included with salable scrap.

Industrial Wastes and Pollution Control.   The preceding discussion of recovery, handling, and storage applied to spoiled goods and scrap materials. Some additional considerations are necessary for waste. For some wastes (via evaporation, theft, etc.) no recovery, handling, or storage is necessary, since the goods have disappeared. Many other wastes consist of worthless residuals to be discarded. Although recovery, handling, and possibly storage are necessary, there is little need for control procedures, because the items have no value. A comprehensive control system may provide for timely removal, so as to maintain a safe and efficient workplace, but protection of value is not at issue.

A different situation exists with respect to items previously defined as "industrial wastes." These items, although worthless, require disposal more costly than routine trash collection. Safety considerations require potentially costly procedures in handling toxic, combustible, or explosive wastes. Examples include radioactive materials, dust in flour mills, and gases in coal mines. In other cases, special handling procedures may be necessary for environmental reasons. Treatment may be necessary before certain wastes may be permitted to be discharged into sewers, waterways, the atmosphere, or even landfills.

A comprehensive control system will be concerned with the following areas with respect to industrial wastes:

1. Control over materials and production methods used, with a view toward minimizing the generation of industrial wastes, and/or reducing their objectionable features

2. Control over recovery, handling, and disposal procedures, to ensure compliance with safety and environmental factors at minimum cost.

In addition, continued search for technological improvement is needed, to reduce occurrence, improve treatment and disposal techniques, and conceivably to find economic uses for these wastes.

Control over Disposition. The primary control objective at this stage is to maximize the value received from the disposition of spoilage and scrap (and to minimize the cost of waste disposal). Thus, specific considerations involved will be (1) preparing the items for sale, (2) selecting the best outlet, (3) control of prices received, and (4) control over quantities.

Preparation for sale has been discussed in the preceding section on recovery and handling. A first step is to determine whether items will in fact be sold, or whether they will be reused or reworked. Then, items must be sorted, and as appropriate, cleaned and bundled. Often, a minimum quantity may need to be accumulated before sale is practical.

Selection of the best outlet involves circularizing potential buyers, and possibly obtaining bids. Bids may be on a specific-lot basis, or on a contract basis covering a period of time. In the absence of competitive bids, prices received may be compared to quoted market prices (which exist for many scrap metals and other materials). Good control suggests that a department not involved in the generation or handling of spoilage and scrap should be responsible for price control. The purchasing department is often chosen for this task.

Finally, physical control must be exercised over the quantities of spoilage and scrap leaving the plant. On an overall basis, these must be compared to the records of quantities generated and recovered. On a more detailed level, weights (or other quantity measures) of outgoing shipments must be determined, verified, and recorded. Again, appropriate separation of duties in the generation, handling, and disposal of spoilage and scrap will aid control.

Overall Review of Control Procedures. In addition to the control aspects of the specific occurrence, recovery, and disposition stages, certain overall control matters may be briefly discussed. These include the interaction of spoilage, waste, and scrap control with other control areas within the firm, the role of internal auditing, and finally, a summary of review procedures for this area of control.

Interaction with Other Areas. The interaction of spoilage, waste, and scrap control with other areas of control within the firm has been mentioned previously. General controls over purchasing, materials handling, and production will include controls over spoilage, waste, and scrap. More specifically, spoilage, waste, and scrap may be reduced by examining controls in the following areas:[6]

1. Job estimates—verification as to proper types and quantities of material (and other inputs)

2. Job planning—procedures for verification of designs and specifications; planning overruns to accommodate expected spoilage

3. Inventory—control over theft or damage of items in inventory; control over ordering procedures and data as to quantities on hand

4. Purchasing—general control procedures to balance use of storage space and wasted labor time due to inavailability of materials against benefits of larger purchase orders

[6]See Clarence Langer, "Control of Waste and Spoilage," *National Public Accountant,* 8, 12 (December 1963), pp. 12–14.

5. Small tools and supplies—control over issuance; maintenance of tools; instruction as to proper use

6. Production—scheduling for efficient workflow, and proper utilization of materials, labor, and other inputs.

Thus, to a great extent, spoilage, waste, and scrap control cannot be considered in isolation, but must be viewed as a part of a general control system.

Internal Auditing.   The internal auditing department is generally responsible for the establishment of control procedures for spoilage, waste, and scrap, and for monitoring compliance with the procedures. The amount of time and effort to be devoted to this area of control, both by operating personnel and by internal auditors, must be carefully evaluated. Control over the occurrence, recovery, handling, storage, and disposition of spoilage, waste, and scrap is important because these items often have value to be realized (or, in the case of wastes, have certain disposal requirements to be met). In addition, the efficiency of day-to-day operations may be improved by effective spoilage, waste, and scrap control. On the other hand, there is danger in devoting too much attention if the potential improvements in profits are small. Thus, each firm must determine the level of control appropriate to its particular situation.

The internal auditing literature presents extensive coverage of audit procedures and other details with respect to the design and evaluation of control systems for spoilage, waste, and scrap. The checklist presented in Exhibit 1 is illustrative of these procedures, and serves to summarize our discussion of control.[7]

Control of Nonmanufacturing Spoilage, Waste, and Scrap.   The preceding discussion, and most of the literature, has dealt with control of spoilage, waste, and scrap in manufacturing contexts. Similar concerns exist in nonmanufacturing activities, such as administrative and service functions. The manufacturing notion of spoilage has little counterpart, but both scrap and waste may exist. Scrap would take the form of used or damaged materials that have a recoverable value, such as paper or used punch cards. Waste is likely to be the most significant area, as there are many opportunities in nonmanufacturing activities for inputs to be consumed without yielding the expected output. Materials, supplies, and equipment may disappear (via theft) or be destroyed (via careless handling). Labor services may be unproductive due to lack of supervision, improper training, excessive staff, or other causes. Because these occurrences may exist in any of the firm's activities, procedures for their control should be part of the general control system. Thus, distinct control procedures will not be discussed here.

The subject of spoilage, waste, and scrap control can also be viewed in terms of organizations other than manufacturing firms. For example, retail stores, service-oriented business, and government agencies each must be concerned with this type of control as it affects their particular circumstances. As an illustration of these more specialized concerns, the following section discusses retail shrinkage control.

Retail Shrinkage Control.   The counterpart of spoilage, waste, and scrap in the retailing industry is known as "shrinkage." This is the loss of merchandise with little or no revenue resulting. Shrinkage may be due to outright disappearance of merchandise by internal theft or shoplifting, damage to merchandise by careless handling, clerical errors such as failure to note shortages in shipments received, and other causes.

Many factors exist in the context of a typical retail store that affect the firm's ability to achieve good shrinkage control.[8] These include the design and layout of the store, merchandise packaging and display practices, money-handling proce-

---

[7] Reprinted from Donald E. Patterson, "Importance of Scrap Control in Reducing Costs," *Price Waterhouse Review*, V, 3 (Autumn 1960), pp. 35–44.

[8] This discussion is based extensively on R. L. Adair, "Shrinkage Control is Everyone's Job," *Financial Executive*, XLI, 4 (April 1973), pp. 36–46.

Exhibit 1   Checklist for Evaluating Controls over Spoilage, Waste, and Scrap

A. Initial reporting of scrap, waste, and defective work
   1. What types of scrap and waste are generated by the company, and how are the quantities measured and reported?
   2. Is scrap recycled in the production process and, if so, how is this reported?
   3. Are reports of defective materials and spoiled work prepared at the point of generation?
   4. Do reports show source and cause of rejection as well as quantity and description of items?
   5. Are copies of all scrap, spoilage, and rework reports sent directly to the accounting department, and are they prenumbered for accounting control?
   6. Who else gets copies of detail reports? Are they put to effective use in minimizing scrap, waste, and spoilage?
B. Accounting department analyses and reports
   1. Are scrap, spoilage, and rework quantities shown in detail reports priced and summarized periodically by the accounting department?
   2. Are losses due to scrap, spoilage, and rework analyzed and segregated by major causes? What are the major causes?
   3. Are all related costs considered in determining amount of such losses? Are records adequate for this purpose?
   4. Is financial responsibility for these losses assigned and reported to individual departments or cost centers?
   5. Are such reports timely, and are they put to effective use in minimizing and controlling scrap, spoilage, and rework?
   6. Are fluctuations in scrap and waste quantities related to changes in production volume, production methods, and products?
   7. Where standard factors are used to relate scrap and spoilage quantities to product yield, how recently were the standards evaluated?
   8. Do the reported quantities of scrap and spoiled work seem reasonable? Excessive?
   9. How do the company's ratios of scrap to material consumption compare with those of other similar plants? With average scrap generation ratios for the industry?
C. Salvage and disposition of scrap and waste
   1. Are scrap and waste accumulated in a physically segregated area, and are physical controls adequate, particularly for high-value items?
   2. Is the physical handling of scrap, waste, and spoiled materials economically efficient?
   3. Are spoiled materials sorted and classified on the basis of ultimate disposition expected?
   4. Are costs, realizable values, and production requirements, as well as the condition of the material, considered in deciding whether to rework, scrap, or sell as seconds? Who makes the decisions?
   5. Are possible uses for obsolete materials and equipment at other company locations considered before disposing of such items as scrap?
   6. Is scrap adequately classified and segregated by basic material content before disposal, and are efforts made to remove contamination?
   7. Is all scrap and waste weighed or measured in some manner at the time of its removal from the plant? If purchaser's or public scales are used, what assurance is there that reported weights are proper?
   8. Are company premises surrounded by appropriate protective devices such as fences, guards, etc.?
   9. What assurance is there that all scrap and waste removed from the plant is reported to the accounting department?
D. Income from scrap and waste
   1. Are competitive bids obtained for sales of scrap? For waste disposal? How frequently?
   2. Are bids also obtained from the vendors from whom materials were originally purchased?
   3. Are bid prices compared with published market quotations wherever possible?
   4. Is full credit obtained from the vendor in all cases where scrap has resulted from existing defects in purchased materials?
   5. What assurance is there that all shipments of scrap and waste are billed and that all income therefrom is recorded?
   6. Are billing, collection, and recording functions segregated from each other and from the physical handling and reporting of scrap?
E. General
   1. Have the company's procedures for controlling scrap and waste been reduced to writing?
   2. Do these procedures clearly define individual responsibilities, particularly with respect to safeguarding company assets and minimizing scrap, waste, and spoilage?
   3. Are established procedures being adhered to and enforced?
   4. Do existing controls provide adequate protection against loss due to fraud, peculation, and theft, and are costs of controls related to risks involved?
   5. Are there areas in which control over scrap, waste, and spoilage appears to be lacking, marginal, or excessive?

dures, security systems, and the quality, training, and supervision of personnel. For example, a self-service store with central checkout counters is likely to be more vulnerable to shoplifting than a store having clerks on duty in each department.

Elements of an effective program for shrinkage control would include the following:

1. Top management must recognize the importance of shrinkage control, and enthusiastically support the control program.

2. Overall internal controls should be reviewed, to identify potential areas of control weakness.

3. Each level of management should have specific, defined responsibilities with respect to shrinkage control. For example:

   a. Department managers must require adherence to company policies and procedures relating to shrinkage control, and ensure that employees are properly trained and supervised;

   b. The office manager must maintain high standards for record keeping and reporting, and carry out necessary internal audit procedures;

   c. The personnel manager must investigate potential employees, and ensure that they are adequately trained before being assigned to regular duty;

   d. The security manager must carry out specified security procedures.

4. Company personnel must be made aware of the importance of shrinkage control, so that they possess both a positive interest and an awareness of procedures to be followed.

5. Appropriate security personnel, devices, and procedures must be provided.

6. Company procedures should be consistently administered, for example, with respect to the prosecution of shoplifters.

7. Standards for shrinkage should be established, and performance should be regularly measured and compared to standard. Corrective actions should be undertaken as appropriate where variances are large.

BIBLIOGRAPHY

Forbes, J. Donald: "Increased Profits Through Scrap Control," *Internal Auditor,* January-February 1970, pp. 62–67.

Hadder, Perry E.: "Operational Audit Approaches to Scrap, Surplus and Salvage," *Internal Auditor,* July-August 1969, pp. 12–21.

Horngren, Charles T.: *Cost Accounting: A Managerial Emphasis,* 4th ed., Prentice-Hall, Englewood Cliffs, N.J., 1977, pp. 603–621.

National Association of Accountants: "Cost Control of Spoiled Work: A Summary of Practice," Accounting Practice Report Number 12, *NAA Bulletin,* June 1961, sec. 3.

Stevenson, Willis C.: "Causal Factors Influencing Manufacturing Scrap Burden," *Internal Auditor,* May-June 1968, pp. 67–79.

———: "An Information Model for Scrap Control," *Management Accounting,* September 1970, pp. 38–40, 47.

Chapter **18**

Joint Products and By-products

HUGO NURNBERG
Professor of Accounting, Michigan State University

INTRODUCTION

Many manufacturing processes are characterized by the production of multiple products from common factor inputs. No special problems arise for multiple products that share common production facilities if the production of one or more products can proceed without the production of the other products. The special condition of the joint product or by-product situation is that the production of one product makes inevitable the production of another product; the one product cannot be produced without the inevitable production of the other product, either in fixed or variable proportions. Certain costing problems are unique to manufacturing processes where the production of one product makes inevitable the production of another product. Although the conceptual and practical issues inherent in the production of multiple products from common factor inputs are equally applicable to distribution processes, this chapter primarily considers manufacturing processes.

Production of multiple products from common factor inputs is a characteristic of the agricultural, extractive, and chemical industries. Examples of such multiple products by industry are indicated in Exhibit 1.

EXHIBIT 1   Multiple Products by Industry

Industry	Multiple products
Agricultural and food:	
Flour milling	Patent flour, clear flour, middlings, bran, wheat germ, cereals
Meat packing	Meat, hides, fertilizer, shortening, hair, bristles
Cotton ginning	Cotton fiber, cotton seed
Fishing	Fresh fish, canned fish, fish meal, fish oil, fertilizer
Cottonseed processing	Cottonseed oil, meal, hulls, linters
Dairy products	Cream, skim milk, whole milk, butter, ice cream, cheese
Fruit, vegetable canning	Various grades of fruits and vegetables
Tobacco	Cigarettes, snuff
Paper products	Paperboard, paper, pulp
Sugar refining	Sugar, molasses, bagasse
Chocolate manufacturing	Chocolate, cocoa, cocoa butter
Extractive:	
Copper mining	Copper, gold, silver, other metals
Sawmill operation	Various grades of lumber, slabs, sawdust
Petroleum refining	Naptha, gasoline, kerosene, diesel and fuel oil, paraffin, tar, petrochemicals
Gold mining	Gold, silver, copper, other metals
Chemical:	
Soap making	Soap, glycerine
Coke manufacturing	Coke, ammonia, coal tar, gas, benzol
Leather tanning	Tanned leather, split leather
Cork manufacture	Cork stoppers, cork shavings, linoleum
Glue manufacture	Various grades of glue, grease, tankage stock

DEFINITION OF TERMS

To clarify the discussion that follows, it is useful to distinguish between *products* and *costs*. The term *products* refers to the goods (or services) resulting from a manufacturing or distribution process, whereas the term *cost* refers to the dollar valuation of these goods (or services).

Product Definitions. *Multiple products* is perhaps the broadest term to refer to the production of two or more products from common factor inputs. More specific terms include *major products, minor products, joint products,* and *by-products.* A variety of somewhat overlapping definitions of these terms is found in the literature, as the following discussion makes apparent.

Whether termed major products, minor products, joint products, or by-products, the single most important characteristic of such multiple products is that the production of one automatically results in the simultaneous production of the others. The products are not distinguishably different until a certain stage in the production process known as the *splitoff point.* Of course, it is often technologically possible to eliminate or discard one of the multiple products at the splitoff point, but it is not economically desirable to do so if it has a sales value in excess of any unique costs of completing and marketing it. For example, Dearden notes (p. 47)[1] that in marble quarrying, it is possible to leave all of the marble except the best grade at the quarry site. However, if the other grades must be quarried in order to obtain the best grade, it is not economically desirable to leave the other grades at the quarry site as long as their sales value exceeds the unique costs of finishing and selling them. Accordingly, the quarrying of marble is a multiple production process and the various grades of marble and marble chips are multiple products because of the inevitability from an economic viewpoint of quarrying several grades of marble simultaneously.

Fixed multiple products refer to products that are produced in fixed proportions due to the nature or quality of the input or the technological process itself. For example, in the electrolytic soda-chlorine-hydrogen process, fixed proportions of caustic soda, chlorine, and hydrogen are produced from specified quantities of salt and water; similarly, in meat packing, once the animals are purchased, nothing can alter the proportion of select to inexpensive cuts of meat. Variations in product yields from fixed production processes are due mainly to variations in the effectiveness with which individual multiple products are recovered. Note, however, that fixed production processes have a time dimension. What is fixed in the short run may well be variable in the long run, although the cost of making the change may be prohibitive.

Variable multiple products refer to products produced in proportions that can be varied significantly by adjusting the production process. For example, gasoline and fuel oil can be produced in varying proportions by varying the extent of fractionalization and distillation; however, even in these situations, the extent to which the proportions can be varied is often limited by technology or market conditions. Thus, the National Association of Accountants suggests (p. 37) that the proportion in which individual multiple products are produced are often effectively fixed by market demand: "In oil refining some variation in product mix is possible but products must be produced in proportions desired by customers." This is not a true case of fixed proportions, however, although the producer does lose the flexibility to vary proportions of joint products produced due to joint demand. Situations where joint demand is invariable may be more conveniently considered equivalent to demand for a single product.

Shillinglaw suggests (p. 243) two basic types of variable joint production processes:

1. Materials-determined yields: the percentage of each of the joint products depends on the quality or composition of the joint materials inputs.

2. Processing-determined yields: the relative yields of the various joint products can be varied by alterations in the processing methods employed.

Within the context of the discussion above, however, only the latter is a variable

---

[1]The page number citations in this chapter refer to publications listed in the bibliography of this chapter.

joint production process; the former is equivalent to a series of different but fixed joint production processes, arising whenever materials (or labor) inputs change in quality. Although this distinction is somewhat arbitrary, it prevails in the literature. Indeed, the very distinction between fixed and variable joint production processes is itself somewhat arbitrary.

Whether multiple products are produced in fixed or variable proportions has important implications for managerial decision making. For inventory valuation and income measurement purposes, however, the accountant usually accepts the actual proportions in which variable multiple products are produced as a given and proceeds thereafter as if they are produced in fixed proportion.

Major Versus Minor Products.   Some writers classify multiple products produced from common factor inputs as either *major products* or *minor products,* the distinction being based on relative economic importance. Thus, multiple products of greater economic importance are referred to as major products and those of lesser economic importance are referred to as minor products. *Main products* and *prime products* are other terms for major products, whereas *by-products* or *recoveries* are other terms for minor products. Obviously, any distinction between major and minor products should be regarded as temporary, to be reconsidered as technology and economic conditions change. The classic example is petroleum refining. Gasoline was originally viewed as a by-product in the manufacture of kerosene, but, with the almost universal use of automobiles and electric lighting, kerosene became the by-product and gasoline became the major product; with the advent of the jet airliner, kerosene once again became a major product. Moreover, as indicated in the list of multiple products by industry in Exhibit 1, a minor product of one industry may be the major product of another industry.

Joint Products.   Both broad and narrow definitions of the term *joint products* are suggested in the literature. Traditionally, most economists and accountants define joint products as distinguishably different major products that are inevitably produced simultaneously from the same common factor inputs. The quantity and sales value of each joint product are such that none of them may be designated as minor products; all joint products are major products. Illustrations of joint products are found in the chemical, lumber, petroleum, mining, and meat packing industries. A meat packing firm does not produce only steak; it incurs materials and labor costs to acquire and slaughter steers which in turn supply various cuts of meat, hides, and trimmings.

Joint products may be further classified by whether their inevitable simultaneous production is in fixed or variable proportions, as discussed earlier. They may be further classified as *complementary* or *substitutable.* If the increase in the production of one joint product leads inevitably to an increase in the production of another joint product, the two are complementary; this is the usual case. In some cases, however, the production of one joint product impedes or precludes the production of another joint product, and the two are called substitutes or alternatives. This is the case in oil refining, where the drawing off of fuel oil at one stage in the fractionalization process reduces the amount of gasoline that could otherwise be obtained.

In a 1957 monograph, the National Association of Accountants favored broadening of the meaning of the term *joint products* to include minor products as well as major products; it argued that both are jointly produced from the same common factor inputs. However, this position has not been widely accepted in the literature or in practice. The term *joint products* continues to refer to major products, with the term *by-products* used to refer to minor products. Both joint products and by-products are the inevitable result of the same production process.

Co-products.   The term *co-products* is occasionally used synonymously with the term *joint products.* Thus, the National Association of Accountants states (p. 7) that "[w]here two or more major products appear in the same group, they are called co-products." However, most authors distinguish co-products from joint products; both are multiple products that share common production facilities, but the production of one or more co-products can proceed without the production of the other co-products, whereas the production of one or more joint products cannot proceed without the production of the other joint products. Thus, co-products are neither joint products nor by-products.

By-products.   It has already been noted that the term *by-products* is often used synonymously with the term minor products to refer to those multiple products that have insignificant sales values relative to those of major products. Otherwise, by-products are the same as joint products. Neuner and Frumer have suggested (p. 409) a rather arbitrary rule to distinguish between the two—if the value of a product is less than 10 percent of the total value of all of the products, it could be considered a by-product rather than a joint product. But note that what may be considered by-products for one firm may be major products for another firm, and vice versa. Thus, in copper mining, copper is the major product whereas gold is the by-product; in gold mining, on the other hand, gold is the major product and copper is the by-product. Time as well as location frequently alters the classification of major products and by-products, as illustrated in petroleum refining, discussed earlier. Ordinarily, the firm has only limited control over the quantity of *by-products* that are produced. Moreover, as Keller and Ferrara note (p. 587), by-products are often sold through different distribution channels than joint products, whereas joint products are frequently sold through the same distribution channels to the same markets. In some situations, only a management directive can resolve the distinction between a joint product and a by-product.

Scrap.   The distinction between scrap (or waste) and by-products is also difficult to establish. Horngren suggests (p. 578) that by-products have relatively more sales value than scrap, and are often subject to additional processing costs beyond the splitoff point, whereas scrap is usually sold outright. There have been numerous instances where changes in technology and economic conditions have made possible the further processing of scrap into more valuable by-products or even major products.

The Kroehler Company, a furniture manufacturer, is cited by Horngren (p. 578) as a good example of the impact of technological change on the importance of products. Historically, there has been a 40 percent wastage of wood in a furniture factory. Two-thirds of the scraps were incinerated at a cost of $2 per ton and the remaining third was used to fire steam boilers. Kroehler now compresses almost all wood scraps into cultured wood, which is used for bottoms and backs of drawers and for other purposes. The basic accounting for scrap and for by-products is the same; accordingly, the remainder of the discussion will be confined to the accounting for by-products. (See also Chapter 17.)

Cost Concepts.   At least three cost concepts are considered in the literature on joint products and by-products: separable costs, common costs, and joint costs.

Separable Costs.   Separable costs are those costs that are readily identified with individual products, invariably because they are incurred after the splitoff point. Examples of separable costs in the meat packing industry include the costs of dressing meat and tanning hides after the animal is slaughtered. Separable costs present no particular accounting problems unique to joint products and by-products; they attach directly to the products to which they relate.

Some writers, however, contend that separable processing costs incurred after the splitoff point should earn the same gross profit rate as the joint costs incurred before the splitoff point, and that the gross profit rates on all multiple products should be identical. (Indeed, this contention underlies the allocation of joint costs to joint products in accordance with relative net realizable value less normal profit margin; see the discussion later in this chapter.) Consistent with this contention, separable processing costs incurred after the splitoff point are treated effectively as joint costs. Lorig, for example, states (p. 634):

> The costs incurred up to the split-off point and the separate processing costs incurred afterward up to the point where sales values are determined are all joint costs. . . . They are unavoidably bound together. . . . Therefore, each dollar invested in such costs must logically be assumed to be equally profitable.

A logical extension of this line of reasoning would be to contend that separable distribution costs incurred after the splitoff point also "must logically be assumed to be equally profitable," and that separable distribution costs as well as separable processing costs are joint costs. Neither contention is followed generally; a distinction is usually maintained between separable, common, and joint costs, and the accounting differs for each.

Common Costs.   Common costs are those costs that are not readily identifiable with individual products and, therefore, are generally allocated. Costs may be common not only to products but also to periods of time, responsibilities, classes of customers, sales territories, and other costing units; costs that are common to products are the major concern of this chapter.

Joint Costs.   There is an important difference between joint costs and common costs, although the terms have been used synonymously. Common costs occur when multiple products are produced together although they could be produced separately, whereas joint costs occur when multiple products must of necessity be produced together and have a definite quantitative relationship to each other such that an increase in the output of one increases the output of the others, although perhaps in variable proportions. Thus, common costs differ from joint costs in that the production of multiple products can be undertaken separately in the case of common costs but not in the case of joint costs. Accordingly, joint costs represent a special type of common cost. Common costs result when management decides to use common factor inputs to produce several products. On the other hand, joint costs result from the production of more than one product due to the nature of the common factor inputs or the production process, not because of a mangement decision. In this chapter, the term *joint costs* is used henceforth to refer to lump-sum costs incurred in the simultaneous production of multiple products that cannot be produced separately.

Joint costs pose two questions for accountants. First, how should they be allocated among the individual multiple products for inventory valuation and income measurement purposes? Second, how should they be treated for decision making? It will be demonstrated that any method of assigning joint costs to individual multiple products produced simultaneously is useful for inventory valuation and income measurement purposes, but is useless for decision making.

For purposes of inventory valuation and income measurement, cost accounting systems generally distinguish between joint products and by-products. Recall that the major distinction between these two classes of products is usually based on relative sales values and is inherently arbitrary. Nevertheless, for a particular firm, the distinction is important for inventory valuation and income measurement purposes, because joint products are costed differently than by-products.

ACCOUNTING FOR JOINT PRODUCTS

Consistent with the historical cost and realization principles, inventories of manufactured goods are reported in terms of the historical cost of the factor inputs sacrificed to obtain them. This cost cannot be ascertained for individual joint products, however, because production costs are joint and apply to the group of joint products as a whole. Because it is not possible to obtain one product without the others, the cost of that product cannot be isolated; all that is known is the cost of producing all of the joint products together.

Because joint products by definition are produced concurrently, any allocation of joint costs among joint products produced in *fixed* proportions is inherently arbitrary. On the other hand, when two or more jointly produced products are produced in *variable* proportions or are not inevitably produced together, it is possible to determine the incremental cost of each by varying the output of one or the other product. In essence, this computation is possible for all substitute or alternative products, although the cost of the computation may make its use uneconomical. For example, assume that 40 units of product A and 60 units of product B are jointly produced at a total cost of $100; by modifying the production process, 50 units of product A and 50 units of product B could be produced at a total cost of $120. The $120 total joint cost can be allocated to products A and B in a totally unambiguous and nonarbitrary manner, as follows: If 50 units of each product are produced, the incremental cost of the last 10 units of product A is $20 plus 10 units of product B, or

$$10A = \$20 + 10B$$

At the same time, the total cost of producing 50 units of each product is $120, or

$$50A + 50B = \$120$$

Solving the two equations, B = $0.20 and A = $2.20. Unfortunately, a different but equally unambiguous and nonarbitrary allocation of total joint cost often results when the proportions of the two products are varied differently. As a result, the accountant usually accepts the proportions in which the joint products are produced as a given and proceeds to allocate joint costs among them as if they were produced in fixed proportions.

Multiple correlation analysis has also been suggested (Chiu and DeCoster, pp. 675–679) as an unambiguous method of allocating joint costs to individual multiple products produced in variable proportions:

> The use of multiple correlation analysis for product cost allocations generates an approximation of the marginal cost of the products . . . multiple correlation analysis frees the accountant from making the assumption that marginal costs per product are always too difficult to unearth. For products that have an output proportion that is variable, multiple correlation allocates costs in a method valuable for decision-making.

Unfortunately, although the regression coefficients (obtainable from regressing periodic measurements of total joint costs against the related periodic measurements of total outputs of the individual multiple products) are approximations of the marginal costs of these individual multiple products, the sum of these marginal costs rarely is the same as the total joint cost due to the presence of the constant in the regression equation. This constant, often referred to as the fixed or standby cost when no products are produced, must itself be allocated to the individual multiple products, at least under full-absorption costing systems. Even under direct costing systems, the constant presumably would be allocated to the individual multiple products when it is negative.

Alternatively, a regression equation could be fitted to the data subject to the restriction that there is no constant—that is, a zero intercept. Although the problem of allocating the fixed or standby cost is now circumvented, the resulting regression coefficients are no longer unbiased. As a matter of fact, because of multicollinearity among the individual joint products—an inherent characteristic of joint production processes—the regression coefficients probably are biased regardless of the presence or absence of fixed or standby costs (see Benston, pp. 666–667). Accordingly, the regression coefficients are not reliable estimates of the marginal costs of the individual joint products, hence multiple correlation analysis does not resolve the joint cost allocation problem; it also suffers from other limitations (see Benston, pp. 662–668).

Nevertheless, some allocation of joint costs to individual joint products must be made for inventory valuation and income measurement purposes. The allocation is trivial if there are no beginning and ending inventories, for there is no effect on income. In the presence of inventories, however, the allocation affects the measurement of income because different amounts of joint costs may be allocated to inventories of numerous joint products under different allocation methods. For this reason, allocation methods must be established for determining reasonable costs for joint products. Additionally, product costs may be required for such special purposes as justifying product prices before governmental regulatory bodies, although the allocation of joint costs for this purpose has long been questioned by accountants and economists.

Several approaches to the allocation of joint costs to individual joint products have been suggested in the literature and are found in practice; these approaches have been classified in a variety of ways.

The National Association of Accountants distinguished (p. 30) between two principal approaches to the allocation of joint costs: (1) according to benefits that individual joint products receive from joint cost factors; and (2) according to ability of individual joint products to absorb joint costs. On the other hand, Devine suggests (p. 115) two apparently different approaches to allocating joint costs to joint products: (1) according to the relative physical qualities of the joint products; and (2) according to relative sales values. Although these two classification schemes may appear to differ from one another, they are essentially the same. Allocation according to benefits that individual joint products receive from joint cost factors is commonly used where a dominant element in the joint cost (usually a raw material) can be traced to each joint product—that is, where the benefits are measured in terms of physical qualities. Allocation according to ability of individual joint products to absorb joint costs is the same as allocation according to relative sales values, for ability to absorb joint costs is measured by sales value. Accordingly, although each approach has many variations, there are two principal approaches to the allocation of joint costs to joint products, one based on relative physical qualities, the other on relative sales values.

Allocation by Relative Physical Characteristics.   There are various methods of allocating joint costs to joint products according to relative physical characteristics; all methods require the computation of some average, and differ primarily by whether a simple average or a weighted average is used.

Simple Average Unit Cost Method.   Perhaps the simplest method of allocating joint costs to joint products is to count the number of units of each of the joint products, add these figures together, and divide the total number of units into the total joint cost to obtain a simple average unit cost; under this method, all of the joint products have the same unit cost. Most commentators refer to this method as the *average unit cost method.* Using an example adapted from Shillinglaw (pp. 236–237), the simple average unit cost method is illustrated as follows: Suppose that it costs $5,000,000 to produce 100,000 units of output that is divisible into five different quality grades as follows:

Grade	Units
First	10,000
Second	20,000
Third	40,000
Fourth	20,000
Fifth	10,000
Total	100,000

The grades represent distinguishably different joint products. In this case, the $5,000,000 total cost is divided by the 100,000 units produced to obtain a $50 unit cost regardless of grade. Obviously, this method can be used only in situations where the joint products can be expressed in terms of the same units.

The logic underlying the simple average unit cost method is that because all joint products are by definition produced in the same process, it is illogical to argue that one product costs more to produce per unit than another. This is true from the viewpoint of the physical handling of the products, but the method is generally unsatisfactory because it ignores two important facts: (1) not all costs are directly related to physical quantities; and (2) some products might not be produced at all were they not physically inseparable, up to a certain point, from the products desired.

Allocation of joint costs under the simple average unit cost method may result in unit costs that have no relationship to their selling prices. That is, the method ignores the cost-value relationship implicit in the accounting measurements of nonmonetary assets. Costs are incurred in the expectation of generating even greater revenues; if the revenue of the group of joint products is greater than the cost of producing them, it follows that no portion of the joint cost is unproductive and no joint product should be assigned a cost in excess of the revenue from that product. Continuing the example adapted from Shillinglaw, suppose that the various grades of output can be sold at the following prices per unit:

Grade	Price
First	$120
Second	90
Third	75
Fourth	60
Fifth	30

Use of the $50 unit cost for all grades implies that some of the joint costs are more productive than others, an economic impossibility. When applied to the poorest grade of output, it produces an even more absurd result—an apparent loss of $20 per unit. Shillinglaw cites (p. 237) evidence that outputs are not equally costly by noting that premiums ordinarily must be paid for higher quality inputs:

> For example, if a given stand of timber is expected to yield a high proportion of the higher valued grades of lumber, the timber rights will command a higher price than if the lower grades predominate. Therefore, since output value affects input cost, it would seem reasonable to reflect value differences in the cost allocation.

Other situations where premiums are paid for higher-quality inputs include fruit and vegetable processing, ore refining—indeed, most processing of raw materials. It is clear that joint products are not equally costly; what is not clear is their individual costs.

Despite the serious limitations of the simple average unit cost method, it is widely used in industries that produce different grades of the same product by a single joint process, such as tobacco, flour milling, and lumber.

Weighted Average Unit Cost Method. Because the simple average unit cost method does not give satisfactory unit cost data, *weight factors* or *points* are often assigned to each joint product based on such diverse characteristics as the size of the unit, the amount of material used, the difficulty of manufacture, the time consumed in manufacture, the quality of labor used in manufacture, or the ultimate sales value. These characteristics and their relative weights are usually combined into a single weight factor, often called a *factor of conversion.* The units of finished joint products are multiplied by their respective weight factors prior to the allocation of total joint costs to the individual joint products.

Elaborating upon the previous example, weight factors assigned to the five grades of output (corresponding to five distinguishably different joint products) might be as follows:

Grade	Points
First	10
Second	8
Third	6
Fourth	4
Fifth	2

The allocation of the $5,000,000 joint cost to the five grades of output then proceeds as indicated in Exhibit 2. Thus, although the cost per unit of output averages $5,000,000/100,000 or $50, it now varies from $83.33 down to $16.67,

EXHIBIT 2   Joint Cost Allocation by Weighted Average Unit Cost Method

Item	Product 1	Product 2	Product 3	Product 4	Product 5	Total
Units produced	10,000	20,000	40,000	20,000	10,000	100,000
Points	10	8	6	4	2	
Equivalent units	100,000	160,000	240,000	80,000	20,000	600,000
Cost per equivalent unit[a]	$8.333	$8.333	$8.333	$8.333	$8.333	$8.333
Total allocated cost[b]	$833,333	$1,333,333	$2,000,000	$666,667	$166,667	$5,000,000
Cost per unit[c]	$83.33	$66.67	$50.00	$33.33	$16.67	
Selling price per unit	$120.00	$90.00	$75.00	$60.00	$30.00	
Profit per unit	$36.67	$23.33	$25.00	$26.67	$13.33	
Profit as a percent of selling price	30.56%	25.93%	33.33%	44.44%	44.44%	

[a]$8.333333 = $5,000,000 total cost/600,000 equivalent units.
[b]$833,333 = 100,000 equivalent units × $8.333333 cost per equivalent unit, etc.
[c]$83.33333 = $833,333 total allocated cost/10,000 units, etc.

depending on the grade. An obvious limitation of the weighted average unit cost method (and one it shares with the simple average unit cost method, though to a lesser degree) is that some of the joint costs appear to be more productive than others, as illustrated in Exhibit 2 where profit rates vary from 25.93 percent to 44.44 percent. Obviously, the weighted average unit cost method, like the simple average unit cost method, can be used only in situations where the joint products are expressed in terms of the same units. Indeed, one major advantage of allocating costs according to relative sales values rather than according to relative physical characteristics is the greater applicability of the former in comparison to the latter; differences in physical units of measurements are no longer important, because all products are expressed in terms of a common unit of measure, the dollar.

Use of weight factors under the weighted average unit cost method is an attempt to allocate joint cost according to the benefits received from each of the joint products. Accordingly, each unweighted unit of raw material or labor time in the final joint product is assumed to cost the same to produce as any other unweighted unit in the same or another final joint product. Weight factors may be expressed in terms of weight, volume, linear measure, atomic weight, or heat units. For example, in wineries, proof gallon has been used as the common denominator for various quantities originally measured in terms of tons, gallons, and cases; in coke manufacturing, the common denominator has often been weight of product per ton of coal; and in beef packing, the common denominator has been the basic grade of beef. In effect, there are many ways to apply the weighted average method of allocating joint costs to joint products, depending on the nature of the production process and the physical characteristics of the products.

One application of the weighted average unit cost method to joint production processes is based on chemical reactions. Specifically, the allocation of joint costs to joint products is based on the atomic weights of the latter, and is illustrated by the electrolysis of salt (NaCl) and water (H_2O) into caustic soda (NaOH), chlorine (Cl), and hydrogen (H). The chemical reaction inherent in this process is represented as follows:

$$NaCl + H_2O = Na\ O\ II + Cl + H$$
$$23\ 16\ 1 \qquad 35 \quad 1$$

The figures under the symbols on the right-hand side of the chemical equation represent the atomic weights of the elements comprising each joint product. Barring moisture and impurities, the joint products are produced in the ratio of 40 pounds of caustic soda (NaOH), 35 pounds of chlorine (Cl), and 1 pound of hydrogen (H), which is allowed to escape.

Two applications of the weighted average unit cost method in the petroleum refining industry are the *barrel-gravity method* and the *gravity-heat unit method*. Both attempt to allocate the joint cost of crude oil to the refined products consistent with certain qualities of the products—namely, their gravity, under the former, and both their gravity and heat content, under the latter. The two methods are illustrated in Exhibit 3, based on an example developed by Griffin (pp. 51–52), in

EXHIBIT 3   Weighted Average Unit Cost Method—Petroleum Refining

			Barrel-gravity method			
Product	Barrel yield	Yield percent	Gravity	Barrel gravity factor	Barrel gravity percent	Allocated cost per barrel
Motor gasoline	50,000	50	50	2,500	69.44	$ 7.74
Kerosene	15,000	15	40	600	16.67	1.86
Fuel oil	25,000	25	20	500	13.89	1.55
Gases and loss	10,000	10	0	0	0.00	0.00
Totals	100,000	100		3,600	100.00	$11.15

		Gravity-heat unit method			
Product	Barrel gravity percent	Allocated crude costs	Heat units percent	Refinery processing costs	Assigned product costs per barrel
Motor gasoline	69.44	$ 6.944	40	$ .460	$ 7.404
Kerosene	16.67	1.667	10	.115	1.782
Fuel oil	13.89	1.389	50	.575	1.964
Gases and loss	0.00	0.000	0	.000	0.000
Totals	100.00	$10.000	100	$1.150	$11.150

which the cost of the crude oil is $10.00 per barrel and the cost of its processing is $1.15 per barrel, or $11.15 in total. Under the barrel-gravity method, this $11.15 total cost per barrel is allocated to the individual refined products consistent with their relative yield and gravity; under the gravity-heat unit method, the $10.00 cost per barrel of crude oil is allocated in this fashion, but the $1.15 processing cost per barrel is allocated consistent with relative heat units. Although not presently in common use, both methods may be more widely used in the future, at least for price justification purposes before regulatory agencies, because they result in allocations of joint costs among regulated and unregulated joint products that often differ significantly from those forthcoming under the presently more common relative sales value methods.

The weighted average unit cost method outwardly appears to result in more reasonable allocations of joint costs to joint products than the simple average unit cost method, because it considers the physical characteristics of the joint products and the technological characteristics of the production process. Nevertheless, physical and technological characteristics may be unrelated to the ultimate sales value of the individual joint products; accordingly, allocations of joint costs under the weighted average unit cost method may also be unrelated to the ultimate sales value of the individual products.

The obvious resolution of this defect is to use weight factors based directly on relative sales values rather than relative quantitative or qualitative characteristics. In the latter case, the weighted average unit cost method closely approximates an allocation of joint costs according to relative sales values rather than according to relative physical characteristics.

Use of the weighted average unit cost method in the glue industry aptly exemplifies the ostensible allocation of joint costs by physical characteristics that nevertheless closely approximates allocation by relative sales values. Raw materials of known cost are placed in production, the outputs of which are several runs of glue. The first run is of the highest grade and highest market value; succeeding runs require further production at additional cost, produce lower grades and lower market values. It is entirely impractical to determine the actual cost of each run and, even if possible, such costs are meaningless because the first run would have the lowest cost but highest quality and market value, whereas the last run would have the highest cost but lowest quality and market value. Instead, the total cost of all glue produced is allocated over the various grades on the basis of their respective tests of purity. This procedure approximates allocation by relative sales values.

Allocation by Relative Sales Values.   As already mentioned, the principal alternative approach to joint cost allocation according to relative physical characteristics is allocation according to relative sales values. The rationale underlying this approach is that the products with the higher sales values should be allocated a larger portion of the joint costs than the products with the lower sales values. In effect, the joint costs are allocated to individual joint products according to the ability of the latter to absorb joint costs, and such ability is measured by sales values. The theory underlying these allocations is that cost would not be incurred unless the joint products generate enough revenue to cover all costs plus a reasonable return. In effect, the cost of each joint product is obtained by the reverse approach of relating costs to sales values. That is, if one product sells for more than another, it is held that more costs were expended to produce it and that more costs should therefore be allocated to it than the product with the lower selling price. On the other hand, allocation by relative sales values "can be considered not primarily as a way of allocating the costs among the products, but, as a way of allocating the profit" (Chiu and DeCoster, p. 674).

Field suggests (p. 91) that the allocation of joint costs to joint mineral products according to relative sales values "appears to be about as reasonable a method as can be devised in the circumstances . . . [because it] avoids carrying forward an allocation of costs disproportionate to expected revenue . . . [and therefore] results in a reasonable matching of costs and revenue." On the other hand, Ijiri notes (p. 59) that there is no logical reason why joint costs should be allocated in proportion to sales values, because joint costs and sales values represent two entirely different aspects of the goods.

Some authors (e.g., Dopuch, Birnberg, and Demski, p. 572) suggest that allocation of joint costs according to relative sales values is the only appropriate method for external financial reporting purposes. Nevertheless, various methods of allocating joint costs according to relative physical characteristics of the individual products are in widespread use, particularly where there are marked fluctuations in the selling prices of the final joint products. As long as such fluctuations are synchronized in terms of their rate of change, joint cost allocations are unaffected; but when the selling prices of some joint products are fairly stable while others fluctuate, allocating joint costs according to relative sales values becomes difficult if not impossible. Field suggests (pp. 91–92) that because of the limitations inherent in any allocation of joint costs to individual joint products, frequent changes in the specific proportions of joint costs allocated to individual joint products should not be made simply to conform to minor fluctuations in relative selling prices. Recall that the weighted average unit cost methods are often surrogates for the relative sales value methods, at least when the weight factors under the former approximate the long-run sales values under the latter.

There are several methods of allocating joint costs consistent with the relative sales values of the individual joint products, depending on the treatment accorded to separable costs incurred beyond the splitoff point.

Allocation by Relative Selling Prices.   From an economic viewpoint, the simplest situation occurs when all of the joint products are sold at the splitoff point without requiring further processing and the incurrence of separable costs of further processing. Under such circumstances, joint costs may be allocated to individual joint products according to the relative selling prices of the individual joint products. This is the equivalent to using individual selling prices as weights under the weighted average unit cost method; indeed, Neuner and Frumer refer (p. 413) to this method as the *weighted average method*, although such use of this term is decidedly uncommon. Allocating joint costs to individual joint products according to relative selling prices is illustrated in Exhibit 4, based on the example adapted from Shillinglaw that was used earlier in this chapter. Other names for this method include the *sales value method*, the *relative sales value method*, the *market price method*, and the *market value method*. In petroleum refining, it is referred to as the *sales allocation, sales realization,* or *Federal Trade Commission method*, and is applied most commonly to relative refinery prices but occasionally to relative wholesale, retail, or transfer prices (American Petroleum Institute, p. 67). Keller and Ferrara find (p. 601) that allocation according to relative selling prices "is an attempt at equality in arbitrariness."

Consistent with the notion that the valuation of inventories should be indicative of their sales-generating capacity, allocation of joint costs according to relative selling prices is generally held to give meaningful results, because such allocations presume that all final joint products should result in some profit margin under typical marketing conditions. Thus, as illustrated in Exhibit 4, where total selling

EXHIBIT 4   Joint Cost Allocation by Relative Selling Prices

Item	Product 1	Product 2	Product 3	Product 4	Product 5	Total
Units produced	10,000	20,000	40,000	20,000	10,000	100,000
Selling price per unit	$120	$90	$75	$60	$30	
Total sales	$1,200,000	$1,800,000	$3,000,000	$1,200,000	$300,000	$7,500,000
Percent of total sales	16%	24%	40%	16%	4%	100%
Total allocated joint cost	$800,000	$1,200,000	$2,000,000	$800,000	$200,000	$5,000,000
Allocated joint cost per unit	$80	$60	$50	$40	$20	
Total profit	$400,000	$600,000	$1,000,000	$400,000	$100,000	$2,500,000
Profit per unit	$40	$30	$25	$20	$10	
Profit as a percent of selling price	33.33%	33.33%	33.33%	33.33%	33.33%	33.33%

price is $7,500,000 and total allocated cost is $5,000,000, the total gross profit margin is $2,500,000 or 33⅓ percent of total selling price. The same gross profit margin pertains to each of the five joint products. Several commentators (e.g., Dearden, p. 51) suggest that the principal advantage of allocating joint costs according to relative selling prices is this purposefully constant gross profit margin for all joint products, which minimizes the effect on monthly income statements of changes in the sales mix of the joint products. Other commentators (e.g., Griffin, p. 47) criticize allocation according to relative selling prices precisely because of its constant gross profit margins.

The problems incident in allocating joint costs to individual joint products requiring processing beyond the splitoff point are illustrated in Exhibits 5, 6, and 7, based on an extension of the example used earlier in this chapter. In addition to the previous information, it is now assumed that four of the five joint products (corresponding to grades of output) require individual processing after the splitoff point prior to their sale, as follows:

Grade	Processing cost per unit
First	$ 0
Second	15
Third	10
Fourth	10
Fifth	10

Under such circumstances, allocating joint costs to individual joint products according to relative selling prices results in some of the joint products appearing to be more profitable than others, as illustrated in Exhibit 5, where profit rates vary from 0 percent to 33.33 percent. Obviously, this variation in individual product profit rates arises because of the separable costs incurred for individual processing after the splitoff point that are not considered in the joint cost allocation method.

EXHIBIT 5   Joint Cost Allocation by Relative Selling Prices in the Presence of Separable Costs to Complete

Item	Product 1	Product 2	Product 3	Product 4	Product 5	Total
Units produced	10,000	20,000	40,000	20,000	10,000	100,000
Selling price per unit	$120	$90	$75	$60	$30	
Total sales	$1,200,000	$1,800,000	$3,000,000	$1,200,000	$300,000	$7,500,000
Percent of total sales	16%	24%	40%	16%	4%	100%
Total allocated joint cost	$800,000	$1,200,000	$2,000,000	$800,000	$200,000	$5,000,000
Allocated joint cost per unit	$80	$60	$50	$40		
Total cost to complete	$-0-	$300,000	$400,000	$200,000	$100,000	$1,000,000
Cost to complete per unit	$-0-	$15	$10	$10	$10	
Total manufacturing cost	$800,000	$1,500,000	$2,400,000	$1,000,000	$300,000	$6,000,000
Manufacturing cost per unit	$80	$75	$60	$50	$30	
Total profit	$400,000	$300,000	$600,000	$200,000	$-0-	$1,500,000
Profit per unit	$40	$15	$15	$10	$-0-	
Profit as a percent of selling price	33.33%	16.67%	20.00%	16.67%	-0-%	20.00%

Allocation by Relative Net Realizable Values.   Given separable processing costs, joint costs are often allocated to individual joint products according to relative net realizable values. Net realizable value is defined in the Committee on Accounting Procedure's *Accounting Research Bulletin No. 43* (p. 31) as "estimated selling price in the ordinary course of business less reasonably predictable costs of completion and disposal." Some commentators (e.g., Horngren, p. 573) favor using relative net realizable values to approximate relative selling prices at the splitoff point if the latter are not explicitly available because there is no market for the joint products at that point. Allocation by relative net realizable values is sometimes referred to as the *hypothetical market value method.* Under this method, some of the joint products appear to be more profitable than others, as illustrated in Exhibit 6, where individual product profit rates vary from 15.38 to 23.08 percent. Nevertheless,

EXHIBIT 6   Joint Cost Allocation by Relative Net Realizable Values

Item	Product 1	Product 2	Product 3	Product 4	Product 5	Total
Units produced	10,000	20,000	40,000	20,000	10,000	100,000
Selling price per unit	$120	$90	$75	$60	$30	
Total sales	$1,200,000	$1,800,000	$3,000,000	$1,200,000	$300,000	$7,500,000
Cost to complete per unit	$-0-	$15	$10	$10	$10	
Total cost to complete	$-0-	$300,000	$400,000	$200,000	$100,000	$1,000,000
Net realizable value per unit	$120	$75	$65	$50	$20	
Total net realizable value	$1,200,000	$1,500,000	$2,600,000	$1,000,000	$200,000	$6,500,000
Percent of total net realizable value	18.46%	23.08%	40.00%	15.38%	3.08%	100.00%
Total allocated joint cost	$923,077	$1,153,846	$2,000,000	$769,231	$153,846	$5,000,000
Allocated joint cost per unit	$92.31	$57.69	$50.00	$38.46	$15.38	
Total manufacturing cost	$923,077	$1,453,846	$2,400,000	$969,231	$253,846	$6,000,000
Manufacturing cost per unit	$92.31	$72.69	$60.00	$48.46	$25.38	
Total profit	$276,923	$346,154	$600,000	$230,769	$46,154	$1,500,000
Profit per unit	$27.69	$17.31	$15.00	$11.54	$4.62	
Profit as a percent of selling price	23.08%	19.23%	20.00%	19.23%	15.38%	20.00%

allocation according to relative net realizable values is an improvement over allocation according to relative selling prices. Both methods may result in some joint products appearing more profitable than others. But if separable costs are very high on some joint products and very low on others, *some* products might appear to be earning profits while *others* appear to be incurring losses if joint costs are allocated according to relative selling prices; *all* joint products appear to be earning profits or suffering losses (although at different rates) if joint costs are allocated according to relative net realizable values. For this reason, Dopuch, Birnberg, and Demski conclude (p. 572) that allocation according to relative net realizable values "relates cost and benefits in the most reasonable and least capricious [manner] . . . by assigning costs to products in proportion to their ability to absorb them."

Allocation by Relative Net Realizable Values Less Normal Profit Margins. When individual joint products require separate processing beyond the splitoff point, the question arises whether all of the profit is attributed to the joint production activities only or to both the joint production activities and the separate processing activities. Allocating joint costs according to relative net realizable values at the splitoff point is predicated on the notion that the separable costs incurred for processing individual joint products beyond the splitoff point are not part of the total cost on which profit is earned. On the other hand, allocating joint costs according to relative net realizable values less normal profit margins is predicated on the notion that the separable costs incurred for processing individual joint products beyond the splitoff point are part of the total cost on which profit is earned, and therefore makes allowance for this profit; this method alone results in all of the joint products appearing to be equally profitable, as illustrated in Exhibit 7, where each joint product profit rate is 20 percent. It is also referred to as the

EXHIBIT 7   Joint Cost Allocation by Relative Net Realizable Values Less Normal Profit Margins

Item	Product 1	Product 2	Product 3	Product 4	Product 5	Total
Units produced	10,000	20,000	40,000	20,000	10,000	100,000
Selling price per unit	$120	$90	$75	$60	$30	
Total sales	$1,200,000	$1,800,000	$3,000,000	$1,200,000	$300,000	$7,500,000
Cost to complete per unit	$-0-	$15	$10	$10	$10	
Total cost to complete	$-0-	$300,000	$400,000	$200,000	$100,000	$1,000,000
Net realizable value per unit	$120	$75	$65	$50	$20	
Total net realizable value	$1,200,000	$1,500,000	$2,600,000	$1,000,000	$200,000	$6,500,000
20% normal profit margin per unit[a]	$24	$18	$15	$12	$6	
Total 20% normal profit margin	$240,000	$360,000	$600,000	$240,000	$60,000	$1,500,000
Net realizable value less 20% normal profit margin per unit (= allocated joint cost per unit)	$96	$57	$50	$38	$14	
Total net realizable value less 20% normal profit margin (= total allocated joint cost)	$960,000	$1,140,000	$2,000,000	$760,000	$140,000	$5,000,000
Manufacturing cost per unit	$96	$72	$60	$48	$24	
Total manufacturing cost	$960,000	$1,440,000	$2,400,000	$960,000	$240,000	$6,000,000
Profit per unit	$24	$18	$15	$12	$6	
Total profit	$240,000	$360,000	$600,000	$240,000	$60,000	$1,500,000
Profit as a percent of selling price	20%	20%	20%	20%	20%	20%

$$^a20\% = 1 - \frac{\$5,000,000 \text{ Total Joint Cost} + \$1,000,000 \text{ Total Cost to Complete}}{\$7,500,000 \text{ Total Sales}} = 1 - 0.80$$

approximated relative-sales-value method, the *modified market price method,* and the *value-added method.* Dearden suggests (p. 53) that allocation by relative net realizable values less normal profit margins is particularly appropriate where (1) the separable costs of the individual joint products differ significantly; and (2) the mix of product sales differs significantly among accounting periods. But whether the resulting uniform markup on all of the joint products of a firm is desirable for inventory purposes is subject to controversy. Such uniform markups surely are not consistent with the facts in many business situations; most firms establish selling prices to meet competition rather than to maintain uniform markups.

Standard Costs.   Until this point, the discussion has been in terms of actual costs. Standard costs, standard mixes, and standard yields may also be used to cost joint production processes in the same manner as they are used to cost other types of production processes. Variances would arise because of variations in the costs and qualities of the inputs as well as the mixes or yields of the outputs, where the standard mixes and standard yields are expressed in terms of the standard output of the joint production process. Thus, the calculation of standard joint cost is analogous to the calculation of actual joint cost except that standard costs, standard mixes, and standard yields are used instead of actual costs, actual mixes, and actual yields. It is still necessary to select one of the allocation methods described previously in order to obtain standard unit costs of individual joint products.

Valuing Joint Products in Excess of Cost. Because the various methods of allocating joint costs to individual joint products are somewhat arbitrary and therefore subject to so many valid criticisms, firms in some industries refrain from making such allocations entirely. For example, in petroleum refining, a small minority of firms use the by-product accounting method; all of the multiple products save one are accounted for as if they were minor products, notwithstanding the relatively great economic importance of some of them. Although this method results in the valuation of some multiple-product inventories in terms of their selling prices, the total valuation of all of the multiple-product inventories does not exceed total cost. (See the following discussion on accounting for by-products.) In other industries, all of the multiple-product inventories are valued in terms of their selling prices or net realizable values, which necessarily involves the recognition of profits at the time of production. Although this practice represents a departure from the historical-cost and realization principles traditionally conceived, such a practice is widespread among firms in the hog packing, canning, and mining industries. For hog packing, valuation of multiple-product inventories at net realizable values is also justified by noting the impracticability of determining unit costs (see, for example, Barden, p. 135). Indeed, such valuations enjoy explicit sanction in the controlling pronouncement on the financial reporting of inventories (Committee on Accounting Procedure, *Accounting Research Bulletin No. 43*, chap. IV, statement 9).

Valuation of inventories at net realizable values is the exception and not the rule for joint products although, as indicated below, such valuation is acceptable for by-products. The rationale for any exception is not obvious; the determination of allocated unit costs is no more impracticable in the hog packing industry than in other joint product industries, such as petroleum refining. Indeed, it is probably more practicable to determine such unit costs in hog packing than in petroleum refining, because joint production is in fixed proportions in hog packing but in variable proportions in petroleum refining. On the other hand, such allocations are probably more arbitrary for fixed-proportion than for variable-proportion joint product industries. Perhaps a more likely explanation for valuing inventories at net realizable values in the hog packing industry but at allocated historical cost in most other joint product industries relates to the readily determinable selling prices and relatively narrow profit margins of the former but not the latter industries. Other joint product industries may now be in the same position as the hog packing industry but do not report inventories at net realizable value, probably because of peculiarities in the historical development of financial reporting prior to the issuance of *Accounting Research Bulletin No. 43,* which otherwise prohibits such valuations.

Because valuation of joint product inventories at net realizable value results in reporting profits prior to the delivery of goods to customers, it has been suggested (Horngren, p. 575) that "the most sensible method is . . . [to] carry . . . inventories at net realizable value less a normal profit margin. . . ." Alternatively, joint product inventories could be reported at net realizable values but offset by an unrealized profit contra valuation account balance to be amortized as the goods are sold. But under either approach, relatively arbitrary allocations are still required to determine either the normal profit margins or the amounts of unrealized profits to be amortized as the goods are sold. In effect, both procedures adjust net realizable value back to historical cost and therefore cannot avoid the allocation problem.

ACCOUNTING FOR BY-PRODUCTS

Both joint products and by-products result inevitably from joint production processes, but whereas joint products are viewed as major products, by-products are viewed as minor products—a secondary result of operations. The distinction between the two is based on the relative economic importance of each and accordingly is subject to change with changes in technology and economic conditions. By-products vary greatly in importance in different industries. Sometimes the sales value of a by-product is so small relative to the other products that the by-product becomes practically synonymous with scrap; on other occasions, the sales value becomes so important that it becomes questionable whether the product is a by-product or a joint product. Such wide variations in the economic importance of by-products explain in part the equally wide variations in the accounting accorded to them. A reasonably complete understanding of the technology and economic conditions underlying the joint production process is essential to determine whether each product should be treated as a joint product or a by-product.

By-products are often classified into two groups depending on their condition at the splitoff point: (1) those requiring no further processing after separation from the major products and therefore marketable (or usable) immediately at the splitoff point; and (2) those requiring further processing after separation from the major products in order to be marketable (or usable). Costs of disposal present accounting problems similar to costs of processing after the splitoff point.

There are two basic approaches to the accounting for by-products. In one, no accounting recognition is given to by-products at the time of production. Rather, accounting recognition is given at the time of sale, when either the revenues or revenues less separable costs are recognized as a separate item in the income statement or as a reduction in the cost of the major products. In the other approach, accounting recognition is given to by-products at the time of production by assigning a portion of the joint costs to them at the splitoff point, thereby reducing the costs assigned to the major products; the subsequent processing (if any) and sale of the by-products are then accounted for separately. Many variations and combinations of these two basic approaches are found in practice, so many that it is difficult to classify certain by-product accounting methods as falling into one or the other of these two basic approaches. The following by-product accounting methods illustrated in comparative form in Exhibits 8 and 9 are representative of those found in practice:

1. Revenue from by-products sold is reported as additional revenue.
2. Revenue from by-products sold less separable costs of processing and disposal is reported as additional revenue.
3. Revenue from by-products sold is reported as other income.
4. Revenue from by-products sold less separable costs of processing and disposal is reported as other income.
5. Revenue from by-products sold is reported as a deduction from the cost of the major products sold.
6. Revenue from by-products sold less separable costs of processing and disposal is reported as a deduction from the cost of the major products sold.
7. Revenue from by-products sold is reported as a deduction from the cost of the major products produced.
8. Revenue from by-products sold less separable costs of processing and disposal is reported as a deduction from the cost of the major products produced.
9. Net realizable value of by-products produced is reported as a deduction from the cost of the major products produced.
10. Net realizable value less normal profit margin of by-products produced is reported as a deduction from the cost of the major products produced.

EXHIBIT 8 Alternative By-product Accounting Methods—19X1

	Methods									
	No. 1	No. 2	No. 3	No. 4	No. 5	No. 6	No. 7	No. 8	No. 9	No. 10
Revenue from major product	$135,000	$135,000	$135,000	$135,000	$135,000	$135,000	$135,000	$135,000	$135,000	$135,000
Revenue from by-product sold	1,050									
Net revenue from by-product sold		840								
Total	$136,050	$135,840	$135,000	$135,000	$135,000	$135,000	$135,000	$135,000	$135,000	$135,000
Cost of major product sold:										
Beginning inventory	$ -0-	$ -0-	$ -0-	$ -0-	$ -0-	$ -0-	$ -0-	$ -0-	$ -0-	$ -0-
Production costs (gross)	100,000	100,000	100,000	100,000	100,000	100,000	100,000	100,000	100,000	100,000
Revenue from by-product sold							(1,050)			
Net revenue from by-product sold								(840)		
Net realizable value of by-product produced									(1,200)	
Net realizable value less normal profit margin of by-product produced										(1,020)
Production costs (net)	$100,000	$100,000	$100,000	$100,000	$100,000	$100,000	$ 98,950	$ 99,160	$ 98,800	$ 98,980
Ending inventory—major product	(10,000)	(10,000)	(10,000)	(10,000)	(10,000)	(10,000)	(9,895)	(9,916)	(9,880)	(9,898)
Cost of major product sold (gross)	$ 90,000	$ 90,000	$ 90,000	$ 90,000	$ 90,000	$ 90,000	$ 89,055	$ 89,244	$ 88,920	$ 89,082
Revenue from by-product sold					(1,050)					
Net revenue from by-product sold						(840)				
Cost of major product sold (net)	$ 90,000	$ 90,000	$ 90,000	$ 90,000	$ 88,950	$ 89,160	$ 89,055	$ 89,244	$ 88,920	$ 89,082
Gross operating margin	$ 46,050	$ 45,840	$ 45,000	$ 45,000	$ 46,050	$ 45,840	$ 45,945	$ 45,756	$ 46,080	$ 45,918
Selling and administrative expenses (gross)	$ 12,000	$ 12,000	$ 12,000	$ 12,000	$ 12,000	$ 12,000	$ 12,000	$ 12,000	$ 12,000	$ 12,000
Amounts pertaining to by-product deducted elsewhere		210		210		210		210	210	210
Selling and administrative expenses (net)	$ 12,000	$ 11,790	$ 12,000	$ 11,790	$ 12,000	$ 11,790	$ 12,000	$ 11,790	$ 11,790	$ 11,790
Net operating margin	$ 34,050	$ 34,050	$ 33,000	$ 33,210	$ 34,050	$ 34,050	$ 33,945	$ 33,966	$ 34,290	$ 34,128
Revenue from by-products			1,050							
Net revenue from by-products				840					-0-	126
Net income for 19X1	$ 34,050	$ 34,050	$ 34,050	$ 34,050	$ 34,050	$ 34,050	$ 33,945	$ 33,966	$ 34,290	$ 34,254

EXHIBIT 9   Alternative By-product Accounting Methods—19X2

	Methods									
	No. 1	No. 2	No. 3	No. 4	No. 5	No. 6	No. 7	No. 8	No. 9	No. 10
Revenue from major product	$15,000	$15,000	$15,000	$15,000	$15,000	$15,000	$15,000	$15,000	$15,000	$15,000
Revenue from by-product sold	450									
Net revenue from by-product sold		360								
Total	$15,450	$15,360	$15,000	$15,000	$15,000	$15,000	$15,000	$15,000	$15,000	$15,000
Cost of major product sold:										
Beginning inventory										
Production costs (gross)	$10,000	$10,000	$10,000	$10,000	$10,000	$10,000	$9,895	$9,916	$9,880	$9,898
Revenue from by-product sold	-0-				(450)					
Net revenue from by-product sold		-0-				(360)				
Net realizable value of by-product produced							(450)		-0-	
Net realizable value less normal profit margin of by-product produced								(360)		-0-
Production costs (net)	$10,000	$10,000	$10,000	$10,000	$9,550	$9,640	$9,445	$9,556	$9,880	$9,898
Ending inventory—major product	-0-	-0-	-0-	-0-						
Cost of major product sold (gross)	$10,000	$10,000	$10,000	$10,000	$9,550	$9,640	$9,445	$9,556	$9,880	$9,898
Revenue from by-product sold										
Net revenue from by-product sold										
Cost of major product sold (net)	$10,000	$10,000	$10,000	$10,000	$9,550	$9,640	$9,445	$9,556	$9,880	$9,898
Gross operating margin	$5,450	$5,360	$5,000	$5,000	$5,450	$5,360	$5,555	$5,444	$5,120	$5,102
Selling and administrative expenses (gross)	$1,000	$1,000	$1,000	$1,000	$1,000	$1,000	$1,000	$1,000	$1,000	$1,000
Amounts pertaining to by-product deducted elsewhere		90		90		90		90	90	90
Selling and administrative expenses (net)	$1,000	$910	$1,000	$910	$1,000	$910	$1,000	$910	$910	$910
Net operating margin	$4,450	$4,450	$4,000	$4,090	$4,450	$4,450	$4,555	$4,534	$4,210	$4,192
Revenue from by-products			450							
Net revenue from by-products				360					-0-	54
Net income for 19X2	$4,450	$4,450	$4,450	$4,450	$4,450	$4,450	$4,555	$4,534	$4,210	$4,246
Net income for 19X1	34,050	34,050	34,050	34,050	34,050	34,050	33,945	33,966	34,290	34,254
Net income for 19X1 and 19X2	$38,500	$38,500	$38,500	$38,500	$38,500	$38,500	$38,500	$38,500	$38,500	$38,500

Under the last two methods, subsequent sales of by-products with initial carrying values equal to either net realizable value or net realizable value less a normal profit margin can be accounted for in a variety of ways analogous to the first eight methods listed above. To simplify the discussion, under the last two methods the illustration assumes that any differences between the revenue from such sales and the sum of the by-product carrying values and separable processing and disposal costs are reported net as other income. Also in order to simplify the discussion, the methods are illustrated for processes involving one major product and one by-product, although they are equally applicable to processes involving several of each.

The following data underlie the comparative illustration of the various by-product accounting methods in Exhibits 8 and 9, adapted from an example offered by Horngren (pp. 579–580):

	19X1	19X2
Major product:		
Beginning inventory	0 units	1,000 units
Production	10,000 units	0 units
Sales	9,000 units	1,000 units
Ending inventory	1,000 units	0 units
Sales revenue (@ $15.00)	$135,000	$15,000
By-product:		
Beginning inventory	0 units	300 units
Production	1,000 units	0 units
Sales	700 units	300 units
Ending inventory	300 units	0 units
Sales revenue (@ $1.50)	$1,050	$450
Disposal costs (@ $.30)	$210	$90

Selling and administrative costs total $12,000 for 19X1, including $210 for the disposal of the by-product, and $1,000 for 19X2, including $90 for the disposal of the by-product. The normal profit margin on the sale of the by-product is 12 percent of selling price, or $.18 per unit. All production occurs in 19X1 at a total cost of $100,000. Given the simplifications inherent in the example, net income for the two years taken together is the same under all methods. Accordingly, as in so many other phases of accounting, the conceptual issue with respect to by-products is one of timing the recognition of revenue and expense. The various methods raise some provocative theoretical problems concerning revenue and expense matching, but expediency usually dictates the method actually used. Accordingly, the discussion of these methods will be brief.

Additional Revenue (Methods 1 and 2). As a matter of expediency, revenues (or, preferably, revenues less separable costs of processing and disposal) from by-product sales are often reported as additional revenue *per se,* and no attempt is made to allocate a portion of the joint costs to the by-products. The major criticisms of these methods relate to the valuation of inventories for balance sheet purposes. Normally, the separable processing cost is the only amount assigned to the by-product inventory, which results in an understatement of by-product cost and an overstatement of the cost of the major product inventory. In addition, as a carryover to this accounting policy, often there is no physical attempt to control the by-product inventory, whereupon losses due to fraud may become important. Finally, these methods are faulted for the incomplete accounting that results prior to the sale of the by-products. Because of such defects, these methods are usually confined to situations where the sales value of the by-product is trivial or indeterminable at the splitoff point, or the use of more detailed methods is too costly relative to perceived benefits derived. These are among the least theoretically sound methods of accounting for by-products.

Other Income (Methods 3 and 4).   Reporting revenues (or, preferably, revenues less separable costs of processing and disposal) from by-product sales as other income is subject to the same criticisms as reporting them as additional revenue: the annual net income figures are the same under both methods; only the components differ. However, by-product activities are reported as nonoperating under the other income methods, whereas they are reported as operating under the additional revenue methods. Because by-products are the inevitable result of a joint production process, their classification as nonoperating may distort the picture of operating results. It follows that the additional revenue methods are preferable to the other income methods.

Revenues from By-product Sold Deducted from Cost of Major Product Sold (Methods 5 and 6).   Consistent with the notion that a by-product is secondary to the major product, revenues (or, preferably, revenues less separable costs of processing and disposal) from by-product sales are often reported as a deduction from the cost of the major product *sold*. An even more consistent application of this notion is to report such revenues (gross or net) as a deduction from the cost of the major product *produced;* see methods 7 and 8. Horngren characterizes (p. 580) methods 5 and 6 as appealing to accountants who prefer expediency but like to recognize conceptual niceties; methods 5 and 6 recognize that by-products somehow reduce the cost of the major product, but they are not precise in timing the recognition of such cost reductions.

Revenues from By-product Sold Deducted from Cost of Major Product Produced (Method 7 and 8).   When the revenues (or, preferably, revenues less separable costs of processing and disposal) from by-product sales are reported as a deduction from the cost of the major product *produced,* the accounting for by-products is virtually identical to the prevalent accounting for waste, scrap, and spoilage. Indeed, it has been suggested (National Association of Accountants, p. 12) that the origin of this method is related to the evolution of by-products from valueless waste:

> Costs of materials, labor, and overhead represented in the waste are of necessity charged against income producing products and additional costs incurred for disposing of the waste are added to other costs of the saleable products. When markets or uses are found, waste materials become by-products. Income realized from the by-products is first applied to reduce the disposal cost of the waste. When income from by-products exceeds the disposal cost, the accounting entry becomes a credit rather than a debit to cost of the main·product. This credit is interpreted as a partial recovery of the major product cost.

Thus, the basic assumption remains that revenues from by-product sales reduce the cost of the major product produced. Because of the close analogy to the accounting for waste, scrap, and spoilage, the methods are favored by many accountants and are in fairly widespread use. Like all previous methods, however, they can be faulted for the incomplete accounting that results prior to the sale of the by-product. The cost of the major product produced is reduced by the revenues (gross or net) of the by-products *sold,* not the by-products *produced,* resulting in a somewhat inconsistent matching of revenues and expense. Moreover, because the joint cost is assigned entirely to the major product, the by-product inventory is not assigned a value or is valued in terms of subsequent separable processing costs only. Accordingly, these methods suggest themselves primarily when the salability of the by-product is uncertain at the time of its production.

Net Relizable Value of By-product Produced Deducted from Cost of Major Product Produced (Method 9).   Reporting the net realizable value of by-product production as a deduction from the cost of the major product produced results in a conceptually consistent matching of revenues and expenses. Moreover, a virtually complete accounting is accorded to both the major product and the by-product at the time of production, whereas the methods described earlier accorded a virtually complete accounting to the major product at the time of production but to the by-product only at the time of sale. The by-product inventory is carried at net realizable value plus any separable processing costs incurred. Although this procedure violates the historical cost and realization conventions, the effect on net income is likely to be immaterial. Obviously, the method works best when net realizable value is readily estimatable; differences between estimates and amounts realized have important managerial implications and should be reported separately. The method is widely used in the beef packing industry. Several authors (Horngren, p. 578; Dopuch, Birnberg, and Demski, p. 577) consider this method to be conceptually superior to all others; indeed, some authors (e.g., Shillinglaw, p. 241) go so far as to limit their textbook discussions of by-product accounting to this method alone.

Net Realizable Value Less Normal Profit Margin of By-product Produced Deducted from Cost of Major Product Produced (Method 10). Reporting the net realizable value less normal profit margin of by-product production as a deduction from the cost of the major product produced, often referred to as the *reversal cost* or *market value method,* is a variation of method 9 where the unadjusted net realizable value is reported as the deduction. Method 10 is favored by those who argue that no inventory item should be assigned a cost that would preclude recognizing a normal profit upon its ultimate sale. Accordingly, the cost assigned to the by-product is obtained by working back from the anticipated selling price and making allowances for the normal profit margin and the separable costs of processing and disposal. An obvious difficulty in applying this method is determining just what constitutes the normal profit margin.

Method 10 is predicated on the assumption that the cost of the by-product is proportional to its selling price. It is the nearest approach to methods used to account for joint products, and is in fact occasionally used for that purpose. Indeed, the major conceptual criticism of this method, as Dopuch, Birnberg, and Demski note (p. 577), is that the costing of the by-product to assure for the subsequent recognition of a normal profit margin upon its sale implies that the by-product is of major significance to the firm, which in turn implies that it is not a by-product at all but rather is a major product. Thus, this method is held to be inconsistent with the very definition of a by-product.

Other Methods. In addition to the 10 methods of accounting for by-products considered above and illustrated in Exhibits 8 and 9, three other methods merit consideration, namely the replacement cost method, the standard cost method, and the joint cost proration method.

Replacement Cost Method. The replacement cost method is often used by firms that consume their own by-products. The by-product is assigned a cost equal to its opportunity or replacement cost, and the cost of the major product is reduced by the same amount.

Perhaps the most prominent use of the *replacement value method,* a variation of the replacement cost method, is in the petroleum industry, where it is used by numerous refineries for statistical studies and comparative operating analyses although, to date, no serious attempts have been made to substitute it for the relative sales value methods for financial reporting purposes (Griffin, p. 49; American Petroleum Institute, p. 67). The assumption underlying the replacement value method is that motor gasoline is the most important refinery product and that its cost should be determined as independently as possible of the other multiple product costs. As Griffin notes (p. 49), in theory, if a crude oil refinery is operated to obtain the maximum gasoline yield, three major products are produced—motor gasoline, fuel oil, and fuel gas; of these, the first two have established market values whereas fuel gas is normally diverted to refinery burner lines, where it becomes a source of power for other operations. The replacement value method assumes a hypothetical processing plan under which crude oil and unfinished stocks are processed in existing facilities to maximize the yields of motor gasoline, fuel oil, and fuel gas. Based on this hypothetical processing, the basic cost of motor gasoline is determined, consisting of the cost of the crude oil plus the estimated processing costs to obtain the maximum gasoline yield, reduced by the estimated market value of the residual fuel oil by-product. However, because actual production does not conform to such hypothetical processing, intermediate stocks of kerosene and distillate fuel and lube are produced, which are evaluated in terms of their motor gasoline and fuel oil content if processed to obtain the maximum gasoline yield.

> For example, kerosene stocks may be converted by appropriate cracking processes to yield maximum gasoline volumes. The cost of this kerosene, or other intermediate stock, is defined as the cost of processing an additional volume of crude oil to replace the gasoline inherent in the kerosene or other stock, lost by not processing it to its maximum gasoline yield, less any operating costs saved by failure to process to ultimate gasoline content. To this value must be added costs necessary to treat and finish the intermediate stock in order to place it in a marketable condition. These costs are referred to as *replacement values* (Griffin, p. 49).

In the final assignment of actual joint costs to the multiple products, these replacement values are assigned to the kerosene, distillate fuel and lube, and fuel oil much as net realizable values are assigned to by-products, and the remaining joint costs are assigned to the motor gasoline. The replacement value method is illustrated in Exhibit 10, based on an example developed by Griffin (pp. 50–51).

EXHIBIT 10   Replacement Value Method

Step 1. Actual production

Products	Barrel yield	Percent yield from crude oil
Motor gasoline	50,000	50
Kerosene	10,000	10
Distillate fuel and lube	25,000	25
Fuel oil	10,000	10
Gases and loss	5,000	5
Totals	100,000	100

Step 2. Theoretical processing to obtain maximum gasoline yields

Products	Percent yield from crude	Percent yield from kerosene	Percent yield distillate
Motor gasoline	60.00	72.00	58.30
Kerosene	—	—	—
Distillate fuel and lube	—	—	—
Fuel oil	31.00	18.00	35.30
Gases and loss	9.00	10.00	6.40
Totals	100.00	100.00	100.00

Step 3. Determination of basic cost of motor gasoline under theoretical processing

Cost of 1 bbl of crude oil, f.o.b. refinery	$10.00
Cost of processing 1 bbl of crude for maximum amount of gasoline, estimated	.44
Total	$10.44
Less: Fuel oil, .31 bbl at market value of $9.50/bbl	2.95
Gases and loss, .09 bbl	—
Net cost of .60 bbl of gasoline	$ 7.49
Basic cost of 1 bbl of gasoline ($7.49/.60)	$12.48

Step 4. Computation of replacement values of intermediate stocks

A. Replacement value of kerosene

.72 bbl of potential gasoline at $12.48/bbl	$ 8.99
.18 bbl of potential fuel oil at $9.50/bbl	1.71
Gross value per barrel	$10.70
Less: Manufacturing cost of making maximum amount of gasoline from 1 bbl of kerosene	.70
Replacement value of kerosene base stock	$10.00
Plus: Cost of finishing base stock to marketable kerosene	.80
Replacement value of finished kerosene per barrel	$10.80

B. Replacement value of distillate fuel and lube

.583 bbl of potential gasoline at $12.48/bbl	$ 7.28
.353 bbl of potential fuel oil at $9.50/bbl	3.35
Gross value per barrel	$10.63
Less: Manufacturing cost of making maximum amount of gasoline from 1 bbl of distillate fuel and lube	.70
Replacement value of distillate fuel and lube stock	$ 9.93
Plus: Cost of finishing base stock to marketable distillate fuel	.45
Replacement value of finished distillate fuel and lube per barrel	$10.38

Step 5. Allocation of actual refinery costs

Delivered costs of crude oil to refinery per barrel	$10.00
Processing costs to convert to actual product yields per barrel	1.15
Total	$11.15

	Yields		
Products	Percent crude	Replacement value per barrel	Total
Kerosene	10	$10.80	$1.08
Distillate fuel	25	10.38	2.60
Fuel oils	10	9.50	.95
Gases and loss	5		
	50		4.63
Motor gasoline	50		$6.52

Step 6. Summary

	Cost per barrel
Motor gasoline	$13.04
Kerosene	10.80
Distillate fuel and lube	10.38
Fuel oil	9.50

According to the Committee on Price Determination (pp. 185–186), "costing of gasoline by the replacement value method provides the closest approximation to the correct economic allocation of joint cost under varying proportions of any of the accounting methods in general use." However, the assumption underlying the replacement value method—namely, that motor gasoline is the most important refinery product—is questionable, given the importance of fuel oil to heating and kerosene to jet aviation. Indeed, in one variation of the replacement value method, fuel oil rather than gasoline is assumed to be the most important refinery product; in another variation, both fuel oil and gasoline are assumed to be more important refinery products than kerosene. Because the market value of fuel oil is considered in the determination of the cost of motor gasoline under the replacement value method, the complete independence that is sought in costing the latter is impaired.

Standard Cost Method. Under those methods discussed previously that assign a cost to the by-product equal to either its net realizable value, its net realizable value less a normal profit margin, or its replacement value, the total cost assigned to the by-product and credited to the major product is based on the actual yield, actual separable processing cost, and actual replacement cost, as applicable. Accordingly, fluctuations in these items result in fluctuations in the cost of the major product, but it is difficult to isolate the cause of the latter fluctuations.

Because of these difficulties, it is sometimes suggested that the reduction in the cost of the major product attributed to the by-product should be measured in terms of a standard unit dollar value and, where possible, a standard yield. No particular complications arise by including by-product standards in a standard cost accounting system, except that additional variance accounts are introduced to cover differences between actual and standard by-product yields and unit dollar values.

Joint Cost Proration Method.   The joint cost proration method allocates a portion of the joint costs to the by-product and reduces the cost of the major product by the same amount; the cost of the by-product for inventory purposes then becomes the sum of the allocated joint costs plus the separable costs of processing, if any. Joint cost proration is sometimes used when the by-product has a relatively high value, equivalent to a major product. Indeed, for this reason, some commentators suggest that it is a method of accounting for joint products, not by-products. The method has been applied to account for the manufacture of coke and various by-products from coal.

EFFECT OF FEDERAL INCOME TAX LAWS AND REGULATIONS

Some accountants have attempted to rely on federal income tax laws and regulations to resolve the joint cost problem, but the laws and regulations are quite broad in recognition of the impossibility of establishing specific rules for every conceivable joint cost situation. Accordingly, tax laws and regulations do not precisely establish the boundaries of acceptable practices. The most pertinent statement is Section 1.471-7 of the Regulations, which states the following:

> *Inventories of miners and manufacturers.* A taxpayer engaged in mining or manufacturing who by a single process or uniform series of processes derives a product of two or more kinds, sizes, or grades the unit cost of which is substantially alike, and who in conformity to a recognized trade practice allocates an amount of cost to each kind, size, or grade of product, which in the aggregate will absorb the total cost of production, may, with the consent of the Commissioner use such allocated cost as a basis for pricing inventories, provided such allocation bears a reasonable relation to the respective selling values of the different kinds, sizes, or grades of product.

Although the above quotation appears to require the allocation of joint costs to the individual multiple products according to their respective sales values, the weighted average unit cost method has been allowed in certain cases. That is, the regulations do not unequivocally authorize allocation according to relative sales values. As Matz and Curry note (p. 709), the regulations stress the use of an allocation method "in conformity to a recognized trade practice . . . with the consent of the Commissioner." Thus, the multiplicity of conceivable joint cost situations is too great to be covered by definite rules that allow or prohibit particular allocation methods.

Rather, before any joint cost is assigned to multiple products, the Commissioner must study the proposed allocation method and inform the producer whether it will be allowed. According to Matz and Curry (p. 709), it is a genuine problem for the Commissioner

> to decide whether or not a cost policy conforms closely enough to the accepted standards of the industry, or whether or not the alleged cost of a joint product or a by-product is

reasonably related to the market values. So much depends upon the judgment of the tax director [Commissioner] that one might justifiably claim that in joint product and by-product costing disputes, the tax director [Commissioner] is virtually the enactor of the law. Of course, decisions may be appealed, but the higher tribunals find themselves beset by the same vague, general statute; and thus they, too, must rely almost entirely upon their own independent discretion and practically *make* the law.

Clearly, the tax laws and regulations have not solved the problem of accounting for joint products and by-products. The tax authorities find themselves in exactly the same predicament as the producer, although their immediate objective is limited to collecting the proper tax.

JOINT PRODUCT ACCOUNTING AND DECISION MAKING

The foregoing discussion of the accounting for joint products has been concerned primarily with the need for inventory valuations in order to measure periodic net income and financial position for financial reporting purposes. Information on joint products is also needed by management for decision making. Some of the decisions for which accounting information on joint products *may* be necessary include the following:

1. How to determine the effect that increases or decreases in the output of joint products as a group have on costs and profits, including whether to expand total product or discontinue total production, and how to ascertain the most profitable mix of jointly produced products

2. How to determine whether it is more profitable to sell a joint product at the splitoff point or to process it further—so-called depth-of-processing decisions

3. What cost data, if any, are useful as a guide for pricing jointly produced products, including the pricing of special orders and price justification for legislative or administrative regulations

4. What cost and profit data are useful for internal control purposes, including the determination and appraisal of efficiency in purchasing and processing and the control of inventories

Although this list is not exhaustive, it is indicative of the range of decisions to be made for which accounting information may be useful. As indicated in succeeding pages, in making decisions relative to products jointly produced, it is essential to remember that the products are necessarily produced together. As Vatter succinctly notes (p. 1704),

> The real problem of cost accounting from this viewpoint is not so much the working out of bases of distributing joint costs but of establishing when and how much cost is relevant to a given question.

Like many other areas of managerial cost accounting, decision making often requires information generated from special studies and statistical analyses. For almost all decisions involving joint products, there is no need to allocate joint costs to individual joint products. The decision to produce the various joint products, the extent of their processing, and their pricing should be based on a comparison of the incremental revenues and the incremental costs. Perhaps the only area in which joint cost allocations are useful, other than for inventory valuation and income measurement purposes, is the area of price justification pursuant to legislative or administrative regulation and, even here, the evidence is inconclusive.

For these reasons, Dearden suggests (p. 48) that the overriding consideration in allocating joint costs to individual joint products is to ascertain that management is not led in using the resulting information to make incorrect decisions. Perhaps the most common mistake is to use allocated joint costs to report profits by individual joint products. Management may be led to discontinue producing or marketing a joint product that is reported to be unprofitable although its incremental revenues exceed its incremental costs. Accordingly, several commentators (Dearden, p. 48; Shillinglaw, p. 245) suggest that profits by individual joint products should never be reported to management because at best they are meaningless and, at worst, they could lead to incorrect decision making. An alternative is to devise allocation methods that are neutral or "sterilized," to use Thomas' phrase (p. 40), with respect to particular decisions. Sterilized allocations do not provide information to managers, but at least avoid the destruction of information that the use of other allocations would cause:

> Although a sterilized allocation is preferable to one that potentially generates poor decisions, it would be even better to make no allocation at all. Decision makers would be no worse off, accounting efforts would be slightly reduced, and the dangers of inappropriately employing the allocation in a context where it was not sterilized would be eliminated. Sterilized allocations, therefore, should be employed only in situations where decisions are better made from allocation-free data, but institutions compel allocations to be made or decision makers insist upon thinking in terms of allocated data. . . . otherwise potentially obnoxious allocations can be rendered harmless if we know exactly what will be done with them. But the best that can be said of a sterilized allocation is that in some circumstances it will be entirely ineffectual (Thomas, p. 46).

Unfortunately, although a joint cost allocation method may be designed to be sterilized with respect to a specific decision, it might not be sterilized with respect to another decision. A large number of different sterilized cost allocation methods would be needed, each one tailored to a limited number of specific decisions. Because the individual firm allocates joint costs to individual joint products only once, it is essential to determine for which decisions the allocations are sterilized and for which decisions they are not sterilized.

Output Decisions.   Joint product output decisions depend on the flexibility of the joint production process—that is, on whether the joint products are produced in fixed or variable proportions. Some joint products are produced in fixed proportions due to the nature or quality of the input or the technological nature of the production process. Other joint products are produced in proportions that can be varied significantly by adjusting the technological nature of the production process. The discussion of output decisions for joint products produced in fixed proportions precedes that for joint products produced in variable proportions.

Fixed Proportion Output Decisions.   For joint products produced in fixed proportions, increases or decreases in the output of one product are inevitably accompanied by proportionate increases or decreases in the output of the others and, therefore, management has no control over the product mix. In such situations, allocating joint costs to individual joint products does not facilitate output decisions and may, in fact, hinder such decision making. Rather, output decisions should be guided by a comparison of the total revenue from the sale of all of the joint products, less any separable processing or distribution costs necessary to place these products in salable form, and the total cost of the joint inputs; for this purpose, historical and forecasted income statements are often prepared for the group of related products.

The preceding may be illustrated using an example developed by Bierman and Dyckman (pp. 166–167), involving the production of two joint products A and B from a joint raw material that costs $2 per pound. For each 10 pounds of this raw material, 4 pounds of A and 6 pounds of B are produced by incurring joint processing costs of $7; subsequent to the splitoff point, additional separable finishing costs of $1.25 per pound of A and $.50 per pound of B are incurred in order to place these products in salable form. Thus, neither the cost of A nor B alone can be determined other than arbitrarily, because the production of either involves the incurrence of joint costs, $20 for materials and $7 for processing. However, the cost of producing 4 pounds of A and 6 pounds of B can be readily determined, as follows:

Raw material cost, 10 pounds @ $2	$20
Joint processing cost	7
Separable finishing cost of A, 4 pounds @ $1.25	5
Separable finishing cost of B, 6 pounds @ $.50	3
Total	$35

Because the separable finishing costs are incremental in nature, if only A was finished and B was discarded at the splitoff point, total costs would be $32, and if only B was finished and A was discarded at the splitoff point, total costs would be $30. Several conclusions are forthcoming from this information that do not depend on the allocation of joint costs: (1) If revenues from the sale of A and B exceed $35, both should be finished. (2) If revenues from the sale of A exceed $32, A should be finished; B should not be finished unless the revenues from the sale of B exceed the $3 cost of finishing B. (3) If revenues from the sale of B exceed $30, B should be finished; A should not be finished unless the revenues from the sale of A exceed the $5 cost of finishing A. (4) If revenues from the sale of A and B are less than $30, neither A nor B should be produced. Thus, although A and B are joint products, a firm may choose not to produce one or the other or both.

Variable Proportion Output Decisions.   In other cases, the proportions in which joint products are produced are variable, subject to the control of management; increasing the production of one will either cause a reduction in the others or have no effect on the production of the others. The extent of control is naturally greater over a long period than over a short period.

Under production processes of variable proportions, changing the proportions in which the joint products are produced and sold usually affects both total sales revenues and total costs. Accordingly, attainment of an optimum product mix is an important objective whenever joint products are produced in variable proportions that are controllable. Allocations of joint costs to individual products do not assist in determining the optimum product mix, however, and output decisions cannot be based on such cost allocations. Once again, it is better to compare the total cost differentials and the total sales differentials for each alternative product mix under consideration. Thus, where increasing the production of one joint product has no effect on the production of the others, the incremental revenues should exceed the incremental costs; and where increasing the production of one joint product causes a reduction in the production of the others, the incremental revenues of the former should exceed the sum of the incremental costs of the former and the net decremental revenues of the latter—an opportunity cost approach characteristic of the replacement cost method of allocating joint costs in petroleum refining.

To illustrate, consider an example suggested by Shillinglaw (pp. 243–244), in which a firm jointly produces two products, X and Y, in a single process. Product X sells for $5 per pound and product Y sells for $2 per pound. Presently, 40 percent of total output of 100 pounds is product X and 60 percent is product Y, but the production process can be modified at a total cost of $45 so that 60 percent of total output is product X and 40 percent is product Y. This is equivalent to exchanging 20 pounds of product Y plus $45 for 20 pounds of product X. The incremental cost of increasing the yield of product X is the sum of the $45 incremental processing cost plus the $40 sales value of the 20 pounds of product Y lost by the process modification, or $85; because this is less than the $100 incremental revenues on the additional 20 pounds of product X, the modification should be made.

Several difficulties hamper efforts to apply this approach in practice. First, incremental cost is not constant per unit of output but varies, depending on relative yields. For example, in refining crude oil, the cost of increasing the yield of gasoline from 35 percent to 36 percent of total output probably differs from the cost of increasing the yield from 40 percent to 41 percent. Accordingly, schedules or tables of incremental costs for different assumed product mixes are required. Second, the opportunity cost of products lost by process modification is the net revenue lost, which is not necessarily equal to the product price. Continuing the previous example, Shillinglaw notes (p. 244) that

> if existing market prices are rigid and increased output of product Y will merely result in increased inventories of product Y, then the opportunity cost component of the incremental cost of product X is zero. (It may even be negative to allow for inventory carrying costs.) Even if market prices are flexible, if the company's share of the market is so large that increases in sales volume can be achieved only by price reductions or greater promotional effort or both, the opportunity cost of product Y will almost certainly be less than its market price.

Where there are a large number of variables to be used in evaluating alternatives, manual computations are often prohibitively expensive and time consuming, and resort is made to operations research techniques, particularly linear programming. Consistent with an analysis by Kaplan and Thompson (pp. 359–361), joint cost allocations according to relative net realizable values are sterilized with respect to product mix decisions based on linear programming models. That is, because such joint cost allocations do not affect the relative profitability of the individual products, the same optimal product mix decisions should be forthcoming whether they are included or excluded in deriving the objective function coefficients of a linear programming model.

Depth-of-Processing Decisions.   Once it is decided to produce joint products, it is frequently also necessary to decide whether to dispose of one or more of the products at the splitoff point or process further. Thus, meat packers may sell meat as cut, or they may smoke, cure, freeze, or can it; petroleum refiners may sell kerosene or subject it to further fractionalization to obtain more gasoline; glue manufacturers may sell a residue as a by-product or process it further into grease and tankage stock, the latter affording the opportunity for still further processing into fertilizer tankage. When a product is the inevitable result of a joint production process, such depth-of-processing decisions should not be influenced by either the amount of the total joint costs or the portion allocated to the particular products for which further processing is contemplated. Costs incurred prior to the splitoff point are incurred regardless of any decision to process further and, for this reason, are not relevant to that decision. Rather, the depth-of-processing decision should be based on the comparison of incremental revenues and incremental separable costs of further processing beyond the splitoff point. Obviously, the amount of incremental revenues from further processing depend on whether the products for which the further processing is contemplated are salable without it; if salable at the splitoff point, the revenues available at that time are an opportunity cost to be considered in the depth-of-processing decision.

This incremental approach to depth-of-processing decisions is illustrated below, adapted from an example developed by Vatter (pp. 1703–1704). Thus, 10,000 pounds of product A and 10,000 pounds of product B are produced jointly at a total cost of $36,000. A has a selling price of $3.00 per pound or a total sales value of $30,000, whereas B has a selling price of $1.50 per pound or a total sales value of $15,000. The depth-of-processing decision to be made is whether to sell A and B at the splitoff point or, by processing the 10,000 pounds of B further at an additional cost of $18,000, convert it into 8,000 pounds of product C that has a selling price of $4.00 per pound or a total sales value of $32,000. Based on these facts, further processing of B into C should not be undertaken:

Sales revenue from C, 8,000 pounds @ $4.00		$32,000
Sales value of B at splitoff, unprocessed, 10,000 pounds @ $1.50	$15,000	
Additional processing costs	18,000	33,000
Decremental profit from further processing		$ 1,000

Comparing the total profit under the two alternatives leads to the same decision; thus, total profit is $9,000 if B is sold without further processing but only $8,000 if B is processed further and converted into C. Note that the consideration of the joint cost allocated to these products might lead to the wrong decision. Thus, if the $36,000 joint cost is allocated according to the relative selling prices of A and B at the splitoff point, the portion allocated to B would be $15,000/$45,000 of $36,000 or $12,000 and, in comparison to the $18,000 cost of further processing and the $32,000 sales value of C, might lead to the decision to process further. For depth-of-processing decisions, however, it is the opportunity cost of the product rather than its allocated joint cost that is relevant; opportunity cost in this instance is the selling price at the splitoff point. This is one reason why an increasing number of accountants favor using selling prices or net realizable values as the basis for valuing joint product inventories.

In some cases, the separable costs of further processing and distribution of individual joint products are relevant to the decision whether to produce the joint products as a group. In making this decision, Shillinglaw notes (p. 235) that the incremental profit from further processing should be considered but incremental losses should be ignored. This may be illustrated using an example developed by Shillinglaw (pp. 235–236), as follows. Suppose that a joint production process yields 2,000 tons of product A and 500 tons of product B at a total joint cost of $60,000. Product A can be sold for $40 per ton, but product B is unsalable without further processing at a cost of $6,000, whereupon it can be sold for $15 per ton. Under such circumstances, the incremental revenues from product A are $80,000, the incremental revenues from product B are $1,500, and the total profit after deducting the $60,000 total joint production cost is $21,500. Now suppose that product B can be sold for only $10 per ton after further processing or, if discarded at the splitoff point, involves a $1 per ton disposal cost. In this case, further processing of product B is no longer justified, and the joint production decision is based on a comparison of total costs with total revenues from product A alone. Product B is obtained along with product A, but is now considered waste and any costs of its disposal are costs of producing product A. However, any losses that would have occurred if product B were processed further can now be ignored, for further processing does not in fact occur.

A related problem is whether to use a joint product as a raw material in operations instead of selling it, and may be evaluated by comparing its sales value with the cost of replacing it with equivalent material from another source. This problem is not a joint cost problem, however, because the alternatives involve separable costs after the splitoff point; the solution is not unique to joint products but rather is applicable to all depth-of-processing decisions for individually pro-duced products.

The simplifying conditions in the previous analyses must be kept in mind. If there are bottleneck resources involved or other complications, the process of determining the incremental revenues and incremental costs under various alter-natives is impossible using incremental analysis alone. Hartley illustrates (1971, pp. 747–754) the use of linear programming for depth-of-processing decisions where there are production and demand constraints, joint production is in variable proportions, and some output is inventoried rather than sold, among other complications; the effect of changes in the selling prices on the quantities of the joint products sold is accommodated in this linear programming model by doing a price-demand analysis, based in part on sensitivity analysis of the optimal solution. Jensen in turn suggests (pp. 768–770) and Hartley concurs (1973, p. 773) that linear programming models do not readily admit demand functions into their structure; that the price-demand analysis on the linear programming model leads to correct decisions if carefully applied and may be more readily accepted in practice by those more familiar with linear than nonlinear programming models; but that the price-demand analysis is awkward relative to reformulation of the depth-of-processing decision as a nonlinear programming model. Thus, depth-of-processing decisions rapidly become far too complex to be handled by the traditional tools of managerial cost accounting alone.

Pricing Decisions. The long-run survival of a firm depends on its ability to obtain prices for its products that exceed all costs and provide an adequate profit margin. But as Shillinglaw aptly notes (p. 661), "[w]hile this is true in the aggregate, the cost of any one product may be a poor basis for pricing that product, partly because cost itself can be calculated in a number of ways and partly because cost calculations completely ignore the effect of price on the number of units sold." These considerations are particularly applicable to joint products. It has already been demonstrated that the costs of individual joint products may be obtained using a variety of allocation methods, each of which is more or less arbitrary. Moreover, pricing joint products on the basis of costs determined by allocations according to relative sales values (or weighted averages if the weight factors reflect relative sales values) is circular, for selling prices have to be known in order to determine the costs. Firms in industries characterized by joint production processes report that costs computed for individual joint products have little bearing on pricing decision. In most cases, pricing decisions are ultimately determined by considering market conditions rather than allocated costs.

Accordingly, although there is a widespread opinion to the contrary, pricing decisions for unregulated firms do not depend on the knowledge of joint product costs except to the extent that the latter gives some indication of the prices of competitors. For pricing decisions, greater reliance should be placed on market guides than on cost guides. As Dun notes (p. 20),

> A purchaser cares nothing for the efficiency or inefficiency of the manufacturer (provided his quality is acceptable), and cares less about the cost allocation policies of his accountant. In normal circumstances, goods or services will be purchased only if the price (however arrived at) is acceptable in the particular circumstances. Although many managements consider that price should bear some relationship to cost, this is simply their "justifiable" starting point. The difficulty of estimating demand does give strength to the cost-based pricing system, since it allows systematic pricing on some definite basis. Management sometimes thinks that it is an indication of what the opposition price might be, but unless experience has shown some reliable relationship, this is wishful thinking. . . . there can be no doubt that for pricing purposes, joint product unit costing is not only unnecessary, but may well be misleading.

Although costs computed for individual joint products may be useful guides for pricing decisions in some circumstances, such decisions require consideration of the entire situation encompassing all of the joint products.

One instance in which joint product unit costs are relevant to pricing decisions involves regulated industries. Unit costs determined by allocating joint costs according to relative sales values have been used to justify prices and existing price relationships to regulatory bodies and others, notwithstanding the well-recognized circularity.

For example, the Natural Gas Act of 1938 provides for the regulation by the Federal Power Commission of the selling price of natural gas sold in interstate commerce. Until the mid-1950s, the Act was interpreted to exclude regulation of firms engaged primarily in producing natural gas. However, the U.S. Supreme Court decision in the Phillips Petroleum Company case of July 1954 held that the sale of natural gas by the producer for transmission and resale in interstate commerce also comes under the jurisdiction of the Federal Power Commission under the Natural Gas Act. By the late 1950s, the Federal Power Commission started to regulate natural gas prices charged by producers in terms of overall production costs and historical pricing patterns, although it did not offer a definition of costs. On the other hand, although the selling price of oil is now regulated by the Federal Energy Office, such regulation is not in terms of cost so much as it is in terms of the May 15, 1973, selling price of oil.

For most producers of natural gas, it is virtually impossible to determine production costs precisely, because oil and natural gas are almost invariably found together; the costs of finding and producing oil and natural gas are jointly incurred up to the splitoff point. If the selling price of natural gas is to be regulated in terms of its cost, it is necessary to determine its cost by allocating a portion of the joint costs to the natural gas. Interestingly, many producing firms do not make such allocations for financial reporting purposes; rather, all of the joint costs are assigned to either the oil or the natural gas, which is treated as the major product, and the other is treated as the by-product.

A major controversy in the regulation of the selling prices of natural gas charged by producer firms arises over the methods used to allocate joint production costs between natural gas and oil; this controversy has exacerbated due to the dramatic increases in the selling price of oil since 1973. The Federal Power Commission traditionally favors allocating joint costs according to relative sales values, and then using the allocated costs as a basis for regulating the selling price of natural gas. As noted previously, allocating joint costs according to relative sales values is often criticized for allowing changes in sales values to cause corresponding changes in allocated costs of individual joint products although total joint costs do not change. In the context of pricing decisions, the method is also criticized for its circularity, whether prices are regulated or unregulated.

Moreover, because the selling price of natural gas but not oil is regulated in terms of cost, it is in the interest of the producer firm to allocate as much of the joint costs to natural gas and as little to oil as possible. From the viewpoint of the producer firm, allocation according to relative sales value is inequitable for regulatory purposes. As Brock aptly notes (pp. 22–23):

> Many gas contracts were negotiated years ago at prices below the current competitive market. As a result, apportionment of present [joint] costs using the low gas prices in effect under these contracts, but using current oil prices, results in a disproportionate amount [of joint costs] being allocated to oil.

Although Brock made these comments in 1963, they are even more applicable to conditions in the late 1970s, due to the dramatic increases in the selling prices of oil since 1973. (See also Accounting Principles Board Committee on Extractive Industries, p. 18.) On the other hand, until the mid-1970s, the selling prices of natural gas were relatively stable, due to the regulatory process itself. It is argued that regulation of selling prices of natural gas in terms of cost is particularly inequitable if joint production costs are allocated between oil and natural gas according to relative sales values because regulation, by restricting the selling price of natural gas, reduces the portion of the joint production costs that are allocated to natural gas and therefore impedes, if not precludes, the ability of producer firms to justify selling price increases due to production cost increases. As a result, producer firms increasingly favor certain weighted average unit cost methods over relative sales value methods of allocating joint costs for regulatory purposes, because a greater portion of the costs is allocated to natural gas under the former than under the latter methods.

Several of these weighted average unit cost methods are illustrated and compared to the relative sales value method in Exhibit 11, based on an example

EXHIBIT 11   Joint Cost Allocation Methods—Oil and Gas

Relative sales value method

Product	Total market value	Fractional part of total market value	Total cost	Cost per unit
Oil	$500,000	5/6	$107,500	$2.150 bbl
Gas	100,000	1/6	21,500	.086 mcf
	$600,000	6/6	$129,000	

British thermal units method

Product	No. of units	Weight assigned	Weighted units	Cost ratio	Total cost allocated	Cost per unit
Oil	50,000 bbl	6	300,000	6/11	$70,364	$1.4073 bbl
Gas	250,000 mcf	1	250,000	5/11	58,636	.2345 mcf
			550,000	11/11	$129,000	

Modified Btu method

		Residual fuel oil
Price per barrel at refinery		$ 9.50
Less: Manufacturing cost	$1.10	
Transportation cost	.15	1.25
Theoretical field price per barrel		$ 8.25
Market value of crude oil		$10.00

Ratio of crude oil price to theoretical price $10.00/$8.25 or 1.212
Modified btu ratio = 6 (normal ratio) × 1.212 = 7.273:1.000

Product	No. of units	Weight assigned	Weighted units	Cost percent	Total cost allocated	Cost per unit
Oil	50,000	7.273	363,650	59.26	$ 76,446	$1.5289 bbl
Gas	250,000	1.000	250,000	40.74	52,554	.21022 mcf
			613,650	100.00	$129,000	

Relative cost method

Product	No. of units	Cost per unit on single-product lease	Total cost if produced on single-product lease	Fractional part	Total cost allocation	Cost per unit
Oil	50,000 bbl	$1.875	$ 93,750	5/7	$ 92,143	$1.84286 bbl
Gas	250,000 mcf	.15	37,500	2/7	36,857	.147428 mcf
			$131,250	7/7	$129,000	

developed by Brock (pp. 22–25). It is assumed that a producer firm incurs joint production costs of $129,000 to produce 250,000 cubic feet of natural gas having the established field price of $.40 per thousand cubic feet; and 50,000 barrels of crude oil having a posted field price of $10.00 per barrel. Allocation of joint costs according to the relative sales value method results in costs of $2.15 per barrel of oil and $.086 per thousand cubic feet of natural gas. Allocation according to the British thermal units method results in costs of $1.4073 per barrel of oil and $.23454 per thousand cubic feet of natural gas; the weight factors reflect the relative heat content of oil and natural gas—specifically, that one barrel of oil contains between 5,000,000 and 6,000,000 Btu's, whereas one thousand cubic feet of natural gas contains about 1,000,000 Btu's. Allocation according to a modified Btu method results in costs of $1.5289 per barrel of oil and $.21022 per thousand cubic feet of natural gas; the weight factors here reflect both the relative heat content of oil and natural gas as well as the higher market value of the former than of the latter due to its more desirable liquid form. Finally, allocation according to the relative cost method results in costs of $1.84286 per barrel of oil and $.147428 per thousand cubic feet of natural gas; the weight factors reflect the relative costs of separately producing the same quantities of oil and natural gas on single-product leases. It should be noted that these methods are illustrated in Exhibit 11 for allocating joint production costs between crude oil and natural gas at the wellhead; variations of these and other methods are used for allocating joint costs of crude oil and its processing among the various joint products derived from crude oil at the refinery.

Like the selling price of crude oil, the selling prices of certain refined petroleum products are now regulated by the Federal Energy Office. Maximum permissible selling prices equal May 15, 1973, selling prices adjusted for the differential purchase cost of crude oil allocated to individual products; the differential cost is allocated consistent with the simple average unit cost method.

Internal Control Decisions.   The presence of joint costs affects the internal organization set up to control costs and evaluate managerial performance. Care must be taken in using costs of individual joint products for internal cost control purposes; joint cost allocations may introduce fluctuations in costs that are unrelated to managerial performance and may focus attention on the allocation method rather than on the cost to be controlled. For this reason, greater attention should be placed on changes in costs or profits over time than on absolute amounts.

Due to the jointness of the production process, inventories of individual joint products are likely to get out of balance unless continuing efforts are made to keep them in line. Increases in sales of one joint product lead to increases in its production as well as to increases in the production and inventories of other joint products whose sales have not increased. The problem might be resolved by adjusting product prices, but this is not always desirable, particularly for firms seeking stable price structures. In the absence of price changes, Shillinglaw considers (p. 245) three alternatives. First, a firm can allow the inventories to increase in the expectation that sales will increase later; if carrying costs are relatively modest, this may be the optimum solution. Second, a firm can reduce production of all products sufficiently to assure that the production of the slower-moving joint products no longer exceeds sales, but this is a drastic solution that is seldom profitable; the question of volume of output is a question of total costs and total revenues rather than one of the profitability of one product alone. Finally, a firm can devote more selling effort to the overstocked products; this is often the optimum solution that is *not* adopted because of the misinterpretation of the costs of joint products. Thus, Shillinglaw reports that unless the margin between selling price and allocated joint cost is sufficient to cover the additional selling expenses, the additional effort will appear to be unprofitable and may not be made. Recalculation of the joint cost allocations in this situation may help, but the firm is still unaware of how much it can afford to spend to sell its excess inventories. For this purpose, the only relevant figures are opportunity costs. To avoid misunderstandings, Shillinglaw suggests (p. 245) that joint costs allocations should not be reported to managers who make decisions on individual joint products. Indeed, for this reason, Dearden suggests (p. 51) a "cardinal rule" for joint product accounting: never report profits by products.

Allocated costs are not useful for determining the adequacy of prices or the profitability of individual joint products. The only reliable measure of the adequacy of prices and the profitability of individual joint products is the contribution it makes to total joint costs after separable processing and distribution costs are deducted from its selling price. This contribution is not the net profit generated by the product and, accordingly, it only indicates profitability of the product relative to other products. For decision making, management must consider the total sales, the total costs, and the total profits of all of the joint products.

The evaluation of the profitability of joint and separable processes should proceed with extreme care or not at all in the absence of bona fide selling prices at the splitoff point. For product costing purposes, joint costs may be allocated according to relative selling prices at the splitoff point or, in the absence of selling prices, according to relative approximate selling prices obtained by subtracting separable processing and distribution costs and perhaps normal profit margins from ultimate selling prices. Horngren cautions (p. 574) against evaluating the relative profitability of joint and separable processes based on approximate selling prices because of the shaky assumptions underlying them; such approximate selling prices may be required for costing joint products but are held to be useless for planning and control. The relative profitability of joint processing and further separable processing should be based on incremental analysis using bona fide selling prices at the splitoff point and after separable processing; if bona fide selling prices are not available, Horngren contends (p. 575) that analysis is impossible. Statistics on physical yields of individual joint products are generally the principal means for evaluating processing efficiency.

BY-PRODUCT ACCOUNTING AND DECISION MAKING

Like the accounting for joint products, the accounting for by-products concerns not only measuring periodic net income and financial position but also generating accounting information that is useful for decision making concerning output, depth-of-processing, pricing, and internal control of by-products. Indeed, the accounting for by-products often significantly influences their use within a firm or their sale to outsiders as opposed to their disposal as waste or scrap.

Output Decisions. In general, the output of by-products is determined by the demand for and output of major products, whether joint production is in fixed or variable proportions. Of course, if joint production is in variable proportions controllable by management, the output of major products is usually maximized relative to the output of by-products because of the higher sales values of the former. Changes in output of major products and by-products should be determined jointly by comparing total incremental revenues and total incremental expenses. These amounts should not be affected by the method of accounting for by-products—specifically, by whether by-product sales are reported as a reduction of the cost of the major products or separately as additional revenues or other income, and by whether or not by-products are assigned a portion of the joint production costs. In practice, however, some firms disregard by-products when making output decisions for major products, particularly when the by-products have insignificant sales values and disposal costs. In summary, there is no separate output decision for by-products, only for major products and by-products considered together; but important decisions remain concerning depth of processing, pricing, and internal control of by-products.

Depth-of-Processing Decisions.   Management seeks to use raw materials completely by converting waste into salable scrap, scrap into more valuable by-products, and by-products into still more valuable by-products or major products. Thus, management is faced with depth-of-processing decisions for waste, scrap, and by-products as well as for joint products, although the presumably greater familiarity of management with major products than with the others may alter perceptions of risk. Comparisons of incremental revenues and incremental expenses are required for depth-of-processing decisions for waste, scrap, and by-products, much as such comparisons are required for depth-of-processing decisions for joint products.

Valuation of by-products at net realizable value usually facilitates comparisons of incremental revenues and incremental expenses incident to depth-of-processing decisions. If by-products are unsalable at the splitoff point without further processing, no value would be assigned prior to the decision to undertake further processing.

Joint cost proration to by-products might impede correct decision making or even lead to incorrect decisions. The correct decision to process a by-product further might be made regardless of the method of accounting employed. But by not allocating joint production costs to by-products, the accounting precludes incorrectly including any portion of the joint costs in comparisons of incremental revenues and incremental expenses and also highlights the ultimate results of the decision to further process for subsequent evaluation purposes. By-products should be valued at net realizable value whenever by-product revenues are considered significant, even though no further processing is required, in order to permit management to determine whether by-products should be sold immediately, scrapped, or held in inventory to be sold through normal distribution channels.

Of course, valuation of by-products at net realizable values precludes reporting profits or losses on their sale except to the extent that the original estimates of net realizable values are incorrect. Thus, the segments of firms that sell by-products are accounted for as cost centers rather than as profit centers. To obtain the motivational benefits inherent in reporting such segments as profit centers, firms frequently make separate profit-and-loss calculations for by-products. This is accomplished in one of several ways: either the by-products are assigned no value, are valued at net realizable values less normal profit margins, or are accounted for as joint products and assigned a portion of the joint production costs.

When by-products are valued either at net realizable values less normal profit margins or at allocated joint costs, the amount of profit varies with the quantities of by-products that are sold, but the gross profit rates are largely determined by either the normal profit margins or joint cost allocations agreed upon by management. The problems encountered here are similar to those encountered by decentralized firms in establishing transfer prices. Valuation of by-products at net realizable values results in accounting for the segments as cost centers, but facilitates correct depth-of-processing decisions from the viewpoint of the firm as a whole; valuation of by-products either at net realizable values less normal profit margins or at allocated joint costs results in accounting for the segments as profit centers with the consequent attainment of some motivational benefits, but may impede correct depth-of-processing decisions, because the segment seeks to maximize segment profit rather than firm-wide profit.

There is a similar trade-off of benefits incident to assigning no value to by-products at the splitoff point. This practice might impede correct depth-of-processing decisions for by-products with positive net realizable values from immediate disposal at the splitoff point. However, the practice eliminates fluctuations in production costs of major products due to fluctuations in net realizable values of by-products. Such fluctuations could also be eliminated by valuing by-products at standard net realizable values.

Utilization Decisions. Closely related to depth-of-processing decisions are decisions concerning the use of by-products within the firm as opposed to their sale to outsiders or their disposal as waste or scrap. In decentralized firms, individual managers make decisions on both the types and quantities of materials to be consumed by considering the costs assigned and the resulting profits reported on their own operations. For by-products that can be sold at established market prices, valuation at net realizable values usually facilitates correct utilization decisions. By-products with greater net realizable values than substitute values should be sold; by-products with greater substitute values than net realizable values should be used rather than the substitute material. In either case, by-products should not be considered as substitutes, and valuation as substitutes would not be reasonable.

For by-products that cannot be readily sold at established market prices but that can be used as substitutes for other raw materials, valuation at replacement cost of equivalent raw materials usually facilitates correct utilization decisions; this valuation should be reduced by the costs of getting the by-product from the point of production to the point of use if such costs are material. Of course, such by-products should be sold whenever their net realizable values exceed the replacement costs of equivalent raw materials.

As a matter of policy, some firms split the incremental profit from using by-products within the firm between the producing and consuming units, in order to provide an incentive to the consuming unit to make the substitution. But such splits may result in incorrect utilization decisions. Moreover, such splits are inherently arbitrary and may result in internal disagreements on the shares given to each unit which must be resolved by top management. To avoid such disagreements, the usual method is to split the incremental profit equally between the producing and consuming units.

Pricing Decisions. Like pricing decisions for joint products, pricing decisions for by-products are ultimately determined by market demand rather than allocated joint costs. To the extent that a firm has some control over by-product prices, pricing decisions should be based on a comparison of incremental revenues and incremental expenses of all of the multiple products.

Internal Control Decisions. The internal control of by-products differs little from the internal control of major products except for the obviously greater emphasis on the latter than on the former. Statistics on physical yields of individual by-products are generally the principal means for evaluating processing efficiency, just as such statistics are used to evaluate processing efficiency of major products. Similarly, continuing efforts should be made to keep by-product inventories from getting out of line. In this regard, management is far more likely to adjust selling prices of by-products than of major products in order to dispose of excess inventories; indeed, in extreme cases, by-products are given away, often with the producing firm incurring the disposal costs. Finally, although it is possible to evaluate the profitability of any separate processing of by-products, it is virtually impossible to evaluate the overall profitability of individual by-products apart from the profitability of the major products.

BIBLIOGRAPHY

Accounting Principles Board Committee on Extractive Industries: *Accounting and Reporting Practices in the Oil and Gas Industry,* AICPA, New York, 1973.

American Petroleum Institute, Division of Finance and Accounting: *Report on Certain Petroleum Industry Accounting Practices,* API, Washington, D.C., 1974.

Barden, Horace G.: *The Accounting Basis of Inventories,* Accounting Research Study No. 13, AICPA, New York, 1973.

Benston, George J.: "Multiple Regression Analysis of Cost Behavior," *Accounting Review,* XLI, 4 (October 1966), pp. 657–672.

Bierman, Harold, Jr., and Thomas R. Dyckman: *Managerial Cost Accounting,* Macmillan Company, New York, 1971.

Brock, Horace R.: "Joint-Cost Allocation—Not a Rate Basis," *NAA Bulletin,* XLIV, 6 (February 1963) pp. 19–26.

Chiu, John S., and Don T. DeCoster: "Multiple Product Costing by Multiple Correlation Analysis," *Accounting Review,* XLI, 4 (October 1966), pp. 673–680.

Committee on Accounting Procedure: *Accounting Research Bulletin No. 43,* AICPA, New York, 1953.

Committee on Price Determination for the Conference on Price Research: *Cost Behavior and Price Policy,* National Bureau of Economic Research, New York, 1943.

Dearden, John: *Cost and Budget Analysis,* Prentice-Hall, Englewood Cliffs, N.J., 1962.

Devine, Carl Thomas: *Cost Accounting and Analysis,* Macmillan Company, New York, 1950.

Dopuch, Nicholas, Jacob G. Birnberg, and Joel Demski: *Cost Accounting: Accounting Data for Management's Decisions,* 2nd ed., Harcourt Brace Jovanovich, New York, 1974.

Dun, L. C.: "Product Costs—The Allocation Problem," *Chartered Accountant in Australia,* December 1972, pp. 18–22.

Field, Robert E.: *Financial Reporting in the Extractive Industries,* Accounting Research Study No. 11, AICPA, New York, 1969.

Griffin, Charles H.: "Multiple Products Costing in Petroleum Refining," *Journal of Accountancy,* CV, 3 (March 1958), pp. 46–52.

Hartley, Ronald V.: "Decision Making When Joint Products Are Involved," *Accounting Review,* XLVI, 4 (October 1971), pp. 746–755.

———: "A Note on Quadratic Programming in a Case of Joint Production: A Reply," *Accounting Review,* XLVIII, 4 (October 1973), pp. 771–774.

Horngren, Charles T.: *Cost Accounting: A Managerial Emphasis,* 3rd ed., Prentice-Hall, Englewood Cliffs, N.J., 1972.

Ijiri, Yuji: *The Foundations of Accounting Measurement: A Mathematical, Economic, and Behavioral Inquiry,* Prentice-Hall, Englewood Cliffs, N.J., 1967.

Jensen, Daniel L.: "Hartley's Demand-Price Analysis in a Case of Joint Production: A Comment," *Accounting Review,* XLVIII, 4 (October 1973), p. 768–770.

Kaplan, Robert S., and Gerald L. Thompson: "Overhead Allocation via Mathematical Programming Models," *Accounting Review,* XLVI, 2 (April 1971), pp. 352–364.

Keller, I. Wayne, and William L. Ferrara: *Management Accounting for Profit Control,* 2nd ed., McGraw-Hill Book Company, New York, 1966.

Lorig, Arthur N.: "Joint Cost Analysis as an Aid to Management," *Accounting Review,* XXX, 4 (October 1955), pp. 634–637.

Matz, Adolph, and Othel J. Curry: *Cost Accounting: Planning and Control,* 5th ed., South-Western Publishing Co., Cincinnati, 1972.

National Association of Accountants: "Costing Joint Products," *Research Report No. 31,* NAA, New York, 1957.

Neuner, John J. W., and Samuel Frumer: *Cost Accounting: Principles and Practice,* 7th corrected ed., Richard D. Irwin, Homewood, Ill., 1967.

Shillinglaw, Gordon: *Cost Accounting: Analysis and Control,* 3rd ed., Richard D. Irwin, Homewood, Ill., 1972.

Thomas, Arthur L.: *The Allocation Problem: Part Two,* Studies in Accounting Research No. 9, American Accounting Association, Sarasota, Fla., 1974.

Vatter, William J.: "Tailor-Making Cost Data for Specific Uses," *NACA Bulletin,* XXXV, 12 (August 1954), pp. 1691–1707.

Chapter **19**

Cost-Volume-Profit Analyses

NICHOLAS DOPUCH
Professor of Accounting, University of Chicago

INTRODUCTION

Cost-volume-profit analysis consists essentially in examining the relationship between changes in volume (output) and changes in profit. The common assumption in the various types of cost-volume-profit analyses is that the firm (department, division, or whatever decision unit is involved) commits itself to holding various forms of capacity for at least another "operating period." Capacity may be held in the form of plants, buildings, equipment, and managerial and other skilled labor (both manufacturing and nonmanufacturing). Inventories that will be carried over from one period to another may also be classified as a capacity.

The commitment to hold capacities results in the incurrence of fixed capacity costs—i.e., costs will be incurred whether the capacities are utilized or allowed to remain idle. The costs incurred may be current cash outlays or allocations of prior period outlays. Examples of the former are salaries for managerial and other skilled personnel, taxes and insurance on properties owned (plant, buildings, equipment, inventories), rentals or lease payments on fixed contracts, and interest and principal payments on existing debt, assuming that the latter will be kept outstanding to finance asset acquisitions of the decision unit. Examples of fixed costs that are allocations of prior period outlays are depreciation on fixed tangible assets, allocations of patent costs and of other intangible assets (advertising, research, etc.). Very often fixed costs represented by cash outlays are quite significant in comparison with the noncash fixed costs, and this is now recognized to be an important factor in CVP analyses under uncertainty.

Of course, capacities are acquired and held primarily because the services they provide are necessary in the production of some commercial output, either tangible products or services. Presumably, the incremental value of the output produced during an operating period will be greater than the incremental costs of producing and selling the output. The incremental costs of production and distribution may be measured as the total incremental cash outlays incurred during the operating period, fixed and variable, plus any opportunity costs incurred in holding and using various forms of capacities. In many CVP analyses the assumption is made that the opportunity cost of using capacities is zero, because the next best alternative to using the capacities is to allow them to remain idle. But this assumption is often made for convenience rather than because it reflects actual situations, as is illustrated below.

This chapter is organized as follows: In the next section, we first examine the short-run (deterministic) economic model of the cost-volume-profit situation. Using linear approximations of nonlinear functions, we then observe how the accountant's familiar breakeven analysis can be constructed from the economic model and illustrate some of the more basic breakeven calculations.

Next, we consider other types of decision situations that are basically extensions of breakeven analysis. In each of these situations, the analyst also relies on the assumption that certain forms of capacity will be held for another operating period.

This section is followed by a discussion of formal programming models for allocating capacities to alternative mixes of outputs. Except where otherwise noted, the typical breakeven "models" assume a single output (or constant output mix).

In the final main section, we briefly consider some of the complications in CVP analysis when uncertainty is recognized. As will be noted, under uncertainty the decision unit faces the possibility of "ruin," because total revenue may not be sufficient to cover the total cash outlays for production and distribution (including cash outlays for both variable and fixed factors).

SHORT-RUN (DETERMINISTIC) ECONOMIC MODEL

Figure 1 shows the nonlinear revenue and nonlinear cost curves typically assumed in the economist's model of a short-run output problem. The specific revenue and cost functions are given above the figure. The revenue curve is nonlinear under the assumption that the decision unit sells its output in an imperfect market wherein additional units of output can be sold only as the output's price is

FIGURE 1 Nonlinear Revenue and Cost Curves

Revenue Function: $TR = 200x - 10x^2$
Cost Function: $TC = 2x^3 - 20x^2 + 100x + 200$

x	$TR(x)$	$TC(x)$
0	$ 0	$ 200
1	190	282
2	360	336
3	490	374
4	640	408
5	750	450
6	840	512
7	910	605
8	960	744
9	990	938
10	1,000	1,200

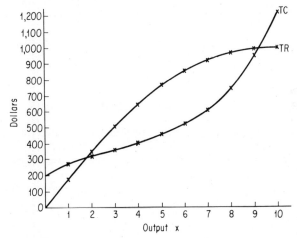

reduced. The cost function is nonlinear to reflect increased economies of scale, up to a point, followed by diseconomies.

In order to maximize a decision unit's profits in the short run, output should be expanded as long as the marginal revenue from additional units of output exceeds the marginal cost of producing and selling these additional units. The optimal output level can be found by differentiating the firm's profit function, $\pi = TR - TC$, with respect to output x, and setting this derivative equal to zero. In this case, we would differentiate:

$$\pi = TR - TC = (200x - 10x^2) - (2x^3 - 20x^2 + 100x + 200)$$

Taking the derivative, $d\pi/dx$, and setting this equal to zero, we have

$$\frac{d\pi}{dx} = (200 - 20x) - (6x^2 - 40x + 100) = 0$$

Solving for x (subject to $x \geq 0$ and assuming that the second-order condition is met) yields an optimal output, denoted by x^*, of 6.0 (closer to 6.1).

At an output of 6.0, the decision unit will receive total revenues of $840 and incur total costs of $512, yielding a profit, π, of $328. Note that a total revenue of $840 at an output of 6.0 implies an average selling price of $140 per unit.

This model for the short-run decision problem is deterministic in the sense that it assumes the decision maker has certain knowledge of the revenue and cost functions over the entire range of feasible outputs. Unfortunately, it is often impractical for the decision maker to generate the type of detailed information about the unit's revenues and costs needed to arrive at an optimal solution to the output problem. It is, however, reasonable to assume that the decision maker possesses at least an intuitive idea about the general behavior of the revenue and cost functions for ranges of output encompassing typical operations. This assumption is the basis for simplifying the economist's model to obtain the accountant's breakeven model, which relies on linear functions.

Using Linear Functions for Revenues and Costs.   Suppose that we restrict our attention to a range between 4 and 8 units. Using the information shown below Figure 1, we note that total revenues will be $640 for an output of 4 units, implying an average price of $160 per unit; at 5 units, total revenues will be $750, implying a price of $150 per unit. For outputs of 7 and 8 units the relevant figures are $910 (average price of $130) and $960 (average price of $120), respectively. Assume that on the basis of other supporting data the decision maker selects the combination of an output price of $140 and expected output of 6 units, by coincidence the optimal output obtained earlier. This will produce an expected total revenues of $840.

Consider now the cost curve for this decision unit. The cost figures for outputs of 4 to 8 units represent the optimal costs for each of these outputs. That is, the decision maker is assumed to adjust the fixed and variable inputs in such a way that the cost of $408 for 4 units, $450 for 5, $512 for 6 units, and so on, is the minimum cost for each of these outputs consistent with the fixed capacities and available technology. Suppose that we draw a line, then, connecting the vertical intercept of the nonlinear cost curve, that is, $200, with the point on the curve for $x = 6$, or $512. This will yield a linear estimate of the total cost curve as shown in Figure 2.

FIGURE 2   Relationship between Actual and Estimated Costs

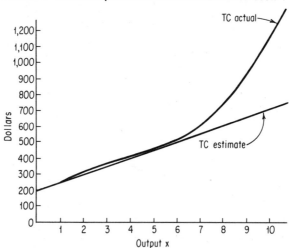

The slope of the linear line is $52, which represents an average of the changes in the total cost per unit from an output of $x = 0$ to $x = 6$. Note that if we take the derivative of the total cost curve at $x = 6$, the estimate of the marginal cost is $76, which indicates that our linear estimate would not be very accurate if we went much beyond $x = 6$ units of output. This is shown in Figure 2.

The Accountant's Breakeven Chart.   The typical breakeven chart merely brings together the linear estimates of a decision unit's revenue and cost curves. Figure 3

FIGURE 3   Relationship between Total Revenues and Total Costs as a Function of Output

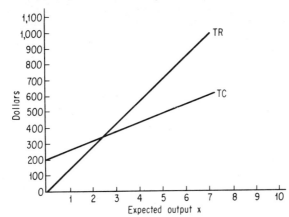

shows a breakeven chart that conforms to the data given above. It shows fixed costs of $200, a revenue line that has a slope of $140 (the average price), and a cost line with a slope of $52. The point at which total revenues equal total costs is $x = 2.27$ (approximately).

The breakeven chart is merely a simplification of a commitment to produce and sell at $140 per unit an output of 6 units, incurring an average variable cost of $52. At no point was any suggestion made that this particular decision unit could produce up to 10 units of output and sell all of these at the same average price of $140 and incur the same average variable costs of $52. If an output of 10 units is contemplated, a new breakeven chart would have to be prepared based on an average selling price of $100 and a linear estimate of the total costs based on that output. The decision maker is not committed once and for all to an output of 6 units, an expected breakeven point of 2.26 units, and an expected profit, π, of $328. The decision maker may adopt new decisions that effectively change the revenue and cost curves of the unit, thereby providing different possible outputs with different expected profits and breakeven points. We consider examples of these changes below.

Profit-Volume Analyses.   Most profit-volume analyses are based on the simple equation

$$\pi = px - bx - a$$

where π = profit
p = average selling price per unit
x = number of units of output
b = average rate of change in total costs as output is increased; for simplicity, this is assumed to measure the average variable costs of production, distribution, and administration per unit of product produced *and* sold
a = an estimate of total fixed costs (for production, distribution, and administration)

Of course, a decision unit breaks even when total revenues equal total costs, or $px - bx - a = 0$. By rearranging this simple "breakeven equation," the breakeven output is $x_{be} = a/(p - b)$. The denominator, $(p - b)$, is called the *contribution margin,* and measures the average change in profit per *unit* of x.

Breakeven in sales dollars (revenues) can be calculated by multiplying both sides of the breakeven equation by p, the selling price per unit. If we then simplify the right-hand side of the result, we observe that breakeven in sales dollars is equal to fixed costs, a, divided by the contribution margin ratio, or $(p - b)/p$. That is,

$$p(x_{be}) = p\,\frac{a}{(p - b)} = \frac{a}{(p - b)/p}$$

Using the previous figures as the basis for illustrations, we have

$$(1)\ x_{be} = \frac{\$200}{(\$140 - \$52)} = \frac{\$200}{\$88} = 2.27$$

$$(2)\ p(x_{be}) = \frac{\$200}{(\$140 - \$52)/\$140} = \frac{\$200}{\$88/\$140} = \frac{\$200}{.63} = \$317.5$$

A more convenient way of displaying the above relationship is to use the profit-volume graph. Such a graph shows the difference between the selling price and the variable cost per unit—the contribution margin—along units of output, thereby indicating the dollar amount of profit for various levels of output. A profit-volume graph defining the relevant concepts of cost-volume-profit analysis is shown in Figure 4; the same graph using the figures above is shown in Figure 5.

FIGURE 4   Profit-Volume Graph. Note: If we used sales dollars on the horizontal axis, the slope of the line would be equal to $(p - b)/p$, the contribution margin per dollar of sales

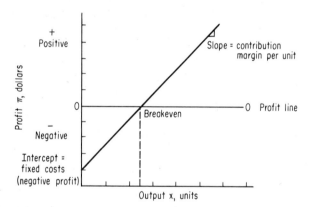

Assessing the Effect on Profit of Changes in Prices, Variable Costs, Fixed Costs, and Units of Output.   Breakeven charts and profit-volume graphs can be used to assess proposed changes contemplated by management. These changes might include an increase or decrease in the selling price per unit, a substitution of fixed for variable factors, or an increase (decrease) in fixed expenditures. In addition to changing the dollar figures of the variables involved, changes in prices and fixed expenditures can affect expected units of output and sales. To illustrate, management might contemplate increasing advertising expenditures in order to increase the number of units sold at a particular selling price. The effect on expected profit could be graphed as shown in Figure 6a, where the dashed line reflects the effect of the contemplated action. Similarly, management might wish to assess the effect of adding more labor (another shift) and cutting back on leased capacities, which would lower the fixed cash costs but increase the average variable cost of produc-

FIGURE 5   Profit-Volume Graph Using Data of Figure 4

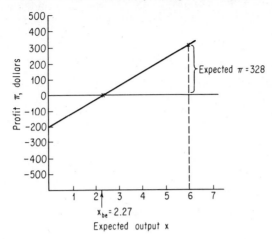

FIGURE 6   Effect on Breakeven Point of Various Changes in the Cost Structure

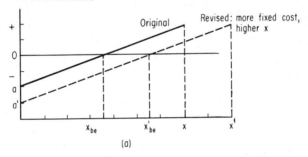

(a)

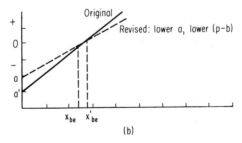

(b)

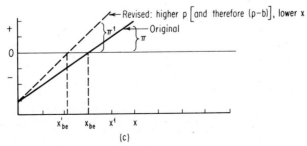

(c)

tion. The latter would be graphed as a decrease in the contribution margin per unit, because $(p - b)$, the original contribution margin, would be greater than $(p - b')$, the new contribution margin. The combined effect of this change is illustrated in Figure 6*b*. Finally, the effect of an increase or decrease in selling prices with the corresponding change in expected output is graphed in Figure 6*c*. There the assumption is that selling price will be increased, raising the contribution margin per unit from $(p - b)$ to $(p' - b)$, but decreasing expected units of output to x'.

The Use of Breakeven Charts and Profit-Volume Graphs in Control. The discussion so far has implied that the main use of breakeven charts and profit-volume graphs is at the planning stage, where management attempts to assess various strategies regarding prices, cost functions, production levels, and so on. The techniques illustrated in Figure 6 may also be used in an after-the-fact or *ex post* manner by labeling one line the "planned line" and the other, the dashed line, as the "actual line." See, e.g., Figure 7, where we assume that actual profit exceeded expected or planned profit because the average contribution margin per unit was higher than planned because (1) average variable costs were less than anticipated,

FIGURE 7   Actual and Planned Financial Outcomes

	Planned	Actual
Average selling price P	$2.00	$2.00
Average variable cost	1.00	.80
Average contribution margin	$1.00	$1.20
Fixed costs a	$5,000	$6,000
Output x_i	10,000	12,000
Profit π	$5,000	$8,400

Difference in π Due to

(a) Change in x: C.M. $(\Delta x) = \$1(2,000)$		$= + \$2,000$
(b) Change in C.M./unit: $\approx 10,000(\Delta\text{C.M.})$		
$= 10,000(\$.20)$	$= + 2,000$
(c) Change in a	$= a - a'$	$= - 1,000$
(d) Joint effect		
$(\Delta x)(\Delta\text{C.M.})$	$= 2,000(\$.20)$	$= + 400$
	Net $\Delta\pi$	$= + \$3,400$

C.M. = contribution margin.

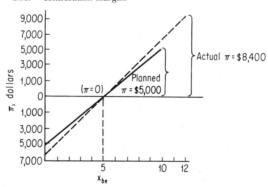

(2) fixed costs were slightly higher than planned, and (3) actual output exceeded planned output, allowing the increased contribution margin per unit to absorb this increased fixed cost. The actual and planned financial data are given in Figure 7.

Breakeven and Profit-Volume Analyses for Multiproduct Firms. The previous discussion relies on the assumption that the decision unit in question either produced a single product or had committed itself to a certain sales mix of products. In the latter case, the revenue and cost lines shown in Figure 3 would reflect a combination of the individual revenue and cost functions, with the slopes of each aggregate line being a weighted average of the slopes of the individual revenue and cost lines. To illustrate, suppose that a decision unit produces three products, A, B, and C, with average selling prices of $200, $120, and $60, respectively. The average variable cost per unit for each product is $60, $50, and $40, respectively, resulting in contribution margins of $140 for A, $70 for B, and $20 for C. Suppose that the contemplated outputs are 24,000 units of A, 24,000 units of B, and 12,000 units of C, giving a total output of 60,000 units. Note that the output of A represents 40 percent of total output, as does the output of B. The output of C, then, represents 20 percent of total output.

If these percentages are used to weight the respective figures above, we shall have a weighted average price used in constructing Figure 3. Similarly, the weighted average variable cost per unit will be .40($60) + .40($50) + .20($40) = $24 + $20 + $8 = $52, as before. This results in a weighted average contribution margin of $88, the same contribution margin used in the previous illustrations. Assume that total fixed costs are estimated at $2 million. Using these figures, we shall merely end up with a breakeven chart (Figure 8a) and profit-volume graph (Figure 8b) that are multiples of our earlier ones, but interpreted now to reflect the decisions of a multiproduct decision unit. Also shown in Figure 8b are the individual contribution margins, to indicate the total contribution to profit of each of the three products. Note that the breakeven point, where the weighted average contribution line crosses the zero profit line, is more a contrived calculation

FIGURE 8   Multiproduct Breakeven Chart (a) and Profit-Volume Graph (b).

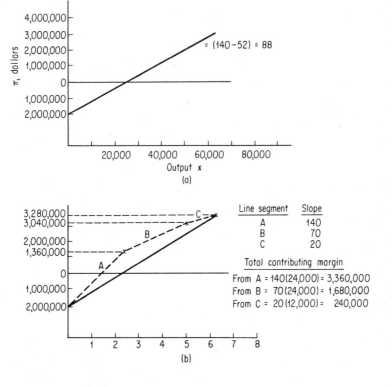

because the firm will not break even with an output of approximately 22,700 units unless these units break down into 40 percent (22,700 units) of A, 40 percent (22,700 units) of B, and 20 percent (22,700 units) of C. This is unlikely, and the assumption of a constant sales mix typically makes breakeven analysis highly questionable in multiproduct situations.

The problem in a multiproduct setting is to choose the output that leads to an optimal profit. Programming models that have been developed for this purpose are illustrated in a later section.

Summary of Breakeven and Profit-Volume Analyses.   The previous discussion dealt with the types of topics that can be found in most texts under the heading of cost-volume-profit analyses—e.g., see the appropriate chapters in Horngren (1977), Shillinglaw (1972), and Dopuch, Birnberg, and Demski (1974). However, less agreement exists with respect to the topics to be discussed in the remaining sections. That is, certain cost accounting texts will treat topics such as adding or dropping a product, make-or-buy decisions, sell now or process further, and programming models for multiproduct firms as separate or special analyses rather than as extensions of cost-volume-profit decisions. The reason they are included as part of this chapter is simply that each of these types of decision situations relies on the assumption that fixed capacities will be held during the subsequent operating period, and that the question of interest centers on the level and/or mix of output for this operating period, given these fixed capacities.

Using linear estimates of revenue and cost curves, cost-volume-profit decisions are resolved in terms of a fundamental notion: as output increases, revenue will increase at a faster rate than costs (the contribution margin is positive), or costs under one alternative will increase at a slower rate than under another alternative. As a result, increases in output contribute to the absorption of fixed costs and ultimately to positive amounts of profit.

Note then that the critical decision variables are units of output, x, the selling price or revenue per unit of output, p, the estimate of the variable cost per unit, b, and an estimate of the total fixed costs, a, that will be incurred because of the decision to hold certain capacities. One of the issues that arises in discussions of the short-run output decision problem is the degree to which accurate estimates can be obtained for these main decision variables. Of course, the optimal degree of accuracy for the estimate of the decision variables is a decision problem in itself, because accuracy can always be increased by investing additional resources in the estimation process. The additional costs from this type of investment must be balanced against the incremental benefits from increased accuracy. A complete analysis of the "value" of information under conditions of uncertainty is complex and is dealt with in more general terms in a separate chapter of this *Handbook*. We might note here, however, that benefits from increased accuracy can come about only if a better estimate leads to a better decision. In some cases, the better estimate will not affect the short-run decision. For example, if we assume that the fixed costs in the earlier illustration will be $250 instead of $200, this does not change the optimal output of 6 units. If we know that fixed costs will be larger, then we can calculate that expected profit is reduced from $388 to $338. The optimal decision of the decision unit to produce 6 units, however, is not affected. The same might hold true for small revisions in selling price and the average variable cost per unit. Illustrations of how the sensitivity of decisions to revised estimates can be assessed will be included in the section on multiproduct models.

Some mention of the methods by which the average variable cost, b, and the fixed costs, a, can be estimated is appropriate. In developing our linear estimate of the cost curve, we used only two points on the curve—the intercept (at $x = 0$) and the total cost at $x = 6$. This method of estimating the cost curve is known as the "account classification method of cost estimation." Suppose that we observe total cost equal to \$512 at $x = 6$ units. In general, the \$512 is made up of fixed and variable costs. If we could classify the cost accounts (which sum to \$512) into fixed costs and variable costs, we would have the basis for determining the two parameter values of the linear cost equation, $TC = a + bx$. Hence, assuming that the fixed cost accounts sum to \$200, then $bx = \$312$, and $b = \$312/x = \$312/6 = \$52$.

Alternatively, we could obtain linear estimates of the cost curve by using all of the observations, and then fit a line to these observations according to some criterion. For example, we could fit the line such that the sum of the squared deviations of the observation from the estimated line is minimized. The least-square regression method achieves this minimum. Another possibility would be to fit the line such that the sum of the absolute deviations is a minimum. These and other methods of cost estimation are discussed in Chapter 5 of this *Handbook*, as well as in various cost accounting texts [Dopuch, Birnberg, and Demski (1974), Shillinglaw (1977), Horngren (1977), Bierman-Dyckman (1971)].

Estimating total costs using the account classification method assumes that all individual cost items are either fixed or entirely variable. Many cost items, however, are mixed items in the sense that they possess both fixed and variable components. The two classes of mixed costs are semifixed costs—those that rise in discrete steps—and semivariable costs—those that have a fixed component and then rise continuously thereafter. Of these, the semifixed, or step costs, present the main problems in cost-volume-profit analyses. For example, in order to increase output significantly, a second shift of workers may be necessary leading to an increase in supervision and other setup costs. It is difficult to graph these and other step costs along the output axis because doing so presupposes knowledge of the optimal production and sales plans as output is continuously expanded. A linear estimate of the total cost curve assumes that the proper decisions will be made regarding how inputs should be acquired to produce different levels of outputs and that an observed cost, say \$512 at $x = 6$ units, represents the results of these input decisions.

Note also that breakeven charts and profit-volume graphs do not provide sufficient information to determine either an optimal output level or output mix. The use of linear estimates of revenue and cost curves suggest that output should be expanded up to the maximum capacity available. But an expansion of output beyond the immediate "relevant" range requires different linear estimates of the revenue and cost curves.

ANALOGOUS CVP DECISION SITUATIONS

Add or Drop a Product. A decision unit will add (drop) a product if the incremental revenues from the product are greater (less) than the incremental costs of producing and distributing the product. In general, the incremental costs consist of the incremental cash outlay costs plus the opportunity costs of using the capacities to produce the product. The opportunity costs will be positive if the capacities could be diverted from the current product and used to produce another product.

The question of whether to add a product generally arises in job-shop operations, where a decision to bid on a new order constitutes a decision to add a new product (the order). The capacity needed to work on the new order is available to the decision unit, and the question is whether to devote the capacity to the new order, to other products (other orders), or let it remain idle.

The decision of whether to add a new product in a continuous processing type of operation is less common, because the capacity needed to produce the new product may have to be acquired through additional investments. If that is the case, the analysis must rely on capital budgeting techniques, such as a discounting model, to resolve the decision (see Chapter 20). The same rule would hold if the decision to drop a product would result in the liquidation of long-lived capacities, such as the sale of fixed assets. The liquidation of long-lived capacities will reduce cash flows—revenues and cash costs—of future time periods beyond the immediate operating period.[1]

In short, the decision to add or drop a product can be treated as a short-run, cost-volume-profit decision only if the level of capacities held does not vary with the decisions. For continuous processing firms this would usually take place only for incidental items. For example, the decision to process a by-product further, given available capacities, is effectively a decision of whether or not to add the product (process further). Similarly, the decision to make a subunit rather than to purchase it is a decision of whether to add the product (make the unit) in order to obtain the subunit at a lower incremental cost than its purchase price from an outside supplier.

Generally, the critical estimates in decisions to add or drop a product are the estimates of the incremental costs of producing and distributing the product. If the product is a new order, there will be uncertainty about the required outlays for materials, labor, and incremental overhead, as well as the opportunity costs of devoting the capacities to the new order. Even though the order calls for an output that the decision unit has previously produced, there will still be uncertainty about the incremental overhead costs associated with the order and the opportunity costs of the capacities. The uncertainty about the incremental overhead remains because many overhead items rise in discrete steps (semifixed costs), making it difficult to determine their new level should a specific order be accepted.

The opportunity cost of using capacity to produce a particular product is difficult to estimate because the estimation requires knowledge of future opportunities that will be available. If a decision unit currently has idle capacity, adding a product that uses only an incidental amount of this capacity does not incur an opportunity cost. (If no future opportunities will have to be rejected because of a new project, then the new project has zero opportunity cost.) However, if the product will use a significant amount of capacity, then it is more likely that acceptance will require the decision unit to reject future profitable opportunities. The difficulty is in predicting which, if any, future opportunities will have to be rejected at the time the present decision to add a product is being made. All we can do here is point out the problem.[2]

If there is uncertainty about the incremental costs when a product is added, there must also be uncertainty about the reduction in costs if a current product is dropped (the order is refused, the by-product is not processed further, the subunit will be purchased, etc.). Quite often the simplifying assumption is made that the incremental outlay costs can be approximated by the variable costs of production and distribution, with some adjustment for changes in significant step costs—e.g., supervision or setup costs. If the spread between the revenue per unit and the total variable cost per unit—the contribution margin—is relatively large, there will be a margin of safety to absorb underestimates of changes in semifixed costs and the opportunity costs of devoting capacities to the product. Once the incremental outlay costs have been classified into variable and relatively fixed items, the same

[1] The decision by a railroad to liquidate passenger rail service is the type of decision that goes beyond the immediate operating period, because the railroad contemplates a liquidation of certain fixed assets in the process (rail cars, stations, etc.).

[2] In the absence of specific knowledge of future opportunities, many managers will require the new product to earn a satisfactory percentage return, in addition to requiring total revenues to absorb all of the product's costs. This effectively forces each product to earn at least the average rate of return over all projects normally accepted by the decision unit.

types of breakeven and profit analyses illustrated earlier may be used to assess the effect of different volume levels on profit.

Make or Buy a Unit. A firm may have capacities available that it can use to manufacture a subunit rather than to purchase the subunit from an outside supplier. This is a decision that can be made each operating period, with the decision being resolved in favor of making the unit in some periods and purchasing it in others. The firm will manufacture the unit if the incremental costs of manufacturing are less than the incremental costs of purchasing. The incremental costs of manufacturing are the incremental outlay costs plus the opportunity costs of devoting the capacities to the subunit. The latter will be zero if the capacities would otherwise stand idle. These costs will be positive if the capacities devoted to the subunit could be used to manufacture another profitable product—e.g., a main product or another type of subunit.

As in the case of a product addition, the incremental outlay costs of manufacturing may be estimated as the total variable costs of production, b', plus any change in semifixed costs. The total variable costs will simply be the variable cost per unit times the number of units to be acquired. Note, then, that the difference between the outside purchase price per unit, p', and the variable cost per unit, b', may be viewed as the contribution per unit from manufacturing, CM'_m. That is, the savings per unit are analogous to the difference between revenue per unit and variable costs per unit in a typical breakeven problem. The firm will "break even" on the decision to manufacture rather than to purchase at an output x'_{be}, where x'_{be} is equal to: incremental fixed costs/CM'_m. Note also that all of the problems encountered in estimating incremental costs for adding a product discussed above apply here as well.

Sell Now or Process Further. In general, a decision unit will process a product further rather than sell it immediately if the incremental revenues from processing exceed the incremental costs of processing. The incremental revenues are measured by the difference between the selling price of the unit after processing and the selling price if sold immediately times the number of units to be processed—that is, ($p_{later} - p_{now}$) total units. The incremental costs are the incremental outlay costs of processing and the opportunity costs of using the capacities to process the product. As noted above, this decision situation is simply a variation of the decision to add a product. Consequently, the analysis is the same except for the measure of incremental revenues, which is based on the increase in selling price after the product has been processed further.

Summary. The three situations described in this section rely on the basic assumption of cost-volume-profit analyses, viz., a decision unit intends to hold a set of capacities during the subsequent operating period that will result in the incurrence of fixed costs whether or not the capacities are utilized in some productive effort. Generally, if the capacities are used, revenues increase at a faster rate than costs. As a result, the decision will be in favor of utilization, e.g., by adding a product. In the three situations the implicit assumption was that only a single other alternative existed for the capacities. When the decision problem involves a consideration of more than one alternative, the simple rules outlined above no longer hold. This problem situation is discussed next.

SHORT-RUN MULTIPRODUCT MODELS—LINEAR PROGRAMMING EXTENSIONS OF COST-VOLUME-PROFIT

In a direct sense, linear programming may be viewed as the multiproduct analogue of the cost-volume-profit analysis (or breakeven model).[3] A linear programming problem develops whenever a firm uses common facilities to produce two or more different types of output. As a rule, the common facilities constrain the maximum amounts of each output that can be produced. In a single-product firm, it is generally profitable to expand output as long as revenues exceed variable costs. In a multiproduct firm, however, an expansion of the output of *one* product usually introduces an additional cost—the opportunity cost of not being able to produce an alternative product or products.

A Graphic Solution to a Linear Programming Problem. To illustrate, suppose that a firm may produce products X_1 and X_2. Product X_1 has a contribution margin (i.e., revenue minus variable costs) of $3; product X_2's contribution margin is $2. The firm has an available capacity of 500 hours. Each unit of output of X_1 requires 2 hours of capacity and each unit of output of X_2 requires 1 hour of this capacity. Thus, the firm can produce 250 units of X_1, 500 units of X_2, or various linear combinations of X_1 and X_2, provided that $2X_1 + 1X_2 \leq 500$ hours.

This problem is simple enough that it may be solved by comparing relative contribution margins. We note that a unit of X_1 uses 2 hours of the scarce resource and returns $3 in contribution margin. Stated alternatively, X_1 returns $1.50 per hour of capacity used. However, X_2 returns $2 per hour of capacity used; therefore, X_2 is relatively more profitable than X_1. Because all the relationships in the problem are linear, it follows that the firm should produce 500 units of X_2 and no units of X_1 (i.e., every unit of X_1 produced forces the firm to forego two units of X_2; the net effect is a loss of $1 of contribution margin). Five hundred units of X_2 yields a total contribution margin of $1,000. This is the maximum contribution margin possible, given the statement of the problem.

This problem can also be solved using graphic techniques. Letting the horizontal axis in the graph in Figure 9 represent output of X_1 and the vertical the output of X_2, the constraint $2X_1 + X_2 \leq 500$ can be graphed as a straight line joining the X_1 and X_2 coordinates of (250, 0) and (0, 500). Any point on this line represents a combination of X_1 and X_2 that is feasible (i.e., does not violate the constraint of $2X_1 + X_2 \leq 500$). The dashed lines shown in Figure 9 represent equal amounts of total contribution margin resulting from combinations of outputs of X_1 and X_2. For example, 300 units of X_2 yields the same total contribution margin ($600) as 200 units of X_1. Similarly, 500 units of X_2 yields the same total contribution margin ($1,000) as 333 units of X_1. However, 333 units of X_1 is not feasible, because this output would require 666 hours of capacity. Hence, the maximum contribution margin possible is $1,000, achieved by producing 500 units of X_2.

Note that the optimal solution occurs at a point where the total contribution margin line (in this case, *cm* = $1,000) touches an extreme point of the feasible region. The feasible region is formed by the triangle with the points moving counterclockwise, (0, 0), (250, 0), (0, 500).

Suppose now that a second constraint is imposed on the problem. For example, assume that the outputs of X_1 and X_2 must pass through a second production department which is constrained as follows: $1.5X_1 + 2X_2 \leq 480$ hours. This constraint implies that the two extremes of either 320 units of X_1 or 240 units of X_2 may be produced in the second department. When this constraint is coupled with the previous one shown in Figure 9, the feasible region is modified as shown in Figure 10. The output of X_1 is still restricted by the first constraint to a maximum output of 250 units of X_1. The primary effect of the second constraint is to reduce

---

[3]This relationship is spelled out more clearly in Robert Jaedicke, "Improving B-E Analysis by Linear Programming Techniques," *NAA Bulletin* (March 1961); and A. Charnes, W. W. Cooper, and Y. Ijiri, "Breakeven Budgeting and Programming to Goals," *Journal of Accounting Research* (Spring 1963).

FIGURE 9

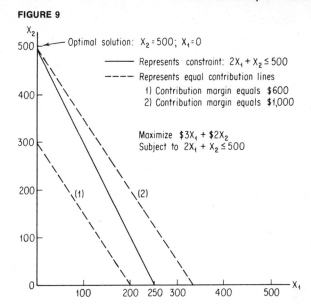

Optimal solution: $X_2 = 500$; $X_1 = 0$

——— Represents constraint: $2X_1 + X_2 \leq 500$

– – – Represents equal contribution lines

1) Contribution margin equals $600
2) Contribution margin equals $1,000

Maximize $3X_1 + \$2X_2$
Subject to $2X_1 + X_2 \leq 500$

the maximum output of X_2 from 500 to 240 units. This constraint remains binding as we move down it to the right, substituting the output of X_1 for X_2, until we reach the intersection of the two constraints ($X_1 = 208$, $X_2 = 84$), after which the first constraint again becomes binding, as shown in Figure 10.

The solution, $X_1 = 208$ and $X_2 = 84$, again occurs where the dashed line representing equal contribution margin touches an extreme point of the feasible region. A contribution margin of $792 is the maximum contribution margin possible with the constraints of $2X_1 + X_2 \leq 500$ and $1.5X_1 + 2X_2 \leq 480$.[4]

Sensitivity of Solution to Accounting Estimation Errors.   The linear programming solution obtained above relies on estimates of the contribution margins of X_1 and X_2 and their technical coefficients of production. The latter are basically engineering data. However, contribution margins are measured using accounting estimates of product variable costs along with estimates of the revenue per unit of output. These accounting measurements are subject to error, and our concern now is the extent to which we can assess the significance of these errors.

The significance of measurement errors in contribution margins may be assessed in part by analyzing the sensitivity of the solution of the linear programming model to changes in contribution margins. If the solution is sensitive to small changes, it may be profitable to obtain more reliable estimates of variable costs and revenue. To illustrate, suppose that past data indicate that the actual variable costs of product X_2 fluctuate in such a manner that its contribution margin may fall anywhere in the range $1.00 to $3.00 (unlikely perhaps, but useful for illustrative purposes).

Referring to Figure 4, we note that if X_2's contribution margin were $1.00, while X_1's remains at $3.00, the new optimal solution will become $X_1 = 250$, $X_2 = 0$. Total contribution margin would be $3(250) + \$2(0) = \$750$. However, if X_2's contribution margin were $3.00, the new optimal solution would be the same as

---

[4]This can be checked by comparing the contribution margin yielded at the other extreme points: $X_1 = 250$, $X_2 = 0$; $X_1 = 0$, $X_2 = 240$; and $X_1 = X_2 = 0$.

FIGURE 10

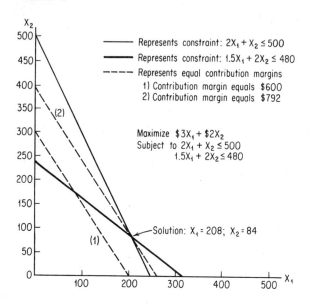

X_2

500 — Represents constraint: $2X_1 + X_2 \leq 500$

450 — Represents constraint: $1.5X_1 + 2X_2 \leq 480$

---- Represents equal contribution margins
1) Contribution margin equals $600
2) Contribution margin equals $792

Maximize $3X_1 + $2X_2$
Subject to $2X_1 + X_2 \leq 500$
$1.5X_1 + 2X_2 \leq 480$

Solution: $X_1 = 208$; $X_2 = 84$

the original one—that is, $X_1 = 208$, $X_2 = 84$, but with a revised total contribution margin of $3(208) + $3(84) = $876.[5]

These "sensitivity" results can be interpreted as follows. If the estimator knew with certainty that X_2's contribution margin would be $1.00 during the next operating period, the decision unit would revise its production plan and produce 250 units of X_1 and 0 units of X_2. In contrast, no revision would be necessary were the actual contribution margin of X_2 to increase to $3.00.

Note, however, that the estimator does not know for sure the contribution margin of X_2 for the next operating period. Instead, the estimation relies on a best estimate, which we assume is $2.00. Suppose, then, that the original production plan is implemented and actual output is $X_1 = 208$, $X_2 = 84$. Unfortunately, the actual contribution margin of X_2 drops to $1.00, so that the decision unit obtains only $3(208) + $1(84) = $708_{(actual)}. Recall that if X_2's contribution margin dropped to $1.00, the optimal solution was $X_1 = 250$, $X_2 = 0$, yielding a total contribution margin of $3(250) = $750.

Hence, the opportunity cost of not knowing in *advance* the actual contribution margin of X_2 is simply $750 − $708 = $42 (that is, the optimal value of the objective function minus the actual value).

The example could be expanded to consider other possible outcomes for contribution margins along with the prior probabilities of their occurrence. This would permit us to calculate the *expected value of perfect information*, by weighting the opportunity cost of each estimation error by the probability of its occurrence. For example, suppose that the probabilities for the contribution margin of X_2 were as follows:

[5]For each case, draw new equal contribution margin lines to reflect the revised relationships. Thus, the first change would yield equal contribution margin lines with a slope of −3/1 = −3, whereas the second results in a slope of −3/3 = −1. The original lines have a slope of −3/2.

Estimate of CM_2	Probability	Opportunity cost of error	Weighted opportunity cost
1.00	.25	$42	.25 ($42) = $10.50
2.00	.50	0	0
3.00	.25	0	0
			Total $10.50

In words, this indicates that the estimator can "expect" to gain only $10.50 on average per operating run with perfect knowledge of CM_2 prior to making the decision. More accurately, the estimator will save $42 once out of every four runs if a perfect estimate of CM_2 were available. This is the upper limit on the value of a perfect estimate of X_2's contribution margin. If the cost of obtaining better estimates of CM_2 exceed an expected value of $10.50 per operating run, then an investment in the estimation process is certainly not warranted. If the cost is less than $10.50, the problem becomes a little more complicated because it is unlikely that a perfect estimate can be obtained. Instead, it is more realistic to assess the value of, say, reducing the range of the estimate from $1.00 to $3.00 to perhaps $1.75 to $2.25.

The difficulty with the above illustration, and with sensitivity analysis in general, is that the selection of the estimate(s) to vary and the ranges in which their observed values might vary are generally based on ad hoc procedures. For example, the estimator will have to decide whether sensitivity analyses should be performed on the contribution margins, the contribution margin components separately (i.e., the individual revenue and cost estimates), the disaggregated costs, the technological constraints, or various combinations of these. The latter would be appropriate if certain sources of variability are correlated, in which case joint probability functions will have to be assessed. The selection process can become so complex that formal methods of sensitivity analyses are too costly to develop. Fortunately, practical methods for performing sensitivity analyses have proved useful, and the above should be taken as an illustration of a simplified approach to the problem.

Using Linear Algebra to Solve Linear Programming Problems

An Algebraic Solution. The previous problem can be used to illustrate how linear algebra may be used to solve complex linear programming problems. First we must convert the two inequality constraints into equations. This can be done by using two slack variables, S_1 and S_2, to represent the physical units of unused capacity of the two constraints. Thus the problem may be formulated as follows:

Maximize
subject to

$$P = \$3X_1 + \$2X_2 + 0S_1 + 0S_2$$
$$2X_1 + X_2 + S_1 + 0S_2 = 500 \quad (1)$$
$$1.5X_1 + 2X_2 + 0S_1 + S_2 = 480 \quad (2)$$

where $X_1, X_2, S_1, S_2 \geq 0$. The last constraint merely indicates that none of the variables can take on negative values. The contribution margins of S_1 and S_2 are assigned a value of 0 because unused capacity has no effect on total contribution margin.

Because there are only two equations, at most we can solve for two unknowns. (The other two variables must be set equal to zero.) One solution is simply $S_1 = 500$ and $S_2 = 480$ ($X_1 = 0$, $X_2 = 0$). This is merely one of six possible solutions to this problem. Other solutions would consist of values of the respective variables that satisfy the following sets of equations.

$$
\begin{aligned}
(X_1, S_1) \quad & 2X_1 + S_1 = 500 \\
& 1.5X_1 + 0S_1 = 480 \\
(X_1, S_2) \quad & 2X_1 + 0S_2 = 500 \\
& 1.5X_1 + S_2 = 480 \\
(X_2, S_1) \quad & X_2 + S_1 = 500 \\
& 2X_2 + 0S_1 = 480 \\
(X_2, S_2) \quad & X_2 + 0S_2 = 500 \\
& 2X_2 + S_2 = 480 \\
(X_1, X_2) \quad & 2X_1 + X_2 = 500 \\
& 1.5X_1 + 2X_2 = 480
\end{aligned}
$$

The number of possible solutions is equal to n factorial divided by $[(n - m)$ factorial $\times m$ factorial]; n is the number of variables, 4, and m is the number of equations, 2. All these solutions will result in nonzero values for the variables indicated. These six solutions are called "basic solutions," those in which the number of nonzero variables is equal to the number of equations. However, some of these basic solutions are not "feasible" because they result in negative values being assigned to some of the variables. For example, the solution to the problem

$$
\begin{aligned}
X_2 + 0S_2 = 500 \\
2X_2 + S_2 = 480
\end{aligned}
$$

implies that $X_2 = 500$ and $S_2 = -520$. Such a solution cannot be implemented.

The simplex method in linear programming consists of a set of rules that ensures that comparisons of the profitability of different solutions will be limited to basic feasible solutions.[6] In terms of the graph in Figure 10, we note that there are four extreme points in the positive quadrant: (0, 0); (250, 0); (208, 84); and (0, 240). Each of these points represents a basic feasible solution. For example, point (0, 0) is equivalent to the solution: $S_1 = 500$, $S_2 = 480$, and $X_1 = X_2 = 0$. Similarly, (250, 0) represents the solution: $X_1 = 250$, $S_2 = 105$, and $X_2 = S_1 = 0$. The procedures for moving from one basic feasible solution to the next will be illustrated with one change only.

The first rule is to begin with a basic feasible solution. One basic feasible solution that is obvious is the solution at the origin. That is, we can start with the problem:

$$
\begin{aligned}
S_1 + 0S_2 = 500 \\
0S_1 + S_2 = 480 \cdot
\end{aligned}
$$

which by inspection has the solution $S_1 = 500$, $S_2 = 480$ (and $X_1 = X_2 = 0$). The contribution margin, $P = \$3(0) + \$2(0) + 0(500) + 0(480) = 0$. P will increase if either X_1 or X_2 is given a positive value. Because X_1 returns $\$3$ per unit, we shall bring X_1 into the solution.

In order to bring X_1 into the solution, we must drop either S_1 or S_2. If we write out both equations in terms of X_1, we note that

$$
\begin{aligned}
2X_1 + X_2 + S_1 + 0S_2 &= 500 \\
2X_1 &= 500 - X_2 - S_1 - 0S_2 \\
X_1 &= 250 - \frac{1}{2X_2} - \frac{1}{2S_1} - 0S_2
\end{aligned} \tag{3}
$$

[6]We are ignoring the problem of "cycling," which may occur when a nonbasic feasible solution is encountered. This is known as the problem of "degeneracy." For solution techniques in degenerate problems, see G. Hadley, *Linear Programming* (Addison-Wesley Publishing Company, Reading, Mass., 1962), chap. 6.

which implies that a maximum of 250 units of X_1 can be produced with X_1 and S_1 equal to zero. Doing the same with the second equation,

$$1.5X_1 + 2X_2 + 0S_1 + S_2 = 480$$
$$X_1 = 320 - 1.33X_2 - 0S_1 - S_2 \tag{4}$$

which indicates that a maximum of 320 units of X_1 can be produced with X_2 and S_2 equal to zero. If we let $X_1 = 320$, S_1 will have to be set equal to a negative value ($= -140$), which would be a nonfeasible solution for equation (3). Hence, the maximum feasible value for X_1 is 250. If we set $S_1 = X_2 = 0$, and $X_1 = 250$ in (3) and substitute (3) in (2), we obtain the following result:

$$1.5(250 - \tfrac{1}{2}X_2 - \tfrac{1}{2}S_1 - 0S_2) + 2X_2 + 0S_1 + S_2 = 480$$

or $\qquad\qquad 375 - .75X_2 - .75S_1 + 2X_2 + S_2 = 480$

Therefore $\qquad S_2 = 105 - 1.25X_2 + .75S_1$
or $\qquad\qquad\; S_2 = 105 \tag{5}$
since $\qquad\quad\; X_2 = S_1 = 0$

The new contribution margin will be

$$P = \$3(250) + \$2(0) + 0(0) + 0(105) = \$750$$

The next step would be to determine whether X_2 should be brought into the solution and, if so, whether in place of X_1 or S_2. (The former is unlikely.) Equation (3) indicates that for every unit of X_2 produced, X_1 will have to be reduced by one-half unit. Similarly, a unit increase in X_2 will require a reduction in S_2 of 1.25 units [equation (5)]. The effect on P of a positive change in X_2 can be summarized as follows:

$$\$2(1) - [\$3(\tfrac{1}{2}) + \$0(1.25)] = \$.50$$

This results in a positive change in P, indicating that X_2 should be brought into the solution. To determine whether X_1 or S_2 should be replaced, we first rewrite equations (3) and (5) in terms of X_2. Thus:

$$\tfrac{1}{2}X_2 = 250 - X_1 - \tfrac{1}{2}S_1 - 0S_2$$
$$X_2 = 500 - 2X_1 - S_1 - 0S_2 \tag{6}$$

and $\qquad\qquad 1.25X_2 = 105 + .75S_1 - S_2$
$$X_2 = 84 + .60S_1 - .80S_2 \tag{7}$$

A comparison of equations (6) and (7) indicates that X_2 must be limited to an output of 84 units, in which case S_2 will equal zero. We may then use (3) and (7) to determine the values of X_1 and X_2 that will satisfy all constraints, leading to the solution

$$S_1 = S_2 = 0$$
$$X_1 = 208$$
and $\qquad\qquad X_2 = 84$

Therefore, $P = \$3(208) + \$2(84) = \$792$, which we know is the optimal solution to this problem.

Simplex Tableaus.   The procedures described above are part of the general solution algorithm for linear programming problems known as the simplex method. Computer programs for this solution technique are provided by most computer manufacturers. Thus, users need only be familiar with the reporting format for the outputs of computer codes. Most of these are in the form of

EXHIBIT 1

Vectors:	x_1	x_2	s_1	s_2		
Contribution margin of each variable:	$3	$2	0	0		Total Contribution
Variables in the solution (prices)						
← S_1 (0)	2	1	1	0	500	$P = 0(500) + 0(480)$
S_2 (0)	1.5	2	0	1	480	$= 0$
Improvement in P if variable is increased (per unit)	$3	$2	0	0		
Insert X_1, remove S_1	↑					I
New tableau						
X_1 ($3)	1	0	0.80	−0.40	208	$P = \$3(208) + \$2(84)$
X_2 ($2)	0	1	−0.60	0.80	84	$= \$792$
Improvement in P if variable is increased (per unit)	0	0	−$1.20	−$0.40		II

"simplex tableaus." The initial and final (optimal) tableaus for our problem are illustrated in Exhibit 1. The simplex tableaus may be viewed as a series of column vectors that indicate the effect of introducing and eliminating different variables in the solutions to the problem. In Tableau I we show the original solution, $S_1 = 500$, $S_2 = 480$; the optimal solution appears in Tableau II.

A Matrix Formulation of the Problem. The final solution consists of the vectors x_1 and x_2 that form the problem:

Maximize $\qquad\qquad \$3X_1 + \$2X_2$
subject to $\qquad\qquad\quad 2X_1 + \quad X_2 = 550$
$\qquad\qquad\qquad\quad 1.5X_1 + \quad 2X_2 = 480$

(i.e., the constraints are now written as equations). Suppose that we define the set of coefficients for X_1 and X_2 as the matrix **B**. Letting **x** be the column vector $\begin{pmatrix} X_1 \\ X_2 \end{pmatrix}$ and **b** the column vector $\begin{pmatrix} 480 \\ 500 \end{pmatrix}$, this problem can be expressed in matrix form as

$$\mathbf{Bx = b}$$

which, when written out, is the following:

$$\begin{bmatrix} 2 & 1 \\ 1.5 & 2 \end{bmatrix} \begin{bmatrix} X_1 \\ X_2 \end{bmatrix} = \begin{bmatrix} 500 \\ 480 \end{bmatrix}$$

In algebra, the expression $ax = b$ can be solved by dividing both sides of the equation by a, the constant. This is the same as multiplying both sides by $1/a = a^{-1}$. Division is not defined in matrix algebra; however, the *inverse* of a matrix performs the same function as a^{-1} in algebra. That is, for the problem above,

$$\mathbf{B^{-1}Bx = B^{-1}b}$$
or $\qquad\qquad\qquad\qquad \mathbf{Ix = B^{-1}b}$
and $\qquad\qquad\qquad\qquad \mathbf{x = B^{-1}b}$

where $\mathbf{B^{-1}}$ is the inverse of **B** and **I** is an identity matrix. (An identity matrix is a square matrix that has 1's down the diagonal and 0's elsewhere.)

There are several methods for finding the inverse of a matrix. One method consists of performing what are known as "elementary" row (and column) operations on an identity matrix which are necessary to transform the original matrix into an identity form. For example, $\mathbf{B}^{-1}$ can be determined by performing the same operation on $\begin{bmatrix} 1 & 0 \\ 0 & 1 \end{bmatrix}$ which will change $\begin{bmatrix} 2.0 & 1.0 \\ 1.5 & 2.0 \end{bmatrix}$ to this identity form. To illustrate, we shall write $\mathbf{B}$ and $\mathbf{I}$ as if we were multiplying:

(1)
(2)
$$\begin{bmatrix} 2.0 & 1.0 \\ 1.5 & 2.0 \end{bmatrix} \; \Bigg\| \; \begin{bmatrix} 1.0 & 0 \\ 0 & 1.0 \end{bmatrix}$$

(a) Divide row (1) by 2 which yields (3) = 1.0, ½ ‖ ½, 0.
(b) Multiply (3) by (−1.5) and add the result to (2). This results in (4) = 0, 1.25 ‖ −.75, 1.00.
   Combining (3) and (4), we have:

(3)
(4)
$$\begin{bmatrix} 1.0 & ½ \\ 0 & 1.25 \end{bmatrix} \; \Bigg\| \; \begin{bmatrix} ½ & 0 \\ -.75 & 1.00 \end{bmatrix}$$

(c) Divide (4) by 1.25, so (6) = 0, 1.0 ‖ −.60, .80.
(d) Multiply (6) by −½ and add the result to (3). This gives (5) = 1.0, 0 ‖ .80 − .40.
   Combining (5) and (6),

(5)
(6)
$$\begin{bmatrix} 1.0 & 0 \\ 0 & 1.0 \end{bmatrix} \; \Bigg\| \; \begin{bmatrix} .80 & -.40 \\ -.60 & .80 \end{bmatrix}$$

so that $\begin{bmatrix} .80 & -.40 \\ -.60 & .80 \end{bmatrix}$ should be $\mathbf{B}^{-1}$. We can check the result by determining whether $\mathbf{B}^{-1}\mathbf{B} = \mathbf{I}$, or whether

$$\begin{bmatrix} .80 & -.40 \\ -.60 & .80 \end{bmatrix} \begin{bmatrix} 2 & 1 \\ 1.5 & 2 \end{bmatrix} = \begin{bmatrix} .80(2) - .40(1.5) = 1.0 & .80(1) - .40(2) = 0 \\ -.60(2) + .80(1.5) = 0 & -.60(1) + .80(2) = 1.0 \end{bmatrix}$$

$$= \begin{bmatrix} 1 & 0 \\ 0 & 1 \end{bmatrix}$$

Therefore, because $\mathbf{B}^{-1}\mathbf{Bx} = \mathbf{B}^{-1}\mathbf{b}$ and $\mathbf{x} = \mathbf{B}^{-1}\mathbf{b}$

$$\mathbf{x} = \begin{bmatrix} .80 & -.40 \\ -.60 & .80 \end{bmatrix} \begin{bmatrix} 500 \\ 480 \end{bmatrix}$$

or
$$\begin{bmatrix} X_1 \\ X_2 \end{bmatrix} = \begin{bmatrix} .80(500) - .40(480) = 208 \\ -.60(500) + .80(480) = 84 \end{bmatrix}$$

that is,
$$X_1 = 208$$
$$X_2 = 84$$

which is the result we obtained earlier.
   Note that $\mathbf{B}^{-1}$ also appears in Tableau II of Exhibit 1 under the column headings s_1, s_2. This is not surprising, for s_1 and s_2 originally formed an identity matrix, and the procedures that transformed this matrix to its final form were essentially the row operations needed to transform

$$\begin{array}{cc} X_1 & X_2 \end{array}$$
$$\begin{bmatrix} 2 & 1 \\ 1.5 & 2 \end{bmatrix}$$

to an identity form in Tableau II.

Algebraic Techniques Used to Assess the Sensitivity of Linear Programming Solutions

Using the Inverse to Assess Changes in Constraints. The inverse is particularly useful in assessing the effect of changes in either or both of the constraints. For example, suppose that we wish to determine the effect of increasing the constraints from 500 and 480 to 600 and 520, respectively. The new solution is

$$\begin{bmatrix} X_1 \\ X_2 \end{bmatrix} = \begin{bmatrix} .80 & -.40 \\ -.60 & .80 \end{bmatrix} \begin{bmatrix} 600 \\ 520 \end{bmatrix}$$

$$= \begin{bmatrix} .80(600) - .40(520) = 272 \\ -.60(600) + .80(520) = 56 \end{bmatrix}$$

The new contribution margin P will be equal to $3(272) + 2(56) = \$928$. The change in P, $928 - \$792 = \$136$, can then be compared to the cost of expanding the capacities to 600 and 520 to determine whether the decision would be profitable.

Note that these increases in capacity will not change the vectors in the optimal solution. That is, the final solution still consists of the vectors x_1, x_2. A change in vectors would have been indicated by a negative value for X_1 or X_2. As an illustration, suppose that we consider the effect of increasing the capacity of the first constraint to 700 hours, while the second remains at 480. Using the inverse of **B**,

$$\begin{bmatrix} X_1 \\ X_2 \end{bmatrix} = \begin{bmatrix} .80 & -.40 \\ -.60 & .80 \end{bmatrix} \begin{bmatrix} 700 \\ 480 \end{bmatrix} = \begin{bmatrix} 368 \\ -36 \end{bmatrix}$$

This is not a feasible solution, because $X_2 = -36$.

Referring to Tableau II of Exhibit 1, we note that a negative sign appears in the second row in the column s_1. This indicates that a feasible solution will result if S_1 is brought into the solution at a value of $-36/-.60 = 60$ in place of X_2. Assigning S_1 the value of 60 will require a downward adjustment in X_1 of $.80(60) = 48$. (See the coefficient in row 1, column s_1.) Thus the new optimal solution is

$$X_1 = 320$$
$$S_1 = 60$$

The new contribution margin is $3(320) = \$960$, which represents an improvement of $960 - \$792 = \$168$. This change could be used to evaluate the decision to expand facility 1 to 700 units.

The Role of Shadow Prices. The figures -1.20 and $-.40$ appearing in the bottom row of Tableau II in the columns s_1 and s_2 represent, respectively, the change in P if S_1 and S_2 are increased. S_1 and S_2 represent the unused capacities of the two constraints. Thus, we may view these figures as the marginal values of having additional units of capacity available. Recall that in the first illustration above, an increase in the capacities of the two facilities from 500 to 600 hours and 480 to 520 hours, respectively, resulted in a new solution of $X_1 = 272$, $X_2 = 56$. The increase in P was $136. This increase of $136 can also be accounted for as follows:

$$\Delta P = \$1.20(\Delta \text{ in capacity 1}) + \$0.40(\Delta \text{ in capacity 2})$$
$$= \$1.20(100 \text{ hours}) + \$0.40(40 \text{ hours})$$
$$= \$120 + \$16$$
$$= \$136$$

$1.20 and $0.40 are called "shadow prices." These shadow prices provide a quick reference to the opportunity costs of not having additional capacity available. They always appear under the columns representing the slack variables. They remain valid as indicators of the marginal value of additional capacity provided that the increased capacity would not require a change in the solution basis (as it did in the second illustration when capacity 1 increased to 700 hours).

Shadow prices can also be used internally to charge divisional managers for the use of scarce resources. However, the use of shadow prices internally is a complex topic that cannot be fully explored here.[7]

Changes in Contribution Margins.   Algebraic techniques also exist for assessing the significance of errors in measuring the contribution margin of the different products. These can be illustrated by the data in Tableau II of Exhibit 1.

The solution appearing in Tableau II is optimal because P cannot be improved by the introduction of S_1 or S_2 into the solution. This is indicated by the negative signs preceding the values $1.20 and $0.40. The value $-$1.20 summarizes the effect of reducing X_1 by .80 units and increasing X_2 by .60 units for every unit increase in S_1. A unit of S_1 yields a zero contribution. Therefore, the effect on P if S_1 is increased by one unit is $0 - (.80 \times \$3 - .60 \times \$2) = -\$1.20$. Similarly, the effect of increasing S_2 is $0 - (-.40 \times \$3 + .80 \times \$2) = \$1.20 - \$1.60 = -\$0.40$.

Suppose that we wish to assess the effect of an error in measuring the contribution margin of X_1, which we shall now denote by C_1. Consider first the effect of a decrease in C_1. The decrease would become significant at the point where either S_1 or S_2 should enter the solution. This will occur when one or both of the values appearing under the $\mathbf{s_1}$ and $\mathbf{s_2}$ columns become positive. A decrease in C_1 will not affect S_2. That is, if C_1 is less than $3, $0 - (-.40 \times C_1 + .80 \times \$2) = .40C_1 - \$1.60$, so that decreasing C_1 will result in a figure that must be more negative than $-\$0.40$. However, a sufficient decrease in C_1 will eventually result in the substitution of S_1 for X_1. For example, suppose that C_1 drops to $1.40. The change in P if S_1 were brought into the solution would be $0 - (.80 \times \$1.40 - .60 \times \$2) = -\$1.12 + \$1.20 = +.08$. The positive value indicates that S_1 should enter the solution. Because it must enter at a positive value, S_1 must replace X_1. The new solution would be $X_2 = 240$, $S_1 = 260$. This is a reasonable effect because a large decrease in C_1 makes X_2 relatively more attractive than X_1. The lower critical value of C_1 can be determined by solving the expression:

$$0 = (.80 \times C_1 - .60 \times \$2)$$
$$\$1.20 = .80\,C_1$$
$$\$1.50 = C_1$$

If C_1 drops below $1.50, the original solution is no longer optimal. The technique described here can be used in problems involving large numbers of variables and equations.

The critical maximum value for C_1 can be determined in a similar manner. An increase in C_1 will make X_1 relatively more profitable than X_2, until eventually X_2 will be replaced by S_2. The critical point occurs when

$$0 - (-.40 \times C_1 + .80 \times \$2) = 0$$
$$.40C_1 = \$1.60$$
$$C_1 = \$4$$

Thus, the critical range for C_1 is $\$1.50 \leqslant C_1 \leqslant 4$.

Applying similar procedures for C_2, we observe that the critical range for C_2 is also $\$1.50 \leqslant C_2 \leqslant \$4$ (a coincidence only). The $4 upper limit is found by solving the expression

$$0 - (\$.80 \times \$3 - .60C_2) = 0$$

---

[7]N. Dopuch and D. Drake, "Accounting Implications of a Mathematical Programming Approach to the Transfer Price Problem," *Journal of Accounting Research* (Spring 1964); and J. M. Samuels, "Opportunity Costing: An Application of Mathematical Programming," *Journal of Accounting Research* (Autumn 1965).

whereas the lower value is the solution to

$$0 - (-.40 \times \$3 + .80C_2) = 0$$

This result, incidentally, is consistent with our earlier example, where we noted that the optimal solution changed when C_2 dropped to \$1.00 ($<$ \$1.50) but remained the same when C_2 increased to \$3.00 (which is less than the upper limit).

Computer codes are available for performing sensitivity analysis on more complex problems and on more complex types of changes in parameter values. As we indicated earlier, sensitivity analysis may be used at the planning stage to assess the value of having improved information about the probability distribution of parameter values. Sensitivity analysis may also be used at the control and evaluation stage, once a particular solution is implemented, to assess the decision significance of variances from anticipated parameter values. The exact procedures for doing so are described elsewhere,[8] so we shall not illustrate them here. The illustrations in the previous sections are sufficient to indicate how linear programming extends incremental analysis to multiproduct situations. These situations may arise in any one of the traditional cost-volume-profit problems, such as expanding output levels, deciding whether to make or buy products, and processing outputs through additional processes.

UNCERTAINTY AND CVP ANALYSES

In the previous sections we assumed either that parameter values—e.g., prices, variable costs, quantities of outputs, etc.—were known with certainty or that certainty equivalent estimates could be used to obtain the same results. In the case of the latter, a summary measure, say the mean, of the probability distributions of possible values for decision parameters would be used as certainty equivalent estimates and the decision rule would be to *maximize the expected level of profits*. A choice of the "best" summary measure might be a problem in itself, depending on the shape of the probability distribution among other things, but that is not what is important at this point. The crucial issue is whether decision makers are willing to maximize the expected level of profit and, in the process, to ignore other aspects of the probability distributions of random variables such as the variance around the mean.

A rule to maximize the expected level of profit under conditions of uncertainty will be optimal for a decision maker who has a neutral attitude toward risk. That is, the utility function for increasing levels of profit would be linear, so that two times the level of profit, 2π, would be worth twice the utility of π, and three times the level, 3π, would be worth three times the utility of π, and so on. The disutility for losses would also be linear, so that the disutility of -2π would be twice the disutility of $-\pi$, etc.

Many economic models under uncertainty, however, assume that decision makers are *risk-averse*—in mathematical terms, the utility function is concave, continuous, and differentiable, with the first derivative greater than zero and the second less than zero.[9] Although merely assuming risk aversion is insufficient for generating specifically how output and pricing policies will be affected by uncertainty,[10] a

---

[8]N. Dopuch, J. Birnberg, and J. S. Demski, "An Extension of Standard Cost Variance Analysis," *Accounting Review* (July 1967); and J. Demski, "An Accounting System Structured on a Linear Programming Model," *Accounting Review* (October 1967).

[9]For example, a utility function of the form $U(\pi) = [1 - e^{-(\pi/\alpha)}]$ reflects a constant level of risk aversion.

[10]For examples relating to firms that face uncertain prices, see A. Sandmo, "On the Theory of the Competitive Firm Under Price Uncertainty," *American Economic Review*, 61 (March 1971), pp. 65–73.

general rule is that risk-averse decision makers require higher expected returns for higher-risk investments. This suggests that knowledge of the degree of riskiness of individual investments or of portfolios of investments would be useful information to a decision maker. Although there is still some disagreement on how best to represent riskiness in uncertainty models, most models use the variance (or standard deviation) around the mean as a surrogate measure of riskiness. Before considering accounting proposals in this area, we shall first review some general results from economics.

Short-Run Decisions Under Uncertainty. The potential effect of uncertainty on short-run decision rules was suggested by Fellner as long ago as 1948, when he linked firm's average cost pricing policies to considerations of uncertainty.[11] In recent years more formal results have been obtained that indicate, for example, that optimal output decisions under uncertainty may be inconsistent with the familiar rule that firms should produce at an output where marginal revenue equals marginal cost (see pp. 19-3). More specifically, the optimal output level of firms' whose decision makers are risk-averse will be lower than the output level at which $MR = MC$.[12] As pointed out above, other specific results may depend on the exact shape of the risk-averse utility function of decision makers. Thus, under the assumption of decreasing absolute risk aversion, an increase in the level of fixed costs can lead to a decrease in the optimal level of output.[13] Recall, though, that in the certainty (equivalent) model, a change in fixed costs would not affect the optimal output.

The effect of fixed costs on optimal short-run policies was examined in more detail by Day, Aigner, and Smith, who considered the effects of various safety margin rules on optimal outputs.[14] In developing their analyses they assumed that safety margin rules could be linked to a firm's concern over recovering fixed overhead costs, where these are assumed to measure the *payments* required for the firm to operate during the next decision period. One of their conclusions was that

> The desire to cover overhead and hence to avoid losses in the presence of uncertainty about price or the position of the monopolist's demand curve result in various output policies which can be most simply characterized as full cost pricing or safety margin pricing . . . (p. 1300).

This conclusion was derived by assuming that firms' decision makers are risk-averse and that they can account indirectly for risk by compromising between expected profits and safety margins.[15] The fact that they did not have to rely on a specific utility function to arrive at this result is important, because very often decision makers cannot operationalize their utility function, especially in cases where they are operating in the best interests of others (e.g., managers operating for owners). In such cases, it is more difficult to develop optimal for decision makers who are presented with information on means and variances, as will become clear as we now review the work done in accounting on this problem.

[11]W. Fellner, "Average-Cost Pricing and the Theory of Uncertainty," *Journal of Political Economy,* 56 (June 1948), pp. 249–252.

[12]A. Sandmo, "On the Theory of the Competitive Firm," and H. E. Leland, "Theory of the Firm Facing Uncertain Demand," *American Economic Review,* 62 (June 1972), pp. 278–291. The former deals with a competitive firm, whereas the latter deals with monopolistic firms.

[13]*Ibid.* A comment by I. Bernhardt on Sandmo's analysis, and Sandmo's reply, appear in the March 1972 issue of the *Accounting Economic Review,* pp. 193–195.

[14]R. H. Day, D. J. Aigner, and K. R. Smith, "Safety Margins and Profit Maximization in the Theory of the Firm," *Journal of Political Economy,* 79 (November–December 1971), pp. 1293–1301.

[15]*Ibid.,* p. 1298.

CVP Analyses Under Uncertainty. Jaedicke and Robichek were among the first to advocate incorporating uncertainty information in CVP models.[16] In their first illustration, they assume that the only uncertain variable is units of sales, Q. Selling price, P, variable cost, V, and fixed costs, F, are assumed to be known with certainty. In a later illustration, these variables are also treated as random variables.

Our interest is in how decision makers might use information about the uncertainty of different decision variables, rather than with the mechanics of the proposed models or their statistical problems. Consequently, we shall ignore various criticisms of the latter aspects and concentrate only on the proposed uses of CVP models under uncertainty.

In line with that, Jaedicke and Robichek propose that information on uncertainty can be used to compare different alternatives, such as different pricing policies (and the corresponding effect on Q), or different products. To illustrate, suppose that the expected profit for a particular product is $450,000, given an expected Q of 5,000 units, expected P of $3,000, expected V of $1,750, and expected F of $5,800,000. Based on the probability distributions of these random variables, the calculated standard deviation for this expected profit (σ_z, in their notation) is $681,500. Two other potential products promise the same expected profit of $450,000 with standard deviations of $500,000 and $1,253,000, respectively. If we assumed that these random profit variables were normally distributed, we could display the essential of the distributions as in Figure 11.

Jaedicke and Robichek do not indicate how managers will make a choice in this situation, stating that "the best alternative cannot be chosen without some statement of the firm's attitude toward risk."[17] However, if we assume that decision makers are risk-averse, then simple rules from investment theory may be formulated for certain types of decision situations. For example, a risk-averse decision maker would choose the alternative with the lowest degree of risk if all alternatives have the same expected return. Letting the standard deviation be a measure of the risks of the above three alternatives, the decision maker would choose the product with the standard deviation of $500,000, which is the lowest of the three, given that each has an expected return of $450,000 in profit. For alternatives with the same standard deviation, a risk-averse decision maker would choose the alternative with the highest expected return (or profit). This situation is not illustrated by Jaedicke and Robichek, but it is intuitively consistent with the first rule.

A more difficult choice to resolve, however, occurs when alternatives differ by expected returns *and* standard deviations. Even here the problem is simplified if the alternative with the highest expected return also has the lowest standard deviation. But this is indeed a rare case in practice. More generally, alternatives with higher expected returns also have higher standard deviations, so the decision maker must make some trade-off between returns and risk. To illustrate, suppose that one alternative has an expected return of $750,000 in profits and a standard deviation of $1,000,000. A second one has an expected return of $500,000 and a standard deviation of $600,000. A decision maker who can specify a trade-off measure between return and risk, say d, could maximize the expression: max $[E(\pi) - d(\sigma\pi)]$. If $d \geq .625$, the decision maker would prefer the second alternative; for $d \leq .625$, the first would be preferred.

In subsequent publications by others, criticisms have been levied against Jaedicke and Robichek for their simplified, and perhaps erroneous, assumptions about the distributions of their random variables, especially profits, which is a

---

[16]R. K. Jaedicke and A. A. Robichek, "Information for Production and Marketing Decisions," *Accounting Review,* XXXIX (October 1964), pp. 917–926.
[17]*Ibid.*, p. 926.

FIGURE 11

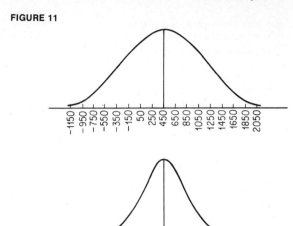

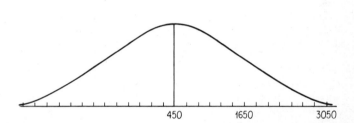

derived variable.[18] However, assuming that we can obtain the "correct" distribution of profit variables, a more important question is whether the proper decision rules can be formulated on the basis of expected values and standard deviations of individual alternatives, as proposed above. In this regard, two criticisms of the basic approach particularly warrant our attention.

In the first, Johnson and Simik criticize the approach because it fails to recognize that the choice of products (or lines) to produce is actually a portfolio choice, rather than a single-product choice.[19] If the products are not completely independent, then the total firm's profit variance will depend on the covariance between the profits of the various product lines.[20] If the profits of products are positively correlated, then the total variance (and standard deviation) of profits will increase; if these profits are negatively correlated, then the total variance will decrease. Once the decision maker has constructed various feasible portfolios and calculated their expected profits and standard deviations, Johnson and Simik

---

[18]See, for example, Jimmy E. Hilliard and Robert A. Leich, "Cost-Volume-Profit Analysis Under Uncertainty: A Log Normal Approach," *Accounting Review* (January 1975), pp. 69–80, as well as some of their references.

[19]G. Johnson and S. Simik, "Multiproduct C.V.P. Analysis Under Uncertainty," *Journal of Accounting Research,* 9 (Autumn 1971), pp. 278–286.

[20]The covariance between two random variables, X_i, X_j, is the *expected value* of the product: $[X_i - E(X_i)] [X_j - E(X_j)] = E[X_i - E(X_i)][X_j - E(X_j)]$, where E is the expectations operator. See Chapter 3 of this *Handbook.*

suggest that a decision on which portfolio to produce can be made using the same criteria as above—i.e., minimize the standard deviation for a given level of *portfolio* profits or maximize the expected profits for a given level of standard deviation of portfolio profits, etc.

We note that with this and the other approaches so far discussed in this section, the assumption is that there exists a single (dominant) decision maker whose utility function will determine the trade-off between risks and returns. A second criticism that has been made is that such an assumption is inappropriate for large corporations, where decisions may be the output of committee deliberations and where decisions should be made in the best interests of a diverse group of owners (shareholders). That is, it is unlikely that there exists a single utility function that can capture the heterogeneous nature of such a situation.

This problem is not unique to short-run decision making under uncertainty. It also arises in capital investment analysis, where long-term investments under uncertainty must be made in the interests of the owners of corporations. The determination of optimal decision rules for long-term investments under uncertainty constitutes a complex theory in itself. Suffice it to note here that the theory assumes that managers attempt to maximize the present value of the wealth of firms' owners so that decision rules can be developed in terms of their effects on the market value of claims to ownership. This in turn requires assumptions about the risk attitude of owners and the nature of the capital market in which ownership shares are traded. Assuming that investors in general are risk-averse and that capital markets are efficient and perfectly competitive, capital asset pricing models have been derived that indicate that the return on an individual asset, and thus its price, will be a function of the returns (prices) of all assets traded in the capital market.[21]

These notions can be extended to indicate how management's decisions will be viewed by owners, given that these decisions will impact on the equilibrium prices of firms' securities. In particular, Magee has relied on these extensions recently to develop an alternative approach to CVP analysis under uncertainty.[22] Under his approach, "the essential variables for the manager's short-run decision problem are not the expected value and variance of profit, but, rather, the expected value of profit *and the covariance of profit with the return on the market portfolio.*" Moreover, consistent with capital market theory, "any tradeoff between expected profit and risk . . . does not depend on the manager's risk preferences, but, rather, the market's tradeoff of risk for return. . . ."[23] In the process of proposing this model Magee has confronted accountants with some difficult estimation problems, because his model cannot be implemented without estimates of the covariance of a firm's profits, say firm *j*, with the return on the market portfolio of assets and/of the "market's" trade-off of risk for return.

Of course, it is possible to make some simplifying assumptions about these estimates, in much the same way that accountants make simplifying assumptions in capital investment analyses.[24] For example, over time managers may be able to

---

[21]See, for example, J. Lintner, "The Valuation of Risk Assets and the Selection of Risky Investments . . . ," *Review of Economics and Statistics,* XLVII (February 1965), pp. 13–37; also, W. F. Sharpe, "Capital Asset Prices: A Theory of Market Equilibrium Under Conditions of Risk," *Journal of Finance,* XIX (September 1964), pp. 425–442; and E. Fama, "Risk, Return and Equilibrium: Some Clarifying Comments," *Journal of Finance,* XXIII (March 1968), pp. 29–40.

[22]R. P. Magee, "Cost-Volume-Profit Analysis, Uncertainty and Capital Market Equilibrium," *Journal of Accounting Research,* 13 (Autumn 1975), pp. 257–266.

[23]*Ibid.,* p. 261.

[24]See, for example, N. Dopuch, J. Birnberg, and J. Demski, *Cost Accounting: Accounting Data for Management Decisions,* 2nd ed. (Harcourt Brace Jovanovich, New York, 1974), pp. 189–193.

ascertain the market's trade-off between risk and return for their decisions, in which case they merely use that measure as if it were their own.[25] Similarly, managers may be able to estimate how the prices of their firm's securities fluctuate as a function of their decision variables—say profit—especially if the operations of the firm are homogeneous (in terms of risk classes) over time. Indeed, that is the type of decision managers must make continuously, or otherwise the owners will exercise their right to replace them.

The above are three types of models that have been proposed to guide managers in making CVP decisions under uncertainty. Other references to this type of problem could have been included, but they too rely essentially on the approaches discussed here, especially the first. Being a relatively new area of concern, it is a difficult one to summarize, because there is not much agreement concerning the different approaches. Perhaps the main message of this section is simply that output decisions under uncertainty are not as straightforward, and simplistic, as implied in the simple rules of incremental analysis presented in the previous sections. If firms' managements are reluctant to accept a new order whose incremental revenues are expected to exceed its expected incremental costs, or to change prices in order to increase expected outputs, this may merely reflect a concern for the additional risks involved, along with a risk-averse attitude. Consequently, what may appear to be an irrational act, on the face of it, may be explained once a measure of risk is introduced into the analysis.

BIBLIOGRAPHY

Bierman, H., and T. R. Dyckman: *Managerial Cost Accounting,* 2nd ed., Macmillan Company, New York, 1976.

Demski, J. S.: *Information Analysis,* Addison-Wesley Publishing Company, Reading, Mass., 1972.

Dopuch, N., J. Birnberg, and J. Demski: *Cost Accounting: Accounting Data for Management's Decisions,* 2nd ed., Harcourt Brace Jovanovich, New York, 1974.

Gass, S. I.: *Linear Programming,* 4th ed., McGraw-Hill Book Company, New York, 1975.

Horngren, C. T.: *Cost Accounting: A Managerial Emphasis,* 4th ed., Prentice-Hall, Englewood Cliffs, N.J., 1977.

Shillinglaw, G.: *Managerial Cost Accounting,* 4th ed., Richard D. Irwin, Homewood, Ill., 1977.

Wagner, H. M.: *Principles of Operations Research,* Prentice-Hall, Englewood Cliffs, N.J., 1969.

[25]Of course, another possibility is to follow the approach taken by economists, which essentially assumes a general form of utility function to relate expected value and variances. This was followed by Adar et al., who assume a risk-averse decision maker faced with a cost-volume-profit decision problem. See Z. Adar, A. Barnea, and B. Lev, "A Comprehensive Cost-Volume-Profit Analysis Under Uncertainty," *Accounting Review* (January 1977), pp. 137–149.

Chapter **20**

Capital Budgeting

ROMAN L. WEIL
Professor of Accounting, University of Chicago

INTRODUCTION

Management must often decide whether to add a product to a line, whether to buy a new machine, or, in general, whether to make investments of funds today in return for benefits that will be received later. Such decisions are based on incremental analysis of future cash receipts and expenditures. This chapter discusses the theory and the mechanism for making investment decisions when cash outlays are required today to create future cash inflows. The proper mode of analyzing investment decisions is one of the most controversial topics in accounting. We first present the most desirable method for making capital expenditure decisions, and then discuss some alternative methods that are less desirable, indicating their shortcomings.

INDEPENDENCE OF INVESTMENT AND FINANCING DECISIONS

A firm faced with a decision such as adding a new product line or buying plant assets must decide both whether to undertake the new project and how to raise the capital required by the new activity. Once a project has been accepted by the firm, the necessary funds can be raised in several different ways or in a combination of ways. Funds can be raised through borrowing, by retaining earnings rather than distributing dividends, or by issuing additional capital stock.

One of the most significant contributions to the theory of finance in recent years has been the discovery that the investment decision should be made independently of the financing decision.[1] That is, the investment decision should be made first, and only after a project gets the go-ahead should management begin to consider how to finance it. All of the assets of the firm are financed by all of its equities. This fact underlies the conclusion that the investment decision is independent of the financing decision for new undertakings. A new project will involve investing capital, but once the project is added to the firm's portfolio of activities, it too is financed by all of the firm's equities.

Raising capital and managing cash are important problems, but they do not concern us here. This chapter discusses only the investment decision, the ranking of investment projects.

CASH FLOWS VERSUS INCOME FLOWS

Rational investment decisions require analysis of cash or fund flows over the life of the investment, not periodic income flows. To illustrate why, and to introduce the investment decision, we examine next a typical project. Consider the decision facing the Garden Winery Company, which is contemplating acquiring equipment that will allow it to bring to market a new variety of wine. The equipment costs $10,000 and is expected to last four years. Exhibit 1 shows information about the new equipment, the cash outlays (required for labor, grapes, and bottles), as well as the revenues expected from the sales of the new variety of wine. The decreasing pattern of revenues over the four years of the machine results in part from the equipment becoming less productive over time and in part by the expected reaction of other wine sellers, who will copy the new wine variety and force down the selling price in the market. For simplicity, assume that Garden Winery Company uses straight-line depreciation, that the equipment has an estimated salvage value of zero, that the Company pays income taxes at the rate of 40 percent of taxable income, and that all cash flows occur at the end of each year.

[1]See, for example, Eugene F. Fama and Merton H. Miller, *The Theory of Finance* (Holt, Rinehart and Winston, New York, 1972), pp. 70–99.

EXHIBIT 1

GARDEN WINERY COMPANY
Revenues, Expenses, Income, and Cash Flows from New Wine Project

End of year (1)	Revenues (2)	Cash outlays (3)	Pretax cash inflow (outflow) (4)	Depreciation charge (5)	Pretax income (6)	Income tax (7)	Net income (8)	Net cash inflows (outflows) (9)
0	—	$10,000	($10,000)	—	—	—	—	($10,000)
1	$ 6,000	1,000	5,000	$ 2,500	$2,500	$1,000	$1,500	4,000
2	5,000	1,000	4,000	2,500	1,500	600	900	3,400
3	4,500	1,000	3,500	2,500	1,000	400	600	3,100
4	4,000	1,000	3,000	2,500	500	200	300	2,800
	$19,500	($14,000)	$ 5,500	$10,000	$5,500	$2,200	$3,300	$ 3,300

(2), (3): Given
(4) = (2) − (3)
(5) = $10,000/4

(6) = (4) − (5)
(7) = .40 × (6)
(8) = (6) − (7)

(9) = (4) − (7)
= (8) + (5) in years 1–4

At the end of year zero, that is to say, at the start of the project, the equipment is purchased for $10,000, as shown in column (9) of Exhibit 1. In each of the next four years, revenues are received as shown in column (2), and current cash outlays for materials (grapes, bottles, and so on) and labor are incurred as shown in column (3). Inflows of funds or cash, as forecast, from operations are shown in column (4). Depreciation charges of $2,500 per year are shown in column (5), and pretax income [columns (2) − (3) − (5)] is shown in column (6). Income taxes, shown in column (7), are 40 percent of pretax income. Column (8) shows net income [= column (6) − column (7)]. Column (9) shows the net cash or funds flows for each of the years and can be derived from either of two computations:

1. Cash inflows, column (2), less cash outflows [= column (3) + column (7)]
2. Net income, column (8), plus expenses (depreciation) not using cash, column (5).

Note that the only effective use of the depreciation amounts in the decision-making process is in the computation of the income taxes payable for a year.

Over the life of the project, the sum of the net income amounts is $3,300, which is exactly equal to the sum of net cash flows. Although the totals over the four years are the same, the timing of the amounts differs. The accounting income figures shown in column (8) for the project being considered by Garden Winery Company are based on an assumed asset expiration of $2,500 each year (for depreciation). The asset requires, however, a cash outlay of $10,000 at the beginning of the first year. Making investment decisions on the basis of accounting income figures, such as those in column (8), ignores the time value of money. The cash flows shown in column (9) accurately depict the time dimension of the economic costs and benefits to the firm.

Once the data on projected cash flows for a project have been compiled (not necessarily an easy task), the capital budgeting problem is to evaluate those data and to decide whether or not to undertake the project. Throughout most of this chapter, we assume that all projected cash flows are equally likely to occur so that there is no problem of relative uncertainty of cash flows.

The Net Present Value Graph. Given the cash flow data for a project, a convenient way to assess the desirability of a project is to construct a *net present value graph*, such as the one shown in Figure 1 for the Garden Winery Company project. The horizontal axis shows the discount rate, and the vertical axis shows the net present value of the cash flows computed for each discount rate. The *net present value* of a series of cash flows is the sum of the discounted present values of each

FIGURE 1   Garden Winery Company—Net Present Value Graph

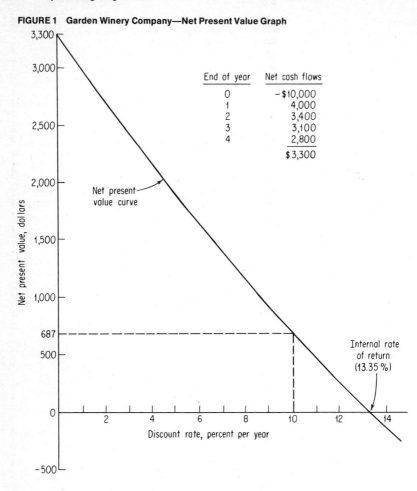

individual cash flow. For example, if the discount rate is zero, then the net present value of the project is the sum of the net cash flows, or $3,300. Thus, the net present value curve shown in Figure 1 intersects the vertical axis at $3,300. To see how the net present value curve is constructed for positive discount rates, consider a discount rate of 10 percent per year and the calculations in Exhibit 2.

EXHIBIT 2

GARDEN WINERY COMPANY PROJECT EVALUATION
Present Values of Cash Flows Discounted at 10 Percent per Year

End of year	Net cash flows		Present value (Discounted at 10%)		
			of $1		of cash flows from project
0	($10,000)	×	1.00000	=	($10,000)
1	4,000	×	.90909	=	3,636
2	3,400	×	.82645	=	2,810
3	3,100	×	.75131	=	2,323
4	2,800	×	.68301	=	1,912
Totals	$ 3,300				$ 687

For each cash flow, for example the $3,400 that flows in at the end of the second year, the present value (at the start of year 1) of that flow is computed ($3,400 × .82645 = $2,810) from the present value of $1 numbers shown in Table 2 of the Appendix. The present value of the initial outlay is, of course, $10,000 regardless of the discount rate. The present values of each of the years' cash flows are computed and the sum of those numbers is found. That sum, $687, is the net present value of the cash flows from the project when the discount rate is 10 percent per year. This net present value of $687 for a 10-percent discount rate is shown explicitly in Figure 1. For any other discount rate, a net present value is similarly computed and a point on the curve can be plotted. (The net present value curve shown in Figure 1 was drawn through the net present value amounts calculated for discounts rates $r = 0, 1, 2, \ldots, 15$ percent. It is *not* a straight line.)

The discount rate, 13.35 percent in the example, where the net present value curve crosses the horizontal axis is called the *internal rate of return*. The internal rate of return of a series of payments is the discount rate that equates the net present value of those payments to zero. One of the alternative methods for evaluating investment projects, discussed later, is based on the internal rate of return.

The net present value graph shows, then, for various discount rates, the net present value of the cash flows from a project. The investment decision rule that managers should use in evaluating investment projects can now be simply stated: If, for the appropriate discount rate, the net present value of the cash flows from a project is positive, then that project should be undertaken. That rule is simple enough once "the appropriate discount rate" is selected. We discuss the determination of that discount rate next.

THE COST OF CAPITAL

The appropriate discount rate to use in evaluating investment projects is the firm's *cost of capital*. The cost of capital is easy to define but, in practice, is difficult to measure. Several definitions of the cost of capital are given below. These definitions do not necessarily appear to be saying the same thing, but the modern theory of finance can demonstrate their equivalence.

The *cost of capital* can be defined by any of the following:

1. The average rate that the firm must pay for funds invested in the firm
2. The average rate the firm would earn if it reacquired its own equity securities and paid off its liabilities in the proportions those liabilities are outstanding
3. The rate of return for new investment projects such that, if all projects undertaken by the firm yield that rate, then the market value of the firm's shares will remain unchanged
4. The stock market's expectation of the rate of return on investment in the company's common shares

The easiest of these definitions to consider is the first. The equities side of the balance sheet (liabilities and shareholders' equity) shows the sources of capital to the firm. Each of the components of capital provided to the firm has a price. Current liabilities, such as accounts payable, provide capital to the firm at no explicit cost. Notes and bonds payable have an explicit, or contractual, interest cost. Preferred shares usually carry a specified dividend rate which, for these purposes, may be considered to be their cost. Because interest on bonds and notes is deductible from otherwise taxable income, the aftertax cost to the firm for interest on notes and bonds is less than the quoted interest rate. The effective price to the firm for preferred stock is the actual dividend rate, because preferred stock dividends are not deductible expenses but aftertax earnings distributions. The price for capital in the form of common stockholders' equity (common stock, additional paid-in capital, and retained earnings) is the rate of discount that equates the present value of the total dividend stream the market expects the firm to distribute over its life to the current market price of the firm's stock. The rate of return on the common stock accounts is, of course, the hardest to compute in practice. The cost of capital for most firms is likely to be between 10 and 20 percent, after taxes.

Another way to think of the cost of capital is to ask, "What can the firm do with new funds without changing the basic nature of the firm?" The firm can purchase marketable securities or additional inventories and can retire some of its debt. The earnings rate from the average investment (with risk and return equal to that from the average project in the firm), regardless of the actual financing method, is its cost of capital.

A firm should undertake an investment project if the net present value of the cash flows is positive when the cash flows are discounted at the cost of capital rate.

Sensitivity of Profits to Estimates.   Among the alternatives for evaluating investment projects, there are essentially two kinds: those that take into account the time value of money and those that do not. Those that do all require an estimate of the cost of capital or, as it is called in other contexts, the "cutoff" or "minimum acceptable" rate of return. Estimated rates of 10 to 20 percent, after taxes, are commonly used. The subtleties of computing the cost of capital rate are discussed in Chapter 22. Here, the emphasis is on using that rate.

When the net present value of a project is computed by using an estimate of the cost of capital, the signal will usually be unequivocal: the new project clearly is or is not worthwhile. Only when the net present value is close to zero would there be concern about the accuracy of the estimate of the cost of capital being used. But when the net present value is nearly zero, then the firm is nearly indifferent to accepting or rejecting the project. Consequently, the firm will make "nearly correct" decisions by using approximations to the cost of capital. The firm's loss from errors caused by an incorrect estimate of the cost of capital is relatively small and almost surely will be smaller than the cost of errors made in estimating cash flows.

The decision rule for evaluating investment projects is to accept a project that has a positive net present value when its cash flows are discounted at the cost of capital rate and to reject it otherwise. In the Garden Winery Company example, the net present value of the cash flows is positive for all discount rates less than 13.35 percent. Consequently, if management felt that its cost of capital was about 10 percent, then the project is worthwhile. At a cost of capital of 10 percent, the net present value of flows from the project is $687. The net present value of $687 is not to be interpreted as the amount of return on investment in the project but the *excess amount* over what the firm normally expects to earn on its investment. If the cost of capital for Garden Winery Company is less than 13.35 percent, the stockholders will be better off if the project is accepted than if it is rejected.

What loss does the firm suffer if it incorrectly calculates its cost of capital? Suppose that Garden Winery's cost of capital is 15 percent, while management acts as though it is 10 percent. Management miscalculates the cost of capital by 50 percent $[= (.15 - .10)/.10]$. That large error still has a small effect on the firm. Mangement believes that the firm will be $687 better off by accepting the project. When the project is accepted and the cost of capital is 15 percent, the firm will actually be $312 worse off, because the net present value at 15 percent is −$312. The total error of the estimate in present value dollars is $999 [= $687 − (−$312)], which is about 10 percent of the initial investment, $10,000. Thus a 50-percent error in the calculation of the cost of capital rate used to make the decision implies only a 10-percent error in terms of the amount of the initial investment. In general, if a project is marginally profitable for a given cost of capital, it will ordinarily not be grossly unprofitable for slightly higher rates. Conversely, projects that are clearly worthwhile when the cost of capital is 10 percent (that is, having a positive net present value) are likely to be worthwhile, or nearly so, even when the cost of capital is 15 percent.

INCOME TAX CONSIDERATIONS

Income taxes are a major expense of doing business. Income tax regulations affect both the *amounts* of cash flows and the *timing* of cash flows, and, consequently, must be considered in making investment decisions. Chapter 23 discusses many of the managerial implications of income taxes, but here we briefly introduce this important topic.

The most obvious effect of tax laws on investment decisions arises from the accelerated depreciation charges that the tax laws permit. Accelerating depreciation charges on the tax returns shifts taxable income to later years from earlier years. Although accelerated depreciation does not change the total tax liability generated by a project over its life, it does influence profitability measured in present-value terms because of the effect on the timing of cash flows.

Suppose, for example, that the Garden Winery Company decides to use the double-declining-balance method to depreciate the machine required by the new wine variety. Then the net cash flows for the project would be as shown in Exhibit 3.

EXHIBIT 3

GARDEN WINERY COMPANY
Cash Flows Assuming Double-Declining-Balance Depreciation

End of year	Revenues less cash expenses (1)	Depreciation charge (2)	Pretax income (3)	Income tax (4)	Net cash inflows (outflows) (5)
0	—	—	—	—	($10,000)
1	$ 5,000	$ 5,000	$ 0	$ 0	5,000
2	4,000	2,500	1,500	600	3,400
3	3,500	1,250	2,250	900	2,600
4	3,000	1,250	1,750	700	2,300
	$15,500	$10,000	$5,500	$2,200	$ 3,300

(1), (2) Given   (4) = .40 × (3)
(3) = (1) − (2)   (5) = (1) − (4)

Compare Exhibit 3 with Exhibit 1. Note that in both cases the net cash flows total $3,300 and the income taxes payable total $2,200. The accelerated method, however, shifts $1,000 of taxes payable from the first year to the third year ($500) and to the fourth ($500). Exhibit 4 compares the net present values from the project at various discount rates. With straight-line depreciation, the project is marginally acceptable at 13 percent and unacceptable at 14 percent, but with double-declining-balance depreciation, it is clearly acceptable for cost of capital rates almost as high as 15 percent. Nothing has changed except the depreciation method used for tax purposes.

Accelerated depreciation is merely one of the tax-delaying and tax-saving aspects of the income tax regulations. Others include the treatment of long- and short-term capital gains, effects of offsetting losses from one project against gains from another, and the off-again, on-again tax-saving device known as the "investment tax credit" used as an instrument of fiscal policy during the 1960s and 1970s. Chapter 23 discusses many of these.

EXHIBIT 4

GARDEN WINERY COMPANY
Net Present Values Using Different Depreciation Methods

Discount rate in percent per year	Depreciation method	
	Straight-line	Double-declining-balance
10	$687	$880
11	474	680
12	268	487
13	68	300
14	(125)	(119)
15	(312)	(57)

The preceding paragraphs emphasized two important points: (1) an investment project should be undertaken only if it has a net present value greater than zero when cash flows are discounted at the cost of capital, and (2) the investment decision should be separated from the financing decision. Alternative methods of deciding whether or not to undertake an investment project will be considered next, followed by illustrations of the separation of the investment and financing decision.

ALTERNATIVE METHODS FOR EVALUATING PROJECTS

Many methods are used for evaluating projects, but most are conceptually inferior to using the net present value method with a discount rate equal to the cost of capital. Some are better than others: some alternatives that take the time value of money into account often give the same decision results as the net present value rule and, in practice, prove to be satisfactory. The alternative methods that do not take the time value of money into account are easy to use, because they do not involve present value computations, but this simplicity is their chief virtue.

Excess Present Value Index.   The excess present value index is the number of present value dollars of cash inflows per dollar of initial outlay. See the example calculations in column (5) of Exhibit 5. For example, project A returns $1.42 (= $17,000/$12,000) in present value of cash inflows for every $1 invested in the project. The excess present value index *rule* calculates the excess present value index for each project and ranks projects according to their score, or index. Projects that result in less than $1 of present value cash inflows per $1 of initial outlay are rejected. The excess present value index rule will give the same results as the net present value rule so long as projects are not mutually exclusive.

EXHIBIT 5   Data for Capital Rationing Illustration

		At cost of capital of 12 percent		
Project name (1)	Initial cash outlay required (2)	Present value of cash inflows (3)	Net present value of cash flows (4)	Excess present value index (5)
A	$12,000	$17,000	$5,000	1.42
B	11,000	15,000	4,000	1.36
C	7,000	10,000	3,000	1.43
D	3,000	5,500	2,500	1.83

(4) = (3) − (2)   (5) = (3)/(2)

Consider projects A, B, C, and D shown in Exhibit 5 when the cost of capital is 12 percent. If only one of these projects can be chosen, then project A is the preferred alternative under the net present value rule because it has the greatest net present value of cash inflows. Project D is the most desirable according to the excess present value index rule but is the least attractive according to the net present value rule. The excess present value index rule pays no attention to the *amount* of capital that can be invested in a project. This so-called *scale effect* is discussed below in connection with the internal rate of return.

The Internal Rate of Return.   The *internal rate of return,* sometimes called the *time-adjusted rate of return,* of a stream of cash flows is defined as the discount rate that makes the net present value of that stream equal to zero. As Figure 1 illustrates, the internal rate of return is the point on the net present value graph where the net present value line crosses the horizontal axis. The decision rule for using the internal rate of return specifies a *cutoff rate* (such as 10 percent for the Garden Winery Company) and states that projects should be accepted when the internal rate of return on the project is greater than or equal to the cutoff rate and should be rejected otherwise.

Advocates of the internal rate of return argue that the method does not require knowing the firm's cost of capital, and is therefore easier to use in practice than the net present value rule. For the internal rate of return rule to give the correct answers, however, the "cutoff" rate must be the cost of capital. Otherwise, some projects that will increase the value of the firm to its owners will either be rejected when they should be accepted or vice versa.

A technical shortcoming of the internal rate of return rule is that a project can have more than one internal rate of return. This surprising mathematical phenomenon can occur when the pattern of yearly net cash flows contains an intermixing of net cash inflows and outflows. For example, if, at the end of a project's life, cash expenditures will be made to return the plant site to its original condition, then individual cash flows can be negative both at the beginning and at the end of a project's life, but positive in between. Projects with intermixing of cash inflows and outflows are likely to have multiple internal rates of return.[2]

The internal rate of return rule ranks projects in the same order as the net present value rule *only* when each of the following four conditions is met:

1. If the cutoff rate used for the internal rate of return rule is equal to the cost of capital
2. If projects are not mutually exclusive
3. If projects have the same life
4. If there is only one internal rate of return.

[2]Solving for the internal rate of return involves finding the roots of a polynomial. Descartes' rule of signs tells how to determine the limit to the number of roots of such a polynomial. It says that a series of cash flows will have a nonnegative number of *internal rates of return.* The number is equal to the number of variations in the sign of the cash flows, the first occurring now and the others at subsequent yearly intervals: -100, -100, $+50$, $+175$, -50, $+100$. The internal rates of return are the numbers for r that satisfy the equation

$$-100 - \frac{100}{(1 + r)} + \frac{50}{(1 + r)^2} + \frac{175}{(1 + r)^3} - \frac{50}{(1 + r)^4} + \frac{100}{(1 + r)^5} = 0$$

The series of cash flows has three variations in sign: a change from minus to plus, a change from plus to minus, and a change from minus to plus. The rule says that this series must have either three or one internal rates of return; in fact, it has only one, about 12 percent. Note, however, that if a reinvestment rate is assumed, there will never be multiple internal rates of return. The *reinvestment rate* is a rate of earnings assumed for cash inflows that occur before the project's completion.

Otherwise, the internal rate of return may lead to a wrong decision. The illustrations considered next show how the internal rate of return can lead to incorrect project rankings.

Shortcomings of the Internal Rate of Return Rule for Choosing Between Investment Projects.

Mutually Exclusive Projects.   Assume that the aftertax cost of capital is 10 percent per year and that only one of the two projects, E or F, as shown in Exhibit 6, can be chosen.

EXHIBIT 6   Data for Projects E and F

Project name	Cash flows by year end of year		Internal rate of return	Net present value at 10%
	0	1		
E	($100)	$120	.20	$ 9.09
F	(300)	345	.15	13.64

Project E provides a simple illustration for calculating the internal rate of return. The internal rate of return on project E is the rate r such that

$$-\$100 + \frac{\$120}{1 + r} = 0$$

Solving for r gives $r = .20$. The internal rate of return in project F is similarly easy to calculate. The internal rate of return rule would rank project E as better than F, whereas the net present value rule prefers project F. To see that project F is better for the firm, consider what the firm must do with the "idle" $200 it will have to invest if project E is chosen. That $200 must be invested, by definition, at the cost of capital of 10 percent and will provide $220 at the end of the first year. So the total flows available at the end of the first year from project E and from the investment of the idle funds of 10 percent will be $120 + $220 = $340, which is less than the $345 available from project F. The firm will prefer the results from choosing project F as the net present value rule signals.

Figure 2 shows the net present value graphs for projects E and F. Note that E crosses the horizontal axis farther to the right than does F, but at 10 percent, the firm's cost of capital, the net present value of F is larger than that of E.

The net present value graph makes the rankings of the two projects clear. The two net present value curves cross at 12.5 percent, which is the rate r that satisfies the equation

$$-\$100 + \frac{\$120}{1 + r} = -\$300 + \frac{\$345}{1 + r}$$

For costs of capital less than 12.5 percent, project F is preferred to project E, and for costs of capital greater than 12.5 percent, project E is preferred to project F.

Perhaps this point can be better understood if you decide whether you would rather invest $.10 today to get $2 a year from now or invest $1,000 today to get $2,500 a year from now. You may not do both. We presume that you would prefer the second alternative even though the internal rate of return on the first is eight times as large as for the second. The internal rate of return rule, applied to mutually exclusive projects, ignores the amount of funds that can be invested at that rate. This shortcoming, sometimes called the *scale effect*, applies to the excess present value index rule as well.

FIGURE 2   Net Present Value Graphs for Projects E and F

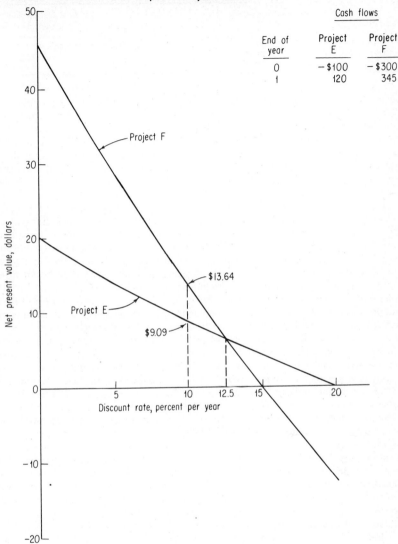

End of year	Cash flows	
	Project E	Project F
0	−$100	−$300
1	120	345

Projects with Different Lifetimes.   Consider projects G and H shown in Exhibit 7. The internal rate of return on project H is the rate r that satisfies the equation

$$-\$100 + \frac{\$50}{(1 + r)} + \frac{\$84}{(1 + r)^2} = 0$$

You can verify that the internal rate of return is 20 percent by using the 20-percent column of Table 2 in the Appendix. The internal rate of return rule ranks project G as better than H, whereas the net present value rule ranks project H better than G. To see why project H is better for the firm, consider what the firm must do during year 2. If project G is accepted, $125 must be invested in the

EXHIBIT 7   Data for Projects G and H

Project name	Cash flows by year end of year			Internal rate of return	Net present value at 10 percent
	0	1	2		
G	($100)	$125	—	.25	$13.64
H	(100)	50	$84	.20	14.87

average investment project available to the firm. The return from such an average project is, by definition, the cost of capital, 10 percent. At the end of year 2, the firm will have $125 × 1.10 = $137.50. If project H is accepted, the $50 cash inflow at the end of the first year will also be invested at 10 percent and will grow to $50 × 1.10 = $55 by the end of year 2. Thus, the total funds available at the end of the second year are $55 + $84 = $139, which is larger than the $137.50 if project G were accepted. The internal rate of return rule ignores the fact that idle funds must be invested at the cost of capital.

Payback Period.   Another rule often used in evaluating investment projects involves the payback period. The *payback period* is the length of time that elapses before total cumulative aftertax cash inflows from the project equal the initial cash outlay for the project. Refer to Exhibits 1 and 3 for data on the Garden Winery Company's project. The Garden Winery Company project has a payback period of about three years for both methods of depreciation, although if the cash flows occur uniformly during each year, then the payback period is shorter for the accelerated depreciation method than for straight line. The payback-period decision rule states that projects be accepted when the payback period is as short as some designated cutoff time period, such as two years, and rejected otherwise.

The weakness in the payback-period rule is that both the time value of money and all cash flows subsequent to the payback date are ignored. One project could have a shorter payback period than another but much smaller net present value. The payback-period rule is designed to emphasize concern with the firm's liquidity and to facilitate calculations when many small, similar projects are considered. The net present value rule, however, also takes liquidity into account because the cost of capital used for discounting cash flows, by definition, accurately measures the costs of securing additional funds should that become necessary.

If the net cash inflows per year from a project are constant and occur for a number of years at least twice as long as the payback period and when the discount rate is reasonably large, say 10 percent per year or more, then the reciprocal of the payback period is approximately equal to the internal rate of return on the project. Thus the payback period will rank projects in the same way that the internal rate of return analysis would if the stated conditions are met.

Discounted Payback Period.   Given the widespread use of the payback-period rule and its inability to yield good decisions for the most general case, some accountants have suggested that firms that want a payback rule should use the discounted payback period. The *discounted payback period* is similar to the ordinary payback period, but it is defined as the length of time that elapses before the *present value* of the cumulative cash inflows is at least as large as the initial cash outlay. The discount rate used in this calculation is most often the cost of capital. The discounted payback period gives some recognition to the time value of funds that flow before payback is accomplished. The ordinary payback periods of projects J and K in Exhibit 8 are the same, three years, but the discounted payback criteria will properly rank K as better than J.

Either payback rule would improperly prefer both J and K to project L. Analysts sometimes recommend the discounted payback rule to firms that are wary of applying the net present value rule to projects like project L. The manager who

EXHIBIT 8   Illustrative Data for Payback Rules, Projects J, K, and L

Project name	Cash flow at end of year					
	0	1	2	3	4	5
J	($10,000)	$2,000	$3,000	$5,000	$3,000	—
K	(10,000)	5,000	3,000	2,000	3,000	—
L	(10,000)	—	—	—	—	$50,000

made the original forecast for $50,000 cash inflow for year 5 may not be around to be held accountable by the time it is learned that the forecast was too optimistic.

Bailout and Discounted Bailout Periods.   The payback period criteria ignore the cash flows after payback has been achieved and the possible residual value of equipment of a project that for whatever reason does not last its estimated life. The *bailout period* is the shortest elapsed time from the start of the project until the cumulative cash inflows from a project plus the residual value of the equipment at the end of the period equal the cash outflows for the project.

Example of Bailout Period.   Assume that a project involving acquisition of equipment requires an initial cash outflow of $100 and yields cash inflows of $25 at the end of each year for seven years. Also assume that the equipment could be sold for $60 at the end of the first year, $50 at the end of the second year, $40 at the end of the third year, $30 at the end of the fourth year, and so on until salvage is zero at the end of the seventh year. The payback period is four years, but by the end of the second year cumulative cash inflows have been $50 and the equipment can be salvaged for $50, so the bailout occurs after only two periods.

The *discounted bailout period* is calculated from the present value of estimated cash flows and the present value of the residual values. In the example above, assuming a discount rate of 10 percent per period, the discounted bailout period is five years. The present value of the cash inflows of $25 per year discounted at 10 percent per year for five years is $95 and the present value of the $20 salvage at the end of the fifth year is $12. At the end of the fifth year is the first time that the sum of these two present values exceeds the initial investment of $100. Thus, the discounted bailout period is five years.

The bailout period (or the discounted bailout period) will always be shorter than the payback period (or the discounted payback period) if the equipment has any residual value at the end of the payback period. Bailout criteria are much superior to payback criteria because bailout takes into account the residual value subsequent to the termination date being considered. Because the estimated residual value at any date incorporates an estimate of the present value of the cash flows from the equipment after that date, the bailout criteria use more of the relevant information available than do the payback criteria.

Accounting Rate of Return.   The *accounting rate of return,* sometimes called the return on investment (ROI) or the *rate of return on book value,* is defined for a project as

$$\frac{\text{Average Yearly Income from the Project}}{\text{Average Investment in the Project}}$$

In the Garden Winery Company example, the total income from the project is $3,300 over four years or an average of $825 per year. The average investment in the project, assuming straight-line depreciation, is $5,000. Hence, the accounting rate of return would be $825/$5,000 = 16.5 percent. The accounting rate of return pays no attention to the time value of money because it uses income, rather than cash flow, data.

The only good things that can be said about the accounting rate of return are that it is easy to compute and, sometimes by coincidence, it gives good answers.

Many companies use the accounting rate of return. One survey indicated that it was the most sophisticated investment decision rule used by about 25 percent of the firms surveyed.[3]

SUMMARY OF EVALUATION RULES

The methods for evaluating investment projects that do not take the time value of money into account should not be used. All the methods that do take the time value of money into account require using a cutoff rate or discount rate. If optimal economic decisions are to result, then the cutoff or discount rate must be set equal to the cost of capital. If the cost of capital rate is to be used at all, then the net present value rule is no more complex than the others, and using it will lead to decisions that will make present value of the firm's wealth equal to or larger than that from using any of the other rules.

SPECIAL PROBLEMS IN EVALUATING AND CHOOSING BETWEEN INVESTMENT PROJECTS

The preceding sections indicate that the best capital expenditures rule is that an investment project should be undertaken when the net present value of the project is positive when the cash flows are discounted at the firm's cost of capital. This section discusses the use of that rule when several projects have positive net present values.

Capital Rationing.   A special problem arises in the context of capital rationing. Suppose that a manager is faced with a set of investment alternatives, each of which requires current cash outlays and has a positive net present value but altogether require more funds this year than have been made available by higher management. For example, assume that a manager has $20,000 to invest in projects, is told to use a 12-percent cost of capital, and may choose from the set of four projects shown in Exhibit 5. Aside from the capital constraint, each of the four projects is independent of the others. (Such constraints on capital are not warranted, but they appear to be used in practice anyway. This point is discussed below.)

All four projects represent worthwhile investments, but the manager, given a $20,000 constraint on first-year cash outlays, may not undertake all of them. Juggling the possibilities, we can see from Exhibit 9 that the manager must choose one from several combinations of projects.

What is the manager to do? To maximize the net present values of the cash flows to the firm, the manager must choose the combination of projects A and C and

[3]See the results of the survey reported by Thomas Klammer, "Empirical Evidence of the Adoption of Sophisticated Capital Budgeting Techniques," *Journal of Business*, 45 (July 1972), p. 393.

EXHIBIT 9   Dilemma Caused by Capital Rationing

Project combinations (1)	Initial cash outlays (2)	Sum of Present value of cash inflows (3)	Net present values (4)	Excess present value index (5)
A, C	$19,000	$27,000	$8,000	1.42
A, D	15,000	22,500	7,500	1.50
B, C	18,000	25,000	7,000	1.39
B, D	14,000	20,500	6,500	1.46
C, D	10,000	15,500	5,500	1.55

reject the others. (Any funds not invested in these four projects must be used elsewhere in the firm and will, presumably, earn the cost of capital.) The most profitable project per dollar of investment, project D, apparently must be rejected if the manager is to act rationally within the capital constraints.

The problem arises from the inherent contradiction in telling a manager to use a cost of capital of, say, 12 percent while simultaneously limiting the capital budget. A limited capital budget implies a high, if not infinite, cost of capital. With a budget constraint, the firm is implicitly telling the manager that the cost of capital for funds in excess of $20,000 per year is so large that extra capital expenditures should not be contemplated. But because all the firm's capital finances all its projects, then the higher cost of capital is the rate the manager (and the firm) should use for evaluating *all* potential investment projects. For these purposes, the cost of capital is not a number that necessarily increases as more capital is used. Using the cost of capital to calculate net present values of cash flows contains the only needed budgeting device: managers will not invest funds in projects returning less than the cost of capital because the net present values of such projects will be negative. Capital rationing has no place in a profit-seeking firm that chooses between investment alternatives by taking the time value of money into account. If management perceives a constraint on funds available for investment, then all managers should be told to use a higher cost of capital than had been used before. If, when the higher discount rate is used by managers in evaluating projects, the total funds required still exceed the perceived constraints, then the discount rate should be increased to a still higher level. If at the higher discount rate not all of the "available funds" would be used, the rate should be reduced. By a series of successive approximations, the discount rate to allocate available funds will be optimally determined.[4]

Ranking Projects. Capital budgeting decisions are often thought of as being one of three kinds:

1. Accept/reject decisions for investment projects—ones whose future cash flows are independent of each other
2. Choosing the best of a set of mutually exclusive projects
3. Ranking investments in order of desirability.

The preceding discussion has dealt with all three of these kinds of decisions. The third kind of decision, ranking investments, is not a solvable problem in general, at least with current knowledge. An investment project is either acceptable or not; for a given discount rate the net present value either is nonnegative, in which case the project is acceptable, or is negative, in which case the project is unacceptable. As between independent projects with nonnegative net present values determined for a given discount rate, it is not posssible to construct a ranking. It is possible, however, as the preceding discussion indicates, to vary the discount rate at the margin so that the analyst can determine which of the acceptable projects for a given discount rate is the first to become unacceptable as the rate is increased.

SEPARATING THE INVESTMENT AND FINANCING DECISIONS—LEASES

The first section of this chapter pointed out that (1) an investment project should be undertaken only if it has a net present value greater than zero when cash flows

---

[4]See H. Martin Weingartner, *Mathematical Programming and the Analysis of Capital Budgeting Problems* (Prentice-Hall, Englewood Cliffs, N.J., 1963), for a discussion of the use of mathematical programming to deal with capital, and other, constraints in capital budgeting analyses. See also Fama and Miller, *The Theory of Finance,* pp. 134–137, for a criticism and discussion of Weingartner's suggestions.

are discounted at the cost of capital and (2) the investment decision should be separated from the financing decision. The preceding sections have analyzed the desirability of the net present value rule. This section illustrates the required separation of the purchase and financing decisions, by analyzing the factors in a decision whether to lease or buy an asset.

Many firms are currently acquiring rights to use assets through long-term noncancelable leases. Leasing transactions pose two separate problems for managers: (1) whether the lease should be entered into and (2) how financial accounting reports the effects of leasing transactions in the financial statements. The issues may be easier to grasp if we first discuss the financial accounting aspects of leases.

We examine the accounting for leases in the context of the Garden Winery Company example introduced earlier. Recall the Garden Winery Company is planning to bring a new variety of wine to the market. In order to do so, it must acquire equipment that costs $10,000, that is expected to last for four years, and that is expected to have no salvage value at the end of the four-year period.

Assume that the Garden Winery Company can borrow for four years at 8 percent per year. The manufacturer is willing to sell the equipment for $10,000 or to lease it for four years on a noncancelable basis. That is, Garden Winery Company must make payments for four years no matter what. Garden Winery Company is responsible for property taxes, maintenance, and repairs of the equipment under either the purchase or leasing plans.

Assume that the lease is signed on December 31, 19X0, and that payments on the lease are due on December 31, 19X1, 19X2, 19X3, and 19X4. In practice, lease payments are usually made in advance, but the computations in the example are simpler if we assume payments at the end of the year. Compound interest computations show that each of the lease payments, rounded to the nearest dollar, must be $3,019. The present value at December 31, 19X0, of $1 paid at the end of 19X1 and each of the next three years is $3.31213 when the interest rate is 8 percent per year. (See Table 4 of the Appendix.) Because the lease payments must have a present value of $10,000, each payment must be $10,000/3.31213 = $3,019.21. The $.21 per payment is ignored in the following discussion.

Operating Lease Method. In a cancelable lease, called an *operating lease,* the owner, or lessor, merely sells the rights to use the property to the lessee for specified periods of time. For example, the telephone company leases telephones by the month, and car rental companies lease cars by the day or week on a cancelable basis. Cancelable leases and some noncancelable leases are accounted for with the *operating lease* method. If the Garden Winery Company lease were accounted for as an operating lease (which it probably would not be, see footnote 5 below), then no entry would be made on December 31, 19X0, when the lease is signed, and the following accounting entry would be made on each of the dates December 31, 19X1, 19X2, 19X3, and 19X4:

Leasing (Rental) Expense	3,019	
Cash		3,019

To recognize annual expense of leasing equipment. The amounts for the 19X4 entry would be $3,020.

Capital Lease Method. If this noncancelable lease were judged to be a form of borrowing to purchase the equipment, then it would be accounted for as a *capital,* or *financing, lease.*[5] This treatment recognizes the signing of the lease as the simultaneous acquisition of a long-term asset, called a *leasehold,* and the incurring

[5] A lease must be accounted for as a capital lease if it meets one of the four criteria spelled out in FASB Statement of Financial Accounting Standards No. 13, November 1976, Paragraph 7. These criteria are:

of a long-term liability for lease payments. At the time the lease is signed, both the leasehold and the liability are recorded on the books at the present value of the liability, $10,000 in the example.

The entry made at the time Garden Winery Company signed its four-year noncancelable lease, to be accounted for with the capital lease method, would be

Asset—Equipment Leasehold	10,000	
Liability—Present Value of Lease Obligations		10,000
To recognize acquisition of asset and assumption of the related liability.		

At the end of each year, two separate entries must be made under the capital lease method. The leasehold is a long-term asset and, like most long-term assets, it must be amortized over its useful life. The first entry made at the end of each year recognizes the amortization of the leasehold asset. Assuming that Garden Winery Company uses straight-line amortization of its leasehold, the entry made at the ends of 19X1, 19X2, 19X3, and 19X4 would be

Amortization Expense (on Equipment Leasehold)	2,500	
Asset—Equipment Leasehold		2,500

The second entry made at the end of each year recognizes the lease payment (identical in amount with the operating lease), which is part payment of interest on the liability and part reduction in the liability itself. The entries made at the end of each of the four years would be

December 31, 19X1:

Interest Expense	800	
Liability—Present Value of Lease Obligations	2,219	
Cash		3,019

To recognize lease payment including interest on liability for year (.08 × $10,000 = $800). The balance of the cash payment, $2,219, reduces the liability. The present value of the liability after this entry is $7,781 = $10,000 − $2,219.

December 31, 19X2:

Interest Expense	622	
Liability—Present Value of Lease Obligations	2,397	
Cash		3,019

To recognize lease payment including interest on liability for year (.08 × $7,781 = $622). The balance of the cash payment, $2,397, reduces the liability. The present value of the liability after this entry is $5,384 = $7,781 − $2,397.

---

    a. The lease transfers ownership of the property to the lessee by the end of the lease term. . . .

    b. The lease contains a bargain purchase option. . . .

    c. The lease term . . . is equal to 75 percent or more of the estimated economic life of the leased property. . . .

    d. The present value of . . . the minimum lease payments. . . , excluding that portion of the payments representing executory costs such as insurance, maintenance, and taxes to be paid by the lessor, equals or exceeds 90 percent of the excess of the fair value of the leased property . . . to the lessor over any related investment tax credit retained by the lessor. . . . A lessor shall compute the present value of the minimum lease payments using the interest rate implicit in the lease. . . . A lessee shall compute the present value of the minimum lease payments using his incremental borrowing rate . . . , unless (i) it is practicable for him to learn the implicit rate computed by the lessor and (ii) the implicit rate computed by the lessor is less than the lessee's incremental borrowing rate. If both of those conditions are met, the lessee shall use the implicit rate.

The lease in our example is a capital lease because it clearly satisfies criterion d and probably satisfies c as well.

December 31, 19X3:

Interest Expense	431	
Liability—Present Value of Lease Obligations	2,588	
Cash		3,019

To recognize lease payment including interest on liability for year (.08 × $5,384 = $431). The balance of the cash payment, $2,588, reduces the liability. The present value of the liability after this entry is $2,796 = $5,384 − $2,588.

December 31, 19X4:

Interest Expense	223	
Liability—Present Value of Lease Obligations	2,796	
Cash		3,019

To recognize lease payment including interest on liability for year (.08 × $2,796 = $223). The rest of the cash payment, $2,796, reduces the liability. The present value of the liability after this entry is zero: liability reductions of $2,219, $2,397, $2,588, and $2,796 total $10,000.

Notice that in the capital lease method, the total leasing expenses over the four years is $12,076, consisting of $10,000 (= $2,500 + $2,500 + $2,500 + $2,500) for amortization expenses of the leasehold and $2,076 (= $800 + $622 + $431 + $223) for interest charges. This is exactly the same as the total expenses recognized under the operating lease method described above. The difference between the operating lease method and the capital lease method is the *timing* of the expense recognition on the income statement and the substantial difference in the disclosure on the balance sheet. The operating lease method requires no entries in balance sheet accounts. It is often described as "off-balance-sheet financing" because it recognizes neither the asset nor the liability. The capital lease method recognizes both the asset and the liability and also recognizes expenses sooner than does the operating lease method, as summarized in Exhibit 10.

EXHIBIT 10

GARDEN WINERY COMPANY
Comparison of Expenses Recognized Under Operating and Capital Lease Methods

	Expenses recognized each year under	
Year	Operating lease method	Capital lease method
19X1	$ 3,019	$ 3,300 (= $ 2,500[b] + $ 800[c])
19X2	3,019	3,122 (= 2,500 + 622)
19X3	3,019	2,931 (= 2,500 + 431)
19X4	3,019	2,723 (= 2,500 + 223)
Total	$12,076[a]	$12,076 (= $10,000[b] + $2,076[c])

[a]Leasing expense.
[b]Amortization expense.
[c]Interest expense.

MANAGERIAL EVALUATION OF LEASES

It is easy to confuse the investment and the financing decisions in the context of making the lease-versus-purchase decision. A long-term noncancelable lease is a form of borrowing which is, in turn, a form of financing. In evaluating an asset acquisition, the implications of borrowing, whether with explicit debt or with a lease, should be examined closely. Under a noncancelable lease, the firm commits itself to payments over the term of the lease whether or not the leased asset is continued in use. A noncancelable lease may be accounted for as a capital lease or as an operating lease, depending on the circumstances. The financial accounting for capital leases should not affect management's evaluation of whether leasing is a preferred form of financing for the particular asset. Cancelable leases, such as for the use of telephones rented by the month or cars rented by the day or week, present no conceptual difficulties because they are not a form of borrowing.

Managerial Evaluation of Noncancelable Leases.   Return to the example of the Garden Winery Company. The Company has decided to acquire an asset with a four-year life, which costs $10,000 and which will be used to help bring a new variety of wine to the market. Assume that the manufacturer of the asset states that it can be leased for four years with annual lease payments based on an 8-percent interest rate to be made at the end of each year. We found in the preceding section that if the interest rate implicit in the lease contract is 8 percent per year, then the annual lease payments are $3,019 at the end of each year. Exhibit 11 shows the schedules of cash flows that will result from buying the asset outright and from leasing it for four years from the manufacturer.

Case I: Purchase.   Case I reproduces the information from Exhibits 1 and 2 that apply when the asset is purchased outright and annual cash flows are discounted at 10 percent per year. The net present value of the investment project when the asset is purchased is $687. Because the net present value is greater than zero, Garden Winery Company concludes that the project is worth undertaking. The initial cash outflow of $10,000 is used to acquire the asset. In each of the following years the cash flows consist of sales less cash operating expenses and income taxes.

Case II: Lease for Four Years.   The second schedule in Exhibit 11 shows the net cash flows each year if the asset is leased with an implicit interest rate of 8 percent per year, which requires four annual payments of $3,019. Column (2) shows the cash revenues less other cash expenses, just as when the asset is purchased. Column (4) shows the annual lease payments, assumed to occur at the end of each year. Column (8) shows the pretax income, revenues minus lease payments. Lease payments are deductible expenses for tax purposes. Column (9) shows income tax expense, 40 percent of pretax income. Column (10) shows net income (for accounting purposes), and column (11) shows net cash inflows and outflows. When the asset is leased, there is no depreciation so that accounting income each year is the same as net cash flow each year. Finally, column (12) shows the present value of each of the cash flows discounted at 10 percent, the discount rate used Garden Winery Company in making investment decisions. Notice that the net present value of the leasing plan is $1,775, more (about 2½ times larger) than the net present value derived in case I for purchasing the asset.

Some managers would note the much larger net present value for the leasing plan and conclude that leasing is surely better for the firm than buying outright. *Comparing the net present values of the results in cases I and II, buying outright versus leasing, is invalid.* The investment decision has been confounded with the financing decision. A noncancelable lease is a form of borrowing. In case I, the firm is not borrowing; in case II it is borrowing. To evaluate the leasing plan, the manager should construct a series of cash flows in which the firm borrows equivalent amounts of funds for the equivalent interest rates that are implicit in the lease contract and then compare a borrow-purchase alternative with the leasing alternative. Correct managerial decisions require comparable financing plans. Because the leasing contract effectively combines the financing and investment decisions, then the valid alternative to leasing is a borrow-purchase alternative equivalent to leasing in terms of financing such as the alternative illustrated in case III.

Case III: Borrow for Four Years and Purchase.   If the leasing company is willing to lend to Garden Winery Company at 8 percent per year, then the Company can presumably borrow from a bank at 8 percent per year. If payments on the loan are

EXHIBIT 11

20-20

GARDEN WINERY COMPANY

Annual Net Cash Flows and Net Present Values of Alternatives Available for Acquiring Asset
(Discount Rate is 10 Percent per Year; Income Taxes are 40 Percent of Pretax Income)

End of year (1)	Revenues less other operating cash expenses[a] (2)	Depreciation[b] (3)	Lease payments (4)	Total = (5)	Interest expense[c] (6)	Principal repayment[d] (7)	Pretax income[e] (8)	Income tax expense[f] (9)	Net income[f] (10)	Net cash inflows (outflows)[h] (11)	Present value of net cash flows at 10%[i] (12)
				Case I: Purchase Asset; No Borrowing (See Exhibits 1 and 2)							
19X0	—									($10,000)	($10,000)
19X1	$ 5,000	$ 2,500	—	—	—	—	$2,500	$1,000	$1,500	4,000	3,636
19X2	4,000	2,500	—	—	—	—	1,500	600	900	3,400	2,810
19X3	3,500	2,500	—	—	—	—	1,000	400	600	3,100	2,329
19X4	3,000	2,500	—	—	—	—	500	200	300	2,800	1,912
	$15,500	$10,000					$5,500	$2,200	$3,300	$ 3,300	$ 687
				Case II: Lease Asset; Lease Payments Imputed at 8 Percent Interest Rate; Four Payments in Arrears							
19X0	—									—	—
19X1	$ 5,000		$ 3,019	—	—	—	$1,981	$ 792	$1,189	$ 1,189	$ 1,081
19X2	4,000		3,019	—	—	—	981	392	589	589	486
19X3	3,500		3,019	—	—	—	481	193[j]	288	288	216
19X4	3,000		3,019	—	—	—	(19)	(8)	(11)	(11)	(8)
	$15,500		$12,076				$3,424	$1,369	$2,055	$ 2,055	$ 1,775
				Case III: Purchase Asset; Borrow $10,000 at 8 Percent to Be Repaid in Four Annual Installments							
19X0	—									0[k]	0[k]
19X1	$ 5,000	$ 2,500	—	$ 3,019	$ 800	$ 2,219	$1,700	$ 680	$1,020	1,301	1,183
19X2	4,000	2,500	—	3,019	622	2,397	878	351	527	630	521
19X3	3,500	2,500	—	3,019	431	2,588	569	228	341	253	190
19X4	3,000	2,500	—	3,019	223	2,796	277	110	167	(129)	(88)
	$15,500	$10,000		$12,076	$2,076	$10,000	$3,424	$1,369	$2,055	$ 2,055	$ 1,806

The footnotes for the exhibit appear on page 20-21.

Footnotes for Exhibit 11:

[a]Refer to Exhibit 1; the amounts shown here are the amounts in column (2) less the amounts shown in column (3) of Exhibit 1.

[b]Straight-line method; $10,000 cost/4-year life.

[c]Eight percent of outstanding loan. Outstanding loan is $10,000 less cumulative principal repayments shown in column (7).

[d]Lease payment ($3,019) less portion allocated to interest expense from column (6).

[e]Amount in column (2) less amounts in columns (3), (4), and (6).

[f]Forty percent of amount in column (8).

[g]Amount in column (8) less amount in column (9); or 60 percent of amount in column (8).

[h]Amount in column (2) less amounts in columns (4), (5), and (9).

[i]Amount in column (11) multiplied by present value factor for 10-percent discount rate: 1,000 for cash flow at end of 19X0, .90909 for cash flows at end of 19X1, .82644 for cash flows at end of 19X2, .75131 for cash flows at end of 19X3, and .68301 for cash flows at end of year 19X4. See Table 2 of the Appendix and Exhibit 2.

[j]By actual multiplication, this number is $192; rounding to the nearest dollar has caused the sum of numbers in this column to be in error by $1. This number has been changed to undo the rounding effects.

[k]At the end of 19X0, $10,000 is borrowed and used immediately to acquire asset; this number is +$10,000 − $10,000 = $0.

---

made in annual installments at the end of the year, then the payments will be $3,019 for each of the four years, just as for the lease. After all, the same amount is being borrowed and at the same interest rate as in the lease. Part of each payment to the bank is for interest and part is principal prepayment. The journal entries presented earlier for the capital lease accounting method show how much of each payment is for interest and how much is for principal. These amounts are shown in columns (6) and (7) of Exhibit 11. Separating the annual payment into interest and principal repayment is required for the computation of income taxes, because the interest expense is a deduction in computing taxable income while repayment of loan principal is not.

If the Company borrows and purchases the asset, it will report depreciation each year identical with that if it purchases without borrowing. Column (3) shows the depreciation charges. In the case of borrow-purchase, pretax income is revenues less other cash expenses, column (2), less interest expense, column (5). Column (9) shows income taxes, which are 40 percent of pretax income. Net cash flow for the period shown in column (11) is revenues less other cash expenses, column (2), less payments to the bank to service the debt, column (5), less income taxes, column (9). Column (12) shows the present values of each of the net cash flows discounted at 10 percent per year.

The net present value of the borrow-purchase alternative is $1,806, which is somewhat larger than the net present value of the lease alternative because of the timing of income tax payments. In this illustration, borrowing turns out to be slightly superior to leasing as a form of financing.

Why Do Leasing and Borrow-Purchase Appear More Attractive than Outright Purchase? Both leasing and borrow-purchase have net present values more than 2½ times as large as the net present alue of the outright purchase. Why? We can rephrase this question to make the managerial implications clearer. Suppose that the analysis in case I, outright purchase, showed a negative net present value, indicating that the project was not worthwhile for the Company, but that the analyses in cases II or III, one of the borrowing plans, showed a positive net present value that indicates that the project is worthwhile when financed with debt. What should the manager conclude?

The answers to both questions involve an understanding of the difference between the interest cost of debt and the cost of capital used in making investment decisions. In the illustration for Garden Winery Company, the aftertax cost of capital is 10 percent, whereas the borrowing rate is 8 percent. (In general, the difference between these two rates can be even larger than in this illustration. A difference of two percentage points is about as small as we would expect to see.) In the net present value of the leasing and borrow-purchase alternatives, the Company is charged with interest on borrowings at 8 percent, but the cash flows are discounted at 10 percent. Any time a series of interest payments is discounted with a higher rate than that specified in the loan contract, the present value of the loan payments will have a lower net present value than the face amount of the borrowing.

The difference between the net present values of borrowing and outright purchase results from showing the expected returns to financial leverage as a part of the return to the specific project. But, of course, the firm always has the option to borrow at the current market rate of interest. The returns and risks of leverage accrue to the firm's financing policy as a whole and should not be attributed to any one investment project.

Thus, we reach the conclusion that if the net present value for outright purchase is negative even though the net present value for one of the borrowing alternatives is positive, then the firm should not undertake the project. Lease contracts by their very nature involve a simultaneous consideration of investment and financing. Because the two aspects cannot easily be separated in general, the manager should first evaluate the project assuming outright purchase. Only after outright purchase appears worthwhile, because the project has a positive net present value, should the form of financing be considered. Once the lease terms are specified, then the manager should ascertain the payment schedule for a straight loan that is as similar as possible in terms of amounts borrowed and timing of repayments as are implicit in the lease. Then the borrowing and leasing alternatives can be compared.[6]

Warning: The Borrowing Plan Must Be Analogous to Leasing. Care should be taken in constructing the borrowing alternative to be compared with the leasing alternative. It is important that the periodic amounts to be paid under the assumed borrowing be roughly equal to (or at least proportional to) the amounts of the assumed lease payments. If they are not, then the method illustrated is likely to give the wrong answer. For example, if the proposed lease requires equal annual payments at the end of the year, then the assumed borrowing should be like a mortgage (with equal annual payments) rather than like a bond (with small periodic interest payments until maturity, when the entire principal is repaid). If bond-type borrowing is compared to leasing, then borrowing would almost always appear preferable to leasing in the kind of analysis illustrated here. In a bond-type borrowing, money is borrowed for a longer period of time on average than in lease-type (or mortgage-type) borrowing. That is, in any period after the first, bond-type borrowing implies borrowing more money than lease-type borrowing. We have seen earlier that when money is borrowed at one rate and the cash flows

---

[6]The nature of leasing contracts can be somewhat more complicated than indicated here. For example, lease payments can be made in advance, with the initial lease payment being immediately deductible for tax purposes. It is not usually possible to arrange a straight loan with interest payable in advance that is deductible for tax purposes. (In theory, there is no such thing as interest paid in advance.) If payments are made before interest has accrued, then theory says that those payments must be a reduction in the principal amount of the loan, not interest. Another complication arises when the manufacturer offers a "package deal" where the combined interest payments and asset cost are together smaller than they would be separately. (Automobile dealers often are willing to sell at a lower price when the buyer borrows from the dealer than when the buyer makes an outright purchase.) The questions raised by some leasing contracts are beyond the scope of this discussion. The reader interested in a fuller discussion is referred to Chapter 8 of the *Handbook of Modern Accounting*, 2nd ed., edited by Sidney Davidson and Roman L. Weil (McGraw-Hill Book Company, New York, 1977).

are discounted at a higher (cost of capital) rate, then the benefits of leverage are confounded with the benefits of a specific project where no (or less) money is borrowed.

WHEN FUTURE CASH FLOWS ARE UNCERTAIN

Throughout this chapter we have assumed that projected cash flows are equally likely to occur, (that is, for example in terms of Exhibit 1, that the $4,000 inflow at the end of Year 1 is exactly as likely to occur as the $2,800 inflow at the end of Year 4), that the investment projects being considered are all of equal risk, and that the risk for any one project being considered is equal to the average risk in all activities of the firm. In practice, of course, such assumptions about the nature of investment projects are not likely to be met. There have been at least three solutions proposed for dealing with the question of how to treat nonconstant risk in investment projects:

1. Change the discount rate used in computing net present values. The more risky the cash flows from a project, the higher the discount rate to be used.

2. Use a risk-free discount rate, rather than the cost of capital, in computing a net present value, and from it subtract a risk premium expressed in dollars.

3. Use the capital asset pricing model developed by Sharpe and others[7] and treat the portfolio of the investment projects in a fashion parallel to a portfolio of equity securities in modern portfolio theory.

Both of the first two methods have drawbacks in that no one has yet specified an analytical method for quantifying the risk in terms of increased discount rates on the one hand or in terms of the dollar risk premium on the other. The third method has stringent data requirements that may not be practicable and, in any case, has not been subject as yet to extensive testing and use. For a description see Chapters 10 through 12 of Bierman and Smidt.[8]

The current state of the art is best summarized by saying that capital budgeting decisions are made under the three assumptions listed at the start of this section and the results are modified, as the decision maker chooses, on the basis of intuition, experience, and judgment.

BIBLIOGRAPHY

Bierman, H., and S. Smidt: *The Capital Budgeting Decision,* 4th ed., Macmillan Company, New York, 1975.

Dean, Joel: *Capital Budgeting,* Columbia University, New York, 1951.

Fama, Eugene F.: "Risk, Return and Equilibrium: Some Clarifying Comments," *Journal of Finance,* 23 (March 1968), pp. 29–40.

———— and Merton H. Miller: *The Theory of Finance,* Holt, Rinehart and Winston, New York, 1972.

Fisher, Irving: *The Theory of Interest.* Macmillan Company, New York, 1930.

Hamada, R. S.: "Portfolio Analysis, Market Equilibrium, and Corporation Finance." *Journal of Finance,* 24 (March 1969), pp. 13–31.

Hirshleifer, Jack: "On the Theory of Optimal Investment Decision." *Journal of Political Economy,* August 1958, pp. 329–352.

[7]J. Lintner, "The Valuation of Risk Assets and the Selection of Risky Investments in Stock Portfolios and Capital Budgets," *Review of Economics and Statistics,* 47 (February 1965), pp. 13–37; J. Mossin, "Equilibrium in a Capital Asset Market," *Econometrica,* October 1966, pp. 768–775; W. F. Sharpe, "Capital Asset Prices: A Theory of Market Equilibrium Under Conditions of Risk," *Journal of Finance,* September 1964, pp. 425–442.

[8]H. Bierman and S. Smidt, *The Capital Budgeting Decision,* 4th ed. (Macmillan Company, New York, 1975), chaps. 10–12.

Klammer, Thomas: "Empirical Evidence of the Adoption of Sophisticated Capital Budgeting Techniques," *Journal of Business,* 45 (July 1972), p. 393.

Lintner, J.: "The Valuation of Risk Assets and the Selection of Risky Investments in Stock Portfolios and Capital Budgets," *Review of Economics and Statistics,* 47 (February 1965), pp. 13–37.

Lorie, J. H., and L. J. Savage: "Three Problems in Capital Rationing," *Journal of Business,* October 1955, pp. 229–239.

Lutz, Friedrich, and Vera Lutz: *The Theory of Investment of the Firm,* Princeton University Press, Princeton, N.J., 1951.

Mossin, J.: "Equilibrium in a Capital Asset Market," *Econometrica,* Ocotober 1966, pp. 768–775.

Sharpe, W. F.: "Capital Asset Prices: A Theory of Market Equilibrium Under Conditions of Risk," *Journal of Finance,* September 1964, pp. 425–442.

Solomon, Ezra, ed.: *The Management of Corporate Capital,* Free Press, New York, 1959.

Weingartner, H. Martin: *Mathematical Programming and the Analysis of Capital Budgeting Problems,* Prentice-Hall, Englewood Cliffs, N.J., 1963.

Chapter **21**

Distribution Costs

HERBERT F. TAGGART

Emeritus Professor of Accounting, Graduate School of Business
Administration, University of Michigan

DEFINITION AND CHARACTERISTICS OF DISTRIBUTION COSTS

Definition. Distribution costs include all costs of (1) creating, stimulating, and directing demand for goods and services and (2) getting goods and services into the hands of consumers, including the costs involved in keeping records of sales and collections. These two main branches of distribution are frequently described as "order getting," and "order filling." The specifics go well beyond a narrow interpretation of these terms. Order getting includes market research, advertising, sales promotion, personal selling, impersonal selling (such as mail-order selling), and in some cases technical services, such as application engineering and the like. Order filling includes the paper work involved in processing customers' orders, issuing shipping documents, passing on credit, inventory control, and customer accounting, as well as the physical operations of picking stock, packing shipments, loading cars or trucks, and similar items. It also includes collection routines and, in many cases, charges for uncollectible accounts.

This broad description of the distributive process will be the foundation for consideration of distribution costs in this chapter. It does not follow, however, that in the typical business entity all these activities are carried on in organizational segments that are under the jurisdiction of distribution executives. Some functions essential to the distributive process are carried on in other branches of the enterprise, such as the general administrative office or the factory. A complete study of distribution costs must take into account such activities.

Production. The term "production" applies equally to goods and services, and the distribution functions for both are identical except that in the usual case services do not require physical handling and delivery. Production shares some service functions with distribution, an example being personnel. This fact gives rise to problems of cost allocation between production and distribution. In certain cases, given operations may qualify and be accounted for as production in one instance and as distribution in another. A good example is packing goods for shipment. If this operation is performed as a continuous part of the production process, it will ordinarily be accounted for as a cost of production. If, on the other hand, goods arrive at a certain state of completion, are placed in storage, and are packed for shipment only after orders are received, the packing function falls in the distribution area.

Finished goods storage is another function that falls somewhere between production and distribution. If the finished goods warehouse is under the supervision of factory executives, its operating costs may be included among factory costs. If, on the other hand, warehousing of finished goods is entirely divorced from the factory, the associated costs will probably be accounted for in the distribution category.

Finance.   Basically, finance involves providing the cash resources necessary for operating the entire business. In some companies finance also embraces the entire accounting establishment, including maintaining all accounts, financial data processing, credit and collections, and related activities. Some of these areas fall into the territory previously described as distribution, and for purposes of this chapter they will be so treated.

Administration.   Administration may be divided into two categories: specific and general. Each substantive business function has its own administrative personnel to see to it that it is carried on efficiently, economically, and in accordance with policy. In addition, the company as a whole requires administration, performed at the top by the board of directors, and under their guidance by the company officers. In practice, "administration" is also a catchall, where functions that may really belong elsewhere but for various reasons are not so assigned may find a home. Partly this may be due to the fact that some functions frequently included in administration jointly serve general or all other functions, just as "general administration" does. Such a function may be personnel, for example, which may have overall responsibility for setting employment standards and hiring policies, devising compensation plans, dealing with employee representatives, and allied activities for all parts of the organization. Any complete statement of the costs of a major function, such as distribution, must include an allowance for such costs.

There is a question whether or not the more general aspects of general administration and of finance should be allocated at all to the operating functions such as production and distribution. Such allocations are bound to be somewhat arbitrary, and for this reason they should always be regarded as being no better than reasonable approximations of the truth. However, if what is desired is a representation of the net income derived from the several segments of the business, such allocations must be made.

It would obviously be impossible to deal with all the cost analysis and control problems of every type of distributive activity in anything short of an encyclopedia. This chapter therefore confines itself to a consideration of those aspects of what is usually thought of as a "typical" manufacturer, wholesaler, and retailer, though recognizing that the description may not fit any specific member of any of these groups. The principles and procedures, however, are adaptable to the particular circumstances of any enterprise that performs the functions to which they relate.

Importance of Distribution Costs.   To belabor the fact that distribution costs are important and worth a great deal more attention than has sometimes been given them is hardly necessary. Exhibit 1 provides an unusually complete breakdown of distribution costs of the same line of products at three levels. A manufacturer of mechanical equipment, from its own records and other sources, prepared a tabulation from which the figures in Exhibit 1 are adapted. They illustrate the functional classification of distribution costs, an analytical device of basic importance in the study and evaluation of costs. They also demonstrate what appears to be a common pattern of distribution cost relationships, as far as such a pattern can

EXHIBIT 1   Analysis of Retail Price

	Manufacturer	Distributor	Dealer	Total
Manufacturing cost plus profit	50.9%	—	—	50.9%
Distribution costs:				
Administrative	1.3%	1.3%	9.1%	11.7%
Selling	.9	1.9	6.9	9.7
Advertising	3.3	1.5	2.9	7.7
Trans. and delivery	1.9	.8	3.3	6.0
Storage and handling	.9	1.3	—	2.2
Order service	.1	.2	—	.3
Market research	.1	—	—	.1
Product planning	.1	—	—	.1
Product service	.1	.2	(1.6)	(1.3)
Occupancy	—	—	3.3	3.3
All other	—	—	4.3	4.3
Net before income taxes	—	2.0	3.0	5.0
Total distribution cost	8.7%	9.2%	31.2%	49.1%
Retail price	59.6%	9.2%	31.2%	100.0%

be traced in published sources. The retailer's costs absorb a substantially greater portion of the consumer's dollar than do those of the wholesaler. The distribution costs of the manufacturer, who relies heavily on the wholesale and retail channels, are apt to constitute a relatively small fraction of the total.

Prevalence of Joint or Common Costs.   One of the most significant characteristics of distribution costs is the relatively large proportion of joint or common costs. Joint costs are those that are common to two or more segments of the business. The segments may be chronological or geographical, or they may consist of customers, customer groups, orders, shipments, products, product lines, distribution functions, or any other significant object of scrutiny. Whenever the analyst attempts to determine the costs of relatively narrow segmental categories, such as individual customers or products, the great bulk of costs will be found to be joint or common, and their application to such segments requires the development of logical methods of allocation. This situation is in contrast to that in manufacturing costs, where direct labor and materials frequently bulk large, and joint costs are confined mainly to overhead items.

Direct and Indirect Costs.   Costs which are not joint or common to more than one distribution segment are usually referred to as direct, whereas joint or common costs are said to be indirect. These terms must be used with care, however, since directness and indirectness always involve a point of view that must constantly be kept in mind. Thus a cost which is direct when looked at in one way is indirect when regarded from a different standpoint. For example, selling cost which can be clearly identified with a particular customer is indirect when considered in relation to the several commodities that the customer buys. Varying degrees of indirectness must also be recognized. The selling cost just referred to is indirect with respect to the commodities by only one step or degree. Only one method of allocation or assignment is necessary to establish its relationship with the individual commodities. The salary of the president of the company, on the other hand, is only remotely related to any significant analytical segment, and, if it is to be allocated at all, must be dealt with in several successive stages.

Directness and indirectness relate also to time periods. The most obvious examples are costs that are chargeable to the operations of a given year, such as most labor service items, as opposed to costs that have to be allocated or assigned to time periods, such as depreciation.

Fixed and Variable Costs.   A concept related to the preceding discussion, but by no means identical in definition or effect, is the dichotomy between fixed and variable costs. Fixed costs are those costs that, for a given period of time, do not fluctuate with changes in the rate of business activity. Variable costs, on the other hand, do increase with increased activity and decrease as activity decreases, though not necessarily at the same rate.

Distribution costs are sometimes spoken of and treated as if they were all fixed. This is particularly true when price policies are under consideration. The expression "selling and administrative overhead" is illustrative of this tendency, because administrative costs, being largely salaries and occupancy cost, do tend to be predominantly fixed. It is an error, however, to think of distribution costs as an essentially fixed category. Large segments are decidedly controllable because they vary with activity.

DISTRIBUTION COSTS IN THE ACCOUNTS AND IN FINANCIAL REPORTING

Distribution Cost Accounts.   The first step in orderly examination of any subject is logical classification. Such classification results in grouping like phenomena and in distinguishing unlike data. It makes possible the drawing of logical conclusions and the taking of appropriate actions, if any action is indicated. In the accounting area these objectives are arrived at by two mechanisms, principally by making comparisons and by establishing responsibility. Proper account classifications promote these objectives by making possible the collection of basic data in a logical manner.

Natural Divisions and Functions.   The most common and useful classifications of costs are in terms of natural divisions and functions. Natural divisions are sometimes called objects of expenditure. The term refers to what is bought, as contrasted with what is accomplished. Functions, on the other hand, represent what is accomplished—the distribution activities. Natural divisions include the items that the average person would probably list when asked to list the costs of doing business: wages, rent, fuel, electricity, insurance, taxes, and so forth. Functions are the operations which are accomplished by means of the services derived from these expenditures: purchasing, production, selling, advertising, delivery, and the like. The functions correspond to the responsibilities for getting these tasks done according to plan. Each function uses personal services, supplies, and the other objects of expenditure.

The most acceptable system of cost classification uses both of these concepts, since both are necessary for attaining the desired objectives. The functional breakdown is controlling, providing the major subheads of the chart of accounts, each function being supported by the natural expenses which it entails. Account classifications that answer to this description vary infinitely in scope and particularity, depending on the organization of the accounting entity and the purposes to be served.

Distribution Costs in Financial Reports.   The usual published financial report contains almost no details of distribution costs. In many cases, in fact, distribution costs are lumped together with cost of goods sold and all other operating expenses in a single conglomerate figure. It is therefore a safe generalization to say that substantially no information about distribution costs can be obtained from the usual published reports except, of course, in the case of merchandising enterprises, where nearly all operating costs are of a distribution nature.

Problems of Timing.   The distribution costs that are in published statements, whether identifiable or not, are all in the income statement. They constitute all such costs incurred during the period included in the report, regardless of their true relationship to the revenues of the period. Distribution costs, in other words, are seldom, if ever, capitalized or deferred to future periods. (This statement, of course, does not apply to distribution facilities, such as warehouses or sales offices, the costs of which are capitalized and depreciated.)

This failure to defer distribution costs, even where they are clearly for the benefit of subsequent periods, constitutes, in some cases at least, an obvious disregard of the general rules that assets should be recognized whenever there are future benefits and that expenses should be matched with the revenues for whose benefit they are incurred.

Schiff[1] points out that transportation of finished goods from plant to warehouse and the cost of storing them to the time of shipment to customers should be added to inventory costs if the matching concept is to be faithfully followed. This is particularly true in businesses where production and sales cycles differ, especially if monthly reports are relied upon for judging executive performance.

Although the arguments for charging such expenditures to expense at once may be sufficiently compelling to condone this infraction of the matching rule, this treatment of such items is likely to present problems in the analysis of distribution costs and the interpretation of their fluctuations from period to period. This is because the objective of a great many such analyses is to relate the costs to concurrent sales of commodities or services to specific classes of customers. If the immediate objective of the expenditure is not current sales, but rather to lay the foundation for future sales, whatever analysis is made must take this fact into account.

PURPOSES OF DISTRIBUTION COST ANALYSIS

Definition.   An authoritative definition of distribution cost analysis is as follows:[2]

> Distribution cost analysis is the assembling of the various items of distribution cost into meaningful classifications and their comparison in this form with alternative expenditures and with related sales volumes and gross margin. More specifically, it is a technique used by individual business concerns for the determination of the costs of performing specific marketing activities and of costs and profits for various segments of the business such as products or product groups, customer classes, or units of sale—and a study of these findings in the light of possible alternatives.

Purposes.   The principal ends to be served by distribution cost analysis may be summed up under two headings: cost control and assistance in consideration of pricing policies. The values of distribution cost analysis for these purposes are summarized in the following manner.[3]

> Distribution cost analysis may be used by businessmen as an aid in determining profitable objectives for the business, in setting policies and procedures of operation, in determining the efficiency of their organization, and in measuring the profitability of operation in individual segments of the business.
>
> More specifically, distribution costs analysis may be used:
>
> 1. To determine the kinds and amounts of expense incurred in each separate marketing activity such as outside selling, billing, warehousing, and delivery.
>
> Availability of such cost data permits effective assignment of responsibility for cost performance to specific individuals supervising the activities. They make it possible also to trace the reasons for changes in cost over a period of time or variations in cost from budget, and the detailed record provides a basis for corrective action. They open the way to development of standard costs where standards are feasible.

---

[1]Michael Schiff, *Accounting and Control in Physical Distribution Management* (The National Council of Physical Distribution Management, Chicago, 1972), pp. 1–8.

[2]"The Values and Uses of Distribution Cost Analysis," a pamphlet published by the American Marketing Association (Chicago, 1957).

[3]*Ibid.*

2. To evaluate marketing methods, policies, and operating procedures.

Distribution cost analysis provides basic data for appraising the value of services (such as credit or delivery), methods of sale (by telephone, mail, or personal solicitation), and company performance of functions as opposed to use of outside organizations (for delivery, warehousing, and the like). It facilitates judgment as to when and where agents, distributors, or other middlemen will be more economical than direct sale.

3. To determine the marketing cost and profitability of the company's various products or customers.

Cost analysis permits calculation of these facts for individual products and customers or for such groups of them as product lines, brands, styles and sizes, classes of trade, sales territories, and the like. Such data are useful, too, in estimating costs and profits for proposed products or for changes in product or customer mix.

4. To determine the relationship between cost and order size—as a basis for diminishing losses on small orders and as a basis for quantity-discount schedules conforming to the Robinson-Patman Act.

Any general use of distribution cost analysis by businessmen for the appraisal of marketing structure, policy, and plans would have significant economic implications. The effect would be to increase the general level of marketing efficiency. Competition, in turn, may be expected to transfer much of the economy gained to the public through lower prices. Thus, widespread use of distribution cost analysis would be the equivalent of a general technological advance in industry. The reduction in unit costs and increase in efficiency from use of distribution cost analysis may be even greater than that attained as a result of the pioneer work in time and motion studies and cost accounting in the factory.

Cost Control. Cost control is basically a matter of people reacting intelligently to the circumstances in which they find themselves. In order to react intelligently, however, they must have a means of understanding and evaluating the circumstances. This is what the mechanics of cost control provides.

Cost control pervades all levels of business enterprise and engages, or should engage, the attention and support of every member of the organization. From the top, the board of directors exercises cost control in making decisions with respect to capital investments, areas of operation, and other basic policies. At the bottom, clerks or laborers exercise cost control in the way they use their time and how they treat company property. In between, the burden of cost control falls on supervisory personnel at all levels. These are the people who are responsible for the efficiency and economy with which business functions are carried out. It is primarily for them that cost analyses are prepared. The cost analysis reports that they receive should therefore be aimed at two basic ends: to provide guidance in carrying out their cost control responsibilities, and to measure their success or failure.

Budgets. Distribution cost budgets must be prepared in the light of the sales forecast, and vice versa. The two are interdependent, because the volume of sales is influenced by the amount of money management is willing to commit to the distribution process, and the amount of expenditures is determined in significant measure by the volume of sales desired. Of course, there is a limit to the capability of added expenditures in any given situation to produce added revenues, and this must be recognized by those charged with preparing both sales plans and budgets. Chapters 6 and 7 should be consulted for a discussion of budget preparation and administration.

Sales Plans and Goals. Cost control of distribution operations (other than top-level decisions made by boards of directors and executive officers) starts with a sales plan or goal based on market research, a study of company history, and surveys of the market and of competition. All levels of the marketing organization should participate in preparing the sales plan, since everyone from the field salesperson to the vice president in charge of sales can make a contribution. The sales plan, like all operating plans and budgets, should not be imposed from above.

It should instead be the joint effort of all concerned, so that when it is adopted all participants will feel that their contributions have been given adequate weight and for that reason will be encouraged to shoulder their share of the responsibility for its success.

Rakes[4] emphasizes this point in describing sales forecasting procedures in his company:

> For a long time, salesmen were not called upon to participate in developing the marketing plan. Planning normally stopped at the sales manager level. If the sales manager is very close to his market area, his forecasts can be most effective. However, if the party submitting the forecast is not committed to making it happen, then the subsequent production and sales plans will be of little value. It is of little benefit to have a sales manager committed to a sales plan if the salesmen in the field . . . are not committed to the same plan. To correct this situation, we decided to have each individual salesman forecast his sales for each product, customer by customer. By comparing forecasts with actual results, a measure of performance can be established for each salesman which can be tied in to bonuses or incentive compensation plans.

In the case of the sales personnel, the sales plan will normally take the form of the quotas they are expected to meet, and hopefully to exceed. Their compensation and their chances for retention and promotion will depend on their success. The sales quotas must be sufficiently detailed to provide the salespeople with guidelines for using their time and placing their emphasis. It should be detailed as to products and product lines. It may be quantified in terms of physical units, dollars of sales, dollars of gross margin, or in other ways.

In the case of sales supervisors, such as district or regional sales managers, the sales plan will consist of a consolidation of the sales quotas of those under their supervision. Their hopes for economic betterment, too, will depend on how well the personnel under their guidance perform.

Other branches of the distribution organization are also affected by the sales plan (as, of course, is true of the production or procurement organization). For example, warehousing and physical handling must be available at the right times and in the right places. Even the clerical staff must be geared to handle the work load that the sales plan will generate.

Distribution Cost Standards.   As in the case of manufacturing, the development and use of cost standards are feasible in certain areas of distribution. This is particularly the case in clerical activities and in warehouse functions. The procedures for developing standards in these areas do not differ from those in manufacturing. Time and motion studies provide the basic data.

In order getting, however, the cost standard concept is, generally speaking, inappropriate. Keller[5] points this out with respect to field selling. Much cost analysis revolves around the concepts of functions and units of functional service. This is all very well in a factory (or an office) where, says Keller, "all circumstances are conducive to accurate recording of measurable work, and substantially accurate unit costs are secured." In selling, says this author,

> . . . cost per call is frequently set forth as one of these unit costs to be established. But what is a call? If the salesman has called upon the Jones Company and found the purchasing agent was not in, was that a call? You might say no. Let us eliminate that and consider only productive calls. But, what is a productive call and who decides that it falls into that category? I do not believe the salesman will record many nonproductive calls, for his innate optimism will lead him to consider all contacts productive to a degree.

[4]Harold W. Rakes, "Grass Roots Forecasting," *Management Accounting,* LVI, 3 (September 1974), p. 33.

[5]I. Wayne Keller, "Relative Profit Margin Approach to Distribution Costing," *NACA Bulletin,* 30, 13 (March 1949).

The concept of cost standards does not readily fit the activities of the salesperson, the creative functions of the advertising copywriter, the consideration of a customer's credit problems, and many other distributive functions. As a matter of fact, trying to straitjacket such operations within the cost standard concept may well defeat its own purpose, since it may result in work badly done and in frustrated and unhappy personnel. Where work is sufficiently routine and repetitive, and under close supervision, however, the use of cost standards is to be recommended.

Responsibility for Cost Control.   As indicated above, cost control is the responsibility of every member of a business organization. Particular onus must be borne by those in supervisory positions at all levels. This is sometimes difficult to achieve in the distribution area, especially in those branches that consider themselves to be creative and artistic rather than humdrum and routine. This attitude characterizes almost the entire area of demand creation and channeling. To secure the cooperation of the persons engaged in these activities requires no small skill in salesmanship on the part of those who are charged with making the cost control mechanics work.

No cost control system will activate itself or motivate those whose cooperation is required unless someone is put in charge of devising suitable reports, making sure that they get into the proper hands, and following up to determine whether necessary actions have been taken. Ordinarily the company controller or someone within his organization is charged with these duties. Regardless of how well this activity is organized and staffed, however, it will be a failure unless top management is wholeheartedly behind it.

Pricing Policy.   It is an economic truism that the individual costs of merchants or producers do not determine their selling prices. Even the monopolist has to consider the factor of demand, and other sellers cannot ignore competition. As Beyer[6] says, "cost is probably the least important of the considerations . . . in a businessman's setting of his product prices." This does not mean, however, that costs can or should be ignored in the establishment of production, selling, and pricing policies. And distribution costs are of the same importance, *ceteris paribus,* as are production or acquisition costs. The common practice of adding a flat percentage to cover selling and administrative expense is a wholly inadequate recognition of this fact.

According to Joel Dean,[7] costs have these valid uses in the establishment of selling prices:

1. To measure the effects of alternative prices upon profits.
2. To guess what people (customers, competitors, and potential competitors) will do in response to a proposed price.
3. To justify a course of price action that has already been decided upon. . . . Examples include satisfying the government that the provisions of the Robinson-Patman Act have been met, justifying prices before a regulatory commission, and convincing customers that the price rise was "necessary."

To these should be added a fourth use, which is to assist in determining whether alternative specifications or methods of production or selling methods and policies might bring about a satisfactory profit objective when price is so fixed by custom or competition that the individual seller can do nothing about it. In this use, price becomes a determinant of cost, rather than the contrary. As Dean puts it, "fre-

[6]Robert Beyer and Donald J. Trawicki, *Profitability Accounting for Planning and Control,* 2nd ed. (Ronald Press, New York, 1972), p. 297.
[7]Joel Dean, "Cost Forecasting and Price Policy," *Journal of Marketing,* 13, 3 (January 1949), pp. 284–285.

quently the relation of cost to price is, in practice, inverted. The practical problem is to tailor costs to fit a predetermined selling price."

Price Differentiation.   Total costs, including manufacturing or procurement as well as distribution, are of importance in consideration of total prices. In thinking about differential prices to classes of customers or in the light of differing quantities or methods of sale, distribution costs are of major significance. The chief exception to this statement is found in custom industries, such as job printing, where the size of an order may have a substantial effect on unit manufacturing as well as distribution costs. Differentiating prices for this reason should not be confused with so-called marginal or incremental pricing, which is founded on the proposition that, in considering the acceptance of a particular order or of business from a particular customer, fixed or "sunk" costs may be ignored. This type of pricing has limited utility in special circumstances (for example, for government contracts or for exports), but it is not acceptable as a built-in feature of pricing policy generally.

Pricing Under the Robinson-Patman Act.   The usefulness of distribution cost analysis in considering price differentials is by no means confined to the matter of compliance with the Robinson-Patman Act, though it is often assumed that this is the case. Manufacturers or merchants who wish to offer price inducements for greater volumes of purchases or larger sizes of orders may do this intelligently only if they have at least an approximate idea of the cost savings involved. Even where such differentials are dictated by competition, sellers should not be content to meet such competition blindly. One obvious aspect of such a situation is that by studying their cost differentials they may discover how to increase them.

The portion of the Robinson-Patman Act which deals with price differentiation is Section 2(a), which generally forbids discrimination in price "between different purchasers of commodities of like grade and quality," with some exceptions. One of the exceptions is the cost proviso, which reads as follows:[8] "That nothing herein contained shall prevent differentials which make only due allowance for differences in the cost of manufacture, sale or delivery resulting from the differing methods or quantities in which such commodities are to such purchasers sold or delivered."

For a law which has been on the statute books since 1936, there are remarkably few reliable guidelines to assure compliance. This is particularly true with respect to the cost proviso. One thing is sure: reliance on the cost proviso after a complaint has been issued or a private suit under Sec. 4 of the Clayton Act has been started is difficult, expensive, and uncertain. The cost proviso has been described, with much justice, as "illusory." It is nevertheless true that sellers who wish to be in compliance with the law are well advised to conduct studies of their distribution costs for this purpose. Such studies have at least two important advantages. They make a favorable impression on the Federal Trade Commission investigator, thus perhaps forestalling formal complaints, and they often uncover uneconomic aspects of the sellers' sales organization and methods that can be corrected.

Cost studies made for Robinson-Patman purposes involve analyses by commodities, customer groupings, order sizes, channels of trade, territories (sometimes, at least), and otherwise. These analyses are described hereafter under appropriate heads. The procedures suitable for managerial purposes do not necessarily differ from those needed for the cost defense, except that the latter must usually be more detailed and objective. Specific comments are reserved until later. Such "rules of the game" as are thoroughly established are detailed in Taggart's *Cost Justification.*[9]

---

[8] Sec. 2(a), 15 U.S.C. 13(a).

[9] Herbert F. Taggart, *Cost Justification* (Bureau of Business Research, University of Michigan, Ann Arbor, 1959).

Financial Reporting by Conglomerate or Diversified Companies. Another area in which distribution cost analysis may be of use is in reporting the results of operations of so-called conglomerate or diversified companies. To the extent that such companies choose or are required to publish figures showing the net results of operating in more than one industrial line, distribution costs common to two or more lines may have to be separated. It is to the advantage of everyone concerned that the methods used for such separations be as logical and defensible as possible.

MECHANICS AND PROCEDURES

Cost Comparisons. In its simplest form distribution cost analysis consists of time-period comparisons of parallel arrays of natural expense items, accompanied by some effort to appraise the changes from period to period. Thus this month is compared with last month, or with the same month last year and this year to date is compared with last year to date. Also the expenses are related to the factor which is presumed to cause or to justify the changes the comparison reveals. In most cases this factor will be sales, generally in dollars, but sometimes in physical units. The expenses that have remained unchanged per dollar of sales or per unit sold are assumed to have been properly controlled, whereas those whose rate has varied appreciably require further study. An attempt is made to ascertain the reason and perhaps fix the blame for costs whose rate has increased, and some effort should be made to seek the causes for decreased rates of expenditure and to encourage their continuance.

In small, uncomplicated enterprises, such as convenience groceries, this analytical procedure has much to recommend it. It is unsophisticated. It requires little more than a reasonably detailed chart of expense accounts and a healthy curiosity on the part of managers to know how well their efforts at expense control are working. It may lead them to attempt a simple form of budgeting, and their comparisons will then take on a new dimension: actual against budget.

As firms grow in size and complexity these measures become inadequate. To cite a simple example, when a convenience grocery takes on a line of fresh meats the relationship of expense levels to sales becomes more complex. In order to understand the forces at work and their effects, it is necessary to sort out the expenses so as to know which pertain to groceries and which to meats. Whatever analytical procedures are in use must then be applied separately to each branch of the business. Also the manager of the grocery department becomes responsible for his expenses and the manager of the meat department for his.

Further increases in size and complexity demand still more sophisticated cost analyses and control measures. Operating functions become identified, and the functional breakdown of costs becomes essential to their study and control. Cost comparisons, whether by time periods or with budgets, are made by functions, so that the manager of the function may be informed and held responsible. Cost standards may be developed in certain areas, and comparisons are made between actual and standard costs. Deviations of actual from standard costs are analyzed to determine their causes and to ascertain appropriate actions. The establishment of branch stores or warehouses or sales offices adds a geographical aspect to the cost comparisons. Each such unit becomes a center to which all the cost comparison techniques may be applied, and in suitable cases the performance of each such decentralized operation may be compared with others in the same category.

Complete Functional Analysis. The logical conclusion to this evolution is arrived at when it is desired to know costs in terms of commodities sold or services performed, customers, channels of trade, order sizes, territories, and so forth. A comprehensive description of what is involved is found in the report of the

Federal Trade Commission's Advisory Committee on Cost Justification.[10] Although this report was prepared with the cost proviso of the Robinson-Patman Act in mind, the analysis procedures are in sufficiently general terms so that they furnish guidance in many circumstances.

Relevant Costs.   Because the purpose of distribution cost analysis is to enable management to arrive at intelligent decisions with respect to business problems, it is essential that the cost data on which management relies be relevant to these problems. That is, the costs which management is asked to take into account must have a logical relationship to the decisions which management must make. This makes it necessary to examine different costs for different purposes.

For the purpose of deciding whether certain actual or proposed differential pricing plans conform to the requirements of the Robinson-Patman Act, for example, all related costs, whether fixed or variable, are pertinent. In view of the interpretation of this law by the Federal Trade Commission and the courts, it is plainly impossible to arrive at a reliable conclusion on the basis of anything short of fully allocated costs.

On the other hand, many business decisions require that certain costs be ignored. These are the costs which would not be affected by the decision in question. The best examples are to be found in connection with decisions to increase or decrease production, to add a product to the line (or delete one from the line), to add or abandon a sales territory, to serve or refuse to serve specific customers or classes of customers. In all these cases the relevant costs are those that would be increased or decreased if the decision is made to take the action proposed. If a cost will be neither increased nor decreased by the decision, it may be ignored, and the decision makers' thinking should not be confused by putting before them tabulations containing irrelevant costs.

Generally speaking, the costs which may be ignored in such cases are the fixed, or relatively fixed, costs, and the costs which must be taken into account are the variable costs. This is the principal reason for attempting to divide all costs between these two categories.

Accountants' opinions differ widely as to the degree to which attention should be concentrated on variable costs. Some would apparently be willing to exclude fixed costs entirely from the decision-making process. Others advocate full costing with equal vigor. Schiff and Mellman[11] report that, in the companies they studied, "The net profit approach, where all costs and expenses are allocated to products is most frequently used. . . ." At the same time they found much use made of cost analyses that were not carried out that far.

Perhaps the best advice is that both variable and full costing have their merits and uses and each should be employed where it best meets the need. It should be kept in mind, of course, that neither of these devices is a matter of absolutes. Costs that would not vary with a small change in volume or over a short period of time may well show variation when larger changes or longer time periods are involved. A cost is neither fixed nor variable because of its name. The only way to tell how to classify it is by a realistic consideration of how it would actually react to the proposed change in circumstances.

COST ANALYSIS IN DISTRIBUTIVE ENTERPRISES

Every concern engaged in retail or wholesale selling of goods or services does some distribution cost analysis if it keeps books at all. The vast majority of such

---

[10]Reproduced in *ibid.,* pp. 551–572.

[11]Michael Schiff and Martin Mellman, *Financial Management of the Marketing Function* (Financial Executives Research Foundation, New York, 1962).

enterprises, being small, neither need nor employ sophisticated analyses. The methods they use are unlikely to go beyond simple cost comparisons, usually by time periods. They may go a step further if there are trade association or similar statistics available, and check to see whether they are doing as good a managerial job as their contemporaries. Larger retail and wholesale enterprises may carry on detailed studies of operating costs and results. Some of these are described below.

Retailing.   Cost analysis in the retail field has been promoted by the National Retail Merchants Association (NRMA) and other trade associations, by the U.S. Department of Commerce, by university bureaus of business research, and by manufacturers who provide accounting advice and assistance to their dealers.

NRMA Expense Accounting.   By far the best-known and most carefully formulated scheme of accounting for costs at the retail level is that of the National Retail Merchants Association. The activities of this Association in this area began with the appointment of a committee in 1916. Its report recommended the creation and adoption of a common expense accounting language. As the committee remarked,[12] "The prime object is to establish a basis of understanding between the stores so that in conversing with one another, or comparing statistics of operation, the terms used and the meaning attached to them may be identical to all." The achievement of this objective made possible the publication by the Controllers' Congress of the Association of an annual compilation entitled "Merchandising and Operating Results of Departmentized Stores," and by Harvard University of the annual reports called "Operating Results of Department and Specialty Stores." (The latter publication was taken over by the NRMA in 1963.) Without the standardization of terminology and classification of accounts these reports would have been unfeasible, or at least much less intelligible and useful. The Association has also published many valuable studies of significant aspects of store operation and cost control.

NRMA Expense Accounting Manuals.   The National Retail Merchants Association has published a series of expense accounting manuals that have contained definitions of terms and instructions to enable participating stores to inform themselves about their own costs and to participate in the joint collection of expense statistics.

Wholesaling.   Distribution cost analyses required by the wholesaler differ neither in scope nor in kind from those suitable for the manufacturer. Retailer, wholesaler, and manufacturer are equally interested in analyses that aid in solving problems of cost control, and each of them has or may have the need to control the operations of branches which are geographically separated from the principal headquarters. Branch accounting is not given specific attention here, for the problems of branch accounting are largely mechanical rather than analytical. Branch accounting involves methods of assuring prompt and accurate communication, maintenance of uniformity in accounting procedures and policies, avoidance of the waste involved in decentralized functions that could be more economically handled at a central location, and similar matters. In the area of analysis, branch accounting involves merely the application at several locations of the same procedures which are used by the unitary enterprise.

With respect to segmented analysis, the retailer is interested primarily in product (merchandise) breakdowns, whereas wholesalers and manufacturers are equally concerned with customer and order-size analyses. The sections covering these subjects which follow are therefore equally applicable to wholesalers and manufacturers.

---

[12]Quoted in 1950 edition of the National Retail Dry Goods Association (NRDGA), *Standard Expense Accounting Manual* (New York), p. 9.

TERRITORIAL COST ANALYSIS

Perhaps the most common form of distribution cost analysis by manufacturers is analysis by territories. Part of the reason for the prevalence of such analyses is the fact that many territorial expenses are direct. All that is required to obtain the data on such costs is a chart of accounts which contains a territorial breakdown. More important, it is difficult to see how a satisfactory territorial sales organization can be established and maintained without knowledge of the costs involved.

A large company is apt to have more than one level of territory. At the lowest level is the district and at the intermediate level the region. The material which follows is couched in terms of sales districts, but, since sales regions are merely groups of sales districts, essentially the same procedures and considerations apply to regions as to districts. The region's costs are the summation of the costs of the districts of which it is composed, with regional management and funtional services added. Regional management and functions (such as, for example, personnel selection and training) supplement and to some extent supplant the related home office activities.

Objectives.   The prinicpal objectives of territorial cost analysis are described in *NACA Research Series No. 21* as follows:[13]

> 1. To determine profitability of each geographical unit in the company's marketing area. In this case, manufacturing costs and sales (or gross margin) must also be analyzed by territories.
> 2. To estimate the effect which a proposed change in territorial operations can be expected to have on profits.
> 3. To measure the effectiveness with which management in charge of an individual territory is doing its work.

Business Decisions Affected by Knowledge of Territorial Costs.   The prime purpose served by an analysis of territorial operating data is to determine whether the territorial executives are doing their jobs. Both revenue and cost data are necessary for this purpose, since territorial managers are charged with adhering to company policies with respect to pricing, product mix, and other matters which affect revenues and gross margins, as well as with the control of costs. Decisions with respect to keeping and rewarding territorial personnel are among the most important served by analysis territorial operations.

Other managerial decisions that require a knowledge of territorial costs are as follows:

1. Changes in intensity of sales coverage. Involved are proposals to add to or subtract from the regular sales force; to utilize the services of special salespeople supplied by home or regional offices, and other methods of contacting larger or smaller numbers of customers or spending more (or less) time with each.

2. Changes in intensity of advertising and sales promotion. Decisions relating to the use of local advertising media are involved, as well as the use of displays, point-of-sale material, samples, demonstrators, and the like.

3. Changes in territorial boundaries. Should new territories be added, or old ones abandoned? Should a territory be split, or combined with all or part of another? Light on such questions is thrown by studies of territorial profitability and the effects on territorial operating costs and effectiveness of changes in population, types of industry, traffic conditions, and other factors which affect the mobility of salespeople and their ability to provide adequate coverage of the area.

---

[13]"The Assignment of Nonmanufacturing Costs to Territories and Other Segments," *NACA Bulletin,* 33, 4, (December 1951), part 3, p. 528. The NACA (National Association of Cost Accountants) changed its name to the NAA (National Association of Accountants) subsequent to the issue of this study.

4. Changes in methods of covering a territory. Customers may be contacted by telephone, by personal visitation, by mail, by local advertising. The relative costs of each form of solicitation are significant, and the proper choice of methods or combinations of methods is dependent to a major extent on cost analyses which demonstrate their economic effectiveness. Methods that are suitable for one territory are not necessarily suitable for another.

Direct Costs. The direct costs of operating a sales territory are those which are generated within the territory and the amount of which is not determined by any sort of proration or allocation. Precisely what the direct costs are will depend on the functions performed by the territorial organization. They will invariably include direct selling costs, such as salespeople's compensation, travel, and customer entertainment. They will include also rent, utilities, supplies, and other operating costs of the district sales office, if there is one. Salespeople's equipment, such as samples, literature, price lists, order forms, and the like, are also direct costs, although some of these items are usually supplied by headquarters and may or may not be charged to the territory on a cost basis. Ideally they should be, but if they are not material in amount they may be included in sales administration overhead and allocated to territories along with other costs of the administrative function.

If the territory has its own warehouse facilities and delivery system, the costs of these functions, too, are direct territorial costs. In such a case the territorial manager becomes more than a sales manager and is responsible for substantially all company activities domiciled in the territory. He may well have, in this event, territorial sales, warehousing, and delivery executives as his immediate subordinates. Another group of activities that may or may not take place within the territory embraces credit and collection, billing, customer accounting, and related clerical functions. Some if not all of these areas are likely to be centralized, however, in a large organization, and especially one which is equipped with a computer.

Readily Allocable Indirect Costs. The costs of such functions as those mentioned in the preceding paragraph, to the extent that they are centralized and shared by two or more territories, can ordinarily be allocated to the respective territories on logical and acceptable bases. Such allocations require measuring the services received by each territory and attaching appropriate unit costs. The receiving and storage portion of warehousing cost, for example, may be charged to territories in terms of territorial sales volumes, measured in physical units if possible, or in dollars if uniformity of sales mix permits. The order picking and packing activities in the centralized warehouse may be assigned to territories on the basis of the number of orders shipped, providing each territory's orders are of approximately equal average size. If they are not, a detailed cost study of picking and packing will disclose the costs of handling various sizes of orders, and an equitable assignment to territories may then be made. It is to be noted, of course, that such a study of order processing costs is necessary for other distribution cost analyses, so that the territorial assignment is not its sole purpose.

Delivery, if by common carrier, should present few difficulties. If delivery is made by company truck fleet, however, and trips cross the boundaries of more than one territory, there will be some problems in an equitable cost assignment. Relative ton-miles or some other physical measurement of service received will probably achieve reasonable equity. Again, the cost of company-operated delivery functions must be analyzed for purposes of control, and the further analysis for allocation to territories may well be justified as a control measure.

The allocation of centralized credit, billing, customer accounting, and related costs to territories can usually be done by using as units of functional service the numbers of customers, orders, shipments, invoice lines, and other appropriate measures. In this area, however, the cost analyst should consider whether the increased accuracy attained by meticulous adherence to logical procedures is worth the time and effort. These costs may be of such relatively minor magnitude that merging them with other administrative items for allocation on a broad base may be satisfactory. It should not be forgotten, however, that a territory which has many small customers and correspondingly small orders requires much more of these services in proportion to sales volume than does the opposite type of territory.

The costs of certain types of regional or home office personnel may also be charged against territorial operations with a good deal of assurance. These are people who provide specialized assistance to all territories and perhaps perform technical supervisory functions. Examples are internal auditors, advertising and sales promotion specialists, product specialists, sales engineers, and the like. Also missionary salespeople, sales training specialists, and others of similar character can be treated the same way. Charges for their travel and a per diem for their services are the appropriate cost assignment method.

Remote Indirect Costs. Many company-wide costs are not so easily assigned to territories. Such a cost may be national, and especially institutional, advertising. Probably the best basis for allocating such costs to territories is relative sales potential, measured by population or in some other suitable way. Territorial sales quotas or goals may also be used. Actual sales dollars is hardly a satisfactory basis. Such advertising is aimed at potential sales, and the territory that does not achieve its potential should not be rewarded by being charged a lower share of general advertising. Neither should the territory which exceeds its quota be penalized.

Home office sales administration obviously must be charged to territories if territorial net profits are to be ascertained. No single basis for such an allocation is ideal. Equal amounts to each territory are sometimes used for this purpose. Other measures are based on the numbers of people supervised, or their total compensation, or the total of direct territorial expenses. The ideal measure, of course, would be the burden on time and energy of the administrative organization imposed by each territory. At least two insurmountable obstacles prevent the use of this factor. One is the extreme difficulty, if not impossibility, of obtaining such a measure. Reliable time reports from such people as the general sales manager are hardly conceivable. Estimates of time spent by the same individuals will be strongly influenced by what happened yesterday. The other obstacle is the fact that the attention required by individual sales districts fluctuates widely from year to year. A territory where the sailing is smooth this year may have to break in a new salesperson next year, or may be threatened by exceptionally keen competition, or have a marked turnover in dealerships. Allocation of this type of cost should be on the basis of long-run considerations not influenced by short-term crises.

Market research falls into the same cost category with general sales administration. It seldom has a discernible connection with specific sales territories. Substantially all market research is forward-looking—devoted to the products or demand-influencing methods of next year or following years. This is a cost that might conceivably be capitalized or deferred and charged against the future periods which it benefits. Orthodox accounting, however, calls for charging it against the revenues of the year in which it is incurred. In any particular year the market research cost incurred and charged immediately to expense is in lieu of charges for earlier years' market research that might have been deferred and charged to this year. This treatment may be the only practical approach and thus makes good accounting sense. The only exception might be a year in which expenditures for this purpose were materially larger than normal. Allocation of this cost to territories may well be on the same basis as the allocation of general marketing administration.

Distribution's share of general company administration is even more remote from the territory. The only purpose served by its allocation is to arrive at a figure of net territorial profit, and the validity of such a figure would be questioned by many authorities. Any allocation method contains a considerable element of arbitrariness. Actual or potential sales or the total of previously assigned costs have approximately equal logical merit.

Territorial Operating Reports.   The results of territorial operations need to be reported to the various levels of management. At the bottom are the territorial managers. Frequently they receive reports on only those items over which they have direct control: sales and direct territorial expenses. *NACA Research Series No. 21* quotes one company executive as follows:[14] "My personal preference is to stop with the 'territorial manager's margin.' Why bother him with items he can't control? In fact, why even show the figures if you do not want an argument on how expenses are distributed?"

And, indeed, if the territorial managers' performance is to be evaluated on the basis of some variety of contribution margin, and especially if their compensation is to be geared to this, there is much to be said for this point of view. On the other hand, some companies routinely charge their field locations with assessments for home office costs. Where this is a long-standing practice, it would be of questionable wisdom not to follow it also in territorial performance reports.

The exact items to be included in the computation of territorial contribution will differ according to company organization and the degree of the territory's autonomy. The figures on the reports should, of course, be accompanied by comparisons with quotas and budgets and with the same figures for other time periods, and perhaps with other territories.

Reports to higher levels of management may be on a net profit basis, or at least something closer to net profit than the territorial contribution. Precisely how such reports should be prepared depends to a great extent on what management wants or what it is used to. The accountant who prepares reports for these people can scarcely afford to ignore these factors. The purpose of such reports is largely to demonstrate whether or not each territory is carrying its full share of the load. If such reports are prepared, they should be accompanied by comparisons with planned or budgeted results. Decisions and conclusions should be based on the degree of success achieved by the territory in carrying out its assigned tasks, and not on absolute profit or loss results.

Robinson-Patman Aspects.   It is not unusual for price discrimination complaints to be limited to certain geographical areas. The areas chosen may not, of course, correspond precisely with the respondent's sales districts. Nevertheless, the existence of territorial cost data, prepared in the ordinary course of business, may be of great assistance to sellers who are attempting to defend their pricing policies. Generally speaking, if a price discrimination complaint is so geographically limited, costs of other areas are excluded from consideration.

Also, the company that wishes to avoid such a complaint by reviewing its costs and prices to see whether a clear case of cost justification could be made will ordinarily select a few representative sales districts in order to keep the scope of the study within reasonable bounds of time and expense. Such a study also is greatly expedited by the existence of a regular scheme of studying district operations for managerial purposes.

CUSTOMER COST ANALYSIS

Purposes.   According to *NACA Research Series No. 21*,[15] the purposes of distribution cost analysis by customers are as follows:

---

[14]*Ibid.*, p. 533.
[15]*Ibid.*, 33, p. 543.

(1) To determine how sales effort should be apportioned among different customers or classes of customers;

(2) To decide whether or not an individual account should continue to be solicited;

(3) To establish price differentials based upon differences in marketing costs incurred to serve various classes of customers; and

(4) To help to explain profit or loss shown on specific products or territories.

This study suggests that cost analysis by customers will ordinarily be done on the incremental basis. "The costs assigned to customers are those which will differ if one alternative is chosen rather than another." This statement reflects the fact that the bulk of the decisions which relate to customers are of the sort which is best served by this limited analysis. This is certainly the case where the analysis relates to individual customers, and also is true for the most part where customer groupings are involved.

If, however, the problem is that of price differentiation, full allocation of costs is essential. The incremental approach is inappropriate and inadequate if the legality of price differences is under consideration, and the adoption of a discount schedule or other scheme of price differences among customers without giving consideration to possible legal consequences is risky at best.

Analysis by Individual Customers.   Complete cost analysis in terms of individual customers is rare. Such analyses on a comprehensive bases would be inordinately costly and unlikely to yield information that would be of much use in making the type of decisions which are commonly made with respect to individual customers. Considerations other than costs will ordinarily determine whether to drop or add a customer or whether to cultivate an existing customer more intensively or less so. The customers' potential, rather than their current performance, is the key question. If they could become profitable customers, sales effort is likely to be spent on them, even though cost analysis might show that business with them is now done at a loss.

The escapable costs of serving an individual customer are apt to be very small. Except for the cost of the merchandise itself, they will probably consist of whatever might be saved by discontinuing the salesperson's calls. And this is apt to be negligible unless the circumstances are unusual. If the customer's place of business lies along the salesperson's regular route, the only cost involved is that of his or her time while calling. Even with respect to that, the question must be asked as to what the salesperson would do with that time if he or she did not spend it in this way. If there exists no more profitable way of spending the time involved, the opportunity cost, at least, is nil.

Analysis by Customer Classes.   The grouping or classification of customers for purposes of making managerial and pricing decisions is a matter of critical importance. Faulty classification can cost a great deal in unnecessary price concessions, in customer goodwill, and in competitive position. It can make cost justification of price differentials impossible and thus lead to a Federal Trade Commission cease-and-desist order or the loss of a treble damage suit.

Customers may be classified along many lines. One is geographical, according to sales districts or territories. Another type of customer classification depends on the function that the customer performs in the distributive process. Thus customers are designated as wholesalers, jobbers, distributors, retailers, industrial users, governmental units, and so forth. A common classification is in accordance with volume of purchases over a period of time—usually a year, but sometimes a shorter period.

Customer classifications other than by volume are somewhat less vulnerable to attack. Territorial price differences, for example, may be clearly justified by differences in transportation cost alone, and injury to competition at the secondary level is rather unlikely. Classification by channels of trade may be shielded from the operation of the Robinson-Patman Act by lack of competitive effect. Such classification is not foolproof, however. Merely calling a customer a wholesaler, for example, does not make him (or her) one.

Excessively wide dispersion of costs within customer volume groups is difficult to prove under ordinary circumstances. A factual situation such as existed in the Standard Motor Products case[16] is unlikely to be repeated. There the respondent had accumulated time data for all sales personnel and all customers for an entire year, as well as data concerning the number and size of orders and shipments. From this unusually complete information a Commission employee was able to compute what he called individual customer costs. Call, order, and shipment data accumulated on a sampling basis could never be put to such a use. They may be entirely adequate to establish average costs for a customer class, but they prove nothing about individual customer costs beyond the limited time period included in the sample, and they are not ordinarily collected in such a way as to make even this information easy to compute. In the fluid milk case, the Supreme Court drew inferences of probably wide dispersion of costs from the characteristics of the dairy business which, in the Court's opinion, made the dairy companies' grouping procedures "like averaging one horse and one rabbit." Other sellers should heed this decision and avoid, as far as possible, customer classifications which are subject to such an attack.

Classification of customers according to the sizes of orders they place is sometimes attempted, but this may not be a valid customer classification. In most lines of business any customer is likely to place orders of varying sizes, so that the only valid customer classification related to order sizes is in terms of the average size of orders placed. In such a classification it will usually be found that the larger customers (those who buy in larger volumes over a period) tend to place larger orders on the average, but this is not necessarily true—they may merely buy more often. In certain lines of business, such as perishable foods, for example, periodic volume and order sizes sometimes go hand in hand. A grocer may, for instance, take roughly the same amount of dairy products day after day. In such cases volume analysis and order-size analysis coincide. For the most part, though, cost analysis in terms of sizes of orders has an uncertain relationship to customers.

Analysis by Distributive Channels.   Where sellers deal with customers at various levels (wholesalers, retailers, consumers), a study of the costs of serving such groups will commonly show distinct differences. To a major extent this is likely to be due to using different selling methods or sales personnel for each customer category. Such practices make possible substantial identification of costs with each customer group (the direct costs of that group) and a correspondingly low amount of indirect costs that must be allocated. As a result, cost analysis by distributive channels is apt to be easier and more reliable than the analysis of customer groups in terms of size. Aside from this factor, however, cost analysis by channels differs not at all from that by size groups.

The business decisions which may be affected by channel analysis are much more apt to be of a managerial character than related to price. Price differentiation by channels is strongly influenced by competition and trade custom, and relative costs have only a remote bearing. Cost analysis is an aid to efficiency in cultivating each channel, however, and is useful in answering problems of method and intensity. It is of importance also in deciding whether to drop or add channels, and in this instance, at least, the incremental approach is the appropriate one.

Analysis by Volume Groups.   The analysis of distribution costs in terms of customers grouped according to their annual (or other periodic) purchase volumes is commonly associated with differential pricing decisions. This is not at all

[16]*In re* Standard Motor Products, Inc., 68 FTC 1248 (1965).

surprising, in view of the fact that a high proportion of all differential pricing schemes are based on annual volumes, and most such analyses adopt the price-differentiating groupings as the framework of the analysis. Such analysis is, of course, essential to determining whether or not the pricing plan conforms to the requirements of the Robinson-Patman Act.

The usefulness of this type of analysis is not wholly confined to the pricing area, however. It throws light on why and to what extent small accounts are unprofitable, and on what to do about this situation. It may also help to explain why certain commodities and territories are exceptionally profitable or unprofitable.

Establishment of Volume Groups for Analytical Purposes.   Uncritically adopting the volume groupings previously established solely for reasons of marketing strategy is to defeat the real purpose of the analysis. The analysis should reveal the strengths and weaknesses of the existing volume groups to the end that they may be defended as being the most suitable, or altered if it is found that they are not. Essential for this purpose is the adoption for analytical purposes of a finer breakdown than would be practical for use in a discount plan. Thus one company, in making such a study to aid in devising a new pricing system, categorized customers into 17 volume groups, nine of which spanned intervals of only $1,000. The plan finally adopted contained six customer classes, the narrowest being $3,000. With the aid of modern data processing equipment a study of this sort presents no serious mechanical difficulties.

There is no royal road to perfection in the choice of volume groups. The groups selected to present the picture of cost-volume relationships will finally be chosen on the basis of judgment, in the light of both accounting and commercial realities. What competitors are doing (if the issue is one of price differences) is bound to have an important effect, though it must be borne in mind that under established policies of administering the Robinson-Patman Act competitors' price schedules cannot merely be copied. If the questions to be answered by the analysis relate to managerial rather than price decisions, the groupings chosen must be such as will throw light on the management problems.

Direct Costs: Selling.   A major segment of distribution costs is direct selling, and a major portion of direct selling is directly chargeable to the business done with specific customers. The cost of the time which salespeople spend on customers' premises or in doing paper work or other service on behalf of specific customers is a direct cost of doing business with those customers. To measure this cost is not simple, however. It requires a knowledge of how the salespeople spend their time, which few employers possess and which many sales supervisors would say is impossible to get. It is a fact, however, that this kind of information has been obtained many times and that it is by no means as burdensome and unreliable as is sometimes claimed.

The best source of information about how salespeople spend their time is the salespeople themselves. Most salespeople make daily or weekly reports of their activities—the places they have been, the customers on whom they have called, the prospective customers solicited, and so forth. Rather seldom, however, are salespeople routinely asked to report time spent in these various activities, and this is the statistic necessary to compute the cost of putting the salesperson into the customer's premises. Nearly always, therefore, when customer costs are to be ascertained, the salesperson's reporting system must be expanded to include an analysis of his or her working time. Exhibit 2 is an example of a time-reporting form devised by one company for this purpose. It is not presented as a model, but merely to show the manner in which this company accumulated the desired information.

Another company, which employs the salespeople's reports for managerial purposes, provides them with punched cards arranged so that the salesperson can

EXHIBIT 2

SALESPERSON'S DAILY TIME REPORT

List all customers and prospects contacted this date. See instructions below.

A. Account name	B. Customer code number	C. Type of account		D. Customer class	Time spent			
					E. Travel		F. Sales	
		Cust-omer	Pros-pect		Hours	Tenths	Hours	Tenths

District _____ Date _____ Signature _____ Salesperson's code no. _____

INSTRUCTIONS

One of these reports is to be completed each workday by each sales manager and sales-person. Negative reports are required on days when no contacts are made. Reports for Saturdays, Sundays and Holidays are required only if contacts with customers or prospects are made on those days. Instructions for each of the lettered columns are as follows:

A. The *account name* of each customer or prospect with whom or for whom time is spent is to be entered in this column.

B. The *customer code number* is to be entered here.

C. Please indicate with a check mark (√) in the appropriate column whether the account listed is a *customer* or a *prospect*. If an account has purchased within the past twelve months, classification should be as a customer.

D. Both customer and prospect accounts are also to be classified and coded on this report so as to distinguish between accounts in the following manner. Use Code Number 1 for *accounts we franchise or endeavor to franchise.* Use Code Number 2 for *direct accounts* or prospective accounts such as builders, mobile home manufacturers, government agencies, etc.

E. *Time spent in travel* from home or office to the first call each day and time spent traveling to subsequent calls will be recorded in this column on the same line on which the name of the account appears. Time spent in travel from home to office and from the place of business of the last customer or prospect called on during the day, to home or office, will not be recorded.

F. *Time spent with or on behalf of each account* is to be recorded in this column. Include all time spent with an account whether it be at his place of business or elsewhere, or time spent on the telephone with him. Also record any office time or other time that can be positively identified as having been spent on behalf of a particular account. Time spent in general office work, sales meetings, product training meetings, etc. will not be recorded.

FORWARD COMPLETED REPORTS TO YOUR DISTRICT OFFICE TO ARRIVE ON THE MONDAY FOLLOWING THE WEEK COVERED BY THE REPORTS.

report in detail on a day's activities by merely making marks at the appropriate places on the cards.

Sampling Procedure. In order to minimize the burden on both salespeople and the clerical staff, considerably less than 100 percent reporting for a full year is likely to be adequate. The company that uses the punched-card procedure described above, for example, receives reports from approximately 20 percent of its sales force covering one assigned day per month throughout the year.

For special cost studies, both temporal and geographical samples should be selected in such a manner that a fair representation of the whole will be achieved. The sampling process for this purpose is not scientific, but judgmental. The time sample must be chosen in such a way as to minimize the effects of seasonality. It may be possible to do this by choosing a month (if one month is adequate) in which sales equal approximately one-twelfth of the annual total. It must be remembered, however, that seasonality of salespeople's activities and seasonality of sales may not coincide. The customer sample must include reasonably proportionate representation of customers of all sizes whose buying habits—as to product mix, order sizes, etc.—are also fairly representative of all customers. This end is usually achieved, or attempted, by assembling a group of sales districts whose sales and expense statistics bear a close resemblance to the corresponding statistics for the entire sales area. Some geographic spread is usually thought to be desirable in this connection.

There is often doubt as to the reliability of time data obtained from salespeople. It is feared that they may tend to report what they think will do them the most good, rather than the truth. There is indeed some danger of this. It can be minimized, however, by three steps. The first is careful instruction in advance, with explanations of the purpose of the study, the need for accurate data, and a plea for cooperation. The second is assurance to the reporting salespeople that the data will not be used in any way to prejudice their advancement or compensation. In some cases the salespeople are given assurance that only financial people will see the individual reports and that they will not be made available to sales management. A typical assurance of this sort is as follows: "We want to emphasize that these reports are *in no way used to appraise your selling performance.* Each report is compiled with the others to establish a general pattern of effort devoted to individual products and activities. Your individual reports will not leave this unit." The third essential step is to put someone in charge of receiving and examining the reports who will take prompt steps to remedy defects or correct omissions.

One alternative to having salespeople do their own reporting is to send someone along with them to observe their operations. This procedure may well achieve superior accuracy in reporting what the salesperson actually does, but it is extremely costly and is likely to alter the salesperson's routines in such a way as to make the information of questionable value.

Where the salesperson is paid a straight commission, it may be thought that time studies are unnecessary, because both customer and commodity costs can be ascertained by merely looking at the commissions earned. This is an erroneous assumption. The salesperson's employer is buying time and directing how it should be spent. The saleperson's instructions are intended to achieve the employer's objectives, such as thorough coverage of a district, and the salesperson is not, therefore, at liberty to maximize income by spending time only on the more fruitful accounts. The commission system is merely a method of computing the compensation for the salesperson's time, not an indication of the cost of obtaining a particular order or of doing business with any particular customer.

Direct Costs: Other.   In addition to the cost of salespeople's time spent with or on behalf of customers, other costs may be identified directly with customer groups. Customer entertainment—meals, drinks, ball-game tickets, and the like—is a good example. Identification of these items is commonly required on salespeople's expense reports and they therefore present no problem. The cost of product samples given to customers may require special reporting or may be reported routinely. In many cases this is not a material item. Some companies keep adequate records of catalogues and literature supplied to customers, but frequently this is not done, and accounting for costs of these items as direct charges becomes difficult if not impossible. They are apt to be highly seasonal, and keeping track of them for a brief period would therefore be inadequate. In the absence of records, the existence of definite policies with respect to the distribution of such materials, together with evidence that the policies are adhered to, may serve the purpose.

Order processing and filling and delivery are also direct costs of serving customers, but there are likely to be difficulties in identification and measurement. In the case of order processing and filling, although it is obviously impossible to observe and report on these activities in the same way as can be done with salespeople, it is feasible to keep track of the numbers and sizes of orders received and shipments made over a representative period and to apply to them costs determined by means of time studies. The direct costs of deliveries by common carrier can be measured readily enough, but if delivery is by seller-owned or leased trucks, delivery costs must be allocated with some degree of indirectness.

Advertising and sales promotion usually include elements of both direct and indirect costs. Advertising allowances are direct customer costs and can be accounted for as such. Point-of-sale advertising materials are also inherently direct costs, but measuring the cost chargeable against a given customer or customer group may not be easy. Records of such materials are apt to be lacking. If definite policies as to the distribution of such materials exist and are adhered to, however, they may substitute for records. If sales promotion activities are carried on at customers' premises, they may be reported on in the same way as salespersons' visits. Sales promotion campaigns are likely to be seasonal or sporadic, however, and therefore to present difficulties in sampling.

Readily Allocable Indirect Costs.   The cost of delivery by company fleet is ordinarily allocable to customer volume groups with reasonable precision. Statistics on the number and sizes of deliveries are essential. Costs of getting the trucks to the customers' premises may be allocated on a stop basis, although the time of delivery personnel while at the delivery points will vary according to the size of the deliveries. Time studies of deliveries of various sizes will probably be necessary. If goods are physically homogeneous, the measurement of delivery size is a simple matter. If they are not, however, some difficulty may be encountered. If all sizes of customers purchase approximately the same product mix, even this problem can be solved. Distance of deliveries does not affect the calculation if customers of various sizes are evenly scattered geographically. If the study were one of individual customer costs, distance might have to be taken into account.

General advertising, particularly that directed toward the ultimate consumer, can be reasonably assigned to customer volume groups only on a dollar sales basis. This cost is usually omitted from Robinson-Patman studies because it produces no cost differentiation.

Customer accounting, credit, and collection may usually be treated on a transaction basis, though some of these activities—for example, the preparation and mailing of monthly statements—are more or less uniform per customer.

Field warehousing of goods may be assignable to customer groups on the basis of dollar sales if the purchases of all groups are reasonably homogeneous. If this is not the case, the costs of warehousing different categories of goods must enter into the calculations. In some cases large orders are shipped from the factory and small orders from field locations. This condition requires a study of the use of field warehousing in order that the cost may be assigned only to those customers who get the benefit.

Remote Indirect Costs.   Supervisory and supporting costs in general follow the personnel or the costs of the functions supervised or supported. Precisely what is appropriate depends on organization and circumstances in each instance, but reasonable approaches are usually not hard to find. When incremental costing is involved, most of these costs will not be allocated, since they tend to be unaffected by rather wide swings in total volume of business. A caveat is required with respect to sales supervisors, such as district and regional sales managers, and even top-ranking home office personnel. Direct customer contacts by these people are not unusual, and if there is an appreciable amount of such activity, it must be properly accounted for. Evidence of the time and cost involved is sometimes difficult to pinpoint, but an effort must be made to do so, because costs of such contacts run high per hour, and may make considerable difference in evaluating the business of the customers who are thus contacted. Such customers tend to be in the upper volume brackets. Customer contacts made by supervisory personnel in the course of routine trips in company with field salespeople need not be accounted for in this way. Such contacts are incidental to the supervisor's normal duties of observing the field force and instructing them in their duties.

Assignment of the cost of cultivating prospective customers to customer volume groups presents serious difficulties. The ideal, perhaps, would be to have reliable estimates of the demand potentials of the prospects called upon, and to assign the cost of calling on each one to the corresponding quantity bracket. Lacking such information, a possible allocation method is to consider the entire cost category as general sales promotional effort, and hence to use dollar sales as the allocation basis. This yields no cost differential among brackets, however, except for a desire to produce a figure of net profits, the cost might well be left out of the calculation. For purposes of one study, a survey was made of the first-year purchases of new customers who had been prospects the year before. The allocation of the cost of prospect calls to customer volume groups was based on this survey.

The dollar sales method is presumably the best treatment of the cost of market research for purposes of customer analysis. This method of allocation assumes that, whatever the current research projects may be, their purpose is to maintain and improve the marketing structure as a whole, and their cost should be borne equally by each sales dollar.

Charges for uncollectible accounts are often insignificant, and it makes little difference how they are allocated, if at all. If they are to be allocated, however, this should be done by taking a long-range view. Bad debts experience over a series of years (perhaps as many as five) should be taken into account. To make allocations, data with respect to which classes of customers give rise to bad debts are required. If such data are unavailable, allocation to customer classes on the basis of sales dollars may be the only feasible procedure.

Robinson-Patman Considerations.   For purposes of testing conformity of differential pricing systems with the Robinson-Patman Act, customer costing and classification are crucial. The customer classification of greatest significance is that in terms of volume, since differential pricing is very generally based on periodic volume. There are, however, many unanswered questions with respect to such grouping of customers. In the Chicago fluid milk case, the Supreme Court[17] called for "the use of classes for cost justification which are composed of members of such self-sameness as to make the averaging of the cost of dealing with the group a valid and reasonable indicium of the cost of dealing with any specific group member."

In similar vein, the report of the Advisory Committee on Cost Justification had this to say about classification of customers and other business segments:[18]

> The privilege of classification is not a license to disregard sound business and accounting concepts. In order to become the basis for cost justification of price differentials, the classification should be logical and should reflect actual differences in the manner or cost of dealing. Great care should be taken in establishing price classes to

[17]*U.S. v. Borden Co. et al.*, 370 U.S. 480.
[18]Report of the Advisory Committee on Cost Justification to the Federal Trade Commission. See note 10.

make sure that all members of the class are enough alike to make the averaging of their costs a sound procedure. Customer groupings may properly be based not only on quantities sold but also according to the way customers place their orders: whether for immediate delivery or later shipment on a fixed schedule; in large or small orders; placed directly at the factory or through a sales branch; for on-peak or off-peak manufacture, etc. These trade factors may all be reflected in cost and as criteria for customer classification.

Some sellers have attempted to meet one challenge to volume classification by adopting a dual discount plan, one discount scale being based on the customer's entire purchases and justified by differences in selling costs, and the other scale being based on deliveries at each receiving point (where the customer takes deliveries at two or more locations) and justified by differences in order processing and filling and delivery costs. No such plan has been tested in any public proceeding before the Federal Trade Commission or the courts, but it has obvious merit, especially in sales to chains and other multiunit customers.

ANALYSIS BY ORDER SIZE

The Small Order Problem. Substantially every business is plagued by the problem of what to do about orders that are too small to pay for the out-of-pocket costs of obtaining and filling them. Cost analysis helps to define the parameters of this problem and should, if properly oriented and devised, point toward viable solutions. A recent study of order-size costs was undertaken for the following purposes:

1. To test the continuing validity of the existing pricing plan used in sales to the replacement trade

2. To accumulate data that would indicate where revisions could be made in sales plans in order to gain in market share and improve profits

3. To provide management with cost and statistical information for the purpose of seeking areas where costs could most effectively be reduced

4. To identify the characteristics of unprofitable customers and orders.

Simple Analysis to Determine Breakeven Point. A relatively simple analysis may suffice to determine the point at which a sales transaction stops losing money out of pocket and starts to make a contribution toward common expenses and profits. Sevin describes one such study:[19] All distribution costs were classified in accordance with the factor by which it was assumed that they varied, with the following results:

1. Overhead and routine costs of handling an order	$ .55
2. Cost of handling the shipping order and invoice	2.60
3. Cost of handling each item or line on the invoice	.15
4. Financial cost per dollar of volume	.08
5. Cost per salesperson's call	4.25
Total cost per order	$7.63

Thus, if a salesperson brought in an order for one item whose selling price was $1, the assignable costs would be $7.63. If the gross margin on this sale is 28 percent, the loss would be $7.35. If the order came in by telephone the loss would still be $3.10. The minimum profitable one-line order received without a salesperson's call would be about $17, or, if obtained by means of a salesperson's call, about $38.

The company that made this study concluded that about 50 percent of its orders

[19]C. H. Sevin, *How Manufacturers Reduce Their Distribution Costs,* U.S. Department of Commerce, Economic Series No. 72 (1948).

were handled at loss. In considering the incremental costs of any such volume of orders as this, the incremental cost category must be defined much more broadly than would be the case if the addition or subtraction of only one order were under study. The elimination of 50 percent of all orders would certainly result in substantial curtailment of clerical and order-handling staff, and, if orders are in large measure obtained by personal solicitation, the sales staff might also be decreased or, at least, put to more profitable employment.

Price Differentiation by Order Size. The adoption of a plan of price differentiation based on sizes of orders is, of course, subject to scrutiny for possible violation of the Robinson-Patman Act, and should for that reason, as well as for management purposes, be preceded by a cost study. One of the goals of the order-size study whose purposes were stated above was to ascertain whether order-size discounts that had been adopted several years before were still legally valid.

Cost Functions and Bases of Allocation—Order Getting. For this study both order-getting and order-filling costs were used. The company manufactured a considerable variety of products of a single general category which were sold to original equipment manufacturers (OEMs) for installation in mechanical and scientific equipment, to distributors for resale to retailers and repair shops for replacement, and to the U.S. government for use by the military and other services.

All salespeople throughout the country were required to submit daily time reports for 20 specified working days. The days selected included a two-week period in early April and ten other days specified for each employee during a 14-week period beginning in April and ending in July. This unusual time sample was intended to eliminate the effects of seasonality, weather, and other influences on the salespersons' activities. Data from the two ten-day reports were separately tabulated and the results compared. Because they were found to be in general agreement, they were consolidated.

The time reports classified the salespersons' time as follows:

Customer-related travel time

Personal call time

Telephone call time

Other customer-related time—e.g., correspondence, reviewing files, preparing reports, entertainment

Other travel—to sales shows and trade meetings, for example

Other work time—e.g., time spent at internal sales meetings, conventions, group entertainment

Personal time—personal errands, meals, etc.

To the salespersons' compensation were added amounts covering support, fringe benefits, supervision, travel costs, and the like. The time reports identified customers in order that they might be placed in the proper categories.

Customers were classified into volume groups that were in turn related to order sizes. Costs were allocated to the customer groups partly on the basis of contact time and partly on the basis of the number of calls. The latter basis was particularly appropriate for the cost of travel, including the cost of time spent in travel.

Order Filling. The study of order-filling costs began with a survey of 8,500 orders randomly selected throughout the year. This survey revealed many interesting facts. From the standpoint of costs, the most important characteristics were size of orders, whether received in the mail or by telephone, and whether they could be filled in standard packs or necessitated breaking packages. The company's products were packed in standard shipping quantities at the end of the production lines. These quantities differed according to the size of the item, ranging from 6 to 100. If an order came in for 10, say, of an item whose standard package contained 100, it was obviously necessary to break a standard package and repack the 10 items for shipment. This increased the handling costs substantially.

Clerical costs of processing orders and the costs of picking items in the warehouse and preparing for shipment were measured by standard time-study procedures. Transportation costs from warehouse or factory to customer were averaged by order sizes. Costs of transporting product from factories to outlying warehouses were not included, because they obviously had no relationship to sizes of orders.

Relation of Order-Getting Costs to Order Sizes. Crucial to the utilization of both order-getting and order-filling costs in identifying the total costs of orders was a measurement of the extent to which customers who bought in large volumes tended to place large orders and those whose purchases over the year were made up of small orders. The survey of order characteristics demonstrated these relationships quite clearly. In the replacement channel, for example, 69 percent of the orders of customers with annual volumes of less than $500 were in quantities of less than $50. The average order of these customers was for $76. At the other end of the scale, 69 percent of the orders of customers with annual volumes of $125,000 or more were in quantities of $18,000 or more. Similar results were observed in the OEM and government channels. From data of this sort it was concluded that it was logical to apply order-getting costs of large customers to the large orders and order-getting costs of small customers to small orders. The result, of course, was a substantial increase in the cost differences between order sizes.

Results of Study. This study unearthed many facts of use to management in addition to the data as to cost of filling orders of various sizes. For example, it was found that the proportion of telephone orders was greatest at the small-order level and smallest for large orders. On the average, 29.9 percent of all orders in the replacement channel were received by telephone. The percentage for orders of less than $10 was 64.7 percent, and for orders of $18,000 and up it was 14.3 percent. It was also discovered by the time studies that it cost about $1 more to process a telephone order than to process orders received in the mail. This obviously had an important bearing on the uneconomic character of small orders.

Another statistic of considerable interest related to the proportion of small orders. Of all invoices studied, 56 percent were for amounts of less than $50. These invoices accounted for only 3.5 percent of sales. The causes of such small invoices were various. Some 27 percent were due to the fact that customers' orders were for less than $50; 25 percent were for back-orders because stock was unavailable, and 48 percent arose out of stocking limitations at the several company plants and warehouses.

Paperwork cost of processing a mail order consisting of one line item shipped on one invoice from a district warehouse ranged from $4.60 to $5.90. If shipped from a factory, the corresponding cost ranged from $9.34 to $9.91. The operations studied included acceptance of the order, editing line items, pricing line items, preparing the shipping memo, and billing the customer.

The cost of handling per standard package in a district warehouse was $.38; for a broken package, $.91. At a plant the corresponding costs were $.08 and $.42.

Outbound transportation costs were 9.5 percent of sales value for orders of less than $10 in the replacement channel. They ranged down to 0.5 percent of sales value for orders between $2,500 and $3,500. Above $3,500 the percentage rose slightly because of a change in product mix at that level. In the OEM channel these percentages were 5.8 percent for orders of less than $10 to 0.25 percent for orders in excess of $18,000.

Total order-filling costs, on the average, were 9.8 percent in the replacement channel, 5.8 percent in the government channel, and 3.3 percent in the OEM channel. In the replacement channel, order filling costs ranged from 138 percent for orders under $10 to about 2 percent for orders in excess of $18,000.

An important part of the study was a breakeven analysis. This analysis included all costs, both fixed and variable, for both manufacturing and distribution. The results showed breakeven points in terms of dollars per order as follows: replacement channel, $80; OEM channel, $300; government channel, $50.

Recommendations. At the conclusion of the study the compilers made 15 recommendations, all of which were intended to reduce costs. For eight of these the compilers quantified the amounts that they thought could be saved, but for the others they did not, because in each case additional evaluation and study would be required to determine the exact parameters of the action required. The recommendations follow. Rather than actual dollar amounts, savings are indicated by index numbers, which show relative sizes of the savings.

1. Establishment of minimum order sizes in the replacement and OEM channels—$75 and $300, respectively. Orders below these amounts would be refused. In the replacement channel, however, this company already was assessing a penalty charge of $7.50 on all orders of less than $50, with satisfactory results. As an alternative to refusal, this penalty might be extended to apply to orders below $75. This recommendation was ultimately adopted, with results that will be shown hereafter. Saving: replacement channel, 15; OEM channel, 160.

2. Establishment of minimum annual volumes per receiving point for all customers. Such minimums would be at levels commensurate with the breakeven points. The company already had minimum annual volume levels for some customers that were higher than the ones recommended, but the study compilers pointed out that such higher minimums were excluding potentially profitable customers. The recommendation also pointed out that many customers were being granted price concessions in order to meet competition or for other reasons. If such concessions were controlled more strictly, some customers now unprofitable could be made profitable. Saving: 150.

3. Adoption of methods of minimizing small invoices, which cost about $3 each. Such methods would include:

a. Reduction of orders under $50, per recommendation 1.

b. Improvement of stock availability.

c. Stocking more items in district warehouses, where the tendency was to stock only fast-moving items. Some of the savings to be derived from this suggestion would be offset by increased cost of carrying inventory, but net saving was estimated at 100.

4. Change in method of obtaining orders from one class of customers. Saving: 70.

5. Installation of a handling charge of $.50 for every broken package quantity order. Saving (added income): 58.

6. "Standard" practice of the company called for refusal of government orders of less than $50. Exceptions were permitted, however, at the discretion of the district sales managers. As a result, this rule was more honored in the breach than in the observance. The study had disclosed 5,000 government orders of less than $50, 2,300 of which were less than $10. (The study had shown that the total cost of a $10 order was $31.50.) The recommendation was that no employee be permitted to accept orders from a government agency of less than $50. Saving: 40.

7. Change in method of billing the government, to consolidate certain operations. Saving: 11.

8. Consolidation of back-order items under $10 until an economic shipping quantity was attained. Saving: 25.

9. Review of the salespersons' time reports with a view to seeing whether more working time might be devoted to direct sales solicitation. Only about 20 percent of the average salesperson's time was so used. Most of the rest was taken up by customer service, travel, and paperwork. If these ancillary activities could be better controlled, the salesperson's productivity might be substantially increased.

10. Better correlation of sales force incentive pay to the profitability of the sales for which it was paid. Incentive pay consisted of commissions paid on certain sales. Varying

rates of commissions should be considered, with a view to rewarding sales personnel for emphasizing the types of sales that yield the largest profit margins.

11. *Review of policies with respect to calls on prospective customers.*   The cost of these
calls ranged from 15 to 20 percent of total direct selling cost. A careful review
might disclose that money for this purpose was being spent too liberally.

12. *A study of the company's standard package program.*   Data from this study might
disclose that the numbers of product units packed in standard packages should be
increased or decreased. Any action in this area would affect the number of
broken-package deliveries. In making this recommendation the study compilers
pointed out that any action in this area would also have an effect on packaging
cost, which might to some extent offset the savings in order handling.

13. *Take action to reduce the number of orders received by telephone.*   The study had
shown that it cost about $1 additional per order to process telephoned orders.

14. *Consider reduction of entertainment expense, especially for certain types of customers.*

15. *The study had shown 1,265 "return" calls during the sample period.*   These were
second or third calls on the same customer within a month. "Can these calls be
minimized?"

The study report also commented on certain proposed changes in pricing
schedules. The most interesting of these was one that would alter some of the
order-size discount brackets and introduce an annual volume rebate that would be
based on differences in order-getting costs.

Solutions to the Small Order Problem.   Although the recommendations listed
above resulted from an analysis of costs on the order-size basis, it is obvious that
most of them might have been derived from any careful and detailed study of
distribution procedures and costs.

Perhaps the best solutions of the small order problem are those that in one way
or another pass the cost of small orders on to the customers. There are many ways
of doing this. The most obvious, of course, is the adoption of progressive order-
size discounts. This may be supplemented by other actions. A dairy company, for
example, adopted the radical step of reducing its deliveries from once per week
day to three times per week. For extremely small orders the adoption of a service
charge has much merit. That this is effective is well illustrated by the figures in
Exhibit 3.

EXHIBIT 3   Order Pattern by Size of Order Range

	Replacement			
Order size range in $	1975	1971	1965	1961
$ 0–$ 49	1%	1%	10%	43%
50– 99	8	31	10	11
100– 249	34	26	18	16
250– 499	16	14	16	12
500– 999	18	16	21	10
1,000– 17,999	22	12	24	8
18,000–up	1	—	1	—
Total	100%	100%	100%	100%

The figures in Exhibit 3 are taken from the records of the company for which
the study described above was made. In 1961 this company exacted no penalty for
small orders. As shown in Exhibit 3, orders less than $50 then constituted 43
percent of the total number of orders. In 1965 a $7.50 penalty for orders less than
$35 was adopted. In that year, the number of orders less than $50 decreased to 10
percent. In 1971 the penalty began to apply to all orders under $50. They then
declined to a mere 1 percent of all orders received. The recommendation to apply

the penalty to orders less than $75 was adopted in 1975. The result was a decline in the proportion of orders between $50 and $100 from 31 percent to 8 percent, The company also reported no apparent effect on sales.

Flat refusal of small orders is, of course, a drastic procedure. It may result in losing customers, but, if the manufacturer has an adequate number of distributors, sales volume may not decline. The distributors must, of course, be recompensed for their services, but they can handle small orders more efficiently than the manufacturer and usually give better service. Refusal of the small orders of large customers, such as the U.S. government, may not be feasible, but other methods of discouraging or penalizing such orders may be available.

COST ANALYSIS BY COMMODITIES

Purposes. *NACA Research Series No. 20* lists the purposes of analysis of distribution costs by commodities as follows:[20]

> 1. To determine profitability of present products under conditions currently prevailing
> 2. To aid in estimating the effects that proposed changes in products, methods of marketing, or selling emphasis will have on product costs and profits
> 3. To provide cost information which management wishes to have when making decisions with respect to selling prices or acceptance of business at a given price

To these purposes may well be added that of assisting in the preparation of operating budgets and their administration. Adequate analysis of costs by products will help to determine the effects on costs of increases or decreases in volume, as well as those of changes in products, methods, and emphasis. Also, when pricing policy is under consideration, budgeted costs may be more appropriate than actual costs.

Individual Commodities Versus Commodity Groups. The same research study concluded that the companies which carry on continuous or repetitive commodity cost analysis apply it to groups of commodities rather than to individual items. The reasons for this are apparent. It costs less to analyze costs by groups, and the results obtained are more reliable and meaningful. This is because the product groupings ordinarily follow organizational lines. Each product department may have its own sales force, its own advertising, its own warehousing. The costs of these functions thus become direct charges to the product groups, and no allocations are necessary. Studies of individual products, on the other hand, are likely to require allocations of substantially all marketing costs.

Furthermore, many of the management decisions that must be made with respect to products relate to a cohesive line of products rather than to individual items, and the costs pertaining to the line are the relevant costs. Studies of the costs related to individual products are likely to be occasional rather than periodic. One such occasion might be the threat or advent of a price discrimination complaint concerning a particular commodity rather than the line as a whole.

Methods of Commodity Grouping. How commodities are classified and grouped for cost study purposes depends mainly on the questions to be answered. Grouping by organizational responsibility is clearly desirable in nearly all cases, but other classifications may also be useful. The organizational classification will usually result in grouping of products that are alike physically or by industry designation. Subgroupings by sizes, grades, and other characteristics may be useful. Packaged goods may be distinguished from the same items sold in bulk; goods sold under

---

[20]"The Assignment of Nonmanufacturing Costs to Products," *NACA Bulletin,* 32, 12 (August 1951). See note 13.

seller-owned brands from goods sold unbranded or under brands owned by buyers; goods sold for use by the buyer from those which the buyer resells to others. Distribution methods and costs may differ significantly along all these lines.

Direct Costs. The amount and variety of costs which may be charged directly in commodity analysis depend primarily on the degree and kind of product grouping that underlies the study. Product groups frequently have their own exclusive sales and promotional personnel, for example, whose entire compensation and expenses are a direct cost of the product group. Similarly, product groups may be the beneficiaries of exclusive advertising, and they may be served by exclusive warehouses.

If entire sales and promotional organizations are not devoted to the product groups under analysis, it may still be possible that certain individuals are product specialists and therefore directly chargeable. Some forms or elements of advertising may similarly be direct, even though entire advertising programs are not.

Outward transportation and delivery costs will probably be direct charges to product lines if warehousing of each line is separate. Where more than one product or product line involved in the study are warehoused together, however, storage and delivery will usually be common costs and will therefore have to be allocated.

Some portions of other expenses may also be identifiable with particular product groups. For example, certain market research projects may relate entirely to specific lines or products. Some caution should be exercised here, however, because market research is a long-run endeavor which goes in cycles, so that the product areas which are under study change from year to year. The benefits which a line of products is currently receiving are generally not from research projects being currently carried on, but from those of last year or the year before. Looked at in this light, market research becomes a general cost that must be allocated to product lines not on the basis of the projects being carried on at any one time but rather with regard to the research program of a number of years. The purpose of the research program may well be to sustain and promote the enterprise as a whole rather than to benefit particular segments at a particular time. If this is the case, direct assignment is inappropriate, and some rather broad allocation base, such as sales dollars, may better reflect the true incidence of these costs.

The general rule with respect to the identification and application of direct costs is that this should be done to the greatest extent feasible where the cost elements are material. The best way to accomplish this is to provide adequate account classification so that such costs may be identified without question.

A special problem arises in the case of mixed accounts, containing both direct and indirect elements of cost. Such an account might be supplies, for example. If it is desired to ascertain the distribution costs associated with a particular product or product group, exclusive of all others, this account may be analyzed to discover any supply items directly related to the segment in question. This should be done only if the added accuracy to be thus achieved is worth the added time and trouble. If it is decided to make such an analysis, the account should also be searched for direct costs pertaining to other products or product groups and these should be eliminated before the residue of indirect costs is allocated on whatever basis may be suitable. This process, known as "double screening," is essential to avoid excessive charges to the segment under study. It is to be noted that the same procedure is applicable in all cost analyses, whether by products or by customers.

Readily Allocable Indirect Costs. Where salespeople sell more than one of the products or product groups under study to the same customers in the course of the same visits, their compensation must be allocated. The fact that they may be paid entirely on a commission basis does not avoid this necessity. The salesperson's time is what is being purchased, and if he or she spends time trying to sell a commodity, even unsuccessfully, some part of his or her compensation is attributable to that commodity, whatever the mode of computing the compensation.

Salespeople's time reports are generally the best indicator of how their time is spent with respect to commodities. The broader the commodity groupings, the more reliable the salespeople's reporting is likely to be. Companies with broad lines of products that attempt to get precise reports of time spent on each item have generally been disappointed.

A sometimes satisfactory substitute for time reports is found in estimates by the salespeople, especially if the reasonableness of such estimates is confirmed by their supervisors. *NACA Research Series No. 20* reports that one company used a variant of this procedure by asking salespeople, supervisors, and executives to rate the company's product lines on the basis of the relative effort required to sell them.[21]

> Successive samples of ratings . . . were taken until several hundred replies had been obtained. While individual rating sheets showed wide variations, when combined a quite consistent pattern was found. It was concluded that this was a reasonably good measure of the relative amounts of effort required to sell the various lines and that it accordingly should serve as a good basis for allocating salesmen's salaries and expenses to product lines.

Unfortunately, the research study does not explain precisely how this was done. A possibility would seem to be to apply these ratings to the sales dollars of the several commodity classifications and to allocate in proportion to such weighted sales dollars.

In commodity analysis, salespeople's travel and other expenses and the costs of supervisory and supplementary selling functions, such as sales offices, should be assigned to product groups in proportion to the assignment of sales compensation. An exception to this rule should be made for any commodity specialists among the supervisory staff whose salaries and expenses are direct charges to the commodities under their charge.

Time studies are the key to the allocation of costs of picking and packing orders for products or product groups if these activities are carried on jointly for several or all lines. Costs of storage can usually be allocated on the basis of floor space occupied by each group or line. Seasonal variations may complicate such calculations, but an annual average can usually be worked out.

Most of the clerical costs of order processing, invoice preparation, customer accounting, inventory control, and so forth, can be allocated on a transaction basis. A count of the number of sales transactions in which each commodity or commodity group is involved may be made for a representative period of time and the results used to assign this group of costs for an entire year. In some highly mechanized accounting systems such counts are extremely easy; in others, special arrangements must be made. Time studies of these operations are ordinarily unnecessary since it is not an unreasonable assumption that a given clerical operation with respect to one commodity item requires the same amount of time as for another. If any of these operations are decentralized, so that they apply to only one commodity segment, the procedure must be modified accordingly.

Delivery costs incurred in common for more than one product group must be allocated. Common carrier charges can usually be prorated on a weight basis, with due allowance for the fact that some items may fall into a different freight classification than others. The distance factor does not enter into the cost allocations, because it may usually be assumed that all products are shipped the average

---

[21]*Ibid.,* p. 1572.

distance, whatever that may be. The sample on which the study of delivery costs is based should be broad enough to neutralize the distance factor.

Costs of operating company truck fleets can usually be assigned to products on the basis of weight or bulk. In this case neither stops nor distance enter into the calculations, except that the sample must be large enough to be sure that the effects of these factors on total costs are adequately represented.

Remote Indirect Costs.   Institutional advertising is a good example of a cost that must be allocated on a more or less arbitrary basis. Such advertising mentions products, if at all, only in a very general terms, or as examples of the advantages of buying our brand instead of brand X. It must be spread over the entire line of commodities and services associated with the company name. Sales dollars, or perhaps gross margin dollars, is the most common basis. The use of gross margin dollars may be particularly appropriate where gross margins differ widely, some goods being carried mostly for the convenience of customers or to fill out a line, whereas profits depend on sales of the products with longer margins.

No advertising cost is applicable to products with which the company name and reputation are not associated. Such products may be the company's own unadvertised and unidentified brands or products made for sale under customers' private brands. A potentially difficult situation arises where it is generally known that Company A manufactures goods for Company B under B's brand name. Should A's advertising be allocated to the B products? Generally speaking, the answer is in the negative unless A's fame and reputation far outshine those of B and B is in effect relying on A's advertising to sell the B brand goods. A negative answer is obvious, for example, if A is a small manufacturer and B is large and widely known for the quality and reliability of the goods it handles. In such a case, B's customer is certainly relying on B's reputation and is not motivated to buy from B because of A's advertising of its own line of brand goods.

In situations where timing of selling activities, even by way of estimates, is too difficult or expensive, relative sales dollars or gross margin dollars may be the best answer for commodity allocation. Which variety of dollars should be chosen depends to some extent on instructions to salespersons as to where and how to expend their efforts, how sales quotas are prepared, and what inducements are provided for maximizing either total sales volume or total gross margin. Particularly in the case of challenge in a Robinson-Patman proceeding, it is important that objective support be provided for the choice of either type of dollars or any other broad basis of allocation.

As in all cost analyses, general administrative costs, if allocated at all, will follow the costs of the personnel and activities administered. Such costs will not be allocated at all, of course, if what is wanted is commodity contribution margins, because these costs are little affected by moderate changes in volume.

Robinson-Patman Considerations.   Price discrimination complaints may relate to specific products or to product lines, and neither may fit the seller's regular pattern for commodity cost analysis. In such cases, a special analysis will be necessary, coupled, of course, with an analysis by customer or order-size classes, depending on which variety of price differentiation is in use. Another reason why a special study may be necessary is that allocation methods entirely satisfactory for management use may not meet the exacting standards insisted upon by the Federal Trade Commission or the courts. Estimates of major elements of cost, such as selling expense, must be bolstered by objective indications that they are not biased. It should be emphasized again, however, that the seller who has made careful cost analyses in the ordinary course of business stands a much better chance of convincing Commission investigators that a complaint should not be issued than does one who has not.

ORGANIZATION FOR DISTRIBUTION COST ANALYSIS

No kind of accounting gets done by itself. Someone has to plan it, be provided with the necessary help, and be given the requisite authority to see that it gets done. Distribution cost analysis is a neglected area in the vast majority of companies. The reasons lie in ignorance of its techniques, failure to appreciate its benefits, and an understandable reluctance to spend money where the return is deemed to be uncertain.

The following description of the functions of the distribution cost accountant is derived from the operating manual of a large industrial company. It not only portrays the responsibilities of this member of the financial staff but suggests the uses to which adequate information about distribution costs may be put.

Basic Responsibilities of the Distribution Cost Accountant

I. Keep abreast of current practices, trends, and developments in distribution cost accounting and other subjects relating to distribution costs—self-development.
   a. Reading—cost accounting and marketing literature
   b. Attend conferences and seminars
   c. Contacts inside and outside company
   d. Contact with distribution operations through level of sale to ultimate customer.
II. Initiate the distribution cost accounting objectives, policies, and plans of the department.
   a. Short-range and long-range plans—analysis and control of costs
   b. Knowledge of basic financial and marketing plans and objectives of department.
III. Prepare special analyses by commodities, channels of distribution, classes of customers, territories, size of orders, etc., to relate costs to results obtained for use by management in the guidance of marketing effort.
IV. Prepare analyses and estimates required for the establishment of prices, discount structures, and promotional plans.
   a. Functional discounts
   b. Quantity discounts
   c. Special promotions
   d. Direct shipments
   e. Special accounts or orders.
V. Prepare special analyses of finished-goods inventories for use in establishing the location and levels of inventories. This would include measuring the effect on profits, residual income, return on investment, etc.
VI. Assist in the development of standards (or indices) where applicable for control of distribution costs, measurement of efficiency of operations or effectiveness of expenditure, and direction of effort.
   a. Joint effort with marketing
   b. Isolate costs by responsibility
   c. Develop basis for measurement—unit of production.
VII. Provide assistance to managers in the preparation of budgets and appropriation requests.
   a. Interpretation of accounting requirements
   b. Comparisons with other similar operations
   c. Estimates of costs of distributing new products or expanding markets for present products, etc.
VIII. Prepare and transmit reports on distribution costs and analyses and interpretation of cost data to aid management in controlling costs.
   a. Responsibility and functional reporting
   b. Comparisons with standards
   c. Reports for special situations.
IX. Advise and counsel, upon request, independent wholesalers on distribution cost accounting matters.
   a. Analysis of operating data
   b. Yardsticks for measurement
   c. Exchange of key information.

BIBLIOGRAPHY

Beyer, Robert, and Donald J. Trawicki: *Profitability Accounting for Planning and Control*, 2nd ed., Ronald Press Company, New York, 1972.

Crowningshield, Gerald R., and Kenneth A. Gorman: *Cost Accounting, Principles and Managerial Applications,* 3rd ed., Houghton Mifflin Company, Boston, 1974, chap. 18.

Dean, Joel: "Cost Forecasting and Price Policy," *Journal of Marketing,* 13, 3 January 1949; pp. 279–288.

Matz, Adolph, and Othel J. Curry: *Cost Accounting, Planning and Control,* 5th ed., South-Western Publishing Company, Cincinnati, Ohio, 1972, chap. 22.

NACA Research Series No. 20: *The Assignment of Nonmanufacturing Costs to Products,* August 1951.

NACA Research Series No. 21: *The Assignment of Nonmanufacturing Costs to Territories and Other Segments,* December 1951.

Schiff, Michael: *Accounting and Control in Physical Distribution Management,* The National Council of Physical Distribution Management, Chicago, 1972.

—— and Martin Mellman: *Financial Management of the Marketing Function,* Financial Executives Research Foundation, New York, 1962.

Shillinglaw, Gordon: *Cost Accounting: Analysis and Control,* 3rd ed., Richard D. Irwin, Homewood, Ill., 1972, chap. 13.

Taggart, Herbert F.: *Cost Justification,* Bureau of Business Research, University of Michigan, Ann Arbor, 1959.

Chapter 22

Divisional Cost Analysis

ALFRED RAPPAPORT
Professor of Accounting and Information Systems, Northwestern
University

INTRODUCTION

The increasing size, geographic dispersion, and diversification of firms have led to an extensive use of decentralized financial control systems. The essential purpose of these management control systems is to assure that resources are acquired and used effectively and efficiently in the pursuit of the firm's objectives. A decentralized financial control system involves, first, a partitioning of the firm into areas of activity that correspond to the decision domain of individual managers and, second, the development of performance evaluation standards for each unit.

"Divisionalization" may be viewed as a special case of the generic phenomenon of "decentralization." Consistent with common business parlance, a segment of an organization will be denoted here as a "division" when the management responsibility for both producing *and* selling products (or services) resides within a given segment. According to the above definition, neither a manufacturing plant responsible for quality of output and level of cost incurred nor a sales branch responsible solely for sales volume and mix would qualify as a division. On the other hand, even the lowest level of the organization to which profit responsibility is delegated would qualify as a division.

Having established the division as the cost object, that is, the part of the organization for which costs are to be determined, there remains the basic question of the purposes of such cost determination or cost analysis. The principal focus in this chapter is on the role of divisional cost analysis in providing management with information useful for decision making and performance evaluation. In addition, the roles of divisional cost analysis in providing information to investors and other external parties assessing the firm and its management are examined.

DECENTRALIZATION AND DIVISIONAL CONTROL SYSTEMS

About 50 years ago, when Alfred P. Sloan was first concerned with the issue of decentralization, it represented a significant management problem for General Motors and perhaps a few other large corporations. Today organization structure is a critical management issue for the *Fortune* 500 companies and undoubtedly many more companies as well. The evolution of such firms to the multidivisional form of organization is attributable not only to the increasing size of firms, but is clearly related to corporate expansion into new product lines and market areas by internal development as well as by mergers and acquisitions. This trend accelerated greatly during the 1960s with the conglomerate merger movement and the emergence of the multinational corporation and has continued in the 1970s.

The Nature of Decentralization. Characterizations of organization structure in terms of the familiar centralization-versus-decentralization dichotomy are unduly restrictive and not particularly useful in theory development. Decentralization is a difficult concept to define in operational terms, because it is not an absolute state, but rather a matter of the *degree* of freedom to make decisions granted within an organization. Furthermore, the binary view of centralization versus decentralization places great emphasis on the issues of formal structure and the delegation of authority, but tends to obscure equally important informational and interpersonal issues that shape interunit relationships in organizations.

Contemporary organizational theory has adopted increasingly a cybernetic view of organization—a view that emphasizes the dynamic interrelationships among the elements of a system and with the system's environment. Consistent with this view, a multidivisional firm has been characterized as

> a complex adaptive system that seeks to survive and grow by coping with changing external conditions and by dealing with its own recurring internal conflicts and performance deviations.[1]

The appropriate degree of decision autonomy to be granted divisional management by headquarters would then depend on the relationships linking the two units, the linkages between the division and other divisions, and the firm's total

[1] Jay W. Lorsch and Stephen A. Allen III, *Managing Diversity and Interdependence: An Organizational Study of Multidivisional Firms* (Harvard University Press, Cambridge, Mass., 1973), p. 6.

environment. Although the systems or cybernetic approach attempts to resolve organizational design problems by taking into account the specific contextual setting, there are, nonetheless, some general observations that can be made regarding the benefits and costs of decentralization.

Benefits and Costs of Decentralization. The ideal of choosing that degree of decentralization that maximizes the excess of benefits over costs is at best difficult to implement, because the quantification of neither benefits nor costs can be accomplished with a satisfactory degree of confidence. An enumeration of the claimed benefits and costs does, however, help to identify the important issues and thereby facilitates organizational choice concerning the appropriate degree of decentralization.

Most lists of the claimed benefits of decentralization include the following:

1. Better decisions are likely to be made when decision-making responsibility is transferred to divisional managers who, because of their greater familiarity with individual markets and product lines, can react to changes in local conditions in a timely and effective fashion.

2. Distributing decision-making responsibility throughout the organization frees top management from detailed involvement in day-to-day operations and enables it to devote more effort to strategic planning.

3. As managers gain more decision-making control over the factors governing their measures of performance, their incentive to do well increases correspondingly.

4. Decision-making freedom at various levels of the organization provides an excellent training ground for preparing executive-level talent.

Relatively greater degrees of decentralization also result in increased communication and coordination costs within the firm. It is commonly believed that, over some broad range of decentralization, these costs are more than offset by the benefits of decentralization. Depending on the internal interdependencies existing within the firm, decentralization can in some cases promote suboptimization, that is, decisions that increase the profit of one division but reduce that of the company as a whole. An improperly designed transfer price system may, for example, lead to just such decisions.

Thompson's[2] classification of interdependencies commonly found in complex organizations is particularly useful for understanding the circumstances under which the net benefits of decentralization are likely to be maximum. Thompson suggests the following types of interdependencies, as succinctly summarized by Lorsch and Allen:[3]

1. *Pooled interdependence,* where major operating units may have virtually no contact with one another but where each unit renders a discrete contribution to the whole organization and in turn is supported by the whole. Under these conditions the units operate independently of one another; but failure of any one unit may jeopardize the whole and, thus, the other parts of the organization.

2. *Sequential interdependence,* where the output of one major unit is the input for another unit. Here the interdependence is *direct* but somewhat *asymmetrical.* That is, the supplier unit must perform its task properly before the recipient can act; and unless the recipient acts, the supplier cannot solve its output problem.

3. *Reciprocal interdependence,* where the outputs of each unit represent inputs for the other units. In this case each unit presents direct contingencies for every other unit.

All organizations have pooled interdependence, whereas increasingly more

[2]James D. Thompson, *Organizations in Action* (McGraw-Hill Book Company, New York, 1967), pp. 54–55.
[3]Lorsch and Allen, *Managing Diversity and Interdependence,* p. 11.

complex organizations have sequential and reciprocal interdependencies. The three types of interdependencies, in the order presented, are increasingly more difficult to coordinate because each in turn represents a greater degree of mutual dependency and contingency.

Decentralization is likely to imply greater net benefits when the subunits in a firm are linked only by pooled interdependence. In the presence of only pooled interdependence, the likelihood is that the pursuit of divisional profit is congruent with the economic objectives of the firm as a whole. In firms characterized by sequential and reciprocal interdependencies, not only do coordination costs rise because of the continuing need for mutual adjustment between divisions, but without a properly designed management control system there may well be a conflict between what is in the best interest of a particular division and the overall interests of the firm.

Purpose and Nature of Divisional Control Systems. Divisional control systems are a critical part of the overall management control system and are designed to assure that resources are acquired and used effectively and efficiently in the pursuit of the firm's objectives. Accounting information is, in turn, an integral part of divisional control systems. Divisional accounting reports should serve to motivate divisional managers to make decisions that are congruent with the interests of the firm as a whole, to evaluate the performance of the divisional management, and to evaluate the performance of the product-market activity encompassed by the division.

Although profit is the dominant standard for the measurement of divisional performance, there are a range of practices in the implementation of the profit measurement for profit centers. In addition to the usual problems associated with profit measurement for the consolidated entity, divisional profit measurement introduces new problems, such as, for example, the question of whether and how common costs ought to be allocated. Although the profit center remains the form most frequently employed for divisional control systems, many companies use the investment center form, which relates profit to the level of divisional investment. In either case, the approach taken to cost analysis is likely to have a profound influence on the final results. In light of this, a brief discussion of alternative approaches to cost analysis will precede the examination of divisional cost analysis for decision making, management performance evaluation, and divisional performance evaluation.

APPROACHES TO COST ANALYSIS[4]

What is cost, and how should it be assigned to various cost objects of interest? Arguments for and against particular cost measurement methods can be found with great frequency in the accounting literature. The direct costing controversy and the various methods proposed for allocating overhead to products or divisions serve as examples of two of the more common issues debated. The discussion in the literature can be usefully classified according to three basic approaches to cost analysis: historical communication approach, user decision model approach, and information evaluation approach.

Historical Communication Approach. Demski and Feltham summarize the historical communication approach as follows:

> This approach focuses on the establishment of principles or rules for the collection and processing of data. These rules might codify current practice, might stem from high authority, or might be derived from some theory or conceptual framework. In any

---

[4]The ideas in this section are adapted from Joel S. Demski and Gerald A. Feltham, *Cost Determination: A Conceptual Approach* (Iowa State University Press, Ames, 1976).

event, there is an underlying belief that a unique set of rules can be established such that the resulting data are understood by any possible user. According to this approach, there are too many diverse uses to justify elaborate information systems tailored to every conceivable need. Potential uses are a consideration, but the best way to serve the user is to formulate clear rules for measuring costs. In this way, there will be minimal ambiguity about the meaning of cost, and the user can make his own adjustments for any shortcomings of the data provided.[5]

This approach, with its heavy reliance on historical cost, is essentially based on the notion that the "true cost" of producing some product or service can be established by following prescribed measurement rules and to the extent the result might be in error the user must necessarily apply the doctrine of *caveat emptor*. Although this approach is more often argued in terms of financial accounting rather than management accounting and is less dominant than, say, 15 or so years ago, it still appears to have wide acceptance in some accounting circles.

User Decision Model Approach. The major shortcoming of the historical communication approach is its failure to take into consideration the different information needs of diverse users. Because only one basic set of information was available, various users were often forced to adapt their problem-solving approach and decisions to the available information rather than tailoring information to meet their respective needs. In light of this situation, the user decision model approach emerged during the late 1950s and gained considerable impetus during the next 10 years in management and financial accounting alike. The approach is summarized by Demski and Feltham as follows:

> The user decision model approach focuses on the decision method or model that, given some assumption, should be (or is) used for various classes of decisions. Models are postulated, and deductive reasoning is used to derive what data are relevant and how the data should be measured. Classes of decisions are identified; examples are capital investment decisions, pricing decisions, and output decisions. Most often, the models are drawn heavily from the classical economic theory of the firm, operations research, and more recently, from the behavioral theory of the firm. In contrast to the absolute truth theme of the historical communication approach, the user decision model approach has a theme of conditional truth. That is, it recognizes the possibility of different decision models leading to the generation of different data.[6]

Information Evaluation Approach. Because neither the historical communication approach nor the user decision model approach explicitly incorporates a cost-benefit analysis, recognizes uncertainty, or considers how the information choice itself might alter events, Demski and Feltham recommend the information evaluation approach, which does in fact incorporate each of the above considerations. A particular measurement of, say, cost is favored to the extent it produces outcomes whose aggregate values exceed that of the resources consumed. Under this approach, accounting measures are treated as an economic commodity evaluated within a specific contextual setting. Thus the "best" measure of cost might well vary from situation to situation, and "true cost" might not be the most cost efficient measure in a particular setting. The decision by the accountant concerning the "relevant cost" to supply depends on his or her perception of the decision situation, the method of analysis employed by the decision maker, and the cost of supplying that information.

To illustrate the information evaluation approach, consider the case of a firm that is considering whether to accept or reject a special order of 1,000 units of product representing a variation of its normal output. Suppose that the incremental revenue will be $20,000, raw materials for the order will cost $5,000, and 800

[5]*Ibid.*, p. 4.
[6]*Ibid.*, p. 6.

and 200 direct labor hours from departments A and B, respectively, will be required as well. Using the positive contribution margin criterion, the special order will be accepted if the expected cost of labor and variable overhead is less than $15,000 (= $20,000 − $5,000).

The plant-wide rate for labor plus variable overhead costs is $16 per hour. On the basis of this rate the order would be rejected, because its acceptance would lead to a −$1,000 contribution margin [$20,000 − $5,000 − $16 per hour × (800 hours + 200 hours) = −$1,000]. Now assume that the accountant believes that the rates for the two departments are not identical. The question thus arises as to whether or not an analysis should be conducted to determine the two departmental rates and the results reported to the decision maker. Although the outcome of the analysis cannot be known with certainty without actually performing it, the accountant believes that one of three findings will materialize: the rates for departments A and B will be, respectively, $12 and $20, $14 and $18, or $16 and $16. The respective contribution margins will then be

Departmental rates (A & B)	$12 & $20	$14 & $18	$16 & $16
Expected incremental revenue	$20,000	$20,000	$20,000
Expected incremental costs			
Raw materials	$ 5,000	$ 5,000	$ 5,000
Labor and variable overhead			
Department A (800 hours)	9,600	11,200	12,800
Department B (200 hours)	4,000	3,600	3,200
Total	$18,600	$19,800	$21,000
Expected contribution margin	$ 1,400	$ 200	−$1,000

Assuming that the decision maker uses the positive contribution margin criterion, the special order will be accepted only if the $12 and $20 or $14 and $18 rates are reported. Performing the analysis could lead to a gain of $1,400, $200, or $0, less the cost of analysis. The decision of whether or not the analysis should be conducted will depend on the accountant's risk attitude, beliefs concerning how likely each of three sets of departmental rates will be, and an estimate for the cost of analysis. Suppose that the accountant is risk-neutral and assigns respective probabilities of .2, .6, and .2 to the three events. The expected value of performing the analysis is, then,

$$.2(\$1,400) + .6(\$200) + .2(\$0) - \text{Cost of Analysis} = \$400 - \text{Cost of Analysis}$$

Thus, the accountant should conduct the analysis if the cost is less than $400.

The foregoing application of the information evaluation approach to the question of whether or not the accountant should provide plant-wide or departmental rates is instructive in illustrating its conceptual superiority over the historical communication approach and user decision model approach. Unlike the other two approaches, the information evaluation approach explicitly considers both the uncertainty surrounding the decision situation and the cost of supplying information. It is, however, the difficulty of modeling an uncertain decision situation that limits its practical application in most instances. Consequently, the information evaluation approach has not to date gained wide acceptance among practicing accountants and managers.

A combination of the user decision model and information evaluation approaches seems to be emerging as a frequently used approach to information choice generally and to managerial cost analysis more specifically. This mixed approach, which might be referred to as the "decision evaluation approach," expands on the user decision model approach by providing recognition of the different needs of heterogeneous users and the varying needs of given users as they use accounting information in different decision situations. All of this analysis is conducted within a broad qualitative cost-benefit framework that presumably is less formal than that demanded by the information evaluation approach.

DIVISIONAL COST ANALYSIS FOR DECISION MAKING AND PERFORMANCE EVALUATION

Periodic divisional profit measurement serves three essential purposes:
1. *Ex ante* decision-making guidance to divisional management
2. *Ex post* evaluation by top management of the performance of divisional management
3. *Ex post* evaluation by top management of the performance of the division as a corporate investment

It is important to emphasize that profit measurements for decision making look to the future, whereas management and divisional performance evaluations look to the past. Thus profit measurements of past periods are useful for decision-making purposes only to the extent that they provide a better understanding of profits likely to be realized in future periods. In the discussion to follow on divisional profit measurement for each of the above-mentioned purposes, revenue measurement is assumed to be straightforward and the principal focus is directed at cost measurement problems.

Cost Analysis for Decision Making.   Cost analysis is commonly defined as the estimation of a cost already incurred or the projection of a cost to be incurred to accomplish some objective. Decision problems arise, and hence the need for cost analysis for decision making, when management sees two or more alternative ways to accomplish a desired objective. In principle, the resolution of a decision problem entails forecasting the net benefits expected for each alternative and selecting the one that promises to convey the highest benefits. The net benefit, in turn, is the difference between the anticipated value to be received and the anticipated costs or resources to be consumed under each alternative. Because the principal task of cost analysis for decision making involves forecasting and comparing costs associated with various alternatives, it stands to reason that it must be concerned with incremental or differential costs, that is the difference in cost that would result from selecting one alternative in preference to another. When one alternative is to do nothing, incremental cost simply refers to the cost change resulting from the decision to do something. For example, consider the case of a television set manufacturer currently producing at an annual level of 2 million sets at a cost of $100 million. If production volume were increased to 2.5 million, total cost is projected to be $110 million. The incremental cost of increasing production by 500,000 units is $10 million. Suppose that the incremental revenue from the additional units is expected to be $30 million, then the net benefit of increasing production is expected to be $20 million.

Before proceeding further, the question of whether cash flow or income figures should be employed in cost analysis for decision making needs to be examined. In many situations there will be no difference between the two figures. When there is, however, the cash flow figure should be used. For example, returning to the television set manufacturer, suppose that the company has 500,000 picture tubes in inventory. The picture tubes were originally purchased at a cost of $20 per unit for a product line that was just discontinued. Although the picture tubes have no scrap value, the production engineer contends that with only minor modification these picture tubes can be used for the planned incremental production of 500,000 sets. This would enable the company to avoid purchasing 500,000 additional picture tubes at the current price of $12 per unit. The cost of picture tubes associated with the 500,000 units of increased production would be $20 per unit for income measurement purposes. For purposes of decision making, the cost analysis should convey to management that using the picture tubes for the increased production requires no cash expenditure except that for the minor modification.

The foregoing example also serves to illustrate the principal that *sunk costs* (the costs of resources previously acquired whose value remains unaffected by a choice among competing alternatives) are not relevant in cost analysis for decision making. Further, the example may be used to illustrate the role of opportunity cost in cost analysis for decision making. The opportunity cost of a resource is the net benefit that could be gained by employing the resource in its best alternative use. To measure the opportunity cost of the picture tubes, we must know the cash that must be foregone to make the picture tubes available for use in the increased production schedule. Because the picture tubes have no alternative use and no scrap value, their opportunity cost is zero. It is this cost, the opportunity cost, that is relevant in cost analysis for decision making. For detailed applications of this approach to such decisions as using idle capacity, rationing scarce capacity, pricing new products, selecting customers, replacing equipment, and selecting an order quantity, the reader is referred to Chapter 4.

Divisional results may be viewed as an aggregation of the various operating decisions made in behalf of the division. Just as in the case of the individual decision, a primary objective of divisional cost analysis is to identify the determinants of cost and to quantify their effects. An important determinant of cost in virtually all organizations is the level or quantity of activity generated during a designated time span. The activity bases may range from general bases, such as units of product manufactured or sold, to more delineated bases, such as miles driven for automobile costs and number of employees for personnel department costs. Variable costs are those costs that vary proportionally to changes in activity, whereas fixed costs are those that are insensitive to wide fluctuations in activity during a designated time period. Viewed from the perspective of the division as a whole, variable costs are relevant to cost analysis for decision making whenever the level (or mix) of activity might be affected by some contemplated management action. In light of this, it is useful to portray divisional results by cost behavior classifications, i.e., variable and fixed. Further, divisional analysis for decision making and performance evaluation is greatly facilitated by a breakdown of divisional activities by major products or markets served. Such a statement is presented as Exhibit 1. Because in this section the concern is with cost analysis for

EXHIBIT 1   A Divisional Income Statement (in thousands of dollars)

	Division as a whole	Unallocated	Segments within the division		
			Product A	Product B	Product C
Net sales	$2,500		$1,000	$600	$900
Less:					
Variable cost of goods sold	$1,200		$ 600	$250	350
Variable selling and administrative expenses	400		150	150	100
Total variable costs	$1,600		$ 750	$400	$450
Contribution margin	$ 900		$ 250	$200	$450
− Controllable fixed costs	250	$ 100	50	50	50
Controllable operating profit	$ 650	$(100)	$ 200	$150	$400
− Interest on controllable investment	100	20	40	20	20
Controllable residual income	$ 550	$(120)	$ 160	$130	$380
− Fixed costs controlled by others	250	150	50	20	30
Net residual income before taxes	$ 300	$(270)	$ 110	$110	$350

decision making, the portion of the divisional income statement up to and including the "contribution margin" will be of primary interest. The remainder of the divisional income statement presented as Exhibit 1 is pertinent to cost analysis for performance evaluation, which is covered in the next section.

Contribution margin is the difference between net sales and total variable costs. The variable costs include not only manufacturing costs, such as direct materials, direct labor, and certain overhead items, but variable selling costs such as sales commissions. In most cases variable costs are traceable to segments within a division such as products or markets. The contribution figure is particularly useful for forecasting the profit impact of decisions that are expected to affect volume or product mix in the short run. More specifically, the profit impact of a decision can be estimated by multiplying the contribution margin ratio, that is, contribution margin divided by net sales, by the forecasted change in dollar sales. For example, suppose that the division is considering the desirability of launching an advertising campaign for product A. The campaign is expected to cost about $30,000 and result in incremental sales of $200,000. Multiplying the expected increase in sales by the contribution margin ratio of 25 percent yields an expected benefit of $50,000. After deducting the $30,000 cost for advertising, the net expected impact on profits is $20,000.

The contribution margin format focuses management attention on disparities in contribution margin ratios earned by various products and provides important information for management decisions impacting on product volume and mix. In the current illustration, the division realizes a 36 percent contribution margin ratio. Assuming that individual product prices and costs remain reasonably stable, one sees that the divisional contribution margin ratio can be quite sensitive to product mix changes. This is so because of the wide range in individual product contribution margin ratios, i.e., 25 percent, 33.3 percent, and 50 percent for products A, B, and C, respectively.

Although it is true that the contribution margin approach enables divisional managers quickly to approximate the short-run profit impact of product volume or mix changes, two precautionary statements need to be made. First, when using the contribution margin approach for estimating probable profit impact, the level of production capacity currently being used needs to be taken into account. If an anticipated increase in volume can be accommodated by existing capacity, estimating profit impact with just contribution margin calculations is entirely satisfactory. On the other hand, if the division is already operating at peak capacity, increased volume would necessarily involve expenditures to increase capacity as well. When this is the situation, the analysis should include not only the incremental contribution margin to be gained, but also the incremental fixed costs required.

The second precautionary statement concerning the use of the contribution margin approach involves its application to product mix decisions when the products use common facilities and the facilities are being utilized at peak capacity. Under these conditions the use of a decision rule that calls for the production of the product with the highest contribution margin per unit, or the highest contribution margin ratio and the production of other products only after the first product's demand has been satisfied, can lead to suboptimal results. To illustrate, consider the following simplified example. A division produces two products, X and Y, with the following per-unit results:

	Product X	Product Y
Selling price	$20	$16
Variable costs	10	12
Contribution margin	$10	$ 4
Contribution margin ratio	50%	25%

Total fixed costs are $400,000, and current capacity allows for a total of 400,000 production hours. Products X and Y require 8 and 2 hours of production per unit, respectively. In this case, the selection of product X on the basis of both its higher contribution margin and contribution margin ratio would lead to a suboptimal decision. This is so because the decision does not consider the amount of scarce factor of production used up in producing each of the products. This can be accomplished by calculating the contribution margin per unit of scarce resource, i.e., per production hour, as follows:

	Product X	*Product Y*
Contribution margin	$ 10	$ 4
Hours of production per unit	8	2
Contribution margin per production hour	$1.25	$2.00

In this particular situation the divisional decision maker would prefer product Y to product X. In fact, in the absence of other constraints, product X would never be produced. The total contribution margin from producing solely product Y would be $800,000, that is, 400,000 production hours times the $2.00 contribution margin per production hour, whereas for product X it would be only $500,000, that is, 400,000 production hours times the $1.25 contribution margin per production hour. When there are several products and a number of constraints, product combination problems are solved most efficiently by the linear programming technique.

Cost Analysis for Performance Evaluation.   In this section the focus is shifted from cost analysis for decision making to cost analysis for performance evaluation of divisional management and of the division as a corporate investment. As will be emphasized, a key criterion of cost analysis for performance evaluation of divisional management is controllability, whereas traceability or attributability represents a critical criterion of cost analysis for assessing the performance of a division as a corporate investment.

As stated earlier, the portion of the divisional income statement up to and including the contribution margin is particularly pertinent for short-run decision-making purposes. Evaluation of the divisional manager may be directed either to "controllable operating profit" or "controllable residual income," whereas evaluation of the division can be conducted in terms of net residual income before taxes. Controllable operating profit, as shown in Exhibit 1, is obtained by subtracting controllable fixed costs from the contribution margin. It is important to emphasize that not all divisional fixed costs are ordinarily controllable at the divisional level. For example, capital investments exceeding some dollar amount, say $10,000, may require approval from corporate headquarters. In this case, the depreciation on all such investments might not be included as part of the controllable fixed costs. The controllable fixed costs would usually include such discretionary items as sales promotion, engineering, research and development, management consulting, management development, and certain advertising costs.

Controllable fixed costs for the division as a whole total $250,000. Notice, however, that at the product level within the division only $150,000 is controllable. This means that product managers have substantial influence over the level of cost incurrence for $150,000 and the division manager exercises effective control over the remaining $100,000. If a manager is to be evaluated on the basis of the planned-versus-actual controllable operating profit, then both a sense of equity and the inducement for positive motivation dictate that the degree of control that the manager exercises over revenues and costs be reasonably substantial. In the absence of that level of control, controllable operating profit has serious limitations as a performance evaluation index and as a positive motivational device.

The question of whether or not controllable operating profit or controllable residual income is the more appropriate performance evaluation criterion for divisional managers depends on the degree to which divisional managers actively influence investment decisions. If the level of investment is effectively governed by division managers, then there is a persuasive argument for charging the managers some imputed interest for the use of their controllable investment. The objective of maximizing controllable residual income motivates the divisional manager to invest only in those resources that promise to yield a rate of return in excess of that charged by corporate headquarters. Companies using the residual income approach often cite the superiority of an index that induces managers to concentrate on maximizing dollars of income after cost of capital charges rather than a percentage return on investment (ROI). If managers of relatively profitable divisions were evaluated on the basis of ROI rather than controllable residual income, they might well be motivated to reject investment projects that from the standpoint of the corporation as a whole ought to be accepted. For example, consider the case of the manager of product A. Assume that the manager has a controllable investment totaling $1,000,000, that the headquarters cost of capital charge is 15 percent, and that the investment currently earns a return of 25 percent. There is an investment project that promises to return 20 percent on investment during each of the first few years of its economic life. Residual income and ROI will clearly motivate the manager to make different decisions in this case. When residual income is the measure of performance evaluation, the manager can be expected to accept the project because its anticipated return of 20 percent exceeds the cost of capital charge of 15 percent. In contrast, the ROI performance evaluation criterion will lead the manager to reject the project because the acceptance of a 20 percent rate of return project will reduce the current overall ROI of 25 percent earned by the division manager for product A.

The use of controllable residual income as an index for management performance evaluation calls for the prior resolution of a number of measurement issues with respect to both how controllable investment is determined and how an appropriate cost of capital charge is developed. On the controllable investment issue, some of the questions that must be considered include the following:

1. Should investment in a division be interpreted to mean the division's total assets, net assets (total assets minus total liabilities), or fixed assets plus net current assets?

2. Whichever of these definitions of investment is used, should fixed assets be included at cost, net book value (i.e., after making a deduction for accumulated depreciation), or at some measure of current value?

3. How should assets shared by two or more divisions, or held by the company as corporate assets (e.g., a central research laboratory), be treated in computing the investment in one of the divisions? Where divisions do not hold separate cash balances of their own, should any part of the central cash balance be imputed to divisions for inclusion in their capital computations? Where receivables are not recorded divisionally, how, if at all, should receivables be included in the division's capital computation?

4. Where inventories of some or all divisions are valued with a LIFO (last-in, first-out) cost-flow assumption, is any adjustment to the balance sheet amounts necessary when computing the investment in a division?

5. Should the investment base for the rate-of-return calculation be taken at the beginning of the period, at the end, at some intermediate point, or should it be an average for the period?[7]

These and other issues, such as the quantification of leased assets, must be

---

[7]David Solomons, *Divisional Performance: Measurement and Control* (Financial Executives Research Foundation, New York, 1965), p. 128.

resolved before the amount of capital employed by a division manager can be determined. Before the cost of capital charge can be ascertained, the rate of interest charged on divisional capital must also be decided. There is perhaps no more controversial and difficult topic in modern finance than the measurement of a firm's cost of capital. Conceptually, it constitutes the minimum return a firm must earn on an investment project to maintain its intrinsic, or long-run market, value. This minimum return is, in turn, based on the rate of return investors could earn on alternative investments of equivalent risk.

Consider, first, the case of companies financed entirely by equity capital. The cost of equity capital, representing the minimum return the firm must earn on new investment to maintain shareholder wealth, is commonly measured as the rate at which the market capitalizes the firm's expected earnings before the contemplated investment. The estimation of this rate results in, at best, a "ballpark" estimate, because of the inherent difficulty of projecting future earnings potential and the shifting forces affecting market valuation. Further, the adoption of this rate implicitly assumes that the decision to invest in a project or set of projects will not change the business risk of the firm and further that the firm's capital structure will not change (i.e., that the firm's financial risk remains constant). "Business risk" is the risk associated with the firm's operations apart from any risk in financing those operations.

When debt is introduced into the firm's capital structure, the cost of equity entails not only the risk-free rate and a premium for business risk, but a premium for financial risk as well. As financial leverage is increased, the risk associated with shareholders returns likewise increases.

The cost of capital for firms financed with debt as well as equity is commonly computed as the weighted average of the costs of debt and equity financing. The basic rationale for using the weighted average cost of capital is that by accepting only projects expected to yield returns greater than that cost, the firm will increase the market price of its stock in the long run and thereby increase shareholder wealth. Once again, there is an implicit assumption that business risk will not change as a result of planned investment and that the firm will continue to raise capital in the same proportions as the present capital structure, i.e., that financial risk will not change.

The mechanics of computing the weighted average cost of capital are illustrated below:

	(1) Amount (in millions)	(2) Weights (%)	(3) Costs (%)	(4) = (2) × (3) Weighted costs (%)
Debt	$10	50	4.6	2.3
Common stock	4	20	15.0[a]	3.0
Retained earnings	6	30	14.0[a]	4.2
Weighted average cost of capital				9.5

[a]These two costs would in principle be the same except for the difference in transactions costs. A company incurs larger transactions costs in raising new funds with stock issues than through the earnings retention process.

Finally, should a single rate or multiple rates be used for cost of capital rates in the various divisions within a company? Some argue that when different divisions experience different degrees of business risk and, in addition, require different degrees of financing, these factors need to be recognized by charging different or multiple cost of capital rates. Those who argue this position further point to the fact that if the divisions were separate businesses, variations in riskiness would mean that they would be required to pay prices for their capital commensurate with the perceived level of risk. Solomons succinctly states the opposing view favoring a single rate for all divisions:

> The answer to these questions is to be found in the fact that the divisions are not separate businesses and their effect on the riskiness of an investment in the parent corporation cannot be assessed by looking at them one at a time. Just as an insurance company reduces the uncertainty of its loss experience by increasing the spread of the risks it insures, just as an investor reduces the uncertainty of his investment income by increasing the size and variety of his portfolio, so diversification in a divisionalized business aims to reduce the risks borne by the corporation. It does this by offsetting the risks associated with the separate divisions. Thus, the addition of a divisional activity which is in itself quite risky might actually *reduce* the riskiness of the whole corporate enterprise. For this reason, the riskiness of a division is not to be assessed by looking at it in isolation from the rest of the business. For this reason, also, a single corporate cost of capital can quite appropriately be used throughout the company, without regard to the supposed riskiness of any division considered as a separate entity.[8]

Before this discussion of performance evaluation of divisional managers can be complete, a word of caution needs to be added. Whether the performance evaluation criterion is controllable operating profit, controllable residual income, or some variant of ROI, each can in some organizations tend to promote short-range thinking that discourages growth and the acceptance of reasonable risk. This is particularly true when divisional projects promising more than the minimum acceptable discounted-cash-flow rate of return are suppressed or rejected because the results during the initial years of the project are expected to impact adversely on operating profit, residual income, or ROI. To maximize the likelihood that divisional managers will consider the best long-run interests of the company as well as the more immediate impact of their decisions, performance evaluation of actual results should be administered within the framework of carefully developed plans and budgets. In such a system, any adverse short-run earnings results expected from a capital investment made in anticipation of longer-term strategic benefits would be explicitly recognized in the division manager's operating profit or residual income budget, and the evaluation would then be conducted in light of the relationship between actual and targeted results.

In cost analysis for performance evaluation of division managers, the critical consideration is controllability. Cost analysis for evaluating the performance of divisions as a corporate investment, on the other hand, involves correlating the incurrence of costs with the activities of specific divisions, i.e., traceability of costs. In drawing the distinction between performance of a manager versus performance of the division, it is important to recognize that the two performances are not necessarily correlated. That is, it is quite conceivable that a division realizes a relatively low profitability and the manager is doing a superb job under difficult circumstances. The reverse is possible as well.

As can be seen in Exhibit 1, performance of divisions and product segments within the division is evaluated in terms of net residual income before taxes, which is controllable residual income minus fixed costs traceable to the segment but controlled by others. For the division as a whole, fixed costs clearly traceable to the division but controlled at the headquarters level are $250,000. Of this $250,000, only $100,000 is traceable to products A, B, and C. The remaining $150,000 of fixed costs are division costs that benefit all three of the products. These are common costs, i.e., costs incurred to benefit more than one segment. The divisional general manager's salary, data processing, certain product advertising, and depreciation on common facilities are representative examples of such costs. Observe that as an organization is further segmented there is a corresponding

[8]*Ibid.,* p. 159.

increase in common costs. Indeed, when a firm is viewed as a consolidated entity, there are no common costs.

It is important to emphasize that in the divisional income statement presented as Exhibit 1 no arbitrary allocations of common costs have been made. The $150,000 of costs traceable to the division as a whole but not to the individual products are segregated in the "unallocated" column. In addition, there are costs incurred at the corporate level for the benefit of the various divisions. Such costs would include the compensation of the company's top executives, financial and legal services, institutional advertising, and pure research carried out in a corporate research facility for the benefit of two or more divisions. The corporate common costs do not appear on Exhibit 1 at all.

The question of whether and how common costs ought to be allocated naturally depends on how the results are expected to be used. In some companies even corporate-level common costs are allocated to divisions. The most frequent argument made is that allocation is necessary to ensure that divisions set prices for their products at a level that will cover not only their own costs but also their share of corporate costs. From the standpoint of assessing a division as a corporate investment, the case for allocating corporate-level common costs to divisions is less persuasive, for in the event an individual division were sold only a relatively small cost savings would ordinarily be realized on corporate common costs. How a company decides to treat its common costs can make a substantial difference in the relative performance evaluation of its various divisions. Mautz[9] reports that, among 238 companies he studied, 114 companies (48 percent of the companies) show total common costs of more than 10 percent of sales. More will be said on the subject of common cost allocation in the next section, dealing with divisional analysis for external reporting.

DIVISIONAL ANALYSIS FOR EXTERNAL REPORTING

Just as the unprecedented rate of corporate diversification in recent years has led to the extensive development of decentralized financial control systems for purposes of management decision making and control, it has also led to a recognition that corporate external reports need to be segmented into meaningful economic categories to facilitate analysis by investors and other interested parties. Active discussion of the idea that diversified firms report their operating results on some segmented basis first received widespread attention during the late 1960s and culminated with the SEC requirement that, starting in 1970, companies report sales and contribution to earnings by segments or lines of business in their 10-K reports.

Up to the present time, financial reporting by segments in corporate annual reports to shareholders has been voluntary. Nonetheless, most companies reporting segment information for purposes of 10-K reports also make similar disclosure in their annual reports. Despite the increasing disclosure of divisional or segment results, a number of difficult-to-resolve issues remain. Once the decision of what segment information to be reported is made, there are, broadly speaking, two classes of accounting problems: (1) the basis for determining a reportable segment, and (2) the basis for attributing economic stocks (balance sheet accounts) and economic flows (income statement accounts) to segments.

Determining a Reportable Segment.   In its Statement of Financial Accounting Standards No. 14, *Financial Reporting for Segments of a Business Enterprise*, the

---

[9]Robert K. Mautz, *Financial Reporting by Diversified Companies* (Financial Executives Research Foundation, New York, 1968), p. 243.

Financial Accounting Standards Board requires a three-step approach to determining reportable segments.[10]

1. Identify the individual products and services from which the enterprise derives its revenue.

2. Group the products and services by industry lines into industry segments.

3. Select those industry segments that are significant with respect to the enterprise as a whole.

Although a number of systems have been developed for classifying business activities by industry, such as the Standard Industrial Classification (SIC) and the Enterprise Standard Industrial Classification (ESIC), they are not necessarily suited to financial reporting purposes. Consequently, management judgement will of necessity play a major role in determining industry segments.

The logical starting point for selecting industry segments is the division, or profit center. That is the smallest unit of activity for which both revenue and expense information is accumulated for internal purposes. In the event some divisions cross industry lines, it may become necessary to disaggregate their activities by industry groupings.

The critical judgment to be made involves how extensive should be the group of products and services included in an industry segment. As the dimensions of an industry segment broaden, the resulting information ordinarily decreases in usefulness, because the segment has become substantially less homogeneous. On the other hand, as the industry segment narrows, the number of industry segments increases and each is less significant in relation to the firm as a whole. In addition, as the number of segments increases, there is often a corresponding increase in the costs that are common to two or more segments. The resolution of an appropriate level of aggregation for industry segments can be guided by taking into account the demand elasticities and production functions governing various divisions or profit centers.

Different revenue patterns appear when demand schedules have varying price and income elasticities. For example, a fall in prices will lead to an increase in revenues when demand is elastic and to a decrease in revenues when demand for products is inelastic. Similarly, an increase in national income will lead to a large increase in revenues when the consumer demand is income elastic, but to a small increase in revenues when demand is income inelastic. Thus, if two products have similar demand elasticities and are sold in similar markets, they can be considered a single activity. If their demand elasticities are different, they usually should be treated as separate activities.

Similar considerations apply to differing behavior of product costs. If costs of one product are stable through time, while those of another vary, the earnings derived from the two products will exhibit different patterns through time. Combining the two activities may once again reduce the value of the report to the investor.

Two products are likely to have different cost trends if their production functions are disparate. Thus, if one product is heavily labor-intensive while another is heavily capital-intensive, each will probably have different pattens of costs through time. Under these conditions, each product should be considered a separate activity. Conversely, if two products have similar production functions, they will probably display similar trends in costs and may be considered a single activity. Aggregating activities with a common production function into a single activity tends to reduce the magnitude of common expenses.

---

[10]Statement of Financial Accounting Standards No. 14, *Financial Reporting for Segments of a Business Enterprise*, December 1976 (Financial Accounting Standards Board, Stamford, Conn.), p. 8.

An exception to the general recommendation is warranted when products with disparate demand characteritics, profitability, and risk are produced with some common capital assets. For example, in compression molding, a firm may produce totally different products using the same machine but different dies. There is little rationale for combining a plastic part for an automobile with a plastic toy.

In summary, if two or more products or services have a common demand elasticity, they may be treated as a single activity, and if two or more products or services use similar production functions, and as such experience parallel cost trends, they may be considered as a single activity. The FASB's request for separate information about foreign operations is, for example, in some measure a recognition of different demand elasticities due to differing business environments in individual countries or groups of countries.

Once the industry segments have been identified, the question then arises as to whether each is significant enough to warrant specification as a reportable segment. The FASB requires that an industry segment be regarded as significant if it satisfies one or more of the following tests in the current period:

1. Revenue (including both sales to unaffiliated customers and intersegment sales or transfers) is 10 percent or more of the combined revenue of all of the enterprise's industry segments.

2. Operating profit or loss is 10 percent or more of the greater, in absolute amount, of:

a. The combined operating profit of all industry segments that did not incur an operating loss, or

b. The combined operating loss of all industry segments that did incur an operating loss.

3. Identifiable assets are 10 percent or more of the combined identifiable assets of all industry segments.

The Board goes on to specify that the reportable segments should aggregate to at least 75 percent of the total corporate revenue, and proposes 10 as a practical limit for the number of reportable segments. For each segment a company would be required to disclose the following:

- Revenue
- Profit contribution (revenue less directly traceable costs)
- Operating profit (profit contribution less allocated operating cost)
- Identifiable assets

These disclosure requirements, in turn, give rise to a number of issues concerning how economic stocks and flows are to be attributed to segments. The focus here will be on attributing costs to segments.

Attributing Costs to Segments.[11]   A format for segmented income statements is presented as Exhibit 2. The analyst using the proposed statement as a basis for earnings projections would naturally begin with the sales figures. If segments are classified according to products with common demand elasticities, the analyst has a basis for projecting probable changes in price and volume, and hence total revenues.

The investor would benefit from the separate reporting of three types of traceable cost—variable, managed, and committed. When variable expenses are deducted from sales, the contribution margin is obtained.

The contribution margin ratio (that is, contribution margin divided by sales) provides the analyst with information for estimating how much segment earnings contributions will increase or decrease with every dollar of projected rise or decline in sales. However, the analyst must consider the assumption that variable expenses

---

[11]This section is largely based on Alfred Rappaport and Eugene M. Lerner, *Segment Reporting for Managers and Investors* (National Association of Accountants, New York, 1972).

EXHIBIT 2   Model Segmented Income Statement (in thousands of dollars)

	Total	Segment X	Segment Y	Segment Z
Sales	$10,600	$4,500	$3,600	$2,500
Variable expenses	6,600	3,000	2,000	1,600
Contribution margin	$ 4,000	$1,500	$1,600	$ 900
Other traceable expenses:				
Managed	$ 850	$ 400	$ 250	$ 200
Committed	1,300	600	400	300
	$ 2,150	$1,000	$ 650	$ 500
Earnings contribution before income taxes	$ 1,850	$ 500	$ 950	$ 400
Income taxes	925	250	475	200
Earnings contribution after income taxes	$ 925	$ 250	$ 475	$ 200
Common expense (net of income taxes)	225			
Net income after taxes	$ 700			

fluctuate proportionally with sales volume over a probable range of near-term volume projections. A segment currently operating at full capacity would have to expand its capacity to meet projected increases in demand. As the company expands, it may well use higher capital-labor ratios and consequently alter the contribution margin ratio.

To promote future sales increases or changes in sales mix, companies incur costs at the discretion of management. This second class of traceable costs, managed costs, includes such items as advertising, sales promotion, product engineering, and new product research. Some managed costs are intended to bring results in the short run, whereas others such as new product research have a long-range expected benefit. They may be positively correlated to sales or earnings levels, but the analyst recognizes that managed costs respond primarily to management judgment. Therefore, the analyst gains some understanding of management strategy for profit projections from those costs classified as managed.

The third class of traceable expenses, committed expenses, is neither responsive to volume nor management decisions in the current period. Committed expenses, sometimes called "capacity expenses," derive principally from capital budgeting decisions of past periods. They include such items as depreciation, property taxes, and insurance, and are essentially fixed amounts under existing operating conditions. As long as a segment uses its current capacity, fluctuations in output will result in stable committed expenses. Projections for committed expenses naturally depend on knowledge of practical capacity and the capital expenditure plans of the segment. After all three classes of traceable expenses are deducted from revenues, each segment's contribution to common expenses and corporate profit is obtained.

Mautz concluded in his study that: (1) common costs are often significant relative to net income of companies, (2) a variety of allocation methods are currently being used by companies in their internal reports, and (3) net income can be highly sensitive to the choice among alternative allocation methods.[12] In light of these findings, and because arbitrary allocations of common costs may obscure important relationships between revenues and earnings, many writers recommend that all common expenses be treated as corporate expenses rather than allocated to individual segments.

Cost analysis to determine whether a cost can properly be viewed as traceable or is more reasonably classified as a common cost is often complex and subject to

[12]Mautz, *Financial Reporting by Diversified Companies*, p. 358.

judgment. To illustrate, the problem of attributing costs to segments is examined for

- Segments with different financing arrangements
- Assignment of income taxes to segments
- Transfer prices

Consider first the case of variable financing arrangements. Comparability between segments in the segmented income statement is difficult when certain segments or basic activities obtain large proportions of their capital resources through leasing arrangements, whereas other segments purchase capital resources outright. This is because some lease rental payments would be classified as an expense traceable to the segment, whereas the interest expense on debt used to finance the purchase is classified as a corporate expense. Many companies compute segment earnings before interest, viewing it as a common expense not directly traceable to individual segments.

Comparability becomes an issue to the financial statement reader when determining whether a company is committing its funds to segments with relatively high or low rates of earnings growth. Unless earnings are computed on a comparable basis, the apparent answer to this and related questions of interest to the investor may be misleading. When disparate depreciation, inventory costing, and other accounting procedures are used in different segments, comparability becomes a problem.

Taxes should be treated as any other expense incurred by the firm. If an expense is traceable to a specific segment, it is properly deducted from the segment's revenues to arrive at the earnings contribution figure. Thus, aftertax earnings contribution should be computed whenever income taxes are traceable to segments, because the investor is interested in differentiating those segments that attract special tax benefits from other segments. However, in some situations income taxes are not traceable to specific segments, and therefore segment income may be reported on a pretax basis.

The treatment of income tax expense in segmented statements is important especially when a company has components operating in industries attracting special tax benefits. Suppose that the company wished to assign income taxes to segments. What approach might be taken? In theory, the company determines the taxes that each segment would have to pay if it were on its own. Assume that the segment with tax benefits, for example, the oil segment, would not only have a zero tax bill if it filed a separate return but would have a loss that could be applied against other income of the corporation in filing a consolidated tax return.

This leads to the question of which segment should be credited with the benefit of these added tax savings accomplished through the use of a consolidated return. Three alternatives are possible:

1. Allocate the savings on a *pro rata* basis to each segment that is in a taxable position.

2. Credit the savings to the oil segment as "other income" (reflected as a negative tax).

3. Credit the savings to corporate expense account and do not allocate to any segments.

Consistent with the fundamental idea that traceable items be associated with individual segments, it is recommended that the savings be credited to the oil company segment. Filing a consolidated tax return and taking advantage of the oil company's special tax status simply represents a means of minimizing the company's overall current tax payments.

The problem of pricing intracompany transactions is similar to the common expense problem in the absence of external competitive markets for transferred goods or services. In each case expense allocations must necessarily be based on subjective judgments. The problem is compounded because companies generally use a number of different transfer pricing methods for internal purposes. Moreover, individual companies commonly employ more than one method within the company. Mautz cites the five methods used most frequently as

1. Cost to the shipping unit
2. Price established by arm's-length transactions to which company is a party
3. Price established by arm's-length transactions to which company is not a party
4. Price established by negotiations between the units concerned, and
5. Cost plus a fixed fee or rate of markup.[13]

For diversified companies whose activities are essentially disparate and autonomous, the transfer problem is either relatively insignificant or nonexistent. The question of how to price intracompany transfers arises primarily in more integrated firms, particularly vertically integrated firms.

Despite extensive literature on the subject, "optimum" transfer pricing methods for management purposes remain a goal rather than a reality. The unresolved problem is one of developing a set of transfer prices that will simultaneously guide a division's decisions in the best long-run interests of the firm and also serve as an equitable price for measuring divisional performance. For purposes of external reporting, the problem is somewhat different and perhaps easier to solve.

Asking all managements to adopt a single uniform pricing method is inappropriate. The uniform adoption of one transfer pricing method by all companies would be difficult to support because of varying organizational and market arrangements among companies. Further, this approach would conflict with current management reporting procedures and would also create additional costs for the firm. On the other hand, it is appropriate to provide guidelines for reporting, because "probably no single accounting method lends itself so fully to the transfer of profits from one component to another, either intentionally or unintentionally, as does the pricing of intracompany transfers."[14]

The pricing of transfers when there is an external competitive market is no particular problem. The absence of arm's-length transactions does pose some problems for developing transfer prices for management planning and control; however, proper structuring of segments can mitigate the problem for external reporting.

One important guideline is that segments should generate both revenue and expense streams. Because revenue is not recognized unless there has been an arm's-length transaction, it follows that parts of a firm that are essentially suppliers to other parts should not be treated as separate segments.

If a unit of the firm has substantial transactions with external parties as well as within the firm, then it would be appropriate to eliminate the intracompany sales and report the results of sales to outsiders as part of a separate segment. Because the intracompany sales total is based on market prices, the need to allocate costs subjectively is effectively bypassed.

BIBLIOGRAPHY

Demski, Joel S., and Gerald A. Feltham: *Cost Determination: A Conceptual Approach,* Iowa State University Press, Ames, Iowa, 1976.

Lorsch, Jay W., and Stephen A. Allen III: *Managing Diversity and Interdependence: An Organizational Study of Multidivisional Firms,* Harvard University Press, Cambridge, Mass., 1973.

[13]*Ibid.,* p. 36.
[14]*Ibid.,* p. 37.

Mautz, Robert K.: *Financial Reporting by Diversified Companies,* Financial Executives Research Foundation, New York, 1968.

Rappaport, Alfred, and Eugene M. Lerner: *Segment Reporting for Managers and Investors,* National Association of Accountants, New York, 1972.

Solomons, David: *Divisional Performance: Measurement and Control,* Financial Executives Research Foundation, New York, 1965.

Statement of Financial Accounting Standards No. 14, *Financial Reporting for Segments of a Business Enterprise,* December 1976, Financial Accounting Standards Board, Stamford, Conn.

Thompson, James D.: *Organizations in Action,* McGraw-Hill Book Company, New York, 1967.

Chapter **23**

Tax Considerations in Cost Accounting

WILLIAM L. RABY
Touche Ross & Co.

MATT G. MINOR
Film Finance Group, Ltd.

THE INCOME TAX AND ACCOUNTING ALTERNATIVES

To sense how tax considerations affect cost accounting alternatives, we must ask first how financial reporting concepts interact with business decisions, how tax considerations influence financial reporting standards, and then how financial reporting standards impact on cost accounting.

How do accounting concepts affect business decisions? The "official" summary of what was accomplished during any given year is contained in the annual financial statements. A management that is concerned about how its action will look must think of how the accounting system will report those actions. If planning and control procedures are integrated by preparing projected financial statements showing operating results and financial position, and are then revised from time to time either as conditions change or in an attempt to produce more acceptable results, the lowest supervisory levels within the company will be affected in their daily decision making by accounting concepts of revenue, expense, and income.

The impact of tax accounting on financial accounting is far less clear. If the company has easy access to capital markets, or management stands to gain by favorable performance of the company's stock (e.g., as the result of stock ownership or of stock options), then the primary concern may be with enhancing the reported earnings per share in both the short run and intermediate term (e.g., three to five years). To the extent that income taxes are an expense, savings that can be effected in the reported expense will be sought, but savings that are merely differences in timing for accounting purposes may not be viewed as of great value unless substantial in amount. For example, the difference between accelerated and straight-line depreciation for a capital-intensive company will be large enough so that accelerated depreciation will be used for tax purposes, but policies as to which repairs are charged to expense and which are capitalized and depreciated may well be determined without regard to tax consequences.

But for the company without ready access to the security markets, including the vast majority of closely held companies, and especially for the company more concerned about cash flow than about reported earnings per share, tax treatment translates into cash flow at the rate of about $.48 per dollar involved. Timing differences make for interest-free loans at worst, and to a going concern that interest-free loan may be viewed as an ideal source of quasi-equity capital—one that has no specific maturity date, requires no interest or dividends, and is available without SEC registration or other similar folderol.

Conclusion: for most business units, tax deductibility (or deferral) equates with cash flow. Tax treatments that reduce taxable income are actively sought. If an accounting treatment and a tax treatment are in conflict, and it is felt that changing the accounting treatment will help in obtaining the favorable tax treatment, there is some degree of pressure exerted on management's accounting decisions. That pressure is in the direction of conforming financial and cost accounting to tax accounting. Needless to say, there are always counter pressures, but the concern here is to understand the tax treatment given items that are of interest in cost accounting in order to grasp better the direction in which the tax treatments available may be pushing the choice among the cost alternatives. The procedure will be to examine some of the areas where the concepts of tax and financial accounting may not be fully in agreement.

However, before examining these individual areas where tax and financial treatment may differ, let us first examine a theoretical model of how the income tax affects the choices among accounting alternatives.

Concept of the Model. Imagine, for the moment, a situation with two similar companies, each managed by competent executives. The primary difference between the two companies is that company A is not subject to income tax whereas company B is subject to both federal and state income taxes at a combined rate of 55 percent.

To illustrate how the model operates, consider two decisions: adoption of LIFO (last-in, first-out) inventory as opposed to retention of FIFO (first-in, first-out), and the purchase of an item where it would be discretionary to either capitalize the cost or to expense it all in the year of purchase.

In both situations, to quantify the differences between alternatives, the model utilizes the "profitability index" method of applying the "discounted cash flow" approach. The basic idea is to equate the time element involved in diverse investments. The use of the present value concept provides a useful tool for reducing dollars at various points in time to a common denominator that makes them comparable to one another.

In the profitability index approach, the company selects a rate of return as its estimated or desired rate of return. It may use its estimated cost of capital, or it may use a target return on investment. The cash inflows and outflows of each alternative are reduced to their present values based on this percentage and the use of present value tables. The cash outflows are then subtracted from the inflows. If the result is exactly zero, then the rate of return is the target rate of return. If the result is less than zero, then the return is unsatisfactory. If the result is greater than zero, the degree to which it is greater than zero measures the relative profitability of the alternative.

Adoption of the LIFO Cost-Flow Assumption for Inventory. In this situation, companies A and B have just completed operations for 19X1, in which beginning FIFO inventory at cost (which was lower than market) was $1,100,000 and ending FIFO inventory was $1,400,000. Costs increased 9 percent during 19X1, and the FIFO results of operations were as given in Exhibit 1.

EXHIBIT 1

(000 omitted)	Company A	Company B
Beginning inventory	$1,100	$1,100
Purchases	5,200	5,200
Goods available for sale	$6,300	$6,300
Ending inventory	1,400	1,400
Cost of goods sold	$4,900	$4,900
Sales less other expenses	7,000	7,000
Pretax profit	$2,100	$2,100
Income tax at 55 percent	—	1,155
Net income	$2,100	$ 945

If these companies were to change from FIFO to LIFO for 19X1, ending inventory would be $1,284 (= $1,400/$1.09) and the operating results under LIFO would look something like those shown in Exhibit 2.

EXHIBIT 2

(000 omitted)	Company A	Company B
Beginning inventory	$1,100	$1,100
Purchases	5,200	5,200
Goods available for sale	$6,300	$6,300
Ending inventory	1,284	1,284
Cost of goods sold	$5,016	$5,016
Sales less other expenses	7,000	7,000
Pretax profit	$1,984	$1,984
Income tax at 55 percent	—	1,091
Net income	$1,984	$ 893

Now let us analyze the FIFO-versus-LIFO decision on the basis that the net income from FIFO operations can be reinvested in the business by each company at a 10-percent aftertax return. Thus, in our analysis (Exhibit 3), the cash available for investment is for company A the $2,100,000 that it earned in 19X1 and for Company B the $945,000 that it earned in 19X1 assuming that FIFO was used.

EXHIBIT 3

	Company A		Company B	
	FIFO	LIFO	FIFO	LIFO
Cash outflow				
Year 1	$2,100	$2,100	$ 945	$ 945
Cash inflow				
Year 1	$ 210	$ 210	$ 95	$ 159
2	231	231	104	110
3	254	254	114	121
4	280	280	126	134
5	307	307	138	147
6	338	338	152	162
7	372	372	167	178
8	409	409	184	195
9	450	450	203	215
10	495	495	223	237
Total	$3,346	$3,346	$1,506	$1,658
Present value	$2,100	$2,100	$945	$1,059
Present value of inflows less present value of outflow	$0.00	$0.00	$0.00	$114

This analysis indicates that, with respect to company A, overall profitability will be unaffected by the change from FIFO to LIFO. This is the expected result since the adoption of LIFO has no impact on the cash flow of company A, which pays no income tax. We have already seen that the reported earnings of company A will decrease from $2,100,000 to $1,984,000 if it adopts LIFO. The manager of company A may not find LIFO attractive, because no benefit will be obtained to offset the decrease in reported earnings.

The manager of company B is faced with a more complex decision. On the one hand, if company B switches to LIFO, reported earnings will decrease by $52,000 from $945,000 to $893,000. On the other hand, over a 10-year period the fact that company B will realize in 19X1 a tax (i.e., cash) savings of $64,000 means that by the end of the 10th year, company B will have $152,000 more cash than it would have if FIFO had been continued. In addition, $88,000 of investment earnings will be reflected in reported earnings under LIFO over the 10-year period that would not have been available under FIFO. Thus, over the 10-year period, total reported earnings under LIFO will actually exceed total FIFO reported earnings by $36,000 (= $88,000 − $52,000). Taking into consideration all of these potential benefits to company B incident to the switch to LIFO, can the manager of company B justify the continuation of FIFO merely because the reported earnings for 19X1 will be less under LIFO than under FIFO? Under the assumptions of our simple model, the answer would appear to be an obvious no. However, in the model we have ignored thus far the impact of an anticipation of continuing inflation in the future. The effect of continuing inflation would be to increase the relative advantage for LIFO, because additional cash flow in the nature of tax savings would be generated not only in the initial year but also in each subsequent year. On the other hand, reported LIFO earnings would continue to lag behind reported FIFO earnings.

For example, if we change the assumptions for company B such that for each subsequent year inventory quantity will remain the same but price levels for costs and sales will increase 5 percent each year, the results will be those in Exhibit 4. If LIFO were adopted, the results would be as shown in Exhibit 5 assuming aftertax earnings of 10 percent on the additional cash flow.

By the end of the 10th year, company B would have accumulated additional cash of $769,000 through the use of LIFO. However, not until the eighth year would reported LIFO earnings finally exceed reported FIFO earnings. Thus, the manager of company B is confronted with answering what appears to be a very difficult question, namely, is the total inflow of cash of $769,000 worth the price of having to report decreased earnings for a period of seven years? As we shall see in the section of this chapter that discusses LIFO in detail, this perplexing situation in which the manager of company B finds himself is a direct result of what we refer to as the *conformity* requirement of the Internal Revenue Code provision dealing with LIFO.

Discretionary Purchase—Capitalize or Expense.   Let us leave company B in its LIFO quandary and turn to what is a simpler decision, namely, whether a purchase should be capitalized or charged to expense.

In this situation both company A and company B have just purchased an item costing $10,000. We assume that the manager of each has complete discretion either to capitalize the item and depreciate it over an eight-year period (SYD method) or to expense the entire amount in the year of purchase. As in the previous example, the cost of capital is estimated to be 10 percent. In this situation, an analysis under the profitability index approach would result in cash inflows and outflows as shown in Exhibit 6.

What does this analysis tell us? First, for company A, which pays no income tax, overall profitability is not affected by the decision to capitalize or to expense the repair costs. The reason, of course, is that the decision has no impact on the flow of dollars; rather, it merely relates to whether the total expense of $10,000 will reduce book income in the first year as opposed to depreciation deductions occurring in each of the eight years. Thus, company A is likely to choose capitalization, because the company's book income for the first year will be greater by $7,778 [= $10,000 − (8/36 × $10,000)].

Note, however, that company B, subject to tax, again has a more difficult decision. In the absence of an investment credit, company B should choose to expense the item rather than capitalize it so long as it anticipates constant tax rates. The reason? The closer to the present the benefit is obtained, the greater the present value of the tax benefit.

EXHIBIT 4 Net Income Using FIFO Cost-Flow Assumption Over 10-Year Period

FIFO	19X1	19X2	19X3	19X4	19X5	19X6	19X7	19X8	19X9	19Y0	Total
Beginning inventory	$1,100	$1,400	$1,470	$1,544	$1,621	$1,702	$1,787	$1,876	$1,970	$2,068	
Purchases	5,200	5,460	5,733	6,020	6,321	6,637	6,968	7,317	7,683	8,067	
Goods available for sale	$6,300	$6,860	$7,203	$7,564	$7,942	$8,339	$8,755	$9,193	$9,653	$10,135	
Ending inventory	1,400	1,470	1,544	1,621	1,702	1,787	1,876	1,970	2,068	2,172	
Cost of goods sold	$4,900	$5,390	$5,659	$5,943	$6,240	$6,552	$6,879	$7,223	$7,585	$7,963	
Sales less other expenses	7,000	7,350	7,718	8,103	8,509	8,934	9,381	9,850	10,342	10,859	
Pretax profit	$2,100	$1,960	$2,059	$2,160	$2,269	$2,382	$2,502	$2,627	$2,757	$2,896	
Income tax at 55 percent	1,155	1,078	1,132	1,188	1,248	1,310	1,376	1,445	1,516	1,593	
Net income	$ 945	$ 882	$ 927	$ 972	$1,021	$1,072	$1,126	$1,182	$1,241	$1,303	$10,671

EXHIBIT 5 Net Income Using LIFO Cost-Flow Assumption Over 10-Year Period

LIFO	19X1	19X2	19X3	19X4	19X5	19X6	19X7	19X8	19X9	19Y0	Total
Beginning inventory	$1,100	$1,284	$1,284	$1,284	$1,284	$1,284	$1,284	$1,284	$1,284	$1,284	
Purchases	5,200	5,460	5,733	6,020	6,321	6,637	6,968	7,317	7,683	8,067	
Goods available for sale	$6,300	$6,744	$7,017	$7,304	$7,605	$7,921	$8,252	$8,601	$8,967	$9,351	
Ending inventory	1,284	1,284	1,284	1,284	1,284	1,284	1,284	1,284	1,284	1,284	
Cost of goods sold	$5,016	$5,460	$5,733	$6,020	$6,321	$6,637	$6,968	$7,317	$7,683	$8,067	
Sales less other expenses	7,000	7,350	7,718	8,103	8,509	8,934	9,381	9,850	10,342	10,859	
Pretax profit	$1,984	$1,890	$1,985	$2,083	$2,188	$2,297	$2,413	$2,533	$2,659	$2,792	
Income tax at 55 percent	1,091	1,040	1,092	1,146	1,203	1,263	1,327	1,393	1,462	1,536	
Net income before return on cash flow	$ 893	$ 850	$ 893	$ 937	$ 985	$1,034	$1,086	$1,140	$1,197	$1,256	$10,271
10% return on LIFO-generated cash flow	—	6	11	16	22	28	36	44	54	65	282
Net income	$ 893	$ 856	$ 904	$ 953	$1,007	$1,062	$1,122	$1,184	$1,251	$1,321	$10,553

EXHIBIT 6 Purchase of an Asset—Capitalized or Charged to Expense

| | Company A pretax analysis | | Company B aftertax analysis | | | | Memo only | | |
| | | | No investment credit | | 10% investment credit | | | | |
	Expense	Capitalize	Expense	Capitalize[a]	Expense	Capitalize[a]	Depreciation	Value @ 50%	Present value
Cash outflow									
Year 1	$10,000	$10,000	$5,000	$10,000	$5,000	$ 9,000			
Assumed cash inflow									
Year 1	$ 1,000	$ 1,000	$ 500	$ 1,611	$ 500	$ 1,611	$2,222	$1,111	$1,010
2	1,100	1,100	550	1,522	550	1,522	1,944	972	803
3	1,210	1,210	605	1,439	605	1,439	1,667	834	627
4	1,331	1,331	666	1,360	666	1,360	1,389	694	472
5	1,464	1,464	732	1,288	732	1,288	1,111	556	345
6	1,611	1,611	805	1,221	805	1,221	833	416	235
7	1,771	1,771	886	1,164	886	1,164	556	278	143
8	1,949	1,949	974	1,113	974	1,113	278	139	65
Total	$11,436	$11,436	$5,718	$10,718	$5,718	$10,718	$10,000	$5,000	$3,700
Present value of inflow	$10,000	$10,000	$5,000	$ 8,700	$5,000	$ 8,700			
Present value of inflow less present value of outflow	$0	$0	$0	($1,300)	$0	($300)			

[a]Aftertax cash flow + cash flow benefit (tax reduction) from tax depreciation.

Note that the example of company B also includes the situation where a 10-percent investment credit is available if the item is capitalized. The introduction of the investment credit injects a new decision element. The analysis shows that the net present value of −$300 is still negative but is not as bad as the −$1,300 when no investment credit was available. In general, the higher the tax rate and the greater the perceived cost of capital, the more advantageous will be the immediate deduction, even at the expense of foregoing the investment credit at the assumed rate; but there is some level of investment credit that for any given set of facts will make capitalization appear more attractive.[1]

INVENTORY

Given the IRS rules (i.e., the basic rules of Code Sec. 446(a) that taxable income be computed in accordance with the *method* of accounting regularly employed in keeping the taxpayer's books, and of Reg. Sec. 1.471-2 that an inventory valuation method must conform to the best accounting practice in the particular trade or business of the taxpayer), it is reasonable to start with the question of why there should ever be any difference between inventory valuation for financial accounting purposes and inventory valuation for tax purposes.

One reason is application of the accounting concept of *materiality* to the method of inventory valuation. The financial accountant might for good business reasons decide to modify the valuation method previously used and, in the absence of materiality, charge any adjustment required as a result of such change to income to the year of change. Unfortunately, the Internal Revenue Service has a different concept of materiality. Regulation Sec. 1.446-1(e)(2)(ii)(a) defines a material item as any item that involves the proper time for inclusion in income or for taking a deduction. Likewise, the financial accountant and the independent auditor have great respect for the doctrine of consistency as it relates to the measurement and determination of periodic income. Not only must consistency be applied to the methods of measuring income, but also any departures from consistent application must be disclosed. Consistency is also important in tax accounting, but in a different way; for consistency represents a tool often used by IRS agents to exact maximum tax dollars from the taxpayer. Thus, if the taxpayer desires to change a method of accounting in order to increase deductions, the Service takes the view that the taxpayer cannot do so because of the consistency requirement. An example of this approach can be seen where individual states have amended their laws so that a tax that previously accrued on, say, July 1 of the year henceforth becomes an actual liability six months earlier, on January 1 of the same year. The IRS position is that the consistency concept bars the taxpayer from accelerating the timing of the deduction for the tax. On the other hand, the Service does not visualize the consistency concept as a bar to its compelling the taxpayer to change from one consistent method to a different method if the new method will increase revenues.

Finally, as we shall examine in detail later, the court system over the years has had great difficulty in answering the related questions of when an item accrues as a deduction for tax purposes and when is taxable income clearly reflected as opposed to materially distorted. The end result of this difficulty is a tax library full of decisions regarding tax accounting, many of which make little accounting sense. Each, however, represents a rule of tax accounting in the sense that a particular court has made a determination regarding the application of the law to a particular factual situation.

[1]For a complete analysis of these problems, see Clyde P. Stickney and Jeffrey B. Wallace, *A Practical Guide to the Class Life (ADR) System,* Lawyers & Judges Publishing Company, Tucson, Ariz., 1977.

Thus, over the years, as a result of the concepts of materiality and consistency and determinations by the Service and the Courts of what "clearly reflects income," differences have arisen in the area of inventory valuation between financial accounting and tax accounting. These differences generally fall into one of seven categories, as described in the sections that follow.

Lower of Cost or Market.   Because the major objective of inventory accounting is to reflect periodic income clearly through the process of matching appropriate costs against revenue, the primary basis of accounting for inventories is cost. However, because inventories are required not only for the purpose of measuring periodic income but also for the statement of financial position, and because, in some cases, the utility of goods may have diminished during a period to such an extent that cost may not be recoverable in future periods, the rule of "cost or market, whichever is lower" has been developed as a departure from the cost basis of pricing inventory.

Financial Accounting Treatment.   *Accounting Research Bulletin No. 43,* Chapter 4, Statement 6, provides:

> As used in the phrase *lower of cost or market* the term *market* means current replacement cost . . . except that:
> (1) Market should not exceed the net realizable value . . . ; and
> (2) Market should not be less than net realizable value reduced by an allowance for an approximately normal profit margin.

Statement 7 adds that the cost-or-market rule may properly be applied either directly to each item or to the total of the inventory or, in some cases, to the total of the components of each major category.

Tax Accounting Treatment.   The tax rule for lower of cost or market is set forth in Reg. Sec. 1-471-4, wherein market is defined as "the current bid price prevailing at the date of the inventory for the particular merchandise in the volume in which usually purchased by the taxpayer." The regulation also provides that in applying the lower-of-cost-or-market rule, the market value of each *article* on hand at the inventory date shall be compared with the cost of the article, and the lower of such values shall be taken as the inventory value of the article.

It should be noted that the lower-of-cost-or-market rule is not available to taxpayers using the LIFO method. Under tax LIFO, inventory must be valued at cost.

Conformity and Consistency.   There is no statutory requirement that the lower-of-cost-or-market rule applied for tax purposes conform to that used for financial purposes. If a taxpayer has consistently applied the lower-of-cost-or-market rule to the total of the inventory, the method in use does not conform to the technical requirements of the regulations. Such a taxpayer should have a reasonable basis for change in its method to conform to the regulations. But such a change, or a change from the cost method to the lower-of-cost-or-market method, would constitute a change in method of accounting for tax purposes that would require the advance permission of the Service. Permission to change would probably be granted only if any foreseeable adjustment resulting were spread over 10 years.

An important point to note is that the tax consistency requirement is a two-edged sword that is usually (but not always) held by the IRS. Thus, if a taxpayer has consistently used an improper method for both tax and financial reporting purposes, a change in the book method will not produce a corresponding change for tax purposes unless an application is made and permission is granted to change the method of accounting. On the other hand, the Service, upon examination of a return, may take the position that the method consistently used is an improper one and that the taxpayer must change to a method that conforms to the regulations.

Overhead Inclusions and Exclusions. On September 14, 1973, the Internal Revenue Service adopted final regulations relating to permissible methods for determining what indirect production costs should be included in inventory valuation of manufacturers. These new rules (known as the "Full Absorption Regulations") appear at Reg. Sec. 1.471-11(a). They provide an illuminating framework that illustrates precisely why financial cost accounting and tax cost accounting often differ. For example, Reg. Sec. 1.446-1(c)(1)(ii) provides that an accounting method used by the taxpayer will be acceptable if it (1) accords with generally accepted accounting principles, (2) is consistently used from year to year, and (3) *is consistent with the Income Tax Regulations* (emphasis supplied). Likewise, Reg. Sec. 1.471-2(b) regarding valuation of inventories provides that greater weight is to be given consistency than to any particular method of valuation "so long as the method or basis used is in accord with Regulations 1.471-1 through 1.471-11." Thus, it is the additional requirement that the tax costing method conform to the regulations that sets it apart from the financial costing method. Moreover, in order to determine acceptable tax costing methods and to determine what alternatives are available to the financial manager to maximize the cash flow of the company, a thorough understanding of the "Full Absorption Regulations" is required.

What, then, do these regulations provide? First, the regulations require that all taxpayers engaged in manufacturing or production operations use a "full absorption" method of inventory costing. Second, the regulations establish separate cost categories and applicable rules that set forth the circumstances under which the various category costs are includable or excludable from the computation of inventoriable costs. And, third, the regulations set forth the acceptable methods that may be used to allocate inventoriable indirect production costs to goods in the ending inventory.

After summarizing all of the definitions, paragraphs, subparagraphs, general rules, exceptions, and cross-references included in the regulations, one is left with the following available tax accounting alternatives in determining inventoriable costs:

A. Regardless of the costing method used for financial purposes, the following costs must be inventoried:
  1. All direct product costs
     Note: This category includes both direct material costs and direct labor costs (e.g., basic compensation, overtime pay, vacation and holiday pay, sick leave pay, shift differential, payroll taxes, and supplemental unemployment benefit payments).
  2. All of the following indirect production costs to the extent that they are incident to and necessary for production or manufacturing operations or processes:
     (a) Repair expenses
     (b) Maintenance
     (c) Utilities
     (d) Rent
     (e) Indirect labor and production supervisory wages [including fringe benefits referred to in A(1) above]
     (f) Indirect materials and supplies
     (g) Tools and equipment not capitalized
     (h) Costs of quality control and inspection
B. Regardless of the costing method used for financial purposes, the following costs are not included in inventoriable costs for tax purposes:
  1. Marketing expenses
  2. Advertising expenses
  3. Selling expenses
  4. Other distribution expenses
  5. Interest

6. Research and experimental expenses including engineering and product development expenses
7. Losses under Section 165 and the regulations thereunder
8. Percentage depletion in excess of cost depletion
9. Depreciation and amortization reported for federal income tax purposes in excess of depreciation reported by the taxpayer in the financial reports
10. Income taxes attributable to income received on the sale of inventory
11. Pension contributions to the extent that they represent past service cost
12. General and administrative expenses incident to and necessary for the taxpayer's activities as a whole rather than to production or manufacturing operations or processes
13. Salaries paid to officers attributable to the performance of services that are incident to and necessary for the taxpayer's activities taken as a whole rather than to production or manufacturing operations or processes

C. If the taxpayer uses a method of accounting for production costs in the financial reports that is *comparable* to the tax accounting method, then the inclusion or exclusion of the following costs shall be determined on the basis of their financial reporting treatment (i.e., they shall be treated as inventoriable costs for tax purposes only if they are so treated for financial reporting purposes):
  1. Deductible taxes other than income taxes
  2. Book depreciation and cost depletion
  3. Pension and profit-sharing benefits and other employee benefits including workmen's compensation expenses, payments under a wage continuation plan, premiums on life and health insurance, and other miscellaneous benefits
  4. Costs attributable to strikes, rework labor, scrap, and spoilage
  5. Factory administrative expenses
  6. Officer's salaries
  7. Insurance costs

D. If the taxpayer uses a method of accounting for production costs in the financial reports that is *not comparable* to the tax accounting method (e.g., if the prime cost method is used for financial reporting), a different rule applies. Inventoriable costs then include:
  1. All direct costs as in A(1) above
  2. All the indirect production costs listed in A(2) above
  3. *None* of the costs listed in B above
  4. *All* of the indirect costs listed in C above with the exception of C(3), employee benefits, and C(4), costs attributable to strikes, rework, labor, scrap, and spoilage

Having once established which costs are properly inventoriable for tax purposes, the regulations also delineate the acceptable methods that may be used to allocate the inventoriable indirect production costs to goods includible in the ending inventory. The acceptable allocation methods include:
  1. The manufacturing burden rate method, and
  2. The standard cost method

Note: Under either method, the practical capacity concept may be used to determine the total amount of *fixed* indirect production costs that must be allocated.

Direct Costing.   Under direct costing, only direct production costs are treated as inventoriable costs (i.e., fixed production costs are treated as period costs and are deducted in total from cost of goods sold). The concept of full absorption costing, of course, involves the capitalization through inventory of both variable and fixed production costs. Accordingly, in view of the "Full Absorption Regulations," discussed in detail in the preceding section, it is clear that the Internal Revenue Service does not accept the use of direct costing for federal income tax purposes. Thus, the use of direct costing for managerial purposes only will generally have no impact at all on the computation of taxable income.

Average Cost.   Unlike the lower-of-cost-or-market rule, the concept of average cost is not a departure from the cost method. Rather, average cost is merely a flow assumption that is employed in order to determine cost. Specifically, it is an assumption as to the flow of costs, just as FIFO and LIFO are assumptions as to the flow of costs.

Financial Accounting Treatment.   The use of average costs in pricing inventories is common. The 1975 edition of *Accounting Trends and Techniques* shows 236 out of a total of 600 companies as using the average cost method. It is commonly applied in one of two ways:

1. The weighted average method (based on a periodic inventory system), whereby the goods on hand at the end of a period are assumed to be the weighted average of the inventory cost of goods on hand at the beginning of the period plus all goods purchased during the period. Under this method the weighted average is computed by dividing the total cost (beginning inventory + purchases) by the total number of units.

2. The moving average method (based on perpetual inventory records), whereby a new average cost is computed after each purchase.

Tax Accounting Treatment.   The tax rules regarding the use of an average cost method are as significant as the full absorption rules discussed above in highlighting why tax accounting often differs from financial accounting. To understand what appears to be the tax rule, we must start with two old cases decided by the now-defunct Board of Tax Appeals and Revenue Ruling 71-234 issued in 1971. The cases, *Ashtabula Bow Socket Co.,* 2 BTA 306 (1925) and *Demarest Silk Co.,* 4 BTA 741 (1926), held that whether the average cost method could be used depended on its application to the goods as a whole and not to a particular class.

The full text of Revenue Ruling 71-234 is set forth below.

1971-1 Rev. Rul. 71-234. CB 148. INVENTORIES—Valuation—change of inventory method. The average cost (rolling average) method of computing inventories used by the manufacturer of a product requiring aging from one to three years does not meet the requirements of Sec. 471; T.B.R. 48 superseded. Ref. ¶20,684.

The purpose of this Revenue Ruling is to update and restate, under the current statute and regulations, the position set forth in T.B.R. 48, C.B. 1, 47 (1919).

The question presented is whether the average cost method of taking inventories (sometimes also referred to as "the rolling average method") may be used by the taxpayer under the circumstances described below.

The taxpayer, a domestic corporation, produces a product that requires aging from one to three years. The materials purchased are not currently consumed in manufacture, but are held for aging purposes. Furthermore, prices are subject to substantial fluctuation. In computing its inventories, materials purchased during a month are added, both as to quantity and cost, to the quantity and cost balance brought forward from the previous month and an average cost to the close of the month is computed by dividing the total quantity into the total money figure. This average is then applied to the quantity of materials used for manufacture during the month and the amount so computed is credited to the material account.

The specific question in the instant case is whether inventories computed under this method form a proper factor for the computation of income for Federal income tax purposes.

Section 471 of the Internal Revenue Code of 1954 provides as follows:

Whenever in the opinion of the Secretary or his delegate the use of inventories is necessary in order clearly to determine the income of any taxpayer, inventories shall be taken by such taxpayer on such basis as the Secretary or his delegate may prescribe as conforming as nearly as may be to the best accounting practice in the trade or business and as most clearly reflecting the income.

Section 1.471–1 of the Income Tax Regulations provides that, in order to reflect taxable income correctly, inventories at the beginning and end of each taxable year are necessary in every case in which the production, purchase, or sale of merchandise is an income-producing factor. The inventory should include all finished or partly finished goods and, in the case of raw materials and supplies, only those which have been acquired for sale or which will physically become a part of merchandise intended for sale. Section 1.471–2(a) of the regulations provides as follows:

(a) Section 471 provides two tests to which each inventory must conform:
(1) It must conform as nearly as may be to the best accounting practice in the trade or business, and
(2) It must clearly reflect the income.

Section 1.471–2(c) of the regulations provides, in part, as follows:

(c) The bases of valuation most commonly used by business concerns and which meet the requirements of section 471 are (1) cost and (2) cost or market, whichever is lower.

In a business requiring goods to be carried for lengthy periods and where an average cost method of inventory valuation is used an overstatement of profit will occur whenever the current market is declining, while on an advancing market the profits on the actual sales of the year will be understated. When the market is stable the average method will reflect with approximate accuracy the true profit. The computation of taxable income upon such a basis results in an assignment of income to a year, not upon the basis of the transactions of the year, but upon the basis of transactions parts of which spread over more than a year. An annual accounting period is a fundamental requirement of the Federal income tax law, and every computation of taxable income must be made in conformity therewith. This the average cost inventory method in the instant case failed to do.

Accordingly, the taxpayer in the instant case may not use the average cost inventory method or rolling average method since this method does not conform to the requirements of section 471 of the Code and the applicable regulations thereunder.

T.B.R. 48 is hereby superseded, since the position stated therein is restated under the current law in this Revenue Ruling.

Note the following items of import that flow from the Service's discussion of average cost in the Ruling:

1. Neither the Code nor the Regulations specifically mention the concept of average cost.

2. The requirement that the method conform to the best accounting practice in the trade or business is apparently outweighed by the requirement that it clearly reflect income (whatever that means).

3. Because the taxable period is one year, the Service appears to be saying that the average cost method cannot result in a clear reflection of income if the components of the average are drawn from a longer period.

LIFO.   The 1974 edition of *Accounting Trends and Techniques* listed 150 of a total of 600 companies as using the LIFO method. This was exactly the same number as the preceding year. The 1975 edition, however, shows that the number had increased from 150 to 303—an increase of over 100 percent in one year. For the first time in history, over 50 percent of the reporting companies now use LIFO for all or a portion of their inventories. Ten of 12 department store chains now use LIFO, but only 4 of 16 grocery store chains do so. Ninety-two percent of all chemical companies now use LIFO, whereas in the prior year only 29 percent did so. This dramatic change, which took place in a climate of high inflation, rising interest rates, and depressed stock prices, emphasizes the value that a large percentage of management places on cash flow even though such increase is achievable only by reflecting reduced earnings in the short run.

Just as is the average cost method, from an accounting viewpoint, LIFO is not a departure from the cost method but is a cost-flow assumption. If market is below cost, then presently accepted accounting practice would be to show the inventory at market rather than cost. LIFO for financial reporting, then, has the tendency to show inventory valuations of LIFO users at the lowest prices that have prevailed since the adoption of LIFO.

LIFO for tax purposes was introduced by the Revenue Act of 1938 for use by tanners and producers of certain nonferrous metals. The Revenue Act of 1939 permitted any taxpayer to use LIFO; however, regulations were so restrictive (i.e., they required the matching of physical units in beginning and ending inventories) that LIFO was not practicable for most companies. In the 1940s the dollar-value concept was developed and was approved by the Tax Court in 1948. In 1961, an explanation of the dollar-value concept was finally added to the regulations. The regulations now provide detailed rules regarding the adoption of LIFO and the computation of LIFO inventories.

The primary benefit achieved by the adoption of LIFO is, of course, the increase in cash flow generated from the reduced taxable income coupled with the additional aftertax earnings that the company can generate as a result of the influx of cash. In addition, some accounting theorists submit that the use of LIFO results in a better matching of current costs against current revenue for the purpose of determining and measuring periodic income.

The potential LIFO benefits, as discussed above, are subject to certain risks, and LIFO adoption has possible disadvantages. For example, there is a requirement that if LIFO is used for tax purposes, it must also be used for financial reporting purposes, thereby, in the short run at least, resulting in a decrease in reported earnings of the company.

Likewise, the use of LIFO can affect reported working capital and may affect the computation of the contributions to bonus, profit-sharing, and other benefit plans. In addition, it should be noted that if future costs decrease rather than increase, LIFO could result in a write-down for financial statement purposes with no corresponding write-down allowable for tax purposes.

Disclosure of Financial Accounting Treatment.   In the case of a change to LIFO, there are disclosure requirements. APB Opinion No. 20, Paragraph 14(d), provides as an example that if the method of pricing inventory is changed from the FIFO method to the LIFO method, it may be assumed that the ending inventory of the immediately preceding year is also the beginning inventory of the current period for the LIFO method.

Tax Accounting Treatment.   In the year LIFO is adopted, the opening inventory must be based on cost, and any previous write-downs to market must be restored by filing an amended return for the year preceding the first LIFO year. The Service has the authority to adjust this opening LIFO inventory to assure that all costs are properly reflected.

For tax accounting under LIFO, the lower-of-cost-or-market valuation basis is not permitted, even though it is used in financial reporting.

Increases in quantities over the base layer are priced under one of the following methods (election of the method to be used must be made in the year LIFO is adopted):

1. Most recent purchases
2. Earliest acquisitions during the year
3. Average cost, or
4. Some other acceptable method

Two methods are permitted in valuing the LIFO inventories:

1. The unit method (i.e., specific goods), or
2. The dollar-value method

If the specific goods method is used, the inventory items must be separated into separate pools and items may be included in the same pool only if they are of a like kind.

If the dollar-value method is used, a manufacturer or processor may establish a single pool for a natural business unit. Once the pools have been established, the regulations provide three methods for computing the value of a dollar-value pool. The first is the "double-extension" method, whereby each item in the pool must be extended both at current-year costs and at base-year costs. The Service provides that this method must ordinarily be used. The second method is the "index" method, whereby a representative portion of the inventory items in the pool may be double-extended at both current-year costs and base-year costs in order to arrive at an index which is then applied to the pool as a whole. The Service provides that this method may be used only where the double-extension method is impractical because of technological changes, the extensive variety of items, or extreme fluctuations in the variety of items in the pool. The third method is the "link-chain" method, whereby all or a representative portion of the inventory items in the pool are double-extended not at both current- and base-year costs but rather at end-of-year and beginning-of-the-year costs in order to arrive at a "current-year's" index which is then multiplied by the cumulative index that existed at the end of the prior year in order to arrive at a new cumulative index. The regulations provide that the "link-chain" method can be used only in those cases where the taxpayer can establish that the use of either an index method or the double-extension method would be impracticable or unsuitable in view of the nature of the pool.

In most cases, in computing the value of a dollar-value pool, the use of the "link-chain" method is far superior to any other method with respect to its ease of application as well as to the quality of its results.

Conformity and Consistency.   Having just urged the use of LIFO and specifically the use of the "link-chain" method, we now issue a note of caution. The first LIFO conformity requirement was issued in the predecessor of what is now Section 472 of the Internal Revenue Code, which imposed the requirement that the LIFO inventory method may be used only if the taxpayer establishes that it has used no procedure other than LIFO in determining income for the year in reports or statements to shareholders, etc., or for credit purposes. That first rule has been followed by many IRS pronouncements regarding what this conformity requirement means.

With respect to consistency, it should be noted that the LIFO inventory method is a method of accounting in the tax sense. If a company does not presently use the LIFO inventory method, it may adopt LIFO by making an election in its tax return and attaching a Form 970 to the return. Once LIFO is adopted, its use may be discontinued only if permitted or required by the Internal Revenue Service.

Standard Cost Variances.   The standard cost method of allocating inventoriable costs to goods in ending inventory has been widely used by business because of the lower clerical costs and the benefits derived from being able to analyze the differences between predetermined costs and actual costs. An analysis of these differences (i.e., variances) can give relevant information as to the causes of excess costs. How does the disposition of these variances for tax accounting purposes differ from their treatment for financial statement purposes?

Financial Accounting Treatment.   In the case of financial statement treatment of variances from standard cost, various methods are commonly used and the proper method probably depends on whom you are asking. Thus, you can find the variances being entirely charged or credited to operations or apportioned between inventory and operations.

Tax Accounting Treatment.   Tax accounting for variances is not as flexible. Regulation Sec. 1.471-11(d)(3) provides that the standard costs can be used to value ending inventory, provided that the taxpayer allocates a *pro rata* portion of any positive or negative variances (whether of overhead or direct production cost) to goods in ending inventory. If the variances are not significant in amount, then they need not be allocated to goods in ending inventory, *provided that* such allocation is not made in the taxpayer's financial reports.

PRACTICAL CAPACITY EXCEPTION.   Allocation is not required where fixed indirect production costs are not absorbed due to failure to produce at practical capacity.

Long-Term Contracts.   That taxable income must be determined on the basis of a taxable year in itself creates problems for tax purposes as well as for financial accounting purposes. The case of long-term contracts is an example. A long-term contract is a construction-type contract where costs are incurred in one year (perhaps interim billings are also issued in that year) but the construction is not completed until a subsequent year. In such a situation, of course, at the end of the first year, the total profit to be realized from the contract is an unknown.

Financial Accounting Treatment.   There are basically two generally accepted methods for recognizing revenue from long-term construction contracts. The first is the completed-contract method, whereby revenue is recognized only in the year of completion. The second is the percentage-of-completion method, whereby percentages are derived by comparing costs incurred with estimated total costs and the calculated percentages are used to allocate anticipated total revenue and cost to each period. *ARB No. 45* provides that the percentage-of-completion method is preferable when estimates of cost to complete and extent of progress toward completion are reasonably dependable. Otherwise, the completed-contract method is preferable.

In the case of the percentage of completion method, *ARB No. 45* states that when the current estimate of total contract costs indicates a loss, in most circumstances provision should be made that period for the total loss on the contract. It also provides that provision should be made for foreseeable losses where the completed-contract method is used.

When the completed-contract method is used, *ARB No. 45* provides that it may be appropriate to allocate general and administrative costs to contract costs rather than charge them to income. On the other hand, it also states that there should be no excessive deferring of overhead costs. The section does not delve into the complex area of specifically what costs should be treated as contract costs and what costs should be treated as period costs.

Tax Accounting Treatment.   Section 451 of the Code provides:

(a) General Rule.—The amount of any item of gross income shall be included in the gross income for the taxable year in which received by the taxpayer, unless, under the method of accounting used in computing taxable income, such amount is to be properly accounted for as of a different period.

Note that the law says nothing about a long-term contract. However, the regulations under Section 451 do deal with the concept of long-term contracts. Specifically, Reg. Sec. 1.451-3 provides:

1. A long-term contract is defined as a building, installation, construction, or manufacturing contract that is not completed within the taxable year in which it is entered into. The inclusion of "manufacturing" contracts in the long-term definition is restricted to those that either are (a) unique items of a type not normally carried in the taxpayer's finished goods, or (b) items that, regardless of the duration of the actual contract, *normally* require more than 12 months to complete.

2. The regulation permits the use of either the percentage-of-completion method or the completed-contract method.

3. The regulation says very little about what costs must be treated as contract costs in using the percentage-of-completion method but does make the point that

other income and expense items such as "investment income or expenses not attributable to such contracts" and service agreement costs should fall outside of the application of the special treatment rules.

4. Costs of taxpayers using the completed contract method are spelled out in detail, as follows:

"Direct material costs" include the costs of those materials which become an integral part of the subject matter of the long-term contract and those materials which are consumed in the ordinary course of building, constructing, installing, or manufacturing the subject matter of a long-term contract.

"Direct labor costs" include the cost of labor which can be identified or associated with a particular long-term contract. The elements of direct labor costs include such items as basic compensation, overtime pay, vacation and holiday pay, sick leave pay (other than payments pursuant to a wage continuation plan under section 105(d)), shift differential, payroll taxes and payments to a supplemental unemployment benefit plan paid or incurred on behalf of employees engaged in direct labor.

The term "indirect costs" includes all costs (other than direct material costs and direct labor costs) which are incident to and necessary for the performance of particular long-term contracts. Indirect costs which must be allocated to long-term contracts include:

(a) Repair expenses of equipment or facilities used in the performance of particular long-term contracts,

(b) Maintenance of equipment or facilities used in the performance of particular long-term contracts,

(c) Utilities, such as heat, light, and power, relating to equipment or facilities used in the performance of particular long-term contracts,

(d) Rent of equipment or facilities used in the performance of particular long-term contracts,

(e) Indirect labor and contract supervisory wages, including basic compensation, overtime pay, vacation and holiday pay, sick leave pay (other than payments pursuant to a wage continuation plan under section 105(d)), shift differential, payroll taxes and contributions to a supplemental unemployment benefit plant incurred in the performance of particular long-term contracts,

(f) Indirect materials and supplies used in the performance of particular long-term contracts,

(g) Tools and equipment not capitalized used in the performance of particular long-term contracts,

(h) Costs of quality control and inspection incurred in the performance of particular long-term contracts,

(i) Taxes otherwise allowable as a deduction under section 164 (other than State and local and foreign income taxes) to the extent such taxes are attributable to labor, materials, supplies, equipment or facilities used in the performance of particular long-term contracts,

(j) Depreciation and amortization reported for financial purposes on equipment and facilities used in the performance of particular long-term contracts,

(k) Cost depletion incurred in the performance of particular long-term contracts,

(l) Administrative costs incurred in the performance of particular long-term contracts (but not including any cost of selling or any return on capital),

(m) Compensation paid to officers attributable to services performed on particular long-term contracts (other than incidental or occasional services), and

(n) Costs of insurance incurred in the performance of particular long-term contracts, such as insurance on machinery and equipment used in the construction of the subject matter of a long-term contract.

Costs which are not required to be included in costs attributable to a long-term contract include:

(a) Marketing and selling expenses, including bidding expenses,

(b) Advertising expenses,

(c) Other distribution expenses,

(d) Interest,

(e) General and administrative expenses attributable to the performance of services which benefit the long-term contractor's activities as a whole (such as payroll expenses, legal and accounting expenses, etc.),

(f) Research and experimental expenses (described in Section 174 and the regulations thereunder),

(g) Losses under section 165 and the regulations thereunder,

(h) Percentage depletion in excess of cost depletion,

(i) Depreciation and amortization on idle equipment and facilities and depreciation and amortization reported for Federal income tax purposes in excess of depreciation reported by the taxpayer in his financial reports,

(j) Income taxes attributable to income received from long-term contracts,

(k) Pension and profit-sharing contributions representing either past service costs or representing current service costs otherwise allowable as a deduction under section 404, and other employee benefits incurred on behalf of labor. These other benefits include workmen's compensation expenses, payments under a wage continuation plan described in section 105(d), amounts includible in the gross income of employees under nonqualified pension, profit-sharing and stock bonus plans, premiums on life and health insurance and miscellaneous benefits provided for employees such as safety, medical treatment, cafeteria, recreational facilities, membership dues, etc., which are otherwise allowable as deductions under chapter I of the Code,

(l) Cost attributable to strikes, rework labor, scrap and spoilage, and

(m) Compensation paid to officers attributable to the performance of services which benefit the long-term contractor's activities as a whole.

"Costs which are properly allocable to a long-term contract" do not include costs incurred with respect to any guarantee, warranty, maintenance, or other service agreement relating to the subject matter of the long-term contract. . . .

In the case of a taxpayer who is required to allocate indirect costs to long-term contracts . . . such costs may be allocated among long-term contracts either—

(i) By a specific identification (or "tracing") method, or

(ii) By a method of allocation utilizing burden rates, such as ratios based on direct costs, hours, or other items, or similar formulas, so long as the method employed for such allocation reasonably allocates indirect expenses among long-term contracts completed during the taxable year and long-term contracts which have not been completed as of the end of the taxable year. Indirect expenses may ordinarily be allocated to long-term contracts on the basis of direct labor and material costs, direct labor costs, direct labor hours, or any other basis which results in a reasonable allocation of such indirect costs.

Conformity and Consistency.   At present, there is no requirement that the tax method used correspond to the method used for financial reporting purposes. However, it would appear that decisions made regarding what costs are treated as contract costs for book purposes would have an impact on the tax accounting treatment, especially if the taxpayer were trying to treat as period costs some items that it capitalized on its financial statements.

With respect to consistency, it is clear that the method used for tax purposes constitutes a "method of accounting" and that if the taxpayer desired to change its method for tax purposes, it could do so only by first obtaining the permission of the Service. This would be true not only in the case of, say, a change from the percentage-of-completion method to the long-term-contract method, but also in the case of changing the treatment of specific items as contract costs.

COST ALLOCATIONS AND SECTION 482

The number of companies doing business both in the United States and abroad continues to increase. These multinational firms conduct their overseas operations in various forms. For example, foreign operations may be conducted through branches or divisions of a U.S. corporation. Alternatively, the foreign operations may be conducted through a separate foreign subsidiary.

Not only may the form in which foreign operations are carried out vary from enterprise to enterprise, but also the very nature of foreign operations assumes a myriad of configurations, from the simple process of manufacturing an item in the

United States and selling it abroad to complex arrangements such as the following. A process may be first developed and designed in the United States and initial production may commence also in the United States until all of the bugs are ironed out. Subsequently, however, with cheaper labor available in many parts of the world, a portion of the manufacturing process may be transferred overseas to the point where goods may be going in and out of various U.S. ports in various stages of production. As this process expands, so, too, does the problem of dealing with the taxing power of each jurisdiction with which these products come in contact. Although it may be true that ultimate profit or loss to be realized from this process will not be known until final sale is made to the consumer, each of these taxing jurisdictions may be concerned in some manner with the costing process used as these goods travel on their circuitous journey so that a determination can be made of the amount of profit realized in each state and country.

Financial Accounting Treatment for Intracompany and Intercompany Transfers. *ARB No. 43* and *ARB No. 51* discuss the purpose, policy, and application involved in the issuance of consolidated financial statements and in the issuance of combined statements. The purpose of such statements is to present the results of operations as if the group were a single company with one or more branches or divisions. Thus, *ARB No. 51* requires with respect to consolidated financial statements that intercompany balances and transactions should be eliminated. Accordingly, any intercompany profit or loss on assets remaining within the group is eliminated. *ARB No. 51* provides that if income taxes have been paid on intercompany profits on assets remaining within the group, such taxes should be reported as deferred taxes. Finally, *ARB No. 51* provides that where combined statements are prepared for a group of unrelated companies, such as a group of unconsolidated subsidiaries, intercompany profits and losses should be eliminated in the same manner as in consolidated statements.

With this background in mind, it can be seen that the book treatment of this flow of goods could be quite simple. For example, costs could just be accumulated until final sale, at which time the total profit or loss would be realized. On the other hand, if each branch, division, or entity in the group is treated as a profit center, a pricing system may be developed so that central management can measure the performance of the managers of each of these profit centers.

Various methods have been employed in this measuring process. With respect to transfer pricing, the methods include:

1. Cost-plus
2. Market prices
3. Negotiated prices

Tax Accounting Treatment. If the flow of goods referred to above takes place within a single corporation, no particular federal income tax problem results because, as in the case of financial accounting, any intracompany profit or loss would be eliminated in determining taxable income of the corporation.

Similarly, if the flow of goods occurs between or among a group of affiliated companies that file a consolidated federal income tax return, there is no major federal income tax problem because under the consolidated return regulations (e.g., Regulations Section 1.1502-13) gain or loss on "deferred intercompany transactions" is not recognized until the goods are disposed of outside the group. In the case of sale of property between members, the amount of deferred gain or loss includes both direct and indirect costs that are properly includible in the cost of goods sold.

It should be noted that the consolidated return filing privilege is specifically not available to foreign corporations. Thus, it is in the situation where the flow of goods journeys through one or more foreign corporations that the cost allocation problem and the impact of Section 482 become important. We have referred above to the various book methods that might be utilized in recording this flow as well as the purposes served. In the tax sense, the purpose of Section 482 is to assure that U.S. taxable income is clearly reflected where goods are transferred between or among a group of controlled entities. The Internal Revenue Service has adopted detailed regulations [Reg. Sec. 1.482-2(e)] regarding the U.S. tax treatment of transactions involving the sale or other disposition of tangible property between controlled members. The more significant provisions of these regulations which should be familiar to the financial manager are summarized below.

Arm's-Length Charge Concept.   The basic premise of the regulation is that the sale or other disposition of tangible property from one group member to another shall be recorded at an "arm's-length price," which is the price that an unrelated party would have paid under the same circumstances for the property involved in the controlled sale. Such a price normally involves a profit to the seller.

If an arm's-length price is not reflected, the Service shall make appropriate adjustments or allocations between the seller and the buyer in order to reflect an arm's-length price.

Comparable Uncontrolled Sales.   In determining what is, and what is not, an arm's-length price, the regulation provides that comparable uncontrolled sales prices must be used if there are any. In the following section we shall discuss the difficulty of distinguishing between a repair and a capital expenditure. The same type of difficulty is involved in determining whether or not an uncontrolled sale is a comparable one. The regulation distinguishes between (1) comparable uncontrolled sales that are identical, (2) comparable uncontrolled sales that are similar so that adjustments can be made to arrive at a comparable uncontrolled sales price, and (3) uncontrolled sales that vary so radically from the controlled sales that they cannot be considered as comparable.

Resale Price Method.   The regulation provides that if there are no comparable uncontrolled sales, then the resale price method must be used if the standards for its application are met.

Under the resale price method, the arm's-length price is determined by adjusting the applicable resale price for an appropriate markup. In this formula, the term "applicable resale price" means the anticipated price the buyer will charge an uncontrolled party when the product is resold.

The regulation also provides that the following standards must exist in order for the resale price method to be applicable:

1. There must be no comparable uncontrolled sales.
2. An applicable resale price must be available within a reasonable time before or after the controlled sale.
3. The buyer must not add more than an insubstantial amount to the value of the property by physically altering the product before resale. Packaging, repacking, labeling, or minor assembly of product does not constitute physical alteration.
4. The buyer must not add more than an insubstantial amount to the value of the property by the use of intangible property.

The use of the resale price method is also permitted even if the buyer adds a substantial amount to the value of the property if such method is more feasible and is likely to result in a more accurate determination of an arm's-length price than the use of the cost-plus method.

Cost-Plus Method.   Under the cost-plus method, the arm's-length price is computed by adding to the cost of producing the property a profit amount computed by multiplying the cost by an appropriate gross profit percentage.

The regulation provides that the gross profit percentage used must be comparable. For example, if the costs used in producing the appropriate gross profit percentage are comprised of the full cost of goods sold, including direct and indirect costs, then the cost of producing the property involved in the controlled sales must be comprised of the full cost of goods sold also. On the other hand, if the costs used in computing the appropriate gross profit percentage are comprised only of direct costs, the cost of producing the property involved in the controlled sale must be comprised only of direct costs.

Conformity and Consistency. As we view the transfer pricing methodology encompassed in Section 482, it appears that it stands outside and apart from the accounting method concepts that are discussed elsewhere in this chapter. Therefore, there is no requirement that the tax allocation method conform to the book allocation method. As a matter of fact, there may be no book allocation method. This is not to say that the book allocation method might not have tax significance. For the determination of what is an arm's-length price is in the largest sense a question of fact. In such a situation, proper documentation and support is all-important. Thus, evidence of the basis used for book allocation may serve as documentation and support for the tax allocations made.

Consistency, on the other hand, does not have much significance in the Section 482 context. If an improper pricing method has been used in the past, the fact is of little value in determining the pricing method applicable in a subsequent year. Likewise, if, for example, the resale price method has been used in prior years in the absence of comparable uncontrolled sales, the existence of a comparable uncontrolled sale in a subsequent year could render the resale price method inapplicable. Thus, if a company has not in the past made uncontrolled sales and is contemplating doing so, it must consider what impact such sales might have on the pricing method used for all of its controlled sales.

CAPITAL EXPENDITURES VERSUS DEDUCTIBLE REPAIRS AND MAINTENANCE

The tax treatment of repairs depends on whether they are classified as ordinary or extraordinary. An ordinary repair is defined as one that does not materially increase the value or extend the life of the asset, whereas an extraordinary repair does, in fact, extend an asset's life.

Financial Accounting for Maintenance and Repairs. In the case of ordinary repairs, proper financial accounting requires that generally such costs should be charged to expense when incurred. Because repairs do not usually occur ratably throughout the year, it is acceptable to account for such repairs by use of a budgetary allowance.

In the case of extraordinary repairs, the expenditures are ideally treated as replacements. A theoretically ideal way of recording extraordinary repairs is to eliminate the cost of the replaced parts from the asset account, relieve the accumulated depreciation account of the depreciation provided thereon, and charge the asset account with the entire cost of the new parts. Not as theoretically correct is the expedient of charging extraordinary repairs to the accumulated depreciation account.

Because of the difficulty of distinguishing between ordinary and extraordinary repairs (as well as between capital and noncapital expenditures), it is common practice to establish a minimum rule whereby all costs below a certain dollar amount (e.g., $500) are treated as current expenses whether or not they have a useful life of more than a year.

Tax Accounting for Maintenance and Repairs. The general tax accounting rule regarding the treatment of repairs is found in the regulations under Section 162 of the Code dealing with ordinary and necessary business expenses. Regulation Sec. 1.162-4 provides for the current deduction of the cost of incidental repairs that neither materially add to the value of the property nor appreciably prolong its life, unless they are treated as part of the cost of goods sold or are added to basis.

On the other hand, repairs that are of the nature of replacements must either be capitalized and depreciated *or* charged against the depreciation reserve account. A special rule applies (see discussion below) if the taxpayer elects to claim depreciation under the "Asset Depreciation Range" system.

In *Union Pacific R.R. Co. v. U.S.,* 99 US 402 (1878), the Supreme Court distinguished repairs from capital expenditures as follows:

> Theoretically, the expenses chargeable to earnings include the general expenses of keeping up the organization of the company, and all expenses incurred in operating the works and keeping them in good condition and repair; whilst expenses chargeable to capital include those which are incurred in the original construction of the works, and in the subsequent enlargement and improvement thereof.

Conformity and Consistency.   There is no technical requirement that the tax method of accounting for repairs conform to financial accounting. However, because of the factual nature of the distinction between what constitutes a repair as opposed to an improvement, it would be difficult to sustain a position that an item constitutes a currently deductible repair for tax purposes if it is capitalized for financial accounting purposes. On the other hand, revenue agents frequently challenge the deductibility of repair items whatever the book treatment of the items.

It would also appear that policies regarding the treatment of repairs should constitute methods of accounting that, if used consistently over a period of years, should not be subject to adjustment by the Service in the ordinary case. However, the courts have never been able to resolve satisfactorily the question of consistency versus capitalization.

Compare, for example, the case of *Cincinnati, New Orleans and Texas Pacific Railway Co.* (Ct. Cl.) 70-1 USTC par. 9344, with the case of *Mountain Fuel Supply Co.* (CA-10) 71-2 USTC par. 9681.

In the *Cincinnati Railway Co.* case, the court held that the Commissioner could not change the taxpayer's consistently applied method of accounting whereby all items costing less than $500 were charged to expense rather than capitalized and depreciated. The Court determined that income was clearly reflected for tax purposes regardless of the fact that, under the minimum rule, some items were expensed that had a useful life in excess of one year.

In *Mountain Fuel,* however, the court held that the Commissioner did not erroneously change the taxpayer's method of accounting by requiring the capitalization of expenditures for the maintenance and repair of the taxpayer's natural gas pipelines instead of allowing it to expense them as it had consistently done.

Asset Depreciation Range and Repair Allowance.   In order to minimize the amount of time wasted in disputes between revenue agents and taxpayers over differences regarding useful lives for purpose of depreciation, Congress in 1971 added provisions to Section 167 of the Internal Revenue Code that established a new elective method that is binding on the Service and the taxpayer. This new system is known as the "Asset Depreciation Range (ADR) System." An additional feature of this new system is the concept of repair allowance. Under the repair allowance provisions, the taxpayer may continue to deduct repair expenses as in the past and, as we have discussed above, run the risk that an examining agent will take a different view as to what constitutes a repair; or the taxpayer who has elected ADR may instead elect to apply the percentage repair allowance rule.

Percentage Repair Allowance Rule.   Under application of the percentage repair allowance rule, a repair allowance percentage is established for each class of property. For example, the repair allowance percentage for tractor units used over the road is presently 16.5 percent. This percentage is then applied by the taxpayer to the average unadjusted basis of the applicable property in order to arrive at a maximum repair allowance. Next the taxpayer must compute the amount of expenditures for the repair, maintenance, rehabilitation, or improvement of the "repair allowance property" within the class. The taxpayer must exclude any expenditures that are clearly capital additions (see below regarding "excluded additions"). If the total nonexcluded expenditures are less than the amount of the repair allowance, the entire amount of expenditures is treated as currently deductible and will not be questioned by the agent. On the other hand, if the total expenditure exceeds the repair allowance, the excess must be treated as a property improvement and must be capitalized.

Excluded Additions.   Expenditures that constitute additions are not covered by the above percentage rule; rather, such expenditures must be capitalized and depreciated. Regulation Sec. 1. 167(a)-11(d)(2)(vi) provides that the following expenditures would constitute excluded additions:

1. An expenditure that substantially increases the productivity of an existing identifiable unit of property over its productivity when first acquired by the taxpayer (note: Whenever we see the term "substantial" used in such a context, we are reminded of the Supreme Court Justice who once defined the term substantial to mean "more than minimal." Thus, if the nature of the repair is to, say, install radial steel tires in place of old nylon ones, thereby increasing the gas mileage of the unit, would an agent come in and take the position that productivity has been substantially increased?)

2. An expenditure that substantially increases the capacity of an existing unit of property over its capacity when first acquired by the taxpayer

3. An expenditure that modifies an existing unit of property for a substantially different use

4. An expenditure for an identifiable unit of property that is either an addition or a replacement

5. An expenditure for replacement of a component of an identifiable unit of property if gain or loss is recognized on retirement of the old one

6. An expenditure for additional cubic or linear space in a building or structure

7. An expenditure for the replacement of a material portion of lines, cables, and poles of certain utilities.

Lease Cost Versus Construction Loss.   A taxpayer purchased land for the purpose of constructing new plant facilities. Because it was unable to obtain customary permanent financing for the project, it entered into a sale-and-leaseback agreement with an insurance company whereby, upon completion, the taxpayer would sell the property to the insurance company for $2,400,00 and lease it back for an initial term of 30 years. Upon completion of the plant, the taxpayer found that its total cost in purchasing the land and constructing the plant was about $3,200,000. What is the result?

Financial Accounting Treatment.   Paragraph 21 of APB Opinion No. 5 concluded that the sale and leaseback usually cannot be accounted for as independent transactions (i.e., neither the sale price nor the annual rental can be objectively evaluated independently of the other). Accordingly, material gains or losses resulting from the sale of properties that are the subject of sale-and-leaseback transactions should be amortized over the life of the lease as an adjustment of the rental cost. The related tax effect should also be amortized over the life of the lease.

Tax Accounting Treatment.   We have referred previously to the fact that the occurrence of transactions gives rise to taxability. In the area of gains and losses, the transactions that trigger the tax effect are sales or exchanges. For example, Section 1002 of the Code states that, except as otherwise provided, on the sale or exchange of property the entire amount of gain or loss (i.e., amount realized less basis) shall be recognized. How does the rule apply to the specific situation? There was a sale for $2,400,000. Cost basis was $3,200,000. Loss recognized is $800,000. In the actual case [see *Leslie Co.* 64 TC 247 (1975) aff'd 76-2 USTC 9553 (CA-3)], the Service admitted the general rule but argued that an exception applied, namely, the provision of Section 1031 that no gain or loss shall be recognized on the exchange of like-kind property, when taken in conjunction with Reg. Sec. 1.1031(a)-1(c) which treats a leasehold of 30 years or more as being equivalent to a fee interest. The court found that a sale and not an exchange had taken place, but six members of the Tax Court dissented.

Conformity and Consistency.   The *Leslie* case is of particular interest with respect to the conformity question—especially in light of what Judge Irwin had to say in the majority opinion regarding the book treatment of the transaction:

> From an accounting standpoint it is true that the loss, being an extraordinary item, may cause a distortion of income. That is probably why petitioner amortized the unrecovered costs over the 30-year term in its financial statements. Petitioner's treatment of the item on the books, however, is not dispositive of the issue for tax purposes. It is not at all uncommon to find that the book and tax treatment of a given transaction differ. Although losses may be amortized for book purposes, nothing in the Code permits such amortization for tax purposes.

OTHER EXPENSES

Research and Development Costs.   According to the background information set forth in Appendix A to Statement of Financial Accounting Standards No. 2 (FASB Statement No. 2), "Accounting for Research and Development Costs," total expenditures in the United States for research and development activities in 1973 were about $30 billion, of which $20 billion were expended by the private sector.

Financial Accounting Treatment.   FASB Statement No. 2 provides that proper financial accounting requires that all research and development costs be charged to expense when incurred.

The definition in FASB Statement No. 2 of "research" and "development" is as follows:

> 1. *Research* is planned search or critical investigation aimed at discovery of new knowledge with the hope that such knowledge will be useful in developing a new product or service (hereinafter "product") or a new process or technique (hereinafter "process") or in bringing about a significant improvement to an existing product or process.
>
> 2. *Development* is the translation of research findings or other knowledge into a plan or design for a new product or process or for a significant improvement to an existing product or process whether intended for sale or use. It includes the conceptual formulation, design, and testing of product alternatives, construction of prototypes, and operation of pilot plants. It does not include routine or periodic alterations to existing products, production lines, manufacturing processes, and other on-going operations even though those alterations may represent improvements and it does not include market research or market testing activities.

Examples and discussion in FASB Statement No. 2 that follow the above definitions indicate that, in the financial accounting sense:

1. The modification of the design on a product or process would be included within the meaning of research and development.

2. Legal work in connection with patent applications would be *excluded*.

3. The costs of intangibles purchased from others for a particular research and development project are research and development costs if they have no alternative future use.

Tax Accounting Treatment.   Code Section 174 provides for special tax treatment of research and development costs. Under this section, a taxpayer has available two alternative methods for treating research and development costs. First, the taxpayer may elect to deduct such costs currently. Second, the taxpayer who does not elect to deduct such costs currently may treat them as deferred items and amortize them over the determinable useful life. If the resulting property has no determinable useful life, they may be amortized over a period of 60 months or more. The amortization period commences in the first month in which the taxpayer realizes benefits from the expenditures.

The types of expenditures that are subject to this special tax treatment are defined in Reg. Sec. 1.174-2 as being expenditures incurred in connection with the taxpayer's trade or business that represent research and development costs in the experimental or laboratory sense. The term includes all such costs incident to the development of an experimental or pilot model, a plant process, a product, a formula, an invention, or similar property, and the improvement of already existing property of the type mentioned. The term does not include expenditures such as those for the ordinary testing or inspection of materials or products for quality control or those for efficiency surveys, advertising, or promotions. However, the term includes the costs of obtaining a patent, such as attorney's fees expended in making and perfecting a patent application. On the other hand, the term does not include the costs of acquiring another's patent, model, production, or process.

Of particular interest to the financial manager of a new company that is developing new products is the 1974 U.S. Supreme Court decision in *Snow v. Comm.*, 416 US 500 (1974), wherein the Court held that the election to currently deduct such expenditures is available to a developing company even though the company has not yet reached the point of making sales of the product. Prior to this decision, the Service had taken the position that such a developing company was not yet engaged in carrying on a trade or business.

Conformity and Consistency.   The alternative tax methods discussed above are available regardless of the method used by the taxpayer in the financial statements.

The election to deduct research and development costs currently is made by claiming the deductions in the income tax return for the first taxable year in which such expenditures are incurred. Once made, the election is binding on all future years unless the taxpayer applies for and obtains the Commissioner's consent either to change the overall method or to apply a different method to particular projects. Likewise, the taxpayer who is currently deferring such costs must, in order to change to the current deduction method, apply for and obtain the consent of the Commissioner. Application for permission to change to a different method is made by filing a letter with the Commissioner not later than the last day of the first taxable year in which the taxpayer proposes to use the new method.

Demolition and Abandonment Losses.   APB Statement No. 4 provides in part that if productive facilities have become worthless, the unamortized cost should be recognized as a current loss. This position is consistent with the basic cost-recovery concept of financial accounting. A review of excerpts in various financial statements as summarized in the 1975 edition of *Accounting Trends and Techniques* indicates that this position is followed in many types of situations, although the current loss is not necessarily taken in the year of abandonment but often in an earlier year when the facts indicate that costs can no longer be recovered through continuing operations.

Because the tax aspects of a situation depend on the occurrence of a transaction or a recognizable event, the tax rules in the case of the timing of losses can often differ from proper financial statement treatment.

Demolition Losses.   Under Section 165 of the Code, the taxpayer is generally allowed a deduction for any loss sustained during the taxable year that is not compensated for by insurance or otherwise. The amount of such loss is limited to the adjusted basis of the property. With respect to the demolition of a building, the obvious tax issue involved should be whether or not a loss has been sustained.

The Internal Revenue Service has consistently taken the position that a loss is generally sustained upon the demolition of a building provided that, at the time the building was purchased, there was no intention to demolish it. On the other hand, if there was such an intention to demolish at the time the building was acquired, the Service is of the view that no loss deduction is allowable. The Courts have generally followed this position with the modification of some, including the Tax Court, that if the purpose of the demolition is to construct a new building, then the adjusted basis of the old building cannot be deducted as a loss but must be added to the basis of the new one and depreciated over the life of the new building.

.It should be recognized that a demolition loss is really different in concept from other types of losses envisaged by Section 165. For example, a casualty loss or a theft loss is triggered by an outside agency, whereas a demolition is a voluntary act. Likewise, in the case of a casualty, it is clear that the economic loss occurs at the time of the casualty. However, in the case of the demolition, it is less clear that an economic loss occurs at the time of the demolition. Rather, the demolition loss is attributable directly to the fact that the economic life of the building has ended sooner than originally estimated. The loss really took place in earlier years,

An example should make this point clearer. Let us assume that a new grocery store was constructed in 1956 at a cost of $1 million. Based on its historical data regarding the economic life of a supermarket, the taxpayer commenced depreciating the building over 20 years; however, the Service upon examining the return changed the life to 40 years. Twenty years later, in 1976, the taxpayer determined that the old supermarket was no longer competitive. Accordingly, it was demolished and replaced by a new modern structure. In this situation, the facts show that the taxpayer's original assessment of the useful life of the building was correct. That is, if a 20-year life had been used, the adjusted basis of the old building in 1976 would be zero and there would be nothing left to deduct upon demolition. However, because the Service had adjusted the life to 40 years, the adjusted basis in 1976 is $500,000 assuming straight-line depreciation. Thus, logic indicates that the taxpayer be entitled to deduct this remaining basis in 1976 when the building is demolished. Note that the allowance of a $500,000 deduction in 1976 does not put the taxpayer in as good a position as would use of the original 20-year life estimate, because the shorter life would have resulted in additional cash flow from 1956 to 1976 as a direct result of larger depreciation deductions.

Abandonment Losses. If an asset is abandoned, the tax loss deduction rules depend on whether or not the asset is depreciable. In the case of nondepreciable property, Reg. Sec. 1.165-2 provides for the allowance of a loss in an amount equal to the basis of the abandoned asset. The loss is deductible in the taxable year in which the loss is sustained regardless of the year in which the overt act of abandonment occurs.

In the case of depreciable property, special rules are provided in the regulations under Section 167 dealing with depreciation. For example, Reg. Sec. 1.167(a)-8(a)(4) provides for the allowance of a deductible loss at the time of actual physical abandonment of a depreciable asset in the amount of the adjusted basis of the asset. This provision applies only in the case of an actual physical abandonment. If the asset is not physically abandoned but is, rather, transferred to a supplies or scrap account, then a loss in the amount of the excess of the adjusted basis over the estimated salvage or fair market value will be allowed only if

1. The retirement is an abnormal retirement, or
2. The retirement is a normal retirement from a single-asset account, or

3. The retirement is a normal retirement from a multiple-asset account in which the depreciation rate was based on the maximum expected life of the longest-lived asset contained in the account.

Vacation Pay. The method used in accounting for vacation pay on financial statements varies over a wide range of alternatives. At one end of the spectrum is the practice of expensing vacation pay only at the time of disbursement of vacation pay. In the middle of the spectrum is the practice of expensing vacation pay as of the eligibility date. At the other end is the practice of accruing vacation pay in the year the employee performs services regardless of whether or not the vacation pay "earned" is vested.

The tax rules regarding the deduction of vacation pay are interesting in their complexity, if for no other reason. For historians, they are also of interest because of the long period of time it took Congress to resolve the problem of the deductibility of contingent vacation pay. The rules as they presently apply consist of the following:

1. Vacation pay should be accrued in advance of the year in which vacations are taken (i.e., in the year services are performed and vacation is "earned") if
   (a) The liability to a specific person has been clearly established, and
   (b) The amount of liability to each person can be computed with reasonable accuracy.

Rev. Rul. 54-608, 1954-2CB8

2. With respect to contingent vacation pay, Code Section 463 provides that accrual-basis taxpayers shall be permitted to elect to accrue such contingent vacation pay in advance of the year of vacation on the following basis:
   (a) The deduction is for reasonable additions to a vacation pay accrual account for vacation pay earned before the close of the year of accrual and payable in the year of accrual or the following 12 months,
   (b) To prevent double deductions, a change to the accrual method permitted by Section 463 requires the establishment of a suspense account in an amount equal to the opening accrual account balance (less possible adjustments),
   (c) The suspense account could trigger an additional deduction in a subsequent year if the ending balance in the accrual account should dip below that of the opening suspense account balance.

Employee Benefit Plans. Business practice is replete with a myriad of plans commonly referred to as "employee benefit plans." It is difficult to categorize them, but for the purpose of analysis we shall use the following categories:

A. Postretirement benefits
   1. Funded
      a. Defined benefits
      b. Defined contributions
   2. Unfunded
      a. Term life insurance
      b. Medical care benefits
      c. Deferred compensation
   3. Stock settlements
B. Preretirement benefits
   1. Relocation expenses
   2. Medical care benefits
   3. Fringe benefits

Financial Accounting Treatment.

PENSION PLANS. APB Opinion No. 8 deals specifically with the problems of financial accounting for the cost of pension plans and concludes that pension cost should be accounted for on the accrual basis and, in most cases, the cost of the plan should be accounted for on the assumption that the company will continue to provide the benefits called for—regardless of whether or not the plan is funded. This financial accounting distinction between accounting for pension costs as opposed to funding the plan is a significant one. It implies that current operations are to be charged with the entire cost of benefit payments. In order to determine the pension costs, an actuarial cost method should be used that is rational, systematic, and consistently applied. Amortization of past service costs should also be rational, systematic, and not in excess of annual tax limitation provisions.

DEFINED CONTRIBUTION PLANS.   In the Case of a defined contribution plan whereby contributions must be made in accordance with a specified formula and benefit payments will be based on the amounts accumulated from such contributions, the cost for each year should be the amount contributed to the plan.

However, if a defined contribution plan also calls for defined benefits and the substance of the plan is to provide the defined benefits, the annual cost must be determined in accordance with the rules applicable to defined benefit plans.

DEFERRED COMPENSATION CONTRACTS.   APB Opinion No. 12 deals with financial accounting for deferred compensation contracts with individual employees and concludes that such contracts should be accounted for under the accrual method whereby the estimated amount to be paid under each contract should be accrued in a systematic and rational manner over the period of active employment.

STOCK SETTLEMENTS.   In the case where the employee benefit plan provides for compensation in the form of stock of the employer (e.g., some stock option, stock purchase, and stock award plans), APB Opinion No. 25 requires that the compensation cost be recognized as an expense of the periods in which the employee performs services.

Tax Accounting Treatment.   You may recall that a primary reason for the difference between tax accounting and financial accounting is that, in many cases, the Code provides specific requirements that must be met in order to obtain a specific tax result. This is especially true in the area of the deductibility of the costs of employee benefit plans. Summarized below are the detailed tax rules relating to various types of employee benefit plans.

PENSION PLANS.   In the case of defined benefit plans, Code Section 404 allows a current deduction for contributions to a trust under a qualified plan that meets the requirements of Section 401. The amount of the deduction is subject to limitations based on actuarially determined normal cost and unfunded past service credits.

If contributions are made to a pension trust and the plan is not qualified, contributions paid are deductible only in the year the amount is includible in income of the employee.

If the pension plan is not funded, no deduction would be allowable until the pension was paid regardless of when accrued and regardless of forfeitability.

DEFINED CONTRIBUTION PLANS.   In the case of defined contribution plans, Code Section 404 also allows a current deduction for contributions to a trust under a qualified plan. The amount of the deduction is subject to limitations based on the amount of compensation paid to the employees covered by the trust. Generally, the limitation is 15 percent of covered compensation.

If the defined contribution plan is not a qualified plan, deduction is permitted only in the year the employee includes in gross income the amount attributable to the employer contribution. The applicable year of deduction and inclusion is the year in which the employee's interest is not subject to a substantial risk of forfeiture.

UNFUNDED DEFERRED COMPENSATION.   Let us assume that a corporation adopts a deferred compensation plan whereby it contracts with certain key employees to defer payment of a portion of their salary until they reach a certain age. We have already seen that proper financial accounting requires accrual of the liability in the year the services are performed. However, for income tax purposes, the corporation will be entitled to a deduction only when payments of the deferred compensation are actually made to the employee.

STOCK SETTLEMENTS.   If the employer corporation provides additional compensation by use of a qualified stock option plan, it will be entitled to no tax deduction unless the employee disposes of the stock prematurely, in which case the corporation is entitled to a tax deduction in an amount equal to the ordinary income that the employee is required to recognize. The 1976 Tax Reform Act eliminated future grants of "qualified" options.

If a nonqualified stock option is granted to an employee, the employer corporation will be entitled to a tax deduction equal to the excess of the fair market value of the option (if it has an ascertainable fair market value) over any amount paid for it.

It should be noted that current tax laws permit a corporate employer to fund a qualified plan by making contributions of employer stock to a qualified stock bonus trust rather than contributing cash. If corporate stock is contributed, the employer corporation receives a tax deduction equal to the fair market value of the contributed stock. Thus, instead of the qualified plan being a cash drain to the employer, it can serve to generate additional working capital because of the tax deduction obtained. In evaluating such a proposed plan, the existing shareholders must be aware of the effect of dilution of their current interests resulting from the buildup of company shares in the trust.

Relocation Expenses.   An employer can generally obtain a deduction for amounts it pays to employees to reimburse them for costs of moving from one job location to another. The tax law requires that the employee must include the amount of reimbursement in gross income. The employee is then entitled to take a deduction for certain moving expenses incurred. However, the amount of the deduction is subject to various limitations. For example, the deduction for temporary living expenses plus house-hunting trips plus expenses incident to the purchase and sale of residences is limited to an overall amount of $3,000. Moreover, the expenses related to house-hunting trips and temporary living expenses may not exceed $1,500 of the $3,000.

Medical Care Benefits.   Under present law, it is possible for a corporation to adopt a medical reimbursement plan whereby the company can agree to reimburse certain employees for medical care costs of the employee, his or her spouse, and dependents. If carefully drawn, the employer corporation will be entitled to a tax deduction in the amount of the reimbursements and the employee will not be required to include such amounts in gross income.

Warranty and Other Anticipated Costs and Revenue Adjustments.   In dealing with these items, the question is when is an obligation recognized as a liability (or when should a revenue overstatement be recognized)? This is a problem both in financial reporting and tax accounting. The answers in tax accounting are frequently perplexing.

Financial Accounting Treatment.   Various types of estimated or contingent liabilities require current accrual in financial accounting. These include:

1. Additions to allowances for uncollectible accounts
2. Additions to allowances for expected cash discounts on outstanding receivables
3. Additions to estimated liabilities for possible future product warranty service
4. Additions to estimated liabilities for estimated, but not contingent, damages for tort claims
5. Accrued bonuses payable to persons who must still be employed at a later date in order actually to receive them
6. Contributions to a trusteed supplemental unemployment plan for employees

7. Estimated costs of performing future services where a prepayment for the services has already been received and included in income
8. Additions to estimated liabilities for nonvested sick pay
9. Estimated employment taxes on accrued compensation

Tax Accounting Treatment.   The tax accounting rule regarding the time of accrual of expenses was long ago established by the Supreme Court in the case of *U.S. v. P. Chauncey Anderson* 1 USTC 154 (1926), in which the Court held that an item accrues for tax purposes in the year in which all events have occurred that determine the fact of liability and the amount is determinable with reasonable accuracy. This rule, although simple to state, has been difficult to apply in many cases. With respect to the types of situations referred to above, interpretation of the "all events" test has led to the following applications:

Description	*Application*
1. Bad debt reserves	Notwithstanding the general rule, Code Section 166(c) permits the use of the reserve method in lieu of the specific charge-off method.
2. Estimated cash discounts	Book reserves set up in anticipation of cash discounts are not deductible for tax purposes.
3. Warranty reserves	Annual additions to warranty reserves are not allowable deductions for tax purposes since the fact of liability to a particular person is not certain.
4. Estimated tort claims	No tax deduction allowable until the fact of liability is certain even if the amount is reasonably ascertainable.
5. Accrued bonuses	No tax deduction for accrued bonuses if the employee must still be employed at some date in the future in order to receive payment.
6. Supplemental unemployment plan	The IRS has ruled that contributions to a trusteed Supplemental Compensation Plan are not deductible at the time the employer makes transfers to a contingency fund. Rather, deduction is permitted only in the year in which the liability to pay is fixed.
7. Estimated costs of future services	The Tax Court has refused to allow advance deduction of estimated costs of performing future services even in dance contract situations where the taxpayer has received prepayment for those services and included the prepayment in income.
8. Reserves for nonvested sick pay	No tax deduction allowable in the year of accrual because the fact of liability is not certain even though the amount of the liability is reasonably ascertainable because it is based on hours worked during the year of the book accrual.
9. Employment taxes on accrued compensation	FICA and FUTA taxes attributable to accrued wages are not deductible in the year the wages are accrued. Rather, they are deductible only in the subsequent year.

COSTS OF TAX-EXEMPT ORGANIZATIONS ALLOCABLE TO UNRELATED BUSINESS INCOME

To this point, we have been discussing differences between tax and financial accounting relating to profit-seeking enterprises and have indicated that the tax accounting treatment must be considered because tax dollars relate to cash flow which, in turn, ultimately affects the overall profitability of the enterprise. We now turn to organizations that do not exist to make a profit. Must these nonprofit organizations also be aware of the intricacies of tax accounting? As we shall see, the answer appears to be a resounding yes.

Financial Accounting Treatment.   Recent industry audit guides have been issued by the AICPA to aid in the examination of such nonprofit organizations as voluntary health and welfare organizations, hospitals, and colleges and universities.

Tax Accounting Treatment.   The importance of tax accounting to the financial manager of a nonprofit organization relates to the question, "When is a nonprofit organization not a nonprofit organization?" The tax answer is that, to the extent the organization has "unrelated business taxable income," it is in business for profit and it must pay a tax on that unrelated income in excess of $1,000 per year.

The term "unrelated business taxable income" is a net concept representing the excess of gross income derived from the carrying on of an unrelated trade or business less deductions directly connected therewith. Summarized below are the concepts that must be applied in order to determine those costs that are directly connected with the gross income from unrelated businesses.

Directly Connected.   As noted above, in order to be deductible, the expenses must be "directly connected" with the carrying on of the unrelated trade or business. The regulations state that, in order for an item to be "directly connected," it must have "proximate and primary" relationship to the carrying on of that business.

1. EXPENSES ATTRIBUTABLE SOLELY TO UNRELATED BUSINESS.   Any expenses that are attributable solely to the conduct of the unrelated business would qualify as being "proximately and primarily" related.

EXAMPLES

(a) Salaries of personnel employed full-time in carrying on the unrelated business

(b) Depreciation of a building used entirely in the conduct of the unrelated business

2. DUAL USE OF FACILITIES OR PERSONNEL.   The regulations provide that where facilities or personnel are used both to carry on exempt functions and to conduct unrelated trade or business, expenses, depreciation and overhead items should be allocated between the two uses on a reasonable basis.

EXAMPLE: The president of the organization, who receives a salary of $20,000, devotes 10 percent of work time to the unrelated business. $2,000 would be deductible from gross income.

3. EXPLOITATION OF EXEMPT FUNCTION.   The exploitation of exempt function provision is an unusual feature of the tax law. It applies in situations where the organization incurs expenses that relate in some manner to the unrelated business but that are incurred primarily in connection with the conduct of the exempt function. Such expenses can be deducted only if they would normally be incurred by a taxable organization. Even so the deduction is limited to the excess of such deductions over exempt activity income. Finally, the allocation of such deductions to unrelated income cannot result in a loss.

Listed below are some examples of activities that it has been held represent an unrelated trade or business of an exempt organization:

1. Advertising in publications: Under Reg. Sec. 1.513-1, the profits of exempt organizations from the sale of advertising in periodicals, journals, and magazines

they publish are unrelated business income unless the advertising activities contribute importantly to the accomplishment of the exempt purpose.

2. Trade shows: The regulation also provides that a trade association's charges to exhibitors and public admission fees in connection with trade shows are exempt from unrelated business income tax so long as the purpose of the show is to promote demand for the industry's products in general. But if the purpose is to provide a sales facility for individual exhibitors, the income is taxable.

3. Public customers of clubs: If an exempt organization regularly operates a club in such a way that not only members but also guests regularly use the facilities, the Service has ruled that the operation of the facility amounts to carrying on of an unrelated trade or business and the income attributable to nonmember use may be subjected to tax.

MISCELLANEOUS TOPICS

Cash-Basis Tax Returns Versus Accrual-Basis Financial Statements.   When the cash basis of accounting is used, the effects of transactions on income and expense of a period are recognized only when cash is actually or constructively received or when expenditures are actually made. On the other hand, the essence of the accrual basis of accounting is to determine periodic income by measuring all economic resources and changes in them rather than simply recording receipts and payments of money. Nevertheless, there is a certain cash orientation in accrual accounting. One good reason for the focus on cash is that if a business is profitable, its income taxes must be paid with cash. The Internal Revenue Service does not like to accept used equipment in payment of taxes, although it will seize it if nothing else is available.

In those situations where the profits of the business represent a buildup in noncash resources (e.g., accounts receivable of a service company), it makes sense to try to compute the income tax on the cash basis so that the noncash resources are not impaired. On the other hand, such a business would continue to measure periodic income for financial accounting purposes under the accrual basis so that its management and those with whom they deal in financial matters can have a better picture of how the business is progressing. Can the cash basis be used for tax and the accrual basis for financial reporting purposes?

Financial Accounting Treatment.   It goes almost without saying that generally accepted accounting principles require the use of the accrual method of accounting. Moreover, certain regulatory agencies require the use of the accrual method for reporting purposes.

This is not to say that cash-basis financial statements cannot be, or are not, prepared. Businesses may prepare such statements and they may be audited. However, such statements are not in accord with generally accepted accounting principles and, if an accountant's opinion were to be rendered, disclosure would be required of the general nature, amount, and net effect of material accruals omitted from the cash-basis statements.

Tax Accounting Treatment.   With respect to the tax rules regarding the overall method of accounting employed by a taxpayer, the Code provides in Section 446 for the use of (1) the cash receipts and disbursements method, (2) the accrual method, (3) any other method permitted (e.g., installment method or long-term contract method), and (4) any combination of the foregoing methods.

Caveat: Section 446 also provides that (1) taxable income shall be computed under the method of accounting on the basis of which the taxpayer regularly computes income in *keeping his or her books,* and (2) the method used must clearly reflect income.

Without a doubt, Section 446 is one of the most anomalous, ambiguous and, perhaps, ill-conceived provisions in the Internal Revenue Code. For example, what are "books"? What does "clearly reflect income" mean when relating to the cash basis of accounting? Generally accepted accounting principles require the use of the accrual method in order to measure periodic income fairly. Finally, is it prudent to provide that tax accounting conform to book accounting when the objectives of the two are different? The answers to these questions, if obtainable, are not easy. However, if the goal is to use the cash method for tax accounting purposes in order to minimize the taxes currently payable and maximize the availability of cash flow and preserve the accumulation of noncash resources, an attempt must be made to answer them.

WHAT IS A "METHOD OF ACCOUNTING"?   Although we are primarily discussing the concept of the overall cash basis of accounting, it should be noted that the Service takes the view in Reg. Sec. 1.446-1(a) that the term "method of accounting" includes not only the overall method but also the "accounting treatment of any item." For this purpose, an "item" would include such things as research and development costs, interest revenue or expense, property taxes, inventory, payroll taxes, depreciation, bad debts, billing policy, sick leave, vacation pay, etc.

What are the "books"? As noted, the Service has stated that the tax accounting method shall conform to the method used in keeping the "books"—not only the overall method but also the method with respect to each item—unless some exception or deviation permits otherwise (e.g., tax accounting for research and development costs). The regulations do not define "books"; however, they do provide that the taxpayer must maintain such accounting records as will enable the filing of a correct return. In turn the accounting records are defined to include the taxpayer's regular books of account and such other records and data as may be necessary to support the entries on the books of account and on the tax return.

An interesting case that discusses this subject is *Patchen v. Commissioner,* U.S. Court of Appeals, 5th Circuit, 58-2USTC par. 9733. In *Patchen,* the partnership (organized in 1946) kept its books and filed tax returns on the cash basis in 1946 and 1947. In 1948 it installed an accrual system for book purposes but continued the consistent practice of filing tax returns on the cash basis by preparing and maintaining adjustments from the accrual to the cash basis. The Court held that the adjusting entries and records were part of the partnership's books and, further, because the cash method clearly reflected income, the Commissioner had no power to force the partnership to use the accrual method.

Patchen appears to be sound law regarding tax accounting and is especially useful in cases where the book and tax methods originally conformed but the taxpayer subsequently changed the book method. On the other hand, it poses some additional questions. For example, if in the initial year of the partnership, the accrual basis books were converted to the cash basis for tax accounting purposes, would the taxpayer's risk be greater? Moreover, if the books were actually maintained and the tax returns filed on the cash basis, but adjusting entries were then made to convert to the accrual basis for financial statement purposes, would the "books" also include these adjusting entries, thereby precluding use of the cash basis for tax purposes? There have been recent situations where the Service has denied applications by taxpayers to change to the cash method where such taxpayers are required to prepare accrual-basis statements for regulatory agencies. The Service's reasoning is that the accrual-basis statements are part of the books and records and the tax accounting method must conform to them.

In conclusion, on this point, it appears that the only safe procedure to follow is to start off using the cash method for both book and financial statement purposes, until at least two tax returns have been filed on the cash basis.

What does "clearly reflect income" mean? We have indicated that in order to use the cash method for tax purposes it must clearly reflect income, but what does this mean?

First, according to regulations, it means that in any case in which the production, purchase, or sale of merchandise is an income-producing factor, inventories must be taken into account. In this regard, it is the Service's position that the cash basis cannot result in a clear reflection of income where inventories are present. Therefore, to the extent that a business' profits are represented by a buildup in inventory, cash must still be generated to pay the taxes. Note: If such inventory buildup is attributable to inflation and does not represent "real earnings," the LIFO method may eliminate any tax thereon; but, as previously discussed, LIFO has its own peculiar conformity requirements.

Second, cash expenditures made for capital items having a life extending substantially beyond the end of the year must, even under the cash method, be charged to a capital account.

Third, with respect to prepaid interest, the tax law requires that the deduction be on the accrual basis.

Fourth, advance rental payments are not deductible on the cash basis.

Conformity and Consistency.   As noted in the *Patchen* case and in the discussion above, Section 446 requires that the tax accounting method conform to the book method, at least at the outset.

A taxpayer who subsequently changes the book method cannot also change the tax accounting method without first obtaining permission from the Service. Such permission generally is obtained by filing Form 3115 within the first 180 days of the taxable year and will ordinarily be approved if the taxpayer agrees to take any necessary adjustments into account ratably over a 10-year (or less) period (Revenue Procedure 70-27).

If a revenue agent raises an accounting method issue in the course of an examination of a return, the taxpayer has the alternative of requesting application of Revenue Procedure 70-27, thereby taking any resulting adjustment into account over a 10-year period.

Appraisals as a Basis for Allocating Cost.   Although acquisition cost is the tax basis of assets, it is sometimes difficult to determine what that acquisition cost is.

Let us take the case of the outright purchase of an operating division for a total purchase price of $10 million. Even in a nontax environment, the allocation of the $10 million has substantial meaning. Depending on whether or not allocations are made to intangible assets, whether or not such intangibles are amortizable, and other factors, the amount of future income reported each period from use of the assets will be affected. The greater the allocation to intangibles that are not amortizable, the greater the reported income.

The introduction of the income tax produces a different result. To the extent that an income tax deduction can be obtained for any portion of the purchase price, additional cash flow is generated for use in the business. In the example above, if the entire $10 million were deductible in the year of acquisition, the true cash outlay would be reduced from $10 million to $5.2 million assuming a 48-percent tax rate. To the extent that a portion of the $10 million is deductible, not in the current year but in subsequent years, the cost of acquisition can be viewed as being reduced by the present value of those future tax deductions.

Financial Accounting Treatment.   APB Opinion No. 16, issued in 1970, discusses in detail the financial accounting aspects of business combinations including application of the purchase method. Paragraphs 68 and 87 of the Opinion provide the method of allocating the cost of the assets acquired in a group. The substance of the allocation method is to assign a fair market value to all identifiable assets and liabilities (e.g., marketable securities, receivables, inventories, plant and equipment, intangible assets that can be identified and named, other assets, liabilities and accruals, etc.). Any excess of cost over the assigned values should be recorded as goodwill and, under APB Opinion No. 17, amortized on a straight-line basis over the estimated life (not to exceed 40 years). The Opinion states that independent appraisals may be used as an aid in determining the fair market values of some of the assets. The Opinion does not require that the appraisal be made prior to the acquisition, and there are many situations in practice where the allocation appraisals have been made subsequent to the acquisition.

Tax Accounting Treatment.   Because the only thing that the Code and Regulations say about allocation of purchase price is that the basis of property acquired is cost, the best way to understand the tax problems involved is to examine a couple of recent cases dealing with the question.

Winn-Dixie is a major food retailer in the southeastern United States. In 1962, Winn-Dixie acquired a chain of 35 supermarkets in Alabama from Hill Grocery Company. The agreement provided for a purchase price equal to book value of the assets acquired plus $4,420,000. No appraisal as such was apparently made at the time of or subsequent to the acquisition. However, Winn-Dixie testified that during the negotiations it requested and received detailed information regarding the occupancy cost for each of Hill's retail outlets. These costs were compared to Winn-Dixie's average occupancy for new locations. These computations produced a total net "premium value" of about $3,375,000 which was allocated to the leasehold interests. The balance of the $4,420,000 was allocated to the excess over book value of equipment, inventory and supplies.

Under these facts the U.S. Court of Appeals for the 5th Circuit held [71-1 USTC 9488] that proper tax allocation of the purchase price required that the entire $4,420,000 be allocated to nondepreciable goodwill.

This decision is of particular interest for many reasons. First, it evidences the fact that a tax allocation case can be decided without reference to the financial accounting employed—witness the fact that in a purchase situation Winn-Dixie reported goodwill of $1,045,000 but ended up with the entire excess of purchase price over Hill's net book value allocated to goodwill. Second, it evidences the lack of weight given to the taxpayer's testimony regarding the propriety of the allocation. The Court disposed of Winn-Dixie's unilateral valuation of the leases as being entirely self-serving. Third, it gives outright acceptance to a tax concept known as the "mass asset" rule. Under this rule, intangible assets are treated as a single entity that, unlike its individual components, is considered to have no determinable useful life and is nondepreciable. Fourth, and perhaps most important, it evidences the disastrous tax consequences that can befall a purchaser of a group of assets if the purchaser has no appraisal to support the allocations made.

Now let us move from Alabama to Texas. In 1964, the Houston *Chronicle* entered into an agreement to purchase the assets of the Houston *Press* for $4,500,000, none of which was allocated among the various assets prior to the sale. However, subsequent to the sale, the purchaser hired a firm of valuation engineers to appraise the various assets acquired from the *Press.* Included in their valuation was an amount of $71,200 allocable to a subscription list which the taxpayer amortized over a five-year period.

Under these facts, the same U.S. Court of Appeals for the 5th Circuit held [73-2 USTC 9537] that the $71,200 was properly allocable to subscription lists and amortizable over a five-year period. This Opinion, as was that of *Winn-Dixie,* is of interest for several reasons. First, it reaffirms the tax accounting rule that goodwill is not amortizable as a matter of law. Second, it points out that not all intangibles that look like goodwill are necessarily goodwill. Rather, if the taxpayer can prove the value and the ascertainable life of the specific intangible, it can be amortized. Third, it recognizes the mass asset rule for what it really is, namely, not a rule of law but "evidentiary failures on the part of the taxpayer." Fourth, and most important, it illustrates the importance of an independent appraisal in substantiating the tax allocation made. Thus, in *Winn-Dixie* the taxpayer without an appraisal lost; whereas, in *Houston Chronicle,* the taxpayer with an appraisal won.

Conformity and Consistency.   Neither of the cases mentioned above discussed the method or the impact of the financial statement allocations. Perhaps this is as it should be. If an allocation is made to goodwill for financial statement purposes, the amount so allocated must be amortized over a period not in excess of 40 years. If the Service does not permit this amortization for tax purposes, why should it be permitted to use the financial statement allocation to goodwill as evidence against the taxpayer? Nevertheless, a taxpayer seeking a tax deduction for amounts allocated to intangibles would be wise not only to obtain an appraisal in order to establish a value for the intangible, but also to determine the estimated useful life of the asset (i.e., shorter than 40 years) and use such life for financial statement purposes. This is so because financial statement treatment of the item as goodwill would likely be considered a type of "admission against interest" and used as evidence against the taxpayer.

Assets Contributed by Stockholders and Others.   As we have just seen, the act of acquiring assets and allocating costs to them can be a complicated process, but let us complicate it a little more. What happens if, instead of purchasing the assets, the assets are contributed to the corporation by either shareholders or nonshareholders? Will the tax accounting treatment differ from that used in the financial statement?

Financial Accounting Treatment.   APB Opinion No. 29, "Accounting for Nonmonetary Transactions," concludes that if a nonmonetary asset is received in a nonreciprocal transfer (e.g., as a contribution by a shareholder or nonshareholder), the cost should be measured by the fair market value of the assets received provided that the fair market value of the asset transferred is determinable within reasonable limits.

Tax Accounting Treatment.   For tax purposes, if a corporation acquires property from its controlling shareholders, the property so acquired keeps the same basis as it had in the hands of the shareholder. This carryover-of-basis rule also applies to property acquired from shareholders as paid-in surplus or a contribution to capital (Code Section 362).

If the transferor is a nonshareholder and property other than money is acquired as a contribution to capital, then the tax basis of the property is zero. Even if money is received as such a contribution, the tax basis of any property acquired within 12 months must be reduced by the amount of the contribution. Any money not expended during the 12-month period reduces the tax basis of the corporation's other assets.

BIBLIOGRAPHY

Bittker, Boris I., and James S. Eustice: *Federal Income Taxation of Corporations and Shareholders,* 3rd ed., Warren, Gorman & Lamont, Boston, 1971.

Commerce Clearing House: *1978 Federal Tax Course,* Commerce Clearing House, New York, 1977.

Prentice-Hall 1978 Federal Tax Course, Prentice-Hall, Englewood Cliffs, N.J., 1977.

Raby, William L.: *The Income Tax and Business Decisions,* 3rd ed., Prentice-Hall, Englewood Cliffs, N.J., 1975.

Stickney, Clyde P., and Jeffrey B. Wallace: *A Practical Guide to the Class Life (ADR) System,* Lawyers & Judges Publishing Company, Tucson, Ariz., 1977.

Chapter **24**

Management Information Systems

FELIX KAUFMAN
Partner, Coopers & Lybrand

INTRODUCTION

To begin with, one has a right to ask, "What is a *management information system?*" This is a contentious question. The term was not widely used until the late 1950s, which might suggest that it refers to something new. That might imply that management information only recently became available in some effective way.

At the same time, if management information has had standing for a long time, why the belated use of the term and the absence of previous literature and discussion? A likely explanation—which I favor—is that an awareness of MIS (management information systems) is a consequence of electronic data processing and computerization.

The awareness developed as the result of an evolution starting in the mid-1950s that is adequately described by this hypothetical sequence:

1. The computer as a data processor was conceived, designed, manufactured, and applied.

2. Even before significant experience was accumulated, designers and prospective users could see that it could provide information systems of greater power. This perception led to references to new system concepts such as "integrated" and "total" systems—never rigorously defined but generally describing concepts that people thought they understood.

3. A substantial first-generation computer experience heavily emphasized the high-volume paperwork processes dealing with employees (payroll), customers (accounts receivable), and the like. These jobs were done better and quicker but not differently and did not characterize the breakthrough we thought the computer could provide.

4. Second-generation hardware came along. It represented a big improvement in capability. We now know that the extra power was needed to expand the role of EDP on the straightforward first-generation applications. At the time, however, hardware providers attempted to titillate the market with the idea that a systems breakthrough was at hand. They promoted the view that companies could use the new computers to achieve unprecedented data processing power by designing management information systems.

There is no proof that this marketing ploy by itself accounts for the introduction of the concept. But the beginning of a formal recognition of the concept of management information systems as a marketing idea tells us something about the current absence of a definition or a well-accepted consensus about what they are. In any case, the unusual beginning does not form the basis for casual treatment of the concept or its dismissal as a "buzz phrase."

Accordingly, we can conclude that *there are management information systems.* It is a fuzzy concept, poorly understood but fairly described, though not defined, by these statements:

- They have "always" existed.
- They had no status (visibility) before the computer.
- They could not be systems of real managerial significance without the computer, because in the era of precomputer data processing the use of information was not (could not be) based on structure, discipline, and a consistent view of the uses of information. Information was fragmented, departmentalized, informal, and disintegrated.
- The concept is unfolding as the EDP technology advances rapidly.

Pursuing Some Related Confusions.   In the preceding narrative several terms were used that it will be useful to discuss further.

What Is an Integrated System?   Every institution has a set of information processes (or flows). Before the computer it was difficult to harmonize two or more of these processes that belonged together to some extent. They belonged together because they worked with some common elements of information or because certain events affected two or more of these processes. The typical precomputer conditions allowed these processes to get "out of synchronization." One file was updated and reflected current operations. Another did not. In those systems a piece of information could appear many times in different places and not be reported as the same amount in each of these places because of scheduling and processing defects. An integrated system is designed to comprehend interaction. It is harmonious. This is easier to deal with in computer-based environments (even though one must acknowledge that integrated systems have been slow to materialize).

An effective information system achieves some respectable level of integration. We cannot as yet express quantitatively the dimensions of "respectable level."

Total Systems. No generally recognized use of the term *total systems* has come to my attention. The term has not had a useful role in the evolution of philosophies that in turn bear on advanced systems design work. In fact, it is a mischievious concept. In theory, a total system comprehends all of the data requirements of a business and all of its information interconnections. It is pure—a perfect system. It does not and cannot exist. In fact, as time passes, the importance of adaptability in an information system asserts itself as a vital consideration. If change is the only certain condition, the ability to design around a comprehensive forward understanding of all needs is not possible.

A management information system should reflect these thoughts. It seeks to be as integrated as possible; it seeks to be as inclusive as possible. It does not have to be the ultimate degree of either.

Accounting's Relation to Management Information Systems. It is appropriate here to state a relationship between information systems and the principles, structural concepts, and procedures that underlie accounting. Accounting is only one part of an information system. It probably is the oldest part of the totality, best defined as a classification system, best understood and more extensively and intricately connected to the other parts. Perhaps for the state of the art as we know it now, accounting is the most important part of an information system.

The other information flows, often not formally handled before the computer, involve diverse kinds of data about operations of a nonfinancial nature and the even more complex and unstructured universe of information from outside the entity—that is, outside the organization that belongs to the management information system.

MIS: A Definition. A *management information system* is a formalized set of activities for collecting, processing, storing, and reporting operations and planning data in a manner useful to management. From a practical standpoint such systems were not sufficiently useful or effective enough to be recognized as such prior to electronic data processing. The practical concept depends on data processing technology and is augmented as technology progresses.

THE PROPERTIES OF DATA PROCESSING SYSTEMS THAT MAKE MANAGEMENT INFORMATION SYSTEMS POSSIBLE

If information systems of stature have come into existence since computers arrived, computers must have properties that information systems need. We can identify information system requirements by identifying these properties. They are:

1. The ability to process, calculate, and manipulate very quickly
2. The ability to make information flows between parts of the system occur automatically and unfailingly
3. The ability to inquire into the records to obtain status information quickly

4. The ability to ask questions that involve relationships among and within records and to obtain results quickly

5. The ability to hold and execute complex algorithms that generate information useful for decisions or in some instances, the decisions themselves

6. The ability to animate the system so that it is responsive to the user in real time, creating a condition analogous to a conversation, wherein the user specifies data, obtains results, changes the data or the program or both, obtains new results, and so on.

Processing Speed. From a management point of view, data ought to reflect the degree of currentness pertinent to the decisions for which it is to be used. For a long time, processing cycles were constrained by the cost of processing resources. To deal with a transaction instantly, at the moment it took place, was usually not technically feasible. When it was, the cost was prohibitively high.

The instant recording of most types of transactions could be accomplished only by moving part of data processing out to the transaction locale. When using manual, or even punchcard, techniques, this results in an impracticable decentralization of record keeping.

The foregoing, however, may be misleading if it causes the reader to infer that the only timely information system is one that captures transaction information instantly. In many cases, instant information capture is not necessary because there is no need to know instantly what that transaction has done to the status of the account it affects. We are going to continue to do a great deal of batch processing. Under *batch processing,* transactions are allowed to accumulate for some period of time, then are put in order according to the sequence of the affected file and processed as a single stream. In short, every updating application has its natural time cycle, the length of which is never determined exactly. Before real-time computing, processing was on a batch basis and the cycle tended to be set by the requirements of batch processing. With new technology the other extreme may become fashionable, with everything processed instantly whether or not the information is useful immediately.

Processing Connections. One illustration of the need for real-time processing can be observed by looking at the characteristics of an airline reservation system. Before the computer, and before significant developments in communications, the seats on a given flight had to be allocated on some estimated basis to the various locations in the airline system that might receive requests for space. Then came the interesting problem of knowing the total situation at any moment. Because this really was not possible, it had to follow that the availability of space could not be known accurately. This perhaps is one of the best examples of the need to move events from wherever they occur to processing at a central control point instantly. The dispersion of the system is made transparent to the user no matter where the body of information of importance is kept.

Connecting Information Flows. Precomputer information flows were significantly less integrated than they are now or can be. When organizations are dispersed or complex, there is a severe problem in making the information systems mesh. Meshing is required when an event or condition arises in one location that affects records in another. It can be a simple requirement, such as one event requiring posting to more than one file. It can also be a bit more complicated, such as one event resulting in a condition that must be reported elsewhere.

Information systems can fail in two ways. First, the parts may not be connected and the records do not mesh or agree. Second, the flows may be late and records are not synchronized in time. Computer-based systems, whose parts interconnect automatically through wire communications, should meet integration requirements smoothly and routinely. The needs are "designed in"; multiple effects are dealt with simultaneously and implied conditions are routed automatically to affected records.

Consider the case that involves inventory activity in many branch locations. Not atypical is the system that lets each unit operate its own inventory management process subject to some rules for meeting certain conditions by the interchange of data. Computers are effective in meeting this need because they allow the simultaneous maintenance of consolidated as well as branch records.

In effect, systems implemented by computers can coordinate separate but related data processing activities.

Inquiry.   An important need in an information system is the ability to obtain the status of a record. We have always had this ability, but because processing systems have been controlled by their characteristics, often we do not get current information when we query. In fact, most of the time we do not know how old that information is. A management information system of worth must give the user the ability to query rapidly. More and more, this is the ability to query instantly and to expect that the information provided thereby is current. Precomputer systems were seriously deficient in this regard. Manual records are easy to read but not accessible to most users. Computer systems using random access memories and display tube outputs appear to meet our ultimate needs in this regard. No one has yet defined a more demanding unmet requirement.

It should be recognized that inquiry frequently involves the use of data at a low level, as for example, to respond instantly to customer queries about their balances. Can such reporting, although necessary managerially, be considered a requirement? Managerial needs stretch along a wide spectrum; my own view is that simple inquiry requirements lie at the least important end of this spectrum.

Flexible Access.   The ability to scan masses of data looking for cases that meet specified conditions is the most important characteristic of the data processing that powers management information systems. In precomputer environments, based on manual and accounting machine methods, it was not practicable to examine large numbers of records in files to obtain all cases that satisfied certain conditions. Scanning was a visual process. If calculations and summarizations had to be performed, the difficulty was compounded.

We met these needs by brute force in the early computer days. Files were usually held on magnetic tape. Information on magnetic tape could move through a computer fast enough for the machine to emulate a person. The computer could look at every record and select those that met specified conditions.

The state of the art now combines random access memories and data base management software so as to make large masses of information amenable to scrutiny on the basis of many associated relationships without requiring the examination of every record that might meet the requirement.

Interactivity.   The features of inquiry, display, and access came together in a powerful union to give the user the ability to interact with the information system. This is another important property. Interaction is the property of a system that allows the user to engage in a question and answer dialogue with the machine. Each question in a string reflects the analysis of previous responses and should indicate a process in which the user gets closer to useful data as the questioning proceeds.

To be interactive, the system must allow:

1. Instant access to a data base in a highly flexible manner
2. Instant access to programs that allow the user to work on the data with an assortment of procedures and algorithms
3. The ability to display results to the user fast enough to maintain the dialogue relationship

Interactive situations vary dramatically as to the amount of data and the number of programs. Accordingly, in some situations, interactive capability can exist without large-scale data processing arrangements. In the simplest case, the user has a small data base, a simple program, and access to a terminal connected to a time-sharing system.

LEVELS OF INTERACTIVITY

The idea of an interactive relationship can best be understood by a progression through the several levels of such a relationship that might be encountered.

The first allows the system to query. The capability in its most primitive form proceeds as follows:

1. The user specifies a record wished to be seen.
2. The system displays that record instantly, that is, at the moment a query occurs at a terminal.

At the next level, the preceding sequence occurs but the user can modify the record just queried, as in the reservation of space on a passenger flight. In short, the user can update the file.

In the third case, the user wishes to operate on a problem, in contrast to updating a record. Accordingly, the sequence followed has this form:

1. Via a remote relationship (that is, from a terminal), the user requests a program.
2. The user follows the direction of the program and provides data as required.
3. The computer provides an output quickly; for practical purposes the response is instantaneous. The output is a specific answer, for example, a return on investment figure, schedules or reports, or even forecast financial statements.
4. The user examines the results and decides whether the needs have been met. In forecasting financial results for example, the user can decide that:
   (a) The results are not good enough.
   (b) The results are achieved only by violating resource limitations. (We do not have enough cash to support these needs.)
5. The user continues the dialogue, perhaps by changing the inputs in order to seek answers consonant with the objectives.
6. The user might call forth a different program to solve a subordinate part of the problem before returning to the main requirement.

All of this constitutes a dialogue.

In the foregoing, at least until the last illustration, the capabilities of the information system are primarily abilities to *provide* information. The relationship of that provider capability to decision making itself is still obscure. Nevertheless, it is clear that a management information system relates to decision making by facilitating it or doing it, and one aspect of how this can happen follows naturally from the earlier discussion about interactive relationships.

At the end of that discussion we talked about programs that solve problems. The solutions thereto may aid decision making. Alternatively, the programs may provide data useful to decision making. The elegance of this process is related to the programs we are discussing here. As a class we can describe these programs as models, so-called because they are written to represent the way a real activity behaves or the way a prospective activity might behave. In either case, the purpose is the same. We wish to study this process not by watching it over time, but by compressing time and space through the use of a computer-powered "shorthand."

Models vary widely in complexity. They help us with important decision processes because they allow us to study different ways of dealing with a situation, as when they forecast the financial consequences of alternative behavior. Models need data; the sources are familiar. Data can be provided by the formal information systems, by a very large number of sources outside of the organization itself, by guesses and estimates, and by staff work that synthesizes data by its complex use of all of these sources.

To what degree is the information system the main conduit through which data flows reach modeling activities? It is difficult to say. Once again, we confront definitional issues that may not be answerable. Nor should this cause concern; one doubts that the definitions need to be clarified. To summarize these thoughts:

- The computer as a driver of models is very powerful. That role will expand indefinitely.
- As more of the data flows in a company are handled by computers, more of the inputs to models will flow from computerized data bases.
- Many of these input requirements are not held in computerized data bases in the form needed and must be worked on first. Over time, our understanding of these needs will sharpen and the information system will deliver better input.
- A good deal of the data needed may come from external data sources. Our ability to use this information increases as these external flows are provided by other computerized systems. In some instances, the ability of one system to deliver such information will be automatic (as when computerized census data needed for marketing studies is obtained directly through electronic linkages).

It is possible, perhaps likely, that the formal processing system will not be an important provider of data to the foregoing process. How should we characterize a situation in which modeling is used effectively but without depending on formal information systems? An attempt to show these relationships is provided by Exhibit 1.

EXHIBIT 1   Relation between Modeling and Formal Information Processes

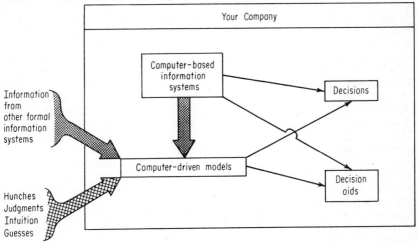

THE RELATIONSHIP OF A MIS SYSTEM TO DECISION MAKING

Most computer-based applications put into operation until now can be described as event or transaction systems. They displace clerical processes that support operations required to produce a product or provide a service. Familiar examples include:

- Processes that pay people for their efforts and keep track of the amounts
- Processes that order materials and services to replenish those used up

- Processes that track the availability of resources
- Processes that bill recipients of materials and services and keep track of payments thereon

These and other familiar examples dominate business data processing and account for the existence of the large bodies of information held in electronic media (called "data bases" and "files").

These systems are not designed to support or make management-level decisions. They exist to help an organization conduct its operations. In many, perhaps most cases, collections of these transaction processing activities are being called "MIS systems." By and large, this is a misuse of the phrase, because decision making is only occasionally being supported, and even less frequently is actually being effected by the system itself. Accordingly, if the typical information system is not a MIS system, characterizations notwithstanding, can it evolve in that direction? It may be simply a matter of time before transaction processing requirements and decision support needs are fused through the more effective use of large bodies of corporate data.

This evolution probably has already started and will probably continue. That view is rooted in two attributes of current transaction processing environments:

1. We have been programming low-level decisions for some time. At some point, the increasing elegance of these processes makes them become more than automated substitutions of clerical activities.

2. Access to files, now data bases, has been improving markedly in producing a flexibility in analyzing data, which in turn significantly improves the linkage between large bodies of information and the decision process. We have discovered better ways to tap into large masses of information.

It is worthwhile to go into these matters in greater detail.

In setting up a record-keeping system, the most primitive condition exists when the ability to evaluate the effect of transaction processing (posting) is not automated in any respect. Low-level decisions as to the presence of special or exception conditions lie outside of the processing system. They are not abetted by any logic applied by the data processing system itself. The first step upward occurs when the information system flags its own attention-requiring cases (as when customers delinquent on payments are identified by a delinquency detection logic).

Readers who are not familiar with computers need to understand that the ability to make simple decisions automatically is possible because the underlying conditions can be stated as strings of arithmetic processes. These processes may be as long and complex as required so long as the elemental steps involve arithmetic. Readers also must appreciate that an overwhelming number of logical processes have this attribute; this is often not appreciated when the logic is implemented by manual methods (or in someone's head).

For example, to detect that a customer payment is late requires comparison of the current date with a due date. People do not perceive that they do this automatically. Computers accomplish the process by comparing the two dates by subtraction (taking the number value of one from the other). The value of the answer describes the condition.

People tell when credit limits have been exceeded by comparing dollar values. Obviously, this is the instant detection of a greater than, equal to, less than condition. Computers do the same thing painstakingly. It is astonishing how much low-level decision making does or can involve strings of simple arithmetic steps. Detection of some condition in a formal automated way is easy.

The next step upward occurs when most of the "treatment" logic for that condition can be integrated into the system. The computer now selects and prints the appropriate dunning letter, frequently provoking an outraged public which personalizes the machine. Even at this point, one might argue that the situation does not have stature as a management problem. The logic can be applied by clerks, and the results are products of a clerical information system.

A higher-order situation involves the reordering of materials. The decision as to *when* and *how much* is often made by clerks but ought not to be because their participation reflects the application of decision rules that are usually too simple for the condition being evaluated.

The development of algorithms to do the job by computer makes the system operate the way it might if a corps of skilled managers made the decisions themselves. But there is still a question as to whether this example and similar ones elevate the system to management information status. Assuming that it does, a management information system exists in rudimentary form when the capability to make low-order decisions relating mainly to daily operations has been integrated into data processing.

Is this what users of the term MIS really mean or understand? That, of course, is not answerable. My perception is that users of the term believe that a management information system serves higher-order decisions. The management information system does this by providing data to *power* the decision process in which the decisions themselves are made by people or by computers (by driving the necessary algorithms in the latter case).

Retrieving Information from Large Masses of Data. We are approaching a general capability to obtain the status of any desired record about as quickly as that information could be useful. This has great value for monitoring and controlling purposes. Although its management-level uses of this capability are less important, it is hard to say how much less. Management itself is not likely to need information that relates to a specific employee or customer.

There is some evidence, however, that systems of recent vintage (late 1970s) making files instantly accessible from terminals are either useful to or intriguing to top executives who find the capability of value to them. The value arises perhaps in making the executives instantly knowledgeable about certain matters, although the need does not concern significant decision processes.

Ad Hoc Analysis. *Ad hoc analysis* for data files, as a use of a decision-support system, means the ability to supply, on demand, information that meets certain criteria which in turn can aid decision processes. Going further, it can mean the user's ability to search data to discover what criteria might be relevant to further ad hoc analysis. Essentially, ad hoc analysis is the ability to get into a large mass of data on an impromptu basis, in contrast to premeditated, designed arrangements, which produce reports of a specified content.

For quite a while, technology would let us generate only standard reports. Major improvements in the organization of records (data bases), in the capacity of electronic storage media, and the speed with which information can be examined are having a dramatic effect on the role of ad hoc analysis.

The principal development involves the organization of records. It is now common to describe this reorganization of data as a data base to differentiate its condition from conventionally organized records. The concept of a data base can be illustrated in an uncomplicated way by noting what its ultimate condition would be if there were no technical restrictions.

Imagine storing unlimited amounts of information as if each discrete unit thereof was a record unto itself. A customer record would not be stored as such. The name, address, amount owed, and every other piece of stored information would exist independently. But if the customer record in its typical form was needed, it could be secured without delay by picking up all of the component elements.

No data base management system can yet do this; nor is there evidence that such fragmentation in record design is valuable. In the current state of the art, however, we can go well beyond the rigid organization of well-understood file arrangements. We can maintain a much larger number of classifications and organize data into these categories without extensive duplication of information.

A Simple Illustration.   A conventional personnel file would probably include the age of the employee. Then, the need to list the names of all employees of a specific age could be accomplished by examining every employee record. The same need could be dealt with more efficiently by maintaining continuously tables of all employees for each age category. With such tables, there is a continuous state of readiness for that question. In a data base environment, the same readiness to answer is achieved through the use of computer programs that direct us through a mass of information and employ associative power to do so.

The foregoing discussion needs to be related in a more precise manner to the way management-level decisions are made. The typical well-understood reporting aspect of an information system is accomplished by issuing standard reports. The standard report is standard because the people who design the system agreed with the people that use the system that certain reports would be needed and that they should be issued on a regular basis at agreed-upon intervals. Do standard reports serve management decision-making requirements? It seems quite clear that they serve management control requirements, because frequently standard reports are reporting on the status of certain matters: amounts owed by customers, inventory levels, and so forth. In this role they meet management control requirements, but they are probably being gradually displaced by systems with the ability to provide the same information by querying the files at the instant a need is recognized. Financial statements, however, also meet the definition of standard reports, and they certainly represent a presentation of information in a more profound way than simple status-level output. Nevertheless one cannot identify a clear connection between the examination of financial statements and management information decision making. Financial statements and many other reports serve fundamentally as management provokers. Such reports indicate conditions (1) that induce management to believe that a problem exists, (2) which in turn requires a decision as to how the problem can be dealt with, and (3) this almost inevitably precipitates a further investigation which is likely to involve substantial additional information requirements.

Such needs are met by ad hoc reporting, which provides the ability to meet a requirement shortly after it has been defined, and does so without transforming the underlying system. Technical developments have tended to move computer-driven information systems in this direction.

A MIS system should contribute significantly to important decision-making processes extending beyond situations that lubricate simple day-to-day operational needs. It goes beyond needs based on simple logic that can be defined and programmed readily. *At the same time, it is not necessarily a capability for bringing computer-programmed order to major executive decisions.*

THE STATUS OF MIS

There is a strong connection between MIS, as the term is used here, and electronic data processing. The assessment of current MIS that follows is in the context of the elegant systems that are now technologically possible. The following assessment represents the opinion of this author.

It is useful to approach the task of assessment first by establishing a model of the environment in which MIS can be applied. The model is general enough in form to illustrate the points to be made and specific enough to allow the reader to use it as a basis for more specific research and evaluation.[1]

Overview of Information Systems.   Before appraising the current status of MIS, we must examine the broad framework in which information systems may exist. Exhibit 2 is an overview of such a framework as it exists in typical large companies. For purposes of further, more detailed analysis, the information systems potential has been broken into six areas by broad business function:

- Marketing/sales
- Production/manufacturing
- Purchasing/procurement
- Finance
- Administration
- Research/development

Within each functional area, three levels of information system activity are denoted: planning, control, and the activity itself.

Planning takes us out of a current time frame. It seeks information that will help us to decide how we want things to happen in the future. The emphasis of this chapter has been and is that the relationship of planning to operations and control from an information standpoint is not as direct or as important as prevailing attitudes imply. Frequently, distilled operational data are not consequential to planning. Accordingly, it is a mistake to equate transaction systems and management information systems.

Control is the monitoring and comparing process that allows management to compare what is happening to what is supposed to be happening. Control is linked directly to activity. Even the most detailed unit of activity accounted for by an operational process can be installed in this way. More likely, however, control is based on some degree of aggregation of activity units.

The *activity* is the paperwork aspect of some operation, payroll, for example. Although such operations provide information to other levels, their purpose is the given operation—to pay people, to procure materials, to receive payment, etc.

The connecting arrows signify the potential interactions among the business functions. Exhibit 3 then, serves as our overall "road map" as we proceed to assess the degree to which progress has been made and to identify the opportunities for information systems design in the future.

Marketing/Sales.   The marketing/sales function, in one form or another, exists in all integrated companies and was often an early target of information systems planners. It was preceded only by applications to the finance function.

Exhibit 3 looks deeper into the components of marketing/sales and introduces a new concept which will apply in all functional areas discussed. This concept is that management interest in information derived from information systems varies with the level and type of responsibility of management itself. Thus a vertical dimension applies which results in four levels of hierarchical interest and responsibility:

- Strategic planning
- Operational planning
- Control reporting
- Transaction systems

---

[1]The information systems schematics in this section are derived from work being done at Occidental Petroleum Corporation and are used with permission of that company whose Corporate Director of MIS, Edward A. Lustig, has been helpful in many ways. Recognition is also given to Arch B. Johnston, Consultant to Occidental, for his assistance in interpreting this material. All evaluations and judgments, however, are the sole responsibility of the author and relate to general practice rather than that of Occidental.

EXHIBIT 2 Information System Schematic: Overview

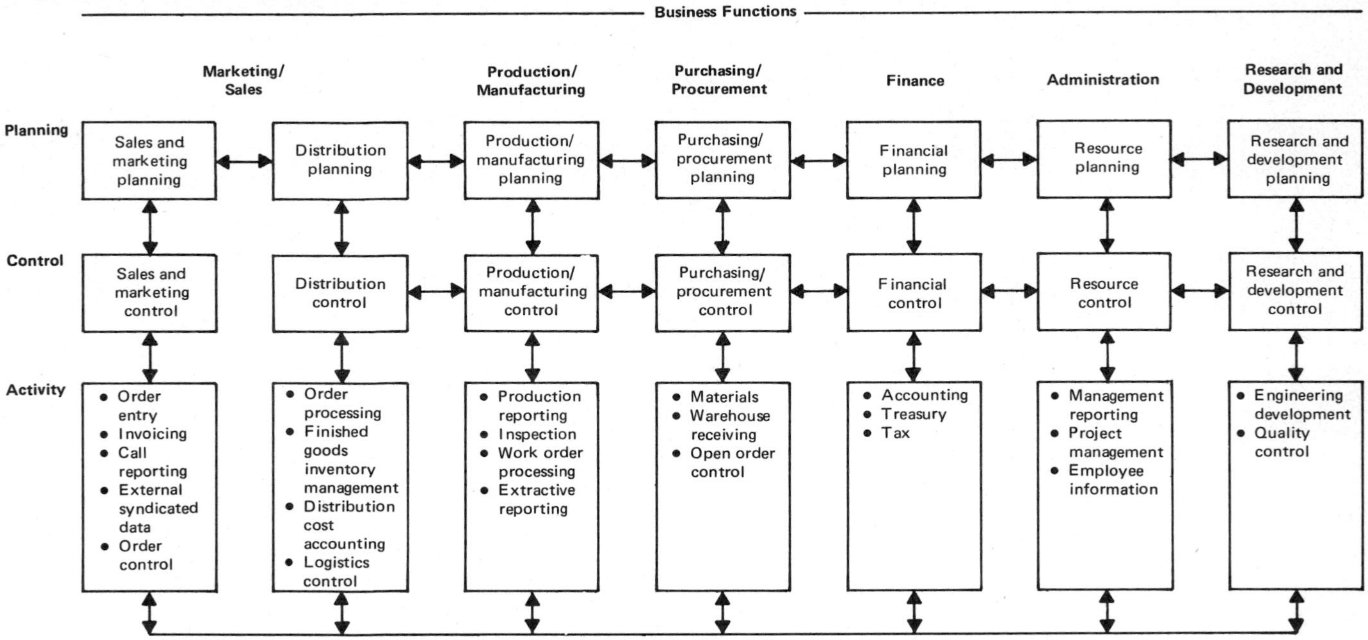

EXHIBIT 3 Information System Schematic: Marketing/Sales

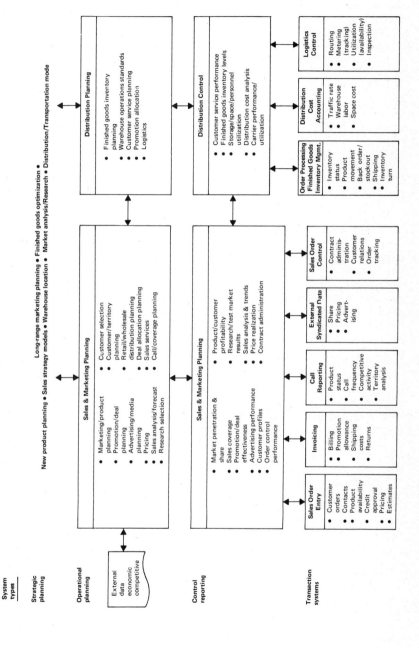

The earliest application of electronic data processing in the marketing/sales function was at the lowest level—in the transaction systems. Often this was an area already assisted by traditional tabulating (punchcard) equipment and the transition to electronic machines represented merely a faster and (sometimes) less expensive way of doing the same information processing job.

As the computer hardware improved, particularly for large volumes of fast-access data storage, applications at the transaction-system level became more pervasive, and the concept of integration grew in favor. Thus began interaction between transaction systems within the function (as when data on customer invoicing simultaneously found its place in the inventory system) and between functions (as when customer orders reached into and generated demand in the manufacturing system).

There is now wide acceptance and successful application of information systems that accomplish integration horizontally within and between functions. There has also been real progress in the upward flow of such information within the marketing/sales function to produce meaningful data at the control reporting level. These data extend beyond conventional sales analyses by areas, products, and salespeople to previously unattainable analyses of individual product and customer profitability, distribution cost analyses, and similar control and planning measures and tools that guide higher levels of management. A key element of this achievement is access to the cost data that arises from cost accounting systems at the transaction level in the production/manufacturing function. This access implies information processing interactivity at the central reporting level that is now contained in the information systems of the larger (and more successful) companies.

In the marketing/sales function, automated management information "applications" are widely in use at the transaction level. Moreover, these provide summary data, producing "applications" at the control level which in turn provide more precise and current information for the monitoring of the business and prompt identification of trouble spots. These applications, at both levels, are frequently interrelated to other applications in the same and other functional areas.

Production/Manufacturing.   Production/manufacturing, perhaps more than marketing/sales, differs widely with the nature of the specific company. Indeed, there are many large organizations in which the function may not really exist, as with those engaged in the sale of services, or resale of products manufactured by others. Where it does exist, the representative information system schematic will be tailored to the type of product(s), dispersion of manufacturing facilities, and other related criteria.

Exhibit 4 represents the type of company that produces both raw materials extractively and finished products, the latter by fabrication and by chemical or other processing.

In this functional area there has long been successful application of electronic equipment at the transaction level. In manufacturing, parts inventories were early candidates for mechanization, first with bookkeeping machines, then with punchcard equipment, and on into the era of electronic data processing. Similarly, many plants added reporting subsystems for labor, then for machine use, and finally for integrating all of these subsystems into a composite system that led to product costing, productivity, and performance reporting.

In the extractive industries, notably petroleum, systems were developed that accurately and cumulatively recorded production—by well, lease, zone, and reservoir. These systems provide both accounting information (the basis for payment of oil royalties, for instance) and operational information (the trend in gas/oil ratios, water content, production per well per day, etc.). As electronic hardware improved, more sophisticated applications became possible. These embraced

EXHIBIT 4   Information System Schematic: Production/Manufacturing

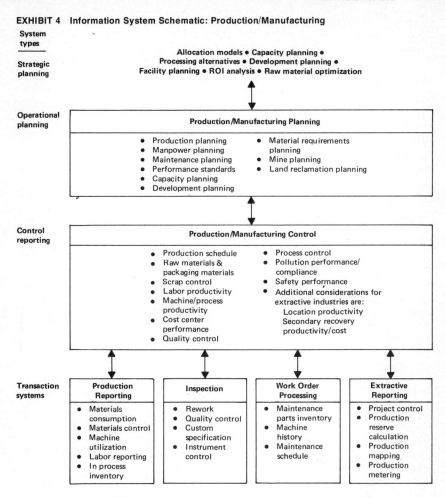

System types

Strategic planning

Allocation models ● Capacity planning ●
Processing alternatives ● Development planning ●
Facility planning ● ROI analysis ● Raw material optimization

Operational planning

Production/Manufacturing Planning

- Production planning
- Manpower planning
- Maintenance planning
- Performance standards
- Capacity planning
- Development planning

- Material requirements planning
- Mine planning
- Land reclamation planning

Control reporting

Production/Manufacturing Control

- Production schedule
- Raw materials & packaging materials
- Scrap control
- Labor productivity
- Machine/process productivity
- Cost center performance
- Quality control

- Process control
- Pollution performance/ compliance
- Safety performance
- Additional considerations for extractive industries are:
  Location productivity
  Secondary recovery productivity/cost

Transaction systems

Production Reporting

- Materials consumption
- Materials control
- Machine utilization
- Labor reporting
- In process inventory

Inspection

- Rework
- Quality control
- Custom specification
- Instrument control

Work Order Processing

- Maintenance parts inventory
- Machine history
- Maintenance schedule

Extractive Reporting

- Project control
- Production reserve calculation
- Production mapping
- Production metering

broader data bases, using more advanced mathematical and statistical methods to forecast the future. Currently, effective systems exist for simulation of behavior under a wide variety of operating practices. The capability of telescoping decades of actual practice under hundreds of combinations of variable operating conditions into minutes, or at most hours, with a large-scale computer makes possible the selection of operating modes to optimize the desired element. In the petroleum industry, for example, this optimal goal may be cost, total recoverable oil, or most oil in shortest time.

Purchasing/Procurement.   The purchasing/procurement function varies in size, complexity, and importance from company to company. In general, however, it has considerable significance and often presents opportunities for substantial cost savings. Exhibit 5 depicts the basic elements, in terms of information systems support required at the various levels.

In companies where large numbers of items are required for recurrent purchase, mechanization has been a necessity. This was an area for early application of ledger-posting machines to maintain perpetual inventories. Punchcard equipment then displaced posting machines—often with mixed results because the necessity

EXHIBIT 5   Information System Schematic: Purchasing/Procurement

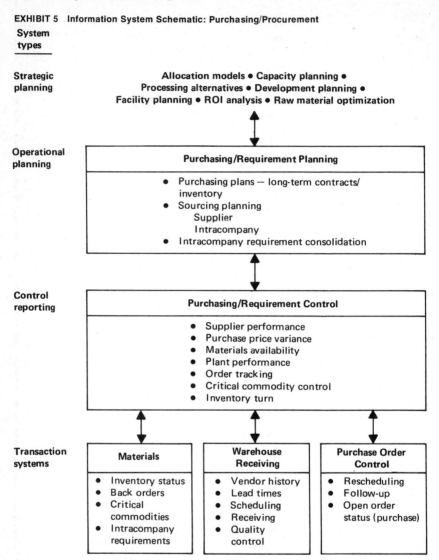

System types	
Strategic planning	**Allocation models • Capacity planning • Processing alternatives • Development planning • Facility planning • ROI analysis • Raw material optimization**
Operational planning	**Purchasing/Requirement Planning** • Purchasing plans — long-term contracts/inventory • Sourcing planning Supplier Intracompany • Intracompany requirement consolidation
Control reporting	**Purchasing/Requirement Control** • Supplier performance • Purchase price variance • Materials availability • Plant performance • Order tracking • Critical commodity control • Inventory turn

Transaction systems:

Materials
- Inventory status
- Back orders
- Critical commodities
- Intracompany requirements

Warehouse Receiving
- Vendor history
- Lead times
- Scheduling
- Receiving
- Quality control

Purchase Order Control
- Rescheduling
- Follow-up
- Open order status (purchase)

for accumulating large batches of transactions before making machine runs sometimes resulted in less current records. There were, however, lower unit processing costs, and the flexibility of machine sorting and tabulating to produce printed reports less expensively and more rapidly. The advent of computers in this functional area dramatically increased these advantages. It became possible to produce reports that not only presented the current inventory status, item by item, but also could include the indicated action, in terms of what to reorder, in what quantitites, and from whom.

Presently, many of the computerized purchasing/procurement systems and their applications are integrated, not only within the function but with the marketing/sales, production/manufacturing, and finance functions.

As computer hardware and software improve in cost effectiveness, as communications become more and more wedded to information processing, we see a major impact in the design of information systems related to the purchasing/procurement function.

It is now possible to deal on a centralized basis with large numbers of widely dispersed inventory locations, bringing to bear the economies of scale in terms of price through national contracts and volume buying with deliveries to multiple points. Many companies with such information systems are also able to engage profitably in reciprocity arrangements to ensure that their vendors, where possible, also become their customers. Other aspects of such information systems lead to better inventory management, control of surplus and slow-moving items, exchanges of critical materials among company units, and lower investment in total inventory. All of this can be seen to have high potential for bottom-line results.

In summary, information systems are widely employed in the purchasing/procurement function, and a substantial number of companies have been able to develop such systems from the grass-roots transaction level up through control reporting into operational planning. In certain industries, where procurement is a major element, there has been success in strategic planning based on inputs available from the underlying information systems.

Looking ahead, we predict more progress in this functional area. The trend toward distributed processing favors additional networks of computer communications involving low-cost, high-performance terminals with limited intelligence and economical local data bases. Thus inventory information can be maintained dynamically at the source (warehouse, plant, etc.), where it is both subject to instant inquiry and also part of a much larger and widely dispersed inventory system, the planning and control of which can be centralized.

Finance. Thus far in our discussion of the probable levels and areas of information systems utilization in business and industry we have dealt with operational functions. The conclusions have been that there is now widespread application of computerized systems and that the outlook for the future is clearly toward more such applications, both quantitatively and qualitatively. Yet the first, and by far the largest, area of company activity to be influenced by information systems concepts and successive generations of processing equipment was that of finance and accounting.

Exhibit 6 depicts a typical aggregation of activities that can be logically grouped under the finance function. Analysis of information systems costs in a typical company today will almost certainly reveal that the finance and accounting function is still one of the largest users of the facilities. Indeed, despite a trend to establish the information systems activity as a separate function within the corporate hierarchy, it is more often than not true that systems design and hardware operations are duties assigned to the chief financial executive. The reasons for this are evident. Nearly all companies exist to make a profit. Profit is usually measured in dollars. The chief financial executive has the final responsibility for developing and operating the systems which provide that measurement.

First, the record-keeping function requires systems capable of processing a large volume of transactions. The traditional accounts receivable and payable, payroll and labor distribution, cost and job accounting, etc., records must be maintained. These activities, required by law or managerial necessity, were the earliest to be mechanized and first to move from posting machines to unit record (punchcard) equipment and then to computers. Virtually all companies beyond the smallest are to some extent computerized in the finance and accounting function. "Service bureaus," whose development has paralleled the development of automated processing equipment over the years, have made information systems processing available to companies not otherwise able to acquire their own computers.

EXHIBIT 6   Information System Schematic: Finance

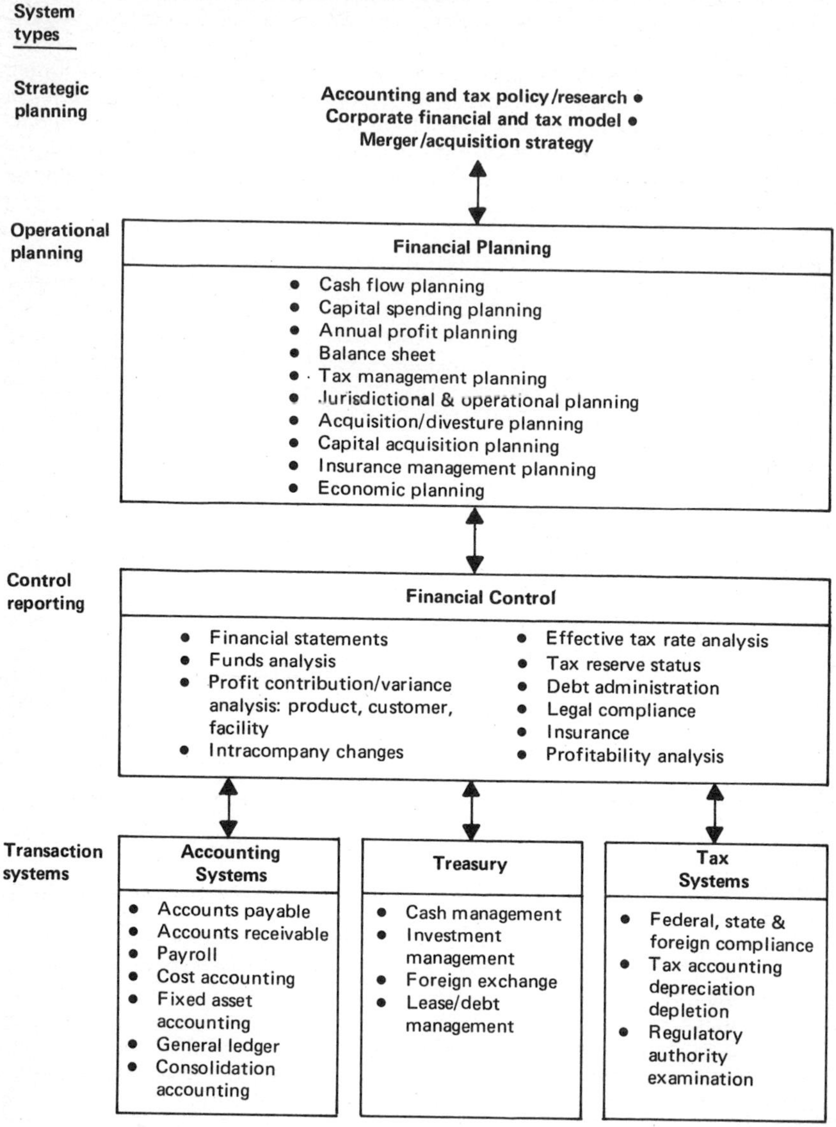

System
types

Strategic
planning

Accounting and tax policy/research ●
Corporate financial and tax model ●
Merger/acquisition strategy

Operational
planning

Financial Planning
● Cash flow planning ● Capital spending planning ● Annual profit planning ● Balance sheet ● · Tax management planning ● Jurisdictional & operational planning ● Acquisition/divesture planning ● Capital acquisition planning ● Insurance management planning ● Economic planning

Control
reporting

Financial Control	
● Financial statements ● Funds analysis ● Profit contribution/variance analysis: product, customer, facility ● Intracompany changes	● Effective tax rate analysis ● Tax reserve status ● Debt administration ● Legal compliance ● Insurance ● Profitability analysis

Transaction
systems

Accounting Systems	Treasury	Tax Systems
● Accounts payable ● Accounts receivable ● Payroll ● Cost accounting ● Fixed asset accounting ● General ledger ● Consolidation accounting	● Cash management ● Investment management ● Foreign exchange ● Lease/debt management	● Federal, state & foreign compliance ● Tax accounting depreciation depletion ● Regulatory authority examination

Information systems are advanced in design and widespread in use in the finance function. In the larger companies at least, information systems are not only at the transaction systems level but also for control and planning. To a large extent the growth in both detail and sophistication of financial information systems has both been caused by and has influenced the changing role of the chief financial executive. As the role grew from record keeper to analyst of the situation, to forecaster of the trends, the financial executive's advice and counsel became more vital to the total management of the enterprise. Success in this ever-expanding role became more and more dependent on the rapid, accurate, and detailed gathering of information, both financial and operational. This gathering has been accomplished by the design of even more complex and pervasive information systems. In large companies, particularly those with a multiplicity of products or services and a wide geographic dispersion, highly automated and properly integrated information systems have become absolute essentials without which the enterprise could not survive.

Conceptually the modern finance and accounting process can be pictured as in Exhibit 7. Present-day systems use computer communications networks, as extensive as needed to embrace the totality of the company, to collect data at the earliest possible time and pass it through the various transaction systems, into the subsidiary and general ledgers, and ultimately in condensed and management meaningful form to financial reports.

EXHIBIT 7   Consolidated Finance and Accounting Process

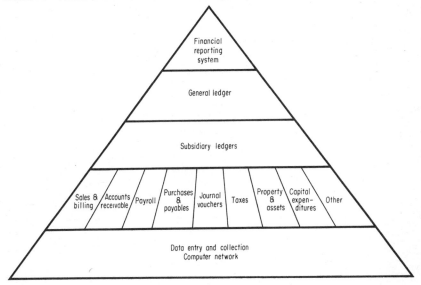

Looking forward to information systems developments in the finance area, we must first recognize that virtually all processing hardware manufacturers are announcing, installing, and then improving equipment at even lower prices for small users. This means that automated information systems are fast becoming economically available to practically all businesses. Thus we can expect a proliferation of small but effective business computers bringing the benefits of information systems to a wide segment of business. Because most of these new users will be employing standard, off-the-shelf, systems for the normal accounting and finance processes, it is likely that the resultant uniformity will, over time, have a profound effect on the way paperwork is handled. Coupling this development with the implications of electronic funds transfer systems (EFTS), we may indeed see a level of automation that crosses company boundaries in many respects. Lower costs should, in the long run, be associated with this trend, as will some displacement of clerical help. In medium or large companies we may expect to see information systems becoming even more dynamic as electronic data storage becomes cheaper and terminal hardware becomes more widely used.

Administration. The administration function takes on different forms and embraces different activities from company to company. One way of looking at the function is displayed on Exhibit 8. This concept considers administration as something beyond the aggregation of relatively unimportant office management chores that often make up the function. Rather, administration is viewed as the focal point for the highest level of business, resource and systems planning.

In this context it can be seen that a wide variety of transaction systems must provide informational inputs to the control process and upward into operational

EXHIBIT 8 Information System Schematic: Administration

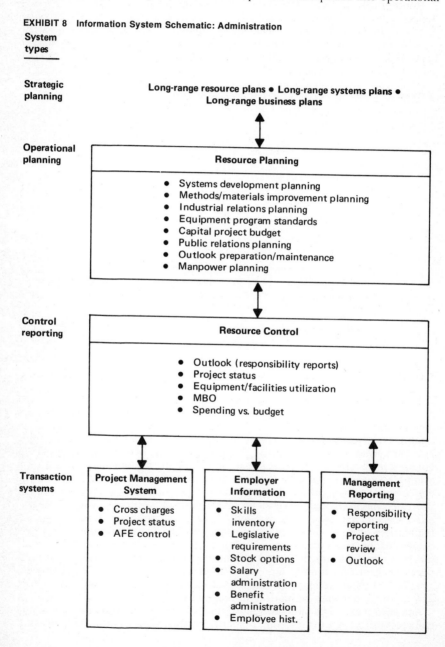

System
types

Strategic planning

Long-range resource plans • Long-range systems plans • Long-range business plans

Operational planning

Resource Planning

- Systems development planning
- Methods/materials improvement planning
- Industrial relations planning
- Equipment program standards
- Capital project budget
- Public relations planning
- Outlook preparation/maintenance
- Manpower planning

Control reporting

Resource Control

- Outlook (responsibility reports)
- Project status
- Equipment/facilities utilization
- MBO
- Spending vs. budget

Transaction systems

Project Management System	Employer Information	Management Reporting
• Cross charges • Project status • AFE control	• Skills inventory • Legislative requirements • Stock options • Salary administration • Benefit administration • Employee hist.	• Responsibility reporting • Project review • Outlook

and strategic planning. Many of these transaction systems are, in fact, in place in the other functions and must interface, at the proper time and level of detail, into the administration flow.

Exhibit 8 shows only three of these transaction system areas, as examples. The project management area deals with large-scale capital projects, line responsibility for which may well reside in the marketing/sales, manufacturing/production, or other functions in which the projects are underway. Likewise the financial, cash-flow impact of each project is developed within the Finance function. The need for bringing all of this together at one point and as rapidly as possible derives from the fact that funds must be made available, as needed, but not before needed. The high cost of borrowing, for instance, demands that acquisition of outside capital be deferred until the last minute. As inevitable delays are encountered in such projects, the effect on cash needs must be promptly signaled. Similarly, such delays (or accelerations) also need to be made known to executive general management, beyond the responsible function, so that company-wide plans related to the project can be kept in synchronization and pressures generated where necessary and possible to get projects that are slipping in time or cost back on course.

In the employee information area, a number of functions are usually involved and information processing may be widely decentralized at the transaction level, especially in divisionalized and geographically dispersed companies. There may be many payroll systems, personnel offices, and records, and benefit plan administrators. Here again it is becoming essential to have in place data flows that bring the right information, at the right time, into a central point not only for overall human resource and financial planning but increasingly for compliance with requirements of government agencies. ERISA and OSHA are examples.

As a final example, many companies are moving toward uniformity in overall management reporting, designing reporting systems that draw from the many and diverse transaction systems in each function to produce necessary control reports and to pass toward the center of the organizational hierarchy the information that is needed. Consistency in report format becomes more necessary as reports reach higher levels, for it is here that information has to be consolidated and the various functions of the company come together in a meaningful way for executive general management review and action.

Research and Development.   The research and development (R&D) function is so different from company to company that it can only be generalized as to information processing in the broadest terms. Exhibit 9 shows some of the activities that might be expected.

In an information processing sense it is likely that future trends will have some influence on R&D. It should be noted first that the research activity is one of the earliest, and heaviest, users of computers. Many large companies were using digital computers in research long before the equipment came into play in business data processing.

This sequence of events derived from the fact that the first computers (circa 1950) were high-speed electronic calculators designed (and limited) to the solution of mathematical equations. Many research problems are stated in equation form and therefore were natural problems to be solved on the early computers. Thus refinery optimization, for example, was possible through linear programming and simulation methods well before the "business" computer arrived. This type of problem solving continues to be a heavy (and profitable) user of present-day computers.

With the advent of equipment and programming systems aimed at the special needs of business data processing, some parallel effect began to be perceived in the approach to the technical uses of the computing facilities. An example of this, where business systems may interface with modeling and simulation systems, is

EXHIBIT 9   Information System Schematic: Research and Development

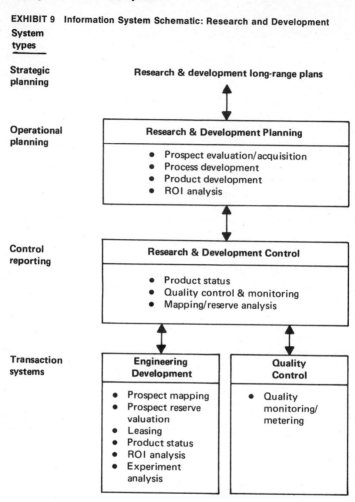

System types

Strategic planning

Research & development long-range plans

Operational planning

Research & Development Planning

- Prospect evaluation/acquisition
- Process development
- Product development
- ROI analysis

Control reporting

Research & Development Control

- Product status
- Quality control & monitoring
- Mapping/reserve analysis

Transaction systems

Engineering Development

- Prospect mapping
- Prospect reserve valuation
- Leasing
- Product status
- ROI analysis
- Experiment analysis

Quality Control

- Quality monitoring/metering

discussed in the following section. Information also flows in the opposite direction, that is, from the technical or operational systems into the business systems. The proliferation of minicomputers and related instrumentation in process control situations provides an example. In plants that make heavy use of electricity in their processes (the chemical industry, for instance), cost of products is directly and significantly influenced by the quantity of electricity used. Pricing structures of the utilities often are stepwise functions, so that the consumption of quantities greater than anticipated by users can lead to higher total and unit costs. Computers installed directly in the process can handle this problem better than humans reacting to reports or to visually interpreted instrumentation. Similar installations are now saving costs in office building heating/air conditioning systems.

INFORMATION SYSTEMS AND INFORMATION REQUIREMENTS IN MODELING AND SIMULATION

Discussions of the development of information systems throw additional attention on the requirements occasioned by strategic planning and to a lesser extent by operational planning. Modeling and simulation have moved to the forefront as structured approaches to the decision processes at these levels. These formal processes must be powered by data. The data can be of three varieties:

1. Guesses, hunches, and judgments unsupported by investigation and documentation
2. Information form outside systems—structured or otherwise
3. Information from internal systems in some state of readiness or acquired through special investigation

At first glance, it seems logical to think that an organization's accounting system would readily provide at least the basic information required for the modeling and simulation of the financial planning activities of an organization. (After all, the accounting system processes all financial transactions and summarizes them into the accounting statements. These statements are used to display financial performance and evaluate the overall financial effectiveness of the organization.) However, an accounting system is concerned primarily with the summarization of transaction details into accounts that may not reflect significant planning needs.

In a service company, for example, employee time and expense transactions are usually processed and summarized by customer, internal projects, etc., which data are used for billing or budgetary control purposes. There is no *accounting* need for summarizing and storing employee time by employee category, or by month of occurrence, etc. In the same environment, however, an employee planning model would certainly be concerned with seasonal variation, which could be ascertained only if monthly (or period) data were stored and maintained for at least three years. Moreover, the employee planning model would require extensive data on the grade or level of employees expended to project or type of service. Because the data would not normally be maintained within the information base of the accounting system, it would have to be extracted from the detailed transaction records or from some form of intermediate level of summarization in the accounting system.

For information systems to be truly effective, the detailed information must be established and maintained so that it can be extracted and properly summarized for use in models. If, for example, analysis of sales by product, region, district, etc., is required for simulation, planning can ensure that required data will be readily available. Without prior consideration, such data will not be automatically accumulated and made a part of the organization's information system.

Should extensive data bases of many detailed transactions be maintained to satisfy possible future simulation and modeling requirements? It could be very costly to maintain, and easily exceed the cost of obtaining the necessary information from less formally organized structures. If certain details are required only once a year, the costs of "researching" the necessary details once a year must be weighed against the cost of maintaining formal data base structures throughout the year.

In actual practice, we have encountered a broad spectrum of accounting systems. In some instances, they involve so much aggregation that very little information is provided for modeling and simulation. The required data must be obtained through exhaustive searches for necessary details, or subjective estimates must be employed in lieu of the desired data. In other cases, even where companies have well structured and extensive information systems using mechanized data bases, certain information required for planning is often either not available in data base form or must be calculated from other data base information. Although this is not a major problem, it does point up the fact that even in "advanced" systems, the data required for modeling and simulation is often not *readily* available.

The conclusion that might be drawn is that the potential need for such information must be taken into consideration and the necessary data provided for through thorough analysis of the transaction and accounting systems. Against this, however, is our inability to forecast these information requirements and the further problem that these decision-making settings are not repetitive in some standard manner. Under the circumstances, standby data bases as on-line repositories of information for high-level decision situations are probably not a cost-effective objective.

BIBLIOGRAPHY

Alexander, M. J.: *Information Systems Analysis,* Science Research Associates, Chicago, 1974.

Blumenthal, Sherman C.: *Management Information Systems: A Framework for Planning and Development,* Prentice-Hall, Englewood Cliffs, N.J., 1969.

Davis, Gordon B.: "The Computer and Modern Accounting," in *Handbook of Modern Accounting,* 2nd ed., Sidney Davidson and Roman L. Weil, eds., McGraw-Hill Book Company, New York, 1977, chap. 7.

————: *Management Information Systems: Conceptual Foundations, Structure and Development,* McGraw-Hill Book Company, New York, 1974.

Kanter, Jerome: *Management-Oriented Management Information Systems,* 2nd ed., Prentice Hall, Englewood Cliffs, N.J., 1977.

Katzan, Harry, Jr.: *Computer Data Management and Data Base Technology,* Van Nostrand Reinhold Company, New York, 1975.

————: *Computer Systems Organization and Programming,* Science Research Associates, Chicago, 1976.

McFarlan, F. Warren, Richard L. Nolan and David P. Norton: *Information Systems Administration,* Holt, Rinehart & Winston, New York, 1973.

Sharpe, William F.: *The Economics of Computers,* Columbia University Press, New York, 1969.

Simon, Herbert A.: *The New Science of Management Decision,* Harper & Row, New York, 1960.

Chapter **25**

Cost Accounting in Nonprofit Organizations

MALVERN J. GROSS, JR.
Partner, Price Waterhouse & Co.

D. EDWARD MARTIN
Manager, Price Waterhouse & Co.

INTRODUCTION

The field of cost accounting as it exists today has been developed entirely in response to the needs of profit-oriented industrial and manufacturing concerns, and it is natural to think of cost accounting only in terms of production processes, goods manufactured, joint products and by-products, overhead variances, etc. Yet cost accounting does have applicability to nonprofit institutions of all types.

As has been discussed earlier in this handbook, the function of cost accounting is to accumulate, record, classify, summarize, allocate (as necessary), and report the costs and expenses incurred by any organization for the purposes of cost control and estimation, as well as to aid in numerous management and planning decisions. These management objectives are as important to nonprofit organizations as to commercial entities, and the cost accounting function is just as applicable to nonprofit organizations, albeit, in many instances, in a far less sophisticated manner.

This chapter, then, will discuss the present state of the art in the use of cost accounting in the nonprofit sector and will point out the many influences that are affecting nonprofit organizations and accelerating their usage of cost accounting.

The Nonprofit Entity.   The American Accounting Association (AAA) has provided a good description of "not-for-profit" in the following excerpts from a report by its Not-for-Profit Committee:

> The usual basis of differentiation into the profit/not-for-profit dichotomy is the presence or absence of a deliberate or conscious profit motive. . . .
>
> An equally important distinguishing characteristic was found in the nature of the respective organizations' equity interests; that is, if the organization operates for the direct financial benefit of its separable stockholders, it is "profit-seeking," even though there may be no intent to increase the organization's net worth per se.
>
> The working definition . . . [is] . . . that a not-for-profit organization is one in which:
> (1) There is no deliberate or conscious profit motive;
> (2) There are no personally or individually owned equity shares or interests;
> (3) Equity interests may not be sold or exchanged; and
> (4) There is no usual or required direct or proportionate financial benefit to contributors of capital or to the patrons.[1]

The AAA included colleges and universities, religious organizations, hospitals, voluntary health and welfare organizations, charitable organizations, and governments within the scope of its not-for-profit definition, while excluding such organizations as cooperatives, trade unions, trade associations, and golf and country clubs. For purposes of this chapter, however, these latter organizations are considered part of the nonprofit sector. On the other hand, because of their unique composition and purposes, governmental and quasigovernmental units have been excluded.

The nonprofit sector is much larger than most realize, as was noted in the report of the Commission on Private Philanthropy and Public Needs (the Filer Commission):

> According to recent extrapolations, there may be as many as six million organizations in America's voluntary sector. . . . One out of every ten service workers in the United States is employed by a nonprofit organization, one out of every six professional workers. One ninth of all property is owned by voluntary organizations.
>
> The last estimate encompasses groups such as labor unions and chambers of commerce, which serve primarily the economic interests of their members. The somewhat

[1]American Accounting Association, "Report of the Committee on Accounting Practice of Not-for-Profit Organizations," *Accounting Review,* Supplement to Volume XLVI (1971), p. 94.

smaller part of the voluntary sector that has been the focus of the Commission's attention is defined for most Commission purposes by Section 501(c)(3) of the Internal Revenue Code, which covers organizations that are both tax exempt and eligible to receive tax-deductible gifts. The code specifically designates charitable, religious, scientific, literary and educational organizations.

The Commission estimates that revenues in these areas, including both government and private funds, add up to around $80 billion a year. This amount does not include non-money resources, such as volunteer work and free corporate services. When these are added in, it is estimated that the voluntary sector accounts for over $100 billion in money and other resources annually.[2]

Accounting Principles. Despite its tremendous impact on the way we live, it has been only in recent years that the accounting profession has paid significant attention to the accounting problems of this increasingly important sector of our society. For instance, in 1972–1974 the American Institute of Certified Public Accountants (AICPA) issued three "industry audit guides" addressed to three segments of the nonprofit sector—hospitals, colleges and universities and voluntary health and welfare organizations. Each of these audit guides is designed to provide general assistance to the specific nonprofit organization and its auditors in recognizing and applying basic accounting principles and in preparing financial statements. Then, in 1974 the Accounting Advisory Committee to the previously mentioned Filer Commission made a number of recommendations, including the suggestion that a single set of accounting principles be adopted and applied by all nonprofit organizations. (It must be noted, however, that the audit guides and the Accounting Advisory Committee's report are only of *indirect* value in dealing with the *costs* incurred by the nonprofit organization, because they deal primarily with general accounting rather than cost accounting principles.)

In 1977, the AICPA distributed a discussion draft containing proposed accounting principles applicable to all those nonprofit organizations not covered by the three previously issued audit guides. This document is expected to be completed in late 1978 and will be issued in the form of a "Statement of Position" addressed to the Financial Accounting Standards Board.

The Financial Accounting Standards Board and the Cost Accounting Standards Board are continuously in the process of producing and refining those accounting concepts that will have varying degrees of impact on accounting for the nonprofit sector. (The latter Board and its contributions to cost accounting principles are discussed in greater detail in another section of this chapter.)

In addition to the efforts begun by the accounting profession, there are a number of national organizations (the National Association of College and University Business Officers, the American Hospital Association, the National Health Council, Inc., the National Assembly of National Voluntary Health and Social Welfare Organizations, Inc., and United Way of America, to name a few), each of which represents a particular sector of the nonprofit community and each of which has been active in formulating accounting and record-keeping principles and systems for their particular nonprofit area. However, as with the audit guides, the recommended accounting principles and reporting formats of these groups vary considerably and, in fact, different principles are recommended in several of their publications for essentially the same basic transactions.

The Potential of Cost Accounting. Further, as might be expected with the relative inattention paid to basic accounting and reporting principles of nonprofit entities, even less concern has been shown for the application of *cost* accounting

[2]Commission on Private Philanthropy and Public Needs, *Giving in America—Toward a Stronger Voluntary Sector* (Commission on Private Philanthropy and Public Needs, Washington, D.C., 1975), p. 11.

principles. Although cost accounting is in its infancy in this sector, its potential for nonprofit organizations has not gone entirely unnoticed, as evidenced by these comments from the AAA's Not-for-Profit Committee:

> While cost accounting has been widely used in the profit-oriented sector, its use by not-for-profit organizations has not been widespread. Yet, cost accounting may be more important in many not-for-profit organizations than in the private sector because: (1) the interests of society as a whole may be involved, (2) the lack of the profit motive as a regulating device or as a measure of operating efficiency, (3) of the lack of an "interested economic group" (such as stockholders) to continually evaluate management's effectiveness and (4) some not-for-profit organizations (particularly governments) have the power to force revenues and thus assure self-perpetuation even if inefficient.
>
> Historically, accounting and reporting for the operations of most not-for-profit organizations have developed largely along lines of accountability for compliance with budgetary and other legal restrictions on an individual fund basis. The emphasis has been on compliance rather than efficiency and upon individual fund entities rather than on total organizational objectives and responsibilities. Budgets are typically prepared on the basis of allowable disbursements or obligational authority; consequently, planning, control, and reporting have tended to emphasize these factors rather than the efficient use of the resources consumed. With the exception of some self-sustaining funds and activities, where cost data have been used to plan, control or evaluate current operations, the cost data have been almost universally produced by cost-finding or cost-analysis studies. Seldom have cost data been produced by cost accounting systems fully integrated with the general accounting system.[3]

It is important to recognize that nonprofit organizations exist to serve the needs of the public or of a particular constituency, and it is reasonable to expect a demand from the public (or its elected officials) that nonprofit organizations report in a manner that will help interested parties, whether they be contributors, potential supporters, or regulatory agencies, to determine if the organization has been effective in meeting its objectives. Likewise, it is fair to ask that nonprofit organizations also provide some measurement to help answer a basic and vital question: "At what cost are the organization's objectives being met?" Once again, the Not-for-Profit Committee of the AAA included some relevant comments in regard to this important issue:

> There is a general tendency among many not-for-profit organizations to play down cost responsibility with statements such as: (1) "There is no need to determine unit costs because revenues are not tied directly to cost," (2) "The benefits or services are so essential to society that any cost can be justified," or (3) "Any amount of funds we can get can be used effectively." Such statements are basically incompatible with the economic concept of limited resources and almost unlimited uses. Regardless of how worthwhile are the purposes of the organization, the limited amounts of resources available will of necessity dictate that some compromises be made in allocating the resources among the several possible objectives to be achieved. The most efficient utilization of resources will maximize the accomplishment of the greatest number of desirable goals.[4]

KEY FINANCIAL CONCEPTS

Before beginning a detailed discussion of cost accounting as it pertains to the nonprofit sector, it is necessary to review certain techniques used in nonprofit accounting. For the most part, accounting for nonprofits has evolved from trust accounting or "stewardship" principles, which emphasized accountability and

---

[3]American Accounting Association, "Report of the Committee on Accounting Practice of Not-for-Profit Organizations," p. 127.
[4]*Ibid.*

dictated a form of reporting that disclosed to the readers of the financial statements whether the trustee had properly accounted for the monies entrusted to him. This reporting form may be basically illustrated as follows:

Cash, beginning of year	$XXX
Add receipts	XX
Less expenses	(XX)
Cash, end of year	$XXX

Although it does emphasize the trustee's responsibility, this method of reporting tells the reader very little in terms of how the money was used to further the objectives of the organization. Thus, over the years stewardship reporting has evolved into an accounting method generally referred to as "fund accounting."

Fund Accounting.   Fund accounting, simply stated, is that accounting activity in which separate, self-balancing records called "funds" are established and maintained for each individual restricted gift received, with individual funds of similar purpose usually being combined as a single "fund" for reporting purposes.

> The resources made available to a not-for-profit organization may be restricted, that is, they may be usable only for certain purposes or specific activities. For example, a church may receive donations for a building addition; a hospital may receive a grant for adding an intensive care facility; ... a university may receive a Federal grant for research purposes or may be the custodian of resources to be used only for making student loans. There may also be instances in which the management decides to designate specific purposes for which certain resources must be used, e.g., they may wish to accumulate resources for equipment replacement or facility enlargement. An essential custodianship obligation in such situations is to use the resources in accordance with stipulations inherent in their receipt and report upon this compliance to others.[5]

Exhibit 1 shows a condensed financial statement, the "Statement of Changes in Fund Balances," for a single organization that keeps a number of separate funds, reporting the activity of each in a separate grouping. It also illustrates the tendency to report in the previously discussed stewardship format, that is, accounting for monies received and spent. It should be observed that no attempt is made to help the reader see an overall picture of the organization, or to see the "net result" of the activity for the period. In practice, many organizations report each of their funds shown in this illustration on separate pages, thereby adding to the reader's difficulty in getting an overview of the activity.

The Single-Entity Concept.   There has been criticism leveled at this form of reporting in recent years, not only because it can be confusing, but also because it provides limited information as to how the funds were utilized, and, more important, as to how adequately and efficiently the expenditures furthered the organization's purpose.

Fund accounting tends to fragment reporting and seems to imply that the organization is a series of separate units called "funds," rather than a single entity. As a result, there has been an increasing tendency to reduce the number of separate fund groupings and to report such groupings in a columnar format along with a "total" column. Many organizations have also started reporting in a format that clearly discloses the activities for the year, including the *net result*—i.e., the *excess* of revenues over expenses (or vice versa). Exhibit 2 illustrates an example of this type of reporting, using the same fund information reported in Exhibit 1.

An example of the sometimes "less-than-fond" feeling toward fund accounting held by many users of nonprofit organizations' financial statements is well expressed in *The Law of Associations:*

[5]Edward S. Lynn and Robert J. Freeman, *Fund Accounting—Theory and Practice* (Prentice-Hall, Englewood Cliffs, N.J., 1974), pp. 7–8. Reprinted with permission.

EXHIBIT 1

TYPICAL NONPROFIT ORGANIZATION
Statement of Changes in Fund Balances
For the Year Ending December 31, 197A

Current Unrestricted Fund

Fund balance, January 1, 197A	$251,010
Contributions	96,517
Service fees	43,819
Investment income	6,753
Salaries	(85,163)
Rent	(25,060)
Utilities	(3,998)
Postage	(4,257)
Printing	(5,950)
Supplies	(15,426)
Transfer to fixed asset fund	(10,000)
Other	(13,606)
Fund balance, December 31, 197A	$234,639

Current Restricted Fund

Fund balance, January 1, 197A	$101,549
Restricted contributions	28,657
Salaries	(16,515)
Supplies	(10,414)
Fund balance, December 31, 197A	$103,277

Endowment Fund

Fund balance, January 1, 197A	$135,060
Endowment gifts	10,150
Capital gains	3,657
Fund balance, December 31, 197A	$148,867

Fixed Asset Fund

Fund balance, January 1, 197A	$105,600
Gifts	25,000
Transfer from unrestricted fund	10,000
Depreciation on vehicles	(8,150)
Fund balance, December 31, 197A	$132,450

Fund accounting is widely used by not-for-profit organizations, principally because of statutory requirements (as in the case of state and local governments), or because many of the assets and receipts of an organization are restricted as to their use (as in the case of educational institutions).

Fund accounting is occasionally used by associations, but with much less justification than in the case of other not-for-profit organizations. Serious consideration should be given to establishing restricted funds as separate entities, and accounting for them separately, or using a fund accounting approach for restricted assets and income, and conventional accounting for all other association activities.

What is most important is that the presence of a few restricted assets and income not be used as an excuse to adopt a fund accounting approach to the basic financial statements of an association.

Fund accounting is a necessary evil born of the legal requirement to segregate and account separately for certain funds, and should never be used when such requirements are not present. It produces complex and confusing financial statements. It can be used by the unscrupulous to shift, create, and conceal income and expense in an accounting version of the old shell game.[6]

[6]Copyright © 1975 by Matthew Bender & Co., Inc., and reprinted with permission from George D. Webster, ed., *The Law of Associations* (Matthew Bender & Co., New York, 1975), chap. 18, p. 18–6.

EXHIBIT 2

TYPICAL NONPROFIT ORGANIZATION
Statement of Revenues, Expenses, and Changes in Fund Balances
For the Year Ending December 31, 197A

	Current fund		Endowment fund	Fixed asset fund	Total all funds
	Unrestricted	Restricted			
Revenues					
Contributions	$ 96,517	$ 28,657	$ 10,150	$ 25,000	$160,324
Service fees.......................	43,819				43,819
Investment income	6,753				6,753
Capital gains			3,657		3,657
Total	$147,089	$ 28,657	$ 13,807	$ 25,000	$214,553
Expenses					
Salaries	$ 85,163	$ 16,515			$101,678
Rent.............................	25,060				25,060
Utilities	3,998				3,998
Postage	4,257				4,257
Printing	5,950				5,950
Supplies	15,426	10,414			25,840
Depreciation				$ 8.150	8.150
Other............................	13,606				13,606
Total	$153,460	$ 26,929		$ 8,150	$188,539
Excess (deficit) of revenues over expenses.......................	$ (6,371)	$ 1,728	$ 13,807	$ 16,850	$ 26,014
Fund balances, January 1, 197A	251,010	101,549	135,060	105,600	593,219
Transfer between funds.............	(10,000)			10,000	
Fund balances, December 31, 197A ...	$234,639	$103,277	$148,867	$132,450	$619,233

It is important to recognize that as long as an organization reports on a segmented, fund-by-fund basis, with the costs spread among a number of funds, it will be difficult to report figures in a manner that will allow the reader of the financial statements to understand what a particular program or activity costs. The use of fund accounting, with multiple fund reporting, has probably been the single largest obstacle to nonprofit organizations' reporting in a manner that tells the reader something about how effective the organization has been in performing its function and at what cost.

Areas of Special Concern. Although nonprofit organizations are often quite similar in organization and structure to profit-oriented business organizations, there can be significant areas of difference which must be considered when dealing with the accounting and financial aspects of nonprofits from a cost accounting standpoint. The following discussion is intended to familiarize the reader with some of the special problem areas that impact cost accounting techniques for this sector of our society.

Cash Versus Accrual Basis Accouting. The cash basis of accounting is simply that system in which an organization records revenues and costs only when they are actually received or paid, respectively, with no attempt to separate them into the time periods to which they apply. The accrual method, on the other hand, allows revenues and costs to be identified with specific periods of time, being recorded as they are realized or incurred. The actual dates of cash receipts and payments are not relevant to the recognition of revenue and cost.

Most small and many medium-sized nonprofit organizations use the cash basis, with some using a "hybrid" of the two, a "modified" cash basis. Despite the simplicity of using only cash transactions as a basis for accounting, the strongest arguments can be made for use of the accrual basis. Essentially, fair presentation of the financial statements normally *requires* that the accrual basis be used. Many nonprofit organizations will have material amounts of unpaid bills or uncollected income at the end of an accounting period, and recognition of these items is necessary to state fairly the results of operations and the financial position of the organization.

Reporting on the accrual basis is also a necessity for those organizations trying to measure the cost of their services. In order to determine accurately the cost of a particular activity during the year, all bills, even those that are unpaid and perhaps even unreceived, must be included in the financial statements. It is not possible to draw valid conclusions about the cost of a particular service or program area unless total expenses can be accumulated. For example, the comparison of actual costs incurred with the amounts budgeted for a particular area is a significant management control, but this comparison is ineffective and misleading unless total costs are used.

Federal Income Taxes.   One area of increasing importance to the nonprofit sector is that of federal income taxes. Nonprofit organizations are normally exempt from federal income taxes once an exemption status has been established by a ruling or determination letter from the Internal Revenue Service. Even though they are exempt from most federal taxes, virtually all nonprofit organizations are required to file annual information returns with the IRS; these annual information returns (Form 990) provide for an allocation of costs into several prescribed categories.

Although qualified nonprofit organizations are exempt from taxes on most categories of income, Congress has imposed a tax on income from any "unrelated trade or business." This tax on unrelated business income is designed to prevent unfair competition with commercial businesses that must pay taxes. Initially, churches were excluded from the unrelated business tax, but now virtually all nonprofit, tax-exempt organizations are covered.

This unique tax situation has particular relevance to cost accounting in that nonprofit organizations are allowed to *allocate* various overhead costs in order to compute the amount of taxable unrelated business income; the methods and bases used in such cost allocations are discussed elsewhere in this chapter.

Capitalization of Fixed Assets and Depreciation.   The subject of fixed asset capitalization has been a controversial one; for historical reasons, many types of nonprofit organizations write off as expense the cost of fixed assets as they are purchased. Other organizations capitalize but do not depreciate their assets. The Accounting Advisory Committee, in its report to the Filer Commission, concluded that fixed assets should be capitalized for *all* nonprofit organizations, citing as justification that capitalizing fixed assets had the following benefits:

(1) Shows the organization's accountability and the resources available to the board for use in carrying out the programs.
(2) Presents a more comparable statement of activity from period to period, not distorted by a large acquisition in any one period.
(3) Permits allocation of the cost of fixed assets to program activities over periods benefited by these assets.
(4) Capitalizing fixed assets is "generally accepted" for other types of organizations, and is generally understood by business people.[7]

From a cost accounting standpoint, it is essential that fixed assets be capitalized and depreciated. Without depreciation, the total costs of rendering the services of the entity are understated. As noted in the AICPA's guide for voluntary health and welfare organizations:

The relative effort being expended by one organization compared with other organizations and the allocation of such efforts to the various programs of the organization are indicated in part by cost determinations. Whenever it is relevant to measure and report the cost of rendering current services, depreciation of assets used in providing such

---

[7]Accounting Advisory Committee, *Report to the Commission on Private Philanthropy and Public Needs* (Accounting Advisory Committee, New York, October 1974), p. 25.

services is relevant as an element of such measurement and reporting process. Although depreciation can be distinguished from most other elements of cost in that it requires no current equivalent cash outlay, it is not optional or discretionary. Assets used in providing services are both valuable and exhaustible. Accordingly, there is a cost expiration associated with the use of depreciable assets, whether they are owned or rented, whether acquired by gift or by purchase, and whether they are used by a profit-seeking or by a not-for-profit organization.

Where depreciation is omitted, the cost of performing the organization's services is understated. Depreciation expense, therefore, should be recognized as a cost of rendering current services and should be included as an element of expense in the statement of support, revenue, and expenses of the fund in which the assets are recorded and in the statement of functional expenditures.[8]

All three of the AICPA's audit guides require that an organization capitalize its fixed assets and two of them require depreciation accounting. (The audit guide for colleges and universities differs from the other two by providing that depreciation accounting is optional.)

Costs of Noncash Transactions.   The areas of consideration discussed thus far contain elements of applicability to both profit and nonprofit entities. The area of noncash contributions of materials and services, however, is essentially unique to nonprofit organizations.

Donations of certain categories of noncash assets, such as investments, supplies, equipment, etc., are usually (but not always) recorded by the nonprofit organization at their fair market values at the date of receipt. Donated supplies and inventories are the two most often omitted from the financial statements; where they are omitted, and where such assets are used in performing the services of the organization, the costs of such services will be *understated.* It is usually fairly easy for the organization to establish a value for such assets, and it is obvious that they should.

The donation of *services* by volunteers is, on the other hand, more difficult to deal with. Few organizations presently record the value of such services, yet the value associated with donated services often has a material impact on the cost of services rendered. Where such values are not recorded, the *total* costs of the program, both cash and noncash, are understated.

One type of nonprofit organization, the museum, has recently considered the impact of contributed services, and the Association of Science-Technology Centers has recommended policies of treatment for these services:

> The extent and nature of contributed services will vary widely among museums, ranging from limited participation in fund-raising activities to regular service as a volunteer worker at the museum. Contributed services should be recognized in financial statements when their value is significant and *all* of the following circumstances exist:
>
>   1. The services performed are a normal part of the museum's program or supporting services and otherwise would be performed by salaried personnel.
>   2. The museum exercises control over the duties of the contributors of the services.
>   3. The museum has a clearly measurable basis for the value placed on the services.
>   In any event, museums should include disclosures regarding the scope and impact of contributed services in a footnote to the financial statements and/or comment regarding this matter in the narrative section of the annual report.
>   Whenever services such as legal, accounting, repair, or construction are contributed either entirely or at a bargain, the value of the contribution can be recorded. . . .[9]

All three AICPA audit guides also follow similar criteria and require such amounts to be recorded.

[8]American Institute of Certified Public Accountants, *Audit of Voluntary Health and Welfare Organizations* (AICPA, New York, 1974), p. 12.

[9]Association of Science-Technology Centers, *Museum Accounting Guidelines* (Association of Science-Technology Centers, Washington, D.C., 1976), p. 8.

Functional Reporting. Traditionally, nonprofit organizations have reported on a basis of "natural" expense classifications, such as *salaries, rent, interest,* etc. Unfortunately this type of classification has told the reader very little about what was accomplished by these expenditures.

In recent years, the accounting profession has been telling these organizations that they should be reclassifying such natural expenses into a functional or programmatic classification, in order to tell the reader how the funds were being used.

The Accounting Advisory Committee, in concluding that functional reporting was the appropriate means for use in the financial statements for nonprofit organizations, listed the following arguments:

(1) Unless an organization classifies expenses by major program services, it is not possible to have a financial basis for an evaluation of the degree to which an organization is achieving its charitable purposes.

(2) Many organizations conduct substantial program activities with their own staff, whereas others conduct program activities principally through grants to individuals or other organizations. The reader cannot make adequate comparisons of the costs of program services of such dissimilar organizations without a functional classification of expenses.

(3) The functional reporting of expense enables the reader to relate fund raising and administrative costs to total proceeds from fund raising campaigns, to total revenue and to program costs.[10]

As will be discussed more fully in a following section of this chapter, functional reporting is essential if meaningful "cost" data are to be developed.

AREAS OF SIGNIFICANT INFLUENCE

There are a number of internal and external influences on nonprofit organizations that will have significant impact on cost accounting for nonprofit entities. Several of these influences have already been felt; others will have their full impact in the future.

Some areas of influence have already been discussed: the AICPA audit guides, the Accounting Advisory Committee's *Report to the Commission on Private Philanthropy and Public Needs,* and the accounting manuals prepared by several of the national associations of certain types of nonprofit organizations (i.e., colleges, museums, etc.). When considering the aggregate effect of these various organizations, however, it is important not to overlook the influence exercised through regulatory aspects of both federal and state governmental units.

The role of the IRS has already been noted in the comments on their reporting format and on taxable unrelated business income. In addition, government influences cost accounting in two other important ways. First, state regulatory agencies regulate nonprofit organizations through the use of required reporting formats and certain ratio limitations. Second, those organizations having federal government grants or contracts are subject to regulation that directly affects costs chargeable under such contracts. Each of these is discussed more fully in the following paragraphs.

Influence of State Requirements. More than half of the states require nonprofit organizations that own property or solicit contributions within that state's boundaries to register and to file periodic reports.[11]

---

[10]Accounting Advisory Committee, *Report to the Commission on Private Philanthropy and Public Needs,* p. 29.

[11]The state of New York, for example, has been one of the leaders in regulating charitable organizations. Approximately 7,000 organizations file with that state's Bureau of Charitable

This registration or licensing often involves financial statements and sometimes these statements must be accompanied by the opinion of an independent accountant. Most states make no distinction between resident and nonresident organizations. Organizations soliciting funds by mail or advertisement usually are subject to these requirements even though they may not have an office or employees in the state.

Most states exempt certain categories of organizations from filing. Unfortunately, with the exception of religious organizations, the exemptions are not consistent from state to state. For example, in New York, organizations receiving less than $10,000 are not required to register. In Arkansas the amount is $1,000. . . .[12]

A significant number of the reports filed under these state requirements contain functional reporting, including the separate disclosure of fund-raising costs and general and administrative expenses. Thus, these organizations find that by law they must allocate costs among programs and supporting functions. This is a significant influence for nonprofit organizations and is facilitating the development of cost accounting techniques by such organizations.

Perhaps equally significant has been the recent increase in state legislation (and proposed *federal* legislation) designed to "protect" contributors through the use of maximum ratio limits on the cost of fund-raising and/or administrative expense. Some legislation has taken the approach of establishing requirements that certain percentages of total income must be used currently for program purposes. The effect of these ratio limitations has been for nonprofit organizations to take a sharp and critical look at the expenses that should be classified in each of these various functional categories.

Limitations on Fund-Raising Costs. Fund raising is expensive to an organization, and some state governments have suggested that charitable organizations should not be allowed to spend more than a certain percentage (usually ranging from 15 to 35 percent) of their contribution income on fund-raising costs. Limitations of this type may appear reasonable to the person having no basis to know what actual costs may be and who thinks of fund raising in the context of a United Way-type campaign, in which the majority of work is handled by volunteers.

The purpose of those who propose limits to fund raising is to cause nonprofit organizations to change their method of fund raising to a less expensive method, but it is based on the underlying assumption that high fund-raising costs reflect inefficiency and can be reduced. Such an assumption may or may not be valid.

Minimum Levels for Program Costs. Another approach frequently being considered as a regulatory measure is to require nonprofit organizations to spend a certain percentage of their income on "program" activities. For example, if an organization's income were $100,000 and the specified spending rate were 50 percent, the organization would be required by law to spend $50,000 for its programs; the remaining $50,000 would be available for supporting costs, such as fund raising and general and administrative expenses.

Government Contracts. Another major influence accelerating the development of cost accounting techniques for nonprofit organizations is the large number of government grants and contracts being given to nonprofit organizations, with the resulting governmental requirements for reporting on the costs of such projects.

---

and Proprietary Organizations; in 1974 these organizations had combined assets of $5.8 billion and had solicited contributions in excess of $1.4 billion (although such solicitations were not exclusively in New York).

New York's filing requirements are also significant in that they require depreciation accounting (with depreciation expense allocated to program and supporting functions), as well as detailed information regarding fund-raising expenses.

[12]Malvern J. Gross, Jr., "State Compliance Reporting for Nonprofit Organizations," *CPA Journal*, April 1975, p. 33.

Government contracts may be categorized as being of two principal types: *fixed-price* contracts, in which the contract price is not subject to adjustment based on the incurrence of costs by the contractor, and *cost-reimbursable* contracts, under the terms of which a contractor is reimbursed for allowable costs, often with a provision for some variety of additional compensation. (These are, of course, greatly simplified definitions, and the reader is directed to more comprehensive published sources for more detailed descriptions of the various kinds of contracts included within these two major categories.) The federal government's procurement regulations, discussed later in this chapter, are designed to govern the reimbursement of costs of contractors under the second type of contract as discussed above.

There are a number of "nonprofit institutes" and educational institutions that perform research-related projects in the natural and social sciences; many receive the support of the government through the government contracts procedure. In the aggregate, nonprofit institutes have historically constituted a small percentage of the federal procurement budget, but, as was reported by the Commission on Government Procurement:

> their importance is far greater if their work in basic and applied research is considered. Although efficiency due to the profit motive, tax base considerations, or competition do not normally apply to this category of resources, the nonprofit organization offers flexibility of operations (particularly in personnel policies), objectivity due to absence of profit or product bias, and ability to attract and hold a high level of scientific and technical talent.
>
> Government agencies predominantly use universities for basic research (in contrast to applied research or development), since this effort most readily correlates with instruction and individual projects by faculty and graduate students. Approximately half of the total ... Federal obligations for basic research were expended by universities and colleges and by FFRDCs (Federally Funded Research and Development Centers) administered by universities.[13]

Procurement Regulations.   The federal government has established regulations to govern the contracting procedures through which the government purchases vast amounts of goods and services. For defense contracts, the applicable guidelines are the "Armed Services Procurement Regulations" (ASPR), found in the *Code of Federal Regulations* (*CFR* Title 32, "National Defense"); the civilian counterpart to these rules are in the "Federal Procurement Regulations" (*CFR* Title 41, "Public Contracts and Property Management").[14]

The composition of total costs applicable to research and development under grants and contracts with educational institutions is defined as being "comprised of the allowable direct costs incident to its performance, plus the allowable portion of

[13]*Report of the Commission on Government Procurement*, E. Perkins McGuire, Chairman (U.S. Government Printing Office, Washington, D.C., 1972), vol. 2, pp. 19–20.
    The Commission also reported on some of the problems such nonprofit institutes face:

> Nonprofit institutions have shared with universities the difficulties caused by cost sharing on R&D projects. In addition, Government agencies tend to pay lower fees to them than to other contractors. Some Internal Revenue Service interpretations of the tax laws lean toward taxation of income earned by independent research institutes, including income from Government-sponsored research. Certain provisions of the Tax Reform Act of 1969 suggest further constraints on the funding capacities of these research organizations that will deter them from bidding on large Government projects. The nonprofit community feels that Government procurement rules and procedures do not recognize them as a separate class of organization with unique characteristics and problems . . . (p. 19).

[14]Part 15 of the above-referenced procurement regulations set forth the basic requirements for government contractors, in terms of accounting principles and practice. Distinction is made as regards contracts and grants with educational institutions in Section 3; other types of nonprofit contractors are covered by the same provisions applicable to the commercial business sector.

the allowable indirect costs of the institution, less applicable credits. . . ." The essential terms, "reasonable costs," "allocable costs," and "applicable credits," as they relate to these contracts are defined in the regulations, which also lists "factors affecting allowability" as follows:

> The tests of allowability of costs under these principles are: (a) they must be reasonable; (b) they must be allocable to research agreements under the standards and methods provided herein; (c) they must be accorded consistent treatment through application of those generally accepted accounting principles appropriate to the circumstances; and (d) they must conform to any limitations or exclusions set forth in these principles or in the research agreement as to types or amounts of cost items.[15]

Another essential consideration for the nonprofit government contractor is the decision as to what items constitute *direct* as opposed to *indirect* costs. A direct cost may be considered to be any cost that can be identified specifically with a particular cost objective, with all other costs being indirect.

The nonprofit contractor will apply indirect costs to specific programs by means of an indirect expense rate based on a computation of allocated indirect costs as a percentage of direct costs. Its total contract costs, including indirect expenses, are then subject to audit and adjustment by the government, usually through an agency of the Department of Health, Education and Welfare (HEW). After the contractor's costs have been reviewed and audited (and possibly a portion disallowed), its indirect cost rates are approved and complete reimbursement of contract amounts are finalized. Although most contractors are subject to the renegotiation process, most nonprofits are not.[16]

Government Management.   In addition to the federal procurement regulations discussed in the preceding section, there is another section of the *Code of Federal Regulations* with applicability to nonprofit organizations (other than state and local governments) and the accounting for their costs under government contracts.

"Government Management" is Title 34 in the federal regulations and deals with procurement management, property management, financial management, and management systems. Part 211 of this Title, "Cost Sharing on Federal Research," establishes guidelines for contractors' "sharing" or *contributing* a portion of the contract project's cost. "Cost sharing" may be defined as a contractor's participating with the government in a research project's costs, and is intended to serve as an incentive for the contractor to perform its work efficiently and to hold costs down.

Proper record keeping and accounting for costs by the nonprofit organization is essential if it is to contribute services or materials to the project at the preestablished percentage rates.

Cost Accounting Standards Board.   Another major governmental influence on nonprofit organizations is the Cost Accounting Standards Board (CASB). If the contractual amount of negotiated contracts and subcontracts is in excess of stated

---

[15]U.S. National Archives and Records Service, *Code of Federal Regulations,* Title 32, "National Defense," subtitle A, chap. 1, subchap. A, part 15.303-2 (U.S. Government Printing Office, Washington, D.C., 1974).

[16]Under the provisions of the Renegotiation Act of 1951, as amended (*CFR,* Title 32, chap. XIV), contractors with the U.S. government are subject to evaluation by the Renegotiation Board. It is the responsibility of this Board to determine the extent to which some portion of the profits earned from contracts with various U.S. government departments and agencies are excessive, and to remove such excess through negotiation with the contractor or through unilateral order by the Board.

Under sec. 106 of the Act (Mandatory Exemptions), however, it is provided that renegotiation will not apply to any contract or subcontract with a nonprofit organization exempt from taxation under the Internal Revenue Code. State and local governments are also specifically exempted.

levels, all contractors, including nonprofit organizations, are subject to the standards of the CASB.

As has been noted in previous chapters of this handbook, the CASB was established under federal regulations to promulgate "cost accounting standards designed to achieve uniformity and consistency in the cost accounting practices followed by . . . contractors." (Originally founded to deal with *defense* contractors in 1970, the rules and regulations of the CASB were extended in 1972 to include negotiated *nondefense* contracts in excess of $100,000 by including them in the "Federal Procurement Regulations System," discussed previously in this chapter.)

The statutory level of coverage was extended in 1975 in order to remove small contractors and business units from CASB coverage. Basically, present contractors must have received a negotiated contract (or subcontract) in excess of $500,000 in order to be subject to the standards, and, once having been awarded a contract of that amount, remains subject to the standards for all negotiated contracts (or subcontracts) in excess of $100,000 that might subsequently be awarded. Thus, many larger nonprofit organizations are subject to the CASB standards.

Certain nonprofit organizations (educational institutions and state and local governments) are specifically *exempted* from coverage of *certain* of the CASB standards:

Standard 403—Allocation of home office expenses to segments
Standard 408—Accounting for costs of compensated personal absence
Standard 409—Depreciation of tangible capital assets
Standard 410—Allocation of business unit general and administrative expense to final cost objectives

One subject currently under study, "indirect costs of colleges and universities," would have direct applications to a specific type of nonprofit organization.

As noted earlier in this handbook, contractors whose dollar volume of prime *defense* contract awards subject to CASB standards are in excess of $10 million in a federal fiscal year are, in addition, required to file a Disclosure Statement (Form CASB-DS-1) with the CASB, documenting the accounting practices in effect. However, qualifying colleges and universities must submit Form CASB-DS-2, which is specially designed to deal with the terminology and accounting practices that are unique to these institutions. Few educational institutions are involved in this filing, however, because of the $10 million requirement.

Third-Party Reimbursement.   Third-party reimbursement has had and will continue to have a significant impact on the development of cost accounting techniques for one major sector of the nonprofit industry—hospitals and similar health care institutions.

Until perhaps the beginning of the 1960s, there had been little emphasis on cost accounting. Financial and accounting positions were often staffed by medical persons with little training or ability for the tasks they faced. Even with the American Hospital Association's *Chart of Accounts for Hospitals* and its *Cost Finding and Rate Setting for Hospitals,* many hospitals had not incorporated the guidelines in these publications into their accounting systems. The application of accounting principles from hospital to hospital was usually nonstandardized and inconsistent.

Beginning in the early 1960s, an increasing percentage of hospital activity involved third-party payors—various welfare agencies, insurance companies, and government agencies, all of which had "insurance" plans or specified arrangements with recipients that included paying at least a portion of the covered individuals' medical expenses, usually directly to the hospitals. Of these, the Blue Cross System (composed of numerous, separate nonprofit "Plans") is the largest. Serving approximately 100 million persons, Blue Cross pays in excess of $5 billion annually for hospital and other health care benefits for its own subscribers. Equally important in recognizing Blue Cross's ability to influence cost accounting is its role as a fiscal agent, through which federal and state governments pay approximately $6 billion a year for services rendered to beneficiaries of Medicare and Medicaid. This is an example of the "golden rule": they who have the gold make the rules. And, in this case, cost accounting rules.

It was the requirements of these third-party payors for supporting information on costs to be reimbursed that gave rise to the first widespread, meaningful cost accumulation and reporting systems in hospitals. The changes were complex and often confusing at first, but great progress has been made. There is little doubt that the pressure for accurate cost accounting and reporting to these third-party payors will continue, as will the need for greater levels of accounting sophistication on the part of hospitals.[17]

Recent Developments of Accounting Principles.   The last of the significant areas of influence on the development of cost accounting for nonprofit organizations is that of the increased interest in, and development of, accounting principles by various organizations within the accounting profession as well as in the separate nonprofit communities. (The reader is directed to the Bibliography at the end of this chapter for a listing of some of the more recent significant publications.)

The last decade has seen important activity in establishing accounting, reporting, and auditing standards for many types of nonprofit organizations, and this activity is expected to continue, and probably to accelerate. This development has been characterized by a trend away from the accounting for funds received and disbursed to the accounting for the use of resources available to the institution in terms of program accomplishment. This results in nonprofit organizations and their accountants becoming increasingly aware of the value of cost data when properly accumulated and analyzed.

ACCUMULATION AND ANALYSIS OF COST DATA

The managements of many nonprofit organizations have resisted suggestions that they attempt to measure the cost of services being rendered because of a concern that this might hamper their ability to render quality service. They seem afraid that emphasis on cost measurement might result in decisions being made that would inhibit their ability to respond effectively to new developments. Others express concern that users of this financial data will compare the costs of two organizations having similar programs and will draw conclusions that would be inaccurate because of nonquantitative, quality differences in the two. Further, some nonprofit managers seem concerned that cost measurement implies there should be revenue to match against each cost or that each program should be self-supporting. In part, these concerns are valid, and yet, in our world of limited resources, it is not only appropriate but necessary for society to ask the cost of services being rendered by the nonprofit sector.

As was stated earlier, a nonprofit organization raises money in order to spend money to provide a service, but with only limited funds available in the nonprofit sector, decisions have to be made as to where these limited funds should be spent. Thus, cost measurement is vital to this decision-making process, whether it be internal (management deciding which of two programs to develop) or external (the contributor deciding which organization has the most effective program and should thus receive the gift).

From a conceptual standpoint, then, cost measurement is important to the nonprofit sector, not as a standard for determining profit, but as a tool to

---

[17]A principal means for dealing with the costs of operations for hospitals is through the method of "cost finding." A detailed discussion and example of this method are included in the next section.

determine how scarce resources should be spent and, once the determination is made, how effectively they have been used.

Developing and Recording Cost Data.   Before an organization's cost information can be collected and properly used, it is necessary that the specific purposes for which the cost information is to be used are clearly defined. There are various acceptable cost collection techniques available, as may be seen from the preceding chapters in this book, and each grouping of nonprofit organizations—and, ultimately, each individual organization—has to determine what its specific goals and needs are to be. Only then can the appropriate costing techniques and systems be decided upon. At the same time, it is necessary for the organization to recognize the various kinds and classifications of costs[18] to be dealt with and to be certain that

[18]For example, "historical costs" represent the amounts of cost actually incurred during some prior time period. "Forecasted" or "estimated" costs represent "educated guesses" about future costs, based on previous results and projected occurrences. "Standard" costs are also estimated or forecasted costs, often recorded directly in the accounts, and are used as a

EXHIBIT 3   Standards for Determining Cost

Costing standard	Explanation
1. The purposes for which cost information is to be used should determine the framework within which cost information is developed.	Costs are determined to satisfy purposes for which cost information is needed. A clear definition of these purposes is needed in order to specify the cost determination approach to be used.
2. Cost information should be based on the accrual method of accounting.	To provide valid and consistent cost, the accrual method of accounting should be used, applying the concept of materiality.
3. Cost data should be reconcilable to official financial accounting data.	Reconciliation to official financial accounting records is necessary to ensure the validity of cost records. (Reconciliation is the process of identifying and giving appropriate consideration to differences in two or more sets of data.)
4. Nonfinancial data should be reconcilable to official institutional records.	Reconciliation of nonfinancial data to the official records of the institution is necessary to ensure the validity of cost data when such nonfinancial data are used in the cost determination process.
5. Definitions used in cost determinations should be applied uniformly.	Uniform definitions should be employed during the cost determination process and from period to period to achieve reliable cost information.
6. Cost information and related costing units should cover the same period.	Cost determination for a particular period should be related to the units of service provided during that same period.
7. Cost information should be consistently determined.	Cost information used in any cost study must be consistently determined for all periods included and for all organizational units included. Cost data will not be comparable unless consistently determined. Consistency depends on uniform definitions, methods, and interpretations as well as judgments exercised in the cost determination process.
8. Cost should be attributed to a cost objective based on a causal or beneficial relationship.	Meaningful and dependable cost determinations require that costs be assigned to cost objectives according to identifiable relationships that logically and reasonably cause the cost to occur or that result in benefits received by the cost objective.

SOURCE: NACUBO's *Administrative Service*, by permission of the National Association of College and University Business Officers, Washington, D.C., 1974, pp. 14–16.

they are being properly understood and utilized effectively in meeting its objectives.

The Costing Standards Committee of the National Association of College and University Business Officers (NACUBO) has formulated 12 "standards" for determining costs (see Exhibit 3), and although the emphasis of NACUBO's analysis naturally was directed to institutions of higher learning, the basic elements of those standards, some of which have already been mentioned, are applicable to many types of nonprofit entities.

---

measurement of an organization's actual incurred costs as determined through an analysis of variances.

Types of costs may be further analyzed and defined, and management must also have a clear understanding and working knowledge of additional classifications of costs, i.e., "direct" and "indirect" costs, "fixed," "variable" and "semivariable" costs, etc. For further details and explanations, the reader is directed to the earlier chapters in this *Handbook*.

Costing standard	Explanation
9. Indirect cost should be allocated based on quantitative measures that can be applied in a practical manner.	The bases of allocation of indirect cost should involve the use of those quantitative measures that best represent the relationship of cost to the cost objective, with the result that indirect costs are equitably distributed. There are instances when the most equitable distribution may not be the most practical, both in terms of time and related expense involved in collecting and tabulating quantitative measures. In such cases, the most practical measure should be selected, provided that the results are not materially different.
10. Common cost incurred to provide two or more services should be allocated in an equitable manner.	Allocation of common costs to joint services, which are cost objectives, should be based on a logical relationship of the several services to one another and to the nature and circumstances of the costs incurred. It should be recognized that separate costing of jointly produced services is subjective and the bases available to allocate joint costs are arbitrary.
11. Capital cost of a cost objective should reflect the applicable expired capital cost of the period.	Capital cost of a cost objective should reflect applicable expired cost determined on the basis of the estimated useful life of the asset being depreciated.
12. Cost information should be accompanied by a disclosure statement.	Explanatory disclosures necessary to provide the user with a clear understanding of the previously established, intended use of cost information should accompany the reporting of such information. Disclosures should encompass the costing method and approach used, the cost definition used, the types of cost included, identification of cost objectives and costing units, and other information pertinent to the cost-determination effort.

Classification by Function. As noted briefly earlier, nonprofit organizations have traditionally maintained their records and reported the results of their operations in terms of the type of "natural" or "objective" expenses incurred—that is, salaries, rent, supplies, utilities, etc. Although many users of the financial statements may be interested in this natural expense classification, it provides them with little useful information to aid in determining how the purposes of the organization were furthered by the expense. Increasingly, therefore, it is being recognized that this form of "natural" reporting is less than adequate.

More and more nonprofit organizations are being urged to report on a functional or "program" basis. A functional basis of reporting classifies the natural expense categories into various functions or program categories, corresponding to the services or programs provided by the organization.

As can be seen from Exhibits 4 and 5, the functional format lays the groundwork for answering such questions as "What did the program cost?" and "Is it cost-effective?" Answers to questions such as these are not available in the natural expense format. (The reader should also look again at Exhibit 2, which shows the final statement for the same organization in a natural expense format.)

EXHIBIT 4

TYPICAL NONPROFIT ORGANIZATION
Schedule of Conversion of Expenses from Natural to Functional Classifications
For the Year Ended December 31, 197A

| | Program | | | Supporting | | |
| | | | | General and admin. | Fund raising | Total |
	A	B	C			
Salaries	$34,533	$23,395	$20,610	$17,570	$ 5,570	$101,678
Rent	11,277	5,263	1,253	6,014	1,253	25,060
Utilities	1,800	838	200	960	200	3,998
Postage		23		415	3,819	4,257
Printing	454	101	69	1,273	4,053	5,950
Supplies	8,000	6,000	500	10,840	500	25,840
Depreciation	4,850	1,260	300	1,440	300	8,150
Other	7,018	3,019	1,681	1,434	454	13,606
	$67,932	$39,899	$24,613	$39,946	$16,149	$188,539
Persons served	16,983					
Home calls made		1,330				
Responses to requests			4,102			
Contributions raised					$160,234	
Unit costs	$4.00	$30.00	$6.00		$ .10	

Although functional reporting does not directly provide unit cost measurement, it does tell readers of the statement a great deal about where the organization spent its money and allows readers the opportunity to make their own judgments. And, to the extent that services rendered can be quantified in terms of "units," it supplies the basic groundwork for unit cost measurement.

The trend to functional reporting has been accelerated in recent years by both professional literature and government regulation. All of the three audit guides issued by the AICPA provide illustrative statements on a functional basis. In addition, three industry books, *Standards of Accounting and Financial Reporting for Voluntary Health and Welfare Organizations* (published jointly by the National Health Council, National Assembly of National Voluntary Health and Social Welfare Organizations, and United Way of America), *Accounting & Financial Reporting—A*

EXHIBIT 5

TYPICAL NONPROFIT ORGANIZATION
Statement of Revenues, Expenses, and Changes in Fund Balances
For the Year Ending December 31, 197A

Revenue (in total)		$214,553
Expenses		
Program		
Project A	$67,932	
Project B	39,899	
Project C	24,613	132,444
Supporting		
General and administrative	39,946	
Fund raising	16,149	56,095
Total expenses		188,539
Excess of revenues over expenses		26,014
Fund balances, January 1, 197A		593,219
Fund balances, December 31, 197A		$619,233

Guide for United Ways and Not-for-Profit Human Service Organizations (published by the United Way of America), and *College and University Business Administration* (Administrative Manual published by NACUBO), have also accented functional reporting.

Government regulation, discussed in greater detail in a previous section, is also playing an important role because the financial reporting statutes of a number of states (including New York, Pennsylvania, Illinois, and Ohio) require reporting formats that are on a functional basis. This government regulation reflects a growing demand by the public for accountability, in a meaningful manner, by nonprofit organizations.

Categories of Functional Reporting. Perhaps the most difficult part of functional reporting is defining the functional or program categories on which to report. Most current literature now provides for two basic categories:

1. *Program services, classified into as many categories as there are major programs.*

2. *Supporting services, usually classified into at least two subcategories, "general and administrative" and "fund raising."* For organizations *not* raising funds from the general public, there are other supporting categories that would be more appropriate than "fund raising," such as "membership development" (in the case of a membership organization), "contract development" (in the case of an organization receiving contracts from government agencies), and "grant development" (in the case of organizations raising funds from private foundations). However, *all* organizations soliciting funds—that is, requesting money for which no *quid pro quo* is involved—should disclose their fund-raising costs.

A number of state legislatures and the Congress have expressed concern that some nonprofit organizations are spending disproportionate amounts of their resources on supporting services or that they are not spending their resources for the purpose for which they were established. Expressed another way, questions are being raised as to whether some organizations are more interested in their own perpetuation than in accomplishing their objectives.

Thus, it becomes important that organizations carefully review the definition of the type of expenses falling in each of these expense categories to make certain that program-oriented expenses are not inadvertently classified as supporting expenses. The following discussion outlines the major categories for classification by function.

Program Services. Expenses for program services are those costs incurred to further the purposes for which the organization exists. They include both direct costs, such as personnel assigned to program activities, and indirect expenses, such as occupancy and overhead costs related to these personnel and to the other direct program costs.

The cost of rendering program services should be broken down among the major programs of the organization in a meaningful manner. For example, although it might be argued that a college has only one program (education), on closer examination it will be seen that most colleges and universities have a number of different program objectives, including research projects and public service. These can and should be separately identified in the financial statements.

General and Administrative Expenses.   General and administrative expenses are those that do not *directly* contribute to the program activities of the organization, but relate primarily to the maintenance of the organizational structure. These expenses include the unallocated time of the executive director and staff, the cost of bookkeeping, purchasing activities, general office functions, board meetings, legal expenses, and the costs associated with maintaining and promoting the public image of the organization. As with program services, this category includes both direct and indirect expenses.

Some types of supporting services, such as typing pools or filing departments, may, in fact, be related more to program activities than to the "maintenance" of the organization. Where this is so, these expenses should be classified as program-related (or, if applicable to both program and supporting categories, should be allocated between both).

A problem exists, however, in that some employees are reluctant to keep the records necessary to provide a basis for allocation of their time among functional categories. They rationalize that by charging all their time to the general and administrative category they have been conservative, and thus have not overstated the program services category. This is a risky approach because, as previously noted, there is an increasing tendency to regulate by legislative limitations on fund raising and administrative costs. Further, the public is becoming increasingly sophisticated in reading financial statements and is therefore questioning why some organizations are apparently spending large proportions of their funds on supporting activities.

The difficulty, of course, is that the notion exists that supporting expenses are somehow not really necessary, that they are wasted money representing "fat" that should be eliminated, or at least cut back. In fact, supporting services are usually essential to the success of the program. It is important, therefore, to draw as tight a definition of supporting services as possible, classifying as supporting expenses only those amounts that are clearly *not* applicable to a specific program.

It can be argued, of course, that every employee or activity of an organization is directly or indirectly aimed at accomplishing program activities, and that there are no such things as "nonprogram" expenses, except possibly those incurred for general fund raising. For example, without an executive director, there would probably be no program, and thus, even an executive director involved in overall management is essential to the success of program activities. There is logic to this argument, but most accountants and nonprofit administrators agree that an organization should report separately, as *supporting* services, those costs that are more directly involved with the survival of the organization than with the accomplishment of program objectives.

Fund Raising.   Fund-raising expenses are those expenses incurred to induce others to contribute money or time for which the contributor will receive no goods or services in return. Fund-raising expenses normally include the costs of personnel, occupancy, maintenance of mailing lists, printing, mailing, and all direct and indirect costs of soliciting funds or services.

Some organizations solicit all or part of their funds in the form of "grants" from private foundations or from a few specific individuals to be used for specific purposes. Usually such solicitation is for substantial amounts. A further characteristic of this form of solicitation is that the organization must report back to the donor on how the funds were spent. This type of "fund raising" should be separately classified in the financial statements to distinguish it from general fund raising, perhaps with the description, "grant solicitation." This is also true of the costs of soliciting research funds from government or business. Membership associations should likewise classify the cost of obtaining new members as "membership development" (under the functional classification of supporting services). The alternative of classifying the cost of all solicitations (or expenses incurred in revenue development) in only a single category may be misleading to the readers of the statements.

FUND RAISING VERSUS PUBLIC EDUCATION. One difficult area for nonprofit administrators and accountants is the distinction between the costs incurred for fund raising and for public education. Some types of organizations have, as one of their program objectives, the education of the public to the dangers of a particular disease or issue. Where this is so, the cost of such public education is considered a *program* expense. The problem is that public education literature often also includes a direct or implied request for funds, thereby giving the literature two objectives—public education and fund raising. It is often difficult to separate the two for purposes of reporting costs.

One authoritative guide, *Standards of Accounting and Financial Reporting for Voluntary Health and Welfare Organizations,* advocates that, where there is any significant element of fund raising, the entire cost of the publication should be classified as fund raising, rather than as *part* fund raising and *part* public education.[19] This approach of charging everything to fund raising has appeal largely because it eliminates the difficult allocation problem. Further, because it leans over backward to report all questionable costs as fund raising, it helps to create credibility for the organization. In the early 1960s there were many organizations not reporting fund-raising costs, and this approach arose as an effort to regain public confidence.

With the increased publicity of the cost of fund raising and administrative costs, nonprofit organizations cannot afford the luxury of overstating these supporting categories. Accordingly, where a piece of literature clearly has both functions, the organization is obligated to use some reasonable basis for allocation to a program category.

FUND RAISING AS A PROGRAM FUNCTION. Although relatively infrequent, for some organizations fund raising can be a program function, and, where this is the case, it should be so classified with an appropriate descriptive caption. For example, one of the program functions of some national organizations may be to educate the staff of their local affiliates on fund-raising techniques, or even to assist in the fund-raising efforts of the affiliate. Under these circumstances, such costs may or may not be a program function of the national depending on the financial arrangements with the affiliate. Where there is no direct benefit to the national (i.e., no direct sharing of the contributions raised by the affiliate), such costs may more appropriately be reported by the national as a "program" function. Where the national receives a direct benefit, such as a percentage of contributions, then these costs would be more appropriately classified as "supporting." Depend-

---

[19]The three sponsoring organizations of this publication issued an "interpretation" in 1976 that softened this position, indicating that in some instances it would be appropriate to allocate costs between these functions.

ing on the facts, it is also possible that such costs could be both program and supporting, in which case an appropriate allocation should be made.

DEFERRED FUND-RAISING COSTS.   Some costs associated with fund raising benefit more than one period, such as the cost of developing mailing lists or the cost of an active program to persuade donors to make bequests. In both examples, these costs will benefit future periods. However, it is difficult to measure the future benefit of such costs, and for that reason they should normally be expensed in full in the year incurred, as opposed to being capitalized and amortized.

Allocation Techniques.   Thus far the discussion has not focused on the techniques for allocating expenses between functions. This is the difficult aspect of functional reporting, although common sense usually provides reasonable answers.

Most nonprofit organizations have relatively few categories of natural costs, with payroll and occupancy often accounting for 75 percent or more of the total costs of the organization. The following discussion includes some of the various categories of costs and the allocation techniques most often used.

Payroll Costs.   The most common method of allocating payroll costs is on the basis of time spent by each employee. This presents no problem for employees spending all of their time on one function, but most organizations have employees who work in more than one functional area.

Each employee should keep a time record of the functions or projects on which time is spent. Unfortunately, many workers are reluctant to keep such time records because they can be bothersome to maintain on a continuous basis (and perhaps in part because it suggests that someone is "looking over their shoulders" to see how they are spending their time). It takes discipline to get employees to keep time records, but there is little choice if accurate functional reporting is the objective.

Ideally, employees should keep track of their time on a *daily* basis; this would then allow the bookkeeper to make a complete and accurate analysis at the end of each period. As desirable as this may be, few nonprofit organizations insist that their employees keep a daily time record throughout the year; instead, they use various alternative procedures to provide a reasonable basis for the allocation, depending on the circumstances:

1. *Periodic recordkeeping:* Detailed records are kept only for certain specific periods—such as for one day of each week or for one week of each month—on the assumption that these periods will be fairly representative and can be used as a basis for allocating all time for the year.

2. *Employee estimates:* Each employee's time is summarized at the end of each time period based on his or her recollection of how his or her time was allocated.

3. *Parallel allocation:* No attempt is made to keep detailed records of secretarial and supporting staff; instead, the salary costs of such persons are allocated on the same basis as the costs of their supervisor.[20]

4. *Allocation by specific nature of task:* There are a number of persons who do not directly work on program functions; examples include file clerks, mailroom staff, telephone operators, receptionists, office managers, janitorial staff, bookkeeping staff, purchasing agents, and stenographic pools. Even with these employees, the nature of the job performed should be carefully reviewed, and where there is a

---

[20]The allocation of time of the executive director and other principal supervisors is usually difficult because they have many duties and functions, and there is the need for more detail than for most other persons in the organization. A nonprofit organization's top officers are often lax in keeping such records, and because they are the "bosses," there is no one to press them to do so. Nevertheless, it is important that their time be allocated as fully as possible, and in particular that it be allocated to program functions.

reasonable basis for allocation to a function other than "general and administrative," they should be so allocated. (For example, the stenographic pool can readily record the time spent working for particular individuals or departments, and thus their time can be allocated on the same basis as the persons they are serving. If file clerks are primarily involved in filing materials relating to program functions, their time should be allocated to these functions.)[21]

Occupancy and Other Office Costs.   Occupancy (rent, heat, light, etc.) and other office costs (supplies, equipment, etc.) should also be allocated, usually on the same basis as the compensation of persons using the space. This is normally done on a square-footage basis, with nonproductive space, such as halls and restrooms, excluded from the allocation formula's denominator. One variation from this method is to allocate these costs on the basis of payroll costs, the presumption being the higher the salary level, the greater the space occupied.

Other Categories of Costs.   Some nonprofit organizations have many categories of expense other than payroll and occupancy. These include travel, publication costs, supplies used in a program, mailings, etc. Each category should be reviewed to determine the appropriate function that should be charged. Again, the reader should keep in mind that the objective is to allocate as much of these expenses as possible to functional categories other than general and administrative.

Unit Costs and Measures.   One of the important aspects of cost accounting for commercial organizations is that costs are categorized and expressed in terms of a *cost per unit*—for example, cost per unit of production, cost per unit of measure (pound, square foot, etc.), cost of machine output per hour, etc. Once calculated, such unit costs are more easily and accurately compared to historical, forecasted, or standard costs for the purpose of determining efficiency and conformity to plan. It follows, then, that cost accounting, when applied to the nonprofit organization, can also be used to derive and calculate meaningful units of measure.

Unit measures have been discussed in a detailed cost study of "NCHEMS," National Center for Higher Education Management Systems (at Western Interstate Commission for Higher Education), as follows:

> Measures describe participants, resources, activities, finances, and outcomes. The use of the term "measure" implies that a unit of measurement can be identified and that these units can be defined, aggregated, and displayed in a standard manner. The . . . [intent] . . . is to develop financial measures, that is, measures that reflect costs of physical and human resources used at a specific level of activity during a stated period of time. Other items of information are required by the costing procedures in addition to financial measures. For example, resource measures, such as full-time equivalent personnel or assignable square feet, typically are used as parameters in the allocation of support costs. Likewise, certain activity measures, such as course enrollments and student contact hours, are useful in calculating unit costs . . . for the Instruction program. The nondollar items of information are referred to collectively as nonfinancial measures.[22]

NCHEMS' study listed and explained various financial and nonfinancial unit measures, including the following:

Financial Measures

1. (Program) personnel compensation
2. Administrative support/personnel compensation

---

[21]Some of these categories of people, on the other hand, are administrative, and their associated costs are not normally allocated. For example, the bookkeeping staff, office manager, and telephone operator are not normally allocated to program categories because their functions relate more to maintaining the organization than to performing the service for which the organization was formed.

[22]James R. Topping, *Cost Analysis Manual,* Technical Report No. 45 (National Center for Higher Education Management Systems at WICHE, Boulder, Colo., 1974), p. 19.

3. Other staff compensation
4. Supplies and services expenditures
5. Capital expenditures (funds actually expended)
6. Capital costs (valuation placed on the services provided by buildings and equipment owned or leased and used during any time period)
7. Scholarships and fellowships
8. Direct costs (expenditures assigned to activity centers, including 1–4 above)
9. Support costs (costs not assigned directly to a final cost objective)
10. Full costs (sum of direct costs, capital costs, and allocated support costs for an activity center or group of centers)

Nonfinancial Measures

1. Semester credit (one student engaged in instructional activity for one semester of credit)
2. Student contact hour (one hour of instruction to one student in one week)
3. Course enrollment (one student enrolled in one course or section)
4. Assignable square feet (sum of all areas of floor space assigned to and functionally usable by an occupant)
5. FTE service months (number of "full-time equivalent" months worked by one person during a fiscal year)[23]

Again, although the above measures are clearly directed toward a specific type of nonprofit organization, other unit bases, similar in intent and tailored for a specific organizational structure and nature of service, could be established for any type of nonprofit entity.

Another major type of nonprofit organization, the hospital, also makes use of unit measures for purposes of establishing specific rates for its services. The American Hospital Association (AHA) has listed the following four generally used methods of determining rates for individual items:

1. Relative values—
   Each test or procedure is assigned a unit value based on the relative time and/or skill required to perform it. Each is multiplied by the number of tests or procedures in the cost period so as to develop weighted values. The total amount to be recovered from rates, divided by total weighted values, produces the unit value. The unit value is then multiplied by the relative units for each test to provide the weighted rate per test. [Examples of] departments to which this technique is appropriate are x-ray [and] laboratory. . . .
2. Cost plus a percentage—
   This method is used in merchandising-type departments, such as pharmacy and central supply.
3. Hourly rates—
   Departments using hourly rates (man-hour or clock-hour) include the operating rooms, anesthesia, and physiotherapy.
4. Routine services—
   Presently related to the type of [patient] accommodation . . . (private, semi-private, ward), to calculate rates, computations are based on fixed and variable costs related to type of accommodation.[24]

Exhibit 6 contains a simple example prepared by the AHA, which reflects the development of individual rates for an operating room through the use of per-unit measures.

The AHA's accounting and financial guide, *Chart of Accounts for Hospitals,* outlines procedures for accounting for actual and expected revenue and expenses, accumulating and classifying them first by appropriate "organizational units" (such as "nursing units," "stations," "departments," or "functions"), then into primary and secondary subclassifications, including "type of patient," "service," "financial status," or "type of accommodation."

[23]*Ibid.*, pp. 19–23.

[24]American Hospital Association, *Cost Finding and Rate Setting for Hospitals* (AHA, Chicago, 1968), p. 94. Reprinted with permission.

EXHIBIT 6   Schedule for Development of Rates for Operating Room

Hours during which operating rooms will be in use	5,000
Average hospital paid personnel per operation	5
Man-hours of usage (5 × 5,000)	25,000
Financial needs (cost finding results for operating rooms plus additional requirements	
for operating margin, etc.)	$400,000
Rate per man-hour ($400,000 ÷ 25,000)	$16.00
Rate per operating room hour (5 × $16.00)	$80.00

SOURCE: Reprinted, with permission, from *Cost Finding and Rate Setting For Hospitals,* 1968 ed., published by the American Hospital Association, p. 94.

The organizational units are referred to as revenue centers and cost centers; some units are both (the laboratory, for example); others produce no revenue and are only cost centers (the housekeeping department, for example).

The routine accounting process, assuming a responsibility accounting system is used, records and reports only the direct, controllable cost of each organizational unit. Indirect and other noncontrollable costs, such as depreciation and interest, are not recorded by organizational units, but are entered in an "unassigned expense" classification. Therefore, the *full* costs of operating an organizational unit or department are *not* shown in the departmental expense accounts of the hospital. In addition, a number of departments exist primarily to serve other departments within the hospital.[25]

The significance of these AHA comments will become more readily apparent in the following comments on cost finding.

Cost Finding. "Cost finding" is a term used by some organizations, and particularly by hospitals. Although variously defined,[26] cost finding is the identifying, classifying, and allocation of costs—costs of many types and for many purposes— as they are included in the expense records of an organization. Simply stated, when the nonprofit organization wishes to determine the costs of a program or service, it "finds" them through a process of analyzing all the expenses of the organization and accumulating those by desired category, allocating as necessary those expenses not directly attributable.

Although cost finding has applications that may relate to many nonprofit entities, it is in the areas of hospitals and similar medical facilities where it has been most widely used, because of the need of these facilities to account for costs to third-party payors. Thus, "cost finding" is in a more developed stage for hospitals than for other types of nonprofit organizations.

In cost finding, the hospital's direct costs and allocated indirect costs are accumulated by type of department, then these "adjusted costs" are allocated from the "non-revenue-producing" departments to each other and to the "revenue-producing" cost centers. The AHA, in its *Cost Finding and Rate Setting for Hospitals,* has described three methods for allocation among departments.

The first method is a "simple" or "direct" allocation process in which costs of non-revenue-producing cost centers or departments are allocated directly to revenue-producing centers, without first being distributed and accumulated in other non-revenue-producing centers. The second method is called the "step-

[25] *Ibid.,* p. 1.

[26] Cost finding may be generally defined as a determination of the total cost accumulated for a process, cost center, etc., through allocation of direct costs and proration of indirect costs. Lynn and Freeman, in *Fund Accounting—Theory and Practice* (p. 645), however, prefer a "narrower definition" in relation to cost accounting: "the term 'cost accounting' ... [refers] ... to a continuous process of analyzing, classifying, recording, and summarizing costs within the discipline and controls of the formal accounting system and reporting them to users on a regular basis. The determination or estimation of costs by more informal procedures and/or on an irregular basis is referred to as 'cost finding.'"

down" method—costs are distributed from non-revenue-producing cost centers to both other non-revenue-producing *and* revenue-producing centers, *closing* each center as it is distributed to others. In the third way of allocating, the "double-distribution" method, non-revenue-producing centers are not permanently closed after allocating their accumulated costs, but remain open to *receive* subsequent cost distributions from other centers. If additional costs are so received, it is necessary to allocate the costs a second time before closing the center. Not surprisingly, the procedure most commonly applied by hospitals is the second of these, the "step-down" method, because it provides a more accurate allocation of costs than the first method, but is easier to utilize than the more complicated "double-distribution" process.

An Illustration of the "Step-Down" Method. There are several basic procedures for an organization to use in the cost-finding process. The first of these is to accumulate accounting data from the financial records, scheduling the direct expenses appropriately on a worksheet, by cost center. An example of such a worksheet, including reclassifications and adjustments, is illustrated in Exhibit 7.

The next step is to allocate the costs in non-revenue-producing cost centers to revenue-producing cost centers, as is demonstrated using the step-down method in Exhibit 8.

In this illustration, the "closing" of each non-revenue-producing cost center can be seen as its accumulated costs and those costs received from other centers, if any, are distributed. Exhibit 9 shows a supporting schedule with the bases of allocation for distributing each center's costs. In this schedule, the number of "allocation units," i.e., square feet, hours, units, and requisitions, are divided into the *total costs to be allocated* to arrive at a "unit cost multiplier." This *multiplier* times each cost center's *allocation units* yields the amount of costs allocated to other centers on the worksheet in Exhibit 8.

The final cost-finding procedure is to summarize the cost data into a report or series of reports for use by management. Such reports would include pertinent revenue data, summarized by revenue-producing cost center, as compared to the costs by cost center determined through cost finding, and would vary in format depending on the needs of management.

Bookkeeping and Cost-Recording Capabilities. After discussions of some of the more important elements of cost accounting and reporting for nonprofit organizations, it is now relevant to comment briefly on some of their personnel and record-keeping aspects. Nonprofit organizations, of course, come in every conceivable size, from the very small to the very large, from those with no paid staff to those with a complex organization of professional employees. Unfortunately, one characteristic that appears to be common to a large majority of them is a lack of accounting sophistication; this must be recognized when considering allocations of costs between functions.

There are several reasons for this lack of sophistication. One factor is that it has only been in recent years that the public has been demanding full disclosure, and so there has been no need for strong, established accounting expertise in the nonprofit sector. In addition, most nonprofit organizations are not large enough to afford (or have enough transactions to warrant) the use of electronic data processing applications for their record keeping and for the end-of-period allocation process. As a result, much of the accounting process is performed manually, with some organizations using individuals not trained or experienced in accounting and finance. (It should be noted, however, that the manual worksheet is an adequate way of performing cost allocation. The schedule in Exhibit 4 is a good example of a simple worksheet for allocation of costs to functional classifications.)

Perhaps the real key, however, is the reluctance (and sometimes the *inability*) to pay the going rate for top-level accounting and financial people. An attitude seems

EXHIBIT 7

TYPICAL SMALL HOSPITAL
Worksheet for Reclassification of Direct Expenses
For the Year Ended December 31, 197A

Cost centers	Per trial balance			Reclassifications*			Reclassified balances		
	Salaries	Other	Total	Salaries	Other	Total	Salaries	Other	Total
Non-revenue-producing									
A (depreciation)		$ 300,000	$ 300,000					$ 300,000	$ 300,000
B	$ 600,000	320,000	920,000	(a)$(20,000)		$(20,000)	$ 580,000	320,000	900,000
C	800,000	900,000	1,700,000				800,000	900,000	1,700,000
D	135,000	650,000	785,000	(a)20,000		20,000	155,000	650,000	805,000
E	220,000	105,000	325,000				220,000	105,000	325,000
Revenue-producing									
F	775,000	700,000	1,475,000				775,000	700,000	1,475,000
G	400,000	350,000	750,000	(b)(50,000)	$(30,000)	(80,000)	350,000	320,000	670,000
H				(b)50,000	30,000	80,000	50,000	30,000	80,000
I	100,000	35,000	135,000				100,000	35,000	135,000
J	500,000	215,000	715,000				500,000	215,000	715,000
	$3,530,000	$3,575,000	$7,105,000	-0-	-0-	-0-	$3,530,000	$3,575,000	$7,105,000

*Bases for reclassifications would naturally vary from organization to organization. Entry (a) above represents a transfer from one cost center to another. Entry (b) represents the establishment of a new cost center that did not exist until *after* the expenses were analyzed.

EXHIBIT 8

TYPICAL SMALL HOSPITAL
Worksheet for Cost Finding ("Step-Down" Method)
For the Year Ended December 31, 197A

Cost centers	Direct costs (Reclassified balances)	A	B	C	D	E	Total
Non-revenue-producing							
A (depreciation)	$ 300,000	$300,000					
B	900,000	$ 50,000	$950,000				
C	1,700,000	30,000	$250,000	$1,980,000			
D	805,000	15,000	50,000	$ 300,000	$1,170,000		
E	325,000	35,000	100,000	460,000	$ 180,000	$1,100,000	
	$4,030,000						
Revenue-producing							
F	$1,475,000	50,000	200,000	580,000	285,000	$ 400,000	$2,990,000
G	670,000	24,000	150,000	260,000	135,000	300,000	1,539,000
H	80,000	60,000	20,000	60,000	255,000	40,000	515,000
I	135,000	16,000	100,000	140,000	150,000	200,000	741,000
J	715,000	20,000	80,000	180,000	165,000	160,000	1,320,000
	$3,075,000	$300,000	$950,000	$1,980,000	$1,170,000	$1,100,000	
Total	$7,105,000						$7,105,000

EXHIBIT 9

TYPICAL SMALL HOSPITAL
Supporting Schedule for Bases of Allocation of Costs in Non-Revenue-Producing Cost Centers to
Revenue-Producing Cost Centers
For the Year Ended December 31, 197A

Cost centers	A	B	C	D	E
	Square feet	No. of hours paid	No. of units used	No. of requisitions processed	No. of hours paid
A (depreciation)	150,000				
B	25,000	95,000			
C	15,000	25,000	495,000		
D	7,500	5,000	75,000	390,000	
E	17,500	10,000	115,000	60,000	55,000
F	25,000	20,000	145,000	95,000	20,000
G	12,000	15,000	65,000	45,000	15,000
H	30,000	2,000	15,000	85,000	2,000
I	8,000	10,000	35,000	50,000	10,000
J	10,000	8,000	45,000	55,000	8,000
No. of allocation units	150,000	95,000	495,000	390,000	55,000
Costs to be allocated	$300,000	$950,000	$1,980,000	$1,170,000	$1,100,000
Unit cost multiplier	$2	$10	$4	$3	$20

Cost centers and basis of allocation

to prevail that people employed by nonprofit organizations should be willing to take part of their pay in "psychic" compensation—a feeling of well-being for a job performed for a worthy cause—and thus to accept a lower rate of pay. This attitude results, of course, in an organization often getting exactly that for which it pays, and the costs can be very high.

CONCLUSION

Cost accounting for nonprofit organizations is still largely a new art that is only now beginning to get the attention it deserves. With perhaps a few major exceptions (hospitals and colleges and universities, for example), cost accounting, as it is traditionally considered, is nonexistent in this sector. For the most part, cost accounting now involves only functional reporting with a clear distinction between program and supporting services; yet functional reporting has only recently begun to be accepted as the desirable form of reporting for most nonprofit organizations.

Except for hospitals, unit cost information is seldom provided even by the largest of nonprofit organizations, although there seems little reason why such data could not be developed. Most nonprofit organizations, if they spend a little time thinking about it (and use a bit of common sense), can determine a reasonable basis for measuring the units of service provided. Although some may argue that unit costs are not meaningful because it is not possible to make valid comparisons of such costs per unit between organizations, they overlook one of the most important uses of unit costs: that of being able to compare the costs of the individual programs *within* a single organization as a management tool for making allocation decisions.

Presently, there are areas of influence having significant impact on the introduction and use of cost accounting techniques, with perhaps the strongest of these being the public's demand to know more about the operations of the nonprofit sector of society. Resources are scarce, and nonprofit organizations can no longer ignore this demand for full accountability. This atmosphere is healthy and, in the coming years, will serve to accelerate the significant shift in emphasis in reporting—from that of a "stewardship" of funds to that of reporting what programs were accomplished, and at what cost.

BIBLIOGRAPHY

Accounting Advisory Committee: *Report to the Commission on Private Philanthropy and Public Needs,* Accounting Advisory Committee, New York, October 1974.

American Accounting Association: "Report of the Committee on Accounting Practices of Not-for-Profit Organizations," *Accounting Review,* Supplement to Vol. XLVI, 1971, pp. 80–163.

American Hospital Association: *Chart of Accounts for Hospitals,* AHA, Chicago, 1976.

——: *Cost Finding and Rate Setting for Hospitals,* AHA, Chicago, 1968.

American Institute of Certified Public Accountants: *Audits of Colleges and Universities,* AICPA, New York, 1973.

——: *Audits of Voluntary Health and Welfare Organizations,* AICPA, New York, 1974.

——: *Hospital Audit Guide,* AICPA, New York, 1972.

——: *A Tentative Set of Accounting Principles and Reporting Practices for Nonprofit Organizations Not Covered by Existing AICPA Audit Guides* (Discussion Draft), AICPA, New York, February 1977.

Association of Science-Technology Centers: *Museum Accounting Guidelines,* Association of Science-Technology Centers, Washington, D.C., 1976.

Bastable, C. W.: "Evaluating Performance of Not-for-Profit Entities," *Journal of Accountancy,* January 1973, pp. 32–34.

Commission on Private Philanthropy and Public Needs: *Giving in America—Toward a Stronger Voluntary Sector,* Commission of Private Philanthropy and Public Needs, Washington, D.C., 1975.

Green, J. L., Jr., and A. W. Barber: *A System of Cost Accounting for Physical Plant Operations in Institutions of Higher Education,* University of Georgia Press, Athens, Ga., 1968.

Gross, Malvern J., Jr.: "Eight Recent Developments Affecting NPO Accounting," *Philanthropy Monthly,* December 1975, pp. 14–17.

———: *Financial and Accounting Guide for Nonprofit Organizations,* 2nd ed., Ronald Press, New York, 1974.

———: "Full Disclosure—A Better Answer," *Philanthropy Monthly,* March 1976, pp. 12–18.

———: "Fund-Raising and Program Cost Ratios," *Philanthropy Monthly,* June 1975, pp. 28–34.

———: "Must College Financial Reporting Be So Hard to Understand?" *Price Waterhouse Review,* 21, 1 (1976), pp. 20–29.

———: "A New Study of the Cost of Fund-Raising in New York," *Philanthropy Monthly,* April 1976, pp. 22–25.

———: "State Compliance Reporting for Nonprofit Organizations," *CPA Journal,* April 1975, pp. 33–36.

Harris, Arthur F. M.: "Association Accounting," chap. 18 of *The Law of Associations,* George D. Webster, ed. Matthew Bender & Co., New York, 1975.

Henke, E. O.: *Accounting for Non-Profit Organizations,* Wadsworth Publishing Co., Belmont, Calif., 1966.

———: "Evaluating Performance of Not-for-Profit Entities," *Journal of Accountancy,* January 1973, p. 34.

———: "Performance Evaluation for Not-for-Profit Organizations," *Journal of Accountancy,* June 1972, pp. 51–55.

Lynn, Edward S., and Robert J. Freeman: *Fund Accounting—Theory and Practice,* Prentice-Hall, Englewood Cliffs, N.J., 1974.

National Association of College and University Business Officers: *College and University Business Administration* (Administrative Manual), 3rd ed., NACUBO, Washington, D.C., 1974.

———: *Fundamental Considerations for Determining Cost Information in Higher Education,* NACUBO, Washington, D.C., 1975.

National Health Council, National Assembly of National Voluntary Health and Social Welfare Organizations, Inc., and United Way of America: *Standards of Accounting and Financial Reporting for Voluntary Health and Welfare Organizations,* rev. ed., NHC, NVHSWO, and United Way, New York, 1974.

Report of the Commission on Government Procedure, vol. 2, E. Perkins McGuire, Chairman, U.S. Government Printing Office, Washington, D.C., 1972.

Skousen, K. Fred, Jay M. Smith, and Leon W. Woodfield: *User Needs: An Empirical Study of College and University Financial Reporting,* National Association of College and University Business Officers, Washington, D.C., 1975.

Topping, James R.: *Cost Analysis Manual,* Technical Report No. 45, National Center for Higher Education Management Systems at WICHE, Boulder, Colo., 1974.

U.S. National Archives and Records Service: *Code of Federal Regulations,* Title 4, "Accounts," chap. 3, revised as of January 1, 1975, U.S. Government Printing Office, Washington, D.C., 1975.

———: *Code of Federal Regulations,* Title 32, "National Defense," subtitle A, chap. I, subchap. A, part 15: "Contract Cost Principles and Procedures," revised as of July 1, 1974, U.S. Government Printing Office, Washington, D.C., 1974.

———: *Code of Federal Regulations,* Title 34, "Government Management," chap. II, subchap. B, part 211, revised as of January 1, 1975, U.S. Government Printing Office, Washington, D.C., 1975.

———: *Code of Federal Regulations,* Title 41, "Public Contracts and Property Management," part 15, "Contract Cost Principles and Procedures," revised as of January 1, 1975, U.S. Government Printing Office, Washington, D.C., 1975.

United Way of America: *Accounting and Financial Reporting—A Guide for United Ways and Not-for-Profit Human Service Organizations,* United Way, Alexandria, Va., 1974.

———: *Budgeting—A Guide for United Ways and Not-for-Profit Human Service Organizations,* United Way, Alexandria, Va., 1975.

———: *UWASIS—United Way of America Services Identification System,* United Way, Alexandria, Va., 1972.

Chapter 26

Human Resource Accounting*

ERIC G. FLAMHOLTZ
Associate Professor of Accounting-Information Systems, and
Director, Accounting-Information Systems Research Program,
Graduate School of Management, University of California,
Los Angeles

*Portions of this chapter are adapted from Eric G. Flamholtz, *Human Resource Accounting* (Dickenson Publishing Company, Encino, Calif., 1974), by permission of the author and publisher.

INTRODUCTION

Human resource accounting (HRA) is a branch of managerial accounting. It involves the application of accounting concepts and methods to the area of personnel management. In addition, HRA can provide information about human resource costs for corporate financial reporting, just as cost accounting provides information about inventory valuation for financial reports. Because currently accepted financial accounting standards do not treat investments in human resources as assets, this chapter focuses on HRA as a managerial tool.[1]

The chapter is organized into four parts. The first section discusses the nature and purpose of HRA. The next section examines the use of HRA in the human resource management process. The third section discusses the methods of accounting for human resource cost and deals with the problems involved in the design of human resource cost accounting systems. The final section presents illustrations of how selected organizations have actually applied HRA to meet their own needs.

NATURE AND PURPOSE OF HUMAN RESOURCE ACCOUNTING

Definition.   Human resource accounting may be defined as the measurement and reporting of the cost and value of people as organizational resources. It involves accounting for investments in people and their replacement cost. It also involves accounting for the economic value of people to an organization.

The primary purpose of HRA is to facilitate the management of people as organizational resources. Thus we might also refer to it as "human resource management accounting"—the application of accounting to the management of human resources.

Assumptions Underlying HRA.   Human resource accounting is based on three basic ideas or assumptions: (1) the notion that people are valuable organizational resources; (2) the belief that the value of people as organizational resources is a function of the way in which they are managed; and (3) the premise that information in the form of measurements of human resource costs and value are necessary to manage human resources effectively and efficiently. Each of these underlying assumptions is examined below.

People Are Valuable Organizational Resources.   The fundamental notion underlying HRA is that people are valuable organizational resources. This means that people are capable of providing current and future services to organizations and that these expected future services have economic value to the enterprise. We can thus refer to people as organizational resources because of their service potential, without the implication that they are *owned* by organizations.

It is not necessary for people to be owned by organizations for us to account for them as resources. First, the management accounting-information system need not be constrained by external reporting conventions. If management perceives the need for human resource accounting information, it can be developed and reported as an adjunct to the financial accounting system, just as some cost accounting information is currently treated. Second, even though people are not owned by organizations and may potentially leave an enterprise, we can still account for investments in them, their replacement cost, and their economic value. The uncertainty involved in the likelihood of turnover can be treated by providing

---

[1]For a discussion of the role of human resource accounting in corporate financial reporting, see Eric G. Flamholtz, *Human Resource Accounting* (Dickenson Publishing Company, Encino, Calif., 1974), chap. 9.

an "allowance for expected turnover" as a contra account to "human resource investments," just as we now provide an "allowance for uncollectible accounts" as a contra to receivables. Third, an organization choosing to account for people as resources parallels the economist's treatment of people as human capital (as a factor of production) in explaining economic growth. To account for something as a resource, it is merely necessary that it provide future benefits and be subject to some degree of control or influence by the organization. People provide future economic benefits to organizations, and they are subject to control or influence through explicit or implicit employment agreements; accordingly, we may account for them as organizational resources.

Human Resource Value Is Influenced by Management Style.   A second important idea underlying HRA is that the value of people as organizational resources can be influenced by the way in which they are managed. The value of human resources can be enhanced, depleted, or conserved as a result of different management actions. For example, management can enhance the value of human resources through training, or the value may be depleted if technological obsolescence occurs. Similarly, some styles of leadership may increase employee motivation and, in turn, productivity—thus enhancing human resource value.

HRA Information Is Needed.   The third assumption is that information about human resource cost and value is necessary for effective and efficient management of people as an organizational resource. Information about human resource cost and value is useful, as discussed below, in various aspects of the human resource management process, including planning and control of the acquisition, development, allocation, compensation, conservation, and utilization of people. In this sense, HRA is intended as a component of the overall managerial accounting-information system.

Two Major Aspects of HRA.   There are two major aspects of human resource accounting: human resource cost accounting (HRCA) and human resource value accounting (HRVA). HRCA deals with accounting for investments made by organizations in acquiring and developing human resources as well as with the replacement costs of people presently employed. The principal focus of this chapter is on HRCA. HRVA deals with the measurement of the value of people as economic resources, a topic that is beyond the scope of the present chapter.[2]

Nature of Human Resource Cost Accounting.   Human resource cost accounting may be defined as the measurement and reporting of the costs incurred to acquire, develop, and replace people as organizational resources. It deals with two related types of costs: (1) costs associated with the functions of *the personnel management process* in acquiring and developing human resources, and (2) costs of people as human resources *per se.*

The first category refers to accounting for personnel activities and functions such as recruitment, selection, hiring, placement, and training. The costs of such activities are elements of the costs of acquiring and developing human assets. Accounting for costs of personnel functions may be termed "personnel cost accounting." It is a prerequisite to HRCA.

The second category refers to accounting for the costs of people as human assets, rather than for the functions of personnel management *per se.* It involves measuring the costs of acquiring and developing different classes of personnel and may be termed "human asset accounting."

[2]For a discussion of accounting for human resource value, see *ibid.,* chaps. 4–7. See also Baruch Lev and Aba Schwartz, "On the Use of the Economic Concept of Human Capital in Financial Statements," *Accounting Review,* January 1971, pp. 103–112; B. Jaggi and H. S. Lau, "Toward a Model for Human Resource Valuation," *Accounting Review,* April 1974, pp. 321–329; and Pekin Ogan, "A Human Resource Model for Professional Service Organizations," *Accounting Review,* April 1976, pp. 306–320.

These two aspects of HRCA and their relation to HRA as a whole are shown schematically in Exhibit 1. In summary, HRA consists of two components: (1) accounting for human resource costs and (2) accounting for human resource value. The first component, in turn, has two parts: (1) personnel cost accounting and (2) human asset accounting.

EXHIBIT 1   The Elements of Human Resource Accounting

```
                    ┌──────────────┐
                    │    Human     │
                    │   resource   │
                    │  accounting  │
                    └──────────────┘
                  ┌──────────┴──────────┐
                  ▼                     ▼
         ┌──────────────┐       ┌──────────────┐
         │    Human     │       │    Human     │
         │   resource   │       │   resource   │
         │cost accounting│      │value accounting│
         └──────────────┘       └──────────────┘
          ┌──────┴──────┐
          ▼             ▼
   ┌──────────┐   ┌──────────┐
   │ Personnel│   │  Human   │
   │   cost   │──▶│  asset   │
   │accounting│   │accounting│
   └──────────┘   └──────────┘
```

Need to Account for Human Resource Costs.   Human resource costs may be defined as the sacrifices incurred to acquire or replace people. Interest in developing methods of accounting for human resource costs first began to receive serious attention during the 1960s.[3]

Primary Reasons for Growth of Interest in HRCA.   The recent growth of interest in HRCA has been caused by several related factors. First, services have become an increasingly important part of gross national product, and yet there is still relatively little in the accounting literature dealing with concepts or methods of accounting for human resources, which are the principal assets of most service firms. This deficiency has resulted, historically, because accounting has evolved to meet the needs of an industrial, not a service-based, economy. Second, as a result of increasing technological complexity, the educational and training period required by people for entry-level organizational positions has increased significantly from prior decades. For example, many people entering management trainee positions now have MBA degrees rather than merely BA degrees or high school diplomas. Thus people bring to organizations a set of knowledge, skills, and experience that constitutes a form of capital—human capital—rather than merely the ability to perform relatively unskilled tasks.[4] As the amount of human capital people bring with them to organizations (manufacturing as well as service firms) increases, it makes sense to account for such corporate "assets." In addition, some organizations are themselves spending substantial sums to train and develop technical, administrative, and interpersonal skills of people. Such organizations obviously recognize that these expenditures are investments with future benefits

[3]See, for example, R. Lee Brummet, Eric G. Flamholtz, and William C. Pyle, "Human Resource Measurement—A Challenge for Accountants," *Accounting Review,* April 1968, pp. 217–224.

[4]See Theodore Schultz, "Investment in Human Capital," *American Economic Review,* March 1961, pp. 1–17.

even though they are accounted for as expenses under conventional financial reporting standards.

Dysfunctional Effects Without HRCA.   Moreover, if organizations do not account for human resource costs, management may underestimate (or ignore) both the investments required to acquire and train human assets and the costs that must be incurred to replace people. Without appropriate information, decisions may be suboptimal. For example, a large aerospace corporation was recently faced with the need to reduce its work force in order to lower expenses. The firm chose to terminate engineers with relatively esoteric specialties and years of experience (engineers who would be difficult, if not impossible, to replace) rather than lower-salaried, more easily replaceable engineers. In effect, the firm was depleting a portfolio of human assets. In that industry the ability to obtain contracts depends, at least in part, on existing capabilities to get the job done. Thus a firm may require that a diverse set of skills be available, even though some may never be used. Although the firm may have made the correct decision, it was made without information about the replacement cost of the engineers, information that might have led to the choice of a different alternative.

MANAGERIAL USES OF HUMAN RESOURCE ACCOUNTING

HRA is intended to be a managerial tool. This section examines its uses in various aspects of human resource management, describes the broad role of HRCA in human resource planning and control, and describes HRCA's specific functions in the acquisition, development, allocation, conservation, and compensation of people.

The purpose of this section, then, is to provide an overview of the managerial uses and applications of HRCA. In a subsequent section, we examine selected case examples of how these methods have actually been applied in human resource management.

Role of HRCA in Planning and Control.   The principal role of human resource cost accounting in personnel management is analogous to the role of accounting in manufacturing, marketing, or financial management. HRCA involves providing information for human resource planning and control. These generic management functions are described below.

Role of HRCA in Planning.   "Planning involves making choices between alternatives and is primarily, if not entirely, a decision-making activity."[5] Human resource planning is the process of planning to satisfy an organization's human resource needs and requirements. It is a process of choosing the organization's human resource objectives and the means (programs) for attaining them.

One of the roles of HRCA is to provide the cost information required in the human resource planning process. Typically, this involves providing the cost information necessary for budgeting. For example, it may involve providing historical cost information to a bank's personnel director about the costs of recruiting and selecting loan officers so that the manager may prepare a budget based on the anticipated level of recruitment for the coming fiscal year. In effect, this information may be used to develop flexible budgets and forecasts of costs for various personnel functions: recruiting, training, etc. At present, this type of information is not typically available, even in large, well-managed organizations.

Another aspect of HRCA's role in planning is to provide the cost information required to assess alternatives in specific human resource management decisions.

[5]Committee to Prepare a Statement of Basic Accounting Theory, *A Statement of Basic Accounting Theory* (American Accounting Association, New York, 1966), p. 44.

Decision making involves choices concerning the acquisition, development, allocation, compensation, and conservation of human resources. For example, faced with a layoff decision, a decision maker may wish to compare the expected payroll savings with the potential replacement costs to be incurred if employees are rehired. HRCA can provide the required replacement cost information. Similarly, management may wish to assess the relative cost of two proposed training programs, and the function of HRCA is to provide such information.

Role of HRCA in Control.   Control may be defined as "the process by which managers assure that resources are obtained and used effectively and efficiently in the accomplishment of the organization's goals."[6] It involves an attempt to motivate people toward achievement of overall organizational goals. Human resource control involves the process through which an organization attempts to assure that its human resource objectives are attained effectively and efficiently.

The role of HRCA is to provide cost information necessary to implement the control function. For example, information may be required about turnover costs in order to assess management's performance in human resource conservation.

Role of HRCA in Functions of Human Resource Management Process.   HRCA plays a role not only in the overall functions of planning and control; it also has specific uses in various aspects of the human resource management process: acquisition, development, allocation, compensation, and conservation. These are examined below.

Acquisition of Human Resources.   Human resource acquisition involves recruiting, selecting, and hiring people to meet an organization's present and future needs. It involves obtaining the human resources required by the organization to attain its overall objectives.

HRCA may be used to provide information required to budget acquisition programs. This is the process of determining the amount to be invested by an organization in recruiting, selecting, and hiring the people required by the firm.

Costs for the personnel function of most firms is typically seen as "burden," "overhead," or unproductive expenses. Yet the acquisition function of personnel departments does have a measurable output—the number of people in different personnel classifications who are hired. It is possible, therefore, to provide information to be used by personnel management in planning the budget and by top management in assessing its reasonableness.

DEVELOPING STANDARD ACQUISITION COSTS.   It is also feasible to develop standard personnel acquisition costs for different classifications of employees. For example, an insurance company might develop standard acquisition costs for claims personnel, including investigators, adjusters, etc., as shown in Exhibit 2. The methods used to obtain this information are described below.

EXHIBIT 2

MIDWESTERN INSURANCE COMPANY*
Standard Acquisition Costs—Claims Personnel

Personnel classifications	Standard acquisition costs
Claims investigator	$ 600
Claims adjuster	600
Officer adjuster	5,600
Field examiner	7,000
Chief adjuster	11,300
Claims manager	14,900

*This is a pseudonym.

[6]Robert N. Anthony, John Dearden, and Richard F. Vancil, *Management Control Systems,* rev. ed. (Richard D. Irwin, Homewood, Ill., 1972), p. 5.

In many organizations, personnel management activities are treated as discretionary expense centers. That is, the firm's expenditure on personnel management is treated as though it is determined solely by management's judgment. However, if standard acquisition costs are developed, the personnel function can be treated as a standard cost center.[7] This is analogous to treating a manufacturing plant as a standard cost center.

PERSONNEL AS A PROFIT CENTER.   The use of HRCA also allows certain aspects of the personnel function to be treated as "profit centers." A profit center involves responsibility for costs and revenues. Because personnel recruiting is a service to other parts of the organization, management may establish a "transfer price" (a price for the transfer of goods or services between organizational units) for recruitment. The transfer price can be a "cost per employee hired" or "cost per employee interviewed."

There are two advantages to this system. First, treating the personnel function as a profit center (crediting it for the revenue generated from its services and charging it for costs incurred) may tend to make personnel management profit-conscious, and increase motivation to provide more cost effective service to the organization. Second, under this system other parts of the organization are charged with the cost of hiring personnel, rather than having it "buried" in the personnel budget. If a manager's budget is not charged with costs of a service activity, there may be a tendency (either conscious or unconscious) to treat it as a "free" good and use it inefficiently. For example, the vice president for personnel for a large financial institution has observed the tendency of managers in the organization to interview an unnecessarily large number of job applicants because the managers "don't have to foot the bill."

Development of Human Resources.   Human resource development is the process of increasing the capabilities of people as organizational resources. It involves various forms of training designed to enhance the skills, attitudes, or motivation of people. This, in turn, increases the value of people to an organization. Development may occur through either formal, off-the-job programs or by on-the-job learning.

Expenditures for human resource development are essentially capital expenditures; they represent investments in developing "human capital." Thus the primary problem faced by management in making human resource development decisions is to assess the cost and value of proposed development programs.

Human resource accounting can facilitate decisions involving the allocation of resources to development projects in two related ways. First, it can provide information about the cost of alternative development programs to permit planning or budgeting of expenditures. Second, it can help measure anticipated cost savings from proposed development expenditures in order to derive a rate of return on proposed investments. For example, an investment in a new method of training machine operators might be based on a comparison of the projected cost savings (differential productivity before and after the training) with the required investment. The cost savings may be measured by comparing the "learning curves" (a graph of the performance of people on a specified task over time) of operators trained under both methods. The value of the differential rates of learning may be calculated by multiplying the different units of performance by their rate of compensation as a measure of the cost to be recovered.

ACQUISITION AND DEVELOPMENT TRADE-OFFS.   A common problem involved in manufacturing management is the "make-or-buy" decision. Similarly, in personnel management a typical issue is whether to acquire a trained person from outside the organization or to recruit untrained people and develop them from within.

[7]*Ibid.*, p. 201.

Some firms follow the policy of hiring experienced people from other firms. This results in reduced training costs, but generally higher salaries must be paid to attract such people. Thus there is a trade-off between the differential salaries required to attract trained personnel and the cost of training their equivalent with a firm.

HRCA can facilitate such acquisition-development trade-off decisions by providing information about the costs to develop people for various positions. These costs can be compared with the differential salaries, if any, needed to attract trained personnel.

Allocation of Human Resources.   The allocation of human resources is the process of assigning people to various organizational roles and tasks. One criterion that managers ought to use in guiding allocation decisions is the expected return on investment, that is, the anticipated return on the human capital committed to a project.

Without HRCA information, managers may have only a vague idea about either the original investment made in human resources or their replacement cost. Thus the function of HRCA in allocation is to provide such information for use in assessing potential projects. For example, a large engineering-construction firm typically faces the problem of determining how much to bid for various types of projects. The firm has three principal classes of projects: heavy construction, design engineering, and hybrids with both construction and engineering. The first category requires substantial commitments of financial resources but relatively little investment of human capital, and the second type involves primarily human rather than financial resources. Information about the investment in human assets and its replacement cost would enable the firm to assess the required revenues to generate a satisfactory return on investment.

Conservation of Human Resources.   The conservation of human resources is the process of maintaining the capabilities of people as individuals and the effectiveness of the human organization as a whole. Depletion of human resources can occur in two different ways. First, individuals can become technologically obsolete. Their technical skills may not be adequate to the new requirements of their jobs. If organizations permit such skill depletion to occur, then there has been a failure to maintain human resources. For example, engineers in the aerospace industry are frequently assigned to very specialized projects that last several years (e.g., the design of a wing of an aircraft). During this period, the engineers may have little opportunity for continuing development, and by the end of the project they may be obsolete.

One way in which top management can control, at least to some extent, the technological obsolescence of personnel is through HRCA. Management may monitor the amount of investments made in employee development. This is a surrogate or proxy measure of the extent to which management is paying attention to this aspect of human resource conservation.

Depletion can also occur if people leave an organization, or if their probability of leaving increases. Concern over this problem was one of the original reasons for the development of human resource accounting.

Many organizations currently use turnover rates to assess human resource conservation. However, as Robert L. Woodruff, Jr., Vice President of Human Resource at R. G. Barry Corporation (a soft goods manufacturing firm that has developed its own system of HRCA) has stated:

> Conventional personnel replacement turnover statistics do not give a manager sufficient information to evaluate the economic impact of the turnover he is experiencing. . . . The difficulty with conventional personnel turnover statistics is that they give equal weight to each "transaction" regardless of: (1) the level of the position within the

organization; (2) the age of the person leaving; (3) the tenure of the person with the organization; (4) the amount of the firm's investment in the person; and (5) the level of performance and/or potential of the person.[8]

Human resource cost accounting, as Woodruff also notes, "can provide the manager with a more accurate representation of the economic nature and consequences of personnel turnover."[9] Turnover rates merely indicate the numbers of people who have left an organization, whereas human resource replacement cost indicates the economic magnitude of the event.

Compensation. Compensation may be defined as the financial rewards paid to people for services rendered to an organization. One of the managerial problems involved in compensation is to evaluate the relative worth of jobs. This function is termed "job evaluation," which may be defined as the process of measuring the value of jobs to an organization. Job evaluation is typically performed using point systems, factor comparison, ranking methods, or grade descriptions.

Human resource cost accounting may be useful either as a supplement or an alternative to traditional job evaluation methods. The basic approach would involve using replacement cost as a measure of job worth to the company. It is

[8]Robert L. Woodruff, Jr., "Accounting for Human Resource Costs," unpublished paper presented at Human Resource Accounting Seminar, Ausschuss für Wirtschaftliche Verwaltung, Bonn, Federal Republic of Germany, 1974, p. 18.

[9]*Ibid.*, p. 19.

EXHIBIT 3   Overview of Human Resource Cost Accounting's Role in the Personnel Management Process

Human resource management functions	Generic management processes	
	Planning	Control
Acquisition	1. Provides cost information to budget acquisition programs: historical and standard costs	1. Provides standard cost of acquisition activities (recruitment, selection, etc.) for cost control 2. Facilitates treatment of personnel acquisition function as a profit center
Development	1. Provides information about cost of development programs for budgetary planning 2. Measures anticipated cost savings from proposed development expenditures 3. Facilitates acquisition development trade-off decisions	1. Provides standard cost information for development activities 2. Can facilitate treatment of training as a profit center
Allocation	1. Provides information about human resource costs for investment decisions and allocation decisions	1. Can use investment in human resources as criterion for evaluating project performance (return)
Conservation	1. Can use expected cost of turnover in turnover control programs	1. Monitors investments in human resources to conserve skills 2. Measures economic cost of turnover
Compensation	1. Can use replacement cost in job evaluation for compensation planning	1. Can use replacement costs to monitor compensation rates set by other methods and control for over- or underpriced jobs

influenced by both the supply of skills available in the external labor market and internal factors such as the degree of training required. By applying human resource replacement cost information as a measure of job worth, management may identify over- and underpriced jobs.

Summary.   This section has examined the uses of HRCA in selected aspects of the human resource management process. As we have seen, HRCA may be used in the acquisition, development, allocation, conservation, and compensation of human resources. Although a full discussion of all of the possible uses of HRCA is beyond the scope of this chapter, some of the major applications have been discussed.

These uses are summarized in Exhibit 3. They are shown classified in terms of planning or control functions.

ACCOUNTING FOR HUMAN RESOURCE COSTS

This section presents the basic concepts and measurement techniques required to account for human resource costs. It provides the terminology and measurement models that are the building blocks of the actual systems of accounting for human resource costs, examples of which are described in a subsequent section.

Nature of Human Resource Costs.   Accounting uses the concept of "cost" in a variety of ways. References are made to "historical cost," "acquisition cost," "outlay cost," "replacement cost," "current cost," "direct and indirect cost," "standard cost," "incremental cost," "sunk cost," "fixed and variable cost," "marginal cost," and "opportunity cost," to cite just some of the more common ways in which the term "cost" is used. Many of these cost concepts are applicable to human resources.

Definition of Cost.   Formally defined, *cost* is a sacrifice incurred to obtain some anticipated benefit or service. A cost may be incurred to acquire tangible objects or intangible benefits.

Conceptually, all costs may have "asset" and "expense" components. An *asset* is the portion of a cost that is expected to provide benefits during future accounting periods. An *expense* is the portion of a cost that has been consumed during the current accounting period. A fundamental accounting problem is, of course, to measure the asset and expense components of costs.

Historical and Replacement Costs.   There are several accounting concepts of cost that are of considerable importance to human resource accounting. Two of these concepts are historical cost and replacement cost. *Historical cost* refers to the sacrifice that was actually incurred to acquire or obtain a resource. This may also be termed "original cost." *Replacement cost* refers to the sacrifice that must be incurred to replace a resource presently owned or employed.

Outlay and Imputed Costs.   Another pair of cost concepts that are important for human resource accounting are outlay and imputed costs, which are components of original and replacement costs. An *outlay cost* refers to the actual cash expenditure that must be incurred to acquire or replace a resource. It is a measure of the cash that must be sacrificed to acquire or replace a resource. *Imputed costs* do not involve actual cash outlays and thus do not appear in the financial records; such costs, nevertheless, involve a sacrifice.[10] For example, if a salesperson devotes time to training a trainee, the sales foregone during this period constitute an imputed cost. Similarly, if a firm is out of merchandise when potential customers call in orders, an imputed cost of lost margin on sales is incurred.

Concepts of Human Resource Costs.   The notion of "human resource cost" is derived from the general concept of cost. *Human resource costs* are incurred to

[10] Imputed costs are often referred to as opportunity costs.

acquire or replace people. Like other costs, they have expense and asset components; and they may be comprised of outlay and imputed costs. In addition, it is possible to account for *standard* as well as *actual* human resource costs. Finally, the conventional accounting concepts of historical and replacement cost also have counterparts in human resource accounting.

Historical Cost of Human Resources. The *historical cost* of human resources refers to the sacrifice that was incurred to acquire and develop people. It typically includes costs of recruitment, selection, hiring, replacement, orientation, and on-the-job training. This is analogous to the concept of historical cost for other assets. For example, the historical cost of plant and equipment is the cost incurred to acquire these resources.

Replacement Cost of Human Resources. The *replacement cost* of human resources refers to the sacrifice that would have to be incurred today to replace human resources presently employed. For example, if an individual were to leave an organization, costs would have to be incurred to recruit, select, and train a replacement.

Human resource replacement cost also typically includes the costs attributable to the turnover of a present employee as well as the costs of acquiring and developing a replacement. For example, it includes costs of separation pay.

In principle, the notion of "human resource replacement cost" can be extended to individuals, groups of people, and to human organization as a whole. At present, however, personnel managers typically think in terms of acquiring a substitute capable of rendering an equivalent set of services in a specified position, rather than in terms of replacing an individual *per se*. In other words, they think in terms of replacing people in relation to specified roles rather than in terms of replacing an individual.

This suggests that there is a dual notion of replacement cost: positional and personal. In this context, *positional replacement cost* refers to the sacrifice that would have to be incurred today to replace a person in a specified position with a substitute capable of providing an equivalent set of services *in the given position*. It refers to the cost of replacing the set of services required of *any* incumbent in a specified position. *Personal replacement cost* refers to the sacrifice that would have to be incurred today to replace a person presently employed with a substitute capable of rendering an equivalent set of services. It is the cost of replacing a set of services provided by one person with an equivalent set to be provided by another. Personal replacement cost is not usually less than positional replacement cost and, in general, is larger. These concepts of replacement cost can be extended to groups as well as to individuals. However, at present there has been virtually no research done on the replacement cost of groups. Instead, the emphasis has been on individuals as the basic unit of analysis.

Measurement Model for Historical Cost of Human Resources. We have previously defined the concept of the historical cost of human resources as the sacrifice that would have to be incurred today to acquire and develop people. Our concern in this section will be with the measurement of this concept.

Exhibit 4 presents a model for the measurement of historical human resource costs. The model shows the elements comprising historical human resource costs at three levels of classification: (1) natural cost classifications, which refer to the primary objects of expenditures such as salaries, advertising, agency fees, etc.; (2) costs of specific personnel management functions such as recruitment, selection, and training; and (3) costs of the basic human resource management functions involved in historical cost of human resources: acquisition and development. Each of these elements is described below. Acquisition and development costs comprise costs of specific personnel activities such as recruitment and selection, which, in turn, comprise various natural cost items.

EXHIBIT 4   Model for Measurement of Historical Human Resource Costs

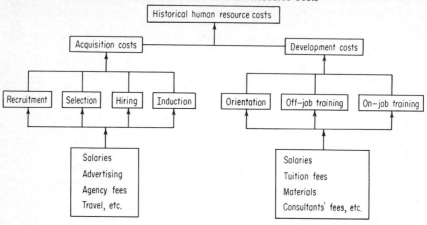

Acquisition Costs.   Human resource acquisition involves recruiting, selecting, and hiring people to meet an organization's present and future human resource needs. Acquisition costs refer to the sacrifices that must be incurred to "acquire" a new employee. They include the costs of recruitment, selection, hiring, and induction of personnel.

RECRUITMENT COSTS.   These are costs incurred to identify possible sources of human resources, including those both inside and outside an organization. They are also incurred to attract possible future members of an organization.

Recruitment costs comprise expenditures for materials, labor, and services incurred as part of the recruitment function. Although the actual classifications of expenditures incurred may differ among organizations, the most common natural expenditures include recruiters' salaries and benefits, advertising costs, agency fees, travel and entertainment, recruiting materials (brochures, etc.), and administrative expenses.

SELECTION COSTS.   These are costs incurred to determine who should and who should not be offered employment. They include all the costs incurred in selecting people for membership in an organization.

The major components of selection costs are interviewing, testing, and the administrative costs of processing applicants. These are made up of various natural expense classifications such as salaries, materials, and consulting fees.

In a particular organization, selection costs will depend on several factors, including the type of personnel being hired and the method of recruitment. The greater the responsibilities of the position for which a person is being selected, the more extensive the selection process and, in turn, the greater the cost of selection. For example, the extent of selection will be greater for managers, engineers, or salespeople than for machine operators, secretaries, or bank tellers. There will also typically be a trade-off between the cost of recruitment and cost of selection. If mass media are used to recruit employees, screening costs will generally be high. The use of agencies tends to minimize preliminary screening but may result in higher selection costs attributable to agency fees.

HIRING AND PLACEMENT COSTS.   These are costs incurred to bring an individual into an organization and place the person on the job. An employee may be hired either from outside the organization or selected from within. If the selection is made from within, the person probably will be either promoted or transferred, although demotions are also possible.

Hiring and placement costs may include agency fees paid after a person has been hired, or costs of relocating employees (moving and travel costs for either new or present employees). They may also include the cost of replacing people who have been promoted or transferred from one position to another. This is termed the "cost of internal acquisition or replacement."

In practice, it may be desirable to treat hiring and placement costs as a single classification. Taken together, their purpose is to bring an individual into the organization and into a position. The magnitude of these costs will also vary in relation to position levels in the organization.

Development Costs. Development costs refer to the sacrifice that must be incurred to train a person either to provide the level of performance normally expected from an individual in a given position or to enhance the individual's skills. Human resource development may be intended to enhance technical, administrative, or interpersonal skills.

Development costs include three components: (1) orientation, (2) off-the-job training, and (3) on-the-job training. They typically include costs such as salaries, tuition, materials, travel, and consulting fees.

ORIENTATION COSTS. These are costs associated with formal orientation of employees. The orientation may involve becoming familiar with personnel policies, company products, facilities, and so on. It may require as little as a few hours to as much as several days.

Orientation costs typically include a mixture of salaries and materials. The salaries are for both the trainer and trainees. Materials may include brochures describing firm policies, history, etc.

OFF-THE-JOB TRAINING. These are costs incurred in formal training not directly connected with actual job performance. Formal training programs may be initial "break-in" training, advanced technical training, or management development programs. They range from relatively brief, simple training for specified tasks to specialized programs held over several years. Special facilities may be used for such training, including machinery for training operators or conference facilities. Formal training may also be purchased as a service from educational institutions or from consultants who use the firm's own facilities.

Off-the-job training costs may include salaries, tuition, meals, travel, facilities costs, consulting fees, and materials. Salaries include the costs of trainers as well as trainees.

ON-THE-JOB TRAINING. These are the costs incurred in training an individual on the job itself rather than in formal training programs. On-the-job training is used not only for production workers but also for professionals such as accountants, engineers, and management trainees.

On-the-job training may range from a relatively short period required to learn a simple, repetitive task to many years required for complex, nonroutine functions. The costs associated with this training include labor and materials costs. One of the labor costs is the imputed cost of "subnormal productivity during training." This cost is incurred by the organization as a result of having a trainee whose performance is less than that normally expected from an experienced person in a given position. It is a cost of productivity foregone, attributable to the negative differential performance of trainees. For example, if a sales trainee generates less revenues than an experienced salesperson, the differential constitutes an imputed cost to the firm.

Specific Measurement Procedures. The previous section presented a model for measuring the historical cost of human resources. This section examines the specific procedures used to measure and account for such costs. In general, the process of measuring these costs involves: (1) a revision in the conventional accounting system to change the chart of accounts and add subsidiary ledgers, and

(2) adding a method of accounting for imputed costs that are not accounted for under conventional accounting.

Revision in Chart of Accounts.   Much of the data required to account for human resource costs can come from the conventional accounting system, if the chart of accounts is revised. At present, the two most common ways of treating human resource costs in the accounts are (1) merely to include them in an aggregate account such as "General or Administrative Expense" or (2) to classify them separately from other general and administrative expenses in an account such as "Recruitment and Employee Relations." The former method provides no information on the magnitude of human resource costs, whereas the latter indicates their magnitude but does not indicate the components of such costs nor provide a way to determine the costs of classifications of human resources (e.g., tellers, loan officers, management associates).

In order to account for human resource costs and apply the model described above, the chart of accounts must be revised, as illustrated in Exhibit 5 for a large

EXHIBIT 5   Revised Chart of Accounts for Human Resource Costs, Eastern City Bank

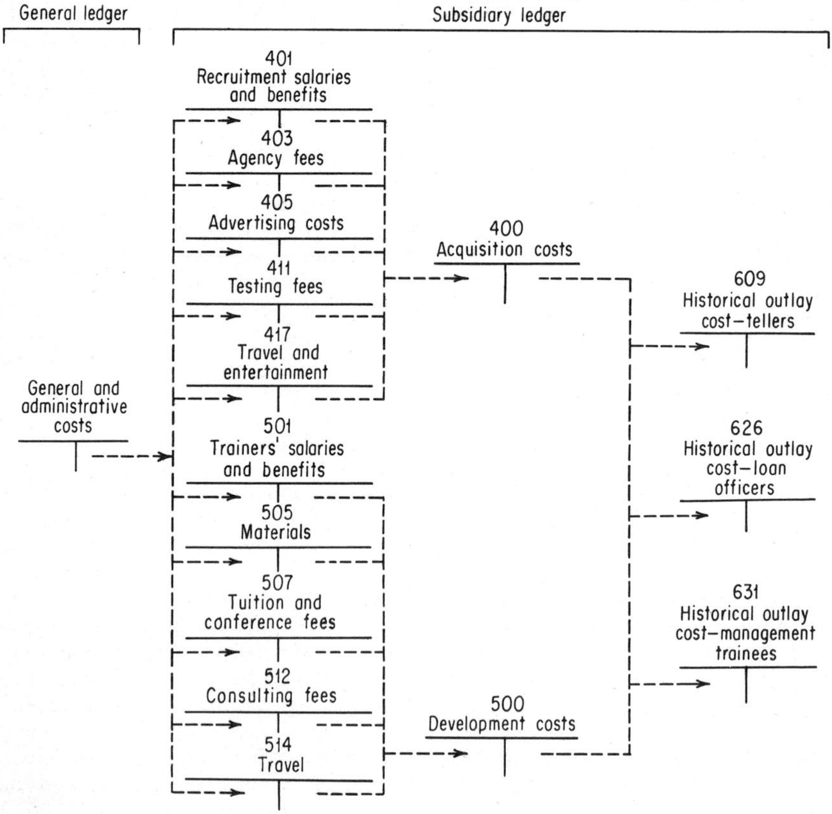

bank. The account for "General and Administrative Expense" in the general ledger must be supplemented by using the subsidiary ledger to record various human resource costs in a set of natural expense classifications. As shown in Exhibit 5, these may include accounts for recruitment salaries, employment agency fees for recruitment and selection, advertising costs, etc. These costs are summarized into two generic human resource management cost accounts: acquisition costs and development costs. These costs are then traced or allocated to accounts reflecting the investment in various groups of personnel. Exhibit 5 illustrates three types of personnel classifications. It shows the accounts for three classes of personnel: tellers, loan officers, and management trainees.

The revised chart of accounts provides a great deal of the information required to account for human resource costs. The specific problems of measuring each type of cost are examined below. It should also be noted, however, that not all of the data required to account for human resource historical costs can be obtained from the conventional accounting system. Only *outlay* cost data can be obtained by this method.

Off-Line System of Accounting for Imputed Costs.   It is also necessary to account for the imputed costs of human resource acquisition and development. To do this, a supplementary subsystem is required.

Imputed costs arise when benefits (typically revenue) are foregone in order to acquire or develop a resource. In the case of human resources, revenue that might have been earned by trainers may be sacrificed in the hope that their efforts will increase the productivity of trainees. For example, a CPA firm's partners may devote time to training that would otherwise be devoted to generating revenue ("chargeable hours"). This represents an investment in human resource development, one that may be measured in terms of the revenue or profit contribution foregone.

The specific subsystem used to account for imputed costs will depend on several factors, including the type and the nature of the imputed costs. It may vary from a relatively simple method of tracing time devoted to training and costing this time invested at an appropriate rate, to more complex attempts to measure the differential reductions in productivity of subordinates when a manager decreases supervision of present personnel in order to train new additions.

Measuring Acquisition Costs—Special Issues.   One important issue involved in accounting for acquisition costs is how to treat the costs attributable to people who are not hired. (An analogous problem arises in accounting for exploration costs of "dry hole" natural resource accounting.) These costs should be treated as costs of acquiring the people actually hired; that is, they should be allocated to the person hired. This principle is the same for all elements of acquisition costs: recruitment, selection, and hiring costs. For example, the Western Michigan Manufacturing Company has decided to hire two machinists. To recruit possible job candidates, it places a newspaper advertisement for one week at a cost of $1,000. As a result of the advertisement, 20 possible candidates are recruited and finally two are selected and hired. The recruitment cost allocated to each machinist is $500. The total recruiting cost was incurred in order to recruit *two* machinists, not the 20 who were interviewed. Similarly, the cost of interviewing 20 candidates for a position as an auditor in a CPA firm may be incurred in order to select two people. Thus, the basic principle in measuring acquisition costs is to allocate the cost of the acquisition activity (recruiting, selection, or hiring) to the number of people it is intended to produce.

Measuring Development Costs—Special Issues.   Just as for acquisition costs, the basic procedure for measuring development costs involves revising the chart of accounts to report the elements of these costs. However, there is also one special issue that involves measuring the cost of on-the-job training.

On-the-job training costs include the costs of the trainee's salary and a trainer's salary, if any. However, it does not necessarily include the total amount of their salaries; rather, it includes only the "unrecovered portion" of their salaries, the amount paid for which productivity has not been received. Operationally defined, the investment in on-the-job training is the percentage of standard productivity *not* achieved by a trainee multiplied by the trainee's salary for the training period plus an analogous amount for the trainer.

Example of Training Cost Measurement.   The following example illustrates the procedure for measuring investments in training.

The Electrosonics Corporation is a manufacturer of radar and other equipment. Its principal customer is the Department of Defense. The firm requires highly trained technicians. An individual may be experienced in the industry but still may require a lengthy period of on-the-job training. The learning curve for one type of technician is shown in Exhibit 6.

EXHIBIT 6   Investment in Training during Learning Period, the Electrosonics Corporation

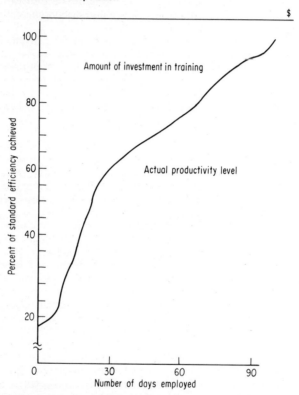

As Exhibit 6 shows, the individual is not expected to achieve standard productivity until the 90th day employed. Assuming that wages are the same during the first 90 days as thereafter, the difference between standard productivity and the actual productivity achieved by an individual is a cost of learning. This learning cost is essentially an investment made by an organization to develop its technicians. It is an investment in human assets.

Another, sometimes hidden, cost of on-the-job training is the differential cost of the lost productivity of people whose own performance is affected by that of a trainee. For example, during the learning period of a new person on an assembly line, the individual may hamper the work of others, causing productivity of several people to be below normal. This too constitutes a cost of lost productivity attributable to training.

Measurement Model for Replacement Cost of Human Resources. This section presents a model for measuring the replacement cost of human resources. It focuses on positional rather than personal cost.

The concept of positional replacement cost refers to the sacrifice that would have to be incurred today to replace a person occupying a specified position with a substitute capable of rendering equivalent services *in the given position*. As shown in Exhibit 7, there are three basic elements of positional replacement cost: acquisition cost, development costs, and separation costs. The first two of these costs have been discussed previously; the third is examined below.

EXHIBIT 7   Model for Measurement of Human Resource Replacement Costs

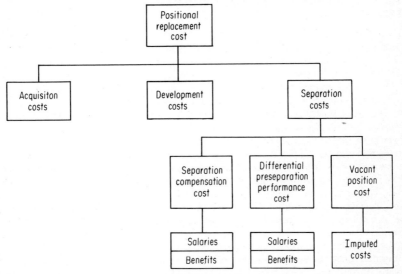

Separation Cost Elements.   Separation cost is incurred as a result of a position holder leaving an organization. It includes three basic elements: separation compensation cost, differential preseparation performance cost, and vacant position cost. These costs should ordinarily be capitalized and amortized, but should be expensed when the employee ceases to be employed. Each of these cost components is discussed in turn.

SEPARATION COMPENSATION COST.   Separation compensation is the cost of severance pay, if any, for personnel. It may range from very little or no cost to a person's salary for one year, and perhaps more.

These costs may be calculated on a basis of an average employee for a given position classification rather than for an individual *per se*. Although these costs may be substantial, organizations sometimes fail to recognize their significance unless they are measured and reported.

DIFFERENTIAL PRESEPARATION PERFORMANCE COST.   Another element of separation costs is the cost of lost productivity prior to the separation of an individual from an organization. There is a tendency for performance to decrease prior to separation. In many cases, it may be difficult to measure for specified individuals but may be measurable from historical performance records by personnel classifications.

VACANT POSITION COST.   During a period of searching for a replacement, an organization may incur an indirect cost of separating a position holder because the responsibilities of the vacant position are not being performed. If performance in one position has an impact on performance in other positions, holders of the latter may perform less effectively when the former is vacant. In an insurance company, for example, the performance of a claims investigator influences the performance of other investigators as well as adjusters, examiners, and the claims manager. The loss of an investigator results in a greater than normal cost during the period in which there is a search for a replacement. This difference can be termed a cost of a vacant position. Similarly, during the period of searching for a new salesperson, an imputed cost may be incurred because of a loss of sales that would otherwise have accrued to the organization. This is also a vacant position cost.

DESIGNING ACCOUNTING SYSTEMS FOR HUMAN RESOURCE COSTS

The previous sections have described the nature, uses, and methods of measuring human resource costs. Although human resource accounting is a relatively new field, some organizations have begun to develop systems of accounting for their human resource costs.

The type of system developed depends on several factors, including the nature of the organization, its size, the types and levels of human resource skills, as well as the degree of sophistication of the organization's personnel management system. Even within the same industry (say, banking), two organizations may wish to develop different degrees of human resource cost accounting capability.

Recognizing that HRA is a relatively new field and the differences in intended uses for systems, it is useful to examine what selected organizations have actually done in designing accounting systems for human resource costs. Accordingly, this section presents some case examples that illustrate how different types of organizations (service and manufacturing organizations) have developed human resource cost accounting. Each case example examines the nature of the firm, the system's intended uses and the measurements developed. It should also be noted that some of these systems are still in an experimental or developmental stage.

Service Organizations: CPA Firms.   The assets of service organizations are mainly human assets—people. Depending on the level of skills required to render services, such firms may have a substantial investment in human assets or human capital.

CPA firms are a classic example of a service organization that is human-capital intensive rather than physical-capital intensive. Such firms invest material amounts in recruiting, selecting, and training personnel. Accordingly, it is not surprising that CPA firms have been among those first to develop human resource cost accounting systems.

Among the CPA firms involved in developing methods of accounting for human resource costs are Touche Ross & Co., whose Montreal office has developed a system, and Lester Witte & Company. The former is one of the largest international CPA firms, whereas the latter is a medium-sized CPA firm, also with an international practice. In this section, the Touche Ross & Co. system will be described. It will also be compared with a model for measuring similar costs at Lester Witte & Company.

The Firm's Motivation.   The rationale for the firm's interest in developing a system of accounting for investments in people has been described by Michael Alexander, a partner involved in its development:[11]

> A public accounting firm is, by its very nature, human resource intensive, and represents an ideal proving ground for the application of human resource accounting

[11]Michael Alexander, "Investments in People," *Canadian Chartered Accountant,* July 1971, p. 40.

concepts. The primary assets of such a firm are its clients and the human capabilities of its people. The financial or physical assets represent a relatively minor part of the firm's total value and consist largely of cash, receivables, financial capital and office equipment. As a result, conventional accounting systems which deal with these elements alone are of limited use for managing the all-important human resources.

Thus the firm believes that, because people are its most important assets, it is necessary to account for investments in people.

Information Desired. To manage human resources effectively in a public accounting firm, certain information is necessary. Information about costs of recruitment, selection, and training is required. These costs constitute an investment, and one that may not be recovered for several years. Information about the cost of turnover and the replacement cost of people is necessary for two reasons. First, turnover rates are typically quite high in public accounting. For example, assume that a firm hired 100 staff accountants in 1976. By 1981 it could expect that no more than 30 would still be with the firm. Turnover in public accounting is high, but the example cited is based on the actual experience of one large, international firm (not Touche Ross & Co.) and may not be typical of CPA firms generally. Second, the investment in people lost as a result of turnover can be substantial. Similarly, the cost of replacing people as a result of turnover can be significant. For these reasons, it is important to CPA firms to monitor the rate and cost of turnover.

Because a CPA firm is human-capital intensive, its long-term survival depends to a great extent on the development of its human resources. Younger members of the professional staff must be effectively trained in order to provide replacements for senior members of the firm as well as to provide for growth in the firm. This means that managers must be motivated to devote time, energy, and resources to training and development. However, there is typically an opportunity cost to training; time devoted to training may require a sacrifice of revenue for the firm that otherwise could have been earned. This suggests that CPA firms require some measure of the return expected to be derived on its investments in people in order to allocate time to be devoted to development. At a minimum, a firm might simply account for the time allocated to various activities. As Alexander has stated:[12]

> The traditional yardstick of performance in a public accounting firm has normally been chargeable hours—the time an employee devotes to client service. Unfortunately, however, the use of this fact as a single measurement may discourage investment in human resources, since the latter is often seen as a feat which is only accomplished at the expense of chargeable hours.

There are, of course, other needs for information about human resources in a CPA firm. For example, information is needed about the effectiveness of hiring and training policies and programs and about the profitability of manpower allocation decisions. For all these reasons, the firm began to develop a system of accounting for investments in people.

The System's Design and Output. The system was designed to measure the investment in people as individuals. Both outlay costs (out-of-pocket expenditures) and opportunity costs (billings foregone) were estimated in measuring the investment in each individual. Unfortunately, the firm has not published data on the amount of its investments in individuals.

The data collection problems were minimized to some extent because the firm was already generating information required as inputs to the human resource accounting system. In Alexander's words:[13]

[12] *Ibid.*
[13] *Ibid.*

The cost of time or opportunity costs were developed from time records regularly filled out by each employee. These records show how each hour of the day was spent and whether or not it was chargeable to a client. The out-of-pocket or outlay costs were easily obtained with only minor reclassification of existing cost accounts.

According to Alexander, the output of the system consists of a set of reports to management. These reports monitor various aspects of the firm's investment in its people.

Four of the reports generated by the firm's systems are cost of time analysis report, summary of human resource investments, statement of human resource flows, and a contribution report. These are presented and described below.

Cost of Time Analysis Report.   The "cost of time analysis report," shown in Exhibit 8, presents the planned and actual allocation of time for a recent time

EXHIBIT 8

COST OF TIME ANALYSIS REPORT
For the Year Ended December 31, 1970

		Total Office		
	Plan	Manpower variance	Hour variance	Actual
Chargeable	$738,952	$(7,230)	$(24,724)	$706,998
Investment				
Recruiting	$11,500	$ 622	$ 868	$12,990
Orientation	11,000	69	1,931	13,000
Counseling and development	10,000	579	1,421	12,000
Formal training courses	35,000	100	7,000	42,100
Research	15,500	42	(284)	15,258
Total investment	$83,000	$ 1,412	$10,936	$95,348
Maintenance				
Practice development	$ 8,694	$ (124)	$ (5,850)	$ 2,720
Professional affairs and public relations	3,064	19	6,825	9,908
Administration	36,864	237	(310)	36,791
Holidays and vacation	102,000	(742)	(25,892)	75,366
Sickness and personal	28,932	(68)	8,877	37,741
Total maintenance	$ 179,554	$ (678)	$(16,350)	$162,526
Total	$1,001,506	$(6,496)	$(30,138)	$964,872

SOURCE: Michael O. Alexander, "Investments in People," *Canadian Chartered Accountant,* July 1971, p. 41.

period. The major reason for such a report is that the services of people in a CPA firm are closely correlated with time. "Chargeable hours," or time billed to clients, represents a direct contribution to a firm's income. "Time" is the common denominator for investment in human asset development. Thus, it is important to monitor the use of time.

As shown in Exhibit 8, the firm has identified three dimensions of the output or product of professional staff time: chargeable, investment, and maintenance. Chargeable time has already been defined. "Investment" time represents the time devoted to building human assets. "Maintenance" time is the portion of time that is an "expense," and that presumably has no future service potential.

This report indicates the planned as well as actual hours for the various activities, and reports variances from two primary causes. The "Manpower Variance" reflects a different number of people actually on the staff than planned, whereas the "Hours Variance" indicates the difference between planned and actual hours for the specified activity.

The main functions of such a report are planning and control of human services. Most likely, the very fact that standards or plans for each component of a person's time must be set will lead to more systematic and rational planning. Similarly, the very fact that variances from plan are recorded and reported will tend to motivate people to pay attention to the allocation of time.

SUMMARY OF HUMAN RESOURCE INVESTMENTS REPORT. The "summary of human resource investments," shown in Exhibit 9, presents the sum of investments made in people during the year. It compares planned with actual investments, and identifies both the outlay and opportunity cost components of investments. The report does not present the variances; but they can be calculated from the data provided.

EXHIBIT 9

HUMAN RESOURCE INVESTMENTS
For the Year Ending December 31, 1970

	Planned			Actual		
	Cash outlay	Opportunity cost	Total cost	Cash outlay	Opportunity cost	Total cost
Recruiting	$ 500	$11,500	$12,000	$1,420	$12,990	$ 14,410
Orientation	2,500	11,000	13,500	2,200	13,000	15,200
Counseling and development	1,600	10,000	11,600	400	12,000	12,400
Formal training courses	5,000	35,000	40,000	3,500	42,100	45,600
Research	1,400	15,500	16,900	1,200	15,258	16,458
Total	$11,000	$83,000	$94,000	$8,720	$95,348	$104,068

SOURCE: Adapted from Michael O. Alexander, "Investments in People," *Canadian Chartered Accountant*, July 1971, p. 41.

The source of outlay costs is the firm's conventional accounting system, modified slightly in order to accumulate human resource costs incurred. The outlay costs are derived from the cost of time report.

The summary of human resource investments can be used to monitor the effectiveness and efficiency of the firm's human resource investment (human capital budgeting) programs. The effectiveness of the firm's plans can be partially assessed in terms of whether stated goals have been achieved. For example, "formal training" was planned at an estimated cost of $40,000, as shown in Exhibit 9. Was this training objective actually achieved? Did the firm, in other words, do what it intended to do? In addition, the efficiency of training can be assessed. Was the actual cost incurred in training greater than, less than, or equal to planned cost of the specified activities? In other words, the variance from plan can be used as a measure of efficiency of human resource investments.

STATEMENT OF HUMAN RESOURCE FLOWS REPORT. The "statement of human resource flows," shown in Exhibit 10, presents changes in human resources during the year. The report measures such changes both in units of manpower and in monetary terms. It compares planned changes with actual changes, but does not report variances.

This report, according to Alexander, is intended to "emphasize the importance of human resource development, and it allows managers to assess their performance in this context."[14] This statement of purpose does not fully describe the report's uses. Basically, the report enables management to monitor the firm's

[14]*Ibid.*, p. 41.

EXHIBIT 10

STATEMENT OF HUMAN RESOURCE FLOWS
For the Year Ended December 31, 1970

	Manpower		Investments	
	Plan	Actual	Plan	Actual
Opening balance	29	29	$112,532	$112,532
Add:				
Transfers in (other offices)	4	3	$ 13,000	$ 10,321
Investments:				
Recruiting	10	10	12,000	14,410
Investments in existing personnel during period	—	—	82,000	89,658
Total	14	13	$107,000	$114,389
Less:				
Transfers out (other offices)	6	5	$ 30,000	$ 26,449
Departures	9	8	34,000	33,498
				36,381
Amortization	—	—	32,000	
Total	15	13	$ 96,000	$ 96,328
Closing balance	28	29	$123,532	$130,593

SOURCE: Michael O. Alexander, "Investments in People," *Canadian Chartered Accountant,* July 1971, p. 41.

inventory of people and the investments associated with that inventory. The "opening balance" represents the stock of human resources on hand at the beginning of the year. During the year, there are specified planned additions such as transfers into the office or new recruits. There are also anticipated reductions in human assets attributable to transfers out and turnover. The "investments" portion of this report deals with the monetary stock of human capital. Changes in investments in people are caused by all of the changes in physical inventory just described; but they are also affected by changes in existing stock of people through training and amortization. In essence, then, this report can more accurately be labeled a "human capital inventory." It is an inventory in both physical quantities and monetary units.

One aspect of this report worthy of special attention is "amortization." In describing the system, Alexander has stated that "human resource amortization is based upon the same principles as those used to systematically record the expiration or depreciation of a firm's other assets."[15] Amortization for any component of investment in human resources is based on either the individual's expected tenure in the organization or the expected useful life of the investment *per se.* For example, an investment in training that is expected to benefit an individual for three years will be amortized during that period if the individual is expected to remain in the firm for *at least* three years. However, if the person were expected to remain for only two years, the investment would be amortized over a two-year period.

CONTRIBUTION REPORT. The "contribution report," shown in Exhibit 11, is based on the notion that the firm's human resources comprise a profit center. Conceptually, the firm is conceived of as a set of service centers, and the contribution of each center is measured and compared against plan. The report identifies variances for manpower and hours.

Perceived Benefits. The system of accounting for investments in people at the office of Touche Ross & Co. serving as a developmental site is thought to provide management with information that will improve the ability to manage human

[15] *Ibid.*

EXHIBIT 11

CONTRIBUTION REPORT
For the Year Ended December 31, 1970

	Plan	Total office		Actual
		Manpower variance	Hours variance	
Chargeable hours × standard billing rates	$738,743	$ (6,537)	$(25,220)	$706,986
Less:				
Salaries and fringe benefits	240,000	(13,107)		253,107
Amortization of human resource investment	32,000	(4,381)		36,381
Departures	34,000	502		33,498
Standard operating contribution before overhead	$432,743	$(23,523)	$(25,220)	$384,000

SOURCE: Michael O. Alexander, "Investment in People," *Canadian Chartered Accountant,* July 1971, p. 42.

resources. Specifically, the system is said to provide information that is necessary for decision making in such areas as employee turnover, optimum staff mix, and hiring policies. For example, the system, according to Alexander, "has provided the firm with a number of facts which have led to some reassessment of its traditional approach to staff mix and resource allocation."[16] The system indicated that profit contributions per employee were somewhat different than what has been assumed. This implies that the firm has changed its manpower allocation decision rules. Thus the firm is now in a better position to determine optimal staff mix because of the information it has about personnel contributions.

Discussion of System.   The "model" used to measure human resource costs in this firm is implicit in Exhibit 8. The firm identifies four major categories of human resource costs: recruitment, orientation, counseling and development, and formal training courses.

In contrast, the generic model shown in Exhibit 4 classified acquisition costs into recruitment, selection, and hiring components. It is possible that the Touche Ross & Co. system either does not account for selection and hiring costs or classifies them under the recruiting category.

Comparison with Lester Witte & Company.   Another CPA firm, Lester Witte & Company, has developed a different model for accounting for human resource costs, as shown in Exhibit 12. It is essentially a variation on the generic model presented in Exhibit 4, but tailored to the specific situation in this firm.

In comparison with the Touche Ross & Co. model, Lester Witte & Company's model provides more detailed information about the costs comprising investment in people. It does not, however, include opportunity costs.

The system can be developed by modifying the firm's present accounting system's chart of accounts. Another necessary ingredient is an adequate method of recording the time devoted by personnel to such activities as recruiting and training.

Service Organizations: Insurance Companies.   This section describes a system developed to measure positional replacement costs in an insurance company, called "Midwestern Insurance Company" (a pseudonym).

Midwestern Insurance Company is a medium-sized mutual insurance company. It is engaged in business throughout the United States and has more than 4,000 full-time employees, about 25 percent of whom are sales personnel. Its assets exceed $250 million.

[16]*Ibid.,* p. 42.

EXHIBIT 12   Model for Accounting for Historical Human Resource Costs, Lester Witte & Company

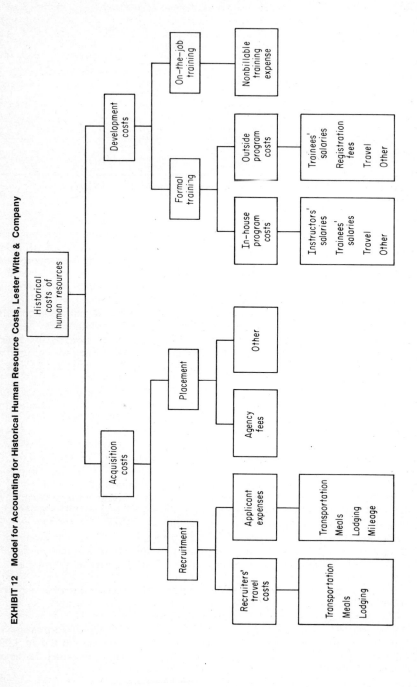

The system of measuring positional replacement costs was developed in a branch of Midwestern Insurance Company. The branch used as a research site is located in the Midwestern part of the United States. It has 110 employees. A partial branch organization chart is presented in Exhibit 13. The branch has four sales teams, each consisting of approximately 15 salespeople and 22 inside and outside claims personnel (investigators, adjusters, examiners, etc.).

EXHIBIT 13 Partial Branch Organization Chart of Research Site, Midwestern Insurance Company

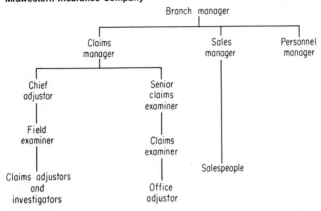

The Company's Motivation.   One of the major reasons for the company's interest in accounting for the replacement cost of its human resources was the high rate and cost of turnover among sales personnel in the insurance industry in general and at Midwestern in particular. The firm typically experienced high turnover among sales personnel and claims investigators during their first year of employment. For example, approximately one-third of all new salespeople left the firm during the first 12 months of employment. Thus, the firm was interested in measuring the cost of replacing sales and claims personnel to determine the magnitude of these costs and the potential for cost savings from reducing turnover. The firm was also interested in the possible use of measures of human resource replacement cost in various personnel policy decisions. For example, management found it difficult to motivate high-performing salespeople to accept promotions to sales manager, because the job change would typically involve a reduction in the individual's earnings. Thus an issue of concern was: How valuable are sales managers to the organization? A related issue was: If they are as valuable as we think they are, how can we modify compensation policy to reflect their value and, in turn, motivate high-potential salespeople to become managers?

The Measurement System.   The measurement of positional replacement costs was based on a model related to the one shown in Exhibit 7 but with some differences, as presented in Exhibit 14.

The model measures three cost components: acquisition, learning, and separation. Unlike the model in Exhibit 7, it distinguishes between "direct" and "indirect" elements of each of these components.

Data Collection.   Information about human resource costs were collected for both claims and sales personnel by methods described above. It should be noted, however, that the firm did not develop an on-line system; rather, the collection was done as a pilot study.

Positional replacement cost data was collected in two forms: anticipated costs and standard costs. *Anticipated positional replacement costs* refer to the costs actually

EXHIBIT 14   Model for Measurement of Human Resource Replacement Costs, Midwestern Insurance Company

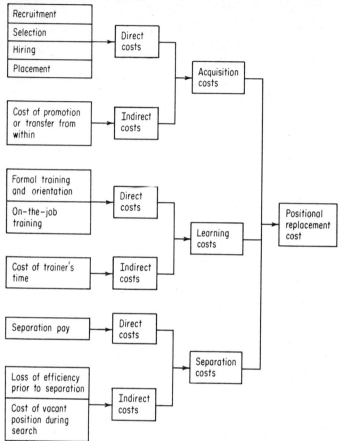

expected to be incurred to acquire "the best available substitute." The best available substitute may or may not be "the most desirable substitute." A *standard positional replacement cost* refers to the cost to replace an individual, assumed to be replaced by the "natural" or "most desirable" substitute. For example, in an insurance company the "natural substitute" for a claims examiner may be an office adjuster. However, it may not be possible to replace the claims examiner with an office adjuster. As a result, it may be necessary to use "the best available substitute," such as a claims adjuster. This may result in a difference between standard positional replacement cost (based on replacement by an office adjuster) and anticipated positional replacement costs (based on replacement by a claims adjuster). The difference between these costs may be attributable to differences in the amount of training required by the two alternative substitutes to effectively replace the examiner.

Selected Data.   The branch collecting these data consisted of 110 employees, including about 60 sales personnel and 22 claims personnel. The positional replacement costs actually obtained for the claims and sales groups, respectively, are presented in Exhibits 15 and 16. These exhibits include estimates of both standard and anticipated positional replacement costs.

EXHIBIT 15

MIDWESTERN INSURANCE COMPANY
Positional Replacement Costs: Sales Personnel

	Positional replacement costs	
Position	Anticipated cost	Standard cost
Salespeople:		
1. Below-average performance	$ 31,600	$31,600
2. Average performance	44,100	44,100
3. Above-average performance	56,800	56,800
Sales manager trainee	51,700	51,700
Sales manager	185,100	90,000

EXHIBIT 16

MIDWESTERN INSURANCE COMPANY
Positional Replacement Costs: Claims Personnel

	Positional replacement costs	
Position	Anticipated cost	Standard cost
Claims investigator	$ 6,000	$ 6,000
Claims adjuster	6,000	6,000
Office adjuster	7,800	7,800
Field examiner	24,700	12,800
Claims examiner	9,700	8,700
Senior examiner	15,900	15,900
Chief adjuster	15,100	15,100
Claims manager	18,700	18,700

As seen in these exhibits, standard and anticipated costs are equivalent in almost all cases, with the exceptions of the field and claims examiners and the sales manager. The differences are attributable to expected difficulties involved in replacing these position holders with their natural or most desirable substitutes. As a result, various components of their respective replacement costs are anticipated to exceed standard costs. These cost differentials are attributable to manpower planning policies and practices. In order to understand the causes of differences between standard and anticipated positional replacement costs, it is helpful to examine the cost elements themselves.

As shown in Exhibit 17, the anticipated cost of replacing a sales manager exceeds standard for two of the three cost components: learning and separation costs. The anticipated training cost exceeds standard by $75,800 and the anticipated separation cost exceeds standard by $19,300, a total of $95,100 more than standard. This difference is attributable to the difficulty (anticipated by management) of obtaining a natural substitute for a sales manager (a sales management trainee), and the corresponding need to replace the manager with a salesperson. First, it will require some time to locate a suitable candidate. In the meantime, the organization will incur imputed costs attributable to the vacant managerial position. Second, while the sales manager's position is vacant during the replacement's training, the company can also anticipate decreased productivity (in sales retention and new business development) of many of its sales people, but especially among its more inexperienced personnel. In addition, the candidate is expected to require a significant amount of time before achieving the normal level of effectiveness as sales manager.

As shown in Exhibit 18, the anticipated cost of replacing a field examiner exceeds standard by $11,900. This differential is expected to arise because of the predicted difficulty of obtaining a natural substitute. More specifically, manage-

EXHIBIT 17

MIDWESTERN INSURANCE COMPANY
Positional Replacement Costs: Standard and Anticipated for Sales Personnel

Position	Standard positional replacement costs				Anticipated positional replacement costs			
	Acquisition	Learning	Separation	Total	Acquisition	Learning	Separation	Total
Salespeople:								
Below average	$ 600	$13,900	$17,100	$31,600	$ 600	$ 13,900	$17,100	$ 31,600
Average	900	19,400	23,800	44,100	900	19,400	23,800	44,100
Above average	1,100	25,000	30,700	56,800	1,100	25,000	30,700	56,800
Sales management								
Trainee	1,000	22,700	27,900	51,700	1,000	22,700	27,900	51,700
Sales manager	51,700	38,300	-0-	90,000	51,700	114,100	19,300	185,100

EXHIBIT 18

MIDWESTERN INSURANCE COMPANY
Positional Replacement Costs: Standard and Anticipated for Claims Personnel

Position	Standard positional replacement costs				Anticipated positional replacement costs			
	Acquisition	Learning	Separation	Total	Acquisition	Learning	Separation	Total
Claims investigator	$ 600	$4,000	$1,400	$ 6,000	$ 600	$ 4,000	$1,400	$ 6,000
Claims adjuster	600	4,000	1,400	6,000	600	4,000	1,400	6,000
Office adjuster	5,600	1,100	1,100	7,800	5,600	1,100	1,100	7,800
Field examiner	8,600	3,300	900	12,800	7,000	16,700	1,000	24,700
Claims examiner	7,100	1,000	600	8,700	6,600	2,500	600	9,700
Chief adjuster	11,300	3,000	900	15,200	11,300	3,000	900	15,200
Senior examiner	11,300	3,500	1,100	15,900	11,300	3,500	1,100	15,900
Claims manager	14,900	3,800	-0-	18,700	14,900	3,800	-0-	18,700

ment estimates a low probability of replacing a field examiner by a transfer of an office adjuster (the natural substitute). If the field examiner is replaced by a claims adjuster, acquisition costs will be $1,600 less than standard, because it is less costly to replace a claims adjuster than a claims examiner. However, $13,400 greater learning costs will be incurred if the replacement is an adjuster rather than an examiner, as a result of a significantly longer period of on-the-job learning. The difference in separation costs between the two positions is only $100, and is not material.

Exhibit 18 also shows that the anticipated cost of replacing a claims examiner exceeds standard by $1,000. This cost differential is also attributable to predicted difficulty in replacing the position holder by the natural substitute.

As already noted, positional replacement costs comprise imputed as well as outlay costs. In this instance, imputed costs are more significant for sales personnel than for claims personnel.

The primary imputed costs are associated with the learning and separation components of positional replacement cost. For example, 55 percent of the learning costs of a salesperson are imputed costs. Similarly, 100 percent of the separation costs of a salesperson are imputed costs. These are costs of a vacant position during a search for a replacement.

The System's Potential Uses.   A system of accounting for positional replacement costs has both direct and indirect uses in the human resource management process. It can be helpful in (1) planning and controlling the use of human resources and (2) developing surrogate measures of a person's value to an organization. The former use is examined below, but the latter is beyond the scope of this chapter.[17]

Measures of positional replacement costs can play a significant role in budgeting manpower requirements, controlling personnel acquisition, learning, and separation costs, and in evaluating the effectiveness of manpower planning policies and practices.

The process of personnel planning involves forecasting not only the number of people required in various staff classifications, but also estimating the monetary costs of recruiting, selecting, hiring, and developing manpower resources in terms of a personnel budget. Anticipated and standard positional replacement costs can facilitate the preparation of such budgets.

In addition, standard positional replacement costs, like all standard costs, can help control personnel costs. Thus the personnel function in organizations can be treated as a cost center, with standard costs to act as criteria for cost control.

The comparisons of standard and anticipated costs can also serve as a means of monitoring the effectiveness of manpower planning policies and practices. For example, in the insurance company previously cited, anticipated positional replacement costs exceeded standard for the field examiner, the claims examiner, and the sales manager positions. The reason in all three cases was the predicted difficulty of obtaining natural substitutes. This is an indication that the organization is incurring an imputed cost attributable to manpower planning practices.

Similarly, analyses of the components of such replacement costs may indicate possible areas for cost savings. For example, 100 percent of separation costs associated with sales personnel are "costs of a vacant position during a search for a replacement." These costs range from $17,100 for a below-average-performing salesperson to $30,700 for an above-average salesperson. The magnitude of these costs, together with the relatively high rate of turnover of insurance sales personnel (about 20 percent annually for new hires) would seem to indicate the desirabil-

---

[17]For a discussion of the use of positional replacement costs as a surrogate measure of human resource value, see Flamholtz, *Human Resource Accounting*, chap. 7.

ity of investigating alternative methods of reducing such costs. The imputed cost that can occur in one year from turnover of new hires can run into hundreds of thousands of dollars. For example, assume that a firm hires 100 salespeople in a given year, and that a first-year turnover rate of 20 percent occurs. Also assume that all of the sales personnel who exit are "below average." Considering only separation costs, the total expected cost attributable to turnover would be $342,000 (= 20 × $17,100). If we now consider total positional replacement cost, expected turnover cost would be $632,000. Of course, these costs would increase if average and above-average salespeople were included in the 20 percent first-year turnover rate, as some undoubtedly are.

Discussion of the System. Midwestern Insurance Company's system of accounting for human resource replacement costs should be viewed as a case study. It is the product of a pilot study to apply a model for measurement of positional replacement costs.

Conventional accounting systems do not report data about imputed costs. Yet, as shown by this example, such costs can be quite significant and, though they may require estimates, they ought to be reported for managerial purposes.

The system also shows the usefulness of standard cost information for human resources. This information can be prepared using methods similar to that for conventional standard costing.

Service Organizations: Banks. Banks are another type of service organization that have applied human resource cost accounting. HRCA has been applied by a few of the largest U.S. banks as well as some smaller banks. Little is currently available in published literature on these applications. However, one application is reported below, for Western States Bank.

The Firm's Motivation. Western States Bank conducted a pilot study involving HRCA. The purpose of the study was to analyze the cost incurred by the bank in replacing an employee. The study was conducted because managers engaged in the personnel function believed that top management did not appreciate the magnitude of such costs.

It was anticipated that knowledge about the magnitude of replacement costs would increase management's awareness of the cost of turnover. It was also felt that this, in turn, would motivate greater attention to controlling turnover costs.

As a focus for the study, the bank chose to deal first with tellers. This is a relatively large, high-turnover population of personnel.

The Measurement Model. The model for measuring positional replacement costs of tellers is shown in Exhibit 19. There are three basic costs (acquisition, development, and separation), just as in the generic model.

ACQUISITION COSTS. The bank identifies two basic components of this cost: employment and hiring costs. Employment costs refer to the costs of recruiting and selecting people; hiring costs refer to costs of actually bringing a person into an organization.

Recruiting costs consist primarily of advertising expenditures and recruiting salaries. There is relatively little travel or entertainment involved in recruiting tellers. Selection costs consist of interviewers' salaries and testing costs. The cost of interviewing is determined by multiplying the interviewer's salary rate by the amount of time devoted to selection. Recruiting costs can be significant, especially for minority employees in connection with affirmative action programs.

New hire processing consists mainly of putting people "on the books." There are certain materials costs as well as labor involved in developing records for new personnel.

DEVELOPMENT COSTS. For tellers, these costs consist of orientation and training components. Orientation costs consist of instructors' salaries and materials. Training costs consist of materials, trainees' salaries, and trainers' salaries. These are comparable to the cost elements in the generic model.

EXHIBIT 19   Model for Measuring Positional Replacements Costs, Western States Bank

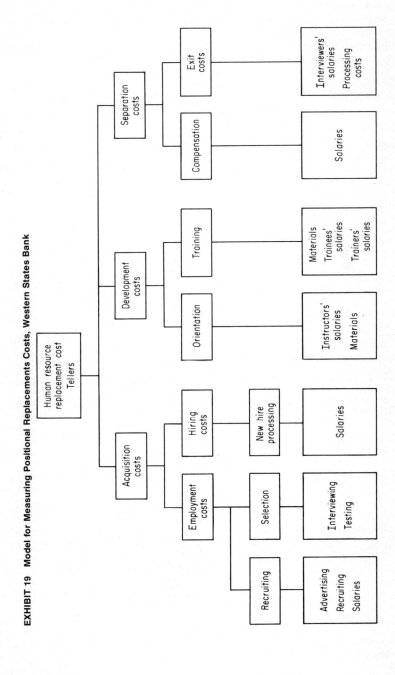

SEPARATION COSTS.   There are two elements of separation costs: compensation and exit costs. The former involves salary costs incurred as severance pay, and the latter relates to the costs of interviewers' salaries (exit interviews) and processing costs incurred in connection with terminations.

Discussion of System.   This system for measuring tellers' positional replacement costs enabled the Western States Bank to determine that the total cost of replacing a teller is $982. The highest cost component is training cost. The magnitude of these costs was surprising to bank officials.

One of the conclusions of the study made to measure these costs was that the bank should try to increase the average tenure of tellers. The bank analyzed its turnover cost of tellers by assuming straight-line amortization of investment over a "normal" expected tenure (service life potential) of 12 months, as illustrated in Exhibit 20.

EXHIBIT 20

WESTERN STATES BANK
Calculation of Unamortized Investment Lost from Turnover of Tellers

Month	Total investment	Service life	Monthly amortization	Allowance for amortization	Net investment
January	982	12	82	82	900
February		11	82	164	818
March		10	82	246	736
April		9	82	328	654
May		8	82	410	572
June		7	82	492	490
July		6	82	574	408
August		5	82	656	326
September		4	82	738	244
October		3	82	820	162
November		2	82	902	80
December		1	80	982	-0-
Total	982		982	982	-0-

This exhibit shows that, for example, if a teller quit at the end of March, the Bank would incur a loss of $736, the amount of the net (unamortized) investment in tellers. If a teller remains for 12 months, the bank amortizes its total investment.

Manufacturing Organizations: Soft Goods.   Although service organizations have shown a great deal of interest in developing human resource accounting, it can also be used by manufacturing organizations. One firm that has developed a system of accounting for its human resource costs is R. G. Barry Corporation. In 1976, Barry's sales exceeded $50 million.

In late 1966 William Pyle, together with the management of R. G. Barry Corporation, initiated a pioneering effort to develop a system of accounting for the firm's investment in its human assets on a current cost basis.[18] Under Pyle's direction, the firm formulated a set of concepts and procedures for measuring recruiting, acquisition, training, development, and other costs incurred as investments in human assets. This section describes the R. G. Barry system.

Company Background.   R. G. Barry Corporation, a public company listed on the American Stock Exchange, produces and manufactures a variety of soft goods. Its

[18]For the full history and description of the R. G. Barry system, see references by William C. Pyle and Robert L. Woodruff in the Bibliography, especially William C. Pyle, "Monitoring Human Resources 'On Line,'" *Michigan Business Review,* July 1970, pp. 19–32; and R. L. Woodruff, "Human Resource Accounting," *Canadian Chartered Accountant,* September 1970, pp. 2–7.

products include slippers and other footwear, robes, and pillows. The company markets its products through manufacturer's representatives in department, specialty, chain, discount, and food store channels of distribution.

Motivation for Human Resource Accounting.   In an article describing the company's human resource accounting system, Robert L. Woodruff, Jr., the firm's Vice President–Human Resources, rhetorically asked:[19]

> Why in the world is a little company with good—but unspectacular—growth, good—but unromantic—products, good—but unsophisticated—technology, good—but un-dramatic—profitability interested in the development of a system of accounting for the human resources of the business? This is a fair question and deserves an answer.

The answer to this question, as we shall see below, is largely attributable to three interrelated factors: (1) the economics of the business in which Barry operates, (2) the company's managerial philosophy, and (3) certain perceived limitations of conventional accounting.

In 1970, 85 percent of R. G. Barry's production was sewn footwear. The basic technology of the industry relies on the use of sewing machines. This means that neither technological change nor financial requirements for new equipment function as a significant barrier to competitive entry into the company's markets. Indeed, apparel companies have the lowest capital per employee and the lowest sales per employee of any of the *Fortune* 500 corporations.[20]

The major component of unit manufacturing costs in apparel companies is labor rather than materials or depreciation costs. Thus the company's management was well aware that the firm's human resources could potentially constitute the competitive difference in its industry. As R. G. Barry's President, Gordon Zacks, stated: "From the very beginning, then, we recognized that if we were to be unique, the only uniqueness we could bank upon was the people power in our company."[21]

Recognizing the crucial role played by human resources in its industry, R. G. Barry adopted a managerial philosophy based on the premise that people are valuable organizational resources. In Woodruff's words: "Like many companies, Barry, over the years, had placed great philosophical emphasis on the value of people to the corporation."[22] Similarly, Zacks stated: "I think that the characteristic philosophy of our firm, and a philosophy that has characterized our company even from the beginning, is one which emphasizes the value of people in the organization."[23] It should be noted, however, that the company's managerial philosophy does not treat people as the only important resource; rather, people are viewed as an integral part of a mix of resources. As Gordon Zacks observed:[24]

> We believe that it is the job of the manager to plan, organize, and control the utilization of three types of assets—*human assets, customer loyalty assets,* and *physical assets*—and to employ these in such a way that he generates a profit by creating new assets. Furthermore, he should manage his profit in such a way as to remain solvent.

This philosophy led Barry to identify five key "result areas" for which managers are held responsible: profit, solvency, physical resources, human resources, and

---

[19]*Ibid.*, p. 2.

[20]*Ibid.*

[21]Gordon Zacks, "Objectives of Human Resource Accounting at the R. G. Barry Corporation," in *Human Resource Accounting: Development and Implementation in Industry,* R. L. Brummet, E. G. Flamholtz, and W. C. Pyle, eds. (Foundation for Research on Human Behavior, Ann Arbor, Mich., 1969), p. 68.

[22]Woodruff, "Human Resource Accounting," p. 2.

[23]Zacks, "Objectives of Human Resource Accounting," pp. 67–68.

[24]*Ibid.*, p. 69.

customer loyalty resources. Thus, the firm's managerial philosophy was consistent with the underlying premise of human resource accounting—that people are valuable organizational resources.

The third factor contributing to Barry's interest in developing a system of accounting for its human resources was the recognition that management did not receive sufficient information to manage its human resources effectively. The company's accounting-information system did not provide information required to facilitate certain decisions involving human resource planning and utilization. Similarly, it did not provide managers feedback to permit the evaluation of the company's effectiveness in utilizing its human resources. Barry also recognized that the behavior of managers is influenced by the kind of feedback they receive about their performance, and that people tend to direct attention toward aspects of their performance on which they are evaluated. This means that if managers do not receive performance reports on their effectiveness in managing people, they are likely to concentrate on the measured aspects of performance while neglecting the unmeasured management of people. Barry's top management was concerned, for example, that a manager could sacrifice long-term profitability for short-term increases in reported net income by either "driving" people or eliminating training expenditures; yet there was no way to monitor the economic impact of such mismanagement.

For all these reasons, Barry's top management felt the need to develop a system of measurements of the cost and value of its human resources. Its ultimate aim was to develop an information system that provided data to help facilitate planning and control of the management of human resources. In late 1966, as noted earlier, the company began to develop its present system.

The System's Objectives and Scope. The company's specific objectives in developing a human resource accounting system, as cited by Woodruff, were:

1. To provide Barry managers with specific feedback information on their performance in managing the organizational assets and customer loyalty assets entrusted to their care

2. To provide Barry managers with additional information pertaining to human resources which would assist in decision making

3. To provide the organization with a more accurate accounting of its return on total assets employed, rather than just physical assets, and to enable management to analyze how changes in the status of the assets employed affect the achievement of corporation objectives.[25]

The system's purpose, in other words, was to provide the information needed by managers to facilitate decisions involving human resources, to provide feedback on their performance in managing human resources, and to reflect investments in human resources in financial statements prepared for internal purposes.

The initial effort was limited to an accounting of approximately "100 exempt salaried employees." (The term "exempt salaried employees" refers to those salaried employees, as opposed to hourly personnel, who are not covered by the U.S. Wage and Hours Law.) The system's scope was limited for three reasons. First, this was done to make the problem more tractable. Second, it was anticipated that the experience gained in accounting for the exempt personnel would probably be helpful in extending the system to other people. Finally, these 100 people were thought to constitute one of the most valuable segments of the company's human resources.

In 1969, the system was extended to include factory and clerical employees in two of the company's plants. In 1970, the R. G. Barry Corporation reported a net

[25]Robert L. Woodruff, "What Price People?", *Personnel Administrator,* January–February 1969, p. 18.

investment of $1,765,000 in human resources.[26] This total was the sum of investments made in 425 factory and clerical personnel.

For reasons of feasibility, the system's scope was limited to accounting for the original cost of human resources. It was felt that there were significantly fewer measurement problems involved in accounting for human resource costs than in measuring human resource value, because the approach used to measure costs could be borrowed from conventional accounting. As Brummet, Flamholtz, and Pyle stated:[27]

> It is significant to note that many of the concepts and much of the terminology being used in developing human resource accounting are being adopted from conventional accounting. They are merely being applied to a problem that has been relatively ignored.

The problem of current valuation was deferred.

The Measurement System Developed.   The system developed to account for the investments made in the firm's managerial (exempt) resources is shown schematically in Exhibit 21. As shown in the schematic, the total costs of the firm are first classified into two components: (1) human resource costs and (2) other costs. The human resource costs are then separated into their expense and asset components. For a cost to be treated as an asset, it must be expected to provide benefits to the company beyond the current accounting period. If its benefits are expected to be fully consumed during the current period, it is treated as an expense. The human assets are then classified into functional categories such as recruiting, acquisition, informal training, development, etc. These functional costs are then traced to specified individuals and recorded in individualized accounts for managers A, B, ..., N. Rules and procedures have been developed to depreciate these investments over their expected future service life.

There are seven functional accounts for exempt personnel in the R. G. Barry system. These are:[28]

1. Recruiting outlay costs—costs associated with locating and selecting new personnel. This category includes search fees, advertising, interviewer or interviewee travel expenses, allocation of personnel, and acquiring department time for internal screening, interviewing, testing, and evaluation expenses. Outlay costs for unsuccessful candidates are allocated to the cost of obtaining the candidate hired. For example, if 10 candidates are interviewed for a salesperson's position, the total recruiting outlay costs incurred are allocated to the one selected and hired.

2. Acquisition costs—costs incurred in bringing a new person "on board." This category includes placement fees, moving costs, physical examination, allocation of personnel, and acquiring department time in placing a person on the payroll and providing the necessary equipment for the job.

3. Formal training and familiarization costs—costs normally incurred immediately after hire or possible transfer from one location to another. These refer to formal orientation programs, vestibule training, etc.

4. Informal training costs—costs associated with the process of teaching a new person to adapt existing skills to the specific job requirements of the new job. The costs related to this process are normally salary allocations only and vary with each position depending on the level of the job in the organization, number of subordinates, interaction patterns outside the department, etc.

5. Familiarization costs—costs associated with the process of integrating a new person into the organization. This cost is incurred while the person is learning the

[26]Pyle, "Monitoring Human Resources 'on Line,'" p. 26.
[27]Brummet, Flamholtz, and Pyle, "Human Resource Measurement," p. 224.
[28]Woodruff, "What Price People?", p. 19.

EXHIBIT 21 Schematic Model of Human Resource Accounting System for Investments in Individuals at R. G. Barry Corporation.

(Adapted from William C. Pyle, "Implementation of Human Resource Accounting in Industry," in R. Lee Brummet, Eric G. Flamholtz, and William C. Pyle, eds., *Human Resource Accounting Development and Implementation in Industry,* Foundation for Research on Human Behavior, Ann Arbor, Mich., 1969, p. 43. Reprinted by permission of Foundation for Research on Human Behavior.)

company's philosophy, history, policies, objectives, communications patterns, and mode of operations. It is incurred during a period of socialization with the people with whom the new position holder will regularly interact. The costs are calculated as a portion of salary during the familiarization period.

6. Investment-building experience costs—costs associated with investments in on-the-job training that occur after the initial familiarization period and that are expected to have value to the company beyond the current accounting period. Investment-building experience is the development of a capability that would not reasonably be expected as a normal part of the person's job.

7. Development costs—costs associated with investments in increasing an individual's capabilities in areas beyond the specific technical skills required by the position. In this category are management seminars, university programs, or courses, etc.

The functional accounts for exempt personnel differ from those used for factory and clerical personnel because both the nature and scale of investments are significantly different. Three functional accounts are used for the latter group: acquisition, orientation, and training costs.

Data Collection.   It was not feasible to determine the actual historical cost incurred as investments in the company's human resources. Instead, the system was developed to account for *future* investments in people, and estimates were made of actual past expenditures. As Robert Woodruff explained:[29]

> Although it was possible to develop the means to accrue and account for future organizational assets [sic] outlay costs, records were not available to reconstruct investments in long-service management members. Consequently, standards were developed for the above seven functional areas in order to establish beginning balances for the individual accounts. As accumulated experience provides accurate actual costs in the functional area, modification of the original standards may become necessary.

The company has modified its existing personnel forms to collect the required input data in the future. For example, "development costs" are collected by means of a "Training and Development Requisition."[30]

Depreciation Methods.   As previously noted, investments in human resources are depreciated over their expected useful life. Certain items such as recruiting and acquisition costs are depreciated over the expected organizational tenure of the individual because they are expected to provide benefits as long as the person remains in the company. Other items such as training and development are depreciated over the period of expected utility, which is typically shorter than the person's expected tenure.

In addition, individual employee asset accounts are reviewed periodically to determine whether obsolescence or health deterioration warrants recognition of a loss of human assets. Clearly, obsolescence is difficult to assess, and it is a judgmental factor. When turnover occurs, the undepreciated balance of a person's account is written off as a charge to current earnings.

Selected Data.   This system provides management with several types of data that were not previously available. First, personnel management now has information

---

[29]*Ibid.,* p. 20.

[30]These forms, together with related instructions, can be found in R. L. Woodruff and R. G. Whitman, "The Behavioral Aspects of Accounting for Performance Evaluation at R. G. Barry Corporation" (with special reference to human resource accounting), in *The Behavioral Aspects of Accounting Data for Performance Evaluation,* Thomas J. Burns, ed. (College of Administrative Science, Ohio State University, Columbus, Ohio, 1970), pp. 23–34. Selected forms can also be found in R. L. Woodruff, "Development of a Human Resource Accounting System at the R. G. Barry Corporation," in *Human Resource Accounting,* Brummet, Flamholtz, and Pyle, eds., pp. 73–84.

on the typical investments made in people. For example, about $3,000 is typically invested in first-line supervisors, whereas more than $30,000 is invested in a top-level manager. Selected investments are shown in Exhibit 22. Management can use this information in planning and controlling certain personnel activities as well as in strategic planning, as discussed subsequently.

The system also provides personnel management with information on the investments being made in different human resource management functions such as recruiting, on-the-job training, and so on. Thus it monitors the company's investment in certain essential personnel functions and can be used for planning and control. Selected data on the company's investment in personnel functions are shown in Exhibit 23.

EXHIBIT 22

R. G. BARRY CORPORATION
Average Investments in Individuals
1969

Types of personnel	Mean investment
First-line supervisor	$ 3,000
Engineer	10,000
Middle manager	15,000
Top manager	35,000

SOURCE: Robert L. Woodruff, Jr., "Human Resource Accounting," *Canadian Chartered Accountant,* September 1970, p. 5.

EXHIBIT 23

R. G. BARRY CORPORATION
Investments in Human Resource Management
Functions
1969

Functions	Investment
1. Acquisition cost*	$110,000
2. On-the-job training	120,000
3. Familiarization	155,000
4. Formal development	50,000

*Cost of new hires, transfers, and promotions.
SOURCE: Robert L. Woodruff, Jr., "Human Resource Accounting," *Canadian Chartered Accountant,* September 1970, p. 5.

The system not only provides personnel management with information, it also provides information to operating people. For example, the company's "Human Resource Accounting Quarterly Reports" inform operating people about the monetary losses attributable to turnover. Management believes that, by representing turnover in monetary terms rather than by rates, the economic losses incurred by the company when people exit "are clearly dramatized to the operating people."

For internal managerial purposes, the company has also developed a set of financial statements that reflect the impact of human resource accounting. This means that expenditures made as investments in people that are expected to have a useful life of more than one year should be capitalized and depreciated rather than expensed during the current accounting period. Woodruff states that, by this method, "the effect of various investments in, and write-offs of, human resources on the income stream is more truly representative of the performance of the company than that which conventional accounting data presently indicate."[31]

Financial statements reflecting the difference between human resource accounting and conventional accounting treatments of income and assets for 1970 and 1971 are shown in Exhibits 24 and 25. These financial statements are taken from the Company's 1970 and 1971 annual reports. (The company published these statements for only a few years for illustrative purposes and does not currently provide this information to stockholders.)

The 1970 balance sheet shows a net investment in human resources of more than $900,000, whereas the 1971 report shows net investments of approximately $1,600,000. This means that total assets as conventionally defined were understated because they were measured according to generally accepted accounting principles.

[31]Woodruff, "What Price People?", p. 5.

EXHIBIT 24

R. G. BARRY CORPORATION AND SUBSIDIARIES
The Total Concept
Pro Forma
(Conventional and Human Resource Accounting)

Balance Sheet

	1970 Conventional and human resource	1970 Conventional only
Assets		
Total Current Assets	$10,944,693	$10,944,693
Net Property, Plant, and Equipment	1,682,357	1,682,357
Excess of Purchase Price of Subsidiaries over Net Assets Acquired	1,188,704	1,188,704
Net Investments in Human Resources	942,194	—
Other Assets	166,417	166,417
	$14,924,365	$13,982,171
Liabilities and Stockholders' Equity		
Total Current Liabilities	$ 3,651,573	$ 3,651,573
Long Term Debt, Excluding Current Installments	2,179,000	2,179,000
Deferred Compensation	77,491	77,491
Deferred Federal Income Taxes Based Upon Full Tax Deduction for Human Resource Costs	471,097	—
Stockholders' Equity:		
Capital Stock	1,087,211	1,087,211
Additional Capital in Excess of Par Value	3,951,843	3,951,843
Retained Earnings:		
Financial	3,035,053	3,035,053
Human Resources	471,097	—
Total Stockholders' Equity	8,545,204	8,074,107
	$14,924,365	$13,982,171

Statement of Income

Net Sales	$28,164,181	$28,164,181
Cost of Sales	18,252,181	18,252,181
Gross Profit	9,912,000	9,912,000
Selling, General and Administrative Expenses	7,546,118	7,546,118
Operating Income	2,365,882	2,365,882
Other Deductions, Net	250,412	250,412
Income Before Federal Income Taxes	2,115,470	2,115,470
Net Increase (Decrease) in Human Resource Investment	(43,900)	—
Adjusted Income Before Federal Income Taxes	2,071,570	2,115,470
Federal Income Taxes	1,008,050	1,030,000
Net Income	$1,063,520	$1,085,470

The information presented here is provided only to illustrate the informational value of human resource accounting for more effective internal management of the business. The figures included regarding investments and amortization of human resources are unaudited and you are cautioned for purposes of evaluating the performance of this company to refer to the conventional certified accounting data further on in this report.

The income statement for 1970 shows a net decrease in human assets of about $44,000. This is the difference between new investments in human resources and depreciation plus write-offs for turnover and other losses. Thus in 1970 net income before income taxes was *lower* under human resource accounting than under conventional accounting by approximately $44,000. The income statement for 1971 shows a net increase in human resource investments of approximately $138,000. In this year, net income under human resource accounting is *greater* than income as calculated under conventional accounting, because the latter treats investments in human capital as expenses of the current period.

These differences in accounting treatments of investments in people have

EXHIBIT 25

R. G. BARRY CORPORATION AND SUBSIDIARIES
The Total Concept
Pro Forma
(Conventional and Human Resource Accounting)

Balance Sheet

Assets	1971 Conventional and human resource	1971 Conventional only
Total Current Assets	$12,810,346	$12,810,346
Net Property, Plant, and Equipment	3,343,379	3,343,379
Excess of Purchase Price over Net Assets Acquired	1,291,079	1,291,079
Net Investments in Human Resources	1,561,264	—
Other Assets	209,419	209,419
	$19,215,487	$17,654,223

Liabilities and Stockholders' Equity

Total Current Liabilities	3,060,576	3,060,576
Long Term Debt, Excluding Current Installments	5,095,000	5,095,000
Deferred Compensation	95,252	95,252
Deferred Federal Income Taxes Based upon Full Tax Deduction for Human Resource Costs	780,632	—
Stockholders' Equity:		
Capital Stock..	1,209,301	1,209,301
Additional Capital in Excess of Par Value	5,645,224	5,645,224
Retained Earnings:		
Financial	2,548,870	2,548,870
Human Resources	780,632	—
Total Stockholders' Equity	10,184,027	9,403,395
	$19,215,487	$17,654,223

Statement of Income

Net Sales	$34,123,202	$34,123,202
Cost of Sales	21,918,942	21,918,942
Gross Profit	12,204,260	12,204,260
Selling, General and Administrative Expenses	9,417,933	9,417,933
Operating Income...................................	2,786,327	2,786,327
Other Deductions, Net	383,174	383,174
Income Before Federal Income Taxes	2,403,153	2,403,153
Net Increase in Human Resource Investment	137,700	—
Adjusted Income Before Federal Income Taxes	2,540,853	2,403,153
Federal Income Taxes.....................................	1,197,850	1,129,000
Net Income	1,343,003	1,274,153

The information presented here is provided only to illustrate the informational value of human resource accounting for more effective internal management of the business. The figures included regarding investments and amortization of human resources are unaudited and you are cautioned for purposes of evaluating the performance of this company to refer to the conventional certified accounting data further on in this report.

important managerial implications, because they affect the calculation of the company's rate of return on investment (ROI). These different accounting conventions affect both the numerator and denominator of ROI. The impact of this difference for the year 1971 is shown in Exhibit 26.

The system also provides a "human resource capital budget" and a report on performance against plans. This information is intended to assist Barry's managers in the management of human resources.

The System's Uses and Benefits.   R. G. Barry's system of accounting for human resource costs has some important applications and benefits. The system can be used in manpower planning because it provides management with historical costs

EXHIBIT 26

R. G. BARRY CORPORATION
Difference in Return on Investment
(Conventional and Human Resource Accounting)
1971 (*Pro Forma*)

Accounting methods	Net income	Total assets	ROI
Conventional	$1,274,000	$17,654,000	7.2%
Human resource	1,343,000	19,215,000	6.9%
Difference	$ 69,000	$ 1,561,000	

SOURCE: R. G. Barry Corporation 1971 Annual Report.

of recruiting, hiring, training, and so on. These historical costs of personnel functions can be used as estimates for budgeting personnel costs. For example, the company may be planning to expand its operations and open a new plant. This may require the addition of personnel, including ten first-line supervisors, two middle managers, and one top manager. Using historical data, the company can budget its personnel activities more reliably, as shown in Exhibit 27.

EXHIBIT 27

CAPITAL BUDGET FOR HUMAN RESOURCES
BASED ON DATA DEVELOPED BY R. G. BARRY CORPORATION

Classification	Number	Cost per individual	Total budgeted cost
First-line supervisor	10	$ 3,000	$30,000
Middle manager	2	15,000	32,000
Top manager	1	35,000	35,000
			$97,000

The system can be used not only in planning manpower activities, it can also be employed in strategic planning for the company as a whole. The company's President, Gordon Zacks, has described the application of human resource accounting in formulating strategy:[32]

> We use human resource accounting information in strategic decision-making. The information is employed in evaluating alternative investment opportunities. We have rejected the conventional return-on-assets approach because it does not recognize human investments. In evaluating a project, we take the physical assets into account as everyone else does, but we also add to that the investment to be made in the human resources required to support the opportunity. And when we develop relationships to profit, it is the relationship of all those resources, tangible and human, to a particular profit opportunity.

Thus, R. G. Barry is attempting to use the notion of expected return on investment on *all* its resources (human as well as conventionally defined assets) as a criterion for strategic decision making. Its human resource accounting system helps management implement this concept by providing data about human resource costs which are essential inputs to this criterion. In contrast, management could not operationalize this criterion if it only had data from a conventional accounting system.

The system is helpful not only in planning but also in control. The system has

[32]Pyle, "Monitoring Human Resources," pp. 26–27.

two different but related control functions: (1) to motivate managers to conserve (or, more properly, not to liquidate unnecessarily) the company's human assets, and (2) to provide a means of evaluating management's conservation of its human resources. As William Pyle has stated:[33]

> In fact, one factor motivating the R. G. Barry Corporation to develop a human resource accounting system was their desire that managers not be rewarded for "spurious" profits obtained at the expense of liquidating their human or customer loyalty assets.

Specifically, the company feared that under conventional accounting managers might be motivated to pressure subordinates in order to increase current profitability at the expense of losing their longer-term motivation and loyalty. As a result of being "driven," people might become increasingly dissatisfied and leave the organization. Thus a manager might show reported increases in earnings while he was actually liquidating the company's human assets and, accordingly, diminishing long-term profitability. This is analogous to using a machine and failing to charge the expired costs to earnings. The result is that net income is overstated. Without human resource accounting, then, managers may have a built-in motivation to liquidate human resources in order to "look good."

This is a classic example of potential unintended dysfunctional effects of a measurement system, and it can be avoided by the existence of a human resource accounting system. With Barry's human resource accounting system, the amortized cost of human resources is written off as a loss when turnover occurs. This reduces reported net income. In principle, this eliminates the potential incentive to deplete human assets in order to increase profitability.

Personnel management can monitor the extent to which human resources have been conserved by means of a quarterly report that accounts for "increases" and "decreases" in human resource investments. Because the monetary loss of human assets attributable to turnover is reported, management can obtain a better understanding of the economic effects of turnover than if merely rates were reported.

Potentially, the system has another major control function—to provide a means of evaluating the personnel department's efficiency. Specifically, the cost standards for the addition and replacement of people can be compared with actual costs. Variances, if any, should be explained.

Discussion of the System. R. G. Barry's system of accounting for investments in people as organizational resources should be viewed as a case study. It is the product of one company's attempt to apply the concepts of human resource accounting. As such, it is most certainly a pioneering effort.

The cost classifications used differ from those of the generic model presented in this chapter. This again illustrates how different companies may develop different human resource cost accounting systems to suit their particular situation.

BIBLIOGRAPHY

Alexander, Michael: "Investments in People," *Canadian Chartered Accountant,* July 1971, p. 40.

Brummet, R. Lee, Eric G. Flamholtz, and William C. Pyle: "Human Resource Measurement—A Challenge for Accountants," *Accounting Review,* April 1968, pp. 217–224.

Flamholtz, Eric G.: *Human Resource Accounting,* Dickenson Publishing Co., Encino, Calif., 1974.

Lau, H. S.: "Toward a Model for Human Resource Valuation," *Accounting Review,* April 1974, pp. 321–329.

Lev, Baruch, and Aba Schwartz: "On the Use of the Economic Concept of Human Capital in Financial Statements," *Accounting Review,* January 1971, pp. 103–112.

[33]William C. Pyle, "Accounting for Your People," *Innovation,* no. 10 (1970), p. 51.

Ogan, Pekin: "A Human Resource Model for Professional Service Organizations," *Accounting Review,* April 1976, pp. 306–320.

Pyle, William C.: "Accounting for Your People," *Innovation,* no. 10 (1970), p. 51.

———: "Monitoring Human Resources 'On Line,'" *Michigan Business Review,* July 1970, pp. 19–32.

Schultz, Theodore: "Investment in Human Capital," *American Economic Review,* March 1961, pp. 1–17.

Woodruff, R. L.: "Development of a Human Resource Accounting System at the R. G. Barry Corporation," in *Human Resource Accounting: Development and Implementation in Industry,* R. L. Brummet, E. G. Flamholtz, and W. C. Pyle, eds., Foundation for Research on Human Behavior, Ann Arbor, Mich., 1969.

———: "Human Resource Accounting," *Canadian Chartered Accountant,* September 1970, pp. 2–7.

——— and Whitman, R. G.: "The Behavioral Aspects of Accounting for Performance Evaluation at R. G. Barry Corporation," in *The Behavioral Aspects of Accounting Data for Performance Evaluation,* Thomas J. Burns, ed., Ohio State University, Columbus, Ohio, 1970.

Zacks, Gordon: "Objectives of Human Resource Accounting at the R. G. Barry Corporation," in *Human Resource Accounting: Development and Implementation in Industry,* R. L. Brummet, E. G. Flamholtz, and W. C. Pyle, eds., Foundation for Research on Human Behavior, Ann Arbor, Mich., 1969.

Chapter **27**

Measurement and Uses of Replacement Costs

DONALD R. BRINKMAN
President, Valuation Systems Corporation

BACKGROUND

The major thrust to current value accounting came from the massive inflation beginning in the early 1970s. This was noted in the AICPA's study: *The Objectives of Financial Statements,*[1] published in 1973. The study group concluded that one objective (No. 7) should be

> ... to provide a statement of financial position useful for predicting, comparing, and evaluating enterprise earning power. This statement should provide information concerning enterprise transactions and other events that are part of incomplete earning cycles. *Current values* should also be reported when they differ significantly from historical cost. Assets and liabilities should be grouped or segregated by their relative uncertainty of the amount and timing of prospective realization or liquidation. (Emphasis supplied.)

The Study Group concluded that another objective (No. 8) should be:[2]

> ... to provide a statement of periodic earnings useful for predicting, comparing, and evaluating enterprise earning power. The net result of completed earnings cycles and enterprise activities resulting in recognizable progress toward completion of incomplete cycles should be reported. Changes in the *values* reflected in successive statements of financial position should also be reported, but separately, since they differ in terms of their certainty of realization.

[1] American Institute of Certified Public Accountants, *Objectives of Financial Statements: Study Groups Report,* AICPA, New York, October 1973.
[2] *Ibid.*

Further movement toward current value accounting came from the Financial Accounting Standards Board publication of objectives of financial statements in 1976, in which it stated:[3]

> Financial statements of a business enterprise should provide information about the *economic resources* of an enterprise, which are sources of prospective cash flows to the enterprise; its obligations to transfer economic measures to others, which are causes of prospective cash outflows from the enterprise; and its earnings, which are the financial results of its operations and other events and conditions that affect the enterprise.

On March 23, 1976, the SEC issued *Accounting Series Release No. 190 (ASR No. 190)*, adopting amendments to Regulation S-X requiring disclosure of certain replacement cost data. The SEC required replacement cost data for fiscal years ending on or after December 31, 1976, for companies with gross property, plant, and equipment plus inventories exceeding $100 million. The $100 million must be greater than 10 percent of total assets at the beginning of the most recently completed fiscal year. The disclosures required under the SEC rule are as follows:

1. The current replacement cost of inventories at each fiscal year end
2. The current replacement cost of goods sold at the times of sale
3. The current cost of replacing (new) the productive capacity together with its depreciated replacement cost at each fiscal year end
4. The depreciation based on current replacement cost of productive capacity, using depreciable lives, identical with that in conventional historical cost accounting, and the straight-line method of depreciation
5. Consideration given in items 1–4 above to the effects on direct labor costs, repairs and maintenance, utility and other indirect costs, changes in salvage values from those presently used for historical cost statements, and extent of usage of depreciation in inventory costs, or cost of sales
6. Additional information such as relationships between cost changes and changes in selling prices, and the difficulty and related costs of replacing productive capacity

ASR No. 190 states:

> The *purpose* of this rule is to provide information to investors which will assist them in obtaining an understanding of the current costs of operating the business which cannot be obtained from historical cost financial statements taken alone. Such information will necessarily include subjective estimates and it may be supplemented by additional disclosures to assist investors in understanding the meaning of the data in particular company situations. A *secondary purpose* is to provide information which will enable investors to determine the current cost of inventories and productive capacity as a measure of the current economic investment in these assets existing at the balance sheet date. (Emphasis supplied.)

ASR No. 190 goes on to explain:

> The Commission views its rule as a first step in a process of providing more meaningful disclosure about current economic costs and values to investors.

In *SAB No. 7*[4] the SEC staff added:

> The staff believes all registrants should disclose replacement cost data. However, the staff will not object if these data are supplemented by data setting forth the net realizable value [*or current disposal value*] and/or the "economic value" [*the present value of the expected future earnings from the asset*] of properties, provided that the basis for such data is fully disclosed. (Clarification supplied.)

[3]Financial Accounting Standards Board, "Tentative Conclusions on Objectives of Financial Statements of Business Enterprises," FASB, Stamford, Conn., 1976.
[4]*SEC Staff Accounting Bulletin No. 7*, 1976.

Definitions and Concepts.   In the context of current value accounting, several value bases must be considered. These bases are historical cost, replacement cost (current cost), reproduction cost, market value (current exit value in orderly liquidation or net realizable value), and present value of future cash flows.

Historical cost is the amount of cash (or its equivalent) paid out to acquire an asset in a past transaction. It is based on the exchange price of goods and services at the time they were acquired.

Replacement cost, as defined in *SEC Staff Accounting Bulletin No. 7,* is:

> ... the lowest amount that would have to be paid in the normal course of business to obtain a *new* asset of *equivalent* operating or *productive capability.* Replacement cost (new) is the total estimated current cost of replacing total productive capacity at the end of the year while depreciated relacement cost is the replacement cost (new) adjusted for the already expired service potential of such assets. (Emphasis supplied.)

This definition assumes maintenance of physical capacity, continuity of the enterprise, and earnings derived from physical capacity.

Staff Accounting Bulletin No. 7 defines productive capacity as

> the measurement of a company's ability to produce and distribute. The productive capacity of a company can be measured by the number of units it can presently produce and distribute within a particular time frame. . . . (Emphasis added.)

One significant clarification in applying the definition of replacement cost of productive capacity is

> The measurement is applied to "what *is* in existence now" as opposed to attempting to measure hypothetical future operating capacity with various re-engineered alternatives.

A good first rule to follow in the measurement process is to ask the question "*What is?*" as opposed to "*What if?*" The next question to ask is: "What is the cost of equivalent *capacity* at the present time."

Replacement cost should not be confused with reproduction cost. *Reproduction cost* represents the cost of an identical asset (as opposed to identical productive capacity) using today's labor and material rates. The key difference between replacement cost and reproduction cost is the factor of technological change. Replacement cost takes changes in technology into consideration, whereas reproduction cost does not.

Market value (current exit value in orderly liquidation) is the amount of cash (or its equivalent) that could be presently received by disposing of an asset based on a present transaction. Market values are *not* forced or distressed sales prices, but are prices obtained by allowing a reasonable time for the sale to occur. Market values assume continuity of the enterprise and the disposal transaction occurring in the normal course of business. As an example, inventory values would be based on market selling prices with allowances for selling costs in the normal quantities sold; machinery and equipment would be based on current exit values in the units or combinations in which they are normally put into service; and land and buildings would be based on selling prices of similiar properties with similar geographic characteristics. This measure is often called *net realizable value.*

Present value is the *net* amount of discounted cash inflows and outflows expected to be received from use of or disposing of an asset in future transactions. Measurement of the net cash inflows and outflows should be based on a probability of 85 percent or more that the cash flows will occur.[5] Beyond the time period at which it is not possible to have 85 percent probability of cash flow, the net realizable value of the asset at that point in time should be determined, discounted

---

[5]The 85 percent cutoff is the opinion of this author, not otherwise determined in the literature.

to present value, and added to the discounted cash flow to determine the current value. The current rate of discount implicit in the amount of cash required to currently obtain an equivalent asset should be used.

The Accounting/Economic Link. Historical costs are based on the exchange prices of goods and services at the time acquired. Replacement cost (new) is based on the exchange prices of goods and services at the current time. During the interim between acquisition and the present, prices may change because of external economic forces and technological developments.

The basic function of a replacement cost measurement system is to measure relative price changes and technological changes. A critical element in this measurement process is the development of a classification system to relate associated price movements with each classification of goods and services. Currently the best classification system is the U.S. Standard Industrial Classification (SIC) as expanded by the U.S. Bureau of the Census. Currently the best specific price movement data are the Wholesale Price Indices (over 2,500) and the Industry Sector Price Indexes available from the U.S. Bureau of Labor Statistics. The classification scheme can be linked to a firm's internal data and linked to available external data to measure replacement costs.

Replacement Cost Background. Professor Theodore Limperg, Jr., of the Amsterdam School of Economics, is credited with most fully developing the concept of replacement cost accounting. The Limperg theory is predicated on continuity of the firm, resulting in a necessity to maintain physical capital. Therefore, assets used or sold will be replaced with assets performing a similar function.

Limperg's theory strongly influenced the accounting developments in the Netherlands after World War I. This development resulted in several major Dutch corporations developing replacement cost accounting systems. The most notable of these is Phillips Industries, which has been practicing replacement cost accounting since about 1936. They have the most sophisticated replacement cost accounting system in the world.

The Inflation Accounting Committee in the United Kingdom, chaired by F. E. P. Sandilands, in its Inflation Accounting Report,[6] described five concepts of profit. Its concept number three was the basis for *ASR No. 190,* issued by the SEC. Concept No. 3 states:

> Profit for the year is regarded as any gains arising during the year which may be distributed while maintaining the productive capacity of assets held by the company. Capital is regarded as the productive capacity of the company.

The SEC staff has indicated that it intends to move toward concept No. 5 in the Inflation Accounting Report, which states:

> Profit for the year is regarded as any gains arising during the year which may be distributed after charging for the "value" of the company's assets consumed during the year. Capital is regarded as the "value to the business" of the company's assets.

REPLACEMENT COST MEASUREMENT TECHNIQUES

There are four generally applicable replacement cost measurement techniques: direct pricing, indexing, unit pricing, and functional pricing.[7]

Direct Pricing. Direct pricing is the application of direct labor and material prices to an asset or group of assets. *Staff Accounting Bulletin No. 11* defines direct pricing as follows:

---

[6]F. E. P., Sandilands, *Report of the Inflation Accounting Committee* (Sandilands Report), Her Majesty's Stationery Office, London, 1975.
[7]*SEC Staff Accounting Bulletin No. 11* refers to the same taxonomy.

Direct pricing applies to assets or groups of assets whereby direct labor and material prices are determined from purchase orders, invoices, engineering estimates, price lists, manufacturers' quotes, internally published labor and material prices, and other direct price sources.

The concept of direct pricing is the assignment of current replacement costs to an item or an aggregate of heterogeneous asset items. It involves collecting replacement prices based on normal order quantities to replace the existing productive capacity with a technologically equivalent asset. It is best utilized for unique or specialized items of material dollar value. The prices should include all factors attributable to replacing the asset, including freight, taxes, installation, and other known costs.

Direct pricing is the most accurate replacement cost measurement, but also the most costly and time consuming. It is required when historical cost records are unavailable. It is often used to price raw material inventory items.

Direct pricing is generally the basis for developing the other three types of replacement cost measurements: indexing, unit pricing, and functional pricing.

Indexing. Indexing adjusts a base cost, which may be an historical cost, original cost, or a recent replacement cost established by direct pricing. *Staff Accounting Bulletin No. 11* defines indexing as follows:

> Indexing provides a valid measurement of replacement cost provided the index is adjusted for technological change or if the asset type has not had technological change. Indexing should be applied to homogeneous asset groups on a vintaged basis and should not be applied to used asset purchases or assets acquired in business combinations accounted for as purchases.

Considerations for applying indexing include:

- The specification for the index reasonably fits the specified items in the historical costs being indexed.
- The historical acquisition costs and dates are available and are based on *new* assets.
- The extent of technological change and its reflection in the index is not material.
- The asset groups to be indexed do not conflict with the index data, depreciation method, or other constraints of management usage.

The concept of indexing is to express a given quantity in terms of relative prices in comparison with a base quantity. A price index is a *ratio* of one price to the price of a specified "equivalent." Most indexes select a base year where the base index value is equal to 100. Future years are then expressed relative to the price in the base year. An example of a price and a price index is as follows:

Year	Price	Index
19X0 (base)	$200	100
19X2	400	200
19X5	500	250

To use the index (e.g., to find the relative price change), divide the current index value by the index value associated with the year being updated. The relative price change in our example from 19X2 to 19X5 is 1.25 (= 250/200).

Indexing is easy to apply, because it is the adjusted ratio of the current index to the index at the time the base cost new was established. For example, assume that we have a machine with a historical cost new of $50,000 and a purchase date of 19X0. The current index ratio for the machine is 2.5 (= 250/100). The base cost ($50,000) is adjusted by the index ratio of 2.5 to establish today's replacement cost at $125,000.

Indexing is a simple tool, inexpensive to apply if the historical cost new data are available. It is good for measuring replacement cost of relatively immaterial dollar amounts, with low technological change, and high volumes of items such as furniture, fixtures, general plant equipment, etc.

Index data are generally available from external sources.[8] External sources such as governmental agencies, engineering and construction associations, are generally the best index sources. Other external sources of index information are private insurance companies, appraisal companies, etc. These private agencies usually do not document the methods used in developing their indices, and the index presentation may be discontinued without advance notice.

Indexes developed within the firm are generated from actual price experiences and can be obtained from purchasing, accounting, research, and engineering divisions. These types of indexes are usually the best for internal usages because they apply to the types of assets the firm is employing in its productive capacity.

Composite indexes are generally individual indexes combined to match the actual productive capacity with the firm. Assume, for example, that an injection molding machine has an index price three times as large as its installation cost. Then a composite index combines the index for injection molding machines with the labor index for the machine's installation in the ratio of 75 for the machine and 25 for labor.

Direct Pricing Used with Indexing.   To construct an index, a specification for an asset is determined, and a direct price for that specified asset is determined annually. Each annual price is calculated as a price relative to the previous annual price to develop the price index. Thus, direct pricing is used in the development of indexes and can also be used in the checking of indexes in use. As an example, if an index is applied to an asset and it is not known if the index is moving in accordance with the asset being measured, an annual direct price can be determined for the measured asset to check the relative price movement of the index.

Unit Pricing.   *Staff Accounting Bulletin No. 11* defines unit pricing as follows:

> Unit pricing is a structured variation of direct pricing whereby a building, inventory lot, or other type of asset is directly priced based upon labor, material, and overhead estimates, then divided into a unit measure (e.g., replacement cost per square foot of building, replacement cost per unit of inventory, etc.).

Under unit pricing, the existing asset is disaggregated into component parts (such as square feet of office space, cubic feet of storage space, tons of cotton) and the replacement cost of the units is determined from direct prices. Unit pricing is best utilized for buildings and inventories. All replacement costs should be included that would be incurred "in the normal course of business." For example, if we have 20 plant locations and could replace them with four plant locations, but this would *not* be done "in the normal course of business," we would not base the measurement on the four plant locations. If, on the other hand, we actually plan to replace five locations with one, the measurement would be made on the basis of the one new replacement. For unit pricing, historical cost data are not necessary, because the base unit price is derived from current replacement prices.

As an example, consider a 1970 office building with 100,000 square feet constructed in Chicago at a historical cost of $3 million. Under current national office construction techniques, the national average unit price for office buildings is $50 per square foot. The national unit price is modified (based on the Construction Specification Institute components) for Chicago to be $52 per square foot. The replacement new office building has 100,000 square feet and would be based on current national office construction techniques. Therefore, the replacement

[8]For an extensive list of indexes see Valuation Systems Corporation, *Replacement Cost Measurement: External Data Sources Reference Guide* (Rolling Meadows, Ill., 1976).

cost would be \$5.2 million (= 100,000 square feet × \$52 per square foot). The date of acquisition and acquisition cost do not enter into the calculation.

Direct Pricing Used with Unit Pricing.   Within unit pricing, direct pricing is used to determine the price new of the base unit. In order to determine the unit price for a building, the direct prices are developed for all the components of the new base building and divided by the square feet of the base building to determine its unit price (price per square foot). The base building unit price (\$/square foot) is used to determine replacement costs for similar types of replacement buildings at different geographic locations and of different sizes.

Functional Pricing.   *Staff Accounting Bulletin No. 11* defines functional pricing as follows:

> Functional pricing is generally used to determine the replacement cost for a processing function, rather than for a specific asset or asset group. Functional pricing can be applied to a heterogeneous group of assets. Functional pricing often combines the techniques of indexing, direct pricing, and unit pricing. It measures the cost of productive capacity based on the number of units which can be produced within a particular time period. For example, a meat packing plant with a replacement cost of \$5 million has the capacity to process 500 head of cattle per day, resulting in a functional replacement cost of \$10,000 per head of cattle per day. Functional pricing may involve the usage of information such as:
> - Engineering studies
> - Recently built processing facilities
> - Design specifications for processing plants
> - Major equipment suppliers
> - Manufacturers' quotes
> - Internal estimates for installation and/or modifications
> - Trade association studies
>
> Functional pricing takes into consideration and adjusts for technological change, but one major consideration is additional adjustments for economies of scale.

Staff Accounting Bulletin No. 12 addresses the problems of measuring economies of scale as follows:

> A linear approach may not be appropriate in all situations. Technical engineering writings provide considerable evidence that costs in many situations tend to change exponentially rather than linearly. Replacement cost computations, which are designed to measure costs attributable to existing capacity, should incorporate methods of attribution that are as realistic as possible if the resulting information is to be useful. Accordingly, the fact that the relationship between cost and capacity may be linear, exponential, etc., should be recognized. The following situations may be distinguished:
>
> (a) When the assumed replacement configuration capacity must be scaled down to existing capacity, engineers frequently employ the following function, called the "six-tenths" rule, as a rough approximation of the cost of a different capacity level:
>
> $$RCE = RCN \times \left(\frac{PCE}{PCN}\right)^{.6}$$
>
> where RCE = replacement cost of existing assets
>   RCN = replacement cost of larger, more efficient assets
>   PCE = productive capacity of existing assets
>   PCN = productive capacity of larger, more efficient assets
>
> Frequently, the estimate resulting from the use of the above formula will be sufficient for compliance with [the replacement cost rulings]. However, the engineering literature also notes that, while this approach in many cases is a significant improvement over use of a linear relationship, mechanical application may result in inaccurate results. Accordingly, consideration must be given to factors such as the following:
>
> (1) Cost for certain types of equipment may follow a different exponential cost curve.

(2) Breaks in cost curves may occur when some specific capacity size is passed.

(3) Different exponents may be applicable to different capacity levels for the same type of equipment.

(b) In other cases, a linear relationship may be appropriate. For example, if a company intends to replace existing capacity by acquiring a new capacity that represents 25% of a new facility built in conjunction with other users, then 25% of the total cost of the new facility would likely be the appropriate measurement. Another instance in which linear computations may suffice is a situation involving a relatively small increase in capacity level—say less than 10% or 20%. In such instances, dependent upon the exponent, the differences between an exponential computation and a linear computation are frequently not material.

In conclusion, an exponential relationship such as the "six-tenths" rule is generally an improvement over linear extrapolation whenever fairly substantial changes in capacity are involved. As a practical matter, this means that some involvement of knowledgeable engineers or others familiar with the measurement of cost behavior will typically be advisable if significant changes in the scale of capacity are part of replacement cost computations. At the same time, it should be noted that any method of rescaling capacity is typically facilitated by using a cost-per-unit-of-output approach.

Relating to technological considerations, *Staff Accounting Bulletin No. 10* states:

The computations should be based upon technology and environmental conditions *existing* as of the determination date. . . .

If technology or environmental factors are undergoing significant change or are presently uncertain, this inherent imprecision in the replacement cost data should be disclosed.

The approach to functional pricing is to review a set of assets (e.g., process line, department, plant, etc.) by the functions they perform and associate the existing assets with the functions. *Staff Accounting Bulletin No. 7* states:

Some re-engineering would normally be necessary even though a complete re-engineering of the entire productive capacity would seldom be required.

Under the functional pricing technique, some redesign of the replacement configuration based upon current technology may have to be made. *Staff Accounting Bulletin No. 7* states:

Replacement costs should be based on the entity's normal approach to replacement of capacity.

Functional pricing will generally take into consideration the other three techniques: direct pricing, unit pricing, and indexing.

Technique Use. In applying the various measurement techniques, *Staff Accounting Bulletin No. 12* states:

If the use of the indices results in a reasonable approximation of replacement cost computed on an item-by-item basis (or other appropriate methods), the use of such indices will be acceptable. It is important to note, however, that in many instances the use of indices will result in *reproduction costs* which may *not* be a reasonable approximation of replacement costs.

Any logical approach to the estimation of replacement cost is acceptable provided it results in a conclusion which reasonably approximates the replacement cost of productive capacity.

The estimation of the replacement cost of productive capacity is basically a two-step process. Management must first decide if existing capacity would be replaced with assets similar to those presently owned or if different assets would be required because of technological advances, new government regulations, or other current economic and operating considerations. The second step is the selection of appropriate methods to price the replacement assets. In many cases, a combination of direct pricing methods and indexing will be required.

Typically, indices do not reflect technological changes to any appreciable extent.

Adjusting the original cost of presently owned assets by appropriate indices results in the current cost to reproduce those assets. Reproduction cost may be equivalent to replacement cost if existing productive capacity would be replaced using assets similar to those presently owned. However, if replacement cost is to be estimated on the basis of using assets different from those presently owned, because of technological change or other factors, measurement techniques other than indexing are usually required.

For those assets which would not be replaced through reproduction, normally some repricing will be required to reflect the replacement cost of productive capacity.

For structures which will be replaced in a different form, unit pricing is one acceptable method of estimating replacement cost. If the structures are an integral part of the manufacturing process, as in a brewery or chemical facility, the functional pricing method may be appropriate.

As with structures, machinery and equipment which has been affected by technological change usually requires specific identification of the replacement or substitute facilities to serve as a basis for estimating replacement costs using a direct, unit, or functional pricing technique. However, because a large number of assets may be involved, this procedure may be costly and time consuming. Sampling techniques may be used in these situations to minimize the number of items requiring direct pricing. The cost of estimating replacement costs of property, plant, and equipment which have undergone technological change can be reduced accordingly.

Using one sampling technique, the estimated replacement cost, based on direct pricing, of the items in the sample divided by the items' indexed original cost results in a factor which approximates the effect of the technological change. If the sample is representative of the total group of assets from which it was taken, the technological change factor computed for the sample may be applied to the indexed historical costs of other items in the group to adjust for the effects of technological change for the entire group.

MATERIALITY, AGGREGATION, AND TECHNIQUE SELECTION

There are three major steps in measuring replacement costs: determining materiality, aggregating assets, and technique selection. The materiality of the assets measured must be considered so that excessive time is not consumed on immaterial measurements. The amount of data aggregation is significant in order to avoid detailed direct price measurements on every asset. On the other hand, the level of aggregation should *not* be so high that, in effect, a single index is applied to the entire enterprise. The last variable is technique selection: direct pricing, indexing, unit pricing, or functional pricing.

Materiality.   Materiality relates the dollar amount of a group of assets to the dollar amount of the total asset structure. The greater the materiality of the group of assets, the more consideration should be given to using a more accurate replacement cost measurement (e.g., direct pricing is the most accurate; indexing is the least accurate). On the other hand, the more accurate the measurement, the more effort and cost are required to make the measurement (e.g., direct pricing is the most costly; indexing is the least costly). Thus, materiality determines the trade-off between a large amount of expensive effort versus a smaller amount of inexpensive effort.

The initial step is to analyze the chart of accounts and determine which inventories and fixed assets are material. After identifying the material elements, an analysis of the further subdivisions of the account can be made. A check is made to be certain external data sources fit the internal data. For example, it would not be worthwhile to segregate desks and chairs if an index exists only for office furniture and fixtures (i.e., desks and chairs combined).

As another example, the records show $100 million in fixed assets, with a group of injection molding machines constituting $35 million or 35 percent of the total.

In this case, because of materiality, the injection molding machines should be separated into specific types. Then direct prices should be used, by obtaining prices from vendor sources for each type at the "lowest amount that would have to be paid in the normal course of business to obtain a new asset of equivalent operating or productive capability." Additionally, another replacement cost measurement technique (e.g., indexing) could be used to verify the accuracy of the calculation.

Assume that within the $100 million fixed assets, there is $500,000 in land improvements. In this case, because of materiality, it is *not* necessary to divide land improvements into various types, nor to use direct pricing, but instead use a land improvement index based on vintage costs for the entire account.

Aggregation. The most accurate replacement cost measurements result from individual asset measurement. But practicability dictates that assets should be aggregated by type, function, and location and different replacement cost measurement techniques applied to each aggregate to minimize the loss of accuracy while reducing costs.

Examples of aggregating assets by type, function, and location are as follows:

▪ By type, group all furniture and fixtures throughout a plant, division, or company. This would be a homogeneous asset aggregation by type.

▪ By function, group all assets together that make up a product line. This would be a heterogeneous grouping of assets that performs a given function.

▪ By location, group all assets together in a plant (e.g., pulp and paper mill). This would be a heterogeneous asset aggregation within a given location performing a given function.

The level of detail selected for asset aggregation is a function of other management uses for the data (e.g., pricing, return on investment, monitoring property taxes, business combinations, etc.). Other management uses of the data can be maximized by aggregating asset replacement costs at the plant level or lower. The following are usually measured at these levels:

▪ Capital investment decisions
▪ Return-on-investment measures
▪ Property tax assessments
▪ Insurance placement

Aggregation categories can usually follow general ledger accounts such as

▪ Raw Materials
▪ Work in Process
▪ Finished Goods
▪ Furniture and Fixtures
▪ Auto/Trucks
▪ Machinery and Equipment
▪ Land Improvements
▪ Buildings

Inventory and property records (whether manual or computerized) can be aggregated by these account categories at a minimum. The records can also be associated with organizational levels of the company. If computerized, the company, subsidiary, or division codes can be used from the records. If manual, the records may be separated by company, subsidiary, division, or plant; have codes by organizational breakdown; or be physically located at the company, subsidiary, divisional, or plant level.

For inventories, records are usually maintained by raw material type with quantities and prices. The work-in-process and finished goods inventory records are usually maintained by product. These records provide the basis for aggregation.

If the property records are mechanized, vintage totals by classification and composite ages and lives by classification can be calculated. If the property records are manual, vintage totals are often kept by account for tax purposes (e.g., guideline lives and asset depreciation range) and by life to calculate depreciation. Therefore, existing manual property records can usually be used to obtain vintage totals, composite ages, and lives.

The discussion above describes the minimal aggregation of assets that exist for companies, with either manual or computerized record keeping. Additional aggregations should be performed for more accurate calculations of replacement cost and to minimize the cost of replacement cost implementation.

Technique Selection. The selection of a replacement cost measurement technique is a function of technological change, asset operating characteristics, replacement in the "normal course of business," assets *not* to be replaced, idle/obsolete assets, asset data availability, internal asset records, internal management policies and procedures, other management uses, and future audit considerations. The following sections discuss these measurement variables as they relate to selecting a measurement technique (e.g., direct pricing, indexing, unit pricing, or functional pricing).

FACTORS AFFECTING TECHNIQUE SELECTION

Technological Change. Technological change is the key differential between replacement cost and reproduction cost. If historical costs are adjusted through indexing and the indices do not reflect technological change, the result will be reproduction cost and not replacement cost. *Staff Accounting Bulletin No. 12* states:

> Because of technological changes or other factors, measurement techniques other than indexing are usually required.

In selecting the measurement technique, future technology should *not* be forecast. *Staff Accounting Bulletin No. 10* states:

> The computations should be based upon technology and environmental conditions existing as of the determination date.

Direct measurement of technological change involves the same concepts and techniques used in capital budgeting. When technological change has occurred, a newer improved asset is available to replace the current asset. The technological improvement manifests itself through lower operating costs per unit of output.

The cost of a production process for a given annual capacity depends on many individual factors. These factors must be explicitly taken into account in formulating the replacement cost of a machine. The following factors are quantified in dollars to determine the operating costs of a machine and its probable replacement:

1. Rate of production
2. Setup time
3. Setup costs
4. Average cost of periodic maintenance
5. Average cost of replacement parts
6. Average time between breakdowns
7. Maximum length of production run
8. Average downtime
9. Average waste and salvage
10. Average percentage of rework
11. Availability and cost of maintenance and service contracts
12. Ease of use and operator efficiency
13. Labor requirements

This list is not exhaustive, because all the costs depend on the production process. Any costs that is material should be included. Most of the data may be obtained from production schedules and budgets.

The operating costs for current machines are derived from the actual costs as reflected in the plant records. The operating costs for the technologically improved replacement are estimated from engineering specifications and the manner in which the machine would be used.

The unit cost of production will be lower for a technologically improved asset. By applying this unit cost to the currently existing production process and determining its present value over the remaining useful life of the asset, the replacement cost for the current asset can be calculated.

Detailed measurement of technological change has been attempted at the asset level for machine tools.[9] For specific machine tools such as horizontal boring and milling machines, vertical turret lathes, jig borers, drills, grinders, and saws, characteristics have been identified that relate to technological changes in the equipment as follows:

- Automatic controls
- Ability to maintain tolerances
- Feeds
- Speeds
- Spindle construction
- Horsepower
- Bed and weigh
- Clutches
- Lubrication

These techniques have not at this time been expanded beyond the machine tool category. The concept is being expanded and developed further by several groups currently researching this measurement problem.

Operating Characteristics.   Operating characteristics of assets affect the choice of a replacement cost measurement technique. It is often difficult to separate assets into homogeneous groups in a production process, because the consideration for replacing one asset in the process may result in the requirement to replace all the assets in the process. An identification of specialized, high-cost equipment is required. The identification of the asset operating characteristics will determine if separate calculations can be made for individual assets or if a functional pricing technique should be used. As an example, in a paint process line, the operation makes it difficult to separate and replace individual assets. Therefore, a functional pricing technique would be used for the paint processing line.

Normal Course of Business.   Replacement in the "normal course of business" is also a criterion for technique selection. Ask the question, "What would be done to replace the asset in the normal course of business?" The answer helps to decide the level of detail (aggregation) and the amount of technological change to consider.

As an example, a retailer who has 20 distribution centers may be able to replace the entire functional capacity with only four distribution centers. But would the retailer actually replace all 20 distribution centers simultaneously? The conclusion is that the retailer would *not* replace all 20 centers with four centers at one time but might experiment by replacing five of them with one new facility. Thus, the criterion of replacement cost in the "normal course of business" dictates that at most five centers would be replaced by the one, resulting in replacement cost measurements on the one combined center (five for one) plus the remaining 15 centers. The 20 centers would not be measured as four, because this would *not* be replacement "in the normal course of business."

[9]Lawrence C. Hackamack, and Les Barnes, "Rating Machine Obsolescence with PCQ," *Automation*, August 1966.

Another example of replacement in the "normal course of business" is a manufacturer with 100 stamping machines that could be replaced in total with an integrated stamping process. The manufacturer would only replace one or two machines at a time in the "normal course of business." Thus, the conclusion is *not* to measure replacement costs in terms of the single, integrated stamping process. As another example, the engineering division has developed a theory on replacing the entire stamping process with a much more sophisticated, technologically advanced process. If management would *not* attempt this technological advancement as its replacement in the "normal course of business," the theoretical replacement should *not* be considered as a basis for replacement cost measurement.

Assets Not to Be Replaced. Whether or not assets are to be replaced is a consideration in selecting a measurement technique. *Staff Accounting Bulletin No. 7* states:

> As long as the company intends to maintain its total productive capacity, disclosure of replacement costs should be made even if particular elements which currently make up the capacity are not going to be replaced. If the company intends to reduce its capacity materially through the abandonment or sale of significant facilities, disclosure of the facts, amounts, and circumstances may be made in lieu of providing replacement cost data. . . .

A key consideration in the selecting of a technique is whether or not definitive plans for abandonment or sale of significant facilities have been established. But if definitive plans have not been established, the replacement cost need not be calculated if management is willing to disclose the circumstances.

As an example, consider a manufacturer of black-and-white television picture tubes. Although there may be a continuing market for black-and-white television sets, the product line is nearing the end of its life. Therefore, the manufacturer may *not* replace the manufacturing capacity for black-and-white picture tubes. At the time when the manufacturer plans to reduce this capacity through abandonment or sale, disclosure of this fact may be made in lieu of measuring the replacement cost of the black-and-white picture tube capacity.

Idle Capacity. Idle assets do not require replacement cost measurements because they are not part of the productive capacity. *Staff Accounting Bulletin No. 7* states:

> The productive capacity of a manufacturer would be measured by the number of units it can presently produce and distribute within a particular time frame;. . .

Therefore, idle capacity does not have to be measured on a replacement cost basis, because it is not currently part of the productive capacity.

Data Availability. *Data Availability* is a consideration in the selection of a measurement technique. The lack of data may prohibit the use of a desired technique. Data availability helps select the level of aggregation for the measurement. Data availability refers to engineering data, purchasing data, internal index data, supplier price lists, manufacturers' quotes, and other published labor and material price data. Examples of data availability criteria for selecting a measurement technique are as follows:

> A manufacturer has a large quantity of expensive welders that may be direct priced. In analyzing the information available, the manufacturer finds an index that tracks the same type of welders as in the plant. Thus, using the index would be less time consuming than direct pricing all the welders.
>
> A machine shop operator has drill presses, benders, shapers, punches, and other items that may be grouped by type. There may be an index available for each type of asset. In lieu of using a detailed index for each type of asset, the manufacturer may find a composite index for machine shop equipment that would be less time consuming to use than indexing all the individual types of assets.

A manufacturer of plastic parts has many injection molding machines and would like to find an index. Lack of index availability related to injection molding machines forces the selection of the direct pricing technique, even though it may be more expensive. An industry group has data for their types of assets based on functional prices. The manufacturers in that industry find they can more easily determine this replacement cost by using the functional price data made available by the association.

Internal Records. The existing level of detail and content of inventory and fixed asset records affect the choice of measurement techniques. As an example, minimum required information for indexing is historical costs, acquisition dates, assurances that the assets were acquired new, that little technological change has occurred, and availability of an index.

A problem arises when a business combination has been accounted for as a purchase. In this case, current values were determined at purchase date and the total purchase price was allocated to the assets based on their individual current values. In this circumstance, indexing is not allowed by the SEC. Therefore, a review of other techniques (e.g., unit pricing for buildings, functional pricing for processes, direct pricing for major equipment, etc.) must be considered. In some instances it may be possible to reconstruct the allocation process used in the business combination, derive the original historical cost (new), and index some of the data.

Other special problems arise from unusual accounting entries, asset modifications, and expensed items. Unusual accounting entries such as IRS revenue agent report adjustments require analysis to determine what has been changed. These types of adjustments often occur when the agent decides that additional costs must be capitalized for given projects. This will indicate that the original costs capitalized may not be appropriate for indexing. Each of these cases requires special attention.

Modifications made to existing assets are often performed to change their capacity. Whenever modifications have been drastic, consideration should be given to using functional pricing. It would not be appropriate to index the original cost and index the modification cost, because the capacity may have been materially altered. In this case the best approach is to utilize functional pricing or direct pricing.

Minor and expensed assets in the replacement cost measurement should follow the same policy as used by management in its historical cost records. *Staff Accounting Bulletin No. 7* states:

> The basis of reporting replacement cost data should be the same as that used for historical cost data. However, if such amounts [minor and expensed assets] are significant, and management believes that their disclosure would be useful to investors, the replacement cost should be reported separately and the fact that such amounts have not been included in historical cost property, plant, and equipment should be disclosed.

Internal Procedures. Internal policies and procedures include the capitalization policies, data consolidation flow, depreciation methods, and inclusion of historical cost elements. Capitalization policies refer to the dollar amount cutoffs at which the company capitalizes assets (e.g., $500 and above for machinery and equipment, $100 and above for furniture and fixtures, all original and subsequent modification costs for buildings, etc.). A review of these policies will indicate the amount and level of detailed data available for selecting a measurement technique.

A separate data consolidation flow for replacement cost measurements should *not* be established. Establishing one will only result in later conflict with the present accounting consolidaton process. Therefore, the present accounting consolidation process should be reviewed to be certain that the replacement cost data can flow through the same process.

Depreciation methods and life assignments are stipulated in *Accounting Series Release No. 190,* which states:

> For purposes of this calculation, economic lives and salvage values currently used in calculating historical cost depreciation, depletion or amortization shall generally be used. For assets being depreciated, depleted or amortized on a time expired basis, the straight-line method shall be used in making this calculation.

The current chart of accounts should be reviewed for present life assignments in order to conform with *ASR No. 190.* Then, using these life assignments and the replacement cost of the productive capacity, the straight-line method of calculation can be used for calculating the depreciation expense.

In discussing the assignment of economic lives and their usage, *Staff Accounting Bulletin No. 7* states:

> Generally accepted accounting principles require that when the original estimate of economic life used for purposes of calculating depreciation no longer reflects the current estimate of the useful life of the asset, the life used in the calculation should be changed to reflect up-to-date estimates and the remaining undepreciated cost of the asset should be allocated on a systematic and rational basis over the remaining life. Therefore, any change in economic life should not result from replacement cost requirements but from changing estimates of economic conditions relating to the asset. The rule does not contemplate any special review of economic lives not otherwise required.
>
> In most cases, therefore, the life of the equipment being replaced should be used with appropriate disclosure of the possible effect on cost of the longer economic life of new equipment. If a registrant feels that because of unusual circumstances such an approach would distort the data presented in terms of the objectives articulated by the Commission for requiring the disclosure, it may make the basic calculation on the basis of the economic life of the *new* equipment with full disclosure of the reasons for this decision and its effect on the data presented.

In reviewing the internal policies and procedures, the inclusion of historical cost elements in the historical statements will help in selecting a measurement technique. As an example, if the company capitalizes only the cost of equipment and expenses the installation cost, indexing the equipment cost would not provide a measurement of the replacement cost of productive capacity. In this case, direct pricing of the equipment plus installation would be appropriate.

Another consideration in the historical cost statements is the extent of fully depreciated assets. Only if the fully depreciated assets are less than 5 percent of gross property, plant, and equipment can they be eliminated from the replacement cost disclosure.

Management Uses of Replacement Cost Data.   Other management uses of the replacement cost data have been identified by many corporate managements. The identified uses will dictate the level of aggregation for the replacement cost measurements. They will also provide a direction as to the measurement technique to be selected. As an example, if a corporation intends to calculate return on investment for its manufacturing plants, replacement cost data should be developed at the plant level from lower-level aggregations. Another example would be companies that intend to monitor property tax assessments. Assessments are generally made at the plant level. Because assessments are based on real property and personal property, the replacement cost aggregates will have to take into account the definition for assessment purposes of real versus personal property.

EXTERNAL MEASUREMENT DATA

Staff Accounting Bulletin No. 11 states that four types of replacement cost measurement techniques are most generally applicable: indexing, direct pricing, unit pricing, and functional pricing. For each technique it is necessary to determine the extent of external data available to make the measurements,[10] and to identify problems in using the data.

Direct Price Sources.   There are many sources of direct price data. Most sellers of commodities, product manufacturers, equipment manufacturers, and even construction companies building manufacturing plants issue direct prices as part of their business activities. For measuring replacement cost, direct price data is required for material, labor, and overhead factors. Direct price sources are categorized as follows:

- Supplier price lists
- Manufacturers' quotes
- Published labor rates
- Published material price books

Unfortunately, quotations for various discounts currently offered are seldom published and direct prices obtained from catalogues or price sheets are likely to be overstatements of replacement costs.

Index Sources.   Index sources are numerous and can be misleading. Therefore, they should be reviewed for the following characteristics:

- Source name
- Time period covered
- Base valuation year
- Frequency of publication
- Publication lag time
- Number of indexes
- Specifications for prices of indexes
- Problems

External index sources are generally classified as domestic (governmental and private) and foreign.

Domestic index sources available for replacement cost measurements include:
Governmental sources:
U.S. Bureau of Labor Statistics
- Wholesale Price Indexes
- Industry Sector Price Indexes
U.S. Bureau of the Census
U.S. Bureau of Domestic Commerce
Private sources:
Boeckh Building Cost Indexes
Chemical Engineering magazine
Engineering News Record magazine
Factory Mutual Engineering
Handy Whitman Utility Indexes
Howard W. Sams and Company, Inc.
Marshall Valuation Service
National Labor News magazine
Oil and Gas Journal magazine
Predicasts Basebook
Foreign index sources available for replacement cost measurements include:
Australian Government
Belgian National Institute of Statistics
British Government
Canadian Government

---

[10]See Valuation Systems Corporation, *Replacement Cost Measurement: External Data Sources Reference Guide* (Rolling Meadows, Ill., 1976).

Economist magazine (Britain)
European Chemical News
European Free Trade Association
German Institute of Statistics
Organization of American States
Organization for Economic Cooperation and Development
Statistical Office of European Communities
United Nations

Measuring replacement cost by indexing is readily computerized. Because of large amounts of data and continuous change occurring throughout the economy, index series can develop into fairly sizable data bases. Index sources should ideally be obtained from publicly available sources. These tend to be the most supportable, available on a frequent basis, and do not have unreasonable time lags between effective date and publication date. Among the most usable index sources for measuring replacement cost are the U.S. Bureau of Labor Statistics Wholesale Price Indexes and Industry Sector Price Indexes.

The Wholesale Price Indexes are organized in a hierarchical structure of five levels as follows:

- Major group
- Subgroup
- Product class
- Subproduct
- Item

The base year for the Wholesale Price Indexes is 1967, unless otherwise specified in the specific index. The indexes are based on weighted averages whereby lower-level indexes are assigned weights (according to amounts of commodities purchased) and combined to form higher-level indexes. The following is an example of the weighting process:

Index identifier	*Description*	*Value*	*Weights*
1111	Farm tractors	100.0	10
1112	Agricultural machinery, excluding tractors	150.0	2

$$\text{Higher-Level Value} = \frac{\Sigma(\text{Weights})(\text{Value})}{\Sigma \text{ Weights}}$$

$$\frac{(10 \times 100) + (2 \times 150)}{10 + 2} = 108.3$$

Thus, we have

Index identifier	*Description*	*Value*	*Weights*
111	Agricultural machinery and Equipment	108.3	1

There are several problems associated with using the Wholesale Price Indexes in the replacement cost measurement process: goodness of fit of the index to the asset measured; technological change; and data discontinuity. The goodness-of-fit problem is paramount in determining how well an index series represents the price movement of the measured asset. First, it is necessary to determine if the description of the index series matches the description of the measured asset. As an example, consider an asset called "pumps." In order to be certain that the index series matches the measured asset, it is necessary to review the specifications for the index series. In this example, the specification for the index series calls for a 10-horsepower industrial pump. Therefore, the fit between an asset and the index depends on whether our pumps are approximately 10-horsepower industrial pumps.

In the Wholesale Price Indexes, technological change is partially accounted for in the higher-level indexes. This is accomplished by weighting the lower-level indexes and adjusting them over time based on the amounts of the commodities purchased. The following is a hypothetical example:

	19X1	19X9
Office machinery and equipment		
Electronic calculator	5%	14%
Adding machines	10	1
Typewriters	60	60
Other machines	25	25
Total	100%	100%

Notice how in the weighting the electronic calculators have increased in the proportion included and the adding machines have decreased in their proportion included in the weight. The result of this weighting is that higher-level indexes reflect some technological change.

Problems in data discontinuity in the Wholesale Price Indexes can be classified as follows:

- Missing data points
- New index series started
- Index series discontinued
- Index specifications changed

In the more than 2,500 index series covering several decades, there are several points in the data that are nonexistent. Computer programs should test for nonexistence and be programmed to interpolate as required.

The problem with new index series being started is that data are not available to measure a vintage cost prior to the start of the specific index. The problem with index series being discontinued is opposite of the index-start problem. A vintage cost for a year after the index was discontinued cannot be measured.

The problem with index specifications changing is that it is difficult to verify usage of an index that matches the measured asset. Approximately 200 to 300 specifications are changed each year.

Data discontinuity problems with the Wholesale Price Indexes can be resolved. An index series that extends only from 1967 to 1976 may be extended backward from 1967 if another more general index series similar to the one to be extended exists. Because the two index series are similar, the price movements among the series will approximate each other. Specific index series for individual items can be averaged with fixed weights to derive the more general index series to be certain that the price trends of the more general index series include the price trends of the specific index series.[11]

Because the grouping of items within an index series is intended to measure related items with similar price trends, the average growth rates between two related series should be approximately the same. Adjusting the differences by the ratio of the annual growth rates provides an additional adjustment to account for the minor variations between the two series. The assumption is that the differences in average growth rates between two index series over a known period where those series can be compared (1967 to 1976 in the above examples) will be the same for periods where the values for one series are unknown.

To illustrate the required transformation, we assume the two index series shown in Exhibit 1.

Over the period 1967 to 1976, index series A had an average growth rate of about 7 percent, calculated as follows:

[11]For example, see *VSCOM User's Guide*, Valuation Systems Corporation (Rolling Meadows, Ill., 1976).

Exhibit 1   Illustrative indexes for Coping with Data Discontinuities

Year	Index A	Index B
1960	81.70	
1961	73.80	
1962	81.20	
1963	80.90	
1964	86.50	
1965	96.30	
1966	97.90	
1967	100.00	100.00
1968	103.90	104.00
1969	112.10	112.20
1970	111.20	111.20
1971	109.90	109.90
1972	114.20	114.20
1973	131.10	131.10
1974	148.00	148.00
1975	163.90	163.90
1976	186.00	162.10

$$\left(\frac{186.00}{100.00}\right)^{1/9} - 1 = 1.07139 - 1 = 7.139 \text{ percent}$$

Index series B had an average growth rate of about 5.5 percent:

$$\left(\frac{162.10}{100.00}\right)^{1/9} - 1 = 1.05514 - 1 = 5.51 \text{ percent}$$

Series B can be extended by using series A by adjusting the differences of series A by the ratio of the growth rates over time as shown in Exhibit 2.

Exhibit 2   Extending Discontinuous Index Series (Based on Data in Exhibit 1)

Year	Index A	Difference	Adjusted difference[a]	Index B[b]
1960	81.70	−7.9	−7.80	81.95
1961	73.80	7.4	7.30	74.15
1962	81.20	−0.3	−0.29	81.45
1963	80.90	5.6	5.52	81.16
1964	86.50	9.8	9.67	86.68
1965	96.30	1.6	1.58	96.35
1966	97.90	2.1	2.07	97.93
1967	100.00			100.00
1968	103.90			104.00
1969	112.10			112.20
1970	111.20			111.20
1971	109.90			109.90
1972	114.20			114.20
1973	131.10			131.10
1974	148.00			148.00
1975	163.90			163.90
1976	186.00			162.10

[a]Adjusted difference = difference × $(162.10/186.00)^{1/9}$ = difference × 1.05514.
[b]New values for index B are developed by subtracting the adjusted differences from the preceding year's value. For example, 97.93 (in 1966) = 100.00 − 2.07; 96.35 (in 1965) = 97.93 − 1.58.

Composite indexes can reduce the amount of computational effort required in the indexing measurement technique. Three steps are necessary in developing a composite index: selecting the indexes to be used, determining their weights, and combining them. The following provides an example of developing a composite index. In this example, a significant portion of the replacement cost of the machine consists of the labor charge for installation.

Components of machine		Weight
Labor installation		30%
Machine		70%
Indexes	1970	1976
Labor	100	160
Machine	100	130
30% of labor index	30	48
70% of machine	70	91
Composite	100	139

Unit Price Sources. For external data sources related to unit price of inventories the data requirements are similar to those required for direct pricing: published labor rates and published materials rates. They must be related to the firm's raw materials, the amount of labor and materials incorporated into work in process, and the amount of labor, materials, and overhead incorporated into the finished goods.

For structures (buildings), external unit price sources are as follows:

- Boeckh Manual
- Building Cost File
- Dodge Building Cost Services
- Means Construction Manual
- National Construction Estimator
- Orr System
- Richardson Engineering Service
- Wood & Tower

In using unit construction costs, it should be noted that significant variations occur over time and significant variations occur due to geographic locations. Buildings should not be indexed for more than a five-year period. Unit price factors that incorporate these variations should be used.

To develop unit price data, additional external sources should be surveyed, such as:

- Recent construction cost estimates
- Costs of construction in progress
- Costs of recently completed construction
- Utilization of professional cost estimations

Unit price data for construction should be modified from its sources. Most sources provide a basic unit price at a given location and time. Therefore, the local material and labor prices are used in the construction of the base unit price. The local labor and material price must be adjusted to the time of the replacement cost valuation, and the unit prices must be adjusted for geographical differences to the location of the structure being measured. These adjustments should both be made on the proportions of the unit prices represented by the components of construction. The components should be classified in accordance with the standards set by the Construction Specifications Institute.

INTERNAL DATA ANALYSIS

Considerations for internal data analysis are data consolidation flow, inventories data, productive capacity data, and auditability.

Data Consolidation Flow. In the process of gathering financial data, the flow is generally from product lines to plants to divisions (companies/subsidiaries), to corporate management. Within this information flow, the basic sources of internal data include:

- Labor rates from the payroll system
- Material costs from the procurement and accounts payable system
- Raw materials from the procurement and accounts payable system
- Work in process from the inventory system, including product costing, cost distribution, burden rate calculation, and overhead distribution
- General-purpose machinery and equipment data from the procurement and accounts payable system and from the property control system
- Special-purpose equipment data from the procurement and accounts payable system, along with the property control system
- Building cost data as vintaged total costs in the property control system and unit prices from construction in progress, from estimates of planned construction, or from professional construction cost estimates

The replacement cost data should follow the present chart of accounts.

Inventories Data. Replacement costs for inventories should be derived from separate measurement of raw materials, work in process, and finished goods. Replacement cost measurement requires a review of the present inventory cost flow assumption (FIFO, LIFO, weighted average, etc.); analysis of sales, cycles, inventory turnover rates and price movements; examination of present classification methods; chart of accounts review, pricing techniques employed; index development; and data collection, summarization, calculation, and replacement cost reporting.

In reviewing the presently used accounting for inventories, it is appropriate to determine if the accounting approximates replacement cost. For example, with a rapid inventory turnover, a FIFO assumption for historical costs may lead to balance sheet amounts approximately equal to replacement cost of inventories at the balance sheet date. On the other hand, a LIFO assumption for historical costs when there is a rapid turnover rate may lead to a cost of goods sold figure approximately equal replacement cost of goods sold. The key determinants in reviewing the present method of accounting are the materiality of the key items affecting the inventory value, their turnover rate, and the price changes of the material items.

The cost-flow assumption used for inventories in the historical records is significant in developing replacement costs. *Staff Accounting Bulletin No. 7* states:

> Frequently the FIFO method of computing year-end inventories will approximate the replacement cost of such inventories and the LIFO method of computing cost of sales will approximate the replacement cost method of computing cost of sales. . . . Any method will be acceptable if it results in amounts which do not *materially* differ from amounts computed using replacement cost. However, it will *not* be acceptable to simply use FIFO and LIFO amounts without assuring that they do not differ materially from replacement cost amounts. (Emphasis supplied.)

A review of the present method of accounting for inventories should also incorporate an identification of handling obsolete or discontinued inventories. *Staff Accounting Bulletin No. 7* states:

> Obsolete or discontinued inventory items should be set forth separately and not included in replacement cost calculations.

In cases where current replacement cost exceeds net realizable value, *Accounting Series Release No. 190* states:

> If current replacement cost exceeds net realizable value at that date, that fact shall be stated and the amount of the excess disclosed.

Sales cycles should be reviewed by product to determine whether the product sales are continuous, cyclical, seasonal, or some other periodic timing. The chart of accounts review should incorporate the following considerations:

- Items to be valued at historical cost
- Exclusions (e.g., long-term contracts, obsolete inventories, etc.)
- Material quantity/price items
- Homogeneous item specifications
- Association to an external index, direct price, or unit price
- Association/development of an internal index

Currently used pricing techniques should be reviewed for providing data. Existing purchase records may be a source of direct prices. Existing inventory, procurement, accounts payable, and payroll records may also be a source of internal data for the development of indexes. Suppliers are an external source of pricing data. An external index source is the Wholesome Price Indexes published by the U.S. Bureau of Labor Statistics.

Internally developed indexes can be either basic or composite. Basic indexes should be of the Paasche type.[12] Development of basic indexes incorporates a detail specification of the index and periodic tracking of prices of the specified items. Composite index development takes two or more indexes, weights them in accordance with the measured items to be indexed, and combines them based on their relative weights. The composite index can be used to index heterogeneous items based on relative weights of usage.

Raw Materials.   Replacement cost of raw materials requires an examination of the accounting records for significant quantity and price categories. Long-term contracts for raw materials must be reviewed for their terms. *Staff Accounting Bulletin No. 7* states:

> If the contract runs for a long term (e.g.) more than two years beyond the balance sheet date), the company should use the contract price in the calculation. It should disclose the nature and terms of the contract if the inventory acquired is a substantial input to the production process. If the supply contract has only a short time to run and the price paid varies materially from year-end market prices, the year-end market prices should be used in determining replacement cost.

Work in Process and Finished Goods.   Replacement cost measurements of work in process and finished goods are similar to those for raw materials, except that additional considerations must be made for standard costs and other cost accounting methods. Standard costs must be reviewed to see if they are current relative to labor, material, and overhead content. Also, the extent to which depreciation is reflected must be considered, because the replacement cost depreciation charge will be different from the historical cost charge. When other cost accounting techniques are used, the extent to which overhead is reflected in the inventory valuations must be considered.

The inclusion of depreciation in inventory cost or cost of sales is considered in Rule 3-17(e) of *Accounting Series Release No. 190* and in *Staff Accounting Bulletin No. 10.* Rule 3-17(e) states:

> If depreciation, depletion or amortization expense is a component of inventory costs or cost of sales, indicate that fact and cross-reference to the answer for this subsection in subsection (b)(Replacement Cost of Sales) in order to avoid potential duplication in the use of these data.

Staff Accounting Bulletin No. 10 clarifies this language as follows:

> The purpose of the above language is to avoid double-counting depreciation expense.
>   Many companies allocate depreciation expense to cost of sales, selling, general and

[12]Sidney Davidson and Roman L. Weil, eds., *Handbook of Modern Accounting,* 2nd ed., (McGraw-Hill Book Company, New York 1977), chap. 46.

administrative expense and other accounts, while other companies report depreciation expense as a single-line item in their income statements. Companies reporting in the former format might inadvertently "double-count" the element of depreciation expense allocated to cost of sales, first when reporting cost of sales (which would include an allocation of depreciation expense) and second when reporting total depreciation. To avoid such double-counting, [the rule] requires a cross reference.

From a composite index developed for the finished goods, a set of composite indexes for the work-in-process categories can be developed. The chart of accounts used in work in process and finished goods will classify products rather than raw materials. Therefore, the classification scheme has to separate the significant product items.

After the appropriate classification and separation process has been made, pricing the finished goods can be performed. It is necessary to direct price each finished good based on replacement prices for raw materials, labor content, and overhead content. A composite index can be developed to generate the relative difference between historical cost and replacement cost for the finished goods. The composite needs to be weighted to the relative content of raw materials, labor, and overhead.

Long-term contracts for finished goods must be reviewed for their terms. *Staff Accounting Bulletin No. 12* states:

> Inventory profits result from holding inventories during a period of rising inventory costs and are measured by the difference between the replacement cost of an item and its historical cost at the date the item becomes specific to the requirements of a particular customer (frequently the date of sale). Different methods of accounting for inventories can affect the degree to which inventory profits are included and identifiable in current income, but no method based upon historical cost always eliminates or discloses this profit explicitly.
>
> Such profits do not reflect an increase in the economic earning power of a business and they are not normally repeatable in the absence of continued price increases. Accordingly, the Staff considers disclosure of the impact of material inventory profits on reported earnings and the trend of reported earnings important information for investors in assessing the quality of earnings and understanding the relationship between cost changes and changes in selling prices.

The final step is to collect the historical cost data and replacement cost data for the work in process and finished goods account, ensuring that exceptions are handled. After the historical costs have been balanced, the data can be summarized, replacement costs calculated, and reports generated.

Cost of Sales.   As with work in process and finished goods, cost of sales must be analyzed to determine if historical costs can approximate replacement costs. *Staff Accounting Bulletin No. 7* states:

> Cost of sales [are to be] computed on the basis of the replacement cost of the goods or services at the time of sale.

Cost of sales should use the same classification as finished goods. Sales trends over the measured period should be identified, and the data points to reflect price changes over the period should be determined. Then collect the price change data for the raw materials and labor, and develop a composite index to relate the cost of sales to the time of sale.

Productive Capacity Data.   Productive capacity data incorporate the following: physical parameters and capacities, management policies and controls, internal asset data, leased asset data, and foreign asset data.

Physical Parameters and Capacities.   Physical parameters and capacities must be reviewed to determine "the number of units [assets] can presently produce and distribute within a particular time frame."[13] This analysis should be by subsidiary or plant location and should provide measurement constraints on aggregation of assets and geographic variables. The first portion of this analysis is to determine whether it is process oriented or not. Examples of nonprocess-oriented facilities would exist in the following industries: automotive, containers, drugs, electronics, foods, machine tools, office and business equipment, retail stores, textiles, and tires. Examples of process-oriented facilities would exist in the following industries: aluminum, brewing, chemicals, fertilizers, forest products, oil refining, paper manufacturing, and steel.

Physical capacity considerations for measuring replacement cost are discussed in *Staff Accounting Bulletin No. 12,* which states:

> In most instances, if management intends to replace existing capacity with different assets, that intent should be recognized in the replacement cost data. The results will then indicate to the extent possible the direction of the company.
>
> Whenever replacement with a new asset configuration is assumed, there are at least two types of situations that can be distinguished:
>
> (a) If management could reasonably assume that it would replace with greater capacity and that such capacity should be utilized, then only the portion of total costs attributable to existing capacity should be disclosed as the replacement cost of existing productive capacity. This allocation would be appropriate even though a replacement opportunity exists with capacity equivalent to that presently owned.
>
> (b) If management expects to produce in the future at the same level as it currently produces but would be required to replace with higher capacity because equivalent capacity replacements were not available, then replacement cost would be the total costs of the higher capacity.

Management Policies and Controls.   Management policies relating to replacement cost measurements are asset capitalization, asset life assignments, depreciation methodology, and capital budgeting.

Asset capitalization policies should include the elements of the cost bases, such as sales price, freight, installation, startup costs, interest, and other indirect charges.

Asset life assignments are important to the computation of replacement cost depreciation and the current depreciated replacement costs. Generally accepted accounting principles require an adjustment to historical lives when economic conditions warrant a change. *SEC Staff Accounting Bulletin No. 7* says that, "Therefore any change in economic life should not result from replacement cost requirements but from changing estimates of economic conditions relating to the asset."

Rather than calculate replacement cost on an asset-by-asset basis with individual lives assigned to each asset, composite life assignments may be made to groups of assets (e.g., assets measured by a functional pricing technique, etc.). *Staff Accounting Bulletin No. 12* states:

> Generally, replacement cost depreciation expense may be computed by using the appropriate composite life of the existing group of assets.
>
> The determination of accumulated replacement cost depreciation may present a special problem. Because of the interaction of changes in prices, composition of assets, and timing of acquisitions, the ratio of total accumulated depreciation to total cost on a historical cost basis may differ from that on a replacement cost basis.
>
> For example, the following tabulation [Exhibit 3] summarizes a group of assets with replacement cost data estimated on an individual asset basis.
>
> If, instead, replacement cost were estimated at $30,000 on a composite basis (e.g., functional pricing), the following illustrates the difference in the accumulated depreciation ratios:

---

[13] *SEC Staff Accounting Bulletin No. 7.*

Estimated replacement of the group	$30,000
Historical ratio of accumulated depreciation to cost ($7,700 ÷ $20,000)	38½%
Indicated replacement cost accumulated depreciation	$11,550
Replacement cost accumulated depreciation computed on an asset-by-asset basis, per above	$14,880

EXHIBIT 3

Year acquired	Cost	Life (years)	Historical depreciation[a]		Cost	Replacement depreciation	
			Provision for 1976	Accumulated at 12-31-76		Provision for 1976[b]	Accumulated at 12-31-76
1961	$ 1,000	20	$ 50	$ 800	$ 3,000	$ 150	$ 2,400
1968	2,000	10	200	1,800	5,000	500	4,500
1969	3,000	10	300	2,400	6,000	600	4,800
1971	5,000	25	200	1,200	7,000	280	1,680
1975	4,000	16	250	500	4,000	250	500
1976	5,000	5	1,000	1,000	5,000	1,000	1,000
Total	$20,000		$2,000	$7,700	$30,000	$2,780	$14,880

[a]Based on a full year's depreciation provision in the year acquired.
[b]Assumed no changes in prices during 1976.

One approach to the computation of replacement cost accumulated depreciation is to make a detailed analysis of the assets for which replacement cost was estimated on a group basis and, to the extent possible, match the replacement assets with the historical assets. The staff, however, believes that in most cases alternative techniques can be applied to reduce clerical effort in making the computations.

For instance, using the data from the example above, a weighted-average life of the historical assets could be computed, as follows [see Exhibit 4].

EXHIBIT 4

Year acquired	Historical cost	Age in years	Age extension
1961	$ 1,000	16	$ 16,000
1968	2,000	9	18,000
1969	3,000	8	24,000
1971	5,000	6	30,000
1975	4,000	2	8,000
1976	5,000	1	5,000
Total	$20,000		$101,000

Divided by total historical cost	20,000
Weighted-average age	5.05 years
Estimated replacement cost of productivity capacity	$30,000
Composite historical depreciation rate ($2,000 ÷ $20,000)	10%
Estimated replacement cost depreciation	$ 3,000
Weighted-average age	5.05 years
Approximate accumulated replacement cost depreciation	$15,150

A review of fully depreciated assets should be made. The materiality "(e.g., less than 5 percent of gross property, plant, and equipment)" of the fully depreciated assets that are still in use but that have been written off the books must be determined.[14] All fully depreciated assets still in use and still on the books are part of productive capacity, and their replacement cost (new) should be determined.[15]

Capital budgeting must be reviewed to determine whether backup data exist for replacement cost measurements. For example, a company may not have purchased new equipment or installed a new process line recently, but it may have measured a replacement cost at a recent date for these productive capacity units.

Management's intention for the short-term and long-term implementation of replacement cost measurements is important. For the short-term implementation, the amount of effort required to measure replacement cost is the greatest; but if proper attention is given to the data collection, analysis, and computations, a large amount of reworking the data in following years will be avoided. Additionally, management's intention to use the data for other purposes will determine constraints on aggregations of the data. For example, if management intends to use the data for pricing, return-on-investment, property tax monitoring, insurance placement, business combination analyses, etc., the data should be maintained at the plant level. Maintenance of more detailed asset-by-asset and asset group data for these purposes may be too burdensome, costly, and time consuming. At higher levels of aggregation, such as divisions or subsidiaries, the data may be too highly aggregated to be usable for other management purposes.

Internal Asset Data.   Internal data should incorporate information regarding the property records, engineering data, insurance appraisal data, purchasing data, and governmental or regulatory filing data. The property records may be manual or computerized. In either case, the records must be amenable to aggregation to higher levels (than asset by asset) for making replacement cost measurements. A review of the records should be made to determine the following types of information:

- Classification codes
- Number of records
- Level of aggregation
- Availability of data by chart of accounts within location
- Allocation of purchase price from prior business combinations
- Purchased new versus used

Engineering data should be reviewed to determine the following:

- Nonprocess versus process orientation
- Special-purpose machinery and equipment
- Size and types of buildings
- Integration of assets (e.g., homogeneous versus heterogeneous)
- Degree of technological change
- Existing replacement cost data
- Availability of external engineering data
- Functional subdivision of assets
- Capital budgeting data
- Governmental requirements (e.g., pollution control equipment, updated safety requirements, etc.)

Insurance/appraisal data should be reviewed to determine the following:

- Date of most recent inventory
- Date of most recent pricing
- Degree of reproduction cost measurement versus replacement cost
- Potential for reconciliation to accounting records
- Amount of indexing utilized

---

[14]*SEC Staff Accounting Bulletin No. 11.*
[15]*SEC Staff Accounting Bulletin No. 7.*

- Itemization of special purpose machinery and equipment
- Definition of size and types of buildings

Purchasing data should be reviewed to determine if direct price information is available: the amount of data available for developing internal indexes; and the amount of items purchased *used* as a general policy. Relative to the purchase of used equipment, *Staff Accounting Bulletin No. 10* states:

> The following conditions would appear to be necessary for basing replacement cost on the current prices of used items:
>   1. Used facilities and equipment are available and, in management's judgment, will continue to be available during the remaining life of its existing productive capacity.
>   2. Under current economic conditions, management would replace its productive capacity with used facilities and equipment. The cost of the used facilities and equipment would become the gross replacement cost for purposes of [this measurement]. Disclosure should be made if used facilities and equipment provide the basis for replacement of a significant portion of productive capacity.

Leased Asset Data.   Leased assets must be reviewed for compliance with *Accounting Series Release No. 190*. The data or leased items may be computerized as part of the property records, or it may be in a manual form. In order to measure the replacement costs, it is necessary to have historical cost (new), purchase date, classification, and other similar data elements as listed above in the property records. This is necessary because *ASR No. 190* states:

> For purposes of this rule, assets held under financing leases as defined in [*ASR No. 147*] shall be included in productive capacity.

Staff Accounting Bulletin No. 9 states:

> [The *ASR No. 147* rule] does not require separate disclosure of non-capitalized financing leases unless the present value of the minimum lease payments is greater than 5% of the sum of long-term debt, stockholders' equity and the present value of the minimum lease commitments.

In general, the rules state that if leased facilities qualify for disclosure under *ASR No. 147*, they should be included in the replacement cost calculation. *Staff Accounting Bulletin No. 10* states the exception:

> In unusual factual circumstances where the replacement cost of such leased assets may have increased so significantly compared to other assets that such assets on a replacement cost basis would constitute a significant part of productive capacity computed on that basis,

then they should be included under *ASR No. 190* disclosures.

Foreign Asset Data.   Foreign assets should be reviewed for the following:
- Materiality
- Level of aggregation
- Availability of local external data[16]
- Compliance with FASB No. 8 for currency translation
- Available internal data relating to classification codes, unusual accounting entries, chart of account schedules, etc.
- Engineering data similar to that specified above

Often U.S. corporations export assets assembled in the United States. In these cases, the functional approach to replacement cost based on the U.S. assets could be used.

---

[16]See Valuation Systems Corporation, *VSCOM-190 Foreign Data* (Rolling Meadows, Ill., 1977).

Auditability. The independent accountant should be involved in the planning and reviewing of the implementation for replacement cost measurements. *Accounting Series Release No. 190* states:

> The independent accountant will be associated with the replacement cost information even though it is unaudited. The Commission urges the Auditing Standards Executive Committee (AUDSEC) of the American Institute of Certified Public Accountants to develop appropriate standards applicable to the auditor in the case of such association.

AUDSEC developed *SAS No. 18* for auditors to follow to "be associated with the replacement cost information." The objectives of the Statement on Auditing Standards developed by AUDSEC are to determine if:

- The replacement cost information is prepared and presented in conformity with Regulation S-X of the Commission, and
- Management's disclosures with respect to the replacement cost information are consistent with management's responses to such inquiries.

The Standard states procedures for auditors to follow in making inquiries about replacement cost measurement methodology, general guidance procedures for the auditor to follow, and the auditor's reports to be rendered. Regarding the nature of the auditor's procedures, AUDSEC stated in *SAS No. 18*:

> a. Inquire of management as to whether the replacement cost information has been prepared and presented in accordance with the requirements of Regulation S-X.
> b. Inquire of management as to the methods selected to calculate replacement cost information and the reasons for selecting them, including considerations given by management to (1) current replacement programs, (2) plans or expressed intentions concerning future replacements, (3) plans or expressed intentions not to replace certain inventories or productive capacity, and (4) technological changes that have occurred in the industry.
> c. Inquire of management as to procedures used to compile the data supporting the replacement cost information and as to the relationship between data supporting the replacement cost information and data supporting the audited financial information. Example of such inquiries follow: Are the useful lives used to calculate depreciation on the historical cost basis the same as those used on the replacement cost basis? Are inventory quantities used in the determination of inventory value for the historical cost financial statements the same as inventory quantities used to calculate the replacement cost information?
> d. Inquire about the methods and bases used by management to calculate any supplemental replacement cost information, such as historical relationships between cost of sales and selling prices or the effect of technologically improved capacity replacements on operating costs.
> e. If management has changed the method of calculating replacement cost information, inquire as to the reasons for using a method different from that used in the previous fiscal period.
>
> The auditor should consider whether disclosures with respect to the unaudited replacement cost information are consistent with management's responses to the above inquiries and other information obtained during the audit of the financial statements. The auditor has no obligation to perform any procedures to corroborate management's responses concerning the unaudited replacement cost information

To comply with these developments, replacement cost measurement techniques should be traceable for future audit considerations. An audit trail should be established for each replacement cost measurement technique with appropriate documentation to the internal and external data sources used. As noted in subparagraph c. above, provision should be made for a reconciliation of the replacement cost data to the data supporting the audited financial information.

A COMPUTERIZED APPROACH TO REPLACEMENT COSTS

A computerized solution to replacement cost measurements should include: a structured approach; access to indexes; links to indexes, unit prices, direct prices, functional prices, and asset lives; computerized aggregation tools; data transmission and teleprocessing capability; data base maintenance; and auditability.[17]

A Structured Approach. A structured approach provides for utilization of any of the generally accepted replacement cost measurement techniques (indexing, unit pricing, direct pricing, and functional pricing). As required by *Accounting Series Release No. 190*, it should provide for all assets throughout the world. It should keep pace with changing SEC requirements, provide continuously updated external data, and be cost effective.

Internal and External Data Links. The internal and external data links should provide the ability to assign a numeric indicator to a commodity, an asset, a group of assets, a labor skill, and materials; and to associate each of these with a selected external index, unit price, direct price, or functional price. The internal or external data links should be hierarchical and provide titles and definitions for each element.

The hierarchy of an internal or external data link might be as shown below:

Internal/external data link	*Level*	*Description*
35	Major group	Machinery, except electrical
356	Group	General industrial machinery
3564	Industry	Blowers and fans
35646	Asset class	Dust collection and other air purification equipment for industrial gas cleaning systems
356465	Asset group	Particulate emission collectors
3564651	Asset	Electrostatic precipitator

Computerized Aggregation Tools. Computerized aggregation tools should have the ability to display selected index series, index series descriptions, index series specifications, internal or external data links, and internal or external data link descriptions. They should be capable of extending an index series backward or forward through time; combining several indexes into one; testing the relationship between the separate index series or price data; and creating index series from price and quantity data. They should be capable of producing unit price data at any geographic location of a structure based upon component cost and quantity data[18] of a recently built structure of the same type. They should also be capable of computing the current replacement cost of an asset by associating it with an asset of equivalent function.

Data Transmission and Teleprocessing Capability. Data transmission and teleprocessing capabilities provide for immediate updating and editing of data and for the creation of data bases which can be built, verified, and edited from remote locations. The processing capability of the system should include the ability to

---

[17]The system mentioned in this section is described in more detail by Valuation Systems Corporation, *VSCOM-190 Management Briefing* (Rolling Meadows, Ill., 1976).

[18]The Construction Specifications Institute, *Uniform Construction Index* (Washington, D.C., 1972).

collect data, analyze aggregation levels, calculate replacement costs, and produce various replacement cost reports (e.g., Historic Cost Detail, Historic Cost Summary, Replacement Cost Detail, and Replacement Cost Summary).

Data Base Maintenance.   Data base maintenance refers to both external and internal data. External data such as indexes can cause problems because of missing data points, late startup of index series, discontinued index series, and changed specifications. External data base maintenance should incorporate solutions to these problems. Internal data base maintenance should incorporate the ability to retain historic cost data for inputting and for future balancing and reconciliation.

Auditability.   Auditability is a key consideration in a computer-based system. All elements of the system should be capable of maintaining the source record or document description for a readily available audit trail. The audit trail should provide for transaction codes, valuation technique codes, depreciation technique codes, inventory valuation method technique codes, asset classes, chart of accounts, country codes, and pointer codes for the internal or external data links and their relationships to indexes, unit prices, direct prices, and functional prices.

REPLACEMENT COST MEASUREMENT APPLICATIONS

To use replacement cost measurements, consideration must be given to the measurement technique selection, materiality of the measured assets, level of aggregation, availability of external data, and availability of internal data. These considerations will be incorporated below in the example of replacement cost measurements for inventories, general-purpose equipment, special-purpose equipment, buildings, and process plants.

Inventories.   In this example, the replacement cost of the inventory is for a manufacturing company using a FIFO cost-flow assumption for inventory. To simplify the example, assume that sales, purchases, production, and price increases were spread evenly throughout the year. Assume that the following historical cost information exists:

	Material	Labor and overhead	Total
Average inventory	$41,000	$ 33,000	$ 74,000
Year-end inventory	37,000	28,000	65,000
Cost of sales	90,000	148,000	238,000

Analysis of wage rates and overhead costs indicates that labor and overhead increased in price by 5.2 percent during the year. Analysis of sample of representative raw materials indicates that materials increased in price by 12 percent during the year.

Adjustment for Cost of Sales.
   1. Compute inventory turnover:

	Material	Labor and overhead
Cost of sales (A)	$90,000	$148,000
Average inventory (B)	41,000	33,000
Inventory turnover (A/B)	2.20	4.48

   2. Determine the percentage adjustment for specific price increases during the approximate time lag between incurring cost and the time of sale:

	Material	Labor and overhead
Annual percentage price change (A)	12%	5.2%
Inventory turnover (B)	2.20	4.48
Adjustment for specific price increases during the time lag between incurring cost and the time of sale (A/B)	5.45%	1.16%

3. Determine the cost of sales adjustment:

	Material	Labor and overhead
Cost of sales	$90,000	$148,000
Approximate adjustment	5.45%	1.16%
Adjustment to cost of sales for specific price change	$4,905	$1,717

4. Cost of sales at replacement cost:

Historic cost of sales	$238,000
Adjustment for price changes	
Material	4,905
Labor and overhead	1,717
Estimated cost of sales at replacement cost	$244,622

Adjustment for Year-End Inventory.

1. Determine year-end inventory adjustment for approximate time lag in recognizing price changes:

	Material	Labor and overhead
Turnover (A)	2.20	4.48
Annual percentage price change (B)	12%	5.2%
Percentage price change in inventory (B/A)	5.45%	1.15%
Approximate adjustment for effect of cost increases to purchases and production ratably throughout cycle	× ½	× ½
Adjustment rate	2.73%	.58%

2. Adjustment to year-end inventory:

	Material	Labor and overhead
Year-end inventory at historical cost	$37,000	$28,000
Adjustment rate	2.73%	.58%
Adjustment to year-end inventory for price change	$ 1,010	$ 162

3. Year-end inventory at replacement cost:

Year-end inventory at historical cost	$65,000
Adjustment for specific price change:	
Material	1,010
Labor and overhead	162
Inventory at estimated replacement cost	$66,172

General-Purpose Equipment.   General-purpose equipment refers to equipment items such as furniture and fixtures, office, mechanical, automotive, laboratory, metalworking, metalcutting, electrical power (e.g., transformers, regulators, etc.), and finished steel (e.g. tools, jigs, dies, etc.). For this example, the classification selected is furniture and fixtures. The technique selected is indexing with aggregations at the vintage year-of-acquisition level. The technique selection and the aggregation level were based on the furniture and fixtures account representing 2 percent of gross historical cost of property, plant, and equipment. The index selected is the Wholesale Price Index Series No. 122 for furniture and fixtures. The computations are given in Exhibit 5.

EXHIBIT 5

Year	Historical cost	Index	Index ratio	Replacement cost
1971	$ 2,000	118.1	$\dfrac{166.9}{118.1}$	$ 2,826
1972	3,000	120.2	$\dfrac{166.9}{120.2}$	4,165
1973	5,000	129.4	$\dfrac{166.9}{129.4}$	6,448
1974	500	152.4	$\dfrac{166.9}{152.4}$	547
1975	4,000	166.9	$\dfrac{166.9}{166.9}$	4,000
Total	$14,500			$17,986

For the depreciation expense, computation, *ASR No. 190* states:

> The approximate amount of depreciation (should be based upon what) would have been recorded if it were estimated on the basis of average current replacement cost of productive capacity. For purposes of this calculation, economic lives and salvage values currently used in calculating historical cost depreciation . . . shall generally be used. For assets being depreciated . . . on a time expired basis, the straight-line method shall be used in making this calculation.

In this example, the furniture and fixtures are assigned an economic life in the historical cost records of 10 years. The depreciation expense is calculated as in Exhibit 6.

EXHIBIT 6

Year	Replacement cost	Life	Depreciation expense
1971	$ 2,826	10	$ 282.60
1972	4,165	10	416.50
1973	6,448	10	644.80
1974	547	10	54.70
1975	4,000	10	400.00
Total	$17,986		$1,798.60

To calculate the accumulated replacement cost depreciation, the computations of Exhibit 7 show the difference between using vintage aging and the ratio of gross replacement cost to gross historical cost.

EXHIBIT 7

Year	Historical cost amount	Accumulated historical cost depreciation	Replacement cost	Accumulated replacement cost depreciation
1971	$ 2,000	$1,000	$ 2,826	$1,413
1972	3,000	1,200	4,165	1,666
1973	5,000	1,500	6,448	1,934
1974	500	100	547	109
1975	4,000	400	4,000	400
Total	$14,500	$4,200	$17,986	$5,522

Using vintage costs, the following accumulated replacement cost depreciation is based on the ratio technique:

$$\$4,200 \times \frac{\$17,986}{\$14,500} = \$5,209$$

This example of using vintage cost computations versus the ratio technique indicates the amount of divergence ($5,522 versus $5,209) that can occur. This divergence becomes more significant as the age and amounts of older historical costs increase.

Another technique for calculating accumulated replacement cost depreciation is based on the composite life. This is calculated as shown in Exhibit 8. The $42,000

EXHIBIT 8

Year	Historical cost	Age	Weighted historical cost
1971	$ 2,000	5	$10,000
1972	3,000	4	12,000
1973	5,000	3	15,000
1974	500	2	1,000
1975	4,000	1	4,000
	$14,500		$42,000

divided by the historical cost of $14,500 provides a weighted average age of 2.9 years. Multiplying the weighted average age of 2.9 years by the depreciation expense on the replacement cost basis, $1,798.60, results in an accumulated replacement cost depreciation of $5,215.94.

The accumulated depreciation on replacement cost as required by *ASR No. 190* based on the three techniques of calculation is summarized as follows:

Calculation technique	Accumulated replacement cost depreciation as of 1975
Vintage aging	$5,522
Ratio	5,209
Composite life	5,216

Special-Purpose Equipment. For most special-purpose machinery, the direct price technique is used in most initial replacement cost measurements because of technological change. Later measurement updates then use indexing until material technological changes again occur. A few items of special machinery will usually represent a large fraction of total machinery and equipment dollars. In this example, the replacement cost for an injection molding machine acquired in 1960 for $61,000 (including installation) is calculated. The price for the replacement machine is obtained from the Industrial Machinery Equipment Company. Based on the December 1976 price, the replacement cost for the machine is as follows:

Injection molding machine	$79,000
Taxes	3,950
Freight	1,000
Installation	11,500
Replacement cost	$95,450

Buildings.   Buildings are generally measured by the unit price technique. They are first classified by category (e.g., light manufacturing, medium manufacturing, heavy manufacturing, warehouse, office, etc.). They are next classified by framing type (e.g., low-rise steel frame, wood frame, multistory steel frame, etc.). Building unit prices should *not* be indexed for more than five years or the results are more likely to be reproduction costs than replacement costs. Replacement costs for buildings are best measured by using a recently constructed building of a given category and type. The model is then adjusted for time, location, and size to measure the productive capacity in question.

The unit price for a replacement building model is developed by classifying the building components into the Construction Specifications Institute classification and calculating a unit price for each classification based upon its unit measure. These unit prices are then adjusted for differences in time and location. Because building costs do not vary linearly with size, a scale factor is used in measuring buildings of a size different from the one used to calculate the unit price.

The unit price multiplied by the unit dimension measures the replacement cost of each building component. Adding the replacement cost of all building components and of the contractor's overhead provides the replacement cost for the total building as shown in Exhibit 9. The unit price is computed from the total replacement cost ($637,727) divided by the building square footage (34,000 square

EXHIBIT 9   Building Replacement Cost

System component	Unit of measure [a]	Dimension	Unit cost	Total cost
Site work	SITSF	408,000	.36	$146,880
Foundation	BLDSF	34,000	.42	14,280
Floor	BLDSF	34,000	1.18	40,120
Interior columns	COLLF	192	12.59	2,417
Exterior walls	WLSF	13,990	2.09	29,239
Exterior glazed openings	OPGSF	663	5.32	3,527
Interior walls	WLSF	8,429	2.17	18,290
Doors	DRSF	758	4.00	3,032
Specialties	BLDSF	34,000	.06	2,040
Plumbing	FIXTR	42	1100.96	46,240
Heat and ventilation	BLDSF	34,000	.65	22,100
Electrical	BLDSF	34,000	.99	33,660
Roof	RFSF	34,000	5.12	174,080
Total direct cost				$535,905
Overhead (19%) [b]				101,822
Total replacement cost				$637,727

[a] See Exhibit 10 for explanation of unit of measure.

[b] Overhead percentage is derived from contractor's records as costs incurred for architectural fees, engineering fees, and other indirect costs.

feet), resulting in a unit price of $18.76 per square foot. For other buildings of a similar framing and type, this unit price is adjusted for time (not more than five years), geographical locations to provide replacement cost of buildings at other locations, and size.

EXHIBIT 10   Units of Measure for Various Components of Buildings

Component	Description	Unit of measure
1. Site work	Measure total square feet of site. For parking areas determine the number of cars or the square feet of paved area. For sidewalks measure the square feet. For streets measure the square feet.	SITSF
2. Foundation	Measure the total building square feet. The measurement does not include basement walls or floors.	BLDGSF
3. Floor	Measure the total enclosed area. Include in the measurement all balconies, porches, and basements.	BLDGSF
4. Interior columns	Measure the columns in linear feet. Include the vertical interior columns and pilasters above the foundation. Do not include loadbearing walls or any loadbearing components of walls or structural members.	COLLF
5. Roof system	Measure total waterproofed roof area.	RFSF
6. Exterior walls	Measure the total square feet of exterior walls including basement walls. Do not deduct for normal doors and windows. This measurement includes all structural members contained in the walls, including exterior finishes, insulation, core, and interior finishes.	EWSF
7. Exterior glazed openings	Measure in total square feet of the actual openings. This measurement includes frames, finishes, and type of glass or panels.	OPGSF
8. Interior walls	Measure in total wall square feet without deduction for normal doors.	IWSF
9. Doors	Measure total square feet of door openings including movable closures.	DRSF
10. Specialties	The inclusions are all the elements that make the building operative for its specific purpose.	BLDGSF
11. Plumbing	Count the number of normal fixtures. This does not include special fixtures for sprinkler systems, etc.	FIXT
12. Heating and ventilating	Measure total enclosed area. Where air conditioning is included, the tonnage of the air conditioning system is measured.	BLDGSF (tons)
13. Electrical	Measure the total enclosed area of the building.	BLDGSF

Process Plant.   Replacement cost of process plants is usually determined by use of functional pricing, which uses direct pricing, indexing, and unit pricing. We illustrate functional pricing for a paper manufacturing plant. The plant has six functional processes: chip handling, refining, screening, pulp mill, paper, and boiler. The individual techniques used to develop the total functional price are as follows:

Chip handling:	direct price new equipment.
Refining:	direct price new equipment.
Screening:	unit price based on current technology.
Pulp mill:	index.
Paper:	direct price new equipment.
Boiler:	index.

Exhibit 11 shows the costs that are connected with these functions. For the idle assets, the original cost of $1,151,000 can produce a net realizable value of

EXHIBIT 11

Function description	Historical cost	Replacement cost	Idle assets	Excess operating costs (annual)
Chip handling	$ 700,000	$ 1,000,000	$ 317,000	$137,000[1]
Refining	2,500,000	6,000,000		
Screening	1,730,000	3,250,000		324,000[3]
Pulp mill	1,201,000	825,000	834,000[2]	
Paper	13,740,000	10,935,000		60,000[4]
Boiler, hog fuel	2,040,000	2,450,000		25,000
Total	$21,911,000	$24,460,000	$1,151,000	$546,000

[1]Plant layout near chip handling area causes extra conveying and storage equipment to be included.
[2]Falling demand for high-grade paper caused shutdown of extra digesters.
[3]Screening equipment is in different building due to lack of space, causing extra piping of screened products.
[4]One $6 million paper machine produces 50,000 tons per year of paper as opposed to two old $4.5 million machines (20,000 tons per year each). Operating costs would be reduced by $60,000.

$240,000 which is disclosed separately. The resulting replacement cost for the functional pricing example is as follows:

1. Unadjusted for capacity	$24,460,000
2. Adjusted for capacity ($24,460,000 × 80%)	19,568,000

The operating cost of $546,000 per year must be disclosed separately in the accompanying narrative.

OTHER MANAGEMENT USES

Dividend Policy. Distribution of all of historical costs profits will generally reduce the real capital of the business and could increase the future reinvestment necessary to replace productive capacity. Under replacement cost, dividends can be determined at current levels required not to impair productive capacity. Management can then better determine the proper allocation between reinvestments and shareholder dividend distributions.

Example

	Historical cost	Replacement cost
Revenue	$1,000	$1,000
Cost of sales (FIFO)	500	
Cost of sales (replacement cost)		600
Gross margin	$ 500	$ 400
Other operating expenses	(200)	(200)
Depreciation	(50)	(100)
Income	$250	$100

In this example, the company has earned less than the historical cost-based statements indicate. If the company were to pay out more than $100 in dividends, it would be paying out more than distributable income; subsequently, additional funds would be needed to maintain current operating levels.

Debt/Equity Analysis.   Historical cost data are *not* ideal for use in planning debt and equity relationships. Generally, equity as a whole is underestimated in a historical cost system. By using data generated from replacement cost, management has better information from which to plan financing requirements, whether they be additional debt offerings or additional equity offerings. This leads to more credible relationships with lenders and investors and a healthier financial structure.

■ Assets and liabilities can be more accurately valued by lenders under replacement cost.

■ Debt/equity ratio calculated under replacement cost is a more accurate barometer of the financial risk of the company.

■ Cash requirements can be better determined using replacement cost rather than historical cost-based statements.

■ Replacement cost statements can be valuable tools in determining the type of financing required because debt and equity are expressed in terms of their current relationships.

Pricing Policy. Using FIFO cost flows in a period of rising costs, management can be misled by the matching of older, lower costs against current, higher selling prices. Replacement cost can be matched against current selling prices, allowing for pricing decisions to become more sensitive to changes in product costs. Even though the market dictates price, management will still be better off relating prices of the market to their pricing based on replacement cost.

Example

	Historical cost	Replacement cost
Revenue	$1,000	$1,000
Cost of sales (FIFO)	500	
Cost of sales (replacement cost)		600
Gross margin	$ 500	$ 400

Notice in the above example that gross margin is 50 percent based on historical cost accounting and only 40 percent based on replacement cost accounting. This provides a truer picture of the pricing strategies for the corporation.

Capital Investment Decisions. Capital investment decisions based on inventories and fixed assets at historical book values can lead to significant underestimates of cash requirements. Under replacement cost measurements the long-range replacement cost requirements can be based on more relevant data.

Return on Investment. Using historical cost data makes it difficult to compare performance of operating units, such as plants, because plants with newer equipment at higher prices will have higher depreciation and lower reported profits. ROI techniques using historical cost data become more difficult to apply or are less than meaningful when applied. Under replacement cost, management can view comparative operating results in the perspective of replacement cost relative to operating revenues and can make better decisions on allocating resources to specific operating units and product lines.

Business Combinations. Both taxable business combinations under the Internal Revenue Code and those to be accounted for as a purchase under generally accepted accounting principles require a determination of current asset values. Under replacement cost accounting, the relevant current value data is available for making realistic analyses of merger and acquisition candidates. The tax impact under a taxable transaction within the Internal Revenue Code and their accounting implications for future profits based on purchase accounting are more easily determinable.

Ad Valorem (Property) Taxes. Throughout the country, assessors base property taxes on current value information. In order for companies to monitor properly the assessment levels for their properties, replacement cost data are needed rather than historical cost data. Often assessors use erroneous historical cost information provided by the company to generate approximations to current value to the detriment (or advantage) of the corporate taxpayer. Replacement cost information can be used to monitor tax assessments.

Insurance Placement and Proof of Loss. Insurance placement and proof of loss have traditionally been based on reproduction cost less physical depreciation. During the last decade, this technique of insurance measurement has been shifting to replacement cost of productive capacity. As such, insurance departments are continually gearing themselves to provide replacement cost data to the insurance carriers in order to determine the amount of insurance to be carried on the corporate properties. In the event of a loss, the burden of proof is on the corporation to prove the replacement cost of its loss. Replacement cost data can better provide information regarding the amount of insurance to carry and provide more realistic data in the event of a loss.

BIBLIOGRAPHY

Accounting Practices Committee of the National Council of Chartered Accountants (South Africa): "Accounting for Inflation and Other Changes in Price Level," National Council of Chartered Accountants, Johannesburg, May 1975.

Accounting Standards Committee: "Background Papers to the Exposure Draft on Current Cost Accounting," London, 1976.

Accounting Standards Committee: "Proposed Statement of Standard Accounting Practice: Current Cost Accounting," London, 1976.

Alexander, Michael O.: *Accounting for Inflation: A Challenge for Business,* Maclean-Hunter, Toronto, Canada, 1975.

American Institute of Certified Public Accountants: "Report of the Study Group on the Objectives of Financial Statements: Objectives of Financial Statements" (Trueblood Report), AICPA, New York, 1973.

Arthur Andersen & Co.: *Accounting Standards for Business Enterprises Throughout the World,* Arthur Andersen & Co., Chicago, 1974.

Backer, Morton: *Current Value Accounting,* Financial Executives Research Foundation, New York, 1973.

Bakker, Pieter: *Inflation and Profit Control,* Methuen Publications, Toronto, 1974.

Boyce, Byrl N.: *Real Estate Appraisal Terminology,* Ballinger Publishing Company, Cambridge, Mass., 1975.

Chambers, Raymond J.: *Accounting Evaluation and Economic Behavior,* Prentice-Hall, Englewood Cliffs, N.J., 1966.

Construction Specifications Institute: "Uniform Construction Index," Construction Specifications Institute, Washington, D.C., 1972.

Davidson, Sidney, James S. Schindler, Clyde P. Stickney, and Roman L. Weil: *Accounting: The Language of Business,* 3rd ed., Thomas Horton & Daughters, Glen Ridge, N.J., 1977.

———: *Financial Accounting: An Introduction to Concepts, Methods, and Uses,* Dryden Press, Hinsdale, Ill., 1976, chaps. 11, 14.

Davidson, Sidney, Clyde P. Stickney, and Roman L. Weil: *Inflation Accounting,* McGraw-Hill Book Company, New York, 1976.

Davidson, Sidney, and Roman L. Weil: "Replacement Cost/Current Value Accounting," in *Handbook of Modern Accounting,* 2nd ed., McGraw-Hill Book Company, New York, 1977, chap. 46.

Edwards, Edgar O., and Phillip W. Bell: *The Theory and Measurement of Business Income,* University of California Press, Berkeley, 1961.

Griliches, Zvi: *Price Indexes and Quality Changes,* Harvard University Press, Cambridge, Mass., 1971.

Institute of Chartered Accountants in Australia and Australian Society of Accountants: "Explanatory Statement: The Basis of Current Cost Accounting," ICA and ASA, Melbourne, 1976.

Largay, James A., III, and John Leslie Livingstone: *Accounting for Changing Prices,* John Wiley & Sons, New York, 1976.

Marston, Anson, Robley Winfrey, and Jean C. Hempstead: *Engineering Valuation & Depreciation,* Iowa State University Press, Ames, 1953.

New Zealand Society of Accountants: "Proposed Statement of Standard Accounting Practice: Accounting in Terms of Current Costs and Values," New Zealand Society of Accountants, Wellington, 1976.

Revsine, Lawrence: *Replacement Cost Accounting,* Prentice-Hall, Englewood Cliffs, N.J., 1973.

Rosen, L. S.: *Current Value Accounting and Price-Level Restatements,* Canadian Institute of Chartered Accountants, Toronto, 1972.

Ross, Howard: *Financial Statements—A Crusade for Current Values,* Pitman Publishing Corporation, New York, 1969.

Securities and Exchange Commission: *Accounting Series Release No. 190,* March 23, 1976; *Staff Accounting Bulletin No. 7,* March 23, 1976; *Staff Accounting Bulletin No. 9,* June 17, 1976; *Staff Accounting Bulletin No. 10,* July 27, 1976; *Staff Accounting Bulletin No. 11,* September 3, 1976; *Staff Accounting Bulletin No. 12,* November 10, 1976; *Staff Accounting Bulletin No. 13,* January 4, 1977; SEC, Washington, D.C.

Stigler, George J., and James K. Kindall: *The Behavior of Industrial Prices,* National Bureau of Economic Research, New York, 1970.

Valuation Systems Corporation: *Replacement Cost Measurement: External Data Sources Reference Guide,* Rolling Meadows, Ill., 1976.

Vancil, Richard F., and Roman L. Weil: *Replacement Cost Accounting: Readings on Concepts, Uses, and Methods,* Thomas Horton & Daughters, Glen Ridge, N.J., 1976.

Appendix

Compound Interest, Annuity, and Bond Tables

TABLE 1   Future Value of $1

$$F_n = P(1 + r)^n$$
r = interest rate; n = number of periods until valuation

Periods = n	¼%	½%	⅔%	¾%	1%	1½%	2%	3%
1	1.00250	1.00500	1.00667	1.00750	1.01000	1.01500	1.02000	1.03000
2	1.00501	1.01003	1.01338	1.01506	1.02010	1.03022	1.04040	1.06090
3	1.00752	1.01508	1.02013	1.02267	1.03030	1.04568	1.06121	1.09273
4	1.01004	1.02015	1.02693	1.03034	1.04060	1.06136	1.08243	1.12551
5	1.01256	1.02525	1.03378	1.03807	1.05101	1.07728	1.10408	1.15927
6	1.01509	1.03038	1.04067	1.04585	1.06152	1.09344	1.12616	1.19405
7	1.01763	1.03553	1.04761	1.05370	1.07214	1.10984	1.14869	1.22987
8	1.02018	1.04071	1.05459	1.06160	1.08286	1.12649	1.17166	1.26677
9	1.02273	1.04591	1.06163	1.06956	1.09369	1.14339	1.19509	1.30477
10	1.02528	1.05114	1.06870	1.07758	1.10462	1.16054	1.21899	1.34392
11	1.02785	1.05640	1.07583	1.08566	1.11567	1.17795	1.24337	1.38423
12	1.03042	1.06168	1.08300	1.09381	1.12683	1.19562	1.26824	1.42576
13	1.03299	1.06699	1.09022	1.10201	1.13809	1.21355	1.29361	1.46853
14	1.03557	1.07232	1.09749	1.11028	1.14947	1.23176	1.31948	1.51259
15	1.03816	1.07768	1.10480	1.11860	1.16097	1.25023	1.34587	1.55797
16	1.04076	1.08307	1.11217	1.12699	1.17258	1.26899	1.37279	1.60471
17	1.04336	1.08849	1.11958	1.13544	1.18430	1.28802	1.40024	1.65285
18	1.04597	1.09393	1.12705	1.14396	1.19615	1.30734	1.42825	1.70243
19	1.04858	1.09940	1.13456	1.15254	1.20811	1.32695	1.45681	1.75351
20	1.05121	1.10490	1.14213	1.16118	1.22019	1.34686	1.48595	1.80611
22	1.05647	1.11597	1.15740	1.17867	1.24472	1.38756	1.54598	1.91610
24	1.06176	1.12716	1.17289	1.19641	1.26973	1.42950	1.60844	2.03279
26	1.06707	1.13846	1.18858	1.21443	1.29526	1.47271	1.67342	2.15659
28	1.07241	1.14987	1.20448	1.23271	1.32129	1.51722	1.74102	2.28793
30	1.07778	1.16140	1.22059	1.25127	1.34785	1.56308	1.81136	2.42726
32	1.08318	1.17304	1.23692	1.27011	1.37494	1.61032	1.88454	2.57508
34	1.08860	1.18480	1.25347	1.28923	1.40258	1.65900	1.96068	2.73191
36	1.09405	1.19668	1.27024	1.30865	1.43077	1.70914	2.03989	2.89828
38	1.09953	1.20868	1.28723	1.32835	1.45953	1.76080	2.12230	3.07478
40	1.10503	1.22079	1.30445	1.34835	1.48886	1.81402	2.20804	3.26204
45	1.11892	1.25162	1.34852	1.39968	1.56481	1.95421	2.43785	3.78160
50	1.13297	1.28323	1.39407	1.45296	1.64463	2.10524	2.69159	4.38391
100	1.28362	1.64667	1.94343	2.11108	2.70481	4.43205	7.24465	19.21863

Periods = n	4%	5%	6%	7%	8%	10%	12%	20%
1	1.04000	1.05000	1.06000	1.07000	1.08000	1.10000	1.12000	1.20000
2	1.08160	1.10250	1.12360	1.14490	1.16640	1.21000	1.25440	1.44000
3	1.12486	1.15762	1.19102	1.22504	1.25971	1.33100	1.40493	1.72800
4	1.16986	1.21551	1.26248	1.31080	1.36049	1.46410	1.57352	2.07360
5	1.21665	1.27628	1.33823	1.40255	1.46933	1.61051	1.76234	2.48832
6	1.26532	1.34010	1.41852	1.50073	1.58687	1.77156	1.97382	2.98598
7	1.31593	1.40710	1.50363	1.60578	1.71382	1.94872	2.21068	3.58318
8	1.36857	1.47746	1.59385	1.71819	1.85093	2.14359	2.47596	4.29982
9	1.42331	1.55133	1.68948	1.83846	1.99900	2.35795	2.77308	5.15978
10	1.48024	1.62889	1.79085	1.96715	2.15892	2.59374	3.10585	6.19174
11	1.53945	1.71034	1.89830	2.10485	2.33164	2.85312	3.47855	7.43008
12	1.60103	1.79586	2.01220	2.25219	2.51817	3.13843	3.89598	8.91610
13	1.66507	1.88565	2.13293	2.40985	2.71962	3.45227	4.36349	10.69932
14	1.73168	1.97993	2.26090	2.57853	2.93719	3.79750	4.88711	12.83918
15	1.80094	2.07893	2.39656	2.75903	3.17217	4.17725	5.47357	15.40702
16	1.87298	2.18287	2.54035	2.95216	3.42594	4.59497	6.13039	18.48843
17	1.94790	2.29202	2.69277	3.15882	3.70002	5.05447	6.86604	22.18611
18	2.02582	2.40662	2.85434	3.37993	3.99602	5.55992	7.68997	26.62333
19	2.10685	2.52695	3.02560	3.61653	4.31570	6.11591	8.61276	31.94800
20	2.19112	2.65330	3.20714	3.86968	4.66096	6.72750	9.64629	38.33760
22	2.36992	2.92526	3.60354	4.43040	5.43654	8.14027	12.10031	55.20614
24	2.56330	3.22510	4.04893	5.07237	6.34118	9.84973	15.17863	79.49685
26	2.77247	3.55567	4.54938	5.80735	7.39635	11.91818	19.04007	114.4755
28	2.99870	3.92013	5.11169	6.64884	8.62711	14.42099	23.88387	164.8447
30	3.24340	4.32194	5.74349	7.61226	10.06266	17.44940	29.95992	237.3763
32	3.50806	4.76494	6.45339	8.71527	11.73708	21.11378	37.58173	341.8219
34	3.79432	5.25335	7.25103	9.97811	13.69013	25.54767	47.14252	492.2235
36	4.10393	5.79182	8.14725	11.42394	15.96817	30.91268	59.13557	708.8019
38	4.43881	6.38548	9.15425	13.07927	18.62528	37.40434	74.17966	1020.675
40	4.80102	7.03999	10.28572	14.97446	21.72452	45.25926	93.05097	1469.772
45	5.84118	8.98501	13.76461	21.00245	31.92045	72.89048	163.9876	3657.262
50	7.10668	11.46740	18.42015	29.45703	46.90161	117.3909	289.0022	9100.438
100	50.50495	131.5013	339.3021	867.7163	2199.761	13780.61	83522.27	828×10^5

TABLE 2   Present Value of $1

$$P = F_n(1 + r)^{-n}$$

r = discount rate; n = number of periods until payment

Periods = n	¼%	½%	⅔%	¾%	1%	1½%	2%	3%
1	0.99751	0.99502	0.99338	0.99256	.99010	.98522	.98039	.97087
2	0.99502	0.99007	0.98680	0.98517	.98030	.97066	.96117	.94260
3	0.99254	0.98515	0.98026	0.97783	.97059	.95632	.94232	.91514
4	0.99006	0.98025	0.97377	0.97055	.96098	.94218	.92385	.88849
5	0.98759	0.97537	0.96732	0.96333	.95147	.92826	.90573	.86261
6	0.98513	0.97052	0.96092	0.95616	.94205	.91454	.88797	.83748
7	0.98267	0.96569	0.95455	0.94904	.93272	.90103	.87056	.81309
8	0.98022	0.96089	0.94823	0.94198	.92348	.88771	.85349	.78941
9	0.97778	0.95610	0.94195	0.93496	.91434	.87459	.83676	.76642
10	0.97534	0.95135	0.93571	0.92800	.90529	.86167	.82035	.74409
11	0.97291	0.94661	0.92952	0.92109	.89632	.84893	.80426	.72242
12	0.97048	0.94191	0.92336	0.91424	.88745	.83639	.78849	.70138
13	0.96806	0.93722	0.91725	0.90743	.87866	.82403	.77303	.68095
14	0.96565	0.93256	0.91117	0.90068	.86996	.81185	.75788	.66112
15	0.96324	0.92792	0.90514	0.89397	.86135	.79985	.74301	.64186
16	0.96084	0.92330	0.89914	0.88732	.85282	.78803	.72845	.62317
17	0.95844	0.91871	0.89319	0.88071	.84438	.77639	.71416	.60502
18	0.95605	0.91414	0.88727	0.87416	.83602	.76491	.70016	.58739
19	0.95367	0.90959	0.88140	0.86765	.82774	.75361	.68643	.57029
20	0.95129	0.90506	0.87556	0.86119	.81954	.74247	.67297	.55368
22	0.94655	0.89608	0.86400	0.84842	.80340	.72069	.64684	.52189
24	0.94184	0.88719	0.85260	0.83583	.78757	.69954	.62172	.49193
26	0.93714	0.87838	0.84134	0.82343	.77205	.67902	.59758	.46369
28	0.93248	0.86966	0.83023	0.81122	.75684	.65910	.57437	.43708
30	0.92783	0.86103	0.81927	0.79919	.74192	.63976	.55207	.41199
32	0.92321	0.85248	0.80846	0.78733	.72730	.62099	.53063	.38834
34	0.91861	0.84402	0.79779	0.77565	.71297	.60277	.51003	.36604
36	0.91403	0.83564	0.78725	0.76415	.69892	.58509	.49022	.34503
38	0.90948	0.82735	0.77686	0.75281	.68515	.56792	.47119	.32523
40	0.90495	0.81914	0.76661	0.74165	.67165	.55126	.45289	.30656
45	0.89372	0.79896	0.74156	0.71445	.63905	.51171	.41020	.26444
50	0.88263	0.77929	0.71732	0.68825	.60804	.47500	.37153	.22811
100	0.77904	0.60729	0.51455	0.47369	.36971	.22563	.13803	.05203

Periods = n	4%	5%	6%	7%	8%	10%	12%	20%
1	.96154	.95238	.94340	.93458	.92593	.90909	.89286	.83333
2	.92456	.90703	.89000	.87344	.85734	.82645	.79719	.69444
3	.88900	.86384	.83962	.81630	.79383	.75131	.71178	.57870
4	.85480	.82270	.79209	.76290	.73503	.68301	.63552	.48225
5	.82193	.78353	.74726	.71299	.68058	.62092	.56743	.40188
6	.79031	.74622	.70496	.66634	.63017	.56447	.50663	.33490
7	.75992	.71068	.66506	.62275	.58349	.51316	.45235	.27908
8	.73069	.67684	.62741	.58201	.54027	.46651	.40388	.23257
9	.70259	.64461	.59190	.54393	.50025	.42410	.36061	.19381
10	.67556	.61391	.55839	.50835	.46319	.38554	.32197	.16151
11	.64958	.58468	.52679	.47509	.42888	.35049	.28748	.13459
12	.62460	.55684	.49697	.44401	.39711	.31863	.25668	.11216
13	.60057	.53032	.46884	.41496	.36770	.28966	.22917	.09346
14	.57748	.50507	.44230	.38782	.34046	.26333	.20462	.07789
15	.55526	.48102	.41727	.36245	.31524	.23939	.18270	.06491
16	.53391	.45811	.39365	.33873	.29189	.21763	.16312	.05409
17	.51337	.43630	.37136	.31657	.27027	.19784	.14564	.04507
18	.49363	.41552	.35034	.29586	.25025	.17986	.13004	.03756
19	.47464	.39573	.33051	.27651	.23171	.16351	.11611	.03130
20	.45639	.37689	.31180	.25842	.21455	.14864	.10367	.02608
22	.42196	.34185	.27751	.22571	.18394	.12285	.08264	.01811
24	.39012	.31007	.24698	.19715	.15770	.10153	.06588	.01258
26	.36069	.28124	.21981	.17220	.13520	.08391	.05252	.00874
28	.33348	.25509	.19563	.15040	.11591	.06934	.04187	.00607
30	.30832	.23138	.17411	.13137	.09938	.05731	.03338	.00421
32	.28506	.20987	.15496	.11474	.08520	.04736	.02661	.00293
34	.26355	.19035	.13791	.10022	.07305	.03914	.02121	.00203
36	.24367	.17266	.12274	.08754	.06262	.03235	.01691	.00141
38	.22529	.15661	.10924	.07646	.05369	.02673	.01348	.00098
40	.20829	.14205	.09722	.06678	.04603	.02209	.01075	.00068
45	.17120	.11130	.07265	.04761	.03133	.01372	.00610	.00027
50	.14071	.08720	.05429	.03395	.02132	.00852	.00346	.00011
100	.01980	.00760	.00295	.00115	.00045	.00007	.00001	.00000

TABLE 3   Future Value of Annuity of $1 in Arrears

$$F = \frac{(1 + r)^n - 1}{r}$$

r = interest rate; n = number of payments

No. of payments = n	¼%	½%	⅔%	¾%	1%	1½%	2%	3%
1	1.00000	1.00000	1.00000	1.00000	1.00000	1.00000	1.00000	1.00000
2	2.00250	2.00500	2.00667	2.00750	2.01000	2.01500	2.02000	2.03000
3	3.00751	3.01503	3.02004	3.02256	3.03010	3.04522	3.06040	3.09090
4	4.01503	4.03010	4.04018	4.04523	4.06040	4.09090	4.12161	4.18363
5	5.02506	5.05025	5.06711	5.07556	5.10101	5.15227	5.20404	5.30914
6	6.03763	6.07550	6.10089	6.11363	6.15202	6.22955	6.30812	6.46841
7	7.05272	7.10588	7.14157	7.15948	7.21354	7.32299	7.43428	7.66246
8	8.07035	8.14141	8.18918	8.21318	8.28567	8.43284	8.58297	8.89234
9	9.09053	9.18212	9.24377	9.27478	9.36853	9.55933	9.75463	10.15911
10	10.11325	10.22803	10.30540	10.34434	10.46221	10.70272	10.94972	11.46388
11	11.13854	11.27917	11.37410	11.42192	11.56683	11.86326	12.16872	12.80780
12	12.16638	12.33556	12.44993	12.50759	12.68250	13.04121	13.41209	14.19203
13	13.19680	13.39724	13.53293	13.60139	13.80933	14.23683	14.68033	15.61779
14	14.22979	14.46423	14.62315	14.70340	14.94742	15.45038	15.97394	17.08632
15	15.26537	15.53655	15.72063	15.81368	16.09690	16.68214	17.29342	18.59891
16	16.30353	16.61423	16.82544	16.93228	17.25786	17.93237	18.63929	20.15688
17	17.34429	17.69730	17.93761	18.05927	18.43044	19.20136	20.01207	21.76159
18	18.38765	18.78579	19.05719	19.19472	19.61475	20.48938	21.41231	23.41444
19	19.43362	19.87972	20.18424	20.33868	20.81090	21.79672	22.84056	25.11687
20	20.48220	20.97912	21.31880	21.49122	22.01900	23.12367	24.29737	26.87037
22	22.58724	23.19443	23.61066	23.82230	24.47159	25.83758	27.29898	30.53678
24	24.70282	25.43196	25.93319	26.18847	26.97346	28.63352	30.42186	34.42647
26	26.82899	27.69191	28.28678	28.59027	29.52563	31.51397	33.67091	38.55304
28	28.96580	29.97452	30.67187	31.02823	32.12910	34.48148	37.05121	42.93092
30	31.11331	32.28002	33.08885	33.50290	34.78489	37.53868	40.56808	47.57542
32	33.27157	34.60862	35.53818	36.01483	37.49407	40.68829	44.22703	52.50276
34	35.44064	36.96058	38.02026	38.56458	40.25770	43.93309	48.03380	57.73018
36	37.62056	39.33610	40.53556	41.15272	43.07688	47.27597	51.99437	63.27594
38	39.81140	41.73545	43.08450	43.77982	45.95272	50.71989	56.11494	69.15945
40	42.01320	44.15885	45.66754	46.44648	48.88637	54.26789	60.40198	75.40126
45	47.56606	50.32416	52.27734	53.29011	56.48107	63.61420	71.89271	92.71986
50	53.18868	56.64516	59.11042	60.39426	64.46318	73.68283	84.57940	112.7969
100	113.44996	129.33370	141.51445	148.14451	170.4814	228.8030	312.2323	607.2877

NOTE: To convert this table to values of an annuity in advance, take one more period and subtract 1.00000.

No. of payments = n	4%	5%	6%	7%	8%	10%	12%	20%
1	1.00000	1.00000	1.00000	1.00000	1.00000	1.00000	1.00000	1.00000
2	2.04000	2.05000	2.06000	2.07000	2.08000	2.10000	2.12000	2.20000
3	3.12160	3.15250	3.18360	3.21490	3.24640	3.31000	3.37440	3.64000
4	4.24646	4.31012	4.37462	4.43994	4.50611	4.64100	4.77933	5.36800
5	5.41632	5.52563	5.63709	5.75074	5.86660	6.10510	6.35285	7.44160
6	6.63298	6.80191	6.97532	7.15329	7.33593	7.71561	8.11519	9.92992
7	7.89829	8.14201	8.39384	8.65402	8.92280	9.48717	10.08901	12.91590
8	9.21423	9.54911	9.89747	10.25980	10.63663	11.43589	12.29969	16.49908
9	10.58280	11.02656	11.49132	11.97799	12.48756	13.57948	14.77566	20.79890
10	12.00611	12.57789	13.18079	13.81645	14.48656	15.93742	17.54874	25.95868
11	13.48635	14.20679	14.97164	15.78360	16.64549	18.53117	20.65458	32.15042
12	15.02581	15.91713	16.86994	17.88845	18.97713	21.38428	24.13313	39.58050
13	16.62684	17.71298	18.88214	20.14064	21.49530	24.52271	28.02911	48.49660
14	18.29191	19.59863	21.01507	22.55049	24.21492	27.97498	32.39260	59.19592
15	20.02359	21.57856	23.27597	25.12902	27.15211	31.77248	37.27971	72.03511
16	21.82453	23.65749	25.67253	27.88805	30.32428	35.94973	42.75328	87.44213
17	23.69751	25.84037	28.21288	30.84022	33.75023	40.54470	48.88367	105.9306
18	25.64541	28.13238	30.90565	33.99903	37.45024	45.59917	55.74971	128.1167
19	27.67123	30.53900	33.75999	37.37896	41.44626	51.15909	63.43968	154.7400
20	29.77808	33.06595	36.78559	40.99549	45.76196	57.27500	72.05244	186.6880
22	34.24797	38.50521	43.39229	49.00574	55.45676	71.40275	92.50258	271.0307
24	39.08260	44.50200	50.81558	58.17667	66.76476	88.49733	118.1552	392.4842
26	44.31174	51.11345	59.15638	68.67647	79.95442	109.1818	150.3339	567.3773
28	49.96758	58.40258	68.52811	80.69769	95.33883	134.2099	190.6989	819.2233
30	56.08494	66.43885	79.05819	94.46079	113.2832	164.4940	241.3327	1181.881
32	62.70147	75.29883	90.88978	110.2181	134.2135	201.1378	304.8477	1704.109
34	69.85791	85.06696	104.1838	128.2588	158.6267	245.4767	384.5210	2456.118
36	77.59831	95.83632	119.1209	148.9135	187.1022	299.1268	484.4631	3539.009
38	85.97034	107.7096	135.9042	172.5610	220.3159	364.0434	609.8305	5098.373
40	95.02552	120.7998	154.7620	199.6351	259.0565	442.5926	767.0914	7343.858
45	121.0294	159.7002	212.7435	285.7493	386.5056	718.9048	1358.230	18281.31
50	152.6671	209.3480	290.3359	406.5289	573.7702	1163.909	2400.018	45497.19
100	1237.624	2610.025	5638.368	12381.66	27484.52	137796.1	696010.5	414×10^6

TABLE 4   Present Value of Annuity of $1 in Arrears

$$P_A = \frac{1 - (1 + r)^{-n}}{r}$$

r = discount rate; n = number of payments

No. of payments = n	¼%	½%	⅔%	¾%	1%	1½%	2%	3%
1	0.99751	0.99502	0.99338	0.99256	.99010	.98522	.98039	.97087
2	1.99252	1.98510	1.98018	1.97772	1.97040	1.95588	1.94156	1.91347
3	2.98506	2.97025	2.96044	2.95556	2.94099	2.91220	2.88388	2.82861
4	3.97512	3.95050	3.93421	3.92611	3.90197	3.85438	3.80773	3.71710
5	4.96272	4.92587	4.90154	4.88944	4.85343	4.78264	4.71346	4.57971
6	5.94785	5.89638	5.86245	5.84560	5.79548	5.69719	5.60143	5.41719
7	6.93052	6.86207	6.81700	6.79464	6.72819	6.59821	6.47199	6.23028
8	7.91074	7.82296	7.76524	7.73661	7.65168	7.48593	7.32548	7.01969
9	8.88852	8.77906	8.70719	8.67158	8.56602	8.36052	8.16224	7.78611
10	9.86386	9.73041	9.64290	9.59958	9.47130	9.22218	8.98259	8.53020
11	10.83677	10.67703	10.57242	10.52067	10.36763	10.07112	9.78685	9.25262
12	11.80725	11.61893	11.49578	11.43491	11.25508	10.90751	10.57534	9.95400
13	12.77532	12.55615	12.41303	12.34235	12.13374	11.73153	11.34837	10.63496
14	13.74096	13.48871	13.32420	13.24302	13.00370	12.54338	12.10625	11.29607
15	14.70420	14.41662	14.22934	14.13699	13.86505	13.34323	12.84926	11.93794
16	15.66504	15.33993	15.12848	15.02431	14.71787	14.13126	13.57771	12.56110
17	16.62348	16.25863	16.02167	15.90502	15.56225	14.90765	14.29187	13.16612
18	17.57953	17.17277	16.90894	16.77918	16.39827	15.67256	14.99203	13.75351
19	18.53320	18.08236	17.79034	17.64683	17.22601	16.42617	15.67846	14.32380
20	19.48449	18.98742	18.66590	18.50802	18.04555	17.16864	16.35143	14.87747
22	21.37995	20.78406	20.39967	20.21121	19.66038	18.62082	17.65805	15.93692
24	23.26598	22.56287	22.11054	21.88915	21.24339	20.03041	18.91393	16.93554
26	25.14261	24.32402	23.79883	23.54219	22.79520	21.39863	20.12104	17.87684
28	27.00989	26.06769	25.46484	25.17071	24.31644	22.72672	21.28127	18.76411
30	28.86787	27.79405	27.10885	26.77508	25.80771	24.01584	22.39646	19.60044
32	30.71660	29.50328	28.73116	28.35565	27.26959	25.26714	23.46333	20.38877
34	32.55611	31.19555	30.33205	29.91278	28.70267	26.48173	24.49859	21.13184
36	34.38647	32.87102	31.91181	31.44681	30.10751	27.66068	25.48884	21.83225
38	36.20770	34.52985	33.47071	32.95808	31.48466	28.80505	26.44064	22.49246
40	38.01986	36.17223	35.00903	34.44694	32.83469	29.91585	27.35548	23.11477
45	42.51088	40.20710	38.76658	38.07318	36.09451	32.55234	29.49016	24.51871
50	46.94617	44.14279	42.40134	41.56645	39.19612	34.99969	31.42361	25.72976
100	88.38248	78.54264	72.81686	70.17962	63.02888	51.62470	43.09835	31.59891

NOTE: To convert this table to values of an annuity in advance, take one less period and add 1.00000.

No. of payments = n	4%	5%	6%	7%	8%	10%	12%	20%
1	.96154	.95238	.94340	.93458	.92593	.90909	.89286	.83333
2	1.88609	1.85941	1.83339	1.80802	1.78326	1.73554	1.69005	1.52778
3	2.77509	2.72325	2.67301	2.62432	2.57710	2.48685	2.40183	2.10648
4	3.62990	3.54595	3.46511	3.38721	3.31213	3.16987	3.03735	2.58873
5	4.45182	4.32948	4.21236	4.10020	3.99271	3.79079	3.60478	2.99061
6	5.24214	5.07569	4.91732	4.76654	4.62288	4.35526	4.11141	3.32551
7	6.00205	5.78637	5.58238	5.38929	5.20637	4.86842	4.56376	3.60459
8	6.73274	6.46321	6.20979	5.97130	5.74664	5.33493	4.96764	3.83716
9	7.43533	7.10782	6.80169	6.51523	6.24689	5.75902	5.32825	4.03097
10	8.11090	7.72173	7.36009	7.02358	6.71008	6.14457	5.65022	4.19247
11	8.76048	8.30641	7.88687	7.49867	7.13896	6.49506	5.93770	4.32706
12	9.38507	8.86325	8.38384	7.94269	7.53608	6.81369	6.19437	4.43922
13	9.98565	9.39357	8.85268	8.35765	7.90378	7.10336	6.42355	4.53268
14	10.56312	9.89864	9.29498	8.74547	8.24424	7.36669	6.62817	4.61057
15	11.11839	10.37966	9.71225	9.10791	8.55948	7.60608	6.81086	4.67547
16	11.65230	10.83777	10.10590	9.44665	8.85137	7.82371	6.97399	4.72956
17	12.16567	11.27407	10.47726	9.76322	9.12164	8.02155	7.11963	4.77463
18	12.65930	11.68959	10.82760	10.05909	9.37189	8.20141	7.24967	4.81219
19	13.13394	12.08532	11.15812	10.33560	9.60360	8.36492	7.36578	4.84350
20	13.59033	12.46221	11.46992	10.59401	9.81815	8.51356	7.46944	4.86958
22	14.45112	13.16300	12.04158	11.06124	10.20074	8.77154	7.64465	4.90943
24	15.24696	13.79864	12.55036	11.46933	10.52876	8.98474	7.78432	4.93710
26	15.98277	14.37519	13.00317	11.82578	10.80998	9.16095	7.89566	4.95632
28	16.66306	14.89813	13.40616	12.13711	11.05108	9.30657	7.98442	4.96967
30	17.29203	15.37245	13.76483	12.40904	11.25778	9.42691	8.05518	4.97894
32	17.87355	15.80268	14.08404	12.64656	11.43500	9.52638	8.11159	4.98537
34	18.41120	16.19290	14.36814	12.85401	11.58693	9.60857	8.15656	4.98984
36	18.90828	16.54685	14.62099	13.03521	11.71719	9.67651	8.19241	4.99295
38	19.36786	16.86789	14.84602	13.19347	11.82887	9.73265	8.22099	4.99510
40	19.79277	17.15909	15.04630	13.33171	11.92461	9.77905	8.24378	4.99660
45	20.72004	17.77407	15.45583	13.60552	12.10840	9.86281	8.28252	4.99863
50	21.48218	18.25593	15.76186	13.80075	12.23348	9.91481	8.30450	4.99945
100	24.50500	19.84791	16.61755	14.26925	12.49432	9.99927	8.33323	5.00000

TABLE 5   **Bond Values in Percent of Par: 6-Percent Semiannual Coupons**
Bond Value = $6/r + (100 - 6/r)(1 + r/2)^{-2n}$
r = yield to maturity; n = years to maturity

Market yield % per year compounded semiannually	Years to maturity							
	½	5	10	15	19½	20	30	40
3.0	101.478	113.833	125.753	136.024	144.047	144.874	159.071	169.611
3.5	101.228	111.376	120.941	128.982	135.118	135.743	146.205	153.600
4.0	100.980	108.983	116.351	122.396	126.903	127.355	134.761	139.745
4.5	100.734	106.650	111.973	116.234	119.337	119.645	124.562	127.712
5.0	100.488	104.376	107.795	110.465	112.365	112.551	115.454	117.226
5.1	100.439	103.928	106.982	109.356	111.037	111.202	113.752	115.293
5.2	100.390	103.483	106.177	108.262	109.731	109.874	112.087	113.411
5.3	100.341	103.040	105.380	107.181	108.445	108.568	110.458	111.578
5.4	100.292	102.599	104.590	106.115	107.180	107.283	108.864	109.792
5.5	100.243	102.160	103.807	105.062	105.935	106.019	107.306	108.053
5.6	100.195	101.724	103.031	104.023	104.710	104.776	105.780	106.359
5.7	100.146	101.289	102.263	102.998	103.504	103.553	104.288	104.707
5.8	100.097	100.857	101.502	101.986	102.317	102.349	102.828	103.098
5.9	100.049	100.428	100.747	100.986	101.149	101.165	101.399	101.529
6.0	100	100	100	100	100	100	100	100
6.1	99.9515	99.5746	99.2595	99.0262	98.8685	98.8535	98.6309	98.5088
6.2	99.9030	99.1513	98.5259	98.0650	97.7549	97.7254	97.2907	97.0546
6.3	99.8546	98.7302	97.7990	97.1161	96.6587	96.6153	95.9787	95.6364
6.4	99.8062	98.3112	97.0787	96.1793	95.5796	95.5229	94.6942	94.2529
6.5	99.7579	97.8944	96.3651	95.2545	94.5174	94.4478	93.4365	92.9031
6.6	99.7096	97.4797	95.6580	94.3414	93.4717	93.3899	92.2050	91.5860
6.7	99.6613	97.0670	94.9574	93.4400	92.4423	92.3486	90.9989	90.3007
6.8	99.6132	96.6565	94.2632	92.5501	91.4288	91.3238	89.8178	89.0461
6.9	99.5650	96.2480	93.5753	91.6714	90.4310	90.3152	88.6608	87.8213
7.0	99.5169	95.8417	92.8938	90.8039	89.4487	89.3224	87.5276	86.6255
7.5	99.2771	93.8404	89.5779	86.6281	84.7588	84.5868	82.1966	81.0519
8.0	99.0385	91.8891	86.4097	82.7080	80.4155	80.2072	77.3765	76.0846
8.5	98.8010	89.9864	83.3820	79.0262	76.3899	76.1534	73.0090	71.6412
9.0	98.5646	88.1309	80.4881	75.5666	72.6555	72.3976	69.0430	67.6520

TABLE 6   Bond Values in Percent of Par: 8-Percent Semiannual Coupons
$$\text{Bond Value} = 8/r + (100 - 8/r)(1 + r/2)^{-2n}$$
$$r = \text{yield to maturity}; \; n = \text{years to maturity}$$

Market yield % per year compounded semiannually	Years to maturity							
	½	5	10	15	19½	20	30	40
5.0	101.463	113.128	123.384	131.396	137.096	137.654	146.363	151.678
5.5	101.217	110.800	119.034	125.312	129.675	130.098	136.528	140.266
6.0	100.971	108.530	114.877	119.600	122.808	123.115	127.676	130.201
6.5	100.726	106.317	110.905	114.236	116.448	116.656	119.690	121.291
7.0	100.483	104.158	107.106	109.196	110.551	110.678	112.472	113.374
7.1	100.435	103.733	106.367	108.225	109.424	109.536	111.113	111.898
7.2	100.386	103.310	105.634	107.266	108.314	108.411	109.780	110.455
7.3	100.338	102.889	104.908	106.318	107.220	107.303	108.473	109.044
7.4	100.289	102.470	104.188	105.382	106.142	106.212	107.191	107.665
7.5	100.241	102.053	103.474	104.457	105.080	105.138	105.934	106.316
7.6	100.193	101.638	102.767	103.544	104.034	104.079	104.702	104.997
7.7	100.144	101.226	102.066	102.642	103.003	103.036	103.492	103.706
7.8	100.096	100.815	101.371	101.750	101.987	102.009	102.306	102.444
7.9	100.048	100.407	100.683	100.870	100.986	100.997	101.142	101.209
8.0	100	100	100	100	100	100	100	100
8.1	99.9519	99.5955	99.3235	99.1406	99.0279	99.0177	98.8794	98.8170
8.2	99.9039	99.1929	98.6529	98.2916	98.0699	98.0498	97.7798	97.6589
8.3	99.8560	98.7924	97.9882	97.4528	97.1257	97.0962	96.7006	96.5253
8.4	99.8081	98.3938	97.3294	96.6240	96.1951	96.1566	95.6414	95.4152
8.5	99.7602	97.9973	96.6764	95.8052	95.2780	95.2307	94.6018	94.3282
8.6	99.7124	97.6027	96.0291	94.9962	94.3739	94.3183	93.5812	93.2636
8.7	99.6646	97.2100	95.3875	94.1969	93.4829	93.4191	92.5792	92.2208
8.8	99.6169	96.8193	94.7514	93.4071	92.6045	92.5331	91.5955	91.1992
8.9	99.5692	96.4305	94.1210	92.6266	91.7387	91.6598	90.6295	90.1982
9.0	99.5215	96.0436	93.4960	91.8555	90.8851	90.7992	89.6810	89.2173
9.5	99.2840	94.1378	90.4520	88.1347	86.7949	86.6777	85.1858	84.5961
10.0	99.0476	92.2783	87.5378	84.6275	82.9830	82.8409	81.0707	80.4035
10.5	98.8123	90.4639	84.7472	81.3201	79.4271	79.2656	77.2956	76.5876
11.0	98.5782	88.6935	82.0744	78.1994	76.1070	75.9308	73.8252	73.1036

Index